O'BRIEN'S

Collecting TOYS

Identification & Value Guide
10th Edition

EDITED BY ELIZABETH A. STEPHAN

What's on the cover?

All values are for toys in C10 condition

Front Cover

Top to bottom:
Fisher-Price Mickey Mouse Xylophone,
  No. 798 .... $975
Kenton Overland Circus Caliope Wagon,........................$700
  Photo courtesy Christie's East
Turner Staek Truck, closed cab, ca. 1940s $400
  Photo from John Taylor

Back Cover

Top row, left to right:
Chein Ride-A-Rocket $600
Schoenhut Clown...$125
Calamity mechanical bank, J. & E. Stevens, 1905 .....$35,000
Bottom Row, left to right:
John Deere Thresher, Vindex...................................... $3,900
Case Combine, Vindex $5,200

Published by

krause publications

700 E. State Street • Iola, WI 54990-0001
Telephone: 715/445-2214

Please call or write for our free catalog of publications. Our toll-free number to place an
order or obtain a free catalog is 800-258-0929 or please use our regular business telephone,
715-445-2214.

Library of Congress Catalog Number: 99-61890
ISBN: 0-87349-242-0

Printed in the United States of America

TABLE OF CONTENTS

INTRODUCTION

The year 2001: the first year of the millennium. It's the year made famous by Stanley Kubrick's movie *2001: A Space Odyssey.* It's the year of the tenth edition of *O'Brien's Collecting Toys.* Is it a stretch comparing Stanley Kubrick's classic and a toy price guide? Probably. But like Kubrick's movie, this book is a classic.

First published in 1978, Richard O'Brien's *Collecting Toys* boasted of 4,000 listings and was the first of its kind on the market. Twenty-plus years later, the tenth edition has more than 20,000 listings and has become the standard-bearer in the industry.

The toy collecting hobby has changed a lot since then. Vintage toys have long been the mainstay of toy collectors. Prewar tin wind-ups, cast-iron banks, and vehicles were often seen as the Holy Grails of the toy world. But by the mid-1980s, it became obvious that the toys of the baby-boom generation were gaining in popularity.

In the fourth edition of *Collecting Toys*, published in 1985, O'Brien wrote, "A number of the toys added in this edition are from the 1950s and 1960s, as these toys are becoming more and more collectible…" If one were to follow the evolution of *Collecting Toys*, one would see the evolution of the toy hobby. O'Brien was able to balance the vintage prewar toys with the newer, postwar toys that began to pick up collectible steam in the mid 1980s.

The sixth edition saw the addition of PEZ dispensers and Schoenhut—two completely different toys. With their colorful plastic bodies and character heads, PEZ dispensers seem to epitomize the baby-boom generation. The Psychedelic Eye dispenser, the Universal Monsters dispensers, they are exactly what many toy collectors are looking for—colorful and whimsical. Made during the first half of the twentieth century, Schoenhut toys are nothing short of classic. Unlike PEZ, finding a piece of Schoenhut's Humpty Dumpty Circus in C10 condition is impossible. Even in C6 condition, the same piece could still be worth a bundle.

Dollhouse furniture, BB guns and Erector Sets were added to the seventh edition. Like PEZ, plastic dollhouse furniture is a classic baby-boomer toy. Made by companies like Ideal, Renwal, and Marx, dollhouse furniture has seen a rise in popularity in the last few years. The classic movie *A Christmas Story* shows the popularity of BB guns with the boomer crowd. (Readers should note that the Red Ryder BB gun Ralphie wanted so badly was never produced; see the BB Guns chapter for more information.) Erector Sets were popular with boomers, but were around long before the postwar generation was born.

By the time the eighth edition of *Collecting Toys* was published in 1997, O'Brien's guide was established as the book for vintage toys. This was the first edition published by Krause Publications; it had more than 16,000 listings, four times that of the original book.

Richard O'Brien retired after the eighth edition was published. During his publishing career, O'Brien authored numerous toy price guides, including *Collecting Toy Cars & Trucks,* *Collecting Toy Trains, Collecting American-Made Soldiers* and *Collecting Foreign-Made Soldiers.* O'Brien wrote the definitive book on the history of American toys—*The Story of American Toys.* Long out of print, it is a book anyone interested in toys should read. In addition to his books on toys, O'Brien has written several novels, including *Evil* and *Never Tell Him You're Alone.*

A New Generation of Collecting Toys

I took over the editing of *Collecting Toys* in 1997. Referred to as "O'Brien's" by most collectors, the name of the book was changed to *O'Brien's Collecting Toys.* The ninth edition saw the addition of Lionel Trains. Not everyone saw this as a necessity, but the addition rounded out the book. Many see train collectors and toy collectors as two different groups. Over the last few years, I have realized this isn't true. Many toy collectors have a few trains, and many train collectors have a few toys. (Toy buildings and vehicles are perfect for train dioramas) Lionel remains in this edition and makes it that much stronger.

I wanted to make sure *O'Brien's* continued to feature vintage toys, but I didn't want to ignore one of the hottest areas of toy collecting today—action figures. While collectors won't find the most recent McFarlane figure or even some of the early Transformers, they will find a comprehensive listing of *Star Wars* figures. To ignore the phenomenon that is *Star Wars* would be a mistake. The introduction of the 3-3/4-inch figures in 1977 forever changed the toy world. The continued popularity of the *Star Wars* figures warrants their inclusion in this book.

The newest addition to *O'Brien's Collecting Toys* is a chapter covering farm toys, an ever growing and often-ignored area of toys. Toy companies like Kansas Toy Novelty Company, Arcade and Vindex have been making cast-iron tractors and implements since the early twentieth century, but it was Fred Ertl who established the farm toy industry that we know today when he made his first tractor in 1945. Collectors know that a single chapter covering farm toys cannot cover the entire genre. I strived to make this new section as representative of the hobby as I could.

Collectors of Japanese tin vehicles and airplanes don't fret, the chapters on these two topics were not deleted, they were moved. The former Japanese Tin Vehicles chapter can now be found under the same name in the Vehicles chapter. Japanese Tin Airplanes are now part of the Aircraft chapter.

O'Brien Numbers

In the introduction of the ninth edition of *O'Brien Collecting Toys*, I explained why I removed the number code, also known as O'Brien numbers, used in several chapters and sections. After hearing from many readers, these numbers have been returned, but I feel they need some explanation.

These numbers are used as a tool to identify a toy and catalog a collection. They were introduced by Richard O'Brien and were never at any time a number found on the toy. For example, Arcade's Yellow Cab, No. 1590Y has an O'Brien number of AR256. This is an alphanumeric code unique to this toy. If you were to look this up in *O'Brien's Collecting Toy Cars & Trucks* or in an earlier edition of *Collecting Toys*, it would have the same code. Readers should also note that not all listings have O'Brien numbers.

The O'Brien numbers can be found at the end of the listings in parenthesis.

A Few Final Thoughts

The Internet has changed the face of collecting forever. A piece that a dealer sold for $1 at a toy show can now be sold for $20 on the Internet. A collector can easily find that ellusive toy in a few minutes without even leaving home and often times at a bargain price.

Will the Internet ruin the value of your toy collection? Will it harm your investment? No. The toys that were an investment in the past are still an investment today. In 2000, Bill Bertoia Auctions sold a Tipp & Company Mickey and Minnie on Motorcycle tin wind-up without box for close to $53,000. (The same toy with a box sold at Randy Inman Auctions for $110,000.) This lone event proves that toy collecting is still an investment, if you spend your money on the right toys.

What are the "right" toys? There isn't an easy answer to that question. For example, Vintage tin, character toys, premiums, mechanical and still banks, and lead toy soldiers keep their values, but just because a toy is old doesn't mean it is valuable. The best way to find the right toy is through research by reading price guides and toy magazines, attending toy shows, and following auction sales.

Pricing

The values listed in this book come from a number of sources—dealers, collectors and auction houses; ads in magazines such as *Toy Shop*; price lists provided by dealers; and toy shows.

Readers should be aware that this is a guide and only a guide. The values listed here are not written in stone. Many things can change the value of a toy: region, condition, time of year, and last but certainly not least, desire. In the end, a toy is only worth what someone is willing to pay for it.

If you are looking for an appraisal for insurance reasons, contact a professional appraiser. To find an appraiser in your area, please contact:

American Society of Appraisers
555 Herndon Pkwy #125
Herndon, VA 20170
703-478-2228
www.appraisers.org

Do note that a professional appraiser will charge for his or her services.

Please remember that although the listings, captions and prices have been checked and double-checked, neither the editor nor Krause Publications can assume responsibility for any typographical errors or losses that might be incurred as a result of consulting this guide.

Acknowledgments

My name may be on the cover of this book, but many people helped me along the way.

Deb Schellin was responsible for much of the data entry involved with this book.

Tom Dupuis designed the cover.

Bonnie Tetzlaff, Kay Sommerfeld and Sally Olson were responsible for the pagination.

A book like this would never be possible without the experts and contributors. I owe many thanks to the following: Stan Alekna, Charles Best, Fred Berecz, Ray Brandes, Jim Buskirk, Jim and Patsy Carlson, Kent Comstock, Reid Covey, Don and Barb DeSalle, Perry Eichor, John Fawcett, John Gibson, Jim Harmon, Judy Izen, Dave Leopard, Richard MacNary, Fred Maxwell, John Murray, Bob Pierce, Randy Prasse, Mark Rich, M. Aaron Roy, Brian Seligman, Scott Smiles, Bob Smith, Ron Smith, John Snyder, Jr., John Taylor, Marcie Tubbs, David Welch, and Randy Welch.

As always, I must thank my co-workers—Mark Williams, publisher of the Toys and Comics and Games Divisions at Krause Publications; Sharon Korbeck, editorial director of *Toy Shop*, *Toy Cars & Models* and *Warman's Today's Collector*; Merry Dudley, editor of *Toy Cars & Models*; Tom Bartsch, associate editor of *Toy Shop*; and Lisa Jacobsen, associate editor of *Warman's Today's Collector*. They are all instrumental in all the books I edit; they offer advice, information and oftentimes some much-needed support.

Elizabeth A. Stephan
Editor
stephane@krause

Abbreviations

n/a Not applicable; if n/a is listed in the C10 column, that toy was not available with a box or package. If n/a is listed in another price column, that item doesn't have any value in that condition.

NPF No Price Found; just because an item is listed as NPF does not mean that it is especially rare, it only means that an accurate value for that toy could not be found.

✳✳✳✳✳✳✳✳

Unless otherwise noted, the pricing grades are as follow:

C6 Good; evident overall wear, well played with but acceptable to many collectors.

C8 Very Good; minor overall wear, very clean

C10 Mint, Mint in Box; like new

ACTION FIGURES

Adventure heroes and superheroes are everywhere, on comic pages, television and movie screens, and, of course, in toy store aisles. The action figure likenesses produced by numerous toy companies are among today's hottest collectibles.

Action figure collecting is one of the fastest growing and potentially largest collectibles areas since the baseball card boom of the 1980s. A stroll through the toy section of any store is proof enough. Plus, it is a given that a percentage of today's teen and preteen action figure buyers will become collectors, and their potential numbers are huge. Action figures could bring more collectors into the hobby than G.I. Joe, Hot Wheels and model kits combined.

Hundreds of figures are for sale currently, and they are commonplace in toy stores. In some places action figures are literally climbing the walls. Why collect them if they can be bought directly from current store shelves? For many collectors, that's exactly how the collecting frenzy begins.

For many action figure collectors, time began in the 1960s. While boys had played with toy soldiers for hundreds of years, these were typically iron or lead figures with no movable parts. The same held true for the hard plastic Marx figures of the 1950s. By definition, however, the term "action figure" was born in the 1960s.

That decade also saw American culture and technologies come of age in ways that changed countless aspects of everyday life, including how toys would be made and sold.

Heroes from the TV screen

By the late 1950s, television had replaced the dinner table and parlor radio as the family hearth. The sturdy cabinet in the living room captivated with a power only hinted at by radio and which has never been challenged since. It was a working window not only into a wide world of people and places, but also, increasingly, of neat things to buy. Youngsters clustered on the floor, soaking up the names and lore of their new friends and heroes—Wonder Woman, Superman, Batman, G.I. Joe.

From 1961 to 1963, toy makers watched with envy and despair as Mattel's Barbie, aided by TV, took the world of girls' toys by storm. Of course, no one would dream of selling dolls to boys, so this barrier seemed insurmountable. But wheels of industry would not be easily stopped, and the simple solution to this dilemma ranks as one of the greatest marketing spins of all time. If boys won't play with dolls, why not rename them "action figures"?

Hasbro's first test of G.I. Joe, the male answer to Barbie, debuted at New York's International Toy Fair in early 1964. Toy Fair is where buyers, retailers and manufacturers meet to view upcoming lines—and in the process, make or break a toy's success.

Buyers met the twelve-inch G.I. Joe with both hopes and reservations. They wanted to believe that a successful "Barbie for boys" had been created, but as much as Hasbro touted Joe as "America's Movable Fighting Man," the buyers still heard "doll."

Virtually no orders were generated at Toy Fair, so in June, with no fanfare or ad support, Hasbro released the new toy into the New York test market. Every test store sold out within a week and the invasion of America was on. By year's end, G.I. Joe had earned Hasbro $17 million, in spite of sales lost to product shortages.

G.I. Joe was the first true-articulated action figure for boys, but he wouldn't be alone for long. A.C. Gilbert introduced James Bond figures in 1965, but for the first time in his career, Ian Fleming's super spy failed in his mission. Marx also entered the ring with the Best of the West series, but G.I. Joe had a seemingly limitless arsenal of battle-geared appeal.

The first reasonably successful challenge to G.I. Joe came from Ideal's Captain Action. While Joe's identity was well established, Captain Action was a man of many faces. Ideal designed Captain Action to establish not only his own identity, but also to capitalize on those many popular superheroes. Joe was just Joe, but Captain Action figures and sets could become Spider-Man, Batman, the Phantom, Green Hornet and others. Today, Captain Action figures and sets command the second highest prices in the action figure market, second only to classic G.I. Joes.

Ideal's brief foray into the world of superhero action figures paved the way for many to come. While G.I. Joe was forced to temper his image and soften it from the quintessential military Green Beret Joe of 1967 into the Adventure Team Joe of 1970, superheroes were largely immune to the Vietnam protests that forced Joe's change of mission. By 1969, Ideal tired of Captain Action's complex licensing agreements and discontinued the series, but another company was waiting in the wings. It was Mego.

Mighty Mego

In 1972, Mego released its first superhero series, the six-figure set of Official World's Greatest Super Heroes. These eight-inch tall cloth and plastic figures were joined by twenty-eight others by the time the series ended ten years later. Mego supplemented this superhero line with licensed film and TV characters from, most notably, *Planet of the Apes, Star Trek* and *The Dukes of Hazzard,* as well as historic figures representing the Old West and the World's Greatest Super Knights.

Another milestone in action figure history took place in 1977. Out of nowhere, George Lucas' *Star Wars* had become a worldwide smash, but nobody except Kenner had bothered to secure rights to merchandise toys. When Kenner realized the magnitude of *Star Wars'* potential, it rushed toys through production, but it didn't have time to get action figures on the shelves by Christmas. Instead, Kenner essentially pre-sold the figures as the mail-order Early Bird set.

By Christmas 1978, the line had grown to seventeen figures and the first wave of a deluge of accessories and related toys. The Star Wars figures also established a third standard size for action figures. G.I. Joes and Captain Action were twelve-inch figures, Mego figures measured eight inches, and Kenner's Star Wars figures were just 3-3/4-inches tall. Their tremendous popularity cemented that size as a new standard that holds to this day.

Next came the six-inch figure, set by Mattel's highly successful and lucrative 1981 Masters of the Universe series. This series was the first to be reverse licensed; in other words, Mattel made the toys first, and then sold the licensing to television and film, not the other way around. Mattel also upped the manufacturing ante by endowing the figures with action features such as punching and grabbing movements, thus enhancing their play value and setting another standard in the process.

Action figures are big business, and hot series like Star Trek and McFarlane's Spawn are now regularly ranked in the top twenty best selling lines by industry trade magazines. An enduring character identity is a key to the continued demand and future appreciation. Star Trek has proven itself a worthy long term franchise and is joining the ranks of Star Wars as the blue chip stocks of the action figure market.

The action figure aisles are now attracting more adults, and they are not always buying for their kids. More adults today buy action figures as collectibles and investments. And those investments will in years hence feed the needs of tomorrow's collectors—the ones who are now sitting on the floor playing with Captain Picard, Batman and Spawn.

Contributors: Action Figures—John Marshall, P.O. Box 340, Rancocas, NJ 08073, Jmars@toyzilla.com, www.toyzilla.com; **Space: 1999**—Corey LeChat, P.O. Box 40135, Pittsburgh, PA 15201, the1999guy@aol.com; **Star Wars**—Chris Fawcett, cfawcett@ix.netcom.com.

Action Jackson (Mego, 1974)

8" Figures	C8	C10
Action Jackson, Black version	25	60
Action Jackson, blond, brown, or black beard	15	30
Action Jackson, blond, brown, or black hair	15	30

Accessories	C8	C10
Parachute Plunge	5	15
Strap-On Helicopter	5	15
Water Scooter	5	15

Outfits	C8	C10
Air Force Pilot	7	15

Outfits (Continued)	C8	C10
Army Outfit	7	15
Aussie Marine	7	15
Baseball	7	15
Fisherman	7	15
Football	7	15
Frog Man	7	15
Hockey	7	15
Jungle Safari	7	15
Karate	7	15

Outfits (Continued)

	C8	C10
Navy Sailor	7	15
Rescue Squad	7	15
Scramble Cyclist	7	15
Secret Agent	7	15
Ski Patrol	7	15
Snowmobile Outfit	7	15
Surf and Scuba Outfit	7	15
Western Cowboy	7	15

Vehicles

	C8	C10
Adventure Set	40	85
Campmobile	40	85
Dune Buggy	30	60
Formula Racer	30	60
Mustang	30	60
Rescue Helicopter	40	85
Safari Jeep	40	85
Scramble Cycle	20	40
Snowmobile	15	30

Alien, 18" figure, Alien, Kenner, $500

Addams Family (Remco, 1964)

Figures

	C8	C10
Lurch	150	450
Morticia	160	500
Uncle Fester	160	500

Alien (Kenner, 1979)

18" Figure

	C8	C10
Alien	200	500

American West (Mego, 1973)

8" Figures

	C8	C10
Buffalo Bill Cody, boxed	40	75
Buffalo Bill Cody, carded	40	100
Cochise, boxed	40	75
Cochise, carded	40	100
Davy Crockett, boxed	70	110
Davy Crockett, carded	70	140
Shadow (horse), boxed	70	140
Sitting Bull, boxed	45	90
Sitting Bull, carded	45	125
Wild Bill Hickok, boxed	40	75
Wild Bill Hickok, carded	40	125
Wyatt Earp, boxed	40	75
Wyatt Earp, carded	40	125

Play Sets

	C8	C10
Dodge City Play Set, vinyl	100	200

Archies (Marx, 1975)

Figures

	C8	C10
Archie	15	75
Betty	15	75
Jughead	15	75
Veronica	15	75

Astronauts (Marx, 1969)

Figures

	C8	C10
Jane Apollo Astronaut	65	125
Johnny Apollo Astronaut	125	200
Kennedy Space Center Astronaut	65	140

Banana Splits (Sutton, 1970)

Figures

	C8	C10
Bingo the Bear	45	125

Jane Apollo Astronaut, Astronauts, Marx, $125

Figures (Continued)

	C8	C10
Drooper the Lion	45	125
Fleagle Beagle	45	125
Snorky the Elephant	45	125

Battlestar Galactica (Mattel, 1978-79)

3-3/4" Figures, Series 1, 1978

	C8	C10
Commander Adama	15	40
Cylon Centurian	15	40
Daggit (brown)	15	30
Daggit (tan)	15	30
Imperious Leader	15	30
Ovion	12	35
Starbuck	15	40

3-3/4" Figures, Series 2, 1979

	C8	C10
Baltar	30	75
Boray	30	75
Cylon Commander	55	110
Lucifer	55	110

12" Figures

	C8	C10
Colonial Warrior	30	85
Cylon Centurian	30	95

Best of the West (Marx, 1960s)

Figures

	C8	C10
Bill Buck, 1967	300	475
Buckboard with Horse and Harness	100	225
Chief Cherokee, 1965	150	200
Daniel Boone, 1965	100	200
Davy Crockett	175	250
Fighting Eagle, 1967	150	225
General Custer, 1965	100	200
Geronimo and Pinto	150	200
Geronimo, 1967	100	150
Jamie West, 1967	50	100
Jane West, 1966	60	120
Janice West, 1967	50	100
Jay West, 1967	50	100

Daggit (brown), Battlestar Galactica, Mattel, $30. Photo courtesy Lenny Lee

Ovion, Battlestar Galactica, Mattel, $35. Photo courtesy Lenny Lee

Lucifer, Battlestar Galactica, Mattel, $110. Photo courtesy Lenny Lee

Boray, Battlestar Galactica, Mattel, $75. Photo courtesy Lenny Lee

Daniel Boone, 1965, Best of the West, Marx, $200

Fighting Eagle, 1967, Best of the West, Marx, $25

Pancho Horse, for 9" figures, 1968, Best of the West, Marx, $75

Accessories (Continued)

	C8	C10
Jungle Truck	15	30
Motorcross Honda	20	50
Rescue Rig	20	50
Rugged Rider	15	30
Sky Commander	20	40
Sport Camper	20	50

Figures (Continued)

	C8	C10
Johnny West Covered Wagon, with horse and harness	100	225
Johnny West with Comanche	80	125
Johnny West, 1965	75	150
Josie West, 1967	50	100
Pancho Horse, for 9" figures, 1968	50	75
Princess Wildflower, 1974	100	175
Sam Cobra, 1972	100	200
Sheriff Garrett, 1973	150	200
Thunderbolt Horse	75	125
Zeb Zachary, 1967	200	300

Big Jim (Mattel, 1973-76)

Accessories

	C8	C10
Baja Beast	10	20
Boat and Buggy Set	10	25
Camping Tent	5	20
Camping Tent	5	15
Devil River Trip	15	30

Sheriff Garrett, 1973, Best of the West, Marx, $200

Big Jack, Big Jim, Mattel, $25

Figures

	C8	C10
Big Jack	7	25
Big Jack	7	25
Big Jeff	7	25
Big Josh	7	25
Dr. Steel	10	30

Big Jim's P.A.C.K. (Mattel, 1976-77)

Accessories

	C8	C10
Beast	45	100
BlitzRig	60	120
Howler	30	60
LazerVette	45	100

Bionic Woman (Kenner, 1976-77)

12" Figures

	C8	C10
Fembot	70	160
Jamie Sommers	40	100
Jamie Sommers with purse	50	125

Accessories

	C8	C10
Beauty Salon	30	70

Accessories (Continued)

	C8	C10
Carriage House	55	140
Classroom	100	200
Dome House	55	140
Sports Car	40	100

Black Hole (Mego, 1979-80)

3-3/4" Figures

	C8	C10
Captain Holland, 1979	5	25
Dr. Alex Durant, 1979	5	25
Dr. Hans Reinhardt, 1979	5	25
Harry Booth, 1979	5	25
Humanoid, 1980	200	750
Kate McCrae, 1979	5	25
Maximillian, 1979	20	75
Old B.O.B., 1980	60	200
Pizer, 1979	10	50
S.T.A.R., 1980	85	350
Sentry Robot, 1980	15	75
V.I.N.cent., 1979	15	70

12" Figures

	C8	C10
Captain Holland	40	75
Dr. Alex Durant	40	75
Dr. Hans Reinhardt	40	75
Harry Booth	45	85
Kate McCrae	50	95
Pizer	40	75

Bonanza (American Character, 1966)

Accessoires

	C8	C10
4 in 1 Wagon	40	100
Ben's Palomino	35	75
Hoss' Stallion	35	75
Little Joe's Pinto	35	75

Figures

	C8	C10
Ben	50	150
Ben with Palomino	80	225
Hoss	70	150
Hoss with Stallion	70	200
Little Joe	50	150
Little Joe with Pinto	70	200
Outlaw	50	150

Buck Rogers (Mego, 1979)

3-3/4" Figures

	C8	C10
Ardella	6	15
Buck Rogers	35	60
Doctor Huer	6	20
Draco	6	20
Draconian Guard	10	20
Killer Kane	6	15
Tiger Man	10	25
Twiki	20	45
Wilma Deering	12	25

3-3/4" Play Sets

	C8	C10
Star Fighter Command Center	35	100

3-3/4" Vehicles

	C8	C10
Draconian Marauder	25	50
Land Rover	20	40
Laserscope Fighter	20	40
Star Fighter	25	50
Star Searcher	30	60

12" Figures

	C8	C10
Buck Rogers	30	90
Doctor Huer	30	80
Draco	30	80

12" Figures (Continued)

	C8	C10
Draconian Guard	30	80
Killer Kane	30	80
Tiger Man	30	125
Twiki	30	60

Butch and Sundance: The Early Days (Kenner, 1979)

Accessories and Vehicles

	C8	C10
Bluff, Butch's horse	20	50
Mint Wagon	25	60
Saloon Play Set	45	110
Spurs, Sundance's horse	20	50

Figures

	C8	C10
Butch Cassidy	12	30
Marshall LeFors	12	30
O.C. Hanks	12	30
Sheriff Bledsoe	12	30
Sundance Kid	12	30

Captain Action (Ideal, 1966-68)

9" Figures

	C8	C10
Action Boy, 1967	275	900
Action Boy, with space suit, 1968	350	1100

12" Figures

	C8	C10
Captain Action, parachute offer on box, 1967	275	700
Captain Action, photo box, 1966	300	900

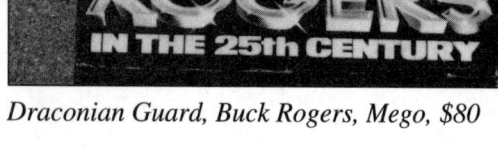

Draconian Guard, Buck Rogers, Mego, $80

Captain Action, parachute offer on box, 1967, Captain Action, Ideal, $700

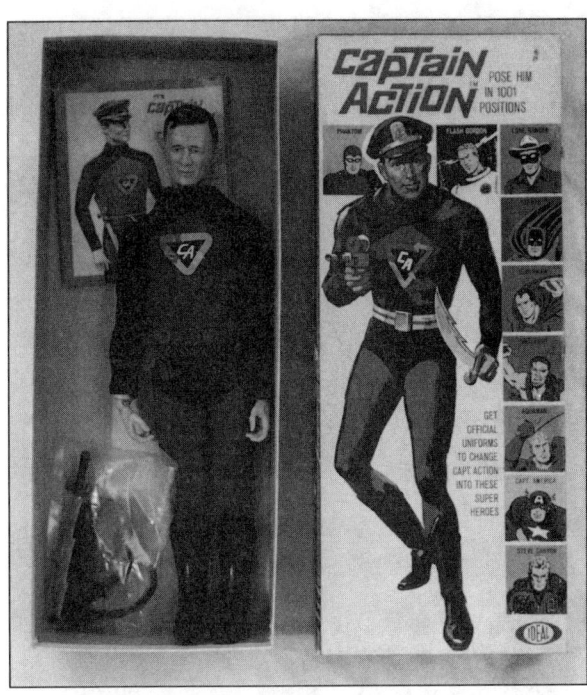

Captain Action, with red-shirted Lone Ranger on box, 1966, Captain Action, Ideal, $500

12" Figures (Continued)

	C8	C10
Captain Action, with blue-shirted Lone Ranger on box, 1966	200	500
Captain Action, with red-shirted Lone Ranger on box, 1966	200	500
Dr. Evil, 1967	300	1200

Dr. Evil, 1967, Captain Action, Ideal, $1200

Accessories

	C8	C10
Action Cave Carrying Case, vinyl, 1967	400	700
Directional Communicator Set, 1966	110	300
Dr. Evil Sanctuary, 1967	2500	3500
Jet Mortar, 1966	110	300
Parachute Pack, 1966	100	225
Power Pack, 1966	125	250
Quick Change Chamber, Cardboard, Sears Exclusive, 1967	750	900
Silver Streak Amphibian, 1967	800	1200
Silver Streak Garage with Silver Streak Vehicle, Sears Exclusive	1500	2000
Survival Kit, twenty pieces, 1967	125	275
Vinyl Headquarters Carrying Case, Sears Exclusive, 1967	200	500
Weapons Arsenal, ten pieces, 1966	110	225

Action Boy Costumes

	C8	C10
Aqualad, 1967	300	900
Robin, 1967	300	1200
Superboy, 1967	300	1000

Captain Action Costumes

	C8	C10
Aquaman, 1966	160	600
Aquaman, with flasher ring, 1967	180	950
Batman, 1966	225	700
Batman, with flasher ring, 1967	250	1100
Buck Rogers, with flasher ring, 1967	450	2700
Captain America, 1966	220	900
Captain America, with flasher ring, 1967	225	1200
Flash Gordon, 1966	200	600
Flash Gordon, with flasher ring, 1967	225	800

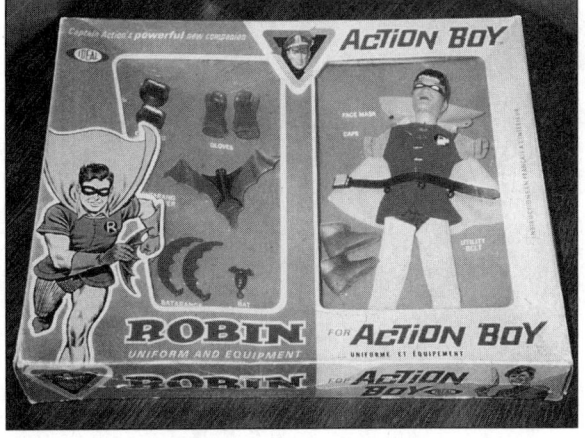

Robin, 1967, Captain Action, Ideal, $1200

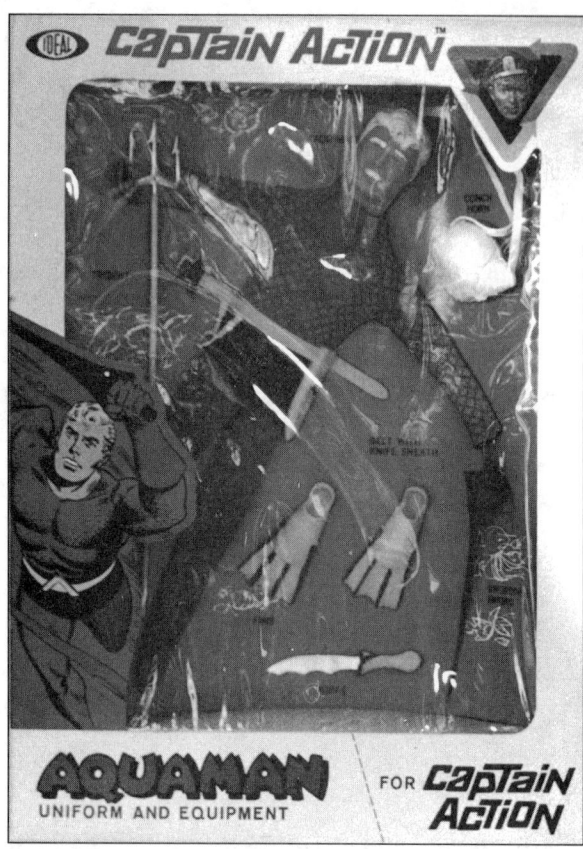

Aquaman, 1966, Captain Action, Ideal, $600

Batman, 1966, Captain Action, Ideal, $700

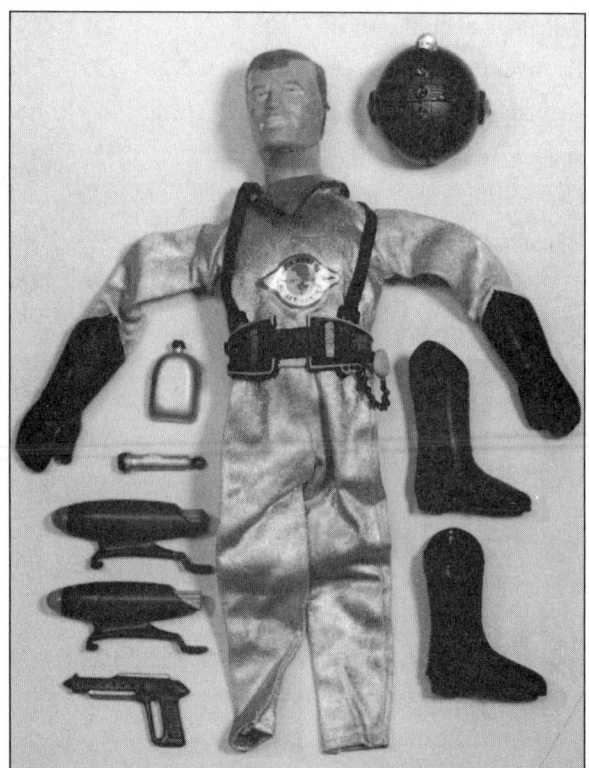

Buck Rogers, with flasher ring, 1967, Captain Action, Ideal, $2700

Green Hornet, with flasher ring, 1967, Captain Action, Ideal, $7500

Captain Action Costumes (Continued)

	C8	C10
Green Hornet, with flasher ring, 1967	2000	7500
Lone Ranger, blue shirt, with flasher ring, 1967	500	1000
Lone Ranger, red shirt, 1966	200	700
Phantom, 1966	200	750
Phantom, with flasher ring, 1967	250	900
Sergeant Fury, 1966	200	800
Spider-Man, with flasher ring, 1967	550	8000
Steve Canyon, 1966	200	700
Steve Canyon, with flasher ring, 1967	225	850
Superman, 1966	200	700
Superman, with flasher ring, 1967	225	1100
Tonto, with flasher ring, 1967	375	1100

Captain Scarlett (Pedigree, 1967)

12" Figure

	C8	C10
Captain Scarlet	150	300

Charlie's Angels (Hasbro, 1977)

8-1/2" Figures

	C8	C10
Jill — Farrah Fawcett	50	100

Phantom, 1966, Captain Action, Ideal, $750

Sabrina—Kate Jackson, Charlie's Angels, Hasbro, $75

8-1/2" Figures (Continued)

	C8	C10
Kelly — Jaclyn Smith	40	75
Kris — Cheryl Ladd	40	75
Sabrina — Kate Jackson	40	75
Sabrina, Kris and Kelly Gift Set	75	200

CHiPs (Mego, 1979)

3-3/4" Figures and Accessories

	C8	C10
Jimmy Squeaks	5	15
Jon	10	20
Launcher with Motorcycle	25	50
Motorcycle, boxed	5	30
Ponch	8	20
Sarge	10	30
Wheels Willie	5	15

8" Figures and Accessories

	C8	C10
Jon	20	50
Motorcycle	30	75

8" Figures and Accessories (Continued)

	C8	C10
Ponch	15	40
Sarge	25	50

Clash of The Titans (Mattel, 1980)

Figures

	C8	C10
Calibos	20	50
Charon	30	75
Kraken	75	250
Pegasus	25	75
Perseus	20	50
Perseus and Pegasus, two-pack	50	105
Thallo	20	50

Comic Action Heroes (Mego, 1975)

3-3/4" Figures

	C8	C10
Aquaman	30	75
Batman	20	75

Batman, Comic Action Heroes, Mego, $75. Photo courtesy Lenny Lee

Captain America, Comic Action Heroes, Mego, $75. Photo courtesy Lenny Lee

3-3/4" Figures (Continued)

	C8	C10
Captain America	20	75
Green Goblin	22	125
Hulk	20	50
Joker	20	75
Penguin	20	75
Robin	20	65
Shazam	20	75
Spider-Man	20	75
Superman	20	65
Wonder Woman	20	65

Accessories

	C8	C10
Collapsing Tower with Invisible Plane & Wonder Woman	100	200
Exploding Bridge with Batmobile	100	200
Fortress of Solitude with Superman	100	200
Mangler	125	300

Penguine, Comic Action Heroes, Mego, $75.

Collapsing Tower with Invisible Plane & Wonder Woman, Comic Action Heroes, Mego, $200. Photo courtesy Lenny Lee

Comic Heroine Posin' Dolls (Ideal, 1967)

12" Boxed Figures	C8	C10
Batgirl, 1967	1000	5500
Mera, 1967	600	4500
Supergirl, 1967	600	4500
Wonder Woman, 1967	600	4500

Robin, Comic Action Heroes, Mego, $65.

Batgirl, Comic Heroine Posin' Dolls (Super Queens), Ideal, $5500

Commander Power (Mego, 1975)

Figure with Vehicle	C8	C10
Commander Power with Lightning Cycle........	20	40

Die-Cast Super Heroes (Mego, 1979)

6" Figures	C8	C10
Batman	30	125
Hulk...	25	75
Spider-Man..	30	125
Superman...	30	95

Doctor Who (Denys Fisher, 1976)

Figures	C8	C10
Cyberman	200	400
Dalek	150	325
Doctor Who (4th)	100	225
Giant Robot	165	375
K-9...	150	300
Leela	200	400

Doctor Who (4th), Doctor Who, Denys Fisher, $225. Photo courtesy Corey LeChat

Vehicles	C8	C10
Tardis..	150	300

Doctor Who (Palitoy, 1976)

Figures	C8	C10
Dalek, Talking..	250	475
K-9, Talking	150	300

Emergency (LJN, 1973)

Figures	C8	C10
John	35	100
Roy	35	100

Vehicles	C8	C10
Rescue Truck...	35	100

Evel Knievel (Ideal, 1973-74)

Figures	C8	C10
Evel Knievel, blue suit	20	50
Evel Knievel, red suit	20	50
Evel Knievel, white suit	20	50
Robby Knievel...	25	60

Cyberman, Doctor Who, Denys Fisher, $400. Photo courtesy Corey LeChat

Giant Robot, Doctor Who, Denys Fisher, $375. Photo courtesy Corey LeChat

Leela, Doctor Who, Denys Fisher, $400. Photo courtesy Corey LeChat

Tardis, Doctor Who, Denys Fisher, $300. Photo courtesy Corey LeChat

K-9, Doctor Who, Denys Fisher, $300. Photo courtesy Corey LeChat

Dalek, Talking, Doctor Who, Palitoy, $475. Photo courtesy Corey LeChat

K-9, Talking, Doctor Who, Palitoy, $300. Photo courtesy Corey LeChat

Vehicles and Accessories	C8	C10
Arctic Explorer set	35	75
Chopper	35	75
Evel Knievel Canyon Stunt Cycle	40	80
Evel Knievel Dragster	50	110
Evel Knievel Stunt and Crash Car	45	100
Evel Knievel Stunt Cycle	35	75
Explorer Set	20	40
Racing Set	20	40
Rescue Set	20	40
Road and Trail Set	50	125
Scramble Van	30	75
Skull Canyon Play Set	50	125
Stunt Stadium	40	100
Tail Bike	35	60

Flash Gordon (Mego, 1976)

9" Figures	C8	C10
Dale Arden	35	85
Dr. Zarkow	55	110
Flash Gordon	55	110
Ming	30	85

Play Sets	C8	C10
Flash Gordon Play Set	55	125

G.I. Joe (Hasbro, 1960-70s)

Action Girl Series Figure Sets	C6	C8	C10
G.I. Nurse, No. 8060, Red Cross hat and arm band, white dress, stockings, shoes, crutches, medic bag, stethoscope, plasma bottle, bandages and splints, 1967	1750	2000	4000

G.I. Nurse, G.I. Joe, Action Girl Series, $4000

Action Marine Series

Figure Sets

	C6	C8	C10
Action Marine, No. 7700, fatigues, green cap, boots, dog tags, insignias and manual, 1964	125	145	375
Marine Medic Series, No. 90711, Red Cross helmet, flag and arm bands, crutch, bandages, splints, first aid pouch, stethoscope, plasma bottle, stretcher, medic bag, belt w/ammo pouches, 1967	325	425	3250
Talking Action Marine, No. 7790, 1967	175	200	850
Talking Adventure Pack and Tent Set, No. 90711, 1968	275	325	3250
Talking Adventure Pack with Field Pack Equipment, No. 90712, 1968	275	325	3250

Uniform/Equipment Sets

	C6	C8	C10
Beachhead Assault Field Pack Set, No. 7713, M-1 rifle, bayonet, entrenching shovel and cover, canteen w/cover, belt, mess kit w/cover, field pack, flamethrower, first aid pouch, tent, pegs and poles, tent camo and camo, 1964	100	175	325
Beachhead Assault Tent Set, No. 7711, tent, flamethrower, pistol belt, first-aid pouch, mess kit w/utensils and manual, 1964	100	200	475
Beachhead Fatigue Pants, No. 7715, 1964	15	30	200
Beachhead Fatigue Shirt, No. 7714, 1964	20	30	225

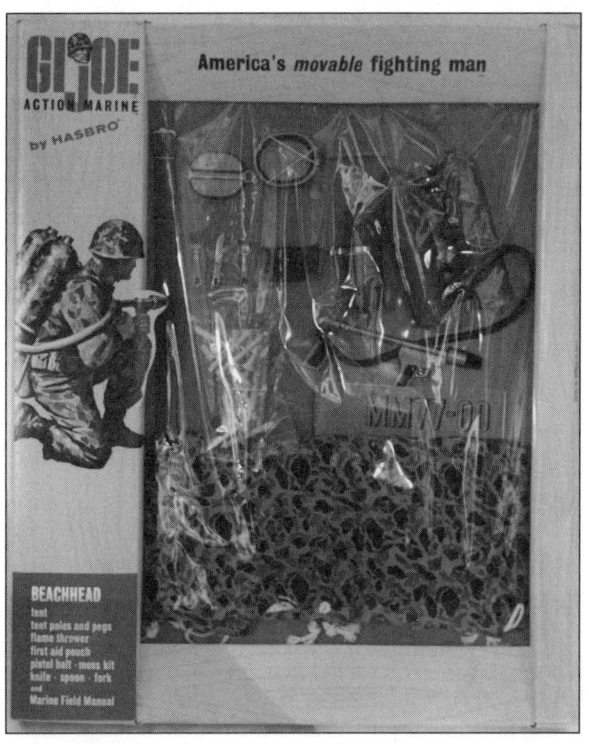

Beachhead Assault Tent Set, G.I. Joe, Action Marine Series, $475

Action Marine Series (Continued)

	C6	C8	C10
Beachhead Field Pack, No. 7712, cartridge belt, rifle, grenades, field pack, entrenching tool, canteen and manual, 1964	40	65	150
Beachhead Flamethrower Set, No. 7718, reissue, 1967	15	30	225
Beachhead Flamethrower Set, No. 7718, 1964	15	30	125

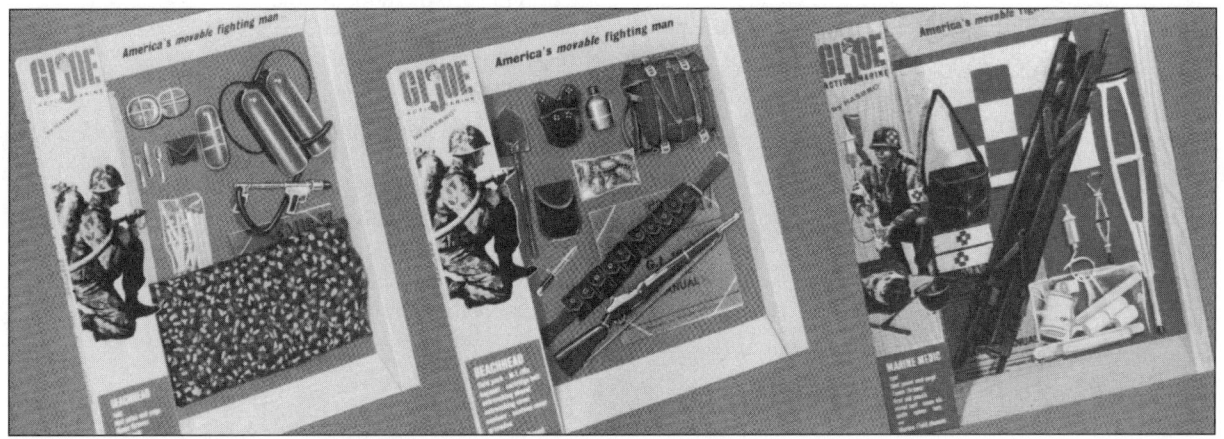

Left to Right: Beachhead Assault Tent Set, G.I. Joe, Action Marine Series, $475; Beachhead Field Pack, G.I. Joe, Action Marine Series, $150; Marine Medic Set with stretcher, G.I. Joe, Action Marine Series, $850. Photo courtesy Hasbro's 1965 Catalog

Action Marine Series (Continued)

	C6	C8	C10
Beachhead Mess Kit Set, No. 7716, 1964	25	40	275
Beachhead Rifle Set, No. 7717, reissue, 1967	30	50	225
Beachhead Rifle Set, No. 7717, bayonet, cartridge belt, hand grenades and M-1 rifle, 1964	30	50	150
Communications Field Radio/Telephone Set, No. 7703, reissue, 1967	35	60	275
Communications Field Set, No. 7703, 1964	35	50	175
Communications Flag Set, No. 7704, flags for Army, Navy, Air Corps, Marines and United States, 1964	200	250	475
Communications Poncho, No. 7702, 1964	35	50	250
Communications Post and Poncho Set, No. 7701, field radio and telephone, wire roll, carbine, binoculars, map, case, manual, poncho, 1964	125	175	475
Dress Parade Set, No. 7710, Marine jacket, trousers, pistol belt, shoes, hat, M-1 rifle and manual, 1964	125	225	450
Dress Parade Set, No. 7710, reissue, 1968	125	225	750
Jungle Fighter Set, No. 7732, reissue, 1968	450	700	2750
Jungle Fighter Set, No. 7732, bush hat, jacket w/emblems, pants, flamethrower, field telephone, knife and sheath, pistol belt, pistol, holster, canteen w/cover and knuckle knife, 1967	450	700	3500
Marine Automatic M-60 Machine Gun Set, No. 7726, 1967	35	75	325
Marine Basics Set, No. 7722, 1966	55	85	275
Marine Bunk Bed Set, No. 7723, reissue, 1967	55	80	475
Marine Bunk Bed Set, No. 7723, 1966	55	80	375
Marine Demolition Set, No. 7730, reissue, 1968	50	100	450
Marine Demolition Set, No. 7730, mine detector and harness, land mine, 1966	50	100	350
Marine First Aid Set, No. 7721, reissue, 1967	45	85	225

Action Marine Series (Continued)

	C6	C8	C10
Marine First Aid Set, No. 7721, first-aid pouch, arm band and helmet, 1964	45	85	125
Marine Medic Set, No. 7720, w/crutch, etc., 1965	25	40	125
Marine Medic Set, No. 7720, reissue, 1967	25	40	225
Marine Medic Set with stretcher, No. 7719, first-aid shoulder pouch, stretcher, bandages, arm bands, plasma bottle, stethoscope, Red Cross flag, and manual, 1964	175	300	850
Marine Mortar Set, No. 7725, 1967	60	80	350
Marine Weapons Rack Set, No. 7727, 1967	75	145	625
Paratrooper Camouflage Set, No. 7708, netting and foliage, 1964	20	35	65
Paratrooper Helmet Set, No. 7707, 1964	20	40	85
Paratrooper Parachute Pack, No. 7709, 1964	30	80	125
Paratrooper Small Arms Set, No. 7706, reissue, 1967	30	75	225
Tank Commander Set, No. 7731, includes faux leather jacket, helmet and visor, insignia, radio w/tripod, machine gun, ammo box, 1967	325	500	1750
Tank Commander Set, No. 7731, reissue, 1968	325	500	1525

Action Pilot Series

Figure Sets

	C6	C8	C10
Action Pilot, No. 7800, orange jumpsuit, blue cap, black boots, dog tags, insignias, manual, catalog and club application, 1964	130	165	600
Talking Action Pilot, No. 7890, 1967	190	245	1500

Uniform/Equipment Sets

	C6	C8	C10
Air Academy Cadet Set, No. 7822, deluxe set w/figure, dress jacket, shoes, and pants, garrison cap, saber and scabbard, white M-1 rifle, chest sash and belt sash, 1967	225	450	1250
Air Academy Cadet Set, No. 7822, reissue, 1968	225	450	1150
Air Force Basics Set, No. 7814, 1966	30	55	200
Air Force Basics Set, No. 7814, reissue, 1967	30	55	275

Action Pilot Series (Continued)

	C6	C8	C10
Air Force Mae West Air Vest & Equipment Set, No. 7816, 1967	85	125	325
Air Force Police Set, No. 7813, reissue, 1967	70	150	325
Air Force Police Set, No. 7813, 1965	70	150	250
Air Force Security Set, No. 7815, Air Security radio and helmet, cartridge belt, pistol and holster, 1967	275	350	590
Air/Sea Rescue Set, No. 7825, includes black air tanks, rescue ring, buoy, depth gauge, face mask, fins, orange scuba outfit, 1967	325	550	2500
Air/Sea Rescue Set, No. 7825, reissue, 1968	325	550	2500
Astronaut Set, No. 7824, helmet w/visor, foil space suit, booties, gloves, space camera, propellant gun, tether cord, oxygen chest pack, silver boots, white jumpsuit and cloth cap, 1967	100	200	3000
Astronaut Set, No. 7824, reissue, 1968	100	200	1250
Communications Set, No. 7812, 1964	55	100	225
Crash Crew Set, No. 7820, fire proof jacket, hood, pants and gloves, silver boots, belt, flashlight, axe, pliers, fire extinguisher, stretcher, strap cutter, 1966	125	250	450
Dress Uniform Jacket Set, No. 7804, 1964	40	65	250
Dress Uniform Pants, No. 7805, 1964	20	35	200
Dress Uniform Set, No. 7803, Air Force jacket, trousers, shirt, tie, cap and manual, 1964	225	450	3000
Dress Uniform Shirt & Equipment Set, No. 7806, 1964	25	40	200
Fighter Pilot Set, No. 7823, reissue, 1968	400	650	2650
Fighter Pilot Set, No. 7823, working parachute and pack, gold helmet, Mae West vest, green pants, flash light, orange jump suit, black boots, 1967	400	650	2500
Scramble Communications Set, No. 7812, poncho, field telephone and radio, map w/case, binoculars and wire roll, 1965	35	75	175
Scramble Communications Set, No. 7812, reissue, 1967	35	75	250

Action Pilot Series (Continued)

	C6	C8	C10
Scramble Crash Helmet, No. 7810, helmet, face mask, hose, tinted visor, 1964	65	90	125
Scramble Crash Helmet, No. 7810, reissue, 1967	65	90	225
Scramble Flight Suit, No. 7808, gray flight suit, 1964	50	300	225
Scramble Flight Suit, No. 7808, 1967	50	75	400
Scramble Parachute Set, No. 7811, 1964	20	40	150
Scramble Parachute Set, No. 7809, reissue, 1967	20	40	250
Scramble Set, No. 7807, deluxe set, gray flight suit, orange air vest, white crash helmet, pistol belt w/.45 pistol, holster, clipboard, flare gun and parachute w/insert, 1964	125	225	950
Survival Life Raft Set, No. 7802, raft w/oar and sea anchor, 1964	45	90	325
Survival Life Raft Set, No. 7801, raft w/oar, flare gun, knife, air vest, first-aid kit, sea anchor and manual, 1964	75	125	550

Vehicle Sets

	C6	C8	C10
Crash Crew Fire Truck Set, No. 8040, 1967	950	1700	3500
Official Space Capsule Set, No. 8020, space capsule, record, space suit, cloth space boots, space gloves, helmet w/visor, 1966	175	225	350
Official Space Capsule Set with flotation, No. 5979, Sears exclusive w/collar, life raft and oars, 1966	200	325	700

Action Sailor Series

Figure Sets

	C6	C8	C10
Action Sailor, No. 7600, white cap, denim shirt and pants, boots, dog tags, navy manual and insignias, 1964	125	225	350
Navy Scuba Set, No. 7643-83, Adventure Pack, 1968	300	450	3250
Talking Action Sailor, No. 7690, 1967	200	330	1250
Talking Landing Signal Officer Set, No. 90621, Talking Adventure Pack, 1968	325	350	3500
Talking Shore Patrol Set, No. 90612, Talking Adventure Pack, 1968	200	450	3500

Annapolis Cadet, G.I. Joe, Action Sailor Series, $1350

Action Sailor Series (Continued)

Uniform/Equipment Sets

	C6	C8	C10
Annapolis Cadet, No. 7624, reissue, 1968	275	375	1350
Annapolis Cadet, No. 7624, garrison cap, dress jacket, pants, shoes, sword, scabbard, belt and white M-1 rifle, 1967	275	375	1350
Breeches Buoy, No. 7625, reissue, 1968	325	425	1450
Breeches Buoy, No. 7625, yellow jacket and pants, chair and pulley, flare gun, blinker light, 1967	325	425	1500
Deep Freeze, No. 7623, white boots, fur parka, pants, snow shoes, ice axe, snow sled w/rope and flare gun, 1967	250	375	1600
Deep Freeze, No. 7623, reissue, 1968	250	375	1500
Deep Sea Diver Set, No. 7620, reissue, 1968	325	425	2000
Deep Sea Diver Set, No. 7620, underwater uniform, helmet, upper and lower plate, sledge hammer, buoy w/rope, gloves, compass, hoses, lead boots and weight belt, 1965	325	425	2000

Action Sailor Series (Continued)

	C6	C8	C10
Frogman Scuba Bottoms, No. 7604, 1964	20	35	100
Frogman Scuba Tank Set, No. 7606, 1964	25	40	100
Frogman Scuba Top Set, No. 7603, 1964	25	45	125
Frogman Underwater Demolition Set, No. 7602, headpiece, face mask, swim fins, rubber suit, scuba tank, depth gauge, knife, dynamite and manual, 1964	175	250	1500
Landing Signal Officer, No. 7621, jumpsuit, signal paddles, goggles, cloth head gear, headphones, clipboard (complete), binoculars and flare gun., 1966	225	350	575
Navy Attack Helmet Set, No. 7610, shirt and pants, boots, yellow life vest, blue helmet, flare gun binoculars, signal flags, 1964	35	75	150
Navy Attack Life Jacket, No. 7611, 1964	20	45	120
Navy Attack Set, No. 7607, life jacket, field glasses, blinker light, signal flags, manual, 1964	60	125	425
Navy Attack Work Pants Set, No. 7609, 1964	25	40	150
Navy Attack Work Shirt Set, No. 7608, 1964	25	40	175
Navy Basics Set, No. 7628, 1966	25	55	125
Navy Dress Parade Rifle Set, No. 7619, 1965	35	65	125
Navy Dress Parade Set, No. 7619, billy club, cartridge belt, bayonet and white dress rifle, 1964	45	80	175
Navy L.S.O. Equipment Set, No. 7626, helmet, headphones, signal paddles, flare gun, 1966	40	80	150
Navy Life Ring Set, No. 7627, U.S.N. life ring, helmet sticker, 1966	25	45	150
Navy Machine Gun Set, No. 7618, MG and ammo box, 1965	40	80	175
Sea Rescue Set, No. 7622, reissued w/life preserver, 1966	95	135	500
Sea Rescue Set, No. 7601, life raft, oar, anchor, flare gun, first-aid kit, knife, scabbard, manual, 1964	95	135	500

Official Sea Sled and Frogman Set, G.I. Joe, Action Sailor Series, $550

Action Sailor Series (Continued)

	C6	C8	C10
Shore Patrol, No. 7612, reissued w/radio and helmet and shoes, 1967	1000	2000	3500
Shore Patrol, No. 7612, dress shirt, tie and pants, helmet, white belt, .45 and holster, billy club, boots, arm band, sea bag, 1964	500	1000	2000
Shore Patrol Dress Jumper Set, No. 7613, 1964	75	125	225
Shore Patrol Dress Pant Set, No. 7614, 1964	40	75	175
Shore Patrol Helmet and Small Arms Set, No. 7616, white belt, billy stick, white helmet, .45 pistol, 1964	40	75	150
Shore Patrol Sea Bag Set, No. 7615, 1964	25	50	125

Vehicle Sets

	C6	C8	C10
Official Sea Sled and Frogman Set, No. 8050, without cave, 1966	150	300	550
Official Sea Sled and Frogman Set, No. 5979, Sears, w/figure and underwater cave, orange scuba suit, fins, mask, tanks, sea sled in orange and black, 1966	175	325	650

Action Soldier, G.I. Joe, Action Soldier Series, $350

Black Action Soldier, G.I. Joe, Action Soldier Series, $2500

Action Soldier Series

Figure Sets

	C6	C8	C10
Action Soldier, No. 7500, fatigue cap, shirt, pants, boots, dog tags, army manual and insignias, helmet, belt w/pouches, M-1 rifle, 1964	100	175	350
Black Action Soldier, No. 7900, 1965	450	800	2500
Canadian Mountie Set, No. 5904, Sears exclusive, 1967	850	1500	4000
Desert Patrol Attack Jeep Set, No. 8030, Desert Fighter figure, jeep w/steering wheel, spare tire, tan tripod, gun and gun mount and ring, black antenna, tan jacket and shorts, socks, goggles, 1967	400	1250	2000
Forward Observer Set, No. 5969, Sears exclusive, 1966	200	375	750
Green Beret, No. 7536, field radio, bazooka rocket, bazooka, green beret, jacket, pants, M-16 rifle, grenades, camo scarf, belt pistol and holster, 1966	275	400	3000

Talking Adventure Pack, Command Post Equipt., G.I. Joe, Action Soldier Series, $3000

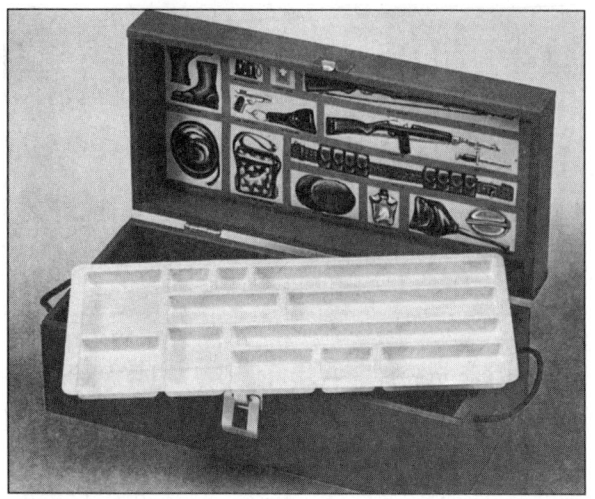

Basic Footlocker, G.I. Joe, Action Soldier Series, $125. Photo courtesy Hasbro's 1965 Catalog

Action Soldier Series (Continued)

	C6	C8	C10
Machine Gun Emplacement Set, No. 7531, Sears exclusive, 1965	150	275	1250
Talking Action Soldier, No. 7590, 1967	85	135	825
Talking Adventure Pack, Bivouac Equipment, No. 90513, 1968	275	325	3000
Talking Adventure Pack, Command Post Equipt., No. 90517, 1968	275	375	3000
Talking Adventure Pack, Mountain Troop Series, No. 7557-83, 1968	375	650	3500
Talking Adventure Pack, Special Forces Equip., No. 90532, 1968	275	500	3500

Uniform/Equipment Sets

	C6	C8	C10
Adventure Pack with fourteen pieces, No. 8008.83, Adventure Pack Footlocker, 1968	75	125	600

Action Soldier Series (Continued)

	C6	C8	C10
Adventure Pack with sixteen items, No. 8007.83, Adventure Pack Footlocker, 1968	75	125	600
Adventure Pack with twelve items, No. 8006.83, Adventure Pack Footlocker, 1968	75	125	600
Adventure Pack with twelve items, No. 8005.83, Adventure Pack Footlocker, 1968	75	125	600
Adventure Pack, Army Bivouac Series, No. 7549-83, 1968	225	450	3500
Air Police Equipment, No. 7813, gray field phone, carbine, white helmet and bayonet, 1964	40	95	200
Basic Footlocker, No. 8000, wood tray w/cardboard wrapper, 1964	35	75	125

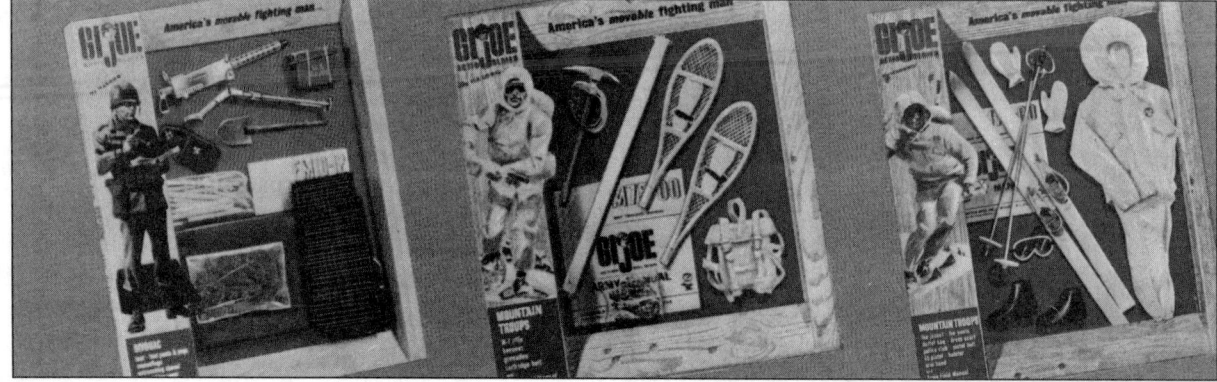

Left to Right: Bivouac Deluxe Pup Tent Set, G.I. Joe, Action Soldier Series, $450; Mountain Troops Set, G.I. Joe, Action Soldier Series, $350; Ski Patrol Deluxe Set, G.I. Joe, Action Soldier Series, $1250. Photo courtesy Hasbro's 1965 Catalog

Left to Right: Combat Field Jacket Set, G.I. Joe, Action Soldier Series, $525; Combat Field Pack Deluxe Set, G.I. Joe, Action Soldier Series, $325; Bivouac Sleeping Bag Set, G.I. Joe, Action Soldier Series, $150. Photo courtesy Hasbro's 1965 Catalog

Action Soldier Series (Continued)

	C6	C8	C10
Bivouac Deluxe Pup Tent Set, No. 7513, M-1 rifle and bayonet, shovel and cover, canteen and cover, mess kit, cartridge belt, machine gun, tent, pegs, poles, camoflage, sleeping bag, netting, ammo box, 1964	115	225	450
Bivouac Machine Gun Set, No. 7514, reissue, 1967	25	40	225

Combat Camouflaged Netting Set, G.I. Joe, Action Soldier Series, $85

Action Soldier Series (Continued)

	C6	C8	C10
Bivouac Machine Gun Set, No. 7514, machine gun set and ammo box, 1964	25	40	125
Bivouac Sleeping Bag, No. 7515, zippered bag, 1964	20	30	125
Bivouac Sleeping Bag Set, No. 7512, mess kit, canteen, bayonet, cartridge belt, M-1 rifle, manual, 1964	25	30	150
Combat Camouflaged Netting Set, No. 7511, foliage and posts, 1964	25	40	85
Combat Construction Set, No. 7572, orange safety helmet, work gloves, jack hammer, 1967	325	400	575
Combat Demolition Set, No. 7573, 1967	65	100	525
Combat Engineer Set, No. 7571, pick, shovel, detonator, dynamite, tripod and transit w/grease gun, 1967	125	175	625
Combat Fatigue Pants Set, No. 7504, 1964	15	25	110
Combat Fatigue Shirt Set, No. 7503, 1964	20	30	125
Combat Field Jacket, No. 7505, 1964	45	65	325
Combat Field Jacket Set, No. 7501, jacket, bayonet, cartridge belt, hand grenades, M-1 rifle and manual, 1964	65	100	525
Combat Field Pack & Entrenching Tool, No. 7506, 1964	25	45	125
Combat Field Pack Deluxe Set, No. 7502, field jacket, pack, entrenching shovel w/cover, mess kit, first-aid pouch, canteen w/cover, 1964	75	125	325

Combat Rifle Set, G.I. Joe, Action Soldier Series, $325

Command Post Field Radio and Telephone Set, G.I. Joe, Action Soldier Series, $135

Action Soldier Series (Continued)

	C6	C8	C10
Combat Helmet Set, No. 7507, w/netting and foliage leaves, 1964 20		35	75
Combat Mess Kit, No. 7509, plate, fork, knife, spoon, canteen, etc., 1964 20		45	85
Combat Rifle Set, No. 7510, bayonet, M-1 rifle, belt and grenades, 1967 55		100	325
Combat Sandbags Set, No. 7508, three bags per set, 1964 10		40	85
Command Post Field Radio and Telephone Set, No. 7520, reissue, 1967 35		70	400
Command Post Field Radio and Telephone Set, No. 7520, field radio, telephone w/wire roll and map, 1964 35		70	135
Command Post Poncho, No. 7519, on card, 1964 30		45	225
Command Post Poncho Set, No. 7517, poncho, field radio and telephone, wire roll, pistol, belt and holster, map and case and manual, 1964 85		125	400
Command Post Small Arms Set, No. 7518, holster and .45 pistol, belt, grenades, 1964 30		60	100

Action Soldier Series (Continued)

	C6	C8	C10
Dress Parade Adventure Pack, No. 8009.83, Adventure Pack w/thirty-seven pieces, 1968 750		1250	3500
Green Beret and Small Arms Set, No. 7533, reissue, 1967 85		100	425
Green Beret and Small Arms Set, No. 7533, 1966 85		110	300
Green Beret Machine Gun Outpost Set, No. 5978, Sears exclusive w/two figures and equipment, 1966 .. 225		450	1500
Heavy Weapons Set, No. 7538, reissue, 1968 175		325	1500
Heavy Weapons Set, No. 7538, mortar launcher and shells, M-60 machine gun, grenades, flak jacket, shirt and pants, 1967 175		325	1750
Military Police Duffle Bag Set, No. 7523, 1964 25		40	85
Military Police Helmet and Small Arms Set, No. 7526, 1964 35		75	125
Military Police Helmet and Small Arms Set, No. 7526, reissue, 1967 35		75	250
Military Police Ike Jacket, No. 7524, jacket w/red scarf and arm band, 1964 ... 40		60	125

Military Police Ike Pants, G.I. Joe, Action Soldier Series, $100

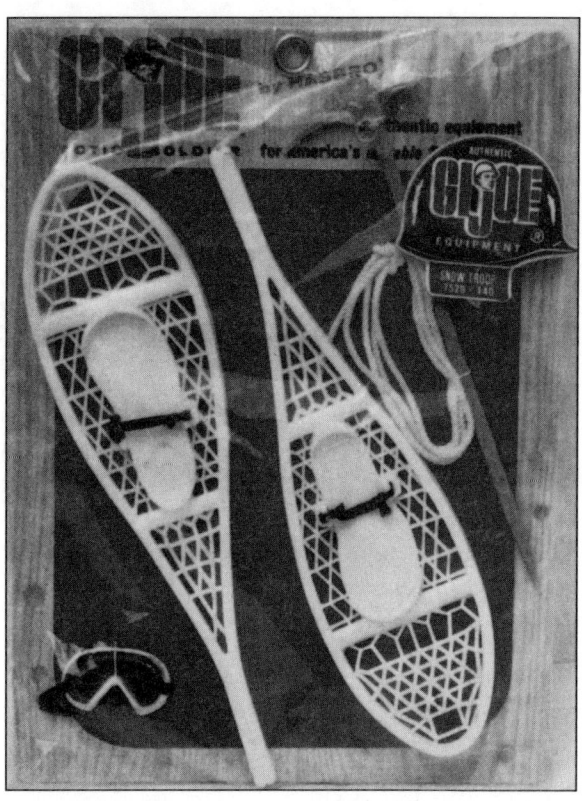

Snow Troop Set, G.I. Joe, Action Soldier Series, $150

Action Soldier Series (Continued)

	C6	C8	C10
Military Police Ike Pants, No. 7525, matches Ike jacket, 1964	20	30	100
Military Police Uniform Set, No. 7539, reissue, 1968	450	900	3000
Military Police Uniform Set, No. 7521, includes Ike jacket and pants, scarf, boots, helmet, belt w/ammo pouches, .45 pistol and holster, billy club, armband, duffle bag, 1964	450	1650	3000
Military Police Uniform Set, No. 7539, includes green or tan uniform, black and gold MP Helmet, billy club, belt, pistol and holster, MP armband and red tunic, 1967	450	1650	3500
Mountain Troops Set, No. 7530, snow shoes, ice axe, ropes, grenades, camoflage pack, web belt, manual, 1964	90	175	350
Sabotage Set, No. 7516, reissued in photo box, 1968	125	250	1700
Sabotage Set, No. 7516, dingy and oar, blinker light, detonator w/strap, TNT, wool stocking cap, gas mask, binoculars, green radio and .45 pistol and holster, 1967	125	250	2000

Action Soldier Series (Continued)

	C6	C8	C10
Ski Patrol Deluxe Set, No. 7531, White parka, boots, goggles, mittens, skis, poles and manual, 1964	170	350	1250
Ski Patrol Helmet and Small Arms Set, No. 7527, reissue, 1967	75	125	250
Ski Patrol Helmet and Small Arms Set, No. 7527, 1965	35	75	135
Snow Troop Set, No. 7529, reissue, 1967	20	45	225
Snow Troop Set, No. 7529, snow shoes, goggles and ice pick, 1966	20	45	150
Special Forces Bazooka Set, No. 7528, 1966	35	45	225
Special Forces Bazooka Set, No. 7528, reissue, 1967	35	45	325
Special Forces Uniform Set, No. 7532, 1966	200	375	1000
West Point Cadet Uniform Set, No. 7537, dress jacket, pants, shoes, chest and belt sash, parade hat w/plume, saber, scabbard and white M-1 rifle, 1967	250	475	1500
West Point Cadet Uniform Set, No. 7537, reissue, 1968	250	375	1200

Action Soldier Series (Continued)

	C6	C8	C10

Vehicle Sets

	C6	C8	C10
Amphibious Duck, No. 5693, Irwin, 26" long, 1967	175	375	700
Armored Car, No. 5397, Irwin, friction powered, 20" long, 1967	150	300	500
Helicopter, No. 5395, Irwin, friction powered, 28" long, 1967	150	300	500
Jet Fighter Plane, No. 5396, Irwin, friction powered, 30" long, 1967	225	475	800
Military Staff Car, No. 5652, Irwin, friction powered, 24" long, 1967	200	400	750
Motorcycle and Sidecar, No. 5651, Irwin, 14" long, khaki, w/decals, 1967	75	150	325
Official Combat Jeep Set, No. 7000, trailer, steering wheel, spare tire, windshield, cannon, search light, shell, flag, guard rails, tripod, tailgate and hood, without Moto-Rev Sound, 1965	200	375	550
Official Jeep Combat Set, No. 7000, w/Moto-Rev sound, 1965	225	400	650
Personnel Carrier/Mine Sweeper, No. 5694, Irwin, 26" long, 1967	300	350	700

Action Soldiers of the World

	C6	C8	C10

Figure Sets

	C6	C8	C10
Australian Jungle Fighter, No. 8205, standard set w/action figure uniform, no equipment, 1966	150	275	1200
Australian Jungle Fighter, No. 8105, action figure w/jacket, shorts, socks, boots, bush hat, belt, "Victoria Cross" medal, knuckle knife, flamethrower, entrenching tool, bush knife and sheath, 1966	250	400	2500
British Commando, No. 8104, deluxe set w/action figure, helmet, night raid green jacket, pants, boots, canteen and cover, gas mask and cover, belt, Sten sub machine gun, gun clip and "Victoria Cross" medal, 1966	300	425	2500
British Commando, No. 8204, standard set w/no equipment, 1966	150	275	1750
Foreign Soldiers of the World, No. 8111-83, Talking Adventure Pack, 1968	750	825	5000

Action Soldiers of the World (Continued)

	C6	C8	C10
French Resistance Fighter, No. 8103, deluxe set w/figure, beret, short black boots, black sweater, denim pants, "Croix de Guerre" medal, knife, shoulder holster, pistol, radio, sub machine gun and grenades, 1966	200	250	2250
French Resistance Fighter, No. 8203, Standard set w/action figure and equipment, 1966	125	225	1250
German Storm Trooper, No. 8100, deluxe set w/figure, helmet, jacket, pants, boots, Luger pistol, holster, cartridge belt, cartridges, "Iron Cross" medal, stick grenades, 9MM Schmeisser, field pack, 1966	275	425	2500
German Storm Trooper, No. 8200, Standard set w/no equipment, 1966	275	325	1300
Japanese Imperial Soldier, No. 8101, deluxe set w/figure, Arisaka rifle, belt, cartridges, field pack, Nambu pistol, holster, bayonet, "Order of the Kite" medal, helmet, jacket, pants, short brown boots, 1966	425	675	2700
Japanese Imperial Soldier, No. 8201, Standard set w/equipment, 1966	300	325	1425
Russian Infantry Man, No. 8102, deluxe set w/action figure, fur cap, tunic, pants, boots, ammo box, ammo rounds, anti-tank grenades, belt, bipod, DP light machine gun, "Order of Lenin" medal, field glasses and case, 1966	275	400	2250
Russian Infantry Man, No. 8202, dtandard set w/no equipment, 1966	315	400	1250
Uniforms of Six Nations, No. 5038, 1967	750	950	2500

Uniform/Equipment Sets

	C6	C8	C10
Australian Jungle Fighter Set, No. 8305, 1966	25	50	250
British Commando Set, No. 8304, Sten submachine gun, gas mask and carrier, canteen and cover, cartridge belt, rifle, "Victoria Cross" medal, manual, 1966	125	200	325
French Resistance Fighter Set, No. 8303, shoulder holster, Lebel pistol, knife, grenades, radio, 7.65 submachine gun, "Croix de Guerra" medal, counter-intelligence manual, 1966	25	50	275

Action Soldiers of the World (Continued)

	C6	C8	C10
German Storm Trooper, No. 8300, 1966	125	175	325
Japanese Imperial Soldier Set, No. 8301, field pack, Nambu pistol and holster, Arisaka rifle w/bayonet, cartridge belt, "Order of the Kite" medal, counter-intelligence manual, 1966	175	275	625
Russian Infantry Man Set, No. 8302, DP light machine gun, bipod, field glasses and case, anti-tank grenades, ammo box, "Order of Lenin" medal, counter-intelligence medal, 1966	175	220	325

Adventure Team

Figure Sets

	C6	C8	C10
Air Adventurer, No. 7403, includes figure w/Kung Fu grip, orange flight suit, boots, insignia, dog tags, rifle, boots, warranty, club insert, 1970	120	375	300
Air Adventurer, No. 7282, w/Kung Fu grip, 1974	95	125	325
Air Adventurer, No. 7282, life-like body figure, uniform and equipment, 1976	75	100	200
Black Adventurer, No. 7404, includes figure, shirt w/insignia, pants, boots, dog tags, shoulder holster w/pistol, 1970	125	150	375
Black Adventurer, No. 7283, w/life-like body and Kung Fu grip, 1976	85	125	225
Bulletman, No. 8026, 1976	50	75	150
Eagle Eye Black Commando, No. 7278, 1976	85	125	250
Eagle Eye Land Commander, No. 7276, 1976	65	80	150
Eagle Eye Man of Action, No. 7277, 1976	65	80	165
Intruder Commander, No. 8050, 1976	50	75	150
Intruder Warrior, No. 8051, 1976	50	75	175
Land Adventurer, No. 7401, includes figure, camo shirt and pants, boots, insignia, shoulder holster and pistol, dog tags and team inserts, 1970	45	75	200
Land Adventurer, No. 7280, w/life-like body and Kung Fu grip and uniform set, 1974	50	65	225

Adventure Team (Continued)

	C6	C8	C10
Land Adventurer, No. 7280, 1976	35	50	150
Land Adventurer, No. 7270, 1976	20	50	180
Man of Action, No. 7284, figure w/life-like body and Kung Fu grip, 1974	45	75	200
Man of Action, No. 7500, includes figure, shirt and pants, boots, insignia, dog tags, team inserts, 1970	50	75	225
Man of Action, No. 7274, 1976	25	45	175
Mike Powers/Atomic Man, No. 8025, figure w/"atomic" flashing eye, arm that spins hand-held helicopter, 1975	20	45	150
Sea Adventurer, No. 7281, 1976	55	85	200
Sea Adventurer, No. 7281, w/life-like body and Kung Fu grip and uniform w/equipment, 1974	55	75	225
Sea Adventurer, No. 7271, 1976	40	75	250
Sea Adventurer, No. 7402, includes figure, shirt, dungarees, insignia, boots, shoulder holster and pistol, 1970	45	70	245
Secret Mountain Outpost, No. 8040, 1975	50	85	150
Talking Adventure Team Black Commander, No. 7406, 1973	150	225	600
Talking Adventure Team Black Commander, No. 7291, w/Kung Fu grip, 1974	85	350	750
Talking Adventure Team Commander, No. 7400, includes figure, two-pocket green shirt, pants, boots, insignia, instructions, dog tag, shoulder holster and pistol, 1970	65	125	400
Talking Adventure Team Commander, No. 7290, w/Kung Fu grip, 1974	75	200	500
Talking Astronaut, No. 7590, 1970	90	175	650
Talking Black Commander, No. 7291, 1976	125	300	600
Talking Commander, No. 7290, 1976	75	115	500
Talking Man of Action, No. 7590, shirt, pants, boots, dog tags, rifle, insignia, instructions, 1970	75	125	350
Talking Man of Action, No. 7292, 1976	75	120	525

Adventure Team (Continued)

	C6	C8	C10
Talking Man of Action, No. 7292, w/life-like body and Kung Fu grip, 1974	75	200	650

Uniform/Equipment Sets

	C6	C8	C10
Adventure Team Headquarters Set, No. 7490, Adventure Team playset, 1972	50	125	200
Adventure Team Training Center Set, No. 7495, rifle rack, logs, barrel, barber wire, rope ladder, three tires, two targets, escape slide, tent and poles, first aid kit, respirator and mask, snake, instructions, 1973	75	125	225
Aerial Reconnaissance Set, No. 7345, jumpsuit, helmet, aerial recon vehicle w/built-in camera, 1971	75	125	225
Attack at Vulture Falls, No. 7420, super deluxe set, 1975	75	150	275
Black Widow Rendezvous, No. 7414, super deluxe set, 1975	125	200	350
Buried Bounty, No. 7328-5, deluxe set, 1975	10	25	85
Capture of the Pygmy Gorilla Set, No. 7437, 1970	100	175	325
Challenge of Savage River, No. 8032, deluxe set, 1975	100	175	350
Chest Winch Set, No. 7313, 1972	10	15	40
Chest Winch Set, No. 7313, reissue, 1974	10	15	75

Danger of the Depths Set, G.I. Joe, Adventure Team, $325

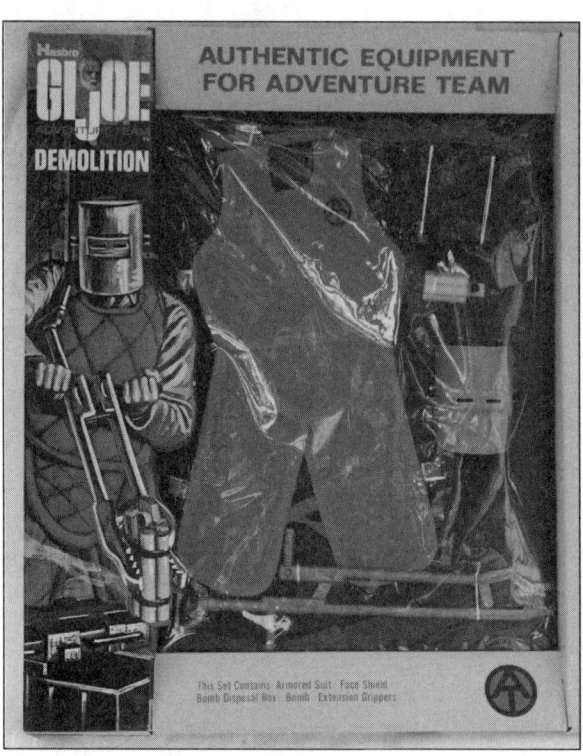

Demolition Set, G.I. Joe, Adventure Team, $125

Adventure Team (Continued)

	C6	C8	C10
Command Para Drop, No. 8033, deluxe set, 1975	200	300	550
Copter Rescue Set, No. 7308-3, blue jumpsuit, red binoculars, 1973	15	20	30
Danger of the Depths Set, No. 7412, 1970	100	175	325
Danger Ray Detection, No. 7338-1, magnetic ray detector, solar communicator w/headphones, two-piece uniform, instructions and comic, 1975	45	90	225
Dangerous Climb Set, No. 7309-2, 1973	20	35	75
Dangerous Mission Set, No. 7608-5, green shirt, pants, hunting rifle, 1973	20	35	75
Demolition Set, No. 7370, armored suit, face shield, bomb, bomb disposal box, extension grips, 1971	20	45	125
Demolition Set, No. 7371, w/land mines, mine detector and carrying case w/metallic suit, 1971	75	100	250
Desert Explorer Set, No. 7309-5, 1973	20	40	80
Desert Survival Set, No. 7308-6, 1973	20	40	80

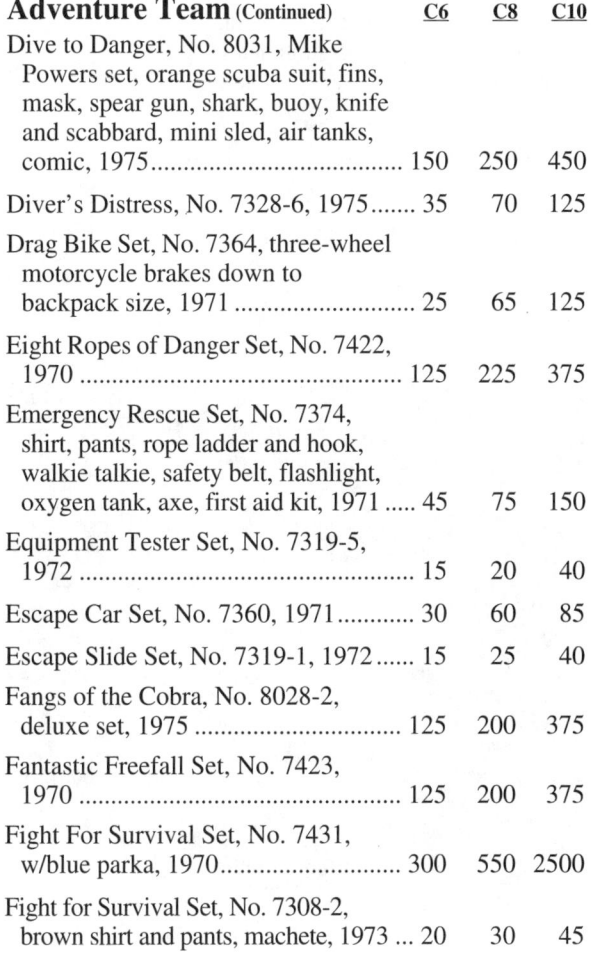

FrontRow: left to right: G.I. Joe Action Marine, Action Marine Series, 1964; G.I. Joe Action Sailor, Action Sailor Series, 1964. Back row, left to right: G.I. Joe Eight Ropes of Danger Set, Adventure Team, 1970; G.I. Joe Fantastic Freefall Set, Adventure Team, 1970

High Voltage Escape Set, G.I. Joe, Adventure Team, $150

Adventure Team (Continued)	C6	C8	C10
Dive to Danger, No. 8031, Mike Powers set, orange scuba suit, fins, mask, spear gun, shark, buoy, knife and scabbard, mini sled, air tanks, comic, 1975	150	250	450
Diver's Distress, No. 7328-6, 1975	35	70	125
Drag Bike Set, No. 7364, three-wheel motorcycle brakes down to backpack size, 1971	25	65	125
Eight Ropes of Danger Set, No. 7422, 1970	125	225	375
Emergency Rescue Set, No. 7374, shirt, pants, rope ladder and hook, walkie talkie, safety belt, flashlight, oxygen tank, axe, first aid kit, 1971	45	75	150
Equipment Tester Set, No. 7319-5, 1972	15	20	40
Escape Car Set, No. 7360, 1971	30	60	85
Escape Slide Set, No. 7319-1, 1972	15	25	40
Fangs of the Cobra, No. 8028-2, deluxe set, 1975	125	200	375
Fantastic Freefall Set, No. 7423, 1970	125	200	375
Fight For Survival Set, No. 7431, w/blue parka, 1970	300	550	2500
Fight for Survival Set, No. 7308-2, brown shirt and pants, machete, 1973	20	30	45

Adventure Team (Continued)	C6	C8	C10
Fight for Survival Set with Polar Explorer, No. 7982, 1969	250	450	850
Fire Fighter Set, No. 7351, 1971	20	30	55
Flying Rescue Set, No. 7361, 1971	35	60	85
Flying Space Adventure Set, No. 7425, 1970	400	600	1000
Footlocker, No. 8000, green plastic w/cardboard wrapper, 1974	35	70	225
Green Danger, No. 7328-4, 1975	30	45	60
Hidden Missile Discovery Set, No. 7415, 1970	100	200	450
Hidden Treasure Set, No. 7308-1, shirt, pants, pick axe, shovel, 1973	15	25	40
High Voltage Escape Set, No. 7342, net, jumpsuit, hat, wrist meter, wire cutters, wire, warning sign, 1971	40	75	150
Hurricane Spotter Set, No. 7343, slicker suit, rain measure, portable radar, map and case, binoculars, 1971	55	80	175
Jaws of Death, No. 7421, super deluxe set, 1975	325	500	650
Jettison to Safety, No. 7339-2, infrared terrain scanner, mobile rocket pack, two-piece flight suit, instructions and comic, 1975	85	200	275

Adventure Team (Continued)

	C6	C8	C10
Jungle Ordeal Set, No. 7309-3, 1973	15	25	45
Jungle Survival Set, No. 7373, 1971	15	25	45
Karate Set, No. 7372, 1971	35	70	125
Laser Rescue Set, No. 7311, hand-held laser w/backpack generator, 1972	20	35	45
Laser Rescue Set, No. 7311, reissue, 1974	20	35	100
Life-Line Catapult Set, No. 7353, 1971	15	25	40
Long Range Recon, No. 7328-3, deluxe set, 1975	10	20	35
Magnetic Flaw Detector Set, No. 7319-2, 1972	10	20	30
Mine Shaft Breakout, No. 7339-3, sonic rock blaster, chest winch, two-piece uniform, netting, instructions, comic, 1975	70	125	250
Missile Recovery Set, No. 7340, 1971	40	55	85
Mystery of the Boiling Lagoon, Sears, pontoon boat, diver's suit, diver's helmet, weighted belt and boots, depth gauge, air hose, buoy, nose cone, pincer arm, instructions, 1973	150	200	225
Night Surveillance, No. 7338-2, deluxe set, 1975	35	45	90
Peril of the Raging Inferno, No. 7416, fireproof suit, hood and boots, breathing apparatus, camera, fire extinguisher, detection meter, gaskets, 1975	85	150	275
Photo Reconnaissance Set, No. 7309-4, 1973	20	30	45
Race for Recovery, No. 8028-1, 1975	20	35	125
Radiation Detection Set, No. 7341, jumpsuit w/belt, "uranium ore," goggles, container, pincer arm, 1971	30	50	85
Raging River Dam Up, No. 7339-1, 1975	60	90	150
Rescue Raft Set, No. 7350, 1971	15	20	65
Revenge of the Spy Shark, No. 7413, super deluxe set, 1975	50	175	400
Rock Blaster, No. 7312, sonic blaster w/tripod, backpack generator, face shield, 1972	10	20	35

Adventure Team (Continued)

	C6	C8	C10
Rocket Pack Set, No. 7315, reissue, 1974	10	20	50
Rocket Pack Set, No. 7315, 1972	10	20	75
Sample Analyzer Set, No. 7319-3, 1972	10	20	45
Search for the Abominable Snowman Set, No. 7439.16, Sears, white suit, belt, goggles, gloves, rifle, skis and poles, show shoes, sled, rope, net, supply chest, binoculars, Abominable Snowman, comic book, 1973	110	175	350
Secret Agent Set, No. 7375, 1971	30	55	175
Secret Courier, No. 7328-1, 1975	45	65	135
Secret Mission Set, No. 8030, deluxe set, 1975	65	95	200
Secret Mission Set, No. 7309-1, 1973	45	65	135
Secret Mission to Spy Island Set, No. 7411, comic, inflatable raft w/oar, binoculars, signal light, flare gun, TNT and detonator, wire roll, boots, pants, sweater, black cap, camera, radio w/earphones, .45 submachine gun, 1970	75	125	250
Secret Rendezvous Set, No. 7308-4, parka, pants, flare gun, 1973	10	20	35
Seismograph Set, No. 7319-6, 1972	10	20	35
Shocking Escape, No. 7338-3, escape slide, chest pack climber, jumpsuit w/gloves and belt, high voltage sign, instructions and comic, 1975	25	65	125

Sky Dive to Danger, G.I. Joe, Adventure Team, $325

Adventure Team (Continued)

	C6	C8	C10
Signal Flasher Set, No. 7362, large back pack type signal flash unit, 1971	15	30	50
Sky Dive to Danger, No. 7440, super deluxe set, 1975	90	150	325
Solar Communicator Set, No. 7314, 1972	10	20	35
Solar Communicator Set, No. 7314, reissue, 1974	10	20	95
Sonic Rock Blaster Set, No. 7312, 1972	10	20	35
Sonic Rock Blaster Set, No. 7312, reissue, 1974	10	20	35
Special Assignment, No. 8028-3, deluxe set, 1975	30	55	135
Thermal Terrain Scanner Set, No. 7319-4, 1972	25	35	50
Three-in-One Super Adventure Set, No. 7480, Danger of the Depths, Secret Mission to Spy Island and Flying Space Adventure Packs, 1971	550	975	1250
Three-in-One Super Adventure Set, No. 7480, cold of the Arctic, Heat of the Desert and Danger of the Jungle, 1971	250	400	750
Thrust into Danger, No. 7328-2, deluxe set, 1975	45	55	175
Trouble at Vulture Pass, No. 59289, Sears exclusive, super deluxe set, 1975	75	125	325
Turbo Copter Set, No. 7363, strap-on one man helicopter, 1971	15	35	65
Undercover Agent Set, No. 7309-6, trenchcoat and belt, walkie-talkie, 1973	15	30	35
Underwater Demolition Set, No. 7310, hand-held propulsion device, breathing apparatus, dynamite, 1972	15	20	40
Underwater Demolition Set, No. 7310, reissue, 1974	10	20	75
Underwater Explorer Set, No. 7354, self propelled underwater device, 1971	15	30	60
Volcano Jumper Set, No. 7344, jumpsuit w/hood, belt, nylon rope, chest pack, TNT pack, 1971	45	80	250

Adventure Team (Continued)

	C6	C8	C10
White Tiger Hunt Set, No. 7436, hunter's jacket and pants, hat, rifle, tent, cage, chain, campfire, white tiger, comic, 1970	80	125	275
Windboat Set, No. 7353, back pack, sled w/wheels, sail, 1971	10	25	55
Winter Rescue Set, No. 7309-4, Replaced Photo Reconnaissance Set, 1973	40	75	150

Vehicle Sets

	C6	C8	C10
Action Sea Sled, J.C. Penney, 13", Adventure Pack, 1973	25	40	85
Adventure Team Vehicle Set, No. 7005, 1970	50	75	225
All Terrain Vehicle, No. 23528, 14" vehicle, 1973	50	75	125
Amphicat, No. 59158, Irwin, scaled to fit two figures, 1973	35	55	125
Avenger Pursuit Craft, Sears exclusive, 1976	100	175	275
Big Trapper, No. 7498, without action figure, 1976	75	105	325
Big Trapper Adventure with Intruder, No. 7494, w/action figure, 1976	100	150	425
Capture Copter, No. 7480, without action figure, 1976	80	175	325
Capture Copter Adventure with Intruder, No. 7481, w/action figure, 1976	110	200	350
Chopper Cycle, No. 59114, 15" vehicle, J.C. Penney's, 1973	30	50	100
Combat Action Jeep, No. 59751, 18" vehicle, J.C. Penney's, 1973	50	65	125
Combat Jeep and Trailer, No. 7000, 1976	80	135	550
Devil of the Deep, No. 7439, 1974	80	135	325
Fantastic Sea Wolf Submarine, No. 7460, 1975	60	100	175
Fate of the Troubleshooter, No. 7450, 1974	50	125	225
Giant Air-Sea Helicopter, No. 59189, 28" vehicle, J.C. Penney's, 1973	50	125	225
Helicopter, No. 7380, 14", yellow, w/working winch, 1973	50	90	150
Helicopter, No. 7380, 1976	50	90	300

Adventure Team (Continued)

	C6	C8	C10
Mobile Support Vehicle Set, No. 7499, 1972	85	150	325
Recovery of the Lost Mummy Adventure Set, Sears exclusive, 1971	125	250	425
Sandstorm Survival Adventure, No. 7493, 1974	125	200	300
Search for the Stolen Idol Set, No. 7418, 1971	120	225	350
Secret of the Mummy's Tomb Set, No. 7441, w/Land Adventurer figure, shirt, pants, boots, insignia, pith helmet, pick, shovel, Mummy's tomb, net, gems, vehicle w/winch, comic, 1970	175	300	600
Sharks Surprise Set with Sea Adventurer, No. 7442, 1970	175	325	550
Signal All Terrain Vehicle, J.C. Penney's, 12" vehicle, 1973	30	65	125
Sky Hawk, No. 7470, 5-3/4-foot wingspan, 1975	65	100	175
Spacewalk Mystery Set with Astronaut, No. 7445, 1970	225	300	550
Trapped in the Coils of Doom, No. 79-59301, J.C. Penney's exclusive, 1974	250	300	550

Adventures of G.I. Joe

Figure Sets

	C6	C8	C10
Aquanaut, No. 7910, 1969	175	550	3000
Challenge at Hawk River, Recreations of Adventure Team series, 1999	5	10	20
Negro Adventurer, No. 7905, Sears exclusive, includes painted hair figure, blue jeans, pullover sweater, shoulder holster and pistol, plus product letter from Sears, 1969	450	750	2750
Peril of the Raging Inferno, 1999	5	10	20
Save the Tiger, 1999	5	10	20
Sharks Surprise Set with Frogman, No. 7980, w/figure, orange scuba suit, blue sea sled, air tanks, harpoon, face mask, treasure chest, shark, instructions and comic, 1969	125	300	750
Talking Astronaut, No. 7615, hard-hand figure w/white coveralls w/insignias, white boots, dog tags, 1969	85	275	1000

Adventures of G.I. Joe (Continued)

Uniform/Equipment Sets

	C6	C8	C10
Adventure Locker, No. 7940, Footlocker, 1969	80	165	350
Aqua Locker, No. 7941, Footlocker, 1969	90	180	375
Astro Locker, No. 7942, Footlocker, 1969	90	180	375
Danger of the Depths Underwater Diver Set, No. 7920, 1969	140	275	500
Eight Ropes of Danger Set, No. 7950, diving suit, treasure chest, octopus, 1969	110	225	525
Fantastic Freefall Set, No. 7951, includes figure w/parachute and pack, blinker light, air vest, flash light, crash helmet w/visor and oxygen mask, dog tags, orange jump suit, black boots, 1969	150	325	675
Flight for Survival Set with o Polar Explorer, No. 7982.83, reissue, 1969	150	300	500
Hidden Missile Discovery Set, No. 7952, 1969	70	135	400
Mouth of Doom Set, No. 7953, 1969	125	250	550
Mysterious Explosion Set, No. 7921, basic, 1969	60	125	425
Perilous Rescue Set, No. 7923, basic, 1969	150	300	500
Secret Mission to Spy Island Set, No. 7922, basic, 1969	110	225	450

Vehicle Sets

	C6	C8	C10
Sharks Surprise Set with Frogman, No. 7980, 1969	175	325	650
Sharks Surprise Set without Frogman, No. 7980.83, 1969	150	300	550
Spacewalk Mystery Set with Spaceman, No. 7981, 1969	150	375	650
Spacewalk Mystery Set without Spaceman, No. 7981.83, reissue, 1969	125	275	550

GI Joe Action Series, Army, Navy, Marine and Air Force

Uniform/Equipment Sets

	C6	C8	C10
Basic Footlocker, No. 8000, 1965	50	75	175
Footlocker Adventure Pack, No. 8002.83, 22 pieces, 1968	70	145	450

Spacewalk Mystery Set with Spaceman, G.I. Joe, Adventures of G.I. Joe, $650

Magna Tools, G.I. Joe, Super Joe, $30

GI Joe Action Series, Army, Navy, Marine and Air Force (Continued)

	C6	C8	C10
Footlocker Adventure Pack, No. 8001.83, 15 pieces, 1968	65	135	450
Footlocker Adventure Pack, No. 8000.83, 16 pieces, 1968	65	135	450
Footlocker Adventure Pack, No. 8002.83, 15 pieces, 1968	65	135	450

Super Joe
Figure Sets

	C6	C8	C10
Gor, No. 7510, 1977	40	70	130
Luminos, No. 7506, 1977	45	70	130
Super Joe, No. 7503, 1977	20	35	70
Super Joe (Black), No. 7504, 1977	35	50	100
Super Joe Commander, No. 7501, 1977	25	45	75

Super Joe (Continued)

	C6	C8	C10
The Shield, No. 7505, 1977	40	65	125

Uniform/Equipment Sets

	C6	C8	C10
Aqua Laser, No. 7528-1, 1977	10	20	30
Edge of Adventure, No. 7518-2, 1977	10	20	35
Emergency Rescue, No. 7518-3, 1977	10	20	30
Fusion Bazooka, No. 7528-3, 1977	10	20	30
Helipak, No. 7538-2, 1977	10	20	30
Invisible Danger, No. 7518-1, 1977	10	20	35
Magna Tools, No. 7538-1, 1977	10	20	30
Path of Danger, No. 7518-4, 1977	10	20	30
Sonic Scanner, No. 7538-3, 1977	10	20	30
Treacherous Dive, No. 7528-2, 1977	10	20	30

Vehicle Sets

	C6	C8	C10
Rocket Command Center, No. 7570, 1977	50	100	200
Rocket Command Center, No. 7571, Super Adventure Set including Gor, 1977	60	115	225

Happy Days (Mego, 1978)

Figures

	C8	C10
Fonzie, boxed	30	100
Fonzie, carded	30	75
Potsie, carded	30	75
Ralph, carded	30	75
Richie, carded	30	75

Play Sets

	C8	C10
Fonzie's Garage Play Set, 1978	60	150

Vehicles

	C8	C10
Fonzie's Jalopy, 1978	40	80
Fonzie's Motorcycle, 1978	40	80

James Bond: Moonraker (Mego, 1979)

12" Figures

	C8	C10
Drax	150	200
Holly	150	200
James Bond	125	150
James Bond, deluxe version	350	500
Jaws	300	500

Figures

	C8	C10
Drax	45	100
Holly Goodhead	45	100
James Bond	45	100
Jaws	200	525

James Bond: Secret Agent 007 (Gilbert, 1965-66)

Figures

	C8	C10
James Bond	190	400
Oddjob	200	550

Gene Simmons, KISS, Mego, $260

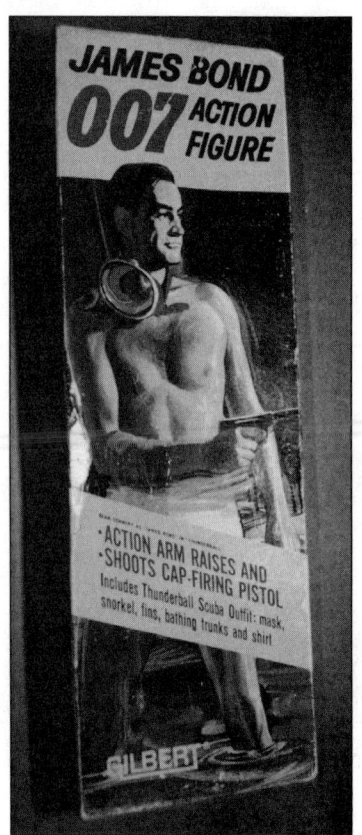

James Bond, James Bond: Secret Agent 007, Gilbert, $400

Paul Stanley, KISS, Mego, $260

Johnny Hero (Rosko, 1965-68)

13" Figures	C8	C10
Johnny Hero	65	100
Johnny Hero, Olympic Hero	65	100

KISS (Mego, 1978)

12" Boxed Figures	C8	C10
Ace Frehley	100	260
Gene Simmons	110	260
Paul Stanley	100	260
Peter Criss	100	260

Laverne and Shirley (Mego, 1978)

12" Boxed Figures	C8	C10
Laverne and Shirley	60	150
Lenny and Squiggy	90	150

Lone Ranger Rides Again (Gabriel, 1979)

Figures	C8	C10
Butch Cavendish	40	75
Dan Reid	25	60
Little Bear with Hawk	25	60
Lone Ranger	20	60
Red Sleeves	25	60
Tonto	20	60

The Monster Frankenstein, Mad Monster Series, Mego, $90

Mad Monster Series (Mego, 1974)

8" Figures	C8	C10
The Dreadful Dracula	80	160
The Horrible Mummy	50	100
The Human Wolfman	75	150
The Monster Frankenstein	45	90

Accessories	C8	C10
Mad Monster Castle, vinyl	300	600

Major Matt Mason (Mattel, 1967-70)

Figures	C8	C10
Callisto, 6"	100	250
Captain Lazer, 12"	125	300
Doug Davis, 6"	100	300
Jeff Long, 6"	150	550

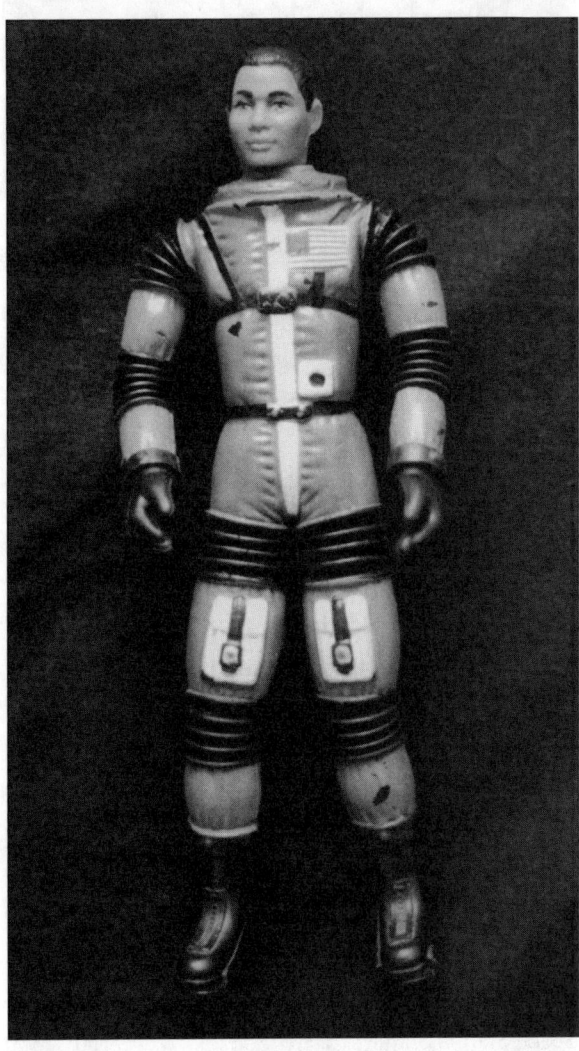

Jeff Long, 6", Major Matt Mason, Mattel, $550. Photo courtesy Corey LeChat

Sergeant Storm, 6", Major Matt Mason, Mattel, $400. Photo courtesy Corey LeChat

Figures (Continued)

	C8	C10
Major Matt Mason, 6"	75	225
Mission Team Four-Pack	350	625
Scorpio, 7"	350	850
Sergeant Storm, 6"	100	400

Vehicles and Accessories

	C8	C10
Astro-Trak	50	150
Firebolt Space Cannon	45	125
Gamma Ray Guard	30	100
Moon Suit Pak	35	100
Reconojet Pak	25	75
Rocket Launch	25	75
Satellite Launch Pak	25	75
Satellite Locker	30	80
Space Power Suit	30	110
Space Probe Pak	25	75
Space Shelter Pak	25	75
Space Station Set	150	350
Star Seeker	85	180

Vehicles and Accessories (Continued)

	C8	C10
Supernaut Power Limbs	30	110
Uni-Tred & Space Bubble	95	175
XRG-1 Reentry Glider	150	395

Micronauts (Mego, 1976-80)

Alien Invaders Carded

	C8	C10
Antron, 1979	15	30
Centaurus, 1980	35	70
Karrio, 1979	10	20
Kronos, 1980	35	70
Lobros, 1980	35	70
Membros, 1979	15	30
Repto, 1979	13	25

Alien Invaders Play Sets

	C8	C10
Rocket Tubes, 1978	23	50

Alien Invaders Vehicles

	C8	C10
Alphatron	5	10
Aquatron, 1977	10	20
Betatron	5	10
Gammatron	5	10
Hornetroid, 1979	20	40
Hydra, 1976	7	15
Mobile Exploration Lab, 1976	17	35
Solarion, 1978	15	30
Star Searcher, 1978	15	40
Taurion, 1978	11	22
Terraphant, 1979	20	40

Boxed Figures

	C8	C10
Andromeda, 1977	10	25
Baron Karza, 1977	15	30
Biotron, 1976	10	25
Force Commander, 1977	10	25
Giant Acroyear, 1977	10	25
Megas, 1981	10	25
Microtron, 1976	5	20
Nemesis Robot, 1978	7	15
Oberon, 1977	10	25
Phobos Robot, 1978	12	25

Carded Figures

	C8	C10
Acroyear II, 1977, red, blue, orange	7	15

Carded Figures (Continued)	C8	C10
Acroyear, 1976, red, blue, orange	10	20
Galactic Defender, 1978, white, yellow	7	15
Galactic Warriors, 1976, red, blue, orange	4	10
Pharoid with Time Chamber, 1977, blue, red, gray	10	20
Space Glider, 1976, blue, green, orange	5	10
Time Traveler, 1976, clear plastic, yellow, orange	3	10
Time Traveler, 1976, solid plastic, yellow, orange	5	15

Micropolis Play Sets	C8	C10
Galactic Command Center, 1978	20	40
Interplanetary Headquarters, 1978	20	40
Mega City, 1978	20	30
Microrail City, 1978	20	40

Play Sets	C8	C10
Astro Station, 1976	10	20
Stratstation, 1976	15	30

Vehicles	C8	C10
Battle Cruiser, 1977	30	60
Crater Cruncher with figure, 1976	5	15
Galactic Cruiser, 1976	7	17
Hydro Copter, 1976	10	25
Neon Orbiter, 1977	6	20
Photon Sled with figure, 1976	5	15
Rhodium Orbiter, 1977	6	20
Thorium Orbiter, 1977	6	20
Ultronic Scooter with figure, 1976	5	15
Warp Racer with figure, 1976	5	15

Mork and Mindy (Mattel, 1980)

Figures	C8	C10
Mindy	20	45
Mork from Ork with egg	20	45
Mork with Talking Spacepack, upside down	20	50

Mork with Talking Spacepack, upside down, Mork and Mindy, Mattel, $50

Gold Knight, Noble Knights, Marx, $150

Noble Knights (Marx, 1968)

Figures	C8	C10
Black Knight	250	550
Bravo Armor Horse	75	150
Gold Knight	75	150
Silver Knight	75	150
Valiant Armor Horse	200	400
Valor Armor Horse	75	150
Victor Armor Horse	75	150

One Million Years, B.C. (Mego, 1976)

Figures	C8	C10
Dimetrodon, 1976, boxed	75	150
Grok, 1976, carded	25	50
Hairy Rhino, 1976, boxed	75	150
Mada, 1976, carded	25	50
Orm, 1976, carded	25	50
Trag, 1976, carded	25	50
Tribal Lair Gift Set (five figures), 1976	70	180
Tribal Lair, 1976	60	120
Tyrannosaur, 1976, boxed	75	150
Zon, 1976, carded	25	50

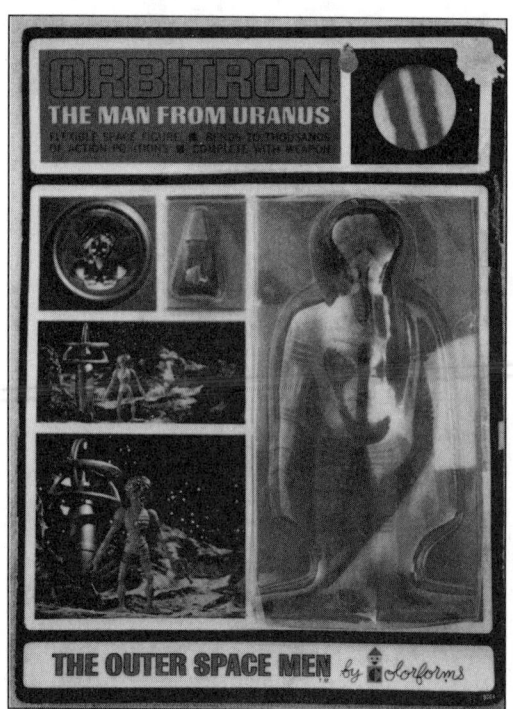

Electron / Man from Pluto, Outer Space Men,
Colorforms, $500

Orbitron / Man from Uranus, Outer Space Men,
Colorforms, $600

Outer Space Men (Colorforms, 1968)

Figures	C8	C10
Alpha 7 / Man from Mars	150	450
Astro-Nautilus / Man from Neptune	300	750
Colossus Rex / Man from Jupiter	300	800
Commander Comet / Man from Venus	200	500
Electron / Man from Pluto	200	500
Orbitron / Man from Uranus	200	600
Xodiac / Man from Saturn	200	500

Planet of the Apes (Mego, 1973-75)

8" Figures	C8	C10
Astronaut Burke, 1975, boxed	50	250
Astronaut Burke, 1975, carded	50	100
Astronaut Verdon, 1975, boxed	50	250
Astronaut Verdon, 1975, carded	50	125
Astronaut, 1973, boxed	50	250
Astronaut, 1975, carded	50	100
Cornelius, 1973, boxed	40	200
Cornelius, 1975, carded	40	100
Dr. Zaius, 1973, boxed	40	200
Dr. Zaius, 1975, carded	40	100

8" Figures (Continued)

	C8	C10
Galen, 1975, boxed	40	200
Galen, 1975, carded	40	100
General Urko, 1975, boxed	50	250
General Urko, 1975, carded	50	100
General Ursus, 1975, boxed	50	250
General Ursus, 1975, carded	50	100
Soldier Ape, 1973, boxed	50	250
Soldier Ape, 1975, carded	50	100
Zira, 1973, boxed	30	200
Zira, 1975, carded	30	100

Accessories

	C8	C10
Action Stallion, brown motorized, 1975, boxed	50	100
Battering Ram, 1975, boxed	20	40
Dr. Zaius' Throne, 1975, boxed	20	40
Jail, 1975, boxed	20	40

Play Sets

	C8	C10
Forbidden Zone Trap, 1975	90	200
Fortress, 1975	85	200
Treehouse, 1975	75	200
Village, 1975	85	200

Vehicles

	C8	C10
Catapult and Wagon, 1975, boxed	75	150

Pocket Super Heroes (Mego, 1976-79)

3-3/4" Figures

	C8	C10
Aquaman, 1976, white card	50	100
Batman, 1976, red card	20	40
Batman, 1976, white card	20	40
Captain America, 1976, white card	50	100
General Zod, 1979, red card	5	15
Green Goblin, 1976, white card	50	100
Hulk, 1976, white card	15	40
Hulk, 1979, red card	15	30
Jor-El (Superman), 1979, red card	10	20
Lex Luthor (Superman), 1979, red card	10	20
Robin, 1976, white card	20	40
Robin, 1979, red card	20	40
Spider-Man, 1976, white card	15	40
Spider-Man, 1979, red card	15	30

Batcave, 1981, Pocket Super Heroes, Mego, $300

3-3/4" Figures (Continued)

	C8	C10
Superman, 1976, white card	15	30
Superman, 1979, red card	15	30
Wonder Woman, 1979, white card	20	45

Accessories

	C8	C10
Batcave, 1981	120	300

Vehicles

	C8	C10
Batmachine, 1979	40	100
Batmobile, 1979, with Batman and Robin	80	200
Spider-Car, 1979, with Spider-Man and Hulk	30	75
Spider-Machine, 1979	40	100

Robin Hood and His Merry Men (Mego, 1974)

8" Figures

	C8	C10
Friar Tuck	25	75
Little John	45	100
Robin Hood	75	150
Will Scarlett	75	150

Figures

	C8	C10
Friar Tuck	25	60
Little John	65	150
Robin Hood	90	300
Will Scarlett	75	275

Shogun Warriors (Mattel, 1979)

24" Figures

	C8	C10
Daimos	75	150
Dragun	75	175
Dragun (2nd figure)	75	150

Maskatron, Six Million Dollar Man, Kenner, $150

24" Figures (Continued)

	C8	C10
Gaiking	75	150
Godzilla	100	200
Godzilla (2nd figure)	150	200
Mazinga	85	175
Mazinga (2nd figure)	75	150
Raydeen	75	150
Rodan	150	300

Six Million Dollar Man (Kenner, 1975-78)

Accessories

	C8	C10
Backpack Radio	10	25
Bionic Cycle	10	20
Bionic Mission Vehicle	25	25
Bionic Transport	10	45
Bionic Video Center	35	100
Critical Assignment Arms	15	45
Critical Assignment Legs	15	45

Accessories (Continued)

	C8	C10
Dual Launch Drag Set with 4" Steve Austin Bionic Bigfoot figure	45	80
Flight Suit	15	30
Mission Control Center	25	75
Mission to Mars Space Suit	15	30
OSI Headquarters	30	70
OSI Undercover Blue Denims	15	30
Porta-Communicator	20	50
Tower & Cycle Set	25	50
Venus Space Probe	125	275

Figures

	C8	C10
Bionic Bigfoot	75	175
Maskatron	40	150
Oscar Goldman	50	100
Steve Austin	50	100
Steve Austin with biosonic arm	75	300
Steve Austin with engine block	50	150
Steve Austin with girder	60	200

Oscar Goldman, Six Million Dollar Man, Kenner, $100

Moonbase Alpha Deluxe Playset with three figures, Space:1999, Mattel, $200. Photo courtesy Corey LeChat

Professor Bergman, Space:1999, Mattel, $60. Photo courtesy Corey LeChat

Moonbase Alpha Playset, Space:1999, Mattel, $80. Photo courtesy Corey LeChat

*Eagle Playset with three 3" figures, Space:1999, **Mattel**, $300. Photo courtesy Corey LeChat*

Commander Koenig, Space:1999, Mattel, $60. Photo courtesy Corey LeChat

Dr. Russell, Space:1999, Mattel, $60. Photo courtesy Corey LeChat

Space:1999 (Mattel, 1976)

Figures	C8	C10
Commander Koenig	30	60
Dr. Russell	30	60
Professor Bergman	30	60
Zython Alien	75	200

Play Set	C8	C10
Eagle Playset with three 3" figures	150	300
Moonbase Alpha Deluxe Playset with three figures	75	200
Moonbase Alpha Playset	35	80

Space:1999 (Palitoy, 1975)

Figures	C8	C10
Alan Carter	200	425
Captain Koenig	150	250

Figures (Continued)	C8	C10
Captain Zantor	75	160
Mysterious Alien	75	160
Paul Morrow	175	300

Star Trek (Mego, 1974-80)

8" Carded Figures	C8	C10
Andorian, 1976	300	650
Captain Kirk, 1974	25	50
Cheron, 1975	85	175
Dr. McCoy, 1974	35	75
Gorn, 1975	80	180
Klingon, 1974	25	50
Lt. Uhura, 1974	50	135
Mr. Spock, 1974	25	50

Alan Carter, Space:1999, Palitoy, $425. Photo courtesy Corey LeChat

Captain Koenig, Space:1999, Palitoy, $250. Photo courtesy Corey LeChat

Captain Zantor in package, Space:1999, Palitoy, $160. Photo courtesy Corey LeChat

Mysterious Alien, Space:1999, Palitoy, $160. Photo courtesy Corey LeChat

Paul Morrow, Space:1999, Palitoy, $300. Photo courtesy Corey LeChat

Cheron, 1975, Star Trek, Mego, $175. Photo courtesy Corey LeChat

8" Carded Figures (Continued)	C8	C10
Mugato, 1976	275	500
Neptunian, 1975	100	225
Romulan, 1976	600	1000
Scotty, 1974	35	80
Talos, 1976	275	500

8" Carded Figures (Continued)	C8	C10
The Keeper, 1975	75	175

Play Sets	C8	C10
Mission to Gamma VI	700	1200
U.S.S. Enterprise Bridge	100	275

Back of Star Trek card. Photo courtesy Corey LeChat

Dr. McCoy, 1974, Star Trek, Mego, $75

Gorn, 1975, Star Trek, Mego, $180. Photo courtesy Corey LeChat

Klingon, 1974, Star Trek, Mego, $50. Photo courtesy Corey LeChat

Star Trek: The Motion Picture (Mego, 1980-81)

3-3/4" Carded Figures

	C8	C10
Acturian	75	150

Acturian, Star Trek: The Motion Picture, Mego, $150

3-3/4" Carded Figures (Continued)

	C8	C10
Betelgeusian	75	150
Captain Kirk	12	35
Decker, 1979	12	35
Dr. McCoy	12	35
Ilia	10	20
Klingon	75	150
Megarite	75	150
Mr. Spock	12	35
Rigellian	75	150
Scotty	12	35
Zatanite	75	150

12" Boxed Figures

	C8	C10
Arcturian, 1979	40	125
Captain Kirk, 1979	40	75
Decker, 1979	45	115
Ilia, 1979	40	75

Dr. McCoy, Star Trek: The Motion Picture, Mego, $35

Mr. Spock, Star Trek: The Motion Picture, Mego, $35

U.S.S. Enterprise Bridge, Star Trek: The Motion Picture, Mego, $105

Klingon, Star Trek: The Motion Picture, Mego, $150

12" Boxed Figures (Continued)	**C8**	**C10**
Klingon, 1979	40	125
Mr. Spock, 1979	40	75

Play Sets	**C8**	**C10**
U.S.S. Enterprise Bridge	45	105

Star Wars (Kenner, 1977-Present) Action Figures, 3-3/4"

Droids	**C8**	**C10**
A-Wing Pilot	25	170
Boba Fett	17	670
C-3PO	45	125
Jann Tosh	8	20
Jord Dusat	8	20
Kea Moll	10	30
Kez-Iban	10	25
R2-D2	40	85
Sise Fromm	35	85
Thall Joben	8	20
Tig Fromm	30	75
Uncle Gundy	8	19

Empire Strikes Back	**C8**	**C10**
2-1B	7	85
4-LOM	9	105
AT-AT Commander	6	50

A-Wing Pilot, Star Wars, 3-3/4" figure, Droids, Kenner, $170

Empire Strikes Back (Continued)	**C8**	**C10**
AT-AT Driver	8	65
Bespin Security Guard, black	8	55
Bespin Security Guard, white	8	60
Bossk	9	95
C-3PO with Removable Limbs	7	55
Cloud Car Pilot	12	70
Dengar	7	65
FX-7	6	60
Han in Bespin Outfit	10	105
Han in Hoth Gear	8	85
Hoth Rebel Soldier	6	55
IG-88	10	115
Imperial Commander	6	45
Imperial TIE Fighter Pilot	10	100
Lando Calrissian	8	70
Leia in Bespin Gown	12	125
Leia in Hoth Gear	15	100
Lobot	5	50

Empire Strikes Back (Continued)

	C8	C10
Luke in Bespin Outfit	15	150
Luke in Hoth Gear	8	70
R2-D2 with Sensorscope	9	60
Rebel Commander	6	50
Snowtrooper	8	70
Ugnaught	6	55
Yoda	16	140
Zuckuss	7	85

Episode I

	C8	C10
Adi Gallia	3	8
Anakin Skywalker (Naboo Pilot)	3	8
Anakin Skywalker (Naboo)	3	8
Anakin Skywalker (Tatooine)	3	8
Battle Droid (four versions)	3	8
Boss Nass	3	8
C-3PO	3	8
Captain Panaka	3	9

Chancellor Valorum, 3-3/4" figure, Star Wars, Episode I, Kenner, $8

Anakin Skywalker (Tatooine), 3-3/4" figure, Star Wars, Episode I, Kenner, $8

Episode I (Continued)

	C8	C10
Captain Tarpals	3	8
Chancellor Valorum	3	8
Darth Maul	3	10
Darth Maul (Jedi Duel)	3	9
Darth Maul (Sith Lord)	3	8
Darth Maul (Tatooine)	3	8
Darth Sidious	3	8
Darth Sidious (Holograph)	3	8
Destroyer Droid	3	8
Destroyer Droid (Battle Damaged)	3	8
Gasgano	3	8
Jar Jar Binks	3	8
Jar Jar Binks (Swamp)	3	8
Ki-Adi-Mundi	3	8
Mace Windu	3	8
Mosespa Encounter—Sebulba, Jar Jar, Anakin	6	12
Naboo Royal Guard	3	8

Darth Sidious, 3-3/4" figure, Star Wars, Episode I, Kenner, $8

Padme Naberrie, 3-3/4" figure, Star Wars, Episode I, Kenner, $8

Gasgano, Star Wars, 3-3/4" figure, Episode I, Kenner, $8

Queen Amidala (Naboo) with Blaster Pistols, 3-3/4" figure, Star Wars, Episode I, Kenner, $8

Episode I (Continued)	C8	C10
Naboo Royal Security	3	9
Obi-Wan Kenobi	3	10
Obi-Wan Kenobi (Jedi Duel)	3	8
Obi-Wan Kenobi (Jedi Knight)	3	8
Obi-Wan Kenobi (Naboo)	3	8
Ody Mandrell with Pit Droid	3	8
OOM-9	3	8
Padme Naberrie	3	8
Pit Droids	3	8
Queen Amidala (Battle)	3	8
Queen Amidala (Coruscant)	3	10
Queen Amidala (Naboo) with Blaster Pistols	3	8
Qui-Gon Jinn	3	10
Qui-Gon Jinn (Jedi Duel)	3	8
Qui-Gon Jinn (Jedi Master)	3	8
Qui-Gon Jinn (Naboo)	3	8
R2-B1	3	8

Episode I (Continued)	C8	C10
Ric Olie	3	8
Senator Palpatine	3	8
Sio Bibble	3	8
Tatooine Showdown—Darth Maul, Qui-Gon, Anakin	6	15
TC-14	3	8
Watto	3	9
Watto's Box—Watto, Graxol Kelvyyn, Shakka	6	20
Yoda	3	8

Ewoks	C8	C10
Dulok Scout	8	18
Dulok Shaman	8	19
King Gornesh	8	18
Logray	10	20
Urgah	8	18
Wicket	11	35

Senator Palpatine, 3-3/4" figure, Star Wars, Episode I, Kenner, $8

Han in Carbonite with coin, 3-3/4" figure, Star Wars, Power of the Force, Kenner, $195

Power of the Force

	C8	C10
Amanaman, with coin	105	230
Anakin Skywalker, with coin	20	2330
AT-AT Driver, with coin	4	550
AT-ST Driver, with coin	5	50
A-Wing Pilot, with coin	45	80
Barada, with coin	35	105
Biker Scout, with coin	6	90
B-Wing Pilot, with coin	4	30
C-3PO with Removable Limbs, with coin	4	70
Chewbacca, with coin	5	100
Darth Vader, with coin	6	115
Emperor Palpatine, with coin	5	60
EV-9D9, with coin	60	140
Gamorrean Guard, with coin	4	240
Han in Carbonite, with coin	80	195
Han in Trenchcoat, with coin	6	490
Imperial Dignitary, with coin	40	70

Yoda with coin, 3-3/4" figure, Star Wars, Power of the Force, Kenner, $340

Power of the Force (Continued)

	C8	C10
Imperial Gunner, with coin	60	130
Jawa, with coin	7	85
Lando as General Pilot, with coin	55	105
Leia in Battle Poncho	10	80
Luke as Jedi Knight with Green Saber, with coin	18	195
Luke as X-Wing Pilot, with coin	6	85
Luke in Battle Poncho, with coin	50	115
Luke in Stormtrooper Disguise, with coin	125	380
Lumat, with coin	8	45
Nikto, with coin	6	590
Obi-Wan Kenobi, with coin	7	95
Paploo, with coin	8	50
R2-D2 with pop-up Lightsaber, with coin	85	155
Romba, with coin	30	55
Stormtrooper, with coin	7	190
Teebo, with coin	6	135
Warok, with coin	30	65
Wicket, with coin	8	135
Yak Face, with coin	175	1500
Yoda, with coin	12	340

Power of the Force 2

	C8	C10
2-1B Medic Droid	2	8
4-LOM	3	10
8-D8 Droid	3	10
Admiral Ackbar	3	10
Admiral Motti	5	9
Anakin Skywalker	3	12
ASP-7 Droid	3	8
AT-AT Driver (Fan Club Four)	3	20
AT-ST Driver	3	10
Aunt Beru	3	14
Ben (Obi-Wan) Kenobi	5	9
Bib Fortuna	3	10
Biggs Darklighter	3	14
Boba Fett	4	15
Boba Fett	5	10
Boba Fett vs. IG-88	6	25
B'omarr Monk	10	15

Cantina Showdown—Obi-Wan Kenobi, Ponda Baba, Dr. Evazan, 3-3/4" figure, Star Wars, Power of the Force 2, Kenner, $12. Photo courtesy Hasbro, Inc.

Power of the Force 2 (Continued)

	C8	C10
Bossk	3	10
C-3PO	3	10
C-3PO with Removable Limbs and Backpack	3	16
C-3PO, Shop Worn	3	8
C-3PO, with Millennium Minted Coin	5	10
Cantina Aliens—Labria, Nabrun Leids, Takeel	6	12
Cantina Greedo	3	7
Cantina Han Solo	3	7
Cantina Showdown—Obi-Wan Kenobi, Ponda Baba, Dr. Evazan	6	12
Captain Piett	3	14
Chewbacca	3	12
Chewbacca (Hoth)	3	8
Chewbacca as Boushh's Bounty	3	18
Chewbacca in Bounty Hunter Disguise	3	6
Chewbacca, with Millennium Minted Coin	5	10
Clone Emperor	3	18
Crowd Control Stormtrooper	5	9
Dagobah with Yoda	6	12
Darktrooper	3	30
Darth Vader	4	13
Darth Vader	3	8
Darth Vader	5	9
Darth Vader with Interrogation Droid	5	7
Darth Vader with Removable Helmet	4	24
Dash Rendar	3	8

Power of the Force 2 (Continued)

	C8	C10
Death Star Droid with Mouse Droid (Fan Club Four)	3	20
Death Star Escape—Luke and Han in Stormtrooper Disguise, Chewbacca	6	22
Death Star Gunner	3	18
Death Star Trooper	3	26
Death Star with Darth Vader	6	12
Dengar	3	10
Droopy McCool and Barquin D'an	6	20
Emperor Palpatine	3	8
Emperor Palpatine	3	10
Emperor Palpatine, with Millennium Minted Coin	5	10
Emperor's Royal Guard	3	12
Emporer Palpatine	5	9
Endor Rebel Soldier	3	14
Endor with Wicket	10	22
EV-9D9	3	10
Falcon with Han Solo	6	8
Falcon with Luke Skywalker	6	8
Figrin D'an (Cantina Band Member)	10	15
Final Jedi Duel—Darth Vader, Luke, Emperor Palpatine	6	24
Gamorrean Guard	3	10
Garindan (Long Snoot)	3	10
Grand Admiral Thrawn	3	20
Grand Moff Tarkin	3	10
Greedo	3	18
Han in Bespin Outfit	3	10
Han in Bespin Outfit, with Millennium Minted Coin	5	10
Han in Carbonite	3	6
Han in Endor Gear	3	12
Han in Hoth Gear	3	12
Han in Stormtrooper Disguise	10	20
Han Solo	3	12
Han Solo with Smuggler's Flight Pack	5	9
Hoth Rebel Soldier	3	10
Imperial Probe Droid	5	9
Imperial Sentinel	3	18
Ishi Tib	3	14

Power of the Force 2 (Continued)

	C8	C10
Jabba the Hutt's Dancers—Rystall, Greeata, Lyn Me	6	16
Jabba's Skiff Guards—Klaatu, Barada, Nikto	8	35
Jawa & Gonk Droid	3	7
Jawas	3	20
Jedi Knight Luke Skywalker	5	9
Jedi Spirits—Anakin Skywalker, Yoda, Obi-Wan Kenobi	6	10
Kyle Katarn	3	35
Lak Sivrak	3	12
Lando as General	3	14
Lando as Skiff Guard	3	10
Lando Calrissian	3	10
Leia and Han	6	12
Leia and Luke	6	12
Leia and R2-D2	6	12
Leia and Wicket the Ewok	6	12
Leia as Jabba's Prisoner	3	10
Leia in Boushh Disguise	3	6
Leia in Endor Gear, with Millennium Minted Coin	5	10
Leia in Ewok Celebration Outfit	3	14
Leia in Hoth Gear (Fan Club Four)	3	22
Leia with All-New Likeness	3	16
Lobot	3	14
Luke as X-Wing Pilot	3	14
Luke in Battle Poncho, with Millennium Minted Coin	5	10
Luke in Bespin Outfit	3	16
Luke in Ceremonial Garb	3	12
Luke in Dagobah Fatigues	3	12
Luke in Hoth Gear	3	11
Luke in Imperial Guard Disguise	3	8
Luke in Stormtrooper Disguise	4	24
Luke Skywalker	3	18
Luke Skywalker	4	12
Luke Skywalker	3	8
Luke Skywalker with T16	3	7
Luke Skywalker's Desert Sport Skiff	5	10
Luke with Blast Shield Helmet	3	16

Power of the Force 2 (Continued)

	C8	C10
Mace Windu	5	10
Malakili (Rancor Keeper)	3	8
Mara Jade	3	35
Max Rebo and Doda Bodonawieedo	6	25
Momaw Nadon (Hammerhead)	2	16
Mon Mothma	3	16
Muftak and Kabe	10	16
Mynock Hunt—Han, Leia, Chewbacca	6	32
Nien Nunb	3	10
Obi-Wan Kenobi	4	12
Obi-Wan Kenobi	3	8
Obi-Wan Kenobi Spirit	10	10
Oola and Salacious Crumb	10	14
Orrimaarko (Prune Face)	3	22
Ponda Baba	3	10
Pote Snitkin (Fan Club Four)	3	20
Prince Xizor	3	6
Prince Xizor vs. Darth Vader	6	15
Princess Leia	3	13
Princess Leia	3	8
Princess Leia (Hood Up)	5	9
Princess Leia Organa Solo	3	18
Purchase of the Droids—Luke, C-3PO, Uncle Owen	6	18
R2-D2	5	9
R2-D2	3	8
R2-D2	3	12
R2-D2 with Datalink and Sensorscope	3	14
R2-D2 with Holographic Princess Leia	5	9
R5-D4	3	11
Rebel Fleet Trooper	3	11
Rebel Pilots—Wedge Antilles, B-Wing Pilot (Ten Nunb), Y-Wing Pilot	6	26
Ree-Yees	3	26
Saelt-Marae (Yak Face)	3	10
Sandtrooper	3	12
Snowtrooper	3	10
Snowtrooper	5	9
Snowtrooper, with Millennium Minted Coin	5	10
Spacetrooper	3	25

Power of the Force 2 (Continued)

	C8	C10
STAP and Battle Droid	10	12
Stormtrooper	5	7
Stormtrooper	3	11
Sy Snootles and Joh Yowza	6	20
Tatooine with Luke Skywalker	10	25
Theater Edition Jedi Knight Luke Skywalker	10	65
TIE Fighter Pilot	3	11
TIE Fighter with Darth Vader	6	15
Tusken Raider	3	13
Ugnaught	3	10
Weequay Skiff Guard	3	10
Wicket and Logray	3	10
Yoda	3	12
Yoda	3	11
Zuckuss	3	14

Return of the Jedi

	C8	C10
8D8	7	25
Admiral Ackbar	8	30
AT-ST Driver	9	25
Bib Fortuna	10	30
Biker Scout	10	45
B-Wing Pilot	7	25
Chief Chirpa	8	30
Emperor Palpatine	8	40
Emperor's Royal Guard	8	35
Gamorrean Guard	7	35
General Madine	7	30
Han in Trenchcoat	11	35
Klaatu	9	25
Klaatu in Skiff Guard Outfit	9	25
Lando Calrissian, Skiff Guard Outfit	9	35
Leia in Battle Poncho	20	45
Leia in Boushh Disguise	12	40
Logray	7	25
Luke as Jedi Knight, blue saber	35	145
Luke as Jedi Knight, green saber	25	90
Lumat	14	35
Nien Nunb	6	30
Nikto	10	30

Return of the Jedi (Continued)

	C8	C10
Paploo	14	40
Pruneface	8	30
Rancor Keeper	9	25
Rebel Commando	8	25
Ree-Yees	7	25
Squid Head	8	35
Sy Snootles and the Rebo Band	25	150
Teebo	10	35
Weequay	10	30
Wicket	13	50

Star Wars

	C8	C10
Boba Fett	25	970
C-3PO	10	195
Chewbacca	9	230
Darth Vader	11	280
Death Squad Commander	9	185
Death Star Droid	8	140

Boba Fett, 3-3/4" figure, Star Wars, Kenner, $970

Chewbacca, 3-3/4" figure, Star Wars, Kenner, $230

Darth Vader, 3-3/4" figure, Star Wars, Kenner, $280

Luke with Telescoping Saber, 3-3/4" figure, Star Wars, Kenner, $4850

R2-D2, 3-3/4" figure, Star Wars, Kenner, $165

Star Wars (Continued)

	C8	C10
Early Bird Figures—Luke, Leia, R2-D2, Chewbacca	220	550
Greedo	7	150
Hammerhead	7	165
Han Solo, Large Head	20	510
Han Solo, Small Head	25	450
Jawa, Cloth Cape	10	200
Jawa, Vinyl Cape	230	2570
Luke as X-Wing Pilot	8	140
Luke Skywalker	25	400
Luke with Telescoping Saber	195	4850
Obi-Wan Kenobi	11	250
Power Droid	6	110
Princess Leia	30	330
R2-D2	9	165
R5-D4	8	110
Snaggletooth, Blue Body, Sears Exclusive	185	n/a
Snaggletooth, Red Body	7	160
Stormtrooper	12	200
Tusken Raider	9	220
Walrus Man	7	125

Action Figures, 12"

Collector's Series

	C8	C10
Admiral Akbar	15	30
AT-AT Driver	15	22
Barquin D'an	15	22
Boba Fett	15	70
C-3PO	15	30
Cantina Band Aliens with Six Members, Wal-Mart Exclusive	15	35
Chewbacca	15	75
Chewbacca (Chained)	15	35
Darth Vader	15	20
Emperor Palpatine	15	18
Grand Moff Tarkin and Imperial Gunner, FAO Exclusive	30	60
Grand Moff Tarkin with Interrogation Droid	15	22
Greedo	15	22
Han and Luke in Stormtrooper Disguise, K-B Exclusive	30	55
Han in Carbonite	15	35

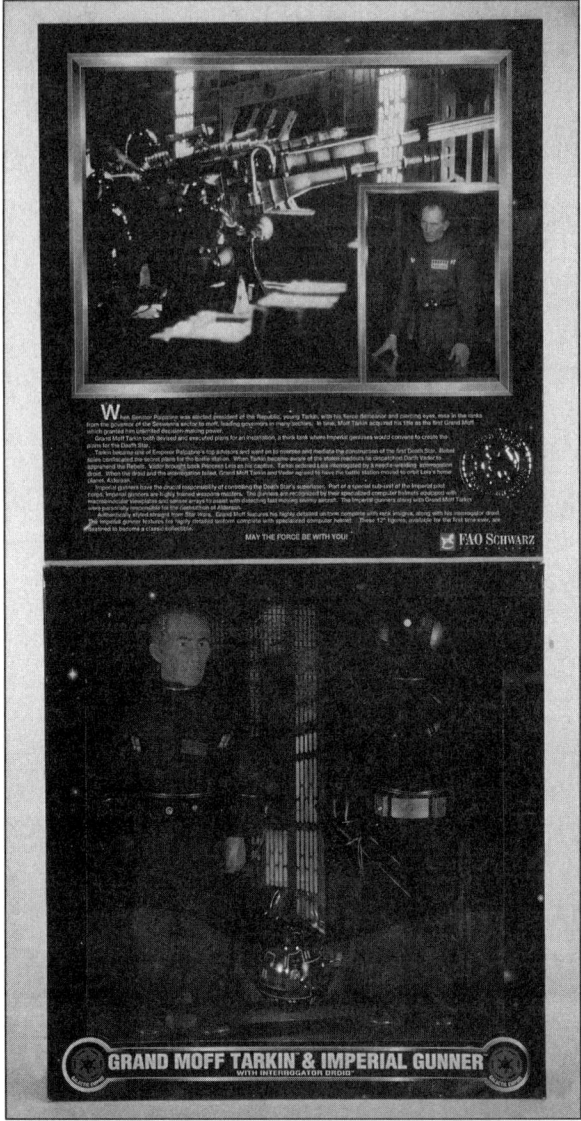

Grand Moff Tarkin and Imperial Gunner (FAO Exclusive), 12" figure, Star Wars, Collector's Series, Kenner, $60

Collector's Series (Continued)

	C8	C10
Han in Hoth Gear	15	18
Han in Hoth Gear with Tauntaun	25	45
Han Solo	15	20
Jawa	15	12
Lando Calrissian	15	20
Leia as Jabba's Prisoner and R2-D2, FAO Exclusive	30	60
Leia in Hoth Gear, Service Merchandise Exclusive	15	20
Luke as Jedi Knight	15	18
Luke as Jedi Knight and Bib Fortuna	30	60

Greedo, 12" figure, Star Wars, Colle1ctor's Series, Kenner, $22

Luke in Hoth Gear with Wampa, 12" figure, Star Wars, Collector's Series, Kenner, $80

Collector's Series (Continued)

	C8	C10
Luke Skywalker	15	20
Luke with Poncho (Tatooine), Han with Flight Jacket, Leia in Boushh Disguise (K-B Exclusive)	20	65
Obi-Wan Kenobi	15	35
Princess Leia	15	45
R2-D2	15	12
R2-D2, Wal-Mart Exclusive	10	15
R5-D4, Wal-Mart Exclusive	10	15
Sandtrooper	15	15
Snowtrooper	15	18
Stormtrooper	15	36
TIE Fighter Pilot	15	28
Tusken Raider	15	35
Wedge Antilles and Biggs Darklighter, FAO Exclusive	30	60
Wicket, Wal-Mart Exclusive	10	15
Yoda	15	20

Empire Strikes Back

	C8	C10
Boba Fett	155	420
IG-88	240	660

Episode I

	C8	C10
Anakin Skywalker	6	10
Battle Droid	6	15
Darth Maul	10	25
Jar Jar Binks	6	20

Collector's Series (Continued)

	C8	C10
Luke as X-Wing Pilot	15	30
Luke in Bespin Outfit	15	35
Luke in Ceremonial Garb	15	15
Luke in Hoth Gear	15	18
Luke in Hoth Gear with Wampa	30	80

Han in Hoth Gear with Tauntaun, 12" figure, Star Wars, Collector's Series, Kenner, $45

Darth Maul, 12" figure, Star Wars, Episode I, Kenner, $25

Episode I (Continued)

	C8	C10
Obi-Wan Kenobi	6	15
Pit Droids	6	10
Qui-Gon Jinn	6	20

Qui-Gon Jinn, 12" figure, Star Wars, Episode I, Kenner, $20

Episode I (Continued)

	C8	C10
R2-A6	6	10
Watto	6	15

Princess Leia Collection

	C8	C10
Princess Leia in Cermonial Gown	10	25

Queen Amidala Collection

	C8	C10
Padme (Beautiful Braids)	8	16
Queen Amidala (Black Travel Dress)	10	40

Queen Amidala (Black Travel Dress), 12" figure, Star Wars, Queen Amidala Collection, Kenner, $40

Queen Amidala (Hidden Majesty), 12" figure, Star Wars, Queen Amidala Collection, Kenner, $16

Luke Skywalker, 12" figure, Star Wars, Kenner, $240

Princess Leia, 12" figure, Star Wars, Kenner, $260

Queen Amidala Collection (Continued)	C8	C10
Queen Amidala (Hidden Majesty)	8	16
Queen Amidala (Red Senate Gown)	10	40
Queen Amidala (Return to Naboo)	10	45
Queen Amidala (Royal Elegance)	8	16
Queen Amidala (Ultimate Hair)	8	16

Star Wars	C8	C10
Boba Fett	160	410
C-3PO	45	125
Chewbacca	55	175
Darth Vader	70	195
Han Solo	170	380
Jawa	80	175
Luke Skywalker	90	240
Obi-Wan Kenobi	115	220
Princess Leia	90	260
R2-D2	45	110
Stormtrooper	90	260

Beasts

Empire Strikes Back	C8	C10
Taun Taun, solid belly	14	40
Taun Taun, split belly	13	45
Wampa	14	35

Return of the Jedi	C8	C10
Rancor	30	60

Patrol Dewback, Star Wars, Kenner, $75

Star Wars

	C8	C10
Patrol Dewback	20	75

Carrying Cases

Empire Strikes Back

	C8	C10
Darth Vader	40	n/a
Mini Figure	30	n/a

Return of the Jedi

	C8	C10
C-3PO	25	n/a
Darth Vader with three figures	220	n/a
Laser Rifle	25	n/a

Star Wars

	C8	C10
24-Figure	30	n/a

Micro Series

	C8	C10
Bespin Control Room	25	25
Bespin Freeze Chamber	20	60
Bespin Gantry	11	25
Bespin World	40	90
Death Star Compactor	20	45
Death Star Escape	17	40
Death Star World	40	100
Hoth Generator Attack	14	30
Hoth Ion Cannon	17	40
Hoth Turret Defense	15	30
Hoth Wampa Cave	14	30
Hoth World	60	120
Imperial TIE Fighter	25	60
Millennium Falcon	140	320
Snowspeeder	90	175
X-Wing Fighter	20	45

Mini Rigs

	C8	C10
AST-5	7	20
CAP-2 Captivator	9	25
Desert Sail Skiff	7	20
Endor Forest Ranger	12	25
INT-4 Interceptor	9	25
ISP-6 Imperial Shuttle Pod	9	20
MLC-3 Mobile Laser Cannon	10	30

Dagobah, Star Wars, Strikes Back, Empire Kenner, $75

	C8	C10
MTV-7 Multi-Terrain Vehicle	9	30
PDT-8 Personal Deployment Transport	10	30
Radar Laser Cannon	8	19
Tri-Pod Laser Cannon	8	17
Vehicle Maintenance Energizer	8	17

Play Sets

Empire Strikes Back

	C8	C10
Cloud City Play Set, Sears Exclusive	100	270
Dagobah	18	75
Darth Vader's Star Destroyer	35	115
Hoth Ice Planet	35	85
Imperial Attack Base	25	80
Rebel Command Center	60	155
Turret and Probot	35	80

Darth Vader's Star Destroyer, Star Wars, Empire Strikes Back, Kenner, $115

Rebel Command Center, Star Wars, Empire Strikes Back, Kenner, $155

Ewoks	C8	C10
Ewoks Treehouse	16	35

Power of the Force	C8	C10
Jabba's Dungeon, with Amanaman, EV-9D9, Barada	220	310

Return of the Jedi	C8	C10
Ewok Village	30	75
Jabba the Hutt Dungeon	25	55
Jabba's Dungeon, with Nikto, 8D8, Klaatu	30	90

Star Wars	C8	C10
Cantina Adventure Set, Sears Exclusive	180	510
Creature Cantina	35	95

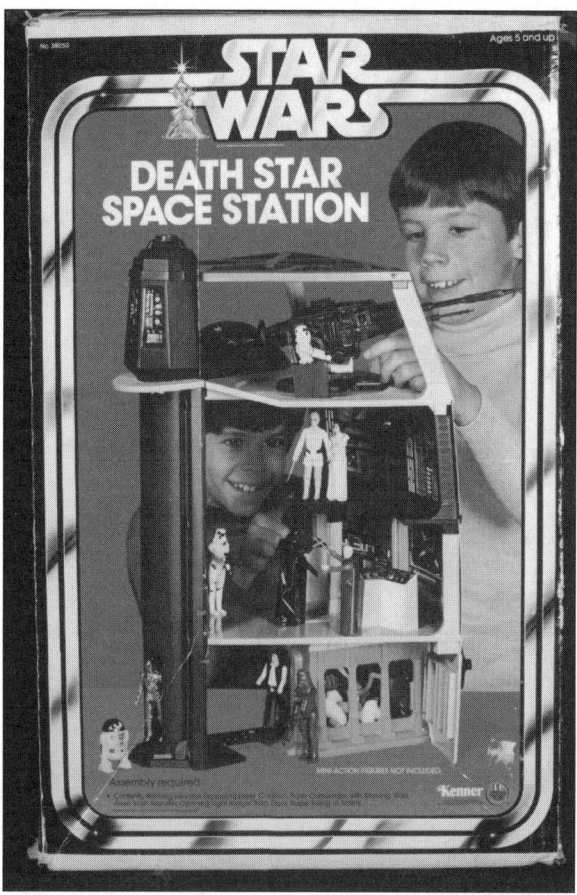

Death Star Space Station, Star Wars, Kenner, $250

Star Wars (Continued)	C8	C10
Death Star Space Station	60	250
Droid Factory	35	115
Land of the Jawas	40	140

Jabba's Dungeon, with Amanaman, EV-9D9, Barada, Star Wars, Power of the Force, Kenner, $310

Land of the Jawas, Star Wars, Kenner, $140

A-Wing Fighter, Star Wars, Droids, Kenner, $400

Vehicles

Droids

	C8	C10
ATL Interceptor	15	45
A-Wing Fighter	195	400
Imperial Side Gunner	18	60

Empire Strikes Back

	C8	C10
AT-AT	75	190
Rebel Transport	45	100
Scout Walker	30	65
Slave I	35	100
Slave I, die-cast	25	75
Snowspeeder	35	75
Snowspeeder, die-cast	25	80
TIE Bomber, die-cast	250	670
Twin-Pod Cloud Car	25	75
Y-Wing Fighter	40	145

Ewoks

	C8	C10
Ewoks Fire Cart	7	18
Ewoks Woodland Wagon	7	40

Power of the Force

	C8	C10
Ewok Battle Wagon	65	220
Imperial Sniper Vehicle	30	70
One-Man Sand Skimmer	25	65
Security Scout Vehicle	30	80
Tatooine Skiff	280	570

Return of the Jedi

	C8	C10
B-Wing Fighter	65	125
Ewok Combat Glider	7	18

Return of the Jedi (Continued)

	C8	C10
Imperial Shuttle	165	330
Speeder Bike	11	30
TIE Interceptor	50	110
Y-Wing Fighter	55	135

Star Wars

	C8	C10
Darth Vader's TIE Fighter	45	105
Darth Vader's TIE Fighter, die-cast	11	55
Imperial TIE Fighter	30	120
Imperial Trooper Transport	30	70
Jawa Sand Crawler, battery-operated	210	540
Land Speeder	16	60
Land Speeder, die-cast	13	60
Millennium Falcon	70	210
Millennium Falcon, die-cast	30	110
Sonic Land Speeder, JC Penney Exclusive	140	470
Star Destroyer, die-cast	45	125
TIE Fighter, die-cast	15	45
X-Wing Fighter	30	110
X-Wing Fighter, die-cast	18	70

Weapons

Droids

	C8	C10
Droids Lightsaber, red or green plastic	75	190

Empire Strikes Back

	C8	C10
Laser Pistol	20	80
Lightsaber, red or green	16	40

Darth Vader's TIE Fighter, Star Wars, Kenner, $105

Empire Strikes Back (Continued)

	C8	C10
Lightsaber, yellow	16	45

Return of the Jedi

	C8	C10
Biker Scout's Laser Pistol	20	55
Lightsaber	20	40

Star Wars

	C8	C10
Han Solo's Laser Pistol	20	90
Inflatable Lightsaber	30	135
Three-Position Laser Rifle	75	240

Starsky and Hutch (Mego, 1976)

8" Figures and Accessories

	C8	C10
Captain Dobey	25	50
Car	65	125
Chopper	25	45
Huggy Bear	25	50
Hutch	20	45
Starsky	20	45

Super Hero Bendables (Mego, 1972)

5" Figures

	C8	C10
Aquaman	50	120
Batgirl	50	120
Batman	35	90
Captain America	35	90
Catwoman	70	175
Joker	60	150
Mr. Mxyzptlk	50	125
Penguin	60	150
Riddler	60	150
Robin	30	75
Shazam	50	125
Supergirl	70	175
Superman	30	75
Tarzan	25	60
Wonder Woman	50	100

Universal Monsters (Remco, 1979)

8" Figures

	C8	C10
Creature from the Black Lagoon	75	200
Dracula	40	100
Frankenstein	20	40

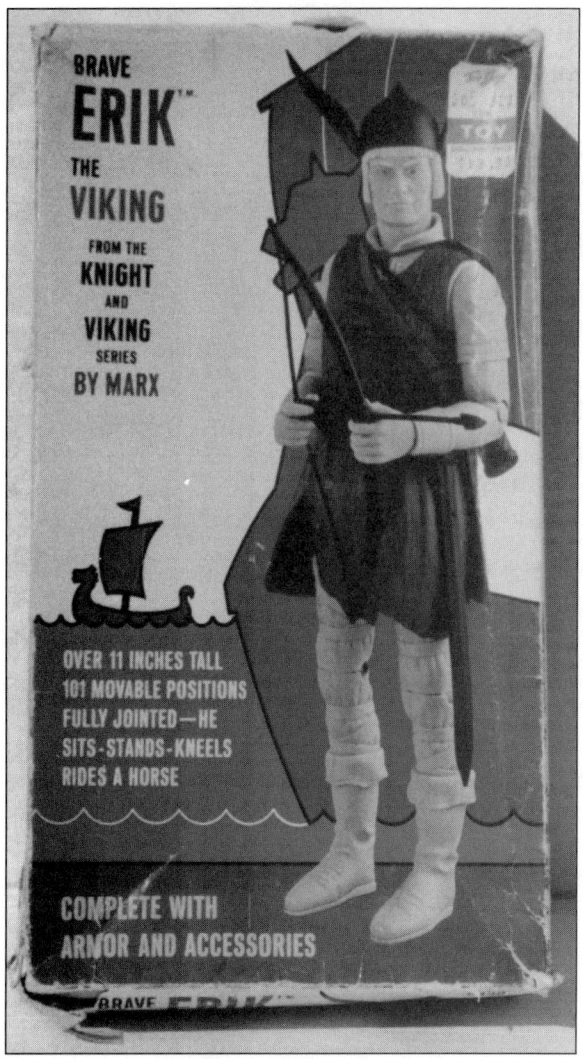

Brave Eric the Viking, Vikings, Marx, $300

8" Figures (Continued)

	C8	C10
Mummy, The	20	40
Phantom of the Opera	100	250
Wolfman, The	55	130

Vikings (Marx, 1960s)

Figures

	C8	C10
Brave Eric the Viking	150	300
Mighty Viking Horse	150	300
Odin the Viking Chieftan	150	300

Waltons (Mego, 1975)

8" Figures

	C8	C10
Grandma and Grandpa	25	50
John Boy and Ellen	25	50

8" Figures (Continued)

	C8	C10
Mom and Pop	25	50

Accessories

	C8	C10
Barn	50	100
Country Store	50	100
Truck	40	80

Play Sets

	C8	C10
Farm House	75	150
Farm House with Six Figures	150	300

Welcome Back, Kotter (Mattel, 1976)

Figures

	C8	C10
Barbarino	40	80
Epstein	20	50
Horshback	20	50
Mr. Kotter	20	50
Washington	20	50

Play Sets

	C8	C10
Welcome Back Kotter Play Set, Deluxe	50	150
Welcome Back, Kotter Play Set	40	100

Wizard of Oz (Mego, 1974)

4" Boxed Figures

	C8	C10
Munchkin Dancer	75	150
Munchkin Flower Girl	75	150
Munchkin General	75	150

4" Boxed Figures (Continued)

	C8	C10
Munchkin Lollipop Kid	75	150
Munchkin Mayor	75	150

8" Boxed Figures

	C8	C10
Cowardly Lion	25	50
Dorothy with Toto	25	50
Glinda the Good Witch	25	50
Scarecrow	25	50
Tin Woodsman	25	50
Wicked Witch	50	100
Wizard of Oz	35	250

Play Sets

	C8	C10
Emerald City with eight 8" figures	125	350
Emerald City with Wizard of Oz	45	100
Munchkin Land	150	300
Witch's Castle, Sears Exclusive	250	450

Wonder Woman Series (Mego, 1977-80)

Figures

	C8	C10
Major Steve Trevor, 1978	26	65
Queen Hippolyte, 1978	40	100

Welcome Back Kotter Play Set, Deluxe, Welcome Back, Kotter, Mattel, $150

Wonder Women with Fly Away Action, Wonder Woman Series, Mego, $250

Figures (Continued)

	C8	C10
Queen Nubia, 1978	40	100
Wonder Woman with Diana Prince Outfit, 1978	100	200
Wonder Women with Fly Away Action	125	250

World's Greatest Super Knights (Mego, 1975)

8" Figures

	C8	C10
Black Knight	90	355
Ivanhoe	65	275
King Arthur	60	200
Sir Galahad	80	300
Sir Lancelot	80	300

Ivanhoe, World's Greatest Super Knights, Mego, $275

Captain America, 8" figure, 1972, World's Greatest Super-Heroes, Mego, $200

World's Greatest Super Pirates (Mego, 1974)

Figures

	C8	C10
Blackbeard	200	500
Captain Patch	175	300
Jean Lafitte	250	550
Long John Silver	250	550

World's Greatest Super-Heroes (Mego, 1972-78)

8" Figures

	C8	C10
Aquaman, 1972, boxed	50	150
Aquaman, 1972, carded	50	150
Batgirl, 1973, boxed	125	300
Batgirl, 1973, carded	125	250
Batman, fist fighting, 1975, boxed	150	350
Batman, painted mask, 1972, boxed	60	150
Batman, painted mask, 1972, carded	60	100
Batman, removable mask, 1972, boxed	200	350

Catwoman, 8" figure, 1973, World's Greatest Super-Heroes, Mego, $350

Left to Right: Captain America, boxed, 1972, $200; Spiderman, boxed, 1972, $100.

8" Figures (Continued)

	C8	C10
Falcon, 1974, boxed	60	150
Falcon, 1974, carded	60	450
Green Arrow, 1973, boxed	150	450
Green Arrow, 1973, carded	150	550
Green Goblin, 1974, boxed	90	275
Green Goblin, 1974, carded	90	650
Human Torch, Fantastic Four, 1975, boxed	25	90
Human Torch, Fantastic Four, 1975, card	25	50
Incredible Hulk, 1974, boxed	20	100
Incredible Hulk, 1974, carded	20	50
Invisible Girl, Fantastic Four, 1975, boxed	30	150
Invisible Girl, Fantastic Four, 1975, card	30	60
Iron Man, 1974, boxed	75	125
Iron Man, 1974, carded	75	450
Isis, 1976, boxed	75	250
Isis, 1976, carded	75	125
Joker, 1973, boxed	60	150
Joker, 1973, carded	60	150
Joker, fist fighting, 1975, boxed	150	400
Lizard, 1974, boxed	75	200
Lizard, 1974, carded	75	450
Lizard, fist fighting, 1974, boxed	200	600
Mr. Fantastic, Fantastic Four, 1975, boxed	30	140
Mr. Fantastic, Fantastic Four, 1975, carded	30	60
Mr. Mxyzptlk, open mouth, 1973, boxed	50	75
Mr. Mxyzptlk, open mouth, 1973, carded	50	150
Mr. Mxyzptlk, smirk, 1973, boxed	60	150

8" Figures (Continued)

	C8	C10
Batman, removable mask, 1972, Kresge card only	200	450
Bruce Wayne, 1974, boxed, Montgomery Ward exclusive	1200	2000
Captain America, 1972, boxed	60	200
Captain America, 1972, carded	60	150
Catwoman, 1973, boxed	150	350
Catwoman, 1973, carded	150	450
Clark Kent, 1974, boxed, Montgomery Ward exclusive	1200	2000
Conan, 1975, boxed	150	400
Conan, 1975, carded	150	500
Dick Grayson, 1974, boxed, Montgomery Ward exclusive	1200	2000

Joker, 8" figure, 1973, World's Greatest Super-Heroes, Mego, $150

Superman, 8" figure, 1972, World's Greatest Super-Heroes, Mego, $125

8" Figures (Continued)

	C8	C10
Penguin, 1973, boxed	60	150
Penguin, 1973, carded	60	125
Peter Parker, 1974, boxed, Montgomery Ward exclusive	1200	2000
Riddler, 1973, boxed	100	250
Riddler, 1973, carded	100	400
Riddler, fist fighting, 1975, boxed	150	400
Robin, fist fighting, 1975, boxed	125	350
Robin, painted mask, 1972, boxed	60	150
Robin, painted mask, 1972, carded	60	90
Robin, removable mask, 1972, boxed	250	400
Robin, removable mask, 1972, solid box	250	1500
Shazam, 1972, boxed	75	200
Shazam, 1972, carded	75	150
Spider-Man, 1972, boxed	20	100
Spider-Man, 1972, carded	20	50
Supergirl, 1973, boxed	300	450
Supergirl, 1973, carded	300	450
Superman, 1972, boxed	50	125
Superman, 1972, carded	50	100

8" Figures (Continued)

	C8	C10
Tarzan, 1972, boxed	50	150
Tarzan, 1976, Kresge card only	60	225
Thing, Fantastic Four, 1975, boxed	40	150
Thing, Fantastic Four, 1975, carded	40	60
Thor, 1975, boxed	150	300
Thor, 1975, carded	150	300
Wonder Woman, boxed	100	350
Wonder Woman, Kresge card only	100	450
Wondergirl	125	400

12-1/2" Figures

	C8	C10
Amazing Spider-Man, 1978	40	100
Batman, 1978	60	125
Batman, magnetic, 1978	75	100
Captain America, 1978	75	150

Captain America, 12-1/2" Figure, 1978, World's Greatest Super-Heroes, Mego, $150

12-1/2" Figures (Continued)

	C8	C10
Hulk, 1978	30	60
Robin, magnetic, 1978	75	100
Spider-Man, web shooting	75	150

Accessories

	C8	C10
Super Hero Carry Case, 1973	40	100
Supervator, 1974	60	120

Play Sets

	C8	C10
Aquaman vs. the Great White Shark, 1978	300	750
Batcave Play Set, 1974, vinyl	150	300
Batman's Wayne Foundation Penthouse, 1977, fiberboard	600	1200
Hall of Justice, 1976, vinyl	125	250

Superman Series

	C8	C10
General Zod, 1978	50	100
Jor-El, 1978	50	100
Lex Luthor, 1978	50	100
Superman, 1978	50	125

Teen Titans, 6-1/2" Figures

	C8	C10
Aqualad	175	350
Kid Flash	175	300
Speedy	300	500
Wondergirl	200	450

Vehicles

	C8	C10
Batcopter, 1974, boxed	75	150
Batcopter, 1974, on display card	55	110
Batcycle, black, 1975, boxed	75	185
Batcycle, black, 1975, carded	60	150
Batcycle, blue, 1974, boxed	75	170
Batcycle, blue, 1974, carded	75	135
Batmobile and Batman	40	100
Batmobile, 1974, artwork box	75	325
Batmobile, 1974, carded	50	120
Batmobile, 1974, photo box	75	395
Captain America, 1976	125	275
Green Arrowcar, 1976	175	350
Jokermobile, 1976	150	300
Mobile Bat Lab, 1975	125	250
Spidercar, 1976	50	125

AIRCRAFT

(See also Tin Wind-Ups, Comic Characters, Premiums and Paper)

The airplane, until the last several years, was one aspect of toy collecting that attracted little interest and even less enthusiasm. Prices of toy airplanes generally reflected this lethargy.

As those of us born and raised during 1920-1940 (the golden age of aviation) acquired the time, the inclination and the means to obtain those objects on which our fantasies were transported during childhood, the scramble began, and demand and prices have been climbing steadily ever since.

Collecting toy aircraft and memorabilia has finally come into its own. As an investment, they seem a good risk, although I find few true collectors who get any joy from acquiring only objects that are guaranteed to appreciate in value. True value lies in the ability of an object to rekindle our memories or stir the imagination.

Those interested in collecting die-cast toy aircraft can choose from Tootsietoy, Hubley, Erie, Manoil, Barclay, Dinky, Mercury, S.R., Solido, Tekno, C.I.J., and a host of others. Cast iron was used by numerous companies before World War II, including Hubley, Arcade, Dent and Kilgore. Pressed steel seemed to be dominated by Wyandotte and Marx for the smaller types, and Keystone, Kingsbury and Steelcraft, among others, produced the larger types. Tin toy aircraft was made by many companies. The pre-war types were made by Marx, Strauss, Chein, Kingsbury, Girard, American Flyer, and numerous European manufacturers. Japanese companies, although having produced some very desirable toys prior to World War II, joined the fray in the 1950s. Some of the later Japanese tin types were very accurate representations of actual aircraft, while others resembled real aircraft as much as Godzilla resembles Snow White.

Some of the nicest toy aircraft ever produced were the "Gnom" series made by Lehmann in the 1930s. These accurate small tin toys were based on two Heinkel aircraft and variations thereof. They are difficult to find and quite a nice display item.

In addition to the above, there are numerous examples of slush-cast items from Barclay, Kansas Toy and Novelty, Tommy Toy, Ralstoy, Lincoln White Metal, Best and perhaps the finest examples of the slush-cast toy industry from C.A. Wood. In addition to the above, some very unique planes were made by the Sun and Auburn rubber companies but well-preserved and undistorted rubber toy aircraft are very rare.

Some excellent plastic types were produced immediately after World War II and into the 1960s. Some items, such as the P-38, B-25, B-17 and P-40 by Renwal and the B-26 by Hubley, were faithful copies as well as those made by Reliable Plastics of Canada, while others, such as the P-39 by Ideal, are so out of proportion that they lack even the symbiotic charm that often accompanies grotesqueness. Other toy manufacturers of plastic toy aircraft were Thomas, Acme, Premier, Lido, and Reliable.

If one collects toy aircraft, it follows that one wants to display toy aircraft, and they really look best on the numerous toy airports depicting structures of the same time period. In addition to airfields and hangars, there were numerous ground support personnel and vehicles.

Interest in aviation continues, and the flight of the Voyager, along with the development of the Stealth and numerous other record-setting craft, will have a dramatic effect on the interest in things related to flight. Consequently, prices will rise and availability will decrease in inverse proportion to interest.

Contributors: Capt. Perry R. Eichor, USAF (retired) and Donna Eichor, 703 North Almond Drive, Simpsonville, SC, 29681. I.D. Planes—Richard L. MacNary, 4727 Alpine Dr., Lilburn, GA 30247. Captain Eichor has been collecting aircraft toys since he was a young officer in the Air Force, his twenty-one years as an Air Force officer only served to deepen his interest in the subject. Today when he is not collecting, researching or writing about aeronautical toys, he works as a criminal justice administrator as well as an appraiser and auctioneer.

A.C. Williams

	C6	C8	C10
UX-166, cast-iron, Lindy-type plane, nickeled engine and wheels, 5-3/4" wingspan	75	112	150
UX83, cast iron, 3-1/4" wingspan	100	150	200
UX-99, cast iron, 4-1/2" wingspan	112	170	225
Zeppelin, cast iron, "Graf Zeppelin," 8" long	100	175	275
Zeppelin, cast iron, "Graf Zeppelin," 5-1/2" long	100	150	200
Zeppelin, cast iron, "Graf Zeppelin," 5" long	50	75	125

American Flyer

	C6	C8	C10
Monoplane, No. 560, "A.F. Lines Air Service," c. 1929, 24" wingspan	350	525	700
Spirit of America, c. 1928, 18" wingspan	150	225	400

Arcade

	C6	C8	C10
Airplane, No. 3640, cast-iron, single engine, pressed-steel wing, body resembles Corsair, red and yellow, or blue and yellow, 10" wingspan	230	345	500

Arcade (Continued)

	C6	C8	C10
Airplane, No. 3630, cast-iron, twin engine, pressed-steel wing, 7" wingspan	175	265	350
Airplane, No. 3620, cast-iron, tri-motor, pressed-steel props, 4" wingspan	50	90	150
Airplane, No. 361, cast iron, twin engine, "United Boeing," 4-7/8" wingspan	50	90	150
Arcadia Airport	600	950	1400
Monocoupe, 5-1/2" long	262	395	525
Monocoupe, No. 357, cast iron, pull toy, 11" wingspan	1300	2100	3200
Monocoupe, No. 355, cast iron, steel wing, 8-1/2" wingspan	475	750	1000
Monocoupe, No. 353, 4-1/2" long	200	250	400

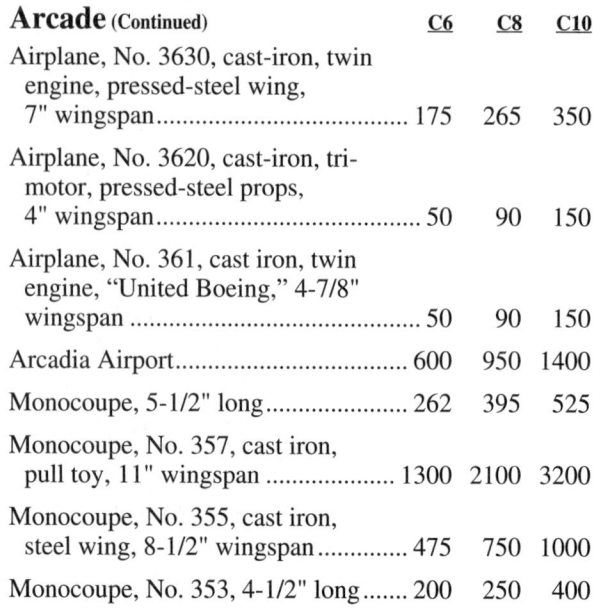

American Flyer Monoplane, No. 560, c. 1929, 24" wingspan, $700. Photo courtesy Wilkinson Collection, Detroit Antique Toy Museum

American Flyer ad from the 1929 Playthings *magazine*

Arcade Arcadia Airport, missing awnings

*Arcade Monocoupe, No. 357, 11" wingspan, $3200.
Photo courtesy Bill Bertoia Auctions*

*Top row, left to right: Auburn Rubber Boeing, No.
1548, 8" wingspan, $115; Auburn Rubber Consoli-
dated A-11 Light Bomber, 4" wingspan, $115. Bottom
row, left to right: Auburn Rubber Army Pursuit Plane,
No. 586, $60; Auburn Rubber Douglas DC2 Trans-
port, $100. Photo courtesy Ed Poole*

*Barclay Aeroplane, No. 195, $110. Photo cour-
tesy Hank Anton*

Auburn Rubber

	C6	C8	C10
Army Pursuit Plane, No. 586, "US 1X2755" on wings, Curtiss P-37, (AA3)	10	30	60
Boeing, No. 1548, "Clipper," 8" wingspan, (AA1)	25	70	115
Consolidated A-11 Light Bomber, 4" wingspan, (AA2)	25	70	115
Douglas DC2 Transport, (AA4)	40	60	100
Jet, marked "XR577," 8", (AA6)	35	52	70
Jet 559, (AA5)	22	33	45

Automatic Toy Co.

	C6	C8	C10
Futurmatic Airport	150	225	300
Rocket and Space Ship, No. 305, tin litho, friction, w/rubber wheels, sparks, 1930s, 9" long, 4-1/2" wide, 3" tall	30	50	75
Silver Eagle, aluminum, wooden wheels, two engine, c. 1930s, 13" wingspan	75	125	200

Barclay

	C6	C8	C10
Aeroplane, No. 195, "U.S. Army," single engine transport, 3-3/4" wingspan, (BA7)	20	30	50
Aeroplane, No. 195, w/Monoplane piggy-backed on it, (BA7a)	50	75	120
Aeroplane, No. 195, w/clip of bombs attached to it, (BA7b)	45	70	110
Altantic Bremen, The, c. 1928, (BA2)	40	75	100
Dirigible, early to mid 1930, 4-3/8", (BA4a)	20	40	60
Giant Zeppelin, No. 57, (BA4)	17	25	35
Lindy-type Plane, No. 52, small, (BA10)	15	20	30
Monoplane, thick-winged, w/oversized wheels; shown in 1935 Barclay Bros. Catalog, approx. 2-1/2" long, (BA9)	20	30	45
Monoplane, No. 307, single engine, (BA1a)	48	72	95
Monoplane, No. 195, single engine, high-wing, Crackerjack size, one-piece, vertical prop, sold w/Aeroplane Carrier and piggy-back on Aeroplane, (BA3)	17	25	35
Rocket Ship, No. 611, (BA6)	100	150	200
Rocket Ship, No. 610, (BA5)	100	150	200

Big Bang

	C6	C8	C10
Bombing Plane, No. 11-P, cast iron, single barrel, die-cast propeller, 13" long	600	900	1500

Big Bang Bombing Plane, No. 11-P, 13" long, $800. Photo courtesy Sotheby's, New York

Buddy "L" Army Tank Transport Plane, No. 959, 1941, 27" wingspan, $925. Photo courtesy Richard MacNary

Big Bang (Continued)	**C6**	**C8**	**C10**
Bombing Plane, No. 11-P, cast iron, double barrel, steel propeller, 13" long	350	600	800

Buddy "L"	**C6**	**C8**	**C10**
Army Tank Transport Plane, No. 959, pressed steel, two detachable tanks under wings, tanks have hum motor device, 1941, 27" wingspan	460	690	925
Monoplane and Catapult Hanger, No. 2007, c. 1930-31	1200	2200	3000
Single High-wing Monoplane, No. 5000, c. 1929-31	400	600	800
Transport Airplane (Ford), No. 603, c. 1946, 27" wingspan	300	450	600
Triple Hangar and Three Planes, No. 5010, (planes are monocoupes), c. 1931	1700	2700	3750

C.A.W. Novelty Company

Charles A. Wood was known as the "Pioneer Birdman" in Clay Center, Kansas. Master aircraft mechanic, early pilot and aviation booster, his emphasis on aircraft in his toy line reflected his lifelong love. Unfortunately his toys have been largely unavailable to collectors.

Wood's line was heavy with miniature airplanes. It was reported he flew his toys to Eastern markets: This could have been true under special circumstances only, for in its best years (over sixty employees and two million toys) the company output would have been too large to ship by air.

In comparing his toys and others, we see that Wood didn't take any shortcuts. He manufactured a Ford Trimotor with the landing gear and outboard motors on struts; pilots' heads showing through open cockpit windows; and a most realistic model of Ben Howard's famous stunt-plane with "Mr. Mulligan" prominently embossed. Wood's early production had metal disk wheels with painted black "tires." Later toys had rubber or plastic wheels. All aircraft had cast propellers, tapered and rounded wings except C.A.W. All of his pieces are more models than toys. His replicas of famous aircraft, local airliners, and mailplanes are miniature souvenirs of history.

Because Wood was such an activist a brief biography may be of interest. He was born about 1891, and went to work for Longren Aircraft Mfg. Co. in Topeka, Kansas in 1915. He opened the toy factory in Clay Center in 1925, and was influential in establishing a local airport in a wheat field in 1929. He received a pilot's license, bought a Waco F biplane, erected a Butler hangar, and opened a repair service in 1930. He was active in persuading Midland Air Express and Western Air Express lines to make route stops in Clay Center, which put this county seat on the air map.

In 1938, during National Airmail Week, Wood flew a commemorative from Morganville to Kansas City. One mail sack was delivered to the airfield by a Pony Express horseman. During the war he was an instructor at a naval training center. Later, he owned a Rearwing plane, was a Piper Cub dealer, and in 1955, designed and built a monoplane dubbed "Little Monster." He continued to fly until 1976—a grand old man of early aviation.

	C6	**C8**	**C10**
Army Pursuit Plane, No. 37, P-37 Monoplane, low-wing, marked "Seversky," under wings is Air Corp mark, "37" and "Made in USA," cowled radial engine, 2-7/8" x 3-1/2", (CWA12)	50	90	150

C.A.W. Novelty Company Army Pursuit Plane, No. 37, 2-7/8" x 3-1/2", $150. Photo courtesy Perry Eichor

C.A.W. Novelty Company Mister Mulligan Airplane, No. 34, c. 1936 production, 3" x 3-1/2", $170. Photo courtesy Perry Eichor

Top row, left to right: C.A.W. Novelty Company Monoplane, 3-1/8" x 3-5/8", $120; C.A.W. Novelty Company Sr. Low-wing Monoplane, No. 29, 3-3/4" x 4", $100; C.A.W. Novelty Company Jr. Low-wing Monoplane, No. 28, 3-5/8" x 3-1/2", $70. Bottom row, left to right: C.A.W. Novelty Company Boeing Bomber, No. 36, 2-58" x 3-1/2", $100; C.A.W. Novelty Company Army Pursuit Plane, No. 37, 2-7/8" x 3-1/2", $150. Photo courtesy Perry Eichor

C.A.W. Novelty Company Monoplane, No. 12, 3-1/8" x 4-3/8", $125. Photo courtesy Gary Fransom

C.A.W. Novelty Company (Continued)

	C6	C8	C10
Boeing Bomber, No. 36, low-wing, marked "Boeing," "NC13361" and "Made in USA," bi-motored, three-bladed props, looks like Boeing model 247 airliner, 2-58" x 3-1/2", (CWA11)	50	75	100
Jr. Low-wing Monoplane, No. 28, Northrop, cowled radial engine, w/two restrooms, six wondows, pilot in open cockpit near tail, 3-5/8" x 3-1/2", (CWA8)	30	50	70
Mister Mulligan Airplane, No. 34, high-wing, marked "Mister Mulligan" and "NR273Y," cowled radial engine, two windows, two doors, c. 1936 production, 3" x 3-1/2", (CWA10)	60	90	170
Monoplane, No. 12, Ford tri-motor model 4, seven cylinder, radial engines, outboards and landing gear on struts, tail wheel, complex molding, 3-1/8" x 4-3/8", (CWA7)	60	90	125

C.A.W. Novelty Company (Continued)

	C6	C8	C10
Monoplane, low-wing cabin or pursuit plane, cowled radial engine, forward cockpit, divided windshield, open windows w/pilot's head inside, 3-1/8" x 3-5/8", (CWA13)	60	80	120
Monoplane, high-wing, Ford Model, V-12 engine, eight window, two restrooms, crew of two in open cockpit behind wing, tail wheel, 3-5/8" x 3-1/2", (CWA3)	30	40	60
Monoplane, high-wing, Ford model 2?, V-12 engine, eight window, w/two restrooms, closed cockpit in front of wing, tail wheel, 3-5/8" x 3-1/2", (CWA4)	20	40	60
Monoplane, high-wing, Ford model 2?, V-12 engine, eight window, w/two restrooms, crew of two in open cockpit behind wing, tail wheel, stubbier wings, possibly CAW copy, 3-5/8" x 3-1/2", (CWA2b)	NPF	NPF	NPF

C.A.W. Novelty Company (Continued)

	C6	C8	C10
Monoplane, large, high-wing Lindy Ryan-type but w/V-8 engine, oversized propeller, five windows and door, probably C.A.W., (CWA14)	20	40	60
Monoplane, large, amphibian, Douglas Dolphin, bi-motored, 3-1/4" x 3-5/8", (CWA6)	40	70	100
Monoplane, small, high-wing racing-type, V-8 engine, closed cockpit in front of wing, six windows, marked "CAW" and "Pat., appld. for" under tail, 2-5/8" x 2-1/2", (CWA2)	30	45	60
Monoplane, small, high-wing Lindy-type, six-cylinder radial engine, negative dihedral in wings, 2-3/8" x 2-1/2", (CWA1)	15	20	30
Monoplane, small, Amphibian, Douglas Dolphin, bi-motored, 2-1/4" x 2-1/2", (CWA5)	400	60	80

C.A.W. Novelty Company (Continued)

	C6	C8	C10
Sr. Low-wing Monoplane, No. 29, Lockheed or Northrup cowled radial engine, six windows, pilot in open cockpit near tail, tail wheel, 3-3/4" x 4", (CWA9)	40	60	100

Dent

	C6	C8	C10
Air Express, cast iron, tri-motor, 11-1/2" wingspan	2500	4000	7000
Air Express, cast iron, green, 12" wingspan	750	1200	1500
Airline Monoplane, cast aluminum, "?" on fuselage, stripes on rudder, 12-1/2" wingspan	700	1050	1400
Airline Monoplane, cast iron, "X5043" cast on rudder, 12-1/2" wingspan	750	1000	1500
Ford, cast iron, tri-motor, "1417" cast on rudder above "Ford," 12" wingspan	2000	3500	5750

C.A.W. Novelty Company Monoplane, 3-1/8" x 3-5/8", $120

C.A.W. Novelty Company Monoplane, high-wing, 3-5/8" x 3-1/2", $60. Photo courtesy Perry Eichor

C.A.W. Novelty Company Monoplane, small, 2-3/8" x 2-1/2", $30

Dent Air Express, 12" wingspan, $1500. Photo courtesy Wilkinson Collection; Detroit Antique Toy Museum

Dent Los Angeles Dirigible, c. 1920s, 10-3/4" long, $1700. Photo courtesy Bill Bertoia Auctions

Erie Boeing B-17, $125. Photo courtesy Perry Eichor

Erie Boeing 247, $70. Photo courtesy Perry Eichor

Erie Northrup Delta, $125. Photo courtesy Perry Eichor

Dent (Continued)	C6	C8	C10
Lindy, cast iron, 12-1/2" wingspan	1000	1900	3000
Los Angeles Dirigible, cast iron, c. 1925, 8-1/2"	450	675	900
Los Angeles Dirigible, c. 1932, 6-3/4" long	150	225	400
Los Angeles Dirigible, cast iron, c. 1925, 13" long	1000	1500	2000
Los Angeles Dirigible, cast iron, c. 1920s, 10-3/4" long	700	1200	1700
Lucky Boy, 4" wingspan	100	200	225
Lucky Boy, cast iron, "X6043" cast on rudder, 12-1/2" wingspan	800	1200	1600
Lucky Boy, cast iron, tri-motor, 7" wingspan	550	800	1200
Lucky Boy Glider, cast iron, high-wing, 6-1/2" wingspan	300	500	800
Question Mark, cast iron, tri-motor, "?" on fuselage, 12" wingspan	3000	6000	8000
Zep Zeppelin, cast iron, 6-1/2" long	150	300	400
Zep Zeppelin, aluminum, 5" long	65	90	140
Zep Zeppelin, cast iron, 5"	100	150	200

Erie	C6	C8	C10
Boeing 247, twin engine, marked "U.S. Army"	25	45	70
Boeing B-17	25	60	125
Northrup Delta, single-engine passenger airliner	30	60	125
Northrup Gamma, single seat, open cockpit	50	80	135
Two-place open cockpit, "U.S. Army" on wings	30	50	75

Gibbs	C6	C8	C10
Biplane, wooden, tin tail, aluminum propeller, pull plane, propeller spin, 7-1/2" wingspan approx.	40	70	200

Girard	C6	C8	C10
High-wing Monoplane, pressed steel, 18" wingspan	150	500	750

Girard (Continued)	C6	C8	C10
High-wing Monoplane, pressed steel, 10" wingspan	150	275	500
Whiz Skyfighter Biplane, early	100	200	300

Hubley	C6	C8	C10
302 DO-X Seaplane, cast iron, high-wing, six engine, 4" wingspan, (H31)	100	200	300
Air Ford, cast iron, two open cockpits, 4" long, (H38)	150	200	275
Air Ford, 3-3/4" wingspan, (H40)	85	125	170
Airplane, No. 467, die-cast, folding wings, retractable landing gear, plastic cockpit, resembles Brewster Buffalo, red and silver w/four-bladed prop in early version, later version was green and yellow w/two-blade prop, 8-5/8" wingspan, (H25)	52	78	105
America, cast iron, largest cast-iron plane made, tri-motor, open cockpit, w/pilot and copilot, 17" wingspan, (H1)	2000	4500	8500

Erie Northrup Gamma, $135

Hubley American Eagle or Flying Circus, $125. Photo courtesy Perry Eichor

Hubley (Continued)	C6	C8	C10
America, cast iron, single engine, wire spring drive, w/two pilots in open cockpit, 17" wingspan, (H15)	3000	7500	12,000
American Eagle or Flying Circus, Early—red and silver, four-bladed prop, no airscoop on top of engine cowl, (H21)	75	100	150
American Eagle or Flying Circus, Mid—two tone blue, red cowl, large airscoop atop engine cowl, four-bladed prop, (H21)	40	75	125
American Eagle or Flying Circus, Late—orange and yellow, large airscoop, either four- or two-bladed prop, (H21)	20	40	75
Attack Bomber, No. 326, plastic, retractable landing gear, Martin B-26 Marauder copy, 7-7/8" wingspan, (H19)	75	125	225
Bell Airacuda XFM-1, die-cast, red and silver, folding landing gear, movable guns in front of twin pusher engines, three-bladed props, new in 1940, (H2)	150	250	425
Bremen, cast iron, 6-1/2" wingspan, (H13)	600	1000	1450
Bremen, cast iron, 7" wingspan, (H13A)	500	1200	1600
Bremen, cast iron, marked "Junkers Bremen" on fuselage, open cockpit w/two pilots, prop turned by wheels, 10" wingspan, (H14)	2000	5000	8000

Hubley Attack Bomber, No. 326, 7-7/8" wingspan, $225. Photo courtesy Perry Eichor

Hubley Bell Airacuda XFM-1, $425. Photo courtesy Perry Eichor

Hubley Bremen, 6-1/2" wingspan, $1450. Photo courtesy Bill Bertoia Auctions

Hubley Friendship Seaplane, 13" wingspan, $10,000. Photo courtesy Bill Bertoia Auctions

Left to Right: Hubley Hellcat, 9-1/4" wingspan, $40; Hubley U.S. Army Monoplane, 6" wingspan, $75. Photo courtesy Perry Eichor

Hubley Lindy, 10" wingspan, $1400. Photo courtesy Perry Eichor

Hubley (Continued)	C6	C8	C10
Bremen, aluminum, 6-1/2" wingspan, (H12)	250	500	1000
Crusader, No. 427, die-cast, twin engine, twinboom, marked, "TAT NC-31," 5-1/8" wingspan, (H27)	40	80	120
Delta Wing Jet, No. 751, die-cast, folding, retractable landing gear, red and silver plastic cockpit, 6-1/8" wingspan, (H26)	30	60	100
DO-X Seaplane, cast iron, high-wing, six engine, 5" wingspan, (H32)	100	270	350
Friendship Seaplane, cast-iron, marked "Fokker" embossed on fuselage, 13" wingspan, (H16)	3000	6000	10,000
Giro Plane, No. 304, cast iron, nickel-plate rotor, prop and engine, (H30)	75	120	200
Hellcat, plastic, 9-1/4" wingspan, (H33)	20	30	40
Jet, No. 430, die-cast, single engine, folding wings, retractable landing gear, cast cockpit, either red and silver or blue and silver, 6" wingspan, (H7)	40	60	80

Hubley (Continued)	C6	C8	C10
Lindy, cast iron, 10" wingspan, (H9)	600	1000	1400
Lindy, cast iron, prop turns via gear attached to wheel, 10" wingspan, (H10)	1000	1500	3000
Lindy, cast iron, w/"Spirit of St. Louis" decals, ratchet drive action noise-maker, has wing struts, (H11)	1250	2500	4000
Lindy, No. 377, cast iron, single engine, 3-1/2" wingspan, (H3)	75	100	150

Hubley (Continued)

	C6	C8	C10
Lindy Glider, cast iron, 6-1/4" long, (H34)	300	700	1200
Lockheed Sirius, marked "Lindy NR-211," 9" long, (H37)	3000	7000	10,500
Monoplane, No. 303, cast iron, low-wing single engine, nickel-plate wings and prop w/various colored body, 5" wingspan, (H28)	50	80	120
Monoplane, No. 305, cast iron, low-wing, single-engine, nickel plate wings and prop, 3-3/4" wingspan, (H29)	30	50	75
Navy Blimp, 4-1/2" long, (H39)	140	210	280
P-38, die-cast, red and silver, retractable landing gear, later versions are yellow and green camouflage, 12-5/8" wingspan, (H24)	100	150	200
P-39, die-cast and tin, "U.S. Army" imprinted on rear horizon stabilizers, tin wings, 5-1/2", (H20)	30	50	75

Hubley Lindy Glider, 6-1/4" long, $1200. Photo courtesy Sotheby's, New York

Hubley Lockheed Sirius, 9" long, $10500. Photo courtesy Bill Bertoia Auctions

Hubley (Continued)

	C6	C8	C10
P-40, die-cast, early version was silver and red w/three-bladed prop, later version orange and yellow w/two-bladed prop, 8" wingspan, (H23)	68	100	135
Piper Club, No. 433, red, also in olive drab L-4 version, 7-7/8" wingspan, (H22)	20	40	60
Question Mark, tri-motor, 12-1/2" wingspan, (H36)	1750	3000	4500
Twin Engine, No. 389, cast iron, painted and nickel plate, marked "TAT NC 431," 5-5/8" wingspan, (H5)	50	75	100
Twin Engine, silver and red or green, 3-3/8" wingspan, (H6)	30	60	80
U.S. Army Monoplane, No. 431, die-cast, white rubber tires, enclosed in cast fairings, single engine, low-wing, 5-1/2" wingspan, (H4)	30	45	70
U.S. Army Monoplane, die-cast, low-wing, single-engine, folding wheels, silver and red (early versions had red wood hubs w/white rubber tires, cast cockpit may have openings or be cast or solid), introduced in 1939, 8" wingspan, (H17)	65	100	130

Hubley P-38, 12-5/8" wingspan, $200. Photo courtesy Roger Johnson

Three cockpit variations of the Hubley U.S. Army Monoplane. Photo courtesy Perry Eichor

Hubley (Continued)

	C6	C8	C10
U.S. Army Monoplane, plastic, low-wing, single-engine, folding wheels, silver and red, folding wheels, "U.S. Army" embossed on horizontal stabilizer, 6" wingspan, (H18)	25	45	75
U.S.N. 3-B-4, die-cast, twin engine, twin vertical stabilizer, retractable landing gear, 5-1/8" wingspan, (H8)	60	80	110

I.D. Planes

Black I.D. planes, as they are popularly known, were manufactured during World War II primarily as training aids for the United States, Navy and later the United States Army. There were also postwar I.D.s. The World War II airplanes covered in this section were all made in 1:72-scale and were usually marked on the bottom in raised lettering with the country of ownership/design (United States, Britain, Germany, etc.), the aircraft type (P-38, Spitfire, FW 189, etc.), and the date of model issue (7-42, 8-42, 5-42, etc.).

The program reportedly started the day after Pearl Harbor, but the earliest marking on any of the known models is May 1942. (The dates so marked on the planes are dates of model issue or copyright, not the date the actual plane became operational.) Some of the early World War II attempts at manufacturing these identification aircraft used materials such as reinforced plaster (too lumpy), papier-mâché (too little detail), a hard rubber-like material (too pliable for long sections like wings), metal, and even cast iron (too heavy for shipping and perhaps needed elsewhere).

The vast majority of I.D. aircraft were molded by the Cruver Company of Chicago. The master molds were made by either the Comet Engraving Company or H & H Specialty Company, also both of Chicago. A few models were molded by Design Center and Leominster.

Although they were manufactured for the U.S. Armed Forces, Polk's Hobbies of New York did sell some domestically under the Aristo-Craft name. Most of the surviving World War II types, though, were probably "midnight requisitioned" by pilot or gunner trainees. The quantity produced during the war was staggering. The February 1944 issue of *Flying* magazine states that Cruver had manufactured over 2,000,000 model aircraft since the spring of 1941 (they meant spring of 1942). Not many remain today.

The following listing of World War II model planes was taken from the most complete compilation known, however, it may not be totally inclusive nor may all of these planes have been made in quantity. The best history of I.D. aircraft made from different materials and in different scales, as well as those of the later Korean War vintage, was written by Robert C. Mikesh in the May/June 1984 issue of *Fine Scale Modeler* magazine.

You will note in the guide that not much distinction is made between the values for similar-size models. There is neither enough buying and selling nor enough large collections to accurately determine which plane is more rare than another. They could all be equally hard to find today.

As to grading, C10 means no scuffs, no warpage, no "prune-skin," no repainting or, in other words, a brand new 45-year-old airplane. C8 covers models that are very nice—planes should be complete with wheels or floats; free of serious defects like "prune-skin" or missing parts, and not repainted. The C6 grade covers everything else and probably includes the majority of the models still in existence. Each model is identified by type and date marked.

A special thanks is still due to master modeler Ray ".43 Magnum" Wheeler of Lilburn, Georgia, for his help in identifying some of the more obscure types listed.

Contributor: Richard McNary, 4727 Alpine Dr. SW, Lilburn, GA 30247

*molded by Design Center
**molded by Leominster
All other molded by Cruver

I.D. Planes (British)

	C6	C8	C10
Albacore, 8-42	30	45	60
Albemarle, 9-44	25	37	50
Barracuda, 2-43	15	22	30
Beafighter 1, 9-42	30	45	60
Beafighter 2, 9-42	30	45	60
Beafighter 6, 5-44	30	45	60
Beaufort, 9-42	25	37	50
Beaufort, none	25	37	50
Blenheim IV, 8-42	25	37	50
Boomerang (Aust.)*, none	15	22	30
Botha, 8-42	30	45	60
Defiant, 8-42	15	22	30
Firefly, 2-43	15	22	30
Fulmar, 8-42	15	22	30
Halifax, 9-42	75	100	125
Hampden, 8-42	25	37	50

I.D. Planes Focke Wulf FW 189, $50. Photo courtesy Richard MacNary

I.D. Planes Focke Wulf FW 189, $50. Photo courtesy Richard MacNary

I.D. Planes (British) (Continued)

	C6	C8	C10
Hastings, none	50	75	100
Horsa, 9-44	25	37	50
Hotspur, 6-43	15	22	30
Hurricane, 8-43	15	22	30
Lancaster, 4-43	75	100	150
Lerwick, 9-42	30	45	60
Lysander, 7-43	25	37	50
Manchester, 8-42	25	37	50
Maryland, 2-43	25	37	50
Mosquito, 3-43	30	45	60
Roc, 8-42	15	22	30
Skua, 8-42	15	22	30
Spitfire, 8-42	25	37	50
Spitfire, 1-44	25	37	50
Spitfire 22, 7-45	25	37	50
Spitfire 9A, 10-44	25	37	50
Spitfire 9B, 10-44	25	37	50
Stirling, 5-42	50	75	100
Sunderland, 9-42	90	120	150
Swordfish, 9-42	40	60	80
Tempest 2, 3-45	15	22	30
Tempest 5, 10-44	15	22	30
Typhoon, 6-43	20	30	40
Walrus, 4-44	25	37	50
Wellington 2, 9-42	30	45	60
Wellington 3, 9-42	30	45	65
Whirlwind, 8-43	25	37	50
Whitley, 9-42	25	37	50
York, 9-44	50	75	100

I.D. Planes (German)

	C6	C8	C10
Arado Ar196, 12-43	25	37	50

I.D. Planes (German) (Continued)

	C6	C8	C10
Blohm & Voss BV138, 5-44	50	75	100
Blohm & Voss BV222, 2-44	100	150	200
Blohm & Voss HA139, 11-42	100	150	200
DFS 230, 8-43	15	22	30
Dornier DO 172, 9-42	25	37	50
Dornier DO 215, 9-42	25	37	50
Dornier DO 217E, 8-42	25	37	50
Fi 156 Storch, none	40	60	80
Focke Wulf 200, 3-44	100	150	200
Focke Wulf FW 187, 8-42	25	37	50
Focke Wulf FW 189, 5-42	25	37	50
Focke Wulf FW 190, 7-42	15	22	30
Focke Wulf FW 190, 12-42	15	22	30
Focke Wulf FW 200K, 9-42	100	150	200
Gotha Go 242, 7-42	25	37	50
Heinkel He 111, 9-42	25	37	50
Heinkel He 112, 7-42	20	30	40
Heinkel He 113, 5-42	20	30	40
Heinkel He 113, 9-42	20	30	40
Heinkel He 115K, 9-42	40	60	80
Henschel Hs 126, 10-42	25	37	50
Henschel Hs 129, 8-44	25	37	50
Junkers Ju 188, 7-44	25	37	50
Junkers Ju 52, 8-42	60	90	120
Junkers Ju 86K, 9-42	25	37	50
Junkers Ju 87B, 8-42	15	22	30
Junkers Ju 88, 9-42	25	37	50
Junkers Ju 90, 9-42	50	75	100
Messers. Me 109E, 7-42	20	30	40

I.D. Planes (German) (Continued)

	C6	C8	C10
Messers. Me 109F, 7-42	20	30	40
Messers. Me 110, 8-42	25	38	50
Messers. Me 210, 7-43	30	45	60

I.D. Planes (Italian)

	C6	C8	C10
Cantiere Z. 1007, 9-42	30	45	60
Cantiere Z. 506B, 9-42	100	150	200
Caproni CA.133, 9-42	75	100	125
Fiat BR. 20, 6-42	25	38	50
Fiat CR. 42, 9-42	40	60	80
Fiat CR. 42, 1-43	40	60	80
Fiat G. 50, 8-42	20	30	40
Macchi C. 200, 8-42	20	30	40
Macchi MC. 202, 3-43	20	30	40
Piaggio P. 32 BIS, 9-42	25	38	50
Reggiane Rc. 2000, 9-42	20	30	40
Reggiane Re. 2001, 3-43	20	30	40
Savoia Marchetti 79, 9-42	50	75	100
Savoia Marchetti 81, 9-42	100	150	200
Savoia Marchetti 82, 9-42	30	45	60
Savoia Marchetti 84, 4-43	30	45	60

I.D. Planes (Japanese)

Note: Japanese abbreviations below—Kawa.=Kawanishi; Mitsu.=Mitsubishi; Naka.=Nakajima

	C6	C8	C10
(Adam) Naka. 97, 11-42	30	45	60
(Ann) Mitsu. T-98, 7-42	30	45	60
(Babs) Mitsu. T-97, 6-42	40	60	80
(Claude) Mitsu. T-96, 6042	50	75	100
(Dave) Naka. T-95-NOB, 7-42	25	37	50
(Ida) Mitsu. T-98 ALB, 6-42	30	45	60
(Kate) Naka. T-97, 6-42	15	45	60
(Mary) T-97 ALB, 6-42	30	45	60
(Mavis) Kawa., 11-42	100	150	200
(Nate) "97" Fighter, 9-42	25	37	50
(Nell) Mitsu. T-96, 6-42	25	37	50
(Sally) Mitsu. T-97, 6-42	25	38	50
(Sonia) Mitsu. T-99, 7-42	15	22	30
(Topsy) Mitsu. MC-20, 10-42	25	37	50
(Val) Aichi T-99, 6-42	40	60	80

I.D. Planes (Japanese) (Continued)

	C6	C8	C10
(Zeke) Mitsu. 00, 9-42	20	30	40
Betty (G4M1), 9-43	50	75	100
Betty (G4M2), 4-45	50	75	100
Dinah (Ki46), 8-44	30	45	60
Emily (H8K2), 3-45	40	60	80
Francis (PIY), 3-45	25	37	50
Frank (Ki84), 5-45	20	30	40
George (NIKI-J), 5-45	15	22	30
Hamp (T-00, Zeke 32), 7-43	15	22	30
Helen (Ki49)	30	45	60
Irving (J1N1), 5-45	30	45	60
Jack (J2M1), 12-44	25	37	50
Jake (E13A), 9-44	25	37	50
Jill (B6N), 5-45	15	22	30
Judy (D4Y), 3-45	30	30	40
Lily (Ki48), 9-43	20	30	40
Myrt (C6N), 3-45	15	22	30
Nell (G3M), 1-44	25	37	50
Nick (Ki45), 8-44	25	37	50
Oscar T-01 (Ki43), 9-43	20	30	40
Paul 14, Exp, 12-44	25	37	50
Pete (F1M2), 6-43	30	45	60
Rufe (A6M2-N), 8-43	40	60	80
Tojo (Ki44), 6-44	15	22	30
Tojo (Ki44), 3-45	15	22	30
Tony (Ki61), 4-45	15	22	30
Val T-99 MK2, 8-43	40	60	80
Zeke 52 (A6M5)*, 12-44	20	30	40

I.D. Planes (Netherlands)

	C6	C8	C10
Fokker T8W, 11-42	50	75	100

I.D. Planes (Russian)

	C6	C8	C10
DB-3F, 4-44	25	50	75
DB-3F, 9-42	25	50	75
I-16, none	15	22	30
I-18 (MiG-3), 2-43	15	22	30
IL-2, 12-43	15	22	30

I.D. Planes (Russian) (Continued)

	C6	C8	C10
IL-2, 9-42	15	22	30
MiG-3, 2-44	15	22	30
MiG-3, 8-42	15	22	30
Pe-2, 9-42	15	22	30
SB-3, 11-43	15	22	30
TB-7*, 4-44	15	22	30

I.D. Planes (United States)

	C6	C8	C10
A-20 Havoc, 6-42	25	37	50
A-24 Dauntless, SBD-3, 7-42	15	22	30
A-26 Invader, 2-44	25	37	50
A-29 Hudson (PBO-16), none	25	37	50
A-30 Baltimore, 2-43	25	37	50
A-31 Vengeance, 7-42	15	22	30
A-31 Vengeance, 7-44	15	22	30
A-35 Vengeance, 4-44	15	22	30
AT17 Bobcat*, 7-43	30	60	90
B-17 Flying Fortress, 7-42	100	150	200
B-24 Liberator, 7-42	100	150	200

I.D. Planes B-29 Super Fortress, $100

I.D. Planes JR2S-1 (S44) Excalibur, $200

I.D. Planes (United States)

(Continued)	C6	C8	C10
B-25 Mitchell, 7-42	75	100	125
B-26 Marauder, 10-42	75	100	125
B-26 Marauder, none	75	100	125
B-29 Super Fortress, 3-44	100	150	200
B-29 Super Fortress, 9-44	100	75	100
B-29 Super Fortress, none	100	75	100
B-32 Dominator, 12-44	150	225	300
C-46 Commando, 3-43	50	75	100
C-47 Skytrain, 3-43	40	60	80
C-47 Skytrain**, 5-43	40	60	80
C-54 Skymaster, 3-43	60	90	120
C60A Lodestar, 3-43	25	38	50
C69 Constellation, 4-44	100	150	200
C78 Bobcat, 6-44	30	45	60
C87 Liberator, 3-44	100	150	200
CG-4A Waco Glider, 6-43	30	45	60
F4F-4 Wildcat, 5-43	15	22	30
F4U-1 Corsair, 3-43	15	22	30
F6F Hellcat, 4-43	15	22	30
GH-1 Nightingale*, 5-43	25	37	50
J2F-4 Duck, 12-42	60	75	90
JR2S-1 (S44) Excalibur, 11-44	100	150	200
JRF OA-09 Goose*, 7-43	60	75	90
JRS-1 (S43), 11-42	30	45	60
L-1 Vigilant, 3-43	25	37	50
L-2 Grasshopper, 7-44	25	37	50
L-4 Grasshopper, 2-43	25	37	50
L-5 Sentinel, 1-44	25	37	50
OS2U (on floats)*, 2-43	25	37	50
OS2U (on wheels)*, 2-43	25	37	50
OS2U-1 (on floats), 7-43	25	37	50
P-38 Lightning, 7-42	25	37	50
P-39 Airacobra, 6-42	15	22	30
P-40 Warhawk, 9-42	15	22	30
P-40 Warhawk, 4-44	15	22	30
P-43 Lancer, 5-43	15	22	30
P-47 (D) Thunderbolt, 2-44	15	22	30
P-47 (N) Thunderbolt, 4-45	15	22	30

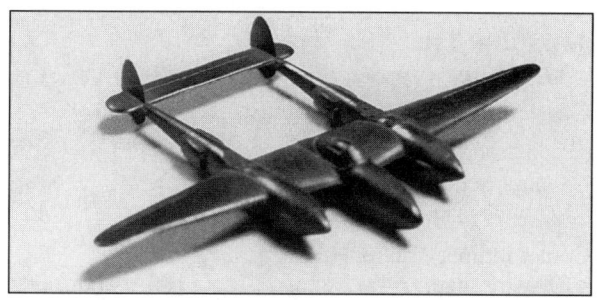

I.D. Planes P-38 Lightning, $50. Photo courtesy Richard MacNary

I.D. Planes (United States)

(Continued)

	C6	C8	C10
P-47 Thunderbolt, 9-42	15	22	30
P-47 Thunderbolt*, none	15	22	30
P-51 Mustang, 6-42	15	22	30
P-51D Mustang, 4-45	15	22	30
P-61 Black Widow, 2-44	25	37	50
P-63 King Cobra, 5-44	15	22	30
P-80 Shooting Star, 4-45	20	30	40
PB2Y-3 Coronado, 4-43	75	100	150
PBM-3 Mariner, 6-43	50	75	100
PBY-5 Catalina, 5-43	40	60	80
PV-1 (B-39) Ventura, 5-43	25	37	50
PV-2 Harpoon, 5-43	25	37	50
SB2A-2 Buccaneer, 5-43	15	22	30
SB2C-1 Helldiver, 3-43	15	22	30
SB2C-2 Helldiver, (floats)*, 3-43	30	45	60
SB2C-2 Helldiver, (wheels)*, 3-43	25	37	50
SB2U-3 Vindicator, 6-43	15	22	30
SB3C-2 Helldiver, 2-45	15	22	30
SNJ-2 Texan, 7-42	15	22	30
SNJ-3 Texan, 7-42	15	22	30
SO3C-1 Seagull (floats), 3-43	30	45	60
SO3C-2 Seagull (wheels), 3-43	25	37	50
SR-10B Reliant, 10-42	25	37	50
TBD-1 Devastator, 5-43	15	22	30
TBF Avenger, 7-43	15	22	30

Ideal

	C6	C8	C10
Electronic Fighter Jet, c. 1959	135	200	270
Globemaster	42	63	85
Helicopter City Play Set	70	105	140

Ideal (Continued)

	C6	C8	C10
U.S. Navy Rescue Float Plane, plastic, wind-up, 10" wingspan	32	48	65

JAPANESE TIN AIRPLANES

Starting with the birth of aviation, toy manufacturers began making toy replicas of anything that flew—old pusher planes through the Spirit of St. Louis, World War I biplanes, World War II fighters and bombers, commercial and military jets and the Concord. Manufacturers stopped using tin in the late 1960s and early 1970s and switched to plastic.

Contributor: Ron Smith, 33005 Arlesford, Solon, OH, 44139, 440-248-7066, fax 440-519-0906. Smith has always loved toy cars and planes, he can still show you his first Dinky Toy his aunt bought him at Fred Harvey's Toy Store in Cleveland's Terminal Tower Building. Smith has collected die-cast cars, trucks and planes, cast-iron toys and plastic promotional cars, but for the past fifteen years he has specialized in tin-plate cars and planes. Smith lives in Ohio with his wife Joan and their two cats, T-2 and Bogart.

	C6	C8	C10
1930s German, wind-up, Tipp, 16" wingspan, (A29)	700	1200	2600
American Airlines Boeing 727, battery, "Y" Co., 16" wingspan, (A39)	125	175	225
American Airlines DC-7, battery, 24" wingspan, (A37)	200	250	450
American Airlines Electra, battery, Linemar, 20" wingspan, (A38)	200	300	400
B-29, friction, "Y" Co., 19" wingspan, (A58)	150	300	500
B-36, friction, "Y" Co., 26" wingspan, (A59)	300	600	1200
B-45 Tornado, friction, Bandai, 16" wingspan, (A60)	100	150	250
B-47 USAF, friction, Daiya, 12" wingspan, (A61)	150	225	325
B50, friction, Bandai, 7-1/2" wingspan, (A14)	40	60	125
B50, friction, Bandai, 7-1/2" wingspan, (A14)	40	60	125
B-50 Superfortress, friction, TCP, 15" wingspan, (A63)	200	300	400

Japanese Tin
Airplanes (Continued)

	C6	C8	C10
B-50 USAF, battery, "Y" Co., 19" wingspan, (A62)	200	300	400
Bluebird Seaplane, friction, S&E, 13" wingspan, (A13)	100	200	300
Boeing 707, battery, 18" wingspan, (A40)	200	300	400
Boeing Stratocruiser, friction, T.N., 20" wingspan, (A41)	300	400	600
Bristol Bulldog, friction, S&E, 14-1/2" wingspan, (A4)	80	150	350
C-120 Pack Plane, friction, 16" wingspan, (A64)	250	500	900
C-124 Globemaster, friction, "Y" Co., 20" wingspan, (A65)	250	600	900

Japanese Tin Airplanes, 1930s German, 16" wingspan, $2600. Photo courtesy Ron Smith

Japanese Tin Airplanes, Bluebird Seaplane, 13" wingspan, $300. Photo courtesy Ron Smith

Japanese Tin
Airplanes (Continued)

	C6	C8	C10
Cessna, friction, T.N., 25" wingspan, (A1)	100	200	350
Cessna, friction, West German, 12" wingspan, (A5)	50	75	150
Comet Jetliner, friction, "Y" Co., 19" wingspan, (A42)	100	200	300
Constellation, friction, Ingap, 15" wingspan, (A11)	100	200	400
Construction, England, 22" wingspan, (A28)	125	175	400

Japanese Tin Airplanes, Bristol Bulldog, 14-1/2" wingspan, $350. Photo courtesy Ron Smith

Japanese Tin Airplanes, Cessna, 25" wingspan, $350. Photo courtesy Ron Smith

Japanese Tin Airplanes, Cessna, 12" wingspan, $150. Photo courtesy Ron Smith

Japanese Tin Airplanes, Constellation, 15" wingspan, $400. Photo courtesy Ron Smith

Japanese Tin Airplanes, De Havilland Comet, 13" wingspan, $500. Photo courtesy Ron Smith

Japanese Tin Airplanes, Construction, 22" wingspan, $400. Photo courtesy Ron Smith

Japanese Tin Airplanes, F3F Biplane, 11-1/2" wingspan, $500. Photo courtesy Ron Smith

Japanese Tin
Airplanes (Continued)

	C6	C8	C10
De Havilland Comet, wind-up, Rico, 13" wingspan, (A20)	100	250	500
Disney Comic Plane, friction, Linemar, 10" wingspan, (A23)	100	200	400
Eastern Constellation, friction, Hadson, 12" wingspan, (A44)	200	350	500
Eastern Constellation, friction, MSK, 7-1/2" wingspan, (A43)	100	150	250
Eastern DC-7, friction, Bandai, 17-1/2" wingspan, (A45)	200	300	500
F-102 USAF, friction, HTS, 11" wingspan, (A69)	125	150	225
F-104 Lockheed, friction, "Y" Co., 16" wingspan, (A70)	125	150	175
F3F Biplane, battery, Cragstan, 11-1/2" wingspan, (A12)	150	250	500
F-80, friction, Bandai, 7-1/2" wingspan, (A22)	40	70	100
F-84 Airforce, battery, Linemar, 13" wingspan, (A66)	100	150	200

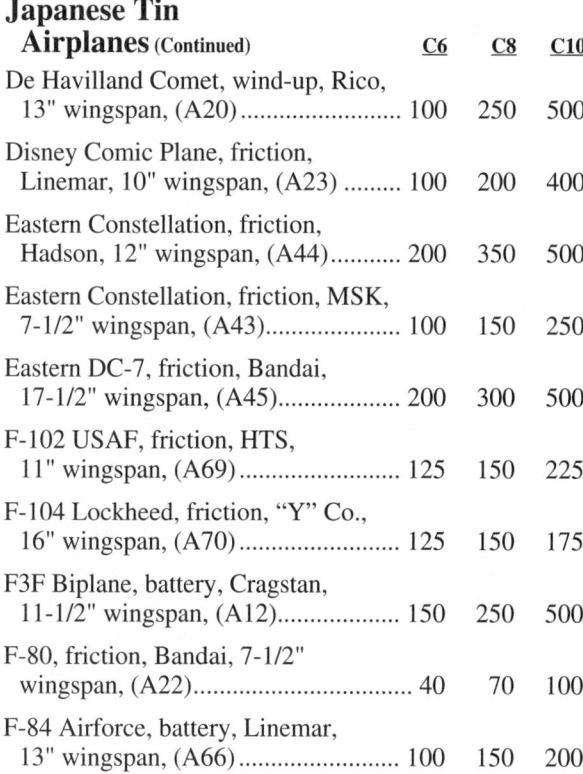

Japanese Tin Airplanes, Farman, 10" wingspan, $1200. Photo courtesy Sotheby's, New York

Japanese Tin
Airplanes (Continued)

	C6	C8	C10
F-86 Airforce, friction, "J" Co., 10" wingspan, (A67)	75	125	175
F-94C Starfire, friction, "Y" Co., 18" wingspan, (A68)	150	300	450
Farman, friction, 10" wingspan, (A36)	400	600	1200

Japanese Tin
Airplanes (Continued)

	C6	C8	C10
Fiat CR-42, wind-up, Ingap, 10" wingspan, (A30)	500	1000	2200
Ford, friction, T.N., 15" wingspan, (A6)	60	150	300
German Biplane, Bar/wind-up, Tipp, 20" wingspan, (A27)	500	1000	2500
Hein, friction, Bandai, 14" wingspan, (A32)	200	350	500
Hospital, Tekno, 14" wingspan, (A26)	400	1000	1800
Jenny Biplane, friction, Haji, 11-1/2" wingspan, (A7)	30	50	100
Jenny Biplane, friction, S&E, 14-1/2" wingspan, (A2)	75	125	250
Lockheed Sirus, friction, 13" wingspan, (A35)	400	800	1000
Northwest DC-7, friction, "Y" Co., 10" wingspan, (A50)	100	150	225

Japanese Tin Airplanes, Fiat CR-42, 10" wingspan, $2200. Photo courtesy Ron Smith

Japanese Tin Airplanes, Ford, 15" wingspan, $300. Photo courtesy Ron Smith

Japanese Tin
Airplanes (Continued)

	C6	C8	C10
Northwest DC-7, friction, Asahi, 19" wingspan, (A52)	300	600	950
Northwest Orient, battery, "Y" Co., 24" wingspan, (A51)	300	500	650
P-47 Thunderbolt, friction, HTC, 10" wingspan, (A18)	100	200	300

Japanese Tin Airplanes, Lockheed Sirus, 13" wingspan, $500. Photo courtesy Tanaka

Japanese Tin Airplanes, Hospital, 14" wingspan, $1800. Photo courtesy Ron Smith

Japanese Tin Airplanes, Jenny Biplane, 11-1/2" wingspan, $100. Photo courtesy Ron Smith

Japanese Tin Airplanes, Hein, 14" wingspan, $1000. Photo courtesy Tanaka

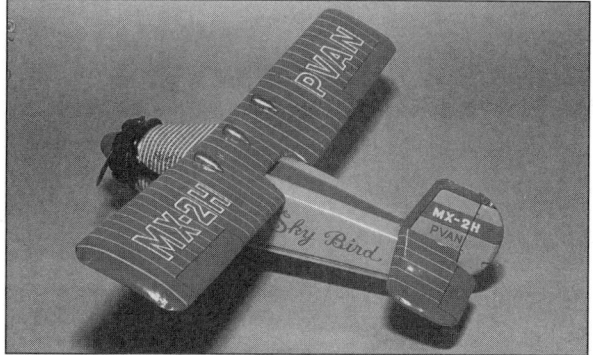

Japanese Tin Airplanes, Sky Bird "Spirit of St. Louis," 9" wingspan, $150. Photo courtesy Ron Smith

Japanese Tin Airplanes, P-47 Thunderbolt, 10" wingspan, $300. Photo courtesy Ron Smith

Japanese Tin Airplanes, WWII Fighter, 8-1/2" wingspan, $400. Photo courtesy Ron Smith

Japanese Tin Airplanes, P-51 Mustang, 10" wingspan, $300. Photo courtesy Ron Smith

Japanese Tin Airplanes, WWII Fighter, 14-1/2" wingspan, $250. Photo courtesy Ron Smith

Japanese Tin Airplanes, WWII Tri-Motor, 9" wingspan, $400. Photo courtesy Ron Smith

Japanese Tin Airplanes, Zero, 14" wingspan, $350. Photo courtesy Tanaka

Japanese Tin
Airplanes (Continued)

	C6	C8	C10
P-47 Thunderbolt, friction, HTC, 10" wingspan, (A18)	100	200	300
P-51 Mustang, friction, HTC, 10" wingspan, (A17)	100	200	300
Pam Am Jet Clipper, battery, Linemar, 18" wingspan, (A49)	200	300	425
Pam Am Stato Clipper, friction, 14" wingspan, (A48)	225	300	450
Pan Am DC-7, friction, T.N., 17" wingspan, (A47)	300	600	800
Presidents Plane, battery, 20" wingspan, (A46)	275	350	500
Ryan Spirit of St. Louis, friction, HTC, 12" wingspan, (A8)	100	250	500
Sky Bird "Spirit of St. Louis," friction, Bandai, 9" wingspan, (A15)	50	80	150
Spitfire, friction, HTC, 10" wingspan, (A16)	80	150	300
Stuka, Dux, 12" wingspan, (A31)	200	500	1000
TWA Constellation, friction, "Y" Co., 12" wingspan, (A53)	200	300	450
TWA DC-2, wind-up, 10" wingspan, (A55)	175	300	425
TWA DC-4, friction, Linemar, 19" wingspan, (A54)	150	350	475
U.N. Hospital Plane, friction, HTC, 12" wingspan, (A9)	70	150	300
United DC-7, friction, 23" wingspan, (A57)	125	250	400
United DC-7 Mainliner, battery, T.N., 19" wingspan, (A56)	150	275	350
WWII Fighter, friction, 14-1/2" wingspan, (A10)	80	150	250
WWII Fighter, wind-up, Spain, 8-1/2" wingspan, (A21)	100	200	400
WWII Tri-Motor, wind-up, Spain, 9" wingspan, (A25)	100	200	400
Zero, friction, Nomura, 14" wingspan, (A33)	150	275	350
Zero, friction, new issue, 15-1/2" wingspan, (A19)	NPF	NPF	150

Kansas Toy & Novelty Company

The years 1920-1940 were decisive for aviation—it was an era of ferment and growth, and was a time of barnstorming and record-breaking; Lindbergh and Earhart made headlines.

The state of Kansas played a large part in the development of airmail and airlines with its manufacturing centers at Topeka and Wichita (Beach, Boeing, Cessna, Laird, Stearman and others), but the toy industry reflected only dimly the excitement of the era.

Listed below are the aircraft said to have been made by KT&N from 1924 to about 1931, using metal disc or wire wheels. Reproductions from Best Toy and Ralstoy will be found with later wheels. Best Toys' later reproductions will have "Made in U.S.A." embossed; and may have small white rubber wheels.

For a more detailed history of Kansas Toy & Novelty, see their section in the Vehicles chapter.

	C6	C8	C10
Airliner, No. 47, "KTN 47," Fokker, similar to No. 45, sometimes reffered to as a seaplane, 3-5/8" x 3-1/2", (KYA9)	NPF	NPF	NPF
Airliner, marked "KTN 47," Fokker, sometimes called a seaplane, similar to No. 45, 3-5/8" x 3-1/2", (KTA10)	30	50	75
Airliner, No. 45, Fokker?, high, oval, corrugated wing and tail, nine circular cabin windows, nine rectangular flightdeck windows, six-cylinder radial engine, large tin propeller, 2-1/2" x 2-1/2", (KTA8)	30	45	75
Cabin Plane, similar to No. 6, Air Service dot-in-circle insignia, V-8 engine, cast propeller, 3-58" x 3", (KTA2)	14	21	35

Kansas Toy & Novelty Company Airliner, No. 47, 3-5/8" x 3-1/2", NPF

Kansas Toy & Novelty Company Airliner, No. 45, 2-1/2" x 2-1/2", $75. Photo courtesy Bill Conover

Left to Right: Kansas Toy & Novelty Company Cabin Plane, 3-58" x 3", $35; Kansas Toy & Novelty Company Cabin Plane, No. 6, 3-3/4" x 3", $60. Photo courtesy Perry Eichor

Kansas Toy & Novelty Company (Continued)

	C6	C8	C10
Cabin Plane, small, similar to No. 32, w/o windows and different rudder, or wingtip, 2-3/8" x 2-1/8", (KTA6)...	20	30	40
Cabin Plane, No. 32, small, high, positive dihedral wing, Air Corps star insignia, six cylinder, radial engine, six oval windows, three metal "wire" wheels, large tine or cast propeller, 2-3/8" x 2-1/8", (KTA5)....	20	30	40
Cabin Plane, No. 6, high-wing w/flaring positive dihedral, Army Air Corps star-in-circle insignia, six cylinder, radial engine, pilot head in open cockpit, eight oval windows, cast prop, lacquer finish, also unnumbered version with large tin propeller, 3-3/4" x 3", (KTA1)	30	40	60
Cabin Plane, large, Lindy-type, high negative dihedral wing w/large stars, six cylinder radial engine, wheels w/black tires, 5", (KTA4)	30	50	75
Cabin Plane, No. 24, high-wing, larger "U.S. Mail" version of above, dot-in-two-circles insignia, V-8 engine, cast propeller, white disc wheels w/painted black "tires," 5-5/8" x 4-3/8", (KTA3)	30	40	75

Kansas Toy & Novelty Company (Continued)

	C6	C8	C10
Glider, No. 56, high oval wing marked "GLIDER," pilot in front, flat lattice fuselage, 2-5/8" x 2-3/8", (KTA11)...............	15	25	40
Zeppelin, No. 44, front and rear cabins, three tail planes, mooring loop on nose, rear axle through rear cabin, 4-1/4", (KTA7).........	50	75	100

Katz Toys

	C6	C8	C10
Pathfinder, The, tri-motor monoplane, 22" wingspan.................	350	600	1200
Red Arrow, The, No. 137, single monoplane, pull toy...........	300	500	1000

Kenton

	C6	C8	C10
Air Mail Plane, 8" wingspan	600	1000	1450
Los Angeles Dirigible, 8" long...........	500	750	1050
Pony Blimp, cast iron, 6" long	125	200	400
United Boeing, cast iron, twin engine .	112	168	225

Keystone

	C6	C8	C10
Airmail Plane, "NC-263"	500	750	1000
Airmail Plane, pressed steel, marked "NX-265," 24" wingspan	800	1500	2130
Ride 'Em Mail Plane, marked "NC-273," 1930s, 23-1/2" wingspan.......	1200	2000	3000
Ride 'Em Riding Plane, No. 293, 28" wingspan....................	400	600	850
Riding Plane, seat over tail, steering bar over cabin, single wing, high, one engine, 23-1/2" long	500	750	1000
Trimotor, 1920s	900	1400	2200

Keystone Airmail Plane, 24" wingspan, $2130. Photo courtesy Calvin L. Chaussee

Kilgore

	C6	C8	C10
Ford, cast iron, tri-motor, "TAT," 13-1/2" wingspan	2000	3000	6000
Kilgore Comet Plane, cap-firing	30	75	100
Monocoupe, high-wing, 5-1/2"	125	200	250
Monoplane, cast iron, marked "N4," open cockpit, 4" long	125	188	250
Monoplane, high-wing, 3-1/2" long	50	75	100
Monoplane, cast iron, bullet, open cockpit, 4" long	100	175	275
Sea Gull, high-wing, pusher prop, 8-1/4" wingspan	625	938	1250
Seagull, high-wing, pusher prop, 4" wingspan	200	300	400
TAT, No. 401, twin-engine passenger monoplane, 4-1/2" long	150	250	325
TAT, largest Kilgore plane	2500	4200	7700
Travel Air Mystery, cast iron, double open cockpits, 6" long	250	375	500

Kilgore Ford, 13-1/2" wingspan, $6000. Photo courtesy Bill Bertoia Auctions

Kilgore Sea Gull, 8-1/4" wingspan, $1250. Photo courtesy Chic Gast

Kingsbury

	C6	C8	C10
Biplane, cast-iron, wind-up, pilot, 16" long	350	525	700
Monoplane, high-wing, tri-motor, clockwork, 15" wingspan	475	715	950
Tin Goose, tri-engine, c. 1930s, 21" wingspan	600	900	1500
Trans Atlantic Monoplane, pressed steel, painted wind-up, c. 1930, 11" long	200	300	500
U.S. Airmail biplane, pressed steel, wind-up, 15" long	200	500	900

Lehmann

	C6	C8	C10
Ikarus, tin and paper, early, 18" wingspan	1200	2000	3000
Shenandoah Dirigible, 7-1/2" long	225	388	750
Zeppelin, No. 652, "EPL 2," c. 1907	400	750	1200
Zeppelin, No. 651, "EPL 1"	400	800	1400

Lincoln White Metal

	C6	C8	C10
Airplane, tri-motored, Fokker F-11(?), tapered high-wings w/wings symbol embossed, seven cylinder, radial engines, outboards mounted in wings, unrealistic window patterns, metal wheels, 2-1/2" x 2-1/2", (LWA1)	30	50	75
Airplane, tri-motored, Fokker F-11(?), tapered high-wings w/wings symbol embossed, seven cylinder, radial engines, outboards mounted on landing gear struts, tin propellers, metal wheels, no windows, 3-1/4" x 4-1/2", (LWA2)	75	100	140

Lincoln White Metal Airplane, 2-1/2" x 2-1/2", $75

Lincoln White Metal (Continued)

	C6	C8	C10
Airplane, steamlined, swallow-shaped, pilot, cowled radial engine, tin propeller, would be called batplane today, c. 3" x 2-1/2", (LWA4)	50	80	125
Airplane, streamlined, swallow-shaped, pilot, cowled radial engine, tin propeller, would be called batplane today, c. 4-1/2" x 3", (LWA3)	75	120	200

Manoil

	C6	C8	C10
Bonanza B-35, No. 519	30	50	75
Ercoupe, No. 520	30	50	75
Lockheed F90, No. 517	30	50	75
Navion, No. 518	30	50	75

Marx

	C6	C8	C10
Air Mail Biplane, four engine, 1930	300	450	600
Air Mail Monoplane, two-engine, 1930	165	248	330

Marx Bomber, 18" wingspan, $200. Photo courtesy Richard MacNary

Marx Bomber, 14-3/4" wingspan, $250. Photo courtesy Perry Eichor

Marx (Continued)

	C6	C8	C10
Airplane, No. 90, light fuselage	100	150	200
Airplane, No. 90, medium fuselage	100	150	200
Airplane, No. 6, U.S. Army two-engine, no guns, 18" wingspan	163	245	325
American Airlines Flagship, 27-1/2"	155	230	310
Army Bomber, No. 1025, three engine, c. 1935, 26" wingspan	75	150	250
Astrojet Airport Set, planes, helicopter, etc.	155	230	310
Bomber, tin litho, sparkling mechanism, camouflaged, four engine, 18" wingspan	60	140	200
Bomber, four engine, drops wooden bombs, 14-3/4" wingspan	80	125	250
City Airport Set	300	500	750
Crop Duster Plane Set	75	125	200
Curtiss Transport, pressed steel, khaki, 9-1/2" wingspan	50	75	100
DC-3 Transport, pressed steel, c. 1939, 10" wingspan	60	80	120
DC-4 type, pressed steel, four-engine passenger, c. 1930s	60	125	250
DC-6 Transport Plane, plastic	75	120	200
Electric Lighted Radio Aiport, 1930s, 5" x 2-1/2" x 3-1/2"	200	350	500
F84 Jet Fighter, remote control	68	100	135
Futuristic Airport	212	318	425

Marx DC-6 Transport Plane, $200. Photo courtesy Perry Eichor

Marx Hangar, c. 1941, $100. Photo courtesy James Apthorpe

Marx P35-type, 15-7/8" wingspan, $210. Photo courtesy Richard MacNary

Marx P35, 13-1/2" wingspan, $120. Photo courtesy Perry Eichor

Marx Pan American Super 7 Clipper, 17-1/2" wingspan, $320. Photo courtesy Perry Eichor

Marx (Continued)	C6	C8	C10
Gyroplane	50	80	120
Hangar, tin litho, c. 1941	50	75	100
Little Lindy Aeroplane, friction, 1930s, 6" wingspan	100	150	200
Lockheed Prop Jet	125	188	250
Mainstream Aiport, c. 1930s	110	165	220
Municipal Airport Hangar, w/plane, early	400	600	800
P35, pressed steel, w/ and w/o wheel skirts, 13-1/2" wingspan	60	90	120
P35-type, two-engine bomber, 15-7/8" wingspan	105	158	210

Marx (Continued)	C6	C8	C10
Pan American, pressed steel, four engine, propeller-driven, also as PAA, 1940, 27" wingspan	200	300	400
Pan American Super 7 Clipper, also as American Airlines, 17-1/2" wingspan	160	240	320
Piggyback Airplane Set	75	125	150
Pioneer Air Express, tin litho, high-wing monoplane, 25-1/2" wingspan	100	125	250
Skycruiser, two-engine transport plane w/siren and whirling propellers, Stratoliner 700, rubber wheels, c. 1940s, 18" wingspan	180	300	450
Skycruiser Stratoliner 700, two-engine	50	75	100

Marx Piggyback Airplane Set, $150. Photo courtesy Richard MacNary

Marx Skycruiser, c. 1940s, 18" wingspan, $450. Photo courtesy Ricahrd MacNary

Marx Skycruiser Stratoliner 700, $125. Photo courtesy Richard MacNary

Left to Right: Marx Trimotor Biplane, 9-1/2" wingspan, $120; Marx Gyroplane, $120. Photo courtesy Perry Eichor

Marx (Continued)

	C6	C8	C10
Skycruiser Stratoliner 700, four-engine	45	75	125
Sparkling Rocket Fighter, No. 1425, tin litho	37	56	75
Swingtail Flying Tiger Transport	300	450	600
Transport, tin litho, friction-powered, four-engine w/whirling propellers	60	90	200
Trimotor Biplane, 9-1/2" wingspan	60	90	120
Universal Airport, w/two metal planes, c. 1940s, 12" long	55	90	200
Zeppelin, "Akron" Marx, c. 1930s, 28" long	100	140	250

Metalcraft

	C6	C8	C10
Build-A-Zep, builds twenty-one different 18" zeppelins	242	365	485
Ford, tri-motor	112	162	225

Metalcraft aircraft construction sets. Photo courtesy December 1929 Butler Bros. Catalog

Metalcraft Spirit of St. Louis, assembled, 9" long, $235. Photo courtesy Mapes Auctioneers

Left to Right: Ralstoy Pursuit Plane, No. P40, 3" x 3-1/4", $50; Ralstoy Cabin Plane, 3-3/8" x 3-3/8", $65; Ralstoy Cabin Plane, 3-5/8" x 3-1/2", $70. Photo courtesy Perry Eichor

Metalcraft (Continued)

	C6	C8	C10
Northrup Alpha Monoplane, marked "PURE the Pure Oil Company," 17" wingspan	600	1000	1800
Riding Rocket, 24" long	100	150	200
Spirit of St. Louis, came as kit, 9" long	118	175	235

Ralstoy

Ralstoy issued new aircraft and reproduced popular Kansas Toy numbers issued during the 1920s. The late 1930s toy reflected the growing awareness of the war in Europe.

	C6	C8	C10
Cabin Plane, No. 32, small, marked "Ralstoy," wings positive dihedral (see Kansas Toy's No. 32 Small Cabin Plane), 2-1/2" x 2-1/4", (RAA1)	20	30	50
Cabin Plane, slim midwing, cowled radial engine, pilot, tin propeller, underside marked "Scout" and "Made in USA," 3" x 3-3/4", (RAA5)	25	35	50
Cabin Plane, marked "NC414" and "Ralstoy," midwing, V-12 engine, tin propeller, 3-3/8" x 3-3/8", (RAA2)	30	40	65
Cabin Plane, large, Lindy-type, high-wing, six-cylinder radial engine, metal wheels, (RAA6)	20	30	40
Cabin Plane, high-wing, cowled radial engine, two doors, six windows, marked "Ralstoy" and "Made in USA," 3-5/8" x 3-1/2", (RAA3)	35	45	70

Top row, left to right: Renwal B-17, No. 777, 1944, 9-1/4" wingspan, $100; Renwal P-38, $100. Middle row, left to right: Renwal B-25, c. 1944, 6-3/4" wingspan, $100; Renwal B-29, No. 29, $100; Renwal C54 Transport, $100. Bottom row. Left to right: Renwal B-17, No. 17, $40; Renwal P40, $100. Photo courtesy Perry Eichor

Ralstoy (Continued)

	C6	C8	C10
Pursuit Plane, No. P40, Curtiss "U.S. Army," midwing, Air Corps star-in-circle insignia, V-12 engine, two machine guns, three-bladed propeller, marked "Made in USA" and "Ralstoy" in diamond, 3" x 3-1/4", (RAA4)	25	35	50

Remco

	C6	C8	C10
Flying Boxcar	50	75	100
Kennedy Airport	58	85	115
Whirlybird Helicopter	20	30	40
WWI "Air Aces" Play Set, 1965	138	205	275

Renwal

	C6	C8	C10
B-17, No. 17, small	10	30	40
B-17, No. 777, plastic, 1944, 9-1/4" wingspan	25	50	100

Renwal DC-4, 7" wingspan, $60. Photo courtesy James Apthorpe

Renwal Martin Mars, No. 15, $120. Photo courtesy James Apthorpe

Renwal (Continued)

	C6	C8	C10
B-25, plastic, c. 1944, 6-3/4" wingspan	30	60	100
B-29, No. 29	30	60	100
C54 Transport, plastic, large	40	35	100
DC-4, 7" wingspan	20	30	60
Martin Mars, No. 15	30	60	120
P38, plastic	20	40	100
P40, plastic	20	45	100
P47, plastic	20	40	100
PB2Y Flying Boat	20	40	100

Savoye

	C6	C8	C10
Blimp, "U.S.N.," 4" long	20	30	60
Monoplane, 3/12" wingspan	30	40	80

Schieble

	C6	C8	C10
Biplane, c. 1920s, 15-1/2" long	300	450	600
Ford, steel, tri-motor, 29-1/2" long	500	900	1550

Steelcraft

	C6	C8	C10
Akron Blimp, pull toy, 25" long	100	150	200
Army Scout Plane, single engine, high-wing monoplane, c. 1920s, 22-1/2" wingspan	700	1100	1825
Army Scout Plane, tri-motor, single high-wing, c. 1920s	300	750	2200
Army Scout Plane, green and orange, 23" wingspan	100	300	500
Graf Zeppelin, pressed steel, pull toy, 30-1/2"	250	375	500

Schieble Ford, 29-1/2" long, $1550. Photo courtesy Wilkinson Collection. Detroit Antique Toy Museum

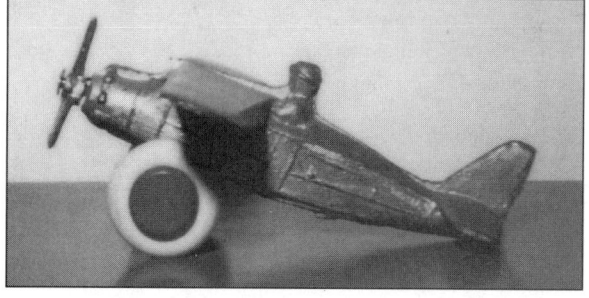

Savoye Monoplane, 3-1/2" wingspan, $80. Photo courtesy Al Lane

Savoye Blimp, 4" long, $60. Photo courtesy Al Lane

Steelcraft Army Scout Plane, c. 1920s, 22-1/2" wingspan, $1825. Photo courtesy Continental Hobby House

Steelcraft Lockheed Sirius, 21-1/2" wingspan, $2000. Photo courtesy Christie's East

Steelcraft (Continued)

	C6	C8	C10
Graf Zeppelin, pull toy, 32" long	300	450	600
Lockheed Sirius, pull toy, 21-1/2" wingspan	650	1400	2000
Macon Zeppelin, 25" long	350	525	700
Monoplane, two open cockpits, c. 1930s, 16" wingspan	250	375	600
NX107, "Little Jim," 23" wingspan	550	825	1300
NX130, blue eagles on wings, 23" wingspan	475	700	950
NX130 U.S. Mail Plane, one engine	388	580	775
NX131 U.S. Mail Plane, tri-motor, pull toy, 26-1/2" wingspan	700	1200	1650
Pan American World Airways Clipper, 26"	135	200	300
Pedal Monoplane, No. 79, high-wing, 32" wingspan, 48" long	1500	2500	4000
Pedal Plane "Pursuit," 1940	1000	1700	3000

Strauss

	C6	C8	C10
Chicago Dirigible, tin litho, 10"	125	188	250
Flying Airship, aluminum, wind-up	275	350	550
Graf Zeppelin, 16" long	240	360	480
Zeppelin, aluminum, "Graf Zeppelin," 16" long	175	250	350

Sun Rubber

	C6	C8	C10
Dual-Control Plane, No. 12010, 4-1/2" long	25	35	50
Pursuit Ship, marked "25-P75," c. 1940-41, 4-1/4" wingspan	20	35	50
Transport, No. 12009, 4" long	40	70	100

Thomas Toys

	C6	C8	C10
Defiant, plastic, 4" long	20	30	40
F-80 Jet Action Rocket Launcher	20	30	40
Warhawk, plastic, 4" long	20	30	40

Steelcraft Pan American World Airways Clipper, 26", $300.

Steelcraft NX130 U.S. Mail Plane, $775. Photo courtesy Calvin L. Chaussee

Thomas Toys F-80 Jet Action Rocket Launcher, $40. Photo courtesy Islyn Thomas

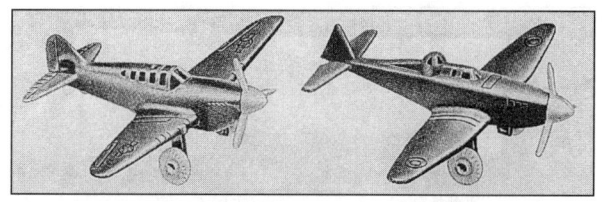

Left to Right: Thomas Toys Warhawk, 4" long, $40; Thomas Toys Defiant, 4" long, $40

Tootsietoy

	C6	C8	C10
Aerodawn Seaplane, No. 4660, rubber tires, 1928	30	55	80
Aerodawn Seaplane, No. 4660	30	60	85
Aerodawn Seaplane, No. 4660, metal tires, 1928	30	60	85
Aeroplane whistle tin-litho, No. 1743, Crackerjack	15	25	40
Air Defense set of ten, No. 1407, die-cast midget series	50	100	150
Airport hanger, two planes, box set	300	600	900
Army Cutlass, 1958-60	8	16	25
Army DC-4 Transport, 1941	40	75	110
Atlantic Clipper, No. 1637, midget series	4	8	12
Autogyro, No. 4659, 1934	40	80	120
Beechcraft Bonanza, 1948	8	16	25
Bellanca, No. 107, high tin wing monoplane, 1932	30	60	90
Biplane, No. 4650, open-spoke tires, 1926	45	85	125
Bi-Wing Plane, No. 4675, closed metal tires	25	50	75
Bi-Wing Seaplane, No. 4675	25	50	75
Bleriot Plane, No. 4482, 1910	40	80	120
Boeing 707, 1958	18	35	55
Boeing Stratocruiser, 1951-54	35	70	105
Coast guard Seaplane, 1950	50	100	150
Crusader, No. 719, twin boom, twin engine, 1937	35	70	100
Curtis P-40 Pursuit, No. 721, olive	85	170	250
Curtis P-40 Pursuit, No. 721, silver, 1941	70	140	200
DC-2 TWA, No. 1636, midget series	4	8	12
DC-4, No. 4550, die-cast charm	1	3	5
Delta, two-piece casting	20	40	60
Delta, 1954-55	15	25	40

Tootsietoy (Continued)

	C6	C8	C10
Dive-Bomber Waco Biplane, 1937	50	95	140
F-40 Skyway, 1956-69	7	13	20
F-86 Sabre Jet, two-casting body, 1950	8	16	25
F-86 Sabre Jet, single casting, 1956	7	13	20
F-94 Army Jet, 1956-69	8	16	25
F-94 Starfire Jet, 1956-69	7	13	20
Fly-N-Giro, No. 720, small-version auto-gyro, 1938	70	140	200
Ford Tri-Motor, No. 4649, 1932	45	85	125
High Wing Monoplane, No. 1353, midget series	5	10	16
High Wing Monoplane, No. 1744, tin-litho, Crackerjack	15	25	40
High Wing Monoplane, tin-litho, two-color, CJ, early	18	35	55
Hiller Helicopter, 1968-69	15	30	45
Lockheed Constellation, 1951	45	90	135
Lockheed Electra twin-engine, No. 125, 1937	25	50	75
Lockheed Sirius, No. 106, tin low wing	30	60	90
Low Wing Monoplane, No. 1747, tin-litho, Crackerjack	15	25	40
Navion, 1948-53	10	20	30
Navy Cutlass, 1956-69	7	13	20
P-38, No. 1638, midget series	10	20	30
P-38 Fighter, twin boom, twin engine, 1950	40	75	110
P-39 Fighter, 1947	50	100	150
P-80 Shooting Star, 1948	10	20	30
Panther Jet, two-casting body, 1953-55	15	25	40
Panther Jet, single casting, 1956-69	7	13	20
Piper Club, 1948-52	8	16	25
Rescue Helicopter, No. 2552, four-blade	8	16	25
Rescue Helicopter, No. 2552, two-blade, 1975-79	6	12	18
Scorpion Helicopter, No. 2220, 1977-79	2	5	8
Sikorsky S-58 Helicopter, 1958-69	30	55	85
Sky fleet, No. 1812, die-cast midget series, set of four	25	50	75

Tootsietoy (Continued)

	C6	C8	C10
TWA DC-2, No. 717, 1937	30	60	90
Twin-Engine Convair, twin engine, 1950	35	65	95
U.S. Army Northrup Alpha Pursuit plane, No. 119, 1936	25	50	75
U.S. Navy Waco C-Model Biplane, No. 718, 1937	45	85	125
United DC-4 Supre Mainliner, 1941	35	65	95
USN Los Angeles Dirigible, No. 1030, 1937	45	85	125

Wyandotte

	C6	C8	C10
Airacuda, pressed steel, twin vertical stabilizers, twin pusher engines, blue or red, 8-1/2" wingspan	45	70	90
Airliner, pressed steel, four-engine, 12-3/4" wingspan	73	110	145
Airliner, two-engine, wooden wheels, WWII-era	75	110	150
Bomber, Army, pressed steel, two-engine	90	135	180

Left tto Right: Wyandotte Airacuda, 8-1/2" wingspan, $90; Wyandotte Airliner, $150. Photo courtesy Perry Eichor

Wyandotte Airliner, 12-3/4" wingspan, $145. Photo courtesy Perry Eichor

Wyandotte China Clipper, No. 207, 13" wingspan, $300. Photo courtesy Wilkinson Collection. Detroit Antique Museum

Left to Right: Wyandotte Crusader, 9-3/4" wingspan, $85; Wyandotte Crusader, 9-3/4" wingspan, $100. Photo courtesy Perry Eichor

Wyandotte (Continued)

	C6	C8	C10
China Clipper, No. 207, 13" wingspan	125	200	300
City Airport, American Airlines, two hangars, control tower, etc., lights up	150	250	375
Crusader, twelve-window version, 9-3/4" wingspan	40	75	100
Crusader, 9-3/4" wingspan	35	55	85
Gyrocopter, twin-engine passenger plane, c. 1930s, 12-1/2" wingspan	100	200	300
Military Air Transport, 13" wingspan	40	60	80
Monoplane, No. 2, Lockheed Vega, high-wing passenger, single engine, bullet nose, 18" wingspan	175	265	350
Mystery Plane, No. 101, twin engine, wings trail backward, 4-1/2" wingspan	30	50	100
Rocket Racer, No. 319, c. 1935	70	120	150
Stratocruiser, 13" wingspan	75	120	150
Super Jet	80	120	160

Wyandotte Gyrocopter, c. 1930s, 12-1/2" wingspan, $300. Photo courtesy Perry Eichor

Wyandotte Rocket Racer, No. 319, c. 1935, $150. Photo courtesy Brian Seligman

Wyandotte Mystery Plane, No. 101, 4-1/2" wingspan, $100. Photo courtesy John Gibson

Wyandotte Stratocruiser, 13" wingspan, $150. Photo courtesy Perry Eichor

Wyandotte (Continued)	C6	C8	C10
U.S. Navy Seaplane, c. 1941, 14-1/2" wingspan	215	322	430

Miscellaneous	C6	C8	C10
Adam Bomb, wood and metal, also "Atom Bomb," c. 1946, 11" wingspan	50	100	150
Aeroplane, No. 321, metal cast, marked "U.S. 256," Air Corps star insignia, 3-1/4" long	15	20	25
Aeroplane, No. 66, metal cast, two engine, lead (some marked "Fred Greene"), c. 1940s, 4-1/2" wingspan	10	15	25
Air Mail Pedal Plane, American National, 1926	3000	5000	9000
Airplane, wood, ride-on	75	100	150

Miscellaneous (Continued)	C6	C8	C10
Airplane, single wing, prop behind tail, pilot, open fuselage, early 1900s	300	450	600
Airplane and Pylon, No. 55, Lionel	300	450	1100
Airplane Kit, wood, "Schoenhut's Airplane Builder"	130	200	300
Airport, No. 88, tin litho, mechanical airport w/early plastic planes that fly, control tower controls for stunts, crash truck pumps water, airport bus, gasoline truck, T. Cohn Co., c. 1940s	75	125	250
Amphibian, two overhead engines, hand-painted, tin wind-up, Bing, 16" wingspan	1400	2500	3400
Biplane Pedal Plane, two motor, 54" long	500	900	1800
Cargo Plane, Eldon, 11" long	20	40	60

Miscellaneous (Continued)

	C6	C8	C10
Champion Monoplane, cast iron, high-wing, 5" long	90	135	180
Dirigible, slush lead, "USN," Tommy Toy, 1930s	25	38	50
Erector Biplane, w/electric motor, A.C. Gilbert	150	260	600
Fighter, tin, single engine, four machine guns mounted on wing, c. 1940	20	30	60
Flagship America airplane, pressed steel, metal Ford tri-motor, c. 1930s, 25" wingspan	175	300	600
Flying Plane, Liberty Playthings, early 1930s	150	225	300
Giant Flyer Monoplane, Tip Top, c. 1920s, 23" long	200	350	500
Helicopter, tin litho, Army, drive, spinning prop, 13" long	40	70	100
Helicopter, friction, Irwin, c. 1950, 15" long	30	45	60
Hillclimber Biplane, c. 1917	225	338	500
Jet, tin litho, USAF, friction powered, 5" wingspan	15	20	35
KD-1 Mak-a-plane, all metal, w/rubber wheels, mechanical, 1940s, 4" long	40	50	70
Lindy, cast iron, nickel prop and wheels, 3-1/2" wingspan	105	158	210
Lindy-type Plane, cast iron, North & Judd, 4-3/8" long	175	265	350
Lindy-type Plane, lead, 2-1/4" wingspan	10	20	30
Luscombe Airplane, 4" long	30	45	60
Monoplane, high wing, marked "U.S.," single engine, open ironwork body, spool wheel works, prop, 8" wingspan	200	300	400
Monoplane, two pilots in open cockpit Liberty V-12 engine, cast propeller, eight oval and two round windows, two painted main gear disc wheels, Midwest, 3-1/8" x 3-5/8"	25	40	70
Monoplane, Liberty V-12 engine, cast propeller, eight oval and two round windows, ailerons and tail surfaces detailed and three disc wheels w/those black painted "tires," 3-3/16" x 3-5/8"	25	40	70

Miscellaneous (Continued)

	C6	C8	C10
Monoplane, No. 700, high-wing, open cockpit and pilot, red, yellow or blue, painted disc wheels, Dayton, 13" wingspan	200	400	600
NX-130, pressed steel, high-wing monoplane, Boycraft, 22" wingspan	350	525	850
Pedal Plane, pursuit plane, 1941	1800	3100	4450
Pyro Jet, plastic, 6" long	10	15	25
Sky Cruiser, tin litho, two-motor transport, engines turn w/friction mechanism, 18" wingspan	40	75	100
Spirit of America Aeroplane, steel and litho, pull-toy, 14' long	30	50	75
Spirit of Columbia, pressed tin, friction, 18" wingspan	500	750	1000
Spirit of St. Louis, pressed steel, go around tower, two planes, electrical, United Electric	800	1200	1600
Spirit of St. Louis, No. 74042, lead, marked "Pat." and "Ancient Art Metal Co., Brooklyn, N.Y.," c. 1927, 5-1/8" wingspan	75	150	200
Swallow Monoplane, high-wing, American National, 24" wingspan	1200	2000	3000
Theodore Hahn Aeroplane, No. 187, lead alloy, 1920s	20	40	75
Turner High-wing Monoplane, one engine, 1930s, 18-1/2" wingspan	275	400	700
Turner High-wing Monoplane, pressed steel, 22-1/2" wingspan	300	450	700
Twin-engine Bomber, No. 43, Metal Cast, B-25?, 5-1/4" wingspan	10	15	20
Watrous Biplane, pressed steel, single engine, bell toy, c. 1915, 8-1/4" wingspan	200	400	750
Zeppelin, "Goodyear" decals, hatch opens, 25" long	125	225	350
Zeppelin, cast iron, "Los Angeles," 12" long	300	750	1500
Zeppelin, cast iron, "Pony DE107," 5-1/2" long	50	100	250
Zeppelin, pot metal, "U.S. Akron," c. 1932, 6" long	25	40	75
Zeppelin, cast iron, "ZEP," 4" long	80	120	160
Zeppelin, cast iron, approx. 3" long	40	60	80
Zeppelin, metal, 25" long	42	64	85
Zeppelin, pull toy, "Little Giant"	50	100	200
Zeppelin, cast iron, pull toy, silver, c. 1920-30s, 6" long	60	90	120

AMERICAN PAPER TOYS

Paper toys and dolls (also called cut-outs, punch-outs and press-outs) have been around since the mid-1600s when they were called Pantins. Dolls as well as forts, planes, and trains, have been produced in paper. Paper toys and dolls were extremely popular from the end of the last century to the period after World War II. Almost every type of toy can be found in a paper or cardboard version.

American companies began turning out paper toys by the thousands around 1900. The most popular manufacturer was the McLoughlin Bros. Company which started out with paper toys in 1857 in New York City. McLoughlin was eventually bought out by Milton Bradley and moved to Springfield, Massachusetts in 1920. McLoughlin/Milton Bradley products included beautifully lithographed covered boxed sets of cardboard figures on wooden stands and sheets of American and foreign soldiers.

During the years 1895 to 1905, almost every major newspaper in America had Sunday Art Supplements which were paper toys for the children. These sheets included a wide range of subjects including armies and navies of the world, historical panoramas, political figures, personalities of the day, and cut-out dolls of celebrities with vast wardrobes. Paper houses and villages were sold by several companies including McLoughlin Bros., Milton Bradley, Built-Rite and Megow. The World War II-era was the golden age of paper toys in the United States.

During the 1940s every conceivable type of toy was available in paper, usually with a patriotic wartime theme. The major paper doll publishers were Merrill and Saalfield and Whitman. They produced paper doll books that were popular with the children of the 1940s through the 1960s.

There are now quite a few books on paper dolls and paper toys, including *Blair Witton: Paper Toys of the World*, Hobby House Press, 1986; *Paper Soldiers* by Edward Ryan, *WWII-Era Paper Toys* by John Matthews, Mary Young has written several books on paper dolls; and Ann Tolstoi Wallach: *Paper Dolls*, Van Nostrand 1982.

Contributor: Judith Izen, P.O Box 623, Lexington, MA 02173. Izen is a noted doll and paper doll authority whose paper doll articles have appeared in several publications. Her books include *Collectors Guide to Ideal Dolls* and *Collectors Encyclopedia of Vogue Dolls* (coauthored with Carol Stover).

Abbott	C6	C8	C10
Blue Feather and Silver Cloud, Native-American dolls, No. 1356, 1940s	25	40	55
Cut-Me-Out Paper Dolls, No. 1358, 1940s	20	30	35
Janet Leigh, No. 1805, 1958	30	55	75
TV Star Time Paper Dolls, No. 1367, c. 1950s	20	25	30

All-Nu	C6	C8	C10
Decal sheet of soldiers, by Frank Krupp, meant to be attached to heavy cardboard backing, c. 1942	60	75	100
Soldiers, heavy cardboard, No. 113, nurse, c. 1942-43, 5" high	4	5	7

All-Nu (Continued)	C6	C8	C10
Soldiers, heavy cardboard, No. 100, officer marching w/sabre, c. 1942-43, 5" high	4	5	7
Soldiers, heavy cardboard, No. 101, marching, slope arms, WWI helmet, c. 1942-43, 5" high	4	5	7
Soldiers, heavy cardboard, No. 102, bugler, campaign cap, c. 1942-43, 5" high	4	5	7
Soldiers, heavy cardboard, No. 103, signalman, WWI helmet, c. 1942-43, 5" high	4	5	7
Soldiers, heavy cardboard, No. 104, officer kneeling w/binoculars, c. 1942-43, 5" high	4	5	7

All-Nu (Continued)

	C6	C8	C10
Soldiers, heavy cardboard, No. 105, kneeling firing rifle w/WWI helmet, c. 1942-43, 5" high	4	5	7
Soldiers, heavy cardboard, No. 106, throwing grenade, WWI helmet, c. 1942-43, 5" high	4	5	7
Soldiers, heavy cardboard, No. 107, fixed bayonet, WWI helmet, c. 1942-43, 5" high	4	5	7
Soldiers, heavy cardboard, No. 108, charging w/gas mask, WWI helmet, c. 1942-43, 5" high	4	5	7
Soldiers, heavy cardboard, No. 109, charging w/rifle, port arms, WWI helmet, c. 1942-43, 5" high	4	5	7
Soldiers, heavy cardboard, No. 110, seated machine gunner, WWI helmet, c. 1942-43, 5" high	4	5	7
Soldiers, heavy cardboard, No. 112, General McArthur, c. 1942-43, 5" high	12	14	16
Soldiers, heavy cardboard, No. 155, truck w/soldiers in rear, WWII helmets, c. 1942-43, 5" high	4	5	7
Soldiers, heavy cardboard, No. 114, two men carrying wounded soldier on stretcher, WWII helmets, c. 1942-43, 5" high	4	5	7
Soldiers, heavy cardboard, No. 115, two men firing rifles from prone position, WWII helmets, c. 1942-43, 5" high	4	5	7
Soldiers, heavy cardboard, No. 116, soldier on wireless radio, c. 1942-43, 5" high	4	5	7
Soldiers, heavy cardboard, No. 117, on heavy cardboard, three soldiers w/rifles leaving boat, WWII helmets, c. 1942-43, 5" high	4	5	7
Soldiers, heavy cardboard, No. 118, on heavy cardboard, two paratroopers, one w/tommy gun, WWII helmets, c. 1942-43, 5" high	4	5	7
Soldiers, heavy cardboard, No. 119, on heavy cardboard, ski trooper, c. 1942-43, 5" high	4	5	7
Soldiers, heavy cardboard, No. 120, on heavy cardboard, soldier advancing w/rifle, WWII helmet, c. 1942-43, 5" high	4	5	7

All-Nu (Continued)

	C6	C8	C10
Soldiers, heavy cardboard, No. 150, on heavy cardboard, three men in jeep, WWI helmets, c. 1942-43, 5" high	4	5	7
Soldiers, heavy cardboard, No. 151, on heavy cardboard, five man team w/cannon, WWI helmets, c. 1942-43, 5" high	4	5	7
Soldiers, heavy cardboard, No. 152, on heavy cardboard, two men manning wheeled AA gun, WWI helmets, c. 1942-43, 5" high	4	5	7
Soldiers, heavy cardboard, No. 153, on heavy cardboard, tank w/three men, c. 1942-43, 5" high	4	5	7
Soldiers, heavy cardboard, No. 154, Ambulance, c. 1942-43, 5" high	4	5	7
Soldiers, heavy cardboard, No. 111, flag-bearer, WWI helmet, c. 1942-43, 5" high	4	5	7

Artcraft

	C6	C8	C10
Dodie from "My Three Sons" A Paper Doll Book, Dodie and Dolly, No. 5115, 1971	30	40	55
Hee Haw, No. 5139, 1971	25	40	45

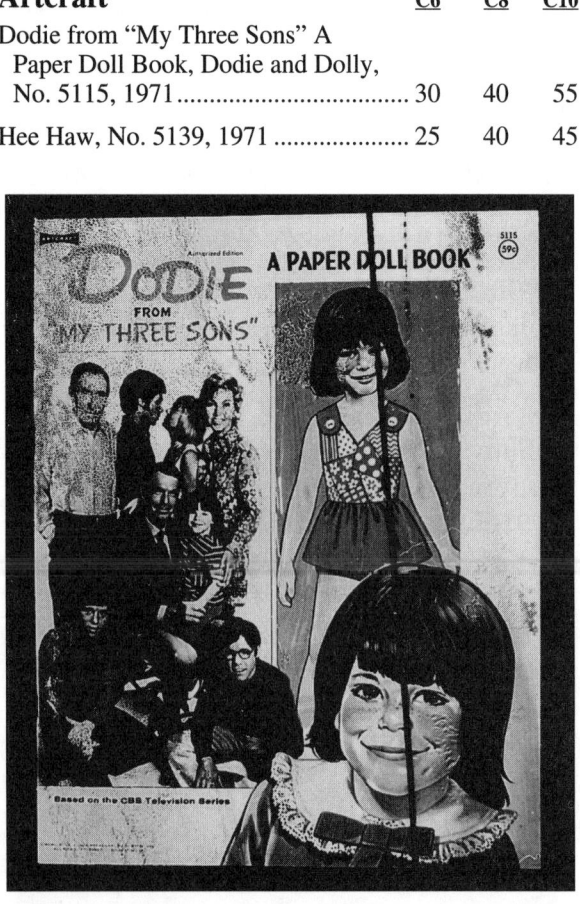

Artcraft, Dodie from "My Three Sons" A Paper Doll Book, No. 5115, 1971, $55

Artcraft, Tricia Paper Doll, No. 4248, 1969, $245

Artcraft (Continued)

	C6	C8	C10
Julia, includes Diahann Carroll, Julia, Corey, Marie and Earl J. Waggedorn, No. 5140, 1968	25	40	50
Little Women, No. 5127, c. 1970	15	25	35
Lost Horizon, No. 5112, 1973	15	20	25
Partridge Family, The, No. 5137, 1971	30	45	60
Patridge Family, No. 5143, 1972	35	45	55
Susan Dey as Laurie (Partridge Family), fashions by Kate Greenaway, 1972	25	35	45
The Flying Nun, The, No. 4417, 1968, 1969	25	40	50
Tricia Paper Doll, No. 4248, 1969	190	225	245

Artfield

	C6	C8	C10
Nanny and the Professor, No. 4283, 1971	25	35	45

Built-Rite

Built-Rite began to produce cardboard construction toys in 1934. Judging by their catalogs, Built-Rite sold its last fort (25A) in 1954 and its last few construction sets in 1956, that is until 1963-64, when the No. 1033 Doll House and No. 1027 Stock Farm appeared. In 1978, Built-Rite added plastic play sets No. 6002 Fort Laredo and No. 6001 Starship Counterforce Action Playset. It dropped the Built-Rite name and became Warren in 1976, and they continue to make card games, games and puzzles under that name. Its greatest period of success was probably enjoyed prior to and during World War II.

	C6	C8	C10
No. 0001 Toy Soldiers, WWI helmets, each	2	3	4
No. 0002 Toy Trench	25	45	60
No. 0004 Armored Car	15	20	30
No. 0007 Army Plane Hangar	48	60	70
No. 0007 Private Garage, brick	35	45	55
No. 0008 House, brick	65	80	90
No. 0009 House, stucco and brick	65	80	90
No. 0010 House, two-story, brick and shingle	65	80	90
No. 0014 Front Line Trench and Soldier Set, w/trench and six WWII soldiers	40	55	60
No. 0015 Commercial Garage	65	80	90
No. 0016 Fort, no ramp	70	90	125
No. 0017 Service Station	65	80	90
No. 0018 Airport	65	80	85
No. 0020 Army Battery Set	90	125	145
No. 0020 Railroad Tunnel	12	22	27
No. 0022 Army Outpost	45	65	75
No. 0025 Fort, one-ramp	90	120	130
No. 0025A Twenty-six-piece Fort and Soldier Set, same fort as No.25, WWII soldiers, two sandbag foxholes and fiberboard pistol, sold through 1954	120	150	175
No. 0026 United Airlines Airport Hangar	60	75	85
No. 0027 Barn, w/animals	30	45	55
No. 0028 Garage and Super Service Station	70	85	95
No. 0029 Three Cart Set	25	40	45
No. 0033 House, Tudor-type	65	80	90
No. 0033 Lokdwood Dolls, paper dolls, 1940s	25	35	45
No. 0034 House, two-story	65	80	90

Built-Rite (Continued)

	C6	C8	C10
No. 0035 Modern Doll House	65	80	90
No. 0036 House	65	80	90
No. 0036F Three-room Furnished Doll House	85	95	105
No. 0037 Farm Machinery Set	35	50	60
No. 0045 Living Room Furniture	45	55	65
No. 0046 Dining Room Furniture	45	55	65
No. 0047 Bedroom Furniture	45	55	65
No. 0048 Bathroom Furniture	45	55	65
No. 0049 Kitchen Furniture	45	55	65
No. 0050 Army Raiders' Victory Unit, twenty-eight pieces, truck, tank, AA gun, jeep, semi-trach and twenty soldiers, WWII	75	90	100
No. 0055 Five Cardboard Miniature Houses	35	55	65
No. 0056 Five Miniature Buildings, church, school, RR station, firehouse and drugstore	35	55	65
No. 0057 Farm Set, eight-piece	40	50	65
No. 0060 Navy Battle Fleet and Coast Artillery Gun	35	60	75
No. 0066 Three-piece Kitchen	30	45	55
No. 0075 Living Room Furniture	45	55	65
No. 0076 Dining Room Furniture	45	55	65
No. 0077 American Ranger Fighters, eight vehicles, WWII soldiers	80	90	100
No. 0077 Bedroom Furniture	45	55	65
No. 0078 Kitchen Furniture	45	55	65
No. 0083 Weapons Carrier	15	20	30
No. 0100 A Fortress, w/two ramps, c. 1938	120	155	180
No. 0105 Farm Set, w/twenty plastic animals	35	45	55
No. 0111 Railroad Accessory Set	25	30	40
No. 0112 American Fighters, includes 100A fortress w/soldiers, cannons, etc., fifty-five pieces, no flag on tower	120	155	180
No. 0115 Doll House, garage set w/car	65	80	90
No. 0119 Farm Set	45	65	75
No. 0120 Five-room Suburban Doll House	65	85	90

Built-Rite (Continued)

	C6	C8	C10
No. 0127 Large Barn, w/animals	30	40	50
No. 0128 Miniature Village and Scenery set	35	48	60
No. 0148 Train Accessory set	30	40	50
No. 0156 Miniature houses and buildings	55	65	70
No. 0178 Train Accessory set	30	40	50
No. 019 Railroad Station	60	70	80
No. 0201 Twenty-six-piece Guardsman set, two trenches, artillery base, cannon, pistol and WWII soldiers	70	90	120
No. 0202 Train Scenery, twenty-eight pieces	45	65	75
No. 0204F Furnished Country Estate	60	80	90
No. 0210 Railroad Station and Accessories	30	40	50
No. 0212 Station and Railroad Accessories	35	45	55
No. 0245 Miniature Village	35	50	60
No. 0252 Fort Set, twenty-six pieces, No. 25 fort, post-war	110	150	180
No. 0298 Train Accessory set	30	40	50
No. 0300 Stock and Grain Elevator	30	35	45
No. 0375 Station and Railroad Set	30	40	50
No. 0415 House, boxed set w/19" house and garage, twenty-seven pieces of furniture, sedan, baby buggy, shrubbery, etc., c. 1943, 13" x 20"	85	110	135
No. 0459 Five rooms of toy furniture	45	55	65
No. 0460 Pocket-size Series of Miniature Paper Doll Set	15	20	24
No. 0498 Train Accessory Set	25	35	45
No. 0566 Village	40	55	65
No. 1001 Modern Stock Farm	50	60	80
No. 1027 Stock Farm	50	60	80
No. 1033 Doll House	50	65	75
No. 1422 Fort and Soldiers, ninety-four pieces, two-ramp fort	110	145	175
No. 2050 Country Estate, house, bushes, dog, cat, baby buggy	70	90	100
Ranch, over 180 pieces	150	185	200

Colorgraphic

	C6	C8	C10
Young Patriot Invasion Set, contains destroyer, amphibian tractor, tank, jeep, anti-tank gun, bomber and diver bomber, boxed set, No. 500, c. 1944, 10-1/2" x 13"	75	80	95
Young Patriot Learn to Know Your Army, includes tank, howitzer, jeep, anti-tank gun, bomber, fighter and soldiers, w/shooting guns and dropping bombs, No. 350, 1943	75	80	95
Young Patriot Learn to Know Your Navy, construction set includes battleship, destroyer, aircraft carrier, mosquito boat, submarine, planes and depth charges, w/moveable parts, No. 360, 1943, 10" x 14"	75	80	95

Grinnel

	C6	C8	C10
American Family Paper-Doll Book, "Costumes for all the family from 1610 to now" No. C1002	40	50	75

Grinnel (Continued)

	C6	C8	C10
Mother and Daughter, by Patrie Winston, includes mother and daughter doll w/two scotties, No. C-1005, 1940, 15" mother, 11" daughter	20	35	45
My Paper Doll's Sewing Kit, by Margot Voight, No. C-1018, 1940	15	20	30

Lowe

	C6	C8	C10
8 Ages of Judy, The, by Fern Bisel Peat, Judy as baby and ages one to seven, No. L1025, 1941	40	60	80
Assemble Nine Model Warplanes, w/four model tanks, 1941	55	75	85
Babysitter Paper Dolls, No. 945	15	20	30
Brenda Lee Teenage Celebrity, No. 2785, 1961	40	60	80
Bride Doll Cut-out Book, No. 1043, 1940s	20	30	40
Cinderella Steps Out, No. 1242	25	35	50

Lowe, Glenn Miller, No. 21041, 1942, $200

Lowe, House For Sale, No. 9042, 1962, $50

Lowe, Judy and Jack, Peg and Bill Cut-out Dolls, No. L1024, 1940, $70

Lowe (Continued)	C6	C8	C10
Clothes Make a Lady, No. 1029, 1941	20	30	40
Dick the Sailor, No. L1074, c. 1942	20	35	45
Down on The Farm, No. 1056, 1940s	15	20	30
Dr. Kildare and Nurse Susan, No. 2740, 1960s	35	55	70
Fashion Cut-outs, w/Sturdibilt dolls, No. 1243, 1940s	15	20	30
Five Little Peppers, Little Women and Annie three-book set, Lauries, No. L1030, 1941	35	55	75
Glenn Miller, Marion Hutton Turnabout Doll Book, No. 21041, 1942	100	150	200
Harry the Soldier, No. L1074, 1941	45	65	75
House for Sale, No. 9042, 1962	35	45	50
Judy and Jack, Peg and Bill Cut-out Dolls, by Pelagie Doane, No. L1024, 1940	35	45	70

Lowe (Continued)	C6	C8	C10
Junior Prom, by Newman, No. 1042, 1942	20	35	45
Model Airplanes, WWII Airplanes, International, No. 1069, 1941	50	65	75
Model Tanks, No. 1065, 1941	50	65	75
Model Tanks Construction Set, boxed, No. 1267, 1942	50	65	75
Model War Planes Construction Set, boxed, No. 1266, 1942	50	65	75
My Very First Paper Doll Book, a Bonnie Book, No. 4732, 1957	10	15	20
On Guard, No. L535, 1942	40	45	50
Over 80 Turn-About, Standup Sailors, No. 140, 1943	45	55	60
Over 80 Turn-About Standup Sailors, No. 141, 1943	45	55	60
Patience and Prudence, No. 2736, 1958	10	15	20
Playhouse Paper Dolls, designed by Doris and Marion Henderson, No. 1028, 1941	20	30	40
Playtime Pals, No. 1045, 1946	10	15	20

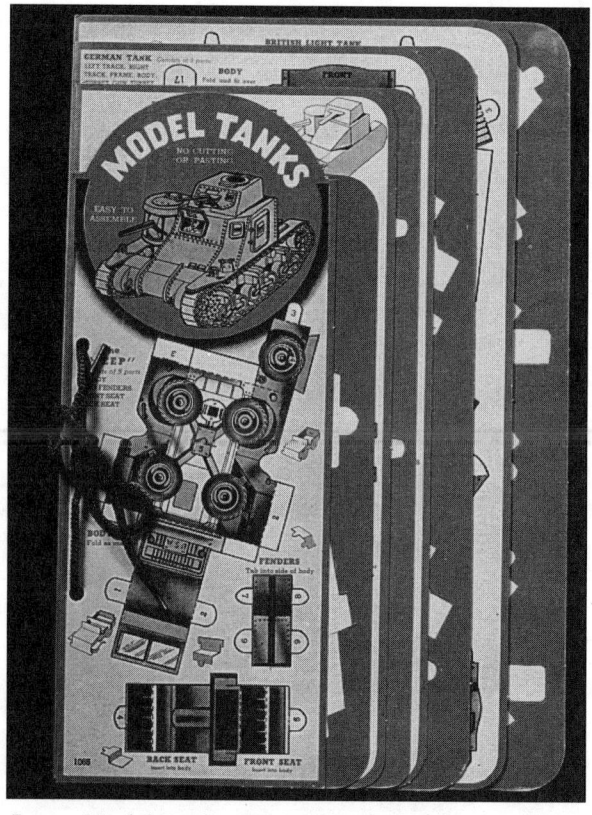

Lowe, Model Tanks, No. 1065, 1941, $75

Lowe, On Guard, No. L535, 1942, $50

Lowe, Over 80 Turn-About Standup Sailors, No. 141, 1943, $60

Lowe, Pressed Board Dolls and Their Dresses, 1942, $45

Lowe, Playhouse Paper Dolls, No. 1028, 1941, $40

Lowe, Sally the Standing Doll, No. 1042, 1940s, $40

Lowe, Toni Hair-do Cut-out Dolls, No. 1284, 1950, $60

Lowe (Continued)

	C6	C8	C10
Polly Patchwork and Her Friends, by Pelagie Doane, No. 1024, 1941 20		30	40
Pressed Board Dolls and Their Dresses, boxed set, No. 1942 25		35	45
Rosemary Clooney, No. 1256 40		50	60
Rosemary Clooney, No. 2487, 1958 40		50	60
Sally the Standing Doll, No. 1042, 1940s 20		30	40
Service Kit of America's Armed Forces-On Land-On Sea-In the Air, No. 265, 1942.. 45		55	60
Square Dance Paper Dolls, by J. VoelzNo. 968-10................................. 15		20	25
The Sue and Tom Cut-out Dolls Book, No. 149, 1946 15		20	25
Tom the Aviator, No. L1074, c. 1942 ... 25		35	45
Toni Hair-do Cut-out Dolls, No. 1284, 1950 35		45	60
Toni Hair-Do Dress-Up Dolls, No. 1251 40		50	60
Toy Models: Warplane and Tank Punch-out, 1941 45		50	65
Turnabouts Dolls Book, The, dolls printed front view on each side, No. 1048, 1940s.. 25		30	35
TV Tap Stars Paper Dolls, No. 99010..... 6		12	25
U.S. Commandos Book, No. 1089, 1943 45		55	60
United States Soldiers, No. L1063, 1942 50		55	60
Victory Girls Arlene the Airline Hostess, c. 1940s................................. 35		45	55
Victory Punch-Out Tanks, soldiers, sailors, planes, No. 848, c. 1943 50		55	60

McLoughlin Bros.

McLoughlin Brothers was the largest American producer of paper soldiers and one of the earliest in the paper doll field. The Brooklyn, New York firm, founded in 1828, began producing paper dolls as early as 1857. Among the other paper toys it sold were dollhouse furniture, toy theaters with actors and scenery, and blocks. The company was sold in 1920 to Milton Bradley.

	C6	C8	C10
02 Series American Indians, kneeling and standing, c. 1904-1910 2		3	4

McLoughlin Bros. (Continued)

	C6	C8	C10
02 Series British Highlanders, c. 1904-1910.. 2		3	4
02 Series U.S. Continentals, c. 1904-1910.. 2		3	4
02 Series U.S. Infantry in Campaign Uniforms, Spanish-American War, c. 1904-1910.. 2		3	4
02 Series U.S. Navy, c. 1904-1910 2		3	4
02 Series U.S. Zouaves, c. 1904-1910..... 2		3	4
02 Series West Point Cadets, c. 1904-1910.. 2		3	4
02 Series West Point Cadets, round base, c. 1915....................................... 2		3	4
100 Soldiers on Parade, second set, c. 1898... 300		350	400
100 Soldiers on Parade, first set, c. 1898... 300		350	400
260 Series Annapolis Cadets, price for each, c. 1889-1895..................... 2		3	4
260 Series Bandsmen, various instruments, price for each, c. 1889-1895... 3		4	5
260 Series Grenadier Guards, price for each, c. 1889-1895..................... 2		3	4
260 Series Navy— USS Boston, c. 1889-1895 2		3	4
260 Series U.S. Infantry, c. 1889-1895... 2		3	4
260 Series U.S. Infantry, c. 1889-1895... 2		3	4
260 Series U.S. Regulars, c. 1889-1895... 2		3	4
260 Series U.S. Regulars, spiked helmet, price for each, c. 1889-1895..... 2		3	4
260 Series West Point Cadets, c. 1889-1895 2		3	4
Big-Girl Paper Dolls, No. 707, 1940..... 20		30	40
Boy Scouts, holding rifles across chests, c. 1915 5		6	7
Brass Band, price for each, 1890............. 4		5	6
British Infantry Red Coats, w/spiked helmets on small wooden blocks, complete set, c. 1898........................ 150		200	250
British Infantry Red Coats, w/spiked helmets on small wooden blocks, price for each, c. 1898, 6" high 4		5	6

McLoughlin Bros. (Continued)

	C6	C8	C10
Diane and Daphne the Round About Dolls Book, large cut-outs by Campbell, No. 545, 1937 30	55	65	
Dutch Paper Doll, boy of the Village of Vollendam, No. 0103, c. 1910, 10-1/2" x 10-1/2" sheet 18	25	30	
Fashion Book of the Round About Dolls, The, by Betty Campbell, eight stand-up dolls plus scissors and pack of paper dolls clothes in package, 1936 35	55	75	
Figures, horizontal sheet of ten figures, uncut, c. 1890 35	50	75	
Grenadiers, price for each, 1890 3	4	5	
Infantry, price for each, c. 1875 3	4	5	
Infantry Soldiers, printed, price for each, 1857 3	4	5	
Landing Party for USS Texas, printed, sailor, 1898, 5-1/4" high 4	5	6	
Little Red School House Kindergarten, The, by Margo Voight, includes two teachers and twenty-three children, 1940 30	45	55	
Mounted U.S. Cavalry, Hussar type, charging, several different poses, price for each, c. 1884 3	4	5	

McLoughlin Bros. (Continued)

	C6	C8	C10
New Folding Doll House, cardboard w/lithographed paper, boxed set, 1897 400	500	575	
New Pretty Village, individual buildings 12	15	18	
New Pretty Village Church Set, 1897 ... 90	125	145	
New Pretty Village School Set, 1897 90	125	145	
Soldiers, seven soldiers plus officer in field uniform, includes Belgium, Italy, France and Britain, price for each, No. 4026, c. 1916, 10-1/2" x 10-1/2" 20	30	40	
U.S. Infantry, Spanish-American War, on wooden blocks, price for each, c. 1898, approx. 6" high............... 4	5	6	
U.S. Regulars, glossy series of figures in full dress, c. 1898, 5" high..... 4	5	6	
U.S. Zouaves, Civil War era, blue coats, red baggy trousers on small wooden blocks, c. 1898, 6" high 4	5	6	
West Point Cadets, small glossy series, price for each, c. 1898, 4-1/2" high 4	5	6	
Winnie's New Wardrobe, by Geraldine Cline, No. 555, 1939 30	32	36	
Zouaves, price for each, 1884.................. 3	4	5	

The box for New Pretty Village from McLoughlin Bros.

McLoughlin Bros., New Pretty Village, $18

McLoughlin Bros., New Pretty Village Church Set, 1897, $145

Merrill

	C6	C8	C10
Alice Faye, No. 4800, 1941	100	150	200
American Beauty Paper Dolls with Dresses Worn by White House First Ladies from 1789-1951, No. 154815, 1951	20	30	40
American Defense Battles Punch-out Book, by George Trimmer, No. 3430, 1940	75	95	105
Ann Blythe, No. 2250-25, 1952	45	55	90

Merrill, Alice Faye, No. 4800, 1941, $200

Merrill, Betty Grable, No. 1558, 1951, $125

Merrill (Continued)

	C6	C8	C10
Army Nurse and Doctor Paper Dolls, No. 3425, 1942	32	40	65
Babyland, No. 3642, 1955	20	35	45
Betty Grable, No. 1558, 1951	55	80	125
Blue Bonnet Paper Dolls, by Florence Salter, No. 3444, 1942	20	35	45
Boarding School Dolls and Clothes, No. 3492, 1942	25	40	55
Bride and Groom, No. 3443, 1949	25	35	50
Bride and Groom, No. 1555, 1949	25	35	50
Bride and Groom Military Wedding Party, set includes sixteen dolls, No. 3411, 1941	40	60	80
Children in the Shoe, No. 1562, 1949	20	30	40
Coke Crowd, The, eight teens w/costumes, No. 3445, 1946	30	45	65
College Style Paper Dolls, Peter and Patsy, No. 3400, 1941	30	45	65
Cowboy and Cowgirl Cut-outs, No. 3449, 1950	25	40	50
Cowgirl Jill and Cowboy Joe, No. 3459	25	35	45
Dancing Dolls with Famous Costumes, ballet dancers, No. 3448, 1954	20	35	45

Merrill, College Style Paper Dolls, No. 3400, 1941, $65

Merrill, Double Wedding 15 Paper Dolls, No. 3472, 1939, $85

Merrill (Continued)	C6	C8	C10
Deanna Durbin, No. 3480, 1940	50	100	165
Dolls from Storyland, by Vivian Robbins, No. 1554, 1948	25	40	50
Double Wedding 15 Paper Dolls, No. 3472, 1939	40	65	85
Esther Williams, three dolls, No. 1563, 1950	55	75	110
Family Princess Paper Dolls, No. 1548, 1958	25	40	55
Frontier Fort, No. 257225, 1952	15	25	30
Gene Autry Ranch Cut-out Book, 1940	65	80	90
Girl Pilots of the Ferry Command, No. 4852, 1943	55	75	115
Gone With the Wind, includes five dolls, No. 3405, 1940	200	300	400
Gone With the Wind, includes eighteen dolls, No. 3404, 1940	200	300	400
High School Girls, No. 1551, 1948	40	45	55
Jack and Jill, six dolls and clothes from Storyland, No. 1561, 1962	15	20	30
Janet Leigh Cut-outs and Coloring Book, No. 2554, 1953	40	55	85

Merrill, Esther Williams, No. 1563, 1950, $110

Merrill, Girl Pilots of the Ferry Command, No. 4852, 1943, $115

Merrill, Paper Doll Family and Their Trailer, No. 3436, 1938, $90

Merrill (Continued)	C6	C8	C10
Jeanette MacDonald, No. 3640, 1941	100	150	200
Karen Goes to College!, No. 1564, 1955	20	30	40
Kitty Goes to Kindergarten, No. 1548, 1956	15	25	35
Liberty Belles Paper Doll Book, No. 3477, 1943	25	35	50
Little Ballerina, No. 154215, 1953........	20	35	45

Merrill (Continued)	C6	C8	C10
Navy Scouts Paper Doll Book, No. 3428, 1942	45	65	85
Our Army and Navy in Action, Cut and Stick, No. 4835, 1942...................	35	45	50
Paper Doll Family and Their Trailer, No. 3436, 1938....................................	70	80	90
Pert and Pretty, No. 1552, 1948	25	30	50
Pig Tails, No. 344410, 1949..................	20	30	40
Pilot and Stewardess Airliner Paper Dolls, No. 3423, 1941	25	30	50

Merrill, Our Army and Navy in Action, Cut and Stick, No. 4835, 1942, $50

Merrill, Pilot and Stewardess Airliner Paper Dolls, No. 3423, 1941, $50

Merrill, Stand-Up Dolls Honey and Bunny, No. 3403, 1936, $70

Merrill (Continued)

	C6	C8	C10
Pink Wedding, The, No. 1559, 1952	45	55	65
Piper Laurie, No. 2551, 1953	55	65	75
Sally's Silver Skates, No. 1549, 1956	25	35	45
Stand-Up Dolls Honey and Bunny, No. 3403, 1936	50	60	70
Sub-Deb Paper Dolls, by Irving Nurick, twelve teenage boy and girl dolls w/clothes, No. 3408, 1941	25	35	45
Teen Town, No. 3443, 1949	25	30	35
Tyrone Power & Linda Darnell, No. 3438, 1941	150	175	200
Umbrella Girls, wrap-around dresses, No. 2562, 1956	30	40	45
Victory Volunteers Dolls with Uniforms, by Merlin, No. 3424, 1942	55	65	75
White House Party Dresses, No. 1550, 1961	25	30	35
Ziegield Girl Paper Dolls, No. 1, No. 3466, 1941	100	150	200

Milton Bradley

	C6	C8	C10
French Infantry, cardboard figures, c. 1915, approx. 6" high	3	5	6
Jean and Joan and their Friends Roundabout Dolls, designed by Betty Campbell, boxed set, No. 4396, 1934	45	65	85

Milton Bradley, Jean and Joan and their Friends Roundabout Dolls, No. 4396, 1934, $85

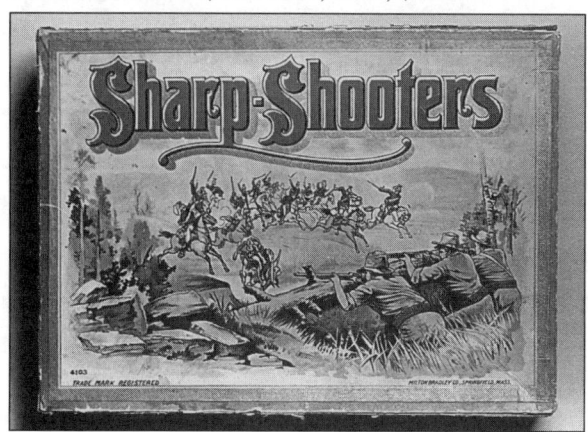

Milton Bradley, Sharp-Shooters, No. 4103, c. 1915, $135

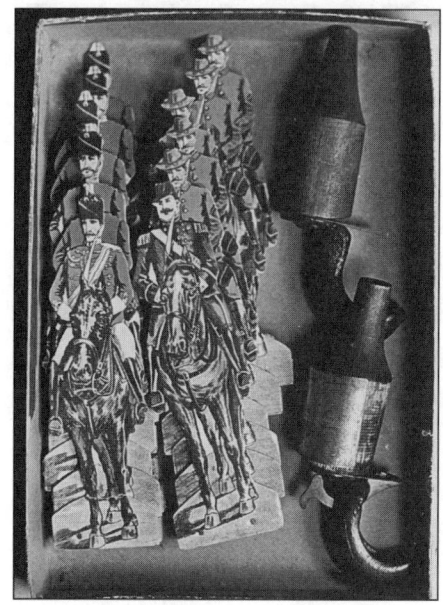

Milton Bradley, Sharp-Shooters, No. 4103, c. 1915, $135

Milton Bradley (Continued)

	C6	C8	C10
Magic Mary, complete w/magnetic doll and strips to put on clothes, boxed set, No. 4010-1, 1955, 10-1/2" x 10-1/2"	10	15	25
Sharp-Shooters, includes two sets of five cardboard soldiers and one officer on stands, boxed, No. 4103, c. 1915	85	100	135
Soldiers Five, five cardboard soldiers, pistol, boxed set, No. 4395, c. 1920	80	100	125
Soldiers on Parade, set of ten No. 4518	55	80	90

Ottenheimer

	C6	C8	C10
My Fair Lady, by Evon Hartman, No. 2960-2, 1965	25	35	50
New York World's Fair Make a Model, includes Unisphere, Swiss Ride, N.Y. Port Authority and Heliport, Spertus, No. 600-50, 1963	25	30	35

Reed

	C6	C8	C10
Model Battleship, c. 1945, 7" x 10"	20	25	30
Model Flat-top, c. 1945	20	25	30
Thrilltown Railroad Pullman Passenger Set, 1943	65	80	90

Saalfield

	C6	C8	C10
A Day With Diane, by Laura Bischoff No. 1770	25	35	45

Saalfield, Bridal Party Paper Dolls, 1963, $35

Saalfield, Cinderella, No. 1610, 1950, $45

Saalfield (Continued)

	C6	C8	C10
Air-Hostess, No. 2546, 1947	30	40	50
Animal Paper Dolls to Dress, includes bear, monkey, pig and kitten, No. 2598, 1950	15	20	25
Animals to Paint, 1910	10	15	23
Army Cut-outs, No. 245, 1937	55	65	80
Barbara Britton Paper Dolls with Magic Stay-on Costumes, boxed set, No. 5190, 1954	50	65	75
Beautiful Paper Dolls by Betty Campbell, has some of same paper dolls as Little Miss Amreica Paper Dolls, No. 242, 1941	20	35	45
Belle of the Ball Paper Dolls, No. 2702, 1948	20	35	45
Book of Paper Doll Cut-outs, No. 2051, 1927	40	55	65
Bridal Party Paper Dolls, 1963	15	25	35
Charming Paper Dolls, No. 1357, c. 1960	10	15	25
Cinderella, by Ethel Hays, No. 1610, 1950	25	35	45
Circus Paper Dolls, No. 2610, 1952	10	15	20
Claudette Colbert, No. 2451, 1943	100	150	200
College Chums, No. 719, 1950s	25	35	45
Colonial Paperdolls, No. 1353	25	40	50

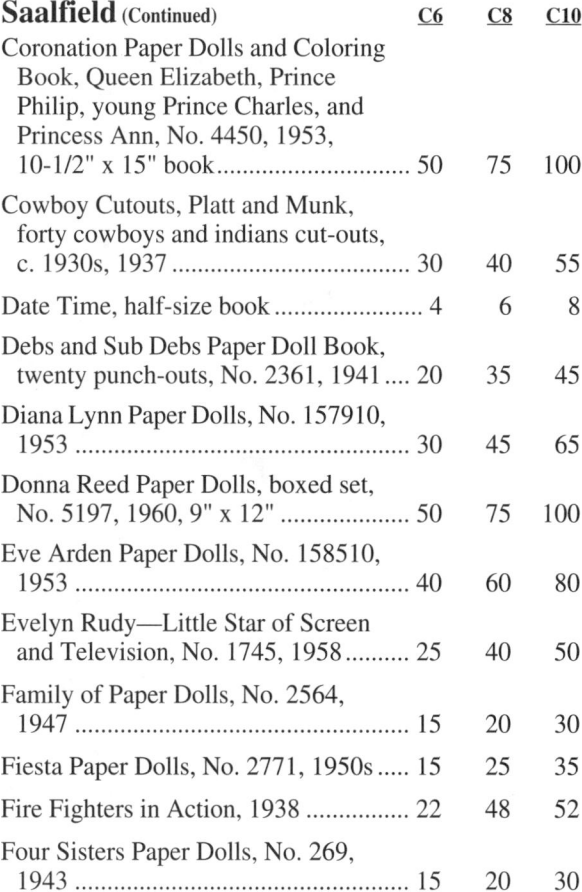

Saalfield, Claudette Colbert, No. 2451, 1943, $200

Saalfield, Diana Lynn Paper Dolls, No. 157910, 1953, $65

Saalfield (Continued)	C6	C8	C10
Coronation Paper Dolls and Coloring Book, Queen Elizabeth, Prince Philip, young Prince Charles, and Princess Ann, No. 4450, 1953, 10-1/2" x 15" book	50	75	100
Cowboy Cutouts, Platt and Munk, forty cowboys and indians cut-outs, c. 1930s, 1937	30	40	55
Date Time, half-size book	4	6	8
Debs and Sub Debs Paper Doll Book, twenty punch-outs, No. 2361, 1941	20	35	45
Diana Lynn Paper Dolls, No. 157910, 1953	30	45	65
Donna Reed Paper Dolls, boxed set, No. 5197, 1960, 9" x 12"	50	75	100
Eve Arden Paper Dolls, No. 158510, 1953	40	60	80
Evelyn Rudy—Little Star of Screen and Television, No. 1745, 1958	25	40	50
Family of Paper Dolls, No. 2564, 1947	15	20	30
Fiesta Paper Dolls, No. 2771, 1950s	15	25	35
Fire Fighters in Action, 1938	22	48	52
Four Sisters Paper Dolls, No. 269, 1943	15	20	30

Saalfield (Continued)	C6	C8	C10
Gigi Perreau, No. 2605, 1951	25	40	55
Gigi Perreau Paper Dolls, No. 1542, 1951	25	40	55
Girl Friend-Boy Friend Paper Dolls, No. 1605, 1955	15	20	30
Gloria Jean Paper Doll Cut-outs, No. 1661, 1940	55	85	115
Good Neighbor Paper Dolls, No. 2487, 1944	10	15	25
Gulliver's Travels Cut-outs, No. 1261, 1939	35	55	75
Hedy Lamarr Paper Dolls, No. 1955	75	115	150
Heidi and Peter, No. 1355, c. 1970	12	15	20
Holiday Paper Dolls, No. 1742, 1950s	10	15	20
Hollywood Fashion Dolls, twelve male and female dolls plus clothes, No. 397, 1939	30	45	60
Hollywood Fashions, No. 1535, 1949	25	35	45
Hour of Charm Paper Dolls, women musicians, No. 2481, 1943	55	80	110
Jane Russell, No. 2611, 1955	40	60	80

Saalfield, Fiesta Paper Dolls, No. 2771, 1950s, $35

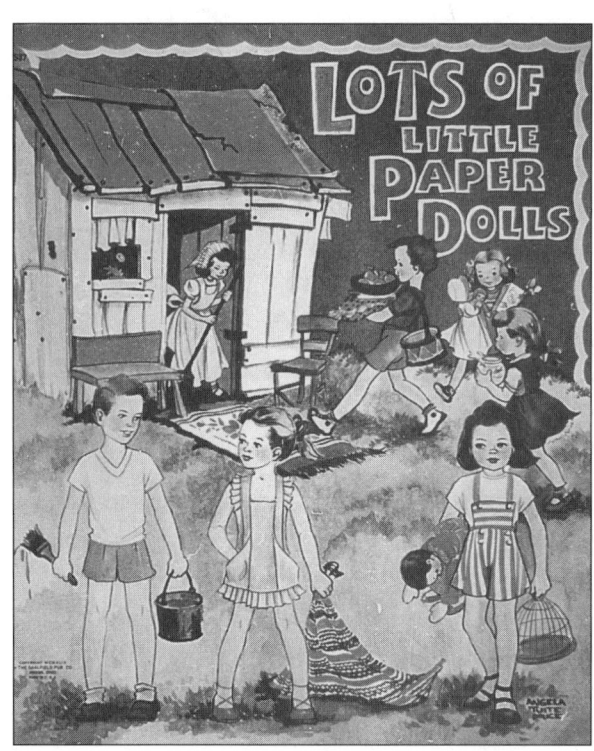

Saalfield, Lots of Little Paper Dolls, No. 1537, 1949, $35

Saalfield, New Shirley Temple in Paper Dolls, The, No. 2425, 1942, $150

Saalfield, Paper Dolls Julia and Marie, No. 1530, 1958, $25

Saalfield (Continued)

	C6	C8	C10
Judy Paper Doll, No. 1713, 1960s	10	15	20
Julia, includes Julia, Earl J. Waggedorn and Corey, 1969	25	35	50
Lilac Time, No. 1362	20	30	40
Little Ballet Dancers, No. 1743, 1950s?	10	15	20
Little Folks' Friends, No. 156, 1915	15	20	25
Little Friends Paper Dolls, No. 1746, 1950s	10	15	20
Little Miss America Paper Doll Book, fifteen punch-outs by Campbell, No. 2358, 1941	25	35	45
Little Women, No. 1377	25	35	45
Lots of Little Paper Dolls, by Angela Tuite Price, No. 1537, 1949	15	25	35
Lucille Ball Paper Dolls, No. 2475, 1944	55	75	110
Martha Hyer Paper Dolls, No. 4423, 1958	30	45	60
Mary Belle Cut-out Doll, by Fern Bisel Peat, four separate sheets, w/three sheets of clothes, No. 2100, 1934, 17" doll	45	55	70
Mary Martin, No. 2427, 1942	115	160	225
Mini Mod PDs with London Fashions, No. 1348, 1966	20	25	35
Modern Miss in Paper Dolls, by Van Swearingen, No. 2397, 1942	30	40	45
Nancy and Her Dolls with 7 Busy Days of Fun, No. 2478, 1944	15	25	35
New Shirley Temple in Paper Dolls, The, No. 2425, 1942	65	90	150
Outdoor Paper Dolls, fourteen dolls and four pages of clothes, No. 1958, 1941	15	20	30
Paper Doll Family and Their House, by Florence and Margaret Hoopes, No. 4125, 1934	60	70	75
Paper Doll Playmates, nurse and nineteen children, costumes, toys, No. 154, 1940	25	35	50
Paper Dolls and Their Dollies, by Mary Knight, No. 1615, 1950s	20	30	40
Paper Dolls from Mother Goose, includes Mary, Bo-Peep, Boy Blue, Bobbie Shaftoe, Miss Muffet and Jack Horner, No. 2758, 1957	15	20	30

Saalfield (Continued)

	C6	C8	C10
Paper Dolls Julia and Marie, by Angela Tuite Price, No. 1530, 1958	15	20	25
Paper Dolls of All Nations New York World's Fair, No. 227, 1939	40	50	60
Paper Dolls of Eve Arden, No. 1706, 1956	45	65	85
Paper Dolls to Cut Out and Paint, No. 1180, 1920s	55	65	75
Paper Dolls United We Stand, by Margot Voight, six children w/uniformsNo. 113	60	65	75
Playhouse Paper Dolls, No. 381, 1947	15	20	30
Popular Paper Dolls, No. 1973, 1942	15	20	25
Pre-Teen Paper Dolls, No. 1366, c. 1960s	10	15	20
Pretty as a Picture, No. 2775, 1950s	20	30	40
Prince and Princess Paper Dolls, No. 2706, 1949	20	25	35
Quiz Kids Paper Dolls, No. 2430, 1942	100	120	140

Saalfield, Paper Dolls of All Nations New York World's Fair, No. 227, 1939, $60

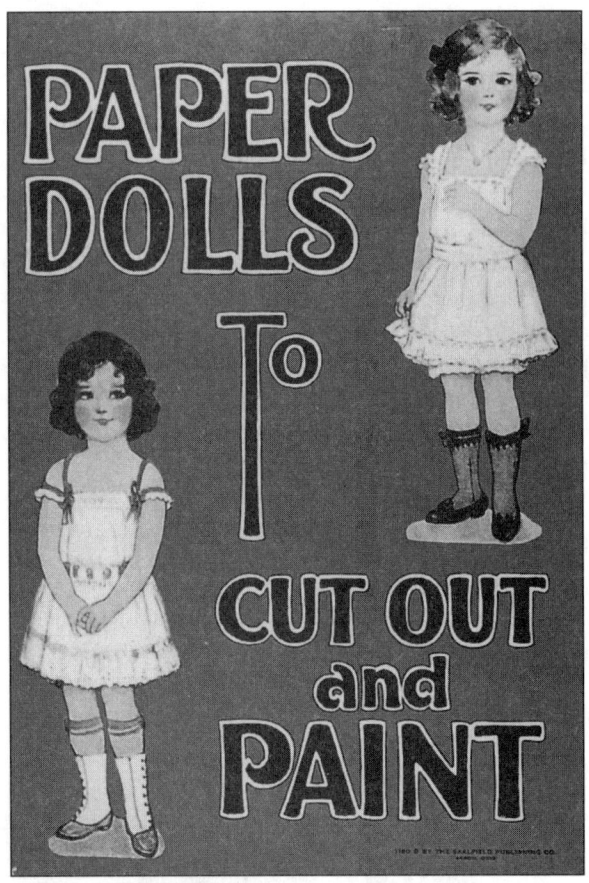

Saalfield, Paper Dolls to Cut Out and Paint, No. 1180, 1920s, $75

Saalfield, Playhouse Paper Dolls, No. 381, 1947, $30

Saalfield (Continued)	C6	C8	C10
Raggedy Ann and Andy, by Ethel Hays, No. 2719, 1953	20	30	40
Raggedy Ann and Andy Paper Dolls, No. 2719-15, 1944	35	45	55
Raggedy Ann and Andy Paper Dolls, by Ethel Hays, No. 2741, 1944	35	45	55
Really Truly Paper Dolls, No. 453	25	35	45
Riders of the West Paper Dolls, No. 2716-15, 1950	10	15	25
Robin Hood and Maid Marian Paper Dolls, No. 1761, 1950s	25	35	45
Rowan & Martin's Laugh-In Punch-Out Paper Doll Book, includes Rowan, Martin, Jo Ann Worley, Arte Johnson, Judy Carne and Goldie Hawn, No. 1325, 1969	30	40	50
Sandra Dee, two dolls and thirty-four costume pieces, boxed, No. 5511, 1959	45	55	65
School Girl Paper Dolls, No. 2400, 1942	20	30	40

Saalfield (Continued)	C6	C8	C10
Schoolmates, No. 1757, 1950s	5	7	10
Sheree North, No. 1728, 1957	45	55	65
Skating Party Paper Doll Book, includes seventeen punch-outs, No. 2328, 1941	20	30	40

Saalfield, Really Truly Paper Dolls, No. 453, $45

Saalfield, Sheree North, No. 1728, 1957, $65

Saalfield, Story Princess—Alene Dalton, No. 1727, 1957, $50

Saalfield (Continued)

	C6	C8	C10
Smart Paper Dolls, No. 1935, 1940	15	25	35
Square Dance Paper Dolls, No. 2717, 1950	15	20	25
Stage Door Canteen, No. 2468, 1943	70	80	90
Star Bright, No. 2797, 1950s	20	30	40
Story Princess—Alene Dalton, No. 1727, 1957	30	40	50
Style Shop Paper Dolls, No. 1516, 1943	20	25	35
Sweetheart Paper Dolls, No. 2458, 1943	20	25	30
That Girl Marlo Thomas, No. 1351, 1967	35	45	55
That Girl Marlo Thomas, No. 1379, 1967	25	35	45
Tom Corbett Space Cadet Punch-Out Book, No. 4304, 1952, 14" long, 10-1/2" wide	40	48	52
Top Notch Paper Dolls, No. 1504, 1948	20	25	30
Tricia Paper Dolls White House Tour Game, White House stand-up doll of Tricia Nixon and costumes, No. 1248, 1970	12	23	45

Saalfield (Continued)

	C6	C8	C10
Tuesday Weld Paper Dolls, two dolls and fifty-eight costume pieces, boxed, No. 5112, 1960	40	50	60
Two Little Charmers	3	5	10
Uncle Sam's Little Helpers Paper Dolls, by Ann Kovach, No. 2450, 1943	35	45	50
Virginia Mayo, No. 4422, 1957	50	60	70
Walking Paper Dolls Family, No. 1074, 1934	55	65	75
Wedding Day, No. 4246, 1970	15	20	25
Wedding Day, No. 4458, 1968	20	25	30

Skyline Mfg.

	C6	C8	C10
This is the Navy, heavy cruiser, No. 501, c. 1942	25	35	40
This is the Navy, includes destroyer and PT boat, No. 500A, c. 1942	25	35	40

Stephens Publishing Co.

	C6	C8	C10
Cheerleader-Teenage Doll, Mary and Elaine, w/four pages of clothes, No. 182, 1950?	10	15	20
Circus Day, by Art Tanchon, animals, clown, circus cages and wagons, No. 135, 1946	18	22	28

Stephens Publishing Co., Circus Day, No. 135, 1946, $28

Stephens Publishing Co. (Continued)

	C6	C8	C10
Glamour Parade Cut-out Dolls, four models and four pages of clothes, No. 184, 1950s?	10	15	25
June Bride, by Art Tanchon, No. 136, 1946	20	35	45
Movie Starlets Paper Dolls, includes Miss Premier, Miss Stardust, Miss Hollywood and Miss Preview plus four pages of costumes, No. 178, c. 1949	15	20	30
Patty's Party Paper Dolls, No. 175, c. 1950	15	20	30

Stephens Publishing Co., June Bride, No. 136, 1946, $45

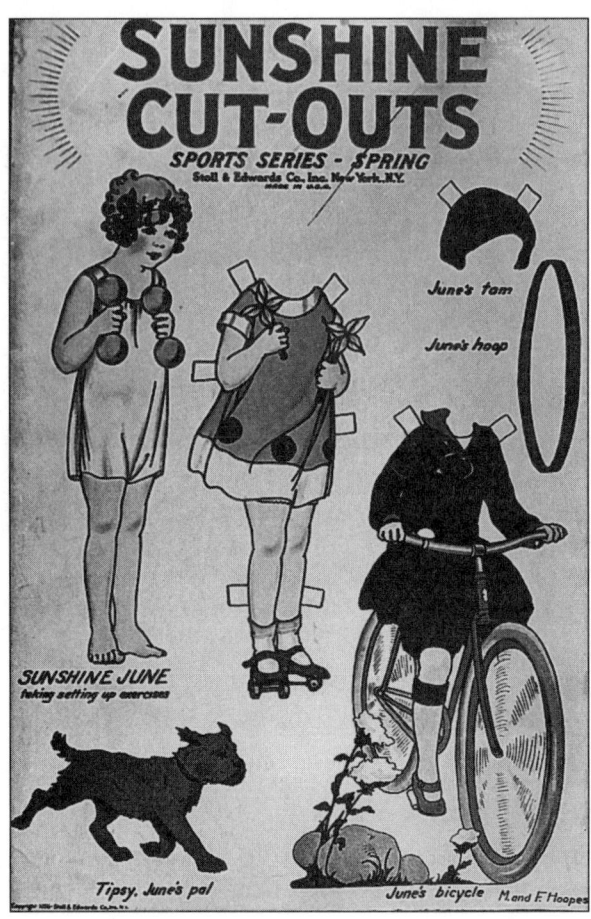

Stroll & Edwards Co., Sunshine Cut-outs Sports Series—Spring, 1926, $90

Stephens Publishing Co. (Continued)

	C6	C8	C10
Playhouse Dolls, four dolls and four pages of clothes, No. 1965, 1949	10	15	25
Scissors Bird Paper Dolls, No. 137, 1946	10	15	20
Six Good Little Dolls, No. 183	13	15	22
Sweetie Pie Twins, Jane and Jean, No. 166, 1949	10	15	25

Stroll & Edwards Co.

	C6	C8	C10
Sunshine Cut-outs Sports Series— Spring, four-part foldout, by M. and F. Hoopes, 1926	70	80	90

Toy Factory

	C6	C8	C10
Welcome Back, Kotter Sweathogs Paper Dolls, 1977	20	25	35

Whitman

	C6	C8	C10
Alice in Wonderland, 1976	5	10	15
Ann and Arthur—Little Paper Doll Books, No. 1146, copyright 1939, 3-1/2" x 7-1/2"	35	40	45

Whitman, Bob Hope and Dorothy Lamour, No. 976, 1942, $250

Whitman (Continued)

	C6	C8	C10
Ava Gardner, No. 119215, 1949, 1952	60	85	125
Baby Brother by Queen Holden, No. 920, 1929	55	85	110
Baby Brother Tender Love, 1977	5	10	15
Baby First Step, (Mattel), No. 1997, 1965	10	15	24
Baby Pat, No. 2072, 1963	10	15	20
Barbie and Ken, boxed set, No. 4797, 1962, 7" x 12"	25	35	55
Barbie and Ken Paper Dolls, No. 1086, 1970	25	30	40
Barbie and Skipper, yachting outfits, No. 1957, 1964	20	30	40
Barbie and Skipper Campsite at Lucky Lake, No. 1836, 1980	7	10	15
Barbie Boutique, No. 1954, 1973	10	15	25
Barbie Costume Dolls, No. 1976, 1964	25	35	55
Beth Ann, No. 1953, 1970	7	10	15
Betsy McCall, No. 4744, 1971	25	35	45
Betty and Joan, Lois and Joan, No. 1015, 1941, 1945	20	30	40

Whitman (Continued)

	C6	C8	C10
Beverly Hillbillies, The: Jed, Jethro, Granny and Elly May, No. 1955, 1964	35	55	75
Big Invasion Punch-out Book, punch-out of beach landing, No. 1936, 1964	25	35	40
Bob Hope and Dorothy Lamour, No. 976, 1942	100	150	250
Bobby Socks Cut-out Dolls, designed by Doris Lane Butler, No. 988, 1945	20	30	40
Bombers by Schomburg, includes B-17, B-25, B-24, Douglas A-20A, short "Stirling," No. 961, 1943	60	75	100
Book of Airplanes, A, No. 923, 1930	20	25	30
Brady Bunch, The, No. 1976, 1973	35	60	90
Bridal Doll Book, No. 1983, 1978	7	10	15
Bridal Party, set contains five dolls, No. 1187, 1950	20	30	40
Bride and Groom, No. 1957, 1968	10	15	25
Brother and Sister Statuette Dolls, heavy cardboard, No. 1182-15, 1950, 7-1/2" dolls	15	25	30
Buffy and Jody (Family Affair), two magic dolls w/stay-on wardrobes, No. 4764, 1970	30	40	60
Buffy Paper Dolls (Family Affair), No. 1955, 1968	32	45	65
Career Girls, w/cloth-like clothes, by Doris Lane Butler, No. 937, 1944	20	30	40
Charmin' Chatty, No. 1959, 1964	20	30	45
Children From Other Lands, eight cut-out dolls w/native costumes, No. 2089, 1961	10	15	20

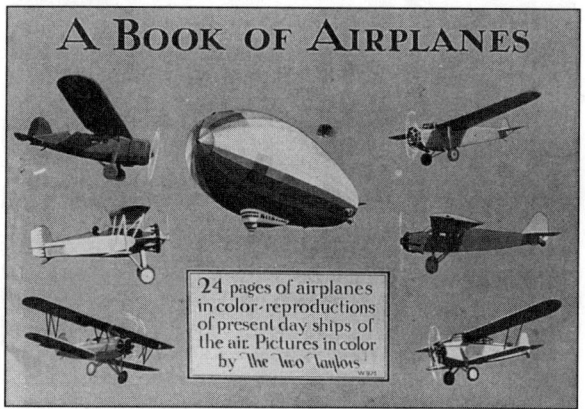

Whitman, Book of Airplanes, A, No. 923, 1930, $30

Whitman (Continued)

	C6	C8	C10
Chrissy Paperdoll with Fun Fashions, 1972	10	15	20
Claire McCardell, designer of the American look, No. 2067, 1956	30	45	65
Cloth-Like Clothes for Three Cute Girls, flocked clothes, No. 1178:15, 1949	20	25	35
Connie Francis, No. 1956, 1963	30	45	65
Cradle Crowd, The, four doll babies w/cloth-like clothes, No. 1173, 1948	25	35	50
Crissy & Velvet Paper Dolls, 1971	15	20	25
Crissy Fashion & Hairstyle Boutique, 1970	15	20	25
Crisy Magic Paper Doll, 1972	10	15	20
Cut-out Dolls, w/paints and clothes to color, book w/four 17" children and sixteen pages of clothing and sheet of paints by Avis Mac, No. 983, c. 1930s, 11" x 18"	30	45	65

Whitman, Cut-out Dolls—Puppies and Kittens, No. 931, 1939, $100

Whitman (Continued)

	C6	C8	C10
Cut-out Dolls—Puppies and Kittens, No. 931, 1939	50	75	100
Cyd Charisse, No. 2084, 1956	50	75	100
Cynthia and Bobby Little Paper Doll Books, No. 1146, copyright 1939, 3-1/2" x 7-1/2"	35	40	45
Dodi Paper Doll, No. 1965, 1966	20	25	35
Dolls that Walk "They Walk-They Dance-They Play," two identical girls and two identical boys, designed by Emily Sprague Wurl, No. 977, 1939	35	50	70
Doris Day, No. 210325, 1952	75	90	125
Dorothy Provine, No. 1964, 1962	35	45	65
Double Date Cut-out Dolls, by Elinee Fon Vaughan, No. 962, 1949	20	30	40
Elizabeth Taylor, No. 973-10, 1950	90	120	160
Eskimo Cut-outs by Milo Winter, No. 1054, 1939	20	35	45
Family Affair, No. 4767, 1968	25	40	55
Family of Paper Dolls, by Queen Holden, mother, father, nurse and six kidsNo. 991	55	75	110
Farm Cut-outs by Milo Winter, six pages of heavy paper cut-outs, No. 1054, 1938, 6-1/2" x 10-1/2"	5	25	35
Fifteen ABC Blocks to Play and Learn, book containing fifteen die-cut blocks to put together, each w/illustrations of nursery rhymes, alphabet letters, animals and numbers on each block, No. 976, 1933	20	30	40
Fourteen Dogs to Cut Out and Stand Up, twelve cardboard punch-out pages of dogs, No. 935, copyright 1930	25	35	48
Freckles & Sniffles, 1977	3	5	8
Gene Autry Melody Ranch Cut-out dolls, No. 990-10, 1950	45	65	95
Ginghams, The, box sets	3	5	10
Girl Friends Paper Dolls, No. 974, 1944	20	30	40
Grace Kelly, No. 2069, 1956	65	95	150
Grace Kelly 2 Cut-out Dolls and Clothes, No. 2049, 1955	60	95	130
Hair-Do Dolls, by Queen Holden, No. 991, 1948	50	75	100

Whitman, Grace Kelly, No. 2069, 1956, $150

Whitman, Kiddieland Village, No. 2004, c. 1935, $95

Whitman (Continued)

	C6	C8	C10
Hayley Mills "The Moonspinners," No. 1960, 1964	30	50	60
Here Comes the Bride, No. 118915, 1952	25	35	45
Here's the Bride, No. 2109, 1953	25	35	45
Howdy Doody Puppet Show Punchout Book, cardboard puppets may be controlled by strings, includes Howdy, Bluster, Inspector, Dilly Dally, Clarabell and Flubadub, No. 211129, copyright 1952	40	65	80
Howdy Doody Sticker Fun, No. 219525, copyright 1951	25	35	40
Howdy Doody Sticker Fun, No. 215825, copyright 1953	25	35	40
Howdy Doody Sticker Fun Circus, No. 2165, copyright 1955	25	35	40
I Love Lucy, Lucille Ball and Desi Arnaz, No. 2101, 1953	55	85	125
It's A Date, No. 1976, 1956	10	15	20
Jimmy & Jane Visit Gene Autry at Melody Ranch, No. 118415, 1951	35	55	70
Joan's Wedding by Florence Sarah Winship, clothes designed by Ruth M. Ruhman, No. 990, 1942	25	35	55

Whitman (Continued)

	C6	C8	C10
Judy and Dick—little paper doll books, No. 1146, copyright 1939, 3-1/2" x 7-1/2"	35	40	45
June Allyson, No. 119015, 1950, 1952	50	65	85
June Allyson, No. 1173:15, 1953	55	65	85
Kiddieland Village, nine buildings and sixty-five cut-out figures, boxed set, No. 2004, c. 1935, 11-1/2" x 15"	65	80	95
Kitty and Billy—Little Paper Doll Books, No. 1146, copyright 1939, 3-1/2" x 7-1/2"	35	40	45
Lazy Dazy, 1973	3	5	10
Lennon Sisters, No. 1979, 1957	25	35	50
Lennon Sisters, No. 1983, 1961	25	35	50
Little Brothers and Sisters, includes Tim, Kay Ann and Pete, No. 971:10, 1953	10	15	25
Lois and Joan Cut-out Dolls, No. 1015, 1941, 1945	20	30	40
Look-a-Like Cut-out Dolls, two mother and daughter pairs of dolls, No. 97210, 1952	15	20	30
Lori Martin in National Velvet, boxed set, No. 4612, 1962, 6" x 11-1/2"	35	45	55
Lucille Ball Desi Arnaz Cut-out Dolls with Little Ricky, No. 2116:25, 1953	86	100	125
Magic Stay-on Dresses, No. 4618	10	15	25
Malibu Skipper, No. 1952, 1973	10	15	25
Margaret O'Brien Paper Dolls, No. 96410	100	135	165

Whitman, Lucille Ball Desi Arnaz Cut-out Dolls with Little Ricky, No. 2116:25, 1953, $125

Whitman (Continued)

	C6	C8	C10
Marge and Gower Champion, 1959	50	75	100
Mary and Joan, No. 1015, 1941, 1945	20	30	40
Mary Jane—A Cut-out Doll, by Florence Winship, w/suitcase for accessories, No. 1010, 1939, 1941	20	35	45
Mary Lee—A Cut-out Doll, No. 1010, c. 1939	20	35	45
Mary of the WACS—A Young American, by Hilda Miloche and Wilma Kane, No. 1012, 1943	30	40	60
Mary Poppins, No. 1977, 1973	20	35	45
Mexican Cut-outs, by Milo Winter, six pages of people, animals and houses, No. 1054, 1938	30	38	48
Midge—Barbie's Best Friend, 1963	30	45	60
Molly Bee, No. 2091, 1962	20	30	40
Mommy and Me, No. 977:10, 1954	15	20	30
Mouseketeer Cut-outs, No. 1974, 1957	25	35	45
Movie Starlets, includes Gail Russell, Diana Lynn, Olga San Juan, Marjorie Reynolds and Joan Caulfield, No. 960, 1946	35	55	75
Mrs. Beasley Paper Doll Book, (Family Affair), No. 1973, 1970	25	35	50

Whitman (Continued)

	C6	C8	C10
Muriel and David—Little Paper Doll Books, No. 1146, copyright 1939, 3-1/2" x 7-1/2"	35	40	45
My Twin Babies with Older Brother and Sister, No. 970, 1940	20	30	45
Nancy and Tommy—Little Paper Doll Books, No. 1146, copyright 1939, 3-1/2" x 7-1/2"	35	40	45
Natalie Wood Paper Dolls, 1958	70	100	130
National Velvet, No. 1958, 1961	30	40	60
Night Before Christmas, w/cut-outs, No. 948	10	15	25
Nineteen Farmyard Animals to Cut Out and Stand Up, twelve pages, No. 935, copyright 1930	35	40	45
Oklahoma with Shirley Jones and Gordon MacRae, No. 1954, 1956	45	60	90
One Hundred Soldiers Punch-out Book, No. 999, 1943	55	60	65
Our Nurse Nancy—A Young American, by Hilda Miloche and Wilma Kane, cut-outs, No. 1012, 1943	25	40	55
Our Sailor Bob Doll, w/uniforms, c. 1943, 10"	25	40	50
Our Soldier Jim, designed by Hilda Milocheand Wilma Kane, standup doll w/uniforms, No. 3980, 1943, 10-1/2"	25	40	50
Our WAVE Joan—A Young American, by Hilda Miloche and Wilma Kane, No. 1012, 1943	35	45	55
Paper Doll "Joan" and Paper Doll "Bobby," by Queen Holden, No. 907, 1928	70	85	100
Paper Dolls Peter and Peggy, by Dixon, sixty-four pages w/very large punch-outs on front and back, No. 965, 1935	45	50	55
Pat Boone, No. 1968, 1959	25	35	45
Pat Crowley, No. 2050, 1955	25	35	45
Patsy a Wooden Doll with Dresses, standup cardboard doll w/wood backing, No. 3037, c. 1938, 10"	20	30	40
Patsy Ann and Her Trunk full of Clothes, by Queen Holden, No. 992, 1939	65	85	110
Peter and Peggy, No. 99210, 1950	15	20	25

Whitman (Continued)

	C6	C8	C10
Peter and Peggy, Jerry and Joan Paper Dolls, by Rachel Taft Dixon, No. 985, 1935	30	45	60
Photo Fashions, No. 973, 1953	10	15	25
Play Time, No. 210525, 1952	10	15	20
Playmates, No. 99510, 1952	15	20	25
Playthings To Cut Out and Stand Up, includes ventriloquist's dummy, floating ships, general's hat, lantern, animals and other moving toys, No. 934, c. 1935	32	36	45
Pollyana Cut-out Dolls, No. 995, 1941	30	40	50
Portrait Girls, w/cloth-like clothes, designed by Hilda Miloche and Wilma Kane, No. 1170, 1947	35	40	45
Power Models Cut-out Dolls Book, six dolls, No. 981, 1942	65	90	110
Pretty Belles, No. 1966, 1965	7	10	15
Prom Time, two dolls and party clothes, No. 2084, 1962	10	15	20
Queen Holden! Betty and Bob, No. 99110, 1952, 12-1/2"	45	55	65
Queen Holden! Hair-Do Dolls, three dolls, clothes and thirty-one different hair-dos, No. 99110, 1948	55	65	75
Raggedy Ann and Andy, No. 1944, 1974	3	5	10
Raggedy Ann and Andy, No. 4740, 1968	7	10	15
Rock Hudson Paper Dolls, No. 2087, 1957	45	55	65
Roy Rogers and Dale Evans, No. 1950, 1954	55	65	75
Roy Rogers and Dale Evans, No. 1186, 1950	55	65	75
Roy Rogers Cut-out Dolls, No. 995, 1948	60	70	80
Rub-A-Dub Doly, No. 1941, 1977	10	15	20
Sally Ann—A Cut-out Doll, No. 1010, c. 1940	15	25	35
Sandra and Sue Statuette Dolls and their Clothes, by Lee Lunzer, No. 1180, 1948	15	25	35
Sandy and Sue, No. 1956, 1963	10	15	20
Shirley Temple Paper Doll Book, 1976	8	12	18

Whitman, Statuette Dolls and Their Clothes, No. 992, 1943, $35

Whitman (Continued)

	C6	C8	C10
Skating Stars, No. 2105, 1954	25	35	45
Snow White and the Seven Dwarfs, No. 970, 1938, 12" x 17"	100	125	150
Snow White and the Seven Dwarfs, No. 1998, c. 1970	15	20	30
Spaceport, U.S.A., 1953	15	20	22
Sports Time, No. 210525, 1952	5	10	15
Statuette Dolls and Their Clothes, two women, No. 992, 1943	15	25	35
Statuette Dolls and Their Clothes, No. 998, 1942	20	30	40
Statuette Dolls and Their Clothes, two girls and a boy, No. 986, 1946	15	25	40
Sunbonnet Sue, No. 2062-29, 1951	15	20	25
Tammy and Her Family, No. 1997, 1964	30	35	45
Tammy and Pepper, No. 1953, 1966	30	35	45
Teen Gal Cut-out Dolls, by Hilda Miloche and William Kane, No. 980, 1943	30	40	50

Whitman, This is Bunny—One of the Five Cut-out Dolly Sisters, 1939, $40

Whitman, This is Patsy—One of the Five Cut-out Dolly Sisters, 1939, $40

Whitman (Continued)

	C6	C8	C10
They Stand Up, by Avis Mac, includes five children, No. 932, 1939, 13" x 18"	40	50	60
Thirty Toy Soldiers, No. 2950, c. 1943	40	50	60
This is Bunny—One of the Five Cut-out Dolly Sisters, 1939	20	30	40
This is Dotty—One of the Five Cut-out Dolly Sisters, 19391	20	30	40
This is Magic—One of the Five Cut-out Dolly Sisters, 1939	20	30	40
This is Patsy—One of the Five Cut-out Dolly Sisters, 1939	20	30	40
This is Peggy—One of the Five Cut-out Dolly Sisters, No. 1002, 1939	20	30	40
Three Bears Cut-out Book, includes Goldilocks and the three bears, No. 1020, copyright 1939	30	40	50
Three Little Girls Who Grew and Grew and This is How They Grew, w/cloth-like clothes, flocked, No. 1176, 1945	25	35	45
Three Little Girls Who Grew and Grew and This is How They Grew, No. 99410, 1945	25	35	45
Three Little Pigs Cut-out Book, includes pigs and Big Bad Wolf, No. 1020, copyright 1939	25	35	45
Three Sweet Baby Dolls to Cut Out and Dress, No. 975, 1954	10	15	20
Tiny Chatty Twins Paper Dolls, No. 1985, 1963	30	35	40
Transfer Pictures, includes 100 decals, No. 1085, copyright 1939	10	15	18

Whitman (Continued)

	C6	C8	C10
Trudy Phillips and Her Crowd, No. 2104, 1954	15	20	25
Twenty-two Animals To Cut Out and Stand Up, includes rabbits, bears, owls, and squirrels, No. 935, Copyright 1930	35	45	50
Twiggy Paper Doll, w/Twiggy dress for small girls, No. 1999, 1967	35	45	55

Whitman, WACS and WAVES, No. 985, 1943, $75

Whitman (Continued)

	C6	C8	C10
WACS and WAVES, No. 985, 1943	55	65	75
Walt Disney Match and Patch Sticker Fun, includes Mickey Mouse, Donald Duck, Pluto, and Goofy, 1953	15	18	20
Walt Disney Presents Hayley Mills in That Darn Cat, No. 1955, 1965	45	50	55
Walt Disney Sticker Fun Book, 1951	10	12	15
Walt Disney Sticker Fun with Peter Pan, 1952	12	15	18
Walt Disney's Cinderella Paper Dolls, 1965	50	60	75
Walt Disney's Let's Build Disneyland, sets for Adventureland, Frontierland, Tomorrowland and Fantasyland, No. 1986, 1957	25	35	40
Walt Disney's Mary Poppins, No. 1982, 1964	40	45	50
Wedding Paper Dolls, No. 1970, 1970	10	15	20
We're a Family Cut-out Dolls, No. 1181, 1954	25	30	35
Whitman Paper Doll Books, four dolls and ten sheets of clothes in folder, No. 3059, 1933	35	40	45
Wispy Walker, 1976	4	7	10
Zoo Cut-outs by Milo Winter, six pages of heavy cut-out animals, No. 1054, 1938	30	38	48

Miscellaneous

	C6	C8	C10
American Beauties Paper Dolls, Reuben Lilja & Co., No. 917, c. 1942	15	20	25
Amos & Andy Cut-out Dolls, cardboard of just Andy, stand-up, 8-1/2" high	5	7	10
Army Air Forces Aircraft Identification, Silhouette Model-Feb., 1:72-scale of Japanese fighter Najajima T-97, A.N.F., 1943, 7" x 11" envelope	16	20	27
Army Ambulance, Handi-Kraft, c. 1942	30	40	48
Around the World with Bob and Barbara, Children's Press, No. 3000, 1946	15	20	30
Betsy McCall Around the World Paper dolls, c. 1962	20	30	40

Betty Bonnet Her Family and Friends, George W. Jacobs & Co., $175

Miscellaneous (Continued)

	C6	C8	C10
Betsy McCall Dress 'n Play Paper Dolls, boxed set, Standard/Toycraft/McCall, No. 802, 1963, 12" x 18"	25	40	50
Betsy McCall Sheets from McCalls magazine	3	5	8
Betsy Ross and Her Friends, boxed set, Platt and Munk, No. 224B, 1963, 7" x 11"	7	10	15
Betty Bonnet Her Family and Friends, by Sheila Young, George W. Jacobs & Co., Phila., 1915 each series includes six sheets and folder; first series	125	150	175
Betty Sue A Cut-out Doll, No. 1010, c. 1940	15	25	35
Bild-A-Set Constructor Kit, Erector-type set of cardboard, boxed No. 85	22	30	35
Binson-Freeman Pre-Flight Trainer, cockpit and how-to-fly course	75	113	150
Birthday Party Stand-up Cut-out Dolls, twenty boys and girls, National Syndicate Displays, Inc., 1944	20	35	45
Brenda Lee, De Journette, No. 4360, 1964, 6-1/2" x 10"	45	55	85

Bild-A-Set Constructor Kit, No. 85, $35

Miscellaneous (Continued)

	C6	C8	C10
Bridal Doll Book, Watkins-Strathmor, No. 1818, 1963	15	20	30
Bride and Groom, Western box set, 1982	3	5	8
Camouflage Defense Force, heavy cardboard, airplanes, soldiers, anti-aircraft guns all hidden within farm buildings, boxed, Jay Line Mfg. Co., No. 431, c. 1943	55	75	90
Career Girls Artcraft, No. 4471, 1960s	15	20	30

Birthday Party Stand-up Cut-out Dolls, National Syndicate Displays,1944, $45

Miscellaneous (Continued)

	C6	C8	C10
Colorgraphic Statue-ettes, three-dimensional and stand-up paper dolls of Marine, Soldier, Sailor, Nurse, WAAC and WAVE, boxed, 1943	25	40	50
Comet Model Airplane Co. Die-Cut Glider, containing die-cut U.S. Army fighter, printed in 1942 by the Comet Model Airplane Co., 5-1/2" x 8" sheet	10	15	18
Commando Machine Gun, thin cardboard cut-out makes model over, 1940s, 25" long	18	22	28
Coronation Cut-out Model Book	55	65	70
Coronation Glitter Model Book	25	40	50
Crepe Paper Doll Outfit, Dennison Manufacturing Company No. 36	55	65	110
Dancing Black Baby, Littauer & Bauer, 1895	75	100	150
Davy Crockett Punch-Out Book, No. 1943, 1955	40	65	85

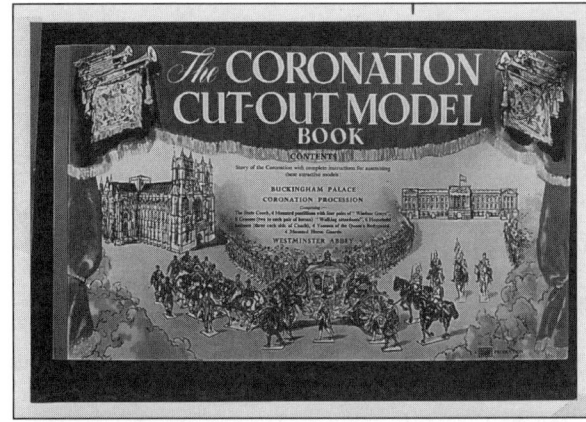

Coronation Cut-out Model Book, $70

Coronation Glitter Model Book, $50

Crepe Paper Doll Outfit, No. 36, Dennison Manufacturing Company, $110

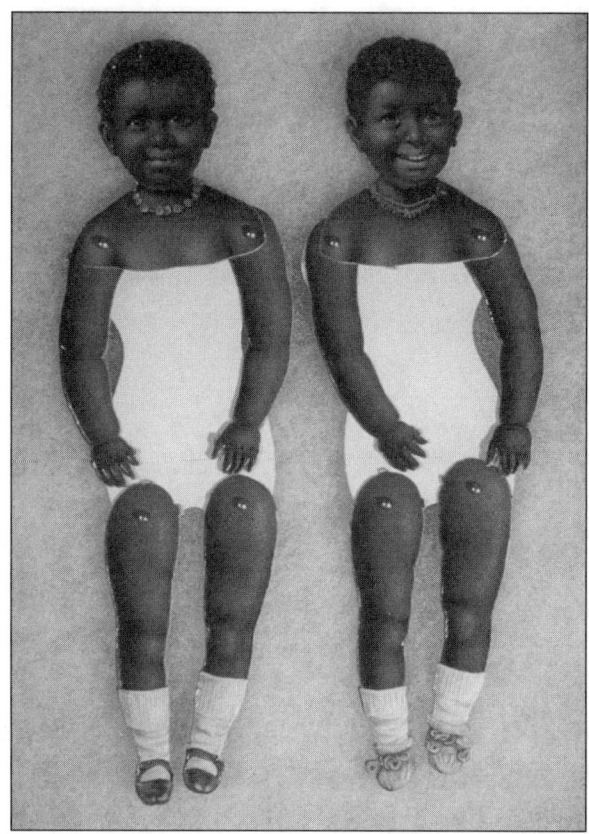

Dancing Black Baby, Littauer & Bauer, 1895, $150

Miscellaneous (Continued)	**C6**	**C8**	**C10**
Decalco-Litho Co. Paper Dolls Sheets, 1) woman and girl and nine outfits; 2) woman and girl and ten outfits; 3) two women and seven outfits; price per sheet, c. 1920s, 8" x 10-1/2" sheets	12	18	25
Dennison's Dolls and Dresses, No. 37, c. 1930	55	65	115
Disneyland Park Punch Out, No. 175, 1960	25	35	50
Dress-Up For the New York World's Fair, by Judy and Barry Martin, Spertus, No. 700, 1963	15	20	30
Dress-Up Paper Doll Cut-outs, Reuben Lilja & Co., 1947	10	15	25
Ellen or the Naughty Girl Reclaimed, S & J Fuller, 1811	150	200	250

Miscellaneous (Continued)	**C6**	**C8**	**C10**
Fabulous High Fashion Models, Bonnie Brooks/Child Craft, No. 2776, 1958	10	15	20
Fairy Folk Cut-out Paper Dolls, by Margaret Carlson, Still & Edwards Co., Inc., 1920s	15	25	35
Fire House P-18, brick firehouse, boxed set, Megow, 1945	35	48	58

Ellen or the Naughty Girl Reclaimed, S & J Fuller, 1811, $250

Fairy Folk Cut-out Paper Dolls, Stills & Edwards, 1920s, $35

Jaunty Juniors, No. 903, 1946, $35

Miscellaneous (Continued)	**C6**	**C8**	**C10**
Fun Farm, Reed and Associates	8	15	18
Gene Autry Ranch Cut-out Book, 1953	50	70	80
Girls in Uniform Paper Dolls Book, No. L1048, c. 1942	35	65	95
Heavy Cruiser "This is the Navy," Skyline Mfg. Co., c. 1943	20	30	40
Historical Dolls To Cut Out and Dress, includes mother, father and two children of heavy cardboard, plus outfits, boxd set, Platt & Munk, No. 226B, 1961, 7" x 11"	20	30	35
House that Jack Built, paper litho, house and story's characters w/stands, c. 1895	400	500	600
Jaunty Juniors, No. 903, 1946	15	25	35
Junior Bombardier, Einson & Freeman Co., No. 202, 1953	25	35	50
Lettie Lane Paper Family, original house folder and six sheets, George W. Jacobs & Co.; third series, 1909	130	155	180
Little Fairy Lightfoot, Chandler's Paper Dolls, Brown, Taggard & Chase, No. 4	150	200	250

Miscellaneous (Continued)	**C6**	**C8**	**C10**
Little Friends from History, by Muriel Wilhoite, Rand McNally, No. 186, 1936	25	40	50
Little Golden Paper Dolls, Golden, Hilda Miloche, 1950s	25	35	45
Little Nurse Cut-out Book, Reuben H. Lilja and Co., Inc., No. 909, early 1940s	20	30	40
Look Who I Am!, by Doris Stelberg, w/fifteen costumes, spiral bound, Hart Publishing Co., 1952, 18" doll	15	20	25
Madame Hattie Fashions, Reuben Lilja, No. 908, 1940s	35	45	48
Make Your Own Battle Set Mechanized Force, Electric Corporation of America, 1942	45	50	55
Maybelle Mercer's Front and Back Dolls, w/wrap-around dresses, by Queen Holden, No. 978	50	75	110
Me and Mimi a Bonnie Story Book Doll, done in the style of the Little Golden Books, a Doll and her Dolly Story Book, plus dolls and their dresses, 1957, 6" x 8"	15	25	35
Mickey and Minnie paper dolls, two figures w/clothes, 1930s, 10"	100	135	175

Lettie Lane Paper Family, George W. Jacobs & Co., 1909, $180

Little Friends from History, No. 186, Rand McNally 1936, $50

Little Fairy Lightfoot, No. 4, Brown, Taggard & Chase, $250

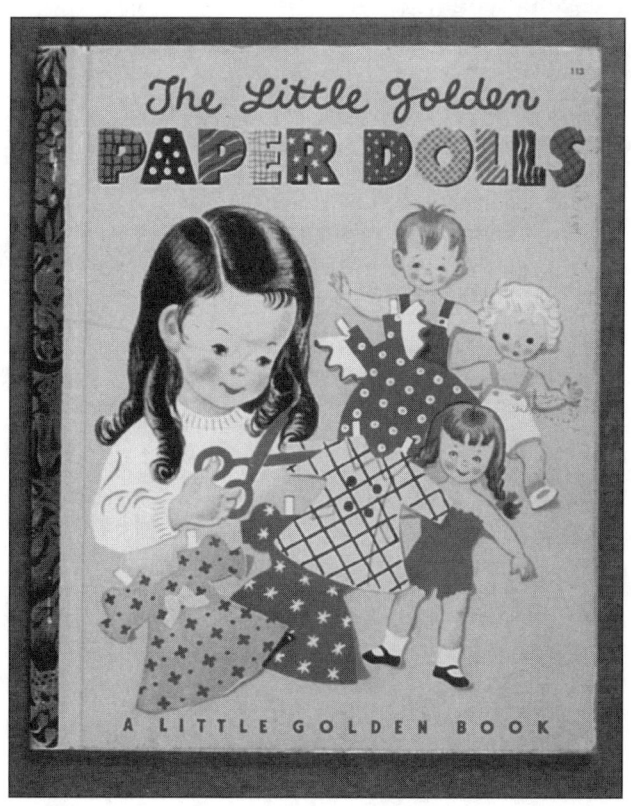

Little Golden Paper Dolls, 1950s, $45

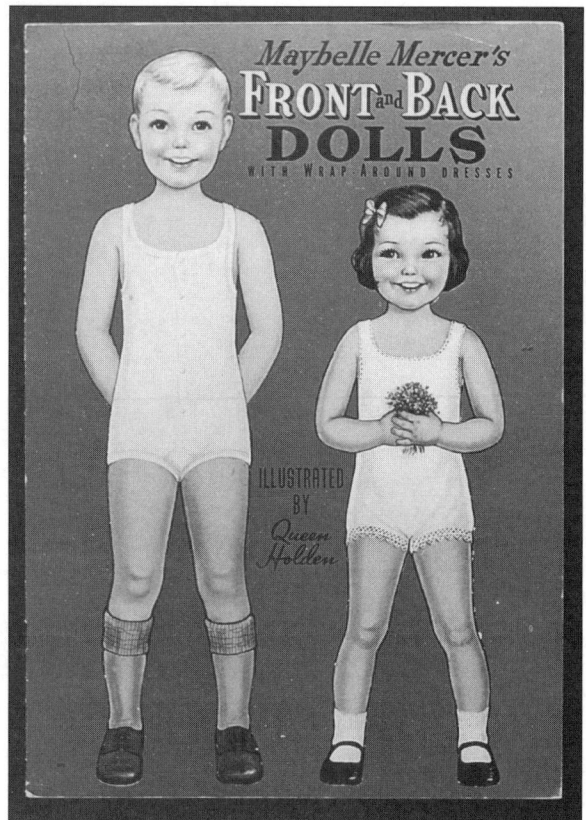

Maybelle Mercer's Front and Back Dolls, No. 978, $110

Paper Doll Outfit Dresses & Hats, No. 102, American Toy Works, $80

Miscellaneous (Continued)

	C6	C8	C10
Our Happy Family Cut-out Sheets, Sam'l Gabriel Sons Co., No. D141, 1928	65	75	90
Our New Home, story by Susan S Popper, pictures by Helen E. Ohrenschall, hardcover book w/six pages of rooms and six gummed pages of people, furniture, etc., Sam'l Gabriel Sons, 1930	80	100	125

Miscellaneous (Continued)

	C6	C8	C10
Paper Doll Outfit Dresses & Hats, American Toy Works, boxed set No. 102	50	65	80
Paper Dolls of the Latest Paris Fashions Brown, Taggard & Chase, 1800s	150	200	250
Patsy, includes Patsy, dog, doghouse, etc., Children's Press, No. 30002, 1946	15	25	35
Patti Page Book of Paper Dolls, 1958	60	70	80
Rap-A-Jap, Woodburn Mfg., No. C1, c. 1943	55	65	72
Ready Cut Village, 1930s	55	70	80
Ricky Nelson Paper Dolls, 1959	35	45	55
Rigby Flying Models of Jet and Rocket Planes, includes ten planes, Garden City Books, 1949	70	80	90

Our Happy Family Cut-out Sheets, No. D141, Sam'l Gabriel Sons Co., 1928, $90

Paper Dolls of the Latest Paris Fashions Brown, Taggard & Chase, 1800s, $250

Royalty Cut-out Books: A Procession of the Knights of the Garter, $70

Miscellaneous (Continued)

	C6	C8	C10
Rigby's Book of Model Ships, 1953	75	85	90
Rigby's Easier to Build Models of Naval Craft, designed by Wallace Rigby, twenty-four models of warships, twenty-seven pages, includes Battleship North Carolina, aircraft carrier, cruiser and destroyer, 1944, 11-1/2" x 14"	95	120	135
Rigby's Easy to Build Models of Fighting Planes	85	95	115
Rigby's Model Book of Flying Clippers, designed by Wallace Rigby, includes two scale models of Douglas DC-Jet Clipper and Douglas DC-7C, 1947, 11" x 14" book	60	70	80

Royalty Cut-out Books: Trooping the Colour, $70

Miscellaneous (Continued)

	C6	C8	C10
Rigby's Model Sports Cars of the World "Sportsracer," includes Chevette, Jaguar, Mercedes-Benz, etc., 1954, 18"	60	70	80
Roy Rogers Sticker Fun Book, No. 2161, 1953	22	30	36
Royalty Cut-out Books: A Procession of the Knights of the Garter	55	65	70
Royalty Cut-out Books: Trooping the Colour	55	65	70
Ruth Newton's Cut-out Dolls and Animals, includes over eighty pieces to cut out and play with, 1934, 11" x 17"	55	65	75
Second series	100	145	175
Six Movie Starlets, including Anne Nagel, Peggy Moran, Jane Frazee, Anne Gwynne, Helen Parrish and Ann Gillis, 1942	85	100	125
Smash the Axis, Electric Corp. of America, 1943	40	55	60
Soldiers, contains nine press-out soldiers, boxed set, wooden cannon and ammunition, Concord Toy Co., c. 1940, 3-1/2" each	50	60	75
Soldiers, cardboard, U.S. Infantry in campaign hats, mounted, approx. 6" high, each	3	4	5
Soldiers Set, contains five cardboard soldiers, and marbles by J. Pressman and Co., Inc., New York, No. 1551, c. 1940, 4-1/2" each	35	50	60
Soldiers—Navy, cardboard, both officer and sailors on wooden blocks, c. 1920, approx. 6" high, each	3	4	5

Soldiers, c. 1940, Condord Toy Co., $75

Miscellaneous (Continued)

	C6	C8	C10
Soldiers—U.S. Sailor, cardboard, on wooden blocks, approx. 6" high, each	3	4	5
Soldiers—West Point Cadets, cardboard, approx. 6" high, each	4	5	6
Stencils Large and Small, by Roy Best, thirty animal punch outs and stencils, w/tiny box of crayons, (Whitman?), No. 954, c. 1935	15	22	28
Stock Farm set, 1,200 die-cut pieces including house, barn, silo, chicken house and tractor, boxed, Concern, No. 123, c. 1944	45	55	60
Story of Cinderella, The, A Fold-A-Way Toy Book, designed by Will Pente, Reilly & Britton Co., c. 1925	30	45	48
Streamline Flyer, contains engine, station, crossing gates, crossing signal, baggage truck, baggage and people, boxed set, Concord Toy Co., No. 122, c. 1940, 10-3/4" x 13-1/2"	45	55	62
Swing-A-Plane, model of a Flying Tiger and on a string, by J.L. Schilling Co., 1944	12	18	20
Tammy, includes paper dolls to cut out and dress, illustrated by Ada Salvi, A Little Golden Story Book, 1963	30	40	75
Tarzan of the Apes, figure set, 1933	40	50	55
The Dress-Up Doll Book, Treasure Books, No. T-167, 1953	8	14	20
The Lone Ranger Rides Again Punch-Out Set, makes fences, figures of LR and Tonto, horses and campfire, DeJournette Mfg. Co.	35	45	55

Miscellaneous (Continued)

	C6	C8	C10
Third series	100	145	175
Three Flying Models of Famous Allied Fighting Planes, by Judd Reed, contains Hell Cat, Spitfire and Stormovik planes, included is "American Ace Spotter," w/turning dial of forty-eight three-view silhouettes of sixteen planes in little windows, 1944, 9" x 12"	30	40	50
Tina and Trudy, by Kathy Lawrence, No. 1967, 1967	20	25	30
Toby Tyler Circus Playbook Punch-Out, No. 1936, 1959	35	45	55
Toy Town, series of fifty different buildings, boxed set, American Color Type Co., 1916	75	100	125
Treasure Hour Puppet Book—The Rustlers of Rocky Ranch, a play of cowboys and Indians in five scenes, cut-out section makes model theater Murray Sales and Service, No. 4, 1968	20	30	35
U.S. Infantry-Spanish—American War, soldier on small wooden block, approx. 6" high	3	4	5
Walt Disney's Babes in Toyland, Golden Punch-Out Book, No. 10363, 1961	40	45	50
Walt Disney's Jane and Michael from Mary Poppins, Watkins/Strathmore, No. 1892-6, 1963	40	45	50
War Between the States, Golden Press, No. GF152, 1959	55	65	75
War Plane Cut-outs, heavy-stock, eight different scale models, 1943, 10" x 14"	35	40	45

ANIMAL-DRAWN

In this category, the toys generally commanding the highest prices are horse-drawn cast-iron pieces. One reason for the eye-opening prices is that horse-drawn cast-iron toys have considerable value apart from their lure as toys—there is an air of genuine Americana about them, and they are likely to attract the interest of many who otherwise pay no attention to toys (decorators figure largely in this area).

Since prices are often so high, reproductions, whether honest or dishonest, can be a problem.

Things to look for when a reproduction is suspected include a rougher surface than an old toy would have (recastings are invariably rougher), uneven fit of pieces, a blurring of details and "aging" that doesn't have the patina of age. Since at least one company, John Wright (formerly Grey Iron), is still manufacturing turn-of-the-century horse-drawn vehicles—some of them from the original molds—it is wise to become familiar with the field before investing heavily.

Althof, Bergmann

Althof, Bergmann began in 1867, when L. Althof teamed with the brothers Bergmann to form a jobbing firm (the brothers were already jobbers). In 1874 the New York company received two patents, one for a bell toy with three soldiers. In addition to bell and animal-drawn toys, they made (or jobbed out) toy furniture, banks and hoop and clockwork toys.

	C6	C8	C10
Fruits and Vegetables, 17-1/2" long..	5000	7500	10,000
Milk Wagon, tin, 13" long..................	600	900	1200
Pull Toy, tin w/iron wheels, wagon, "Express," 26"................................	3000	5000	8000
Pure Milk Milk Cart, c. 1880, 14" long..	500	750	1000

Arcade

All Arcade toys are cast iron.

	C6	C8	C10
Bakery Wagon, cast iron, 13" long......	300	450	600
Big Six Circus & Wild West Wagon, cast iron, 14-1/2" long......................	425	638	850
Cart, wicker and cast iron, horse, driver	100	150	200
Circus Wagon, cast iron, c. 1917.........	400	600	800
Coal Car, cast iron, w/horse	150	225	300
Contractors Dump Wagon, cast iron, w/two horses and driver, 1930s, 13-1/4"...	230	345	460
Contractors Dump Wagon, cast iron, w/horse team and driver, 14" long	250	375	500

Althof, Bergmann Milk Wagon, $1200. Photo courtesy Sotheby's, New York

Althof, Bergmann Pull Toy, $8000. Photo courtesy Sotheby's, New York

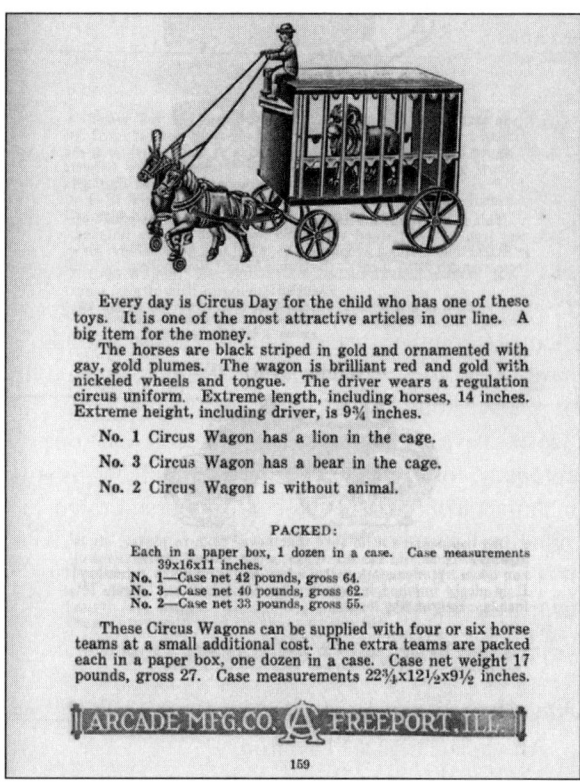

A page form the No. 33 Arcade catalog shows the Arcade Circus Wagon

Arcade (Continued)

	C6	C8	C10
Sulky Plow, cast iron, w/one horse, 10-1/2"	150	250	350

Barclay

	C6	C8	C10
Animal Cage Circus Wagon, lead and tin, c. 1930s, 9-7/8"	30	45	60
Coach, slush lead, c. 1930s, approx. 10-1/4"	30	45	60
Covered Wagon, "1849," w/oxen, 1930s, 7" long	30	40	55

Bliss

Bliss was founded about 1832 by Rufus Bliss, and by 1871 they were advertising their toys. Most were made of wood, and the range was wide, including dollhouses, trains, Noah's arks and ships. In 1883 Bliss made what might have been the first toy telephone set. The brilliant color lithography of Bliss's toys has made many of them prime collectibles.

	C6	C8	C10
Cinderella Coach, paper litho on wood, w/two horses and two coachmen, lift off roof, blocks inside tell Cinderella story, 1890, 26" long	1000	3500	5500

Bliss Fire Hook and Ladder, $4000. Photo courtesy Wilkinson Collection; Detroit Antique Museum

Bliss (Continued)

	C6	C8	C10
Fire Hook and Ladder, paper litho on wood, 30" long	1500	2500	4000
Fire Hook and Ladder, w/two firemen and two horses, 29" long	2000	3000	4000
Pansy Four-horse Stagecoach, paper litho on wood, 1890, 31"	1000	1500	2500
Rough and Ready Fire Engine, w/two horses, 30" long	1600	2700	4000

Carpenter

Carpenter (Francis W.) of Harrison and Port Chester, New York, was in business from 1844 to 1925. Malleable iron was its trademark because it was less fragile. Its two predominant lines were horse-drawn toys and trains.

	C6	C8	C10
Cart, w/two horses, 12" long	635	950	1270
Cart, two-wheel, w/one horse and no driver, pat. 1882	250	400	500
Cart, cast iron, animated, c. 1902, 10-1/2" long	450	675	900
Coal Cart, iron	2000	3000	4000
Delivery Wagon, pat. 1881, 12" long	200	300	400
Doctor's Cart	400	600	800
Dump Cart, w/two horses	350	600	800
Dump Cart, w/one horse, 12"	400	600	800
Fire Patrol, cast iron, w/two horses, one driver and three figures, 1885, 16-1/2" long	900	1400	1900

Carpenter (Continued)

	C6	C8	C10
Fire Wagon, w/one horse and one fireman	350	500	750
Hook and Ladder, w/two horses, and two firemen in standard helmets, early	800	1200	1600
Hook and Ladder, cast iron, w/two horses, one driver and rear man, ladders, c. 1883-1890, 26-1/2"	700	1050	1400
Horse and Carriage, painted cast iron, 1880, 14" long	750	1000	1500
Horse Cart, cast iron, w/one horse and two men, c. 1880, 14-1/2" long	800	1200	1600
Ox Cart, cast iron, w/two oxen, c. 1880-1903, 11" long	400	600	800
Pumper, w/two horses, No. 33, 18" long	1100	1850	2800
Tally-ho, cast iron, w/four horses and seven festive riders in coach, 27-1/2"	4000	9500	12,000
Wagon, w/two horses, 10" long	550	850	1300

Converse

	C6	C8	C10
Delivery Wagon, wood seat, w/one horse, c. 1915	350	525	700
Milk 16 Wagon	70	1100	1700
U.S. Mail 17 Wagon	700	1100	1700

Dent

	C6	C8	C10
Buckboard, w/rider, one horse	125	190	250
Cart, w/horse and driver, 10" long	125	190	250

Dent (Continued)

	C6	C8	C10
Cart, w/lady driver and horse, 11" long	150	225	300
Contractors Dump Wagon, w/two horses, 15" long	150	225	300
Coupe, w/one horse and driver, 9-3/4"	125	190	250
Dray, w/two horses and driver	550	980	1300
Dump Cart, w/black man and mule	300	450	600
Fire Engine Pumper, silver w/two horses, 21" long	400	750	1000
Fire Engine Steam Pumper, three horses, 21" long	1000	1700	2400
Fire Hook and Ladder, 27" long	1000	1700	2400
Fire Patrol, cast iron, w/three horses, w/driver and six riders, c. 1905, 22" long	1200	2000	2800
Fire Patrol, w/three horses and firemen figures, 15-1/2" long	400	1000	2000
Fire Pumper, paint and nickel plate, w/three horses and driver, c. 1908, 15-1/2"	500	800	1100

Dent Fire Hook and Ladder, $2400. Photo courtesy Christie's East

Carpenter Tally-ho, $12000

Dent (Continued)

	C6	C8	C10
Fire Snorkle Wagon, w/three horses and driver	500	750	1000
Hansom Cab, cast iron, w/driver and lady passenger, c. 1905, 14" long	700	1150	1600
Hansom Cab, two-wheeled, w/one horseNo. 57	175	260	350
Hook and Ladder, w/three horses, extra large	500	1000	1500
Hook and Ladder, painted cast iron, mechanized horses, 1915, 14" long	250	400	800
Horse and Cart, cast iron, low sides	125	190	250
Horse and Cart, tin	150	225	300
Hose Reel, w/figures and three horses, figures, 24" long, 10" horse	1200	2000	2900
Ice Wagon, w/two horses, 12" long	100	200	300
Ice Wagon, w/one horse, 14" long	300	500	750
Ice Wagon, cast iron, black horse pulling yellow and orange ice wagon, w/driver, c. 1910, 15-1/2"	675	1000	1350
Ladder Wagon, w/four horses, 1890, 43-1/2" long	3000	4500	6500
Ox Cart, stake sides, w/one ox	125	190	250
Ox Wagon, cast iron, w/driver and two oxen, 16" long	250	500	600
Police Patrol, w/driver, policeman and three horses, 21" long	800	1350	1875
Pony Cart, w/driver and team of horses, stake sides on cart, No. 20	125	190	250
Pumper, painted cast iron, moving horses, 1915, 14-1/2" long	650	1000	1500
Road Car, w/driver in top hat, two seats and one horse, 16" long	450	675	900
Sleigh, w/one horse, c. 1905, 16-1/4"	900	1500	2200
Small Truck Wagon, stake sides	200	300	400
Sulky, w/jockey	150	225	300
Surrey, horse w/wheel attached to one leg	200	300	400
Transfer Wagon, w/two horses, 21" long	450	750	1150
Transfer Wagon, w/driver and two horses, 26" long	500	850	1200
Truck Wagon, w/driver and one horse stake sides, 16" long	200	300	400
Water Tower, w/two horses, c. 1910, 31" long	900	1500	2200

George Brown

In 1856 George W. Brown together with Chauncey Goodrich, founded George W. Brown and Company. Brown, an innovator, introduced the American clockwork toy (he'd spent eleven years in the clockmaking business). He invented many of his toys' mechanisms and may also have designed all or most of his toys. Brown worked primarily in tin, jobbing some of the work out to companies like Union Manufacturing Company in Clinton, Connecticut. Necessarily simple because of the material and manufacturing techniques employed, Brown's toys made up for it with brilliant hand-painted color and stenciling. Tops, rattles, flutes, wagons, fire engines, swords, trains and toy buckets were among the many items put out by the firm. The company merged with Stevens in 1868 and was dissolved in 1880.

	C6	C8	C10
Cab, w/driver and one horse, 8-1/2" long	560	840	1120
Cart and Horse, painted and stenciled tin, 1880, 7-1/2" long	200	300	500
Delivery Cart, 12"	1100	1800	2600
Doctor's Buggy, tin and cast iron, 14" long	650	975	1300
Dog Cart, c. 1870	400	700	1000
Dump Cart, painted tin, 1885, 8-1/4" long	100	150	200
Dump Cart, tin, back gate lifts out for dumping, 1880, 13"	200	300	400
Eagle Chariot, painted tin, 1870, 11" long	500	1000	2500
Express Wagon, tin, w/iron wheels, 10-1/2" long	300	450	600

George Brown Wagon, $600. Photo courtesy Sotheby's, New York

George Brown (Continued)

	C6	C8	C10
Fine Groceries Cart, w/horse	1250	1875	2500
Gig, tin, w/one horse, 10" long	150	225	300
Gig, tin, 9" long	300	450	600
Goat Coat, 7" long	300	450	600
Grand Central Depot Trolley, tin, w/two horses, 13-1/2" long	600	950	1350
Horse Cart, tin, 1870, 11-1/2" long	125	190	250
Ox Cart, painted tin, 1880, 9" long	500	1000	2000
Peddle Wagon, tin, wheeled horses, driver andawning, c. 1880, 2 20" long	1000	2500	5000
Rockaway Passenger Cart, w/two horses, 13" long	1850	2500	4500
Sulky, 8-3/4" long	250	375	500
Sulky, clockwork, 13" long	3000	5500	9000
Yankee Notions Peddler Wagon, 16-1/2" long	3000	7000	10,000

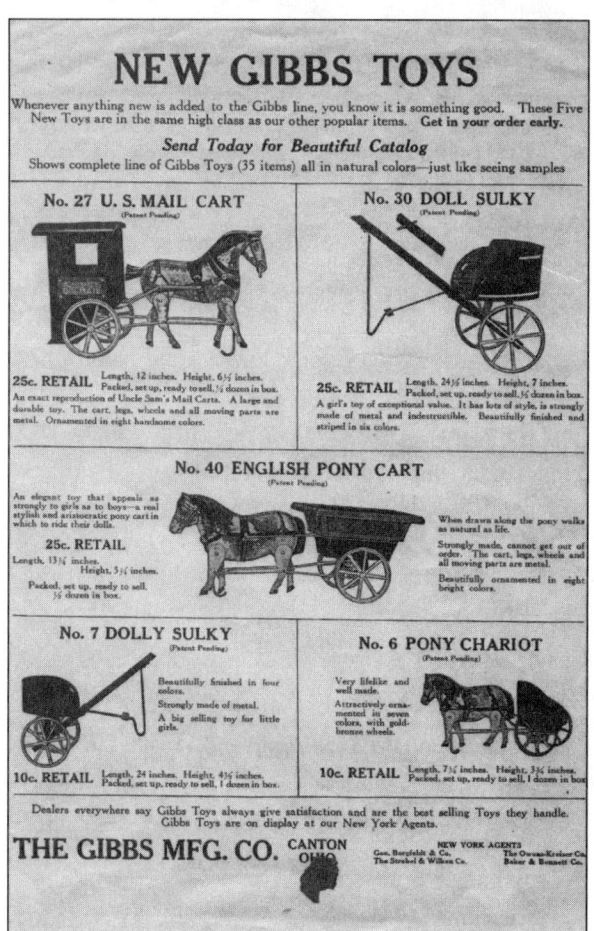

George Brown Wagon, $600. Photo courtesy Sotheby's, New York

Gibbs

After manufacturing wooden barrels and tubs and metal plows since about 1830, Gibbs Manufacturing Company of Canton, Ohio, began turning out toys in 1896. The company's first toy was a political give-away for William McKinley who was from Canton. The first toy was a spring-operated top, and variations of it remained in the firm's catalogs until 1969, when it stopped making toys. Most Gibbs toys were wood or tin, with much use made of lithographed paper for decoration. Many of Gibbs' playthings were of the push and pull variety.

	C6	C8	C10
Cart and horse, paper litho on wood, 13" long	150	225	300
Delivery, No. 14	150	225	300
Dog Cart, boy driver	375	560	750
English Pony Cart, No. 40	110	165	220

Gibbs U.S. Mail Cart, No. 27, $600. Photo courtesy Detroit Antique Museum

Gibbs English Pony Cart, No. 40, $220

Gibbs (Continued)

	C6	C8	C10
Gray Beauty Pacers, No. 50	150	225	300
Groceries The Great Atlantic and Pacific Tea Co. Cart, mule-drawn, 12" long	350	500	1000
Gypsy Wagon, No. 57	250	375	500
Pacing Joe, No. 35	175	263	350
Pioneer Wagon, No. 32	65	100	130
Pony Chariot, No. 6	165	250	350
Pony Circus Wagon, No. 53	200	300	400
Pony Pacer, No. 15, 7" long	115	170	230
Tea Co. Mule Cart	350	500	1000
U.S. Mail Cart, No. 27	300	450	600
Yankee Dump Cart, No. 56	225	338	450

Harris

Harris Toy Company of Toledo, Ohio, seems to have begun production of cast-iron toys during the late 1880s. The firm, which also jobbed for Dent, Hubley and Wilkins, stopped making toys in 1913.

	C6	C8	C10
Brownie Shell Cart, cast iron, 1903	225	340	450
Cart, w/mule driver, 10" long	250	500	750
City Truck, w/two horses and driver, 15" long	1200	1900	2700
City Truck, w/one horse and driver	1300	2000	3150
Dog Cart, cast iron, w/girl driver, 7" long	275	360	550
Fire Patrol Wagon, w/driver, three riders and two horses, 19" long	800	1400	1900
Goat Coat, w/rider, 9-1/2" long	800	1425	1950
Goat Coat, cast iron, shell-type, w/driver, 5" long	100	250	350
Hook and Ladder, cast iron, w/three horses, 19" long	140	210	280
Transfer Wagon, w/three horses, 1903, 18-1/2" long	400	650	850
Wagon, mule, 12" long	300	450	600

Hubley

	C6	C8	C10
Brake, four-seat, w/four horses and eight articulated passengers, 28"	2000	3500	5625
Brake, cast iron, three-seat, w/two horses, 18" long	4000	7000	12,500
Brake, cast iron, three-seat, w/four horses, 18" long	4200	7300	13,000

Hubley Brake, $5625. Photo courtesy Sotheby's, New York

Front to Back: Hubley Brake, $7500; Hubley Brake, $12,500. Photo courtesy Sotheby's, New York

Hubley (Continued)

	C6	C8	C10
Brake, cast iron, two-seat, w/driver and three women passengers, 16-1/2" long	2500	5000	7500
Brake, cast iron, two-seat, 16" long	1600	2700	4000
Brougham, cast iron, w/nickeled, horse and driver, 16" long	300	1000	1500
Brougham, w/top-hatted driver and one horse, 17" long	550	850	1300
Cab, cast iron, w/driver cast in, w/one horse	300	500	750
Cab, 14" long	300	500	700
Cane Wagon, 15" long	600	900	1200
Cart, w/driver, 5-1/2" long	150	225	300
Cart, w/horse and driver, 8" long	155	232	310
Cart, wood, w/iron wheels and iron horse, 1910, 10-1/2" long	175	265	350
Chariot, cast iron, 8-3/4" long	500	750	1000
Chariot, w/driver and two horses, 9-1/2"	600	900	1200
Chariot, cast iron, w/clown and three horses, early, 12-1/2" long	800	1200	1600

Hubley Brake, $4000. Photo courtesy Sotheby's, New York

Hubley Hose Reel, $1000. Photo courtesy Bill Bertoia Auctions

Hubley Cab, $700. Photo courtesy Sotheby's, New York

Hubley Hose Tower Wagon, c. 1915, $1800. Photo courtesy Sotheby's New York

Hubley Coal Wagon, $1000. Photo courtesy Sotheby's, New York

Hubley Ice Wagon, $2000. Photo courtesy Sotheby's New York

Hubley Fire Pumper, $2090

Hubley Landau Carriage, 1905, $2800. Photo courtesy Sotheby's, New York

Hubley Police Patrol, $2200. Photo courtesy Sotheby's, New York

Hubley Royal Circus Bandwagon, $3000. Photo courtesy Sotheby's, New York

Hubley Royal Circus Bear Wagon, $3000. Photo courtesy Sotheby's, New York

Hubley Royal Circus Farmer Van, 1920, $4250. Photo courtesy Bill Bertoia Auctions

Hubley Royal Circus Lion Cage, $750. Photo courtesy Bill Bertoia Auctions

Hubley (Continued)	C6	C8	C10
Chariot Bank, elephant-drawn, 13" long	650	1100	1600
Coal Wagon, w/mule, 9" long	300	450	600
Coal Wagon, w/two horses, 16"	500	750	1000
Conestoga Wagon, tin, w/cloth canopy, w/two horses, 15" long	550	825	1350
Dray Barrel Wagon, w/barrels and barrel ramp, w/driver and two horses, 23" long	1100	1750	2500
Eagle Milk & Cream Wagon, 12" long	500	750	1000
Essex Trap, cast iron, driver and horse, 1890, 13" long	500	1500	2500

Hubley (Continued)	C6	C8	C10
Fire Patrol, cast iron, driver, w/four firemen and prancing horse team, 21" long	700	1100	1500
Fire Patrol, cast iron, driver, w/four riders, all in standard helmets, 13" long	750	1200	1750
Fire Pumper, cast iron, white painted, w/two horses, c. 1906-1910, 19" long	500	775	1100
Fire Pumper, cast iron, w/two horses, driver and two firemen, 20" long	750	1125	1500
Fire Pumper, cast iron, w/three horses and driver, c. 1906-1910, 20-1/2" long	800	1200	1600
Fire Pumper, cast iron, w/American eagle, w/two horses, c. 1905-1910, 21" long	500	1000	1500
Fire Pumper, cast iron, w/three horses, 22" long	800	1400	2090
Fire Pumper, cast iron, w/two horses and driver, c. 1910, 14" long	200	400	600

Hubley (Continued)

	C6	C8	C10
Gig, cast iron, horse-drawn w/lady driver, 15" long	350	650	950
Hook and Ladder, cast iron, w/two horses, 28" long	700	1200	1650
Hook and Ladder, cast iron, w/eagle on shield on side, w/three horses, 33" long	1000	1700	2450
Hook and Ladder, cast iron, w/three horses, two firemen and two wooden ladders, c. 1906-1910, 27-3/4" long	550	850	1300
Hook and Ladder, cast iron, "126," w/three horses, 33-1/2" long	438	657	875
Hose Reel, cast iron, w/three horses and driver, c. 1906, 19" long	750	1200	1700
Hose Reel, cast iron, w/one horse and three figures, 13" long	500	750	1000
Hose Tower Wagon, cast iron, c. 1915, 28" long	800	1300	1800
Ice Wagon, cast iron, w/two black horses pulling green wagon and driver, c. 1906, 15-1/2" long	800	1300	2000
Ice Wagon, cast iron, 8" long	100	150	200
Ice Wagon, cast iron, 1920s, 9-1/2"	175	265	350
Ice Wagon, cast iron and nickel plated, painted, w/driver and horse, 1910, 14"	400	850	1200
Ice Wagon, cast iron, w/one horse, 15"	800	1300	2000
Ice Wagon, cast iron, w/two horses and driver, 16-1/2" long	1000	1650	2200

Hubley (Continued)

	C6	C8	C10
Ice Wagon, cast iron, w/two horses, 15" long	500	800	1200
Landau Carriage, cast iron, painted, 1905, 16-1/2" long	1400	2100	2800
Log Wagon, cast iron, w/two oxen and driver, c. 1905, 15" long	500	750	1100
Log Wagon, w/one horse, 19" long	400	600	800
Milk Cart, cast iron, 12-1/2" long	425	640	850
Milk Wagon, 5" long	140	210	280
Monkey Trapeze Circus Mirror Van, 12-1/2" long	500	800	1300
Phaeton, cast iron, w/one horse	1200	2000	3000
Police Patrol, cast iron, w/driver and riders, 17-1/2" long	600	950	1430
Police Patrol, cast iron, w/driver and six cops, 21" long	1000	1600	2200
Police Patrol, cast iron, w/driver and three riders, early, 13" long	500	750	1000
Roman Chariot, cast iron, w/three large horses	600	900	1200
Roman Chariot, w/driver and three horses, 16" long	200	300	400
Roman Chariot, cast iron, w/three small horses	425	637	850
Royal Circus, cast iron, w/animals, driver and two horses, 15" long	500	1000	1200
Royal Circus Bandwagon, cast iron, w/eight musicians and driver, 1920, 30"	1500	2250	3000
Royal Circus Bandwagon, cast iron, w/four horses and seven riders, 22"	1000	2000	3000
Royal Circus Bandwagon, cast iron, w/two horses and seven riders, c. 1920, 22-1/2"	1800	2900	4000

Hubley Royal Circus Lion Wagon, $1650. Photo courtesy Christie's East

Hubley Royal Circus Polar Bear Cage, 1920s, $1375. Photo courtesy Bill Bertoia Auctions

Left to Right: Hubley Royal Circus Rhino Wagon, $2500. Hubley Royal Circus Tiger Wagon Cage, 1920, $1000; Photo courtesy Sotheby's, New York

Hubley Santa Claus Sleigh, 1910, $1500. Photo courtesy Sotheby's, New York

Hubley (Continued)

	C6	C8	C10
Royal Circus Bear Wagon, cast iron, 15" long	1500	2250	3000
Royal Circus Calliope, cast iron, 12-3/4" long	1400	2400	3400
Royal Circus Clown on Trapeze Van, cast iron, oval-mirrored sides, 1920, 16-1/2"	1600	2700	4000
Royal Circus Farmer Van, cast iron, head revolves and disappears in top of wagon as toy pulled, 1920, 16" long	1700	1850	4250
Royal Circus Giraffe Cage, cast iron, w/large and small giraffes and driver, 1920, 27" long	3000	5500	9200
Royal Circus Lion Cage, cast iron, 9"	375	565	750
Royal Circus Lion Wagon, cast iron, w/rare gray horses and wagon, 15-3/4"	700	1100	1650
Royal Circus Polar Bear Cage, cast iron, 1920s, 11-3/4" long	600	1000	1375
Royal Circus Rhino Wagon, 16" long	850	1700	2500

Hubley Stanhope Gig, $400. Photo courtesy Sotheby's, New York

Hubley (Continued)

	C6	C8	C10
Royal Circus Tiger Wagon Cage, cast iron, w/driver and two tigers, 1920, 16" long	500	750	1000
Santa Claus Sleigh, cast iron, early, 17" long	800	1300	2000
Santa Claus Sleigh, cast iron, w/one reindeer, early, 15" long	1500	2500	4000
Santa Claus Sleigh, cast iron, w/two reindeer, 1910, 16" long	600	1000	1500
Shell Cart and Horse, cast iron, 1905, 7" long	250	375	500
Sleigh, cast iron, w/one horse and woman w/movable arms, early, 14-3/4" long	700	1200	1700
Sleigh, cast iron, nickel plated and painted, w/one horse, 1900, 15" long	250	375	500
Sleigh, cast iron, nickel plated and painted, w/two horses, 1910, 15" long	800	1300	2000
Sleigh, cast iron, painted, w/one horse, 1910, 14-1/2" long	500	800	1200
Spring Wagon, cast iron, w/horse and driver	200	300	400
Stanhope Gig, cast iron, 11-1/2"	200	300	400
Sulky, 8-1/2" long	187	280	375
Surrey, cast iron, two-seat w/driver, woman passenger and two horses, 13-3/4" long	600	900	1200
Surrey, cast iron, w/two horses and driver, 18"	400	600	800
Surrey, two horses, woman driver, 13-3/4" long	750	1125	1500
Surrey, cast iron, w/two horses, driver and rider, c. 1900, 12" long	240	360	480

Hubley (Continued)

	C6	C8	C10
Surrey, cast iron, clockwork w/brass works, 1894, 9" long	500	1000	1500
Surrey, cast iron, w/one horse and lady driver, 13-3/4" long	318	475	635
Trotter, cast iron, w/horse and driver, 1900, 8-3/4" long	200	300	400
Trotter Gig, cast iron, w/lady driver, 11"	150	225	300
Wagon, cast iron, w/horse, 12"	150	225	300
Wagon, cast iron, expandable, w/wood ben, w/two horses and driver, 26"	750	1125	1500

Hull & Stafford

	C6	C8	C10
Dump cart	700	1000	1600
Express Wagon	350	550	750
Gig, w/china doll, c. 1885, 12" long	650	1150	1500
Prospect Park Omnibus, w/two horses and driver, c. 1880, 16-1/2"	5000	10,000	15,000
Wagon, 9" long	800	1400	2000

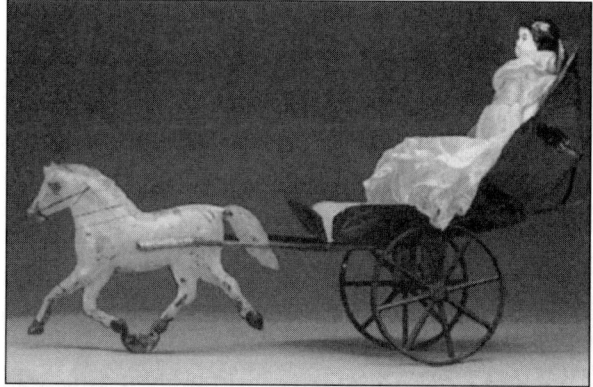

Hull & Stafford Gig, c. 1885, $1500. Photo courtesy Christie's East

Hull & Stafford Prospect Park Omnibus, c. 1880, $15000. Photo courtesy Christie's East

Hull & Stafford Prospect Park Omnibus, c. 1880, $15000. Photo courtesy Christie's East

Ideal

	C6	C8	C10
Fire Department, cast iron, three horses, 30" long	500	1000	1500
Fire Patrol, cast iron, marked "Patrol," 21" long	1000	1700	2500
Fire Pumper, cast iron, two horses, two riders, 20-1/2" long	250	500	750

Ives

Ives is one of the fabled companies in American toy history. Founded by Riley Ives as a metal stamping shop in the late 1850s in Bridgeport, Connecticut, it was around 1856 when Ives began making tin whistles for New York Rubber's squeak toys. This seems to have led to Ives' first true toys—hot air playthings. These were toys put into motion by the hot air from stoves, lanterns, etc., and were first sold in 1868. Ives' son Edward joined the company around 1860, and his son, Harry, took the reins in 1895. Harry Ives was ousted in 1929, and the firm was dissolved in 1932.

During its heyday, which lasted about 40 years, Ives put out a deluge of toys of every type, and quality was its watchword. Toy making was carried on in Bridgeport, Connecticut, from about 1870 until the end.

	C6	C8	C10
Adams Express, w/two horses, 21"	750	1300	1800
Bandwagon, cast iron, w/nine passengers, 31-1/2" long	2500	4000	6000
Brewery Wagon, w/two horses, 18-1/2" long	1000	1700	2500
Caisson, w/driver, cannon, rider and two horses, 21" long	1700	3000	4000
Chief Fire Dept., 15-1/2" long	400	700	1000
Coal Dump Cart, w/donkey and black driver	363	545	725
Coal Dump Wagon, w/donkey and black driver	375	560	750

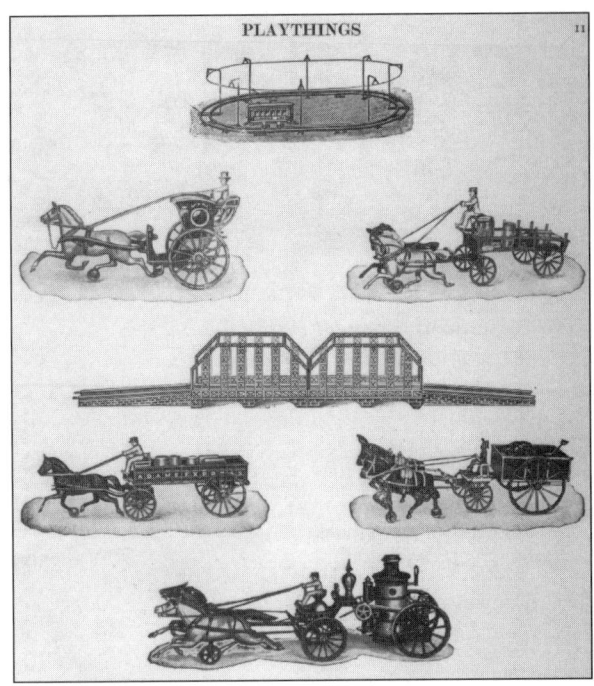

An early advertisement from Playthings *magazine*

Ives Chief Fire Dept., shown with incorrect driver, $1000. Photo courtesy Sotheby's, New York

Ives Coal Dump Wagon, $750. Photo courtesy Sotheby's, New York

Ives Dray Wagon, $3000. Photo courtesy Sotheby's, New York

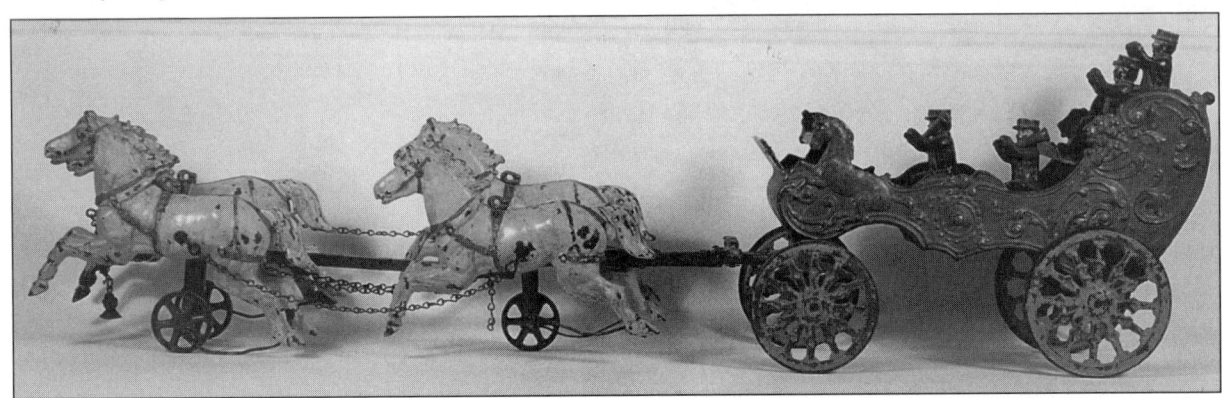

Ives Bandwagon, $6000. Photo courtesy James Maxwell/Virginia Caputo

Ives Fire Patrol, c. 1880-1910, $2200. Photo courtesy Sotheby's, New York

Ives Hansom Cab, $4000. Photo courtesy Bill Bertoia Auctions

Ives Hook and Ladder, c. 1885, $2100. Photo courtesy Christie's East

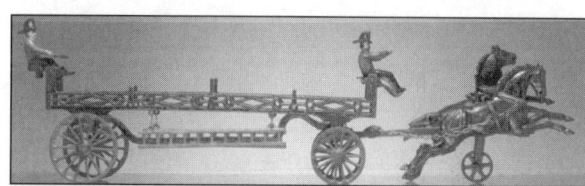

Ives Hook and Ladder, c. 1890, $2200. Photo courtesy Sotheby's, New York

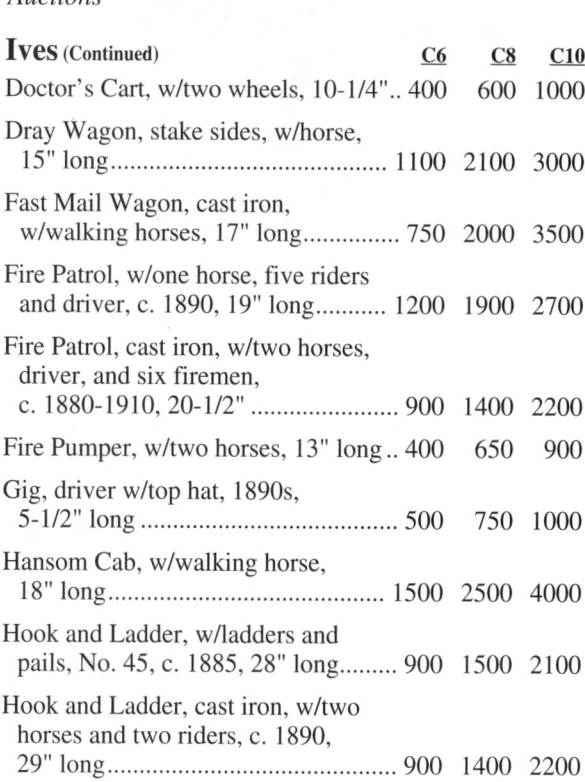

Ives Hook and Ladder, c. 1890, $2200. Photo courtesy Sotheby's, New York

Ives (Continued)

	C6	C8	C10
Doctor's Cart, w/two wheels, 10-1/4"	400	600	1000
Dray Wagon, stake sides, w/horse, 15" long	1100	2100	3000
Fast Mail Wagon, cast iron, w/walking horses, 17" long	750	2000	3500
Fire Patrol, w/one horse, five riders and driver, c. 1890, 19" long	1200	1900	2700
Fire Patrol, cast iron, w/two horses, driver, and six firemen, c. 1880-1910, 20-1/2"	900	1400	2200
Fire Pumper, w/two horses, 13" long	400	650	900
Gig, driver w/top hat, 1890s, 5-1/2" long	500	750	1000
Hansom Cab, w/walking horse, 18" long	1500	2500	4000
Hook and Ladder, w/ladders and pails, No. 45, c. 1885, 28" long	900	1500	2100
Hook and Ladder, cast iron, w/two horses and two riders, c. 1890, 29" long	900	1400	2200

Ives (Continued)

	C6	C8	C10
Hook and Ladder, cast iron, w/driver and two horses, 34" long	1500	2400	3700
Hook and Ladder, Phoenix, c. 1890, 28" long	1500	2400	3600
Horse Cart, tin, 1870, 10" long	600	950	1400
Horse Cart, w/two horses, 1883, 17-1/2"	750	1200	2500

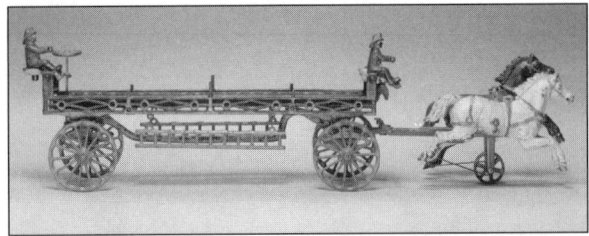

Ives Hook and Ladder, c. 1890, $3600. Photo courtesy Sotheby's, New York

Ives Phoenix Pumper, $2300. Photo courtesy Bill Bertoia Auctions

Ives Hose Reel Wagon, $1300. Photo courtesy Sotheby's, New York

Ives Phoenix Pumper, $2300. Photo courtesy Bill Bertoia Auctions

Ives Patrol Fire Wagon, $2050. Photo courtesy Sotheby's, New York

Ives (Continued)	C6	C8	C10
Hose Reel Wagon, w/driver, rider, and one horse, very low back platform	2000	4000	7000
Hose Reel Wagon, w/one horse and driver, 16" long	600	950	1300
Ox Cart, w/two oxen	400	750	1150
Patrol Fire Wagon, 22" long	800	1350	2050
Phoenix Hose Reel Wagon, cast iron, w/one horse and driver, c. 1880-1910, 15" long	1600	2400	3200
Phoenix Pumper, cast iron, w/driver and two horses, 17-1/2" long	950	1600	2300

Ives (Continued)	C6	C8	C10
Phoenix Pumper, cast iron, clockwork, rarest of Ives pumpers, c. 1890, 19" long	900	1500	2200
Police Patrol Wagon, w/six patrolmen and driver, 1890s, 20-1/2" long	1000	2000	3000
Pull Toy, walking horse, horse walks by means of wheel mechanism, pulls two-wheeled cart, late 19th century	1800	2800	4000
Pumper, 23" long	2000	3200	4500
Stake Wagon, w/two donkeys, 15-1/2"	400	600	800

Ives Stake Wagon, $800. Photo courtesy Sotheby's, New York

Ives (Continued)

	C6	C8	C10
Steam Pumper, w/two horses, 20-1/2"	4000	6000	8000
Wagon, w/mules, 1896	600	950	1400

James Fallows

James Fallows was a foreman at the early American tin toy company Francis, Field and Francis. In 1874 he formed James Fallows & Company in Philadelphia. Most of Fallows' toys were tin, though often with cast-iron wheels many were marked "IXL." Papier-mâché was another primary material in a toy line that consisted of over 200 items.

	C6	C8	C10
4th Avenue Streetcar, tin, w/one horse	500	800	1200
Cart, tin, 12" long	500	750	1000
Cart and Horse, painted tin, 1870, 8-1/2" long	100	200	400
Covered Wagon, painted tin w/litho paper, scenes on sides, 12"	800	1000	1500
Dump Wart, tin, w/one horse, c. 1890, 16" long	600	1000	1200
Fancy Goods and Toys, 21" long	1750	2625	3500
Fine Groceries Delivery Wagon, 7-1/2" long	1250	1875	2500
Fire Pumper, tin, very early, 24" long	5000	10,000	15,000
Fire Pumper, w/two horses, very early, 18" long	5000	8500	10,000
Horse and Carriage, painted and stenciled tin, 1890, 12-1/2" long	500	750	1000
Pure Milk Wagon, painted and stenciled tin, 1895, 12-1/2"	800	1200	2000
Streetcar, w/two horses, 10" long	350	500	800
Streetcar, 9" long	400	600	900
Wagon, cast iron, w/donkey, 10-1/2" long	175	260	350

Kenton

Kenton Lock Manufacturing Co. was incorporated in May 1890, in Kenton, Ohio. In November of 1894 it became the Kenton Hardware Manufacturing Company, and around this period the company began producing toys. It ceased production of horse-drawn toys in the early 1920s (except for a 1930s beer wagon), but in 1939 introduced a completely new line of horse-drawn pieces. This line continued through 1954.

	C6	C8	C10
Aerial Fire Tower, w/three horses and driver, 30" long	800	1400	1900
Ambulance, 2nd Regiment, w/driver and one horse, 15" long	1200	2400	3600
Back to Back Trap, w/driver and woman rider, 12-1/2" long	1100	1900	2750
Bakery Wagon, 1941	325	500	650
Band Wagon, w/musicians, driver and rider on horse	150	225	300
Beer Delivery Wagon, cast iron, (3.2), w/two horses, driver and ten wooden kegs, 1930s, 14-1/2" long	350	525	700
Beer Wagon, cast iron, w/driver and two horses, 15" long	500	800	1200
Boar Cart, cast iron, w/Egyptian driver, c. 1910, 8" long	350	500	750
Cairo Express Egyptian Cart, elephant drawn, 10" long	500	800	1100
Cement Mixer, w/driver and horse, 14" long	350	750	1000
Chariot, cast iron, 6" long	150	225	300
Chariot, cast iron, w/comic driver, 1910, 7-1/2" long	250	375	500
Chariot, camel-drawn w/clown driver, 11" long	700	1200	1600
Chariot, cast iron, w/three horses	600	900	1200
Chief Wagon, w/horse and driver, 12-1/4" long	500	800	1500
Circus Cage Wagon, w/two horses, two riders, driver and animal in cage	350	700	1000
City Express Wagon, w/driver and one horses, 17" long	500	750	1045
Coal Cart, w/donkey and black driver	365	550	725
Contractor's Wagon, w/black driver and two horses, 15-1/2" long	500	800	1200

Kenton (Continued)

	C6	C8	C10
Covered Wagon, cast iron, w/two horses	130	195	260
Cupid in Horse-drawn Slipper, w/one horse, 10-1/2" long	550	950	1400
Cupid in Slipper, cast iron, w/one-horse cart, 8-1/2" long	450	800	1100
Delivery Cart, cast iron, w/donkey	150	225	300
Delivery Wagon, w/driver and two horsesNo. 5, 15" long	250	375	500
Dog Cart, greyhound pulling dog riding in cart, 7" long	250	375	500
Dray, cast iron, w/two black and white horses pulling green dray w/driver, 13-1/2"	300	450	600
Dray, cast iron, painted, No. 5, 1930, 14-1/2" long	175	265	350
Dray, cast iron, w/two horses pulling a green cart w/driver, late 1940s, 14-3/4" long	95	140	190
Dump Wagon, w/two horses, lever releases bottom wagon	250	375	500

Kenton (Continued)

	C6	C8	C10
Dump Wagon, early 1900s, 10-1/4" long	150	225	300
Egyptian Cart, elephant drawn	300	450	600
English Trap, w/two horses, woman and dog, c. 1895, 14" long	1600	2700	4000
Express Wagon, cast iron, w/horse and driver, 12" long	200	300	400
Fire Ladder Wagon, w/front driver only, 12" long	150	225	300
Fire Ladder Wagon, horse drawn, w/drivers front and rear, 17" long	135	200	270
Fire Patrol Wagon, w/driver and three riders, 12" long	360	535	714
Fire Pumper, w/two horses and driver, 20" long	175	260	350
Fire Pumper, cast iron, 26-1/2" long	600	1000	1400

Kenton Hook and Ladder, $3200. Photo courtesy Sotheby's, New York

Kenton Hook and Ladder, $3200. Photo courtesy Sotheby's, New York

Kenton Log Wagon, early 1900s, $1100. Photo courtesy Sotheby's, New York

*Kenton Overland Circus Calliope Wagon, $700.
Photo courtesy Sotheby's, New York*

Kenton (Continued)

	C6	C8	C10
Fire Wagon, nickel plated wagon, w/two horses, driver, equipment and bell, 23" long	200	300	400
Goat Cart, figure w/large cars, 7" long	250	375	500
Gravel Wagon, w/two horses, 3" long	150	225	300
Hansom Cab, 12" long	500	750	1000
Hansom Cab, cast iron, w/top-hatted driver and lady rider	700	1050	1400
Hansom Cab, w/top-hatted driver, 8" long	150	225	300
Hansom Cab, w/figures and horse, 15-1/2" long	300	500	700
Hansom Cab, w/one horse and top-hatted driver, 10" long	1000	1500	2000
Hook and Ladder, cast iron, w/three horses, 16" long	300	450	650
Hook and Ladder, w/three horses, 17" long	250	375	500
Hook and Ladder, cast iron, w/three horses, c. 1910, 19" long	150	225	300
Hook and Ladder, nickel-plated, w/two horses and driver, 20" long	200	300	400
Hook and Ladder, cast iron, painted, w/ladders, 1915, 26" long	600	1000	1400
Hook and Ladder, 30" long	1400	2200	3200
Hook and Ladder Wagon, w/two horses and driver, 20" long	250	375	500
Hose Reel, cast iron, painted, 1920, 13-1/2" long	500	750	1000
Hose Reel, cast iron, w/two horses, c. 1905, 14-1/2" long	600	900	1200

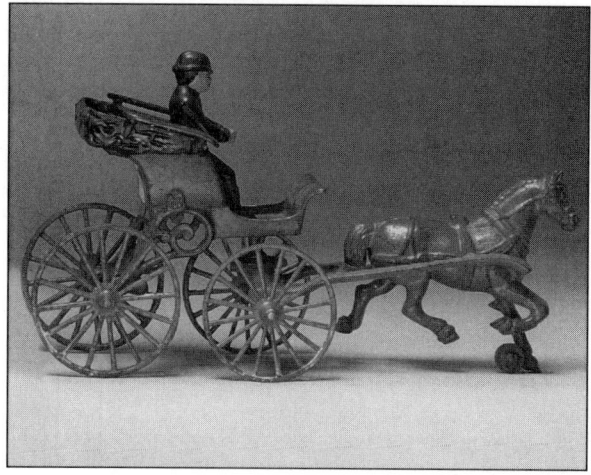

*Kenton Spider Phaeton, $2000. Photo courtesy
Sotheby's, New York*

Kenton (Continued)

	C6	C8	C10
Ice Wagon, cast iron, w/two horses and driver, 1920s, 15" long	250	375	500
Landau, cast iron, white horse pulling green carriage w/driver, c. 1910, 15" long	600	900	1200
Log Wagon, cast iron, black man w/two oxen, early 1900s, 15" long	500	800	1100
Log Wagon, w/one horse and driver, 14-1/2" long	425	640	850
Milk Wagon, w/horse and driver, 12-1/2" long	280	420	540
Overland Circus Bandwagon, w/six musicians and driver, 15-3/4"	500	800	1210
Overland Circus Bear Wagon, cast iron, w/two horses, driver and cage containing cast-iron bears, 1940s, 13"	235	350	470
Overland Circus Calliope Wagon, 14-1/2" long	300	500	700
Ox Cart, 7" long	110	165	220
Ox Cart, 12-1/2" long	385	575	770
Ox Cart, cast iron, 5" long	100	150	200
Ox Wagon, w/two oxen, 18" long	400	600	800
Patrol, w/two horses, driver and ridersNo. 526, 17" long	650	1100	1500
Patrol Wagon, w/driver and rider, 12" long	275	415	550
PlantationCart, Black driver, mule, 1910, 10" long	500	800	1210
Police Patrol, w/mule team, 16"	500	750	1000
Pumper, w/three horses, 18" long	400	600	800

Kenton (Continued)

	C6	C8	C10
Rabbit pulling two-wheeled cart, cast iron, 5" long	200	300	500
Rhino Cart, 8" long	100	200	300
Sand and Gravel Dump Wagon, w/driver and two horses, 10" long	180	270	360
Sand and Gravel Dump Wagon, w/driver and two horses, 15" long	175	260	350
Spider Phaeton, cast iron, 11-1/2" long	850	1350	2000
Stake Wagon, w/two horses and driver w/reins, 15" long	83	125	165
Sulky, driver cast to sulky, 6" long	75	112	150
Sulky, cast iron, w/driver, 7" long	250	375	500
Surrey, w/fringe top, w/driver, passenger and two horses, 1952, 13" long	145	220	290
Surrey, w/one horse, c. 1940, 16" long	150	225	300
Surrey, cast iron, w/two horses, driver and passenger, 12-1/2"	263	395	525
Team of Horses, w/log and black driver	500	750	1000
Transfer Wagon, w/two horses and driver	650	975	1300
Victoria Cab and Horse, cast iron, w/driver and woman, 15-1/2" long	150	225	300
Wagon, w/one-horse and driver No. 3, 15" long	125	190	250
Wagon, w/one horse, No. 5, 15"	125	190	250
Wagon, w/two horses, 15" long	90	135	180
Wagon, w/driver and two horses, 10-1/4"	100	150	200
Water Tower Wagon, driver and two horses, c. 1915, 32" long	440	660	880

Kingsbury

	C6	C8	C10
Dray, cast iron, w/two horses, 20-1/4" long	300	450	600
Hook and Ladder, w/two horses, driver and three ladders, 27" long	600	900	1200
Hook and Ladder, cast iron and pressed steel, w/three horses and two riders, rubber covers on wheels, 25-1/2"	400	600	800
Ladder Truck, cast iron, tin and wood, 1900, 13" long	300	450	600

Lancaster

	C6	C8	C10
Hook and Ladder, cast iron, w/three horses and two drivers, 28" long	250	375	500
Hook and Ladder, cast iron, w/two horses and two drivers, 28" long	200	300	400
Hook and Ladder, cast iron, w/two horses, 25" long	150	225	300
Surrey, w/one seat, driver and horse, Hubley, No. 174	150	225	300
Surrey, no driver, Hubley, No. 58	75	115	150

Mason & Parker

	C6	C8	C10
Buckboard, pressed steel, painted, w/one horse, 1910, 31"	500	750	1000
Cart, painted pressed steel, w/horse, mechanical action from axle, 1910, 13" long	500	750	1000

Pratt & Letchworth

Pratt & Letchworth of Buffalo, New York, was in operation from c. 1880 into the 1890s and sold its toys under the name Buffalo Toy Works. Iron and steel were its main materials, and all of its most prominent toys seem to have been horse-drawn.

	C6	C8	C10
Barouche, w/driver and two horses, 17" long	750	1400	2000
Brake, four-seat, w/four horses, driver and seven passengers, 28" long	4000	7000	11,000

Top to Bottom: Pratt & Letchworth Surrey, c. 1890, $1100; Pratt & Letchworth Hansom Cab, c. 1892, $1800. Photo courtesy Sotheby's, New York

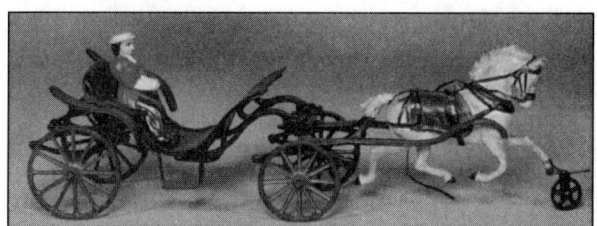

Pratt & Letchworth Pony Phaeton, c. 1892, $1500. Photo courtesy Sotheby's, New York

Pratt & Letchworth Pumper, $2000. Photo courtesy Bill Bertoia Auctions

Pratt & Letchworth (Continued)

	C6	C8	C10
Chemical Wagon, w/three horses and driver	3000	6000	9000
Chief's Wagon	1100	1650	2200
City Delivery Wagon, w/driver, barrels and horse, c. 1885	1100	1700	2500
Doctor's Cart, w/one horse and driver, 11" long	650	1100	1550
Double Surrey, 15" long	450	750	1100
Dray, cast iron and wood, w/one horse, 1890, 12" long	80	1450	2200
Dray, w/one horse and driver, 14-1/2" long	500	850	1500
Fire Chief's Wagon, w/figure and horse, c. 1885, 12" long	700	1100	1500
Gig, cast iron and pressed steel, w/one horse and one rider, 10-1/2" long	400	600	800
Hansom Cab, cast iron, c. 1892, 13" long	700	1200	1800
Hay Cart, 10-1/2"	500	750	1000
Hose Reel, w/one horse and driver in standard helmet	900	1350	1800
Hose Reel, w/one horse, 14-1/4" long	900	1350	1800
Pony Cart, 11" long	413	620	825
Pony Phaeton, w/driver and one horse, c. 1892, 15-1/4" long	600	1000	1500
Pratt & Letchworth Cart, 10" long	150	225	300

Pratt & Letchworth (Continued)

	C6	C8	C10
Pumper, w/driver, rider and two horses, 17" long	750	1400	2000
Sulky, 8-1/2" long	700	1200	1820
Sulky, 15" long	550	850	1300
Surrey, rear seat, w/one horse, c. 1890, 15-1/2" long	500	850	1100

Reed

	C6	C8	C10
Band Chariot, paper on wood, w/fourteen band members, c. 1895, 28-1/2" long	800	1200	2000
Band Chariot, w/fourteen bandsmen, 28-1/2" long	800	1200	2000
Bowery & Central Park Trolley, paper on wood, w/two horses, 1895, 28" long	1500	2300	3500
Cinderella Coach, twin horse-drawn	1100	1700	2760
Mammoth Show Circus Wagon, paper on wood, w/three animals and two trainers, c. 1890, 14" long	1100	1700	2500
Pansy Stage Coach, w/four horses, driver and litho alphabet blocks, 28"	1000	1500	2000

Reed Band Chariot, $2000. Photo courtesy Christie's East

Reed Trolley, 1895, $3500. Photo courtesy Christie's East

Rich Toys

Rich Toys, founded by E.M. and M.E. in 1921, added toys to their line around 1923. Their first toys were manufactured in Morrison, Illinois, and then moved to Clinton, Illinois. In 1953, Rich moved to Tupelo, Mississippi, where, about 1962, a flood put an end to the business.

	C6	C8	C10
Borden's Golden Crest Dairy Cart, wood, 18" long	240	360	480
Budweiser Beer Wagon	300	500	800
National Biscuit Company Wagon, w/one horse	400	600	800
Sand and Gravel Wagon, cast iron, w/driver and two horses, 15" long	150	225	300
Sand and Gravel Wagon, cast iron, w/driver and two horses, 14-3/4" long	100	150	200
Sand and Gravel Wagon, cast iron, w/driver, 9-1/2" long	150	225	300
Streetcar, w/two horses, No. 59, c. 1925, 20" long	600	900	1200

Rich Toys Dairy Cart, $480. Photo courtesy Joe and Sharon Freed

Rich Toys Streetcar, No. 59, c. 1925, $1200. Photo courtesy Wilkinson Collection; Detroit Antique Toy Museum

Shimer Choice Family Groceries Tea, Coffee & Spices, $1200. Photo courtesy Sotheby's, New York

Shimer

	C6	C8	C10
Choice Family Groceries Tea, Coffee & Spices, 12-1/2" long	500	800	1200
Ice Wagon, cast iron, w/driver and two horses, 13" long	375	560	750
Lumber Wagon, cast iron, w/two horses, 26" long	358	535	715
Patrol, cast iron, animated, w/black prisoner and five policemen, 21" long	3500	6500	9000
Surrey, woman driver	375	560	750

Welker & Crosby

	C6	C8	C10
Hose Reel, 13-1/2"	800	1400	1900
Ox Cart, w/two oxen and black driver	600	900	1200

Wilkins Toy Company

Wilkins Toy Company, founded by James S. Wilkins in Keene, New Hampshire, began as the Triumph Wringer Company. The tiny model Wilkins produced to promote his product proved so intriguing to prospective customers and their children that requests for the toys outnumbered the actual product. Wilkins quickly forgot his original idea and turned to toy making. Wilkins' toys were generally cast iron and steel. The firm was acquired by Kingsbury in 1894, and they are still in business as a tool and die maker.

	C6	C8	C10
Aerial Fire Wagon, cast iron, w/three horses and driver, 43" long	2000	3500	5150
Artillery, w/rider on caisson and two horses, seat top lifts off, cannon, c. 1895, 10" long	1000	1500	2000
Boys Express Co. Wagon, cast iron, w/two horses, 16-1/2" long	700	1200	1600

Wilkins Toy Company Aerial Fire Wagon, $5150. Photo courtesy Phillips, New York

Wilkins Toy Company Streetcar, $2800. Photo courtesy Wilkinson Collection; Detroit Antique Toy Museum

Wilkins Toy Company Streetcar, $2400. Photo courtesy David W. Mapes, Inc.

Wilkins Toy Company Fire Pumper Wagon, $5000. Photo courtesy Sotheby's, New York

Wilkins Toy Company (Continued)	C6	C8	C10
Broadway Car Line 75 Streetcar, horse-drawn	900	1600	2400
Buckboard, cast iron	120	180	240
Caisson, horse-drawn, 18"	650	1000	1500
Cane Wagon, w/mule and driver, 11" long	300	450	600
Carriage, w/driver in derby, passenger and one horse	1000	1500	2000
Cart, animated, 6" long	250	375	500
Cart and Horse, 10" long	450	700	1000
Cart and Horse, w/driver, 12"	750	1200	1600
Chariot, w/four horses, 7" long	180	270	360
Chariot, cast iron, woman driver w/three horses, 10-1/2" long	400	600	800
City Truck, cast iron, w/two horses and driver	1000	1500	2000
Coal and Wood Wagon	750	1125	1500
Consolidated Street R.R. 712 Streetcar, cast iron, 14" long	1200	1900	2800
D.P.W. Street Sweeper, w/one horse, brush and driver, 13" long	2000	3200	5700
Delivery Wagon, w/driver and prancing horse team, 21" long	600	900	1200
Doctor's Cart, c. 1900, 10-1/2" long	500	750	1100
Dog Cart, cast iron, 1890, 7-1/2" long	150	225	300

Wilkins Toy Company (Continued)	C6	C8	C10
Dog Cart, cast iron, w/St. Bernard-type dog and rider in cap, c. 1890, 10-1/2" long	600	950	1400
Donkey Cart, 11" long	237	355	475
Donkey Cart, 13-1/4" long	350	525	700
Dray, w/driver and two mules, 17-1/2" long	600	900	1250
Dray, cast iron and tin, drawn by two horses, w/driver in derby hat, c. 1910, 20-1/2" long	900	1350	2200
Dray, cast iron, w/six horses, 16" long	325	500	700
Dray, cast iron, 15" long	300	450	600
Dray, cast iron, w/black driver, and one horse, 12" long	500	750	1100
Fire Chief Buggy, w/one horse and rider, 12" long	650	1050	1500
Fire Chief Engine Pumper, w/two horses, 19" long	500	750	1000
Fire Hose Reel, 10-1/2" long	350	550	750
Fire Ladder Truck, cast iron, w/three horses and two firemen, c. 1910, 20"	415	620	830
Fire Patrol, w/six firemen and three horses, 20" long	500	750	1050
Fire Patrol Wagon, w/firemen, 12" long	450	675	900

Wilkins Toy Company (Continued)

	C6	C8	C10
Fire Patrol Wagon, cast iron, w/two horses and two firemen, 20-1/2" long	550	825	1200
Fire Pumper Wagon, w/driver and three horses, 25" long	1800	3200	5000
Fire Pumper Wagon, w/driver and two horses, 20" long	600	900	1200
Fire Pumper Wagon, horizontal chemical tank, w/two horses, 19-1/2" long	1700	2800	4000
Fire Pumper Wagon, w/two horses, 18"	1700	2800	4000
Gentlemen's Cart, w/gentlemen driver and white horse, 1900, 10"	300	450	600
Gig, fancy, w/driver, 10"	150	225	300
Goat Cart, driver, c. 1900, 9-1/2" long	900	1350	2200
Groceries Wagon, w/one horse, c. 1900, 13-1/2" long	200	300	400
Hansom Cab, cast iron, 15" long	600	950	1400
Hook and Ladder, w/two horses and two firemen, 19-1/2" long	385	575	770
Hook and Ladder, w/two horses, ladders and figures; horses sit on pegs	1000	1500	2000
Hook and Ladder, 24" long	700	1100	1700
Hook and Ladder, cast iron, w/prancing team, 27" long	600	925	1350
Hose Reel, w/two horses and two firemen in standard helmets, 16" long	1500	2500	3500

Wilkins Toy Company (Continued)

	C6	C8	C10
Hose Reel, cast iron, w/one horse, c. 1890, 18" long	800	1300	1900
Huckster's Wagon, w/two horses and driver	800	1450	1950
Ice Wagon, tin and cast iron, 10" long	150	225	300
Landau, cast iron, w/articulated horses, two coachmen and opening doors, 15-1/4" long	1200	2000	3100
Ox Cart, cast iron	300	500	700
Panama Earth Mover, w/driver and two horses, 1903, 20" long	400	600	800
Phaeton, w/driver in top hat and gray pony	450	750	1100
Phaeton, w/woman driver, late 1800s, 16" long	1000	2500	4000
Plantation Cart, cast iron and pressed steel, 1910, 11"	460	690	920
Police Patrol, w/driver, two horses and six policemen, 1911, 20" long	1700	2700	3700
Pony Cart, w/one horse and driver, 7-1/2" long	400	600	800
Pony Cart, w/one horse and driver, 9-1/2" long	500	750	1075
Pumper, w/two horses and two firemen	1100	1650	2200
Spring Wagon, w/driver and horses	300	450	600

Wilkins Toy Company Hook and Ladder, $770. Photo courtesy Bill Bertoia Auctions

Wilkins Toy Company Ox Cart, $700. Photo courtesy Sotheby's, New York

Top row: Wilkins Toy Company Fire Pumper Wagon, $4000; Bottom row, left to right: Wilkins Toy Company Fire Pumper Wagon, $4000; Wilkins Toy Company Hose Reel, $3500. Photo courtesy Christie's East

Wilkins Toy Company (Continued)

	C6	C8	C10
Stake Wagon, 1907	500	675	1000
Steam Engine, w/two horses and driver, 17" long	600	900	1300
Transfer Wagon, tin and cast iron, 15" long	500	850	1200
Wagon, w/driver and mule, 9" long	300	450	600
World's Fair Street R.R. 372 Streetcar, cast iron, w/one horse and six passengers, 15"	900	1600	2400

Miscellaneous

	C6	C8	C10
Africa, two-wheeled cart with driver being pulled by Ostrich, Lehmann	NPF	NPF	NPF
Bakery Wagon, cast iron, w/one horse, 13" long	100	200	300
Barnum and Bailey Circus Cage, stained and litho wood, painted, elephant drawn, 1930, 35" long	400	600	800
Bowery & Central Park Trolley, paper on wood, w/two horses, 28" long	1500	2300	3500
Bread and Cakes Wagon, w/driver and tin horse, 12-1/2" long	350	525	700
Brewery Wagon, cast iron and pressed steel, w/two horses and driver, 20-1/2"	350	525	700
Buckboard, cast iron, w/one horse and driver, 14" long	200	300	400
Buggy, cast iron, w/driver, 6-1/2"	70	100	140
Buggy, pressed steel, w/cast-iron wheels and horse	40	60	80
Buggy, tin, w/horse, 7" long	175	265	350
Cab and Horse, painted and stenciled tin, Merriam, 1880, 8-1/2" long	1300	2700	4000

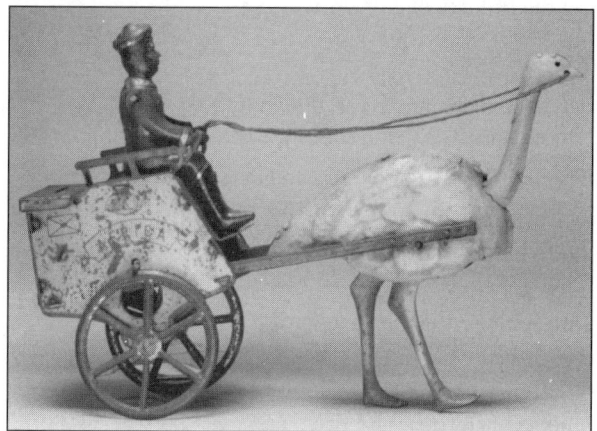

Africa, $0. Photo courtesy Sotheby's, New York

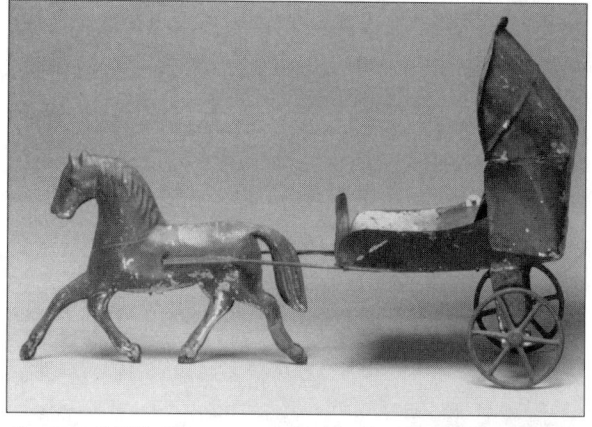

Buggy, $350. Photo courtesy Sotheby's, New York

Doctor's Cart, $2000. Photo courtesy Sotheby's, New York

Miscellaneous (Continued)

	C6	C8	C10
Carriage, metal and wood, w/horse, malleable iron horse w/articulated legs and tail	300	450	600
Cart, tin, w/one horse, 8" long	200	300	400
Cart, tin, painted, w/one horse, 1890, 15" long	250	500	750
Cart, cast iron, stake sides, w/one horse, 7" long	150	225	300
Cart, cast iron, 7" long	125	190	250
Cart, cast iron, w/woman and prancing horse, 10-1/4" long	500	750	1200
Cart, cast iron, w/one horse, 9" long	75	115	150
Cart, cast iron, w/driver and buffalo, 7-1/2" long	400	600	800
Cart, cast iron, two-wheeled cart pulled by lions, 8" long	125	190	250
Cart, cast iron, two-wheeled cart pulled by bulls	100	150	200
Chariot, drawn by tin horse, 13-1/2" long	125	190	250
Chariot, cast iron, w/clown and camel	1000	1600	2400

Dog Cart, c. 1875, $800

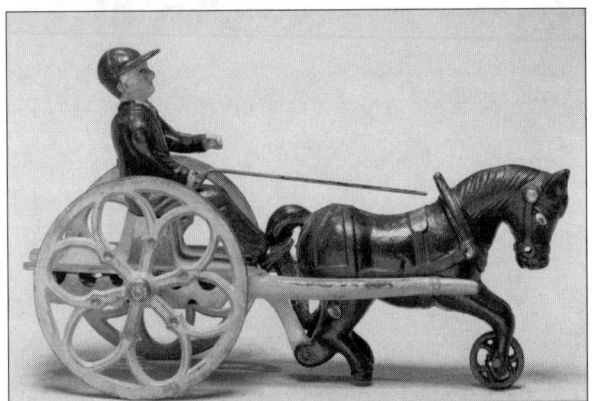

Donkey Cart, $400. Photo courtesy Sotheby's, New York

Fire Patrol, c. 1890, $1300. Photo courtesy Sotheby's, New York

Miscellaneous (Continued)	C6	C8	C10
Chief Fire Wagon, cast iron, w/one horse, 15-1/2" long	350	525	700
Chief's Wagon, cast iron, "Chief," w/one horse, c. 1915-1920, 12" long	150	225	300
Circus Wagon, iron and tin, w/two horses and lion cage, 9" long	200	300	400
Circus Wagon, cast iron and wood, contains carved wood bear, 13" long	250	340	500
Coal Wagon, cast iron, w/driver and coal shovel, 9-1/4"	137	200	275
Conestoga Wagon, cast iron, w/cloth cover and two horses, 12-1/2" long	50	75	100
Conestoga Wagon, litho, w/walking horses and iron wheels, 18" long	140	210	280
Covered Wagon, cast iron, w/cloth top, w/one horse and driver, 13" long	170	255	340
Covered Wagon, tin, Indian head litho on side, w/driver and horse	40	60	80
Dispatch Wagon, w/one horse, Chein, 11-1/2" long	90	135	180
Doctor's Cart, cast iron, 11" long	850	1450	2000
Dog Cart, tin, baby carriage, c. 1875, 10" long	400	600	800

Miscellaneous (Continued)	C6	C8	C10
Donkey Cart, cast iron, w/driver, Stevens	200	300	400
Donkey Cart, tin, w/iron star wheels, 8" long	300	450	600
Donkey Cart, tin, 8-1/2" long	250	375	500
Dray, cast iron, w/one black horse pulling dray, 14" long	150	225	300
Dray Wagon, cast iron, w/driver and two horses, 18" long	250	375	500
Dump Truck, cast iron and tin, w/one horse	200	300	400
Fine Groceries Wagon, tin, w/two horses, 14" long	400	600	800
Fire Hose Reel, cast iron, horse-drawn, 6" long	150	225	300
Fire Patrol, cast iron, w/two horses, three firemen and driver, c. 1910, 19"	1250	1875	2500
Fire Patrol, cast iron, w/two horses, three firemen and one driver, c. 1890, 20-1/2" long	600	950	1300
Fire Patrol, cast iron, wagon contains two firemen and driver, drawn by three horses, 17" long	900	1350	1800
Fire Pumper, cast iron, w/two horses and driver, 13" long	600	900	1200
Fire Pumper, cast iron, w/three horses, 14-1/2"	650	1050	1500
Fire Pumper, cast iron, w/three horses, c. 1910, 17-1/2" long	500	750	1000
Fire Pumper, cast iron, w/three horses, w/driver, and fireman, c. 1910, 18-1/4" long	425	640	850

Miscellaneous (Continued)

	C6	C8	C10
Fire Pumper, cast iron, w/two horses and driver, 19-3/4" long	500	750	1000
Fire Pumper, cast iron, w/three horses, 11-1/4"	500	750	1000
Friendship 1774 Fire Pumper, cast iron, w/rubber hose, 16" long	375	565	750
Goat Cart, tin, early, 10-1/2" long	150	225	300
Goat Cart, iron goat and wheels w/tin cart, 7-1/2" long	100	150	200
Golden Pasture Farm Products, Milk & Cream Wagon, wood, painted and stenciled, steering mechanism for child to ride, 1915, 30" long	500	750	1000
Grass Cutter, cast iron, two-wheeled cart w/two horses and driver	1000	1500	2000
Hansom Cab, cast iron, w/driver, 9-1/2"	120	188	250
Hansom Cab, tin, movable legs on horse, 15-1/2" long	175	265	350
Hard and Soft Coal-Coke and Kindlings Dump Cart, tin, 19" long	500	750	1000
Hook and Ladder, cast iron, w/three horses and driver, 25" long	500	750	1000
Hook and Ladder, cast iron, w/three horses, two drivers and four ladders, c. 1910-1914, 31-1/4" long	1000	1500	2000
Hook and Ladder, wood, ladder, w/figurines and three horses, 29-1/2" long	750	1125	1500
Hook and Ladder, cast iron, w/three horses, 25-1/2" long	600	900	1200
Hook and Ladder, cast iron, w/two horses, 22-3/4" long	1000	1650	2000
Hook and Ladder, cast iron and tin, w/three horses, two firemen and ladders, 21"	175	265	350
Hook and Ladder, cast iron, tin and wood, w/two horses, driver and three ladders, 16-1/2" long	150	225	300
Hook and Ladder, pressed steel and iron, w/figures, ladders, unusual hanging horses	250	375	500
Hook and Ladder, w/three horses, driver, 27-1/2" long	750	1125	1500
Horse and Cart, litho paper, on wooden horse, tin cart	150	225	300
Horse and Cart, tin, open carriage w/driver in top hat, 5-1/2" long	150	225	300

Miscellaneous (Continued)

	C6	C8	C10
Hose Reel, cast iron, w/three horses, one driver and fireman, c. 1910-1914, 21"	1000	1500	2000
Hose Reel, cast iron, w/one horse and driver, 11" long	1000	1650	2500
Hose Reel, cast iron, w/one horse and driver, 12" long	1000	1650	2500
Hose Reel, cast iron, w/one horse and driver and cord fire hose, 12-1/2" long	500	750	1000
Hose Reel, cast iron, w/driver, two horses and man standing on rear bumper, 21" long	750	1125	1500
Hose Reel, cast iron, w/three horses, c. 1910, 19" long	600	900	1200
Hose Wagon, cast iron, w/two firemen, three horses and bell, 21-1/2" long	750	1125	1500
Ice Wagon, cast iron, w/one horse, 12"	500	750	1000
Ice Wagon, cast iron, w/two horses, 12"	600	900	1200
Klondike Ice Co., New York Wagon, tin, w/two horses, 17-1/2"	350	525	700
Ladder Wagon, cast iron, w/two horses and three sections of ladder, w/bell, 25-1/2"	250	375	500
Ladder Wagon, cast iron, w/two drivers and three horses, four sections of ladder, dart type, 30-1/2" long	800	1400	2100
Ladder Wagon, cast iron, w/two ladders and three galloping horses, 13-1/2"	150	225	300
Log Wagon, cast iron, w/driver and two oxen, 15-1/4" long	450	675	900
Mail Cart, tin, horse drawn	140	210	280
Mail Wagon, tin, w/two horses, 17"	175	260	350
Mess Cart, tin, WWI-type, painted, w/two horses	100	150	200
Milk Wagon, tin, painted, goat-drawn, possibly George Brown, 6"	150	225	300
Milk Wagon, w/driver and one horse, 12-3/4" long	200	300	400
Mower, cast iron, w/two horses and driver, 10" long	150	225	300
National Express Wagon, tin litho, w/one horse, 15" long	250	375	500

Miscellaneous (Continued)

	C6	C8	C10
People's Omnibus, tin, w/two horses and driver, c. 1880s-1890s	4000	6000	8000
Police Patrol, cast iron, w/one horse, 12"	150	225	300
Police Patrol Wagon, cast iron, w/driver, five policemen and two horses, 15"	1700	2800	4000
Police Patrol Wagon, cast iron, w/one horse, figures and driver, 11-1/2" long	100	150	200
Produce Wagon, tin, painted, w/one horse, possibly George Brown, 12-1/2" long	350	525	700
Pull Toy, tin, horse and cart w/iron wheels, 11" long	250	375	500
Pull Toy, wood, horse-drawn wagon w/articulated legs, "Borden's Farm Products"	315	470	625
Pull Toy, tin, w/iron wheels, horse pulling water wagon, 7-1/4" long	125	190	250
Pull Toy, tin, w/iron wheels, horse pulling water wagon, 6-3/4" long	350	525	700
Pull Toy, tin, horse-drawn carriage, 12"	150	225	300
Pull Toy, tin, horse and covered delivery wagon, 5-1/4" long	150	225	300
Pull Toy, "Dump Cart," horse pulling cart, 7-3/4" long	80	120	160
Pull Toy, cloth and wood, "Dry Goods," c. 1860, 26" long	400	600	800
Pull Toy, tin, horse and two-wheeled wagon, 9-1/4" long	125	190	250
Pumper, cast iron, w/three horses and figure, 13" long	300	450	600

Produce Wagon, $700. Photo courtesy Sotheby's, New York

Miscellaneous (Continued)

	C6	C8	C10
Pumper, driver part of casting, w/two horses, 15-1/2" long	200	300	400
Pumper, cast iron, w/driver and two horses	125	188	250
Santa Claus and Sleigh, two reindeer pulling a white sled containing black-painted Santa Claus	500	800	1200
Santa Claus and Sleigh, wooden sleigh, composition Santa and plush reindeer, 25" long	1500	2250	3000
Sheep, cast iron and tin, sheep pulling two-wheeled wagon, 8" long	125	200	300
Sheffield Farms Company Wagon, wood, horse w/articulated legs, 21" long	250	400	650
Spring Wagon, cast iron, w/driver and horse, 11" long	150	225	300
Spring Wagon, cast iron, w/driver and horse, 14-1/2" long	150	250	350
Spring Wagon, cast iron, w/driver and two horses, 14-1/2" long	150	275	400
Spring Wagon, cast iron, w/driver and two horses, plus miniature pick, shovel and sledgehammer, 14-1/4" long	600	900	1200
Spring Wagon, cast iron, w/two horses, 15"	150	225	300
Stagecoach, cast iron, w/cowboy driver and two horses, 11" long	130	195	260
Stagecoach, cast iron, w/six horses, 27" long	60	90	120
Stakebed Wagon, cast iron, w/one horse, 14-3/4" long	400	700	1000
Stanley Surrey, w/driver, lady passenger and two horses, 14-3/4" long	100	150	200
Steam Pumper, cast iron, w/two horses and w/driver, 18" long	600	1000	1500
Steam Pumper, cast iron, w/driver and two horses, 20-1/2" long	800	1300	2000
Steam Pumper, cast iron, w/stationary driver, and two horses, 15" long	500	750	1000
Steam Pumper, cast iron, w/stationary driver and three horses, 10-1/2" long	150	225	300
Steam Pumper, cast iron, w/stationary driver and two horses, 9-1/4" long	100	150	250

Miscellaneous (Continued)

	C6	C8	C10
Steam Pumper, cast iron, w/driver and three horses, bell, 17-1/2" long	600	900	1200
Sulky, cast iron, w/driver, 7-1/4" long	150	225	300
Sulky, cast iron, Williams, c. 1920, 8" long	150	225	300
Sulky, cast iron, w/driver, c. 1890s, 8-1/2" long	250	400	550
Sulky, cast iron, w/horse and rider, cart mounted w/four bells, 6-1/2" long	200	300	400
Sulky Racer, plastic wind-up, Wolverine	55	80	110
Transfer Wagon, cast iron, w/three horses and driver, wagon bolted to team, 19"	325	488	650
Transfer Wagon, cast iron, w/driver and two horses, 19-1/2" long	400	600	800
Transfer Wagon, cast iron, w/two horses, driver, 18" long	300	450	600

Miscellaneous (Continued)

	C6	C8	C10
Trolley, cast iron, w/jockey and horse, 6" long	150	225	300
Trotter, lead alloy, All-Nu, 1941, approx. 4" long	30	45	60
Uncle Sam Eagle Head Chariot, cast iron, w/two horses, Jones & Bixler	3000	5000	8000
United States Transfer Co. No. 7 Wagon, wood w/cast-iron wheels, w/two stuffed horses, 31" long	300	450	600
Wagon, cast iron, two-wheeled w/driver, 7-1/4" long	100	150	200
Wagon, cast iron, two-wheeled w/mule and driver, 9-1/2" long	300	450	600
Wagon, cast iron, two-seater, w/one horse	150	225	300
Wagon and Horse, tin, painted and stenciled, Merriam, 1890, 19-1/2" long	2500	3375	5000

BANKS

Mechanical Banks

After trains, mechanical banks are perhaps the most avidly pursued of all the toys cataloged in this book. The most collectible remain those that were produced in cast iron from around 1870 to 1908—over three hundred different types were produced during that period. One factor that adds to their interest is that many were manufactured with an eye toward adults as well as children (the "Tammany" bank, for instance). As a result, prices are high—and they were high long before any of the other toys in this book were thought of as collector's items. Because of their rarity, several of the banks listed have only auction prices, and these prices may seem astronomical. This was done to demonstrate how high mechanical banks can sell for; please keep in mind that not all mechanical banks will sell for such prices.

With such valuable items the problem of counterfeiting arises, and care is strongly urged in the purchase of any high-priced bank. Counterfeits tend to be rougher, to fit together less smoothly, and to lack the patina or "look" of age.

	C6	C8	C10
Acrobat Bank, 1883, 5" high	2000	3000	10,500
Alligator in Trough, patented, 1867	10,000	20,000	35,000

	C6	C8	C10
Always Did Despise A Mule, African-American jockey on mule, 1879, 10" long	800	1200	2800
Always Did Despise A Mule, African-American on bench being kicked by mule, 1897	800	1200	2800
American Bank Sewing Machine	3000	6000	10,000
Artillery Bank, Union Officer w/mortar, firing into fort, 1892	500	1100	2600
Astronaut's Bank, gold moon w/rocket on stand, has rings showing orbit of space capsule, ring has astronauts' names— "Shepard, Grissom, Glenn, Carpenter, Schirra, Cooper," little plane up side of rocket shoots money into moon, pot metal, 11" high	25	38	50
Atlas Bank	1000	1750	3000

Always Did Despise A Mule (Mechanical Banks), J. & E. Stevens, 1879, $2800. Photo courtesy PB Eighty-Four, New York

Always Did Despise A Mule (Mechanical Banks), J. & E. Stevens, 1879, $2800. Photo courtesy PB Eighty-Four, New York

Bad Accident Mule (Mechanical Banks), J. & E. Stevens, 1880s-90s, $4200. Photo courtesy PB Eighty-Four, New York

Boy on Trapeze (Mechanical Banks), J. Barton & Smith, 1891, $6500. Photo courtesy PB Eighty-Four, New York

Mechanical Banks (Continued)	**C6**	**C8**	**C10**
Bad Accident Mule, mule and African-American on two-wheeled cart, 1880s-90s	850	1500	4200
Bank Teller, The, 1876	10,000	30,000	96,000
Bear Hugging Tree	450	675	900
Bill E. Grin, 1887	500	900	2200
Bird on Roof, 1978	650	1000	2200
Book of Knowledge Reproduction of Original Banks, Artillery Bank; Bulldog Bank; Creedmore; Eagle and Eagles; Jonah & Whale; Magician; Man and Pig; Man milking Cow; Teddy and the Bear; Trick Dog; Trick Pony, Tree Trunk and Buffalo; price for each. Note: The original markings are sometimes filed away from the bottom in an attempt to pass one of these banks off as an original, c. 1950	195	295	390
Boy on Trapeze, 1891	600	1500	6500
Boy Robbing Bird's Nest, 1906	1000	3000	10,500

Boy Robbing Bird's Nest (Mechanical Banks), J. & E. Stevens, 1906, $10,500. Photo courtesy Bill Bertoia Auctions

Boy Scout Camp (Mechanical Banks), J. & E. Stevens, 1912, $12,000. Photo courtesy Sotheby's, New York

Boy Stealing Watermelons (Mechanical Banks), $2500. Photo courtesy Christie's East

Mechanical Banks (Continued)

	C6	C8	C10
Boy Scout Camp, 1912	1500	3500	12,000
Boy Stealing Watermelons	750	1500	2500
Bread Winner, 1886	3500	7000	20,000
Bull & Bear, brass model, 1930s	800	1200	1800
Bulldog, 1880s	400	1200	3500
Bulldog, c. 1887	350	600	1200
Bulldog Savings Bank, 1878	1000	2000	3000
Butting Buffalo	500	800	1800
Butting Goat In Tree Stump, c. 1887	600	1000	2000
Calamity, three football players, 1905	3000	8000	35,000
Called Out, 1900	4000	10,000	20,000

Mechanical Banks (Continued)

	C6	C8	C10
Cat and Mouse Bank, 1891	1000	2200	4200
Charlie McCarthy, sitting w/legs crossed on top of trunk, drop coin in back and mouth moves, pot metal, copyright 1938, 5-3/4" high	75	125	200
Chein Monkey, tin litho, seated, tips hat when coin dropped in, 5" high	70	105	140
Chief Big Moon, Indian in teepee, 1899	1200	2200	6000
Chimpanzee, red version, 1880	1400	2200	3200
Chinese Reclining, 1882	2900	4300	8800
Circus Bank, 1888	5000	8000	45,000
Circus Ticket Taker, 1830	550	850	1500
Clown & Harlequin	10,000	30,000	90,000
Clown on Bar	10,000	20,000	70,000
Clown on Globe, 1890	900	1500	4500

Bulldog mechanical banks, manufacturer unknown. Photo courtesy Sotheby's, New York

Cat and Mouse Bank (Mechanical Banks),
J. & E. Stevens, 1891, $4200. Photo courtesy
PB Eighty-Four, New York

Circus Bank (Mechanical Banks), Shepard Hardware,
1888, $45,000

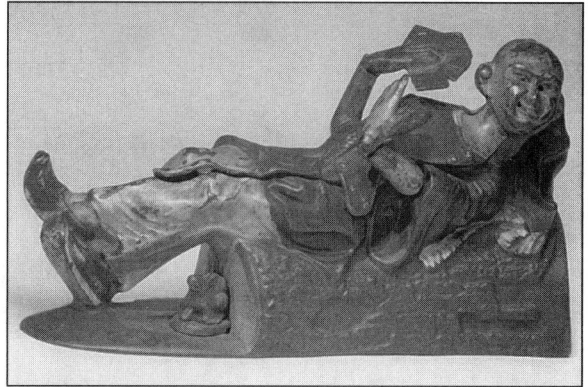

Charlie McCarthy (Mechanical Banks), copyright
1938, $200. Photo courtesy Christie's East

Left to Right: Clown on Globe (Mechanical Banks),
J. & E. Stevens, 1890, $4500; Eagle and Eaglets
(Mechanical Banks), J. & E. Stevens, 1883, $1800.
Photo courtesy PB Eighty-Four, New York

Chimpanzee (Mechanical Banks), Kyser & Rex, 1880,
$3200. Photo courtesy PB eighty-Four, New York

Confectionary (Mechanical Banks), Kyser & Rex, 1881, $8500. Photo courtesy Bill Bertoia Auctions

Cow Kicking (Mechanical Banks), $25,000. Photo courtesy Sotheby's, New York

Creedmore Bank (Mechanical Banks), J. & E. Stevens, 1877, $1500. Photo courtesy Sotheby's, New York

Darktown Battery (Mechanical Banks), J. & E. Stevens, 1888, $8000. Photo courtesy PB Eighty-Four, New York

Mechanical Banks (Continued)

	C6	C8	C10
Columbus	300	450	600
Confectionary, 1881	2000	4000	8500
Cow Kicking, cow kicks over boy	7500	15,000	25,000
Creedmore Bank, man firing into tree, 1877, 10" long	600	900	1500
Crowing Rooster, 1937	500	800	1200
Dapper Dan, 1910	300	500	900
Darktown Battery, African-American pitcher and catcher, 1888	1200	2800	8000
Darky and Cabin, 1885	500	750	1000
Darky and Watermelon, (Foot Ball Bank), Stevens Co., 1888	50,000	100,000	354,500
Darky Football	25,000	75,000	250,000
Dentist Bank, white dentist working on African-American patient, 1880	2000	5500	9500

Darky and Cabin (Mechanical Banks), 1885, $1000. Photo courtesy PB Eighty-Four, New York

Advertisement for Eagle and Eaglets mechanical banks. Photo courtesy James Maxwell/Virginia Caputo

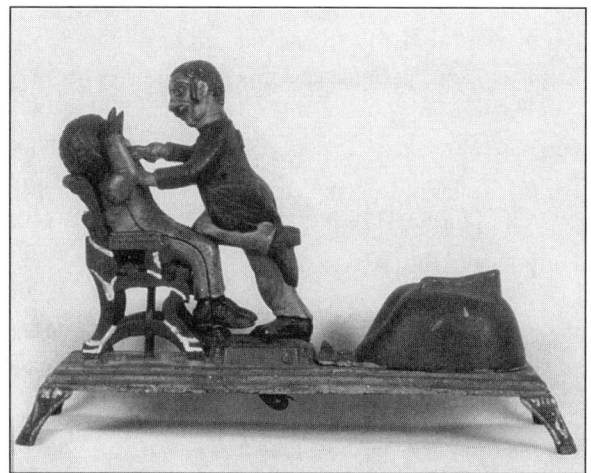

Dentist Bank (Mechanical Banks), J. & E. Stevens, 1880, $9500

Dog on Turntable (Mechanical Banks), Judd, 1870s, $1200

Mechanical Banks (Continued)

	C6	C8	C10
Dinah, bust of African-American woman, 1911, 6-1/2"	600	900	1450
Ding Dong Bell, tin, 1888	10,000	20,000	74,000
Dog Charges Boy, bronze finish	400	700	1000
Dog on Turntable, 1870s	400	800	1200
Dog Standing	150	350	500
Eagle and Eaglets, 1883	600	1200	1800
Elephant, cast iron, Three Star, trunk flips up to catch coin, 1884, 5" high	300	650	1250
Elephant and Clowns, 1883	600	1200	2800

Mechanical Banks (Continued)

	C6	C8	C10
Elephant Howdah Bank, cast iron, 1934	300	500	1250
Ferris Wheel	1000	2000	3000
Fortune Teller, safe, complete w/roll of fortunes, 1901	500	800	1400
Forty-Niner, The, donkey moves ear and tail	100	225	400
Fowler, sportsman shoots bird	6500	14,000	20,000
Freedman	50,000	100,000	300,000
Frog and Snake in Pond, tin litho, in the form of a snake striking at a frog which opens its mouth to receive the coin	3000	4500	6500
Frog on Arched Track	10,000	20,000	35,000
Frog on Lattice, 1870s	450	675	900
Frog on Rock, 1920s	200	400	900
Frog on Round Base, 1872	350	550	1000
Frog, Goat and Old Man	1500	3500	6000
Frogs, two	1200	2400	4000
Gem, Dog and Building, 1893	600	1200	3000
Giant, holding a club	10,000	15,000	20,000
Girl Skipping Rope, w/key, 1890	10,000	20,000	45,000
Globe Savings Fund Bank	250	375	500

Mechanical Banks (Continued)

	C6	C8	C10
Guessing Bank, 1877	1200	2000	3500
Hall's Excelsior Bank, monkey cashier, 1869	300	600	850
Hall's Lilliput, 1875	300	600	850
Hen and Chick, Stevens, 1901	1100	1700	5500
Hindu, 1882	800	1300	1850
Hold the Fort, five-hole, c. 1877	3000	5000	9500

Frog and Snake in Pond (Mechanical Banks), $6500. Photo courtesy PB Eighty-Four, New York

Elephant and Clowns (Mechanical Banks), J. & E. Stevens, 1883, $2800. Photo courtesy PB Eighty-Four, New York

Fortune Teller (Mechanical Banks), Nickel, Baumgarter & Co., 1901, $1400. Photo courtesy PB Eighty-Four, New York

Frogs (Mechanical Banks), J. & E. Stevens, $4000. Photo courtesy PB Eighty-Four, New York

Gem, Dog and Building (Mechanical Banks), J. & E. Stevens, 1893, $3000. Photo courtesy PB Eighty-Four, New York

Giant (Mechanical Banks), $20,000. Photo courtesy PB Eighty-Four, New York

Girl Skipping Rope (Mechanical Banks), J. & E. Stevens, 1890, $45,000. Photo courtesy PB Eighty-Four, New York

Hall's Excelsior Bank (Mechanical Banks), J. & E. Stevens, 1869, $850. Photo courtesy PB Eighty-Four, New York

Home building (Mechanical Banks), $460. Photo courtesy PB Eighty-Four, New York

Horse Race (Mechanical Banks), J. & E. Stevens, 1870, $8000. Photo courtesy Christie's East

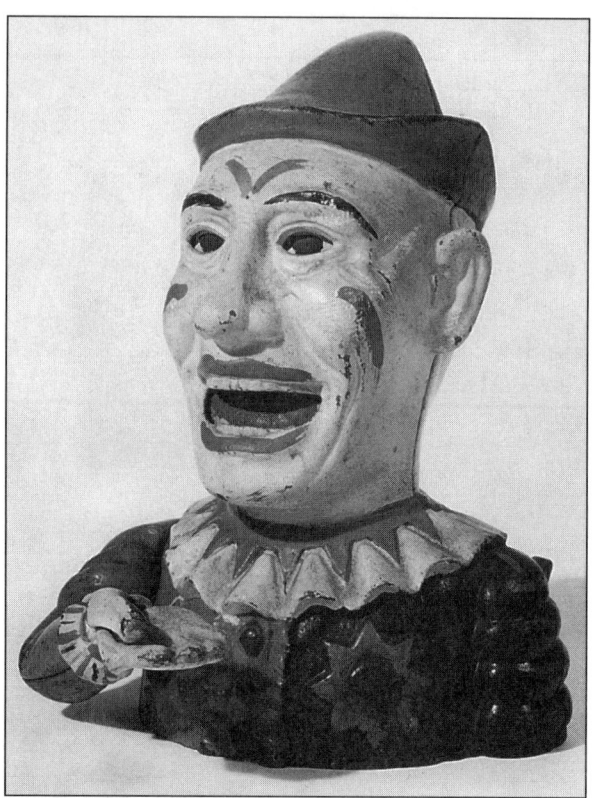

Humpty Dumpty (Mechanical Banks), Shepard Hardware, 1882, $4000. Photo courtesy PB Eighty-Four, New York

Initiating Bank First Degree (Mechanical Banks), Mechanical Novelty Works, 1880, $9000

Mechanical Banks (Continued)	C6	C8	C10
Home building, tin, w/two pillars, teller at window	230	345	460
Horse Race, straight base, 1870	3500	5500	8000
Humpty Dumpty, 1882	800	2200	4000
Independence Hall, 1875	350	550	1050
Indian Shooting Bear, 1883	900	2500	5500
Initiating Bank First Degree, 1880	5000	7000	9000
Jolly Nigger, string tie, England, 1890s	175	300	500
Jolly Nigger, high hat, 1880s, 8" high	250	400	650

Mechanical Banks (Continued)	C6	C8	C10
Jolly Nigger, moves ears, 1920	250	400	650
Jonah and the Whale, cast iron, Jonah in boat, 1890s	1200	2500	5500
Jonah and Whale, Jonah emerges, 1880s	12,000	20,000	55,000
Jumbo on Platform	850	1700	2500
Keeping 'Em Flying, tin, dime register	25	37	50

Mechanical Banks (Continued)

	C6	C8	C10
Kick Inn, litho paper and wood, a mule standing in front of a small building, Presto, 1921	200	500	900
King Aqua	15,000	30,000	95,000
Leap Frog Bank, two boys and tree, 1891	750	1500	5500
Liberty Bell	200	300	500
Lighthouse Bank, 1891	1200	1800	5500
Lion and Monkeys, 1883	650	1400	4200
Lion Hunter, 1911	2000	5000	10,000
Little Jocko, 1912	500	1200	2200
Little Joe, 1910	150	350	575
Locomotive	300	600	900
Magic, 1873	800	1400	2800
Magician Bank, 1901	2500	3500	6500
Mama Katzenjammer and the Kids, 1908, 5-3/4"	3000	5000	7500
Mammy Feeding Child, 1884	3000	4500	6500

Mechanical Banks (Continued)

	C6	C8	C10
Mason and Hod Carrier, 1887	2000	4000	7500
Merry-Go-Round, 1888	7500	11,000	15,000
Meyers No. 84, Jumbo Elephant	100	250	350
Mikado Bank, The, 1886	15,000	25,000	55,000
Money Box Bank, hand-carved on wood base, 10-1/4"	800	1200	1600
Monkey and Coconut, 1886	350	900	2500
Mosque, 1880s	600	1400	2600

Lion Hunter (Mechanical Banks), J. & E. Stevens, 1911, $10,000. Photo courtesy PB Eighty-Four, New York

Jonah and the Whale (Mechanical Banks), Shepard Hardware, 1890s, $5500. Photo courtesy PB Eighty-Four, New York

Left to Right: Lion and Monkeys (Mechanical Banks), Kyser & Rex, 1883, $4200; Indian Shooting Bear (Mechanical Banks), J. & E. Stevens, 1883, $5500. Photo courtesy Sotheby's, New York

Magician Bank (Mechanical Banks), J. & E. Stevens, 1901, $6500. Photo courtesy PB Eighty-Four, New York

Mammy Feeding Child (Mechanical Banks), Kyser & Rex, 1884, $6500. Photo courtesy PB Eighty-Four, New York

Novelty Bank (Mechanical Banks), J. & E. Stevens, 1873, $2250. Photo courtesy Sotheby's, New York

Lion Hunter (Mechanical Banks), J. & E. Stevens, 1911, $10,000. Photo courtesy PB Eighty-Four, New York

Mule Bucking (Mechanical Banks), $1000. Photo courtesy Sotheby's, New York

Mule Entering Barn (Mechanical Banks), Kyser & Rex, 1880, $3500. Photo courtesy Sotheby's, New York

New Bank (Mechanical Banks), c. 1875, $340. Photo courtesy Sotheby's, New York

Mechanical Banks (Continued)

	C6	C8	C10
Mule Bucking, African-American man riding a mule	500	750	1000
Mule Entering Barn, 1880	600	1200	3500
National Bank, 1873	2000	3500	6000
Naughty Girl Bank, modern	25	50	75
New Bank, cast iron, brass policeman in building, c. 1875, 4-1/2" long	170	255	340
New Creedmore, 1891	550	950	1850
North Pole, Eskimos and dog sled	10,000	15,000	25,000
Novelty Bank, house-like bank, 1873	550	1000	2250
Old Woman in the Shoe	50,000	100,000	426,000
Organ Bank, monkey and revolving cat and dog, 1882, 7-1/4" high	500	850	1650
Organ Bank, monkey only, 1881	350	500	850
Organ Boy and Girl, monkey flanked by boy and girl holding tambourine, pat. June 13, 1882, 1882	500	850	1650
Organ Grinder And Bear, 1890s	2300	3500	8500
Organ Grinder And Monkey, 1929	330	485	600
Owl, cast iron, turns head, 1880	250	500	900

Organ Bank (Mechanical Banks), Kyser & Rex, 1882, $1650. Photo courtesy PB Eighty-Four, New York

Organ Grinder And Monkey (Mechanical Banks), 1929, $600. Photo courtesy Sotheby's, New York

Mechanical Banks (Continued)

	C6	C8	C10
Owl, cast iron, slot in book, 1926	350	650	1200
Owl, slot in head, 1926	350	650	1200
Paddy and His Pig, 1882	900	2500	6500
Panorama Bank, 1882	2500	4500	6500
Patronize the Blind Man and His Dog, 1878	2000	3000	4500

Organ Grinder And Monkey (Mechanical Banks),
1929, $600. Photo courtesy Sotheby's, New York

Owl (Mechanical Banks), J. & E. Stevens, 1880, $900.
Photo courtesy PB Eighty-Four, New York

Pegleg Beggar (Mechanical Banks), Judd, 1875,
$1700. Photo courtesy Sotheby's, New York

Patronize the Blind Man and His Dog (Mechanical
Banks), J. & E. Stevens, 1878, $4500. Photo courtesy
Sotheby's, New York

Picture Gallery (Mechanical Banks), 1885, $20,000.
Photo courtesy PB Eighty-Four, New York

Mechanical Banks (Continued)	C6	C8	C10
Pegleg Beggar, 1875	750	1200	1700
Pelican, cast iron, "Boy thumbs nose"	775	1550	2310
Perfection Registering	4500	7000	10,000
Piano, c. 1900	250	500	750
Picture Gallery, 1885	4500	7500	20,000
Pig, Bismarck, 1883	1800	3500	6000
Pig in High Chair, 1887	350	550	1400
Preacher in Pulpit	30,000	40,000	50,000
Presto, shape of building, 1894	250	525	950
Presto-Mouse on Roof, litho paper on wood	7500	12,000	17,500
Professor Pug Frog's Great Bicycle Feat, 1886	1500	3500	10,000
Pump, Bucket	300	700	1000
Punch and Judy, 1884	600	2500	5500
Rabbit, tall	600	1200	2000
Rabbit, small, circular base	450	850	1250
Rabbit in Cabbage Patch, 1925	200	650	1400
Red Riding Hood, 1880s	8500	14,000	18,000
Roller Skating, 1880s	12,000	18,000	45,000
Rooster, 1900s	600	900	1800
Santa Claus at Chimney, 1889	800	1800	5500

Picture Gallery (Mechanical Banks), 1885, $20,000.
Photo courtesy PB Eighty-Four, New York

Picture Gallery (Mechanical Banks), 1885, $20,000.
Photo courtesy PB Eighty-Four, New York

Professor Pug Frog's Great Bicycle Feat (Mechanical Banks), J. & E. Stevens, 1886, $10,000. Photo courtesy Sotheby's, New York

Roller Skating (Mechanical Banks), Kyser & Rex, 1880s, $45,000. Photo courtesy PB Eighty-Four, New York

Speaking Dog Bank (Mechanical Banks), Shepard Hardware, 1885, $4500. Photo courtesy PB Eighty-Four, New York

Punch and Judy (Mechanical Banks), Shepard Hardware, 1884, $5500. Photo courtesy PB Eighty-Four, New York

Santa Claus at Chimney (Mechanical Banks), Shepard Hardware, 1889, $5500. Photo courtesy PB Eighty-Four, New York

Stump Speaker (Mechanical Banks), Shepard Hardware, 1886, $4500. Photo courtesy PB Eighty-Four, New York

Tammany Bank (Mechanical Banks), J. & E. Stevens, 1873, $3000. Photo courtesy Sotheby's, New York

Mechanical Banks (Continued)	**C6**	**C8**	**C10**
See Him Frisk	10,000	20,000	55,000
Shoot the Chute	12,500	17,500	25,000
Speaking Dog Bank, 1885	850	1500	4500
Springing Cat, lead alloy, 1882	3500	6000	8000
Squirrel and Tree Stump, 1881	850	1250	2250
Standing Bear	100	165	220
Strato Bank, pot metal, rocket and planet, 1950s, 8" long	10	15	25
Stump Speaker, cast iron, 1886	850	2200	4500
Tabby, 1887	250	650	1050
Tammany Bank, 1873, 5-3/4" high	400	800	3000
Tank and Cannon, 1919	650	900	1500

Tabby (Mechanical Banks), 1887, $1050

Teddy and The Bear (Mechanical Banks), J. & E. Stevens, 1907, $4500. Photo courtesy PB Eighty-Four, New York

Tabby (Mechanical Banks), 1887, $1050

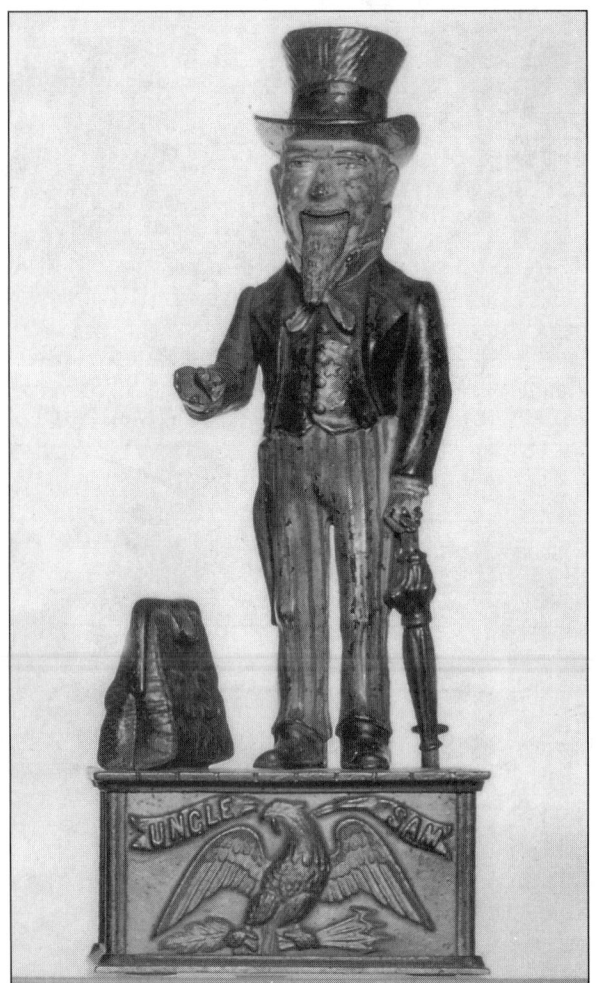

Uncle Sam (Mechanical Banks), Shepard Hardware, 1886, $9200. Photo courtesy PB Eighty-Four, New York

Tabby (Mechanical Banks), 1887, $1050

Tabby (Mechanical Banks), 1887, $1050

Mechanical Banks (Continued)	**C6**	**C8**	**C10**
Teddy and The Bear, Teddy Roosevelt firing at bear in tree, 1907	1000	2200	4500
Telephone	150	300	450
Trick Dog, clown w/hoop, dog and barrel w/six-part base, 1888	750	1500	2500
Trick Dog, clown w/hoop, dark dog and dark barrel, 1929	200	450	1000

Mechanical Banks (Continued)	**C6**	**C8**	**C10**
Trick Pony, 1885	900	1250	4500
Turtle Bank, 1920s	7500	12,000	20,000
U.S. and Spain, 1898	2000	4500	7500
U.S. Building, boy and dog in windows, J. & E. Stevens ?, 1878	3100	4650	6200
Uncle Remus, 1891	1700	2300	3500
Uncle Sam, bust	300	450	600
Uncle Sam, w/umbrella in left hand, 1886	2000	5000	9200

William Tell (Mechanical Banks), J. & E. Stevens, 1896, $2800. Photo courtesy PB Eighty-Four, New York

Watchdog Safe (Mechanical Banks), J. & E. Stevens, 1890s, $1250. Photo courtesy Sotheby's, New York

Zoo (Mechanical Banks), Kyser & Rex, 1890s, $2250. Photo courtesy Sotheby's, New York

World's Fair (Mechanical Banks), J. & E. Stevens, 1893, $2400

Mechanical Banks (Continued)

	C6	C8	C10
Uncle Tom, w/lapels, one star, brass base, 1891	250	650	1250
Uncle Tom, w/lapels and one star	250	650	1250
United States Bank, Stevens, 1880	800	2200	4000
Watchdog Safe, 1890s	350	675	1250
Weeden's Plantation, tin, 1888	750	1250	1850
William Tell, 1896	600	1250	2800
Wireless Bank, 1926	350	650	850
Woodpecker	1500	2800	4000
World's Fair, 1893	850	1250	2400
Zig Zag, cast iron, tin and papier-mache	40,000	80,000	190,000
Zoo, 1890s	850	1650	2250

Still Banks

The same companies that made mechanical banks often made still banks as less expensive alternatives. Several banks can be found in both still and mechanical versions. Companies such as Arcade, Ives, Kenton and Stevens are familiar to still and mechanical bank collectors alike.

Building-shaped banks are perhaps the single largest type of still banks, with others fashioned as animals, people and busts, and appliances like safes, clocks, mail boxes and globes.

One notable class of still banks is the registering bank. Often in the shape of a safe or cash register, these banks typically accept certain coins, such as dimes or nickels. They keep a running tally of deposits and pop open once the bank is filled, typically at $5 or $10. While their delayed reaction mechanism has earned them places in some mechanical collections, they are generally classified as still banks.

As in many other areas of collecting, restoration of banks is strongly discouraged in the marketplace. Unless undertaken by an experienced professional, the restoration of a bank can result in irreparable damage to its collector value.

	C8	C10
$100,000 Money Bag, silver-gray finish, 3-5/8" tall	300	650
1 Pounder Shell Bank, artillery shell, "1 Pounder Bank," 1918, 8"	NPF	NPF
1876 Bank, Large, building bank w/bronze/copper finish, 1895, 3-3/8" tall	75	250
1926 Sesquicentennial Bell, 1926, 3-3/4" x 3-7/8" diameter	75	200

	C8	C10
A.A.O.S.M.S. Shriner's Fezm, red fez w/tassle and gold lettering, 1920s, 2-3/8"	250	650
Administration Building, unpainted, 1893, 5"	250	650
Air Mail Bank on Base, red, 1920, 6-3/8" tall	375	1400
Alamo, unpainted bronze finish, 1930s, 1-7/8" tall, 3-3/8" wide	200	450
Alphabet Bank, octagonal, 3-1/2"	1200	3500
Amish Boy, painted, 1970, 5" tall	10	65
Amish Boy in White Shirt, blue coveralls, black hat, 1971, 5" tall	10	65
Amish Girl, painted, 1970, 5" tall	10	65
Andy Gump, Andy sits reading a paper, painted, 1928, 4-3/8" tall	500	1200
Apollo, plain, unpainted, 1968, 4-1/4"	NPF	NPF
Apollo 8, red, white and blue, 1968, 4-1/4"	20	75
Apple, painted apple on twig w/leaves, 1882, 5-1/4" tall	600	2400
Arabian Safe, 1882, 4-9/16" x 4-1/4"	100	300
Armoured Car, red car on gold wheels, 1900s, 6-3/4" long, 3-3/4" tall	650	3500
Art Deco Elephant, red, 4-3/8" tall	100	225
Aunt Jemima, also called Mammy with Spoon, 1900s, 5-7/8"	125	325
Auto, black, red wheels, four passengers, 1910?, 5-3/4" long	500	1200
Baby in Cradle, rocking cradle, 1890s, 3-1/4" tall	500	1500
Bank of Columbia, unpainted, "Bank of Columbia," 1800s, 4-7/8"	150	375
Bank of England Safe, identical to Egyptian Safe except front is embossed Bank of England, 1882	350	750
Barrel, 1873, 2-3/4" tall	100	225
Baseball on Three Bats, 1914, 5-1/4"	350	1850
Baseball Player, gold, 1909, 5-3/4"	100	550
Baseball Player, several colors, 1910s, 5-3/4" tall	200	750
Basket Puzzle Bank, unpainted, 1894, 2-3/4" tall, 3-1/2" wide	300	650
Basket Registering Bank, woven, 1902, 2-7/8" x 3-3/4"	50	125
Basset Hound, bronze finish, 3-1/8"	650	1500
Battleship Maine, "Maine," 1800s, 5-1/4" tall, 6-5/8" long	650	4500

Bear Seated on Log (Still Banks), $950

Bear, Begging (Still Banks), A.C. Williams, 1900s,

Still Banks (Continued)

	C8	C10
Battleship Maine, white, 1901, 6" tall, 10-1/4" long	500	6000
Battleship Oregon, silver finish, 1890s, 4-7/8" long	200	450
Be Wise Owl, 1900s, 4-7/8" x 2-1/2"	150	375
Bear Seated on Log, 7"	400	950
Bear Stealing Pig, painted, 1913, 5-1/2" tall ..	400	1000
Bear with Honey Pot, painted, 6-1/2" tall	75	175
Bear, Begging, bronze finish, 1900s, 5-3/8"	75	150
Beehive Bank, 1882, 2-3/8"	250	500
Beehive Registering Saving Bank, 1891, 5-3/8" x 6-1/2"	200	425
Beehive with Brass Top, unpainted, 5-1/2" tall on base	350	750
Bethel College Administration Building, 1935, 2-7/8" x 5-1/4"	175	350
Bicentennial Bell, 1976, 4" x 4"	25	45
Billiken, on square base, bronze finish, red cap, 1909, 4-1/4" tall	55	125

Still Banks (Continued)

	C8	C10
Billiken on Throne, 1909, 6-1/2" tall	65	175
Billy Bounce, silver painted body, 1900s, 4-11/16" tall	375	1200
Billy Possum ("Possum & Taters"), on base "Billy Possum," 1909, 3" x 4-3/4"	1200	5500
Bird Bank Building, unpainted cupola building w/bird on top, "Bank New York," 5-7/8"	650	3500
Bird Cage Bank, similar to Crystal Bank, No. 926, but glass is replaced by open mesh, 1900s, 3-7/8" tall	50	125
Bismark Bank (Pig), "Bismark Bank," 1883, 3-3/8"	100	300
Bismark Pig with Rider, bronze finish, 1880s, 7-1/4" tall, 6-1/2" long	1000	3500
Boss Tweed, 1870s, 3-7/8" tall	1500	3500
Boston State House, painted, 1800s, 6-3/4" tall	3000	6000
Boxer Bulldog, seated, bronze finish, 1900s, 4-1/2"	125	225

Still Banks (Continued)

	C8	C10
Boy Scout, A, brown finish, 1910s, 5-7/8" tall	50	150
Boy with Large Football, brown, 1914, 5-1/8" tall	2000	3200
Buckeye (SBCCA), painted, "Ohio The Buckeye State," "SBCC 1973," 1973, 3-1/2"	25	100
Buffalo Bank, gold, 1900s, 3-1/8" x 4-3/8"	50	175
Buffalo Nickel, 1970s, 3-7/8"	35	100
Building with Belfry, in browns, 8" tall	550	4500
Bull on Base, unpainted, 4" tall	200	450
Bull with Long Horns, painted, 3-11/16" tall	50	125
Bulldog, Large, painted, 1960s, 6"	25	65
Bulldog, Seated, 1928, 3-7/8"	200	400
Bulldog, Standing, painted, 1900s, 2-1/4"	250	450
Bungalow Bank, white cottage w/green roof, 1900s, 3-3/4" x 3"	225	650
Bust of Man, 5"	100	350
Buster Brown & Tige, 1900s, 5-1/2"	100	375
Cadet, blue uniform w/gold trim, 1905, 5-3/4" tall	300	750

Still Banks (Continued)

	C8	C10
Camel, Kneeling, 1889, 2-1/2" tall, 4-3/4" long	350	1050
Camel, Large, 1900s, 7-1/4" x 6-1/4"	200	650
Camel, Small, 1920s, 4-3/4" x 3-7/8"	100	225
Camera, 1888	1000	5000
Camera Bank, bronze finish bellows camera on tripod, 1800s, 4-5/16" tall	2500	5000
Campbell Kids, 1900s, 3-5/16" x 4-1/8"	150	350
Cannon, black cannon on red wheels, 1914, 3" tall, 6-7/8" long	2500	5000
Capitalist, The (Everett True), painted, 1913, 5" tall	1200	2000
Capitol Bank, 1981, 5-1/8"	25	50

Buster Brown & Tige (Still Banks), A.C. Williams, 1900s, $375

A Boy Scout (Still Banks), A.C. Williams, 1910s, $150

Camel, Large (Still Banks), A.C. Williams, 1900s, $650

Captain Kidd (Still Banks), 1900s, $850

Still Banks (Continued)   C8   C10

Captain Kidd, Kidd stands by tree trunk
w/shovel, base reads "Captain Kidd,"
1900s, 5-5/8" tall..275   850

Carpenter Safe, 1907, 4-3/8" 2500 5000

Cash Register Savings Bank, unpainted,
"Cash Register Savings Bank," 1906,
4-3/4" 500   750

Cash Register Savings Bank, round face on
three claw foot feet, "Cash Register
Savings Bank," 1880s, 5-5/8" tall...............350   850

Cash Register with Mesh, red finish w/gold-
bronze mesh, 1900s, 3-3/4" tall 50   125

Castle Bank, Small, 1882, 3" x 2-13/16" 200   650

Cat on Tub, bronze finish, 1920s, 4-1/8" tall ..100   200

Cat with Ball, 1900s, 2-1/2" tall.....................200   375

Cat with Bow, 1930s, 4-1/8" 275   575

Cat with Bow, Seated, brown finish, 1922,
4-3/8" tall 225   475

Cat with Bow, Seated, painted, white body,
red bow, 4-3/8" x 2-7/8" 25   50

Cat with Long Tail, 1910s, 4-3/8" tall,
6-3/4" long 375 1250

Cat with Soft Hair, Seated, 1900s,
4-1/4" x 2-7/8" 85   225

*Century of Progress Building (Still Banks), Arcade,
1933, $3000*

City Bank with Chimney (Still Banks), 1870s, $3500

Still Banks (Continued)   C8   C10

Century of Progress Building, white, "A
Century Of Progress" building from
Chicago World's Fair, 1933, 4-1/2" x 7" 800 3000

Champion Heater, green and black,
"Champion," 4-1/8" 125   500

Chanticleer (Rooster), bronze finish, painted
face and comb, 1911, 4-5/8" 850 7500

Chicken Feed Bag, "Chicken Feed," 1973,
4-5/8"...35   350

Chipmunk with Nut, black, 4-1/16" 300   950

Church Towers, 6-3/4" 850 1900

Church Window Safe, 1890s, 3-1/16".............50   165

City Bank with Chimney, painted, 1870s,
6-3/4" tall 650 3500

Still Banks (Continued)

	C8	C10
City Bank with Crown, 1870's, 5-1/2" tall	600	4500
City Bank with Teller, bronze finish, 5-1/2"..	400	750
Clown, gold and red w/tall curved hat, 1908, 6-1/4"	125	250
Clown Bust, painted, 1973, 4-7/8"	100	350
Coca-Cola Bank, red and green w/logo, 3-3/8" tall	600	2200
Coin Registering Bank, w/red doors and dome, 1890, 6-3/4"	2500	6500
Colonial House with Porch, Large, white, 1900s, 4" tall	100	375
Colonial House with Porch, Small, brown finish w/red, green or gold roof, 1910s, 3" tall...	75	250
Columbia, silver finish building bank, 4-1/2" tall	600	900
Columbia Bank, unpainted silver finish, 1890s, 5-3/4" tall..	300	700
Columbia Bank, bronze finish, 1890s, 8-3/4" tall	600	1000
Columbia Magic Savings Bank, unpainted, "Columbia Magic Savings Bank," 1892, 5"..	300	700
Columbia Tower, unpainted three-story tower, 1897, 6-7/8"	450	950
Covered Bridge, white w/red roof, 1960s, 2-1/2" tall, 6-1/8" long	35	75
Covered Wagon, unpainted, 6-5/8" long..........	10	25
Cow, brown or red finish, 1920, 3-3/8" x 5-1/4"	75	550
Crosley Radio, Large, green w/gold highlights, 1930s, 5-1/8" tall.........................	650	1800
Crosley Radio, Small, green, 1930s, 4-5/16" tall	150	700

Still Banks (Continued)

	C8	C10
Cross, dark finish, "God Is Love" on base, 9-1/4" tall	750	2200
Crown Bank on Legs, Small, painted, 4-5/8" ..	600	950
Crown Bank on Legs, Small, painted, 4-5/8".	600	950
Cupola Bank, red and gray, 1872, 4-1/4" x 3-3/8"	100	850
Cupola Bank, black, 1870s, 3-1/4" tall.............	75	425
Cupola Bank, painted building w/center roof cupola, 1869, 5-1/2" tall...............................	300	1250
Cutie Dog, painted, 1914, 3-7/8"......................	65	175

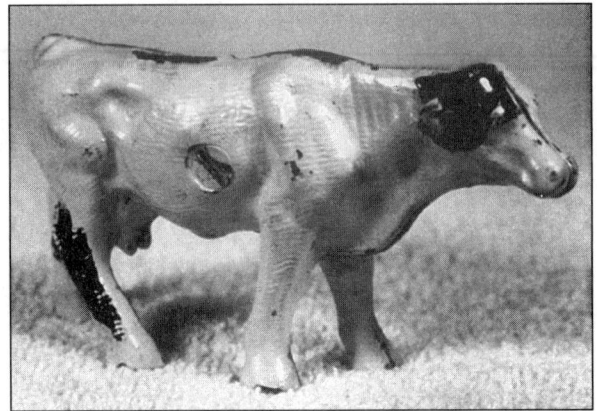

Cow (Still Banks), A.C. Williams, 1920, $550

Columbia Tower (Still Banks), Grey Iron Casting, 1897, $950

Dolphin Boat Bank (Still Banks), Grey Iron Casting, 1900s, $850

Still Banks (Continued)

	C8	C10
Daisy, red safe bank, 1899, 2-1/8" tall	50	175
Darkey Sharecropper, toes visible on one foot, 1900s, 5-1/2" tall	75	375
Decker's Iowana (Pig), unpainted, 2-5/16"	75	200
Derby, "Pass Around the Hat," 2-5/16"	100	325
Dime Registering Coin Barrel, unpainted, 1889, 4" x 2-1/2"	125	225
Dime Savings, "Dime Savings," 1899, 2-1/2" safe	200	425
Dog on Tub, bronze finish, 1920s, 4-1/16" x 2" diameter	125	200
Dog Smoking Cigar, painted, white body, red bow tie, 4-1/4"	450	850
Dolphin Boat Bank, sailor boy in boat holds anchor, 1900s, 4-1/2" tall	500	850
Domed Bank, 1899, 3" tall	20	95
Domed Mosque Bank, gold/bronze finish, 1900s, 4-1/4" tall	85	175
Domed Mosque Bank, bronze finish, 1900s, 3-1/8" tall	65	145
Donkey, black w/red yoke, 3-1/4" tall	100	200
Donkey, "I Made St. Louis Famous," gray finish, 1903, 4-11/16" tall	800	1800
Donkey with Blanket, painted, gray w/red blanket, 1930s, 3-7/8" tall	450	950
Donkey, Large, painted, 1920s, 6-13/16" tall	150	450

Dutch Girl (Still Banks), Grey Iron Casting, $850

Still Banks (Continued)

	C8	C10
Donkey, Small, blue, gold or gray finish, 1910s, 4-1/2" tall	85	200
Dormer Bank, painted building bank w/red roof, 4-3/4" tall	3500	6000
Double Door, building w/two doors, painted white w/gold highlights, 1900s, 5-7/16"	200	425
Doughboy, painted World War I soldier, 1919, 7" tall	350	850
Dry Sink, dark finish, 1970, 3" x 2-3/4"	25	45
Duck, white painted body, 1930s, 4-3/4"	150	275
Duck Bank, unpainted, 1900s, 4-7/8"	150	275
Duck on Tub, "Save for a Rainy Day," 1930s, 5-3/8"	95	450
Duck, Round, painted, yellow body, red beak and top of head, 1930s, 4" tall	225	650
Dutch Boy, 6-3/4" tall	600	850
Dutch Boy, doorstop conversion, 8-1/4" tall	150	275
Dutch Boy on Barrel, 1930s, 5-5/8"	75	275
Dutch Girl, bronze finish, 6-1/2" tall	600	850

Still Banks (Continued)

	C8	C10
Dutch Girl Holding Flowers, painted, iron trap in base, 1930s, 5-1/2" tall	100	275
Eagle Bank Building, painted building w/gold eagle on roof, 9-3/4" tall	450	1250
Eagle with Ball, Building, building w/eagle and ball on roof, 10-3/4" tall	850	6500
Edison Bust, 1972, 5-5/16"	35	65
Eggman (Wm. Howard Taft), 1910, 4-1/8" tall	850	3000
Egyptian Tomb, safe on base, decorated w/Sphinx and obelisk on front, sides show, pyramid, walled ruins and urn w/flowers, gold, 1882, 6-1/4" square	450	750
Electric Railroad, 1893, 8-1/4" long	2500	6000
Elephant, "GOP 1936," 1936, 3-1/2" tall	750	1200
Elephant on Bench on Tub, 1920s, 3-7/8"	125	225
Elephant on Tub, in bronze finish, 1920s, 5-3/8"	100	185
Elephant on Tub, Decorated, painted version of No. 483, 1920s, 5-3/8"	125	200
Elephant on Wheels, unpainted, 1920s, 4" tall	150	300
Elephant Trumpeting, black finish, 1971, 7-1/4" tall	15	35
Elephant with Bent Knee, tan finish, 1904, 3-1/2"	200	375
Elephant with Chariot, Large, also made w/o chariot, 1900s, 4-3/4" tall	2000	3000
Elephant with Chariot, Small, gray elephant, red chariot, yellow wheels, 1906, 7" long	1400	2200
Elephant with Howdah, Large, 1900s, 4-7/8" x 6-3/8"	65	125

Elephant with Swivel Trunk (Still Banks), $250

Still Banks (Continued)

	C8	C10
Elephant with Howdah, Large, gold, 1900s, 6-3/4"	85	150
Elephant with Howdah, Short Trunk, painted gray w/red belt, 1910, 3-3/4" tall	125	275
Elephant with Howdah, Small, 1900s, 3-1/2" x 5"	65	125
Elephant with Raised Slot, gray body, gold blanket, 4-1/2" tall	150	350
Elephant with Swivel Trunk, black finish w/gold swivel trunk, 2-1/2"	125	250
Elephant with Tin Chariot, red chariot, 1900s, 8" long	1000	1600
Elephant with Tucked Trunk, red or green, 1900s, 2-3/4" x 4-5/8"	65	125
Elephant with Turned Trunk, Seated, unpainted, 4-1/4"	450	950
Elephant, Circus, painted, w/lavender pants and red dotted white shirt, 1930s, 3-7/8"	150	350
Elf, painted, converted doorstop, 10" tall	150	450
English Setter, black, 1970, 8-1/2" tall	125	275
Fidelity Safe, Large, green w/gold trim, "Fidelity Safe," 1880, 3-5/8" tall	150	300
Fidelity Trust Vault, Lord Fauntleroy, 1890, 6-1/2" x 5-7/8"	300	650
Fido, painted, white body, black eyes and ears, red collar, 1914, 5"	60	225
Fido on Pillow, painted, 1920s, 7-3/8" long	100	550
Finial Bank, building bank w/single finial on roof, 1887, 5-3/4" tall, 4-3/8" wide	275	1400
Flags Bank (SBCCA), white pyramid w/color US flags, 1976, 3-1/4" tall, 6" square	75	125
Flat Iron Building Bank, silver, 1900s, 5-1/2" tall	135	350
Floral Safe (National Safe), 1898, 4-5/8" x 4-1/8"	125	350
Football Player, 1910s, 5-7/8" tall	250	550
Fort, unpainted bronze finish, 1910s, 4-1/8"	125	275
Four Tower, unpainted w/gold highlights, 5-3/4"	125	450
Four Tower, painted white building w/red roof, 1949, 5-3/8"	35	85
Foxy Grandpa, painted, 1920s, 5-1/2" tall	150	375
Frog, deep green finish, 1973, 4-1/8"	75	125
Frowning Face, hanging bank, chin drops below surface level, 5-5/8" tall	850	1750

Still Banks (Continued)

	C8	C10
G.E. Radio Bank, brown cabinet radio on four legs, 1930s, 3-3/4" tall	125	325
G.E. Refrigerator, Small, blue, 1930s, 3-3/4"	75	225
Gas Pump, red, 5-3/4" tall	275	650
Gem Stove, brown finish, 4-3/4"	75	175
General Butler, 1880s	1000	3500
General Butler, painted head on frog body, 1884, 6-1/2" tall	1500	3500
General Butler, cast iron, 1880s	1800	3500
General Pershing Bust, bronze finish, 1918, 7-3/4" tall	75	175
General Sheridan on Base, General seated on rearing horse, 1910s, 6" tall	250	650
George Washington Bust on Safe, 1903, 5-7/8" tall	1000	2500
Gettysburg Bank, gray monument w/reclining soldier, 1960, 4-3/4" x 7-1/4"	75	200
Give Me A Penny, African-American figure in hat, painted, 1900s, 5-1/2" tall	200	450
Globe Bank with Eagle, red w/eagle on globe, 1875, 5-3/4"	125	450
Globe in Wire Arc, painted, spinning globe, red continents, 1900s, 4-5/8" tall	125	450
Globe on Arc, red, 1900s, 5-1/4" tall	100	300
Globe on Claw Feet, 6"	175	375
Globe on Hand, bronze finish, 1893, 4"	375	1275
Globe Safe with Hinged Door, 1900s, 5"	100	250
Globe Savings Fund Bank, painted "Globe Savings Fund 1888," 1889, 7-1/8"	1800	4000
Gold Eagle, 1970, 5-3/4"	5	20
Good Luck Horseshoe, Buster Brown and Tige w/horse inside horseshoe, 1908, 4-1/4" tall	150	550
Goose Bank, unpainted, 1920s, 3-3/4"	85	175
Graf Zeppelin, silver-gray finish, 1920s, 6-5/8" long	85	375
Graf Zeppelin on Wheels, silver pull-toy bank, 1934, 7-3/4" long	150	475
Grandpa's Hat, top hat, 2-1/4" tall, 3-7/8" wide	225	450
Grenade with Pin, 4-1/4"	85	175
Gunboat, blue hull, white top, twin masts, 8-1/2" long	650	1800
Hall Clock, brown finish, paper face, 1900s, 5-1/4" tall	275	475

Home Savings Bank (Still Banks), Shimer Toy, 1899, $525

Still Banks (Continued)

	C8	C10
Hall Clock, dark finish w/gold highlights, 1923, 5-5/8" tall	300	700
Hall Clock with Cast Face, 1920s, 5-3/26" tall	275	425
Hanging Mailbox, green, wall mount mailbox replica, gold lettering, 1920s, 5-1/8" tall	65	175
Hanging Mailbox on Platform, red box hangs on post in platform base, 1800s, 7-1/4" tall	650	1500
Hard Hat, white w/red lettering, 1970s, 1-15/16" tall	100	250
Harleysville Bank, white w/gray roof, 1959, 2-5/8" tall, 5-1/4" long	75	225
Hen on Nest, bronze finish w/red highlights, 1900s, 3"	100	1750
High Rise Building, 7" tall	200	550
High Rise, Tiered, 5-3/4"	125	350
Hippo, bronze w/red highlights, 2" tall, 5-3/16" long	3500	6000
Holstein Cow, black finish, 1910s, 2-1/2" tall, 4-5/8" long	125	650
Home Bank, dark finish, 1890s, 4" x 3-1/2"	175	500
Home Bank with Crown, painted, "Home Bank," 1872, 5-1/4"	475	1400
Home Savings Bank, painted, 9-5/8" tall	175	650

Still Banks (Continued)

	C8	C10
Home Savings Bank, "Property of Peoples Savings Bank, Grand Rapids, Mich.," 10-1/2" painted	175	650
Home Savings Bank, painted, 1899, 5-7/8"	150	525
Home Savings Bank with Dog Finial, 1891, 5-3/4" tall	125	550
Home Savings Bank with Finial, mustard finish, 1891, 3-1/2" tall	125	375
Honey Bear, silver finish unpainted bear sits eating honey, 2-1/2"	675	1200
Hoover/Curtis Elephant "GOP," ivory finish, 1928, 3-3/8"	675	1600
Horse on Tub, Decorated, 1920s, 5-5/6"	135	300
Horse, "Beauty," black w/raised letters on side, 1900s, 4-1/8" x 4-3/4"	85	175
Horse, Prancing, black w/gray hooves, 1910s, 4-1/4" tall	55	150
Horse, Prancing with Belly Band, light bronze finish, 4-1/2"	175	375
Horse, Prancing, Large, bronze finish, 1910s, 7-3/16" tall	75	165
Horse, Rearing on Oval Base, 1920s, 5-1/8" x 4-7/8"	95	250

Indian with Tomahawk (Still Banks), Hubley, 1900s, $550

Still Banks (Continued)

	C8	C10
Horse, Rearing on Pebbled Base, gold finish, 7-1/4" x 6-1/2"	85	165
Horseshoe with Mesh, horse head inside horseshoe that forms end of mesh coin cage, bronze finish	65	145
Hot Point Electric Stove, white, on legs, 1925, 6"	350	1250
House with Basement, painted, 1893, 4-5/8" square	850	1800
House with Bay Window, painted, 1874, 5-5/8" tall	900	2200
House with Chimney Slot, painted, 2-7/8" x 2-13/16"	275	850
House with Knight, unpainted "Savings Bank" w/knight figure on roof peak, 7-1/4"	375	950
Hub, 1892, 5" x 5-1/4" x 1-5/8"	300	850
Humphrey-Muskie Donkey, pale silver finish, "Humphrey Muskie 68," 1968, 4-1/2" tall	10	35
Humpty Dumpty, painted, white egg, red brick wall, 1930s, 5-1/2" tall	375	850
Humpty Dumpty, Seated, painted, 1974, 5-3/8" tall	75	125
Husky, 1910s, 5"	200	550
I Made Chicago Famous, Large Pig, 1902, 2-5/8" x 5-5/16"	250	550
I Made Chicago Famous, Small Pig, 1902, 2-1/8" x 4-1/8"	200	400
Ice Box, white, "Save For Ice," 4-1/4" tall	175	650
Independence Hall, mustard building on base w/bell tower, 1875, 8-1/8" tall, 15-1/2" long	1800	3500
Independence Hall, deep red/brown finish, Enterprise Mfg., 1875, 10" tall	450	1150
Independence Hall Tower, 1876, 9-1/2"	225	525
Indian Chief Bust, unpainted, 1978, 4-7/8"	35	85
Indian Family, unpainted, 1905, 3-5/8" x 5-1/8"	850	2200
Indian Head Penny, 1972, 3-1/4" diam.	35	85
Indian Seated on Log, unpainted, 1970s, 3-5/8" tall	85	150
Indian with Tomahawk, 1900s, 5-7/8"	175	550
Indiana Paddle Wheeler, black w/red trim, 1896, 7-1/8" long	4000	8000
International Eagle on Globe, unpainted, 8" x 8"	1200	2800

Little Red Riding Hood Safe (Still Banks), J.M. Harper, 1907, $4000

Still Banks (Continued)

	C8	C10
Ironmaster's House, unpainted, 1884, 4-1/2"	600	2200
Japanese Safe, 1882, 5-3/8" tall	100	300
Japanese Safe, painted, 1883, 5-1/2" tall	125	375
Jarmulowsky BuildingJarmulowsky Building, bronze finish building bank, 7-3/4" tall	1200	2800
Jewel Safe, unpainted, 1907, 5-3/8"	125	350
Junior Cash Register, Small, elaborate cast w/slot at top, 1920s, 5-1/4" x 4-5/8"	175	375
Kelvinator Bank, white w/grey trim replica refrigerator, No. 832, 1930s, 4-1/2" tall	150	375
Key, silver finish skeleton key, 1905, 5-1/2" long	250	650

Still Banks (Continued)

	C8	C10
Key, St. Louis World's Fair, dark finish, 1904, 5-3/4" long	275	700
King Midas, painted, 1930s, 4-1/2" tall	1250	2500
Kitty Bank, painted, white body w/blue bow, 1930s, 4-3/4" tall	65	150
Kodak Bank, "Kodak Banks," 1905, 4-1/4" tall, 5" wide	200	450
Labrador Retriever, black finish w/gold collar, 4-1/2"	125	375
Lamb, painted white w/black highlights, 1970, 3-1/4" tall	35	75
Lamb, Small, painted white, 3-3/16"	200	375
Laughing Pig, painted, 2-1/2"	125	275
Liberty Bell, 1905, 3-3/4"	275	550
Liberty Bell with Yoke, 1920s, 3-1/2"	25	65
Liberty Bell, Minniature, 3-1/2" x 1-3/4"	20	35
Lighthouse, "Light of the World," 1950s, 9-1/2" tall	125	250
L'il Tot, 1982, 5-7/8"	125	175
Limousine, black w/white rubber tires, 1920s, 8-1/16" long	750	2500
Limousine, same as No. 1478, but w/steel wheels, 1921	1200	2800
Limousine Yellow Cab, repaint of No. 1478, 1921	1400	2800
Lincoln High Hat, black finish, "Pass Around the Hat," 1880s, 2-3/8" tall	125	225
Lion on Tub, Decorated, 1920s, 5-1/2" tall	125	225
Lion on Tub, Plain, bronze finish, 1920s, 7-1/2" tall	100	200
Lion on Tub, Small, brown or green finish, 1920s, 4-1/8" tall	85	175
Lion on Wheels, gold, 1920s, 4-1/2" x 5-1/2"	145	225
Lion, Ears Up, 1930s, 3-5/8" x 4-1/2"	75	125
Lion, Small, 1934, 2-1/2" x 3-5/8"	85	150
Lion, Tail Between Legs, 3" x 5-1/4"	85	145
Lion, Tail Left, bronze finish, 1910s, 3-3/4" tall	100	175
Lion, Tail Right, 1900s, 4" tall	55	100
Lion, tail Right, 1920s, 3-1/2" x 4-15/16"	55	100
Lion, Tail Right, bronze finish, 1900s, 5-1/4" tall	55	150
Little Red Riding Hood Safe, painted, 1907, 5-1/16" tall	2000	4000

Still Banks (Continued)

	C8	C10
Log Cabin, painted, 1882, 2-1/2" x 3-1/4"	175	425
Lost Dog, unpainted, 1890s, 5-3/8"	275	850
Lucky Cabin, painted w/horseshoe over door, 1970, 4-1/8" tall	35	65
Mailbox on Legs, Large, green street corner box replica, 1920s, 5-1/2" tall	85	225
Mailbox on Legs, Small, green replica street corner mailbox, 1928, 3-3/4" tall	35	100
Main Street Trolley with People, bronze finish, 1920s, 3" x 6-3/4"	175	475
Main Street Trolley without People, 1920s, 6-3/4" long	175	400
Majestic Refrigerator Bank, in red, green or blue w/gold trim, replica of single door fridge on four legs, coin slot in back, w/key lock, 1930s, 4-1/2" tall	375	600

Still Banks (Continued)

	C8	C10
Majestic Radio Bank, mahogany finish replica of a floor standing radio on four legs, coin slot in back, w/key, 1930s, 4-1/2" tall	125	200
Mammy, doorstop conversion, red dress, white apron, 1970s, 8-1/4" tall	10	25
Mammy with Hands on Hips, red dress, white apron, 1900s, 5-1/4" tall	85	400
Man in Barrel, painted, 1890s, 3-3/4" tall	175	550
Man on Cotton Bale, painted darkie sits on hay bale, red scarf, yellow pants, 1898, 4-7/8" tall	1500	3500
Marietta Silo, gray finish, 5-1/2"	275	850
Marshall Stove, red, 3-7/8"	125	225

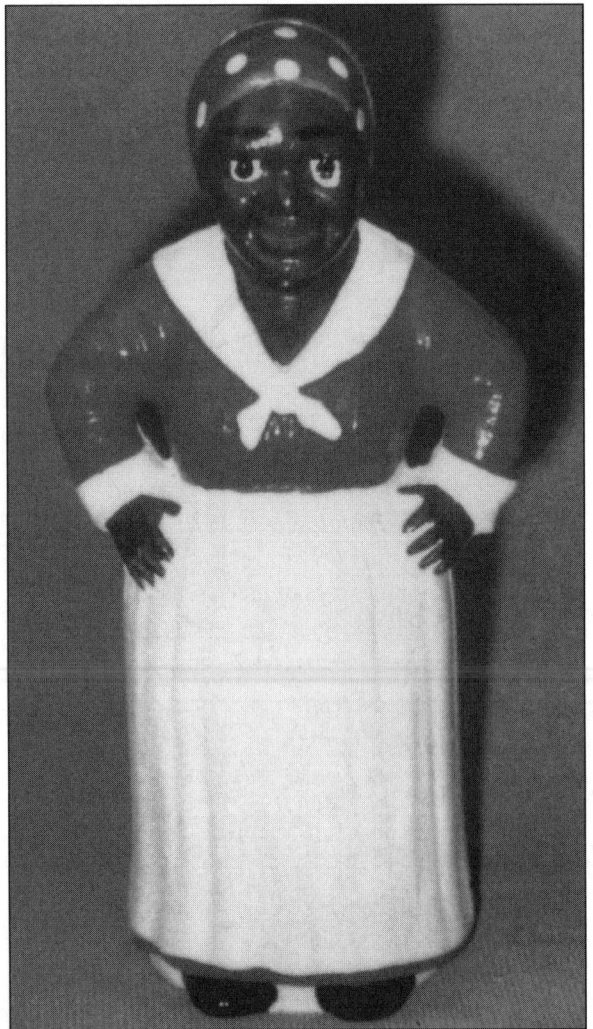

Mammy with Hands on Hips (Still Banks), Hubley, 1900s, $400

Minuteman (Still Banks), Hubley, 1905, $650

Palace (Still Banks), Ives, 1885, $3500

Still Banks (Continued)

	C8	C10
Mary & Little Lamb, painted white w/red trim, 1901, 4-3/8" tall	350	1500
Mascot, boy stands on baseball, 1914, 5-3/4" tall	850	2400
McKinley/Teddy Elephant, bronze finish, 1900, 2-1/2" tall	650	2200
Mean Standing Bear, 5-1/2"	100	225
Mellow Furnace, brown finish, 3-9/16" x 3-1/8"	125	225
Mermaid Boat, companion piece to Dolphin, girl in boat holds fish, 1900s, 4-1/2" tall	350	850
Merry-Go-Round, unpainted, 1920s, 4-5/8" tall	175	550
Metropolitan Bank, "Metropolitan Bank," 1872, 5-7/8"	125	275
Mickey Mouse, bookend bank, painted, 1970s, 5" x 3-3/4"	85	150
Mickey Mouse, Hands on Hips, painted, 9" tall	125	450
Middy with Clapper, brown finish, 1887, 5-1/4"	150	350
Minuteman, painted, 1905, 6" tall	200	650
Model T Ford, black, 1920s, 4" tall	650	1250
Moody & Sankey, painted, two oval portraits on front, 1870, 5"	800	3500
Mosque, Large, Three-story, 1920s, 3-1/2" tall	45	125
Mosque, Small, Two-story, 2-7/8" tall	35	115
Mother Hubbard Safe, 1907, 4-1/2" tall	1500	5000

Still Banks (Continued)

	C8	C10
Mulligan Policeman (Keystone Cop), painted, 1900s, 5-3/4"	175	400
Multiplying Bank, painted building, 1883, 6-1/2"	700	3500
Mutt & Jeff, gold, 1900s, 4-1/4" x 3-1/2"	75	275
National Safe, unpainted, 1800s, 3-3/8" tall	65	125
Nest Egg, bronze finish egg on side, "Horace," 1873, 3-3/8" tall on base	450	850
Nesting Doves Safe, bronze finish, 1907, 5-1/4"	1500	3500
New Heatrola Bank, green finish w/red trim, 1920s, 4-1/2" tall	85	375
Newfoundland Dog, blue or green finish, 1930s, 3-5/8" x 5-3/8"	100	225
Newfoundland Dog with Pack, 4-11/16" tall	85	175
Nixe, silver boy in boat, "Nixe," 4-1/2" tall	350	1450
Nixon Bust, 1972, 5-5/16"	45	85
Nixon/Agnew Elephant, 1968, 2-5/8"	15	35
North Pole Bank, unpainted, "Save Your Casting Money And Freeze It," 1920s, 4-1/4"	375	775
Oak Stove, unpainted, 1899, 2-3/8" tall	125	475
Old Abe with Shield, Eagle, unpainted, 1880, 3-7/8"	450	1300
Old South Church, bronze finish, 10" tall	2000	5000
One Car Garage, painted, 1920s, 2-1/2"	125	350
One Story House, 1900s, 3" tall	65	175
Oregon Gunboat, blue hull, gray guns, black and red stacks, "Oregon," 11" long	850	1800
Organ Grinder, painted, 6-3/16" x 2-1/8"	125	350
Oriental Boy on Pillow, painted, 1920s, 5-1/2" tall	85	200
Oriental Camel, on rockers, 3-3/4" tall	300	875
Ornate Hall Clock, tan finish, paper face, 1900s, 5-7/8" tall	200	425
Osborn Pig, "You can bank on the Osborn...," 2" x 4"	100	350
Oscar the Goat, black w/silver hooves and horns, 7-3/4" tall	75	175
Owl, painted, 1930, 4-1/4"	75	325
Owl on Stump, red, 3-5/8"	65	125
Ox, painted, 4-3/8"	85	150
Palace, 1885, 8" wide, 7-1/2" tall	850	3500
Park Bank Building, 4-3/8" painted	450	2200

Still Banks (Continued)

	C8	C10
Parlor Stove, gray and black, 6-7/8"	275	425
Parrot on Stump, painted, 6-1/4"	125	450
Pavillion, 1880, 3-1/8" x 3"	225	500
Pay Phone Bank, unpainted, 1926, 7-3/16"	450	1800
Pearl Street Bank, unpainted, silver finish, 4-1/4"	350	1800
Pelican, painted white, 1930s, 4-3/4"	350	1500
Penny Register Pail, unpainted, 1889, 2-3/4"	125	250
Penthouse Building, silver finish, 5-7/8" tall	350	850
Peters Weatherbird, 4-1/4" tall	750	2500
Phoenix Dime Register Trunk, steamer trunk, 1890, 3-3/4" x 5"	125	250
Pig, A Christmas Roast, 3-1/4" x 7-1/8"	85	250
Pig, Seated, 1900s, 3" x 4-9/16"	35	125
Plymouth Rock 1620, "1620," 3-7/8" long	650	1850
Polar Bear, Begging, white, 1900s, 5-1/4"	275	450
Policeman Bank, blue w/aluminum finish on gloves and star, gold buttons, black shoes, flesh face and hands, 1930s, 5-5/8" tall	250	1000
Policeman Safe, 1907, 5-1/4"	1250	4500
Polish Rooster, painted, 5-1/2" tall	850	2200
Pooh Bank, 5" x 4-7/8"	5	15

Still Banks (Continued)

	C8	C10
Possum, silver finish, 1910s, 2-3/8" tall, 4-3/8" long	125	575
Postal Savings Mailbox, 1920s, 6-3/4"	85	275
Pot Bellied Stove, flat black finish, 1968, 5-3/4" tall	25	65
Potato, "Bank," 1897, 5-1/4" long	850	1650
Presto Bank, silver finish w/gold dome, 1900s, 3-5/8" tall	85	175
Presto Bank, silver finish, "Bank," 3-1/4" tall	65	150
Presto Bank, building, silver w/gold dome, 4-1/4" tall	85	175
Presto Trick Bank, red doors and roof, 1892, 4-1/2" tall	250	950
Professor Pug Frog Bank, 1900s, 3-1/4"	75	550
Pugdog, Seated, painted, 1889, 3-1/2"	250	475
Puppo, painted bee on body, 1920s, 4-7/8" tall	125	250
Puppo on Pillow, painted brown, cream, black, pink, 1920s, 5-5/8" x 6"	150	275

Pavillion (Still Banks), Kyser & Rex, 1880, $500

Pavillion (Still Banks), Kyser & Rex, 1880, $500

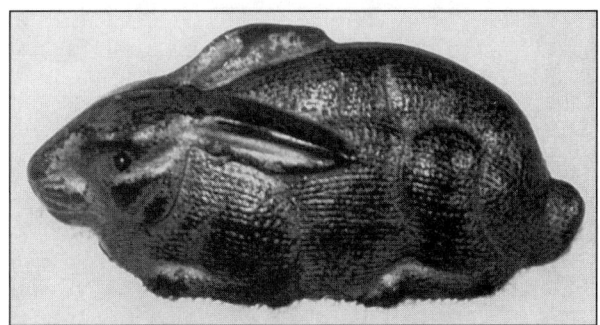

Rabbit Lying Down (Still Banks), $575

Rabbit Standing, Large (Still Banks), A.C. Williams, 1908, $325

Still Banks (Continued)

	C8	C10
Put Money in Thy Purse, change purse, black, 1886, 2-3/4" tall	625	950
Puzzle Try Me, safe, "Puzzle Try Me," 1868, 2-11/16" tall	475	975
Quadrafoil House, Several Makers, 1900s, 3-1/8" tall	125	225
Queen Stove, "Queen" on oven door, 1975, 3-3/4" to cook top	25	65

Still Banks (Continued)

	C8	C10
Quilted Lion, bronze finish, 3-3/4" tall, 4-3/4" long	185	450
Rabbit Lying Down, unpainted, 2-1/8" x 5-1/8"	175	575
Rabbit Standing, Large, brown metal finish, 1908, 6-1/4" tall	125	325
Rabbit with Carrot, painted white, orange and green carrot, 1972, 3-3/8"	85	200
Rabbit, Begging, 1900s, 5-1/8"	85	275
Rabbit, Large Seated, painted white w/pink highlights, 1900s, 4-5/8" tall	125	375
Rabbit, Small, Seated, 1910s, 3-5/8" tall	125	325
Radio Bank, metallic blue, 1928, 3-5/16" tall	100	375
Radio Bank with Three Dials, red, 1920s, 3" tall, 4-5/8" long	100	350
Radio with Combination Door, metal sides and back, 1930s, 4-1/2" red	125	375
Reclining Cow, black, 2-1/8" tall, 4" long	100	400
Recording Bank, 6-5/8" x 4-1/4"	200	575
Red Ball Safe, red ball on base, 3"	175	425
Red Goose Shoes on Base, on pedestal w/base, 1920s, 5-1/2"	300	750
Red Goose Shoes on Pedestal, red goose on bronze base, 4-7/16"	175	350
Red Goose Shoes, Squatty, red body, yellow feet, 1920s, 4" tall	275	500
Reindeer on Base, 1973, 10" x 8"	75	125
Reindeer, Large, bronze finish, 1900s, 9-1/2" tall	125	250
Reindeer, Small, bronze finish, 6-1/4" tall	75	150
Republic Pig, painted pig in business suit, 1970s, 7" tall	35	85
Rhesus Monkey, converted doorstop, painted, 8-1/2"	35	125
Rhino, gold, 1910s, 2-5/8" tall, 5" long	225	650
Rochester Clock, w/working clock, 5" tall	225	750
Rocking Chair, brown finish, 1898, 6-3/4" tall	1500	2750
Rocking Horse, white w/red saddle, "SBCC," 1975, 5-5/8"	350	550
Roller Safe, 1882, 3-11/16" x 2-7/8"	125	245
Roof Bank, 1887, 5-1/4" x 3-3/4"	125	450
Roof Bank, 1900s, 5-1/4"	125	300
Rooster, black w/red comb, 1910s, 4-5/8"	125	400

Still Banks (Continued)

	C8	C10
Rooster, brown finish, w/red comb and wattle, 1910s, 4-3/4"	125	350
Rooster, Large, unpainted except for red comb and wattle, 1913, 6-3/4"	550	1250
Rumplestiltskin, 1910s, 6" x 2-1/4"	200	500
Saddle Horse, 1928, 4-3/8" tall	375	650
Safe Deposit, "Safe Deposit," 1899, 3-5/8"	85	150
Safety Locomotive, gray, 1887, 3-1/4" tall	650	2200
Sailor, Medium, 1910s, 5-1/4" tall	225	475
San Gabriel Mission, painted, musical building, 4-5/8" x 3-3/4"	2000	7500
Santa Claus, painted w/arms folded in front, 1900s, 5-3/4"	450	950
Santa Claus with Tree, w/arms folded in front, tree at back, painted, 1910s, 5-3/4"	450	950

Rooster (Still Banks), Arcade, 1910s, $400

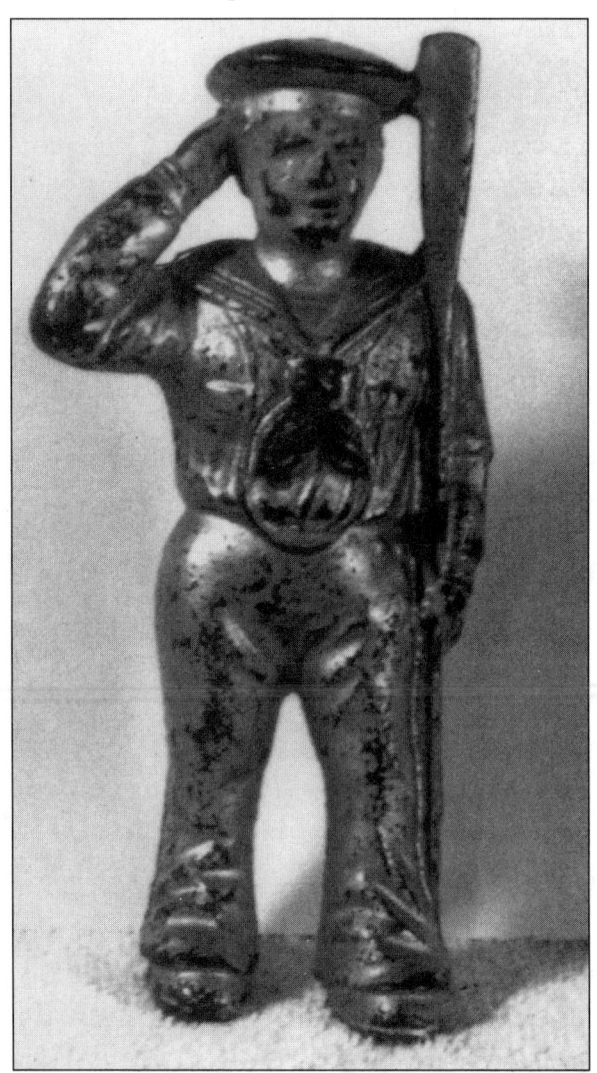

Sailor, Medium (Still Banks), Hubley, 1910s, $475

Santa Claus with Tree (Still Banks), Hubley, 1910s, $950

Still Banks (Continued)

	C8	C10
Santa with Wire Tree, w/removable ornate tree, 1890s, 7-1/4" tall	875	1500
Scottie, Seated, black finish, red collar, 1930s, 4-7/8" x 6"	125	300
Scrollwork Safe, 1900s, 2-3/4" tall	85	225
Seal on Rock, black, 1900s, 3-1/2"	175	500
Security Safe, red door, 1894, 4-1/2" tall	125	275
Security Safe Deposit, 1881, 3-7/8" tall	95	150
Shell Out, conch shell on base, off white, 1882, 4-3/4" long	225	700
Show Horse, 1973, 5-7/8" tall	75	150
Six-Sided Building, unpainted, 2-3/8" tall	225	650
Six-Sided Building, Two Story, 3-3/8" tall	100	275
Skyscraper Bank, silver building, four gold posts, 1900s, 4-3/8" tall	85	125
Skyscraper Bank, silver building, four gold posts, 1900s, 5-1/2" tall	85	150
Skyscraper with Six Posts, silver building, gold posts, 1900s, 6-1/2" tall	125	450
Songbird on Stump, bronze finish, 1900s, 4-3/4"	300	800
Space Heater with Bird, English, 1890s, 6-1/2" tall	175	375
Space Heater with Flowers, English, Far East motif, red finish, 1890s, 6-1/2" tall	175	375
Spaniel, large, painted, 1960s, 10-1/2" long	65	125
Spitz, bronze finish, 1928, 4-1/4"	225	575
Squirrel with Nut, 4-1/8"	425	1250

Three Wise Monkeys (Still Banks), A.C. Williams, 1900s, $550

Still Banks (Continued)

	C8	C10
St. Bernard with Pack, Large, 1900s, 5-1/2" x 7-3/4"	125	225
St. Bernard with Pack, Small, 1900s, 3-3/4" x 5-1/2"	85	175
Star Safe, 1882, 2-5/8" tall	150	450
State Bank, bronze finish, 1910s, 4-1/8" tall	85	175
State Bank, unpainted building bank, 1890s, 3" tall	95	200
State Bank, 1900, 8" x 7"	550	1200
State Bank, bronze building bank, 1890s, 5-1/2" tall	125	325
Statue of Liberty, silver finish w/gold highlights, 1900s, 6-3/8" tall	100	175
Statue of Liberty, 1900s, 6-1/16" tall	85	125
Statue of Liberty, 6-3/8" tall	85	125
Statue of Liberty, Large, silver gray finish, gold highlights, 1900s, 9-1/2" tall	350	1200
Steamboat, brown finish, 1900s, 7-5/8" long	125	375
Steamboat with Small Wheels, silver finish, 7-7/16" long	175	425
Stop Sign, green w/red and gold highlights, 1920, 5-5/8" tall	325	1450
Stork Safe, 1907, 5-1/2"	850	1750
Street Car, painted, 1891, 4-1/2" long	250	650
Sun Dial, 1900s, 4-5/16" tall	650	2200
Sunbonnet Sue, painted, 1970, 7-1/2"	65	165
Tabernacle Savings, unpainted, 2-1/4" x 5"	850	1250
Taft-Sherman Bust, one side Smiling Jim, other side Peaceful Bill, 1908, 4" tall	1000	2000
Tank Bank 1918, Large, gold finish, 1920s, 3" tall x 3-11/16" long	100	200
Tank Bank 1918, Small, gold finish, 1920s, 2-3/8" long	65	150
Tank Bank 1919, silver finish, "1919," 3" x 5-1/2"	125	350
Tank Savings Bank, "Tank Savings Bank," 1919, 9-1/2" long	175	525
Teddy Bear, 1900, 2-1/2" x 3-7/8"	125	350
Teddy Roosevelt Bust, 1919, 5" tall	175	450
Templetone Radio, red, 1930s, 4-1/2"	275	650
Thoroughbred, bronze finish, 1946, 5-1/4"	75	150
Three Wise Monkeys, 1900s, 3-1/4" tall, 3-1/2" wide	225	550

Tower Bank (Still Banks), 1890s, $2200

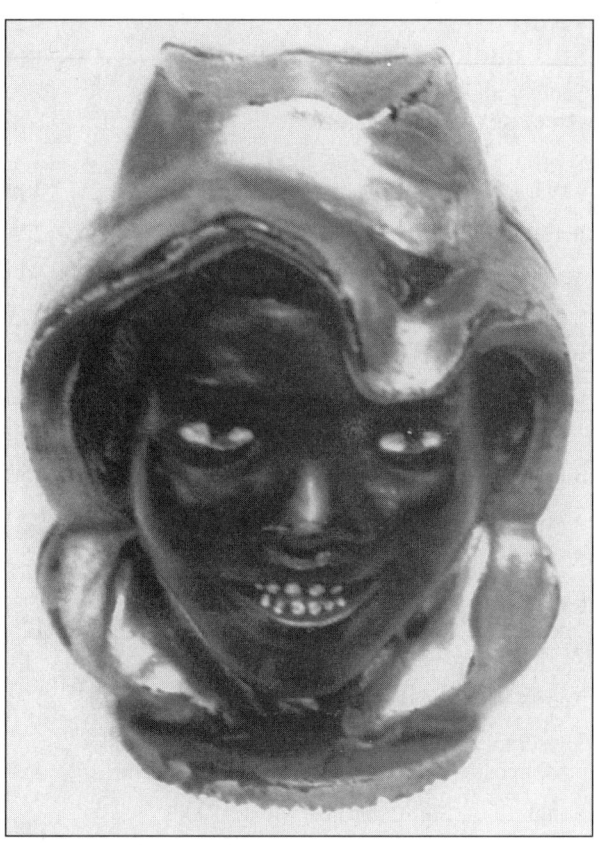

Two-Faced Black Boy, Large (Still Banks), A.C. Williams, 1900s, $350

Still Banks (Continued)

	C8	C10
Time Is Money Clock Bank, alarm clock shaped, gold finish, "Time Is Money," 1910s, 3-1/2" tall	125	200
Time Safe, unpainted, 7" tall, 3-3/4" wide	375	750
Tower, unpainted, 1915, 4-1/8"	175	375
Tower Bank, unpainted, brown finish, J.M. Harper, 1900s, 9-1/4" tall	175	375
Tower Bank, building w/tower rising from roof, "Tower Bank 1890," 1890, 6-7/8"	1200	2200
Town Hall Bank, red, "Town Hall Bank," 1882, 4-5/8"	375	950
Toy Soldier, painted, "SBCCA," 1982, 7-1/2" tall	15	65
Treasure Chest, smaller version is No. 928, 1970, 2-3/4" x 4"	60	135
Triangular Building, "Bank," 1914, 6" tall	325	675
Trick Buffalo, black, 5-1/2" tall	750	1500
Trolley Car, painted, silver, 1900s, 5-1/4" long	225	650
Trunk on Dolly, 1890, 2-5/8" x 3-9/16"	175	350
Trust Bank, 1800s, 7-1/4"	1800	3500
Tug Boat, red, pull toy, 5-1/2" long	4500	7500

Still Banks (Continued)

	C8	C10
Turkey, Large, painted wattle, 1900s, 4-1/4" x 4"	250	550
Turkey, Small, red head and wattle, 1900s, 3-3/8" tall	150	275
Turtle Bank, 1" tall, 3-7/16" long	2000	3500
Two Car Garage, painted, 1920s, 2-1/2"	125	350
Two Goats Butting, two goats on tree stump, "Two Kids" on base, 4-1/2"	950	2000
Two Story House, brown finish w/red roof, 1930s, 3-1/16" tall	75	150
Two-Faced Black Boy, Large, 1900s, 4-1/8" tall	125	350
Two-Faced Black Boy, Small, 1900s, 3-1/8" x 2-3/4"	85	300
Two-Faced Devil, deep red, 1904, 4-1/4" tall	550	1250
Two-Faced Indian, bronze finish w/painted highlights, 1900s, 4-5/16" tall	1500	2750
U.S. Bank, Eagle Finial, green w/gold trim, 1890s, 4-5/16" tall	850	1500
U.S. Mail, silver gray w/red lettering, 1900s, 4-3/4" tall	100	375

Woolworth Building (Still Banks), Kenton, 1915, $225

Still Banks (Continued)

	C8	C10
U.S. Mail Bank with Combination Lock, silver gray w/red lettering, 1903, 6-7/8" tall	225	775
U.S. Mail with Eagle, 1930s, 4-1/8" x 3-1/2"	85	175
U.S. Mail with Eagle, 1906, 4" x 4"	175	325
U.S. Mail, Small, silver or green mail box w/red lettering, 1900s, 3-5/8" x 2-3/4"	75	150
U.S. Navy Akron Zeppelin, silver finish, "US Navy Akron," 1930, 6-5/8" long	175	500
U.S. Treasury Bank, painted, 1920s, 3-1/4"	250	475
Ulysses S. Grant Bust, 1976, 5-1/2" tall	125	250
Ulysses S. Grant Bust on Safe, 1903, 5-5/8" tall	1750	3000
Uncle Sam Hat, red, white and blue, 2" x 3"	125	350
United Banking and Trust, Building Bank, bronze finish, 3" tall	225	450
Victorian House, unpainted deep gray finish, 1892, 4-1/2"	175	375
Victorian House, gray metallic finish, 3-1/4" tall	150	275
Villa, unpainted except for red finial, 1894, 5-9/16"	375	850
Villa Bank, "1882," 1882, 3-7/8" x 3-3/8"	375	700
Vindex Bulldog, painted, "Vindex Toys," 1931, 5-1/4" tall	125	275
Washington Bell with Yoke, red, 1932, 2-3/4"	125	325
Washington Monument, 1900s, 6" tall	150	325
Washington, George, Bust, bronze finish, 1920s, 8" tall	850	1450
Watch Dog Safe, w/brass handle, dog stands guard on front, 5-1/8"	1850	4000
Water Spaniel with Pack (I Hear a Call), 1900, 5-3/8" x 7-7/8"	225	450
Weaver Hen, white w/red comb and wattle, "Weaver," 1970s, 6"	20	50
Westside Presbyterian Church, silver finish, 1916, 3-3/4" x 3-5/8"	350	950
Whale of a Bank, "A Whale of a Bank," 1975, 2-3/4" x 5-3/16"	85	200
Whippet on Base, gold finish, 3-1/2" tall	75	125
White City Barrel No. 1 on Cart, unpainted, "White City Puzzle Savings Bank, A Barrel of Money," 1894, 5" long	275	475
White City Barrel, Large, silver finish barrel, 1893, 5-1/8" tall	175	275

Still Banks (Continued)

	C8	C10
White City Pail, silver finish pail w/handle, 1893, 2-5/8" tall	125	225
White City Puzzle Safe No. 10, unpainted, 1893, 4-5/8"	125	225
White City Puzzle Safe No. 12, unpainted, 1893, 4-7/8"	150	325
White Horse on Base, 1973, 9-1/2" tall	125	225
Wirehaired Terrier, painted, 1920s, 4-5/8"	125	275
Wisconsin Beggar Boy, "Help the Crippled Children of Wisconsin," 6-7/8" tall	525	900
Wise Pig, The, painted off-white pig holding plaque, 1930s, 6-5/8" tall	85	225
Woolworth Building, bronze finish, 1915, 7-7/8" tall	100	225
Woolworth Building, 1915, 5-3/4" x 1-1/4"	85	150
Work Horse on Base, painted white, 9" tall	75	125
Work Horse with Flynet, 1910s, 4" tall	300	800
World's Fair Administration Building, painted, 1893, 6" x 6"	1400	2250

Still Banks (Continued)

	C8	C10
Yellow Cab, orange and black, rubber tires, 1921, 7-7/8" long	1500	2400
York Stove, unpainted, "York Stove," 4" tall	225	525
Young America, Kyser & Rex, 1882, 4-3/8" x 3-1/8" safe	125	275

Yellow Cab (Still Banks), Arcade, 1921, $2400

World's Fair Administration Building (Still Banks), 1893, $2250

BATTERY-OPERATED TOYS

"Made in Japan" are the words toy collectors look for in their pursuit of high-quality mechanical tin toys.

Before World War II, these same words were synonymous with cheap, poor-quality, drab-looking toys made from recycled materials and ideas. Most of the toys were people-animal-oriented with less emphasis on vehicle, nautical, or aircraft-type toys. They were powered either by a spring or a flywheel and didn't last very long or do very much as far as play-value goes. These inexpensive, poor-quality toys kept Japan a third-rate toy manufacturing nation until after the second World War, when Japan's surrender resulted in economic chaos for this industrial nation.

In their quest for economic recovery and to compete in a toy market already dominated by Germany and America, the Japanese knew they had to come up with a new, different and exciting type of toy that would be more desirable than those produced by their competitors.

The Japanese toy designers concentrated their technology on a different type of toy operation. Not satisfied with the limited action and short duration of spring-driven or flywheel-propelled toys, the toy engineers developed a small electric motor powered by flashlight batteries. This mini-motor took up less room than other mechanisms, had a longer-running duration and enabled the toy to perform more functions. This development opened up an entirely new dimension in toy design—it introduced the concept of the battery-operated toy.

The toy designers integrated this new concept into hundreds of automaton-like toys, capable of as many as eight different types of actions in one cycle. These unique toys were an instant hit with the foreign market, especially the United States. These clever, unusual and high-quality toys made Japan the dominant toy producer and exporter for the next twenty to thirty years.

It should be noted that Japan flooded the market with these ingenious, well-made toys while quality control remained a high priority. These merits were not only apparent in their figural toys, but also in their vehicle line. The Japanese toy makers concentrated on very fine detail and quality, especially in their scale-model passenger cars. Their ultimate goal was to produce toys that looked like the real thing. They succeeded. Their workmanship carried over into their other vehicle lines—motorcycles; emergency and construction vehicles; and novelty (silly) and comic character cars; trucks; and space toys.

No other nation was able to equal (much less surpass) the impetus and determination of the Japanese toy makers until Japan relinquished its domination by redirecting its economy.

Now that they are approaching middle age, it is no wonder that these fine toys remain in great demand today and often command a very high price.

The value of a battery-operated toy depends not only on its desirability, rarity and complexity, but very much on its condition. A toy in Mint condition is generally worth twice as much as a toy in Good condition. A toy in Very Good condition will be priced about halfway between Good and Mint.

C-10: Mint. A Mint toy is in the condition in which it was originally issued (perfect) regardless of age. It will also be in perfect mechanical condition, complete with all accessory parts when applicable, and will look brand new. The cloth or fur (plush) covering on some battery toys may reveal some discoloration (yellowing) due to age, but this should not affect its value as a Mint toy as long as it is clean. All toys in this category must be in perfect working condition. The original box in Mint condition will significantly enhance the value.

C-8: Very Good. A battery toy that has seen some use and is starting to show its age is described as Very Good. It will still be in perfect working order and have all its accessory parts when applicable. It will have some age soiling, but will have no rust or corrosion. Overall, it will have an appearance of freshness and still be highly desirable to the fussy collector.

C-6: Good. The term Good applies to a battery toy that has seen considerable use, wear and tear, and some age-soiling, but is still in perfect working condition with no missing parts or accessories. The wet toys may show some slight surface rust that can be easily removed. A toy in Good condition is still a welcome addition to any toy collection, but will be targeted for upgrading by a piece in better condition.

Any battery toy below the condition of Good will reflect a drastic reduction in value. Toys in good shape, but missing accessory parts, will not lose as much value as those that are severely rusted, corroded, painted over, have parts broken off, or are totally inoperable. These toys in Poor condition are usually collected for their scrap value by the toy repairer and seldom are they worth more than $10.

The key to grading is to use common sense and avoid wishful thinking. Grading the condition of a toy may be difficult at times, and consulting with an expert in the field can help dispel doubts about your judgment or your purchase. (See Collectors & Dealers for more information.)

To keep it in Excellent condition, your prized battery toy needs some tender loving care. If it stops working, you could have frustration, if not a disaster, on your hands. The following suggestions should be of some help in avoiding this.

Battery toys, like other mechanical toys, should be operated periodically to keep them loosened up. A lightweight spray lubrication now and then will help considerably if the mechanism is accessible. Do not over lubricate as the excess may stain any cloth or fur covering on the toy.

A quality car wax or polish will keep the lithographed and bare metal parts looking like new, especially on the "wet" toys. Always test an obscure lithographed area to make sure the polish doesn't soften or dissolve the paint. Care should be exercised when polishing metal parts adjoining any cloth or plush covering, as the cleaning substance may stain the coverings. Light surface rust usually disappears with a careful polishing. Nothing can be done for deep rust or corrosion without further ruining the value of the toy. Repainting will only further reduce the value and is not recommended.

Should your battery toy fail to operate, the following steps might be helpful.

1. Make sure it is not gunked-up and that no moving parts are binding.

2. Make sure the battery contacts are not dirty or corroded. If they are, clean them with crocus cloth. **Always use fresh batteries!**

3. Lightly tap the toy with your finger or **lightly** nudge one of the moving parts while the switch is in the "on" position.

If none of the above steps work, then your toy needs major surgery. This means the toy must be completely torn down, repaired and reassembled. Most battery toys are repairable as long as they have not been destructively tampered with and no parts are missing or corroded beyond repair. This job is best left to an expert in toy repair and should never be attempted by one who doesn't know what he or she is doing. Expert repairs will not affect the value of a battery toy as long as the repair is undetectable and the toy looks and functions exactly as it did before the repair. Such repairs are acceptable in toy collecting circles. Expert repairs are expensive but well worth the investment if it means the difference between a highly-prized Mint toy and one below the grade of Good. An inoperable toy is practically worthless, regardless of condition.

	C6	C8	C10
007 Aston-Martin, includes ejectable passenger, eight actions, 1966, 11-1/2" long	210	315	420
007 Secret Agent's Car, (Impala), five actions, 1960s, 15" long	170	255	340
4 Prop Airplane, four actions, 1960s, 17" long, 16-1/4" wingspan	140	210	280
A-B-C Fairy Train, one piece, four actions, 1950s, 14-1/2" long	80	95	160
Accordion Bear, six actions, 1950s, 10-1/2" tall	220	330	440
Accordion Bear, (Flare Toy), five actions, 1950s, 9-1/4" high	150	225	300
Accordion Player Bunny, six actions, 1950s, 12" tall, 9" long	200	325	450
Accordion Player Hobo, with Baby Monkey Playing Cymbals, six actions, 1950s	275	425	525
Acro Chimp Porter, minor toy, 1960s, 8-1/2" tall	50	75	100
Acrobat Clown, minor toy, 1960s, 9" tall	60	90	120
Acrobat Robot, three actions, 1970s, 4-1/2" tall	225	338	450
Air Cargo Prop-Jet Airplane, Seaboard World Airlines, five actions, 1960s, 12" long, 14-1/2" wingspan	150	300	425
Air Control Tower, includes detachable airplane and helicopter, four actions, 1960s, 11" high, 37" span extended	210	315	450

	C6	C8	C10
Air Defense Pom-Pom Gun, five actions, 1950s, 14" long	115	175	260
Air Taxi Helicopter, three actions, 1960s	50	75	100
Aircraft Carrier, eight actions, 1950s, 20" long	200	300	400
Aircraft Carrier, six actions, 1950s, 20" long	275	450	625
Aircraft Carrier Forrestal, includes detachable plastic airplane, three actions, 1950s, 13-3/4" long	200	300	400
Airport Saucer, four actions, 1960s, 8" diameter	100	150	200
Airport Saucer, four actions, 1960s, 9" diameter	100	150	200
All Stars Mr. Baseball Jr., includes eight plastic balls, three actions, rare, 1950s	500	750	1000
Alley the Exciting New Roaring Stalking Alligator, five actions, 1960s, 17-1/2" long	150	225	300
American Airlines 4 Prop Airliner, four actions, 1960s, 12" long, 16-1/2" wingspan	120	180	240
American Airlines Airliner DC-7, seven actions, 1960s, 17-1/2" long, 19" wingspan	200	325	450
American Airlines Airliner DC-7 Multiaction, seven actions, 1960s, 21" long, 23-1/2" wingspan	195	285	380
American Airlines DC-7, w/automatic turnover propellers, seven actions, c. 1950s, 19" wingspan	200	300	400
American Airlines Electra, 1950s, 18" long, 19-1/2" wingspan	175	300	450
American Airlines Flagship Caroline, three actions, 1950s, 18" long, 19-1/2" wingspan	175	300	400
American Circus Television Truck, includes detachable metal antenna, six actions, rare, 1950s, 9-1/4" long	600	900	1200
Amphibian Navy Patrol Plane, w/flashing lights, five actions, rare, 1950s, 13" long, 15" wingspan	900	1350	1800
Amtrak Locomotive, minor toy, 1960s, 16" long	60	90	120
Andy Gard Brink's Armored Car-Bank, minor toy, 1950s, 6-3/4" long	40	60	80

Amphibian Navy Patrol Plane, Alps Co., 1950s, $1800. Photo courtesy Don Hultzman and Ron Chojnacki

	C6	C8	C10
Andy Gard Combat Knight, No. 143, includes lance, stanchion, three plastic rings, and helmet plume, three actions, 1960s, 10-1/4" high	50	75	100
Animated Santa on Rotating Globe, five actions, 1950s, 15" high	400	600	800
Animated Squirrel, eight actions, rare, 1950s, 8-1/2" tall	100	150	200
Answer Game Machine Robot, educational toy, eight actions, 1960s, 14-1/2" tall	400	600	800
Anti-Aircraft Jeep, five actions, 1950s, 9-1/2" long	100	150	200
Anti-Aircraft Jeep, includes detachable tin radar antenna, six actions, 1950s, 11" long	250	375	500
Anti-Aircraft Unit, No. 1, three electrical actions and three manual actions, 1950s, 12-1/2" long	150	225	300
Antique Gooney Car, four actions, 1960s, 9" long	100	125	150
Apollo II-American Eagle Lunar Module, includes detachable plastic antenna, seven actions, 1960s, 10" high	200	300	400
Apollo Lunar Module, mostly plastic, four actions, 1970s, 6" high	170	205	240
Apollo Space Ship USA NASA, four actions, 1960s, 9" long	100	125	150
Apollo Spacecraft, includes detachable astronaut, four actions, 1960s, 10" long	200	300	400

	C6	C8	C10
Apollo Super Space Capsule, five actions, 1960s, 9" high	100	150	200
Apollo-X Moon Challenger Rocket, six actions, 1960s, 16" long	150	225	300
Armored Attack Set, includes fifteen 2" plastic figures, 1960s, jeep 6-1/4" long and tank 5-1/4" long	150	225	300
Army Helicopter, Huey by Bell, six actions, 1960s, 10-1/2" long	90	135	180
Army Radio Jeep J1490, four actions, 1950s, 7-1/4" long	75	125	165
Arthur A-Go-Go, includes detachable cymbals and drum set, six actions, 1960s, 10" high	130	200	295
Astro Captain, three actions, rare, 1960s, 6-1/2" tall	300	450	600
Astro Dog, three actions, 1960s, 11" tall	90	135	180
Astro Dog, (looks like Snoopy), two cycles, five actions, 1960s, 11" high	100	150	200

Atom Rocket 7, M-T Co., 1950s, $240. Photo courtesy Don Hultzman and Ron Chojnacki

	C6	C8	C10
Astrobase, motorized, six actions, 1960s, 20" high	140	210	280
Atom Motorcycle, five actions, 1950s, 11-3/4" long	500	750	1000
Atom Rocket 7, vehicle with fins, four actions, 1950s, 9-1/2" long	120	180	240
Atomic Boat, minor toy, 1950s, 15" long	150	225	300
Atomic Fighter Robot, five actions, 1950s, 11" tall	100	150	200
Atomic Rocket X-1800, three actions, 1960s, 9" long	150	225	300
Atomic Rocket X-1800, three actions, 1960s, 9" long	150	225	300
Attacking Martian Robot, seven actions, two cycles, 1950s, 11-1/2" tall	150	200	250
Attacking Martian Robot, seven actions, two cycles, 1950s, 11-1/2" tall	150	200	250
Automated Santa, three actions, c. 1960s, 10-1/4" tall	100	150	200
Automated Santa, three actions, c. 1960s, 10-1/4" tall	100	150	200
Automatic Toll Gate, includes 8" tin Valiant, six actions, 1955, 16" x 17" base	150	225	300

Arthur A-Go-Go, Alps Co., 1960s, $295

	C6	C8	C10
Auto-Top Ferrari Convertible, three actions, 1960s, 11" long	450	675	900
Auto-Top Ferrari Convertible, three actions, 1960s, 11" long	450	675	900
B-58 Hustler Jet, four actions, 1950s, 21" long, 12" wingspan	425	650	925
Baby Carriage, includes plastic baby bottle to activate switch, minor toy, 1950s, 11-3/4" long, 7" high	60	90	120
Ball Blowing Clown, w/ball, three actions, 1950s, 11" tall	200	300	400
Ball Playing Bear, includes five celluloid balls and one umbrella, no marking, six actions, rare, 1940s, 10-1/2" tall	200	300	400
Ball Playing Dog, three actions, 1950s, 9" high	125	200	250
Balloon Blowing Monkey, five actions, w/balloon, 1950s, 11-1/8" tall	100	150	200

Barber Bear, T-N Co., 1950s, $400. Photo courtesy Don Hultzman and Ron Chojnacki

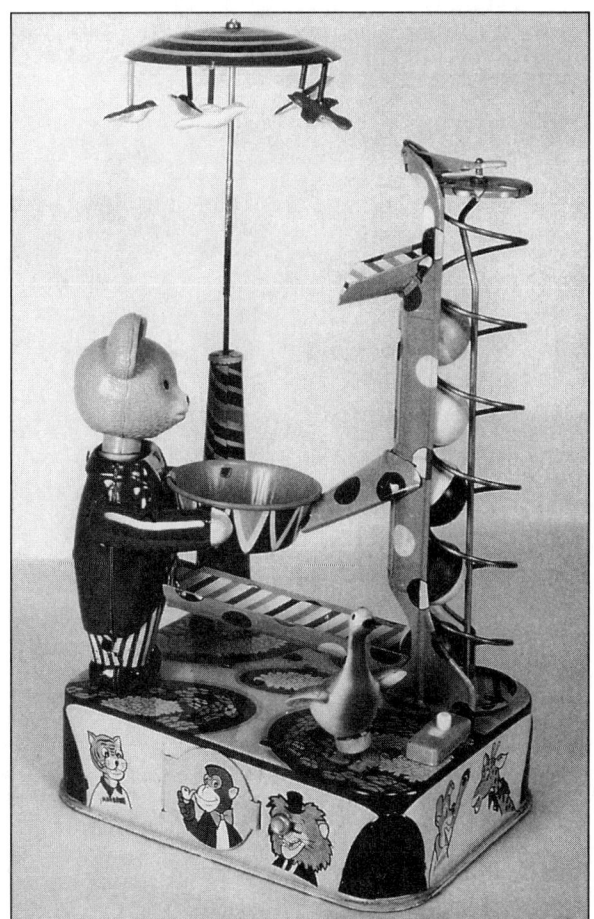

Ball Playing Bear, 1940s, $400. Photo courtesy Don Hultzman and Ron Chojnacki

	C6	C8	C10
Balloon Blowing Teddy Bear, six actions, w/balloon, 1950s, 11-1/8" tall	100	150	200
Balloon Vendor, includes four plastic balloons and tin tray, four actions, 1960s, 12" tall	130	195	260
Baragon, (Godzilla), three actions, 1960s, 10" tall	290	435	580
Barber Bear, five actions, 1950s, 9-1/2" tall	175	300	400
Barking Boxer Dog, minor toy, 1950s, 7" long	45	65	85
Barking Dog, four actions, two cycles, 1950s, 7" long, 7" high	50	75	100
Barking Spaniel Dog, minor toy, 1950s, 7" long	50	75	100
Barney Bear Drummer, five actions, resembles Steiff bear, 1950s, 11" tall	130	195	260
Barnyard Rooster, five actions, 1950s, 10" high	100	150	200
Bartender, six actions, 1960s, 11-1/2" tall	50	75	100

Bartender, T-N Co., 1960s, $100

	C6	C8	C10
Batmobile, 1972 National Periodical Publications, three actions, 12" long	200	300	400
Battery Locomotive, No. 123, three actions, 1950s, 10" long	30	45	60
Bear Chef, (Cutey Cook), includes chef hat and tin litho egg, five actions, 1960s, 9-1/2" tall	175	250	325
Bear Target Game, includes gun, rubber-tipped darts, detachable drum, four actions, 1950s, 8-3/4" high and 4" x 5" base	180	280	375
Bear the Cashier, five actions, 1950s, 7-1/2" high	200	300	400
Bear the Magician, nine actions, rare, 1950s, 12-1/2" tall	1000	1500	2000
Beauty Parlor Bear, seven actions, rare, 1950s, 9-1/2" high	600	900	1200
Begging Pubby, six actions, 1960s, 9" long	40	60	80

	C6	C8	C10
Bengali the Exciting New Growling, Prowling Tiger, Linemar Division, from nose to end of tail, three actions, two cycles, 1961, 18-1/2" long	100	150	200
Big Dipper, includes three tin cars, minor toy, 1960s, 21" long, 11" high	100	150	200
Big Hunter Automatic Gun, three actions, 1950s, 21" long extended	50	75	100
Big John, three actions, 1960s, 12" high	60	90	120
Big John the Indian Chief, five actions, c. 1960s, 12-1/2" tall	100	150	200
Big Loo Your Friend from the Moon, includes ball, darts, compass, etc., twelve actions, 1960s, 38" tall	950	1500	2200
Big Max Robot, four actions, 1958, 8" long, 7" tall	80	125	175
Big Parade, The, includes detachable gun and baton, four actions, 1963, 11-1/2" tall, 15" wide	120	180	240

Beauty Parlor Bear, S&E Co., 1950s, $1200. Photo courtesy Don Hultzman and Ron Chojnacki

	C6	C8	C10
Big Ring Circus Truck, three actions, 1950s, 13" long	140	210	280
Big Shot Cadillac, four actions, rare, 1950s, 10" long	200	300	400
Big Wheel Coca Cola Truck, three actions, 1970s	80	120	160
Big Wheel Family Camper, three actions, 1970s, 10" long	60	90	120
Big Wheel Ice Cream Truck, three actions, 1970s, 10" long	60	90	120
Biller Train, No. 573, includes rubber cable track and two hopper cars, a minor toy, rare, 1950s, 13" long	70	105	140
Billy Blastoff Space Scout, four actions, 1960s, 16" long	90	135	180
Billy the Kid Sheriff, four actions, two cycles, 1950s, 10-1/2" tall	200	300	400
Bimbo the Clown, includes detachable hat, three actions, 1950s, 9-1/4" tall	190	325	400
Bingo Clown, three actions, 1950s, 13" tall	200	300	400
Black Smithy Bear, four actions, rare, 1950s, 9" high	150	200	250
Blacksmith Bear, six actions, 1950s, 9-1/2" tall	200	300	400
Blink-A-Gear-Robot, five actions, 1960s, 14-1/2" tall	400	600	800
Blinky-the-Clown, includes multicolor paper hat, no marking, five actions, 1950s, 10-1/2" tall	300	450	600
Blow-Up-Ball Locomotive, includes celluloid ball, minor toy, 1950s, 9-1/2" long	80	120	160
Blushing Willie, four actions, 1960s, 10" tall	65	85	110
Bobby Drinking Bear, six actions, 1950s, 10" tall	200	300	400
Bobby the Drumming Bear, four actions, 1950s, 10" tall	175	275	380
Boeing 727 Jet Liner, three actions, 1960s, 17-1/2" long, 16-1/4" wingspan	140	210	280
Boeing 727 Jet Plane, three actions, 1960s, 12-1/2" long, 10-3/8" wingspan	150	225	300
Bomber Pilot, six actions, 1960s, 10-1/2" long, 9" wingspan	190	285	380

	C6	C8	C10
Bongo Player, four actions, 1960s, 10" tall	80	120	160
Bongo, Drumming Monkey, includes plastic hat, three actions, 1960s, 9-1/2" high	80	120	160
Bowling Bank, three actions, 1960s, 10" long	100	150	200
Brave Eagle, five actions, 1950s, 11" tall	100	150	200
Breakfast Chef, includes plastic egg and coffee maker, minor toy, 1960s, 8-1/4" tall	70	105	140
Brewster the Rooster, five actions, 1950s, 9-1/2" high	150	200	250
Bristol Bulldog Airplane T-360, four actions—lights, prop spins and stop and go, noise, 12" long, 14-1/2" wingspan	160	240	320
Bruno the Accordion Bear, five actions, 1950s, 10-1/2" tall	150	225	300
Bubble Blowing Bear, four actions, 1950s, 9-1/2" high, 4" x 5" base	150	225	300

Bubble Blowing Monkey, Alps Co., 1950s, $225.
Photo courtesy Don Hultzman and Ron Chojnacki

	C6	C8	C10
Bubble Blowing Boil Over Car, three actions, 1950s, 10" long	100	150	200
Bubble Blowing Boy, four actions, 1950s, 7" high	100	200	300
Bubble Blowing Bunny, four actions, 1950s, 7" high	100	150	200
Bubble Blowing Dog, three actions, 1950s, 8" high	100	150	200
Bubble Blowing Kangaroo, three actions, rare, 1950s, 9" high (base to tip of ears)	200	300	400
Bubble Blowing Lion, four actions, 1950s, 7-1/2" high, 3-1/2" x 7" base	100	150	200
Bubble Blowing Monkey, includes plastic bowl for bubble solution, four actions, 1950s, 10" tall	125	150	225
Bubble Blowing Musician, three actions, 1950s, 11" tall	250	350	450
Bubble Blowing Popeye, five actions, 1950s, 11-3/4" tall	750	1200	2500
Bubble Blowing Washing Bear, includes plastic washtub, three actions, 1950s, 8" high	200	275	350
Bubbling Bull, w/plastic bowl, five actions, 1950s, 6-1/2" long, 8" high	100	150	200
Bulldozer, five actions, 1950s, 7-1/2" long	60	80	120
Bulldozer, six actions, 1950s, 11" long	70	105	140
Bunny the Cashier, five actions, 1950s, 7-1/2" high	150	225	300
Bunny the Magician, includes card-ribbon apparatus for card trick, five actions, 1950s, 14-1/2" tall	300	400	500
Burger Chef, includes chef's hat and tin-litho hamburger, eight actions, 1950s, 9" tall	150	225	325
Busy Bizzy Friendly Bug, three actions, 1950s, 6-1/4" long	60	90	120
Busy Cart Robot, includes plastic wheelbarrow, four actions, c. 1960s, 11" high	200	300	400
Busy Housekeeper, The, four actions, 1950s, 8-1/2" tall	175	300	375
Busy Housekeeper, The (bunny), four actions, 1950s, 10" tall	175	250	325

	C6	C8	C10
Busy Secretary, seven actions, 1950s, 7-1/2" high, 7-1/4" long	125	200	300
Busy Shoe Shining Bear, five actions, 1950s, 10" high	110	175	240
Butt Stompin' Ashtray, includes tin manhole cover, ashtray insert and 4-1/2" high plastic shoe, four actions, 1977, 7-1/4" high	40	60	80
Buttons, Puppy with a Brain, also called Buttons the Push Button Pup, eight actions, 1960s, 12" high	200	300	400
B-Z Porter Baggage Truck, includes three pieces of luggage, minor toy, 1950s, 7-1/2" long, 6-1/2" high	140	210	280
B-Z Rabbit, four actions, c. 1950s, 7" long	60	90	120
B-Z Vendor, ice cream cart, three actions, rare, 1950s, 7-1/2" long	450	675	900
Cabin Cruiser, three actions, c. 1950s, 21-1/2" long	150	225	300
Cabin Cruiser with Outboard Motor, minor toy, 1950s, 12" long	100	135	200
Cable Train, four-piece set; minor toy, 1940s, 12" long	80	120	160
Cadillac Car, three actions, 1949, 10" long	150	225	300
Calypso Joe, four actions, rare, 1950s, 11" tall	190	310	400
Camera Shooting Bear, includes plastic worms, five actions also called Cine-Bear, 1950s, 11" tall	350	475	700
Candy Vending Machine Bank, five actions, rare, 1950s, 9" high	600	900	1200
Capitol Airlines Viscount, four actions, 1950s, 11" long, 14" wingspan	160	240	320
Cappy the Baggage Porter Dog, four actions, 1960s, 12" high, 11" long	100	150	200
Captain Blushwell, six actions, 1960s, 11" tall	80	120	160
Captain Hook, includes tin sword and felt hat, three actions, rare, 1950s, 10-3/4" high	800	1200	1600
Caterpillar, three actions, 1950s, 16" long	90	135	180
Caterpillar Tank M-1, five actions, 1950s, 8-1/2" long, 11" long with barrel extended	150	225	300

	C6	C8	C10
Central Choo Choo, three actions, 1960s, 15" long	40	60	80
Champion Weight Lifter, five actions, 1960s, 10" tall	100	150	200
Change Man Robot, astronaut, four actions, rare, 1960s, 13-1/4" tall	4000	6000	8000
Chaparral 2F car, five actions, 1960s, 11" long	80	120	160
Charlie the Drumming Clown, includes detachable drum and cymbals, six actions, 1950s, 9-1/2" tall	150	225	300
Charlie Weaver, six actions, 1962, 12" tall	75	100	125
Charm the Cobra, three actions, 1960s, 6" high	90	130	175
Chee Chee Chihuahua, five actions, 1960s, 8" high	50	75	100
Chef Cook, includes tin litho egg and hat, five actions, 1960s, 11-1/2" tall w/hat	100	225	300

Chef Cook, "Y" Co., 1960s, $300

	C6	C8	C10
Chemical Fire Engine, four actions, 1950s, 10" long	100	150	200
Chief Robotman, four actions, 1950s, 12" tall	450	675	900
Chimp and Pup Rail Car, four actions, 1950s, 8" high	90	135	180
Chimp with Xylophone, includes four records and hammer, minor toy, 1970s, 12" long, 8" high	100	150	200
Chimpee the One-Man Drummer, includes detachable drum and cymbals, six actions, 1950s, 9" high	70	105	140
Chippy the Chipmunk, (nosetip to tail tip), four actions, 1950s, 12" long	75	120	155
Christmas Time, three actions, rare, 1950s, 10" high, 7" base diameter	400	600	800
Cindy the Meowing Cat, (nosetip to tail tip), four actions, two cycles, 1950s, 12" high	50	75	100
Circus Elephant with Blowing Ball and Parasol, includes celluloid ball and tin litho umbrella, three actions, rare, 1950s, 9-3/4" high	200	275	350
Circus Fire Engine, four actions, 1960s, 11" long	110	175	235
Circus Jet, three actions, 1950s, 9" high assembled	90	135	180
Circus Lion, includes whip and flannel carpet w/levers, four actions, two cycles, 1950s, 11" high	300	450	600
Clancy the Great, includes plastic hat and test coin, three actions, 1960s, 19-1/2" tall without hat	85	135	200
Climbing Donald Duck On His Friction Fire Engine, four actions, 1950s, 12" long	300	525	700
Climbing Fireman, includes three tin ladder sections, five actions, 1950s, 24" high assembled	200	300	400
Climbing Linesman, includes three tin pole sections, three actions, rare, 1950s, 24" high when assembled	250	375	500
Clown and Lion, four actions, 1960s, 11-3/4" high from base to top of tree	250	375	500
Clown Circus Car, five actions, 1960s, 8-1/2" long, 9" high	100	175	235
Clown on Unicycle, three actions, 1960s, 10-1/2" high	180	280	375

	C6	C8	C10
Clown the Magician, No. 40244, includes card-ribbon apparatus for card trick, six actions, 1950s, 12" tall	200	300	400
Clown with Lion, includes spiral apparatus, four actions, 1950s, 12" high	200	300	400
Clowns Bank, The, all plastic, unmarked, minor toy, 1940s, 10" high	80	120	160
Coca-Cola Dispenser Bank, includes four plastic Coke glasses and rubber stopper, minor toy, 1950s, 9-1/2" tall	450	675	900
Cock-A-Doodle-Doo Rooster, four actions, 1950s, 8" high	80	120	160
Colonel Hap Hazard Robot, four actions, 1968, 11-1/4" tall	300	440	600
Combi-O-Mixer, mixer-blender, minor toy, 1950s, 9" long, 9" high	30	45	60
Comic Hungry Bug, VW auto, five actions, 1970s, 7-3/4" long	40	60	80
Comic Musical Car, four actions, 1960s, 6" long, 8-1/2" tall	70	105	140
Comic Road Grader, four actions, 1950s, 9" long	70	105	140

	C6	C8	C10
Comic Road Roller, four actions, 1960s, 9" long	70	105	140
Coney Island Penny Machine, includes plastic prizes, minor toy, 1950s, 13" high	90	130	300
Coney Island Rocket Ride, four actions, 1950s, 13-1/2" high	300	450	600
Continental Blue Locomotive, four actions, 1960s, 12-1/2" long	30	45	60
Corvair Bertone, four actions, 1970s, 12" long	50	75	100
Cowboy Riding Horse, three actions, 1950s, 7" high	70	105	140
Cragstan Astronaut, four actions, 1950s, 14" tall	400	600	800
Cragstan Beep Beep Greyhound Bus, three actions, 1950s, 20" long	100	150	220
Cragstan Biplane 7F18, five actions, 1950s, 12" long, 14-3/8" wingspan	220	330	440
Cragstan Biplane 7F7, U.S. Navy, four actions, 1950s, 9-1/2" long, 11-1/2" wingspan	200	300	400

Comic Musical Car, T-N Co., 1960s, $140. Photo courtesy Don Hultzman and Ron Chojnacki

Box for Cragstan Crapshooter

Cragstan Crapshooter (loose), "Y" Co., 1950s, $200

Cragstan Mother Goose, "Y" Co., 1960s, $200.
Photo courtesy Don Hultzman and Ron Chojnacki

	C6	C8	C10
Cragstan Crapshooter, includes pair of small dice, four actions, 1950s, 9-1/2" tall	100	150	200
Cragstan Crapshooting Monkey, includes pair of small dice, three actions, 1950s, 9" tall	100	150	200
Cragstan Dishwasher Automatic, includes twenty-four-piece dish set, two dish baskets and metal tray, minor toy, 1960s, 9" high	50	75	100
Cragstan Firebird III, three actions, 1950s, 11-1/2" long	400	600	800
Cragstan Flying Plane with Pylon Tower, minor toy, 1950s, plane 8" long, 9-1/2" wingspan, tower 26" high	120	180	240
Cragstan Great Astronaut, five actions, 1960s, 14" tall	500	750	1000

	C6	C8	C10
Cragstan Mother Goose, six actions, 1960s, 8-1/4" high	100	150	200
Cragstan Mr. Robot, four actions, 1960s, 10-1/2" tall	350	525	700
Cragstan One-Arm Bandit, three actions, includes 3" x 3-1/4" sign, 1960s, 6-1/4" high	100	150	200
Cragstan Peanut Vendor, includes felt hat, five actions, 1950s, 8" tall	180	270	360
Cragstan Playboy, five actions, 1960s, 13" high	75	150	200
Cragstan Roulette, A Gambling Man,, includes steel ball, chips, tin table, game sheet, five actions, 1960s, 9" tall	150	225	300
Cragstan Satellite, 1950s, 8" diameter, 5-1/2" high	90	135	180
Cragstan Smoking Jet Plane - U.S.A.F., four actions, 1950s, 11-1/2" long, 7-1/2" wingspan	120	180	240
Cragstan Talking Robot, three actions, 1960s, 10-1/2" tall	400	550	800
Cragstan Telly Bear, six actions, 1950s, 8" high	240	360	480
Cragstan Tootin'-Chugging Locomotive, longest single-piece battery toy made, three actions, 1950s, 24" long	70	105	140
Cragstan Tugboat, three actions, 1950s, 12-3/4" long	140	210	280

Cycling Daddy, Bandai Co., 1960s, $225

	C6	C8	C10
Cragstan Two Gun Sheriff, includes tin hat, five actions, 1950s, 9-1/2" tall	175	225	300
Cragstan Vertol 1107 Helicopter Soldiers, includes rotors, four actions, 1950s, 13-1/2" long	120	180	240
Cragstan Western Locomotive, four actions, 1950s, 12" long	60	90	120
Crane Tractor, 1950s, 7-1/2" long, 11-1/2" high extended	70	105	140

Cymbal Playing Turnover Monkey, T-N Co., 1960s, $100

	C6	C8	C10
Crawling Baby, minor toy, 1940s, 11" long, 8-1/2" high	50	75	100
Crazy Car, five actions, 1950s, 9" long	60	90	120
Cycling Daddy, four actions, 1960s, 10" high	125	175	225
Cyclist Clown, five actions, 1950s, 9" high	200	300	400
Cyclist Clown, seven actions, 1950s, 7" high	200	300	400
Cyclist Clown, six actions, 1950s, 6-1/2" high	200	300	400
Cymbal Playing Turnover Monkey, three actions, 1960s, 8" tall	50	75	100
Daisy the Jolly Drumming Duck, includes detachable drum and cymbals, seven actions, rare, 1950s, 9" high	150	200	275
Dalmatian One-Man Band, No. 90262, includes cymbals and stand, six actions, 1950s, 9" high	120	180	240
Dancing Merry Chimp, five actions, 1960s, 11" tall	100	150	200

Dancing Merry Chimp, Kuramochi Co. (C-K), 1960s, $200

Left to Right: Dennis the Menace (Playing London Bridge), 1950s, $240; Chimp with Xylophone, "Y" Co., 1970s, $200. Photo courtesy Don Hultzman and Ron Chojnacki

	C6	C8	C10
Dancing Sweethearts, minor toy, 1950s, 7" tall	90	135	180
Dandy the Happy Drumming Pup, includes detachable drum and cymbals, six actions, 1950s, 8-1/2" high	85	150	200
Dapper Jigger Dancer, minor toy, 1950s, 12" tall	150	225	300
Dennis the Menace (Playing London Bridge), includes xylophone Rosko, three actions, 1950s, 9" high	120	180	240
Dentist Bear, includes detachable head, seven actions, 1950s, 9-1/2" tall, 6-3/4" x 4-1/4" base	300	450	600
Desert Patrol Jeep, includes turret gunner, four actions, 1960s, 11" long	90	135	180

	C6	C8	C10
Destroyer 206 Boat, includes detachable antenna and five depth charges, six actions, 1950s, 14" long	110	165	220
Diesel Locomotive, minor toy, 1950s, 16-1/2" long	30	45	60
Dino Robot, five actions, 1960s, 11" tall	500	750	1000
Disney Acrobats (Mickey, Donald and Pluto), minor toys, 1950s, 9" high	300	625	800
Disney Fire Engine, four actions, 1950s, 11" long	425	660	880
Disneyland Fire Engine, five actions, 1950s, 18" long	350	550	750
Docking Rocket, includes plastic radar antenna, six actions, 1960s, 16" long, 24" extended	100	150	200
Dog Family, four actions, 1960s, 11" long	50	75	100
Dog Sled, four actions, rare, 1950s, 14" long	300	450	600
Dolly Dressmaker, includes cloth sample, Dolly Seamstress on box, ten actions, rare, 1950s, 7" high	175	250	325
Donald Duck, four actions, 1960s, 8" tall	200	300	400
Donald Duck Locomotive, three actions, 1970s, 9" long	150	225	300
Donald Duck Trolley, three actions, 1960s, 11" high	160	240	320

Dentist Bear, S&E Co., 1950s, $600. Photo courtesy Don Hultzman and Ron Chojnacki

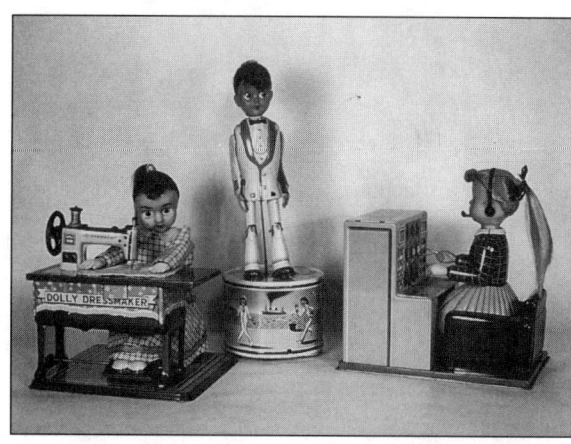

Left to Right: Dolly Dressmaker, T-N Co., 1950s, $325; Strutting My Fair Dancer (Dancing Sailor Girl), Haji Co., 1950s, $200; Switchboard Operator, Linemar, 1950s, $800. Photo courtesy Don Hultzman and Ron Chojnacki

	C6	C8	C10
Douglas C-124 Globe Master, eight actions, c. 1950s, 20-1/2" wingspan, 18" long	300	450	600
Douglas DC-9TWA Jet Plane, four actions, 1960s, 14" long, 17" wingspan	100	150	200
Doxie the Dog, five actions, 1950s, 9" long	20	25	45
Dozo the Steaming Clown, Rosko toys, five actions, 1960s, 10" tall	200	300	400
Dream Boat Hot Rod, four actions, c. 1950s, 7" long	140	210	280
Drill, includes attachments, minor toy, 1950s, 6" long	20	30	40
Drinker's Savings Bank, minor toy, 1960s, 9" high	90	135	180
Drinking Bear, six actions, c. 1970s, 12" high	75	125	150
Drinking Captain, six actions, 1960s, 12" tall	100	150	200
Drinking Dog, four actions, 1950s	90	135	180
Drinking Licking Cat, six actions, 1950s, 10" high, 4" x 4" base	120	180	240
Drum Bear, five actions (walks, lights, beats drum, noise), c. 1950s, 7-3/4" tall	150	225	300

Drinking Captain, S&E Co., 1960s, $200

	C6	C8	C10
Drum Monkey, three actions, 1970s, 8" high	40	60	80
Drummer Bear, six actions, 1950s, 10" tall	140	210	280
Drumming Mickey Mouse, four actions, rare, 1950s, 10" tall	800	1000	1600
Drumming Polar Bear, three actions, 1960s, 12" tall	75	120	165
Ducky Duckling, four actions, 1960s, 8" high	35	55	85
Dump Truck, No. 7343, seven actions, 1960s, 10-1/4" long	60	90	120
Dynamic Fighter Robot, five actions, 1960s, 10" tall	70	105	140
Earthman-Astronaut, five actions, rare, 1950s, 9-1/2" tall	900	1300	1800
El Toro-Cragstan Bullfighter, includes detachable tin matador, four actions, 1950s, 9-1/2" long	90	145	200
Electric Powered TV and Radio Station, three actions, 1950s, 30" long	80	120	160
Electric Remote Control Robot, four actions, rare, 1950s, 7-1/2" tall	500	750	1000
Electric Robot, five actions, 1950s, 14-1/2" tall	300	450	600
Electric School Bus, minor toy, 1950s, 9-1/2" long	70	105	140
Electric Vibraphone, three actions, 1950s, 7-1/2" long, 5-1/2" high	70	105	140
Electro Special Racer, three actions, 1950s, 10" long	500	750	1000
Electro Train Transcontinental, three pieces, three actions, 1950s, 20-1/2" long	90	135	180
Electronic Countdown, six actions, 1959, 24" long	60	90	120
Electronic Fighter Jet 4800, eleven actions, 1950s, 19" long	120	180	240
Electronic Fire House, includes plastic fire engine, minor toy, 1940s, 7" square	70	105	140
Electronic Periscope (Nautilus) Firing Range, three actions, 1950s, 11" high on tripod	100	150	200
Electronic Twin Train Set, No. 372, includes two three-piece trains, minor toy, 1950s, 28" long, 11" wide	100	150	200

	C6	C8	C10
Engine Robot, four actions, 1960s, 9-1/2" tall	100	150	200
Excavator Robot, four actions, 1960s, 10" tall	200	300	400
Expert Motor Cyclist, five actions, rare, 1950s, 12" long	600	900	1200
F.D. Fire Engine, four actions, 1960s, 10" long, 12" high when ladder is extended	110	165	220
F-101A Voodoo Fighter, minor toy, 1960s, 15" long, 14" wingspan	100	150	200
F-14-A Navy Jet Fighter, six actions, 1960s, 13" long, 13" wingspan	200	300	400
Fairyland Loco, locomotive, four actions, 1950s, 9" long	60	90	120
Farm Truck, three actions, 1960s, 11" long	120	180	240
Farm Truck, five actions, 1950s, 9" long	120	180	240
Feeding Bird Watcher, includes detachable tin branch and bird, five action, rare, 1950s, 9" high	300	350	600
Ferris Wheel Truck, four actions, c. 1950s, 11" long	400	600	800
Fido the Xylophone Player, includes detachable xylophone, six actions (body sways, head turns, arms activate lights and sound), c. 1950s, 8-3/4" high	115	170	240

Left to Right: Fighting Spaceman, S-H Co., 1960s, $300; Turn Signal Robot Auto Accessory, T-N Co., 1960s, $320. Photo courtesy Don Hultzman and Ron Chojnacki

	C6	C8	C10
Fighter (airplane), six actions, 1960s, 10-1/2" long, 9" wingspan	160	240	320
Fighter Airplane, four actions, c. 1960s, 7" wingspan	60	90	120
Fighter Jet, four actions, c. 1960s, 7" wingspan	60	90	120
Fighting Bull, five actions, 1960s, 9-1/2" long	100	125	150
Fighting Bull, four actions, two cycles, 1970s, 12" long nose to tail tip	100	150	200
Fighting Robot, all plastic, four actions, 1970s, 10" tall	70	105	140
Fighting Spaceman, five actions, 1960s, 12" tall	150	225	300
Fire Boat, five actions, 1950s, 15" long	150	225	300
Fire Chief, No. 8, three actions, 1960s, 11-1/4" long	90	135	180
Fire Chief Mystery Action Car, four actions, 1960s, 9-3/4" long	130	195	260
Fire Command Car, five actions, 1950s	170	255	340
Fire Engine, four actions, 1950s, 9" long	120	180	240
Fire Engine, three actions, 1950s, 9" long, ladder extends 13"	150	225	300
Fire Engine, three actions, c. 1950s, 8" long	100	150	200
Fire Engine, six actions, 1950s, 12" long, ladder extends 16"	100	150	200
Fire Patrol Boat, three actions, 1950s, 12" long	110	165	220
Fire Tricycle, four actions, 1950s, 9-1/2" long	180	270	360
Firebird Racer, four actions, 1950s, 14-1/4" long	300	450	600
Fishing Bear (also Fishing Panda Bear, Polar Bear, Forest Bear), includes detachable pond, tin fish, six actions, 1950s, 10" high	200	300	400
Fishing Bears Bank, six actions, rare, 1950s, 9-1/2" tall	500	750	1000
Flashing Jet-FC-657 Airplane-U.S.A.F. 7452, four actions, 1950s, 7" long, 6" wingspan	100	150	200
Flashy Jim, minor toy, rare, 1950s, 7-3/4" tall	1100	1650	2200

	C6	C8	C10
Flashy Ray Space Gun, minor toy, 1950s, 18-1/2" long	50	75	100
Flintstone Yacht, 1961, 17" long	90	145	200
Floating Satellite Target Game, The, includes tin gun, rubber-tipped darts and celluloid ball, 1960s, 8-1/2" high	100	150	200
Flutter Birds, includes detachable pulley assembly, six actions, rare, 1950s, 26-1/2" high when assembled	300	450	600
Flying Dutchman-PH-KLM Airliner, five actions, 1950s, 11" long, 14" wingspan	100	150	200
Flying Jet Plane-Boeing 747P, five actions, 1960s, 13" long, 12" wingspan	90	135	180
Flying Platform, includes detachable tin soldier, four actions, rare, 1950s, 5-1/2" diameter, 9" high	200	300	400
Flying Tiger Airplane, four actions w/remote control, 1960s, 7" long, 7" wingspan	60	90	120
Ford Model T, includes detachable tin roof, four actions, 1950s, 10-1/4" long	60	90	120
Ford Mustang 2 x 2, four actions, 1960s, 16" long	60	90	120
Ford Skyliner, four actions, 1950s, 9" long	100	150	200
Fork Lift Truck, minor toy, 1960s, 10-1/4" high	80	120	160
Foto Finish, racehorse, minor toy, 1950s, 12" long	120	180	240
Frankenstein, w/five actions, remote control, 1950s, 12" tall	600	900	1200
Frankenstein Monster, six actions, 1960s, 14" tall	125	175	225
Frankie the Rollerskating Monkey, 1950s, 12" tall	150	225	300
Fred Flintstone Bedrock Band, four actions, 1962, 9-1/2" high	500	650	1000
Fred Flintstone on Dino, eight actions, 1961, 22" long	400	600	800
Friendly Jocko My Favorite Pet, includes detachable cymbals, plastic cup, five actions, 1950s, 8" high	110	175	245

	C6	C8	C10
Fruit Juice Counter, includes plastic barrel, lid, glasses and tin tray, three actions, 1960s, 8" long, 8" high	90	135	180
FS-059 Fighter Plane, jet w/prop, five actions, 1950s, 11" long, 13" wingspan	170	255	340
Funland Cup Ride, includes six umbrellas, three actions, 1960s, 7" tall, 6" x 6" base	100	150	200
Galloping Cowboy Savings Bank, minor toy, rare, 1950s, 8" high, 6-1/2" long	450	675	900
Gama Mercedes-Benz 220 SE Sedan, three actions, 1960s, 9" long	150	225	300
Gear Robot, four actions, 1960s, 10" tall	250	375	500
Gino the Neapolitan Balloon Blower, includes bubble solution plastic tray, five actions, 1960s, 10" tall	100	150	200
Girl with Baby Carriage, three actions, 1960s, 8" high	100	150	200
Godzilla, five actions, 1960s, 10-1/2" tall	300	450	600
Godzilla Monster, three actions, 1970s, 11-1/2" tall	150	200	300
Go-Go Girl, (bar toy), minor toy, risqué toy, PG-rated, 1969, 15-1/4" tall	40	60	80
Go-Kart, includes control wire w/steering key, minor toy, 1960s, 6-1/2" long	90	135	180

Gino the Neapolitan Balloon Blower, Tomiyama Co. (Rosko), 1960s, $200

Go-Go Girl, Poynter Prod. Co., 1969, $80. Photo courtesy Don Hultzman and Ron Chojnacki

	C6	C8	C10
Go-Kart, includes detachable head, three actions, 1950s, 10" long	90	135	180
Golden Gear Robot, five actions, 1960s, 9" tall	300	450	600
Golden Locomotive, minor toy, 1950s, 10-1/2" long	40	60	80
Golden Roto Robot, five actions, 1960s, 8-1/2" tall	100	150	200
Gomora Monster, includes plastic missiles, four actions, 1960s, 8" tall	150	225	300
Good Time Charlie, seven actions, 1960s, 12" tall	100	150	200
Gorilla, white or brown, five actions, 1950s, 9-1/4" tall	200	300	400
Go-Stop Benz Racer, three actions, 1950s, 11" long	150	225	300
Grace Ocean Liner, three actions, 1950s, 15" long	250	375	500
Grandpa Bear, includes rocking chair, five actions, 1950s, 9" tall	175	250	325
Grand-Pa Car, four actions, 1950s, 9" long	75	100	125

	C6	C8	C10
Granpa Panda Bear, five actions, 1950s, 9" tall	100	175	245
Great Garloo, The, includes chain and medallion, seven actions, 1960s, 23" tall	300	450	600
Green Caterpillar, three actions, 1950s, 19-1/2" long	150	250	350
Greyhound Bus, minor toy, 1950s, 7-1/4" long	90	135	180
Greyhound Bus Scenicruiser, three actions, 1950s, 16" long	90	135	180
Greyhound Bus with Headlights, three actions, 1950s, 10-1/4" long	100	150	200
Grumman F9F Navy Jet, Cougar, three actions, 1950s, 11-1/2" long	150	225	300
Guided Missile Launcher, includes plastic missiles, three actions, 1950s, 8" long, 3" tall, 5" wide	110	165	220
Gypsy Fortune Teller, includes twenty fortune cards, five actions, rare, 1950s, 12" high w/hat, 5-3/4" x 7" base	1100	1700	2200
Hamburger Chef, includes tin frying pan, hamburger, plastic bottles, three actions, 1960s, 8" long, 8" high	125	200	275
Handy Hank Mystery Tractor, four actions, 1950s, 9" long	75	100	125
Happy Band Trios, seven actions, rare, 1970s, 12" high	400	600	800

Gypsy Fortune Teller, Ichida Co., 1950s, $2200. Photo courtesy Don Hultzman and Ron Chojnacki

	C6	C8	C10
Happy Clown Car, three actions, 1960s, 6-1/2" long	100	150	200
Happy Clown Theater, w/Pinocchio-like puppet, three actions, 1950s, 10" tall	200	300	400
Happy Fiddler Clown, The, includes tin litho violin, four actions, 1950s, 9-1/2" high	200	300	425
Happy Miner, three actions, 1960s, 11" tall	110	165	220
Happy 'N' Sad Face Cymbal Clown, five actions, 1960s, 10" tall	120	180	200
Happy Naughty Chimp, four actions, 1960s, 9-1/2" high assembled	75	100	150
Happy Plane, three actions, 1960s, 9" long, 10-1/2" wingspan	100	150	200
Happy Santa, three actions, 1960s, 11" tall	100	150	200
Happy Santa (walking), five actions, 1950s, 11" tall	150	225	300
Happy Santa One-Man Band, includes cymbals and stand, six actions, 1950s, 9" high	100	185	245
Happy Singing Bird, three actions, 1950s, 9" high, bird 3" long, 5-5/8" diameter base	60	90	120

Haunted House Mystery Bank (Disneyland promotion), Brumberger Co., 1960s, $550. Photo courtesy Don Hultzman and Ron Chojnacki

	C6	C8	C10
Happy the Clown Puppet Show, w/Pinocchio-like puppet, three actions, 1960s, 10" tall	190	285	380
Happy Tractor, four actions, 1960s, 8" long	40	60	80
Happy'n Sad Magic Face Clown, five actions, 1960s, 10" tall	150	225	300
Harbor Queen Boat, minor toy, 1950s, 12" long	150	225	300
Hasty Chimp, four actions, 1960s, 9" high	50	75	100
Haunted House Mystery Bank (Disneyland promotion), four actions, 1960s, 7-5/8" high	300	425	550
Heavy Machine Gun, includes detachable tripod and plastic ammo belt, four actions, 1950s, 24" long, 13" high on tripod	100	150	200
Hi Bouncer Moon Scout Robot, includes five plastic balls, five actions, rare, 1968, 11-1/4" tall	450	675	900
High Jinks of the Circus, six actions, 1950s, 14" high, extends to 29"	250	350	450
Highway Drive, includes tin magnetic car, three actions, 1950s, 15-1/2" long	70	105	140
Highway Patrol Jeep, four actions, 1950s, 10" long	70	105	140
Highway Patrol Police Special, five actions, 1960s, 11-1/2" long	100	150	200
Highway Skill Driving, three actions, 1960s, 13" long	70	105	140
Hiller Hornet Helicopter, four actions, 1950s, 12-1/4" long, 15" two-piece metal rotor	120	180	240
Hippo Chef (Cuty Cook), includes chef hat and tin litho egg, five actions, 1960s, 10" tall	100	160	300
H-O Gauge Electric Train Set with Real Smoke, seventeen-piece set, 1960s, 23" long	70	105	140
Hobo Clown with Accordion (with cymbal-playing monkey), six actions, 1950s, 10-1/2" high	275	425	525
Hole-in-One Bank, includes marked test coin and golfer, no marking, minor toy, 1960s, 8-1/2" long x 3-1/2" wide	70	105	140

	C6	C8	C10
Holiday Sink-Stove Combination, includes three-piece pan set, minor toy, 1950s, 9" high	40	60	80
Hoop Zing Girl, minor toy, 1950s, 11-1/2" tall	115	185	245
Hoopy the Fishing Duck, includes magnetic fish and detachable pond, seven actions, 1950s, 10" high	275	375	525
Hootin' Hollow Haunted House, eight actions, 1960s, 11" high	500	750	1000
Hooty the Happy Owl, six actions, 1960s, 9" tall	65	100	145
Hot Rod Car, minor toy, 1950s, 10" long	160	240	320
Hot Rod Custom 'T' Ford, four actions, 1960s, 10-1/2" long	180	270	360
Hot Rod Limousine, four actions, 1960s, 10-1/2" long	180	270	360
Hungry Baby Bear, six actions, 1950s, 9-1/2" tall	200	300	400
Hungry Cat, includes tin tray and plastic fish, seven actions, 1960s, 9" high	250	450	700

Hysterical Robot, The (a.k.a. Hysterical Harry and Happy Harry), S-H Co., 1960s, $300. Photo courtesy Don Hultzman and Ron Chojnacki

	C6	C8	C10
Hungry Hound Dog, six actions, 1950s, 9-1/2" high	150	275	300
Hungry Sheep, three actions, two cycles, 1950s, 9" long	100	150	200
Hy Que Monkey, six actions, 1960s, 17" tall	150	225	300
Hysterical Robot, The (a.k.a. Hysterical Harry and Happy Harry), seven actions, 1960s, 13-1/2" tall	150	225	300
Ice Cream Baby Bear, three actions, rare, 1950s, 9-1/2" high	200	300	400
Ice Cream Truck, five actions, 1960s, 10-1/2" long	100	150	200
Indian Joe, four actions, 1960s, 12" tall	75	110	150
Indian Signal Choo Choo, four actions, 1960s, 9-1/2" long	80	120	160
Interceptor, target game, four actions, 1950s, 13" high, 16" wingspan	150	225	300
Interplanetary Rocket, five actions, 1960s, 14-3/4" tall	120	180	240
JDN 7673 Sedan-4-door, minor toy and one of the earliest battery-operated toys, rare, 1920s, 14" long	400	600	800
Jeep, No. 10560, minor toy, 1950s, 5-1/2" long	70	105	140
Jeep USA, minor toy, 1950s, 12-1/2" long	70	105	140
Jet Airport with 4 Jet Airplanes, seven actions, 1960s, 12-1/2" long	200	275	350
Jet Plane Base, includes crank, seven actions, rare, 1950s, 7-1/4" x 11" base, plane 9" long, 7" wingspan	450	675	900
Jig-Saw-Matic, minor toy, 1950s, 7-1/4" high, 4-1/2" x 8-1/2"	40	60	80
Jocko the Drinking Monkey, includes top hat, four actions, 1950s, 11" tall	100	150	200
John's Farm Truck, seven actions, 1950s, 9" long	100	150	200
Jo-Jo the Flipping Monkey, minor toy, 1970s, 10" high	35	75	80
Jolly Bambino, includes candy pieces, five actions, 1950s, 9" high	200	300	400
Jolly Bear Peanut Vendor, The, includes felt hat, five actions, 1950s, 8" high	250	285	500
Jolly Bear the Drummer Boy, five actions, 1950s, 7" tall	100	150	200

	C6	C8	C10
Jolly Bear with Robin, three actions, rare, 1950s, 10" high	400	600	800
Jolly Daddy, four actions, 1950s, 8-3/4" tall	160	240	350
Jolly Drummer Chimpy, includes cymbals and stand, six actions, 1950s, 9" high	100	125	150
Jolly Drumming Bear, four actions, 1950s, 7" tall	100	125	150
Jolly Penguin, five actions, 1950s, 7" tall	100	150	200
Jolly Pianist, five actions, 1950s, 8" high	100	150	200
Jolly Santa on Snow, includes tin skis, four actions, two cycles, 1950s, 12-1/2" tall	150	225	300
Josie the Walking Cow, seven actions, two cycles, 1950s, 14" long, 8-1/2" high	125	175	225
Journey Pup, four actions, remote control, c. 1950s, 7-1/2" long	75	100	125
Jumbo the Bubble-Blowing Elephant, includes plastic bowl for bubble solution, three actions, 1950s, 7-1/4" high	55	85	115
Jungle Jumbo, six actions, two cycles, hunter resembles Teddy Roosevelt, 1950s, 10" high	200	300	400
Jungle Trio, includes tin litho whistle, eight actions, 1950s, 8" high	400	600	800

Jungle Jumbo, B.C. Co., 1950s, $400. Photo courtesy Don Hultzman and Ron Chojnacki

Jolly Penguin, T-N Co., 1950s, $200. Photo courtesy Don Hultzman and Ron Chojnacki

	C6	C8	C10
Jupiter Robot, four actions, 1950s, 12-3/4" tall	150	225	300
Jupiter Rocket Launching Pad, 1960s, 8-1/2" long, 7" high	190	285	380
K-55 Electric Tractor, three actions, c. 1950s, 7" long	70	105	140
King Flying Saucer, three actions, 1960s, 7-1/2" diameter	70	105	140
King Size Fire Engine, three actions, 1960s, 12-1/2" long	150	225	300
Kissing Couple, five actions, 1950s, 10-3/4" long	150	200	300
Kitchen-ette Stove and Sink, no marking, minor toy, includes kitchen utensils and side tray and stoppers, 1940s, 6-1/2" long x 6-3/4" high	50	75	100
Knight in Armor, five actions, rare, 1950s, 10" tall	1100	1650	2200
Knight in Armor Target Game, includes crossbow and rubber tipped darts, three actions, 1950s, 12" tall	200	300	400
Knitting Grandma, three actions, 1950s, 8-1/1" tall	175	250	350
Kooky-Spooky Whistling Tree, w/two color schemes, six actions, 1950s, 14-1/4" tall	450	760	1600
Ladder Fire Engine, five actions, 1950s, 13" long	170	255	340
Lady Pup Tending Her Garden, five actions, 1950s, 8" high	200	275	400

	C6	C8	C10
Lambo with Magnetic Trunk and Light, includes two tin logs and trailer, seven actions, rare, 1950s, 16" long w/trailer	250	375	500
Laughing Clown, The, seven actions, 1960s, 14" tall	160	240	320
Lectric Revolver, three actions, 1950s, 11-1/2" long	40	60	80
Leo the Growling Pet Lion with Magic Face Change, three actions, two cycles, 1970s, 9" long	100	150	200
Light House, includes detachable spin-ball tower, five actions, rare, 1950s, 8-1/2" high, 6-3/4" x 6-3/4" base	600	900	1200
Lighted Freight Train, five pieces w/eight-section track, four actions, 1950s, 25-1/2" long	70	105	140
Lighted Space Vehicle with Floating Satellite, includes celluloid ball, three actions, 1960s, 8-1/2" long	150	225	300
Linda Lee Laundromat, washing machine, minor toy, 1940s, 6-1/2" high	30	45	60
Linemar Music Hall, four actions, 1950s, 8" high, 7-3/4" x 5-1/2" base	100	120	200
Lion, four actions, 1950s, 9" long	100	150	200
Lion Target Game, includes dart gun and darts, four actions, 1950s, 7-1/2" high	120	180	240
Locomotive Continental Blue, four actions, 1970s, 13" long	40	60	80
Loop the Loop Clown, minor toy, 1960s, 10" high	60	120	175

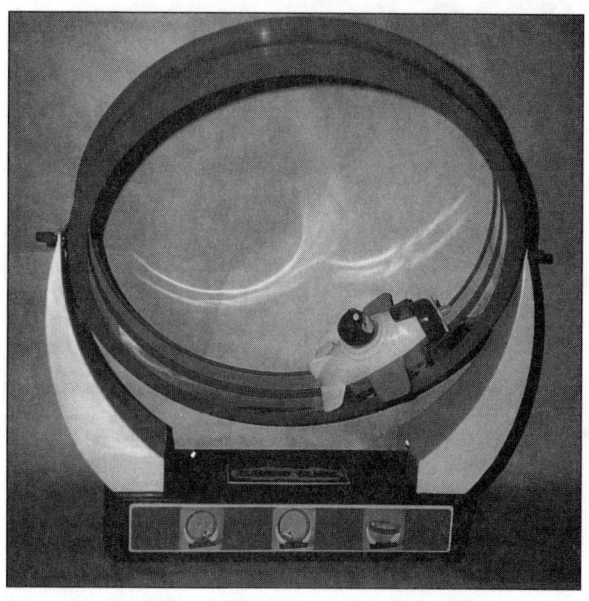

Looping Airplane, "Y" Co. Sears (distributor), 1960s, $80. Photo courtesy Don Hultzman and Ron Chojnacki

	C6	C8	C10
Looping Airplane, minor toy, 1960s, 14-1/2" high, airplane 5" long	40	60	80
Looping Space Tank, five actions, 1960s, 8" long	300	450	600
Los Walky-Son, includes detachable rifles and baton, 1960s, 11-1/2" high, 15" wide	120	180	240
Loser, The (Bar Toy), three actions, c. 1971, 13" high	40	60	80
Lost in Space Robot, three actions, 1966, 13" tall	200	300	400
Love-Beetle-Volks, three actions, 1960s, 10" long	60	90	120
Lucky Crane, includes tin prizes, five actions, rare, 1950s, 8-1/1" high	400	600	800
Lucky Locomotive, four actions, 1950s, 8" long	40	60	80
Lucky Seven Dice-Throwing Monkey, includes plastic straw hat, five dice, two game sheets, twenty chips, five actions, 1960s, 11-1/2" tall	50	75	100
Lufthansa Jet Airplane, three actions, 1960s, 19-1/2" long, 18-1/2" wingspan	110	165	220
Lunar Captain, five actions, 1960s, 13-1/2" long extended	110	165	220

Linemar Music Hall, Linemar Co., 1950s, $200. Photo courtesy Don Hultzman and Ron Chojnacki

Mac the Turtle, "Y" Co., 1960s, $185. Photo courtesy Don Hultzman and Ron Chojnacki

	C6	C8	C10
Lunar Loop/Swing and Orbiting Action, three actions, 1960s, 14" high, 12" diameterhoop	100	150	200
M-101 Aston-Martin Secret Ejector Car, includes ejectable passenger, six actions, 1960s, 11" long	200	300	400
Mac the Turtle, five actions, 1960s, 8" high	85	135	185
Magic Action Bulldozer, three actions, 1950s, 9-1/2" long	100	150	200
Magic Color Moon Express, four actions, 1960s, 13" long	100	150	200
Magic Man Clown, five actions, 1950s, 11" tall	260	385	525
Magic Snowman, includes detachable tin broom, plastic pipe, and styro ball, four actions, 1950s, 11-1/4" tall	125	190	265
Magnet Rail Moon Orbiter, minor toy, 1960s, 14" high, 12" diameter	70	105	140
Main Street, three actions, rare, 1950s, 19-1/2" long	600	1000	2000
Major Tooty, includes drum and hat, three actions, 1960s, 14" tall	85	130	175
Make Up Bear, four actions, rare, 1960s, 9" high	500	750	1000
Mambo the Jolly Drumming Elephant, includes cymbals and stand, six actions, 1950s, 9-1/2" high	90	150	200

	C6	C8	C10
Man in Space Astronaut, minor toy, 1960s, 6" tall	100	150	200
Mars Explorer, astronaut, six actions, 1960s, 10" tall	250	375	500
Mars Explorer, robot, seven actions, 1950s, 9-1/2" tall	200	300	400
Mars King Robot, No. 12101, four actions, 1960s, 9-1/2" tall	210	315	420
Marshal Wild Bill, includes tin cowboy hat, four actions, two cycles, 1950s, 10-1/2" tall	180	280	375
Martian Robot, four actions, 1970s, 12" tall	75	100	125
Marvelous Car, T-Bird, three actions, 1956, 11" long	250	375	500
Marvelous Fire Engine, four actions, 1960s, 11" long	100	150	200
Marvelous Mike, four actions, 1950s, 17" long	100	175	245
Maxwell Coffee-Loving Bear, five actions, 1960s, 10" tall	100	150	200
McGregor, six actions, 1960s, 12" tall when standing	125	175	225
Mechanic Robot, five actions, 1960s, 12" tall	150	225	300

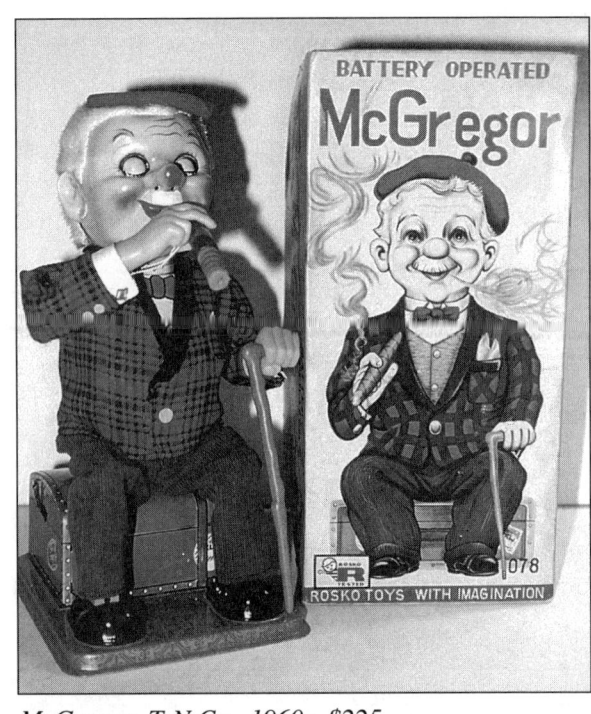

McGregor, T-N Co., 1960s, $225

	C6	C8	C10
Mechanized Robot, The (Robby), our actions, rare, 1950s, 13-1/2" tall	600	900	1200
Mercury Explorer, five actions, 1960s, 8" long	120	180	240
Mercury X-1 Space Saucer, four actions, 1960s, 8" diameter	70	105	140
Merry Christmas Santa In His Rockin' Chair, includes detachable tree and stocking, three actions, rare, 1950s, 21" tall assembled	500	750	1000
Merry Ice Cream Truck, five actions, 1960s, 10-1/2" long	90	135	180
Mexicali Pete-Drum Player, three actions, 1960s, 10-1/2" high	60	90	120
Mickey Mouse and Donald Duck Fire Engine, three actions, 1960s, 16" long	300	450	600
Mickey Mouse Locomotive, six actions, 1960s, 9" long	200	300	400
Mickey Mouse Melody Railroad, includes four circular rails w/xylophone bars, minor toy, rare, 1960s, handcar 6-3/4" long	800	1200	1600
Mickey Mouse on Handcar, three actions, 1960s, 9-3/4" long, 7-3/4" high	350	500	650
Mickey Mouse Sand Buggy, four actions, 1960s, 11" long	150	225	300
Mickey Mouse Trolley, three actions, 1960s, 11" high	150	225	300
Mickey the Magician, includes tin rabbit, four actions, 1960s, 10" tall	785	1200	2500
Mighty Kong, five actions, 1950s, 11" tall	250	375	500
Mighty Mike the Barbell Lifter Bear, four actions, 1950s, 10-1/2" tall	150	225	300
Mighty Robot, four actions, 1960s, 11-1/2" tall	900	1350	1800
Military Air Defense Truck, four actions, 1950s, 15-1/4" long	100	150	200
Military Command Car, five actions, 1950s, 11" long	150	225	300
Military Jet Plane, three actions, 1960s, 16" long, 14" wingspan	100	150	200
Military Police Car, six actions, 1950s, 8-1/2" long	100	150	200

	C6	C8	C10
Million Bus, three actions, rare, 1950s, 12" long	1250	1875	2500
Mimi Poodle with Bone, includes plastic bone, five actions, two cycles, 1950s, 11" long, 10" high	50	75	100
Mischievous Monkey, includes tree and monkey, six actions, 1950s, 18" tall	200	300	400
Mischievous Monkey with Bulldog, four actions, 1950s, 12" high	220	330	440
Miss Friday the Typist, w/removable head, six actions, 1950s, 8" tall	150	225	300
Missile Robot Mr. 45, five actions, 17-1/2" tall	100	150	200
Mix-ette Mixer, includes mixer stand and bowl, minor toy, 1940s, 9" high when assembled	30	45	60
Mobile Satellite Tracking Station, includes detachable antenna, six actions, 1960s, 9" long	400	600	800
Mobile Space TV Unit with Trailer, six actions, rare, 1960s	500	750	1000
Mod Monster Blushing Frankenstein, five actions, 1960s, 13-1/4" tall	150	225	300
Modern Robot, four actions, rare, 1950s, 12" tall	450	675	900
Monkee Mobile, minor toy, 1967, 12" long	300	450	600
Monkey Handcar, three actions, 1950s, 7" high	70	105	140
Monkey on a Picnic, seven actions, 1950s, 9-1/2" high	150	225	300
Monorail Rocket Ship, minor toy, 1950s, 10" long w/supports and rail rods	140	210	280
Monster Robot, three actions, 1970s, 10" tall	100	125	150
Moon Astronaut, four actions, 1950s, 9" tall	500	750	1000
Moon Explorer Robot, five actions, rare, 1960s, 17-1/2" tall (feet to antenna top)	600	900	1200
Moon Explorer Vehicle, five actions, 1960s, 11" long	150	225	300
Moon Express, Magic Color, three actions, 1950s, 12" long	120	180	240

	C6	C8	C10
Moon Globe Orbiter, rocket orbits globe, noise, lights, three actions, c. 1960s, 10-1/2" high	100	150	200
Moon Orbiter, includes six sections of track and trestles, minor toy, 1960s, 4" long	120	180	240
Moon Patrol Space Rover, five actions, 1960s, 11-1/2" long	140	210	280
Moon Rocket, three actions, rare, 1950s, 15-1/4" long	400	600	800
Moon Traveler Apollo Z, five actions, 1960s, 12" long, 15" extended	120	180	240
Mother Bear Sitting and Knitting in Her Old Rocking Chair, four actions, 1950s, 9-1/2" high	170	255	340
Motorcycle Cop, five actions, 1950s, 10-1/2" long, 8-1/4" high	350	500	650
Mountain Cable Car, includes cable, minor toy, 1950s, 9" long	60	90	120
Movieland Drive-In Theater, includes six small cars, ad cards, filmstrips, minor toy, 1959, 14" long	60	90	120
Mr. Atom the Electronic Walking Robot, six actions, 1950s, 17" tall	400	600	800
Mr. Atomic, robot, three actions, rare, 1950s, 11" tall	2500	3750	5000
Mr. Baseball Jr., w/game box, three actions, 1950s, 7" high	500	750	1000
Mr. Chief Robot, four actions, 1950s, 12" tall	450	675	900

Mr. MacPooch Taking a Walk and Smoking His Pipe, SAN Co., 1950s, $300. Photo courtesy Don Hultzman and Ron Chojnacki

	C6	C8	C10
Mr. Fox, the Magician with the Magical Disappearing Rabbit, includes plastic rabbit, five actions, 1960s, 9" tall	400	600	800
Mr. Hustler Robot, six actions, 1960s, 11" tall	200	300	400
Mr. MacPooch Taking a Walk and Smoking His Pipe, four actions, 1950s, 8" tall	150	200	300
Mr. Magoo Car, includes cloth roof top, five actions, 1961, 9" long	175	260	350
Mr. Mercury Type I, seven actions, 1960s, 13" tall	400	600	800
Mr. Mercury Type II (lighted), seven actions, 1960s	400	600	800
Mr. Robot the Mechanical Brain, three actions, rare, 1950s, 8" tall	600	900	1200
Mr. Strong Pup Weight-Lifting Dog, five actions, 1950s, 9" tall	130	195	260
Mr. Traffic Policeman, four actions, 1950s, 14" tall, 6" x 6" base	175	270	365

Movieland Drive-In Theater, Remco Co., 1959, $120. Photo courtesy Don Hultzman and Ron Chojnacki

Mr. Mercury Type I (left) and Type II (right), Marx Co., 1960s, $800 each. Photo courtesy Don Hultzman and Ron Chojnacki

Musical Jolly Chimp, C-K Co., 1960s, $125

	C6	C8	C10
Mr. Zerox, four actions, 1960s, 9-1/2" tall	150	225	300
Multi Action Electra Jet KLM Royal Dutch Airlines PH-DSF, three actions, 1960s, 14" long, 17" wingspan	110	165	220
Mumbo Jumbo, Hawaiian drummer, three actions, 1960s, 9-3/4" high	85	120	160
Musical Bank Organ Grinder & Monkey, includes test coin and detachable celluloid monkey, four actions, rare, 1950s, 8" tall	500	750	1000
Musical Bear (drum and cymbals), includes detachable tin horn, six actions, 1950s, 10" tall	200	300	400
Musical Bulldog Playing Piano, four actions, 1950s, 8-1/2" tall, 6" x 9" base	600	900	1200
Musical Cadillac Car, minor toy, 1950s, 9" long	200	300	400
Musical Clown (New Adventures of Clown), three actions, 1960s, 9" tall	150	225	300
Musical Comic Jumping Jeep, six actions, 1970s, 12" long	70	105	140
Musical Drummer Robot, three actions, rare, 1950s, 8-1/4" tall	4000	6000	8000
Musical Jackal, six actions, rare, 1950s, 10" tall	150	225	600
Musical Jolly Chimp, five actions, two cycles, 1960s, 10-1/2" high	75	100	125
Musical Marching Bear, includes detachable tin horn, four actions, 1950s, 11" tall	115	170	600

	C6	C8	C10
Musical Showboat, includes two detachable smokestacks, minor toy, 1960s, 13" long	100	150	200
My Fair Dancer, minor toy, 1950s, 10-1/2" tall	100	150	200
Mystery Fire Chief Car, No. 81, three actions, 1950s, 9-1/4" long	100	150	200
Mystery Plane, four actions, 1950s, 10" long, 10-1/2" wingspan	120	180	240
Mystery Police Car, three actions, 1960s, 9-3/4" long, 6" wide, 4" high	100	150	200
NAR Television Truck, includes six film strip inserts, four actions, 1950s, 12" long	300	450	600
NBC Television Truck, five actions, 1950s, 9" long	300	450	600
Neptune Tugboat, four actions, 1950s, 15" long, 7" high	90	135	180
New Astronaut Robot, six actions, 1970s, 9-1/2" tall	80	120	160
New Bell Ringer Choo Choo, locomotive, three actions, 1960s, 10" long	50	75	100
New Space Capsule, six actions, 1960s, 9" long	120	180	240
News Service Car, four actions, 1960s, 10" long	150	225	300
Non-Stop Robot, three actions, rare, 1960s, 15" tall	600	900	1200
Nutty Mad Indian, four actions, 1960s, 12" tall	100	150	200
Nutty Mads Car (Drincar), three actions, 1960s, 9-1/4" long	175	250	325

	C6	C8	C10
Nutty Nibs, includes litho bowl of nuts and steel ball, minor toy, rare, 1950s, 11-1/2" tall	700	850	1400
Ol' MacDonald's Farm Truck, includes plastic pig, cow and chicken, four actions, 1960s	100	150	200
Ol' Sleepy Head RIP, seven actions, 1950s, 9" long	150	250	320
Old Fashioned Car, four actions, 1950s, 10" long	50	75	100
Old Fashioned Fire Engine, four actions, 1950s, 12-1/2" long	120	180	240
Old Fashioned Telephone Bear (?), four actions, 1950s, 9-1/2" high	125	175	225
Old Ford Touring Car, four actions, 1950s, 10" long	40	60	80
Old Time Automobile, includes detachable tin-litho driver and steering wheel, three actions, 1950s, 8-3/4" long	80	120	160
Old Timer Car, three actions, 1950s, 9" long	100	150	200
Oldtimer Automoball, includes celluloid ball, three actions, 1950s, 10" long	90	135	180
Oldtimer Sunday Driver, four actions, 1960s, 9" long	70	105	140
Overland Choo Choo Express Locomotive, minor toy, 1950s, 14" long	30	45	60
Overland Stage Coach, four actions, 1960s, 18" long	100	150	200
P.D. Police Patrol Car (Buick), No. 5, three actions, 1960s, 11-1/2" long	80	120	160
P-51 Mustang Shooting Figher Plane, minor toy, 1950s, 9" long, 9" wingspan	90	135	180
Pacific Piping Express Locomotive, four actions, 1960s, 14" long	40	60	80
Pam Am Sky Taxi Helicopter, three actions, 1960s, 11" long	70	105	140
Pan American World Airways 'Seven Seas' DC-7, five actions, 1950s, 15" long, 19" wingspan	140	210	280
Panda Bear, mostly plastic, four actions, 1970s, 10" long	30	45	65
Papa Bear Reading & Drinking in His Old Rocking Chair, four actions, 1950s, 10" high	150	225	300

	C6	C8	C10
Passenger Bus, four actions, 1950s, 16" long	230	345	460
Pat O'Neill, standing, six actions, 1960s, 12" tall	150	225	300
Pat the Dog, five actions, two cycles, 1950s, 9-1/2" long	30	45	60
Pat the Roaring Elephant, w/attached baby elephant, four actions, 1950s, 9" long	100	160	225
Patrol Auto Tricycle, four actions, 1960s, 19" long, 7-1/2" high	200	300	400
Patrol Helicopter No. 7, four actions, 1960s, 11" long	70	105	140
Penguin on Tricycle, three actions, 1950s, 6-1/2" high	100	150	200
Pepi Tumbling Monkey, minor toy, 1960s, 9-1/2" high	40	60	80
Peppermint Twist Doll, minor toy, 1950s, 12" tall	150	225	300
Peppy Puppy, includes tin-litho bone, seven actions, two cycles, 1950s, 8" long, 6-1/2" high	50	75	100
Pet Turtle, four actions, two cycles, 1960s, 7" long	70	105	140
Pete the Space Man (Walking Mate Series), minor action, 1960s, 5" tall	60	90	120
Peter the Drumming Rabbit (VIA-Cragstan), five actions, 1950s, 13" tall	150	225	300

Picnic Bear, Alps Co., 1950s, $200

	C6	C8	C10
Phillips '66' Power Yacht, includes plastic parts for yacht and dock, unmarked, minor toy, 1950s, 18" long	70	105	140
Pick-Up Truck, four actions, 10" long	100	150	200
Picnic Bear, w/Coke, Pepsi and generic logo, five actions, 1950s, 10" high	100	150	200
Picnic Bunny, four actions, 1950s, 10" tall	100	150	200
Picnic Monkey, four actions, 1950s, 10" high	100	150	200
Picnic Poodle, four actions, two cycles, 1950s, 7" long, 7" high	40	60	80
Pierrot Monkey Cycle, five actions, 1950s, 8" long, 10-1/2" high	325	460	650
Piggy Barbecue, includes chef's hat and tin-litho fried egg, five actions, 1950s, 9-1/2" tall	150	225	300
Piggy Cook, includes chef's hat and tin-litho fried egg, five actions, 1950s, 9-1/2" tall, 4" x 6" base	150	225	300
Pinkee the Farmer, seven actions, 1950s, 9-1/2" long	90	100	180
Pinky the Clown, includes tin-litho propeller, ball on nose, five actions, rare, 1950s, 10-1/4" tall	200	300	400
Pinocchio Playing London Bridge, includes xylophone, three actions, 1962, 10" tall	150	225	300
Pioneer Covered Wagon, includes detachable canopy and driver, four actions, 1960s, 14-1/2" long	120	180	240

Piston Action Robot, T-N Co., 1950s, $1800. Photo courtesy Don Hultzman and Ron Chojnacki

Playful Pup in Shoe, "Y" Co., 1960s, $80. Photo courtesy Don Hultzman and Ron Chojnacki

	C6	C8	C10
Pipie the Whale, minor toy, 1950s, 12" long	250	270	500
Pistol Pete, includes tin hat, five actions, 1950s, 10-1/4" high	250	270	500
Piston Action Bulldozer, two cycles, 1960s, 7-1/2" long	90	135	180
Piston Action Robot, resembles Robbie, three actions, 1950s, 8-1/4" tall	900	1350	1800
Piston Head Robot, three actions, 1960s, 10" tall	150	225	300
Piston Robot, four actions, 1960s, 10-1/2" tall	110	165	220
Planet Explorer, four actions, 1950s, 9" long	150	225	300
Planet Rover, wheeled tank, six actions, 1960s, 9" long, 6-1/2" high	140	210	280
Planet 'Y' Space Station, three actions, 1960s, 9" diameter	140	210	280
Playful Pup in Shoe, three actions, 1960s, 10" long	40	60	80
Playful Puppy, four actions, 1950s, 7-3/8" long, 5" high	100	150	200
Playing Monkey, The, includes detachable hat and tin yo-yo, six actions, 1950s, 10" tall	200	300	400
Pluto, five actions, 1960s, 10" long	300	450	600
Polar Bear, three actions, 1970s, 8" long	50	75	100
Police Auto Cycle, motorcycle w/plastic driver and remote control, five actions, 1960s	150	225	300

Popcorn Eating Bear, M-T Co., 1950s, $200. Photo courtesy Don Hultzman and Ron Chojnacki

	C6	C8	C10
Police Motorcycle, seven actions, 1950s, 11-3/4" long	200	300	400
Police No. 5 Police Car, four actions, 1950s, 9-1/2" long	90	135	180
Police Patrol Jeep, four actions— lights, bump and go, noise and smoke, 1960s, 9-1/4" long	100	150	200
Pom Pom Tank, five actions, 1950s, 12" long	160	240	320
Popcorn Eating Bear, five actions, 1950s, 9" high	100	150	200
Popcorn Vendor, No. 4035, includes litho umbrella, six actions, 1960s, 8" high, 7" long	200	300	400
Popcorn Vendor Truck, three actions, 1960s, 9" long	150	225	300
Popeye and Rowboat with Moving Oars, three actions, rare, 1950s, 10" long	5000	7500	10,000
Porsche with Visible Engine, three actions, 1964, 10" long	90	135	180
Poverty Pup, bank, three actions, 1966, 6" long, 4-1/4" high	60	90	120
Power Shovel, six actions, 1950s, 15" long extended	90	135	180

	C6	C8	C10
Pretty Peggy Parrot, six actions, 1950s, 11" long	250	375	500
Princess the French Poodle, no markings, five actions, 1950s, 9" long, 8" high	40	60	80
Professor Owl, includes two disks, five actions, 1950s, 8" high	200	300	400
Project Yankee Doodle, includes plastic missiles, rockets and accessories, six actions, 1959, 15" long	60	90	120
Puffy Morris, five actions, uses real cigarette, 1960s, 10" tall	125	175	225
Puzzled Puppy, five actions, 1950s, 7-1/2" long, 5" high	100	150	200
Queen of the Sea, inlcudes detachable antenna and flag, four actions, 1950s, 21-1/2" long	300	450	600
R.R. Line Locomotive, four actions, 1950s, 6-1/2" long	40	60	80
R-35 Robot, five actions, 1950s, 7-1/2" tall	300	450	600
Rabbits and Carriage, The, four actions, 1950s, 10" tall	150	225	300
Racecar #25, three actions, rare, 1950s, 9" long	800	1200	1600
Radar Jeep, four actions, 1950s, 11" long	150	225	300
Radar Robot, remote robot w/face control box, three actions, 1960s, 9" tall	600	900	1200
Radar Robot, five actions, 1970s, 12" tall	70	105	140
Radar Scope Space Scout, three actions, 1960s, 9-1/4" tall	140	210	280
Radio Rex, includes celluloid dog, minor toy, 1920s, 5" x 7" dog house	100	150	200
Railroad Hand Car, includes rubber track, minor toy, 1950s, 8" long	90	135	180
Railway Yard Shuttle Train, includes locomotive boxcar and track, three actions, 1950s, 8" long, 28" long track	100	150	200
Ranger Robot, six actions, 1950s, 11" tall	400	600	800
Ray Gun, machine gun, includes tripod, three actions, 1950s, 17-1/2" long	50	75	100

	C6	C8	C10
RCA NBC Mobile Color TV Truck, four actions, 1950s, 9" long	300	450	600
Reading Bear, five actions, 1950s, 9" tall	100	175	225
Rembrandt Monkey Artist, five actions, 1950s, 8" high	170	240	365
Reversible Diesel Electric Tractor, minor toy, 1950s	50	75	100
Ricki the Begging Poodle, five actions, 1950s, 9" long, 8" high	30	45	60
River Queen Sidewheeler, three actions, 1950s, 13-1/2" long	140	210	280
Riverboat, includes detachable tin smokestack, three actions, 1950s, 12-3/4" long	130	195	260
Road Construction Roller, four actions, 1950s, 8-1/2" long	60	90	120
Road Grader, three actions, 1960s, 12" long	50	75	100
Road Roller, four actions, 1950s, 9" long	60	90	120
Roarin' Jungle Lion, four actions, two cycles, 1950s, 16" long nose to tail tip	175	250	325
Roaring Gorilla Shooting Gallery, includes fold-outtarget box, tin gun, plastic darts, three actions, 1950s, 9-1/2" tall	200	300	400
Robby Space Patrol, five actions, rare, 1950s, 12-1/2" long	2000	3000	4000
Robert the Robot, three actions, 1950s, 14" tall	120	180	240
Robert the Robot Mechanical Bulldozer, four actions, rare, 1950s, 9" long	300	450	600
Robot, minor toy, rare, 1950s, 6" tall	600	900	1200
Robot, three actions, 1960s, 10-1/2" tall	400	600	800
Robot 2500, four actions, 1970s, 10-1/2" tall	60	90	120
Robotank TR-2, four actions, 1960s, 5" high	140	210	280
Robotank Z Space Robot, five actions, 1960s, 10-1/4" high	300	450	600
Rock 'N' Roll Hotrod (Dreamboat), three actions, 1950s, 7" long	150	225	300

	C6	C8	C10
Rock 'N' Roll Monkey (three variations), includes plastic hat, five actions, 1950s, 13" tall	140	200	280
Rocket Express Rocket Ship Monorail, twenty-piece rail and girder set, three actions, 1950s, 10" long	100	150	200
Rocket Launching Pad, includes tin-litho satellite and rocket, five actions, 1950s, 8-1/2" high	160	240	320
Rocking Chair Bear, five actions, 1950s, 10" high	125	175	200
Rocking Santa, four actions, rare, 1950s, 10" high	300	450	600
Roller Skater, minor toy, 1950s, 12" tall	100	150	200
Rollerskating Clown, minor toy, rare, 1950s, 6" tall	500	750	1000
Romance Car M-841, three actions, 1950s, 8" long	90	135	180
Rootbeer Counter, includes plastic barrel, glasses, and tin tray, three actions, 1960s, 8" long, 8" high	100	160	230
Rosko Robot, five actions, 1950s, 13" tall	500	750	1000
Rotate-O-Matic Super Astronaut, six actions, two cycles, 1960s, 11-1/2" tall	100	150	200
Rover the Poodle Bell Ringer, three actions, two cycles, 1960s, 10-1/2" tall	60	90	120
Roy Rogers Western Telephone, three actions, 1950s, 9" high	90	135	180
Royal Club in Buggy, pushed by Mama Bear, six actions, 1940s, 8" long, 8" high	140	210	280
Rudy the Robot, four actions, 1968, 16-1/4" tall	110	165	220
Sam the Shaving Man, includes metal mirror, seven actions, 1960s, 11-1/2" tall	140	200	285
Sammy Wong the Tea Totaler, four actions, 1950s, 10" tall	100	140	200
Santa Bank (Trim a Tree), four actions, 1960, 11" high	150	225	300
Santa Claus (Sitting on House), No. M-750, four actions, 1950s, 8" high	125	175	225

	C6	C8	C10
Santa Claus Bellringer, five actions, 1950s, 13" tall	100	150	200
Santa Claus on Handcar, three actions, 1960s, 10" high	100	140	200
Santa Claus on Scooter, four actions, 1960s, 10" high	100	140	180
Santa Claus Phone Bank, includes remote 4-3/4" high pay phone, seven actions, 1950s, 8" high	400	600	800
Santa Claus Stands & Sits, six actions, 1960s, 10" tall	150	225	300
Santa Copter, three actions, 1960s, 8-1/2" long	100	150	200
Santa Fe Diesel Battery Cable Train with Headlight (two-piece hookup), minor toy, 1950s, 13-1/2" long	80	120	160
Santa Sled, four actions, rare, 1950s, 14" long	300	450	600
Santa the Bellringer, electromagnet activated and Blinker bulb, minor toy, 1950s, 7" high	100	150	200

	C6	C8	C10
Satellite Interceptor, two-piece target set w/two darts and styro ball, minor toy, 1950s, 6-1/2" long gun-telescope, 5" high blower	200	300	400
Satellite Target Game, includes celluloid ball and special gun, minor toy, 1960s, 8" high, 10-1/2" wide	100	150	200
Saxophone Playing Monkey, four actions, 1950s, 9-1/2" high	200	300	400
School Bus, minor toy, 1950s, 20-1/2" long	70	105	140
Sea Bear #7 Racing Boat, minor toy, 1950s, 10" long	60	90	120
Seascape Tugboat, three actions, 1950s, 6-1/2" long	50	75	100
Secret Service Action Car (Green Hornet motif), four actions, rare, 1960s, 11" long	400	600	800
Serpent Charmer, four actions, 1950s, 7" high	175	300	425
Shaggy the Friendly Pup, three actions, 1960s, 8" long	35	45	65
Shaking Classic Car, four actions, 1960s, 7" long	50	75	100
Shaking Old-Timer Car, No. 2511-1, includes plastic driver, four actions, 1960s, 9" long	60	90	120

Santa the Bellringer, Chase Import Co., 1950s, $200. Photo courtesy Don Hultzman and Ron Chojnacki

Shoe Maker Bear, T-N Co., 1960s, $250. Photo courtesy Don Hultzman and Ron Chojnacki

	C6	C8	C10
Shark-U-Control Racing Car, all plastic, minor toy, 1961, 19" long	80	120	160
Sheriff Car, four actions, 1950s, 10" long	80	120	160
Shoe Maker Bear, three actions, 1960s, 8-1/2" high	125	200	250
Shoe Shine Bear, five actions, 1950s, 9" tall	150	225	300
Shoe Shine Joe, six actions, 1950s, 11" high	150	225	300
Shoe Shine Monkey, five actions, 1950s, 9" high	150	225	300
Shoe-Shaking Dog, five actions, 1950s, 8" long, 6" tall	40	60	80
Shooting Bear, six actions, 1950s, 10" tall	160	240	320
Shooting Gorilla, includes tin gun and darts, four actions, 1950s, 12" high	200	300	400
Shutterbug, photographer, five actions, 1950s, 9" tall	500	700	900
Shuttling Freight Train, includes locomotive, lumber car, four pieces of track, platform and logs, six actions, 1950s, 51" long assembled	150	200	250
Shuttling Train and Freight Yard, includes locomotive, baggage car, two platforms and litho luggage, four actions, 1950s, 11" long, track 51" long	120	180	240
Sight Seeing Bus, four actions, 1960s, 14-1/2" long	100	150	200
Sight Seeing Bus, minor toy, 1950s, 9" long	140	210	280
Sikorsky Rescue Army Helicopter, four actions, 1950s, 11" long	90	135	180
Silver Bell Choo Choo, three actions, 1950s, 12" long	40	60	80
Silver Mountain Express Locomotive, four actions, 1960s, 15-3/4" long	50	75	100
Silver Mountain Locomotive, three actions, 1950s, 16" long	50	75	100
Silver Ray Secret Weapon Space Scout, six actions, rare, 1960s, 9" tall	750	1075	1500
Silver Streak Locomotive No. 6682, four actions, 1950s, 16" long	50	75	100

	C6	C8	C10
Sing Tail Cargo Plane Flying Tiger, five actions, 1960s, 14" long, 14" wingspan	300	450	600
Singing Bird in Cage, four actions, 1950s, 9" high, 4" x 6" rectangular base	100	150	200
Siren Fire Car, four actions, 1950s, 9" long	130	195	260
Siren Patrol Car, four actions, 1960s, 12-1/2" long	90	135	180
Siren Patrol Motorcycle, three actions, 1960s, 12" long	250	350	450
Skating Circus Clown, minor toy, rare, 1950s, 6" tall	450	595	800
Skiing Santa, includes tin skis, four actions, 1960s, 12" tall	150	225	300
Skipping Monkey, minor toy, 1960s, 9-1/2" tall	40	60	80

Skipping Monkey, T-N Co., 1960s, $80. Photo courtesy Don Hultzman and Ron Chojnacki

	C6	C8	C10
Sky Patrol Flying Saucer, includes detachable antenna, seven actions, 1950s, 7-1/2" diameter	100	150	200
Sky Patrol Space Cruiser, five actions, 1950s, 13" long	150	225	300
Sky Taxi-Panam-Boeing Vertol 107, includes two detachable rotors, three actions, 1970s, 12-3/4" long	120	180	240
Slalom Game, includes plastic skier, minor toy, 1960s, 15-1/4" long	100	160	225
Sleeping Baby Bear, includes detachable alarm clock, six actions, 1950s, 9" long	195	285	400
Sleeping Pup, five actions, 1960s, 9" long	45	75	100
Slurpy Pup, four actions, 1960s, 6-1/2" long, 4" high	50	75	100
Smilex Deluxe Coffee Set, includes four sets of cups, saucers, and spoons, plastic, minor toy, 1950s, 12" high assembled	60	90	120

Smoking Elephant, Marusan Co., 1950s, $225. Photo courtesy Don Hultzman and Ron Chojnacki

Smoking Bunny, SAN Co., 1950s, $200. Photo courtesy Don Hultzman and Ron Chojnacki

	C6	C8	C10
Smokey the Bear Jeep, four actions, 1950s, 10" long	220	330	440
Smoking Bulldozer, four actions, 1960s, 9" long	90	135	180
Smoking Bunny, four actions, 1950s, 10-1/2" tall	125	150	200
Smoking Elephant, four actions, 1950s, 8-3/4" tall	115	165	225
Smoking Grandpa (in Rocking Chair), Type I-eyes open, four actions, 1950s, 8" tall	175	250	325
Smoking Grandpa (in Rocking Chair), Type II-eyes closed, four actions, 1950s, 8" tall	200	300	400
Smoking Jet Plane, four actions, 1950s, 12" long, 11" wingspan	150	225	300
Smoking PaPa Bear, four actions, 1950s, 8" tall	150	200	250
Smoking Pop Locomotive: The General, four actions, 1950s, 10-1/4" long	70	105	140
Smoking Popeye, five actions, rare, 1950s, 9" tall	800	1200	1600
Smoking Robot, all plastic, four actions, 1960s, 10" tall	90	135	180
Smoking Spaceman, six actions, 1950s, 12" tall	750	1200	1600

Smoking PaPa Bear, SAN Co., 1950s, $250

	C6	C8	C10
Smoking U.S.A.F. Jet, four actions, 1950s, 13" long, 12" wingspan	150	225	300
Smoking Volkswagen, four actions, 1960s, 10-1/2" long	60	90	120
Smoky Bear, includes detachable tin hat, four actions, 1950s, 9" tall	250	300	500
Smoky Bill on Old-Fashioned Car, four actions, 1960s, 9" long	120	180	240
Smoky Joe Fancy Mobile, four actions—smokes, lights, bump and go and noise, 1960s, 9" long	100	150	200

Snake Charmer (and Casey the Trained Cobra), Linemar Co., 1950s, $500. Photo courtesy Don Hultzman and Ron Chojnacki

	C6	C8	C10
Snake Charmer (and Casey the Trained Cobra), four actions, 1950s, 8" high	250	375	500
Snappy the Dragon, six actions, rare, 1960s, 30" long	2000	3000	4000
Sneezing Bear, five actions, 1950s, 9" high	200	300	400
Snoopie the Non-Fall Dog, three actions, 1960s, 8" long	50	75	100
Snoopy Sniffer, four actions, 1960s, 8" long	40	60	80
Somersaulting Pup with Bark, four actions, two cycles, 1960s, 9" long	50	75	100
Sonicon Space Rocket, minor toy, 1960s, 13" long	250	375	500
Space Capsule, includes styrofoam saucer and astronaut, four actions, 1960s, 10" long	100	150	200
Space Capsule, four actions, 1960s, 10-1/2" long	150	225	300
Space Commando Space Station, four actions, 1960s, 10" diameter	150	225	300
Space Commando Spaceman, four actions, 1960s, 7-3/4" tall	500	750	1000
Space Explorer #1041, six actions, rare, 1960s, 7-3/4" high, extends to 11-1/2" high	600	900	1200
Space Explorer Ship (saucer), six actions, 1950s, 11" diameter	100	150	200
Space Fighter, robot, six actions, 1970s, 9" tall	70	105	140

Space Fighter, S-H Co., 1970s, $140. Photo courtesy Don Hultzman and Ron Chojnacki

	C6	C8	C10
Space Frontier Saturn 5 Rocket, six actions, 1960s, 18" long	100	150	200
Space Patrol 3 Saucer, five actions, 1950s, 7-1/2" diameter	100	150	200
Space Patrol Car, four actions, 1950s, 9-1/2" long	300	450	600
Space Patrol Car, w/lighting guns, three actions, 1950s, 9" long	450	675	900
Space Patrol Robot, six actions, 1950s, 11" tall	140	210	280
Space Patrol Rocket, three actions, 1970s, 11" long	70	105	140
Space Patrol Snoopy, four actions, 1960s, 11" long	100	150	200
Space Patrol Tank, includes detachable tin jet plane, five actions, 1950s, 9" long	150	225	300
Space Patrol Vehicle, four actions, 1950s, 9" long	130	195	260
Space Patrol Vehicle, three actions, 1960s, 9-1/2" long	100	150	200
Space Pioneer Vehicle, three actions, 1960s, 12" long	100	200	300
Space Robot (X-70), five actions, 1960s, 12" tall	500	750	1000
Space Robot Car, six actions, rare, 1950s, 9-1/4" long	1000	1500	2000
Space Robot Trooper, three actions, rare, 1950s, 7-1/2" tall	500	750	1000
Space Rocket Blue Eagle, 1950s, 15" long from tail to probe tip	150	200	250
Space Rocket Solar X, five actions, 1960s, 15-1/12" tall	150	225	300
Space Scooter, three actions, 1960s, 10-1/2" high, 8" long	100	150	200
Space Scooter, Snoopy or Astro-Dog, three actions, 1960s, 8" long	80	120	160
Space Ship, four actions, 1950s, 9-1/2" diameter	180	270	360
Space Ship, three actions, 1970s, 9" long	90	135	180
Space Ship X-5, four actions, 1970s, 8" diameter	60	90	120
Space Ship X-8, four actions, 1960s, 8" long	100	150	200
Space Station, four actions, 1950s, 9" diameter	100	150	200
Space Station, five actions, 1950s, 11-3/4" diameter	500	750	1000
Space Tank, four actions, 1950s, 8" long	120	180	240
Space Tank Robbie Type, four actions, 1960s, 6" long	2000	3000	4000
Space Tank-M41, includes detachable plastic antenna, four actions, 1950s, 9" long	100	150	200
Spaceman Robot, three actions, 1950s, 7-1/2" tall	350	525	700
Spaceman Robot, four actions, 1950s, 9-1/4" tall	400	600	800
Spad XIII S-7 Stunt Biplane, three actions, 1960s, 9" long, 10-3/8" wingspan	130	195	260
Spanking Bear, six actions, 1950s, 9" high	160	200	320
Sparking Burp Gun, three actions, 1950s, 24" long	40	60	80
Sparkling Mike the Robot, three actions, rare, 1950s, 7-1/2" tall	1000	1500	2000
Sparky Savings Bank, electromagnet action, includes 4" long composition dog, minor toy, 1930s, 4" long, 4-1/2" high doghouse	60	90	120
Sparky the Seal, includes celluloid ball, four actions, two cycles, 1950s, 6" high, 7" long	100	150	200
Spirit of 1776, No. 4406, locomotive, five actions, 1976, 15-3/4" long	40	60	80
Sports Car Race Set, includes four plastic race cars, minor toy, 1960s, 8" x 14" base	80	120	160
SSN-571 Submarine, Skate, minor toy, 1950s, 16" long w/rudder extended	120	180	240
SSN-571 Submarine Nautilus, minor toy, 1950s, 16" long w/rudder extended	120	180	240
Star Strider Robot, six actions, 1980s, 12" tall	110	165	220
Steam Roller, includes tin trailer, four actions, 1950s, 8" long	100	150	200
Steam Roller (Road Roller), four actions, 1950s, 12" long w/trailer	90	135	180
Steerable Tank, five actions, 1950s, 9" long	60	90	120

	C6	C8	C10
Strange Explorer, four actions, 1960s, 7-1/2" long	300	450	600
Strato Jet U.S.A.F., three actions, 1950s, 13" long, 14" wingspan	120	180	240
Struttin' Sam, minor toy, 1950s, 10-1/2" tall	250	350	450
Strutting My Fair Dancer (Dancing Sailor Girl), two pieces, minor toy, 1950s, 12" tall	100	150	200
Sunbeam Jeep, No. 1, three actions, 1940s, 10" long	100	150	200
Sunday Driver, includes detachable driver, four actions, 1950s, 10" long	55	90	125
Super Astronaut Robot, four actions, 1960s, 12" tall	150	225	300
Super Astronaut Robot, five actions, two cycles, 1960s, 11-1/2" tall	110	165	220
Super Giant Robot, six actions, 1960s, 15-1/2" tall	200	300	400
Super Jet, three actions, 1950s, 12" long, 8" wingspan	250	375	500
Super Space Capsule, four actions, 1960s, 9" high	100	150	200
Super Space Commander, three actions, 1960s, 10" tall	70	105	140
Super Susie, six actions, 1950s, 9" high	350	625	700
Surrey Jeep, three actions, 1960s, 11" long	90	135	180
Suzette the Eating Monkey, includes tin litho steak, five actions, rare, 1950s, 8-3/4" high, 7" x 5" base	300	450	625
Suzy-Q Automatic Ironer, four actions, 1950s, 7" high	90	135	180
Swingtail Airplane Flying Tigers, seven actions, 1960s, 19-1/2" long, 21" wingspan	300	450	600
Switchboard Operator, four actions, rare, 1950s, 7-1/2" high	250	380	800
Swivel-O-Matic Astronaut Robot, five actions, two cycles, 1960s, 11-1/2" tall	80	120	160
Talking Parrot (called Pete), six actions, 1950s, 18" high	250	350	450
Talking Police Car Mystery Action, three actions, 1960s, 14" long	70	105	140
Talking Robot, three actions, rare, 1960s, 10-3/4" tall	600	900	1200

Suzette the Eating Monkey, Linemar Co., 1950s, $625. Photo courtesy Don Hultzman and Ron Chojnacki

Swivel-O-Matic Astronaut Robot, S-H Co., 1960s, $160. Photo courtesy Don Hultzman and Ron Chojnacki

	C6	C8	C10
Tank 392 U.S. Tank Division, three actions, 1950s, 9-1/2" long	100	125	150
Tank Daisy-Matic, No. 80, includes darts, five actions, 1965, 8-1/2" long	100	150	200
Tank Daisymatic Rapid Fire Tank, No. 64, four actions, 1960s, 8" long	120	180	240
Tank 392 U.S. Tank Division, three actions, 1950s, 9-1/2" long	100	125	150
Tank Daisy-Matic, No. 80, includes darts, five actions, 1965, 8-1/2" long	100	150	200
Tank Daisymatic Rapid Fire Tank, No. 64, four actions, 1960s, 8" long	120	180	240
Tank M-103, three actions, 1950s, 7" long	100	150	200
Tank M-107 U.S. Army, includes four missiles, four actions, 1950s, 6" long	120	180	240
Tank M-35, three actions, 1950s, 8" long	100	150	200
Tank M-4 Combat Tank, five actions, 1960s, 11-1/2" long, 13" w/gun barrel extended	100	150	200
Tank M-41, four actions, 1970s, 8-1/4" long	100	150	200
Tank M-48-T, four actions, 1960s, 8-1/4" long	100	150	200
Tank M-56, wheel drive, seven actions, 1940s, 7-1/2" long	100	150	200
Tank M-81, seven actions, 1960s, 8-1/2" long	100	150	200
Tank M-X, five actions, 1950s, 8-1/2" long	70	105	140
Tank Robot, five actions, 1960s, 10" tall	300	450	600
Tank T-5, includes detachable radar antenna, three actions, 1950s, 8-1/2" long	110	165	220
Tank X-3 (explorer defense), includes six cartridge shells, five actions, 1950s, 7-3/4" long	130	195	260
Tank X-75, includes tin gun and darts, three actions, 1950s, 9" long	110	165	220
Tarzan, four actions, 1966, 13" tall	500	765	1000

	C6	C8	C10
Taxi, yellow cab, five actions, 1950s, 7-1/2" long	100	150	200
Taxi Cab, five actions, 1950s, 8-1/2" long	90	135	180
Taxi Cab, four actions, 1960s, 9" long	90	135	180
Teddy Bear Circus Acrobat, includes detachable bear flyer, three actions, rare, 1950s, 15" high	500	750	1000
Teddy Bear Swing, includes four wire supports and tin sign, three actions, two cycles, 1950s, 17" high	300	380	600
Teddy the Artist, includes removable tray and nine patterns, three actions, 1950s, 8-1/2" high, 5-1/4" x 7" base	300	450	600
Teddy the Boxing Bear, five actions, 1950s, 9" tall	115	190	240
Teddy the Rhythmical Drummer, three actions, 1960s, 11" tall	100	150	200
Teddy-Go-Kart, four actions, 1960s, 10-1/2" long	75	125	160
Telephone Bear, six actions, 1950s, 7-1/2" high	200	300	400
Telephone Bear Ringing and Talking in His Old Rocking Chair, four actions, 1950s, 10" high	250	350	450
Telephone Bunny Ringing and Talking in His Old Rocking Chair, four actions, 1950s, 10" high	170	255	340
Television Spaceman, six actions, 1960s, 14-1/2" high to tip of antenna	400	600	825
Television Truck, three actions, 1950s, 11" long	250	375	500
Thunder Jet Boat, three actions, 1950s, 9-3/4" long	130	195	260

Teddy the Artist, "Y" Co., 1950s, $600

	C6	C8	C10
Tin Man, robot, all plastic, four actions, 1960s, 21" tall	100	150	200
Tinkling Trolley, includes two plastic cowcatchers, four actions, two cycles, 1950s, 10-1/2" long	150	200	250
Tiny Jeep, minor action, 1950s, 4-1/4" long	30	45	60
Tiny Tank, minor action, 1950s, 4-1/4" long	30	45	60
Tom and Jerry Car, three actions, rare, 1960s, 13" long	400	600	800
Tom and Jerry Choo Choo, five actions, 1960s, 10-1/4" long	125	185	255
Tom and Jerry Handcar, three actions, 1960s, 7-3/4" high, 7-3/4" long	150	225	300
Tom and Jerry Handcar, three actions, 1960s, 9-3/4" high, 7-3/4" long	150	225	300

Tin Man, Remco Industries, Inc., 1960s, $200. Photo courtesy Don Hultzman and Ron Chojnacki

	C6	C8	C10
Tom and Jerry Helicopter, three actions, 1960s, 9-1/2" long	125	175	250
Tom and Jerry Highway Patrol, three actions, 1960s, 8" long	120	180	240
Tom and Jerry Jumping Jeep, three actions, 1960s, 9" long	120	180	240
Tom-Tom Indian, four actions, 1961, 10-1/2" tall	80	120	160
Topo Gigio Playing the Xylophone, three actions, 1960s	265	440	525
Torpedo Boat-PT 107, three actions, 1950s, 11-1/2" long	110	165	220
Tractor, three actions, 1960s, 6" long	50	75	100
Tractor, includes litho tin driver, four actions, 1950s, 7-1/2" long	60	90	120
Tractor on Platform, minor toy, 1950s, 9" long tractor w/7" trailer long	80	120	160
Train Robot, four actions, rare, 1950s, 15-1/2" tall	1500	2250	3000
Traveler Bear, three actions, 1950s, 8" high	100	150	200
Treasure Chest Bank, five actions, two cycles, risqué toy, PG-rated, 1960s, 11" tall	90	135	180
Tric-cycling Clown, five actions, 1960s, 12" high	300	450	600
Tricky Dog House, No. 673, four actions, 1960s, 6-3/4" high, 7-1/4" long, 6-3/4" wide	60	90	120
Trumpet Playing Bunny, four actions, 1950s, 10" high	150	225	300
Trumpet Playing Monkey, includes tin horn, four actions, 1950s, 9" high	150	225	300
Tubby the Turtle, three actions, 1950s, 7" long	50	75	100
Tugboat, minor toy, 1950s, 6-1/2" long	50	75	100
Tugboat, three actions, 1950s, 13-1/2" long	110	165	220
Tumbles the Bear, includes porter's hat, minor toy, 1960s, 8-1/2" tall	100	150	200
Turn Signal Robot Auto Accessory, five actions, 1960s, 11" tall	160	240	320
Turn-O-Matic Gun Jeep, five actions, 1960s, 10" long	100	150	200

	C6	C8	C10
Turntable Xylophone Melody Train, three actions, 1960s, 29-1/2" long assembled	50	75	100
TWA Multiaction DC-7C Airliner, seven actions, 1960s, 22-1/2" long, 23-1/4" wingspan	200	300	400
Twin Coupled Tram Cars, two cars, minor toy, 1950s, 11-1/2" long	100	150	200
Twin Racing Cars, three actions, 1950s, 7" long, 10" long w/coupling rod	400	600	800
Twirly Whirly, four actions, 1950s, 13-1/2" high	290	450	600
Twist Dancer (Let's Twist), includes two plastic-rubber rockets, no manufacturer mark, minor toy, 1960s, 15" high	100	150	200
Two Stage Rocket Launching Pad, three actions, 1950s, 7" long, 4" wide, 8" high	250	375	500
U.S Navy Pom Pom Gun, four actions, 1950s, 20" long	80	120	160
U.S. Air Force Military Airlift Command Jet, four actions, 1960s, 14" wingspan	130	195	260

U.S. Royal Tire Mechanical Toy (ferris wheel), Ideal, 1964-65, $200. Photo courtesy Don Hultzman and Ron Chojnacki

Twist Dancer (Let's Twist), 1960s, $200. Photo courtesy Don Hultzman and Ron Chojnacki

	C6	C8	C10
U.S. Air Force Smoking Jet, No. 75029, three actions—smokes, engine noise and bump and go, rare, 1950s, 12" wingspan	200	300	400
U.S. Army Machine Gunner, unmarked, four actions, 1960s, 10" long	100	150	200
U.S. Royal Tire Mechanical Toy (ferris wheel), includes plastic figures, souvenir from the 1964-65 New York World's Fair, minor toy, 1964-65, 10" high	100	150	200
UFO-X05, three actions, 1970s, 7-1/2" diameter	50	75	100
Union Mountain Cable Lines, Monorail set, minor toy, 1950s, 8" long car w/22" x 32" 16-piece oval track	80	120	160
United DC7 Mainliner, five actions, 1950s, 14" wingspan	200	300	400
United Mainliner Stratocruiser, four actions, 1950s, 19-1/2" long, 13" wingspan	190	285	380
United States Ocean Liner, three actions, 1950s, 18-1/2" long	300	450	600
United States Ocean Liner, three actions, 1950s, 14" long	200	300	400
Universal Machine Gun, three actions, 1950s, 14-3/4" long	70	105	140

	C6	C8	C10
USA NASA Apollo Space Ship, four actions, 1960s, 9" long	150	225	300
USA NASA Gemini Space Capsule, includes detachable astronaut, four actions, 1960s, 9" long	120	180	240
V.I.P. the Busy Boss, six actions, 1950s, 8" high	225	325	425
Video Robot, three actions, 1960s, 10" tall	150	175	225
Visible Ford Mustang, four actions, 1960s, 10" long	80	120	160
Vision Robot, five actions, 1960s, 11-3/4" tall	150	225	300
Voice Control Astronaut Base, includes plastic missiles and phonograph records, four actions, 1969, 19" long	90	135	180
Volkswagen, No. 7653, three actions, 1960s, 10" long	90	135	180
Volkswagen Convertible, three actions, 1950s, 9-3/4" long	250	375	500
Volkswagen with Visible Engine, three actions, 1960s, 7" long	80	120	160
Volkswagen with Visible Engine, No. 4049, three actions, 1960s, 8" long	90	135	180
Volkswagen-Elektrik, three actions, 1950s, 8-1/2" long	70	105	140
Wagon Master, four actions, 1960s, 18" long	120	180	240
Walking Bear with Xylophone, seven actions, 1950s, 10" high	175	270	365
Walking Elephant, three actions, 1950s, 8-1/2" long	100	150	200

Walking Bear with Xylophone, Linemar Co., 1950s, $365. Photo courtesy Don Hultzman and Ron Chojnacki

	C6	C8	C10
Walking 'Esso' Tiger, four actions, 1950s, 11-1/2" tall	250	350	450
Walking Itchy Dog, five actions, 1950s, 9" long	45	75	100
Warpath Indian, three actions, 1950s, 12" tall	100	150	200
Wash-O-Matic washing machine, includes lid, minor toy, 1940s, 5-3/4" high, 4-1/4" diameter	30	45	60
Water Spouting Whale with Flopping Tail, minor toy, 1950s, 13" long	100	150	200
Wester Express, Locomotive, four actions, 1960s, 14" long	50	75	100

V.I.P. the Busy Boss, S&E Co., 1950s, $425

Walking Elephant, Linemar Co., 1950s, $200. Photo courtesy Don Hultzman and Ron Chojnacki

	C6	C8	C10
Western Badman Red Gulch Bar, includes three plastic bottles and two plastic glasses, eight actions, 1960s, 9-3/4" high	300	450	600
Western Locomotive, four actions, 1950s, 10-1/2" long	45	65	80
Western Special Locomotive, five actions, 1950s, 12" long	50	75	100
Wheel-A-Gear Robot, five actions, 1960s, 14" tall	250	375	500
Whirlybird Helicopter, three actions, 1960s, 25" long	80	120	160
Whistling Showboat, three actions, 1950s, 14" long	120	180	240
WHOH Skyway Patrol Helicopter, four actions, 1950s, 18" long	100	150	200
Wild West Rodeo, includes plastic bowl for bubble solution, five actions, 1950s, 6-1/2" long, 8" high	100	150	200
Windy the Elephant, includes celluloid ball and tin litho umbrella, three actions, 1950s, 9-3/4" high	150	200	250
Winner 23, Rocket, includes rubber track, minor action, 1950s, 5-1/2" long	150	225	300
Winner of the West Overland Stagecoach with Four Galloping Horses, four actions, 1950s, 18" long	200	300	400
Winston the Barking Bulldog, three actions, two cycles, 1950s, 10" long	70	105	140
Worried Mother Duck and Baby, three actions, 1950s, 11" long, 7" high	100	150	200
X-1800 Space Vehicle, includes detachable plastic antenna, five actions, 1960s, 9" long	140	210	280
X-7 Space Explorer Ship, four actions, 1960s, 7" diameter	90	135	180

X-70 Robot, T-N Co., 1960s, $1000. Photo courtesy Don Hultzman and Ron Chojnacki

	C6	C8	C10
X-70 Robot, five actions, rare, 1960s, 12-1/4" tall	500	750	1000
X-F 160 Jet Airplane, 1960s, 8" wingspan	80	120	160
Yeti the Abominable Snowman, four actions, 1960s, 12" tall	250	335	500
Yo-Yo Clown, includes plastic yo-yo, three actions, 1960s, 9" high	150	190	300
Yo-Yo Monkey, includes plastic yo-yo, three actions, 1960s, 9" tall	100	185	245
Yo-Yo Monkey, minor toy, 1960s, 12" tall, spring extension to 32"	85	135	180
Yummy Yum Kitty, five actions, 1950s, 9-1/2" high	170	270	325
Zero Fighter Plane, three actions, 1950s, 12-1/2" long, 15" wingspan	150	230	300
Zoom Motorboat, three actions, 1950s, 12" long	100	150	200
Zoomer the Robot, three actions, 1950s, 8" tall	250	375	500

BB GUNS

Spring Air BB guns, sometimes referred to as air rifles, are simple in design and operation. They cannot be pumped up to high pressures and their muzzle velocity is usually in the neighborhood of 400 feet per second. Operation is simple: a one-stroke cocking action compresses a spring and draws a piston back through a cylindrical air chamber. Locked in this position, the BB gun is ready to fire. Meanwhile a BB has been placed in the breech, either manually or by an automatic feed mechanism. When the trigger is pulled the piston is driven forward, forcing the air in the cylinder out through the barrel, driving the BB ahead of this blast of air.

A BB gun is not a toy in the traditional sense. If improperly handled it can be dangerous and cause injury. Yet it was conceived, designed, manufactured and advertised for use by children. Common sense tells us that a BB gun should not be placed in the hands of a child too young to understand its dangers or who has not been properly instructed in its safe use.

Daisy and Markham/King both went into the BB gun business in the late 1880s. Located just across the railroad tracks from one another in Plymouth, Michigan, they were in vigorous competition for years. By the early 1930s, Daisy not only owned King but the King guns were being produced in the Daisy plant. During that period of about forty years, as many as thirty companies tried their hand at the BB gun business. Few made a great success of it; none have survived. By the 1930s, "Daisy" and "BB Gun" had become pretty much synonymous terms.

Daisy started life as the Iron Windmill Company in 1882. Iron windmills weren't great sellers, and when windmill designer C.J. Hamilton brought in a small prototype BB gun to be considered for manufacture, the board of directors was cool toward the idea. Eventually it was decided that the little gun would be made as a premium to be given to windmill purchasers. But as Cass Hough, grandson of one of Daisy's founders, said in his 1976 book *It's A Daisy,* "It didn't take long for the tail to begin to wag the dog." A few months later production started in earnest and the first Daisy was on the market.

The people who were running the Iron Windmill company didn't realize their BB gun was only the first of hundreds of models that would be produced over the next century. Neither that first Daisy nor the variations and new models that followed over the next few years were assigned a letter or number designation. Finally, in 1900 Daisy produced a variation with the designation "Model B." The designations such as "first model, second model," etc. are informal terms used by collectors. The BB guns are not so marked. The first Daisy was simply marked "DAISY MFD. BY IRON WIND MILL CO. PLYMOUTH MICH. PAT. APD. FOR." After that, Daisy produced BB guns with names, letters, numbers, or combinations of the same. Their system, or more accurately, lack of system, is confusing to the average collector, and even the advanced collector cannot answer questions about the chronology of Daisy BB guns with absolute certainty every time. Daisy didn't know they were making "collectibles," or that anyone would care a hundred years later when a particular model was manufactured. Some guns have no special marking except a name, which may be shared with several models. Some have a single letter or number designation; still others may have a combination of letters and numbers. Many of Daisy's guns from the late 1930s, have a number and a model number such as "No. 111 Model 40," in addition to a name, in this case "Red Ryder." A classic case is the No. 50 Golden Eagle of 1936. This out of sequence number was used because the gun was made to commemorate Daisy's 50th anniversary.

To make it easy for the reader, the Daisy listings have been broken down into several sections. Name-only guns are in the first section. Those identified by a letter (alphabet guns) are next, followed by numbered guns. Guns with a combination of letters and numbers will be listed according to whichever appears first, the letter or the number.

With a few exceptions, the listing are limited to guns made between 1888 and early 1942. BB guns made after World War II have not yet aroused much collector interest. That is not to say that none of the postwar guns are collectible or that some collectors do not collect these later models, but most collector interest is focused on the prewar era. This eliminated most of the plastic-stocked guns from this chapter and most of the guns from Daisy's facility at Rogers, Arkansas. Daisy switched to plastic stocks around 1950 and moved to Rogers in 1958.

Like the prices of all collectibles, BB gun prices are somewhat subjective and actual prices paid can vary widely. Many factors have to be considered. Supply and demand, nostalgia, condition, how badly the buyer wants the item, and the thickness of the buyer's wallet are all-important factors in the collectibles game. There is no infallible guide to BB gun values. The prices listed are based on collecting, buying and selling BB guns over the past few years and may not reflect prices in every area.

One last word on the listing method used in this book: the term C10 means a piece that is in exactly the condition it was in on the day it was made. In the case of many of the early BB guns, no such piece will ever be found. Just because it is the best example you have ever seen or heard of does not make it a C10.

There have been many contributors to this chapter, far too many to list here, but two deserve mention. Jim E. Thomas of Tulsa, Oklahoma, has long been my mentor in learning the intricacies of Daisy BB gun chronology. In addition, Bill and Lynn Johnson

of Rosamond, California, have been a great assistance in sorting out the very early Daisys and Kings. Much of this early information is very obscure. Daisy did not bother to keep complete records of early model changes or production. Bill, who has studied the subject for many years and has a fine collection of old Daisy/King ads and other paper, was nice enough to go over the evaluations and lend his personal input prior to publication.

Two other important sources of information have been Arni Dunathan's 1971 book *The American BB Gun,* and *It's A Daisy,* by Cass S. Hough. Hough, grandson of one of Daisy's founders, was mainly responsible for developing the great Daisy character guns of the 1930s. The Buck Jones, Buzz Barton, and that most famous of all BB guns, the Daisy Red Ryder, were all Hough creations.

Abbreviations Used

LA:	Lever Action
BA:	Break Action
PA:	Pump Action
SS:	Single Shot
RPTR:	Repeater
WDS:	Wood Stock
PLAS:	Plastic Stock
NIC:	Nickel Finish
BLU:	Blued Finish
PNTD:	Painted Finish

Contributor: Jim Buskirk, c/o TGCA, 3009 Oleander Ave., San Marcos, CA 92069. A casual BB gun collector for years, Buskirk began collecting in earnest in 1985, and in 1989 he began publishing *The Toy Gun Collectors of America Newsletter*, a quarterly magazine for toy gun buffs. His collection of cap guns, BB guns and related items number several hundred pieces and consists of mostly of pre-WWII items, and its main focus is the 1930s era. The Daisy Red Ryder BB guns are of special interest, and his collection includes what is believed to be the first Red Ryder ever made—a factory prototype that was hand-built on a King Model 5536 frame.

Daisy

Daisy with Names	C6	C8	C10
1000 Shot Daisy, marked, "1000 Shot Daisy" on top and/or side of frame, LA, RPTR, WDS, NIC, 1903	150	175	250
20th Century, marked, "20th Century," BA, SS, WDS, NIC, w/cast-metal grip frame, 1899	180	210	300
500 Shot Daisy, marked "500 Shot Daisy" on top and/or side of frame, LA, RPTR, WDS, NIC, 1905	150	175	250

Daisy with Names (Continued)	C6	C8	C10
Daisy, repeater variation of BA, SS, WDS, NIC, marked "Daisy" in indented rectangle on side of grip frame, also marked "Pat. Aug 13, 1889, July 14, 91, Jan. 21, 92, March 26, 1901," frame is all sheet metal, referred to by collectors as the "20th Century sheet metal," but not so marked, 1901	120	140	200

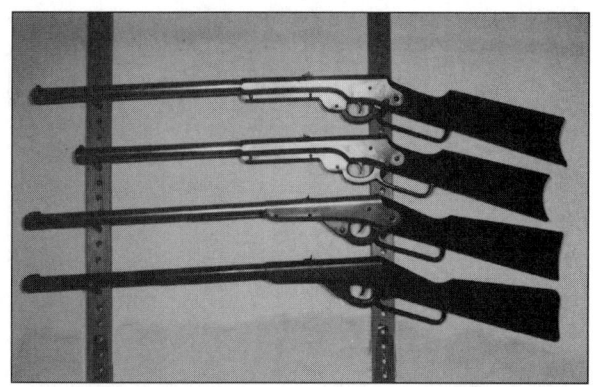

Top to Bottom: Daisy 1000 Shot, 1903, $250; Daisy 500 Shot, 1905, $250; two versions of Daisy Model B, 1909, $75-120. Photo courtesy Jim Buskirk

Daisy with Names (Continued)

	C6	C8	C10
Daisy, BA, SS, WDS, NIC, marked "Daisy" in indented rectangle on side of grip frame, also marked "Pat. Aug 13, 1889, July 14, 91, Jan. 21, 92, March 26, 1901," frame is all sheet metal, referred to by collectors as the "20th Century sheet metal," but not so marked, 1901	100	115	175
Daisy, third model, marked "Daisy Pat May 6, 90," July 14, 91, BA, SS, stock may be wire or wood, NIC, cast-metal grip frame may have checkering, wire stock may have wood insert, 1891	210	275	375
Daisy, second model, marked "Daisy Imp'd Pat May 6, 90," BA, SS, wire stock, NIC, cast-metal grip frame, 1890	300	350	500
Daisy, first model, marked "Daisy Pat Apd For" or "Daisy Pat Aug 13, 89," LA, SS, wire stock, NIC, cast-metal grip frame, 1889	360	420	600

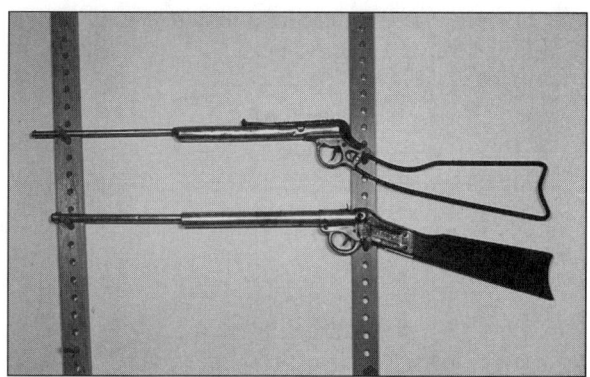

Top to Bottom: Daisy, 1889, $600; Daisy 20th Century, 1899, $300. Photo courtesy Jim Buskirk

Daisy with Names (Continued)

	C6	C8	C10
Sentinel, marked, "Sentinel," BA, SS, WDS, NIC, Daisy's first all sheet metal gun, somewhat streamlined in appearance compared to the earlier guns, semi pistol-grip stock and grip frame, 1899	100	115	175
Sentinel, marked, "Sentinel," BA, RPTR, WDS, NIC, repeater variation, 1899	100	115	175

Daisys with Letter Designations

	C6	C8	C10
Model A, BA, SS, WDS, NIC, 1907	120	140	200
Model A, BA, RPTR, WDS, NIC, 1907	90	105	150
Model B, LA, RPTR, WDS, NIC (500 shot), 1909	55	65	90
Model B, LA, RPTR, WDS, NIC (1000 shot), 1909	60	75	120
Model B, LA, RPTR, WDS, BLU (500 shot), 1909	40	50	70
Model B, LA, RPTR, WDS, BLU (1000 shot), 1909	35	50	75
Model C, BA, RPTR, WDS, NIC, repeater variation (350 shot), 1912	60	75	120
Model C, BA, SS, WDS, NIC, 1910	60	75	120
Model H, LA, RPTR, WDS, NIC (350 or 500 shot), 1914	75	90	125
Model H, LA, RPTR, WDS, BLU (350 or 500 shot), 1914	55	65	90
Model H, LA, SS, WDS, NIC, 1913	75	90	125
Model H, LA, SS, WDS, BLU, 1913	55	65	90

Top to bottom: Daisy Number 111 Model 40 Red Ryder, 1951, $60; Daisy Model 21, 1968, $300. A Christmas Story Red Ryder BB Gun, 1983—due to a screenwriter's error, the Red Ryder was described in the movie as having a compass and sundial in the stock, which it never had. Daisy went along and produced a special prop gun for use in the movie and also produced a limited number of these Red Ryders for sale. Photo courtesy Jim Buskirk.

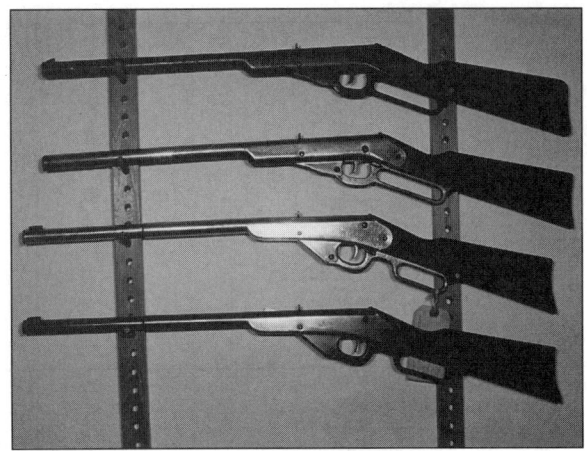

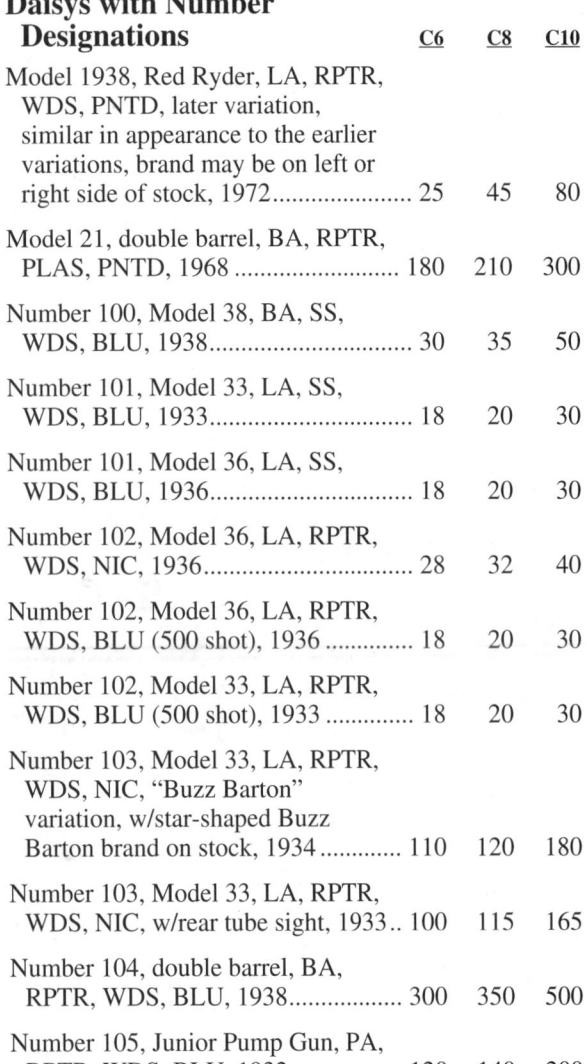

Top to Bottom: Daisy Number 101 Model 33, 1933, $30; Daisy Number 102 Model 33, 1933, $30; Daisy Number 12, 1918, $125; Daisy Number 11, 1917, $90. Photo courtesy Jim Buskirk

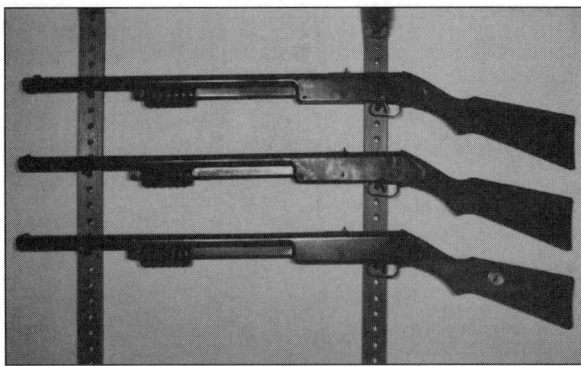

Top to Bottom: Markham/King BB Guns Number 5 Pump Gun, 1931, $150; Daisy Number 105 Junior Pump Gun, 1932, $200; Daisy Number 107 Buck Jones Special, 1934, $110. Photo courtesy Jim

Daisys with Number Designations

	C6	C8	C10
Model 1938, Red Ryder, LA, RPTR, WDS, PNTD, later variation, similar in appearance to the earlier variations, brand may be on left or right side of stock, 1972	25	45	80
Model 21, double barrel, BA, RPTR, PLAS, PNTD, 1968	180	210	300
Number 100, Model 38, BA, SS, WDS, BLU, 1938	30	35	50
Number 101, Model 33, LA, SS, WDS, BLU, 1933	18	20	30
Number 101, Model 36, LA, SS, WDS, BLU, 1936	18	20	30
Number 102, Model 36, LA, RPTR, WDS, NIC, 1936	28	32	40
Number 102, Model 36, LA, RPTR, WDS, BLU (500 shot), 1936	18	20	30
Number 102, Model 33, LA, RPTR, WDS, BLU (500 shot), 1933	18	20	30
Number 103, Model 33, LA, RPTR, WDS, NIC, "Buzz Barton" variation, w/star-shaped Buzz Barton brand on stock, 1934	110	120	180
Number 103, Model 33, LA, RPTR, WDS, NIC, w/rear tube sight, 1933	100	115	165
Number 104, double barrel, BA, RPTR, WDS, BLU, 1938	300	350	500
Number 105, Junior Pump Gun, PA, RPTR, WDS, BLU, 1932	120	140	200

Daisys with Number Designations (Continued)

	C6	C8	C10
Number 107, Buck Jones Special, PA, RPTR, WDS, BLU, engraved frame, compass and sundial stock, 1934	70	80	110
Number 108, Model 39 Carbine, LA, RPTR, WDS, BLU, 1939	45	55	75
Number 11, LA, RPTR, WDS, BLU, may also have model number (500 shot), 1917	55	65	90
Number 11, LA, RPTR, WDS, NIC, may also have model number (500 shot), 1917	75	90	125
Number 111, Model 40, Red Ryder, LA, RPTR, WDS, BLU, w/aluminum cocking lever, 1947	40	50	75
Number 111, Model 40, Red Ryder, LA, RPTR, PLAS, BLU or PNTD, both stock and forestock are plastic, 1951	38	48	60
Number 111, Model 40, Red Ryder, LA, RPTR, WDS, BLU, w/cast-iron cocking lever and copper plated barrel bands, 1940	75	90	125
Number 111, Model 40, Red Ryder, LA, RPTR, WDS, BLU, w/cast-iron cocking lever, 1941	50	63	90
Number 111, Model 40, Red Ryder, LA, RPTR, WDS, BLU, w/plastic forestock, 1950	40	50	75
Number 12, LA, SS, WDS, NIC, may also have model number, 1918	75	90	125
Number 12, LA, SS, WDS, BLU, may also have model number, 1918	55	65	90

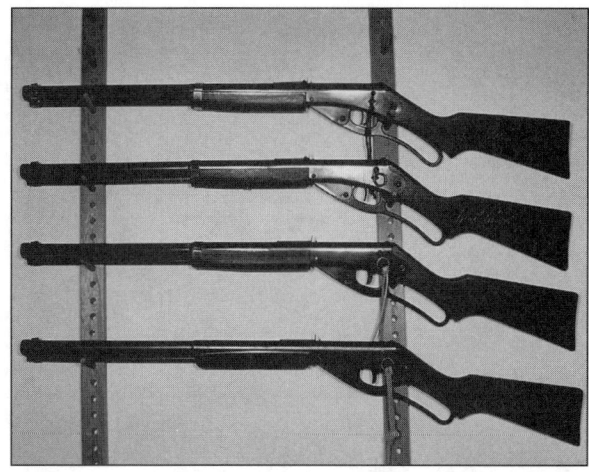

Four examples of the Daisy Number 111 Model 40 Red Red Ryder. Top to Bottom: two examples of the Number 111 with an iron lever, $90-$125; aluminum lever, $75; plastic forestock, $60. Photo courtesy Jim Buskirk

Daisys with Number
Designations (Continued)

	C6	C8	C10
Number 140, Defender, LA, RPTR, WDS, BLU, w/long wooden forestock, dummy bolt and bolt handle and sling, 1941	120	140	200
Number 195, Buzz Barton Special, LA, RPTR, WDS, BLU, w/oval Buzz Barton brand on stock, 1932	70	90	125
Number 195, Model 36 Buzz Barton Special, LA, RPTR, WDS, BLU, w/oval Buzz Barton brand on stock, 1936	60	70	100
Number 20, Little Daisy, BA, SS, WDS, NIC, w/no grip frame, 1908	75	90	125

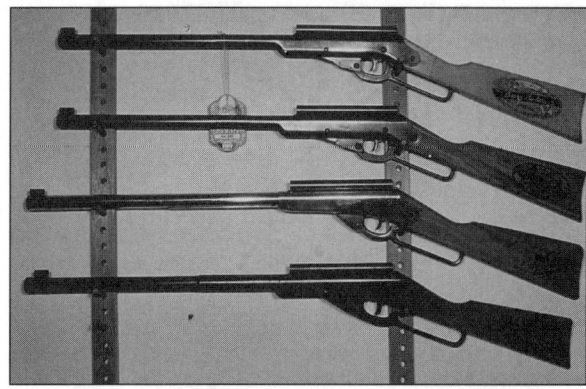

Top to Bottom: Daisy Number 195 Model 36 Buzz Barton Special with paper label, 1936, $100; Daisy Number 195 Buzz Barton Special, 1932, $125; Daisy Number 103 Model 33, 1934, $180; Daisy Number 195 Model 36 without paper label. Photo courtesy Jim Buskirk

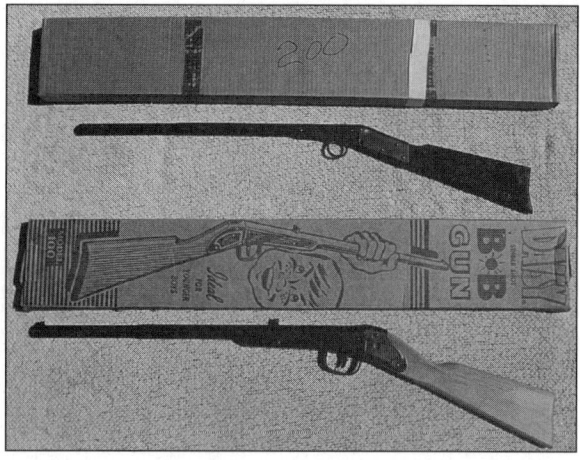

Top to Bottom: Daisy Number 20 Little Daisy, 1908, $90-125; Daisy Number 100 Model 38, 1938, $50. Photo courtesy Jim Buskirk

Daisys with Number
Designations (Continued)

	C6	C8	C10
Number 20, Little Daisy, BA, SS, WDS, NIC, two screws in grip frame, 1912	75	90	125
Number 20, Little Daisy, BA, SS, WDS, NIC, w/three rivets in grip frame and "ring" trigger, 1915	70	80	110
Number 20, Little Daisy, BA, SS, WDS, BLU, w/three rivets in grip frame and "ring" trigger, 1915	55	65	90
Number 25, pump gun, PA, RPTR, WDS, BLU, w/pistol grip stock, 1925	40	50	75
Number 25, pump gun, PA, RPTR, WDS, BLU, w/straight stock, 1914	40	50	75
Number 25, pump gun, PA, RPTR, WDS, BLU, w/pistol grip stock and engraved frame, 1936	30	35	50

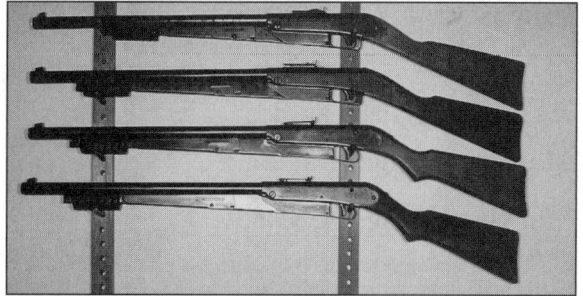

Four different versions of Daisy's Number 25, $50-$75. Top to Bottom: Early version with shot cocking lever and straight stock; long lever with straight stock; long lever with pistol grip stock; long lever and pistol grip stock with hunting scene stamped on frame. Photo courtesy Jim Buskirk

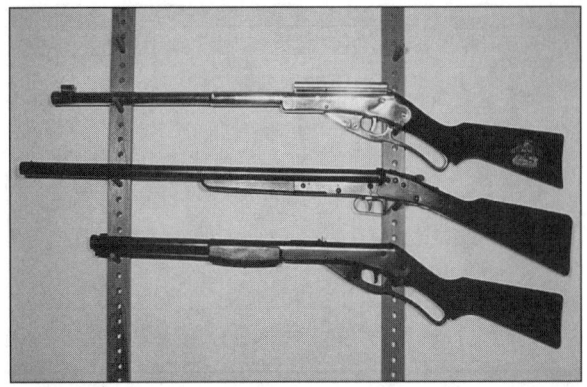

Daisy Number 50 Golden Eagle, 1936, $125. Photo courtesy Jim Buskirk

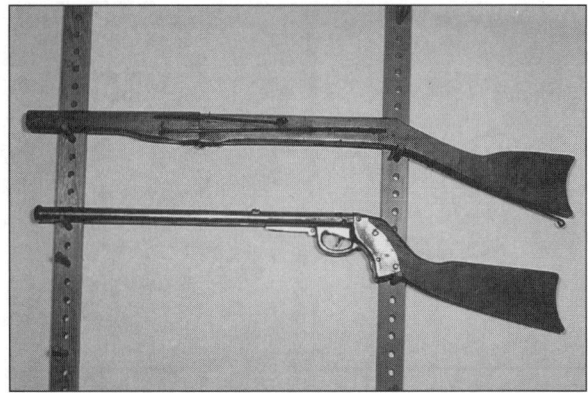

Top to Bottom: Markham/King BB Guns Chicago, 1888, $150; Markham/King BB Guns New King, 1895, $135. Photo courtesy Jim Buskirk

Daisys with Number Designations (Continued)

	C6	C8	C10
Number 25, BB Gun, Daisy's Centennial Commemorative Model, comes in colorful litho box, w/medallion in stock, 1986	40	50	75
Number 30, LA, RPTR, WDS, BLU, may also have model number (500 shot), 1925	34	38	40
Number 30, LA, RPTR, WDS, NIC, may also have model number (500 shot), 1925	44	48	60
Number 3B, LA, RPTR, WDS, black nickel finish, came in colorful lithographed box marked "Daisy Special" (1000 shot), 1914	90	105	150
Number 40, LA, RPTR, WDS, BLU, Daisy's WWII military-styled gun, w/full-length wood stock, sling and bayonet, 1916	150	175	250
Number 50, Golden Eagle, LA, RPTR, WDS, entire gun is copper plated, stock painted black and w/special eagle decal, w/rear tube sight, 1936	75	90	125
Number 94, Red Ryder, LA, RPTR, PLAS, PNTD (1000 shot), 1955	28	32	40

Markham/King BB Guns

Markham/King All Wood Guns

	C6	C8	C10
Challenge, under-barrel cast-iron cocking lever, sheet metal trigger guard, single shot, may have no markings, 1887	225	265	375
Chicago, break action, single shot, outside cocking rods on both sides, oval Markham logo on stock, 1888	90	105	150

Markham/King All Wood Guns (Continued)

	C6	C8	C10
Junior No. 10, BA, SS, WDS, NIC, 1910	60	70	100
Model C, repeater variation, 1905	45	55	75
Model D, BA, SS, WDS, NIC, grip frame wraps around wrist of stock, streamlined shape without pistol grip stock, 1905	45	55	75
New Chicago No. 24, BA, SS, WDS, BLU, 1923	75	90	125
New King, BA, SS, WDS, NIC, stock stained red, pistol grip stock is stamped "New King Patent 483153" in oval logo, 1895	80	95	135
New King, repeater, BA, RPTR, WDS, NIC, repeater variation of the above gun, w/small lever on muzzle cap used to allow a BB to drop into the shot tube, 1896	90	105	150
Number 1, same as "Model D" above, redesignated No. 1 in 1910, 1910	45	55	75
Number 17, BA, SS, WDS, BLU, w/outside cocking rods, 1917	65	80	115
Number 2, same as "Model C" above, redesignated No. 2 in 1910, 1910	45	55	75
Number 21, LA, SS, WDS, NIC, 1916	60	70	100
Number 2136, LA, SS, WDS, BLU, 1936	18	21	30
Number 22, LA, RPTR, WDS, BLU, 1916	60	70	100
Number 2236, LA, RPTR, WDS, BLU (500 shot), 1936	18	21	30

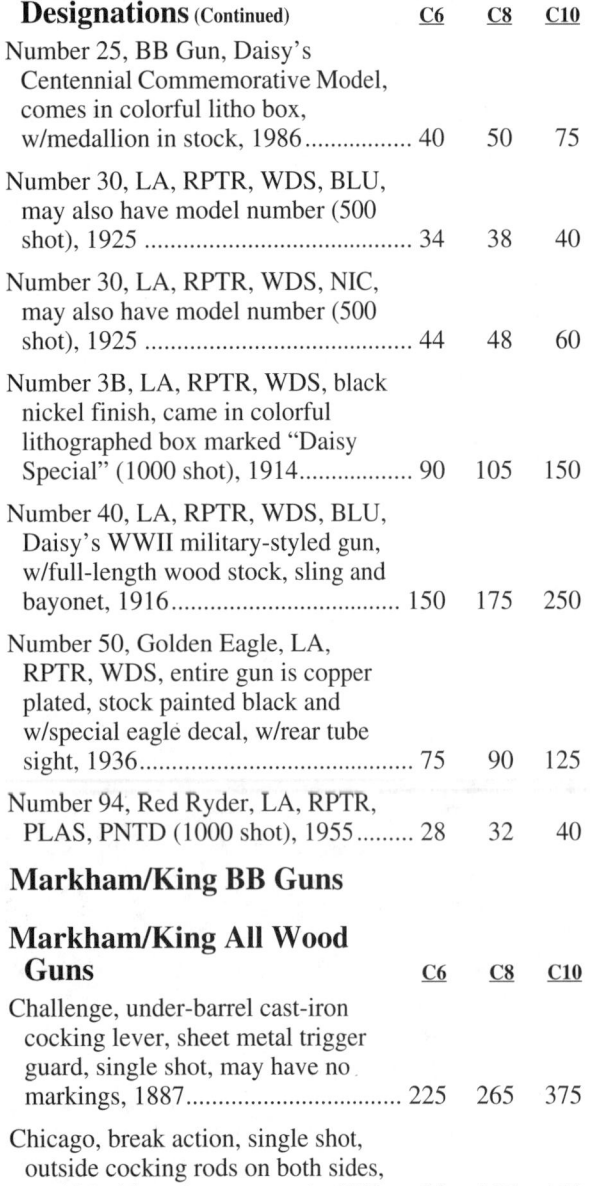

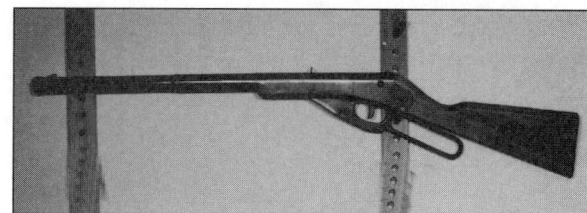

Markham/King BB Guns Number 2236, 1936, $30. Photo courtesy Jim Buskirk

Markham/King All Wood
Guns (Continued)

	C6	C8	C10
Number 4, LA, RPTR, WDS, NIC, frame w/octagon shape (500 shot), 1908	100	115	175
Number 5, LA, RPTR, WDS, NIC, frame w/octagon shape (1000 shot), 1908	100	115	175
Number 5, Pump Gun, PA, RPTR, WDS, BLU, 1931	75	100	150
Number 55, LA, RPTR, WDS, BLU, may have straight or curved lever (1000 shot), 1921	38	42	60
Number 5533, LA, RPTR, WDS, BLU (1000 shot), 1933	38	42	60

Markham/King All Wood
Guns (Continued)

	C6	C8	C10
Number 5536, LA, RPTR, WDS, BLU (1000 shot), 1936	45	55	75
Number 5B, LA, RPTR, WDS, BLU, a deluxe variation of the No. 5, came in a lithographed box, 1910	120	140	200

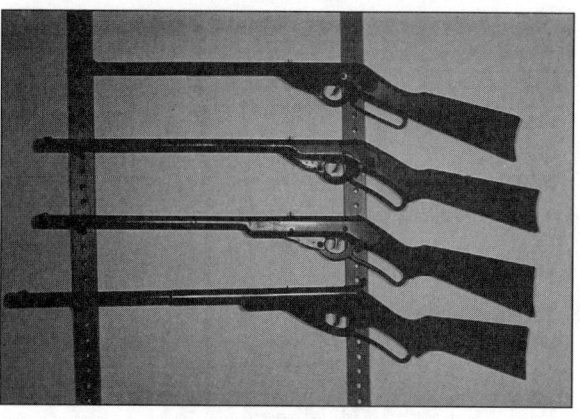

Top to Bottom: Markham/King BB Guns Number 21, 1916, $100; Markham/King BB Guns Number 55, 1921, $60; Markham/King BB Guns Number 5533, 1933, $60; Markham/King BB Guns Number 5536, 1936, $75. Photo courtesy Jim Buskirk

BELL TOYS

	C6	C8	C10
Acrobats Holding Bells, No. 54, Gong Bell Mfg. Co.	310	465	620
Alligator Ridden by Black Boy, 1910, cast iron, N.N. Hill Brass Co., 5-1/2" long	1000	1700	2300
Alligator Snapping at Teasing Boy, cast iron, 9-1/4" long	1500	2400	3500
Althof Bergmann, "Chime & Design Patd. May 19th 1874," three soldiers, one w/flag, two w/rifles, tin	1600	2400	3200
Are You a Buffalo, Gong Bell Mfg. Co.	800	1200	1600
Bear, bounces on air, iron	800	1100	1600
Bear on Tricycle, 4" long	150	225	300
Billy Goat, No. 51, goat mechanically butts bell, 1900, cast iron, Gong Bell Mfg. Co., 7-1/2" long	750	1125	1500
Bird and Bell, tin and iron, 6" long	600	900	1200
Boy and Goat, tin, Althof Bergmann, 9" long	600	900	1200
Boy Scouts, heart-shaped tin wheels, iron, rest pressed steel, 13-1/2" long	750	1125	1500

	C6	C8	C10
Boys Eating Bananas, cast iron	700	1050	1400
Camel with Rider, c. 1874, tin, Althof Bergmann, 9" long	1200	2000	2800
Cat and Dog, Gong Bell Co. Mfg. Co.	2000	3200	4500
Cinderella Chariot, 9-1/4" long	425	638	850
Clown, Gong Bell Mfg. Co., 5-3/4" long	262	393	525
Clown and Black Man on See-Saw, six color, c. 1905, cast iron, Watrous, 6-1/2" long	600	900	1200
Clown and Pig, 1900	325	488	650
Clown Bell-ringers Riding Back to Back on a Mule	1000	1500	2000
Comic Characters, two, three bells, pierced heart wheels, pressed steel and iron	700	1125	1400
Daisy, Gong Bell Mfg. Co., 9" long	600	1000	1400
Darky Fishing, Stevens, 8" long	440	660	880
Ding Dong Bell, Pussy's Not in The Well, c. 1880, cast iron, Gong Bell Mfg. Co., 9-1/2" long	600	925	1235
Dog on Platform, Fallows	400	650	900

Are You a Buffalo, Gong Bell Mfg. Co., $1600. Photo courtesy James Maxwell/Virginia Caputo

Cat and Dog, Gong Bell Mfg. Co., $4500. Photo courtesy James Maxwell/Virginia Caputo

Daisy, Gong Bell Mfg. Co., 9" long, $1400. Photo courtesy Sotheby's, New York

Ding Dong Bell, Pussy's Not in The Well, Gong Bell Mfg. Co., c. 1880, 9-1/2" long, $1235. Photo courtesy Sotheby's, New York

Elephant on Platform, Fallows, 6-3/4" long, $850. Photo courtesy Detroit Antique Toy Museum; courtesy Wilkinson Collection

	C6	C8	C10
Eagle, c. 1906, cast iron, Gong Bell Mfg. Co., 5-1/4" long	550	850	1200
Elephant & Rider in Howdah, driver on elephant's head, cast iron, 4-1/2" long	700	1100	1500
Elephant on Platform, Fallows, 6-3/4" long	425	638	850
Elephant with Bell in Trunk, c. 1905, N.N. Hill Brass Co.	700	1050	1400
Eskimo & Bear, pressed steel body, iron figures	750	1125	1500
Evening New Baby Quieter, man reading paper to baby, 1890s, cast iron, Stevens, 8" long	1100	1700	2450
Goat, 1880, painted tin, Fallows, 14"	1100	1650	2200
Goat, small woman at left leg of goat, c. 1890, tin, either Althof Bergmann or Ives, 7-1/2" high	500	750	1000
Goat, Lamb and Girl on Platform, early, tin, George Brown, 11" long	550	850	1200

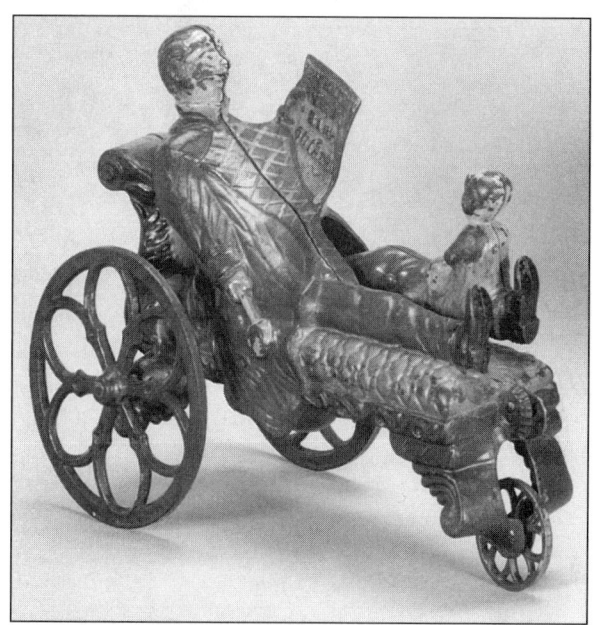

Evening New Baby Quieter, Stevens, 1890s, 8" long, $2450. Photo courtesy Christie's East

	C6	C8	C10
Goats, two, butting, Gong Bell Mfg. Co.	1200	2000	3000
Hello, Hello Telephone Chimes, w/monkey, Gong Bell Mfg. Co.	2000	3000	4000
Horse and Rider, heart-shaped wheels, tin, 9" long	750	1125	1500
Hunter and Rabbit, 1900, cast-iron rabbit pops out, N.N. Hill Brass Co.	750	1125	1500
Jack and Jill on Seesaw, cast iron and tin, Watrous, 7-1/2" long	440	660	880
Jockey on Horse, early, 7-1/2" long	200	300	400

Jonah and Whale, N.N. Hill Brass Co., 5" long, $2000. Photo courtesy James Maxwell/Virginia Caputo

Hello, Hello Telephone Chimes, Gong Bell Mfg. Co., $4000. Photo courtesy James Maxwell/Virginia Caputo

Goat, either Althof Bergmann or Ives, c. 1890, 7-1/2" high, $1000. Photo courtesy PB Eighty-Four, New York

	C6	C8	C10
Jonah and Whale, N.N. Hill Brass Co., 5" long	800	1400	2000
Landing of Columbus, 7" long	492	740	985
Liberty Bell Centennial, Gong Bell Mfg. Co., 8" long	800	1200	1600
Mary and Her Little Lamb, Gong Bell Mfg. Co., 8" long	600	900	1250
Monkey and Coconut, "Monkey Mobile," N.N. Hill Brass Co., 6" long	350	525	700
Monkey and Dog, heart wheels, cast iron and tin, 7" long	500	750	1000
Monkey and Horse, No. 23, cast iron and tin, Gong Bell Mfg. Co.	1500	2250	3000

Liberty Bell Centennial, Gong Bell Mfg. Co., 8" long, $1600. Photo courtesy Sotheby's, New York

Landing of Columbus, 7" long, $985. Photo courtesy Sotheby's, New York

Monkey and Coconut, N.N. Hill Brass Co., 6" long, $700. Photo courtesy Sotheby's, New York

Monkey in Wheeled Chariot, Gong Bell Co. (?), $4000. Photo courtesy James Maxwell/Virginia Caputo

Monkey and Horse, Gong Bell Mfg. Co., $3000. Photo courtesy James Maxwell/Virginia Caputo

	C6	C8	C10
Monkey in Wheeled Chariot, Gong Bell Co. ?	2000	3000	4000
Monkey on a Log, c. 1900, cast iron, Gong Bell Mfg. Co.	750	1125	1500
Monkey on a Velocipede, cast iron, 8" high	1500	2400	3800
Monkey Riding Elephant, clockwork, tin, Fallows, 10" long	1400	2100	2800
Oriental Clown & Poodle, No. 44, cloth in hoop, poodle jumps through hoop and back, 1900, painted cast iron, 13" long	1250	1875	2500
Pig with Clown Rider, Gong Bell Mfg. Co., 6" long	418	625	835

Top row: Saw the Watermelon, Gong Bell Mfg. Co., 8-1/2" long, $2800. Bottom row, left to right: Pig with Clown Rider, Gong Bell Mfg. Co., 6" long, $835; Monkey on a Velocipede, 8" high, $3800. Photo

	C6	C8	C10
Poodle Dog Bell Ringer with Clown, Gong Bell Mfg. Co.	1200	2800	4200
Rough Rider, Watrous, early, 6-1/2" long	123	185	245
Saw the Watermelon, Gong Bell Mfg. Co., 8-1/2" long	1100	1700	2800

Poodle Dog Bell Ringer with Clown, Gong Bell Mfg. Co., $4200. Photo courtesy James Maxwell/Virginia Caputo

Trick Elephant, Gong Bell Mfg. Co., 7-3/4" long, $1600. Photo courtesy James Maxwell/Virginia Caputo

Top row, left to right: Tramp, Gong Bell Mfg. Co., 6" long, $875; Acrobats Holding Bells, Gong Bell Mfg. Co., $620. Bottom Row, left to right: Mary and Her Little Lamb, Gong Bell Mfg. Co., 8" long, $1250; Trick Pony, Gong Bell Mfg. Co., 1893, 8" long, $1350. Photo courtesy Christie's East

Uncle Sam and The Don (missing bell), Gong Bell Mfg. Co., $4500. Photo courtesy James Maxwell/Virginia Caputo

	C6	C8	C10
Steeplechase, two jockeys on horses, Hubley	600	900	1200
Tramp, cast iron, Gong Bell Mfg. Co., 6" long	438	655	875
Trick Elephant, Gong Bell Mfg. Co., 7-3/4" long	800	1200	1600

	C6	C8	C10
Trick Pony, "39," 1893, cast iron, Gong Bell Mfg. Co., 8" long	600	1000	1350
Uncle Sam and The Don, Gong Bell Mfg. Co.	2250	3375	4500
Victory in a Shell-form Chariot, mounted w/bell and eagle, cast iron	1500	2250	3000
Watermelon, c. 1905, N.N. Hill Brass Co., 8-1/2" long	600	900	1200
White Horse Pulling Heart-shaped Wheels, c. 1896, Ives, 9-1/2" long	1000	1500	2000
Wild Mule Jack, cast iron	750	1125	1500
Young America, c. 1880, cast iron, Gong Bell Mfg. Co., 6" long	450	675	900

CATALOGS

FIFTY-FIRST EDITION

The
A. C. WILLIAMS CO.
TOYS
House Furnishing Specialties
and
HARDWARE

RAVENNA, OHIO
U. S. A.

This Catalog Supercedes All Other Catalogs
WRITE FOR PRICES.

A.C. Williams, $90

	C6	C8	C10
A.C. Williams, 1908	220	330	440
A.C. Williams, 1934	45	68	90
A.C. Williams, 1930	45	68	90
A.J. Fisher, New York, illustrating cap pistols, etc., 1877	18	27	36
Aldens Christmas, 1946	40	60	80
Arcade, 1900	115	172	230
Arcade, 1940	100	150	200
Arcade, 1931	125	188	250

	C6	C8	C10
Arcade, 1924	150	225	300
Arcade, 1917	500	750	1000
Arcade, 1901	375	562	750
Arcade, 1899	105	158	210
Arcade, 1889	100	150	200
Arcade, 1902-03	85	128	170
Auburn Rubber, pre-World War II	50	75	100
Aurora, value is for each item, 1971, 1972	17	26	35
Aurora, 1960	27	41	55
Aurora, value is for each item, 1965, 1967	55	82	110
Aurora, 1973	27	41	55
Aurora, 1975	25	38	50
Aurora, 1977	22	33	45
Aurora, value is for each item, 1963, 1964	50	75	100
Baltimore Price Reducer, illustrated w/toys, games, etc., 1928	15	22	30
Barclay, pre-World War II	200	300	400
Bilt E-Z, 1924	5	8	10
Buddy L, 1940	125	188	250
Buddy L, flier, 1926	175	263	350
Buddy L, 1929	275	352	550
Buddy L, Robotoy flier, 1932	125	188	250
Buddy L, 1935	175	262	350
Buddy L, 1941	135	202	270
Buddy L, 1961	22	33	45
Buddy L, value is for each item, 1952, 1953, 1956, 1957, 1959	7	11	15
Buddy L Jr., 1930	150	225	300
Buffalo Toy, 1939	75	112	150
Butler Bros., value is for each item, 1935, 1936	40	60	80

	C6	C8	C10
Butler Bros., tin toys, squeak toys, etc., 1889	30	45	60
Butler Bros., illustrated w/mechanical banks, toys, dolls, etc., 1891	30	45	60
Butler Bros., November, 1899	40	60	80
Butler Bros., June, 1917	70	105	140
Butler Bros., Christmas, 1931	35	52	70
Butler Bros., Spring, 1941	60	90	120
Butler Bros., Christmas, 1930	35	52	70
Carpenter, Francis, 1880s	900	1350	1800
Champion, four pages and cover	150	225	300
Chein, value is for each item, 1956, 1960	50	75	100
Corgi, value is for each item, 1966, 1967	10	15	20
Daisy, 1975	22	33	45
Dayton, 1929	150	225	300
Dent Hardware Co., Fullerton, Pa., 1930	32	48	65
Dent Hardware Co., Fullerton, Pa., undated	30	45	60
Dent Hardware Co., 1910	37	56	75
Dent Hardware Co., 1905	37	56	75
Dent Hardware Co., forty pages, 1900	40	60	80
Dinky, 1950s	27	41	55
Dunham, Buckley & Co., New York, toys, etc., 1895	40	60	80
Durable Toy & Novelty, 1920s	10	15	20
Ehrich Bros., New York, illustrations of banks, toys, dolls, etc., 1892	40	60	80
Eldon, autos, 1961	6	9	12
Eldon, boats, 1961	6	9	12
Erector Set, thirty-eight pages, 1938	15	22	30
Ertl, 1974	3	5	6
Eureka Trick & Novelty Co., thirty-two pages, 1875	20	30	40
Ewing Merkle Catalog, 1903	21	35	70
Fisher-Price, 1954	6	9	12
Fisher-Price, 1966	25	38	50
Garton Pedal Cars, 1940	100	150	200

	C6	C8	C10
Gendron, 1927	600	900	1200
Gilbert, 1966	27	41	55
Gould, L., Christmas, 1922	125	188	250
Gould, L., 1940	55	83	110
Grey Iron, No. 24, 1920s	115	172	230
Hasbro, 1975	27	41	55
Hasbro, 1987, 1989	20	30	40
Howdy Doody Merchandise, 1955	27	41	55
Hubley, 1914-15	55	83	110
Hubley, 1939	60	90	120
Hubley, 1966	16	24	32
Hubley, 1969	11	16	22
Hubley, 1974	22	33	45
Ideal, 1973	12	18	25
Ideal, 1976	12	18	25
Ives and Williams, illustrated brochure of cap pistols and animated cap pistols, 18" x 24"	20	30	40
Ives Yachts, Ships and Shipping, twenty-four pages, 1915	50	75	100

Fisher-Price, 1966, $50

	C6	C8	C10
Ives, Blakeslee & Williams, two-sided broadside, 1890	70	105	140
JC Penney, Christmas, value is for each item, 1975 through 1980	27	41	55
JC Penney, Christmas, value is for each item, 1963, 1964, 1965	68	102	135
JC Penney, Christmas, value is for each item, 1966 through 1970	50	75	100
JC Penney, Christmas, value is for each item, 1971 through 1975	35	52	70
Jones & Bixler, 1912	100	150	200
Kenton Hardware Co., 112 pages, No. 16, 1920s	70	105	140
Kenton Hardware Co., color illustrations, 1934	50	75	100
Kilgore, 1977-78	22	33	45
Kingsbury, 1919	55	82	110
Kingsbury, value is for each item, 1920, c. 1925	32	48	65
Kingsbury, small size, 128 pages, 1930s	100	150	200
Kingsbury Toys, motor driven, sixteen pages, 1936	40	60	80
Knapp Electric Toys, No. 35	10	15	20
Knickerbocker, 1961	8	12	17
Lionel Catalog, 1911	21	35	70
Lionel Catalog, 1968	1	2	4
Lionel Catalog, 1907	21	35	70
Lionel Catalog, 1904	21	35	70
Lionel Catalog, 1906	21	35	70
Lionel Catalog, 1908	21	35	70
Lionel Catalog, 1905	21	35	70
Lionel Catalog, 1914	21	35	70
Lionel Catalog, small, 1913	15	25	50
Lionel Catalog, small, 1914	15	25	50
Lionel Catalog, 1913	21	35	70
Lionel Catalog, 1912	21	35	70
Lionel Catalog, 1969	1	2	4
Lionel Catalog, 1915	21	35	70
Lionel Catalog, 1922	21	35	70
Lionel Catalog, 1955	10	15	20
Lionel Catalog, 1956	5	8	16
Lionel Catalog, 1957	3	6	11
Lionel Catalog, 1958	4	6	12
Lionel Catalog, 1959	4	7	13
Lionel Catalog, 1953	7	12	24
Lionel Catalog, 1961	4	6	12
Lionel Catalog, 1952	9	15	30
Lionel Catalog, 1962	3	6	11
Lionel Catalog, 1963	2	3	5
Lionel Catalog, 1964	2	3	5
Lionel Catalog, 1965	1	2	4
Lionel Catalog, 1916	21	35	70
Lionel Catalog, 1917	21	35	70
Lionel Catalog, 1966	1	2	4
Lionel Catalog, 1960	3	5	10
Lionel Catalog, 1941	14	23	45
Lionel Catalog, 1903	21	35	70
Lionel Catalog, 1934	15	24	48
Lionel Catalog, 1935	17	28	55
Lionel Catalog, 1936	15	24	48
Lionel Catalog, 1937	11	18	35
Lionel Catalog, 1938	14	23	45
Lionel Catalog, 1954	5	9	17
Lionel Catalog, 1940	12	20	40
Lionel Catalog, 1923	15	25	50
Lionel Catalog, 1942	14	23	45
Lionel Catalog, 1945	5	8	16
Lionel Catalog, 1947	20	25	35
Lionel Catalog, 1948	9	15	30
Lionel Catalog, 1949	50	80	110
Lionel Catalog, 1950	25	40	55
Lionel Catalog, 1951	15	25	35
Lionel Catalog, 1939	11	18	35
Lionel Catalog, 1925	21	35	70
Lionel Catalog, 1932	22	38	75
Lionel Catalog, 1910	21	35	70
Lionel Catalog, 1931	21	35	70
Lionel Catalog, 1927	22	38	75
Lionel Catalog, 1933	16	28	55
Lionel Catalog, 1930	21	35	70

	C6	C8	C10
Lionel Catalog, 1929	21	35	70
Lionel Catalog, 1920	21	35	70
Lionel Catalog, 1924	21	35	70
Lionel Catalog, 1926	18	30	60
Lionel Catalog, 1909	21	35	70
Lionel Catalog, 1928	22	38	75
Manoil, 1935-39	100	150	200
Marx, 1976	12	18	25
Marx, 1969	110	165	220
Marx, 1966	100	150	200
Marx, 1964	125	188	250
Marx, thirty-six pages, 1930s	225	338	450
Matchbox, 1970	4	6	8
Matchbox, 1973	11	16	22

	C6	C8	C10
Matchbox, 1969	6	9	12
Matchbox, 1968	7	11	15
Matchbox, 1966	15	22	30
Matchbox, 1965	22	33	45
Matchbox, 1964	25	38	50
Matchbox, 1978	13	19	26
Mattel, 1967	150	225	300

Mattel, 1967, $300

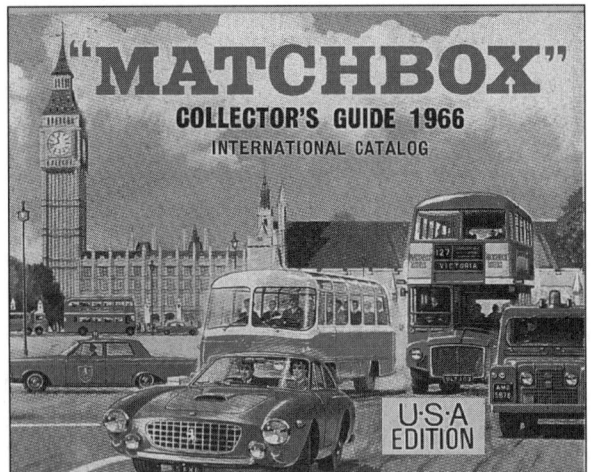

Matchbox, 1966, $30

Matchbox, 1969, $12

Matchbox, 1968, $15

Schoenhut Circus, 1918, $225

	C6	C8	C10
McCadden & Bros. Philadelphia, illustrated iron and tin toys, banks, mechanical toys, dolls, games, etc.	50	75	100
Mego, value is for each item, 1967-69	50	75	100
Mickey Mouse Merchandise Catalog, by Kay Kamen Co., eighty pages, hundreds of illustrations of Mickey Mouse items, 1935	300	450	600
Montgomery Ward, Christmas, value is for each item, 1976 through 1980	27	41	55
Montgomery Ward, Christmas, value is for each item, 1971 through 1975	35	52	70
Montgomery Ward, Christmas, value is for each item, 1966 through 1970	50	75	100
Montgomery Ward, Christmas, value is for each item, 1941 through 1965	68	102	135
Montgomery Ward, Christmas, value is for each item, 1934 through 1940	82	123	165
Montgomery Ward, Christmas, value is for each item, 1981 through 1985	20	30	40

	C6	C8	C10
Nicol & Co., illustrating banks, etc., 1895	27	41	55
Ohio Art, 1961	8	12	17
Popsicle Pete Radio News and Premium catalog, early	40	60	80
Popsicle Pete's, four-page gift list, 1949	10	15	20
Pyro, each, 1966, 1967	19	28	38
Pyro, 1970	9	13	18
Rel Toy Boats foldout, 1958	20	30	40
Revell, 1957-58	37	56	75
Revell, 1958-59	25	38	50
Revell, 1969	10	15	20
Schoenhut, 1903	100	150	200
Schoenhut Circus, 1918	112	168	225
Schoenhut Circus, 1928	100	150	200
Schoenhut Humpty Dumpty Circus, (includes other toys), many illustrations, 1915	100	165	220
Sears, Fall-Winter, 1919	30	45	60
Sears Christmas, each, 1961 through 1965	82	123	165
Sears Christmas, 1933	60	90	120
Sears Christmas, each, 1976 through 1980	30	45	60
Sears Christmas, each, 1971 through 1975	45	68	90
Sears Christmas, each, 1966 through 1970	60	90	120
Sears Christmas, each, 1956 through 1960	82	123	165
Sears Christmas, each, 1951 through 1955	82	123	165
Sears Christmas, each, 1946 through 1950	82	123	165
Sears Christmas, each, 1936 through 1940	82	123	165
Sears Christmas, 1926	67	100	135
Sears Christmas, value is for each item, 1941 through 1945	82	123	165
Selchow & Righter, games and toys, illustrated trains, boats, bell toys, mechanical banks, etc., 1894-95	120	180	240
Selchow & Righter, 108 pages, 1908-1909	80	120	160

	C6	C8	C10
Selchow & Righter, 1921	32	48	65
Shure, N., 1940	85	128	170
Smith-Miller, 1954	40	60	80
Spiegel, Christmas, value is for each item, 1981 through 1985	20	30	40
Spiegel, Christmas, value is for each item, 1986 through 1990	15	22	30
Spiegel, Christmas, value is for each item, 1971 through 1975	35	52	70
Spiegel, Christmas, value is for each item, 1941 through 1965	68	102	135
Spiegel, Christmas, value is for each item, 1976 through 1980	27	41	55
Spiegel, Christmas, value is for each item, 1966 through 1970	50	75	100
State Adams & Dearborn Sts., Chicago, illustrated	10	15	20
Steelcraft, forty-four pages, 1934	300	450	600
Steelcraft, 1936	350	525	700
Stern, Carl P., illustrating cap pistols, etc.	15	22	30
Stevens, J.E. Co., illlustrations of iron toys and mechanical banks, 1906	40	60	80
Stevens, J.E. Co., No. 51, export	40	60	80

	C6	C8	C10
Strauss, tiny, thiry-two pages, 1926	37	56	75
Structo Toys, eight pages, 1931	10	15	20
Supplee-Biddle of Philadelphia, 174 pages, many toys, 1930	90	135	180
Thorsen & Cassady, guns, etc., 1894	20	30	40
Tinkertoy, 1926	6	9	12
Tom Mix Premium Catalog, 1936	30	45	60
Toy Yearbook, value is for each item, 1952-53, 1956-57, 1957-58,1958-59	12	18	25
Transogram, 1949	15	22	30
Vindex, 1932	275	365	550
Walt Disney Character Merchandise, 1930s	250	375	500
Walt Disney Character Merchandise, 1940-41	250	375	500
Western Auto, each, 1960 through 1969	32	48	65
Williams, Charles, 1928	22	33	45
Woolworth's Christmas, 1951	30	45	60
Woolworth's Christmas, 1952	15	22	30
Woolworth's Christmas, 1954	15	22	30
Woolworth's Christmas Catalogs, pre-World War II	30	45	60

Woolworth's Christmas, 1954, $30

Woolworth's Christmas, 1952, $30

COMIC CHARACTERS

(See also Battery-Operated, Mechanical Banks, Paper, Premiums, Movies, Ramp Walkers, Vehicles - Tootsietoy, Wood & Composition Toys)

Collecting, like most other human endeavors, came into a unique focus in the year 2000. The end of the century and the millennium gave people a natural pause to evaluate what they've been interested in and an obvious starting point for new beginnings. And as far as new beginnings go, the results in the marketplace in 2000 were spectacular.

More people entered the market and for anyone interested in comic character collectibles there was more information than ever to go around. There were numerous record setting sales, and many established auctions set record prices as well.

The continued growth in online auction activity on services such as eBay fueled the on-going revolution in accessibility. Price, of course, is still a very important factor, but now a collector in the most isolated rural setting can compete on an even playing field with his or her fellow collectors in our largest cities. While there is great uncertainty in many areas of the dot.com world, the attractiveness of the access it offers is a sure thing.

The accessibility of the product alone would not sustain the present expansion if it were not closely coupled with a similar growth in the amount of information available about collectibles. Whether it is specialized information about a particular niche or a broader overview of pop culture history, there is a dizzying sum of knowledge to be had in the form of newsletters, web sites, books and price guides such as this. It doesn't stop there.

As noted in the last edition, history is now at your fingertips. All one has to do is turn the page in a book, click a computer mouse or a TV remote control, and the past opens up to us instantly. A dozen or more cable channels are functioning from the same basic impulse: We want to know more. When we get to know more, we want to know even more. As a society we seem bent on documenting everything, and as we document we understand. As we understand, we tend to see items we overlooked or passed by in a different light. What was just "there," is now intriguing or even "cool."

For the historians among us, perhaps the most exciting element of this is that this is not just limited to collectors recapturing their own childhood. The demographics of those cable channels, the expanding use of the Internet, and the proliferation of books on collecting correctly suggest just the opposite. The same young people who are leading the vanguard of the Internet are now finding themselves interested in Hopalong Cassidy, Howdy Doody, The Beatles, and other icons of yesteryear.

There is a tangible link—a hold-it-in-your-hands understanding of what was going on "way back when"—provided by comic character collectibles and the knowledge and understanding that comes with them. Beware anyone spending a lot of time trying to convince you that the interest in a certain type or area of collecting will fade as a generation passes on. Folks espousing these types of views have either entirely missed the boat or they're trying to buy your collection cheap. Unlike fads that explode onto the scene, fade out, return, and fade out again, the interest in both nostalgia and history is going to expand into the foreseeable future.

The process of breaking down, identifying, recording and researching these vast areas of collectibles began less than 30 years ago, and it's only in the last decade that we've really accelerated the process. If you consider the huge amount of information available on current products as it is released, you can get an inkling of the amount of information that was missing when we started getting organized as collectors.

The market varies based on region and a number of other factors, but as with other areas in collecting, condition is king. High-grade comic character collectibles represent one of the best investments you could have made in the past few years. The record prices realized this past year for such items, particularly those in their original packaging, is not a fluke. The attention to items from our past is growing and it is going to keep growing as more pieces of the puzzle fit together.

Contributor: John Fawcett, P.O. Box 1156, 3506 Atlantic Highway, Waldoboro, ME 04572

John K. Snyder, Jr. Snyder is President of Diamond International Galleries and is a leading expert on comic character collectibles. He serves as a pricing advisor to *Hake's Price Guide To Character Toys, The Overstreet Comic Book Price Guide, The Overstreet Toy Ring Price Guide, Tomart's Radio Premiums Price Guide, Krause's Radio Premiums Price Guide* and *Toys & Prices,* and the *Original Comic Art Price Guide.*

Alphonse Nodder, Hubley, $780. Photo courtesy Christie's East

Alphonse

	C6	C8	C10
Nodder, in horse-drawn carriage, nodder toys, Hubley, c. 1910, 10-1/2" long	500	850	1250
Nodder, cast iron, movable arms and hands in a goat-pulled cart, Hubley, early 1900s, 13-3/4" long, 7-1/2" high	350	475	780
Nodder, cast iron, mule pulling wagon, Hubley, 7" long	250	475	780
Nodder, cast iron, movable arms and hands, two goats pulling wagon, Hubley, early 1900s, 13-3/4" long, 7-1/2" high	200	310	525

Archie

	C6	C8	C10
Archie and Veronica Jalopy, tin wind-up, w/illustration on side, Spanish, 7"	145	218	350
Archie Hand Puppet, vinyl, Ideal, 1973	25	38	50

Barney Google

	C6	C8	C10
Barney Google and Sparkplug Pull Toy, tin litho, Sparkplug in barn	1500	2250	3600
Barney Google and Sparkplug Scooter Race, pull toy, Nifty Toy Co., 1920s, 8" long	3000	5000	7250

Barney Google (Continued)

	C6	C8	C10
Barney Google and Sparkplug Tin Wind-up, Nifty	650	985	1350
Barney Google Candy Container, glass	150	290	400
Barney Google Doll, wood, w/composition head and movable arms and legs, 9" high	175	350	500
Barney Google Hand Puppet, Gund	45	80	175
Barney Google Riding Sparkplug Paperweight, metal, 3"	75	150	250
Barney Google Tin Wind-up, c. 1923	350	775	1050
Rudy the Ostrich, tin, Nifty, 1924	450	750	1050
Snuffy Smith Hand Puppet, cloth w/rubber head, "King Features," Gund	35	52	85
Sparkplug Candy Container	145	218	350

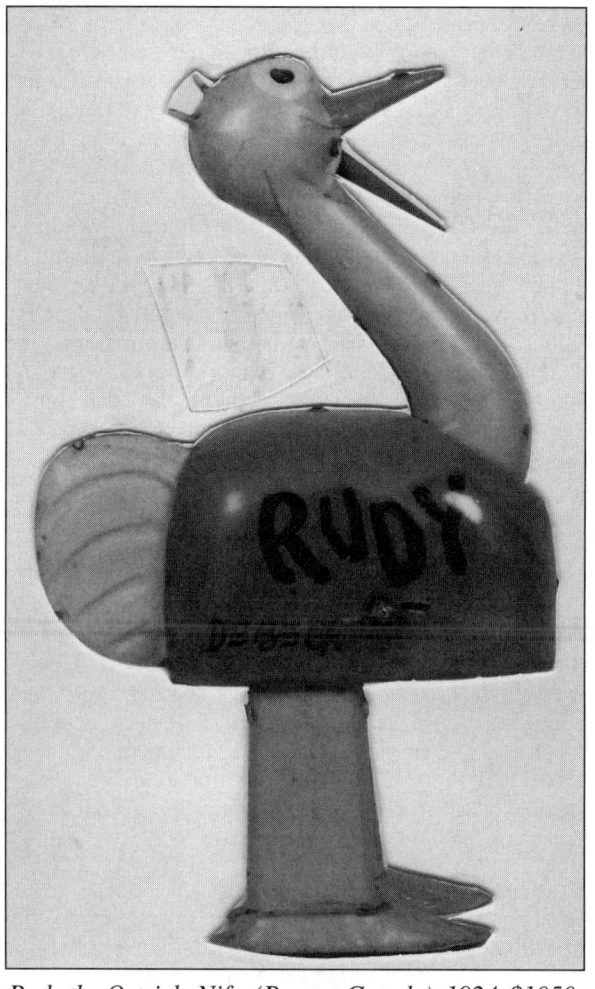

Rudy the Ostrich, Nifty (Barney Google), 1924, $1050. Photo courtesy James Maxwell/Virginia Caputo

Barney Google (Continued)

	C6	C8	C10
Sparkplug Doll, stuffed cloth	125	200	325
Sparkplug on Wheels, 3-1/4" high	225	338	475
Sparkplug Wa-Gee Walker, cloth, felt and metal, wind-up, 9" long	295	460	700

Batman

	C6	C8	C10
Bat Grenade, 1966................................	50	65	80
Bat Ray, Remco, 1977...........................	25	38	65
Batchute, in box add $300, 1966..........	30	125	225
Batmobile, No. 267, Corgi	55	125	200
Batmobile, Batman driver, Marx, 1966	65	98	175
Batmobile, Robin driver, Marx, 4" long..	65	98	150
Bullhorn, Bayshore Ind., 1966	75	150	300
Escape Gun, Lincoln, c. 1966	42	63	125
Flying Batman, inflatable, Ideal, 1966, 12"..	10	15	30
Glasses, 1966...	4	12	25
Hand Puppet, vinyl, Ideal, 1965	27	50	85
Hand Puppet, cloth body	27	50	85
Helmet and Cape, helmet fits over whole head, Ideal, 1966	145	225	375
Hot Line Batphone, Marx....................	250	375	600
Pay Set, Ideal, 1973............................	25	50	75
Picture Pistol, Marx, 1966....................	225	350	525
Robin Hand Puppet, Ideal, 1966	70	105	140
Robin Soaky	40	60	150
Soaky	30	40	75
Thingmaker Set, on original card, 1960s...	250	350	500
Utility Belt, w/belt-radio buckle, on original card, 1960s...........................	50	125	200
Utility Belt Set, Remco, 1979	50	125	200

Beetle Bailey

	C6	C8	C10
Beetle Bailey, tin litho, "Pop Up Beetle Bailey," Linemar	180	270	375
Beetle Bailey Figure, vinyl, 3"...............	8	12	20
Beetle Bailey Hand Puppet, Gund.........	45	68	100
Beetle Bailey's Camp Swampy Play Set, MPC...	115	172	250
Sergeant Snorkel Hand Puppet.............	37	56	75
Zero Hand Puppet, vinyl and cloth, Gund, 1960s	30	45	75

Blondie

	C6	C8	C10
Blondie Hingees Set, 1944	20	30	50
Blondie Paper Cut-Outs, "Blondie's Jalopy," 16" long............................	1200	2000	2800
Blondie Paper Cut-Outs, No. 982, Whitman, 1940...................................	60	125	200
Blondie Paper Cut-Outs, No. 967, Whitman, 1947...................................	37	65	100
Dagwood Aeroplane, "Dagwood's Solo Flight," Marx, 1935	350	550	800
Dagwood Marionette, wood body w/plastic head, hands, feet and life-like hair, marked "Hazelle's," 1940s, 15"	60	90	175
Dagwood the Driver Crazy Car, Marx, 1935, 8" long	500	800	1200

Bringing Up Father

	C6	C8	C10
Bringing Up Father Hingees, 1944........	17	26	40
Jiggs Doll, wood-jointed, Jaymar, 5"	80	120	175
Jiggs Doll, hard plastic, 1960s, 3" high..	6	9	20
Jiggs Jazz Car, wind-up, Nifty, 1920s, 6-1/2" long...........................	1200	3200	5750
Jiggs Stick Puppet, 12" high..................	80	120	160
Maggie and Jiggs, seated on four-wheeled platform, Nifty, 1920s, 8" long...	750	1100	1600

Jiggs Jazz Car (Bringing Up Father), Nifty, 1920s, $5750. Photo courtesy Christie's East

Maggie and Jiggs Squeeze Toy (Bringing Up Father), German, c. 1925, $850. Photo courtesy Christie's East

Bringing Up Father (Continued)

	C6	C8	C10
Maggie and Jiggs Squeeze Toy, tin litho, German, c. 1925, 8"	400	600	850
Maggie and Jiggs Wind-up, Strauss, 1924, 7-1/4" long	800	1200	1750
Maggie Doll, hard plastic, 1960s, 3" high	6	12	20

Buck Rogers

	C6	C8	C10
Atomic Pistol U-235, with box, add $500, Daisy, 1946	150	350	500

Buck Rogers (Continued)

	C6	C8	C10
Battle Cruiser, two grooved wheels on top to run on string, Tootsietoy, 1937	100	150	250
Casting Set, Junior Caster, Rapaport Bros., 1930s	325	500	750
Chemical Laboratory, large set, Gropper Toys, 1937	800	1250	1650
Chemical Laboratory, small set, Gropper Toys, 1937	600	1000	1300
Disintegrator Pistol, w/box $500, Daisy, 1936	200	350	550
Figure, Tootsietoy, 1-3/4" high	38	90	150
Flash Blast Attack Ship, two grooved wheels on top to run string, Tootsietoy, 1937, 4-1/2" long	225	338	500
Flying Saucer, paper, 1940s	75	112	175
Helmet, leather, Daisy, 1933	300	550	775
Liquid Helium Water Pistol, w/box add $1,000, Daisy, 1936	1050	1200	2100
Pop Pistol, 1930s	112	300	400
Rocket Pistol XZ-31, w/box add $500, Daisy, 1934, 9-1/2" long	132	300	500
Rocket Police Patrol, wind-up, Marx, 1939	800	1300	1800
Rocket Ship, wind-up, Marx, 1934, 12" long	358	535	750
Rubber Band Gun, 1940, 5" x 10"	50	75	125
Sonic Ray Gun, yellow plastic, with box, 1952	65	175	300
Strato Kite, 1946	37	56	75

Buck Rogers Atomic Pistol U-235, Daisy, 1946, $500. Photo courtesy Hake's Americana and Collectibles

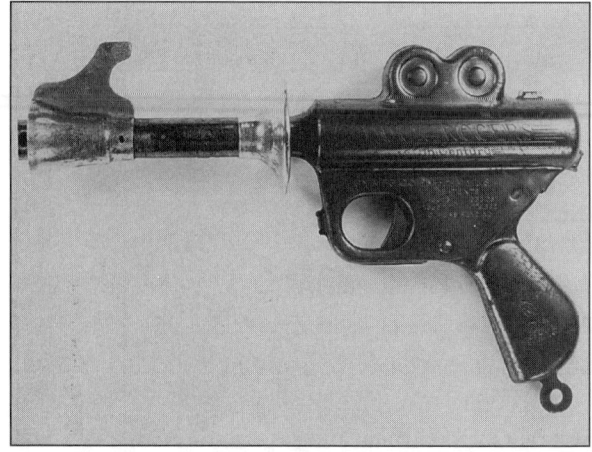

Buck Rogers Rocket Pistol XZ-31, Daisy, 1934, $500. Photo courtesy Hake's Americana and Collectibles

Buck Rogers (Continued)

	C6	C8	C10
Super Sonic Glasses (binoculars), 1953 ... 70		105	140
Super Sonic Ray Gun, w/box 150		200	350
Super-Scope, w/adjustable plastic telescope, Norton-Honer Mfg. Co., 1952, 8-1/2" long 92		138	185
U-238 Atomic Pistol and Holster set, w/box add $500, 1948 400		700	1000
U-238 Atomic Pistol and Holster set, adventure book and coupon, w/box, Daisy, 1946 800		1000	1500
USN Los Angeles, Tootsietoy, 5" long 117		175	235
Venus Duo Destroyer, two grooved wheels on top to run on string, Tootsietoy, 1937 170		255	340
Walkie Talkie, 1950s........................... 110		165	220
Wilma Pistol and Holster Set, small version of Buck Rogers "Pop" pistol, 1930s 200		400	600

Buster Brown and Tige

	C6	C8	C10
Buster Brown and Tige, cast iron, Buster in cart pulled by Tige, 7-1/2" long 500		750	950
Buster Brown and Tige Paper Dolls, w/envelope, dolls, Tige, four suits and hats, and hat for Tige, J. Ottman Lith. Co. N.Y. 150		200	300

Buster Brown and Tige, $950. Photo courtesy Christie's East

Buster Brown and Tige (Continued)

	C6	C8	C10
Buster Brown and Tige Ring, brass, 1930s 35		50	100
Buster Brown and Tige Tin Wind-up, w/street lamp and bell, c. early 1900s 2000		3500	5500

Buster Brown and Tige Tin Wind-up, c. early 1900s, $5500. Photo courtesy Christie's East

Buster Brown Seesaw Tin Wind-up, German, $1600. Photo courtesy Christie's East

Buster Brown
and Tige (Continued)

	C6	C8	C10
Buster Brown Doll, Ideal, 1929	125	175	200
Buster Brown Doll, 1920s, 23" high	200	300	450
Buster Brown Figure, lead	20	35	50
Buster Brown Secret Agent Periscope, c. 1950, 20" long	25	40	60
Buster Brown Seesaw Tin Wind-up, w/Buster and Tige, German, 9-1/2"	600	1100	1600

Captain Marvel Buzz Bomb, $50. Photo courtesy Continental Hobby House

Captain Marvel Comic Hero Punch-outs, Samuel Lowe, 1942, $250. Photo courtesy Bruce Bergstrom-Artman Originals

Buster Brown
and Tige (Continued)

	C6	C8	C10
Buster Brown Tin Wind-up, drives horseless carriage, Lehmann	500	850	1300

Captain America

	C6	C8	C10
Captain America Hand Puppet, 1966	30	50	85
Captain America Jailhouse Lock Set, Larami, 1974	10	15	20
Captain America Utility Set, Remco, 1977	16	25	50

Captain Marvel

	C6	C8	C10
Billy Batson Magic Box	75	100	150
Buzz Bomb	20	30	50
Captain Marvel Lightning Racing Cars, four tin wind-up race cars, box turns into race track with fans in the stand, track is held up by metal supports; individual cars are valued at between $450-$500, 1947	2000	3500	5000
Comic Hero Punch-outs, includes two Captain Marvels, Captain Marvel Jr., Bulletman, Bulletgirl, Spy Smasher, Ibis, two Golden Arrows, Minute Man, Freddy Freeman, Mr. Scarlet, Commando Yank, Pinky, Bulletdog, Samuel Lowe, 1942	150	200	250
Flying Captain Marvel, paper, Reed, 1944-47, 7" x 10"	15	20	35
Gun, movie gun w/film	175	263	350
Hoppy the Flying Marvel Bunny, paper, Reed, c. 1944-47	10	15	30
Magic Eyes, Reed, c. 1945	15	30	50
Magic Flute, copyright picture of Captain Marvel on side, on original card, 1946	100	150	175
Magic Picture, Reed, c. 1944	50	70	90
Porsche Car No. 262, Corgi, 1979	37	56	75
Rocket Raider, Reed, c. 1944-47	15	30	40
Three Flying Marvels, paper, Reed, c. 1944-47	15	30	50
Toss Bag	50	60	80

Dennis the Menace

	C6	C8	C10
Dennis the Menace Figure, Hall, 1970s, 7" high	42	63	85
Dennis the Menace Squirt Gun Figure, plastic, 1954, 5-1/2" high	40	60	80

Dick Tracy

	C6	C8	C10
Air Detective Wings, c. late 1930s	65	75	100
Automatic, w/picture of Eagles, Hubley	90	125	200
B.O. Plenty Holding Sparkle Plenty Tin Wind-up, Marx, mid-1940s	150	270	375
Baby Sparkle Plenty Paper Dolls, No. 1510, Saalfield	35	75	125
Bonny Braids, Ideal, 1951	75	100	125
Bonny Braids Walker, Ideal, 1953	50	75	100
Click Pistol, No. 36, Marx	105	160	300
Click Pistol, aluminum, No. 78, Marx	45	75	150
Copmobile, plastic, Ideal, 1963	35	52	70
Crime Stoppers Lab, Porter Chem Co., 10" x 12" box	150	225	375
Crimestoppers Set, includes badge, handcuffs, billy club, John Henry	45	68	90
Detective Badge with Secret Compartment, metal, large, leather pouch on back, late 1930s	50	75	150
Detective Fingerprint Set, 1933	100	150	250
Dick Tracy and B.O. Plenty with Crimestopper Whistle and Clue Detector	40	60	80
Dick Tracy Doll, painted composition, mouth moves, 13-1/2" high	275	500	650
Dick Tracy Junior Pinback Button, Parisian Novelty Company, 1930s	75	225	400
Double Target Game, 1941, 9-1/2" square w/8" tin gun and darts	150	300	400
Electronic Wrist Radio, Remco	35	52	75
G-Man Gun, wind-up, Marx	150	210	275
Hand Puppet, Ideal, 1961	37	56	75
Handcuffs for Junior, No. 700, John Henry Products, c. 1946	50	75	100
Hingee Paper Figures, set of six, 1940s	20	30	50
Inspector General Badge	600	800	1000
Moon Maid's Daughter Doll, w/space helmet, Ideal, 1965, 16-1/2"	92	140	250
Pen-Lite, 1939	75	85	150
Police Car Tin Wind-up, 1949, 7" long	175	275	375
Police Station, w/7" long automatic siren car, w/box add $250, 1950s	200	350	500

Dick Tracy (Continued)

	C6	C8	C10
Power Jet Squad Gun, Mattel, 1962, 28" long	72	108	150
Shootin' Shell Snubnose .38 Pistol and Holster	NPF	NPF	NPF
Siren Pistol, red w/blue siren, c. late 1930s	40	75	150
Siren Police Whistle, tin, No. 64, Marx	40	60	80
Space Coupe, Aurora, 1966	375	600	850

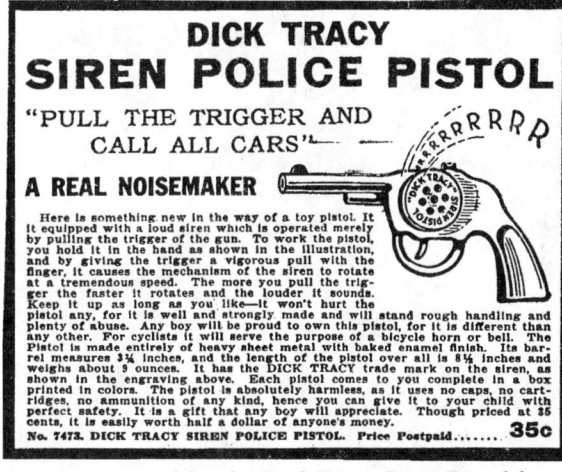

A newspaper ad for the Dick Tracy Siren Pistol from late 1930s. The pistol is valued at $150.

Dick Tracy Riot Car, Marx, c. 1946, $275. Photo courtesy Gary Linden

Dick Tracy Police Station, 1950s, $500. Photo courtesy Ron Chojnacki

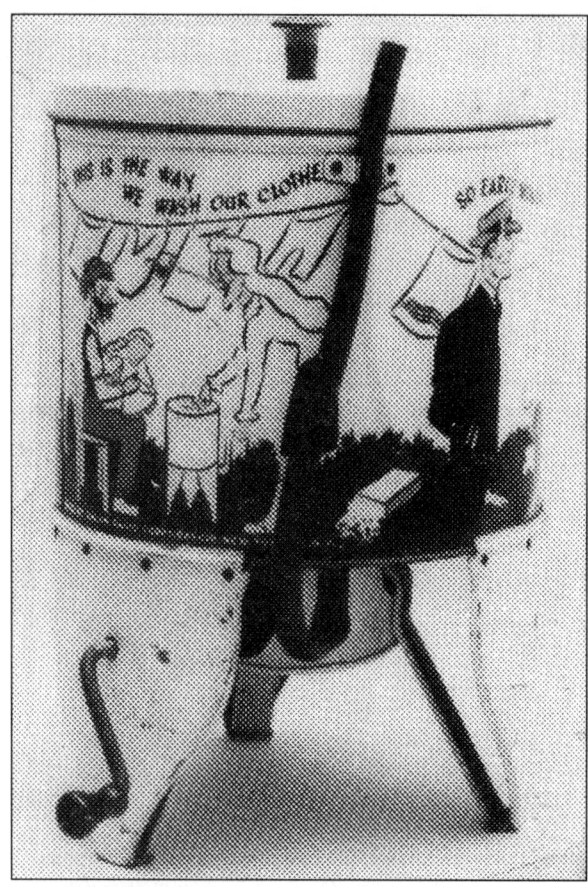

Sparkle Plenty Washing Machine (Dick Tracy), Kalon Radio Corp., c. 1947, $250. Photo courtesy Lloyd W. Ralston Auctions

Dick Tracy (Continued)	C6	C8	C10
Sparkle Plenty Paper Doll Set, No. 5160, Saalfield, 1948	40	60	100
Sparkle Plenty Washing Machine, tin litho, w/crank action, Kalon Radio Corp., c. 1947, 13" tall	100	150	250
Sparkling Pop Pistol, tin litho, No. 96, Marx	125	200	300
Squad Car, heavy tin or sheet metal, convertible, friction motor w/siren and battery-powered flashing light, Dick Tracy and Sam Catchum in plastic, Marx, c. 1948, 20" long	250	375	500
Squad Car No. 1, friction, Marx, 6-3/4" long	110	175	250
Squad Car No. 1, friction, Marx, 11" long	200	275	350
Sub-Machine Gun, "Raider," 1946	150	200	300
Target Game, G34, Marx	150	200	300
Target Game, G25, Marx	150	200	300

Dick Tracy (Continued)	C6	C8	C10
Telephone, Marx, 1967	37	56	75
Water Pistol, plastic, 1955	50	75	125

Felix the Cat	C6	C8	C10
China Set	75	125	200
Doll, stuffed cloth w/rubber hands, Gund, c. 1950, 15" high	80	140	200
Felix Chases Mice Pull Toy	525	900	1300
Felix on Fire Truck Pull Toy, Gong Bell	110	180	250
Felix on Tricycle Pull Toy, Gong Bell	220	350	500

Felix the Cat on Scooter, Nifty, $1650. Photo courtesy Phillips, New York

Dick Tracy Squad Car No. 1, Marx, $350. Photo courtesy Gary Linden

Dick Tracy Squad Car No. 1, Marx, $250. Photo courtesy Gary Linden

Front to Back: Felix the Cat Figure, $500; Felix the Cat Speedy Felix, $2750. Photo courtesy Christie's East

Felix the Cat (Continued)

	C6	C8	C10
Felix the Cat on Scooter, Nifty	600	1000	1650
Figure, wood, jointed w/rubber head, 1940s, 9" high	100	175	300
Figure, cast iron, Dent, 1923, 2" high	180	270	375
Figure, cast iron, w/tin umbrella, 2-1/2" high	200	350	500
Figure, composition, c. 1930s, 13" high	275	425	650
Figure, lead, 2-1/2" high	188	285	375
Figure, wood, 12" high	300	500	700
Nodder, pot-metal, w/Pat Sullivan copyright on bottom of feet, 2" high	100	150	275
Pull Car, Borgfeldt, 1925, 12" long	300	475	650
Soaky	35	52	75
Speedy Felix, in car	1000	1700	2750
Squeeze Toy, rubber, Eastern Moulded Products, 6-1/2"	75	125	175
Walker, tin wind-up, German	325	500	750

Flash Gordon

	C6	C8	C10
Air Ray Pistol, shoots blast of air using rubber diaphragm, 10"	125	188	300
Arresting Ray, picture of Flash on handle, Marx	133	200	325
Automatic Disintegrator, Hubley	200	300	500
Belt, large plastic buckle showing rocket ship flight, 1950s	70	105	150
Casting Set, w/original box, Home Foundry, 1934	800	1000	1350
Click Ray Pistol, w/original box, Marx, 1950s, 10" long	400	600	775

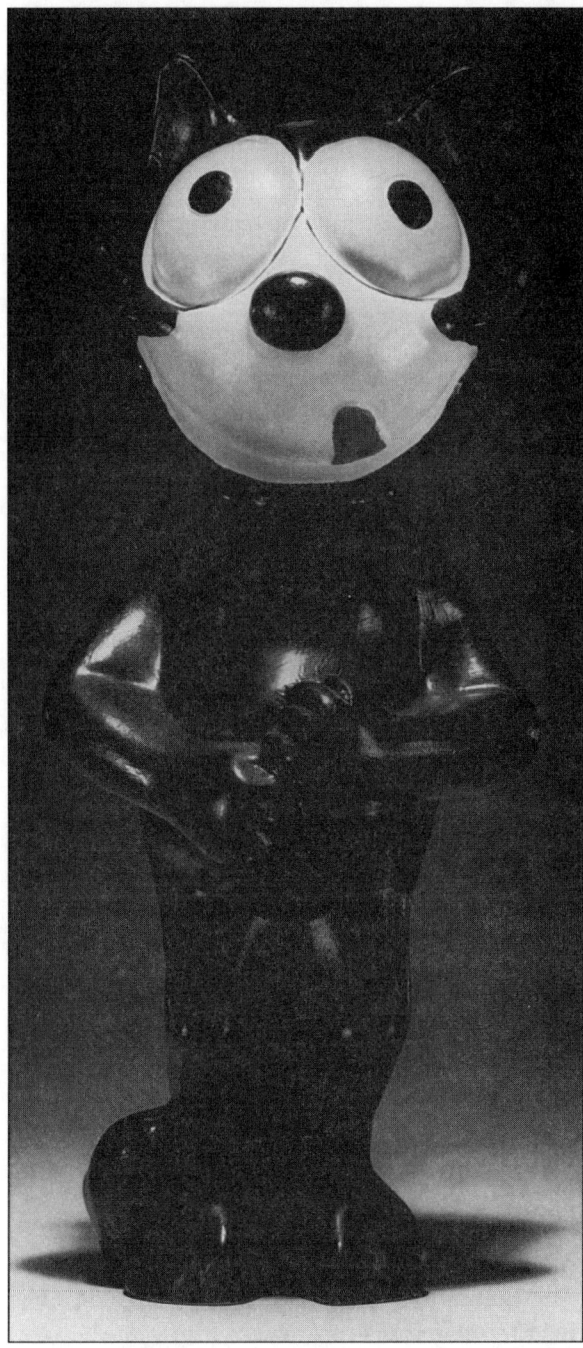

Felix the Cat Figure, c. 1930s, $650. Photo courtesy Christie's East

Flash Gordon (Continued)

	C6	C8	C10
Jet-propelled Kite	27	41	55
Play Set, Mego	58	87	115
Play Set, die-cast, No. 1793, w/original box, Tootsietoy, 1978	27	41	55
Radio Repeater Clicker Pistol, No. 58, add $200 for box, Marx, 1950s, 10" long	205	308	500

Flash Gordon (Continued)

	C6	C8	C10
Rocket Fighter, wind-up, Marx, 1939, 12" long	265	400	650
Signal Pistol, tin litho, No. 74, with box, Marx, 1940s	600	900	1250
Solar Commando, three plastic space men and one ship, 1950s	80	90	150
Space Cruiser, 1952	50	75	120
Space Outfit, Esquire Novelty, 1952	90	135	180
Space Target, metal, standup, Alex Raymond illustration, 12" x 14"	100	160	225
Sparkling Battle Rocket, 1969	40	60	80
Strat-O-Wagon, Wyandotte, 9" long	100	150	200
Two-Way Telephone, Marx, c. 1940	100	150	275
Water Gun, plastic, w/original box add $175, Marx, 7" long	175	325	425

Foxy Grandpa

	C6	C8	C10
Bell Toy, cast iron, vehicle pulled by two boys, 7" long	425	650	925
Doll, cloth and composition, 17" long	450	675	1000
Figure, tin, clockwork, German, 8-1/4" high	300	450	650
Foxy Grandpa Button, 1902	25	65	80
Grandpa Riding Donkey Pull Toy, composition, 9" long platform	450	685	925
Jack-in-the-Box, papier-mâché and paper litho on wood, 1900, 4" square	200	300	400
Nodder, papier-mâché, 1900, 6" tall	150	210	325
Nodder, cast iron, large-headed Grandpa in cart pulled by donkey, Hubley, c. 1910, 6-1/2"	500	800	1150
Nodder, cast iron, in donkey cart, Harirs, 7-1/4" long	225	350	525

Gasoline Alley

	C6	C8	C10
Gasoline Alley Garage and Auto Racer, tin litho, garage and "Bearcat Racer" car, Girard, 1924	400	750	1000
Mrs. Blossom Doll, oilcloth, Live Long Toys, 17" high	100	180	300
Pal Doll, oilcloth, cotton-stuffed, Live Long Toys, 1923	90	140	190
Rachel Doll, cotton-stuffed oilcloth, Live Long Toys, 1923	150	200	325

Gasoline Alley (Continued)

	C6	C8	C10
Skeezix Doll, cotton-stuffed oilcloth, Live Long Toys, 1924	100	150	225
Skeezix Doll, cotton-stuffed oilcloth, as boy, Live Long Toys, 1924	125	175	250
Skeezix Radio, tin litho, Live Long Toys, c. 1924, 5" high	1000	1500	2200
Sunshine X Riding Sparkplug Platform Toy, 9" long	1400	2300	3450
Uncle Walt Doll, oilcloth, Live Long Toys, 26" high	80	120	160

Gumps, The

	C6	C8	C10
Andy Gump Dancing Doll, wooden w/tin legs, 9" high	125	188	285
Andy Gump Roadster, "348," Arcade, 7" long	750	1900	3000
Andy Gump Roadster, "348," deluxe version, Arcade	2000	3500	6500
Chester Gump Cart with Horse, open two-wheel cart w/Chester driving, Arcade, 1920s	280	420	600
Chester Gump Doll, oilcloth, Live Long Toys, c. 1920s, 13" high	150	175	325

Happy Hooligan

	C6	C8	C10
Clown Doll, w/bisque face	600	900	1500
Cymbals Player	300	450	650
Doll, bisque face, dressed as clown, 9-1/2" high	700	1100	1600

Andy Gump Roadster (The Gumps), Arcade, $6500.
Photo courtesy Christie's East

Happy Hooligan Clown Doll, $1600. Photo courtesy Christie's East

Gloomy Gus in Horse Cart (Happy Hooligan), Harris, $3500. Photo courtesy Christie's East

Happy Hooligan in Car (Happy Hooligan), Hill Brass, c. 1903, $5000. Photo courtesy Christie's East

Happy Hooligan (Continued)

	C6	C8	C10
Donkey Cart, c. 1925, 10" long	240	360	500
Gloomy Gus Figure, cast iron, Harris Toy Co., 1903, 5" tall	150	225	400
Gloomy Gus in Goat Cart, cast iron, 14" long	400	700	900
Gloomy Gus in Horse Cart, cast iron, Harris, 14" long	1600	2600	3500
Gloomy Gus in Mule Cart, cast iron, Harris	300	450	600
Hand Puppet, cast iron and cloth, 9-1/4"	50	70	100
Happy Hooligan in Car, Cast iron, Hill Brass, c. 1903, 5-3/4"	1400	3200	5000
Happy Hooligan in Cart, cast iron, horse-pulled and head nods, Kenton, early 1900s, 10-1/4" long, 7-1/2" high	700	1100	1600

Happy Hooligan (Continued)

	C6	C8	C10
Happy Hooligan in Donkey Cart, wind-up, Ingap Co., 1930s, 6-3/8" long	600	1000	1400
Happy Hooligan in Goat Cart, cast iron, 7-1/2" long	200	350	525
Happy Hooligan in Horse Cart, cast iron, Wilkins, 17" long	500	850	1150
Happy Hooligan in Horse-drawn Wagon, cast iron, w/Gloomy Gus and driver, Harris, c. 1905	1800	3000	4000
Happy Hooligan Jigger, w/crank action, Kiddee Metal Toys, 1920s, 10" tall	900	1400	1700
Happy Hooligan Jigger, tin litho, dressed as clown, tap dances on drum, wind-up, Kiddies' Metal Toys Co., 9"	750	1100	1400

Happy Hooligan in Horse-drawn Wagon, Harris, c. 1905, $4000. Photo courtesy Christie's East

Happy Hooligan Police Patrol, Kenton, $3500. Photo courtesy James Maxwell/Virginia Caputo

Left to Right: Henry and His Brother Wind-ups, Japanese, $1600; Henry Henry's Mahout on Donkey, $800; Henry Henry on Trapeze Wind-up, $700. Photo courtesy Christie's East

Henry on Elephant Wind-up, Japanese, $1650.

Happy Hooligan (Continued)	C6	C8	C10
Happy Hooligan on a Ladder	300	400	550
Happy Hooligan on Donkey, celluloid	325	425	550
Happy Hooligan Walking Toy, wind-up, Chein, 1932, 6" high	400	600	850
Happy on Rabbit Candy Container, composition, 7-1/2"	1000	1500	2000
Police Patrol, Happy hit by cop as Gloomy Gus drives, Kenton	1400	2200	3500
Roly-Poly	75	100	175

Henry	C6	C8	C10
Henry and His Brother Wind-ups, celluloid, on wheels, Japanese	700	1100	1600
Henry and his Swan, celluloid mechanical	200	3400	4600
Henry Eating Candy, Linemar, 1950s	500	750	950
Henry on Elephant Wind-up, celluloid and tin, Henry sits on elephant's trunk, w/Mahout, Japanese	700	1150	1650

Henry (Continued)	C6	C8	C10
Henry on Trapeze Wind-up, celluloid	365	525	700
Henry Rubber Squeeze Toy, 1950s, 9-1/2" high	30	50	85
Henry Trapeze Wind-up, part celluloid, Henry, brother and Mahout, Japanese	900	1400	1900
Henry's Mahout on Donkey	450	625	800

Joe Palooka	C6	C8	C10
Championship Belt Buckle, heavy gold-plated brass, buckle shows Palooka w/hands raised in victory, early 1950s	75	100	125
Doll, wood-jointed, 4" high	45	60	100
Doll, wood-jointed, 5-1/2" high	60	85	175
Filmatic, twelve different comic strips	30	45	75

Humphrey Mobile Tin Wind-up (Joe Palooka), Wyandotte, c. mid-1940s, $675. Photo courtesy Christie's East

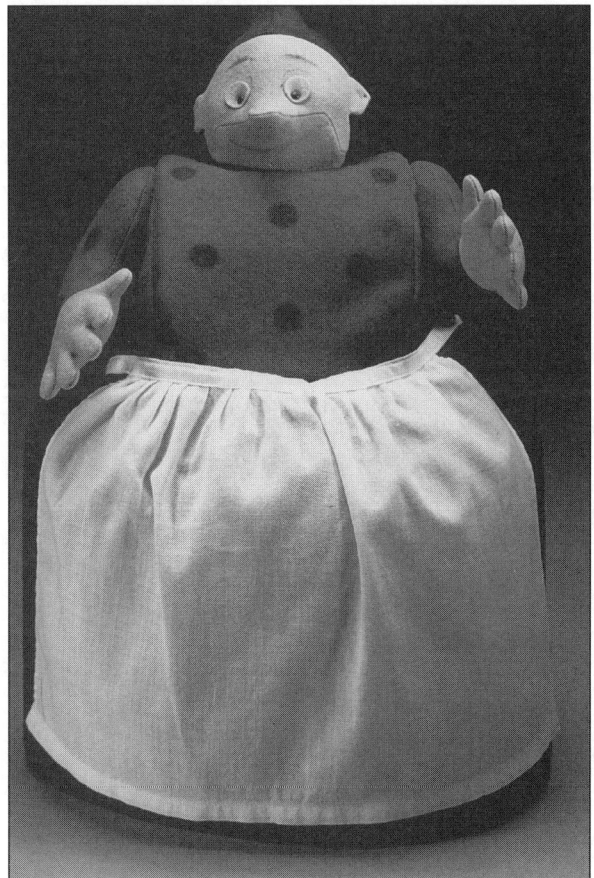

Mama Katzenjammer Doll, Steiff, c. 1908, $2000. Photo courtesy Christie's East

Joe Palooka (Continued)

	C6	C8	C10
Humphrey Doll, cloth and composition, with tag, pinback and apron, Ideal, 14-1/2" high	225	400	750
Humphrey Mobile Tin Wind-up, Wyandotte, c. mid-1940s, 7-1/2" high w/smokestack	350	525	675

Joe Palooka (Continued)

	C6	C8	C10
Joan Palooka Doll, Ideal, 1953	50	75	100
Little Max Speshul Tin Wind-up	3500	5250	7000
Punching Bag, c. 1950	30	45	60

Katzenjammer Kids

	C6	C8	C10
Katzenjammer Kids Hingees, 1945	16	24	40
Katzenjammer Kids See-Saw Bell Toy, Kenton	900	1500	2000
Mama Katzenjammer Doll, felt, Steiff, c. 1908	700	1200	2000
Mama Spanking Kid, other kid standing, as sailor drives mule cart, Kenton, 1911, 12" long	1050	1850	3500

Krazy Kat

	C6	C8	C10
Ignatz Figure, 6" high	150	200	325
Krazy Kat Platform Toy Tin Wind-up, Nifty, 1920s, 7-1/2" long	600	1100	1750
Krazy Kat Teacup and Saucer, Chein, 1930s	30	40	75

Krazy Kat Platform Toy Tin Wind-up, Nifty, 1920s, $1750. Photo courtesy Christie's East

Ignatz Figure (Krazy Kat), $325. Photo courtesy James Maxwell/Virginia Caputo

Little Lulu Doll, Georgene Novelties, $800. Photo courtesy Christie's East

Li'l Abner

	C6	C8	C10
Daisy Mae and Li'l Abner Paper Dolls, w/Mammy and Pappy Yokum, No. 2360, Saalfield, 1941	75	120	180
Daisy Mae and Li'l Abner Paper Dolls, No. 280, Saalfield, 1942	75	120	180
Daisy Mae Dogpatch Family Doll, c. 1950s	100	140	275
Daisy Mae Marionette, stringless, National Mask & Puppet Corp., 1940s	70	105	150
Dogpatch Family Doll, c. 1950s	110	165	250
Flyin' Saucer, Brian Specialties, 1962	42	63	100
Li'l Abner and His Dogpatch Band, wind-up, Unique, 1945	350	550	750
Li'l Abner Hand Puppet, Baby Barry, 1957	42	63	90
Li'l Abner Stringless Marionette, National Mask & Puppet Corp., 1940s	40	60	85

Li'l Abner (Continued)

	C6	C8	C10
Lonesome Polecat Rubber Squeak Toy, Reinert, 1950s	50	75	125
Mammy Yokum, Dogpatch Family Doll, Baby Barry Co., 1957	30	60	100
Mammy Yokum Hand Puppet, Baby Barry Co., 1957	42	75	125
Pappy Yokum Doll, Dogpatch Family Doll, Baby Barry Co., 1957	100	150	225
Pappy Yokum Hand Puppet, Baby Barry, 1957	42	63	85
Shmoo Doll, vinyl, inflatable, 1940s, 15" high	60	90	150

Little Lulu

	C6	C8	C10
Doll, w/mask face, M.H. Buell, 1944, 14" high	55	90	125
Doll, stuffed, Georgene Novelties, 14" high	365	545	800
Doll, felt, 10" high	100	150	250
Shape Book, No. 1970, Whitman, 1971	10	15	25

Little Lulu Doll, $250. Photo courtesy Toy Collector News

Dr. Primm Rolly Dolly (Little Nemo), Schoenhut, $5000. Photo courtesy Christie's East

Flip Bell Toy (Little Nemo), $850. Photo courtesy Christie's East

Sandy with Suitcase in Mouth Tin Wind-up (Little Orphan Annie), $500. Photo courtesy Christie's East

Little Nemo	C6	C8	C10
Dr. Primm Rolly Dolly, Schoenhut, 11-1/2" high	2500	4000	5000
Flip Bell Toy, cast iron, 6-1/2" long	400	600	850
Little Nemo and Mr. Flip Bell Toy	435	650	900

Little Orphan Annie	C6	C8	C10
Annie, Sandy, Daddy, Punjab Hingees, price per set, 1944	20	50	75
Commandos, No. 299, Saalfield, 1943	50	75	125
Little Orphan Annie and Sandy Figures, celluloid	450	675	1000
Little Orphan Annie and Sandy Pull Toy, wood, 1930s, 8"	130	195	275

Little Orphan Annie (Continued)	C6	C8	C10
Little Orphan Annie and Sandy Tin Wind-up, two-piece set, Marx, 1930s, 4-1/2" long	450	675	1000
Little Orphan Annie Doll, oilcloth, c. 1920s, 16-1/4"	150	200	300
Little Orphan Annie Doll, printed fabric, 1930s, 9-1/2"	100	150	225
Little Orphan Annie Doll, wood jointed, Jaymar, 5" high	65	100	175
Little Orphan Annie Skipping Rope Tin Wind-up, Marx, 1930s, 5" high	425	638	875

Sandy's Dog House (Little Orphan Annie), Marx, $700. Photo courtesy Christie's East

Little Orphan Annie Stove, $175. Photo courtesy James Maxwell/Virginia Caputo

Little Orphan Annie (Continued)	C6	C8	C10
Little Orphan Annie Soaky	14	30	50
Sandy Dog with Magic Tail, Marx, 1930s, 7" long	162	245	375
Sandy Doll, oilcloth, Live Long Toys, c. 1920s, 10-1/2" long	140	210	280
Sandy with Suitcase in Mouth Tin Wind-up	215	350	500
Sandy's Dog House, w/wheeled Sandy, Marx	300	450	700
Stove, 4-3/8" high	62	93	175
Stove, Marx, c. 1930s, 8" high	80	120	200
Water Pistol	90	150	175

Looney Tunes	C6	C8	C10
Bugs Bunny & Porky Pig Talking Toy, 1940s	95	143	190

Looney Tunes (Continued)	C6	C8	C10
Bugs Bunny Hand Puppet, early 1950s	22	33	45
Bugs Bunny Soaky, 10" high	12	18	25
Elmer Fudd Hand Puppet, 1950s	35	52	85
Elmer Fudd Soaky, 1960s, 10" high	18	25	50
Porky Pig Cowboy Tin Wind-up, w/lariat, Marx, 1949, 9" high	325	550	825
Porky Pig Hand Puppet, 1950s, 8" high	30	45	60
Porky Pig Soaky, 1960s, 9" high	20	30	50
Porky Pig SqueezeToy, hollow w/squeaker, has hands behind back, Sun Rubber, c. 1940, 6" high	68	125	190
Porky Pig Tin Wind-up, holding umbrella, raises hat, Marx, 1939, 8"	500	750	1250

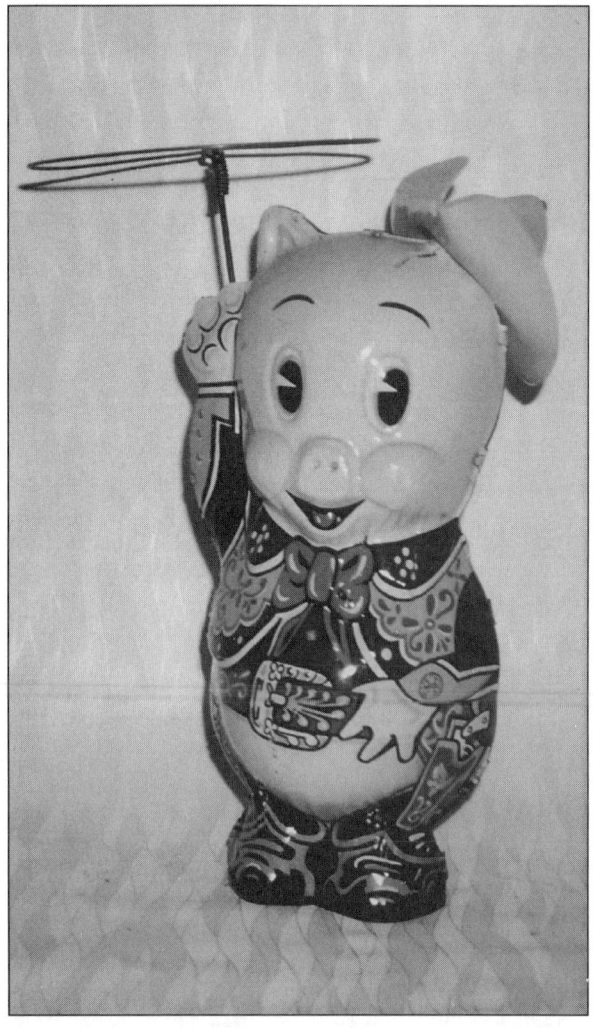

Looney Tunes Porky Pig Cowboy Tin Wind-up, Marx, 1949, $825. Photo courtesy Don Hultzman and Ron Chojnacki

Looney Tunes Porky Pig Tin Wind-up, Marx, 1939, $625. Photo courtesy Detroit Toy Museum; Wilkinson collection

Looney Tunes (Continued)

	C6	C8	C10
Porky Pig Tin Wind-up, holding umbrella, Marx, 1939, 8-1/2" high	250	375	625
Sylvester, cloth, 1971, 15" high	30	45	60
Sylvester Hand Puppet, early 1950s	50	75	100
Sylvester Soaky	16	24	32
Tweety Bird Soaky	15	22	50
Tweety Bird Squeeze Toy, rubber, 1950s	15	22	50
Wile E. Coyote, Dakin, 1970s	12	18	25
Yosemite Sam Squeak Toy, Dakin, 1970, 4" high	16	24	33

Mighty Mouse

	C6	C8	C10
Mighty Mouse Doll, vinyl, 1950	125	160	200
Mighty Mouse Doll, rubber head w/oilcloth body, 1942, 12" high	400	800	1000
Mighty Mouse Soaky	25	35	65

Moon Mullins

	C6	C8	C10
Kayo Doll, oilcloth, 9-3/4"	100	150	200
Kayo Doll, wood-jointed, Jaymar, 5" high	56	90	150
Kayo Figure, head swivels, Sun Rubber, c. 1937, 10" high	200	300	450
Moon Mullins and Kayo on Handcar, tin wind-up, Marx, 1930s, 6" long	395	600	875
Moon Mullins and Mamie Face Masks, price for each, 1933	20	30	60

Moon Mullins (Continued)

	C6	C8	C10
Moon Mullins Doll, wood jointed, Jaymar, 5" high	55	85	150
Moon Mullins Doll, stuffed, Famous Artists Synd., 1930s, 11-1/2" high	55	85	150

Mutt & Jeff

	C6	C8	C10
Jeff Figure, bendable, 1946	120	180	240
Jeff Stick Puppet, 12" high	40	60	80
Mutt Dancing Doll, wooden	40	60	90
Mutt Doll, composition w/ball joints, felt clothes, 8" high	188	300	475
Mutt Figure, bendable, 1946	140	210	280

Peanuts

	C6	C8	C10
Charlie Brown Bobbing Head, composition, possibly first Peanuts toy, 1950s	80	110	160
Charlie Brown Figure, plastic jointed, marked "1952,"	14	21	35
Lucy Doll, plastic, jointed, marked "1952,"	14	21	40
Lucy Squeeze Doll, vinyl, 1950s	15	22	40
Lucy Squeeze Toy, vinyl, 1950s, 8-3/4" high	15	22	40
Lucy Squeeze Toy, 1950s, 7-3/4"	12	18	30
Peanuts Figures: Charlie Brown, Lucy, Linus, Schroeder, Snoopy, Avon, price for each	10	15	25
Schroeder Squeeze Toy, rubber, c. 1960	10	15	45
Snoopy Astronaut Doll, vinyl, 1969, 9-1/2" high	30	50	75
Snoopy Bus, tin litho, 1960s	16	30	45
Snoopy Squeeze Toy, rubber, 1958	25	40	60

Pogo

	C6	C8	C10
Albert Alligator Figure, plastic, 1969, approx. 5" high ("Duz")	5	11	20
Beauregard Figure, plastic, 1969	7	11	15
Churcy Figure, plastic, 1969, 4-1/2" high	14	21	28
Howland Owl, plastic, 1969, 4-1/2" high	8	10	15
Pogo Figure, plastic, 1969, 4" high	7	11	18
Pogo Pogomobile	200	325	500
Porky Figure, plastic, 1969	7	11	14

Bluto Dippy Dumper Truck (Popeye), $1350. Photo courtesy Christie's East

Popeye

	C6	C8	C10
Bluto Dippy Dumper Truck, celluloid and tin, 9-1/2"	500	800	1350
Bluto on Horse Cart Wind-up, celluloid and tin, 7-1/2"	400	650	950
Brutus Mask, cardboard, 1940s	40	75	100
Jeep Doll, wood-jointed, 1930s, 7-1/4"	350	525	750
Jeep Doll, wood-jointed, rare, 1930s, 8"	750	1100	1600
Jeep Doll, wood-jointed, rare, 1930s, 6"	425	650	900
Jeep Doll, wood-jointed, 1930s, 14"	800	1400	2000
Juggling Popeye and Olive Oyl, (marked "Linemar"), T.P.S., 1950s, 9-1/2" high	1000	1500	2000
Olive Oyl and Swee' Pea Handcar, Marx, 1930s	240	400	600
Olive Oyl Ballet Dancer, tin, mechanical, Linemar	250	400	650
Olive Oyl Doll, jointed wood, Jaymar, c. 1940s, 5" high	92	150	200
Olive Oyl Figure, cast iron, 2-1/2" high	175	300	400
Olive Oyl Hand Puppet, Gund, c. 1938	60	90	150
Olive Oyl Hingees Paper Punch-outs, No. 102, Reed & Associates	12	20	40
Olive Oyl Marionette, Gund, 11"	37	56	85

Popeye (Continued)

	C6	C8	C10
Olive Oyl Mask, cardboard, 1940s	20	40	60
Olive Oyl Squeeze Toy, rubber, 1950s	90	135	180
Olive Oyl Wind-up, riding tricycle, Linemar, 4"	1400	2200	3200
Popeye Acrobat Tin Wind-up, Marx	2700	4050	5600
Popeye and Mean Man Mechanical Fighters, rare, Linemar Co., 1950s, 6" long	6000	9000	12,000
Popeye and Olive Oyl Ball Toss Tin Wind-up, Linemar, c. 1950, 19" long	600	1000	1500
Popeye and Olive Oyl Handcar, hollow rubber figures, 6" long	700	1500	2500

The Popeye Jeep Doll from the 1930s can range from $900 to $2000. Photo courtesy Christie's East

Popeye Acrobat Tin Wind-up, Marx, $5600. Photo courtesy Christie's East

Popeye and Olive Oyl Ball Toss Tin Wind-up, Linemar, c. 1950, $1500. Photo courtesy Christie's east

Popeye (Continued)

	C6	C8	C10
Popeye and Olive Oyl Jiggers, Popeye dancing on roof, Olive Oyl Playing Concertina, Marx	900	1600	2350
Popeye and Olive Oyl Sand Toy, tin litho, T. Cohn, 8-1/4" high	450	700	1000
Popeye and Olive Oyl Slinky Handcar Pull Toy, Linemar, 1950s	500	850	1200
Popeye Basketball Player Tin Wind-up, Linemar	700	1000	1500
Popeye Bifbat Paddle Toy, 1929	46	85	175
Popeye Bo Lo Paddle, 1929	20	50	100
Popeye Dippy Dumper Truck, Marx	550	1100	1500
Popeye Doll, stuffed cloth, Knickerbocker, 1930s, 17" high	187	250	400

Popeye (Continued)

	C6	C8	C10
Popeye Doll, jointed wood, c. 1932, 10-1/4" high	225	350	600
Popeye Doll, wood and composition, jointed arms and legs, "1935," 14" high	200	300	425
Popeye Doll, stuffed body w/rubber arms and head, Gund, c. 1950s, 20" high	70	105	150
Popeye Doll, jointed wood body, w/composition head, 8" high	90	135	200

Popeye and Olive Oyl Sand Toy, T. Cohn, $1000. Photo courtesy James Maxwell/Virginia Caputo

Left to Right: Popeye and Olive Oyl Jiggers, Marx, $2350; Popeye Popeye Express, Marx, 1935, $1250

Popeye and Olive Oyl Slinky Handcar Pull Toy, Linemar, 1950s, $1200. Photo courtesy Christie's East

Popeye Dippy Dumper Truck, Marx, $1500. Photo courtesy Christie's East

Popeye Doorstop, Hubley, $3400. Photo courtesy Bill Bertoia Auctions

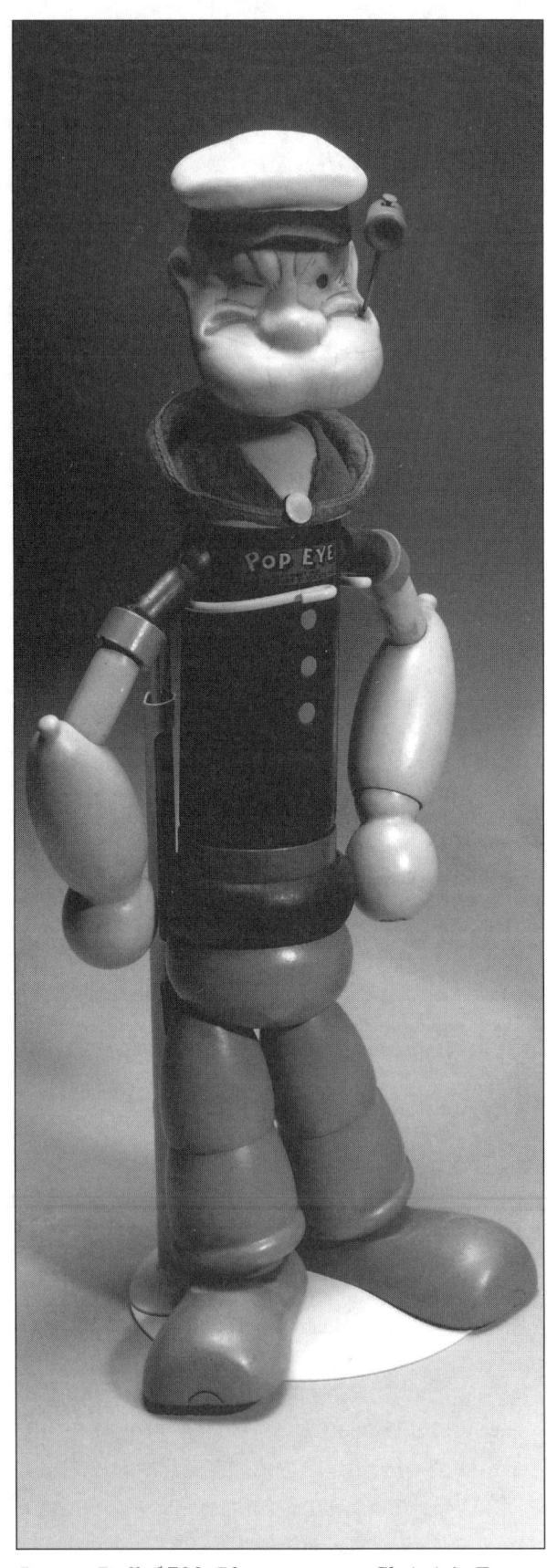

Popeye Doll, $700. Photo courtesy Christie's East

Popeye (Continued)

	C6	C8	C10
Popeye Doll, composition, "Popeye 1935 King Features Syn," 14" high	300	500	700
Popeye Doll, Chein, c. 1935, 11" high	293	440	650
Popeye Doll, hard rubber, "Cameo," jointed at neck, hips and shoulders, 14" high	115	172	250
Popeye Doll, jointed wood, c. 1935, 11" high	300	450	650
Popeye Doll, composition, Popeye is rolling up sleeve, 15" high	100	150	250
Popeye Doorstop, cast iron, Hubley, 10" high	1500	2300	3400
Popeye Drummer, Chein, 7-1/8" high	550	1000	1400
Popeye Eccentric Plane Wind-up, Marx, 1940, 8" long	375	650	950
Popeye Express, overhead airplane flies over train, Marx, 1935	500	850	1250
Popeye Express Wind-up, Popeye pushing box w/parrot, Marx, 1935	500	650	1250
Popeye Figure, cast iron, c. 1930, 3-1/2" high	175	300	425
Popeye Figure, hollow rubber, dated "1935" on back, 7" high	90	135	200
Popeye Figure, jointed wood, Jaymar, 5" high	68	125	160

Popeye in a Barrel, Chein, $825. Photo courtesy Don Hultzman

Popeye (Continued)

	C6	C8	C10
Popeye Figure, solid celluloid, 1930s, 4" high	90	150	222
Popeye Hand Puppet, Gund	20	30	50
Popeye Heavy Hitter Tin Wind-up, Chein, 11-1/2"	2500	4100	6350
Popeye Hingee Paper Figures, No. 102, Reed, 1945	50	80	100
Popeye in a Barrel, Chein, 7" high	350	525	825
Popeye in a Barrel Wind-up Walker, celluloid, Japan, 5-1/2" high	700	1100	1650
Popeye in a Horsecart, celluloid and tin, Marx, c. 1935, 7-1/2"	1500	2600	3850
Popeye in a Rowboat, Hoge, 1935	2500	4200	5850
Popeye Jack-in-the-Box, tin, Popeye pops out of spinach can, mechanical, Mattel	45	75	100
Popeye Jigger Wind-up, Marx, 9-1/2" high	500	850	1250
Popeye Knockout Bank, Straits Mfg. Co., 1935	1000	1500	2300
Popeye Lantern Toy, Linemar, 1950s, 7-1/2" high	400	600	800

Popeye Express Wind-up, Marx, 1935, $1250. Photo courtesy PB Eighty-Four, New York

Popeye in a Barrel Wind-up Walker, Japan, $1650.
Photo courtesy Christie's East

Popeye Rollerskating, Linemar, $1350.

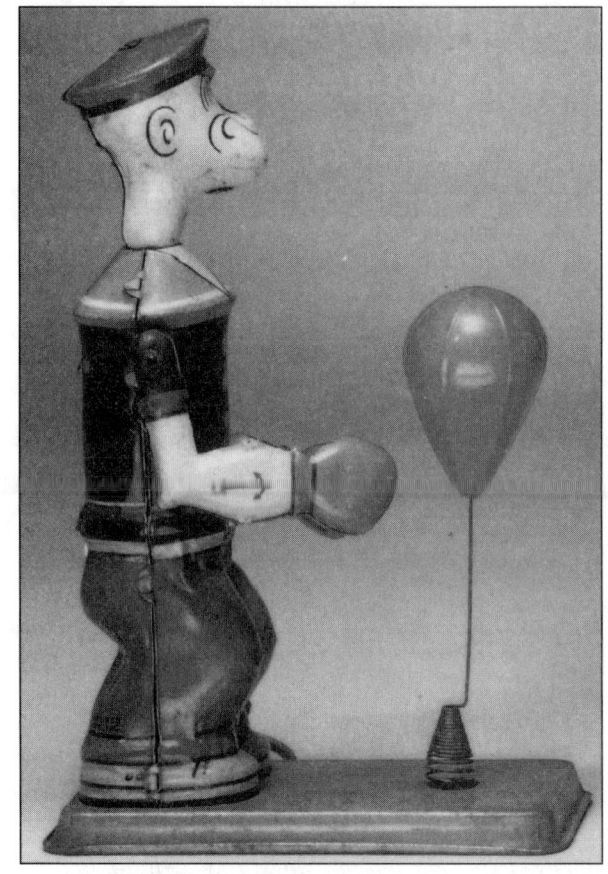

Popeye Puncher, Chein, $6900.

Popeye (Continued)	C6	C8	C10
Popeye Mask, cardboard, 1940s	30	45	75
Popeye Moving Van, tin, friction, Linemar	400	600	875
Popeye on a Tricycle, metal and celluloid, Linemar	370	555	825
Popeye on a Unicycle Wind-up, Linemar, 1950s	600	1000	1400
Popeye One-Man Band, pole with drum and cymbals, rubber Popeye head on top, 1950s, 69" high	100	150	210
Popeye Patrol, Hubley, 8-1/2" long	2500	4500	6200
Popeye Pirate, click pistol, with box add $250, No. 68, Marx	175	375	500
Popeye Puncher, overhead bag, Chein	2050	4000	6900
Popeye Puncher, tin and celluloid, w/floor bag, Chein, 1930	800	1450	1900
Popeye Rollerskating, Linemar	550	825	1350
Popeye Roly Poly, celluloid, Japan, 3-1/2"	150	200	350
Popeye Roly Poly Target Game, Knickerbocker, 1958	95	143	225

Popeye (Continued)

	C6	C8	C10
Popeye Sand Toy, tin litho, teeter-totter, w/Popeye, Swee'Pea, Oyl and Jeep	500	800	1250
Popeye Shadow Boxer, Chein, 1930s, 7" tall	700	1200	1900
Popeye Soaky	22	33	55
Popeye Sparkling Popeye Wind-up, Chein, 1959, 5" long	173	260	345
Popeye Spinach Patrol, Hubley	1400	2500	3800
Popeye Spinach Wagon	1000	1650	2500
Popeye Spinning Olive Oyl in a Chair, Linemar, 1950s, 9" high	800	1400	1900
Popeye Strength Tester, Holgate, 14"	65	98	150
Popeye the Champ, Marx	1100	1900	2900
Popeye the Pilot Wind-up, later version, 8" long	490	800	1150
Popeye the Pilot Wind-up, early version, Marx, 1930, 8" long	500	900	1300
Popeye the Sailor Tin Wind-up, Hoge Mfg. Co., c. 1935	2000	3800	6000

Popeye the Champ, Marx, $2900. Photo courtesy Phillips, New York

Popeye the Pilot Wind-up, $1150. Photo courtesy Sotheby's, New York

Popeye Turnover Tank Tin Wind-up, Linemar, 1950s, $850. Photo courtesy Don Hultzman

Popeye (Continued)

	C6	C8	C10
Popeye Transit Co. Truck, Linemar	650	1100	1700
Popeye Tumbling Popeye Wind-up, Linemar, 5" high	450	700	1100
Popeye Turnover Tank Tin Wind-up, Linemar, 1950s, 6" long	360	600	850
Popeye Walker, plastic walker, Popeye pushing wheelbarrow, Marx, c. 1950s	50	75	100
Popeye Walker Tin Wind-up, Chein, 6-1/2" high	340	525	700
Popeye Whistle Pipe, cardboard bowl w/illustration of Popeye characters, metal stem w/whistle at base, Northwest Products of St. Louis, 3-1/2" long	70	105	150
Popeye Wind-up, celluloid, neck goes up and down, c. 1930, 9" high	475	700	975

Popeye (Continued)

	C6	C8	C10
Popeye Wind-up, Popeye carrying parrots in cages, Marx, 1935, 7-3/4" high 268	450	650
Popeye Xylophone Player, American Preschool Co., 1957, 9" long 263	395	650
Popeye Yazoo Pipe, Northwestern Productions, St. Louis, Mo., 1934 80	120	200
Swee'Pea Hingees Paper Punch-outs, No. 102, Reed, 1944 20	30	50
Swee'Pea Mask, cardboard, 1940s 10	20	40
Thimble Theatre Mystery Playhouse, composition figures w/wooden shuffle feet (ramp walkers), copyright 1939, "Starring Popeye with Wimpy and Olive Oyl," Philadelphia, 12" x 10" x 3"; individual figures sell for $350 in Mint condition, Harding Products .. 1500	2500	3500
Wimpy Dippy Dumper 500	800	1100
Wimpy Figure, cast iron, Hubley, 3-1/8" high 175	263	400
Wimpy Figure, hard plastic, 1960s, 3" ... 12	18	24
Wimpy Figure, jointed wood, "by K.F.S.," 4" high................................ 100	150	250
Wimpy Figure, jointed wood, Jaymar, 5" high 100	150	250
Wimpy Hand Puppet, Gund 29	44	75
Wimpy Mask, cardboard, 1940s 20	30	60
Wimpy Motorcyclist, Linemar 400	700	925
Wimpy Squeeze Toy, rubber, 8" high ... 60	100	175
Wimpy Tricyclist, Linemar 550	900	1200

Prince Valiant

	C6	C8	C10
Prince Valiant Castle Fort, boxed set w/knights, Marx 225	340	450
Prince Valiant Crossbow Pistol Game... 22	33	60
Prince Valiant Shield, tin litho 30	45	75
Prince Valiant Sword and Scabbard, tin, Mattel, 1950s 29	45	65

Red Ryder

	C6	C8	C10
Little Beaver Archery Set, 1951 30	45	75
Red Ryder Molding Set, 1948 40	75	150
Red Ryder Target Game, w/box add $150, 1939.. 40	110	200

Sad Sack

	C6	C8	C10
Sad Sack Doll, vinyl, 1950, 15-1/2" 105	170	230
Sad Sack Doll, vinyl w/cloth uniform, Sterling Doll Co., c. 1952, 20" high.. 70	120	200

Skippy

	C6	C8	C10
Skippy Figure, oilcloth, w/hat, 12" high.. 75	100	150
Skippy Figure, celluloid, 5-1/2" high .. 150	250	400

Smitty

	C6	C8	C10
Smitty Doll, oilcloth, 9-3/4" high........ 125	175	225
Smitty on a Scooter Tin Wind-up, Marx, c. 1930, 8" high 1100	1800	2150

Popeye Thimble Theatre Mystery Playhouse, Harding Products, $3500. Photo courtesy Mapes Auctioneers and Appraisers

Smitty on a Scooter Tin Wind-up, Marx, c. 1930, $2150. Photo courtesy PB Eighty-Four, New York

Smokey Stover

	C6	C8	C10
Smokey Stover, Hingees, 1944	8	15	25
Smokey Stover Figure, hard plastic, 1960s, 3" high	12	20	50

Spider-Man

	C6	C8	C10
Spider-Man Hand Puppet, Ideal, 1966	42	63	90
Spider-Man Walker Wind-up, Marx, 1966	125	188	250
Spider-Man Webmaker, Chemtoy, 1977	16	25	40

Steve Canyon

	C6	C8	C10
Steve Canyon Glider Bomb Truck, Ideal	88	132	175
Steve Canyon Jet Helmet, 1959	50	75	125
Steve Canyon Space Goggles, Rock Industries, c. 1950s	25	38	60

Superman

	C6	C8	C10
2 in 1 Hand Puppet, one side Superman, other Clark, early 1950s	200	300	500
Bendee, Mego, 1973, 5" high	22	33	45
City of Metropolis Adventure Set, Corgi, 1979	65	100	150
Colorforms, 1964	25	40	65
Cut-outs, blue or red, No. 177, Saalfield, 1940	25	1750	2200
Figure, composition, Syroco	900	1750	3000
Figure, wood and composition, Ideal, 1940, 13" high	600	1000	1400
Flying Toy, Transogram, 1954	68	102	150
Hand Puppet, Ideal, 1965	32	48	64
Krypton Rockets, c. 1939	150	225	350

Superman (Continued)

	C6	C8	C10
Kryptonite Rock, 1978	10	15	20
Krypto-Ray Gun, w/seven filmstrips and box, No. 94, Daisy, 1939	750	1250	2000
Movie Viewer, Acme, 1965	30	45	60
Movie Viewer, Acme, 1940	333	500	665
Movie Viewer, w/film, Acme, 1955	60	90	150
Movie Viewer, w/film, Acme, 1947	95	200	350
Play Set, Ideal, 1973	34	51	68
Rollover Airplane, various colors, Marx, 1940s, 6-1/2" long	1000	1500	2500
Rollover Tank, Japan, 1940s, 4" long	290	435	600
Rollover Tank, silver version, Marx, 1940s, 4" long	550	850	1300
Soaky	27	41	75

Superman Rollover Airplane, Marx, 1940s, $2500. Photo courtesy Christie's East

Superman Tank, Linemar, 1958, $2000. Photo courtesy Christie's East

Superman (Continued)

	C6	C8	C10
Superman Button, 1939	35	150	200
Superman Holding Airplane, wind-up, Marx, 1940	800	1750	2500
Superman Tank, tin, battery operated, Linemar, 1958, 10-1/4" long	600	1200	2000
Tricky Trapeze, Kohner, 1966	75	100	150
Water Pistol, in the shape of Superman flying, c. 1950s	35	75	100

Tarzan

	C6	C8	C10
Dart Board Game Tarzan in the Jungle, large, 1935	130	195	260
Gift Set, figures and truck w/cage trailer, No. 36, Corgi	40	60	80
Mask of Akut the Ape, paper, Northern Paper Mills, 1933	60	90	140
Mask of Numa the Lion, paper, Northern Paper Mills, 1933	60	90	140
Mask of Tarzan, paper, Northern Paper Mills, 1933	70	125	200
Target Game Tarzan in the Jungle, battery operated, 1935	140	220	300
Thingmaker Kit, Mattel, 1966	44	66	88

Toonerville Trolley

	C6	C8	C10
Powerful Katrinka Tin Wind-up, tin, raises and lowers Jimmy in her hand, Nifty, 1925, 6-3/4" high	900	1600	2400
Powerful Katrinka Tin Wind-up, boy in wheelbarrow, Lehmann, 1925, 6-1/2" long	1300	2450	3500

Left to Right: Toonerville Trolley Powerful Katrinka Tin Wind-up, Lehmann, 1925, $3500; Toonerville Trolley Powerful Katrinka Tin Wind-up, Nifty, 1925, $2400. Photo courtesy Sotheby's, New York

Toonerville Trolley, Dent, $925. Photo courtesy Don Hultzman

Toonerville Trolley, $600. Photo courtesy Detroit Antique Toy Museum; Wilkinson Collection

Toonerville Trolley (Continued)

	C6	C8	C10
Toonerville Candy Container, glass, 3-1/4" long	250	375	500
Toonerville Trolley, wood, includes six people, 7" long	125	188	300
Toonerville Trolley, lead, c. 1923	100	150	210
Toonerville Trolley, cast iron, Dent	450	675	925
Toonerville Trolley, aluminum, Dent	357	562	775
Toonerville Trolley, Crackerjack size, 1-7/8" high	275	410	600

Toonerville Trolley (Continued)   **C6**   **C8**   **C10**

Item	C6	C8	C10
Toonerville Trolley Wind-up, tin, marked "Copyright 1922 by Fontaine Fox," Skipper driving, Nifty, 7-1/2" high	500	850	1150
Toonerville Trolley Wind-up, rare, Strauss, 1921	375	450	650

Toots and Casper   **C6**   **C8**   **C10**

Item	C6	C8	C10
Buttercup & Spareribs, Buttercup beats Spareribs with broom, Nifty, 1920s, 7-1/2" long	700	1200	1600
Buttercup Doll, cloth, 14"	450	700	1000
Buttercup Doll, stuffed cloth, jointed head, arms, legs, c. 1924, 18" high	250	375	500

Buttercup & Spareribs (Toots and Casper), Nifty, 1920s, $1600. Photo courtesy Christie's East

Uncle Wiggily Crazy Car, Distler (Germany), c. 1922, $6000. Photo courtesy Detroit Antique Toy Museum; Wilkinson Collection

Toots and Casper (Continued)   **C6**   **C8**   **C10**

Item	C6	C8	C10
Buttercup Tin Wind-up, crawls, German, 4-1/4"	650	1100	1750

Uncle Wiggily   **C6**   **C8**   **C10**

Item	C6	C8	C10
Uncle Wiggily Crazy Car, Marx	438	700	1000
Uncle Wiggily Crazy Car, Distler (Germany), c. 1922, 9-1/2" long	2200	4500	6000

Willie the Worm   **C6**   **C8**   **C10**

Item	C6	C8	C10
Willie the Worm and Sammy Fish-n Fun	10	15	25
Willie the Worm and Sammy Flying Machine	12	18	30
Willie The Worm and Sammy in Car Trouble, paper, Fawcett Comics characters, Reed, c. 1944-47	10	15	25

Woody Woodpecker   **C6**   **C8**   **C10**

Item	C6	C8	C10
Walter Lantz Ink Stamp Character Set, includes twelve different rubber stamps	12	18	30
Woody Woodpecker Figure, rubber, "Walter Lantz," 6-1/2" high	10	15	25
Woody Woodpecker Hand Puppet, rubber head, cloth body, "W. Lantz," Mattel, 1962	20	30	60
Woody Woodpecker Soaky	20	25	50

Yellow Kid   **C6**   **C8**   **C10**

Item	C6	C8	C10
Cap Bomb, cast iron, 1-1/2" high	100	150	210
Doll, "Design copyrighted 1894 and 1896," Arnold Printworks, 8" high	250	450	600

Yellow Kid Cap Bomb, $210. Photo courtesy James Maxwell/Virginia Caputo

*Yellow Kid Ladder Toy (missing some figures), $1400.
Photo courtesy James Maxwell/Virginia Caputo*

*Yellow Kid Figure, $1200; Yellow Kid in Cart being
pulled by mule, Kenton, early 1900s, $2500. Photo
courtesy Christie's East*

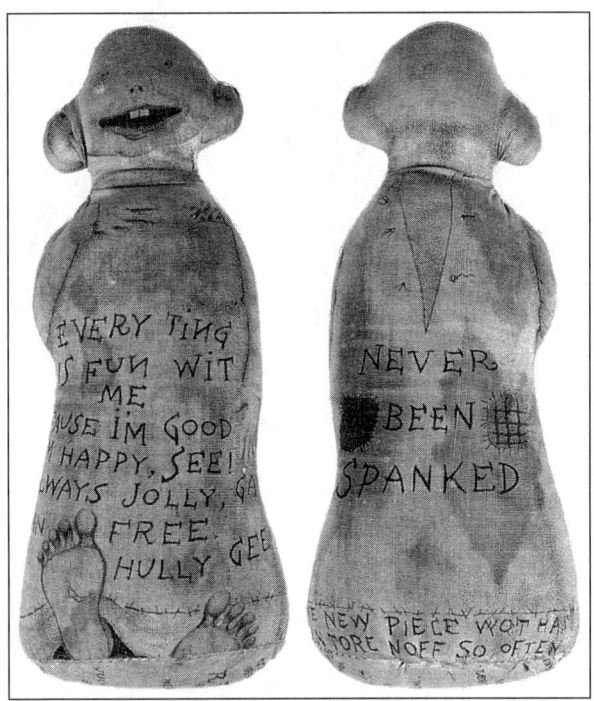

*Front and back view of the Yellow Kid Doll, $600.
Photo courtesy James Maxwell/Virginia Caputo*

Yellow Kid (Continued)

	C6	C8	C10
Doll, papier-mâché and wood, early 1900s, 11" high	500	850	1200
Figure, cast iron, burlap gown, movable arms, 6-1/2" high	600	850	1200
Ladder Toy, 16-1/2" high	700	1100	1400
Yellow Kid Doll, Ideal, 1907	200	350	500
Yellow Kid in Cart, cast iron, he is being pulled by mule, Kenton, early 1900s, 10" long, 6" high	900	1650	2500
Yellow Kid in Goat Cart, cast iron, painted, Kenton, 1890, 7-1/2" long	500	850	1200

Miscellaneous

	C6	C8	C10
Alfred E. Neumann Figure, vinyl, Effanbee, 1960	75	188	250
Baby Snookums Doll (The Newlyweds), fabric, 5-1/2" high	100	250	425
Boob McNutt Tin Wind-up, Strauss	450	675	900
Boots and Her Buddies Paper Dolls, No. 2460, Saalfield, 1943	35	50	75
Broom Hilda Figure, Knickerbocker, c. 1970, 14" high	38	53	75
Comic Strip Rings, Blondie and Barney Google, includes Phantom, King Features, 1953	15	30	50
Comics Paper Doll Cut-Out Book, page each of Popeye, Katzenjammers, Just Kids, Blondie, Dumb Dora, Annie Rooney, Polly and Her Pals, Saalfield, 1935	150	270	375
Dan Dunn Det. Corps Secret Operative 28 Tin Badge, c. 1930s	35	75	125
Don Winslow Flashlight Gun	70	105	140
Ella Cinders Doll, cloth and composition, 1925, 17" high	100	175	250
Famous Komics Film Viewer, w/three boxes of films, Acme, 1940	150	275	400
Favorite Funnies Rubber Print Set, Dick Tracy, Orphan Annie, etc., fourteen stamps, pad, booklet, large size	45	75	125
Harold Teen Ukulele, wood, 1930s, 21"	125	200	250

Humpty Dumpty Doll, Steiff, $2000. Photo courtesy Christie's East

Miscellaneous (Continued)

	C6	C8	C10
Herby Doll, oilcloth, 10"	30	60	100
Herman Nodder (Harvey Comics character), rare, Linemar, 1950s, 4-1/2" high	300	500	650
Hi-Way Henry Wind-up, jalopy w/man, woman, laundry above roof, 1920s	1500	2800	3900
Humpty Dumpty Doll, cloth, Steiff, 10" high	700	1200	2000
Jane Arden Paper Dolls, No. 2408, Saalfield, 1942	45	65	100
Komic Kamera, without filmstrips	24	36	48
Komic Kamera, all metal viewer, w/set of five filmstrips, c. mid-1930s	80	120	175
Little King Pull Toy, wood, Jay-Mar, 1938, 4" high	70	110	175
Little Mary Mixup and Her Friend Peggy Paper Dolls, No. 294, Saalfield, 1922	60	75	100

Hi-Way Henry Wind-up, 1920s, $3900.

Make Your Own Funnies Set, Jaymar Specialty Company, $1300. Photo courtesy Christie's East

Miscellaneous (Continued)

	C6	C8	C10
Make Your Own Funnies Set, jointed wooden figures of Popeye, Chinaman, Konical Kop, Orphan Annie, Sandy, Kayo, Funny Frog, Comical Mouse and Mon Mullins, price for the set, Jaymar Specialty Company	500	800	1300
Mandrake the Magician Magic Kit, Transogram, 1949	75	125	200
Movie Komics, reels of film for toy viewers, c. 1940s	14	30	50
Nancy Doll (Nancy and Sluggo), stuffed, Georgene Novelties, 14" high	90	175	300
Peter Rabbit Chickmobile	312	500	725
Roosevelt Bear on Bicycle, tin litho, c. 1920, 9" long	225	300	500
Secret Agent X-9 Gun and Billy Club	25	50	75
Sight Seeing Auto 899, cast iron, w/Mama Katzenjammer, Uncle Heine, Alphonse, Gloomy Gus, Happy Hooligan, Kenton, c. 1910, 10-1/2" long	2500	5250	7000

Roosevelt Bear on Bicycle, c. 1920, $500. Photo courtesy Detroit Toy Museum; Wilkinson Collection

Miscellaneous (Continued)

	C6	C8	C10
Snowflakes and Swipes Platform Toy, tin litho, c. 1929, 7-1/2" long....	800	1350	1850
Terry and the Pirates Hingees, set includes Terry, Flip Corkin, Pat Ryan, Burma, Taffy Tucker, 1944......	22	33	55

Miscellaneous (Continued)

	C6	C8	C10
Western Thrills with Billy The Kid, paper, character from Funny Animals Comics, Reed, c. 1944-47.....	12	18	30
Wonder Woman String Puppet, Madison, 1977.....................................	37	56	85

Sight Seeing Auto 899, Kenton, c. 1910, $7000. Photo courtesy Christie's East

Snowflakes and Swipes Platform Toy, c. 1929, $1850. Photo courtesy Christie's East

DISNEY

(See also Paper, Premiums, Fisher-Price)

Walt Disney was involved in animation as early as 1920, but his first truly notable character was Oswald the Rabbit, introduced in 1927. Disney did not own the rights to Oswald, however, and he eventually fell into the hands of another animator, Walter Lantz. Although Mickey Mouse first appeared in the 1928 short "Plane Crazy," the third Mickey cartoon, "Steamboat Willie," seems to have been the first released (on November 18, 1928). Mickey was a success from then on. Minnie Mouse also appeared in "Steamboat Willie," and Pluto emerged in 1930 but was not known by that name until 1931. Goofy debuted in 1932 and Donald Duck came along in 1934. Mickey Mouse toys were first produced in 1930 and since then the stream of Disneyana (apparently all of it deemed collectible) has been endless.

Contributor: John Fawcett, P.O. Box 1156, 3506 Atlantic Highway, Waldoboro, ME 04572

Alice in Wonderland

	C6	C8	C10
Alice in Wonderland Marionette, Peter Puppet	85	128	185
Mad Hatter Doll, Gund	200	300	450
Mad Hatter Puppet	85	130	170
Mad Hatter's Taxi, Linemar, 1950s, 5" long	300	475	650

Babes in Toyland

	C6	C8	C10
Indian on Rollerskates Tin Wind-up, Linemar, 1950s, 6-1/2" tall	100	150	200
Soldier, tin wind-up, Linemar, 1950s, 6-1/2" tall	175	263	350
Wood Officer on Horseback, wheeled, Jaymar	175	263	350

Babes in Toyland Soldier, Linemar, 1950s, $350. Photo courtesy Scott Smiles

Babes in Toyland (Continued)

	C6	C8	C10
Wood Soldier, w/rifle, Jaymar, 9" high	60	90	120
Wood Soldier, w/cannon, Jaymar	210	315	420

Bambi

	C6	C8	C10
Bambi Soaky	15	30	50
Flower, tin friction, Linemar, 1950s, 3" long	115	172	250
Jumping Bambi, trigger action, Linemar, 1950s, 6" high	250	375	525
Thumper, tin friction, Linemar, 1950s, 3" long	60	110	160
Thumper, Marx, 1950s, 6" high	100	150	225
Thumper Doll, Gund, early 1940s, 17" high	80	150	200
Thumper Doll, Gund, 1950s, 14" high	38	65	100
Thumper Soaky	11	30	50
Thumper Squeeze Toy, rubber, Sun Rubber, 7" high	30	50	75

Cinderella

	C6	C8	C10
Cinderella and Prince Dancing Wind-up, plastic, No. 7000, Irwin Co., 1950s, 5" high	65	100	150
Hand Puppet, "1957"	22	33	60
Handcar, Jaq and Gus, 8" long	383	575	775
Soaky, w/movable arms, 1960s	15	30	50
Umbrella Wind-up, spins and dances, Irwin, 4-3/4" high	62	95	140

*Davy Crockett Powder Horn, Daisy, $40. Photo
courtesy* Toy Collector News

Davy Crockett

	C6	C8	C10
Alamo Play Set, Marx	250	375	500
Auto-Magic Picture Gun	42	63	85
Badge, "Frontier Marshal," 1950s	27	41	55
Coonskin Hat	22	33	60
Doll, vinyl, Gund, 20" high	60	90	150
Doll, Fortune Toy, 1950s, 8" high	60	90	150
Flying Arrows, balsa wood, to be made into flying arrows, copyright 1955	25	40	65
Frontierland Davy Crockett Outfit, coonskin hat, gun, etc.	70	105	175
Handgun, tin litho, pop-action, 1950s	40	60	100
Play Knife, 1950s	22	40	60
Powder Horn, Daisy	20	30	40
Prairie Wagon, 5" long	26	39	65
Wagon Train, plastic, Marx, 1950s, 14" long	150	225	325

Disneyland

	C6	C8	C10
Casey Jr. Disneyland Express, tin and plastic, locomotive, three cars, Marx	73	110	175
Concert Xylophone, Tudor, 18" long	30	45	75
Ferris Wheel Tin Wind-up, Chein, c. late 1956, 17" high	350	525	850
Happy Birthday Carousel, Ross Co., 1950s, 6" high	80	120	200
Jeep, push toy, Marx, 1960s, 10" long	100	150	225
Melody Player, w/four rolls, Chein, 1950s, 7"	95	150	225
Melody Player Extra Paper Rolls, different songs, price for each, 1950s	10	15	20

*Disneyland Ferris Wheel Tin Wind-up, Chein, c. late
1956, $850. Photo courtesy Hake's Americana &
Collectibles*

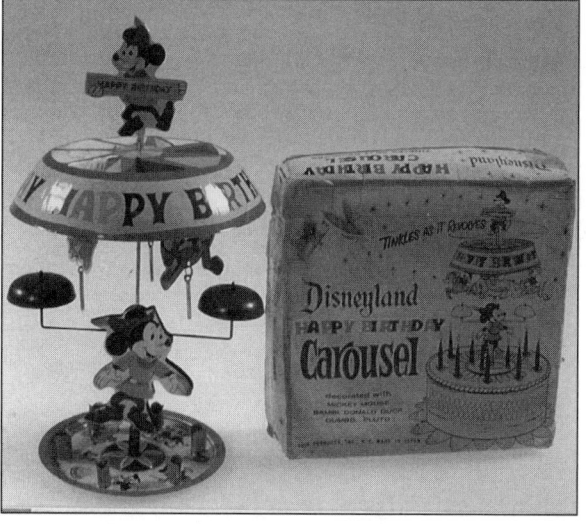

*Disneyland Happy Birthday Carousel, Ross Co.,
1950s, $200. Photo courtesy Continental Hobby
House*

Disneyland Roller Coaster, Chein, 1950s, $600. Photo courtesy Continental Hobby House

Donald Duck Climbing Fireman Wind-up, Linemar, 1950s, $650. Photo courtesy Don Hultzman

Donald Duck Doll, $2500. Photo courtesy Christie's East

Disneyland (Continued)

	C6	C8	C10
Play Set, Marx	425	700	950
Roller Coaster, two tin cars, Chein, 1950s, 10" high	250	400	600

Donald Duck

	C6	C8	C10
Acrobat, Linemar, 1950s, 8-1/2" high	325	525	750
Band Leader Marionette, Madame Alexander, 1938, 9-1/2" tall	150	250	500
Captain Push Puppet, wood and plastic, Kohner, 1950s	100	150	200
Climbing Fireman Wind-up, Linemar, 1950s, 13-1/2"	300	475	650
Convertible, tin, friction, Linemar, 1950s, 5" long	263	410	575
Crawler Wind-up, celluloid, 9-3/4" long	650	1100	1600
Delivery Tricycle, tin and plastic, Marx, 5"	450	750	100
Dipsy Car, tin car w/plastic Mickey or Donald, Marx, 1950s, 5-1/4" long	385	575	770
Disney Flivver, Linemar, 1950s, 5-1/2" long	300	450	600
Doctor Kit	60	90	150
Doll, composition and cloth, long-billed, in Russian costume, 9" high	1000	1750	2500
Doll, stuffed, long-billed, Knickerbocker, 1930s, 13" high	150	250	400
Doll, composition, long-billed, Knickerbocker, 1930s, 9" high	250	375	500
Doll, Gund, c. 1949, 13-1/2" high	110	200	300
Doll, long-billed, 1930s, 16" high	75	160	250
Donald Duck and His Nephews, pull-string action, Linemar, 1950s, 5-1/2" high	400	600	800

Donald Duck and His Nephews Wind-up, Marx, 1950s, $450. Photo courtesy Don Hultzman

Donald Duck (Continued)	**C6**	**C8**	**C10**
Donald Duck and His Nephews Wind-up, plastic, Marx, 1950s, 11" long	225	338	450
Donald Duck and Huey, w/voice, string pull toy, Linemar, 1950s, 7" long	500	750	1000
Donald Duck and Pluto in Roadster, Sun Rubber, 1930s, 6-1/2" long	80	120	200
Donald Duck Duet Tin Wind-up, small Donald w/large Goofy, Marx, c. 1945	440	660	950
Donald Duck Figure, Sun Rubber, 10" high	21	32	60
Donald Duck Figure, long billed, Seiberling Rubber, 1930s, 6" high	150	225	350

Donald Duck Figure, Seiberling Rubber, 1930s, $350. Photo courtesy Hake's Americana & Collectibles

Donald Duck Duet Tin Wind-up, Marx, c. 1945, $950

Donald Duck on Rocking Horse Wind-up, Japan, $6200. Photo courtesy James S. Maxwell and Virginia Caputo

Donald Duck Riding Mule Wind-up, $2000

Donald Duck (Continued)	C6	C8	C10
Donald Duck Figure, celluloid, long billed, Borgfeldt (Japan), 1930s, 5" high	262	395	550
Donald Duck Figure, celluloid, 1940s, 13" high	135	198	300
Donald Duck in His Convertible, friction, Linemar, 1950s, 6" long	275	415	650
Donald Duck Jigger Wind-up, papier-mâché, 11" high	800	1200	1600
Donald Duck Mouseketeers Hat	15	30	50
Donald Duck on Pluto Wind-up, celluloid	1400	2200	3400
Donald Duck on Rocking Horse Wind-up, celluloid and tin, Japan, 3-3/8" long	3000	4500	6200
Donald Duck on Tractor, plastic, friction, Marx, 1950s, 3-1/2" long	120	200	300
Donald Duck on Trapeze, Borgfeldt, 1930s, 9" high	275	362	650
Donald Duck Pulled by Pluto, celluloid w/tin cart, long billed, Japan, 1930s	1750	2625	3600

Donald Duck (Continued)	C6	C8	C10
Donald Duck Rail Car, w/Pluto and doghouse, No. 1107, Lionel, 1930s, 10" long	413	625	875
Donald Duck Riding Mule Wind-up, celluloid, long billed, 7-3/4"	850	1400	2000
Donald Duck Roly-Poly, 1940s, 3-3/4"	187	280	400
Donald Duck Rowboat, wood and paper litho, Chad Valley (England), 12-1/4" long	300	450	700
Donald Duck Skier, plastic, Marx, 1940s	375	675	1000
Donald Duck Skier, Linemar	300	550	800
Donald Duck Swimmer Wind-up, celluloid, 6-1/2"	650	1000	1650
Donald Duck Tricycle, w/twirling parasol, M-T Co. (Japan), 1950s, 7-1/2" high	200	375	500
Donald Duck Tricycle Wind-up, Linemar, 1950s, 3-1/2" long	285	450	650

Donald Duck (Continued)

	C6	C8	C10
Donald Duck Wind-up, hard plastic, Marx, 1960s, 7" high	30	45	75
Donald Duck Wind-up, tin, w/umbrella, Linemar, 4" high	300	450	625
Donald Duck Wind-up, "984," Schuco (German), 6" high	158	235	375
Donald Duck with Whirling Tail Tin Wind-up, Linemar, 1950s, 5-1/4" high	300	450	600
Donald Duck with Whirling Tail Wind-up, plastic, Marx, 1950s, 6-1/2" high	92	135	185
Donald Duck Zylophone, Tudor, 10" long	55	83	125
Donald Race Car Wind-up, celluloid, Occupied Japan	225	338	500
Donald the Driver, friction car, Linemar, 1950s, 6-1/2" long	225	338	500
Donald the Drummer Wind-up, rocker, Linemar, 1950s, 6" high	250	375	525
Donald the Drummer Wind-up, walker, Linemar, 1950s, 6" high	265	400	530
Donald the Drummer Wind-up, Marx, 1950s, 9" tall	275	363	550
Dump Truck, Linemar, 1950s, 5" long	300	450	650
Fire Chief Crazy Car Tin Wind-up, extremely rare, Linemar	700	1500	2000
Huey - Louie - Dewey Locomotive, plastic friction, Marx, 1950s, 3-1/2" long	50	75	120
Rubber Boat, Sun Rubber Co., c. 1940s	40	60	100
Soaky	11	40	65
Straight Shooter, plastic wind-up, 1960s, 6-1/2" high	187	280	450
Teapot, Ohio Art	30	45	75
Tractor, Sun Rubber	112	188	225
Waddler, tin and celluloid, long-billed, "K" Co. (Japan), 1930s, 3-1/4" high	600	900	1200
Waddler, "K" Co., 1930s, 3-1/2" tall	600	900	1200
Walker Wind-up, celluloid, Japan, 3-1/2" high	400	600	825
Washing Machine, M-T Co. (Japan), 1950s, 7-1/2" high	400	600	825

Dumbo the Acrobatic Elephant Tin Wind-up, Marx, 1941, $650. Photo courtesy Don Hultzman

Dumbo

	C6	C8	C10
Dumbo Hand Puppet, Gund, c. 1955, 10"	25	38	75
Dumbo Squeeze Doll, vinyl, 1960s, 9"	22	33	60
Dumbo The Acrobatic Elephant Tin Wind-up, Dumbo flips over, Marx, 1941, 4" high	300	450	650
Timothy Mouse Doll, stuffed, Character Novelty, 1942, 17" high	150	225	350

Ferdinand the Bull

	C6	C8	C10
Doll, jointed wood, 9"	125	188	300
Ferdinand and Matador Wind-up, tin, Marx, 1938	600	1000	1500
Ferdinand the Bull Wind-up, tail whirls, body shakes, Marx, copyright 1938	212	320	450
Figure, hard rubber, Seiberling, late 1930s, 6" long, 3-1/2" high	102	160	240

Ferdinand and Matador Wind-up, Marx, 1938, $1500. Photo courtesy Don Hultzman

Ferdinand the Bull Wind-up, Marx, copyright 1938, $450. Photo courtesy Don Hultzman

Ferdinand the Bull (Continued)	C6	C8	C10
Hand Puppet, Crown, 1938	55	82	110
Pull Toy, Hill, 8-3/4" long	170	255	340

Goofy	C6	C8	C10
Figure, tin, 1930	400	600	850
Goofy on a Unicycle Wind-up, tin, Linemar, 5-1/2" high	500	750	1100
Goofy the Walking Gardener Wind-up, tin, Marx	482	625	965
Goofy Tricycle Wind-up, Linemar, 1950s, 4" tall	650	975	1300
Goofy with Whirling Tail Wind-up, plastic, Marx, 1950s, 8" high	92	140	185
Goofy with Whirling Tail Wind-up, Linemar, 1950s, 5" tall	300	450	600
Goofy's Disneyland Stock Car Wind-up, Linemar, 1950s, 6" long	200	300	425
Goofy's Stock Car Wind-up, Linemar, 1950s, 6" long	200	300	425
Soaky	20	30	60

Goofy the Walking Gardener Wind-up, Marx, $965. Photo courtesy Christie's East

Jiminy Cricket Tin Wind-up, Linemar, 1950s, $650. Photo courtesy Don Hultzman

Jiminy Cricket	C6	C8	C10
Doll, jointed wood, Ideal, 1940, 9" high	225	375	500
Doll, latex head, hands and feet w/cloth body, 13" high	60	90	150
Doll, Knickerbocker, c. 1940, 10" high	300	450	650
Doll, felt and cloth, Crown Toy, 14" high	150	225	325
Doll, felt and cloth, Crown Toy, 15-1/2" high	150	225	325
Doll, cloth body w/rubber head and wooden feet, Gund, 12"	22	40	65
Face Mask, Gillette, 1939	25	38	65
Hand Puppet, vinyl and cloth, Gund	32	48	65
Jiminy Cricket Pushing Bass Fiddle Walkie, Marx	15	22	45
Jiminy Cricket Tin Wind-up, Linemar, 1950s, 5-1/2" tall	300	450	650
Soaky	10	30	50

Lady and the Tramp	C6	C8	C10
Si-Am Doll, stuffed w/vinyl face, Gund, c. 1955, 16" high	40	75	100
Tramp Hand Puppet, Gund	35	52	100
Tramp the Dog, friction, Linemar, 1960s, 4" high	90	135	200

*Ludwig Von Drake Tin Wind-up, Linemar, 1950s,
$580. Photo courtesy Don Hultzman*

Ludwig Von Drake

	C6	C8	C10
Ludwig Von Drake Go-Cart, friction, Marx, 1961	158	235	315
Ludwig Von Drake Squeeze Toy, rubber, Dell, c. 1960, 7"	58	90	115
Ludwig Von Drake Talking Doll	50	75	100
Ludwig Von Drake Tin Wind-up, Linemar, 1950s, 6" tall	290	435	580
Professor Von Drake Go Mobile, wind-up, Linemar, 1950s, 6" long	150	225	300

Mickey and Minnie Mouse

	C6	C8	C10
Acrobats, Borgfeldt, 1934, 11" high	500	750	1150
Bell Toy, wood and metal, Gong Bell, c. 1933, 10-3/4" long	1050	1575	2200
Drum Set, tin and cardboard, shows Minnie watching Mickey juggle, c. 1940	240	360	525

Mickey and Minnie Mouse (Continued)

	C6	C8	C10
Handcar, red, orange and green, Lionel Co., 1930s, 7" long	650	1100	1900
Mickey and Minnie Mouse on Motorcycle Tin Wind-up	13,000	33,000	65,000
Mickey and Minnie Mouse Playland, celluloid, Japan	3000	5500	10,000
Organ Grinder, depicts Minnie Mouse dancing on organ pushed by Mickey, German	1200	1800	2500
Piano, wooden, grand piano w/decal showing Mickey playing, Minnie listening, c. 1935	200	300	400
Swing Toy, celluloid, w/red and green flag, 11-1/2" tall	420	630	900
Tambourine, heavy paper head, depicts Mickey juggling while Minnie watches, Noble & Cooley Co., 1936, 9"	310	500	750
Tea Set, thirteen pieces, c. 1935	140	210	375

Mickey Mouse

	C6	C8	C10
Acrobat, wood, Strombecker, 1950s	45	68	100
Acrobat, clockwork trapeze w/celluloid Mickey, Japan, 1930s, 9" high	243	365	485

*Mickey Mouse Acrobat, Japan, 1930s, $485. Photo
courtesy PB Eighty-Four, New York*

Mickey Mouse Bandleader Doll, Knickerbocker, 1935, $1850. Photo courtesy Don Hultzman

Mickey Mouse Cowboy Mickey Doll, Knickerbocker, c. 1935, $4000. Photo courtesy Christie's East

Mickey Mouse (Continued)

	C6	C8	C10
Bandleader Doll, Knickerbocker, 1935, 12" high	650	1200	1850
Banjo, 1930s, 17" long	140	210	300
Bank, brass, figure of Mickey Mouse, French	2000	5000	10,000
Bank, cast iron, figure of Mickey Mouse, France, c. 1931	1500	2800	5000
Bubble Buster Gun, cast iron, Mickey standing at gun sight, Kilgore, 6" long	75	150	200
Circus, two wood figures revolving on swinging mechanism, 6/3785, Geo. Borgfeldt, 1931, 11" long	500	850	1300
Clicker, tin litho, Mickey showing teeth while playing violin, c. 1930	90	135	225
Cowboy Mickey Doll, Knickerbocker, c. 1935, 19-1/2" high	1400	3000	4000
Cowboy Mickey Doll, Knickerbocker, 1936, 12" high	2000	5000	8000

Mickey Mouse Bank, France, c. 1931, $5000. Photo courtesy James S. Maxwell and Virginia Caputo

Mickey Mouse Doll, $750. Photo courtesy Hakes Americana & Collectibles

Mickey Mouse Drum, Ohio Art, $300. Photo courtesy Hakes Americana & Collectibles

Mickey Mouse (Continued)	C6	C8	C10
Doll, felt, Steiff, early 1930s, 12" high	600	950	1350
Doll, wooden, w/jointed hands, arms, legs and wire tail, leather ears, first toy made by Borgfeldt of NY, marked "Copyright 1928-1930 by Walter E. Disney," 1930	550	825	1100
Drum, tin, Ohio Art, 6" diameter	130	195	300
Figure, cast iron, Mickey Holding Flag, 1930s	140	210	350
Figure, celluloid and wood, Mickey on Hobby Horse, c. 1935, 4-1/2"	1050	1800	2500
Figure, celluloid, w/fat head, 5" high	150	225	300

Mickey Mouse Figure, Fun-E-Flex, $675

Mickey Mouse (Continued)	C6	C8	C10
Dipsy Car, Linemar, 1950s, 5-1/4" long	300	450	600
Dipsy Car, Mickey, tin car w/plastic, Marx, 1950s, 5-1/4" long	318	475	635
Doll, Borgfeldt, 12" high	625	938	1350
Doll, cloth, marked "Walt Disney Mickey Mouse Geo. E. Borgfeldt & Company New York" on bottom of one foot, 11" high	337	505	750
Doll, felt, Character Co., c. 1939-40, 18" high	70	105	200
Doll, felt, dressed in black jacket w/yellow buttons, red pants, bells on toes of yellow shoes, storage space in back, 1950s, 31" high	120	180	240
Doll, Knickerbocker, 1930s, 12" high	325	488	750
Doll, Knickerbocker, 1935, 22" high	500	750	1150
Doll, felt, Mickey has toothy grin, Dean's Rag, 6"	125	200	350

Mickey Mouse (Continued)

	C6	C8	C10
Figure, Fun-E-Flex, 1930s, 3-1/2" high	150	225	300
Figure, lead, Allied Toys, 1933, 2-1/2" high	70	105	160
Figure, rubber, Seiberling, c. 1935, 6" high	150	250	400
Figure, rubber, Dell, 9-1/2" high	50	75	120
Figure, rubber, Sun Rubber, 1940s, 10" high	30	45	75
Figure, Sun Rubber, 8" high	65	98	150
Figure, wood, Fun-E-Flex, 7-1/2" high	300	500	675
Figure, jointed wood, Borgfeldt, early, 7" high	300	450	625
Figure, wood, w/leather ears, Fen-E-Flex, 5" high	250	375	525
Figure, wood, w/jointed arms and legs, c. 1933, 8" high	600	900	1300
Figure, rubber, Lakeside Mfg. Co.	80	120	180
Figure, rubber, Seiberling, 1930s, 3-1/2" high	90	135	240

Mickey Mouse (Continued)

	C6	C8	C10
Flute, tin	40	60	100
Gym Toys Acrobats, includes Mickey, Donald, Minnie, price for each, Linemar, 1950s, 8-1/2" high	200	300	400
Handcar, "Santa Car with Mickey Mouse and His Gift Pack," No. 1105, Lionel, 1935	900	1350	2000
Hingees, 1944	25	40	65
Jazz Drummer, finger-activated tin toy, Nifty, 4-3/4" high	1500	2700	4200
Kaleidoscope, 1950s	32	50	80
Marionette, Madame Alexander, 1938, 9-1/2" high	150	250	500
Marionette, Peter Puppet Playthings Co., 1952, 14" tall	55	90	130
Mask, cardboard, c. 1935	60	90	120
Mickey Mouse Bus Lines - Walt Disney Stars, riding toy, Gong Bell, c. 1960, 19-1/2" long	150	225	350

Mickey Mouse Handcar, Lionel, 1935, $2000

Mickey Mouse Figure, Borgfeldt, early, $625

Mickey Mouse Bus Lines - Walt Disney Stars, Gong

Mickey Mouse Circus Train Set (incomplete set), No. 1536, Lionel, $5000. Photo courtesy PB Eighty-Four, New York

Mickey Mouse (Continued)	C6	C8	C10
Mickey Mouse Circus Train Set, engine, Mickey in tender, three tin-litho cars (dining, band and circus); set includes large paper circus tent and multiple paper accessories, a composition Mickey "Narker" figures and track, No. 1536, Lionel..	1300	2500	5000
Mickey Mouse Express Tin Wind-up, train set, Marx, 1950s, 14" long, base 21" x 13"	700	1100	1700
Mickey Mouse Express Wind-up, Mickey in airplane, Marx, 1950s, 9" diameter	425	638	850

Mickey Mouse Express Wind-up, Marx, 1950s, $850. Photo courtesy Don Hultzman

Mickey Mouse (Continued)	C6	C8	C10
Mickey Mouse Meteor Five-Car Train Tin Wind-up, Marx, 43" long..	800	1000	1500
Mickey Mouse Motorcycle, tin friction, Linemar, 1950s, 3" long	200	300	400
Mickey Mouse Motorcycle, tin friction, Linemar, 1950s, 3-1/2" long	150	225	300
Mickey Mouse on Handcar Wind-up, basket on back, Japan, 8" long	130	210	300
Mickey Mouse on Tricycle Tin Wind-up, 1940s, 3-1/2" long	450	700	900
Mickey Mouse Pirate Ship, Ideal	138	210	275
Mickey Mouse Racing Car Tin Wind-up, w/Mickey at the wheel, metal or rubber wheels, 1930s, 4" long	400	650	900
Mickey Mouse Rollerskater Wind-up, Linemar, 1950s, 6" high	450	750	1130
Mickey Mouse Trapeze, wood, c. 1930s	34	60	100
Mickey Mouse Trapeze, celluloid, Borgfeldt, 1930s	500	750	1150
Mickey Mouse Tricycle, Linemar, 1950s, 4" tall	500	775	1100
Mickey Mouse Tumbler, pie-eyed, Schuco, 1930s, 4" long	150	225	325
Mickey Mouse Tumbling, Marks Bros., 1947, 8" high	42	63	85
Mickey Mouse Wind-up, tin, vibrates, Linemar, 1950s, 5-1/2" high	300	450	600
Mickey Mouse wth Twirling Tail Wind-up, Linemar, 1950s, 5-1/2" high	130	195	275

Mickey Mouse Racing Car Tin Wind-up, 1930s, $900. Photo courtesy PB Eighty-Four, New York

Mickey Mouse Tumbler, Schuco, 1930s, $325. Photo courtesy Christie's East

Mickey Mouse Xylophone Player Tin Wind-up, Linemar, 1950s, $665. Photo courtesy Don Hultzman

Mickey on Scooter Tin Wind-up, Linemar, 1950s, $725. Photo courtesy Don Hultzman

Mickey Mouse (Continued)

	C6	C8	C10
Mickey Mouse Xylophone Player Tin Wind-up, Linemar, 1950s, 6" high	333	500	665
Mickey on Scooter Tin Wind-up, rare, Linemar, 1950s, 4-1/2" high	350	525	725
Mickey on Unicycle Wind-up, Linemar, 1950s, 5" high	650	975	1300
Mickey Race Car Wind-up, celluloid, Occupied Japan	250	375	500
Mickey the Driver, friction, Marx (Japan), 1950s, 6-1/2" long	400	600	850
Mickey the Magician, battery-operated, Linemar, 10"	500	800	1200
Mickey the Musician - I Play the Xylophone Wind-up, Marx, 1950s, 10" high	312	465	625
Mickey Walker, Borgfeldt, 1934, 8" high	2100	3700	5750

Mickey Mouse (Continued)

	C6	C8	C10
Mickey Wouse Waddle Book, Blue Ribbon Book, Inc, 1934	800	2000	6500
Mickey, Minnie and Goofy Sand Pail, tin litho, Ohio Art, 1938	112	168	250
Mickey-in-the-Box, 7" high	260	390	520

Mickey the Magician, Linemar, $1200. Photo courtesy Christie's East

Mickey Mouse Rower, Fun-E-Flex, $4000. Photo courtesy Christie's East

Mickey Mouse (Continued)

	C6	C8	C10
Mickey's Delivery Tin Wind-up, tin litho, celluloid head on Pluto, Pluto on tricycle cart, Linemar, 1950s, 5-1/2" long	375	565	750
Mickey's Mousekemovers Wind-up, Linemar, 1950s, 13" long	500	750	1025
Mickey's Service Truck, plastic friction, Marx, 1950s, 3-1/2" long	50	85	150
Mickey's Tractor, Mickey's head turns, Sun Rubber, 1930s, 4-1/2" long	65	100	150
Movie Fun Optical Toy, Mastercraft, 1950s, 7" x 7" x 5"	150	225	300
Movie Projector, No. E-18, Keystone, 1930s, 10" high	125	210	375
Movie-Jector, 1935	135	200	350
Newsreel, includes three records and five films, Mattel, 9-1/2" high	110	165	225
Parade Roadster, tin litho wind-up, convertible car decorated w/Mickey and other Disney characters, Donald is at the wheel w/Pluto, Mickey and Minnie as passengers, Marx, 1950s, 11-1/4" long	350	525	700
Pencil Box, Dixon Pencil Co., 1930s	110	225	350
Piano, Marks Bros., c. 1935, 10"	1250	2200	3000
Pocket Knife, 1935	40	100	150
Puppet, cloth body w/composition head, hands and feet and cloth ears, early 1940s style	175	263	350
Puppet, Gund, 10" high	11	16	35
Puppet, rubber legs and arms, wood body, Pelham, 24" high	40	80	120

Mickey Mouse (Continued)

	C6	C8	C10
Push Puppet, Gabriel, 1977	10	15	30
Push Puppet, Mickey Mouse Drummer, Kohner, 1950s	100	150	200
Race Car, add $250 for box, T.M. Co., 1930s, 3" long	300	450	650
Rocking Mickey Mouse on Pluto Wind-up, Linemar	800	1400	2000
Roly-Poly, celluloid, early, 4" high	187	280	400
Rower, Fun-E-Flex, 10-3/4"	1700	2750	4000
Running Mickey on Pluto Wind-up, celluloid, M-T Co., 1940s, 5-1/2" long	2000	3750	6750
Saxophone Player, 1930s	800	1500	2200
Scooter Jockey Wind-up, plastic, Mavco Co., 1950s, 6" high	400	600	800
Snow Shovel, Mickey and Pluto, shows them building a snowman, 26" long	90	135	225
Soaky	20	40	60
Soda Jerk Hat, felt, shows Mickey from shoulders up saying "have one on me," c. 1930, 5" x 11"	60	90	150
Soldier Set, cardboard soldiers, gun	500	1000	1500
Sparkler Toy, Nifty, 1930s, 5-1/2" tall	325	490	750
Squeeze Toy, w/red shirt and yellow pants, Sun Rubber, 1950	34	51	85
Squeeze Toy, rubber, large size w/clothes, Sun Rubber, 1950	30	45	75
Tea Service, tin, twenty-four pieces, Chein, 1930s	120	225	350
Tool Chest, complete, Hamilton Metal, 1935	170	325	400
Tumbler, Schuco, 4" high	200	300	425

Mickey Mouse and Donald Duck Handcar, Marx, 1948, $425. Photo courtesy Don Hultzman

Mickey Mouse (Continued)

	C6	C8	C10
Viewer, w/film of "Brave Little Tailor," 1946	60	90	120
Washboard Set, tin, complete, c. 1935	80	120	175
Washing Machine, tin litho, shows two scenes w/Mickey, Minnie, Pluto, Ohio Art Co., 1932 or 1933, 7" high	100	150	220

Mickey Mouse and Donald Duck

	C6	C8	C10
Handcar, plastic, wind-up, Marx, 1948	200	300	425
Mickey Mouse and Donald in Fire Truck, Sun Rubber, late 1930s, 6-1/2" long	75	125	200
Mickey Mouse and Donald on Boat, celluloid	1050	1700	2450
Walker, plastic, both on back of alligator, Marx, 1950s	60	90	120

Mickey Mouse Club

	C6	C8	C10
Auto-Magic Picture Gun, projects films, 1946	35	52	85
Bow and Arrow Set, c. 1955	20	30	50
Mouseketeer Electric TV Story Teller, tin litho, includes TV, record player, records and film reels, T. Cohn, late 1950s	160	240	320
Mouseketeer Hat, wool and rayon, Benay-Albee, 1950s	5	10	20
Mouseketeer Play Outfit	75	112	150
Mouseketeer Soaky	17	35	60
Newreel Projector	68	102	135
Pinback, W.E. Disney, 1928-30	55	110	160

Mickey Mouse Club (Continued)

	C6	C8	C10
Snap-on Ears, plastic, 1950s	10	15	20
Television Playhouse Play Set, w/thirty-nine characters, Marx	232	348	465

Minnie Mouse

	C6	C8	C10
Doll, wearing dress and high heels, 1930, 12" high	225	350	500
Doll, cloth, early 1930s, 16" high	650	975	1300
Figure, wooden, jointed, 1940s, 3" high	200	300	400
Figure, celluloid, string tail, 1930s, 6" high	425	638	875
Figure, cloth, dressed in a red and white polka dot skirt, wearing composition high-heeled shoes, 14-1/2" high	300	450	625
Figure, Fun-E-Flex, 7" high	300	450	625
Figure, lead, Allied Toys, 1933, 2-1/2" high	70	105	140
Figure, Sun Rubber, 1940s, 10-1/2" high	85	125	185
Figure, celluloid, w/fat head, 1930s, 5" high	225	338	475
Figure, wooden, 1930s, 5-1/2" high	187	286	400
Figure, wooden, Fun-E-Flex, 4" high	140	210	300
Hand Puppet, Peter Puppet Playthings, c. 1952	100	150	200
Marionette, Madame Alexander, 1938, 9-1/2" high	150	250	500
Marionette, wood and composition, 1950s, 13"	150	225	300

Minnie Mouse Knitter Tin Wind-up, Linemar, 1950s, $775. Photo courtesy Don Hultzman

Minnie Mouse (Continued)

	C6	C8	C10
Mask, cardboard, c. 1935	40	60	80
Minnie Mouse Cowgirl Doll, Knickerbocker, 1936, 18" high	470	725	960
Minnie Mouse Knitter Tin Wind-up, Linemar, 1950s, 7" high	375	600	775
Minnie Mouse Wind-up, hard plastic, Marx, 1960s, 7" high	70	105	150
Puppet, wood body w/rubber legs and arms, Pelham, 24" high	195	292	390
Roly-Poly, celluloid, 4"	60	90	120
Tricycle, Linemar, 1950s, 4"	450	675	900
Walker, plastic	20	30	40
Washing Machine, Precision Specialties Inc., 1950	100	150	225

Peter Pan

	C6	C8	C10
Captain Hook Hand Puppet, Gund, 1950	17	26	35
Captain Hook Marionette, Peter Puppet Playthings	95	143	190
Peter Pan Figure, Sun Rubber, c. 1952, 9-3/4" high	30	45	75
Peter Pan Jolly Roger Pirate Ship	17	26	35
Peter Pan Marionette, Peter Puppet Playthings, c. 1952	70	105	140
Peter Pan Tea Set, twenty-three pieces, c. 1953	275	363	575
Peter Pan Train Car, 1977	22	33	45
Tinkerbell Hand Puppet, Gund	32	48	65
Wendy Hand Puppet, Gund	14	21	28
Wendy Marionette, 1950s	75	112	150

Pinocchio

	C6	C8	C10
Cleo Mask, Gillette, 1939	10	30	50
Cleo the Goldfish Squeeze Toy, Sun Rubber	23	35	60
Donkey Doll, stuffed, Knickerbocker	95	142	225
Donkey Figure, rubber, Seiberling Rubber, 1940, 4"	70	105	160
Figaro, tin friction toy, Linemar, 1950s, 3" long	70	105	150
Figaro Mask, paper, Gillette, 1939	15	38	50
Gepetto Figure, wood, holding his chin, Multi Products, 1940, 5-1/2"	70	105	140
Gepetto Mask, Gillette, 1939	12	33	45

Pinocchio (Continued)

	C6	C8	C10
Jiminy Cricket, 1940	100	200	300
Pinocchio, plastic, "Walking Pinocchio," Marx, 1950s	40	60	100
Pinocchio Delivery, Marx	250	375	500
Pinocchio Doll, jointed wood and composition, Ideal, 10-1/2" high	250	375	525
Pinocchio Doll, jointed wood and composition, Ideal, 12" high	300	450	625
Pinocchio Doll, jointed, c. 1940, 19-3/4" high	400	600	830
Pinocchio Doll, jointed, c. 1940, 11" high	200	300	420

Pinocchio, Marx, 1950s, $100. Photo courtesy Ed Hyers Antique Toys

Donkey Figure (Pinocchio), Seiberling Rubber, 1940, $160

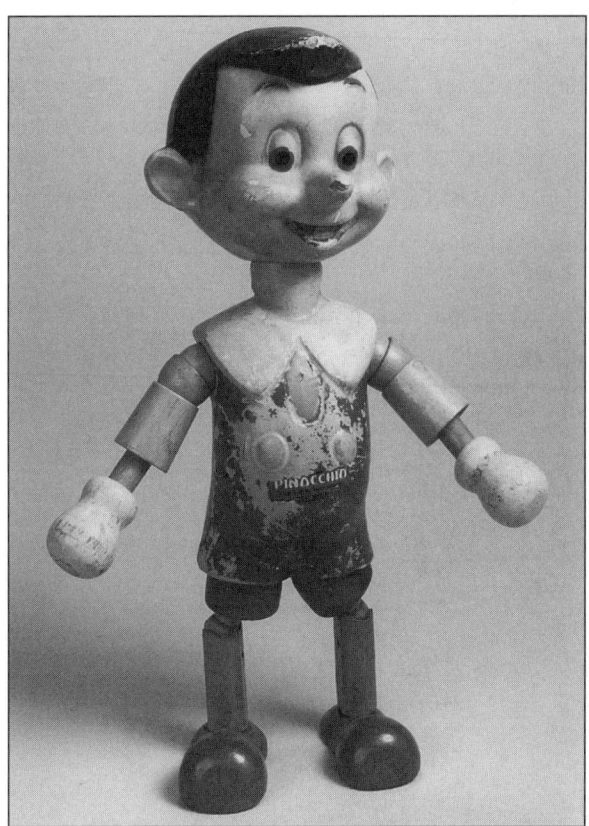

Pinocchio Doll, Ideal, $525

Pinocchio (Continued)

	C6	C8	C10
Pinocchio Doll, jointed, Ideal, 1940, 7-1/2" high	150	225	310
Pinocchio Doll, soft cloth, c. 1940s, 18" high	125	188	275
Pinocchio Doll, stuffed, Knickerbocker, 15" high	92	138	200
Pinocchio Figure, molded wood fiber, Multi Products, 1940, 5" high	100	150	200
Pinocchio Figure, molded wood fiber, Multi Products, 1940, 2-1/2" high	100	150	200
Pinocchio Figure, rubber, Seiberling, 5-1/2" high	27	41	65
Pinocchio Figure, Ideal, 8" high	132	198	300
Pinocchio Figure, cloth and wood, jointed, Kreuger	160	240	330
Pinocchio Hand Puppet, Gund, 1950s	10	15	35
Pinocchio Mask, paper, Gillette, 1939	10	30	50
Pinocchio Soaky	12	30	50
Pinocchio the Acrobat Tin Wind-up, "Watch Him Go!," Marx, 1939	385	575	770

Pinocchio (Continued)

	C6	C8	C10
Pinocchio Tin Wind-up, Linemar Co., 1950s, 5-1/2" tall	350	525	725
Pinocchio Tin Wind-up, w/litho eyes, Marx, c. 1940, 8-1/2" high	300	450	625

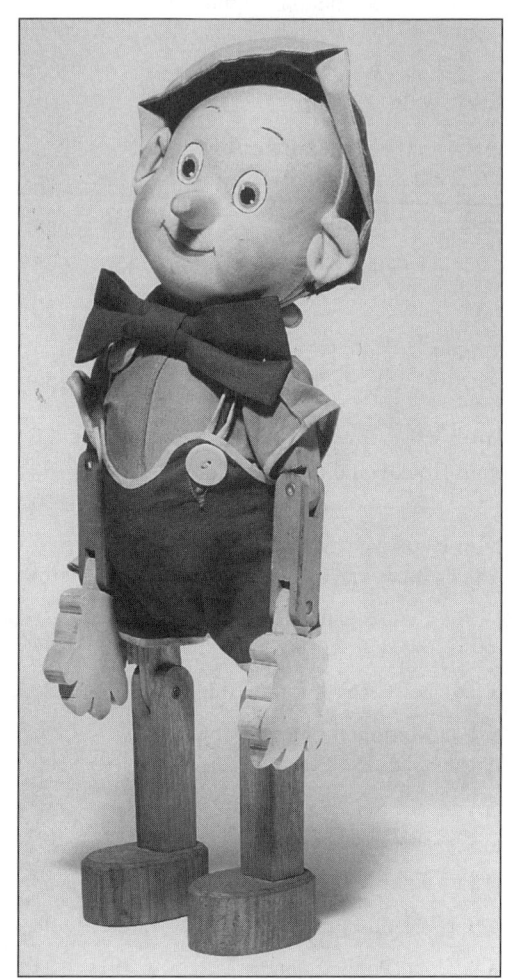

Pinocchio Figure, Kreuger, $330. Photo courtesy PB Eighty-four, New York

A 1940 ad/offer for the Pinocchio Mask by Gillette. Photo courtesy Rex and Richard Grey

Pinocchio Tin Wind-up, Linemar Co., 1950s, $725. Photo courtesy Don Hultzman

Pinocchio (Continued)	C6	C8	C10
Pinocchio Tin Wind-up, w/moving eyes, Marx, 1939, 8-1/2" high	312	470	650
Pinocchio Wind-up, wood and papier-mâché, George Borgfeldt, 1940, 10-1/2" high	318	475	700

Pluto	C6	C8	C10
Begging Rollover Pluto Wind-up, Linemar, 1950s, 6-1/2" long	100	150	200
Drum Major Tin Wind-up, Linemar, 1950s, 6-1/2" tall	250	400	600
Figure, wood, Borgfeldt, 6"	175	263	375
Figure, lead, Allied Toys, 1933, 2-1/2" high	60	90	150

Pluto (Continued)	C6	C8	C10
Figure, wooden w/bendable legs, c. 1934, 3"	140	210	30
Figure, jointed wood, 9"	250	375	500
Figure, Seiberling, c. 1935, 4"	60	90	150
Figure, Seiberling, 7-1/2"	65	98	160
Hand Puppet, Gund, 1950s	15	22	50
Marionette, Madame Alexander, 1938, 6" tall	100	150	250
Musical Pluto, plastic, Marx, 1960s, 8" x 8" base	400	600	850
Mysterious Pluto, Marx	150	225	325
Playful Pluto & Goofy Wind-up, two-piece set, Linemar, 1950s	800	1300	2000
Pluto in His Sports Car, plastic friction drive, 1950s, 4" long	50	75	150
Pluto Motorcycle, tin friction, Linemar, 1950s, 3-1/2" long	300	450	650

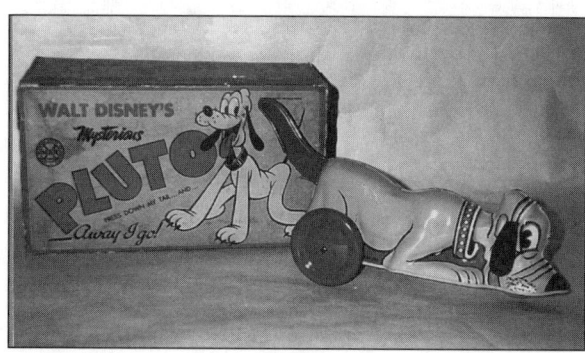

Mysterious Pluto, Marx, $325. Photo courtesy Don Hultzman

Pluto Drum Major Tin Wind-up, Linemar, 1950s, $600. Photo courtesy Don Hultzman

Playful Pluto & Goofy Wind-up, Linemar, 1950s, $2000. Photo courtesy Don Hultzman

Pluto Pulling Cart, Linemar, 1950s, $785. Photo courtesy Ed Hayes

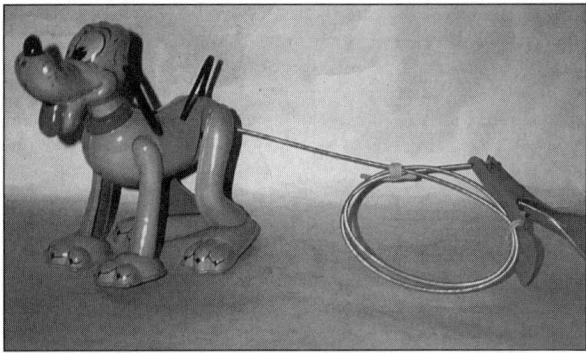

Pluto Squeeze Action Toy with Cable, Linemar, 1950s, $400. Photo courtesy Don Hultzman

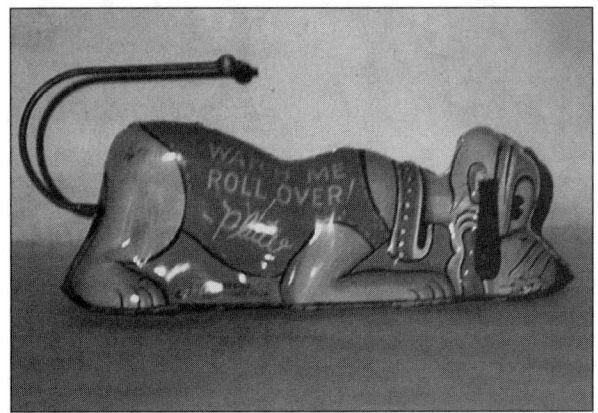

Pluto Watch Me Roll Over Wind-up, Marx, 1939, $300

Wise Pluto Wind-up, Marx, 1939, $475. Photo courtesy Don Hultzman

Pluto (Continued)	**C6**	**C8**	**C10**
Pluto on Rockers, wooden, c. 1930s ...	150	225	325
Pluto Pulling Cart, friction, Linemar, 1950s, 8-1/2" long	392	588	785
Pluto Tricycle, Linemar, 1950s, 4" tall	278	415	555
Pluto with Whirling Tail Wind-up, Linemar, 1950s, 4" high	235	350	500
Soaky	11	30	50
Squeeze Action Toy with Cable, tin litho, Linemar, 1950s, 4-1/4" tall	200	300	400
Squeeze Toy, rubber, in sitting position, 1960s	20	30	50
Squeeze Toy, rubber, No. 11520, Sun Rubber, 1930s	30	45	75
Watch Me Roll Over Wind-up, Marx, 1939	130	195	300

Pluto (Continued)	**C6**	**C8**	**C10**
Wise Pluto Wind-up, Marx, 1939, 8" long	212	318	475

Sleeping Beauty	**C6**	**C8**	**C10**
Sleeping Beauty Hand Puppet, Gund, 1950s	31	50	75
Sleeping Beauty Squeeze Toy, sitting w/animals, 6-1/2"	44	66	100

Bashful Doll (Snow White and The Seven Dwarfs), Ideal, 1938, $200

Snow White and The Seven Dwarfs

	C6	C8	C10
Bashful Doll, stuffed	60	90	150
Bashful Doll, Ideal, 7" high	125	188	275
Bashful Doll, Ideal, 1938, 12" high	80	120	200
Bashful Figure, Seiberling, 5-3/4" high	90	135	200
Bashful Figure, lead, Britains, 1-1/2"	40	60	85
Bashful Marionette, Madame Alexander, 1938, 9-1/2" tall	100	150	250
Bashful Party Mask, 1937	20	30	50
Doc Doll, composition w/velvet clothes, Knickerbocker, 9" high	100	150	225
Doc Doll, Ideal, approx. 7" high	125	188	275
Doc Doll, Ideal, 1938, 12" high	82	123	190
Doc Figure, lead, Britains, 1-1/2" high	60	90	120
Doc Figure, Seiberling, 1938, 5-3/4"	50	75	125
Doc Marionette, Madame Alexander, 1938, 9-1/2" tall	100	150	250

Snow White and The Seven Dwarfs (Continued)

	C6	C8	C10
Doc Party Mask, 1937	14	21	50
Dopey and Doc Pull Toy, 14" long	200	300	425
Dopey Doll, Ideal, 7" high	125	188	300
Dopey Doll, Ideal, 1938, 12" high	150	225	350
Dopey Doll, composition w/velvet clothes, Knickerbocker, 9" high	175	263	425
Dopey Figure, lead, Britains, 1-1/2"	40	60	85
Dopey Hand Puppet, composition w/bell and buckling belt, Crown Toys, 1938	90	135	225
Dopey Hand Puppet, Gund, 1950s	12	18	35
Dopey Marionette, Peter Puppet Playthings, c. 1952	80	120	200
Dopey Marionette, Madame Alexander, 1938, 9-1/2" tall	100	150	250
Dopey Party Mask, 1937	20	50	75
Dopey Soaky	17	30	50
Dopey Squeeze Toy, rubber, 1950s, 10" high	10	15	35
Dopey Tin Wind-up, Marx, 1938	263	395	575

Doc Doll (Snow White and The Seven Dwarfs), Ideal, 1938, $190

Dopey Doll (Snow White and The Seven Dwarfs), Ideal, 1938, $350

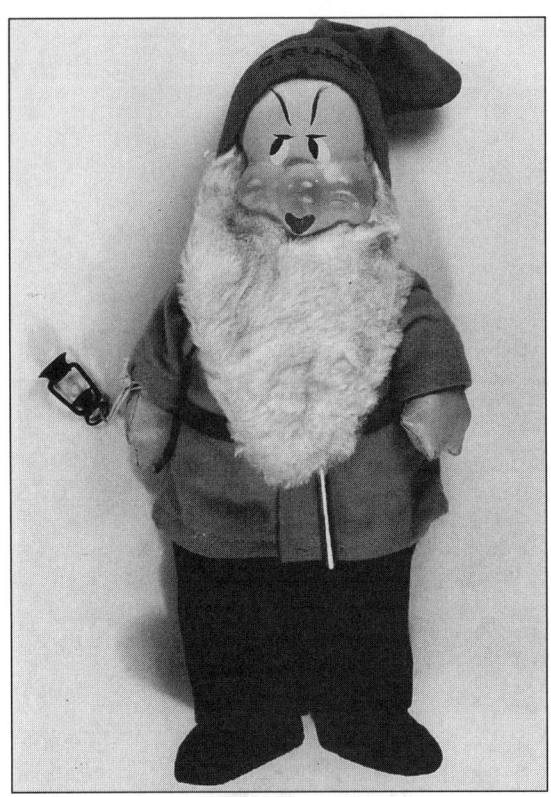

Grumpy Doll (Snow White and The Seven Dwarfs), Ideal, 1938, $185

Snow White and The Seven Dwarfs (Continued)

	C6	C8	C10
Grumpy, stuffed w/molded oilcloth face, Ideal, 11-1/2" high	90	135	200
Grumpy Doll, Ideal, 1938, 11" high	80	120	185
Grumpy Doll, composition w/velvet clothes, Knickerbocker, 9" high	100	150	250
Grumpy Figure, Ideal, 7" high	140	210	300
Grumpy Figure, lead, Britains, 1-1/2" high	40	60	100
Grumpy Marionette, Madame Alexander, 1938, 9-1/2" tall	100	150	250
Grumpy Par-T Mask, 1937	10	30	50
Grumpy Squeeze Toy, rubber, 1950s	10	15	35
Happy Doll, Ideal, 1938, 12" high	110	165	250
Happy Doll, Ideal, 7" high	130	195	300
Happy Figure, lead, Britains, 1-1/2"	30	45	85
Happy Figure, Seiberling, 1938, 5-3/4"	60	90	150
Happy Marionette, Madame Alexander, 1938, 9-1/2" high	110	155	250
Happy Party Mask, 1937	40	60	80

Happy Doll (Snow White and The Seven Dwarfs), Ideal, 1938, $250

Seven Dwarfs Dolls (Snow White and The Seven Dwarfs), Sieberling, 1938, $850. Photo courtesy Stan Alekna

Snow White and The Seven Dwarfs (Continued)

	C6	C8	C10
Happy Squeeze Toy, rubber, 1950s	10	15	35
Horace Horsecollar Hand Puppet, Gund, c. 1960	17	25	50
Huntsman, Madame Alexander, 1938, 9-1/2" tall	100	150	250
Prince, Madame Alexander, 1938, 9-1/2" tall	100	150	250
Seven Dwarfs Dolls, price for the set, Sieberling, 1938, 5-1/2" high	350	525	850
Seven Dwarfs Puppet-Marionettes, price for the set, Pelham	1500	2250	3500
Seven Dwarfs Squeeze Toy, vinyl, price for each, 1950s, approx. 8"	30	45	75
Sleepy Doll, Ideal, 1938, 12" high	120	180	300
Sleepy Doll, Ideal, 7" high	125	188	300
Sleepy Figure, lead, Britains, 1-1/2" high	45	68	100

Snow White and The Seven Dwarfs (Continued)

	C6	C8	C10
Sleepy Marionette, Madame Alexander, 1938, 9-1/2" tall	100	150	250
Sleepy Party Mask, 1937	20	35	60
Sneezy Doll, Ideal, 1938, 12" high	120	180	300
Sneezy Doll, Ideal, 7" high	125	188	300

Sleepy Doll (Snow White and The Seven Dwarfs), Ideal, 1938, $300

Seven Dwarfs Puppet-Marionettes, Pelham, $3500

Sneezy Doll (Snow White and The Seven Dwarfs), Ideal, 1938, $300

Snow White Doll (Snow White and The Seven Dwarfs), Ideal, 1938, $350

Snow White and The Seven Dwarfs (Continued)

	C6	C8	C10
Sneezy Figure, Seiberling, 1938, 5-1/8" high	60	90	150
Sneezy Figure, lead, Britains, 1-1/2" high	45	68	100
Sneezy Marionette, Madame Alexander, 1938, 9-1/2" tall	100	150	250
Sneezy Party Mask, 1937	20	35	60
Sneezy Squeeze Toy, rubber, 1950s	10	15	20
Snow White and the Seven Dwarfs Blocks, set of eighteen w/box	175	263	350
Snow White and the Seven Dwarfs Dining Set, includes dishes, china, with cups, creamer, sugar bowl, plates, 4-1/2" dishes, 6" plate	210	315	420
Snow White and the Seven Dwarfs Drum, tin litho, 1930s	125	188	275
Snow White and the Seven Dwarfs Figures, each, No. 1654, Britains	20	60	100
Snow White and the Seven Dwarfs Figures, lead, by Lincoln Logs, price for the set	500	850	1200

Snow White and The Seven Dwarfs (Continued)

	C6	C8	C10
Snow White and the Seven Dwarfs Musical Top, Chein, 6-1/2" across	110	165	250
Snow White and the Seven Dwarfs Sewing Set, Hasbro	20	30	65
Snow White Doll, Ideal, 1938, 15" high	150	225	350
Snow White Doll, Knickerbocker, 1940s, 12" high	187	300	425
Snow White Doll, Madame Alexander, 1938, 13" high	120	200	300
Snow White Figure, Seiberling, 8-3/4"	250	375	550
Snow White Figure, lead, Britains, 2-1/2"	45	68	125
Snow White Kitchen Set, Wolverine	60	90	150
Snow White Marionette, Madame Alexander, 1938, 9-1/2" tall	150	250	300
Snow White Party Mask	20	30	60
Snow White Sink and Stove, Wolverine	40	60	100

A 1938 ad for the Snow White and The Seven Dwarfs figures by Seiberling

Snow White and The Seven Dwarfs (Continued)

	C6	C8	C10
Snow White Soaky	17	30	50
Snow White Washing Machine, Revell Pastics, c. 1950, 7-1/2" high w/wringer	80	120	200
Wicked Witch, Madame Alexander, 1938, 9-1/2" tall	100	150	250
Witch Party Mask	20	30	50

Three Little Pigs

	C6	C8	C10
Big Bad Wolf, stuffed toy in tux w/carnation, glass eyes, 20" tall	450	675	1000
Big Bad Wolf and The Three Little Pigs, four-piece set, Linemar, 1950s, 4-1/4" tall	750	1125	1500
Big Bad Wolf Halloween Costume, 4" high	60	90	150
Big Bad Wolf Pinback, celluloid, 1-1/4"	38	100	150
Three Little Pigs Acrobats, celluloid, Japan	312	465	675
Three Little Pigs Clothes Washer, Chein	102	153	250
Three Little Pigs Drummer, Schuco, 1930s, 4-1/2" tall	175	300	400
Three Little Pigs Figures, wood w/fiber arms and legs, Borgfeldt, c. 1933, 3-1/4" high	120	180	275
Three Little Pigs Flutist, Schuco, 1930s, 4-1/2" tall	175	263	375
Three Little Pigs Par-T Mask, 1933	40	60	80
Three Little Pigs Sand Bucket, 3" tall	30	45	75
Three Little Pigs Violinist, Schuco, 1930s, 4-1/2" tall	212	318	450
Three Little Pigs Walkers Tin Wind-up, price for each, Linemar	130	195	300

Uncle Scrooge

	C6	C8	C10
Uncle Scrooge Hand Puppet, wearing high hat, 1960s	20	50	75
Uncle Scrooge Limousine, w/"$" on back fender	110	185	275
Uncle Scrooge Squeeze Toy Bank, vinyl, c. 1960, 7" high	40	85	125

Walt Disney

	C6	C8	C10
Character Carousel, Linemar Co., 1950s, 7" high w/3" characters	300	450	600

Walt Disney (Continued)

	C6	C8	C10
Character T.V. Set, Automatic Toy Co., 1950s, 5" cubic	150	225	300
Friction Delivery Wagon, features Mickey, Donald, Pluto, etc., Linemar, 1950s, 6" long	450	675	900
Friction Go-Mobile, features Mickey, Pluto, Donald, etc., Marx, 1960s, 6" long	150	225	300
Mechanical Tricycle, features Pluto, Mickey, Donald, etc., Linemar, 1950s, 4" high	200	300	400
Stars Bus, Gong Bell, 19" long	450	675	900
Television Car, Marx, 1950s, 7-1/2" long	275	365	550

Winnie the Pooh

	C6	C8	C10
Eeyore Squeeze Doll, vinyl, 1960s	37	56	100
Piglet Squeeze Doll, vinyl, 1960s	9	16	25
Tigger Squeeze Doll, 1960s, 9"	9	13	25

Zorro

	C6	C8	C10
Flintlock Pistol, Marx	35	75	125
Hand Puppet, Gund	50	75	100
Hat, hideaway mask and gloves, 1950s	46	70	100
Play Set, Marx	400	600	800
Ring, black top w/"Z" and "Zorro" name	22	40	60
Sword, 1960s, 24" long	5	20	35
Zorro on Rearing Horse, Marx	160	240	320

Miscellaneous

	C6	C8	C10
101 Dalmatians, set of six wooden nodders, 1959	125	200	300
Disney Show Boat, plastic, Playworld Toys, 1981	4	10	20
Disney Showboat, large, 1960	62	100	150
Disneykins, Marx	105	158	210
Elmer Elephant, rubber, w/moveable head, Seiberling	162	243	375
Elmer Elephant Figure, celluloid and string, 1930s, 5"	120	180	300
Frontierland Logs, No. 915, Halsam	45	80	120
Johnny Tremain Flintlock Cap Pistol, Marx	60	100	150
Jungle Book Dancing Bear Wind-up, plastic, Marx	80	150	200

Miscellaneous (Continued)

	C6	C8	C10
Nautilus Submarine, (20,000 Leagues Under the Sea)	155	250	375
Oswald the Rabbit, celluloid, crib toy, c. 1927, 6-1/2" long	250	400	600
Pecos Bill Wind-up, plastic, Marx, 1950s	200	300	400
Practical Pig, tin litho wind-up, Linemar	260	390	520
Practical Pig Doll, Gund	112	180	250

Elmer Elephant, Seiberling, $375. Photo courtesy Hakes Americana & Collectibles

Pecos Bill Wind-up, Marx, 1950s, $400. Photo courtesy Don Hultzman

Disneykins, Marx, $210. Photo courtesy Don Hultzman. Photo by Ron Chojnacki

DOLLHOUSES AND MINIATURE FURNITURE

As World War II ended, consumers had a huge pent-up demand for goods, which had been scarce during the war. The peacetime economy boomed as American industry became the supplier to the rest of the war-ravaged world. Unlike the Depression years, which had immediately preceded the Second World War, employment surged, as did disposable family income. The population surged as well, creating the now well-documented Baby Boom. Newly affluent parents were able to provide their children with much more than the bare necessities. The American toy industry, with excess capacity built to serve the war effort and utilize materials developed during the war, answered the demands of the Baby Boomers and their parents by making low cost toys available through five-and-dime stores and through the catalogs of Sears and Montgomery Wards.

Dollhouses and the miniature furniture and accessories to fit them were originally made, not as toys, but to assist in the education of refined young women of the Victorian era. As "pictures of the times" they were designed to be looked at, not played with. They were often made by German toymakers, for the English market. Following the pattern established in the early part of the twentieth century by companies like Converse, Bliss and Schoenhut, postwar toy manufacturers utilized mass production techniques to produce toys with play value. Prewar houses were often made of heavy printed cardboard or of wood covered with brightly and highly detailed lithographed paper. Furniture was usually made of wood by companies like Strombecker or of cast-metal by companies like Tootsietoy.

World War II had shown the utility of plastic materials, and industries had honed their thermoplastic molding and sheet-metal stamping skills. Plastic toys could be made in high-speed processes with minimal need for hand finishing. Toys could be produced in any color of the rainbow as well as in combinations of colors. They were hygienic, and could be formed with amazing details. Dollhouse furniture and accessories could be produced to resemble their real life counterparts. Couches could be made with wood-toned bases and brightly colored upholstery. Swings could be made to hold and move little family members. Sewing machines had moving parts as did trash cans, lawn mowers and ironing boards. The toys were aimed at little homemakers eager to be just like their parents.

Companies like Renwal, Ideal and Plasco made a wide range of furniture, while manufacturers like Acme/Thomas, Irwin and Commonwealth produced numerous accessories that complemented the furniture lines. During the mid-fifties the Marx Toy Company began to dominate the market for dollhouses and furniture. Marx furniture was molded in one color and generally did not have moving parts. The furniture was packaged and sold with Marx dollhouse play sets. Later, manufacturers like Superior and Wolverine produced one-piece molded furniture usually from polyethylene, a soft flexible plastic, also for inclusion with their dollhouse play sets.

As suburbia grew, so did the types of miniature dollhouses to hold the plastic furniture and accessories. The postwar dollhouses generally were produced from two different materials—fiberboard and sheet steel. The more expensive fiberboard houses, first actually produced before the War, were most often silk screened in four colors. The number of colors and the screening method limited the interior and exterior detail. The flat sides and roofs were screwed together, forming sturdy houses capable of withstanding a lot of play. Windows frames of plastic or metal were sometimes inserted in the exterior walls. Hinged wooden doors generally opened and closed, and a few of the houses contained staircases and closets. The houses were roughly 3/4 inch to one foot in scale, making it easy for little hands to rearrange dolls and furniture inside the four-to-six-room houses. Rich Toys, Keystone and Jayline Toys are the best known of the fiberboard manufacturers. Many of these durable homes survive today.

Sheet metal provided toy manufacturers with a more flexible material with which to design houses, copying the styles of the day. The metal walls, floors and roofs, prior to being stamped from large sheets of the thin metal, were lithographed with the designs of the interiors and exteriors of the houses. As time progressed the detail became quite elaborate as the manufacturers moved beyond four-color lithography to use six, eight or more colors. Perhaps the first of the postwar steel houses, were the two houses produced by National Can Company and marketed under the Playsteel name. In 1948 T. Cohn introduced a now well-recognized house with a red tiled roof. The house had five rooms and an upstairs patio. Each of these earlier houses was 3/4 inch to one foot in scale and well matched the furniture of Renwal, Ideal and Plasco. Soon thereafter, Meritoy of Boston introduced an interesting two-story Cape.

In 1949, the market changed dramatically when Marx Toys first introduced a dollhouse packaged with its own furniture, car and play yard selling for $3.95. Although Marx produced large and well-detailed dollhouses in its 3/4-inch-scale deluxe and "Marxie Mansion" lines, the majority of its houses were 1/2 inch to one foot in scale. They ranged in style from two-story colonials with or without attached family room to L-shaped ranches and split-levels. Interior

lithography changed from time to time, reflecting "modern" decorating trends. The smaller 1/2-inch-scale caught on and dominated the market in the 1950s and sixties as companies like T. Cohn and Wolverine introduced 1/2-inch-scale houses, following the Marx example.

There are still many examples of Baby Boomer miniature furniture and houses to be found at antique shops, flea markets and through online markets. Prices have continued to rise, as toys in Good to Excellent condition become scarce. Condition and rarity continue to be the factors that determine price. A piece of unscratched, unbroken or repaired plastic toy without melt marks will command a higher price than a well played with piece. Toys with moving parts and opening drawers and cabinet doors are generally priced higher than one-piece toys. Collectors will find many paths to follow in assembling their collections. Besides the better known companies like Renwal, Ideal and Marx, manufacturers such as Kleeware of Great Britain, Reliable of Canada, Jaydon, Allied, Best and Mattel all produced miniature furniture and accessories which continue to be fun to play with fifty years later.

Contributor: Marcie Tubbs, 6405 Mitchell Hollow Rd., Charlotte, NC 28277, e-mail: CARDAD@aol.com. Tubbs began collecting an eclectic assortment of Baby Boomer dollhouses, dollhouse furniture and figures after purchasing a furnished T. Cohn dollhouse at the Brimfield, Mass. antique shows a number of years ago; she has been hooked ever since. Tubbs not only enjoys collecting, but also researching the history of the subject. She and her husband, Bob, have written several articles on dollhouses and their inhabitants. She is always interested in adding unusual examples to her ever-growing collection and enjoys hearing from others about the hobby.

Acme/Thomas Toy

Acme Plastics Manufacturing Co., originally founded in 1935, merged with and became the marketing arm of Thomas Toy Company in 1945. Acme/Thomas never attempted to produce a line of dollhouse furniture with the breadth of Renwal, Ideal Plasco or Marx, but instead focused on toys with high play value. These pieces were brightly-colored nursery and outdoor toys in 3/4-inch-scale that complemented the toys of the other manufacturers. Acme/Thomas also produced a number of dollhouse dolls from the rubber-like Vinylite, which are often found with Baby Boomer plastics. Unfortunately, the chemicals from the Vinylite causes melt marks when the dolls come in contact with hard polystyrene toys. The hard plastic pieces are generally marked either Acme or Thomas along with one or more mold numbers.

Various Acme/Thomas Toy playground and nursery pieces, clockwise left to right: Baby Carriage ($7); Hammock ($20); Horsehead Stroller ($10); Slide ($15); Single Swing ($15); Dogsled with harness and dog ($40); Express wagon ($12); Horsehead Seesaw ($10); Tommy Horse ($15). Photo Courtesy Marcie Tubbs

	C10
Baby Carriage, No. I-139	7
Dogsled with Harness and Dog, No. I-184	40

Acme/Thomas Toy (Continued)

	C10
Double Swing, No. I-154	30
Express Wagon, No. I-144	12
Ferris Wheel, No. I-163	40

Birdcage, Commonwealth, $30. Photo Courtesy Marcie Tubbs

Acme/Thomas Toy (Continued)

	C10
Hammock, No. I-166	20
Horsehead Seesaw, No. I-159	10
Horsehead Stroller, No. I-156	10
Horsehead Swing, No. I-154	70
Single Swing, No. I-154	15
Slide, No. I-171	15
Tommy Horse, No. I-179	15
Triple Swing, No. I-154	50

Commonwealth

Commonwealth Plastics Corporation of Leominster, Mass. started as a manufacturer of buttons and costume jewelry. It branched into the production of a small line of party favors and dollhouse accessories that are quite collectible today. The reel-type electric motor makes a "motor" sound as it is rolled along, and the lovebird cage on a stand complements the furniture of the larger toy manufacturers.

	C10
Birdcage	30
Lamppost with Mailbox	18

Commonwealth (Continued)

	C10
Lawn Mower	15
Watering Can and Garden tools	15
Wheelbarrow	10

Ideal

Established in 1903 the Ideal Toy and Novelty Company—the originator of the "Teddy Bear"—was the largest of the postwar American toy and doll manufacturers. They introduced four different lines of dollhouse furniture for Baby Boomers. In 1947 they introduced a line of beautifully detailed 3/4-inch-scale furniture from brightly-colored hard plastic. The toys generally are marked with the Ideal trademark and one or more mold numbers. Early boxed sets included room box walls or an outdoor setting. In later boxed sets, the furniture could be seen through cellophane panels. The nursery and outdoor pieces tend to bring higher prices today than the more common living, dining and bedroom pieces. Two different kitchen lines were sold during this period, a standard and the more desirable deluxe version. The slightly

This plastic Garden Furniture from Ideal, valued at $700-750, is the most highly sought-after Ideal boxed set. The set includes: Patio Umbrella, Plastic Pole, Lawn Bench, Doghouse, Black Scottie Dog, Pool, Birdbath, Circular Lawn Table, Lawn Chair, Picnic Table, Trellis and Lawn Chair. Photo Courtesy Marcie Tubbs

larger and more detailed deluxe line also included a dishwasher, a front opening washing machine and a mangle with a rotating drum. The 3/4-inch-scale furniture was produced until 1952.

In 1950 and 1951, Ideal produced a set of furniture known as Young Decorator. The Young Decorator furniture was almost 1-1/2-inch to one foot in scale making it easy to rearrange and play with on a blueprint-styled playmat included in each box.

In 1964 the Ideal Toy Corporation (the name having been changed in 1951) introduced another line of dollhouse furniture in 3/4-inch to one-foot scale. The Petite Princess Fantasy Furniture with real cloth upholstery had glass and metal details and accessories to highlight the plastic furniture. The furniture was too expensive to appeal to the mass toy market, and in 1965 the line was reintroduced as Princess Patti furniture. The materials used to decorate the Princess Patti furniture were not as expensive as the Petite Princess line. With some nod to reality, the Princess Patti line included the now rare kitchen, bathroom and TV set. Much of this Fantasy furniture is found individually packaged in boxes today.

Ideal

	C10
Bed, No. I-0959	20
Birdbath	20
Black Scottie Dog	90
Carpet Sweeper, No. I-1563	20
Chinese Modern Red Dining Table, No. I-0980	25
Circular Lawn Table, No. I-1003	20
Coffee Table	8
Doghouse, No. I-1016	40
Lawn Bench, No. I-1008	20
Lawn Chair, No. I-1018	15
Lawn Lounge Chair, No. I-1115	20
Lawn Mower, No. I-1315	35

Ideal (Continued)

	C10
Octagonal Sanbox with Pole and Umbrella, No. I-1312	100
Patio Umbrella, No. I-1004	20
Petite Princess, Boudoir Chaise Lounge, No. 44081	15
Petite Princess, Little Princess Royal, Bed, No. 4416-4	30
Petite Princess, Lyre Table with Lamp and Painting, No. 4426-3	20
Petite Princess, Palace Chest with Picture, No. 4420-6	15
Petite Princess, Royal Dressing Table and Stool, No. 4417-2	30
Picnic Table, No. I-1000	35
Plastic Pole	5
Pool, No. I-1060	100
Red Breakfront, No. I-0979	20
Red Buffet, No. I-0983	15
Red Dining Chair with Arms, No. I-0948	12
Red Dining Chair without Arms, No. I-0948	10
Seesaw, No. I-1329	60
Sofa, No. I-0942	15
Trellis, No. I-1012	100
Vaccuum Cleaner, No. I-1559	25
Well Pump, No. I-1084	40

Left to Right: Sofa, Ideal, $15; Coffee Table, Ideal, $8; Sofa, Renwal, $23; Pedestal End Table, Renwal, $8. Photo courtesy Marcie Tubbs

Young Decorator furniture from Ideal. Left to Right: Television, $40; Coffee Table, $10; Torchiere Lamp, $30; Sectional Sofa, individual pieces, $15. Photo courtesy Marcie Tubbs

Ideal (Continued)

	C10
Young Decorator Bathinette, No. I-2082	40
Young Decorator Bathtub, No. I-2172	20
Young Decorator Bed, No. I-2057	15
Young Decorator Blue Bathroom Chair, No. I-2098	15
Young Decorator Buffet, No. I-2034	15
Young Decorator China Cabinet, No. I-2036	20
Young Decorator Coffee Table, No. I-2089	10
Young Decorator Crib, No. I-2109	25
Young Decorator Diaper Pail/Waste Can, No. I-2170	20
Young Decorator Dining Chair, No. I-2045	8
Young Decorator Dining Table, No. I-2040	15
Young Decorator High Chair, No. I-2179	25
Young Decorator Kitchen Chair, No. I-2098	12
Young Decorator Kitchen Table, No. I-2100	20
Young Decorator Living Room Sofa Center Curved Section, No. I-2079	15
Young Decorator Living Room Sofa Center Square Section, No. I-2078	15
Young Decorator Living Room Sofa End Section, No. I-2077	15
Young Decorator Nightstand, No. I-2076	10
Young Decorator Playpen, No. I-2108	25
Young Decorator Range, No. I-2052	30
Young Decorator Refrigerator, No. I-2048	25
Young Decorator Sink, No. I-2062	60
Young Decorator Sink, No. I-2164	20
Young Decorator Television Set, No. I-2090	40
Young Decorator Toilet, No. I-2168	40
Young Decorator Torchiere Lamp, No. I-2081	30
Young Decorator Tricycle with Bell	30
Young Decorator Vanity, No. I-2086	15
Young Decorator Vanity Stool, No. I-2060	8
Young Decorator Wardrobe, No. I-2084	15

Keystone

Among the nicest of the postwar fiberboard homes, were those made by Keystone Manufacturing Company of Boston, Mass. between 1940 and the early 1950s. In the forties, Keystone shipped their dollhouses already assembled, a big plus for harried parents on Christmas Eve. The Keystone fiberboards

Two-story lithographed masonite house with six rooms, fireplace, stairs and closet, 3/4-inch-scale, Keystone, $175. Photo Courtesy Marcie Tubbs

generally have three distinct features—a curving staircase, a fireplace and an upstairs closet. The interior walls often have silk-screened wallpaper and floor designs. The windows are either metal or plastic framed, depending on the age of the house. Unique to Keystone were three "Put-A-Way" houses with one or two extensions that folded back into the house when play was finished. The dollhouses were often marketed with 3/4-inch-scale plastic furniture. Many of the Keystone houses are marked with the company name, and some have a turntable attached to the bottom. The fiberboard houses often cost two to three times the price of a tin counterpart and manufacturing of these well-constructed toys ceased before the end of the Baby Boomer era.

Keystone, 3/4"-scale

	C10
Two-story Lithographed Masonite with Eight Rooms, Double Wing "Put-A-Way"	250
Two-story Lithographed Masonite with Six Room, Single Wing "Put-A-Way"	200
Two-story Lithographed Masonite with Six Rooms, Fireplace, Stairs and Closet	175

Marx Toys

The Louis P. Marx Company became a dominant manufacturer of toys during the postwar era. Originally formed in 1917, Louis Marx applied modern mass production methods to the making of toys. The efficiencies he achieved both in manufacturing and marketing made affordable toys with great play value available to all. In 1949 Marx, attempting to fill up his manufacturing facilities, introduced a two-story brightly lithographed tin dollhouse filled with six rooms of hard plastic dollhouse furniture. The house and furniture were produced in 1/2-inch-scale. While the detail of the lithography was enhanced by the use of ten-color lithography, the furniture was of a single color, one-piece construction with no moving parts. During the twenty-five years that the Marx Company marketed dollhouses, approximately fifteen different styles were produced, although there are many decorating and packaging variations of each style as Marx constantly sought appropriate price points for each distribution channel. While the majority of the houses were 1/2-inch-scale, the houses in the 3/4-inch-scale deluxe and Marxie Mansion lines have some of the best of the Baby Boomer-era dollhouses. The large-scale mansions came in six and seven room versions, electrified and non-electrified, with and without cloth curtains, cornices, awnings, shutters and doorbells.

As the Marx dollhouses changed over time, so did the furniture packaged with them. The early hard polystyrene pieces were replaced with softer, less breakable polyethylene. Styles for the 1/2-inch-scale furniture included "overstuffed" traditional, French Provincial and contemporary. Furniture was made for the primary living areas of the houses as well as for laundry rooms, family rooms, patios, gardens and swimming pools. The hard plastic pieces are often marked with the Marx logo, but the matching soft plastic pieces sometimes are not. In 1964 Marx introduced a beautiful line of all plastic furniture known in the United States as Marx Little Hostess and in Canada as Little Miss Deb. The furniture was often multi-

Kitchen appliances by Marx, $3-5, each. Photo Courtesy Marcie Tubbs

colored or had gilt detailing and was accompanied by plastic or metal accessories. In 1976, after the sale of Marx, the line was reintroduced in England as Amanda Ann.

Marx Toys, 1/2"-scale

	C10
Captain's Chair	5
Circular Couch	10
Coffee Table, hard plastic	5
Common Hard Plastic Furniture, price for each	4
Common Soft Plastic Items, price for each	4
Juke Box	20
Kitchen	8
Kitchen Appliances, Pots and Pans, price for each	4
Kitchen Chair	5
Milk Bar	20
Piano	10
Piano Bench	5
Ping-Pong Table	25
Refrigerator	5
Round Table	5
Sink	5

Marx 1/2-inch-scale furniture. Left to Right: Milk Bar, $20; Stools, $20 each; Round Table, $5; Kitchen Charis, $5 each; Ping-Pong Table, $25; Circular Couch, $10; Coffee Table, $5; Piano, $10; Piano Bench, $5; Juke Box, $20. Photo courtesy Marcie

Two-story house with attached breezeway and rumpus room, 1/2-inch-scale, Marx, $140. Photo Courtesy

Colonial Mansion with Florida room, 3/4-inch-scale, Marx, $175. Photo Courtesy Marcie Tubbs

Marx Toys, 1/2"-scale (Continued)   **C10**

Soft Plastic Furniture 1

Stool 20

Stove.. 5

Marx Houses   **C10**

L-shaped Ranch with TV Antennae, Cupola,
    Chimney and Room Divider 125

Split Level with Front and Back Steps, Railings,
    Fireplace and Chimney.. 125

Marx Houses, 1/2"-scale   **C10**

Two-story with Attached Breezeway and Rumpus
    Room 140

Two-story with Disney Nursery and Garage 125

Two-story with Tin Soldier Nursery......................... 50

Marx Houses, 3/4"-scale   **C10**

Colonial Mansion with Florida room....................... 175

Marx Little Hostess   **C10**

Bench 15

Folding Screen 20

Hamper and Mirror 20

Medicine Cabinet 25

Sink/Vanity Combination 30

Toilet 15

Tub/Shower.. 30

Meritoy

Among the first of the postwar tin dollhouses is an easily recognized Cape Cod with three dormers produced by Meritoy Corporation of Boston. The six-room house was close to 1/2-inch to one foot in scale, and the furnished versions were sold with either Allied or Kleeware half-scale, hard plastic furniture.

Two-story Cape Cod, 1/2-inch-scale, Meritoy, $150. Photo Courtesy Marcie Tubbs

The windows were made of a silk-screened sheet of plastic and are difficult to find intact today.

Plastic Art Toy Corporation of America (Plasco)

The Plastic Art Toy Corporation of America produced the Little Homemaker line of dollhouse furniture from 1947 until nearly the end of the Baby Boomer era. The 3/4-inch-scale furniture owed much of its popularity to its affordable price and broad product line. The inside covers of early boxed sets included room-like settings. As time progressed, Plasco was sold in cellophane window boxes and on blister packs. Later versions of the furniture were cheaply produced and marketed without bases, legs or headboards. This later furniture is not as highly valued as the older, more detailed pieces. As with many

Left to Right: Television Set, Plasco, $30; Grandfather Clock, Plasco, $15. Photo Courtesy Marcie Tubbs

lines of dollhouse furniture, the nursery pieces are among the most prized. Plasco made three dollhouses, all of which are hard to find today. The two ranch houses were made primarily of plastic and the round, futuristic "Open House" was made of fiberboard.

Meritoy, 1/2"-scale

	C10
Two-story Cape Cod	150

Plastic Art Toy Corporation of America (Plasco)

The Plastic Art Toy Corporation of America produced the Little Homemaker line of dollhouse furniture from 1947 until nearly the end of the Baby Boomer era. The 3/4-inch-scale furniture owed much of its popularity to its affordable price and broad product line. The inside covers of early boxed sets included room-like settings. As time progressed, Plasco was sold in cellophane window boxes and on blister packs. Later versions of the furniture were cheaply produced and marketed without bases, legs or headboards. This later furniture is not as highly valued as the older, more detailed pieces. As with many lines of dollhouse furniture, the nursery pieces are among the most prized. Plasco made three dollhouses, all of which are hard to find today. The two ranch houses were made primarily of plastic and the round, futuristic "Open House" was made of fiberboard.

Plastic Art Toy Corporation of America (Plasco)

	C10
Bathinette	30
Club Chair	7
Coffee Table	5
Crib	25
Fireplace	15
Grandfather Clock	15
Highboy	10
Nightstand	5
Sofa	10
Television Set	30
Vanity Chair	3
Wing Chair	7

Playsteel

Playsteel was the toy division of National Can Company. Immediately after World War II they introduced two five-room tin dollhouses, a two-story red roofed, brick and clapboard Colonial, and a two-story

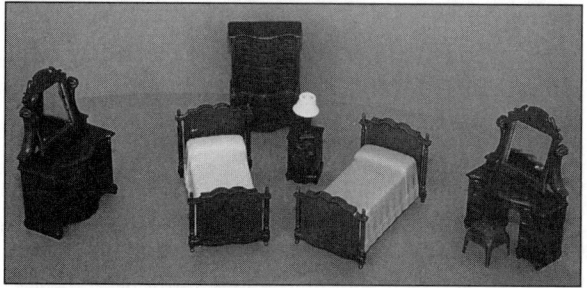

Left to Right: Reliable Bedroom set—Dresser with mirror ($17); Highboy ($15); Twin Bed ($18, each); Nightstand ($10); Table Lamp ($20); Vanity Dresser with Mirror ($17); Vanity Stool ($8). Photo Courtesy Marcie Tubbs

"Buck's County Farmhouse" with a fieldstone exterior and blue slate roof. The houses were originally packed in boxes that were meant to unfold to serve as landscaped yards. The interiors of the two homes were identical. The panes of the windows were cut from the steel and the front door of the Buck's County house opened. The farmhouse was also packaged with two window boxes that attached to the second-story windows. The 3/4-inch-scale was perfect for the furniture of Renwal, Ideal and Plasco, and mail-order catalogues and dimestores often featured the homes packaged with Renwal.Playsteel

Playsteel, 3/4"-scale

	C10
Two-story "Bucks County" with Blue Roof	150
Two-story Colonial with Red Roof	150

Reliable

The needs of Canadian Baby Boomers were met nicely by the Reliable Plastics Company, Limited of Toronto. Reliable produced a wide range of hard plastic dollhouse toys. Many of the well-detailed pieces appear to be made from Ideal molds or molds made from Ideal toys, but many of the toys are quite individual in their styling. Most of the toys are hallmarked and fit the then-common 3/4-inch scale.

Reliable

	C10
Dresser with Mirror	17
Highboy	15
Nightstand	10
Table Lamp	20
Twin Bed	18
Vanity Dresser with Mirror	17
Vanity Stool	8

Renwal

Founded in 1939, Renwal is one of the best recognized of the postwar manufacturers. Besides cars, trucks and other "boys toys," Renwal produced a wide selection of dollhouse furniture, accessories and dolls. The toys, made from the hard plastic polystyrene, were approximately 3/4-inch to one foot in scale. Almost all the pieces were hallmarked with the Renwal name and bear an item number. Introduced in 1945, early Renwal boxed sets contained a cardboard box room for displaying the furniture. Later versions of the furniture had opening drawers and doors. These, together with the later stenciled versions of the toys, bring higher prices today. Renwal stopped producing the furniture in 1956, and eventually the molds were sold. The more common pieces of furniture reappeared in the 1980s marked as made in Hong Kong.

Renwal accessories without original cards. Left to Right: Vacuum ($22), Mop ($50), Trash Can with Flip-top Lid ($12), Dustpan ($15), Carpet Sweeper with Rollers ($95) and Broom ($125). Photo Courtesy Marcie Tubbs

Left to Right: Dresser without opening drawers, Renwal; Twin Bed, Renwal No. B23, $10; Dresser with opening drawers, Renwal No. B23, $9. Photo Courtesy Marcie Tubbs

Renwal accessories. Left to Right: Stool ($11); Trash can with Flip-top Lid ($12); Dustpan ($15); Scale ($12); Vacuum Cleaner ($22); Broom ($125); Mop ($50); and the Carpet Sweeper with Rollers ($95). Photo Courtesy Marcie Tubbs

Left to Right: Father, Mother and Brother, Renwal, $25 each. Photo Courtesy Marcie Tubbs

Left to Right: Sewing Machine, Renwal, $25; Sewing Machine, Ideal, $25. Photo Courtesy Marcie Tubbs. Photo Courtesy Marcie Tubbs

Left to Right: Kiddie Car, Renwal, $35; Tricycle, Renwal, $7

Renwal

	C10
Bathtub, No. T95	10
Broom, No. 121	125
Carpet Sweeper with Rollers, No. 116	95
Dresser with Opening Drawer, No. B23	12
Dresser without Opening Drawer, No. B23	9
Dustpan	15
Family Members, price for each, No. 041-44	25
Hamper, No. T98	5
Highboy, No. B85	8
Mop, No. 117	50
Night Stand, No. B84	5
Pedestal End Table, No. L73	8
Scale, No. 010	12
Sewing Machine, No. 089	25
Sink, No. T96	5
Sofa, No. L78	12
Stool, No. 012	11
Toilet, No. T97	10
Trash Can with Flip-Top Lid, No. 064	12
Tricycle, No. 007	17
Twin Bed, No. B81	10

Two-story Lithographed Fiberboard with Four Rooms, Front Stoop with Benches, 3/4-inch-scale, Rich, $100. Photo courtesy Marcie Tubbs

Renwal (Continued)

	C10
Vaccuum Cleaner, No. 037	22
Vanity Bench, No. L75	3
Vanity with Elaborate Filigree, No. B82	16
Vanity without Elaborate Filigree, No. B82	10

Rich

Rich Toy Manufacturing Co. enjoyed a prominent position among toy manufacturers for a period between 1935 to the early 1960's. Originally designed to match the 1-inch-scale wooden furniture of companies like Strombecker, these fiberboard homes, when made in 3/4-inch-scale, worked perfectly with the plastic furniture introduced in 1946. Rich houses can be found in many different styles ranging from two-room cottages to a curved Art-Deco style. Exteriors were generally applied with four-color silk screens. Early models had metal window frames that were replaced by plastic in later models. Interiors were sparsely decorated. Larger houses occasionally had staircases and the most elaborate had rudimentary lighting and doorbells. Rich rarely marked its houses, although they can often be identified by the pine tree design found on the window shutters.

Rich, 1"-scale

	C10
Two-story Lithographed Fiberboard with Six Rooms, Arts and Crafts-style Bungalow	250
Two-story Lithographed Fiberboard with Six Rooms, Interior Staircase	175

Rich, 3/4"-scale

	C10
Two-story Lithographed Fiberboard with Four Rooms, Front Stoop with Benches	100

T. Cohn/Superior

The single patio Spanish-styled dollhouse with red tiled roof is among the most recognizable of the Baby Boomer dollhouses. Produced by T. Cohn of Brooklyn, NY, it was introduced in time for the 1948 Christmas season. The house was sold both furnished with furniture made by Plasco or Renwal and in an unfurnished version. The scale matched nicely with the furniture of Renwal and Ideal and the dollhouse is often found with an eclectic mix of the postwar furniture. The windows were made of metal and opened, casement style. T. Cohn continued to market a slightly smaller scaled Superior line through the 1960s, introducing several additional house styles. Houses produced before about 1957 were packaged with hard-plastic, one-color furniture marked Superior. After that time, the houses were sold with inferior 1/2-inch-scale soft plastic furniture, reportedly made for Superior by Marx.

T. Cohn/Superior   __C10__

Common Hard Plastic Furniture 5

Common Soft Plastic Furniture.................................. 1

T. Cohn/Superior (Continued)   __C10__

Patio Bench 50

Tin Swimming Pool 50

T. Cohn Houses   __C10__

Common Hard Plastic Furniture 5

Common Soft Plastic Furniture.................................. 1

Modern-style Pastel with Single Patio 60

Patio Bench 50

Spanish-style with Double Patio 125

Three-room Ranch.. 45

Tin Swimming Pool 50

T. Cohn Houses, 3/4"-scale   __C10__

Common Hard Plastic Furniture 5

Common Soft Plastic Furniture.................................. 1

Patio Bench 50

Spanish-style with Single Patio.............................. 150

Tin Swimming Pool 50

Spanish-style house with Single Patio, 1/2-inch-scale, T. Cohn/Superior, $45. Photo Courtesy Marcie Tubbs

ERECTOR SETS

Erector Set collecting has recently come to the forefront as people tire of modern toys. Very few modern toys stimulate the imagination as the toys of old. Imagine the questions posed by a chemistry set, an Erector set or a microscope set. If you think Nintendo can supply the mental stimulation that these toys of yesteryear could, well . . . you're just not in the right gear!

A.C. Gilbert, the inventor of Erector sets, was a medical doctor (1908 graduate of Yale University) as well as the winner of the gold medal for the pole vault at the 1908 World Olympics in London. In addition to his many other skills, A.C. Gilbert was an accomplished professional magician and an outgoing, gregarious individual.

Erector went through three development stages. From 1913 to 1923 (StageI) the sets featured plenty of large, strong girders. Ads showed boys sitting on the bridges built with Erector sets-and it was no exaggeration. After the trauma of World War I and the consequent inflation in the United States (and worse in Europe), Erector was redesigned and slimmed down. Girders were smaller, narrower and lighter, but Gilbert also introduced countless other shapes to make the Erector system more versatile and more capable of building unique and beautiful models. Thus in 1924 Stage II was born, and continued on until the advent of Stage III in 1963, which really signaled the end of the Gilbert company. Although true collectors are interested in the total history of the once great company, most are more familiar with, and desire, the products of Stage II (1924 to 1962). One may call this the shining hour of the most successful scientific toy company in the United States.

A.C. Gilbert ceased to be a major toy producer after 1962. The decline was somewhat agonizing, ending with the purchase of the rights to the famous name "Erector" by Meccano, SA of France, which also acquired Gilbert's old competitor in England.

Before launching into a discussion on value, consider some common sense rules. Of about 45 million Erector sets produced, ninety percent probably went to people who didn't take very good care of them.

That leaves about 4.5 million fairly nice sets in a good state of preservation, but you should figure that about half of these were thrown out or otherwise disposed of. Now we have about 2.25 million pretty nice Erector sets left.

Where are they? Most of us are inclined toward flea markets and garage sales, but this is probably not your best source. You may get lucky, but in most cases this represents the low end of the market. Many sets from these sources are what we in the business call "mixed trash." Whether intentional or not, a set may be only fractionally complete and usually will contain a variety of parts from different years mixed together. If you are looking for fine quality sets in the C10 category, carefully watch for estate auctions, look for high-quality dealers, or buy from established collectors who are continually refining their collections.

Estate auctions are listed in your local newspaper. Many avid collectors are members of the A.C. Gilbert Heritage Society (1440 Whalley, Suite 252, New Haven, CT 06515) or the Southern California Meccano and Erector Club (Box 7653, Porter Ranch Sta., Northridge, CA 91327), or both. The former is the larger of the two; together they represent 500 of the largest collections in the world. Some members have over 1,000 Erector sets, and many have several hundred.

Keep in mind that unless a set was carefully preserved in a dry climate, there is little chance of acquiring a set that is in truly C10 condition (meaning in the same condition as it left the factory). Standard grading categories are listed below.

C10: 100 percent complete. All parts pinned with the original T clips; all cardboards present; no rust or white rust; manual present, near perfect, labels near perfect; only the lightest of scratches, parts may show very light cloudy oxidation (dingy).

C8: 98 to 100 percent complete. Some or all cardboards present but may not be all correctly pinned; manual present (may have folded corners); motor must be present and working; less than five percent of the parts may show the very slightest real rust (like in corners, the type that auto chrome polish can easily remove).

C6: 90 to 95 percent complete. Probably no cardboard; motor there and working; acceptable manual, labels may show serious wear; considerable scratching on bottom, some on top; minor dents in metal box, some signs of rust on five to ten percent of parts.

Since most of what you will come across in flea markets is well below C6 condition, a new category has been introduced-C4. You will need a great deal of help, skill and new parts to restore these sets.

C4: 50 to 75 percent complete. Considerable rust; parts from other sets or brands; possibly a working motor or tattered manual; dents, scratches and torn labels needing total restoration.

Contributors: W.S. (Bill) Harrison III, 223 Boa Vista Street, Punta Gorda, FL 33983-5644; Paul Piontkowski, Pandy's Collectibles (successor to Marion's Designs), 16 Palmer Street, Medford, MA 02155; Francis Usinski, 11612 Ketchum Road, Lawtons, NY 14091. Harrison boasts of an engineering background that spans more than forty years. He has engineered and designed machinery and special equipment in aerospace, executed project management assignments with Monsanto and was chief engineer in metal forging and rubber molding companies. Harrison also has a love of Erector sets. In the past he restored and sold over 1,000 Erector sets before selling his company, Marion Designs, to Pandy's Collectibles in 1996. He has now permanently retired to Florida.

n/a: prices not applicable

WB: wood box

Type I: 1913 to 1923
(the era of girders 1-1/8" wide)

Most of the more valuable sets came in oak boxes with jointed corners. Smaller sets in cardboard boxes are not often seen, but can be quite valuable if discovered. Sets from 1913, the first year, have a unique motor and girder and are the most valuable.

1913

	C4	C6	C8	C10
Mysto #04, w/motor, wood box	125	225	350	500
Mysto #08, largest, three layer, wood box	650	1000	2200	5000
Mysto Erector #01, cardboard	150	300	500	700

1914-16

	C4	C6	C8	C10
Mysto #04, w/motor, wood box	65	90	125	180
Mysto #08, largest, three layer, wood box	800	1000	1800	4000
Mysto Erector #01, cardboard	75	125	200	325

1917-23

	C4	C6	C8	C10
Erector #01, Now called Gilbert Erector	60	100	150	275
Erector #04, w/motor, wood box, metal cover	80	175	300	525
Erector #04, w/motor, wood box	80	150	250	400
Erector #07, '23 wood box, metal cover	175	275	400	700
Erector #08, two layer, wood box	150	225	500	1000

1917-23 (Continued)

	C4	C6	C8	C10
Erector #08, three layer, wood box	500	750	900	2500
Erector #10, three layer, wood box	900	1500	2300	5000

Type II: 1924 to 1962 (the era of girders 5/8" wide)

These sets have a greater variety of parts and are capable of building more complex models. Sets from No. 4 up continued in wooden boxes (four with cardboard cover) until 1933, when metal boxes were introduced to the larger sets (except the Hudson, which went metal in 1934). Half numbers were introduced, confusing some collectors.

1924-26

	C4	C6	C8	C10
Erector #0, (50 cent original)	n/a	60	95	170
Erector #00, (25 cent original)	n/a	50	75	125
Erector #01	n/a	40	60	100
Erector #04, w/motor, wood box	75	120	160	300
Erector #07, '26 steam shovel, brown box	125	200	350	500
Erector #07-1/2, '26 white trk., brown box	150	300	500	750
Erector #08	300	500	1100	2500
Erector #10, multi-drawer	n/a	1200	2500	5000

1927-28

	C4	C6	C8	C10
Erector "B," giant red ferris wheel	300	500	750	1000
Erector #07, steam shovel, red wood box	70	130	180	320

1927-28 (Continued)

	C4	C6	C8	C10
Erector #07-1/2, white trk., red wood box	125	200	300	550
Erector #10, multi-drawer, wood box	1500	2700	4000	6500

1929-30

	C4	C6	C8	C10
2nd Zepplin Set	600	1200	2500	2600

1931-32

	C4	C6	C8	C10
Erector #09 Zeppelin Set	600	1200	1800	2600
Erector #10 "Climax," largest set ever made, 150 lbs	n/a	5000	10,000	20,000
Erector Hudson #08 engine only, w/seven pts.	700	1250	1800	2300
Erector Hudson #08-1/2 engine and Tend+WT	800	1200	2500	4000
Erector Hudson Loco. "A" engine, only	600	1100	1600	2000
Erector White Trk., rec. lid w/picture	175	300	400	650

1933

	C4	C6	C8	C10
Erector Hudson #08-1/2, wood box	1000	1500	2600	6000
Erector Sensa 7, automotive parts	125	250	400	600
Erector Super 6, w/P56G, 110V motor	90	175	275	500

1934

	C4	C6	C8	C10
Erector #07-1/2 Automotive Set	125	250	450	650
Erector #08 Hudson and Tend., blue met	1000	1200	2500	4000
Erector Sensa 7, no automotive parts, red box	100	200	350	550
Erector Super 6, w/P56G, 110V motor, green box	90	175	275	500

1935

	C4	C6	C8	C10

Sets this year only featured architectural panels. If present, sets are more valuable. Many new parts were introduced.

	C4	C6	C8	C10
Erector 07-1/2, Classic Ferris Wheel	125	275	400	600
Erector 08-1/2, Automotive Set	150	300	475	700
Erector 09-1/2, Hudson Set	1000	1900	3600	6500
Erector Super 06-1/2, P51 motor, boiler	n/a	225	300	550

1936

	C4	C6	C8	C10
Erector 05-1/2, w/A52 110V motor	100	200	275	425
Erector 08-1/2, Classic Ferris Wheel	80	83	220	400
Erector 09-1/2, Automotive Set	175	335	500	675
Erector 10-1/2, Hudson Set	1000	1500	2900	5800

1938

	C4	C6	C8	C10
Erector 10-1/2 became Electric Train Set with American Flyer engine and track, plus NN, NM, NP	750	1000	1500	3300

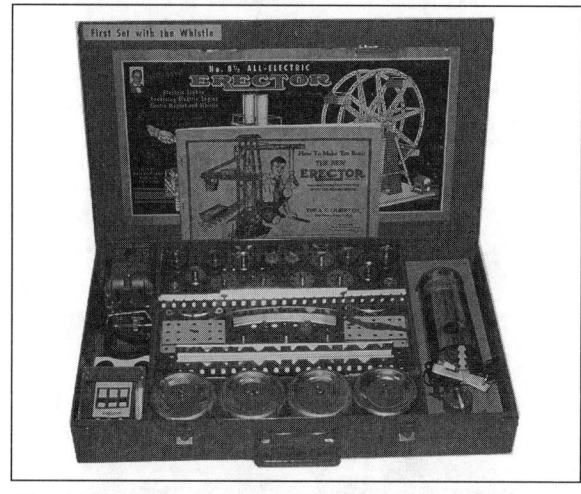

The 1939 #8-1/2 , Classic Ferris Wheel Set. This was the first set with a whistle; it was dropped after 1941. Valued at $400 in C10 condition. Restoration by William S. Harrison III.

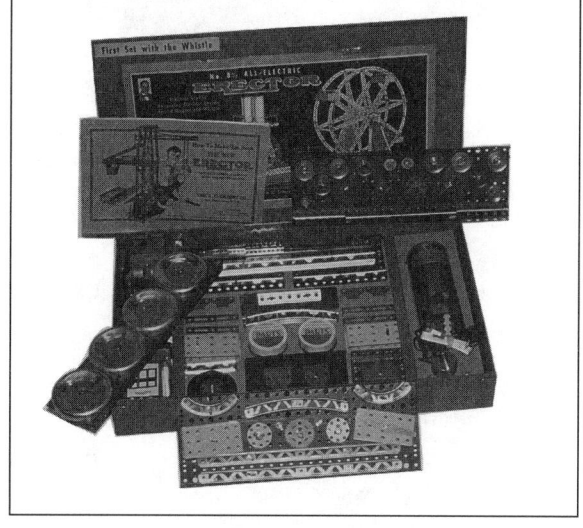

The contents of the 1939 #8-1/2. It should have a large nickel-plated magnet.

The 1937 #8-1/2, Classic Ferris Wheel Set. Introduced in 1936, the 1937 is valued at $400 in C10 condition. Restored by William S. Harrison III.

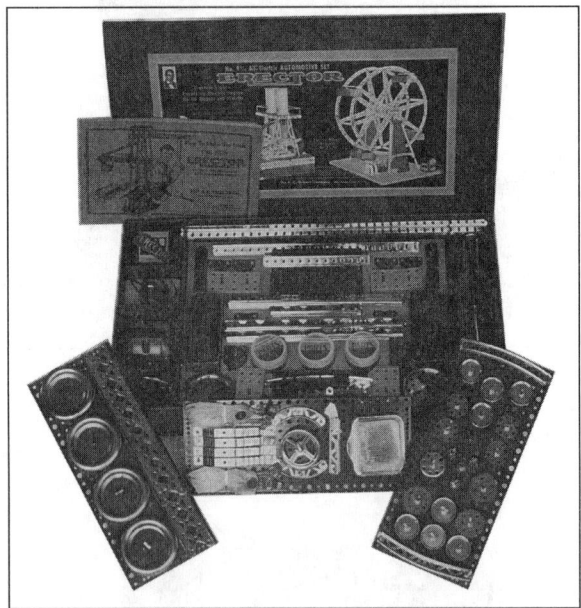

The 1948 #9-1/2 Automotive Set makes the manual contol P-jump but not the Merry-Go-Round. In C10 condition the 9-1/2 is valued at $675. Restored by William S. Harrison.

1948

	C4	C6	C8	C10
Erector 10-1/2 becomes the 12-1/2, remote control/robot set w/P55 motor, full tray, A-48 and A-49 350	500	900	1500

1949

	C4	C6	C8	C10
10-1/2 intro in 09-1/2 box with Merry-Go-Round, capability and continuos parachute jump 150	300	500	800

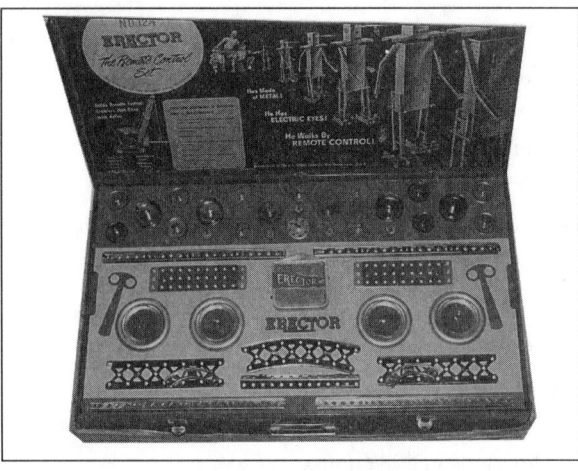

The late 1948 #12-1/2 does not make the Merry-Go-Round or the continuous running parachute jump. In C10 condition the #12-1/2 is valued at $1,500. Restored by William S. Harrison III.

1957

Two momentous changes occurred in 1957—metal boxes up through 8-1/2 had lithographed covers with pictures of the featured model, and the set numbers became a five-digit computer code. Unfortunately, the gauge of metal in the boxes was thinned out and these do not survive as well. The small plastic DC-3 motor of inadequate power was also a 1957 creation.

	C4	C6	C8	C10
10041 Erector 05-1/2 "Motorized" (DC-3) 20	40	75	125
10051 Erector 06-1/2 "Electric Engine" 25	55	85	130
10061 Erector 07-1/2 "Engineer's" 35	70	110	190

Erector's #8-1/2 (left) and #7-1/2 (right) from 1950 show the heavy cardboard boxes an aluminum baseplates used during the Korean War era. In C10 condition the 8-1/2 is valued at $800 and the 7-1/2 and $600. Restored by William S. Harrison III.

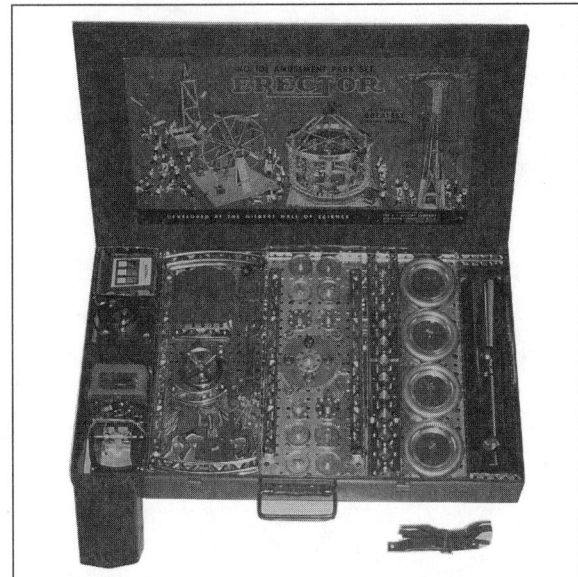

The 1950-51 #10-1/2 Amusement Park set. The Aluminum baseplates and A-47 motor are, once again, due to the Korean War. The #10-1/2 is valued at $800 in C10 condition. Restored by William S. Harrison.

1957 (Continued)

	C4	C6	C8	C10
10071 Erector 08-1/2 "All Electric," Ferris Wheel	60	150	225	350
10080 Erector 10-1/2 "Amusement Park"	100	200	350	600
10091 12-1/2 "Master Builder"	250	475	900	1350

1958

	C4	C6	C8	C10
10041 "Power Model," same as 5-1/2	20	40	75	125
10052 "Rocket Launcher," same as 6-1/2	25	55	85	135
10062 "Steam Engine"	35	70	110	190
10072 "Musical Ferris Wheel," w/music	n/a	150	225	400
10082 "Amusement Park," w/music	n/a	250	475	750
10092 "Master Builder," w/music	n/a	650	900	1500

1959

	C4	C6	C8	C10
10042 "Automatic Radar Scope," same as 10041	20	40	75	125
10053 "Rocket Launcher," same as 10051 $30 premium if gold label intact	25	55	85	135

1959 (Continued)

	C4	C6	C8	C10
10063 "Automatic Conveyo," same as 10062, premium $20 if one belt present	35	70	110	190
10073 "Musical Ferris Wheel," same as 10072, w/music, $20 premium if one belt present	n/a	150	225	400
10083 "Amusement Park," same as 10082, w/music, $20 premium if one belt present	n/a	250	475	750
10093 "Master Builder," same as 10092 w/music, $20 premium if one belt present	n/a	650	900	1500

1960

	C4	C6	C8	C10

Musical parts were dropped and Styrofoam packing introduced this year. Amusement Park and Master Builder used metal boxes made by joining two smaller boxes. Sets retained earlier prices due to scarcity. Production and sales fell sharply in 1960.

	C4	C6	C8	C10
10042 "Automatic Radar Scope"	20	40	75	125
10053 "Rocket Launcher"	25	55	85	135
10063 "Automatic Conveyor"	35	70	110	190
10074 "Ferris Wheel"	80	150	250	350
10084 "Amusement Park," same as 10083, double box	n/a	250	475	750
10094 "Master Builder," same as 10093, double box	n/a	650	900	1500

1962

	C4	C6	C8	C10

This year saw the demise of the "classic" Erector set with trussed girders.

	C4	C6	C8	C10
10094 "Master Builder," double box	n/a	650	900	1500
10181 "Action Helicopter," same as 10042	20	40	75	125
10201 "Rocket Launcher," same as 10053	25	55	85	135
10211 "Cape Canaveral," same as 10063	35	70	110	190
10221 "Lunar Drilling Rig," same as 10074	80	150	250	350
10231 "Astronaut," same as 10084, double box	n/a	250	475	750

Type III: 1963

In 1962 the Gilbert Company was in receivership and production and sales continued to drop. Tooling was worn out, with little money to replace it. The system was redesigned, eliminating the truss configuration. This easily cut the cost of new tooling in half, as any tool engineer can tell you. Thus was born Type III Erector, a bit flimsier and not as realistic but still challenging to the young mind. At present, sets from this era are not much in demand compared to the classic sets of Type I and II. This could change as more collectors dry up the supply. Most of the smaller sets were presented in containers not given to survival such as corrugated boxes, tubes, etc.

The following sets were in metal boxes with a sliding plastic cover. An overcover of cardboard was included with colorful scenes of the models in action on the moon or somewhere in space. The C10 prices include these covers, which did not survive well. If really nice, add twenty percent to C10 prices. All three sizes had foam inserts to hold the parts, and these are impossible to duplicate. The next two years, 1964 and 1965, saw a continuation of these three sets. After 1965 the company was sold to Gabriel Industries, hence Type III sets are many times referred to as Gabriel Era trash.

1963	C4	C6	C8	C10
10127 "Lunar Vehicle Set"	30	60	90	150

1963 (Continued)	C4	C6	C8	C10
10128 "Planetary Probe Set"	50	80	150	200
10129 "Master Power Set"	100	150	225	500

Vital Parts and Accessory Sets

	C10
1E Square Girder Kit, 20-"C," 8-"B," 14-7/8" sc and nt	85
A-48 Mechanical Motor with Key, check for spring slip	40
A-49 Motor and Gearbox, 115 volt AC, running, EXC	40
A-52 Motor, 115 volt AC, running	85
Illumination Kit	150
Musical Parts, comp. reproducer, record, mechanism	200
P-51 Motor and Gearbox, 115 volt AC, running	110
P-55 Motor and Remote Control, 12 volt AC/DC, runs	150
P-56G Motor, 115 volt AC, tapered ends, running	125
P-58 Motor, 6-12 volt AC/DC, "basket case," not running	10
P-58 Motor, "Joe Long" rebuilt	50
Smoke and Choo-Choo Kit, 7-15 volt AC	125
Whistle Kit, 7-15 volt AC	100

FARM TOYS

Allis-Chalmers

	C6	C8	C10
Pedal Tractor, Model 190, orange, winged decal, Ertl	550	800	1000
Pedal Tractor, Model 190 XT, orange, winged decal, Ertl	450	600	750
Pedal Tractor, Model 200, orange, Ertl	475	650	900
Pedal Tractor, Model 7045, orange and black, Ertl	275	375	450
Pedal Tractor, Model 7080, orange and maroon, Ertl	275	375	550
Pedal Tractor, Model 8070, orange and black, Ertl	275	375	550
Pedal Tractor, Model C, orange, Eska	700	1000	1400
Pedal Tractor, Model CA, orange, Eska	700	1100	1500
Pedal Tractor, Model D14, orange, Eska	675	950	1250
Pedal Tractor, Model D17, orange, with white wheels, Ertl	675	950	1250
Tractor and Dump Trailer, No. 2660, Arcade Manufacturing Company, 1937, 8-1/4" long	150	200	300
Tractor and Dump Trailer, No. 2657, Arcade Manufacturing Company, 1937, 12-3/4" long w/trailer	200	345	460
Tractor and Trailer, No. 2650, Arcade Manufacturing Company, 1936, total length 13" long	200	300	450
Tractor Trailer, No. 2650, Arcade Manufacturing Company, 1937, 13" long w/trailer	250	375	500
Tractor, Model B-112, Ertl	70	110	165
Tractor, Model WC, Arcade Manufacturing Company, 1941, 7-3/4" long	425	675	1000

Avery

	C6	C8	C10
Tractor, very early, Hubley, 4-3/4" long	120	180	240

Avery Tractor, Hubley, $240. Photo courtesy Rod Carnahan

Avery (Continued)

	C6	C8	C10
Tractor, stack, no hood, Arcade Manufacturing Company, 1923, 4-1/2" long	50	75	110

Case

	C6	C8	C10
Hay Loader, Vindex, 9" long	3000	4500	5200

Case Hay Loader, Vindex, $5200. Photo courtesy Bill Bertoia Auctions

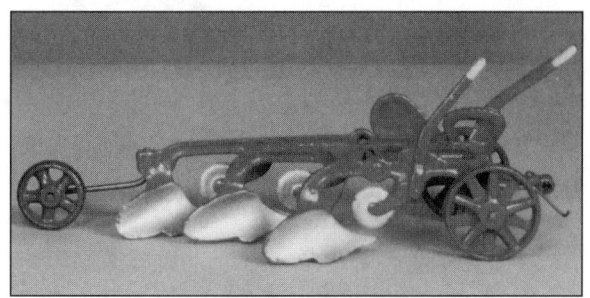

Case Tractor Plow, three-bottom, Vindex, $3700.
Photo courtesy Bill Bertoia Auctions

Caterpillar Tractor, No. 6100, Courtland, $450.
Photo courtesy Joe and Sharon Freed

Case (Continued)

	C6	C8	C10
Manure Spreader, Vindex, 12" long....	500	1250	2000
Pedal Tractor, white and orange, Ertl..	100	150	250
Pedal Tractor, white and black, Ertl....	100	150	250
Pedal Tractor, Agri King, white and orange, Ertl.........	250	400	500
Pedal Tractor, Agri King 1070, desert tan and orange, Ertl	300	450	550
Pedal Tractor, Model 30 Pleasure King, beige and orange, Ertl	550	700	900
Pedal Tractor, Model 400, beige and orange, Eska.....................	800	1300	2000
Pedal Tractor, Model 800 Case-O-Matic, beige and orange, Eska..........	750	950	1500
Pedal Tractor, Model VAC, orange, Eska..........................	500	700	1750
Steam Tractor, crew of two, tow-loop, small version of No. 25, No. 71, Kansas Toy & Novelty Company, 2-1/2" long....................	30	40	60
Steam Tractor, crew of two, tow loop, large front, small rear metal open-spoke wheels and flywheel, No. 25, Kansas Toy & Novelty Company, 3"........................	25	40	60
Tractor Plow, three-bottom, Vindex, 10-1/4" long	1000	2500	3700
Tractor, Model L, Vindex, 6-1/2" long	500	750	1030
Tractor, Model L, Ertl	42	63	85

Caterpillar

	C6	C8	C10
Dozer, Model D-6, Ertl	93	140	195
Dozer, Model D7, die-cast, Reuhl, 1:24-scale	300	475	750
Dozer, Model D7, plastic kit, could be purchased assembled, Reuhl, 1:24-scale	200	375	675

Caterpillar (Continued)

	C6	C8	C10
Grader, die-cast, No. 12, Reuhl, 1:24-scale	650	900	1350
Tractor, No. 271, Arcade Manufacturing Company, 1930, 7-1/2" long	450	800	1300
Tractor, No. 266X, Arcade Manufacturing Company, 1931, 3" long........................	50	75	100
Tractor, No. 267X, Arcade Manufacturing Company, 1931, 3-7/8" long	225	325	500
Tractor, No. 268X, Arcade Manufacturing Company, 1931, 5-5/8" long	500	800	1350
Tractor, No. 269X, Arcade Manufacturing Company, 1931, 6-7/8" long	650	1100	1550
Tractor, No. 270Y, later No. 2700Y, Arcade Manufacturing Company, 1936, 7-3/4" long	750	1250	2200
Tractor, slush lead, Barclay Vehicles, 2-5/8" long	17	26	35
Tractor, mechanical, w/rubber treads, tin wind-up, No. 6100, Courtland, 6" long, 3" wide, 4-1/2" high	250	350	450
Tractor, wind-up, Kingsbury, 8-1/2" ...	225	340	450
Tractor, w/stack, Savoye Pewter Toy Company, 2-3/4" long........................	10	15	20
Tractor, w/cast-iron driver, early, Structo, 8-1/2" long...........................	275	415	550
Tractor (Model D6) and Bulldozer, No. 2012, Doepke "Model Toys," 15" long..............................	300	450	575

Caterpillar Tractor (Model D6) and Bulldozer, No. 2012, Doepke "Model Toys," $575. Photo courtesy Calvin L. Chausee

Caterpillar Tractor with Trailer, No. 46, Structo, $400. Photo courtesy Randy Prasse

Caterpillar (Continued)	C6	C8	C10
Tractor with Trailer, steel treads, heavy spring clockwork motor, No. 46, Structo	200	300	400
Tractor with Treads, No. 4646, Tootsietoy, 1931	27	41	55
Tractor, Model D-7, Reuhl, Miscellaneous Vehicles	312	468	625
Wheel Tractor, Model DW 10, die-cast, Reuhl, 1:24-scale	325	475	750

David Bradley	C6	C8	C10
Cultipacker (Disc Harrows?), Auburn Rubber, 4-3/8" long	22	33	45
Manure Spreader, Auburn Rubber, 4-3/4" long	20	30	40
Plow, Two Furrow, Auburn Rubber, 4-3/8" long	20	30	40

Farmall	C6	C8	C10
Pedal Tractor, Model 560, red w/ white decal, Eska & Ertl Co	350	650	1200
Pedal Tractor, Model 806, red w/ white decal, Ertl	300	500	1000
Tractor, Model A, No. 7050, Arcade Manufacturing Company, 1941, 7-1/2" long	600	1000	1500
Tractor, Model M, No. 7070, Arcade Manufacturing Company, 1941, 7-1/4" long	300	450	700

Ford	C6	C8	C10
Backhoe, Model 7500, Ertl	37	56	75
Pedal Tractor, Commander 6000, blue and gray, later style grille and decal, Ertl	800	1100	1500
Pedal Tractor, Commander 6000, blue and gray, early style grille and decal, Ertl	1500	2000	3000
Pedal Tractor, Model 8000, blue, Ertl	175	250	400
Pedal Tractor, Model 900, red and gray, stamped steel fenders, available w/two or three bolt axle mounting bracket, Graphic Reproductions	1000	2900	3700
Pedal Tractor, Model 901, red and gray, die-cast fenders, bar grille, Graphic Reproductions	1900	2900	3800
Pedal Tractor, Model TW-20, blue, Ertl	125	225	375
Pedal Tractor, Model TW-35, blue, Scale Models	100	225	300
Pedal Tractor, Model TW-5, blue, has dark TW-5 decal w/red trim, Ertl	125	225	375
Pedal Tractor, Model TW-5, blue, has light blue TW-5 decal, Ertl	125	225	375

Ford Powermaster, Model 961, Hubley, NPF

Ford Tractor, Farmall, No. 279, Arcade Manufacturing Company, $1100. Photo courtesy Perry Eichor

Ford (Continued)

	C6	C8	C10
Powermaster, Model 961, Hubley	NPF	NPF	NPF
Tractor, No. 46, Matchbox, 1978	5	7	9
Tractor, No. 39, Matchbox, 1967	10	15	25
Tractor, Farmall, No. 279, Arcade Manufacturing Company, 1929, 6" long	500	750	1100
Tractor, Model 6000, steam boiler in front, Hubley, early 1920s, 4-3/4" long	125	188	250
Tractor, Model 6000, Hubley	150	225	300
Tractor, Model 8000, early, Ertl	25	40	60

Fordson

	C6	C8	C10
Tractor, w/driver, rear wheels larger, visible engine, marked and "Made in USA," Craftoy, 2-1/2" long	15	30	45
Tractor, cast iron, w/driver, Miscellaneous Vehicles, 5-3/4" long	140	210	280
Tractor, driver, horizontal grille pattern, crank, no tow hook, large 1-1/4" and 3/4" metal disk wheels w/four holes in disks, also found w/same size six spoke wheels, No. 17, Kansas Toy & Novelty Company, 2-7/8" long	25	35	45
Tractor, rubber wheels, No. 2730X, Arcade Manufacturing Company, 1934, 3-1/2" long	75	125	175
Tractor, No. 274, Arcade Manufacturing Company, 1928, 4-3/4" long	112	190	250

Graham-Bradley Tractor, Auburn Rubber, $50. Photo courtesy Dave Leopard's book, Rubber Toy Vehicles

Fordson (Continued)

	C6	C8	C10
Tractor, No. 273, Arcade Manufacturing Company, 1928, 3-7/8" long	90	150	200
Tractor, Arcade Manufacturing Company, 1923, 5-3/4" long	150	225	325

Graham-Bradley

	C6	C8	C10
Tractor, Auburn Rubber, 4-1/2" long	25	38	50

International

	C6	C8	C10
Backhoe, Ertl	50	75	100
Trac-Tractor, No. 7120, Arcade Manufacturing Company, 1941, 7-1/2" long	1500	2500	3750

International Trac-Tractor, No. 7120, Arcade Manufacturing Company, $3750. Photo courtesy Tomas G. Nefos

International Harvester

	C6	C8	C10
Cub Tractor, Farmall, plastic, could be purchased assembled, Reuhl, 1:16-scale	175	350	575
Pedal Tractor, Model 1026, red w/white decal, Ertl	300	400	800
Pedal Tractor, Model 50, plastic, red and black, Eska	60	125	175
Pedal Tractor, Model 66, red w/white decal, Ertl	160	400	500
Pedal Tractor, Model 856, red w/white decal, Ertl	300	475	900
Pedal Tractor, Model 86, red w/black stripe decal, Ertl	175	400	500
Trac-Tractor, No. 277, Arcade Manufacturing Company, 1937, 8-1/4" long	600	950	1300

International Harvester Farmall

	C6	C8	C10
Pedal Tractor, Model 400, red, Eska	400	800	1700
Pedal Tractor, Model 450, red w/decal grille, Eska	400	800	1800
Pedal Tractor, Model H, small version, red, open grille, Eska	700	1000	2500
Pedal Tractor, Model H/M, mid size, red, has open grille, Eska	700	1000	1500
Pedal Tractor, Model H/M, mid size, red, closed grille, low steering post, rear seat mounting bracket is about 2-1/2" from the rear of main tractor casting, Eska	700	1000	1500
Pedal Tractor, Model H/M, mid size, red, high steering post, closed grille, Eska	700	1000	1500

John Deere

	C6	C8	C10
Bulldozer with Blade, Model 500, Ertl	50	75	100
Bulldozer, Model 440, Ertl	20	30	40
Combine, Model 6600, Ertl	70	105	140
Farm Wagon, w/two horses, Vindex, 7-1/2" long	800	1300	1900
Lanz Tractor, No. 50, Matchbox, 1963	15	25	35
Manure Spreader, horse-drawn, Vindex	500	1100	1800
Pedal Tractor, Model 10, green, four holes in engine compartment, Ertl	300	450	800
Pedal Tractor, Model 10, green, three holes in engine compartment, Ertl	300	450	800

John Deere Pedal Tractor, Model 20, Ertl, $650. Photo by Jon Jacobson

John Deere (Continued)

	C6	C8	C10
Pedal Tractor, Model 20, green, Ertl	200	300	650
Pedal Tractor, Model 30, green, can be found w/metal or plastic front wheel rims, seat and steering wheels, Ertl	175	250	500
Pedal Tractor, Model 40, green, Ertl	175	250	450
Pedal Tractor, Model 60, large version, green, Eska	400	800	1000
Pedal Tractor, Model 60, small version, green, Eska	300	550	950
Pedal Tractor, Model 620, green, Eska	325	675	1100
Pedal Tractor, Model 730, green, Eska	300	550	900
Pedal Tractor, Model 730, green, variation in body casting, Eska	400	850	1900
Pedal Tractor, Model A, green, Eska	1000	2000	5500
Pedal Tractor, Model A, red w/yellow wheels, block type engine design, Eska	5000	11,000	15,000

John Deere Tractor Plow, three-bottom, Vindex, $2400. Photo courtesy Bill Bertoia Auctions

John Deere Tractor, Model A, Auburn Rubber, $45. Photo courtesy Dave Leopard's book, Rubber Toy Vehicles

John Deere (Continued)

	C6	C8	C10
Pedal Tractor, Model LGT, green, plastic grille, tin fenders and seat, Ertl	400	700	1000
Thresher, Vindex, 15" long	1500	2800	3900
Tractor Plow, three-bottom, Vindex, 9" long	900	1400	2400
Tractor, Model A, Auburn Rubber, 5" long	22	33	45
Tractor, Model D, Vindex, 6-1/2" long	950	1700	2600

Kubota

	C6	C8	C10
Pedal Tractor, Model M6950, orange, Scale Models	150	225	350

Loadstar

	C6	C8	C10
Grain/Cattle Stake Truck, Ertl	60	90	120

Lorain

	C6	C8	C10
Shovel, Reuhl	700	1250	1900

Massey-Ferguson

	C6	C8	C10
Farm Tractor, w/driver, No. 1011, Tootsietoy, 1941, 4" long	200	300	400
Pedal Tractor, Model 390, red, Ertl	150	200	400

Massey-Harris

	C6	C8	C10
Combine, Pull-type, die-cast, made to fit 44 tractor, Reuhl, 1:20-scale	275	400	600
Disc Harrow, die-cast, made to fit 44 tractor, Reuhl, 1:20-scale	175	300	575
Loader, die-cast, made to fit 44 tractor, Reuhl, 1:20-scale	200	475	675

Massey Harris Pedal Tractor, Model 44, Eska, $3100. Photo by Jon Jacobson

Massey-Harris (Continued)

	C6	C8	C10
Pedal Tractor, Model 44, small version, red, open grille, Eska	3000	4000	5500
Pedal Tractor, Model 44, large version, red, closed grille, Eska	1200	2200	3100
Roadmaster Wagon, die-cast, made to fit 44 tractor, Reuhl, 1:24-scale	150	275	550

McCormick-Deering

	C6	C8	C10
Farmall Tractor, Arcade Manufacturing Company, 1937, 6-1/4" long	250	400	600
IH Farmall M Tractor, Auburn Rubber, 4" long	22	33	45
Manure Spreader, cast iron, w/team of horses, Arcade, 14" long	375	560	750
Plow, cast iron, animal drawn, Arcade	175	265	350
Thresher, Arcade Manufacturing Company, 1930, 9-1/2" long	200	300	400
Thresher, Arcade Manufacturing Company, 1927, 12" long	300	450	650

McCormick-Deering Farmall Tractor, Arcade Manufacturing Company, $600. Photo courtesy Liz Isham Cary

McCormick-Deering IH Farmall M Tractor, Auburn Rubber, $45. Photo courtesy Dave Leopard's book, Rubber Toy Vehicles

McCormick-Deering (Continued)

	C6	C8	C10
Tractor, No. 10-20, Arcade Manufacturing Company, 1925, 6-3/4" long	400	600	850
Weber Wagon, cast iron, w/two horses, Arcade	400	600	800

Minneapolis-Moline

	C6	C8	C10
Tractor, Model R, later style, Auburn Rubber, 7-1/4" long	40	60	85
Tractor, Model R, early style, Auburn Rubber, 7-1/2" long	40	60	85
Tractor, Model Z, Auburn Rubber, 4" long	22	33	45

McCormick-Deering Thresher, Arcade Manufacturing Company, $650. Photo courtesy Liz Isham Cory

Oliver

	C6	C8	C10
Pedal Tractor, Model 1800, green w/white wheels, plastic grille, Ertl	600	900	1500

Minneapolis-Moline Tractor, Model R, Auburn Rubber, $85. Photo courtesy Dave Leopard's book, Rubber Toy Vehicles

Minneapolis-Moline Tractor, Model R, Auburn Rubber, $85. Photo courtesy Dave Leopard's book, Rubber Toy Vehicles

Minneapolis-Moline Tractor, Model Z, Auburn Rubber, $45. Photo courtesy Dave Leopard's book, Rubber Toy Vehicles

Oliver (Continued)

	C6	C8	C10
Pedal Tractor, Model 1850, green w/white wheels, plastic grille, Ertl	550	750	1200
Pedal Tractor, Model 1850, green w/white wheels, plastic grille, Ertl	550	750	1200
Pedal Tractor, Model 1855, green w/white wheels, plastic grille, Ertl	550	750	1200
Pedal Tractor, Model 88, small version, green w/red wheels, w/open grill, Eska	1200	2200	3500
Pedal Tractor, Model 88, small version, green w/red wheels, w/closed grille, Eska	900	1600	2200
Pedal Tractor, Model 880, green w/white wheels, Eska	800	1000	1600
Plow, No. 4230X, Arcade Manufacturing Company, 1941, 6-1/4" long	150	2225	300
Plow, Arcade Manufacturing Company, 1923, 6-1/2" long	250	375	550
Row Crop "70" Tractor, Auburn Rubber, 8" long	45	65	85
Superior Spreader, No. 7140, Arcade Manufacturing Company, 1941, 10-1/4" long	600	950	1400
Tractor, No. 356, Arcade Manufacturing Company, 1937, 7-1/2" long	325	500	700

Reliable

	C6	C8	C10
Front-Lift Seeder, Auburn Rubber, 5" long	25	35	50

White

	C6	C8	C10
Pedal Tractor, gray, Scale Model	150	225	300

Oliver Tractor, No. 356, Arcade Manufacturing Company, $700

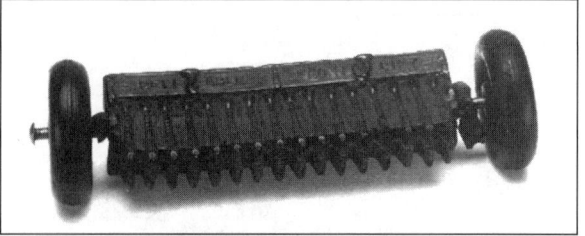

Reliable Front-Lift Seeder, Auburn Rubber, $50. Photo courtesy Dave Leopard's book, Rubber Toy Vehicles

White Pedal Tractor, Scale Model, $300. Photo by Jon Jacobson

White Oliver

	C6	C8	C10
Pedal Tractor, Model 1855, green with white wheels, plastic grille, Ertl	550	750	1200

Whitewater

	C6	C8	C10
Farm Wagon, w/two horses, Vindex	1400	2400	3700

Miscellaneous

	C6	C8	C10
Cattle Truck, plastic, Hubley, postwar, 12"	85	128	170
Cattle Truck, Kingsbury, 1930s, 19" long	215	325	450

Cattle Truck, Hubley, $170

Disk Harrow, Auburn Rubber, $45. Photo courtesy Dave Leopard's book, Rubber Toy Vehicles

Miscellaneous (Continued)

	C6	C8	C10
Cattle Truck, cast iron, Kenton, c. 1938, 8" long	150	225	325
Combine Harvester, No. 51, Matchbox, 1979	4	6	8
Combine, self-propelled, die-cast, made to fit 44 tractor, Reuhl, 1:20-scale	325	475	675
Corn Harvester, No. 4180, Arcade Manufacturing Company, 1939, 5" long	130	200	300
Corn Harvester, No. 702, Arcade Manufacturing Company, 1939, 6-1/2" long	175	275	400
Corn Planter, Arcade Manufacturing Company, 1939, 4-1/2" long	60	90	125
Disk Harrow, eight disk on same 1-5/8" wide frame as No. 61, thirteen pieces, includes disks and wheels, four colors, No. 62, Kansas Toy & Novelty Company, 4" long	40	60	80
Disk Harrow, Auburn Rubber, 4-1/2" long	22	33	45
Farm Cart, mule, black driver, Kenton, 10-1/2" long	375	562	750
Farm Mower, No. 4210X, Arcade Manufacturing Company, 1939, 4" long	60	90	125
Farm Set, w/Ford Truck and Tractor, Huber StarBox Trailer, and Huber Star Scraper-Raker, No. 7003, Tootsietoy, 1928	135	205	275

Miscellaneous (Continued)

	C6	C8	C10
Farm Stake, No. 004, Tonka, 1961	85	175	370
Farm Stake and Horse Trailer, No. 035, Tonka, 1960	125	180	350
Farm Stake and Horse Trailer, No. 735, Tonka, 1962	75	125	225
Farm Stake Truck, Tonka, 1957	190	375	480
Farm Stake Truck, No. 004, Tonka, 1958	100	150	300
Farm Stake Truck, No. 004, Tonka, 1960	100	200	325
Farm Stake Truck, No. 404, Tonka, 1962	50	95	150
Farm Stake Truck, No. 404, Tonka, 1963	60	90	150
Farm Stake Truck and Horse Trailer, No. 035, Tonka, 1961	100	180	350
Farm Stake with Two-horse Trailer, No. 035, Tonka, 1958, 21-3/4" long	125	250	450
Farm Trailer, No. 289, Arcade Manufacturing Company, 1929, 3-3/4" long	50	100	200
Farm Trailer, No. 286, Arcade Manufacturing Company, 1929, 6-3/8" long	150	200	325
Farm Trailer, No. 288, Arcade Manufacturing Company, 1929, 4-5/8" long	50	100	200
Farm Wagon, w/two horses and driver, Kenton, 15" long	325	490	650
Farm Wagon, w/driver and one horse, early, Kenton, 15" long	300	450	600
Farm Wagon, cast iron, w/two horses and figure, Kenton, 14-1/2" long	500	750	1100
Farm Wagon, cast iron, w/two horses, 10"	200	300	400
Farm Wagon, cast iron, w/driver and two unusual horses, 14" long	250	375	500
Farm Wagon, cast iron and wood, large heavy horses, 25-1/2" long	300	450	600
Farm Wagon, w/driver and one horse, Kenton, 14" long	500	750	1100
Farm Wagon, cast iron, w/two horses and driver, Arcade, 10-3/4" long	463	695	925
Farm Wagon, cast iron, w/one horse, Hubley, c. 1915, 12-1/2" long	400	600	800
Farm Wagon and Team, Auburn Rubber	50	70	95

Grain Hauler, Dunwell, $100. Photo courtesy Tim Oei

Miscellaneous (Continued)

	C6	C8	C10
Grain Hauler, Dunwell	50	75	100
Grain Hauler Semi, No. 550, Tonka, 1952, 22-1/4" long	125	180	350
Harrow, Auburn Rubber, 4-1/2" long	20	30	40
Harvester, open top, Auburn Rubber, 5-1/2" long	35	50	75
Hay Wagon, w/two horses, Gibbs, 19" long	100	150	200
Hay Wagon, cast iron, w/driver and two steers, Kyser & Rex, 13" long	700	1200	1700
Hay Wagon, cast iron, w/driver and one steer, Kyser & Rex, 11-1/2" long	550	850	1300
Livestock Hauler Semi, No. 500, Tonka, 1952, 22-1/4" long	100	150	350
Livestock Transport, Dunwell	90	135	180
Livestock Truck, Kilgore, 9" long	500	800	1200
Livestock Truck, Kilgore, 1930s, 7" long	500	700	975
Livestock Truck, Tonka, 1955	110	200	350

Harrow, Auburn Rubber, $40. Photo courtesy Dave Leopard's book, Rubber Toy Vehicles

Harvester, Auburn Rubber, $75. Photo courtesy Dave Leopard's book, Rubber Toy Vehicles

Miscellaneous (Continued)

	C6	C8	C10
Mechanical Farm Tractor, w/o scraper, rear tires are large rubber and front are small rubber tires, tin wind-up, No. 6050, Courtland, 7-1/2" long, 4-3/4" wide, 4-1/2" high	75	100	150
Mechanical Farm Tractor, w/scraper, rear tires are large rubber and front are small rubber tires, tin wind-up, No. 6000, Courtland, 8-3/4" long, 4-3/4" wide, 4-1/2" high	100	150	200
Mechanical Farm Tractor, w/o scraper, rear tires are large tin litho while the front are small rubber tires, tin wind-up, No. 6075, Courtland, 7-1/2" long, 4-3/4" wide, 4-1/2" high	250	350	450
Mini-Tonka Livestock Van, No. 090, Tonka, 1964, 16" long	50	75	100

Mechanical Farm Tractor, No. 6050, Courtland, $150. Photo courtesy Joe and Sharon Freed

Miscellaneous (Continued)

	C6	C8	C10
No. 63 Freeway Gas Tanker, Matchbox, 1973	10	15	20
Planter, marked "KTN No. 61," vee-blade plough w/seed hopper, four pieces includes wheels and three colors, No. 61, Kansas Toy & Novelty Company, 4" long	40	60	80
Plough, single blade on same shaft as No. 61, No. 63, Kansas Toy & Novelty Company, 4" long	40	60	80
Plow, cast iron, w/one horse, cast iron, 10-3/4" long	150	225	300
Plow, cast iron, w/one horse and driver, Wilkins Toy Company, 10-1/2"	1200	1900	2800
Separtor-Thresher, tow hook, auto-type metal open-spoke wheels (not tractor rims), lacquer or enamel, also un-numbered version, No. 27, Kansas Toy & Novelty Company, 3" long	25	40	50
Tipping Farm Trailer, No. 51, Matchbox, 1963	8	10	12
Tractor, "Baby Tractor," friction, marked "patented June 20, 1916," American Metal Toys	100	150	200
Tractor, has hood, no stack, Arcade Manufacturing Company, 1926, 4-1/2" long	125	200	325
Tractor, No. 3560, Oliver, 1941, 7-1/2" long	500	800	1200
Tractor, solid rubber, two dimensional, (part of set), Judy Company, The, 3-1/2" long	15	20	25
Tractor, yellow w/red seat, No. 250, Tonka, 1963	75	112	150
Tractor, No. 250, Tonka, 1962, 8-5/8" long	50	75	100
Tractor, No. 64, Caterpillar, 1981	3	5	7
Tractor, plastic, Manoil	12	18	25
Tractor, plain front, Manoil	12	18	25
Tractor, loop front, Manoil	12	18	25
Tractor, Hubley, 9" long	62	93	125
Tractor, mechanical w/driver, Kingsbury, 8" long	250	375	500

Miscellaneous (Continued)

	C6	C8	C10
Tractor, plastic, Ideal, 1948, 4" long	20	30	40
Tractor, No. 472, Hubley	30	45	60
Tractor, rubber wheels, No. 7240, Arcade Manufacturing Company, 1941, 3-1/8" long	100	150	200
Tractor, black rubber wheels, No. 4060, Arcade Manufacturing Company, 1941, 6-1/4" long	325	500	700
Tractor, No. 7200, Arcade Manufacturing Company, 1941, 6-1/2" long	175	275	400
Tractor, Hubley, 1930s, 5" long	365	545	725
Tractor, wood wheels, No. 7341, Arcade Manufacturing Company, 1941, 6-1/4" long	400	600	850
Tractor, No. 42, Barclay Vehicles, 1931, 2-3/16" long	12	18	25
Tractor, No. 7, Barclay Vehicles, late 1920s-early 1930s	15	22	30
Tractor, driver in cab, Hubley, 3-1/4" long	100	150	200
Tractor and Carry-All Trailer, w/No. 50 Steam Shovel, No. 120, Tonka, 1949	155	280	475
Tractor and Carry-All Trailer, w/No. 100 Steam Shovel, No. 125, Tonka, 1949	150	250	550
Tractor and Carry-All Trailer, No. 130, Tonka, 1949, 30-1/2" long	100	150	350
Tractor and Carry-All Trailer, w/No. 150 Crane and Clam, No. 170, Tonka, 1949	200	300	525
Tractor and Cart, tin, w/iron driver, white rubber wheels, Kingsbury, c. 1930s, 11-1/2" long	200	300	400
Tractor and Dump Trailer, No. 7300, Arcade Manufacturing Company, 1941, 15-1/2" long	600	950	1300
Tractor and Plow, No. 7220, Arcade Manufacturing Company, 1941, tractor 6-1/2" long, overall length 8-3/4"	350	550	850
Tractor and Wagon 8600, Ertl	44	66	88
Tractor, Heavy Gauge, No. 926, Marx Toy Co.	100	150	200

FIGURE KITS

In the 1960s—the golden age of figure kits—Aurora lead the way in diversity of product and demand. Their line of original and glow Universal Studios monsters are today's most sought-after figure kits.

Rating the condition of a figure kit can be difficult because value can be drastically affected by factors such as assembled parts, painted parts, missing pieces, missing instructions, box condition and country of origin.

C10 SEALED. Mint in Box with original factory shrink wrap. Collectors may pay a premium over the C10 price if the box is not damaged. Beware of resealed kits.

C10. A complete, unused kit with an excellent box and instructions and no glue or paint on pieces. Most collectors insist that plastic trees that held pieces be present with pieces still attached. Prices listed in the chapter are based on kits in C10 condition.

PARTIAL ASSEMBLY. A partially-built kit with Excellent box/instructions and no paint is worth eighty-five percent of the C10 price. The more assembly, the more the price decreases. Old styrene glues actually melted pieces together, and white glues (Elmers) do not decrease value as much as Styrene glues because they can be removed.

PARTIAL PAINTING. A complete, partially-painted kit with Excellent box/instructions and no glue is worth eighty-five percent of the C10 price. Painting is not as serious as gluing because most experienced modelers know how to strip paint. Again, the more painting, the more price decreases because stripping takes time and is not always completely successful.

PARTIAL ASSEMBLY/PAINTING. Together these two factors can make pricing very difficult. A general value guideline would be seventy percent of the C10 price with Excellent box/instructions.

BUILT-UP. A fully assembled, complete kit with no box/instructions has a value of fifteen to forty-five percent of the C10 price. The more desirable the C10 kit, the more desirable the built-up. If a kit was issued several times, built-up value decreases. For example,

Aurora's design of Frankenstein was issued four times—Aurora 1961, 1969, 1972, and Monogram 1983. Thus its value is about fifteen of the C10 kit. Vehicles such as Batmobiles and UFOs go toward low percentages because of low visual appeal. Without instructions a novice kit builder will find it virtually impossible to determine if a built-up is complete. Except for very high-priced kits incomplete built-ups have little value.

MISSING PIECES. One missing piece from a kit will result in a large decrease in value regardless of all other combined factors. Even a kit missing one piece is worth only eighty percent of a complete C10 kit. Simply put, many collectors will not buy a kit missing a piece.

INSTRUCTIONS. Missing instructions reduce the C10 price by five to ten percent. Instruction sheets from the sell in the $5-$10 range. Sheets for rare, expensive kits such as Aurora's Gigantic Frankenstein can bring over $35!

BOXES. The market for empty figure kit boxes is almost exclusive to Aurora boxes. A box in Excellent condition box has no split corners, tape, paint, glue, punctures, severe creases or scuffs. Excellent boxes alone have maximum value of forty percent of a kit in C10 condition. Aforementioned box defects decrease value on C10 kits by twenty percent or more.

FOREIGN ISSUE. This factor is an issue primarily with Aurora kits. Because Aurora had branches in Canada, England and Holland they sometimes issued boxes and instructions with wording in other languages and plastic parts in colors other than what American issues had. Ninety percent of the kits you'll ever see will not be foreign issue, but just in case, some collectors devalue C10 foreign issue kits to about seventy-five percent of American C10 prices.

If you're more confused about how to price a kit now than you were before, don't feel bad! Even experienced dealers have a difficult time pricing kits when faced with missing pieces, painted parts, box wear, etc. These guidelines are just that—guidelines.

It should be noted that kit values vary widely due to the geographic region and local collector demand. There is strong interest in American kits in Europe and Japan. The values listed here are conservative, mid-range prices that are indicative of what most collectors would be willing to pay. Obviously, some collectors will pay more and some will pay less.

Special thanks to Greg Roccaro of Staten Island, New York. Some kit numbers and dates were taken from *Science Fiction and Figure Kits* by John Burns of Edmond, Oklahoma. Though not a price guide, it serves as an excellent reference regarding all known kits of this genre.

Contributor: David Welch, P.O. Box 714, Murphysboro, IL 62966. Welch is a nationally known dealer in cartoon, comic, and TV character items. He has been collecting and/or dealing since the age of 13. He has contributed information for various price guides including *Tomart's Disneyana (condensed edition), Tomart's Space Adventure Collectibles,* and *Overstreet's Comic Book Price Guide.*

Addar

Founded by former Aurora employees in 1973, Addar was acquired the license to produce Planet of the Apes figural kits. Although they were known for their Planet of the Apes kits, Addar also issued Super Scenes—dioramas that looked like they were built in a bottle. They also made kits based another popular 1970s character—Evel Knievel.

The popularity of Planet of the Apes wore off sooner than the people of Addar assumed or wanted, and they closed their doors in 1977.

Addar

	C10
Caesar, No. 106, Planet of the Apes, 1974	60
Cornelius, No. 101, Planet of the Apes, 1973	60
Cornfield Roundup, No. 216, Super Scenes, 1975	60
Dr. Zaius, No. 102, Planet of the Apes, 1973	60
Dr. Zira, No. 105, Planet of the Apes, 1974	60
General Aldo, No. 104, Planet of the Apes, 1974	60
General Ursus, No. 103, Planet of the Apes, 1974	60
Jail Wagon, No. 217, Super Scenes, 1975	60
Soldier on Stalion, No. 107, Planet of the Apes, 1975	75
Spirit in a Bottle, No. 227, Super Scenes, 1975	60
Tree House, No. 215, Super Scenes, 1975	60

AMT

Celebrating their fiftieth anniversary in 1998, AMT is known for their vehicle model kits. In the 1960s they began producing Star Trek-related models. Over the years they have expanded their line of figure kits to include Bigfoot and Leonard DaVinci's Invention series.

AMT was purchased by Matchbox in 1978 and again by Ertl in 1984. Currently AMT/Ertl produces only a handful of figural kits.

AMT

	C10
Bigfoot, No. 7701	25
Dragula, No. 905, Munsters TV car, 1964	250
Exploration Set, No. 958, 1974	75
Fred Flintstone's Family Sedan, No. 496, 1974	45
Fred Flintstone's Rock Cruncher, No. 497, 1974	60
Fred Flintstone's Sports Car, No. 495, 1974	60
Galileo 7, No. 959, 1974	45
K-7 Space Station, No. 955, 1975	40
Klingon Cruiser, No. 922, 1967	120
Klingon Cruiser, No. 952	65
Klingon Cruiser, No. 971, 1979	28
Klingon Cruiser, No. 6682, 1985	13
Mr. Spock with Snake, No. 973, 1979	30
Mr. Spock with Snake, No. 956, 1975	60
Munsters Koach, Munsters TV car, 1964	200
Romulan Ship, No. 957, 1975	45
Spaceship Set, No. 953, 1975	60
Spaceship Set, No. 6677, 1984	28
USS Enterprise, No. 970, 1979	28
USS Enterprise, No. 6676, 1983	18
USS Enterprise, No. 6675, 1985	18
USS Enterprise Bridge, No. 950, 1975	28
USS Enterprise with Lights, No. 931, 1967	175
USS Enterprise without Lights, No. 951, 1976	50
Vulcan Shuttle, No. 6679, 1985	15
Vulcan Shuttle, No. 5112, 1979	24
Vulcan Shuttle, No. 972, 1980	24

Aurora

Aurora Plastics Corporation began in 1950 when Abe Shikes made a plastic bow and arrow from a faulty plastic hanger. It was in 1952 that Aurora intoduced their first model kit, The gumann Panther F9F Jet Fighter.

It wasn't until 1955 that Aurora made figure kits. They made a series titled Guys and Gals of All Nations. They were highly-detailed 1:8-scale figure kits designed to draw girls into the world of model kits. Although the series was a success, it did not attract many girls model building. Aurora's marketing shifted back to boys and young men. Aurora's monster figure kits were introduced in 1960 and established Aurora as a pop culture icon of the Sixties.

Aurora was purchased in 1971 by Nabisco. Wanting to avoid any controversy, only "cute" toys were produced under Nabisco. Kits were not completely abandoned, but gone were the days of monster figures.

Nabisco closed Aurora in 1977. Aurora's molds were purchased at auction by Monogram.

For the Aurora line in general, it is the kit name and kit number that are most relevant, dates listed may vary a year either way. Please note that different kits carried identical numbers (i.e., King Kong Glow, 465 and Frankenstein's Flivver, 465).

Some clarification may be needed on the Aurora Frankenstein listing. Frankenstein was first issued in 1961 in a long, rectangular box. The 1969 Frightening Lightning issue was the same kit with optional duplicate glow parts. The box was the same shape, and a lightning bolt was added to the artwork. In 1969 and 1972 the optional glow format continued and square boxes with altered artwork were introduced. The 1969 glow boxes are thicker and sturdier than the 1972 glows. In many cases, the color of the plastic of the original was different from the color of the glow issues. The plastic kit itself will always carry the date of its original issue. The Monster Scenes and Monsters of the Movies Frankensteins are completely different kits from the 1961, 1969 and 1972 issues.

Many of these rare and valuable kits are being reissued in beautifully done boxes. Listed below are Aurora kits being reissued by other manufacturers. How can you tell a reissue from an original? Look carefully at the box. Current issues are marked with a UPC code, a 1990s copyright date and a company name other than Aurora. None of these kits were produced to deceive; however, some people have attempted to sell them as originals.

Aurora Reissues		
Monogram	**Polar Lights**	
Frankenstein	Bride of Frankentstein	
Dracula	Creature from the Black Lagoon	
Wolfman	King Kong Thronster	
Mummy	Addams Family Haunted House	
Creature	The Munsters Living Room Scene	
Godzilla	Wolfman's Wagon	
	Mummy's Chariot	
	Frankensteins Flivver	
Cinemodels	Lost in Space No. 420	
Prisoner	Lost in Space No. 419	
Phantom of	Lost in Space Robot	
the Opera	Undertakers Dragster	

	C10
Addams Family House, No. 805, 1965	750
Alfred E. Neumann, No. 802, 1965	200
Allosaurus, No. 736, 1972	125
American Astronaut, No. 409, 1967	80
Ankylosourus, No. 744, 1974	125
Apache Warrior, No. 401, 1961	300
Aramis, No. K10, 1958	100
Archie's Car, No. 582, 1969	85
Athos, No. K8, 1958	100
Babe Ruth, No. 862, 1965	250
Banana Splits Buggy, No. 832, 1969	350
Batboat, No. 811	500
Batcycle, No. 810, 1967	500
Batman, No. 467, 1964	250
Batman Comic Scenes, No. 187, 1974	85
Batmobile, No. 486, 1966	300
Batplane, No. 487, 1966	200
Black Beauty, No. 489, Green Hornet, 1967	500
Black Knight, various issues	15
Blackbeard, No. 463, 1965	125

Aurora Batboat, No. 811, $500

Aurora Batman, No. 467, $250

Aurora Bride of Frankenstein, No. 482, $800

Aurora (Continued)   **C10**

Blue Knight, various issues.. 12

Bride of Frankenstein, No. 482, 1964 800

Captain Action, No. 480, 1966 300

Captain America, No. 476, 1966............................. 300

Captain America Comic Scenes, No. 192, 1974........ 80

Captain Kidd, No. 464, 1965 125

Cave, No. 732, 1972.. 50

Cave Bear, No. 738, 1972.. 65

Chinese Girl, No. 416, 1957 35

Chinese Mandarin, No. 415, 1957 35

Chitty Chitty Bang Bang, No. 828, 1968................... 80

Confederate Raider, No. 402, 1959.......................... 350

Aurora (Continued)   **C10**

Creature from the Black Lagoon, No. 654,
    Monsters of the Movies, 1975 150

Creature from the Black Lagoon, No. 426, 1963 350

Creature from the Black Lagoon, No. 483, glow,
    1969/1972 150

Cro Magnon Man, No. 730, 1971 50

Cro Magnon Woman, No. 731, 1971 50

Crusader, No. K7, 1959... 100

Customizing Monster Kit No. 1, No. 463, 1963 175

Customizing Monster Kit No. 2, No. 464, 1963 175

D'Artagnan, No. 410, 1966....................................... 90

Dempsey vs. Firpo, No. 861, 1965.......................... 100

Dick Tracy, No. 818, 1968....................................... 165

Aurora Captain Action, No. 480, $300

Aurora Captain Action, No. 480, $300

Aurora (Continued)   <u>C10</u>

Dick Tracy Space Coupe, No. 819, 1968 135

Dimetrodon, No. 745, 1974 125

Dr. Deadly, No. 631, Monster Scenes, 1971 120

Dr. Deadly's Daughter (The Victim), No. 632,
Monster Scenes, 1971 90

Dr. Jekyll, No. 654, Monsters of the Movies, 1975 ... 75

Dr. Jekyll, No. 482, glow, 1969/1972 100

Dr. Jekyll, No. 460, 1965 325

Dracula, No. 424, 1962 300

Dracula, No. 424/454, Frightening Lightning,
1969 350

Dracula, No. 454, glow, 1969/1972 100

Dracula, No. 656, Monsters of the Movies, 1975 165

Dracula's Dragster, No. 466, 1966 425

Dutch Boy, No. 413, 1957 35

Dutch Girl, No. 414, 1957 35

Flying Reptile, No. 734, 1974 100

Aurora (Continued)   <u>C10</u>

Flying Saucer, No. 256, 1975 95

Flying Sub, No. 254, 1975 100

Flying Sub, No. 817, 1968 175

Forgotten Prisoner, No. 422, (repros say "1992
Tomy"), 1966 450

Forgotten Prisoner, No. 422/453, Frightening
Lightning, 1969 500

Forgotten Prisoner, No. 453, glow, 1969/1972 135

Frankenstein, No. 423, 1961 295

Frankenstein, No. 423/449, Frightening Lightning,
1969 325

Frankenstein, No. 449, glow, 1969 135

Frankenstein, glow, 1972 80

Frankenstein, No. 633, Monster Scenes, 1971 175

Frankenstein, No. 651, Monsters of the Movies,
1975 175

Frankenstein's Flivver, No. 465, 1964 400

Aurora Confederate Raider, No. 402, $350

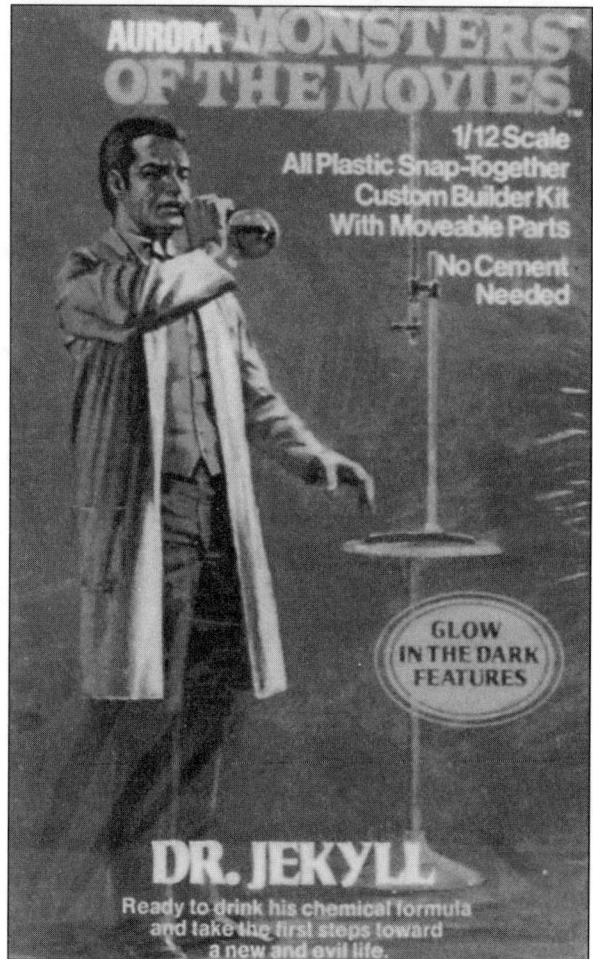

Aurora Dr. Jekyll, No. 482, $100

Aurora Dr. Jekyll, No. 654, $75

Aurora Dracula, No. 454, $100

Aurora (Continued)   C10

Frog, The, No. 451, 1966 225

George Washington, No. 852, 1965 100

Ghidrah, No. 658, Monsters of the Movies, 1975.... 325

Giant Bird, No. 739, 1972 75

Giant Woolly Mammoth, No. 743, 1972 100

Aurora (Continued)   C10

Gigantic Frankenstein "Big Frankie," No. 470,
    w/three bottles paint and brush, 1964 1500

Gladiator, No. 405, w/sword, 1959 175

Gladiator, No. 406, w/trident, 1959 175

Gladiator, No. 469, 1964 500

Godzilla, No. 466, glow, 1969/1972 150

Godzilla's Go-Cart, No. 485, 1966 1500

Gold Knight on Horseback, No. 475/1957, K5,
    1965 200

Aurora Dutch Boy, No. 413, $35

Aurora Dutch Girl, No. 414, $35

Aurora Forgotten Prisoner, No. 422, $450

Aurora The Frog, No. 451, $225

Aurora Ghidrah, No. 658, $325

Aurora (Continued)   **C10**

Green Beret, No. 413, 1966 100

Gruesome Goodies, No. 634, Monster Scenes,
    1971 100

Guillotine, No. 800, 1964.................................... 500

Hanging Cage, No. 637, Monster Scenes, 1971 100

Hercules, No. 481, 1965.. 175

Horned Dinosaur, No. 741, 1972 100

Hulk, No. 421, 1966... 250

Hulk, No. 184, Comic Scenes, 1974 75

Hunchback, No. 461, 1964.................................... 250

Hunchback of Notre Dame, No. 481, 1969/1972 100

Illya Kuryakin, No. 412, 1966 200

Indian Chief, No. 417, 1957................................... 75

Indian Squaw, No. 418, 1957................................. 75

James Bond, No. 414, 1966 300

Jerry West, No. 865, 1965...................................... 110

Jesse James, No. 408, 1966.................................... 200

Aurora Hulk, No. 421, $250

Aurora (Continued)   **C10**

Jimmy Brown, No. 863, 1965 90

John F. Kennedy, No. 851, 1964............................. 150

Aurora James Bond, No. 414, $300

Aurora Jesse James, No. 408, $200

Aurora (Continued)	**C10**
Johnny Unitas, No. 864, 1965	90
Jungle Swamp, No. 740, 1972	100
King Kong, No. 465, glow, 1969/1972	100

Aurora (Continued)	**C10**
King Kong, No. 468, 1964	500
King Kong's Thronester, No. 484, 1966	1500
Land of the Giants, No. 816, Snake Scene, 1968	400

Aurora Mr. Hyde, No. 655, $75

Aurora Mummy's Chariot, No. 459, $550

Aurora Nutty Nose-Nipper, No. 806, $175

Aurora (Continued)

	C10
Land of the Giants Spaceship, No. 830, 1968	400
Lone Ranger, No. 808, 1967	125
Lone Ranger, No. 188, Comic Scenes, 1974	35
Lost in Space, No. 419, 1966	750
Lost in Space, No. 420, 1966	1000
Mad Barber, No. 455	1000
Mexican Caballero, No. 421, 1957	75
Mexican Senorita, No. 422, 1957	75
Mod Squad Woodie, No. 583, 1970	100
Moon Bus, No. 829, 2001: A Space Odyssey, 1968	210
Mr. Hyde, No. 655, Monsters of the Movies, 1975	75
Mummy, No. 427, 1963	250
Mummy, No. 427/452, Frightening Lightning, 1969	400
Mummy, No. 452, glow, 1969	100

Aurora (Continued)

	C10
Mummy, glow, 1972	65
Mummy's Chariot, No. 459, 1965	550
Munsters Family, No. 804, 1965	950
Napoleon Solo, No. 411, 1966	175
Neanderthal Man, No. 729, 1972	50
Nutty Nose-Nipper, No. 806, 1965	175
Odd Job, No. 415, 1966	375
Orion, No. 252, 1975	95
Pain Parlor, No. 635, 1971	125
Pan Am Space Clipper, No. 148, 2001: A Space Odyssey, 1968	150
Pendulum, The, No. 636, Monster Scenes, 1971	120
Penguin, No. 416, 1967	550
Phantom of the Opera, No. 428, 1963	275
Phantom of the Opera, No. 451, 1969	100
Phantom of the Opera, 1972	65
Phantom of the Opera, No. 428/451, Frightening Lightning, 1969	350
Porthos, No. K9, 1958	100
Pushmi-Pullyu, No. 814, Dr. Doolittle, 1968	100
Rat Patrol Diorama, No. 340, 1967	100
Red Knight, various issues	30
Robin, No. 193, Comic Scenes, 1974	75

Aurora Odd Job, No. 415, $375

Aurora Robin, No. 488, $100

Aurora (Continued)   **C10**

Robin, No. 488, 1966 100

Robot, No. 418, Lost in Space, 1968 700

Rodan, No. 657, Monsters of the Movies, 1975 325

Sabre Tooth Tiger, No. 722, 1972 90

Aurora (Continued)   **C10**

Scotch Lad, No. 419, 1957 40

Scotch Lassie, No. 420, 1957 40

Seaview, No. 707, 1966 250

Seaview, No. 253, 1975 100

Silver Knight, various issues 15

Aurora Rodan, No. 657, $325

Aurora (Continued)   **C10**

Spartacus, No. 405, 1965 180

Spider-Man, No. 477, 1966 325

Spider-Man, No. 182, Comic Scenes, 1974 100

Spiked Dinosaur, No. 742, 1972 90

Spindrift, No. 255, 1975 100

Steve Canyon, No. 404, 1966 125

Superboy, No. 478, 1965 300

Superboy, No. 186, Comic Scenes, 1974 95

Superman, No. 562, 1963 300

Superman, No. 185, Comic Scenes, 1974 65

Tar Pit, No. 735, 1971 100

Tarzan, No. 820, 1967 175

Tarzan, No. 181, Comic Scenes, 1974 24

Tonto, No. 809, 1967 135

Tonto, No. 183, Comic Scenes, 1974 20

Tyrannosaurus Rex, No. 746, 1974 400

U.F.O., No. 813, 1968 200

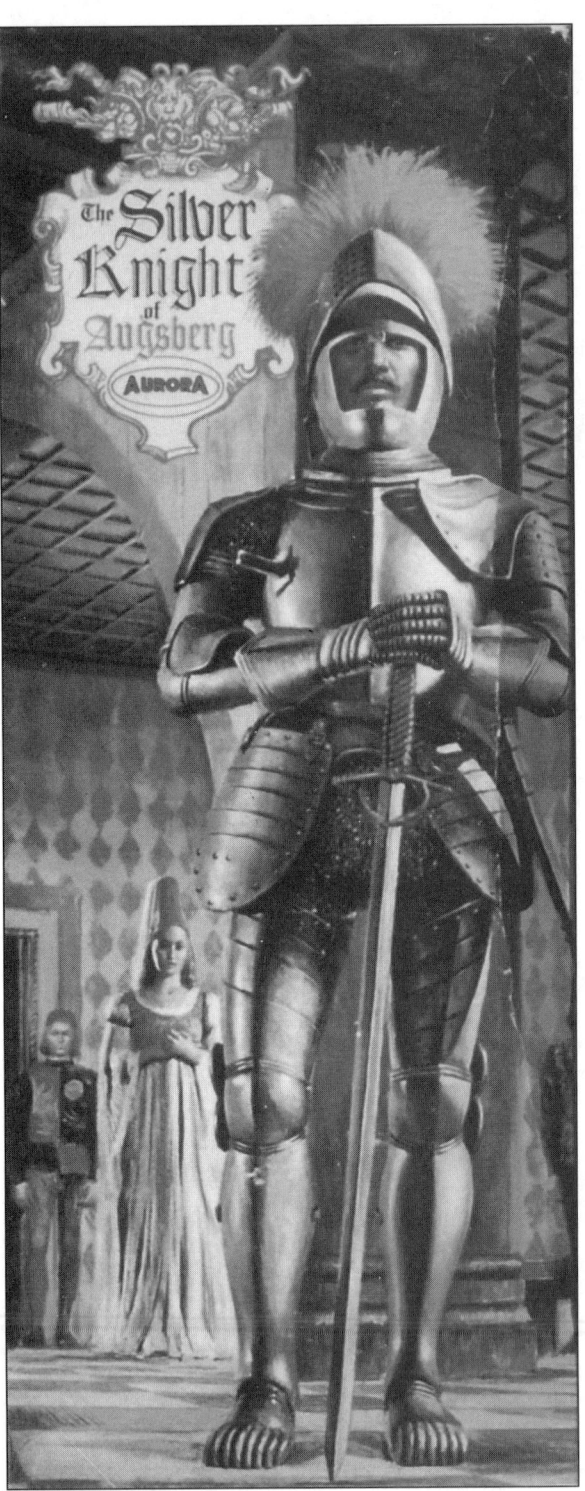

Aurora Silver Knight, $15

Aurora (Continued)   **C10**

U.S. Infantryman, 1956 75

U.S. Marine, No. 412, 1956 75

U.S. Marshall, No. 408, 1959 100

U.S. Sailor, No. 410, 1958 75

Aurora Spartacus, No. 405, $180

Aurora Steve Canyon, No. 404, $125

Aurora Superboy, No. 478, $300

Aurora (Continued) <u>C10</u>

Undertakers Dragster, No. 570 200

Vampire, No. 452, 1966 250

Vampirella, No. 638, Monster Scenes, 1971 175

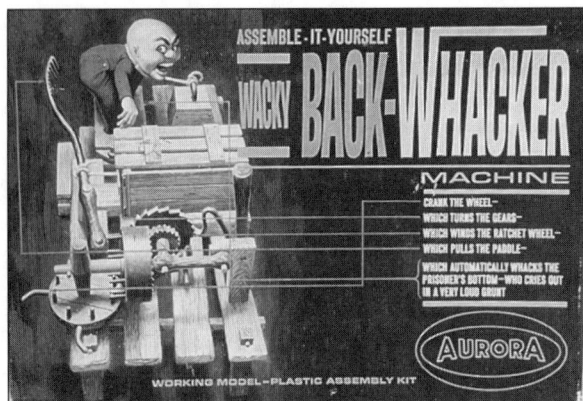

Aurora Wacky Back-Whacker, No. 807, $200

Aurora Witch, No. 470, $120

Aurora (Continued) <u>C10</u>

Viking, No. K6, 1959 120

Voyager, No. 831, Fantastic Voyage, 1969 500

Wacky Back-Whacker, No. 807, 1965 200

Willie Mays, No. 860, 1965 200

Witch, No. 470, glow, 1969/1972 120

Witch, No. 483, 1965 350

Wolfman, No. 425, 1962 300

Wolfman, No. 425/450, Frightening Lightning,
    1969 400

Wolfman, No. 450, glow, 1969 100

Wolfman, glow, 1972 65

Wolfman, No. 652, Monster of the Movies, 1975 ... 175

Wolfman's Wagon, No. 458, 1965 550

Aurora Wonder Woman, No. 479, $550

Aurora (Continued)   **C10**

Wonder Woman, No. 479, 1965 550

Zorro, No. 801, 1965 200

Hawk Daddy the Swingin Suburbanite, No. 532, $65

Hawk Drag Hag, No. 536, $65

Hawk Endsville Eddie, No. 537, $65

Hawk   **C10**

Beach Bunny Catchin' Rays, No. 542, 1964 65

Daddy the Swingin Suburbanite, No. 532, 1963 65

Davey the Psycho Cyclist, No. 531, 1963 65

Digger the Way Out Dragster, No. 530, 1963 65

Drag Hag, No. 536, 1963 65

Endsville Eddie, No. 537, 1963 65

Francis the Foul, No. 535, 1963 30

Frantic Banana Punishing Skins, No. 548, 1965 75

Frantic Cats, No. 549, 1965 75

Freddie Flameout, No. 533, 1963 75

Hot Dogger Hangin Ten, No. 164, glow, 1970 45

Hot Dogger Hangin Ten, No. 541, 1964 75

Huey's Hut Rod, No. 163, glow, 1969 45

Huey's Hut Rod, No. 538, 1963 75

Killer McBash, No. 539, 1963 75

Leaky Boat Louie, No. 534, 1963 75

Hawk Steel Pluckers Havin' a Bash, No. 547, $75

Hawk (Continued)

	C10
Riding Tandem, No. 544, 1965	75
Sling Rave Curvette, No. 637, 1964	25
Steel Pluckers Havin' a Bash, No. 547, 1965	75
Totally Fab, No. 550, 1965	75
Wade A. Minit, No. 636, 1964	75
Weirdsville Customizing Kit, No. 301, 1964	300
Woodie on a Surfari, No. 165, 1970	40
Woodie on a Surfari, No. 540, 1964	75

Lindberg

Founded in 1933, Lindberg is one of the oldest model kit companies in the United States, although they are best known for a series of kits made in the 1906s—Lindy Looneys. These were creepy hot rod models made to cash in on the 1960s weird character craze.

	C10
Big Wheeler, No. 277, 1965	100
Blurp, No. 280, 1964	45
Creeping Crusher, No. 273, 1965	100
Glob, No. 281, 1964	45
Green Ghoul, No. 274, 1965	100
Krimson Terror, No. 272, 1965	150
Mad Maestro, No. 284, 1965	175
Mad Mangler, No. 275, 1965	100
Road Hog, No. 276, 1965	100
Satan's Crate, No. 279, 1965	250
Scuttle Bucket, No. 278, 1965	100
Voop, No. 283, 1964	45
Zopp, No. 282, 1964	45

Monogram

Monogram's first models were balsa wood ships from 1945, and nine years later the company produced their first plastic kits. As modelers know, they expanded their line to include vehicles and figures in the subsequent years.

When Aurora ceased production, Monogram acquired their molds, and they reissued a number of Aurora's kits.

Revell and Monogram—two of the largest manufacturers of plastic model kits—merged in 1986. Revell-Monogram continues

	C10
Dracula, No. 6008, reissue of Aurora kt, 1983	25
Flip Out, No. 105, Fred Flypogger, 1965	200
Frankenstein, No. 6007, Aurora reissue	25
Godzilla, No. 6300, Aurora reissue, 1978	40
Mummy, No. 6010, Aurora reissue, 1983	25
Speed Shift, No. 106, Fred Flypogger, 1965	200
Super Fuzz, No. 104, Fred Flypogger, 1965	200
Superman, No. 6301, Aurora reissue, 1978	15
Wolfman, No. 6009, Aurora reissue, 1983	25

MPC

MPC produced some of the best non-Aurora kits during the 1960s. Like many kit manufacturers, MPC started with vehicles and later moved into figures. Their early figure kits include Stroker McGurk and Hot Curl. Cashing in on the popularity of the sixties TV show Dark Shadows, MPC released two model kits based on characters from the show, Barnabas and the Werewolf.

MPC continued to produce kits into the 1970s, including Star Wars and Alien kits.

	C10
Alien, No. 1961, movie, 1979	95
Barnabas Collins, No. 1550, Dark Shadows, 1969	250
Barnabas Vampire Van, No. 1626, Dark Shadows, 1969	195
Batman, No. 1702, Aurora reissue, 1984	20
C3PO, No. 1913, Star Wars, 1978-1980	15
C3PO, No. 1935, Star Wars, 1983	10
Condemned to Chains, No. 5003, Disney Pirates of Caribbean, 1973	100
Curl's Gurl, No. 103, 1965	75
Curl's Gurl with Hot Shot, No. 103, 1965	75
Darth Vader, No. 1916, 1978/1980	20
Dead Man's Raft, No. 5005, Pirates of Caribbean, 1973	125
Dead Men Tell No Tales, No. 5001, Disney Pirates of Caribbean, 1973	100
Escape from the Crypt, No. 5053, Disney Haunted Mansion, 1974	100
Fate of the Mutineer, No. 5004, Disney Pirates of Caribbean, 1974	100
Freed in the Nick of Time, No. 5007, Pirates of Caribbean, 1973	100
Ghost of America with Stroker McGurk, No. 104, 1964	110
Ghost of the Treasure, No. 5006, Pirates of Caribbean, 1973	80
Grave Robbers Reward, No. 5050, Disney Huanted Mansion, 1974	100
Hoist High the Jolly Roger, No. 5002, Pirates of Caribbean, 1973	100
Hot Curl, No. 101, 1965	75
Hot Shot with Hot Dog, No. 103, 1965	75
Incredible Hulk, No. 1932, 1979	20

MPC (Continued)

	C10
Play It Again Sam, No. 5052, Disney Haunted Mansion, 1974	125
R2-D2, No. 1912, Star Wars, 1978-1980	20
R2-D2, No. 1934, Star Wars, 1983	10
Raiders Coach, No. 0622, Paul Revere & Raiders, 1969	225
Spider-Man, No. 1931, 1978	20
Stroker McGurk and Surf Rod, No. 100, 1964	65
Superman, No. 1701, Aurora reissue, 1985	20
Tall T with Stroker McGurk, No. 102, 1964	65
Vampire Midnight Madness, No. 5051, Disney Haunted Mansion, 1974	100
Werewolf, No. 1552, Dark Shadows, 1969	250
Yellow Submarine, No. 617, Beatles, 1968	275

Multiple

Multiple Products, Inc., a division of Loral Corporation, was known for their toys—the Fireball XL-5 Space City and Daniel Boone toys to name a few. The few kits they did produce were of exceptional quality.

Their original figure kit series was the Crazy Invention line. It included such kits as A Simple Way to Feed a Baby and A Painless Tooth Extractor, they were based on ideas created by comic-strip great Rube Goldberg.

Other Multiple series included Ripley Believe it or Not and World's Greatest Stage Illusions.

	C10
Automatic Baby Feeder, No. 955, 1965	50
Back Scrubber and Hat Remover, No. 958, 1965	50
Disappearing Lady, No. 1257, 1966	100
Floating on Air, No. 1256, 1966	100
Iron Maiden, No. 981, 1966	200
Painless Tooth Extractor, No. 956, 1965	50
Saw the Lady in Half, No. 1258, 1966	100
Signal for Shipwrecked Sailor, No. 957, 1965	50
Torture Chair, No. 980, 1966	200
Torture Wheel, No. 979, 1966	200

Pyro

Beginning in the early Fifties, Pyro produced both vehicle and figure kits. Some of their best-known figure kits include Ghost Rider, Li'L Corporal, Surf's Up and Wyatt Earp.

Pyro Rawhide, No. 276, $60

Pyro Restless Gun, No. 277, $60

Pyro Wyatt Earp, No. 278, $60

Pyro's molds were acquired by Life-Like in the 1970s, and Lindberg reissued many of Pyro's molds in the early 1980s.

Pyro   C10

Curler, The, No. 177, 1970	50
Der Baron, No. 166, 1970	50
Ghost Rider, No. 167, 1970	50
Gladiator, The, No. 175, 1970	50
Lil Corporal, No. 168, 1970	50
Rawhide, No. 276, 1958	60
Restless Gun, No. 277, 1958	60
Surf's Up, No. 176, 1970	40
Wyatt Earp, No. 278, 1958	60

Remco

Remco produced Flintstone kits while the TV show was at the height of popularity. Easily classified as half-toy half-model, these kits were comprised of numerous gears and mechanical parts.

	C10
Flintstones Paddy Wagon, No. 452, 1961	175
Flintstones Sports Car, No. 450, 1961	175
Flintstones Yacht, No. 451, 1961	175

Revell

Revell has been involved in the production of model kits since the Forties, and behind Aurora, Revell is probably the most-recognized name in the model kit industry.

Revell was noticed when they introduced an all-plastic model of the 1910 Maxwell, the car driven by comedian Jack Benny. During the 1960s Revell ven-

Revell Brother Rat Fink, No. 1304, $75

Revell Norval the Bashful Blinket, No. 2003, $300

tured into he area of figure kits with models of The Beatles and the now-famous Ed "Big Daddy" Roth Rat Fink series.

Revell merged with Monogram in 1986.

Many of the Rat Fink kits were reissued by Revell from 1993-1995, depressing the values of the original issues.

Revell   C10

Angel Fink, No. 1307, 1965	150
Beatnik Bandit, No. 1279, Ed Roth, 1963	100
Birthday Bird, No. 2051, Dr. Seuss, 1960	300
Bonanza, No. 1931, 1966	175
Brother Rat Fink, No. 1304, 1964	75
Busby the Afghan Yak, No. 2006, Dr. Seuss, 1959.	300
Cat in the Hat, No. 2000, Dr. Seuss, 1958	300
Cat in the Hat with Thing 1 & 2, No. 2050, Dr. Seuss, 1960	300
Dragnut, No. 1303, Ed Roth, 1963	95
Fink Eliminator, No. 1310, Ed Roth, 1965	200
Flash Gordon and Martian, No. 1450, 1965	120
Flipper and Sandy, No. 1930, 1965	90
Game of the Yertle, No. 2100, Dr. Seuss, 1960	250
George Harrison, No. 1353, 1964	200

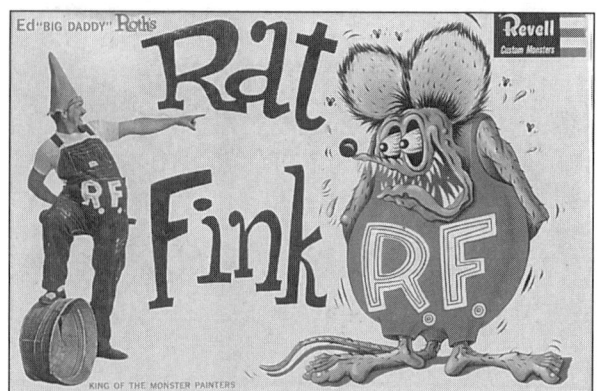

Revell Rat Fink, No. 1305, $40

Revell (Continued)   C10

Gowdy the Dowdy Grackle, No. 2002, Dr. Seuss, 1958	300
Grickily the Gractus, No. 2005, Dr. Seuss, 1959	300
Grickily, Busby and Rosco, No. 2081, Dr. Seuss, 1960	450
Horton the Elephant, No. 2052, Dr. Seuss, 1960	300
John Lennon, No. 1352, 1964	200
Mother's Worry, No. 1302, Ed Roth, 1963	100
Mr. Gasser, No. 1301, Ed Roth, 1963	100
Norval the Bashful Blinket, No. 2003, Dr. Seuss, 1959	300
Outlaw, Ed Roth	100
Paul McCartney, No. 1350, 1964	175
Phantom and Witch Doctor, No. 1451, 1965	120
Rat Fink, No. 1305, 1963	40
Ringo Starr, No. 1351, 1964	200
Robin Hood Fink, No. 1270, Ed Roth, 1965	300
Roscoe the Many Footed Lion, No. 2004, Dr. Seuss, 1959	300
Scuz Fink, No. 1308, 1964	300
Superfink, No. 1308, 1964	300
Surfink, No. 1306, 1965	100
Tingo the Noodle Topped Stroodle, No. 2001, Dr. Seuss, 1958	300
Tingo, Gowdy, and Norval, No. 2080, Dr. Seuss, 1960	450
Tweedy Pie with Boss Fink, No. 1271, Ed Roth, 1965	300

FISHER-PRICE

On October 1, 1930, in East Aurora, New York, the Fisher-Price Toy Company began operation. Located on a small side street of a small town, it would eventually be considered one of the major manufacturers of toys.

Herman Fisher and Irving Price shared their names to develop a name for their new company. Herman Fisher, a past employee of the FairChild Company (a manufacturer of games), and Irving Price, who had sound experience with the Woolworth Company, formed the guidelines by which they would run their new company.

The first manufacturing facility was located on Church Street in East Aurora. It would be considered small for any type of manufacturing today, but it served as the only facility for Fisher-Price toys for the company's first twenty years. It still exists, but was sold by Fisher-Price in the 1970s due to lack of use.

The most important factor in constructing this new company was to create a work force that could contribute their efforts towards a smooth, profitable venture. Among the most important employees were Helen M. Schelle and Margaret Evans Price.

Helen M. Schelle was the first secretary and treasurer of Fisher-Price toys. She developed her skills in the retail management field in the Walker Toy Shop in Binghamton, New York. Given the opportunity to manage the company's early activities, Schelle proved to be a great asset to the advancement of Fisher-Price toys.

Margaret Evans Price was the company's first artist and designer for their new line of toys. She developed her skills as a writer and illustrator for Rand McNally and Harper & Brothers, and as a creator of children's art for Strecher Lithography Company of Rochester, New York. Much of Price's artwork can still be found on early postcards, Valentines and children's books. These early paper collectibles are most often marked "M.E.P." Price created the early artwork for the reproduction of color lithography for the toys. She was also talented in drawing, produced designs for early toys, and contributed to the development of her concepts for Fisher-Price's early line of toys.

The Roycroft Printers contributed their skills to produce the sales catalogs that prospective retailers would use to choose the toys that they would market.

The company began to build a labor force to construct the new toy line, to be sold to the public in 1931. The initial work force was approximately 25 employees. Typical of any small town, most employees were neighbors, friends and relatives who took great pride in the product that they made, since many of the operations were done by hand. Many of the early operations—band sawing, drilling, nailing, and painting—were shared by these early employees.

As Fisher-Price began toy making, numbers were assigned to each toy. This number system started at Number 5 and went up into the thousands. To add to the confusion for collectors today, many of the numbers have been used more than once on various toys.

Because pine was abundant and easy to work with, it was the main wood used in construction of Fisher-Price toys. During the 1930s another material was used—heavy cardboard with inserted brass eyelets used prevent wear from spinning axles.

Creating action from child power was of great importance. The use of bellows was common to produce sound and, as time passed, the introduction of bells was added to create sound and action.

Because of the immense amount of time required to assemble various toys, cottage-type industries were set up by employees, families and residents of East Aurora. Toys such as the Pop-up Kritter were completely hand assembled in area homes. This would prove to be a quick and efficient method of assembly.

As the demand for Fisher-Price toys rose, the company began to use the skills of freelance designer Edward Savage. A mechanical engineer from the University of Minnesota, Savage created some of Fisher-Price's most successful toys. In his home in Rochester, New York, Savage created such toys as the Pop-Up Kritters, Snoopy Sniffer—one of the most popular toys he created—and many of the wind-up toys.

After almost two decades of growth in the 1930s and 1940s, Fisher-Price faced the challenge of limited production. When the United States entered World War II, Fisher-Price, like many companies, turned to a different type of manufacturing. Fisher-Price was set up to create and produce wood products, and this dictated which essential goods they produced for the war. Ship fenders, first-aid kits, cots, bomb crates, and glider ailerons were among the items produced from 1943-1946.

The toys from this period were made from scraps of wood, with bells and some metal parts painted instead of plated. Parts from similar toys were used, this resulted in odd and sometimes unusual variations.

As World War II came to an end, normal production began to resume. Well into the 1950s, Ponderosa pine, with its proven durability, was the main source of material in Fisher-Price toys. As wood became more difficult to obtain, the experimentation with plastics began. The first toy to use this new material successfully was the Busy Bee. Because of the ease of molding, durability and bright colors, plastic was more prevalent in toys of the 1950s.

In 1951, Fisher-Price moved to its new manufacturing facility on Girard Avenue in East Aurora. This facility handled most operations for most of the 1950s. In 1957, Tri Mold, a plastics manufacturer of Kenmore, New York, became a subsidiary and main molding facility of Fisher-Price. As the demand for plastics grew, a new molding facility was built in Holland, New York, in July 1962. The Holland Plant produced many of the plastic parts used in the construction of a more plastic-dominated toy line, and as the 1960s advanced, plastic eventually took over as the main material used to produce toys.

In 1966, Herman Fisher had resigned as president of the company; although, he was chairman of the board until the Quaker Oats acquired Fisher-Price three years later. Quaker expanded the company by building a new plant in Medina, New York and numerous other plants and facilities were created both nationally and internationally.

Considered one of the oldest and largest manufacturers of toys, Fisher-Price still has its main offices at the Girard Avenue address in East Aurora, New York.

ToyTown USA has created a large following with their limited edition (under 5,000) toys manufactured for the Toyfest celebration held in East Aurora each year. This event attracts collectors of toys from all over North America and Europe. The toys manufactured for this event are as follows:

#6550 Buzzy Bee, 1987
#6558 Little Snoopy, 1988
#6575 Toot Toot Engine, 1989
#6590 Prancing Horses, 1990
#6592 Teddy Bear Parade, 1991
#6599 Molly Bell, 1992
#6145 Jingle Elephant, 1993
#6464 Gran'pa Frog, 1994
#76593 Squeeky the Clown, 1995
#76594 Woodsy-Wee Zoo, 1996
#76880 Raggedy Ann and Andy, 1997, also made in 200 numbered special limited edition
#980750 Space Blazer, 1998, also made in 200 numbered special limited edition
#990705 Popeye Cowboy, 1999, also made in 200 numbered special limited edition

The second year toy has sold for well over $500 MIB, and others are moving upwards in value because of the limited availability.

The Fisher-Price Collectors Club is a great opportunity for fellow collectors to advance their knowledge, buy, sell and communicate with other collectors. Collectors are encouraged to join the club, as information on new and old Fisher-Price toys is plentiful in the newsletter. For information, contact the Fisher-Price Collector's Club, Attn: Jeanne Kennedy, 1442 North Ogden, Meza, AZ 85205.

Many factors may contribute to the value of a Fisher-Price toy. The most important factor to consider is the paper lithography. Most Fisher-Price toys found have edge wear. Most toys found with edge wear may also be called normal-wear toys. Toys in this condition often fall in a value class of Good/Very Good. When determining condition of a toy, other areas of importance to the lithography would include the amount of soil on the artwork and the extent to which it has faded and/or lost its color. These areas may be considered less important, unless there is more than slight soiling or discoloration. When a Fisher-Price toy has advanced wear, soiling or missing lithography, the toy is considered to be in Poor condition.

Paint is also important when determining a toy's value. Toys with slight paint wear on wheels, bases and handles fall into the Good/Very Good condition category. Any parts missing—especially lithography parts—also affects the value of the toy. Once the lithography is gone, there is no means of replacement. Missing wheels and axles also lessen the value of a toy.

A toy that is in Mint condition has absolutely no wear or damage. Lithography, paint, wheels, etc. are complete. Boxes—depending on its condition, of course—for older Fisher-Price toys may add up to twenty percent to the value of a Mint toy. Because of their age and scarcity, boxes from the 1930s are of the highest value.

Comic character toys and toys displaying other companies' names demand higher prices. Just because a toy features Disney characters, Popeye or other comic figures does not necessarily mean that it is a rare toy. Rarity is based on the amount of toys produced over a given period of time and the amount still in existence.

Toys that had accessories or figures that were often misplaced will also bring higher values. Often these accessories and/or figures are difficult to locate separately from the toy itself. If a toy is found mint in the box with accessories, it most certainly will demand a higher price. The Fisher-Price toy prices listed in this guide were established by averaging toy prices taken from toy shows, flea markets, dealers, and collectors.

Contributors: John J. Murray, Box 29, Eden, NY 14057. Murray, orginally from Buffalo, New York, presently lives in Eden, New York with his wife Mary and daughter Amanda. Currently employed at Fisher-Price, Murray is part of the Research and Devlopment Art Production Department where he is responsible for creating new color development and decoration for photo and TV models. Murray also serves as Chairman of the Board and CEO of the ToyTown USA Foundation which oversees the ToyTown USA Museum and ToyFest, the largest toy gathering in the United States.

	C6	C8	C10
Allie Gator, No. 653	85	120	150
American Airlines Flagship, No. 170, w/original propellers	600	900	1200
Baby Chick Tandem Cart, No. 50	85	125	170
Barky Dog, No. 462	85	125	175
Big Bill Pelican, No. 794, w/cardboard fish-add $25	65	85	120
Big Performing Circus, No. 900, w/all accessories	375	500	700

	C6	C8	C10
Blackie Drummer, No. 785	500	600	1000
Boom-Boom Popeye, No. 491	450	800	1100
Bossy Bell, No. 656	40	60	80
Bouncing Bunny Cart, No. 307	45	60	90
Bouncy Racer, No. 8	40	60	80
Bucky Burro, No. 166	115	175	230
Buddy Bullfrog, No. 728	85	100	125
Bunny & Cart, No. 406	45	60	90
Bunny Basket Cart, No. 301	40	60	80
Bunny Basket Cart, No. 303	95	140	190

Boom-Boom Popeye, No. 491, $1100. Photo courtesy John Murray; photo by Ross MacKearnin

Circus Wagon, No. 156, $800. Photo courtesy John Murray; photo by Ross MacKearnin

Bucky Burro, No. 166, $230. Photo courtesy John Murray; photo by Ross MacKearnin

	C6	C8	C10
Bunny Bell Drummer, No. 508	85	125	160
Bunny Cart, No. 487	225	325	450
Bunny Cart, No. 10	95	135	180
Bunny Cart, No. 401	200	300	400
Bunny Egg Cart, No. 28	85	150	170
Butch the Pup, No. 333	85	125	170
Buzzy Bee, No. 325	15	25	35
Cackling Hen, No. 123, red	40	65	80
Cackling Hen, No. 120, white	40	65	80
Cement Mixer, No. 926	260	325	485
Chatter Monk, No. 798	85	125	160
Chick & Cart, No. 407	40	60	80
Chick Basket Cart, No. 302	40	60	80
Chug Chug, No. 168, w/two cars	30	45	60
Chuggy Pop-Up, No. 616	85	125	170
Circus Wagon, No. 156	425	600	800
Cookie Pig, No. 476	40	50	60
Dandy Dobbin, No. 765	200	275	400

	C6	C8	C10
Dashing Dobbin, No. 742	450	650	850
Dizzy Donkey, No. 433	75	115	155
Doc & Dopey Dwarfs, No. 770	750	1000	1500

Dandy Dobbin, No. 765, $400. Photo courtesy John Murray; photo by Ross MacKearnin

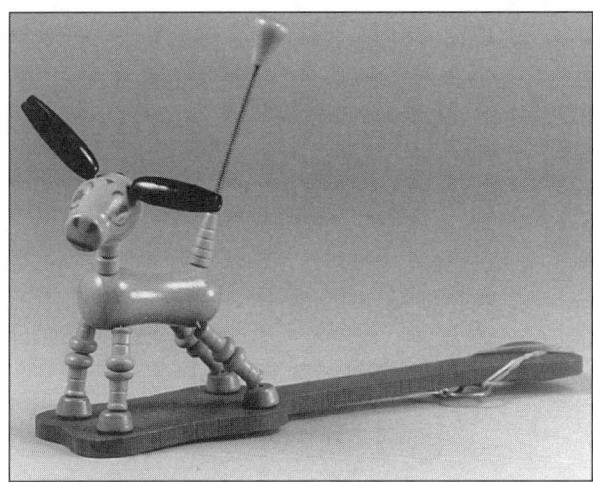

Dizzy Donkey, No. 433, $155. Photo courtesy John Murray; photo by Ross MacKearnin

Doc & Dopey Dwarfs, No. 770, $1500. Photo courtesy John Murray; photo by Ross MacKearnin

Donald Duck Xylophone, No. 177, $360. Photo courtesy John Murray; photo by Ross MacKearnin

Donald Duck Drum Major, No. 400, $270

	C6	C8	C10
Donald Choo-Choo, No. 450	185	275	370
Donald Duck & Nephews, No. 479, w/two nephews	400	500	600
Donald Duck Cart, No. 544	225	325	425
Donald Duck Drum Major, No. 400	135	200	270
Donald Duck Drummer, No. 454	225	325	450
Donald Duck Xylophone, No. 177	180	270	360
Donald Duck Xylophone, No. 185	400	600	800
Dr. Doodle, No. 132	170	255	340
Dr. Doodle, No. 477	225	350	450
Ducky Cart, No. 11	85	125	170
Ducky Cart, No. 16	85	125	170
Dumbo Circus Racer, No. 738, original arms	800	1100	1600

	C6	C8	C10
Elsie's Dairy Truck, No. 745, w/two milk bottles, add $50 for each bottle	475	600	800
Ferdinand the Bull, No. 434	600	900	1200

Ferdinand the Bull, No. 434, $1200. Photo courtesy John Murray; photo by Ross MacKearnin

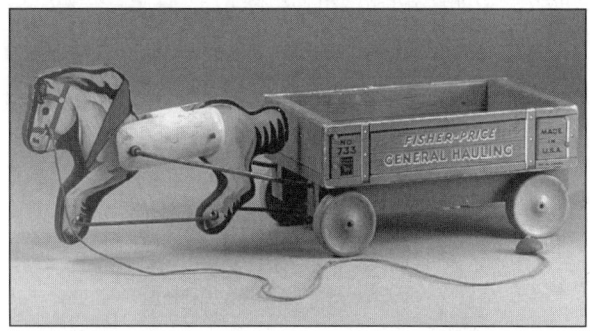

Fisher-Price General Hauling, No. 733, $330. Photo courtesy John Murray; photo by Ross MacKearnin

	C6	C8	C10
Fido Zilo, No. 707	85	110	150
Fisher-Price General Hauling, No. 733	225	250	330
Fuzzy Fido, No. 444	225	325	450
Gabby Goofies, No. 775	40	60	80
Gabby Goofies, No. 776	40	60	80
Gold Star Stage Coach, No. 175, w/baggage	190	285	375
Golden Gulch Express, No. 191	85	125	170
Go'n Back Mule, No. 350, w/original ears	700	1100	1400
Goofy Gertie, No. 440	300	425	575
Happy Helicopter, No. 498	225	285	375

Fuzzy Fido, No. 444, $450. Photo courtesy John Murray; photo by Ross MacKearnin

Gold Star Stage Coach, No. 175, $375. Photo courtesy John Murray; photo by Ross MacKearnin

Hot Dog Wagon, No. 750, $800. Photo courtesy John Murray; photo by Ross MacKearnin

	C6	C8	C10
Happy Hippo, No. 151	85	150	170
Hot Dog Wagon, No. 750	400	600	800
Hot Dog Wagon, No. 445	225	300	400
Huffy Puffy Train, No. 999, w/four cars	110	150	225

	C6	C8	C10
Humpty-Dumpty, No. 755	160	240	325
Jingle Giraffe, No. 472	225	300	375
Jolly Jumper, No. 450	85	125	170
Juggling Jumbo, No. 735	225	300	400
Jumbo Rollo, No. 755	225	300	400
Katy Kackler, No. 140	120	180	240
Kitty Bell, No. 499	65	90	120
Kriss Kricket, No. 678	100	150	200

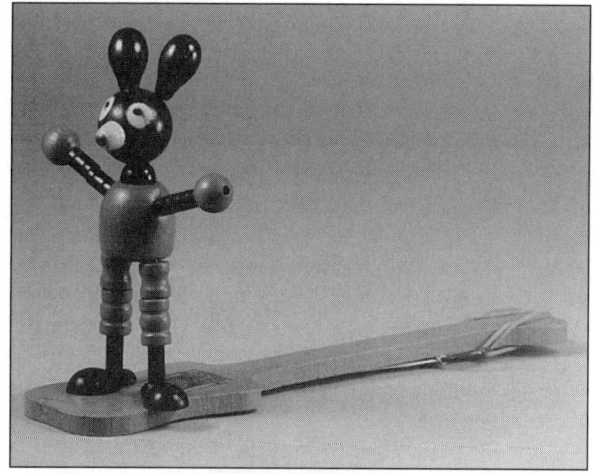

Lop-Ear Looie, No. 415, $450. Photo courtesy John Murray; photo by Ross MacKearnin

Katy Kackler, No. 140, $240. Photo courtesy John Murray; photo by Ross MacKearnin

Mickey Mouse Choo-Choo, No. 432, $1300. Photo courtesy John Murray; photo by Ross MacKearnin

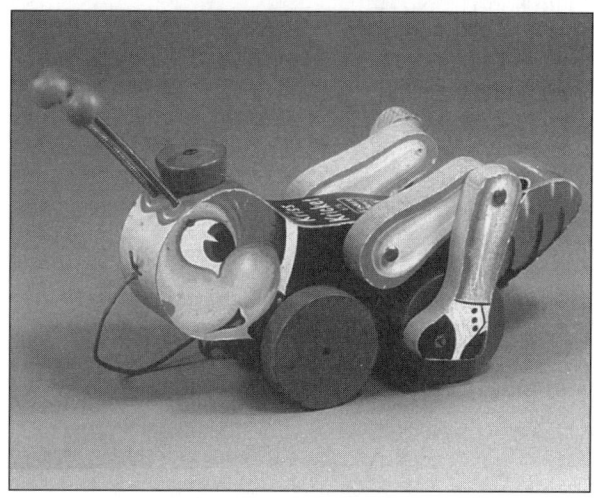

Kriss Kricket, No. 678, $200. Photo courtesy John Murray; photo by Ross MacKearnin

	C6	C8	C10
Lady Bug, No. 658	45	60	80
Leo the Drummer, No. 480	225	280	375
Looky Chug-Chug, No. 220	95	125	170
Looky Chug-Chug, No. 161, w/tender	90	135	180
Looky Fire Truck, No. 7	85	125	170
Looky Push Car, No. 875, w/steering wheel push stick	95	125	165
Lop-Ear Looie, No. 415	225	335	450
Merry Mousewife, No. 662	40	60	80
Merry Mutt, No. 473	85	125	150
Mickey Mouse Choo-Choo, No. 485	95	140	175
Mickey Mouse Choo-Choo, No. 432, early version	650	975	1300

Mickey Mouse Safety Patrol, No. 733, $500. Photo courtesy Kent M. Comstock

Nifty Station Wagon, No. 234, $650. Photo courtesy John Murray; photo by Ross MacKearnin

Nosey Pup, No. 445, $145. Photo courtesy John Murray; photo by Ross MacKearnin

	C6	C8	C10
Mickey Mouse Drummer, No. 476	275	350	475
Mickey Mouse Puddle Jumper, No. 310	90	150	190
Mickey Mouse Safety Patrol, No. 733..	250	375	500
Mickey Mouse Xylophone, No. 798 ...	300	600	975
Molly Moo-Moo, No. 190..................	225	275	350
Moo-oo Cow, No. 155..........................	85	105	140
Mother Goose, No. 164	65	95	135
Musical Duck, No. 795	85	125	165
Musical Elephant, No. 145, w/original ears....................................	250	375	500
Musical Sweeper, No. 230	85	125	170
Musical Sweeper, No. 100	160	225	240
Musical Sweeper, No. 225	85	125	185
Nifty Station Wagon, No. 234, w/roof and four figures.................................	350	450	650

	C6	C8	C10
Nosey Pup, No. 445...............................	75	120	145
Perky Pot, No. 686.................................	85	110	140
Peter Bunny Cart, No. 472	250	325	400
Peter Bunny Engine, No. 721	225	325	450
Pinky Pig, No. 695.................................	85	110	140
Pinocchio Express, No. 720..................	650	850	1150
Playful Puppy, No. 625	45	55	65
Playful Puppy, No. 626	45	55	65
Playland Express, No. 192.....................	85	125	170
Plucky Pinocchio, No. 494	450	600	800
Pluto Pop-Up, No. 440	90	135	185
Pluto the Pup, No. 210..........................	400	525	625
Pony Chime, No. 137	40	60	80
Pony Chime, No. 138	30	40	50
Pony Chime, No. 758	165	250	335
Poodle Zilo, No. 739	85	120	180
Popeye Spinach Eater, No. 488	650	950	1200
Popeye the Sailor, No. 703	800	1200	1600
Pudgy Pig, No. 478................................	40	60	80
Puffy Engine, No. 444	45	70	95
Quacky Family, No. 799	65	90	120
Queen Buzzy Bee, No. 314	40	65	85
Racing Rowboat, No. 730	225	260	300
Riding Horse, No. 237, w/original tail..	600	900	1200

Queen Buzzy Bee, No. 314, $85. Photo courtesy John Murray; photo by Ross MacKearnin

Squeaky the Clown, No. 777, $325. Photo courtesy John Murray; photo by Ross MacKearnin

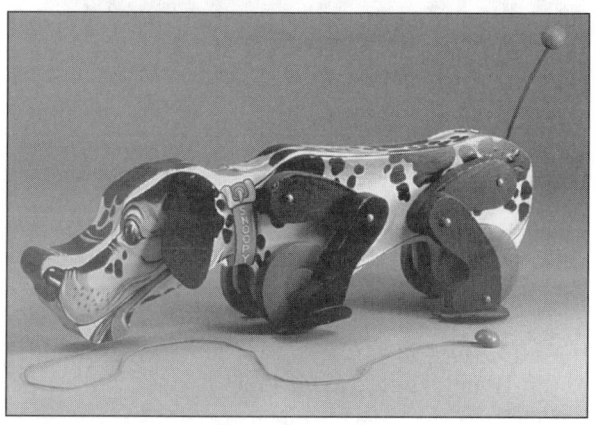

Snoopy Sniffer, No. 180, $140. Photo courtesy John Murray; photo by Ross MacKearnin

	C6	C8	C10
Roller Chimes, No. 123, w/push stick...	85	120	155
Safety School Bus, No. 984, w/all figures	225	350	550
Safety School Bus, No. 983, w/all figures	500	750	1000
Shaggy Zilo, No. 738	85	120	180
Sleep Sue, No. 495	45	55	70
Smokie Engine, No. 642	40	60	75
Snoopy Sniffer, No. 180........................	70	105	140
Snorky Fire Engine, No. 168, w/all figures	85	125	170
Snorky Fire Engine, No. 169, w/all figures	85	125	170

Super-Jet, No. 415, $220. Photo courtesy John Murray; photo by Ross MacKearnin

	C6	C8	C10
Space Blazer, No. 750	265	400	530
Sports Car, No. 674	85	125	150
Squeaky the Clown, No. 777	160	250	325
Stoopy Storky, No. 410, w/original cardboard feet....................................	275	375	550
Streamliner Express, No. 215	900	1300	1800
Super-Jet, No. 415	110	165	220
Suzie Seal, No. 621, ball	40	50	60
Suzie Seal, No. 623, umbrella	40	50	60
Tailspin Tabby, No. 455	85	125	170
Tailspin Tabby, No. 610.......................	70	105	140

Talking Donald Duck, No. 76, $140. Photo courtesy John Murray; photo by Ross MacKearnin

	C6	C8	C10
Tailspin Tabby, No. 400, original pull loops	90	135	180
Tailspin Tabby Pop-Up, No. 600	225	275	325
Talking Donald Duck, No. 76	70	105	140
Talky Parrot, No. 698	95	140	165
Tawny Tiger, No. 654	85	100	125
Teddy Bear Parade, No. 195	600	900	1200
Teddy Bear Zilo, No. 777	85	125	160
Teddy Tooter, No. 712	225	250	300
Teddy Xylophone, No. 752	160	240	320
Thumper Bunny, No. 533	425	575	800
Timber Toter, No. 810	85	110	150
Timmy Turtle, No. 150	85	135	180
Tiny Teddy, No. 635	30	45	65
Tiny Teddy, No. 636	60	90	120

Teddy Bear Zilo, No. 777, $160. Photo courtesy John Murray; photo by Ross MacKearnin

	C6	C8	C10
Tiny Teddy, No. 634	40	65	85
Toy Wagon, No. 131	225	325	450
Tuggy Turtle, No. 139	85	125	160
Uncle Timmy Turtle, No. 125, w/glasses	85	120	150
Walking Duck Cart, No. 305	45	60	90
Walt Disney's Elmer the Elephant, No. 211	400	525	625
Whistling Engine, No. 617	95	140	175
Wiggily Woofer, No. 640	85	120	145
Winky Blinky Fire Truck, No. 200	85	120	150

GUNS

(See also Premiums, Comic Characters)

It can be argued that guns have changed and shaped the course of history in the United States. Throughout every conflict, beginning with the Revolutionary War, guns played a major role in the outcome of battles, both here and abroad. Important in a historical context, guns are a vital and important category of toy collecting. When toys began to be mass-produced after the Civil War, toy guns were among the first to appear on the market. Their success was instantaneous, and toy guns remained among the most popular selling toys through the 1960s.

Although toy guns were patented in the 1850s, they were not manufactured in any quantity until a decade later due to the wartime shortages. These early toy guns were, for the most part, pea shooters and cork poppers and were usually made of wood with metal hardware, although iron and lead types may occasionally be found among them. These early examples are hard to find today and most are known only through their patent drawings. By 1870, inventors, trying to add realism to these toy guns, began using paper caps. This invention had been developed just prior to the Civil War and was known as the Maynard Tape Primer. The tape primer was originally intended to detonate muzzle-loading arms and closely resembled a roll of modern paper caps. For the first time, toy guns could make a loud noise, yet still be relatively safe and harmless. Naturally this spurred the demand for these new toys and designers worked overtime to create new and appealing guns. Their output was prolific, and today the period from 1870 to 1900 is regarded as the "golden age" of the toy gun—especially the toy cap pistol.

By 1880 the cast-iron cap pistol had become the most popular type of toy gun by far, and the various toy makers—primarily J. & E. Stevens and Ives—were competing among themselves to see who could produce the most unique and appealing designs. A glance at any collection of these early toy pistols will show that realism was secondary to artistic imagination. Many pistols from this period were covered with ornamentation and, in some cases, any resemblance

to a real gun was purely coincidental. Leaf-and-scroll designs were the most popular, but pistols can also be found with numerous other designs, including two- and three-dimensional figures, and animated figures. Guns with moving figures, though not as rare as some, are worth much more to a collector than an ordinary-looking pistol from the same period.

Another very desirable pistol from the same era is known as the head pistol. It featured a head, either animal or human, placed at the breech end of the barrel with the mouth open to receive the cap. Over two-dozen varieties of head and animated pistols are known to exist, but are so much in demand that they are seldom offered for sale.

The most popular material used to make these early toy pistols was cast iron, which continued to be used heavily into the twentieth century, until the demands of World War II cut off the supply. Many varieties of old toy guns were, however, made from such diverse materials as paper, wood, steel, tin, lead, rubber, zinc, glass and even wax. During World War II toy guns were even made of molded sawdust mixed with glue. After the war, a few cast-iron pistols were produced and assembled, using both new and old parts, but the cost proved to be prohibitive, and makers soon turned to less expensive metals such as steel and die-cast zinc. By 1950 most toy pistols were being made of die-cast material and plastic, both of which continue to be used today.

From almost the very beginning, toy gun makers have felt the need to personalize their products; hundreds of different names can be found embossed on these little guns. Some examples that come to mind are Excelsior, Victor, American Bulldog, Acorn, Sun, Boom, Darb, Ace, Daisy, Cowboy King, Polo, Triumph and Terror. Many names were used only once on one particular gun and then dropped, while others have reappeared time and again on different models over the years. This custom of naming toy guns still goes on today; a visit to any toy store will turn up names such as Cowhand, Top Gun Jr. and 007. Many of these names seem to reflect current events or personalities, but the meanings of others have become obscure.

Collectors of toy guns can choose from a large array of models and styles, and because of the tremendous historical popularity of these toys, collectors have the opportunity to acquire interesting and unusual examples at an affordable price. Guns from as far back as the 1920s and 1930s can still be found at flea markets, garage sales and second-hand stores, often at a price that is only a fraction of what other toys from these same years will sell for.

Contributor: Charles W. Best, 11523 Pine Valley Dr., Franktown, CO 80116. Best is a leading authority on toy weapons and has been collecting them in earnest since 1966. His collection is regarded as one of the finest and most comprehensive in existence and has won many awards at various gun shows. In addition to writing a number of articles on the subject in such magazines as *Gun Report* and *Antique Toy World,* he is also the author of *Cast-Iron Toy Pistols* and co-author, with Sam Logan, of *Cast-Iron Toy Guns and Capshooters,* both of which are now out of print.

Note: Measurements given, in general, are from one end of the gun to the other, rather than on a diagonal from grip to muzzle. Dates of manufacturers can vary within five years, though most of the later dates are considerably more accurate.

	C6	C8	C10
.45 Smoker, blows cap smoke, c. 1946	30	45	60
101 Ranch Pistol, 1930, 11-1/2"	150	200	250
1776-1876 Cap Pistol, produced for America's centennial, 1876, 5-1/4"	150	225	300
2 in 1 Cap Pistol, 9-1/4"	85	125	175
2 Monkeys Animated Cap Pistol, maker unknown, monkey hits head against coconut held by another monkey, 1882, 4-1/2"	600	850	1250
25 Jr. Cap Automatic, "Made in U.S.A., Patented," 1930, 4-1/8"	25	35	50

	C6	C8	C10
25-50 Cap Automatic, "Made in U.S.A.; Pat, Appld.," 1935, 4-1/2"	22	33	45
25-50 Cap Automatic, "Oil Moving Parts; Made in U.S.A., Patented," 1935, 4-1/2"	25	38	50
25-50 Cap Automatic, "Oil Moving Parts; Made in U.S.A., Patented," can be fired rapidly w/crank, hole near muzzle holds removable crank, 1935	65	90	135

25-50 Cap Automatic, 1935, Stevens, $45. Photo courtesy Charles W. Best

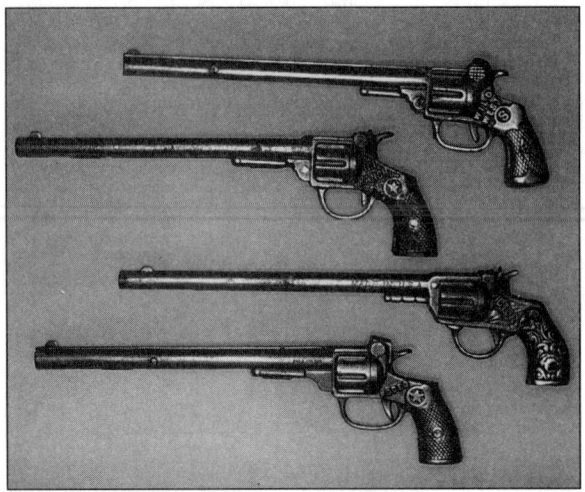

Top to Bottom: Wild West Cap Pistol, Kenton, 1926, $225; 101 Ranch Pistol, 1930, Hubley, $250; Victor Cap Pistol, Stevens, 1924, $250; Rodeo Cap Pistol, Hubley, 1924, $200. Photo courtesy Charles W. Best

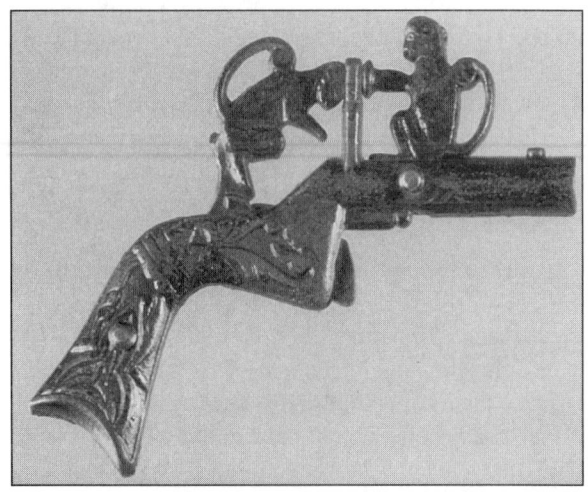

2 Monkeys Animated Cap Pistol, 1882, $1250. Photo courtesy Sotheby's, New York

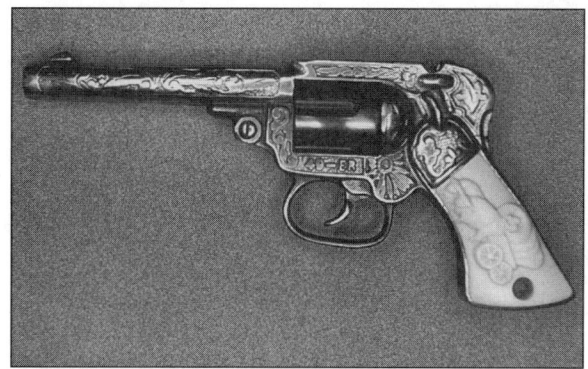

49-ER Cap Pistol, 1940, Stevens, $285. Photo courtesy Charles W. Best

6-Shot, 1932, Stevens, $80

6-Shot Cap Pistol, 1895, Stevens, $450. Photo courtesy Charles W. Best

	C6	C8	C10
25-50 Cap Automatic, "Pat. Appl'd. For, Made in U.S.A.," 1928, 4-1/2"....	30	45	60
25-50 Target Automatic, w/silencer-type barrel, "Oil Moving Parts; Made in U.S.A., Patented," 1935......	150	200	300
49-ER Cap Pistol, 1940, 9"	150	215	285
5-Star Dart Pistol..................................	15	22	30
6-Shot, 1932, 6-1/4"	45	60	80
6-Shot Cap Pistol, "Pat. U.S.A., Jan. 22, 1895," 1895, 6-3/4".....................	250	325	450

Ace Cap Pistol, 1935, Kilgore, $45. Photo courtesy Charles W. Best

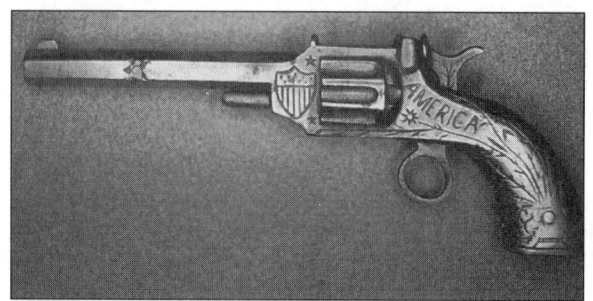

America, 1880, Stevens, $275. Photo courtesy Charles W. Best

	C6	C8	C10
6-Shot Rapid Load Cap Pistol, "Made in U.S.A.," 1932, 6-1/2".....................	60	75	100
Ace Cap Pistol, 1935, 5" long	25	35	45
Ace Cap Pistol, "Made in U.S.A.," 1930, 5" long.....................................	25	35	45
Acme Automatic, repeater, c. 1930.......	15	25	35
Acorn Pistol..	75	100	150
Admiral Dewey Cap Bomb	150	200	300
Aeromatic Glider Gun, shoots balsa airplanes, c. 1940	50	75	100
Agitator, The, cap and torpedo shooter, John Fox, 1908, 8-1/4"........	125	188	250
Aim to Save, c. 1909	150	225	300
Air Blaster, shoots burst of air..............	40	60	80
Air Raid Warning Signal Pistol.............	40	60	100
America, 1880, 8-3/4"	135	200	275
America Cap Pistol, w/shield, pat. 1873...	150	225	300
American Bulldog .22 Blank Shooter, second trigger tips barrel to load, handle curves inward, 1920, 4-1/2" long..	55	75	100

American Bulldog .22 cal. Blank Shooter, 1910, Kenton, $95

Army 45 Cap Automatic, 1940, Hubley, $160. Photo courtesy Charles W. Best

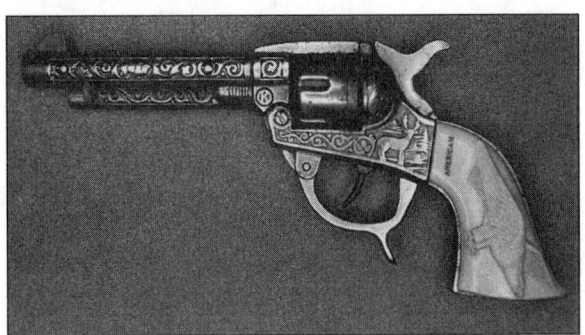

American Cap Pistol, 1940, Kilgore, $550. Photo courtesy Charles W. Best

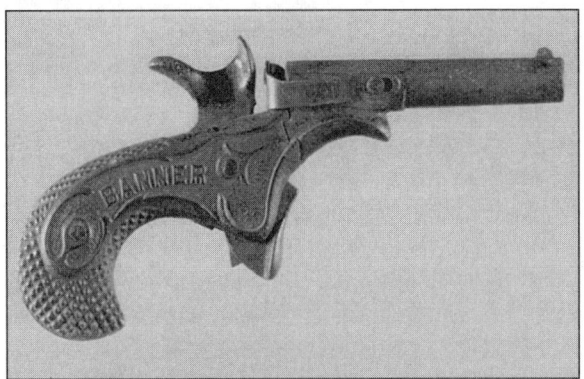

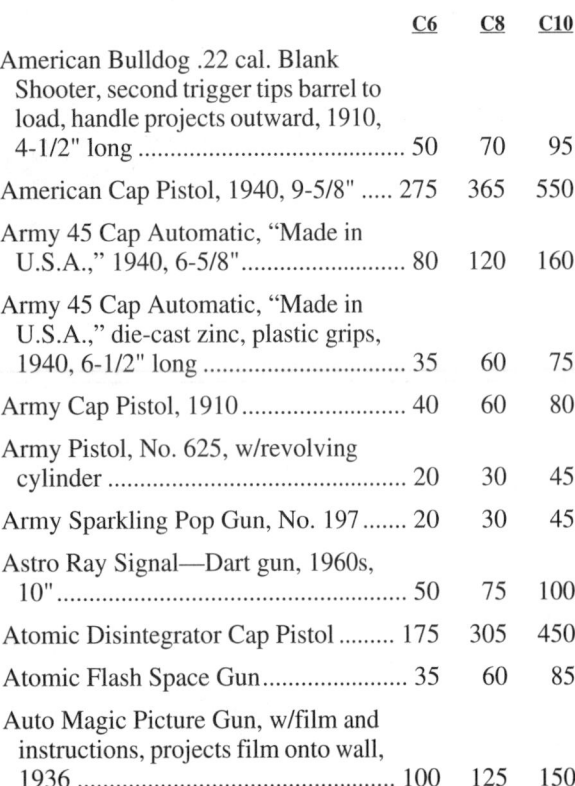

Banner, Ives, $300. Photo courtesy Sotheby's, New York

	C6	C8	C10
American Bulldog .22 cal. Blank Shooter, second trigger tips barrel to load, handle projects outward, 1910, 4-1/2" long	50	70	95
American Cap Pistol, 1940, 9-5/8"	275	365	550
Army 45 Cap Automatic, "Made in U.S.A.," 1940, 6-5/8"	80	120	160
Army 45 Cap Automatic, "Made in U.S.A.," die-cast zinc, plastic grips, 1940, 6-1/2" long	35	60	75
Army Cap Pistol, 1910	40	60	80
Army Pistol, No. 625, w/revolving cylinder	20	30	45
Army Sparkling Pop Gun, No. 197	20	30	45
Astro Ray Signal—Dart gun, 1960s, 10"	50	75	100
Atomic Disintegrator Cap Pistol	175	305	450
Atomic Flash Space Gun	35	60	85
Auto Magic Picture Gun, w/film and instructions, projects film onto wall, 1936	100	125	150

	C6	C8	C10
Auto Repeating Cap Exploder	45	68	90
Automatic Cap Pistol, No. 290, 6-1/2"	25	50	70
Automatic Repeater, No. 40, 1920s, 7" long	25	30	35
Automatic Repeater Paper Pop Pistol, No. 74	25	30	35
Bang Cap Pistol, "Made in U.S.A.," 6" long	25	38	50
Bang-O Cap Pistol, "Made in U.S.A.," 1938, 7" long	50	65	100
Banner, blank-shooting pistol, 5"	150	200	300
Bell Pistol	15	25	35
Benjamin Pump Early BB Gun, before 1910	75	112	150
Biff Cap Automatic, "Made in U.S.A. Pat. Apld. For," 1935, 4-1/2"	42	63	85
Biff Jr. Cap Automatic, "Made in U.S.A. Pat. Apld. For," 1935, 4-1/8" long	30	45	60

	C6	C8	C10
Big Band Pistol, No. 6P, 7-7/8" long	175	275	350
Big Bang Rifle, No. 21-60, 21-3/16" long	750	2000	3500
Big Bill Cap Pistol, 1925, 5-1/2" long	25	35	45
Big Bill Cap Pistol, large hammer, "Made in U.S.A.," 1935, 4-7/8"	20	30	40
Big Bill Cap Pistol, large hammer, "Made in U.S.A.," 1930, 5-3/4"	25	35	45
Big Buster Cap Automatic, w/two-piece trigger, "Patd Jul 2 1907, Made in U.S.A.," 1915, 5"	75	120	150
Big Chief Cap Pistol, "Made in U.S.A.," 1930, 3-1/2"	22	25	35
Big Chief Cap Pistol, marked w/star and "K," 1935, 6"	22	33	45
Big Chief Cap Pistol, 1935, 6" long	20	30	45
Big Clip Cap Pistol, "Made in U.S.A.," 1930, 6-3/4"	25	38	50

	C6	C8	C10
Big Horn Cap Pistol, revolving cylinder, 1939, 8-3/8"	175	275	365
Big Injun, hammerless	150	225	300
Big Noise, The, c. 1922	45	68	90
Big Scout, 1935	30	45	60
Big Scout, engraved, 1940	30	45	60
Bigger Bang Cap Pistol, large hammer, 1930, 6" long	32	48	65
Billy the Kid Cap Pistol, 1938, 6-3/4"	75	125	150
Black Jack Cap Pistol, long barrel, "Pat. Sept. 11-23," 1930, 11"	125	200	250
Blaze Away Dart Pistol, No. G23	15	22	30
Bob Cap Pistol, 1930, 5" long	25	38	50
Bobcat Cap Pistol, 1950s, 4-1/4"	15	20	35
Border Patrol, 1940	35	52	70
Border Patrol Cap Automatic, 1930, 4-1/4" long	30	40	50

Top to Bottom: Pluck Cap Pistol, Stevens, 1930, $25; Big Chief Cap Pistol, 1930, Dent, $35. Photo courtesy Charles W. Best

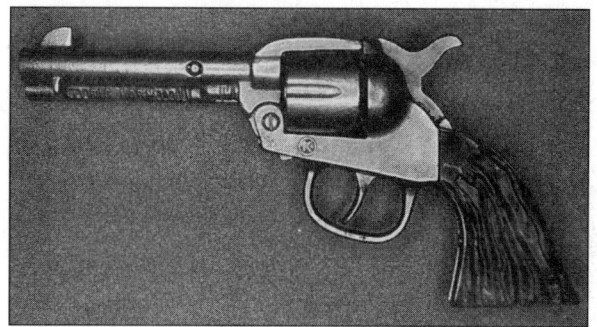

Big Horn Cap Pistol, 1939, Kilgore, $365. Photo courtesy Charles W. Best

Bigger Bang Cap Pistol, 1930, Kilgore, $65. Photo courtesy Charles W. Best

Border Patrol, 1940, $70. Photo courtesy Sotheby's, New York

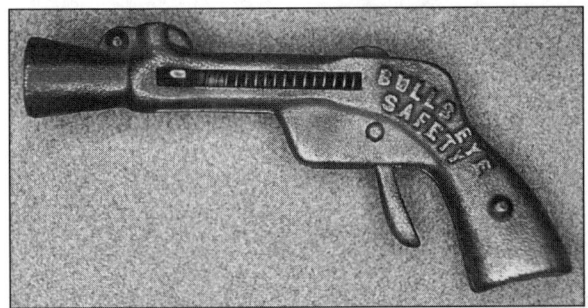

Bulls Eye Safety Pistol, 1910, Stevens, $175

Buster Pistol, unknown maker, $325. Photo courtesy Charles W. Best

Cannon Animated Cap Pistol, $500. Photo courtesy Sotheby's, New York

	C6	C8	C10
Border Patrol Cap Automatic, "Pat. Apld. For, Made in U.S.A.," 1935, 4-1/2" long	30	40	50
Boss Mammoth Cap Pistol, 1925, 6-1/4"	30	45	60
Boy's Delight Cap Pistol, pat. June 1891	225	300	400
Boy's Police Automatic Pop Gun, c. 1940s, 8"	8	12	15
Brat Cap Pistol	30	45	60
Brevet Depose	300	450	600
Bronc Cap Pistol, "Kenton Made in U.S.A.," 1935, 6"	30	45	60
Buc-A-Roo Cap Pistol, 1940, 7-3/4"	50	75	100
Buccaneer Flintlock Pistol, fires plastic bullets, 1958, 3-1/2"	37	56	75
Buck Pistol, 1930, 3-1/4"	40	60	90
Buckle Gun, w/bullets	48	72	95
Buddy, 1935	25	38	50
Buddy, 1930	25	38	50
Buffalo Bill, single shot, 1890	200	300	400
Buffalo Bill Cap Pistol, "Made in U.S.A.," 1940, 7-3/4" long	72	110	145

	C6	C8	C10
Buffalo Bill Cap Pistol, long barreled, "Pat. Sept. 11-23," 1925, 11-3/8"	150	225	300
Buffalo Bill Cap Pistol, long barreled, "Pat. Sept. 11-23," 1930, 13-1/2"	150	225	300
Buffalo Cap Rifle	82	125	165
Bull Cap Pistol, "Pat Appld. For Pat. Mch. 25, '24," 1940, 6-1/4"	25	38	50
Bull Dog Cap Pistol, "Pat 1,488,046," 1935, 6-1/4" long	25	35	45
Bulldog Cap Pistol, 1923, 5-1/2"	37	56	75
Bulldozer Cap Pistol, six-shooter, July 1874	200	275	350
Bulls Eye Safety Pistol, flare barrel w/spring, 1910, 5-1/2"	100	125	175
Bunker Hill Cap Pistol, 1925, 5-1/4" long	30	45	60
Burp Gun, 1956, 13" long	45	68	90
Buster, maker unknown, "Pat. May 28 1901," 6"	195	250	325
Buster Cap Automatic, 1910, 5-1/2"	45	68	90
Butting Match Mechanical Pistol	300	400	600
Cannon Animated Cap Pistol	250	375	500
Cap Bomb, head shape	150	200	250
Cap Bomb, dog's head	150	200	250
Cap Bomb, double-faced	150	200	250
Cap Pistol, double-barrel, dated 1880	125	188	250
Cap Pistol, revolving cylinder, 1887	150	200	250
Cap Pistol, marked w/"W" on one side, "S" on other, normal size barrel	20	25	30
Cap Pistol, repeating, red, 8" long	15	22	30

	C6	C8	C10
Cap Pistol, six-shot, dated 1895	150	200	300
Cap Pistol, hammerless w/four revolving triggers, "Pat. Appl'd For," 1892, 7-1/4"	250	300	400
Cap Pistol, ornate, 1878	50	75	125
Captain Cap Automatic, 1940, 4-1/4" long	30	40	50
Cavalier Cap Automatic, "Pat. Appld. For, Made in U.S.A.," 1935, 4-1/2"	35	52	70
Challenge, 1890...................................	150	225	300
Champ Automatic, 1940, 5"	30	45	60
Chief, 1900-1910...................................	35	45	55
Chief .22 cal. Blank shooter, second trigger tips up barrel to load, 1915, 6" long..	75	100	125
Chief Cap Pistol, single shot	30	45	60
Chief Cap Pistol, "Pat. 1,488,046," 1930, 6-1/8"	25	38	50
Chieftain Cap Pistol, 1920, 11" long.....	75	112	150
Chinese Must Go Cap Pistol, mechanical	350	450	700

Champ Automatic, 1940, Hubley, $60. Photo courtesy Charles W. Best

Click Pistol, Marx, $30. Photo courtesy Charles W. Best

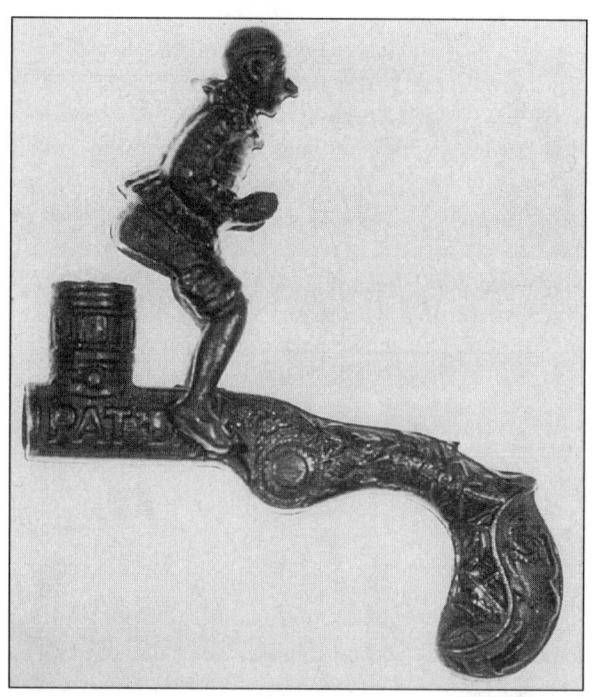

Clown on a Barrel, $1000. Photo courtesy Charles W. Best

Columbia Cap Pistol, 1890, Stevens, $400. Photo courtesy Charles W. Best

	C6	C8	C10
Click Pistol, No. 36	15	22	30
Click Pistol, approx. 7-3/4" long...........	15	22	30
Clicker Pistol, plain black, late 1930s-early 1940s	15	22	30
Clip 50, 1940, 4-1/4"	60	90	120
Clip Jr. Cap Pistol, 1935, 5-1/4"............	25	38	50
Clipper Cap Automatic, 1935, 4-1/8"....	48	72	95
Clown and Mule Pistol, animated	600	800	1500
Clown on a Barrel................................	500	700	1000
Colt .45	100	150	200
Colt Cap Pistol, "Patented June 17, 1890, Made in U.S.A.," 1920, 5-1/2"..	50	75	100
Colt Cap Pistol, 1935, 6-1/2".................	30	45	60
Columbia Cap Pistol, 1890, 8-3/4"......	200	300	400

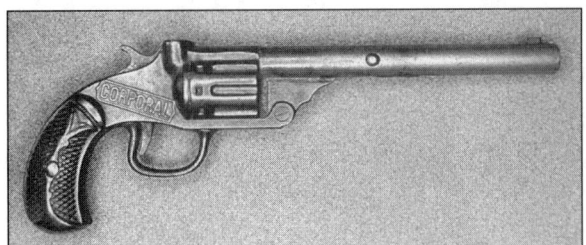

Corporal, 1900, unknown maker, $150. Photo courtesy Charles W. Best

Dagger Derringer, 1955, Hubley, $90. Photo courtesy Charles W. Best

Daniel Boone Wilderness Scout Derringer, Marx, $50. Photo courtesy Gary L. Linden

	C6	C8	C10
Columbia Cap Pistol, pat. June 1891 ..	200	300	400
Columbia Cap Pistol, 1885	200	300	400
Columbia Junior, early BB gun	250	375	500
Comet, 1885, 5-1/2"	150	225	300
Comet, 1925, 7-1/8"	40	60	80
Cop Cap Pistol, "Pat. 1,488,046" or "Pat. Mch. 25 '24," 1930, 5"	25	35	50
Cork-popper Pistol, spur trigger	15	20	30
Cork-shooting Rifle, No. 232, double-barrel	50	75	100
Cork-shooting Rifle, No. 206	15	20	30
Corn Shooter Cap Pistol	65	90	130
Corporal, maker unknown, 1900, 8-7/8"	75	100	150
Cowboy Cap Pistol, "Made in U.S.A.," 1935, 3-1/2"	15	22	30
Cowboy Cap Pistol, "Made in U.S.A.," 1940, 8"	85	125	175
Cowboy Cap Pistol, 1890, 7-5/8"	125	188	250
Cowboy Cap Pistol, long barrel, "Made in U.S.A.," 1930	175	263	350
Cowboy King, 1940	175	250	325
Coyote	40	60	85
Crack, 1925, 5"	40	60	80

	C6	C8	C10
Cupid, 1900, 5-1/4"	62	93	125
Dagger Derringer, 1955	45	65	90
Dandy Cap Pistol, w/a variety of markings, 1935, 5-3/4"	35	52	70
Daniel Boone Wilderness Scout Derringer	25	38	50
Darb Cap Pistol, "Pat. Sept. 11-23," 1930, 5-1/2" long	30	45	60
Dart Pistol, colorful w/fancy lithographing	15	20	30
Dart Pistol, 1950s	27	41	55
Dead Shot, 8-3/4"	125	188	250
Defence, 1896	85	130	175
Derby Cap Pistol, 1930, 7"	30	45	60
Desert Patrol Luger & Silencer, 1960s, 10"	20	25	35
Detroit Cap Pistol, 1910, 6-5/8" long	85	110	150
Dick Cap Automatic, "Made in U.S.A.," 1940, 4-1/8"	30	45	60
Dick Cap Automatic, 4-1/4"	20	25	30
Dick Cap Pistol, 1930, 6"	30	45	60
DIK Cap Pistol, "Pat. Sept. 11-23," 1935, 4-3/4"	27	41	55
Dixie, 1888-1890	75	112	150
Dixie Cap Pistol, "Made in U.S.A. Pat. Appld. For," 1935, 6-1/4"	42	63	85
Doc Cap Pistol, "Pat. Sept. 11-23," 1926, 4-1/2"	40	50	60
Dolphin Cap Pistol, animated	400	600	800
Double-barrel Shotgun, c. 1935, 25"	52	78	105
Doughboy Cap Automatic, "Made in U.S.A.," 1920, 5"	45	68	90

	C6	C8	C10
Dragnet Detective Special Repeating Revolver Cap Gun, c. 1955	27	41	55
Duck Cap Pistol, animated, 1884, 3-3/4" long	2500	3000	5000
Dude Cap Pistol, 1941, 6-1/2"	40	60	80
Dude Pistol, "Pat. Mar. 22 '87," 1887, 3-1/2"	75	112	150
Eagle, c. 1940	40	60	80
Eagle Cap Pistol, "Pat. June 17, 1890," 1995, 7-1/2"	100	150	200
Echo Cap Pistol, "Made in U.S.A.," 1930, 4-1/2"	30	40	50
Echo Cap Pistol, six-shooter, 1881	350	450	550
Echo Cap Pistol, 1920, 4-1/4"	30	40	50

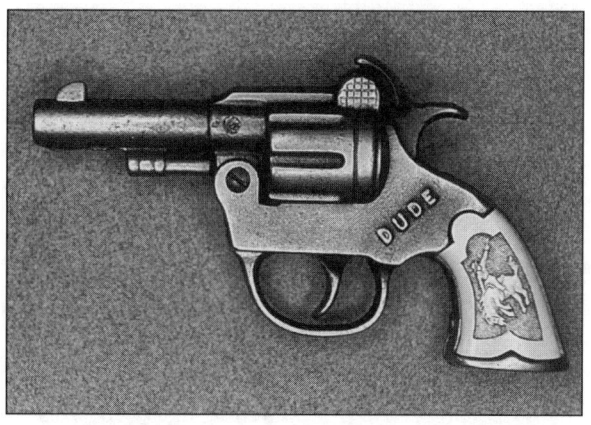

Dude Cap Pistol, 1941, Kenton, $80. Photo courtesy Charles W. Best

Doughboy Cap Automatic, 1920, Kilgore, $90. Photo courtesy Charles D. Richards

Dragnet Detective Special Repeating Revolver Cap Gun, c. 1955, $55. Photo courtesy Hakes Americana & Collectibles

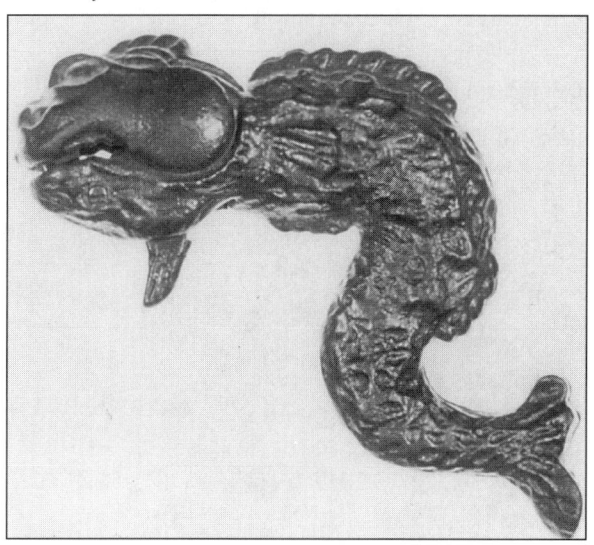

Dolphin Cap Pistol, unknown maker, $800. Photo courtesy Sotheby's, New York

Duck Cap Pistol, 1884, unknown maker, $5000. Photo courtesy Sotheby's, New York

Federal-Kilgore No. 1 Cap Pistol, 1925, Kilgore, $50. Photo courtesy Sotheby's, New York

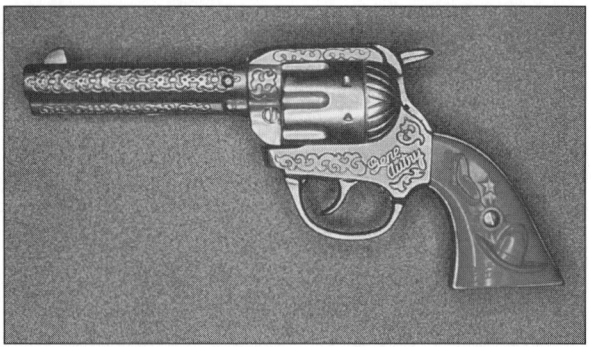

Gene Autry Cap Pistol, 1939, Kenton, $250. Photo courtesy Charles W. Best

Top to Bottom: Flintlock, Hubley, $70; Flintlock Jr. Pistol, Hubley, $35; Flintlock Midget Pistol, Hubley, $30. Photo courtesy Chalres W. Best

	C6	C8	C10
Electronic Space Gun, w/flashlight gun	37	56	75
Excelsior Cap Pistol, "Pat'd Apr. 22, '73," 1875, 5-1/4"	125	188	250
Federal Cap Automatic, w/removable clip to hold caps, 1940, 4-7/8"	45	70	90
Federal Cap Pistol, "Pat. Dec. 14; Made in U.S.A.," 1920	37	56	75
Federal Cap Pistol, 1920, 5-1/2"	25	38	50
Federal No. 2 Cap Pistol, 1925, 6-3/8"	60	90	120
Federal-Kilgore No. 1 Cap Pistol, 1925, 5-1/4"	25	38	50
Fido, 1910, 4"	50	60	70
Firecracker Pistol, w/filigree handle	100	150	200
Firecracker Pistol, five-barrel, 1877	500	800	1200

	C6	C8	C10
First No. 1, 1920, 6-3/4"	150	200	250
Flash Cap Pistol, "Pat'd," 1934, 6-1/4"	45	55	75
Flintlock, No. 280, 9-1/4"	35	52	70
Flintlock Junior	17	26	35
Flintlock Midget	15	22	30
Flying Saucer Gun, 1964	15	25	30
Forty-five Cap Pistol, The, "Made in U.S.A.," unusual shape, 1928, 11-1/8"	75	100	125
Four Way Cap Pistol, "Pat. Appld. For," shoots pea or dart, rubber band and cap, 1930	150	225	300
Fox Cap Pistol, 1935, 4-1/2"	30	40	50
Frontier Cap Pistol, dog's head a top the barrel facing hammer, "Pat. June 21, 1887 and June 17, 1890," 1890	200	300	400
Gang Busters Crusade Against Crime Sub-Machine Gun	125	188	250
Gem Pistol, 1900, 3"	30	45	60
Gene Autry Bull's Eye Cap Pistol, "Gene Autry" signature on grips, 1950s, 6-1/2"	125	188	250
Gene Autry Cap Pistol, 1939, 8-3/8"	125	175	250
Gene Autry Cap Pistol, "Made in U.S.A.," 1940, 6-1/2"	130	185	275
Gene Autry Cap Pistol, "Made in U.S.A. Pat. Appl'd For," 1939, 6-1/2"	125	175	250
Gene Autry Cap Pistol, "Made in U.S.A.," red grips, 1940, 6-1/2"	125	175	250
Gip, 1900	25	38	50
G-Man Automatic Sparkling Pistol, No. 43	65	100	130

	C6	C8	C10
G-Man Automatic Sparkling Pistol, No. 44	65	100	130
G-Man Cap Automatic, looks like German Luger, removable magazine holds caps, 1935, 6"	100	150	200
G-Man Cap Automatic, 1940, 6"	50	75	100
G-Man Clicker Pistol, black	25	35	45
G-Man Gun, No. 707	37	56	75
G-Man Silent Alarm Pistol, No. 54	25	35	45
G-Man Sparkling Sub-Machine Gun, 26" long	100	175	250
G-Man Sparkling Tommy Gun, 1936	175	275	375
G-Man Wind-Up Machine Gun, miniature, 1940s	20	30	40
G-Man Wind-up Spark Pistol, w/painted finish	60	100	125
G-Man Wind-up Spark Pistol, w/nickel finish and jewels on grip	60	100	125
Go Bang	100	150	200

Hopalong Cassidy Revolver, 1950s, Wyandotte, $400. Photo courtesy Charles W. Best

	C6	C8	C10
Guard Cap Pistol, "Made in U.S.A.," 1935, 6-1/4"	30	45	60
Hanson-Lindsborg K.S. Firecracker Pistol, "Pat. Appl'd For," fires firecracker, 1905, 6-3/8"	75	110	150
Hawk Automatic Cap Pistol, No. 2343, 5-3/4"	20	30	40
H-Bar-O Cap Pistol, "Made in U.S.A.," 1925, 7-1/2"	60	75	125
Hero Auto Cap Automatic, 1920, 4-3/4"	45	65	85
Hero Cap Pistol, 1937, 5-1/4"	25	35	50
Hi-Ho Cap Pistol, 1940, 6-1/2"	37	56	75
Hi-Ho Cap Pistol, "Made in U.S.A.," 1940, 7"	35	45	60
Hi-Ho Cap Pistol, "Made in U.S.A.," 1940, 7"	37	56	75
Hi-Ho Cap Pistol, "Pat. Sept. 11-23," 1940, 5-1/8"	35	45	60
Hi-Ranger Cap Pistol, 1940, 7-3/4"	50	70	90
Hopalong Cassidy Revolver, "Hopalong" on both sides of handle, 1950s, 9"	200	300	400
Hopalong Cassidy Revolver, with bust of Hopalong, 1950s, 10"	160	225	325
Hub Cap Pistol, 1940, 6-1/4"	25	38	50
Hustler Pistol	55	82	110
Ibex, 1895, 4-1/2"	60	90	120
Imperial Cap Pistol, 1935, 5-1/4"	60	80	110
Indian Cap Pistol, 1931, 8-1/8"	60	90	120
Invincible Cap Pistol, "Pat. Dec. 14," 1935, 5-1/4"	30	45	60

G-Man Cap Automatic, 1935, Kilgore, $200. Photo courtesy Charles W. Best

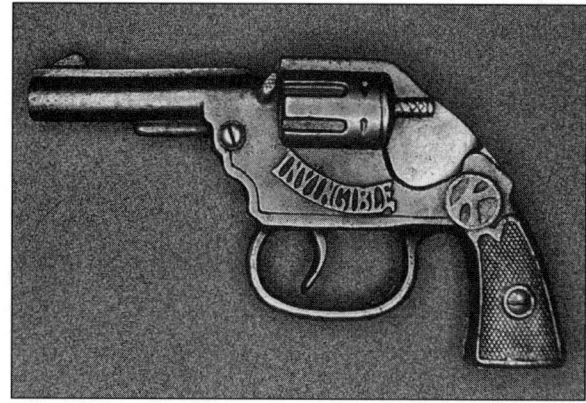

Invincible Cap Pistol, 1935, Kilgore, $60. Photo courtesy Charles W. Best

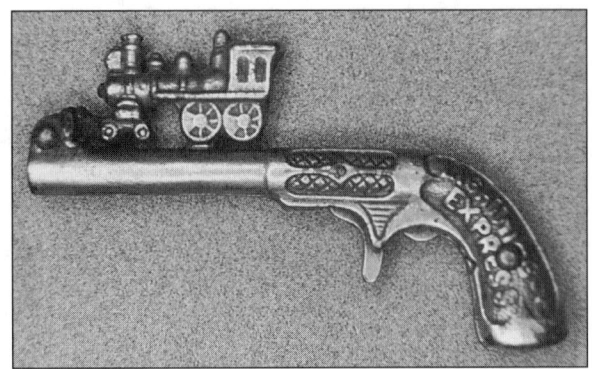

Lightning Express Mechanical Cap Pistol, 1913, Arcade or Kenton, $300. Photo courtesy Charles W. Best

	C6	C8	C10
Invincible New 50 Shot, 1930	30	45	60
Jack Armstrong airplane gun, 1936	50	70	125
Jax Cap Pistol, "Pat. Sept. 11-23," 1930, 4"	25	35	45
Jet Jr. Space Cap Gun, 1949, 6-1/2"	110	165	220
Johnnie's Little Gun	700	1100	1700
Jr. Police Chief Cap Automatic, "Made in U.S.A.," 1938, 3-7/8"	30	45	60
Jr. Ranger .32 cal., 1925	35	50	65
Jumbo Cap Pistol, "Pat. June 17, 1890: Made in U.S.A.," 1895, 9-1/2"	110	165	220
Junior Police .32 Cap Pistol, "Hubley; Pat'd. 2088891," 1940, 5-1/4"	30	45	60
Junior Six-shooter Cap Pistol, 1935, 5-1/2"	35	50	65
Just Out Animated Cap Pistol, 1880s	1500	3000	5000
Kido Cap Pistol, "Kenton Made in U.S.A.," 1936, 5-3/8"	25	38	50
Kilgore Cap Pistol, 1910, 5"	42	63	85
Kilgore Cap Pistol, 1912, 5-1/4"	42	63	85
King Cap Pistol, Pat. Aug. 1879	100	150	200
King Cap Pistol, "Made in U.S.A.," 1925, 4-3/4"	50	60	75
Kit Carson Cap Pistol, "Pat. Sept. 11-23," 1928, 9"	50	75	100
Las Cap Pistol	80	120	160
Lasso 'Em Bill Cap Gun, red rubies in handle w/turning cylinder, 1930, 9"	150	225	300
Lawmaker Cap Pistol, 1941, 8-3/8"	125	175	250

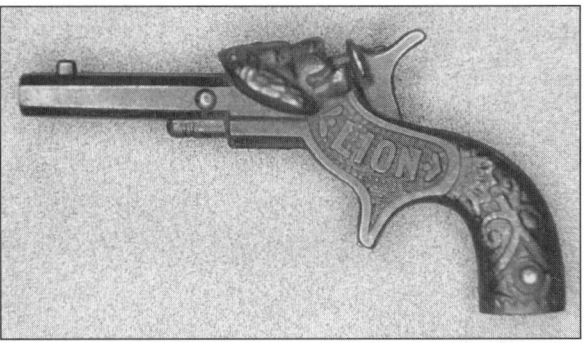

Lion, 1887, Ives, $400. Photo courtesy Charles W. Best

Top to Bottom: Lone Eagle Cap Pistol, 1929, Kilgore, $150; Patrol Cap Pistol, 1939, Hubley, $55. Photo courtesy Charles W. Best

	C6	C8	C10
Liberty, 1875	150	200	250
Liberty, ornate, c. 1912	35	52	70
Lightning Express Mechanical Cap Pistol, train slides forward along barrel to explode cap at end, 1913, 5"	150	225	300
Lion, 1887, 3-3/4"	200	300	400
Lion, 1890, 5-1/4"	175	225	300
Lion Head Cap Pistol, Pat. 1890, 5-1/4"	175	225	300

	C6	C8	C10
Little Bill Cap Pistol, 1925, 5"	30	40	55
Little Chief Firefighter Water Squirt Gun	15	20.	25
Lone Eagle Cap Pistol, 1929, 5-1/4"	60	100	150
Lone Ranger .45 Flasher Flashlight Pistol	45	60	85
Lone Ranger Cap Pistol, 1938, 8-1/2"	170	255	340
Lone Ranger Click Pistol, 9"	55	82	110
Lone Ranger Pop Gun, w/picture of Lone Ranger on handles, 1950s	50	60	85
Lone Ranger Sparkling Pop Pistol, No. 096	50	65	100
Lone Ranger Western Gun Collection, six miniature guns mounted on a card w/history of guns on back, c. 1939	85	125	200
Long Boy Cap Pistol, "Made in U.S.A.," 1922, 11"	80	120	160
Long Tom Cap Pistol, 1939, 10-3/8"	250	375	500
Look Out Cap Pistol, dogs head	300	450	600
Luger Water Pistol, 1960s, 7"	15	20	25

	C6	C8	C10
M&L Water Pistol, w/rubber ball	15	20	25
Machine Gun Cap Automatic, w/crank, "Ra-Ta-Ta-Tat," caps fired rapidly when the crank is turned, 1938, 5"	150	200	250
Magic .22 cal. Blank Pistol, ornate, has second trigger to open barrel for loading, "Pat'd Oct. 17, '99," 1900, 6-1/4"	85	130	170
Man from U.N.C.L.E. Cap Gun, c. 1965	35	52	70
Marx Miniatures of Famous Guns: Civil War Revolver, Mare's Leg, Tommy Gun, Saddle Rifle, price for each	25	40	55
Mascot Cap Automatic, 1936, 3-7/8"	30	40	50
Master Cap Automatic, 1930, 4-5/8"	50	60	70
Master Cap Automatic, 1922, 4-5/8"	30	40	50
Match-shooting Pistol, double-trigger, large, 1873	125	188	250
Mauser, The, maker unknown, 1915, 6-3/4"	250	375	500
Me and My Buddy Animated Pistol, w/figure	55	82	110
Medrick Repeater	75	112	150
Mick, 1930	30	40	50
Minute Man Cap Rifle, "Pat. Appl'd For, Made in U.S.A.," 1936, 20"	200	300	400

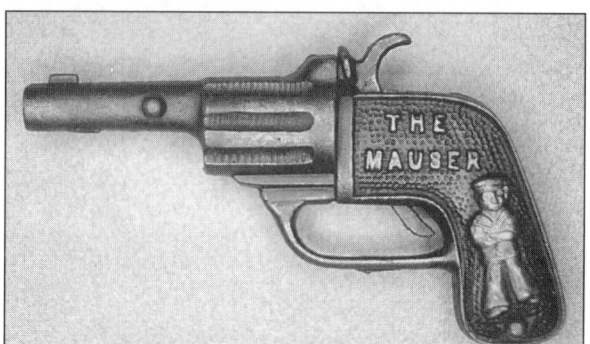

The Mauser, 1915, unknown maker, $500. Photo courtesy Charles W. Best

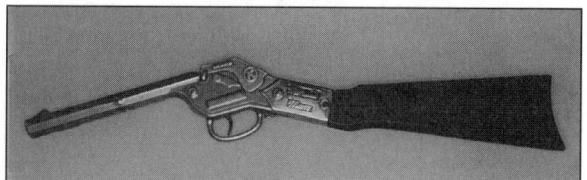

Minute Man Cap Rifle, 1936, Kilgore, $400. Photo courtesy Charles W. Best

Lone Ranger Cap Pistol, 1938, Kilgore, $340. Photo courtesy Charles W. Best

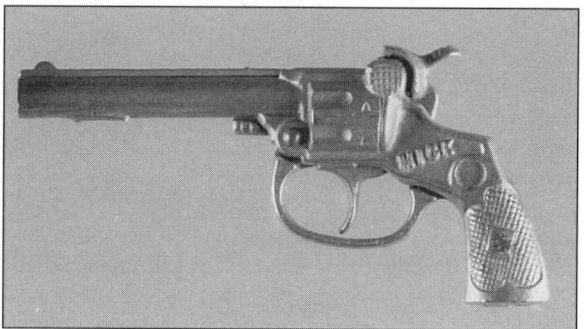

Mick, 1930, unknown maker, $50. Photo courtesy Charles W. Best

Monkey and Coconut Animated Cap Pistol, 1870s-1880s, unknown maker, $850. Photo courtesy Charles W. Best

Moonface Capshooter, c. 1880, Stevens, $1000. Photo courtesy Charles W. Best

	C6	C8	C10
Monkey and Coconut Animated Cap Pistol, 1870s-1880s, 4-1/4"	450	650	850
Monkeys Animated Cap Pistol, 1882, 4-1/4"	550	825	1100
Moonface Capshooter, c. 1880	500	750	1000

Mordt Cap Pistol, 1930, unknown maker, $120. Photo courtesy Charles W. Best

National Cap Automatic, 1925, National, $55. Photo courtesy Sotheby's, New York

	C6	C8	C10
Mordt Cap Pistol, maker unknown, 1930, 8"	60	90	120
Mountie Cap Automatic, No. 6, 1950, 6"	20	30	40
National Cap Automatic, 1915, 3-3/4"	35	50	65
National Cap Automatic, 1925, 4-1/4"	35	45	55
National Cap Automatic, "Made in U.S.A.," 1925, 5-1/4"	35	45	55
National Cap Pistol, 1920, 3-5/8"	35	45	55
National Cap Pistol, 1911, 5"	35	45	55
National Cap Pistol, 1909, 4-7/8"	35	45	55
National Liquid Pistol, 1900, 4-7/8"	55	82	110
National No. 350 Cap Automatic, 1928, 5-1/2"	45	55	65
National No. 380 Cap Pistol, 1930s, 7"	40	55	70

National Liquid Pistol, 1900, Parker/Stearns, $110. Photo courtesy Charles W. Best

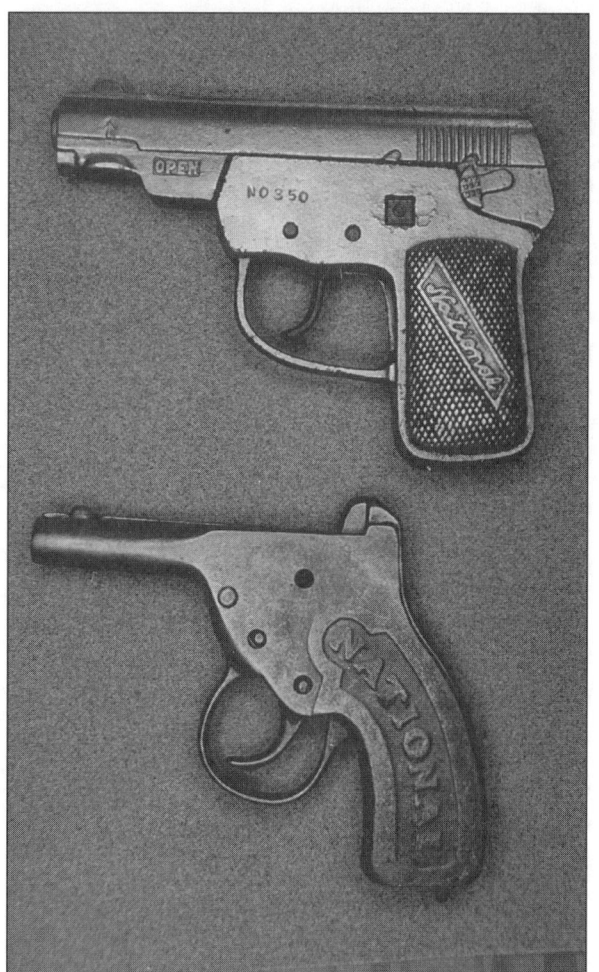

National No. 350 Cap Automatic, 1928, National, $65; National Cap Pistol, 1911, National, $55. Photo courtesy Charles W. Best

	C6	C8	C10
Navy, 1878	125	188	250
Navy, 1907	75	112	150
Navy, 1925	35	52	60
Navy Cap Pistol, "Pat. Sept. 11-23," 1930, 5-1/2"	35	45	55
Navy Double-barrel Cap Pistol	150	225	300
Nemo Cap Pistol, maker unknown, 1910, 6-5/8"	45	68	90
New 50-Shot Invincible Cap Pistol, 1930, 5-1/2"	35	50	65
Nigger Head Cap Pistol, 1887, 4-1/2"	400	500	600
No. 500 (like Luger), 1935	55	82	110
Novelty Cap Pistol, "Pat. Appl'd For," 1885, 5"	150	225	300
Nu-Matic Paper Buster Gun, 7"	25	35	50
Officer Pistol Cap Automatic, modeled after German Luger, 1940, 6"	62	93	125

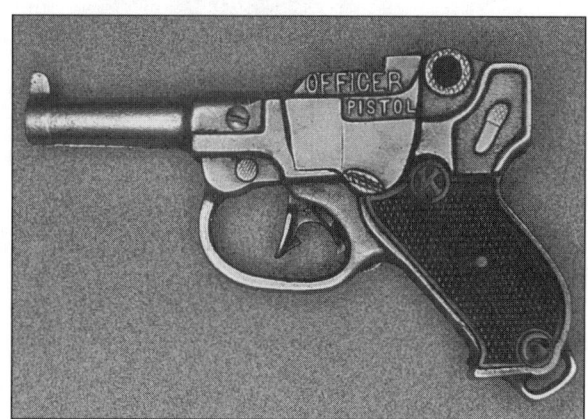

Officer Pistol Cap Automatic, 1940, Kilgore, $125. Photo courtesy Charles W. Best

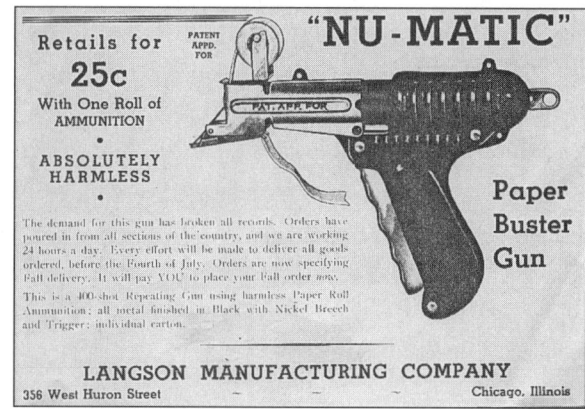

Ad for Langson Manufacturing's Nu-Matic Paper Buster Gun; currently valued at $50, the Numatic originally retailed for 25 cents.

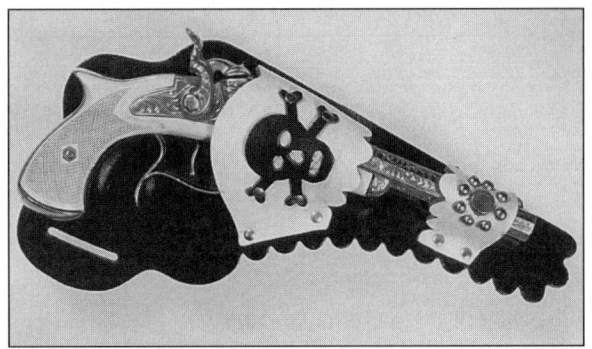

Pirate Cap Pistol with holster, 1941, Hubley, $125.
Photo courtesy Charles W. Best

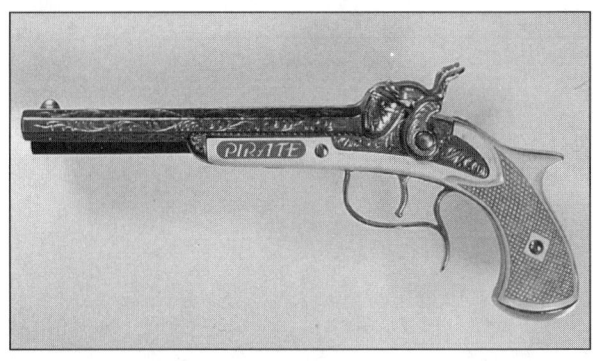

Pirate Cap Pistol without holster, 1950, Hubley,
$120. Photo courtesy Charles W. Best

	C6	C8	C10
Official Detective-Type Sub-Machine Gun, No. 2146	60	85	125
Oh Boy Automatic Cap, "Made in U.S.A.; Pat'd., Aug. 8, 1933," works both as automatic and crank-operated rapid-fire gun, 1933, 4-1/8"	85	128	170
Oh Boy Cap Pistol, 1922, 5-1/2"	35	45	60
Oh Boy Cap Pistol, "Pat. Sept. 11-23," 1930, 5-1/8"	30	35	40
OK Cap Automatic, maker unknown, 1935, 3-3/4"	35	45	55
Old Ironsides Cap Pistol, 10-3/4"	65	98	130
Our Army Forever	175	263	350
P-38 Steel Clicker Pistol, c. 1945	20	30	40
Padlock Cup Pistol, w/key, 4-1/4"	75	125	175
Pal Cap Automatic, 1930, 4"	25	35	50
Pal Cap Pistol, 1930, 4"	20	30	45
Pat Pistol, "Pat. Sept. 11-23," 1935, 6-1/8"	25	35	45
Patrol Cap Pistol, "Made in U.S.A.," 1939, 6"	35	45	55
Pawnee Bill, c. 1940	150	200	300
Pea Matic Pea-shooting Repeater	20	25	35
Pea Shooter, highly embossed handle	35	52	70
Peacemaker Cap Pistol, "Made in U.S.A.," 1940, 8-1/2"	68	100	135
Peerless, 1905, 5-1/2"	60	90	125
Persuader Cap Pistol, "Made in U.S.A., Pat. Appld. For," 1939, 6-3/8"	60	90	125
Pet, 4-1/4"	5	10	15
Ping-Pong Rifle	25	30	35

	C6	C8	C10
Pioneer	60	90	120
Pirate Cap Pistol, two-barrel, two hammers that cock, 1941, 9-3/8"	45	75	125
Pirate Cap Pistol, nonfiring, 1950	60	90	120
Pistol Packin' Mama, four revolving triggers, shoots wooden pegs, c. 1944, 8-1/2"	40	50	75
Pluck Cap Pistol, "Made in U.S.A.," 1930, 3-1/2"	15	20	25
Pluck Cap Pistol, 1895	62	93	125
Police Automatic, 1935	40	60	80
Police Automatic Cap Pistol, 8"	20	30	40
Police Cap Automatic, 1940, 5-1/4"	55	83	110
Police Chief, 1938, 4-5/8"	40	50	65
Police Chief Gun, w/leather shoulder holster set, c. late 1940s	45	55	75
Polo, 1878, 6"	75	90	125
Pono Cap Pistol, "Pat. Sept. 11-23," 1936, 5-1/8"	30	40	50
Pop Gun—Rifle, No. 230, double-barrel	50	75	100
Powder Keg Cap Bomb	85	128	170
Premier Safety, 1914	40	60	85
President Cap Pistol, 1925, 8-3/4"	40	60	80
Presto Cap Automatic, 1940, 5-1/8"	30	45	60
Private Eye Cap Pistol, 6-1/2"	15	25	35
Punch and Judy Animated Cap Pistol, Punch explodes cap w/nose on Judy's back, 1880, 5"	550	700	850
Ranger, 1890-1900	80	120	160
Ranger Cap Pistol, 1940, 8-1/2"	45	60	85
Ranger Cap Pistol, 1939, 8-1/2"	85	130	175

President Cap Pistol, 1925, Kilgore, $80.

Presto Cap Automatic, 1940, Kilgore, $60. Photo courtesy Charles W. Best

Punch and Judy Animated Cap Pistol, 1880, Ives, $850. Photo courtesy Charles W. Best

	C6	C8	C10
Ranger Cap Pistol, 1920, 5-3/8"	50	60	75
Red Ranger Clicker Pistol, black, red "jewel," c. 1939, 8"	40	60	80
Red Ranger Clicker Pistol, c. 1941, 8"	30	45	60

	C6	C8	C10
Red Ranger Rifle	30	50	65
Red Ranger Six-shooter Repeater	40	60	75
Remington .36	50	70	95
Repeating Cap Pistol, No. G375	20	30	40
Rex Cap Automatic, 1914, 4-1/8"	35	50	65
Rex Cap Automatic, 1939, 3-7/8"	35	52	70
Rex Mars Planet Patrol X-92 Gun	100	150	200
Rifleman Flip Special Cap Rifle, 32-1/2"	82	125	165
RIP, c. 1909	75	100	125
Rob Roy, c. 1875	150	225	300
Rocket Ship Space Pistol, late 1940s	35	50	70
Rodeo Cap Pistol, 1938, 7"	35	55	75
Rodeo Cap Pistol, 11-1/4"	125	165	200
Rotor Fifty Cap Pistol, 1930, 6-1/8"	50	70	95
Roy Rogers Cap Pistol, 1940, 8-1/4"	250	375	500
Roy Rogers Cap Pistol, 1940, 10-1/4"	300	450	600

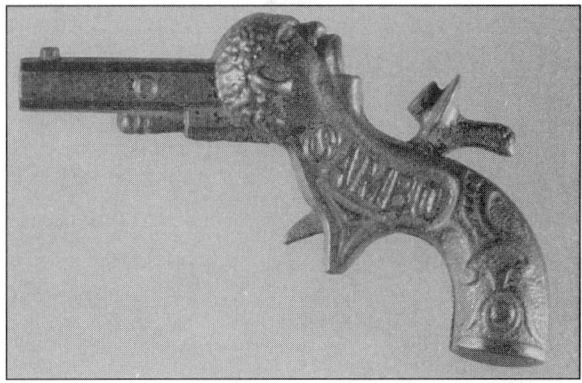

Sambo Cap Pistol, 1887, Ives, $500. Photo courtesy Sotheby's, New York

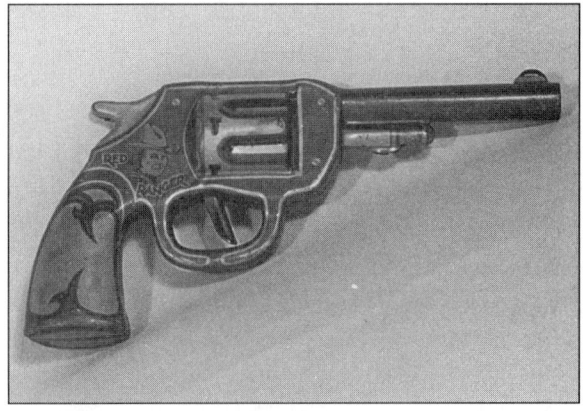

Red Ranger Clicker Pistol, c. 1941, Wyandotte, $60. Photo courtesy Charles W. Best

The Royal Pistol, 1878, Iver Johnson, $800. Photo courtesy Charles W. Best

Scout Cap Pistol, 1890, Stevens, $80

	C6	C8	C10
Royal Pistol, The, mechanical cap, "Pat. Apr. 23, '78," fires spring-loaded top that is attached to bottom of the barrel, 1878, approx. 5"	400	600	800
S & W Cap Gun, 6"	20	25	30
Safety Cap Pistol, "Pat. Mch. 25, '24," 1924, 5"	30	40	50
Safety First Cap Automatic, "Safe," maker unknown, 1920, 3-3/8"	30	45	60
Sambo Cap Pistol, "Pat. June 21, 1887," hammer hits head, 1887, 4-3/8"	250	350	500
Say I Bomb	100	130	175
Scout Cap Pistol, "Made in U.S.A.," 1935, 6-3/4"	35	50	65
Scout Cap Pistol, "Pat. June 17, 1890," 1890, 7"	40	60	80
Scout Cap Pistol, 1940, 6-1/8"	35	50	65
Scout Cap Pistol, automatic, 1914	30	40	50
Scout Jr. Cap Pistol, "Made in U.S.A.," 1935, 6"	35	50	65

	C6	C8	C10
Scoutmaster, 6-3/4"	65	98	130
Senator Cap Pistol, marked w/star and "K," 1925, 7"	50	75	100
Sharpshooter Cap Rifle, 37"	75	112	150
Sheriff Cap Pistol, The, 1940, 8-1/2"	75	125	175
Shoo Fly Cap Pistol	100	150	200
Shoot the Hat Mechanical Cap Pistol	500	800	1000
Shootin' Shell Buckle Gun, 1959	42	63	85
Shotgun, double-barreled, both barrels break down, cock and shoot, 28"	35	52	70
Siren Signal Pistol, 1950s	25	35	50
Siren Signal Pistol, 1940s	30	40	60
Siren Sparkling Pistol, No. 164	50	80	110
Six Shooter Cap Pistol, "Made in U.S.A." on hammer, 1938, 6-1/2"	40	60	80
Six Shooter Cap Pistol, "Made in U.S.A." on hammer, 1938, 6-1/2"	60	80	100
Six Shooter Cap Pistol, 1935, 6-1/2"	60	80	100
Six Shooter Cap Pistol, 1930, 7"	40	60	80
Six Shooter Cap Pistol, 1935, 6-1/2"	40	60	80
Six-shooter Automatic Cap Pistol, (not an automatic), 1934, 6-1/2"	65	85	110
Sliko Cap Pistol, "Pat. Sept. 11-23," 1930, 6-1/4"	30	45	55
Snappy, 1930, 5"	35	45	60
Snappy Jack, c. 1935	50	65	85
Space Gun	30	50	65
Space Rocket Gun, fires two Space Rocket Spheres, 9"	65	100	150

Snappy, 1930, Dent, $60

	C6	C8	C10
Sparkling Atom Buster, No. 46	40	60	85
Sparkling Pop Gun, No. 198	30	45	60
Sparkling Space Gun	50	75	125
Sparkling Sure Shot	25	35	50
Spitfire Cap Automatic, "Made in U.S.A.," 1940, 4-5/8"	40	50	60
Sport, 1875, 4"	175	263	350
Sport Cap Pistol, "Made in U.S.A.," 1930, 7-1/2"	35	50	65
Spud Gun, No. 504, Hollywood, Calif.	30	45	60
Spud Gun, automatic, c. 1940	25	35	45
Spy Cap Pistol, "Made in U.S.A.," 1936, 4-1/4"	30	40	50
Star Cap Pistol, 1910, 6-1/4"	35	52	70
Star Cap Pistol, steer on handle	10	15	20
Stephans, Pat., 1873, 5"	120	180	240
Streamline Siren Sparkling Pistol, No. 155	40	60	75
Sun Cap Pistol	150	175	200
Super Cap Pistol, "Pat. Sept. 11-23," 1930, 8-3/4"	45	60	75
Super Nu-Matic Paper Buster Gun	25	35	50
Sure Shot, 1870-1880	150	175	200
Sure Shot Cap Automatic, 1940, 4-1/4"	35	45	60
Target Cap Pistol, "Pat. 1,488,046," 1935, 8"	60	85	125
Targeteer Pistol	45	68	90

	C6	C8	C10
Teddy Cap Pistol, 1938, 5-5/8"	35	45	60
Terror, 1925	30	45	60
Terror, 1888	250	375	500
Terror Cap Automatic, "Pat. Jan 16 '15," 1915, 4-1/4"	40	60	80
Terror Cap Pistol, w/people embossed, 1882	250	350	450
Texan Cap Pistol, "Pat. Sept. 11-23," 1930, 6-5/8"	45	68	90
Texan Cap Pistol, "Pat. No. 1993916," 1936, 5-3/4"	60	90	125
Texan Cap Pistol, "Made in U.S.A.," 1940, 9-1/4"	125	175	225
Texan Jr. Cap Pistol, "Made in U.S.A.," 1941, 8-1/8"	100	150	200
Texas Centennial, 1936, 11"	225	338	450
Texas Jack, 1886, 9-3/8"	250	300	450
Thunder-Burp Machine Gun, 1960s	40	60	80
Thundergun Rifle, 36" long	100	150	200
Tiger Cap Pistol, 1935, 6-7/8"	35	50	65
Tiger Cap Pistol, 1915, 6-3/4"	40	55	70
Tin Tin Gun, turn crank and it makes noise, 3 x 5"	20	30	40
Tip Top Cap Pistol, 1880, 3-1/2"	175	200	225
Trapper Cap Automatic, fires only single shot, but roll of caps can be carried in the grip, 1935, 4-1/2"	50	75	100
Triumph, 1878, 5-1/8"	165	225	300
Trooper Cap Pistol, 1938, 5-1/8"	30	40	50

Sport, 1875, Ives, $350. Photo courtesy Charles W. Best

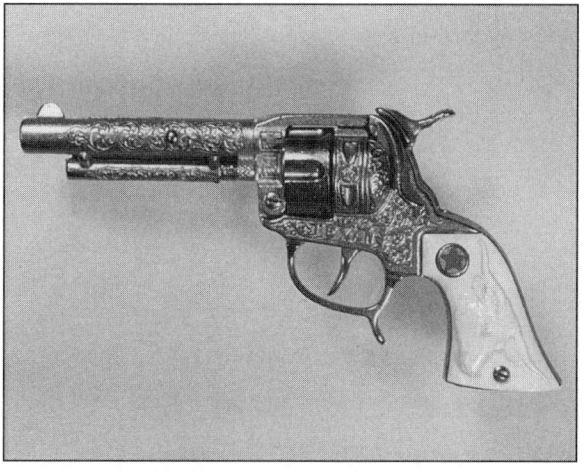

Texan Cap Pistol, 1940, Hubley, $225. Photo courtesy Charles W. Best

Tip Top Cap Pistol, 1880, Stevens, $225. Photo courtesy Charles W. Best

	C6	C8	C10
Trooper Safety Cap Pistol, "Pat. Pend; Made in U.S.A.," operates either as straight cap pistol or can be fired w/crank, 1930, 10"	100	150	200
Trooper Safety Cap Pistol, 1925, 10-1/4"	75	112	150
Two Time Pistol, "Pat. Appld. For," 1930, 9-1/4"	100	150	200
U.S. Navy, 1885, 6-1/2"	75	100	150
U.S.A. Liquid Pistol Water Pistol, "Pat. June 30, 1896," 1896, 4-3/4"	75	100	150
Victor Pistol	125	150	175
Victor Pistol, 1924, 12"	150	200	250
Villa Cap Pistol, "Made in U.S.A.," 1934, 4-3/4"	40	50	60
Volunteer Cap Pistol, "Pat. April 22, '73," 1873	125	188	250
War Cap Pistol, "Pat. Sept. 11-23," 1930, 4-1/4"	35	50	65

	C6	C8	C10
Warrior Cap Pistol, "Pat. Appld. For, 1926," maker unknown, 1926, 9"	100	125	175
Water Pistol, unmarked	30	45	60
Water Pistol, No. 41	30	45	60
Western Cap Pistol, "Made in U.S.A.," 1939, 7-1/2"	30	45	60
Western Cap Pistol, 1931, 7-1/4"	65	98	130
Western Cap Pistol, "Pat. Sept. 11-23," 1935, 7"	35	48	65
Westo Cap Pistol, "Kenton," 1936, 7"	40	50	75
Westo Pistol, "Kenton," 1938, 7"	40	50	75
Whoopie Cap Pistol, 1932, 5-7/8"	35	45	60
Wild West Cap Pistol, "Made in U.S.A.," 1930, 6-1/2"	40	60	75
Wild West Cap Pistol, 1926, 11-1/2"	125	175	225
Wild West Cap Rifle, w/sight, 30"	50	75	110
Winner Cap Automatic, 1940, 4-3/8"	35	45	60
Woodsman Cap Automatic, "Patented; Made in U.S.A.," 1938, 5-1/4"	60	85	110
Xtra Pistol, "Made in U.S.A.," 1936, 5"	30	45	55
Yank Cap Pistol, 1880	125	175	225
Yankee Cap Pistol, 1895, 5-1/2"	125	175	225
York Cap Pistol, "Pat. Sept. 11-23," 1930, 7"	40	55	75
Young Sportsman, c. 1868	75	112	150
Zip Cap Pistol, 1930, 5"	30	45	55
Zip Cap Pistol, 1938, 6"	30	45	55
Zulu Cap Pistol, w/decoration of African warrior with spear pursuing bird, maker unknown, 1890, 6-5/8"	150	225	300

IDEAL DOLLS

Ideal Toy Corporation, one of America's largest and oldest manufacturers of dolls and toys, produced high quality dolls for over eighty years. Each decade of this century saw a wildly popular Ideal doll. Doll collectors, depending on their age may remember playing with such Ideal dolls as Flossie Flirt (1920s), Shirley Temple and Betsy Wetsy (1930s), Toni (1940s), Miss Revlon (1950s), Patti Playpal and Tammy (1960s) or Crissy (1970s). Many of the Ideal dolls are now very desirable to doll collectors and, since they were mass-produced, affordable.

Always an innovator, Ideal used new technology to produce their dolls. Ideal dolls come in materials ranging from cloth, celluloid, composition, hard rubber, latex "magic skin" rubber, hard plastic, injection-molded vinyl, rotation-molded vinyl and blow-molded vinyl. Ideal is responsible for many of the technological breakthroughs in doll manufacturing and holds dozens of patents for innovations such as flirty eyes (eyes that roll from side to side), "ma-ma" voices, "magic skin" latex rubber and blow-molded vinyl dolls (example Patti Playpal).

Ideal was also a forerunner in licensing—tying in with comic-strip characters, merchandisers and movie stars in promoting their dolls. The company started when Morris Michtom named a stuffed bear after President Theodore Roosevelt and called it the Teddy Bear. Ideal was the first American dollmaker to tie-in with a cartoon character—the 1907 comic Yellow Kid. Their first tie-in with a merchandiser was the Uneeda Kid of the National Biscuit Company in 1914. Ideal was the first to strike it big licensing a movie star when they obtained the rights to produce a Shirley Temple doll in 1934. Ideal was a family business owned by the Michtoms until the 1980s when it was sold to C.B.S, which subsequently sold it to View-Master who sold it to Tyco in 1989. The trademark is currently held by the Mattel Toy Corporation.

Contributor: Judith Izen, P.O. Box 623, Lexington, MA 02173. Izen is a noted doll and paper doll authority whose paper doll articles have appeared in several publications. Her books include *Collectors Guide to Ideal Dolls* and *Collectors Encyclopedia of Vogue Dolls* (coauthored with Carol Stover).

	C10
Addams Family Puppets, The, 1964	65
Angel Babies, 1982	15
Archie Bunker's Grandson, 1976	40
Baby Baby-A Handful of Love, 1976	15
Baby Beautiful, 1938	175
Baby Big Eyes, 1954	80
Baby Coos, 1948	150
Baby Crissy, 1973	65
Baby Doll, vinyl head and limbs, cloth body, 1950s	100
Baby Dreams, 1975	45
Baby Giggles, 1968	50
Baby Jesus, 1958	125

	C10
Baby Kiss-a-Boo, 1981	30
Baby Snooks, 1938	200
Belly Button Baby, 1971	40
Betsy McCall, 1953	300
Betsy Wetsy, hard rubber head, 1938	150
Betsy Wetsy, hard plastic head, 1954	150
Betsy Wetsy, all vinyl, 1959	80
Betty Big Girl, 1969	100
Betty Jane, 1940	185
Big Baby Betsy Wetsy, 1960	100
Bizzie Lizzie, 1971	45
Blessed Event, 1950	90
Bonnie Baby, 1960	100

Baby Doll, 1950s, $100. Photo courtesy Robin Randall

Belly Button Baby, 1971, $40. Photo courtesy Judy Izen

	C10
Bonnie Play Pal, 1960	350
Bonny Braids, See Comic Characters	
Bonny Braids Walker, See Comic Characters	
Boopsie, 1950	30
Brandi, 1972	60
Brandi & Andy Gibb, 1979	45
Bride, 1939	200
Bridesmaid, 1939	200
Bud, 1965	85
Butterick Designing Set Mannequin, 1953	50
Bye-Bye Baby, 1960	325
Campbell Kids, 1955	100
Carol Brent, 1961	75
Chew, Chew, Chew Suzy Chew Doll, 1980	35

	C10
Chipettes, includes Jeanette, Brittany, Eleanor, 1984	25
Chipmunks, includes Simon, Alvin, Theodore, 1984	35
Cinderella, 1938	300
Cinnamon, 1972	70
Clarabelle, 1954	200
Composition Baby Dolls, 1910-1940s	175
Country Fashion Crissy Dolls, 1982, 15"	30
Cream Puff, 1959	125
Cricket, 1971	65
Crissy, 1969	45
Cross Patch, 1938	125
Crown Princess, 1957	85
Cuddles, 1928	175
Daddy's Girl, 1961	1200
Deanna Durbin, 1938	600
Derry Daring, 1975	35
Diana Ross, 1969	300

Bride, 1939, $200. Photo courtesy Marge Meisinger

Cinderella, 1938, $300. Photo by Carol Stover; doll courtesy Marge Meisinger

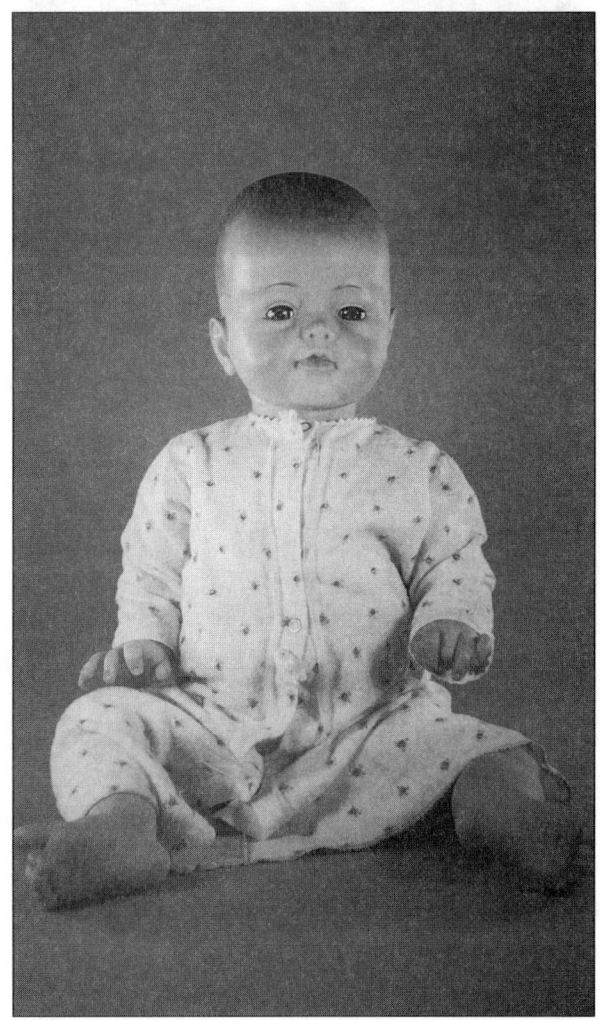

Bye-Bye Baby, 1960, $325. Photo courtesy Judy Izen

Honey Moon, 1965, $80. Photo courtesy Judy Izen

	C10
Dina, 1972	55
Dodi, 1964	40
Dorothy Hamill, 1978	35
Dracky, 1966	65
Ducky, 1932	90
ElectroMan, 1977	45
Fantasy Family—Mom, Dad, Boy, and Girl, price for each, 1964	55
Fashion Flatsy, 1973	45
Flatsy, 1972	45
Flexy Dolls, 1939	200
Flossie Flirt, 1924	150
Franky, 1966	65
Fred Muggs, 1957	70
Giggles, 1967	65
Ginger, 1938	300
Girl Doll, composition, 1910-1940s	175
Girl Doll, hard plastic, 1950s	200
Glamour Misty, 1965	45
Goody Two Shoes, 1965	85
Grown Up Pos'n Tammy, 1965	45
Happi Returns, 1983	25
Hara, 1984	30
Harmony, 1972	50
Harriet Hubbard Ayer, 1953	175
Honey Moon, 1965	80
Honeybunch, 1956	70
Honeysuckle, 1956	70
IDENITE Dolls, 1936	250
In-A-Minute Thumbelina, 1971	55
Jackie, 1962	900
Jay J. Armes, 1976	50
Jelly Belly Dolls, 1982	30
Jim and Dandy, 1985	30
Jody The Old-fashioned Doll, 1975	30
Johnny Play Pal, 1960	350
Judy Garland Teen, 1940	600
Judy Splinters, 1950	200
Karen and Her Magic Carriage, 1980	35
Katie Kachoo, 1966	50

Miss Ideal, 1961, $325. Photo courtesy Judy Izen

	C10
Kerry, 1971	60
Kindles, 1985	20
Kissy, 1979, 3"	25
Kissy, 1961	125
Liberty Boy, 1918	250
L'il Honest Abe, 1953	100
Little Betsy Wetsy, 1957	65
Little Lost Baby, 1968	65
Little Miss Revlon, 1959	125
Little Wingy, 1953	200
Little Women, 1984	45
Liz, 1962	75
Lori Martin, 1961	800
Magic Hair Crissy, 1977	45
Magic Lips, 1955	125
Magic Skin Baby Doll, 1941	100

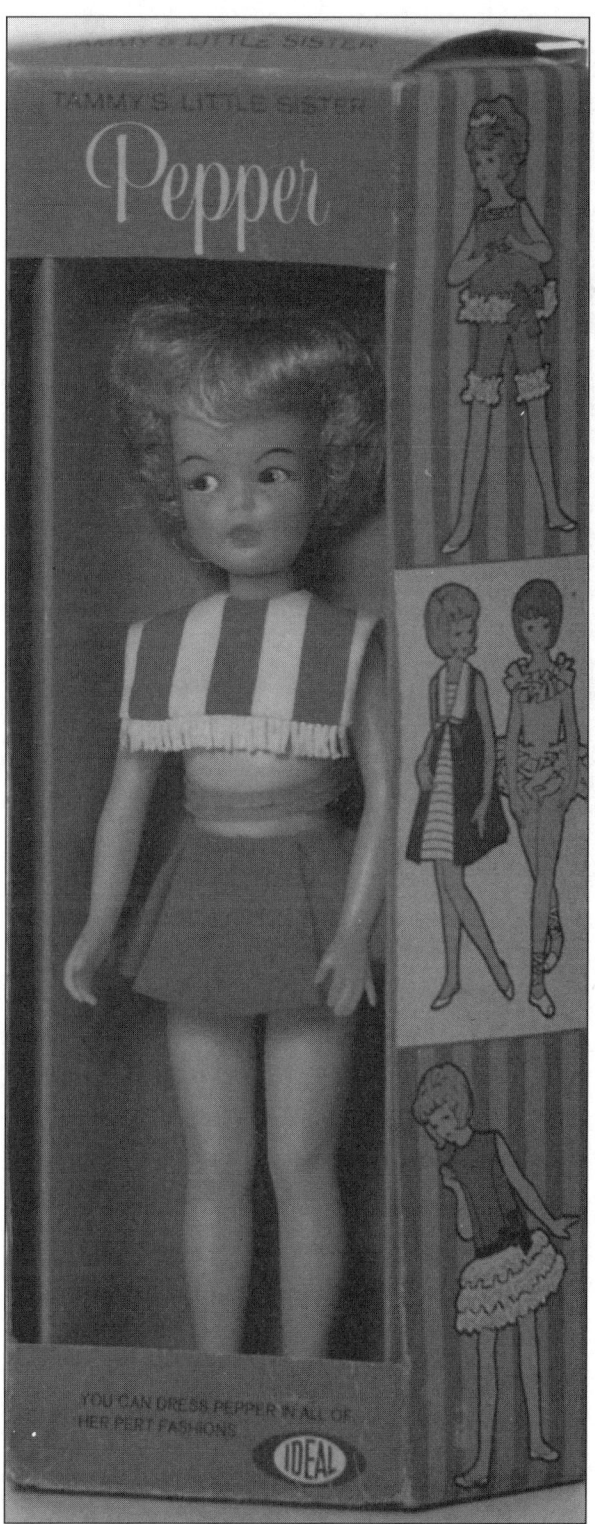

Pepper, 1963, $35. Photo courtesy Judy Izen

	C10
Marama, 1940	800
Mary Hartline, 1952	500
Mayfair, 1939	150

	C10
Mera, Queen of Atlantis, 1967	600
Mia, 1971	55
Mighty Mouse, 1957	60
Mini Monsters, 1966	65
Miss Curity, 1953	350
Miss Ideal, 1961	325
Miss Liberty, 1940s	300
Miss Revlon, 1956	250
Mistress Mary-Quite Contrary, 1938	150
Mitzi, 1961	150
My Bottle Baby, 1979	35
National Velvet, 1961	800
Nursery Tales, 1984	25
Orange Juice Boy, 1928	150
Pam's Pram, 1954	40
Patti Partridge, 1971	70
Patti Play Pal, 1959	350
Patti Play Pal, 1981	150
Patti Playful, 1973	65
Patti Prays, 1957	60
Pattite, 1960	350
Peggy's Snap-On Magic Wardrobe, 1953	40
Penny Play Pal, 1959	300
Pepper, 1963	35
Pete and Repete, 1951	45
Peter Playpal, 1960	850
Plassie, 1942	150
Play 'N Jane, 1971	40
Playtex Dryper Baby, 1960	250
Posie, hard plastic, 1954	150
Posie, bendable vinyl, 1969	50
Pos'n Pete, 1965	45
Pos'n Salty, 1965	45
Princess Beatrix, 1938	250
Princess Mary, 1955	175
Queen of the Ice, 1938	150
Raggedy Ann and Andy, the set, 1983	100
Rub-A-Dub Dolly, 1974	35
Ruth, 1953	125
SallyKins, 1934	175

Sara Stimson, 1980, $40. Photo courtesy Judy Izen

	C10
Samantha the Bewitching Doll, 1965	600
Sara Ann, 21"	300
Sara Ann, 1951, 15"	250
Sara Stimson, 1980	40
Saralee, 1951	300
Saucy Walker, hard plastic, 1953	250
Saucy Walker, vinyl, 1960	200
Shirley Temple, porcelain, 1984	200
Shirley Temple, vinyl, 1960, 36"	1200
Shirley Temple, vinyl, 1984	50
Shirley Temple, vinyl, 1982, 8"	40
Shirley Temple, vinyl, 1974	80
Shirley Temple, vinyl, 1957-61, 12"	200
Shirley Temple, vinyl, 1957-61, 17"	225
Shirley Temple, composition, 1939, 25"	825
Shirley Temple, vinyl, 1957-61, 19"	250

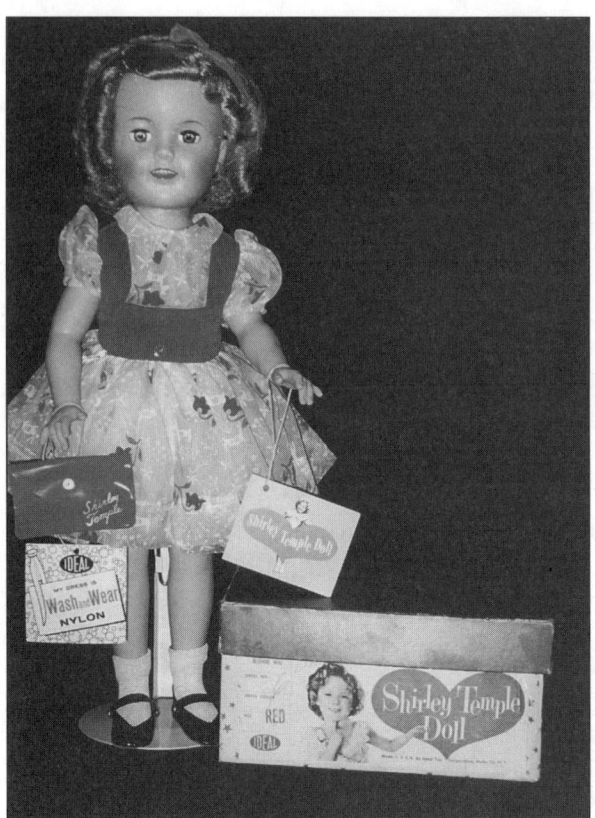

Shirley Temple, 1957-61, $225. Doll courtesy Donna Carr

	C10
Shirley Temple, composition, 1939, 22"	800
Shirley Temple, composition, 1939, 17"	650
Shirley Temple, composition, 1939, 15"	625
Shirley Temple, composition, 1939, 13"	600
Shirley Temple, composition, 1939, 11"	650
Shirley Temple, 1982, 12"	60
Shirley Temple, composition, 1939, 27"	900
Shirley Temple Baby, 1935	800
Smokey the Bear, 1953	150
Snoozie, 1933	150
Snuggles, 1978	30
Soldier, 1940s	150
Soozie Smiles, 1923	125
Storybook Dolls, 1938	100
Stretchie, 1973	25
Suntan Dodi, 1977	30
Suntan Eric, 1977	40
Suntan Tuesday Taylor, 1977	35
Suzy, 1936	150

Tickletoes, 1931, $150. Photo courtesy Judy Izen

	C10
Suzy Play Pal, 1959	350
Tabatha, 1966	500
Talkypot, 1950	90
Tammy, 1962	45
Tammy's Dad, 1963	55
Tammy's Mom, 1963	55
Tara, 1976	75
Tearie Dearie, 1963	30
Ted, 1963	40
Teddy Bear, porcelain, 1984	80
Teddy Bear, cloth, 1907	900
Terry Twist, 1962	150
Thumbelina, 1961	200
Tickletoes, 1931	150
Tiffany Taylor, 1974	65
Timmy Tumbles, 1977	40
Tiny Tears, vinyl, 1984	35
Tiny Tears, porcelain, 1984	60
Tippy Tumbles, 1977	40

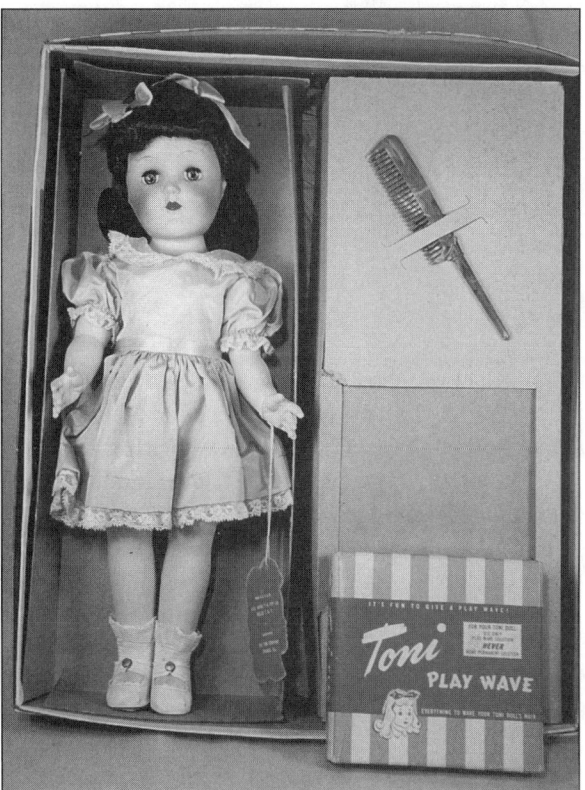

Toni, 1949-53, $300. Doll courtesy Ann Tandle

	C10
Toni, 1949-53, 14"	300
Toni, 1949-53, 22-1/2"	800
Toni Walker, 1954-56, 14"	300
Toni Walker, 1954-56, 21"	500
Tressy, 1970	70
Trilby, 1951	150
Tubsy, 1967	50
Tuesday Taylor, 1976	45
Twinkle Eyes, 1957	60
Uneeda Kid, 1914	250
Upsy Dazy, 1973	35
Vampy, 1966	65
Velvet, 1974	40
Victorian Ladies, 1984, 8"	25
Victorian Ladies, 1984, 12"	30
Vinyl Doll, all vinyl body, 1955	80
Wake-Up Thumbelina, 1976	35
Whoopsie, 1978	45
Wolfie, 1966	65
Zu-Zu Kid, 1916	275

LIONEL TRAINS

Lionel is unquestionably the greatest name in the history of toy trains. Founded in 1902 by Joshua Lionel Cowen (born August 25, 1877), it was incorporated as the Lionel Manufacturing Company on March 13.

In his teens Cowen had worked for New York's Acme Electric Lamp Company as a battery-lamp assembler, and he enjoyed experimenting in his spare time. In 1901, Cowen developed what was to become the first Lionel train—a battery-powered "Electric Express." It was originally designed to be used as a showpiece in a shop window. Customers were curious about the Electric Express, and eventually twelve of the showpieces eventually were sold. Cowen was on his way.

In 1902, Cowen added a trolley car to the display, manufactured for him by Massachusetts' Morton E. Converse. At the same time, six barrels were added to the Electric Express. Other accessories in the first 1902 Lionel catalog included a suspension bridge, a track with a switch, a crossover track that allowed a figure-eight layout and a bumper for the end of a track. The Electric Express, like the trolley, could now be powered by batteries or electricity.

By 1909, Lionel was advertising its trains as "The Standard of the World." Cowen had a knack for advertising, and much of Lionel's early success can be attributed to the companies colorful and punchy ad campaigns and catalogs.

The next twenty years saw tremendous growth for Lionel. In 1915, O-gauge cars were introduced, and they eventually became the most popular scale of train. By the 1920s electricity was found in more homes, and no toy benefited more from electricity than the train. In 1927, Lionel's profits were almost a half-million dollars.

In 1930, the first full year of the Depression, Lionel's profits were down to $82,000, and in 1931 they lost $207,000. The firm temporarily went into receivership in 1934.

That same year the Streamlined Union Pacific diesel M10000 was released. Lionel orchestrated a major publicity campaign timed to coincide with the M10000's release. Sales soared. It was in the fall of this year that Lionel developed the Mickey and Minnie Mouse hand car. It sold more than a quarter million units, and it is very likely the thing that saved the company from bankruptcy. By the next year his company was in the black by $154,000.

Standard gauge was discontinued in 1940, and with the interruption of World War II, Lionel's only war years toy was a cardboard train set as the company fulfilled government contracts.

Lionel's postwar line, known by many as the golden years of Lionel train, was introduced by a sixteen-page catalog contained in the November 23, 1946 issue of Liberty magazine. Though competition with American Flyer soon became fierce, Lionel was able to stay ahead. Bakelite and other plastics became prominent, along with such innovations as knuckle couplers, smoke units, a battery-operated diesel horn (1948) and "Mangnetraction" (Magnetized wheels and axles, which gave stronger pulling power) in the 1950s.

However, by the mid 1950s Lionel began to teeter. In 1957, Lionel introduced HO-scale trains, but that year was the last profitable one for the company. Ever sagacious, Cowen retired the next year and sold all of his Lionel stock the following year.

Cowen died at the age of 85 on September 8, 1965

	C6	C8	C10
90 degrees Crossing, O scale, 1962	4	6	8
Bulb, 8 volt, clear, 1939	n/a	n/a	1
Caboose, O72 scale, 1940	165	275	550

	C6	C8	C10
Electronic Control, instruction booklet, 1946	5	10	15
Electronic Control Unit, 1946	40	60	80

	C6	C8	C10
Fiber Pins, O scale, dozen, 1962 ....n/a	n/a	1
Half Section Curved Track, O scale, 1966 1	1	1
Half Section Straight Track, O scale, 1966 ....n/a	n/a	1
Lockton, O scale, 1947.........................n/a	n/a	1
Lockton, universal, 1937.....................n/a	n/a	1
Lockton, O27 scale, w/light, 1950 10	15	20
Lockton, standard scale, 1921 ....n/a	n/a	1
Lockton, O scale, 1921.........................n/a	n/a	1
Mechanical Key, square, 1934 3	5	10
Steel Pins, O scale, dozen, 1962............n/a	n/a	1
Steel Pins, O/standard scale, dozen, 1937 1	2	2
Straight Track, O scale, 1962................n/a	n/a	1
Switches, O scale, remote control, 1962 35	53	70
Track, straight, mechanical, 1933 ....n/a	n/a	1
Track, curved, mechanical, 1933 ....n/a	n/a	1
Track, standard scale, curved racing car-type 36" diameter, 1912................ 28	42	55
Track, standard scale, curved half section, 1906 ....n/a	1	2
Track, O scale, curved, 1915................n/a	n/a	1
Track, standard scale, straight, 1906.....n/a	1	2
Track, standard scale, curved, w/battery connections, 1915 1	2	3
Track, standard scale, curved, racing car-type, 36" dia., 1915...................... 28	42	55
Track, O scale, curved, w/battery connections, 1915 1	2	3
Track, O scale, curved w/insulated rails, 1926.............................n/a	n/a	1
Track, standard scale, straight half section, 1906 ....n/a	1	2
Track, O scale, straight, 1915................n/a	n/a	1
Track, standard scale, straight w/battery connections, 1915 1	2	3
Track, O scale, straight, w/battery connections, 1915 1	2	3
Track, curved, insulated, mechanical, 1935 ....n/a	n/a	1
Track, curved, mechanical, 1935 ....n/a	n/a	1

	C6	C8	C10
Track, standard scale, straight w/insulated rails, 1926 1	2	3
Track, O scale, straight w/insulated rails, 1926.............................n/a	n/a	1
Track, standard scale, curved racing car-type, 30" dia., 1912 25	38	50
Track, O scale, curved, 1962 ....n/a	n/a	1
Track, O scale, remote control, 1938 3	4	5
Track, standard scale, curved, 1906 .....n/a	1	2
Track, curved, mechanical, 1933..........n/a	n/a	1
Track Clip, O scale, 1937 ....n/a	n/a	1
Track Clip, standard scale, 1937 ....n/a	n/a	1
Transformer, 50 watt, 1942 10	15	20
Transformer, 110 watt, 1948 48	66	85
Transformer, 90 watt, 1947 40	55	75
Transformer, 125 watt, 1956 105	125	140
Transformer, 100 watt, 1939 25	38	50
Transformer, 75 watt, 1939 7	11	14
Transformer, 40 watt, 1916 20	30	40
Transformer, 50 watt, 1915 10	15	20
Transformer, 75 watt, 1939 7	11	14
Transformer, 50 watt, 1915 10	15	20
Transformer, 150 watt, 1948 98	125	150
Transformer, 135 watt, 1961 55	82	120
Transformer, 75 watt, 1915 10	15	20
Transformer, 115 watt, 1953 77	100	145
Transformer, 50 watt, 1933 10	15	20
Transformer, 275 watt, 1953 177	225	295
Transformer, 250 watt, 1948 140	200	275
Transformer, 75 watt, 1923 13	23	45
Transformer, 75 watt, 1933 5	8	10
Transformer, 75 watt, 1938 10	15	20
Transformer, 150 watt, 1939 55	83	110
Transformer, 75 watt, 1914 10	15	20
Transformer, 190 watt, 1950 115	155	195
Transformer, 50 watt, 1917 13	23	45
Transformer, 75 watt, 1922 15	25	50
Transformer, 60 watt, 1930 10	15	20
Transformer, 150 watt, 1914 40	60	80
Transformer, 250 watt, 1939 80	120	160

	C6	C8	C10
Uncoupling Track, O scale, remote control, 1949	8	10	145
1 Bild-A-Motor, O scale, 1928	150	225	300
1 Bild-A-Motor, small, 1928	75	113	150
00-1 Locomotive, OO scale, steam, 4-6-4 Hudson full scale, three-rail w/either 001T tender without whistle or 001W w/whistle, 1938-42	120	200	400
1 Trolley, standard scale, motor car, four wheel, powered, blue body w/blue roof, marked "No. 1 Electric-Rapid Transit No. 1," 1906-1910	1050	1750	3500
1 Trolley, standard scale, motor car, four wheel, powered, cream body w/blue roof, marked "No. 1 Electric-Rapid Transit No. 1," 1906-1910	1260	2100	4200
1 Trolley, standard scale, trailer, non-powered, white body w/blue roof, 1907	1050	1750	3500
1 Trolley, standard scale, trailer, non-powered, cream body w/blue roof, 1907	1050	1750	3500
1 Trolley, standard scale, motor car, four wheel, powered, cream body w/blue roof, "No. 1 Electric-Rapid Transit No. 1," 1906-1910	750	1250	2500
1 Trolley, standard scale, motor car, powered, four wheel, white body w/blue roof, marked "No. 1 Electric-Rapid Transit No. 1," 1906-1910	1110	1850	3700
0-20X 45 Degrees Crossing, O scale, 1915	10	15	20
0-20 90 Degrees Crossing, O scale, 1915	6	9	12
2 Bild-A-Motor, O scale, large, 1928	200	300	400
00-2 Locomotive, OO scale, steam, 4-6-4 Hudson, semi-scale, three-rail w/either 002T tender without whistle or OO2W w/whistle, 1938-42	105	175	350
002W Tender, w/whistle	120	200	400
2 Trolley, standard scale, motor car, four-wheel, powered, No. 2 Electric-Rapid Transit No. 2 red body, cream windows and doors, 1906-1915	1050	1750	3500
2 Trolley, standard scale, trailer, non-powered, cream body w/red windows and doors, 1906-1915	750	1250	2500
2 Trolley, standard scale, motor car, four-wheel, powered, No. 2 Electric-Rapid Transit No. 2 cream body, red windows and doors, 1906-1915	1050	1750	3500
2 Trolley, standard scale, trailer, non-powered, red body, cream windows and doors, 1906-1915	750	1250	2500
00-3 Locomotive, OO scale, steam, 4-6-4 Hudson semi-scale, three-rail w/either 002T Tender without whistle or 002W w/whistle, 1938-1942	120	200	400
0-30 Roadbed, curved, rubber, 1931	3	4	5
3 Trolley, standard scale, eight-wheel, trailer, non-powered, light orange body, dark orange roof, 1906-1909	1200	2000	4000
3 Trolley, standard scale, eight wheel, motor car, powered, No. 3 Electric-Rapid Transit No. 3, cream body, orange roof, 1906-1909	1200	2000	4000
3 Trolley, standard scale, eight wheel, motor car, powered, No. 3 Electric-Rapid Transit No. 3, dark green body and roof, 1906-1909	1350	2250	4500
3 Trolley, standard scale, eight wheel, motor car, powered, No. 3 Electric-Rapid Transit No. 3, light orange body, dark orange roof, 1906-1909	1200	2000	4000
4 Locomotive, O scale, 0-4-0, electric, orange, 1928-1932	270	450	900
4U Locomotive, O scale, 0-4-0, electric, orange only, marked "You build it," unassembled and complete w/instructions in original box, 1928	850	1275	1700
4 Locomotive, O scale, 0-4-0, electric, gray, 1928-1932	300	500	1000
00-4 Locomotive, OO scale, steam, 4-6-4 Hudson semi-scale, two-rail w/either 004T Tender without whistle or 004W w/whistle, 1938-1942	120	200	400
4 Trolley, standard scale, eight-wheel, motor car, cream body and green roof, powered, double motor, "No. 4 Electric-Rapid Transit No. 4," 1908-1910	2700	4500	9000

	C6	C8	C10
4 Trolley, standard scale, eight-wheel, motor car, green body and roof, powered, double motor, "No. 4 Electric-Rapid Transit No. 4," 1908-1910	2700	4500	9000
5 Locomotive, standard scale, 0-4-0, steam, no tender, black cab and boiler, red window trim, "Pennsylvania," 1906-1926	900	1500	3000
5 Locomotive, standard scale, 0-4-0, steam, no tender, black cab and boiler, red window trim, marked "B&ORR," 1906-1926	360	600	1200
5 Locomotive, standard scale, 0-4-0, steam, no tender, black cab and boiler, red window trim, marked "NYC&HRRR," 1906-1926	780	1300	2600
5 Special Locomotive, standard scale, 0-4-0, steam, no tender, black cab and boiler, red window trim w/tender, 1910-1911	450	750	1500
5 Trolley, standard scale, motor car, powered, four wheel, No. 1 Electric-Rapid Transit No. 1, cream body, orange roof, 1906-1910	1200	2000	4000
5C Test Set	1500	2500	4000
5D Repair Station	800	1400	1900
6 Locomotive, standard scale, 4-4-0, steam w/tender, black cab and boiler, red window trim, marked "B&ORR," 1906-1923	630	1050	2100
6 Locomotive, standard scale, 4-4-0, steam, w/tender, black cab and boiler, red window trim, marked "Pennsylvania," 1906-1923	705	1175	2350

	C6	C8	C10
6 Locomotive, standard scale, 4-4-0, special, steam, w/tender, black cab and boiler, red window trim, non-lettered, 1908-1909	450	750	1500
6 Locomotive, standard scale, 4-4-0, steam w/tender, black cab and boiler, red window trim, marked "NYC&HRRR," 1906-1923	300	500	1000
0-60 Telegraph Pole, O scale, set of six, 1929	24	40	80
6-16137 Tank Car, O27 scale, Ford Single-Dome tank car, 1994	10	15	35
6-19212 Boxcar, O27 scale, Pennsylvania boxcar, 1989	10	15	35
6-19232 Boxcar, O27 scale, Rock Island double-door boxcar	10	15	25
6-19243 Boxcar, O27 scale, Clinchford boxcar, 1991	10	15	30
6-9438 Boxcar, O27 scale, Ontario Northland boxcar	10	20	45
00-70 90 Degree Crossing, OO scale, three-rail, 1939	8	11	15
7 Locomotive, standard scale, 4-4-0, steam, brass boiler, nickel cab and tender, 1910-1923	1050	1750	3500
8 Locomotive, standard scale, 0-4-0, electric, olive, 1925-1932	45	75	150
8 Locomotive, standard scale, 0-4-0, electric, mojave, 1925-1932	60	100	200
8 Locomotive, standard scale, 0-4-0, electric, red, 1925-1932	45	75	150
8 Locomotive, standard scale, 0-4-0, electric, peacock, 1925-1932	75	125	250

No. 6 Locomotive, 4-4-0, $1,500. Photo courtesy T.W. Sefton

No. 7 Locomotive, 4-4-0, $3,500. Photo courtesy T.W. Sefton.

No. 9U Locomotive, $1,500.

	C6	C8	C10
8 Locomotive, standard scale, 0-4-0, electric, maroon, 1925-1932	30	50	100
0-80 Semaphore, O scale, 1926-1935	50	75	100
8 Trolley, standard scale, eight wheel, motor car, powered, cream or dark green, marked "Pay as you enter No. 8," 1908-1909	1170	1950	3900
8E Locomotive, standard scale, 0-4-0, electric, mojave, 1926-1932	95	162	325
8E Locomotive, standard scale, 0-4-0, Macy, electric, pea green, cream stripe, 1926-1932	150	250	500
8E Locomotive, standard scale, 0-4-0, electric, peacock, 1926-1932	110	180	360

	C6	C8	C10
8E Locomotive, standard scale, 0-4-0, electric, olive, 1926-1932	60	100	200
8E Locomotive, standard scale, 0-4-0, electric, red, 1926-1932	80	135	270
9 Locomotive, standard scale, electric, dark green, 1929	600	1000	2000
9U Locomotive, standard scale, electric, orange, assembled, 1928	450	750	1500
9U Special Locomotive, standard scale, kit form w/original box, orange, unassembled, 1929	1200	1800	2400
9 Trolley, standardl scale, eight wheel, motor car, powered, cream or dark green, marked "Pay as you enter No. 9," 1909	2100	3500	7000

	C6	C8	C10
9E Locomotive, standard scale, 0-4-0, electric, 242, two-tone green, 1928	472	785	1575
9E Locomotive, standard scale, 2-4-2, electric, gray, 1931	420	700	1400
10 Interurban, standard scale, motor car, powered, marked "Interurban," "New York Central Lines," "10 WB&B&A 10," 1910	1500	2500	5000
10 Interurban, standard scale, motor car, powered, maroon or dark green, "Interurban" and "New York Central Lines," 1910	600	1000	2000
10 Locomotive, standard scale, 0-4-0, electric, peacock blue, mojave, gray, 1925-1929	85	140	280

	C6	C8	C10
10 Macy Locomotive, standard scale, 0-4-0, electric, red, 1930	180	300	600
10E Locomotive, standard scale, 0-4-0, electric, brown, green frame, 1926-1930	90	135	275
10E Locomotive, standard scale, 0-4-0, electric, peacock or gray, 1926-1930	74	122	245
10E Locomotive, standard scale, 0-4-0, electric, peacock or red, w/Bild-a-Loco Motor, 1926-1930	158	260	525
10E Macy Locomotive, standard scale, 0-4-0, electric, peacock w/orange stripe, uncataloged, 1930	85	140	280
11 Flatcar, standard scale, 1906-1926	33	55	110

No. 9E Locomotive, 0-4-0, $1,575.

Part of an early ad for the No. 9 Trolley.

Part of an early ad for the No. 18 Pullman.

	C6	C8	C10
0-11 Switches, O scale, electric, nonderailing, pair, 1933	50	75	100
12 Gondola, standard scale, 1906	30	50	100
0-12 Switches, O scale, electric, 1927	30	50	100
13 Cattle Car, standard scale, 1906	45	75	150
0-13 Switches, O scale, panel board set, 1929	25	38	50
14 Boxcar, standard scale, 1906-1926	60	100	200
00-14 Boxcar, OO scale, yellow and Tuscan, 1938	24	40	80
14 Harmony Boxcar Car Creamery Special, standard scale, uncataloged, 1920	120	200	400
15 Oil, standard scale, 1906-1926	48	80	160
00-15 Tank Car, OO scale, 1938	27	45	90
16 Ballast, standard scale, dark green, 1906-1926	65	108	215
00-16 Hopper, OO scale, 1938	66	110	220
17 Caboose, standard scale, 1906-1926	105	175	350
00-17 Caboose, OO scale, 1938	25	41	82
18 Pullman, standard scale, light orange, marked "New York Central Lines," 1916-1917	360	600	1200
18 Pullman, standard scale, dark olive, marked "New York Central Lines," 1906-1910	360	600	1200
18 Pullman, standard scale, dark olive, marked "Parlor Car" and "New York Central Lines," 1918-1923	210	350	700
19 Combine, standard scale, 1906-1927	300	500	1000

	C6	C8	C10
19 Combine, standard scale, 1906-1927	180	300	600
19 Combine, standard scale, 1906-1927	300	500	1000
20 90 Degrees Crossing, standard scale, 1909	6	9	12
20 Direct, current shunt resistor, 1906	2	4	6
21 Crossing, standard scale, 1906	4	6	8
21 Switch, standard scale, w/light, 1915	12	18	25
0-21 Switch, O scale, w/light, 1915	12	18	25
0-22 Switches, O scale, electric, 1946-1949	26	39	125
0-23 Bumper, O scale, 1915	4	6	8
23 Bumper, standard scale, red or black, 1906	9	13	18
00-24 Boxcar, OO scale, 1939	20	32	65
24 Bulb, eight volt, 1915	n/a	n/a	1
24 Station, standard scale, 1906	350	525	700
25 Bulb, 3-1/2 volt, DC, 1911	n/a	n/a	1
25 Bulb, pear shaped, 1924	n/a	n/a	5
0-25 Bumper, O scale, 1928	17	25	35
25 Bumper, standard scale, cream or black, 1928	20	30	40
25 Station, standard scale, 1906	375	562	750
00-25 Tank Car, OO scale, 1939	30	50	100
26 Bulb, 14 volt AC, 1911	n/a	n/a	1
26 Bumper, O scale, red, 1948	32	48	65
26 Bumper, O scale, gray, 1948	65	98	130
26 Passenger Foot Bridge, standard scale, 1906	100	150	200

	C6	C8	C10
27 Bulb, 12 volt, red, green or clear, 1927 ....n/a	n/a	1
00-27 Caboose, OO scale, 1939 21	35	70
27 Lighting, standard scale, set for cars, 1911 37	52	75
27 Station, standard scale, 1909 250	375	500
27-3 Bulb, 14 volt, clear, 1950 ....n/a	n/a	1
27-6 Bulb, 12 volt, clear, 1940 ....n/a	n/a	1
28 Bulb, 18 volt, red, green, amber or clear, 1927 ....n/a	n/a	1
28-3 Bulb, 18 volt, clear, 1939 ....n/a	n/a	1
28-6 Bulb, 18 volt, red, 1939 ....n/a	n/a	1
29 Bulb, 3-1/2 volt, 1915 ....n/a	n/a	1
29 Day Coach, standard scale, dark olive, 1909 112	188	375
29 Day Coach, standard scale, maroon, 1909 180	300	375
29-3 Bulb, 18 volt, yellow, 1932 ....n/a	n/a	1
30 Bulb, 14 volt, 1915 ....n/a	n/a	1
30 Curved Rubber Roadbed, standard scale, 1931 3	4	5
30 Water Tank Car, gray support structure, 1947-1950 70	150	250
30 Water Tank Car, black support structure, 1947-1950 125	250	500
31 Combine, standard scale, orange, green and maroon, 1921...................... 48	80	160
0-31 Roadbed, O scale, straight, rubber, 1931 3	4	5
31 Straight Rubber Roadbed, standard scale, 1931 3	4	5
31 Track, Super O scale, curved, 1957 ....n/a	2	4
00-31 Track, OO scale, curved, two-rail, 1939 3	5	6
32 Baggage Car, standard scale, maroon, dark olive, brown, orange, 1921 67	112	225
32 Miniature Figures, standard scale, set of twelve, 1910 150	225	300
0-32 Roadbed, O scale, 90-degree crossing, rubber, 1931........................... 3	4	5
32 Rubber Roadbed, standard scale, 90-degree crossing, 1931 3	4	5
32 Track, Super O scale, straight, 1931 5	10	15
00-32 Track, OO scale, straight, two-rail, 1939 5	10	15
33 Half Curve Track, Super O scale, 1957...n/a	2	4
33 Locomotive, 0-6-0, electric, engine only, dark green, 1913 240	400	800
33 Locomotive, standard scale, 0-4-0, electric, dark olive or black, 1913-1924 50	82	165
33 Locomotive, standard scale, 0-4-0, electric, maroon, 1913-1924 120	200	400
33 Locomotive, standard scale, 0-4-0, electric, red, 1913-1924 150	250	500
33 Locomotive, standard scale, 0-4-0, electric, peacock, 1913-1924 75	125	250
33 Locomotive, standard scale, electric 0-4-0, gray, 1913-1924........... 60	100	200
0-33 Roadbed, standard O scale, 45-degree crossing, rubber, 1931.......... 3	4	5
0-33 Roadbed, standard O scale, 45-degree crossing, rubber, 1931.......... 3	4	5
33 Rubber Roadbed, standard O scale, 45-degree crossing, 1931 3	4	5
34 Locomotive, standard scale, 0-6-0, electric, dark green, 1912................. 150	250	500
34 Locomotive, standard scale, 0-4-0, electric, dark green, uncataloged, 1913.. 120	200	400
0-34 Roadbed Switch, O scale, rubber, 1931 3	4	5
34 Rubber Roadbed Switch, standard scale, 1913.. 3	4	5
34 Track, Super O scale, half, straight, 1957.................................n/a	2	4
00-34 Track Connection, OO scale, for curved track, 1939 3	4	5
35 Lamp Post, gray or silver, 1940........ 15	25	50
35 Pullman, standard scale, dark olive, maroon or brown, 1915............. 21	34	68
35 Pullman, standard scale, orange, 1915.. 49	65	130
36RM Controller, standard scale, 1937...n/a	2	3
36 Observation Car, standard scale, dark olive, maroon or brown, 1912..... 21	35	70
36 Observation Car, standard scale, orange, 1912................................... 60	100	200

	C6	C8	C10
37 Uncoupling Track, Super O scale, 1957 8	15	20
38 Accessory Adapter, Super O scale, 1957 ....n/a	1	2
38 Locomotive, standard scale, 0-4-0, electric, pea green, 1913-1924 96	160	320
38 Locomotive, standard scale, 0-4-0, electric, red, 1913-1924 150	250	500
38 Locomotive, standard scale, 0-4-0, electric, brown, 1913-1924 120	200	400
38 Locomotive, standard scale, 0-4-0, electric, black or gray, 1913-1924 75	125	250
38 Water Tower, red roof, 1946-1947 .. 225	338	430
38 Water Tower, brown roof, 1946-1947 175	255	450
39 Bulb, 12 volt, frosted, 1927..............n/a	n/a	1
HO-039 Track Cleaning Car, HO scale, 1961 36	60	120
39-25 Operating and Upcoupling Set, Super O scale, 1960 3	4	5
39-3 Bulb, 12 volt, frosted, 1939 ....n/a	n/a	1
39-5 Operating Unit Set, Super O scale, 1957 3	4	5
40 Bulb, 13 volt, 1927 ....n/a	n/a	1
40-25 Four Conductor Cable and Reel, 1950 ....n/a	1	2

	C6	C8	C10
40-3 Bulb, 8 volt, 1939........................ n/a	n/a	1
40-50 Three Conductor Cable and Reel, 1960 .... n/a	1	2
41 Accessory Contactor, 1936.............. n/a	1	2
41 Locomotive, O27 scale, army switcher, black shell small motorized unit, 1955 130	150	200
42 Locomotive, standard scale, 0-4-4-0, electric, square body, dark green, 1912.. 450	750	1500
42 Locomotive, standard scale, electric, dark green, gray and black, 1913-1923 142	237	475
42 Locomotive, standard scale, electric, peacock, 1913-1923 825	1375	2750
42 Locomotive, standard scale, electric, maroon, 1913-1923 240	400	800
42 Locomotive, standard scale, electric, mojave, 1913-1923 173	288	575
42 Locomotive, O27 scale, Picatinny Arsenal switcher, olive shell, small motorized unit, 1957 135	225	450
0-42 Switch, O scale, manual, single, 1938... 12	18	25
43 Bild-A-Motor, standard scale, gear set, 1929 75	108	150

No. 42 Locomotive, electric, $475.

Archies from Marx, 1975 (Action Figures). Left to Right: Archie, $75; Jughead, $75

Battlestar Galactica from Mattel, 1978-79 (Action Figures). Left to Right: Colonial Warrior, $85; Cylon Centurian, $95

Battlestar Galactica from Mattel, 1978-79 (Action Figures). Left to Right: Imperious Leader, $30; Daggit, tan, $30

Best of the West from Marx, 1960s (Action Figures). Left to Right: Best of the West Johnny West, $150; Johnny West Covered Wagon with horse and harness, $225

Black Hole from Mego, 1979-80 (Action Figures). Left to Right: Kate McCrae, $95; Dr. Alex Durant, $75; Dr. Hans Reinhardt, $75

Black Hole from Mego, 1979-80 (Action Figures). Left to Right: Maximillian, $75; Sentry Robot, $75; V.I.N.cent, $70

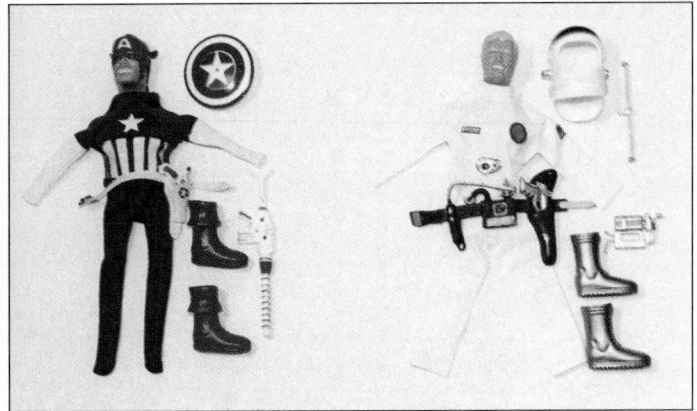

Captain Action from Ideal, 1966-68 (Action Figures). Left to Right: Captain America, $900; Flash Gordon, $600

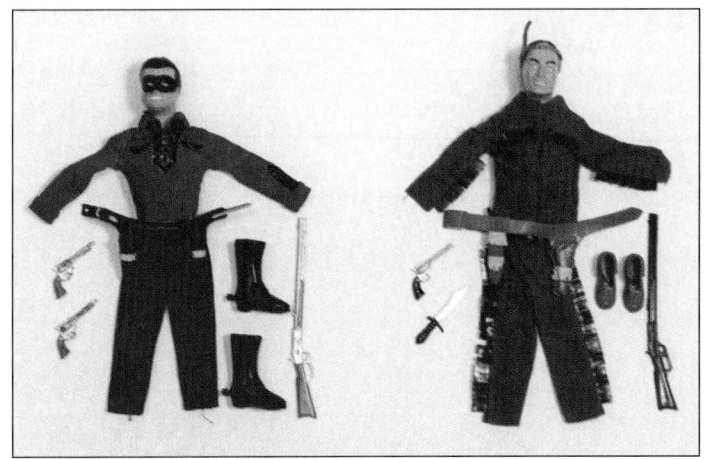

Captain Action from Ideal, 1966-68 (Action Figures). Left to Right: Lone Ranger, red shirt, $700; Tonto, $1100

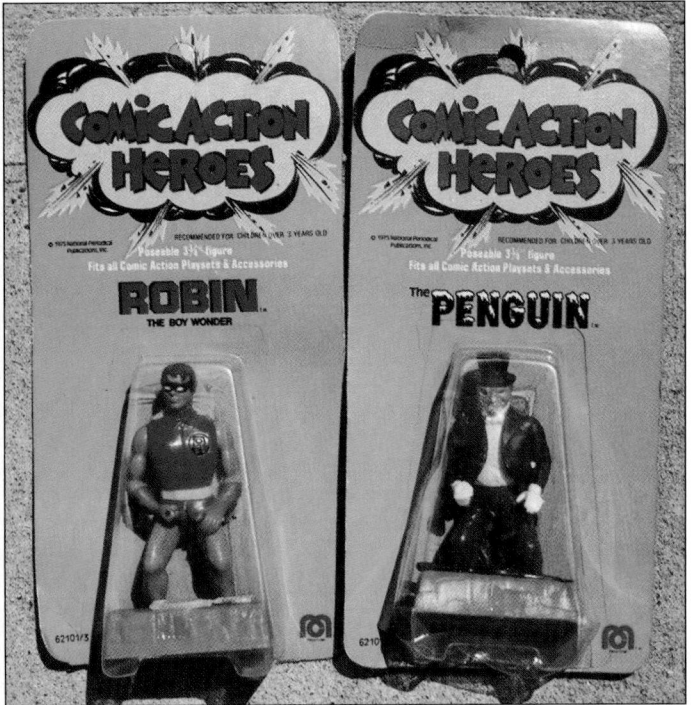

Comic Action Heroes from Mego, 1975 (Action Figures). Left to Right: Robin, $65; Penguin, $75

Comic Heroine Posin' Dolls (Super Queens) from Ideal, 1967 (Action Figures). Left to Right: Supergirl, $4500; Batgirl, $5500; Mera, $4500; Wonder Woman, $4500

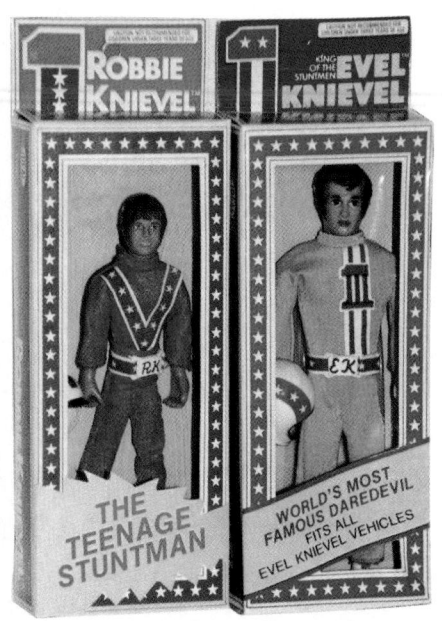

Evel Knievel from Ideal, 1973-74 (Action Figures). Left to Right: Robby Knievel, $60; Evel Knievel with blue suit, $50

Major Matt Mason from Mattel 1967-70 (Action Figures). Back row, left to right: Callisto, $250; Doug Davis, $300. Front row, left to right: Scorpio, $850; Major Matt Mason, $250

Planet of the Apes by Mego, 1973-75 (Action Figures). Left to Right: Cornelius, carded, $100; Galen, carded, $100; Soldier Ape, carded, $100

Star Trek: The Motion Picture from Mego, 1974-80 (Action Figures). Left to Right: Scotty, $35; Ilia, $20; Captain Kirk, $35

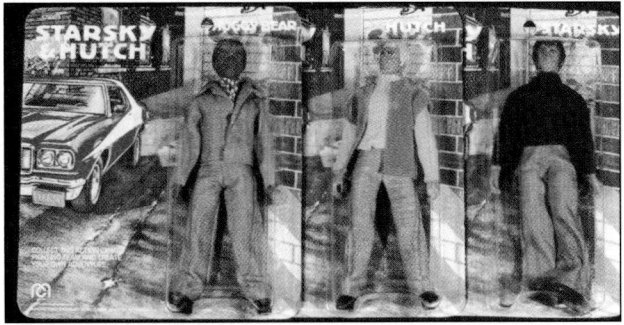

Starsky and Hutch from Mego, 1976 (Action Figures). Left to Right: Huggy Bear, $50; Hutch, $45; Starsky, $45

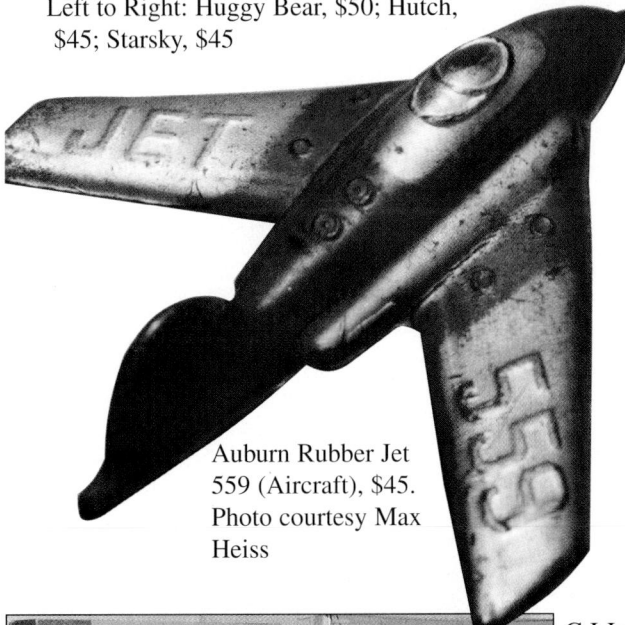

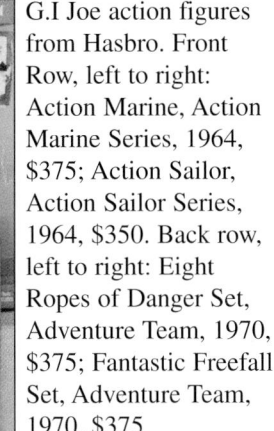

Auburn Rubber Jet 559 (Aircraft), $45. Photo courtesy Max Heiss

World's Greatest Super-Heroes from Mego, 1972-78 (Action Figures). Left to Right: Robin, magnetic, $100; Batman, magnetic, $100

G.I Joe action figures from Hasbro. Front Row, left to right: Action Marine, Action Marine Series, 1964, $375; Action Sailor, Action Sailor Series, 1964, $350. Back row, left to right: Eight Ropes of Danger Set, Adventure Team, 1970, $375; Fantastic Freefall Set, Adventure Team, 1970, $375

World's Greatest Super-Heroes from Mego, 1972-78 (Action Figures). Left to Right: Robin with painted mask, boxed, $150; Robin with painted mask, carded, $90

Pratt & Letchworth Brake (Animal-Drawn), 28" long, $11,000. Photo courtesy Christie's East

Reed Band Chariot (Animal-Drawn), 28-1/2" long, $2000. Photo courtesy Christie's East

Reed Cinderella Coach (Animal-Drawn), $2760. Photo courtesy Christie's East

J. & E. Stevens Calamity Mechanical Bank, $35,000

Marx Dapper Dan Mechanical Bank, $900. Photo courtesy Bill Bertoia Auctions

Freedman Mechanical Bank, $300,000. Photo courtesy Bill Bertoia Auctions

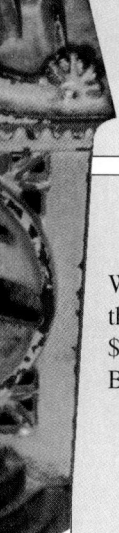

J. & E. Stevens Hall's Lilliput Mechanical Bank (Banks), $850

W.S. Reed Co. Old Woman in the Shoe Mechanical Bank, $426,000. Photo courtesy Bill Bertoia Auctions

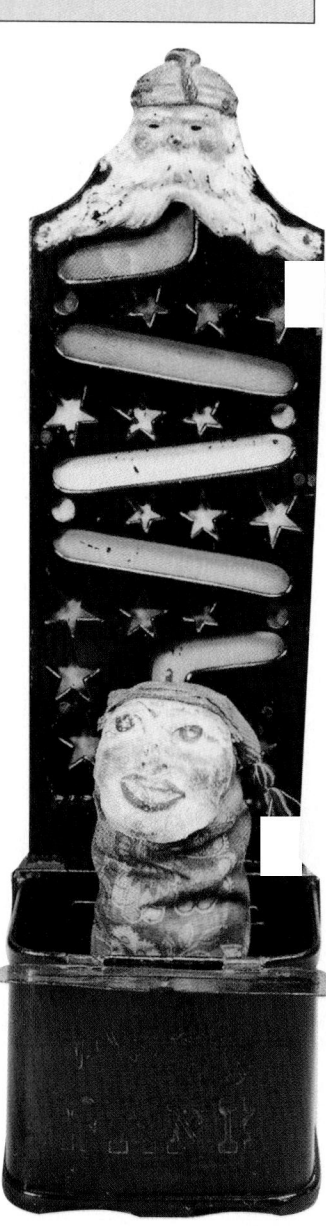

Zig Zag Mechanical Bank, $189,500. Photo courtesy Bill Bertoia Auctions

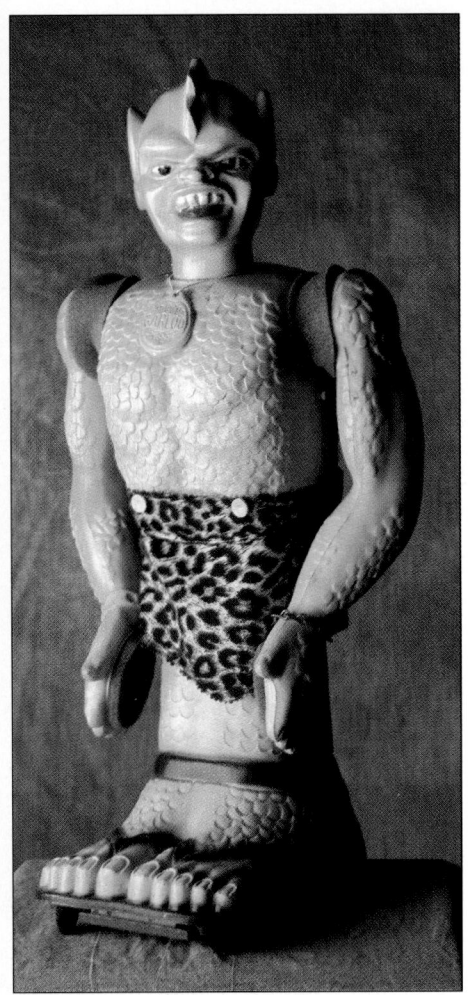

Marx Co. The Great Garloo (Battery-Operated Toys), 23" tall, $600

T-N Co. Marvelous Car, T-Bird (Battery-Operated Toys), 11" long, $500

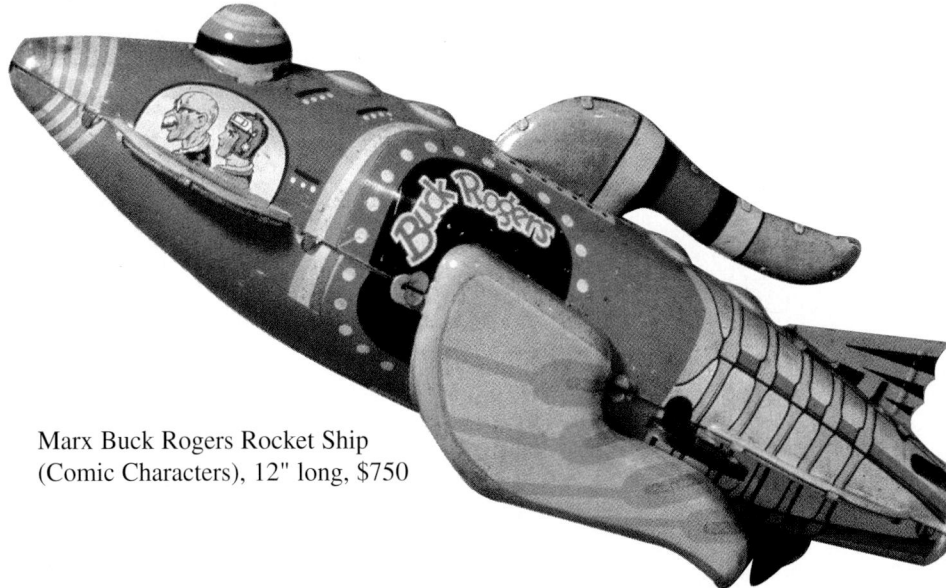

Marx Buck Rogers Rocket Ship (Comic Characters), 12" long, $750

Daisy Superman Krypto-Ray Gun (Comic Characters), $2000. Photo courtesy Danny Fuchs

Peter Rabbit Chickmobile (Comic Characters), $725. Photo courtesy Richard MacNary

Blue Ribbon Book, Inc.
Mickey Mouse Waddle Book
(Disney), $6500

Linemar Rocking Mickey Mouse
on Pluto Wind-up (Disney),
$2000. Photo courtesy Don
Hultzman

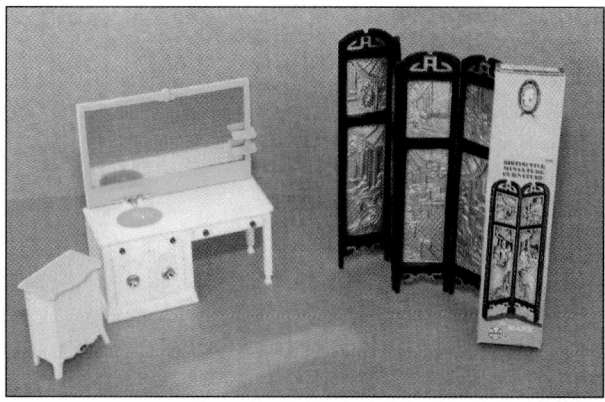

Marx Little Hostess (Dollhouse and Miniature Furniture).
Left to Right: Marx Little Hostess Hamper, $20; Marx
Little Hostess Sink/Vanity Combination, $30; Marx Little
Hostess Folding Screen, $20. Photo courtesy Marcie
Tubbs

Dunwell Livestock Transport (Farm Toys), $180. Photo courtesy Tim
Oei

T. Cohn/Superior Three-room Ranch (Dollhouses And
Miniature Furniture), 3/4-inch-scale , $45. Photo courtesy
Marcie Tubbs

Revell Dragnut (Figure Kits), No. 1303,
$95

Aurora Mod Squad Woodie (Figure Kits),
No. 583, $100

Hawk Sling
Rave
Curvette
(Figure
Kits), No.
637, $25

Fisher-Price Donald Duck Cart, No. 544, $425

Fisher-Price Kitty Bell, No. 499, $120

Diner Kit (Plasticville), $55. Photo courtesy Gary Linden

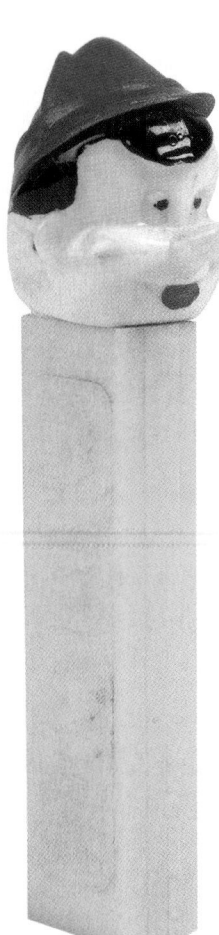

Pinocchio PEZ, $200

Frosty Bar (Plasticville), $40. Photo courtesy Gary Linden

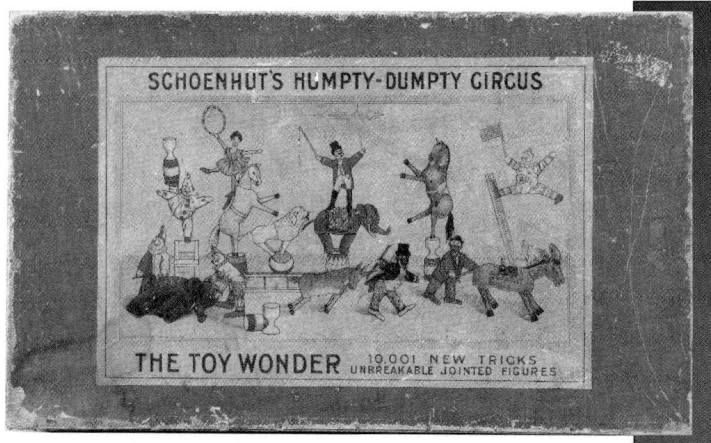

Box for Humpty Dumpty Circus (Schoenhut),
No. 2036. Photo courtesy Christie's East

Humpty Dumpty Circus, (Schoenhut), c. 1925. Photo courtesy Christie's East

Group shot of Teddy
Roosevelt's Adventures in
Africa figures (Schoenhut).
Photo courtesy Blossom Abel

Barclay Podfoot Figures (Soldiers). Khaki soldiers are the most common whereas the green figures are rare. The red figures are very scarce. The dark blue figure with the white helmet (front row, center) is by far the rarest of the Podfoot figures. Photo courtesy Stan Alekna

T.P.S. Bear Playing Ball (Tin Wind-Ups), 19" long, 4" high, $375. Photo courtesy Don Hultzman

T.P.S. Circus Parade (Tin Wind-Ups), 11-1/2" long, $400. Photo courtesy Scott Smiles

T.P.S. Gay 90s Cyclist (Tin Wind-Ups), 7" high, $375. Photo courtesy Scott Smiles

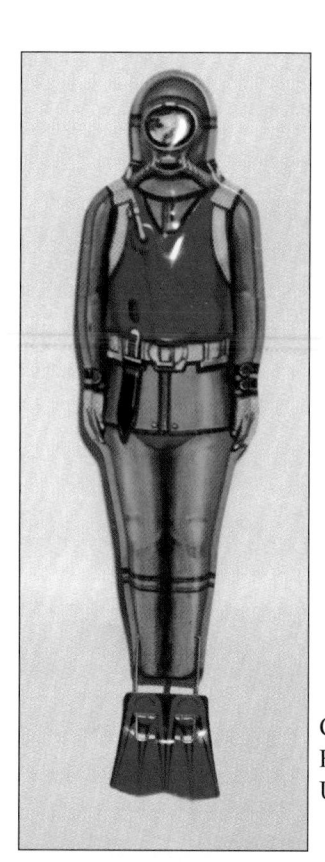

Chein Mechanical Frog Man (Tin Wind-Ups), 11" long, $200

Left to Right: Arcade Manufacturing Company Mack Ice Truck (Vehicles), No. 257, 10-3/4" long, $4200; Arcade Manufacturing Company Mack Ice Truck (Vehicles), No. 257, 10-5/8" long, $1000. Photo courtesy Bill Bertoia Auctions

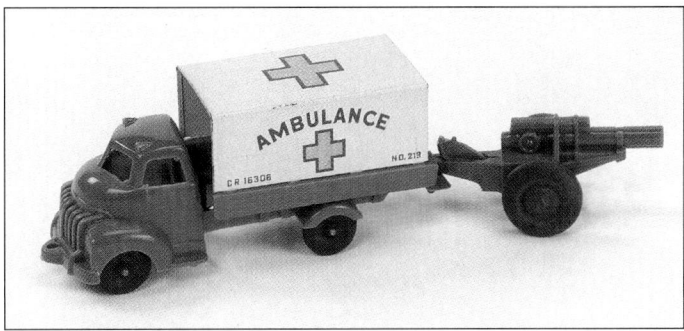

Banner Army Ambulance (Vehicles), 6" long, $40

Buddy "L" Baby Ruth/Butterfinger Curtiss Candies Tandem Truck (Vehicles), $2000. Photo courtesy John Taylor

Chein Hercules Mack Dump Truck (Vehicles), 20" long, $375

Top to Bottom: Buddy "L" Large Trucks Hydraulic Dump Truck (Vehicles), No. 201A, $1700; Buddy "L" Large Trucks Dump Truck (Vehicles), No. 201, 25", $1250. Photo courtesy Tim Oei

Chein Woodie Sedan (Vehicles), 5-1/4" long, $95 (garage not included with car). Photo courtesy Dave Leopard

Courtland Mechanical Operation No. 51 Crane Truck (Vehicles), No. 5000, 13" long, 3-5/8" wide, 5" high, $400. Photo courtesy Bob Smith

Ertl International Scout (Vehicles), $195

Courtland Space Rocket Patrol Car (Vehicles), No. 4060, 7-1/4" long, 3-1/4" wide, 2-3/4" high, $250. Photo courtesy Joe and Sharon Freed

Dunwell Red Star Express Lines Truck (Vehicles), $600. Photo courtesy Tim Oei

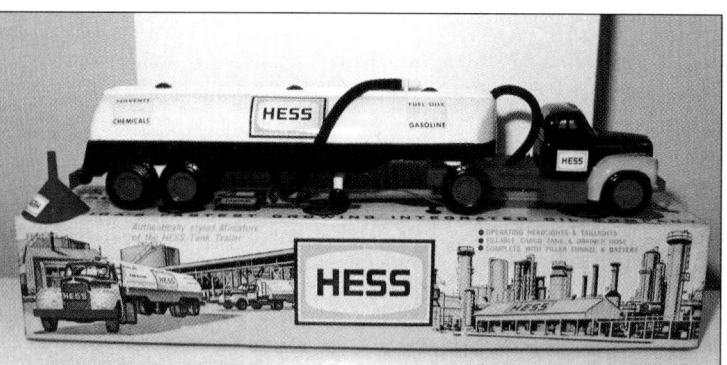

Hess 1964-5 B-Line Mack Tanker Truck (Vehicles), $2000. Photo courtesy Thomas G. Nefos

Hess 1991 Race Car Transporter (Vehicles), $50. Photo courtesy John and Suzanne Adivari

Hess 1970 Pumper Fire Truck (Vehicles), $695. Photo courtesy Thomas G. Nefos

Hot Wheels Cockney Cab
(Vehicles), No. 6466, $160

Hot Wheels Custom Volkswagen (Vehicles), No. 6220, $125

Hot Wheels Fire Chief Cruiser
(Vehicles), No. 6469, $45

Hot Wheels Twinmill
(Vehicles), No. 6258, $50

Hubley Auto Transport (Vehicles), 13" long, $250

Ideal Shell Oil Truck (Vehicles), 12-1/2"
long, $50. Photo courtesy Terry Sells

Bandai Japanese Tin Airplanes F-80 (Aircraft), 7-1/2" wingspan, $100. Photo courtesy Ron Smith

S&E Japanese Tin Airplanes Jenny Biplane (Aircraft), 14-1/2" wingspan, $250. Photo courtesy Ron Smith

Japanese Tin Cadillac Sedan (Vehicles), Bandai, 12", $185. Photo courtesy Ron Smith

Japanese Tin Chevrolet Corvair (Vehicles), Bandai , 8", $125. Photo courtesy Ron Smith

Japanese Tin Ford Thunderbird (Vehicles), Bandai, 7", $150. Photo courtesy Ron Smith

Japanese Tin Ford Thunderbird Retractable (Vehicles), Yonezawa, 11", $200. Photo courtesy Ron Smith

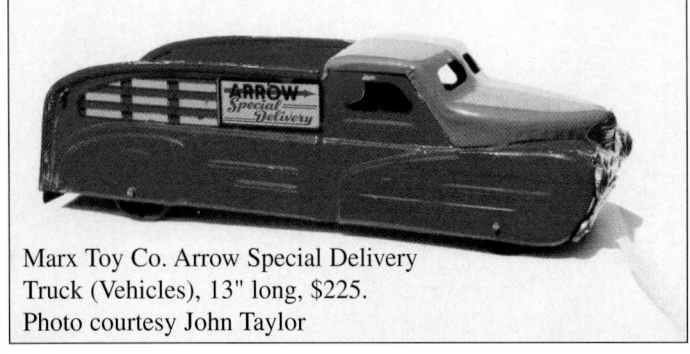

Marx Toy Co. Arrow Special Delivery Truck (Vehicles), 13" long, $225. Photo courtesy John Taylor

Marx Toy Co. Bud Bowman's Milk Express Truck (Vehicles), $350. Photo courtesy John Taylor

Marx Toy Co. Easter Stake Truck (Vehicles), 7" long, $325. Photo courtesy John Taylor

Matchbox No. 25 Bedford Dunlop Van (Vehicles), $55. Photo courtesy Gary Linden

Marx Toy Co. Lonesome Pine Trailer and Convertible Sedan (Vehicles), 13" long, $700. Photo courtesy Bob Smith

Smith-Miller Toys Coca-Cola Truck (Vehicles), No. 206-C, 14" long, $900. Photo courtesy Richard MacNary

Smith-Miller Toys L Mack Army Materials Truck (Vehicles), $925. Photo courtesy Bob Smith

Smith-Miller Toys GMC Mobilgas Tanker (Vehicles), No. 409-G, $750. Photo courtesy Tim Oei

Steelcraft City Fire Dept.
Ladder Truck (Vehicles), $1200.
Photo courtesy Tim Oei

Two examples of Structo's Motor Express Stake Truck
(Vehicles), No. 601, $110. Photo courtesy Randy Prasse

Tonka Dump Truck (Vehicles), No. 006, 1961, $250.
Photo courtesy Don and Barb DeSalle

Structo Package Delivery (Vehicles), No. 603,
$200. Photo courtesy Randy Prasse

Tootsietoy '48 Buick Super Estate Wagon (Vehicles), postwar,
6" long, $65. Photo courtesy John Gibson

Tootsietoy Kayo Ice Wagon (Vehicles), No. 5105, prewar, $400.
Photo courtesy John Gibson

Left to Right: Wyandotte Dump Truck (Vehicles), No. 315,
4-7/8" long, $85; Wyandotte Dump Truck (Vehicles), No.
315, 5-1/4" long, $85. Photo courtesy Brian Seligman

Wyandotte Coupe,
two-door (Vehicles),
8-1/4" long, $135.
Photo courtesy Brian
Seligman

Top to bottom: No. 45 U.S. Marine Missile Launcher Locomotive, $340; No. 2037 Locomotive, $125. Photo courtesy 1961 Lionel catalog.

	C6	C8	C10
0-43 Bild-A-Motor Gear Set, O scale, 1929	32	48	64
43 Pleasure Boat, cream, red and white, 1933-1936, 1939-1941	400	600	800
43 Power Track, Super O scale, 1957	n/a	1	2
00-44 Boxcar, OO scale, 1939	25	42	85
00-44K Kit, OO scale, original box, 1939	110	165	220
44 Locomotive, Super O scale, US Army Missile Launcher, 1959	72	120	240
44 Race Boat, green, white and dark brown, 1935-1936	450	675	900
44-80 Missiles, Super O scale, four, 1959-1962	2	3	4
45 Locomotive, O scale, U.S. Marine Missile Launcher, olive shell w/white missiles, 1960-1962	190	225	340
00-45 Tank Car, OO scale, 1939	21	85	70
00-45K Tank Kit, OO scale, 1939	100	150	200

	C6	C8	C10
45/45N/045 Automatic Gateman, green base, creame house, red roof w/cream chimney, 1935-1936, 1937-1942	16	27	55
46 Bulb, 8 volt, 1936	n/a	n/a	1
00-46 Hopper, OO scale, 1939	25	41	82
00-46K Hopper Kit, OO scale, 1939	100	150	200
46 Single Arm Crossing, cream and green base, lantern on tip of gate, 1939-1942	45	75	150
47 Bulb, 6 volt, 1916	n/a	n/a	1
00-47 Caboose, OO scale, 1939	24	40	80
00-47K Caboose Kit, OO scale, 1939	100	150	200
47 Double Arm Crossing Gates, w/two crossing gates on each side, 1937-1942	70	105	140
47-40 Bulb, 18 volt, red, 1937	n/a	n/a	1
47-73 Bulb, 12 volt, 1942	n/a	n/a	1
48 Bulb, 21 volt, 1936	n/a	n/a	1

No. 52 Fire Fighting car, $300. Photo courtesy Steve Hintze

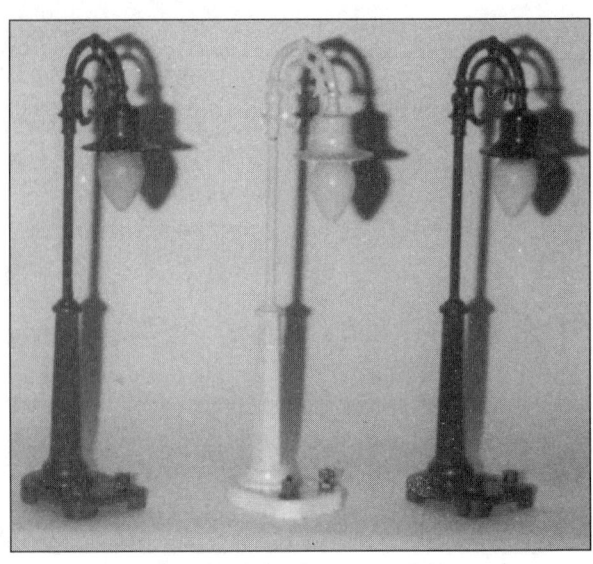

Three version of No. 58 Lamp post, $48, each.

	C6	C8	C10
48 Track, Super O scale, straight, insulated, 1958	4	8	12
48W Whistle Station, lithographed building, red base housing whistle, 1937-1942	10	18	36
49 Lionel Airport, printed cardboard base w/airplane and controls, 1937-1939	1000	1250	1500
49 Track, Super O scale, curved, insulated, 1958	4	8	12
50 Airplane, 1936	400	600	800
50 Gang Car, O27 scale, 1954	45	55	70
HO-050 Gang Car, HO scale, 1959	30	50	100
50 Locomotive, standard scale, electric, maroon, 1924	105	175	350
50 Locomotive, standard scale, electric, dark green, 1924	105	175	350
50 Locomotive, standard scale, electric, mojave, 1924	105	175	350
50 Locomotive, standard scale, 0-4-0, electric gray, 1924	90	150	300
50 Paper Train Set, uncataloged, 1943	90	157	315
51 Airport, printed cardboard base for center control and airplane, 1936-1939	300	450	600
51 Locomotive, standard scale, 0-4-0, steam, "5 Special," 1912-1923	380	650	1300
51 Locomotive, O27 scale, Navy switcher, blue shell small motorized unit, 1956-1957	150	190	250
00-51 Track, OO scale, curved, three-rail, 1939	n/a	1	2
52 Fire Fighting Car, O27 scale, red shell w/man, 1958-1961	165	225	300

	C6	C8	C10
52 Lamp Post, aluminum, 1933	35	52	70
00-52 Track, OO scale, straight, three-rail, 1939	6	8	10
53 Lamp Post, gray, aluminum, mojave, 1931	37	56	75
53 Locomotive, standard scale, 0-4-0, electric, mojave, maroon, dark olive, 1912-1914	360	600	1200
53 Locomotive, standard scale, 0-4-0, electric, mojave, maroon, dark olive, 1920	150	250	500
53 Snow Plow, O27 scale, DRG, Rio Grande, black and yellow, "a" in Grande backwards, 1957	180	250	330
53 Snow Plow, O27 scale, DRG, Rio Grande, black and yellow, 1957	520	680	900
53-8 Bulb, 18 volt, 1932	n/a	n/a	1
54 Ballast Tamper, O27 scale, yellow shell, small motorized unit, w/track trips, 1957	100	160	225
54 Lamp Post, double light, dark green, 1929	35	52	70
54 Locomotive, standard scale, 0-4-4-0, electric, brass, single or double motor, 1913-1923	750	1250	2500
54 Locomotive, standard scale, 0-4-4-0, electric, square body, brass, 1912	1050	1750	3500
00-54 Track Connection, OO scale, for curved track, 1939	n/a	1	2
55 Airplane, red and silver w/control, 1937-1939	250	375	500

	C6	C8	C10
55 Bulb, 14 volt, 1924	n/a	n/a	1
HO-055 Locomotive, HO scale, M&StL switcher, 1961	30	50	100
55 Tie Ejector, O27 scale, red shell w/wooden track ties, small motorized unit and track trips, 1957-1961	72	122	245
55-150 Ties, O27 scale, set of twenty-four, 1957	4	6	8
56 Lamp Post, gray, green, mojave, 1925-1949	32	48	65
HO-056 Locomotive, HO scale, A.E.C. Switcher, 1959	45	75	150
56 Locomotive, O27 scale, M&StL Mining, red shell, small motorized unit, 1958	250	480	580
57 Lamp Post, yellow, "Broadway & Main," 1924-1942	30	50	100
57 Lamp Post, orange, "Broadway & Main," 1924-1942	25	42	85
57 Lamp Post, orange, "Broadway & Fifth Ave.," 1924-1942	24	40	80
57 Lamp Post, orange, "Broadway & 42nd Street," 1924-1942	30	50	100
57 Locomotive, O27 scale, A.E.C. Switcher, cream-red shell, small motorized unit, 1959-1960	325	500	750
HO-057 Locomotive, HO scale, U.P. Switcher, 1959	30	50	100
58 Lamp Post, green, maroon, cream, 1922-1950	14	24	48

Left to right: No. 57 Boulevard Lamp post with silver lettering, $100; No. 56 Lamp post, $65; No. 53 Lamp post, $75; No. 61 Lamp post, $50; No. 57 Lamp post, $100.

	C6	C8	C10
HO-058 Locomotive, R.I. Switcher, 1960	24	40	80
58 Locomotive, O27 scale, rotary snow plow, green shell, 1959-1961	325	450	650
59 Lamp Post, green, 1920-1936	15	25	50
59 Lamp Post, olive, 1920-1936	22	37	75
59 Locomotive, O27 scale, U.S. Air Force Switcher, Minute Man, white shell, 1963	172	288	575
59 Locomotive, U.S. Air Force switcher, white cab	300	425	600
HO-59 Locomotive, HO scale, U.S. Air Force Switcher, 1960	30	50	100
60 Automatic Trip Reverse, standard scale, 1906	3	5	6
60 Locomotive, standard scale, 0-4-0, electric, F.A.O. Schwarz Special, uncataloged, 1913	360	600	1200
60 Telegraph Pole, standard scale, set of six, 1920	66	110	220
60 Trolley, O27 scale, red lettering, rare, 1955-1958	900	1500	3000
60 Trolley, O27 scale, yellow w/red roof, blue lettering, 1955-1958	100	150	195
60 Trolley, O27 scale, moving silhouettes, motor man in front w/direction of movement, 1955-1958	135	225	450
60 Trolley, O27 scale, black lettering, 1955-1958	150	220	300
61 Ground Lockon, Super O scale, 1957	n/a	2	4
61 Lamp Post, dark green, maroon, mojave, olive, 1914-1936	15	25	50
61 Locomotive, standard scale, 0-4-4-0, electric, F.A.O. Schwarz Special, uncataloged, 1913	450	750	1500
00-61 Track, OO scale, curved, three-rail, 1938	3	5	6
62 Automatic Reversing Trip, standard scale, 1914	3	4	5
62 Locomotive, standard scale, 0-4-0, electric, F.A.O. Schwarz Special, uncataloged, 1913	360	600	1200
62 Semaphore, 1920-1932	12	20	40
00-62 Track, OO scale, straight, three-rail, 1939	3	5	6

	C6	C8	C10
63 Lamp Post, double globe, silver, 1933-1942	81	135	270
63 Semaphore, 1915-1921	30	45	60
00-63 Track, OO scale, half-curve, three-rail, 1939	3	5	6
63-10 Opal Globe, 1933	3	4	5
63-11 Bulb, 18 volt, opal, 1935	n/a	n/a	1
64 Lamp Post, green, 1940-1942	14	24	48
64 Semaphore, 1915-1921	21	35	70
00-64 Track Connection, curved, three-rail, 1939	5	8	10
64-15 Bulb, 12 volt, clear, 1940	n/a	n/a	5
64-26 Bulb, 12 volt, opal, 1941	n/a	n/a	5
65 Motorized Hand Car, O27 scale, yellow, two rubber men, small motorized unit, yellow or dark yellow, 1962	135	225	450
65 Semaphore, 1915-1926	30	45	60
65 Semaphore, 1915-1926	35	52	70
00-65 Track, OO scale, half-straight, three-rail, 1939	n/a	1	2
65 Whistle Controller, 1935	6	9	12
00-66 Straight, OO scale, straight, three-rail, 1939	n/a	1	2
66 Whistle and Reversing Controller, 1936	3	5	6
67 Lamp Post, 1915-1926	30	50	100
67 Whistle and Reversing Controller, 1936	4	5	7
68 Executive Inspection Car, red DeSoto, small motorized unit, 1958-1961	200	250	350
HO-068 Inspection Car, HO scale, 1961	30	50	100
68 Warning Signal, standard scale, non-operative, 1926-1939	7	11	14
0-68 Warning Signal, O scale, 1926-1942	7	11	14
69 Motorized Maintenance Car, O27 scale, gray platform, black frame, w/blue man and red danger sign, 1960-1962	175	240	310
69N Warning Bell, standard/O scale, 1936-1942	25	38	50

	C6	C8	C10
0-69 Warning Bell, O scale, 1921-1935	25	38	50
69 Warning Bell, standard scale, 1921-1935	20	34	68
69-7 Fiber Track Pins, 1933	n/a	n/a	1
70 Accessory Set, consists of two No. 62, one No. 68 and one No. 59, 1921	75	112	150
70 Lamp Post, yard light, 1949-1950	17	29	58
71 Lamp Post, crackle gray, 1949-1959	12	15	22
71 Telegraph Pole Set, set of six, 1921	54	90	180
071 Telegraph Poles, O scale, set of six, 1929	63	105	210
00-72 Switches, OO scale, electric, three rail, pair, 1939	150	225	300
072 T-Rail, curved track, per section	n/a	2	3
00-74 Boxcar, OO scale, two-rail, 1939	22	38	75
75 Bulb, 12 volt, 1924	n/a	n/a	1
75 Lamp Set, black plastic, set of two, 1961-1969	17	26	35
75 Low Bridge Sign, 1921	35	52	70
00-75 Tank Car, OO scale, two-rail, 1939	21	35	70
76 Block Signal, standard scale, 1923	25	42	85
76 Boulevard Lights, green plastic, set of three, 1959-1969	9	12	24
76 Warning Bell and Shant, red base, orange roof, black bell fastened to cross gate sign post, similar in appearance to forty-five gateman, no watch man bell inside shanty, 1939-1942	95	143	190
0-77 Automatic Crossing Gate, O scale, 1923-1939	20	30	40
00-77 Caboose, OO scale, two-rail, 1939	28	48	95
77N Crossing Gate, standard/O scale, automatic, 1936-1939	25	38	50
77 Crossing Gate, standard scale, automatic, 1923-1939	35	52	70
0-78 Train Control Block Signal, O scale, red or orange base, 1924	45	68	90

Left to right: No. 184 Bungalow, $90; No. 78 Train Control Block Signal, $80; Two versions of the No. 35 Lamp post, $80, each.

	C6	C8	C10
78 Train Control Block Signal, standard scale, red base, orange base, 1924	40	60	80
79 Flashing Signal, cream or aluminum, 1928-1942	60	90	120
79-23 Bulb, Bulb scale, 12 volt, red, 1939	n/a	n/a	1
80N Semaphore	62	93	125
80 Semaphore, standard scale, 1926-1935	75	112	150
80/81 Race Car Set, includes car, driver, eight sections of curve track, 1912-1916	750	1125	1500
00-81 KW Kit, OO scale, locomotive and tender, three-rail, 1938	600	900	1200
81 Rheostat, 1927	7	11	15
82N Train Control Semaphore, standard/O scale, 1936-1942	92	138	185
82 Train Control Semaphore, standard scale, yellow and green, 1927-1935	55	82	110
0-82 Train Control Semaphore, O scale, 1927-1935	60	90	120
83 Traffic Crossing Signal, red base 35-42	155	225	310
83 Traffic Crossing Signal, tan base 27-34	155	225	310
00-83 W Locomotive and Tender, OO scale, three-rail, 1939-1942	180	300	600

	C6	C8	C10
84 Racing Cars, 1912	2000	3000	4000
0-84 Semaphore, O scale, 1928-1932	60	90	120
84 Semaphore, standard scale, 1927-1932	60	90	120
85 Racing Cars, 1912	2000	3000	4000
85 Telegraph Pole, standard scale, orange, 1929-1942	15	22	30
86 Telegraph Poles, standard scale, set of six, including original box, 1932	82	138	185
87 Crossing Signal, orange or green base, 1927	105	158	210
88 Direction Controller, 1933	3	4	5
88 Rheostat, battery, 1915	7	11	15
89 Flag Pole, 1956-1958	22	33	45
89 Flagstaff and Flag, 1923-1934	50	75	100
90 Flagstaff and Flag, w/round grass plot, 1927-1942	25	38	50
90-93 W Locomotive, OO scale, tender, two rail, 1939	180	300	600
91 Circuit, automatic, breaker, brown w/red light bulb, 1930-1942	38	56	75
91 Circuit Breaker, brown w/red light, 1957-1960	8	11	12
00-91 W Locomotive and Tender, OO scale, two-rail, 1939	180	300	600
92 Circuit Breaker, w/controller, 1959	11	16	23

	C6	C8	C10
92 Floodlight Tower, red, silver, 1931	92	138	185
92 Floodlight Tower, terra-cotta, green, 1931	90	135	180
93 Water Tower, O scale, silver, 1932	47	71	95
93 Water Tower, O scale, green, 1932	20	30	40
94 High Tension Tower, gray, terra-cotta, silver and red, 1932	200	300	400
95 Rheostat, 1934	12	18	25
96 Coal Elevator, manual control, 1938-1940	95	132	190
97 Coal Elevator, electric, 1938-1942, 1946-1950	125	188	250
0-97 Telegraph Pole Set, O scale, 1934	25	38	50
97C Contactor, 1938	5	8	10
0-99 Train Control Block, O scale, 1930	75	112	150
99 Train Control Block Signal, standard scale, red or black base, 1932	85	128	170
99N Train Control Block Signal, standard/O scale, red or black base, 1936	85	128	170
100 Bridge Approaches, standard scale, 1920	20	30	40
100 Locomotive, 2-7/8" scale, 1901	100	2000	4200
HO-100 Power Pack, HO scale, 1961	10	15	20
100 Trolley, standard scale, motor car, blue or red, marked "100 Electric Rapid Transit 100," 1910	600	1000	2000
HO-101 Power Pack, HO scale, 1961	10	15	20
101 Summer Trolley, standard scale, motor car, blue or red, manual, "101 Electric Rapid Transit 101," 1910	600	1000	2000
101 Three Section Bridge, standard scale, cream and green, 1920	55	82	110
102 Bridge, standard scale, four section, 1920	35	52	70
103 Bridge, standard scale, five section, 1913	90	135	180
HO-103 Power Pack, HO scale, 1959	10	15	20
HO-103-800 Power Pack, HO scale, 1961	10	15	20
104 Bridge, standard scale, center span, 1920	15	22	30

	C6	C8	C10
HO-104 Power Pack, HO scale, 1961	10	15	20
104 Tunnel, standard scale, 1909-1914	50	75	100
105 Bridge, standard scale, three section, 1913	25	38	50
105 Bridge, standard scale, five section, 1911	40	60	80
105 Bridge Approaches, O scale, 1920	7	11	15
106 AC Current Reducer, 110 or 120 volts, 1911	3	4	5
106 Bridge, O scale, three section, 1920	25	38	50
107 DC Current Reducer, 220 volts, 1911	10	15	20
107 DC Current Reducer, 110 volts, 1911	10	15	20
108 Battery Rheostat, 1912	3	4	5
108 Bridge, O scale, four section, 1920	48	72	95
109 Bridge, O scale, five section, 1920	40	60	80
109 Tunnel, standard scale, 1913	50	75	100
110 Bridge, O scale, center span, 1920	15	22	30
110 Trestle Set, O scale, twenty-four pieces, 1955-1969	10	15	20
HO-110 Trestle Set, HO scale, 1958	10	15	20
111 Light Bulb Set, 1920	10	15	20
111 Trestle Set, O scale, ten pieces, 1956-1969	13	17	22
HO-111 Trestle Set, HO scale, 1959	10	15	20
111 Trolley, standard scale, trailer, 1910	600	1000	2000
111-100 2 Piers, O scale, two pieces, 1960-1963	10	15	20
112 Gondola, standard scale, 1910	135	225	450
112 Gondola, standard scale, 1913	24	40	80
112 Station, standard scale, cream, 1931-1935	162	243	325
112 Switch, Super O scale, w/controls, pair, 1957-1960	42	63	95
113 Cattle Car, standard scale, 1912-1926	33	55	110
113 Station, standard scale, cream, 1931-1934	275	362	550

	C6	C8	C10
114 Boxcar, standard scale, 1912	36	60	120
HO-114 Engine House, HO scale, w/horn, 1958	50	75	100
114 Newstand, O scale, w/horn, 1957-1959	52	78	120
114 Station, standard scale, cream, 1931-1934	750	1125	1500
HO-115 Kit, HO scale, engine house, 1961	35	52	70
115 Station, cream, red or green trim, 1935	215	322	450
115 Station, cream, red or green trim, 1949	155	200	310
116 Ballast, standard scale, 1910	54	90	180
116 Station, cream, double station, 1935	600	900	1200
117 Caboose, standard scale, 1912-1926	27	45	90
HO-117 Engine House, HO scale, 1959	45	68	90
117 Station, no outside lights, 1936-1942	175	262	350
117 Station, 1936-1942	175	262	350
HO-118 Engine House, HO scale, w/whistle, 1958	50	75	100
118 Newstand, O scale, w/whistle, 1958	42	63	90
118 Tunnel, O scale, 1915-1920	45	68	90
118L Tunnel, O scale, lighted, 1927	40	60	80
119 Tunnel, standard/O scale, 1915	40	60	80
HO-119 Tunnel, HO scale, 1959	7	11	15

	C6	C8	C10
119 Tunnel, O scale, 1957	40	60	80
119L Tunnel, standard/O scale, lighted, 1927	50	75	100
120 90 Degree Crossing, Super O scale, 1957	8	12	16
120L Tunnel, standard/O scale, lighted, 1927	67	100	135
120 Tunnel, standard/O scale, 1915	62	93	125
121 Special Station, standard scale, 1909	300	450	600
121 Tunnel, O scale, 1959-1966	20	30	40
121x Station, standard scale, w/lights, 1917	300	450	600
122 Station, standard scale, 1920	62	93	125
123 Station, standard scale, 1920	125	188	250
123 Tunnel, O scale, curved, 1933	90	135	180
124 Station, standard scale, 1933	137	207	275
124 Station, standard scale, 1920	250	375	500
125 Station, standard scale, 1923	30	45	60
125 Track Template, 1938	5	8	10
125 Whistle Station, gray or green base, 1950-1955	22	33	45
126 Station, standard scale, 1923-1936	135	202	270
127 Station, 1923-1936	117	175	235
128 Newsstand, animated, 1957-1960	85	127	220
128 Tunnel, O scale, lighted, 1920	55	83	110
129 Station and Terrace, standard scale, 1929-1940	800	1200	1600
129 Terrace, standard scale, 1928	900	1350	1800
129 Tunnel, standard/O scale, lighted, 1920	70	105	140
130 60 Degrees Crossing, O scale, 1957	10	15	20
130L Tunnel, O scale, lighted, 1927	125	188	250
130 Tunnel, O scale, 1920	150	225	300
131 Corner Elevation, 1924-1928	350	525	700
131 Tunnel, O scale, curved, 1959-1966	35	53	70
132 Grass Plot, corner, 1924-1928	200	300	400
132 Station, O scale, 1949-1955	45	55	105
133 Grass Plot, heart shaped, 1924-1928	200	300	400

No. 115 Station, $450. Photo courtesy Steve Hintze

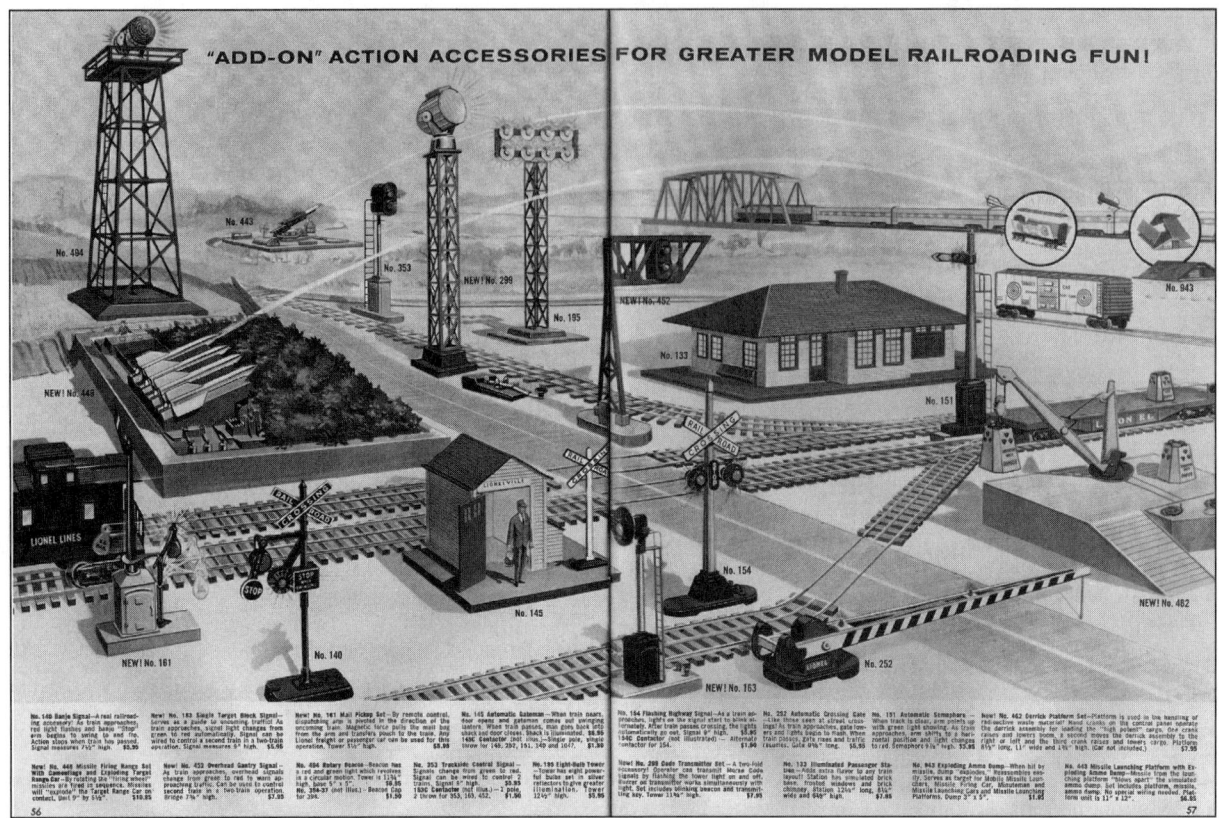

Top of page, left to right: No. 494 Rotary Beacon, $50; No. 443 Missile Launching Platform, $60; No. 353 Trackside Signal, $40; No. 195 Floodlight Tower, $60. Middle of page: No. 448 Missile Firing Range set, $140. Bottom of page, left to right: No. 161 Mail Pickup set, $70; No. 140 Banjo Signal $50; No. 145 Automatic Gateman, $49. Photo courtesy 1961 Lionel catalog.

	C6	C8	C10
133 Station, O scale, 1957-1966	30	45	85
134 Grass Plot, oval, 1924-1928	200	300	400
134 Stop Station, brown w/red roof, 1937-1942	175	263	350
135 Grass Plot, oval, small, 1924-1928	200	300	400
136 Stop Station, lighted, 1937-1942	150	225	300
137 Stop Station, lighted, 1937-1942	112	168	225
138 Water Tank, operating, 1953-1957	75	80	145
140 Banjo Signal, O scale, 1954-1966	25	38	50
HO-140 Banjo Signal, HO scale, 1962	22	33	45
140L Tunnel, standard scale, lighted, 1927-1932	400	600	800
142 Switches, Super O scale, manual, price per pair, 1957	15	23	30

	C6	C8	C10
145 Automatic Gateman, O scale, 1950-1966	26	32	49
HO-145 Gateman, HO scale, automatic, 1959	30	45	60
145C Contactor, O scale, 1950	6	9	12
147 Whistle Controller, O scale, 1961	3	4	5
148 Dwarf Signal, O scale, 1957	30	45	60
148-100 Double Pole Switch, 1957	4	6	8
150 Locomotive, O scale, electric, 0-4-0, dark green, 1918-1925	60	100	200
HO-150 Rectifier, HO scale, 1958	2	3	4
150 Telegraph Poles, O scale, set of six, 1947-1950	19	29	45
151 Semaphore, O scale, 1947-1969	22	35	46
151-51 Bulb, 14 volt, clear, 1950	n/a	n/a	1
152 Crossing Gate, O scale, 1945-1948	21	32	42

	C6	C8	C10
152 Locomotive, O scale, light gray, 1917-1927	113	187	375
152 Locomotive, O scale, peacock or mojave, 1917-1927	135	225	450
152 Locomotive, O scale, electric, dark gray or dark green, 1917-1927	75	125	250
152-33 Bulb, O scale, 12 volt, red, 1940	n/a	n/a	1
153 Block Signal, O scale, 1945-1969	22	34	45
153 Locomotive, O scale, electric, mojave, 1924	75	125	250
153 Locomotive, O scale, dark green, 1924	60	100	200
153 Locomotive, O scale, gray, 1924	60	100	200
153-23 Bulb, 6 volt, red, 1940	n/a	n/a	1
153-24 Bulb, 6 volt, green, 1940	n/a	n/a	1
153C Contactor, O scale, 1940	5	8	10
153-48 Bulb, 14 volt green, 1940	n/a	n/a	1
153-50 Bulb, 14 volt, red, 1940	n/a	n/a	1
154 Highway Signal, O scale, 1940-1942	19	27	38
154 Locomotive, O scale, 0-4-0, electric, dark green, 1917-1923	75	125	250
154-18 Bulb, 12 volt, red, 1942	n/a	n/a	1
154C Contactor, O scale, 1940	4	5	7
155 Freight Shed, yellow base w/maroon roof, 1930-1939, 1940-1942	220	330	440
155 Freight Shed, ivory base w/gray roof, 1930-1942	175	263	350
155 Signal Light, W.M. Bell, 1955-1957	50	75	100
156X Locomotive, O scale, without pilot trucks, 1923-1924	300	500	1000
156 Locomotive, O scale, 4-4-4, electric, gray, olive and maroon, 1917-1923	225	425	850
156 Station Platform, O scale, 1939-1940, 1946-1951	52	78	105
156-13 Bulb, 18 volt, clear, 1939	n/a	n/a	1
157 Hand Truck, standard scale, red, 1930-1932	15	25	50
157 Station Platform, O scale, 1952-1959	37	56	75
158 Locomotive, O scale, 0-4-0, electric, gray, 1919-1923	120	200	400
158 Locomotive, O scale, 0-4-0, electric, black, 1919-1923	135	225	450
158 Platform Set, lighted, two 156 platforms and one 136 station, w/original box, 1940-1942	165	275	550
159C Block Signal contractor, 1940	4	5	7
160 Unloading Bin, 1938	n/a	1	2
161 Baggage Truck, standard scale, green, 1930-1932	30	50	100
161 Mail Pickup Set, O scale, 1961-1963	35	52	70
162 Dump Truck, standard scale, red or gray, 1930-1932	28	48	95
163 Block Signal, O scale, single target, 1961-1963	20	25	38
163 Freight Accessory, includes two 157 hand track, one 161 baggage car and one dump bin, w/original box, 1930	145	217	290
164 Lumber Loader, 1940-1942, 1946-1950	102	170	340
164-64 Logs, set of five, 1952	n/a	n/a	5
165 Magnetic Crane, 1940-1942	75	125	250
165C Controller, 1940	32	48	65
165-53 Bulb, 18 volt, red, 1940	n/a	n/a	1
166 Controller, three button, 1938	3	4	5
167 Whistle and Reverse Controller, O scale, 1945	5	8	10
167X Whistle Controller, OO scale, 1940	3	4	5
168 Controller, 1940	3	4	5
169 Uncoupling and Reversing Controller, 1940	n/a	2	3
170 DC Current Reducer, 220 volts, 1914	5	8	10
171 Inverter, DC to AC, 1936	5	8	10
172 Inverter, DC to AC, 220 volts, 1937	5	8	10
175 Rocket Launcher, O scale, 1958-1960	105	150	300
175-50 Extra Rockets, O scale, 1958	10	15	20
180 Pullman, standard scale, maroon, brown and orange, 1911	50	85	170

	C6	C8	C10
180 Trailer Truck, standard scale, 1915	600	1000	2000
HO-181 Cab Control, HO scale, 1958	7	13	25
181 Combine, standard scale, maroon, brown and orange, 1911	60	100	200
182 Magnet Crane, w/165C controller, 1946-1949	110	150	255
182 Observation Car, standard scale, maroon, brown and orange, 1911	66	110	220
184 Bungalow, lighted, 1923	45	68	90
185 Bungalow, no lights, 1923	40	60	80
186 Bungalow Set, set of five, 1923	300	450	600
186 Log Loading Outfit, log loader, car, bin and uncoupler, 1940	120	200	400
187 Bungalow Set, set of five, 1923	300	450	600
188 Coal Elevator Outfit, 1938	120	200	400
189 Villa, lighted, 1923	162	243	325
190 Observation Car, standard scale, 1907-1927	300	500	1000
190 Observation Car, standard scale, 1907-1927	180	300	600
190 Observation Car, standard scale, 1907-1927	300	500	1000
191 Villa, lighted, 1923	145	217	290
192 Railroad Control Tower, 1959-1960	90	135	200
193 Automatic Accessory Set, O scale, includes one #69, one #76, one #78, one #77, one #80, 1927-1929	175	263	350
193 Water Tower, 1953-1955	62	93	125
194 Automatic Accessory Set, standard scale, includes one #69, one #76, one #78, one #77, one #80, 1927-1929	175	263	350
195 Floodlight Tower, 1957-1969	30	45	60
195 Terrace, standard scale, includes one #191 villa, one #189 villa, one #184 bungalow, one #90 flagpole, two #56 lamp posts, 1927	600	900	1200
195-75 Spare Tower Head, add lights and holder for #195 floodlight tower, 1957	10	15	25
196 Accessory Set, standard/O scale, Includes #127 station, six #60 telegraph poles, #62 semaphore, #68 warning signal, two #58 lamp posts, w/original box, 1927	150	225	300

	C6	C8	C10
196 Smoke Pellets, 100 pellets in bottle/package, price for complete package, 1946	15	25	38
197 Radar Antenna, O scale, gray w/gray base, 1957-1959	30	53	105
HO-197 Radar Antenna, HO scale, 1958	20	30	40
197-75 Replacement Radar Head, 1958	9	15	30
199 Microwave Tower, 1958-1959	37	56	75
199 Scenic Railway Set, standard scale, 1924	120	200	400
200 Gondola, 2-7/8" scale, motorized, auctioned in 1994 in Good to Very Good condition	1000	1500	300
200 Trolley, standard scale, trailer, non-powered, 1910	1200	2000	4000
200 Turntable, standard scale, green and tan, 1928	175	263	350
201 Locomotive, O scale, 0-6-0, steam, switcher, w/2201 B bell tender, 1940	280	475	950
201 Locomotive, O scale, 0-6-0, steam, switcher, w/2201 Tender, no bell, 1940	210	350	700
202 Locomotive, O27 scale, UP Alco A diesel, orange w/black lettering, 1957	30	50	100
202 Summer Trolley, standard scale, motor car, marked "202 Electric Rapid Transit 202," 1910	900	1500	3000
203 Locomotive, O scale, 0-4-0, armored, cannon, prewar, oriented locomotive, 1917	690	1150	2300
203 Locomotive, O scale, steam, switcher, 0-6-0, no bell, similar to 201, 1940	225	375	750
204 Locomotive, O27 scale, A.T.S.F., Alco AA, diesel, 1957	75	109	150
204 Locomotive, O scale, 2-4-2, steam, black, uncataloged, 1940-1941	43	72	145
204 Locomotive, O scale, 2-4-2, steam, gunmetal gray, uncataloged, 1940-1941	67	113	225
205 L.C.L. Merchandise Containers, standard scale, dark green, each, 1930-1938	75	112	150

No. 203 Locomotive, $2,300. Photo courtesy Richard MacNary.

Top row, left to right: No. 6804 Flatcar, $205; No. 6803 Flatcar, $205. Middle row: No. 6806 Flatcar, $175. Bottom row: No. 212 Locomotive, $300.

	C6	C8	C10
205 Locomotive, O27 scale, M.P., Alco AA, diesel, 1957	75	120	170
208 Locomotive, O27 scale, A.T.S.F., Alco diesel AA, 1958	78	100	165
208 Tool Set, gray box, includes tools, sledge hammer, pick, rake, shovel and ax, 1934-1942	60	90	120
208 Tool Set, silver box, includes tools, sledge hammer, pick, rake, shovel and ax, 1934-1942	50	75	100
209 Barrels, standard scale, wooden, set of four, 1934-1942	10	15	20
0-209 Barrels, O scale, wooden, set of six, 1934-1942	17	26	35
209 Locomotive, O27 scale, N.H., Alco AA, diesel, two units, 1958	270	450	900
210 Locomotive, O27 scale, Texas Spec. Alco diesel AA, 1958	110	160	210
210 Switch, standard scale, automatic, pair, 1926	15	22	30
211 Flatcar, standard scale, w/wooden load, 1926-1940	34	57	115

	C6	C8	C10
211 Locomotive, O27 scale, Texas Spec. Alco AA, diesel, 1962	80	130	180
212 Gondola, standard scale, green and maroon, 1926-1940	45	75	150
212 Gondola, standard scale, gray, 1926-1940	60	100	200
212 Locomotive, O27 scale, Alco diesel A, Marine, 1958	90	150	300
212 Locomotive, O27 scale, A.T.S.F. Alco diesel AA, 1964	78	100	150
213 Cattle Car, standard scale, mojave body w/maroon roof, 1926-1940	200	300	400
213 Cattle Car, standard scale, terra-cotta, orange body w/pea green roof, 1926-1940	100	200	300
213 Cattle Car, standard scale, cream body w/maroon roof, 1926-1940	300	450	600
213 Locomotive, O27 scale, M&StL Alco AA, diesel, 1964	75	125	175
214 Boxcar, standard scale, cream body w/orange roof, 1926-1940	100	200	300

	C6	C8	C10
214 Boxcar, standard scale, yellow body w/brown roof, 1926-1940	300	400	500
214 Boxcar, standard scale, terra-cotta, orange body w/green roof, 1926-1940	200	300	400
HO-214 Girder Bridge, HO scale, 1958	5	10	15
214 Girder Bridge, HO scale, light or dark gray, 1953-1969	10	20	30
214R Refrigerator Car, standard scale, ivory body w/peacock roof, 1929-1940	300	400	500

	C6	C8	C10
214R Refrigerator Car, standard scale, white body w/light blue roof, 1929-1940	500	750	1000
215 Tank Car, standard scale, pea green, 1926-1940	75	125	150
215 Tank Car, standard scale, ivory, Sunoco decal, 1926-1940	100	200	300
215 Tank Car, standard scale, silver, Sunoco decal, 1926-1940	200	350	500
216 Hopper Car, standard scale, dark green, 1926-1940	100	200	300

Top row, left to right: No. 217 Caboose, $230; No. 219 Crane, $240. Middle row, left to right: No. 212 Gondola, $200; No. 220 Floodlight, $400. Bottom row, left to right: No. 400E Locomotive with tender, $2,250.

	C6	C8	C10
216 Locomotive, O27 scale, Burlington Alco A, diesel, 1958 100	200	310
216 Locomotive, O27 scale, Minneapolis & St. Louis, Alco diesel A 75	100	140
217 Caboose, standard scale, orange and maroon, 1926-1940 90	150	300
217 Caboose, standard scale, red and peacock, 1926-1940 69	115	230
217 Lighting Set, standard scale, for cars, eight volts, 1914 30	50	100
217 Locomotive, O27 scale, B&M Alco AB, diesel, 1959 75	100	185
218 Dump Car, standard scale, mojave, 1926-1940 78	130	260
218 Locomotive, O27 scale, A.T.S.F. Alco AA, diesel, 1959 70	100	185
218 Locomotive, O27 scale, A.T.S.F. Alco AB, diesel, 1961 70	100	170
218C Locomotive, O27 scale, A.T.S.F. Alco B, diesel, 1961 40	50	80
219 Crane, standard scale, peacock cab, 1926 72	120	240
219 Crane, standard scale, yellow cab, 1926 115	192	385
219 Crane, standard scale, white, ivory cab, 1926 135	225	450
220 Floodlight, standard scale, terra-cotta base, 1931 75	125	250
220 Floodlight, standard scale, green base, 1931 120	200	400
220 Locomotive, O27 scale, A.T.S.F. Alco A, diesel, 1961 75	100	135
221 Locomotive, O27 scale, Alco A, diesel, Marine, uncataloged, 1963 124	207	415
221 Locomotive, O27 scale, A.T.S.F. Alco A, diesel, uncataloged, 1963 175	250	420
221 Locomotive, O27 scale, D&RGW Alco A, diesel, 1963 36	60	120
221 Locomotive, O27 scale, steam, gray, 1946 48	80	160
221 Locomotive, steam, black, 1946..... 60	100	200
HO-222 Deck Bridge, HO scale, 1961 10	15	20
222 Switches, standard scale, price per pair, 1926 30	45	60

	C6	C8	C10
223 Switches, standard scale, non-derailing, price per pair, 1932 46	78	155
223-50 Locomotive, O27 scale, A.B.A.T.S.F. Alco, diesel, 1963 85	125	185
HO-224 Girder Bridge, HO scale, 1961 7	11	14
224 Locomotive, O27 scale, Alco AB, diesel, Navy, 1960 100	150	200
224 Locomotive, steam, paper train, w/original box, uncataloged, 1943 100	150	200
224 Paper Train Set, includes: #224 locomotive, #2224 tender, #2812 red gondola, #61100 yellow boxcar w/brown roof, #47618 red caboose, crossing signal, crossing gate, three figures, baggage car, paper track 300	450	600
224/224E Locomotive, 2-6-2, steam, gunmetal gray, w/2689 sheetmetal tender, 1938-1942 66	110	220
224/224E Locomotive, 2-6-2, steam, black w/plastic tender, 1938-1942 43	72	145
224/224E Locomotive, 2-6-2, steam, black w/2224 die-cast tender, 1938-1942 54	90	180
224/224E Locomotive, 2-6-2, steam, gunmetal gray w/2224 die-cast tender, 1938-1942 110	183	365
225 Locomotive, O27 scale, C&O Alco A, diesel, 1960 65	100	120
225/225 E Locomotive, O scale, 2-6-2, steam, black, w/2235, 2265, 2225 or 2245 tenders, 1939-1940 114	190	380
225/225 E Locomotive, O scale, 2-6-2, steam, gunmetal gray, 1939-1940................ 105	175	350
HO-226 Truss Bridge, HO scale, 1961...................... 7	11	14
226E Locomotive, O scale, 2-6-4, steam, w/2226 tender, 1938-1941 150	250	500
227 Locomotive, O scale, 0-6-0, steam, switcher scale, w/tender 2227T, marked "8976" under cab window, no bell, 1939 375	625	1250
227 Locomotive, O scale, w/tender 2227B bell, 1939 378	630	1260
227 Locomotive, O27 scale, C.N. Alco A, diesel, Canadian market distribution, uncataloged, 1960........... 78	100	160

Top to bottom: No. 229 Locomotive, $120; No. 233LTS, $105. Photo courtesy 1961 Lionel catalog.

	C6	C8	C10
228 Locomotive, O scale, 0-6-0, steam, w/2228B tender, w/bell, 1939	480	800	1600
228 Locomotive, O27 scale, C.N. Alco A, diesel, Canadian market distribution, uncataloged, 1961	70	100	150
228 Locomotive, O scale, 0-6-0, steam, switcher scale, similar to 227, w/228T tender, no bell, 1939	318	530	1060
229 Locomotive, O27 scale, M&StL Alco A, diesel, 1961	60	90	120
229P Locomotive, O27 scale, M&StL Alco A, diesel, 1962	90	90	120
229/229E Locomotive, O scale, 2-4-2, steam, black, 1939	48	80	160
229/229E Locomotive, O scale, steam, gunmetal gray, 1939	30	50	100
229C Locomotive, O27 scale, M&StL Alco B, diesel, 1962	27	45	90
230 Locomotive, 0-6-0, steam, switcher scale, 1939	600	1000	2000
230 Locomotive, O27 scale, C&O Alco A, diesel, 1961	55	80	105

	C6	C8	C10
231 Locomotive, O scale, 0-6-0, steam, switcher scale, 1939	600	1000	2000
231 Locomotive, O27 scale, R.I. Alco A, diesel, 1961	50	75	100
232 Locomotive, O scale, 0-6-0, steam, switcher scale, 1940	465	775	1550
232 Locomotive, O27 scale, N.H. Alco A, diesel, 1962	65	109	130
233 Locomotive, O scale, 0-6-0, steam, switcher scale, 1940	600	1000	2000
233 Locomotive, O27 scale, 2-4-2, steam, w/233W tender, 1961	50	85	105
235 Locomotive, O27 scale, 2-4-2, steam, uncataloged, 1962	80	125	160
236 Locomotive, O27 scale, 2-4-2, steam, 1961	18	30	60
237 Locomotive, O27 scale, steam, 1963	25	35	60
238 or E Locomotive, O scale, P.R.R., steam, black or gunmetal gray, torpedo-type, w/222T, 2225W or 265W tender, 1936-1940	113	188	375

	C6	C8	C10		C6	C8	C10
238 Locomotive, O27 scale, steam 2-4-2, 1963	75	125	150	241 Locomotive, O27 scale, 2-4-2, steam, uncataloged, 1963	75	125	165
239 Locomotive, O27 scale, steam, 2-4-2, 1965	65	90	140	242 Locomotive, O27 scale, steam, 2-4-2, 1962	20	40	60

No. 248 Locomotive, $165.

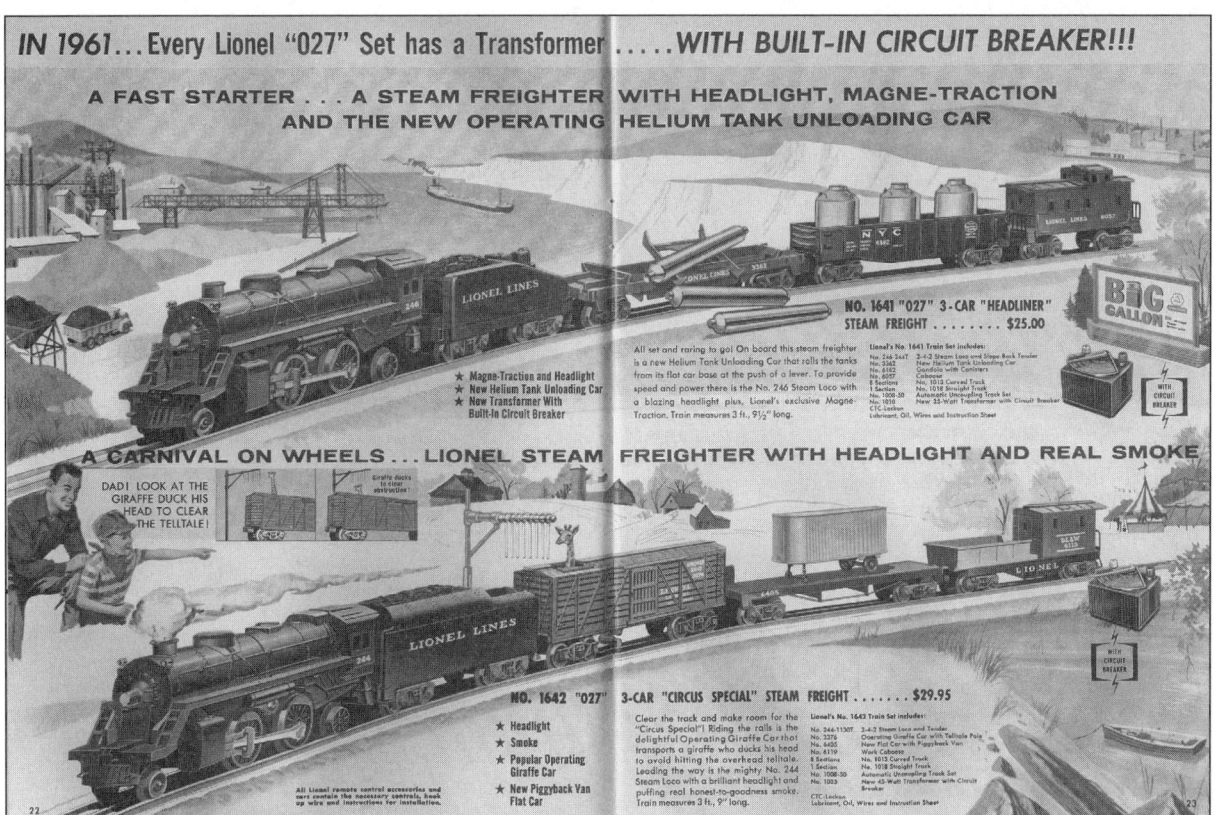

Top to bottom: No. 246 Locomotive, $40; No. 244 Locomotive, $40. Photo courtesy 1961 Lionel catalog.

No. 250E Locomotive, Hiawatha, $1,500.

	C6	C8	C10
243 Locomotive, O27 scale, 2-4-2, steam, 1960	70	100	150
244 Locomotive, O27 scale, 2-4-2, steam, 1960	25	30	40
245 Locomotive, O27 scale, 2-4-2, steam, 1959	125	175	300
HO-245-200 Contactor, HO scale, 1960	4	5	7
246 Locomotive, O27 scale, 2-4-2, steam, 1959	25	35	45
247 Locomotive, O27 scale, 2-4-2, B&O, steam, 1959	30	35	65
248 Locomotive, O scale, electric, red, orange, dark green and olive, 1926-1932	49	83	165
249 Locomotive, O27 scale, 2-4-2, P.R.R., steam, 1958	20	30	50
249 or E Locomotive, O scale, steam, gunmetal gray, 1936	80	133	265
249 or E Locomotive, O scale, steam, black, 1936	120	200	400
250 Locomotive, O scale, 0-4-0, N.Y.C., electric, dark green, peacock and orange, 1926	90	150	300
250 Locomotive, O scale, electric, 0-4-0, orange and terra-cotta, uncataloged, 1934	60	100	200

	C6	C8	C10
250 Locomotive, O27 scale, 2-4-2, P.R.R., steam, 1957	21	35	70
250E Locomotive, O scale, Hiawatha, steam, w/250W, 250WX or 2250W tenders, 1935	450	750	1500
251 Locomotive, O scale, 0-4-0, NYC, electric, box cab, gray or red cabs, 1925	100	168	335
251E Locomotive, O scale, 0-4-0, NYC, electric, box cab, gray or red cabs, 1927	100	168	335
HO-252 Crossing Gate, HO scale, 1959	20	30	40
252 Crossing Gate, O scale, 1950-1962	20	30	40
252 Locomotive, O scale, 0-4-0, NYC, electric, peacock, olive and dark green, 1926	60	100	200
252 Locomotive, O scale, 0-4-0, NYC, electric, terra-cotta and orange, 1926	75	125	250
252 Locomotive, O scale, 0-4-0, NYC, electric, maroon, Macy's Special, 1926	120	200	400
252E Locomotive, O scale, 0-4-0, electric, terra-cotta or orange, 1933-1935	84	140	280

	C6	C8	C10
253 Automatic Block Sign Signal, O scale, 1956	30	45	60
253 Locomotive, O scale, 0-4-0, electric, maroon, 1924	150	250	500
253 Locomotive, O scale, 0-4-0, electric, terra-cotta, 1924	120	200	400
253 Locomotive, O scale, 0-4-0, electric, red, 1924	135	225	450
253 Locomotive, O scale, 0-4-0, electric, peacock, mojave and dark green, 1924	60	100	200
253E Locomotive, O scale, 0-4-0, electric, green, 1931	125	213	425

	C6	C8	C10
253E Locomotive, O scale, 0-4-0, electric, terra-cotta, 1931	120	200	400
254 Locomotive, O scale, 0-4-0, electric, mojave, olive, dark and pea green, 1924	83	138	275
254 Locomotive, O scale, 0-4-0, electric, apple green, 1924	120	200	400
254 Locomotive, O scale, 0-4-0, electric, red, 1924	150	250	500
254E Locomotive, O scale, 0-4-0, electric, olive green, 1927	60	100	200
254E Locomotive, O scale, 0-4-0, electric, apple green, 1927	90	150	300

No. 256 Locomotive, $500.

No. 252 Locomotive, 0-4-0, $200.

Front: No. 264E Locomotive, 2-4-2, Red Comet, $750. Back: No. 263E Locomotive, 2-4-2, Blue Comet, $800.

	C6	C8	C10
255E Locomotive, O scale, 2-4-2, steam, gunmetal gray w/263W tender, 1935	300	525	1050
256 Freight Shed, 1950-1953	27	41	55
256 Locomotive, O scale, electric, orange, rubber-stamped "Lionel," 1924-1930	150	250	500
256 Locomotive, O scale, electric, orange, marked "Lionel," 1924-1930	210	350	700
257 Freight Station, w/horn, 1956-1957	32	45	82
257 Locomotive, O scale, 0-4-0, steam, w/257T or 259T tender, 1930	90	150	300
258 Locomotive, O scale, 2-4-0, steam, 1930	75	125	250
258 Locomotive, O scale, 2-4-2, steam, w/1689T tender, uncataloged, 1941	48	80	160
259 Locomotive, O scale, 2-4-2, steam, 1932	54	90	180
259E Locomotive, O scale, steam, black, 1933	34	73	115
259E Locomotive, O scale, steam, gunmetal gray, 1933	48	80	160
260 Bumper, O scale, 1952	10	15	20
260E Locomotive, O scale, steam, black, w/260T tender, 1930	150	250	500
260E Locomotive, O scale, steam, gunmetal gray, w/263 tender, 1930	180	300	600
261 Locomotive, O scale, 2-4-2, steam, w/257T tender, 1931	75	125	250
261E Locomotive, O scale, steam, w/261T tender, 1935	84	140	280

	C6	C8	C10
262 Crossing Gate, O scale, 1962	21	32	42
262 Locomotive, O scale, 2-4-2, steam, w/262T tender, 1931	90	150	300
262E Locomotive, O scale, 2-4-2, steam, w/262T or 265T tender, 1933	84	140	280
263E Locomotive, O scale, 2-4-2, steam, gunmetal gray, 1936	255	425	850
263E Locomotive, O scale, 2-4-2, steam, Blue Comet, blue, 1936	240	400	800
264 Operating Forklift Platform Assembly	85	142	285
264-150 Boards, set of twelve, 1957	6	8	10
264E Locomotive, O scale, 2-4-2, Red Comet, steam, streamlined, red, 1935	225	375	750
264E Locomotive, O scale, 2-4-2, steam, streamlined, black, 1935	120	200	400
265E Locomotive, O scale, 2-4-2, steam, Blue Streak, streamlined, blue, 1935	180	300	600
265E Locomotive, O scale, 2-4-2, steam, streamlined, black, 1935	87	145	290
265E Locomotive, O scale, steam 2-4-2, streamlined, gunmetal gray, 1935	105	175	350
270 Bridge, O scale, maroon or red, 1931	52	78	105
270 Lighting Set, standard scale, for two cars, 3-1/2 volt, 1915	40	60	80
271 Bridge, O scale, two span, 1931	30	45	60
272 Bridge, O scale, three span, 1931	60	90	120
280 Bridge, standard scale, 1931	45	68	90
281 Bridge, standard scale, two span, 1931	45	68	90
282 Bridge, standard scale, three span, 1931	50	75	100
282 Gantry Crane, O scale, 1954	72	120	240
289E Locomotive, O scale, 2-4-2, steam, streamlined, black, 1689 tender, 1937	52	88	175
289E Locomotive, O scale, 2-4-2, steam, streamlined, 1689 tender, gunmetal gray, 1937	45	75	150
299 Code Transmitter Set, 1961-1963	65	80	145
300 Bridge, standard/O scale, white, silver and red base, marked "Hellgate," largest single span bridge Lionel ever made, 1928	810	1350	2700

	C6	C8	C10
300 Bridge, standard/O scale, ivory, green, orange base, marked "Hellgate," 1928	925	1390	1850
HO-300 Lumber Car, HO scale, operating, 1960	8	14	28
300 Trolley, standard scale, trailer, powered, 1910	1080	1800	3600
300 Trolley, standard scale, marked "City Hall Park 175," 1901	2100	3500	7000
HO-301 Dump Car, HO scale, operating, 1960	12	20	40
HO-301-16 Cargo Bin, HO scale, 1960	4	5	7
303 Summer Trolley, standard scale, motorcar, marked "303 Electric Rapid Transit 303," 1910	1230	2050	4100
308 Metal Sign Set, O scale, five piece, 1945-1949	13	20	28
309 Plastic Sign Set, nine piece, 1950-1959	12	19	28
309 Pullman, standard scale, blue, apple green, pea green, maroon, light brown, mojave, 1926	43	73	145
309 Trolley, standard scale, 1901	1500	2000	4250
310 Baggage Car, standard scale, blue, apple green, pea green, maroon, light brown, mojave, 1926	54	70	140
310 Baggage Car, standard scale, blue, apple green, pea green, maroon, light brown, mojave, 1924-1929	40	68	135

	C6	C8	C10
310R Billboard, O scale, racing, 1963	15	22	30
310 Billboard Set, O scale, billboard and five different inserts, 1950-1968	15	22	30
310 Track, standard scale, 1903	5	8	10
312 Observation Car, standard scale, blue, apple green, pea green, maroon, light brown, mojave, 1926	54	70	140
313 Bascule Bridge, O scale, gray, 1940-1942	312	468	625
313 Bascule Bridge, silver, 1946-1949	240	375	550
314 Girder Bridge, O scale, gray, 1946-1950	23	34	45
315 Trestle, O scale, bridge, illuminated silver, 1946-1947	100	175	250
315-20 Bulb, 12 volt, clear, 1940	n/a	n/a	1
317 Trestle Bridge, gray	35	52	70
318 Locomotive, standard scale, 0-4-0, electric, state brown, 1924	140	238	475
318 Locomotive, standard scale, 0-4-0, electric, mojave, pea green, gray, 1924	110	185	370
318E Locomotive, standard scale, 0-4-0, electric, pea green, mojave, gray, 1926	100	170	340
318E Locomotive, standard scale, 0-4-0, electric, state brown, 1926	180	300	600
318E Locomotive, standard scale, 0-4-0, electric, black, 1926	240	400	800

No. 322 Observation Car, $190.

Top row, left to right: No 341 Observation car, $90; No. 339 Pullman car, $90. Bottom row, left to right: No. 10E Locomotive, $275; No. 332 Baggage car, $95. Photo courtesy PB Eighty-Four, New York

	C6	C8	C10
HO-319 Helicopter Car, HO scale, operating, 1960	16	27	55
319 Pullman, standard scale, 1924	54	85	170
320 Baggage Car, standard scale, 1925	60	100	200
320 Switch, standard scale, 1903	20	30	40
321 Trestle Bridge, O scale, 1958	15	22	30
322 Observation Car, standard scale, 1924	57	95	190
330 90 Degrees Crossing, standard scale, 1903	10	15	20
332 Arch Bridge, O scale, gray, 1959-1966	20	30	46
332 Baggage Car, standard scale, gray, red, peacock, olive, 1926	28	48	95
332 Baggage Car, standard scale, beige body w/maroon roof, 1926	90	150	300
332 Macy Baggage Car, standard scale, uncataloged, 1930	60	100	200
334 Operating Dispatching Board, O scale, 1957-1960	100	150	250
HO-337 Giraffe Car, HO scale, operating, 1961	15	25	50

	C6	C8	C10
337 Macy Pullman, standard scale, red, uncataloged, 1930	60	100	200
337 Pullman, standard scale, pea green, olive, red, mojave, 1925	40	65	130
338 Macy Observation Car, standard scale, uncataloged, 1930	60	100	200
338 Observation Car, standard scale, pea green, olive, red, mojave, 1925	33	55	110
339 Macy Pullman, standard scale, red, uncataloged, 1930	60	100	200
339 Pullman, standard scale, peacock, brown, gray, 1925	27	45	90
339 Pullman, standard scale, beige body, maroon roof, 1925	90	150	300
340 Bridge, standard scale, 1903	175	262	350
341 Macy Observation Car, standard scale, red, uncataloged, 1930	60	100	200
341 Observation Car, standard scale, peacock, brown, gray, 1925	27	45	90
341 Observation Car, standard scale, beige body, maroon roof, 1925	90	150	300
342 Culvert Loader, O scale, 1956-1958	115	150	285

	C6	C8	C10
345 Automatic Culvert Unloader, O scale, 1957	165	190	365
348 Manual Culvert Unloader, O scale, 1966	70	100	185
HO-349 Turbo Missile Firing Car, HO scale,	30	50	100
350 Bumper, standard scale, 1903	25	38	50
350 Transfer Table, O scale, 1957-1960	155	200	350
350-50 Transfer Table Extension, O scale, 1957-1960	53	88	175
352 Ice Depot, O scale, red or brown base, 1955-1957	120	160	260
352-55 Ice Blocks, O scale, set of seven, 1955	10	15	20
353 Trackside Signal, O scale, 1960-1961	14	25	40
356 Freight Station, O scale, w/green and orange carts, 1952-1957	50	75	110
356-25 Baggage Truck, O scale, set of two, 1952	9	14	18
HO-357 Cop and Hobo Car, HO scale, 1962	12	20	40
362 Barrel Loader, O scale, 1952-1957	39	65	130
362-78 Barrels, O scale, set of six, 1952	7	11	15
364 Lumber Loader, O scale, smooth or crackle gray, 1948-1967	85	100	125
364C On-Off Switch, 1959	n/a	n/a	15

	C6	C8	C10
365 Dispatching Station, O scale, 1958-1959	70	105	140
HO-365 Missile Launching Car, HO scale, 1962	12	20	40
HO-366 Milk Car, HO scale, operating, 1961	18	30	60
HO-370 Sheriff and Outlaw Car, HO scale, 1962	12	20	40
375 Turntable, O scale, motorized, 1962-1964	120	185	245
380 Elevated Pillars, standard scale, each, 1903	30	45	60
380 Locomotive, standard scale, 0-4-0, electric, maroon, 1923	192	320	640
380 Locomotive, standard scale, 0-4-0, electric, mojave, dark green, 1923	180	300	600
380E Locomotive, standard scale, 0-4-0, electric, maroon, 1926	180	300	600
380E Locomotive, standard scale, 0-4-0, electric, mojave or dark green, 1926	180	300	600
381 Locomotive, standard scale, 4-4-4, electric, green body, 1928	1200	2000	4000
381U Locomotive, standard scale, electric, kit includes tools, track and original box, 1928	2300	3450	4600
381E Locomotive, standard scale, 4-4-4, electric, green body and frame, 1928	1260	2100	4200
384 Locomotive, standard scale, 2-4-0, steam, w/384T tender, 1930	180	300	600

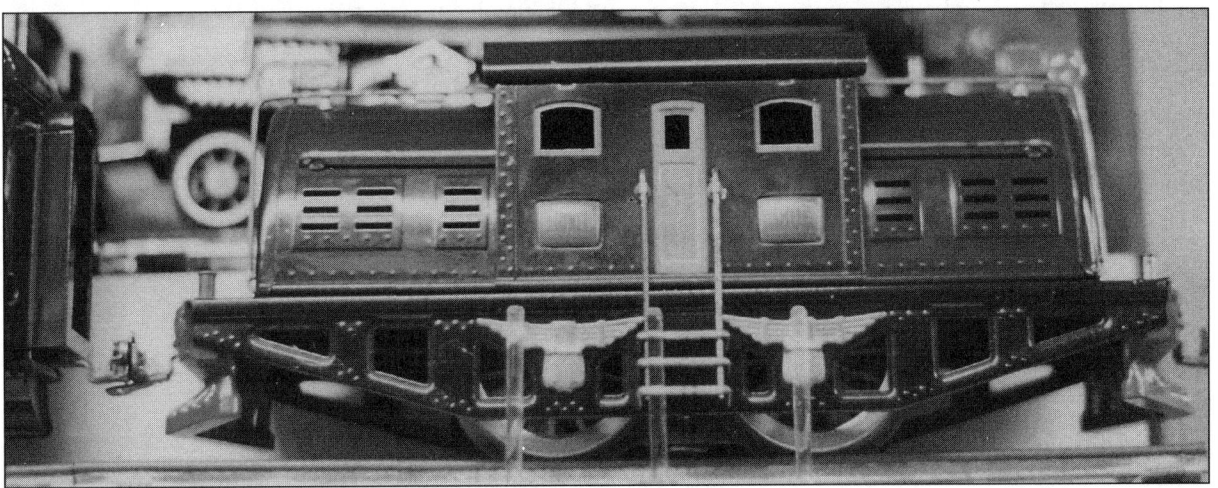

No 380E Locomotive 0-4-0, electric, $600.

No. 381E Locomotive, 4-4-4, electric, $4,200.

No. 384 Locomotive, $600.

	C6	C8	C10
384E Locomotive, standard scale, 2-4-0, steam, w/384T tender, 1930	175	293	585
385E Locomotive, standard scale, 2-4-2, steam, gunmetal gray w/384T, 385T, 385TW or 385W tender, 1933	295	490	980
390 Locomotive, standard scale, 2-4-2, steam, w/390T, black, 1929	250	420	840
390C Control Switch, O scale, 1960	3	6	9
390E Locomotive, standard scale, steam, black, w/tender 390T, 1929	300	500	1000
390E Locomotive, standard scale, two-tone blue, w/tender, 1930	420	700	1400
390E Locomotive, two-tone green	540	900	1800
392E Locomotive, standard scale, 4-4-2, steam, black, 1932	380	630	1260
392E Locomotive, standard scale, 4-4-2, steam, gunmetal gray, 1932	495	825	1650
394 Rotary Beacon, aluminum, red or green tower frame, 1949-1953	22	33	45
394-10 Bulb, 14 volt, clear, 1951	n/a	n/a	1

	C6	C8	C10
394-37 Beacon Cap, 1953	5	10	15
395 Floodlight Tower, four lights, yellow tower, 1949-1956	48	80	160
395 Floodlight Tower, four lights, red tower, 1949-1956	50	75	85
395 Floodlight Tower, four lights, green tower, 1949-1956	32	48	65
395 Floodlight Tower, four lights, silver tower, 1949-1956	25	35	55
397 Diesel Type Coal Loader, yellow diesel motor cover, 1948-1957	120	200	400
397 Diesel Type Coal Loader, later model, blue diesel motor cover, 1948-1957	90	100	165
400 Budd RDC Car, O scale, powered, 1956-1958	125	150	270
400 Gondola, 2-7/8" scale, trailer, 1901	720	1200	2400
400E Locomotive, standard scale, 4-4-4, steam, w/400T tender, black	675	1125	2250

	C6	C8	C10
400E Locomotive, standard scale, 4-4-4, steam, gunmetal gray, w/400T tender	900	1500	3000
400E Locomotive, standard scale, 4-4-4, steam, w/400T tender, blue	855	1425	2850
402 Locomotive, standard scale, 0-4-4-0, electric, mojave, 1923	200	330	660
402E Locomotive, standard scale, 0-4-4-0, electric, mojave, 1926	180	300	600
404 Budd RDC Baggage Car, O scale, powered, 1957-1958	165	200	370
404 Summer Trolley, standard scale, motor car, 1910	1500	2500	5000
408E Locomotive, standard scale, 0-4-4-0, electric, state brown, 1927	660	1100	2200
408E Locomotive, standard scale, 0-4-4-0, electric, green, 1927	1080	1800	3600

	C6	C8	C10
408E Locomotive, standard scale, 0-4-4-0, electric, apple green or mojave, 1927	385	640	1280
410 Billboard Blinker, 1956-1958	22	35	44
HO-410 Suburban Ranch House, HO scale, 1959	10	15	20
HO-411 Figure Set, HO scale, 1959	10	15	20
HO-412 Farm Set, HO scale, 1959	10	15	20
412 Pullman, standard scale, California State Car, light green, 1929	600	1000	2000
412 Pullman, standard scale, California State Car, light brown, 1929	660	1100	2200
413 Countdown Control Panel, 1962	38	50	72

Top row, left to right: No. 512 Gondola, $120; No. 517 Caboose, $100. Middle row: two No. 511 flatcars, $115, each. Bottom row, left row: No. 385E Locomotive with 384T, 385T, 385TW or 385W tender, $980. Photo courtesy PB Eighty-Four, New York

No. 400E Locomotive, $3,000.

No. 402E Locomotive 0-4-4-0, $600.

	C6	C8	C10
413 Pullman, standard scale, Colorado State Car, light green, 1929	600	1000	2000
413 Pullman, standard scale, Colorado State Car, light brown, 1929	660	1100	2200
HO-413 Railroad Structure Set, HO scale, 1959	10	15	20
414 State Car, Illinois, light green, 1930	600	1000	2000
414 State Car, light brown, 1930	660	1100	2200
HO-414 Village Set, HO scale, 1959	10	15	20
415 Diesel Fueling Station, 1955-1967	100	150	200
416 Observation Car, standard scale, light brown, 1929	310	515	1030
416 Observation Car, standard scale, New York State Car, light green, 1929	320	533	1065
418 Pullman, standard scale, mojave, 1923	63	105	210

	C6	C8	C10
418 Pullman, standard scale, apple green, 1923	105	173	345
419 Combine, standard scale, mojave, 1923	60	100	200
419 Combine, standard scale, apple green, 1928-1932	130	250	360
419 Heliport, control tower, 1962	125	188	250
420 Pullman, standard scale, Blue Comet car, light blue body, dark blue roof, marked "Faye," 1930	245	410	820
421 Pullman, standard scale, Blue Comet car, light blue body, dark blue roof, "Westphal," 1930	245	410	820
422 Observation Car, standard scale, Blue Comet car, light blue body, dark blue roof, marked "Tempel," 1930	245	410	820
424 Pullman, standard scale, Stephen Girard set, light green, marked "Liberty Bell," 1931	155	258	515

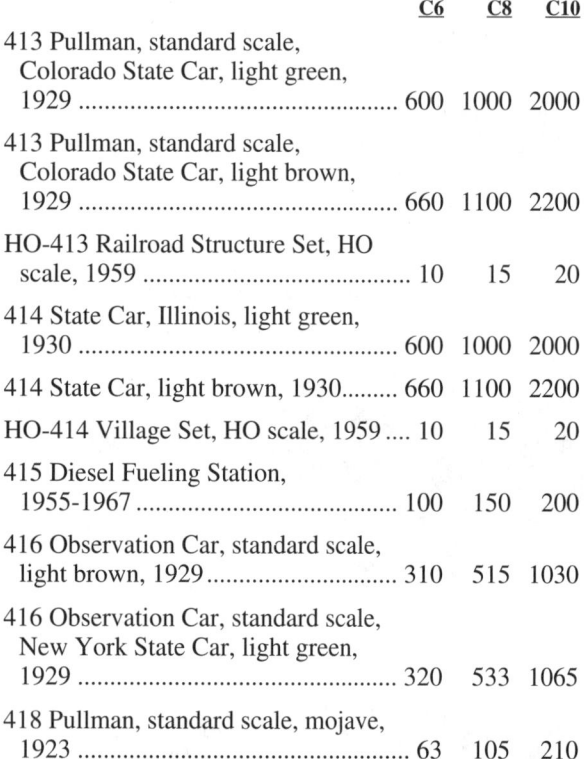

No. 408E Locomotive, $1,280.

No. 414 State Car, $2,000.

	C6	C8	C10
HO-425 Figure Set, HO scale, 1962	7	11	14
425 Pullman, standard scale, Stephen Girard set, light green, 1932	150	272	515
426 Observation Car, standard scale, Stephen Girard set, light green, "Coral Isle," 1931	150	272	515
428 Pullman, standard scale, dark green, 1926	90	150	300
428 Pullman, standard scale, orange, 1926	150	250	500
429 Combine, standard scale, dark green, 1926	135	225	450
429 Combine, standard scale, orange, 1926	105	175	350
430 Observation Car, standard scale, dark green, 1926	90	150	300
430 Observation Car, standard scale, orange, 1926	105	175	350
HO-430 Tree Assortment, HO scale, 1959	6	9	12
431 Diner, standard scale, mojave, 1927	180	300	600
431 Diner, apple green, orange, dark green, 1928-1929	190	317	635
HO-431 Landscape Set, HO scale, 1959	10	15	20
HO-432 Tree Assortment, HO scale, 1961	7	11	14
435 Power Station, 1926	83	138	275
436 Power Station, 1926	95	155	310
437 Signal Tower, orange roof, 1926	180	300	600
437 Signal Tower, green roof, 1926	150	255	510
437 Signal Tower, peacock roof, 1926	125	212	425
438 Signal Tower, orange, red, 1927	200	300	400
438 Signal Tower, white, red, 1927	235	350	470
439 Panel Board, maroon, 1928	90	135	180
439 Panel Board, red, 1928	100	150	200
439 Panel Board, silver, rare, 1928	150	225	300
0440 Signal Bridge, standard scale, 1932	235	350	470
440N Signal Bridge, O/standard scale, 1936	175	262	350
440C Panel Board	62	93	125
441 Weighing scale, Platform, standard scale, green base, cream building, 1932-1936	300	500	1000
442 Diner, 1938	120	180	240
443 Missile Launching Platform, 1960-1962	30	45	60
444 Roundhouse Section, standard scale, 1932-1935	1700	2550	3400
445 Switch Tower, operating, 1952-1957	42	63	85
448 Missile Firing Range Set, 1961-1963	70	75	140
450 Macy Special Locomotive, O scale, electric, 0-4-0 red w/black frame, uncataloged, 1930	300	500	1000
450 Signal Bridge, gray or tan base, 1952-1958	35	52	70
450L Signal Light Head, 1952	20	25	35
452 Gantry Signal, 1961-1963	65	80	120
455 Electric Range, 1932-1933	700	1100	1500

No. 444 Roundhouse Section, $3,400.

	C6	C8	C10
455 Oil Derrick, red base, 1950-1954 .	110	165	220
455 Oil Derrick, green base, 1950-1954	90	135	180
456 Coal Ramp and Hopper Car, 1950-1955	75	125	250
460 Piggyback Terminal, 1955-1957	75	112	150
460-150 Two Trailers, 1956	80	90	100
461 Piggyback, w/truck and trailers, most include, "Midge Toy Tractor," red, 1957	300	450	600
462 Derrick Platform Set, 1961-1962	135	165	290
464 Lumber Mill, 1956-1960	87	130	175
464-150 Boards, set of six, 1956	5	10	15
465 Sound Dispatching Station, 1956-1957	75	112	150
470 IRBM Missile Launch, 1959-1962	105	125	155
HO-470 Missile Launching Platform, HO scale, 1960	34	51	68
479-1 Lionel Trucks, accompanies 6362, 1955	5	10	15
HO-480 Missile Firing Range Set, HO scale, 1961	7	11	14
480-25 Conversion Coupler, 1950	n/a	n/a	4

	C6	C8	C10
490 Observation Car, standard scale, mojave, 1923	75	125	250
490 Observation Car, standard scale, apple green, 1923	109	180	360
494 Rotary Beacon, silver, red, 1954	25	38	50
497 Coaling Station, 1953-1958	100	150	200
500 Motorized Derrick, standard scale, 1903	4000	5000	7000
511 Flatcar, standard scale, dark green, 1927	34	58	115
511 Flatcar, standard scale, medium green, 1927	30	50	100
512 Gondola, standard scale, bright green, 1927	36	60	120
512 Gondola, standard scale, peacock, 1927	22	38	75
513 Cattle Car, standard scale, nickel trim, 1927	150	250	500
513 Cattle Car, standard scale, 1927	39	65	130
514 Boxcar, standard scale, yellow/brown, 1929	50	85	170
514 Boxcar, standard scale, ivory and brown, 1929	57	95	190
514R Refrigerator, standard scale, ivory body, peacock roof, 1929	60	100	200

	C6	C8	C10
514R Refrigerator, standard scale, nickel trim, 1929	123	208	415
514 Refrigerator, standard scale, Lionel ventilated refrigerator, 1927	52	88	175
515 Tank Car, standard scale, Sunoco logo, terra-cotta, ivory and silver, 1927	54	90	180
515 Tank Car, standard scale, Shell, orange, 1927	240	400	800
516 Hopper, standard scale, 1928	72	120	240
517 Caboose, standard scale, red, nickel trim, 1927	30	50	100
517 Caboose, standard scale, red and black, coal train, nickel trim, 1927	90	150	300
517 Caboose, standard scale, pea green, 1927	24	40	80
520 Locomotive, O27 scale, diesel, eighty ton, original pantograph must not be broken, 1956	60	100	200

	C6	C8	C10
520 Search Light, standard scale, terra-cotta platform, 1931	50	85	170
520 Search Light, standard scale, green platform, 1931	75	128	255
529 Pullman, O scale, olive green or terra-cotta, 1926	13	21	42
HO-530 Locomotive, HO scale, DRGW, diesel F-3 powered A, 1958	20	32	65
530 Observation Car, O scale, olive green or terra-cotta, 1926	10	17	35
HO-531 Locomotive, HO scale, C.M. St. P&P, diesel F-3 powered A, 1958	20	32	65
HO-532 Locomotive, HO scale, diesel F-3 powered A, B&O, 1958	20	32	65
HO-533 Locomotive, HO scale, New Haven, diesel F-3 powered A, 1958	20	32	65
HO-535 Locomotive, HO scale, Santa Fe, diesel Alco, AB, 1962	20	32	65

Top row, left to right: No. 514 Refrigerator car, $175; No 517 Caboose, $300. Middle row, left to right: No. 512 Gondola, $75; No. 515 Tank car, $180; No. 516 Hopper, $240. Bottom row, left to right: No. 390E Locomotive, $1,000. Photo courtesy PB Eighty-Four, New York

	C6	C8	C10
HO-536 Locomotive, HO scale, Sante Fe, diesel Alco, 1963	20	32	65
HO-537 Locomotive, HO scale, diesel Alco, AB Santa Fe, 1966	20	32	65
HO-540 Locomotive, HO scale, DRGW, diesel F-3, Dummy B, 1958	15	25	50
HO-541 Locomotive, HO scale, CMST P&P, diesel F-3, Dummy B, 1958	15	25	50
HO-550 Locomotive, HO scale, DRGW, diesel F-3, Dummy A, 1958	15	25	50
550 Miniature Figures, set of six, includes original box, 1932	125	188	250
551 Miniature Figure, engineer, 1932	15	22	30
552 Miniature Figure, conductor, 1932	15	22	30
553 Miniature Figure, porter, 1932	15	22	30
554 Miniature Figure, male passenger, 1932	15	22	30
HO-555 Locomotive, HO scale, Santa Fe, diesel F-3 powered A, 1963	19	32	64
555 Miniature Figure, female passenger, 1932	15	22	30
556 Miniature Figure, red cap, 1932	15	22	30
HO-561 Rotary Snowplow, HO scale, MSTL, 1959	60	100	200
HO-564 Locomotive, HO scale, C&O, diesel Alco, powered A, 1960	19	32	64
HO-565 Locomotive, HO scale, Santa Fe, diesel Alco, powered A, 1959	19	32	64
HO-566 Locomotive, HO scale, Texas special, diesel Alco, powered A, 1959	19	32	64
HO-567 Locomotive, HO scale, Alaska, diesel Alco, powered A, 1959	19	32	64
HO-568 Locomotive, HO scale, Union Pacific, diesel Alco, powered A, 1962	19	32	64
HO-569 Locomotive, HO scale, Union Pacific, diesel Alco, powered A, 1963	19	32	64
HO-571 Locomotive, HO scale, PRR, diesel Alco, powered A, 1963	19	32	64
HO-576 Locomotive, HO scale, Texas special, diesel F-3, Dummy B, 1959	19	32	64
HO-577 Locomotive, HO scale, Alaska, diesel F-3, Dummy B, 1959	19	32	64
HO-581 Locomotive, HO scale, PRR, rectifier, 1960	19	32	64
HO-586 Locomotive, HO scale, Texas special, diesel F-3, Dummy A, 1959	15	25	50
HO-587 Locomotive, HO scale, Alaska, diesel F-3, Dummy A, 1959	15	25	50
HO-591 Locomotive, HO scale, New Haven, rectifier, 1959	19	32	64
HO-592 Locomotive, HO scale, Santa Fe, diesel GP9, 1966	19	32	64
HO-593 Locomotive, HO scale, Northern Pacific, diesel GP9, 1963	19	32	64
HO-594 Locomotive, HO scale, Santa Fe, diesel GP9, 1963	19	32	64
HO-595 Locomotive, HO scale, Santa Fe, diesel F-3, Dummy A, 1959	15	25	50
HO-596 Locomotive, HO scale, NYC, diesel GP9, 1959	19	32	64
HO-597 Locomotive, HO scale, Northern Pacific, diesel GP9, 1961	19	32	64
HO-598 Locomotive, HO scale, NYC, diesel GP7, 1961	19	32	64
600 Derrick Trailer, standard scale, 1903	2000	4500	9000
600 Locomotive, O27 scale, diesel SW2, MKT, 1955	54	90	180
600 Pullman, O scale, four wheel, maroon, dark green, brown, 1915	18	30	60
600 Pullman, O scale, eight wheel, red w/red roof, 1933	54	90	180
600 Pullman, O scale, light blue w/silver roof, 1933	18	30	60
600 Pullman, O scale, gray w/red roof, 1933	45	75	150
601 Locomotive, O27 scale, diesel, Seaboard, 1956	60	100	200
601 Observation Car, O scale, red w/red roof, 1933	45	75	150
601 Observation Car, O scale, gray w/red roof, 1933	40	65	130

	C6	C8	C10
601 Observation Car, O scale, light blue w/silver roof, 1933	18	30	60
601 Pullman, O scale, seven, dark green, 1915	25	42	85
602 Baggage Car, O scale, dark green, 1915	21	35	70
602 Baggage Car, red w/red roof, 1933	63	108	215
602 Baggage Car, light blue w/silver roof, 1933	54	90	180
602 Baggage Car, gray w/red roof, 1933	37	63	125
602 Locomotive, O27 scale, diesel SW2, Seaboard, 1957	62	105	210
HO-602 Locomotive, HO scale, steam, 1960	15	25	50
603 Pullman, O scale, later, orange, 1920	19	32	64
603 Pullman, O scale, late, red, green, orange, maroon, 1931	30	50	100
603 Pullman, O scale, orange, uncataloged, 1921	21	35	70
604 Observation Car, O scale, red, green, orange, maroon, 1931	25	43	85
604 Observation Car, O scale, orange, 1920	24	40	80
HO-605 Locomotive, HO scale, steam, 1959	20	32	64
605 Pullman, O scale, orange, 1925	48	80	160
605 Pullman, O scale, red, 1925	48	80	160
605 Pullman, O scale, olive, 1925	48	80	160
605 Pullman, O scale, gray, 1925	30	50	100
606 Observation Car, O scale, gray, 1925	48	80	160
606 Observation Car, O scale, orange, 1925	48	80	160
606 Observation Car, O scale, red, 1925	48	80	160
606 Observation Car, O scale, olive, 1925	48	80	160
606 Observation Car, O scale, Macy, uncataloged, 1930	48	80	160
607 Pullman, O scale, Macy, uncataloged, 1931	80	135	270
607 Pullman, O scale, 1926	25	43	85
608 Observation Car, O scale, 1926	25	44	88
608 Observation Car, O scale, Macy, uncataloged, 1931	90	150	300
609 Pullman, O scale, uncataloged, 1937	27	45	90
610 Locomotive, O27 scale, diesel SW2, Erie, 1955	85	120	160
610 Pullman, O scale, early, 1915	45	78	155
610 Pullman, O scale, late, 1926	21	35	70
610 Pullman, O scale, Macy, uncataloged, 1926	24	40	80
611 Locomotive, O27 scale, diesel SW2, CNJ, 1957	66	110	220
611 Observation Car, O scale, uncataloged, 1937	18	30	60
612 Observation Car, O scale, Macy, 1926	21	35	70
612 Observation Car, O scale, late, 1926	21	35	70
612 Observation Car, O scale, early, 1915	40	68	135
613 Locomotive, O27 scale, U.P., diesel, SW2, 1958	125	200	415
613 Pullman, O scale, red, aluminum roof, 1931	60	100	200
613 Pullman, O scale, blue, Blue Comet set, 1931	180	338	675
613 Pullman, O scale, terra-cotta, 1931	85	140	280
614 Locomotive, O27 scale, Alaska, diesel, SW2, blue, yellow structure on roof, 1959-1960	65	110	220
614 Observation Car, O scale, red, aluminum roof, 1931	60	100	200
614 Observation Car, O scale, Blue Comet set, blue, 1931	66	112	225
614 Observation Car, O scale, terra-cotta, 1931	63	105	210
615 Baggage Car, O scale, terra-cotta, 1933	75	125	250
615 Baggage Car, O scale, red, aluminum roof, 1933	75	125	250
615 Baggage Car, O scale, Blue Comet set, blue, 1933	60	100	200
616 E or W Diesel Type Power Car, O scale, Streamliner, Flying Yankee, black cast frame, chrome shells, 1935	60	105	210

	C6	C8	C10
616 Locomotive, O27 scale, diesel, SW2, ATSF, 1961	66	110	220
616T Vestibule, O scale, 1935	12	20	40
616-13 Bulb, 12 volt, clear, 1935	n/a	n/a	1
617 Coach, O scale, Streamliner, black and chrome, 1935	24	39	78
617 Coach, O scale, blue and white, Blue Streak, 1935	36	60	120
617 Locomotive, O scale, ATSF, diesel, SW2, black, 1963	90	150	300
618 Observation Car, O scale, Streamliner, black and chrome, 1935	25	43	85
618 Observation Car, O scale, Blue Streak, blue and white, 1935	45	75	150
619 Combine, O scale, Blue Streak, Streamliner, blue and white, 1935	90	150	300
620 Floodlight, O scale, 1937	30	45	60
621 Locomotive, O27 scale, diesel, SW2, CNJ, 1956	60	75	145
622 Locomotive, diesel, SW2, Santa Fe, black, 1949	150	175	325
623 Locomotive, O scale, diesel, SW2, ATSF, black, 1952	73	123	245
624 Locomotive, O scale, diesel, SW2, C&O, blue, yellow stripe, 1952	110	150	270
625 Locomotive, O27 scale, diesel, forty-four ton, LV, 1957	75	120	150
HO-625 Locomotive, HO scale, steam, 1959	27	45	90
HO-626 Locomotive, HO scale, steam, 1963	19	33	65
626 Locomotive, O27 scale, B&O, diesel, forty-four ton, 1957	135	225	450
627 Locomotive, O27 scale, diesel, 45 ton, LV, red body, white stripe, 1956	80	110	145
628 Locomotive, O27 scale, diesel, 45 ton, NP, black w/yellow stripe, 1956	50	83	165
629 Locomotive, O27 scale, Burlington, diesel, forty-four ton, silver, red stripe, 1956	105	175	350
629 Pullman, O scale, four wheel, 1924	20	32	65
629 Pullman, O scale, eight wheel, uncataloged, 1934	39	65	130

	C6	C8	C10
630 Macy Observation Car, O scale, four wheel, uncataloged, 1931	24	40	80
630 Observation Car, O scale, eight wheel, uncataloged, 1934	27	45	90
630 Observation Car, O scale, four wheel, 1924	16	28	55
633 Locomotive, O scale, diesel, SW2, Santa Fe, 1962	100	150	215
634 Locomotive, O scale, diesel, SW2, Santa Fe, blue body, 1962	18	30	60
HO-635 Locomotive, HO scale, steam, 1961	19	32	65
636W Diesel Type Power Car, O scale, U.P., Streamliner, yellow and brown, marked "City of Denver," 1936	42	70	140
HO-636 Locomotive, HO scale, steam, 1963	19	33	65
636-13 Bulb, 8 volt, clear, 1936	n/a	n/a	1
637 Coach, O scale, Streamliner, marked "City of Denver," 1936	30	50	100
637 Locomotive, Super O scale, 2-6-4, steam, 2046W tender or 2040W tender, 1959	52	88	175
638 Observation Car, O scale, Streamliner, yellow and brown, marked "City of Denver," 1936	30	50	100
HO-642 Locomotive, HO scale, steam, 1961	19	33	65
HO-643 Locomotive, HO scale, steam, 1963	19	33	65
HO-645 Locomotive, HO scale, steam, 1962	19	33	65
645 Locomotive, O27 scale, diesel, SW2, Union Pacific, yellow body, 1963	41	68	135
HO-646 Locomotive, HO scale, steam, 1963	19	33	65
646 Locomotive, O scale, 4-6-4, steam, 2046W tender, 1954	88	148	295
HO-647 Locomotive, HO scale, 1966	19	33	65
651 Flatcar, O scale, 1935	15	25	50
652 Gondola, O scale, 1935	16	28	55
653 Hopper, O scale, 1934	19	33	65
654 Tank Car, O scale, silver, orange, 1934	15	25	50
655 Boxcar, O scale, 1934	16	28	55

	C6	C8	C10
656 Cattle Car, O scale, 1935	30	50	100
657 Caboose, O scale, 1934	10	18	35
659 Dump Car, O scale, 1935	24	40	80
665 Locomotive, O scale, 4-6-4, steam, w/6026W or 2046W tender, 1954	100	160	235
671 Locomotive, O scale, steam, 6-8-6, 671W tender, 1946	70	115	230
671 Locomotive, O scale, steam, 6-8-6, w/2671 tender, 1946	90	150	300
671 R&R Locomotive, O scale, steam, 671W tender, 1952	75	125	250
671-75 Smoke Bulb, 14 volt, 1946	5	10	15
675 Locomotive, O scale, 2-6-2, steam, w/2466W, 2466WX or 6466WX tender, 1947	70	115	230
681 Locomotive, O scale, 6-8-6, steam, 2671W tender, 1950	78	130	260
682 Locomotive, O scale, 6-8-6, steam, w/2046W tender, 1954	140	233	465
685 Locomotive, O scale, 4-6-4, steam, w/6026W tender, 1953	85	142	285
700K Locomotive, O72 scale, 4-6-4, steam kit, gray, six kits all original boxes, 1939	2800	4200	5600
700 Locomotive, O scale, 0-4-0, electric, dark green NYC Lines, 1913-1916	225	375	750
700 Window Display Set, standard scale, 1904	n/a	n/a	n/a
700E Locomotive, O72 scale, 4-6-4, steam, black, w/700/700W twelve-wheel cast tender, 1937	750	1250	2500
700EWX Locomotive, O72 scale, steam, black, w/700/700W twelve-wheel cast whistle tender, 1937	1200	2000	4000
700E250 Display Stand and Track, w/Lionel ID plate, 1938	810	1350	2700
701 Locomotive, 0-4-0, electric, dark green, 1913-1916	270	450	900
703 Locomotive, O scale, 4-4-4, electric, dark green, 1913-1916	660	1100	2200
703-10 Smoke Bulb, O scale, 1946	15	25	30
HO-704 Baggage Car, HO scale, Texas Special, 1959	18	30	60
HO-705 Pullman, HO scale, Texas Special, 1959	18	30	60

	C6	C8	C10
706 Locomotive, O scale, 0-4-0, electric, dark green, 1913-1916	420	700	1400
HO-706 Vista Dome, HO scale, Texas Special, 1959	18	30	60
HO-707 Observation Car, HO scale, Texas Special, 1959	18	30	60
HO-708 Baggage Car, HO scale, Pennsylvania, 1960	5	10	20
708 Locomotive, O72 scale, 0-6-0, steam, scale, switcher, "8976" cast in boiler front, 1939	900	1500	3000
HO-709 Vista Dome, HO scale, Pennsylvania, 1960	8	13	26
HO-710 Observation Car, HO scale, Pennsylvania, 1960	6	10	20
710 Pullman, O scale, green, orange, 1924	75	125	250
710 Pullman, O scale, red, 1924	60	100	200
710 Pullman, O scale, two-tone blue, 1924	67	112	225
HO-711 Baggage Car, HO scale, Pennsylvania, 1960	6	10	20
711 Switches, O72 scale, electric, pair, 1935	75	112	150
HO-712 Baggage Car, HO scale, Santa Fe, 1961	14	22	45
712 Observation Car, O scale, green, orange, 1924	72	120	240
712 Observation Car, O scale, red, 1924	60	100	200
712 Observation Car, O scale, two-tone blue, 1924	66	110	220
HO-713 Pullman, HO scale, Santa Fe, 1961	14	22	45
714 Boxcar, O72 scale, 1940	120	200	400
714K Boxcarcar, O72 scale, kit, new only, 1940	n/a	n/a	1000
HO-714 Vista Dome, HO scale, Santa Fe, 1961	8	13	26
HO-715 Observation Car, HO scale, Santa Fe, 1961	6	10	20
715 Tank Car, O72 scale, 1940	120	200	400
715K Tank Car, O72 scale, kit, new only, 1940	n/a	n/a	1000
716K Hopper, O72 scale, kit, new only, 1940	n/a	n/a	1000

No. 763E Locomotive, 4-6-4, $1,850.

	C6	C8	C10
716 Hopper, O72 scale, 1940	97	163	325
717K Caboose, O72 scale, kit, new only, 1940	n/a	n/a	500
717-54 Bulb, 18 volt, clear, 1940	n/a	1	n/a
720 90 Degrees Crossing, O72 scale, 1935	2	5	8
721 Switches, O72 scale, non-electric, pair, 1935	42	70	140
HO-723 Pullman, HO scale, Pennsylvania, 1963	6	10	20
HO-725 Observation Car, HO scale, Pennsylvania, 1963	6	10	20
726 Locomotive, O scale, 2-8-4, steam, w/2426W tender, 1946	200	330	660
726 Locomotive, O scale, 2-8-4, steam, w/2046W tender, 1946	210	330	385
00-72-70 Bulb, O scale, 12 volt, yellow, 1939	n/a	n/a	1
730 90 Degrees Crossing T-Rail, O72 scale, 1935	15	22	30
731 Switches, O72 scale, electric, T-rail, pair, 1935	175	263	350
HO-733 Pullman, HO scale, Santa Fe, 1964	6	10	20
HO-735 Observation Car, HO scale, Santa Fe, 1964	6	10	20
736 Locomotive, O scale, 2-8-4, steam, w/2046W tender, 1950	250	300	400
746 Locomotive, O scale, 4-8-4, steam, w/746W tender w/short stripe, marked "Norfolk & Western," 1957	500	850	1195
746 Locomotive, O scale, 4-8-4, steam, w/long stripe, 1957	580	900	1500

	C6	C8	C10
752E or W Streamliner Power Car, O scale, 1934	140	235	470
752-9 Bulb, 18 volt, clear, 1934	n/a	n/a	1
753 Coach, O scale, streamliner, 1934	42	70	140
754 Observation Car, O scale, streamliner, 1934	42	70	140
760 Pack of Curved Track, sixteen sections, 1935	16	24	32
761 Track, O72 scale, curved, 1934	n/a	1	2
762S Track, O72 scale, straight, insulated, w/lock-on, 1934	n/a	2	3
762 Track, O72 scale, straight, 1934	n/a	1	2
763E Locomotive, O scale, 4-6-4, steam, gunmetal gray, w/2226W or 2226WX tender, 1937	720	1200	2400
763E Locomotive, O scale, 4-6-4, steam, semi-scale, Hudson, black, w/2226WX tender or gunmetal gray 263 or 2263W tender, 1937	555	925	1850
771 Track, O72 scale, curved, T-rail, 1935	n/a	2	3
772 Track, O72 scale, straight, T-rail, 1935	n/a	2	3
772S Track, O72 scale, straight, insulated, T-rail, 1940	3	4	5
773 Fish Plate Set, O72 scale, 100 bolts, 100 nuts, fifty fishplates and wrench, 1936	25	38	50
773 Locomotive, O scale, 4-6-4 steam, Hudson, w/2426W tender, 1950	700	650	1530
773 Locomotive, 4-6-4, Hudson, w/2046W tender, 1964	455	650	900

	C6	C8	C10
782 Streamliner Front Coach, O72 scale, part of articulated Hiawatha set, gray roof, orange sides and maroon underframe, marked "The Milwaukee Road," 1935	150	250	500
783 Coach, O72 scale, streamliner, part of articulated Hiawatha set, gray roof orange sides and maroon underframe, marked "The Milwaukee Road," 1935	150	250	500
784 Observation Car, O72 scale, streamliner, part of articulated Hiawatha set, gray roof, orange sides and maroon underframe, marked "The Milwaukee Road," 1935	150	250	500
792 Front Coach, O72 scale, streamliner, part of Rail Chief set, w/700E Loco, maroon roof, red sides, red underframe, marked "792 Lionel Lines 792," 1937	150	250	500
793 Coach, O72 scale, streamliner, part of Rail Chief set, marked "793 Lionel Lines 793," 1937	150	250	500
794 Observation Car, O72 scale, streamliner, part of Rail Chief set, maroon roof, red sides, red underframe, marked "794 Lionel Lines 794," 1937	150	250	500
800 Boxcar, O scale, 1915	33	55	110
800 Express Motor Car, standard scale, 1904	1000	2000	4000
HO-800 Flatcar, HO scale, w/airplane, 1958	18	30	60
801 Caboose, O scale, 1915	19	33	65
HO-801 Flatcar, HO scale, w/boat, 1958	9	15	30
802 Stock, O scale, 1915	21	35	70
803 Hopper, O scale, dark green, 1923	15	25	50

	C6	C8	C10
803 Hopper, O scale, peacock, 1923	25	43	85
803 Hopper, O scale, 1929	15	25	50
804 Tank Car, O scale, 1929	21	35	70
804 Tank Car, O scale, early, dark gray, 1923	20	33	65
804 Tank Car, O scale, Sunoco, silver, 1923	21	35	70
804 Tank Car, O scale, terra-cotta, 1923	20	33	65
HO-805 AEC Car, HO scale, w/light, 1959	12	20	40
805 Boxcar, O scale, orange, maroon, 1927	15	25	50
805 Boxcar, O scale, pea green, orange, 1927	23	38	75
806 Cattle Car, O scale, 1927	30	50	100
HO-806 Flatcar, HO scale, w/helicopter, 1959	15	25	50
807 Caboose, O scale, 1927	14	23	45
HO-807 Flatcar, HO scale, w/bulldozer, 1959	14	23	45
HO-808 Flatcar, w/tractor	14	23	45
809 Dump Car, O scale, 1931	18	30	60
HO-809 Helium Transport Car, HO scale, 1961	11	19	38
810 Crane, O scale, 1930-1940	60	100	200
HO-810 Generator Transport Car, HO scale, 1961	8	13	26
811 Flatcar, O scale, silver, 1926	40	68	135
811 Flatcar, O scale, maroon, 1926	13	21	42
HO-811-25 Flat, HO scale, w/stakes, 1958	6	10	20
812 Gondola, O scale, 1926	24	40	80
812T Tool Set, O scale, 1937	16	24	32
813 Cattle Car, O scale, 1926	36	60	120

Left to right: No. 806 Cattle car, $100; No. 805 Boxcar, $75; No. 807 Caboose, $45. Photo courtesy Richard MacNary

	C6	C8	C10
HO-813 Mercury Capsule Car, HO scale, 1962 10		16	32
HO-814 Auto Transport Car, HO scale, 1958 15		25	50
814 Boxcar, O scale, nickel plate, 1926 66		110	220
814 Boxcar, O scale, orange body, brown roof, 1926 30		50	100
814R Refrigerator, O scale, white body, brown roof, 1929 85		143	285
814R Refrigerator, O scale, w/rubber-stamped lettering, 1929 360		600	1200
815 Tank Car, O scale, aluminum, silver, 1926 57		95	190
815 Tank Car, O scale, Shell, orange, 1926 40		68	135
HO-815 Tank Car, HO scale, 1958 11		18	35
HO-815-50 Tank Car, HO scale, 1964 8		13	25
HO-815-75 Tank Car, HO scale, 1963 8		13	25
HO-815-85 Tank Car, HO scale, 1964 8		13	25
816 Hopper, O scale, red, olive green, 1927 37		63	125
816 Hopper, O scale, black, 1927 75		125	250
HO-816 Rocket Fuel Tank Car, HO scale, 1962 8		13	25
HO-816-50 Rock Fuel Tank Car, HO scale, 1962 8		13	25
817 Caboose, O scale, 1926 28		48	95
817 Caboose, O scale, flat red, brown roof, rubber-stamped lettering, 1926 .. 60		100	200
HO-817 Caboose, HO scale, 1958 7		12	24
HO-817-150 Caboose, HO scale, Santa Fe, 1960 6		10	20
HO-817-200 Caboose, HO scale, AEC, 1959 6		10	20
HO-817-225 Caboose, HO scale, Alaska, 1959 6		10	20
HO-817-250K Caboose, HO scale, Texas Special, 1959 6		10	20
HO-817-275 Caboose, HO scale, New Haven, 1959 6		10	20
HO-817-300 Caboose, HO scale, Southern Pacific, 1959 6		10	20

	C6	C8	C10
HO-817-350 Caboose, HO scale, Rock Island, 1960 6		10	20
HO-819-1 Work Caboose, HO scale, P.R.R., 1958 8		13	25
HO-819-100 Work Caboose, HO scale, B&M, 1958 8		13	25
HO-819-200 Work Caboose, HO scale, B&M, 1959 8		13	25
HO-819-225 Work Caboose, HO scale, Santa Fe, 1960 8		13	25
HO-819-250 Work Caboose, HO scale, NP, 1960 8		13	25
HO-819-275 Work Caboose, HO scale, C&O, 1960 8		13	25
HO-819-285 Work Caboose, HO scale, C&O, 1963 8		13	25
820 Boxcar, O scale, dark olive, rubber stamped "ATSF" and "48522," 1915 60		100	200
820 Boxcar, O scale, orange or maroon, 1915 27		45	90
820 Floodlight, O scale, terra-cotta base, 1931 45		75	150
820 Floodlight, O scale, green base, 1931 68		113	225
821 Cattle Car, O scale, 1915 27		45	90
HO-821 Pipe Car, HO scale, 1960 8		13	25
HO-821-100 Pipe Car, HO scale, 1963 10		16	32
HO-821-50 Pipe Car, HO scale, 1964 8		13	25
822 Caboose, O scale, 1915 22		38	75
HO-823 Twin Missile Car, HO scale, 1960 21		35	70
HO-824 Flatcar, HO scale, w/two cars, 1958 14		22	45
HO-827 Caboose, HO scale, Lionel, 1961 6		10	20
HO-827-50 Caboose, HO scale, AEC, 1963 6		10	20
HO-827-75 Caboose, HO scale, Lionel, 1963 6		10	20
HO-830 Flatcar, HO scale, w/two vans, 1958 12		20	40
831 Flatcar, O scale, 1927 18		30	60
HO-834 Poultry Car, HO scale, 1959 13		21	42

	C6	C8	C10
HO-836 Hopper, HO scale, 1961	6	10	20
HO-836-100 Hopper, HO scale, Lionel, 1964	6	10	20
HO-836-60 Hopper, HO scale, Alaska, 1966	6	10	20
HO-837 Caboose, HO scale, M&StL, 1961	5	8	15
HO-837-100 Caboose, HO scale, M&StL, 1963	6	10	20
HO-838 Caboose, HO scale, Lackawanna, 1961	6	10	20
HO-840 Caboose, HO scale, NYC, 1961	6	10	20
HO-841 Caboose, HO scale, 1961	6	10	20
HO-841-175 Caboose, HO scale, Santa Fe, 1962	6	10	20
HO-841-50 Caboose, HO scale, Union Pacific, 1962	6	10	20
HO-842 Culvert Pipe Car, HO scale, 1960	8	12	25
HO-845 Gold Bullion Car, HO scale, 1962	10	16	32
HO-847 Exploding Target Car, HO scale, 1960	6	9	18
HO-847-100 Exploding Target Car, HO scale, 1960	17	29	58
HO-850 Missile Launching Car, HO scale, 1960	11	18	35
HO-850-100 Missile Launching Car, HO scale,	11	19	38
HO-860 Derrick, HO scale, 1958	10	16	32
HO-861 Timber Transport Car, HO scale, 1960	6	10	20
HO-861-100 Timber Transport Car, HO scale, 1961	8	13	26
HO-862-25 Gondola, HO scale, 1958	3	5	10
HO-863 Rail Truck Car, HO scale, 1960	8	13	26
HO-864-1 Boxcar, HO scale, Seaboard, 1958	6	10	20
HO-864-100 Boxcar, HO scale, New Haven, 1958	6	10	20
HO-864-125 Boxcar, HO scale, Rutland, 1958	6	10	20
HO-864-150 Boxcar, HO scale, M&StL, 1958	6	10	20

	C6	C8	C10
HO-864-175 Boxcar, HO scale, Timken, 1958	6	10	20
HO-864-200 Boxcar, HO scale, Monon, 1958	6	10	20
HO-864-225 Boxcar, HO scale, Central of Georgia, 1958	6	10	20
HO-864-25 Boxcar, HO scale, NYC, 1958	6	10	20
HO-864-250 Boxcar, HO scale, Wabash, 1958	6	10	20
HO-864-275 Boxcar, HO scale, State of Maine, 1962	6	10	20
HO-864-300 Boxcar, HO scale, Alaska, 1959	6	10	20
HO-864-325 Boxcar, HO scale, D.S.S.A., 1959	6	10	20
HO-864-350 Boxcar, HO scale, State of Maine, 1959	9	15	30
HO-864-400 Boxcar, HO scale, B&M, 1960	6	10	20
HO-864-50 Boxcar, HO scale, State of Maine, 1958	6	10	20
HO-864-700 Boxcar, HO scale, Santa Fe, 1961	6	10	20
HO-864-900 Boxcar, HO scale, NYC, 1959	6	10	20
HO-864-925 Boxcar, HO scale, NYC, 1964	6	10	20
HO-864-935 Boxcar, HO scale, NYC, 1963	6	10	20
HO-865 Gondola, HO scale, w/canisters, 1958	10	16	32
HO-865-225 Gondola, HO scale, w/scrap iron, 1960	8	13	25
HO-865-250 Gondola, HO scale, w/crates, 1960	8	13	25
HO-865-300 Gondola, HO scale, w/crates, 1963	8	13	25
HO-865-350 Gondola, HO scale, NYC, 1963	6	10	20
HO-865-375 Gondola, HO scale, NYC, 1963	6	10	20
HO-865-400 Gondola, HO scale, NYC w/crates, 1963	6	10	20
HO-865-435 Gondola, HO scale, 1964	6	10	20

	C6	C8	C10
HO-866-1 Cattle Car, HO scale, M.K.T., 1958	6	10	20
HO-866-200 Circus Car, HO scale, 1959	10	16	32
HO-866-25 Cattle Car, HO scale, Santa Fe, 1958	6	10	20
HO-870 Maintenance Car, HO scale, w/generator, 1959	9	15	30
HO-872-1 Reefer, HO scale, Fruit Growers, 1958	6	10	20
HO-872-200 Reefer, HO scale, Railway Express, 1959	6	10	20
HO-872-25 Reefer, HO scale, Illinois Central, 1958	6	10	20
HO-872-50 Reefer, HO scale, El Capitan, 1958	6	10	20
HO-873 Rodeo Car, HO scale, 1962	6	10	20
HO-874 Boxcar, HO scale, NYC, 1964	15	25	50
HO-874-25 Boxcar, HO scale, NYC, 1965	6	10	20
HO-874-60 Boxcar, HO scale, B&M, 1964	6	10	20
HO-875 Flatcar, HO scale, w/missile, 1959	10	17	34
876 Helios 21 Spaceship, 1965	12	20	40
HO-877 Miscellaneous Car, HO scale, 1958	6	10	20
HO-879 Derrick, HO scale, 1958	8	13	26
HO-880 Maintenance Car, HO scale, w/light, 1959	18	30	60
900 Boxcar, O scale, ammunition, part of armored train set, 1917	150	250	500
900 or B Catalog, O scale, number for 230 and tender, 0-6-0, similar to loco 227, 1939	450	750	1500
900 Express Trail Car, 2-7/8" scale, 1904	1000	2000	4500
HO-900 Operating Platform, HO scale, 1960	11	18	36
901 Gondola, O scale, gray or maroon, 1919	20	33	65
902 Gondola, O scale, apple green, 1927	8	13	25
902 Gondola, O scale, peacock, 1927	8	13	25
902-5 Rocks, 1958	n/a	n/a	3

	C6	C8	C10
HO-903 Track, HO scale, straight, 3", 1958	n/a	n/a	1
HO-905 Track, HO scale, straight, 1-1/2", 1958	n/a	n/a	1
HO-906 Track, HO scale, straight, 6", 1968	n/a	n/a	1
909 Smoke Fluid, full bottle, 1957	n/a	n/a	5
HO-909 Track, HO scale, straight, 9", 1958	n/a	n/a	1
910 Grove, eleven trees, 1932	150	225	300
911 Country Estate, 191 villa, shrubbery and trees, 1932	450	675	900
912 Suburban Home, 189 villa, shrubbery and trees, 1932	375	525	750
913 Bungalow, w/garden, flowers and trees, 1932	250	375	500
914 Formal Garden Park, two grass plots, centerpiece, flowering bushes, cream base, 1932	175	268	350
915 Curved Tunnel Mountain, O scale, large, 1932	200	300	400
916 Tunnel, O scale, curved, 1932	175	263	350
917 Mountain, medium, 1932	200	300	400
918 Mountain, small, 1932	175	263	350
919 Park Grass, 8 ounces, 1932	9	14	18
920 Scenic Display Set, 1957	57	76	95
920 Scenic Park, small, 1932	2000	3000	4000
920-2 Tunnel Portals, 1958	15	23	30
920-8 Lichen, 1958	n/a	n/a	3
921 Scenic Park, large, 1932	1400	2100	2800
921C Scenic Park, center section, 1932	400	600	800
922 Lamp Terrace, 1932	175	263	350
HO-922 Remote Control Switch, HO scale, right, 1958	n/a	2	3
HO-923 Remote Control Switch, HO scale, left, 1958	n/a	2	3
923 Tunnel, standard scale, 1933	200	300	400
924 Tunnel, O72 scale, curved, 1935	150	225	300
HO-925 Terminal Track, HO scale, straight, 1958	n/a	1	2
HO-925-10 Insulating Clip, HO scale, 1960	n/a	n/a	1
926 Tube of Lubrication, full, 1955	n/a	n/a	3

	C6	C8	C10
927 Flag Plot, 1937-1942	40	60	80
927 Lubrication and Maintenance, kit, 1950-1953	10	17	33
927-3 Liquid Track Cleaner, full can, 1955	n/a	n/a	5
928 Maintenance Kit, 1960-1963	31	36	40
HO-929 Upcoupling Track, HO scale, 9", 1958	2	3	4
HO-930 30 Degrees Crossing, HO scale, 1960	2	3	4
HO-939 Uncoupler, HO scale, 1958	n/a	2	3
HO-942 Manual Switch, HO scale, right, 1958	n/a	2	3
943 Exploding Ammo Dump Car, 1959	20	30	40
HO-943 Manual Switch, HO scale, left, 1958	n/a	2	3
950 Railroad Map, 1958-1966	25	38	50
HO-950 Re-railer, HO scale, 1958	n/a	2	3
951 Farm Set, plastic, thirteen pieces, 1958	8	15	38
952 Figure Set, plastic, thirty pieces, 1958	8	15	34
953 Figure Set, plastic, thirty-two pieces, 1959	8	15	35
954 Swimming Pool and Playground Set, plastic, thirty pieces, 1959	10	15	35
955 Highway Set, plastic, twenty-two pieces, 1958	10	15	30
956 Stockyard, plastic, eighteen pieces, 1959	10	15	30
957 Farm Building and Animal Set, plastic, thirty-five pieces, 1958	10	15	30
958 Vehicles, plastic, twenty-four pieces, 1958	10	20	31
959 Barn Set, plastic, twenty-three pieces, 1958	6	15	33
960 Barn Yard Set, plastic, twenty-nine pieces, 1959	6	15	33
HO-960 Bumper Track, HO scale, 1960	n/a	n/a	1
HO-961 Bumper Track, HO scale, illuminated, 1961	n/a	n/a	1
961 School Set, plastic, thirty-six pieces, 1959	10	15	32

	C6	C8	C10
962 Turnpike Set, plastic, twenty-four pieces, 1958	10	15	38
963 Frontier Set, plastic, eighteen pieces, 1959	10	15	40
964 Factory, plastic, twenty-two pieces, 1959	10	15	50
965 Farm Set, plastic, thirty-six pieces, 1959	13	15	35
966 Firehouse, plastic, forty-five pieces, 1958	13	15	35
967 Post Office, plastic, twenty-five pieces, 1958	10	15	35
968 TV Transmitter, plastic, twenty-eight pieces, 1958	10	15	34
969 Construction Set, plastic, twenty-three pieces, 1960	10	15	30
970 Ticket Booth, cardboard, 1958-1960	65	98	130
971 Box of Lichen, 1959	2	5	10
972 Trees, 1959	2	5	10
973 Landscaping Set, 1959	7	11	15
974 Scenery Set, 1962	11	17	22
HO-975 Terminal Track, HO scale, curved, 1958	1	1	1
980 Ranch Set, plastic, fourteen pieces, 1960	10	15	36
981 Freight Yard Set, plastic, ten pieces, 1960	10	15	34
982 Surburban House, plastic, eighteen pieces, 1960	10	15	34
HO-983 Curved Track, HO scale, curved, 3", 18" radius, 1958	n/a	n/a	1
983 Farm Set, plastic, seven pieces, 1960	10	15	34
HO-984 Curved Track, HO scale, 4-1/2", 18" radius, 1958	n/a	n/a	1
984 Railroad Set, plastic, twenty-two pieces, 1961	10	15	30
HO-985 Curved Track, HO scale, 9", 15" radius, 1958	n/a	n/a	1
985 Freight Area Set, plastic, thirty-two pieces, 1961	13	15	32
986 Farm Set, plastic, twenty pieces, 1962	10	15	33
HO-986 Track, HO scale, curved, 4-1/2", 15" radius, 1958	n/a	n/a	1

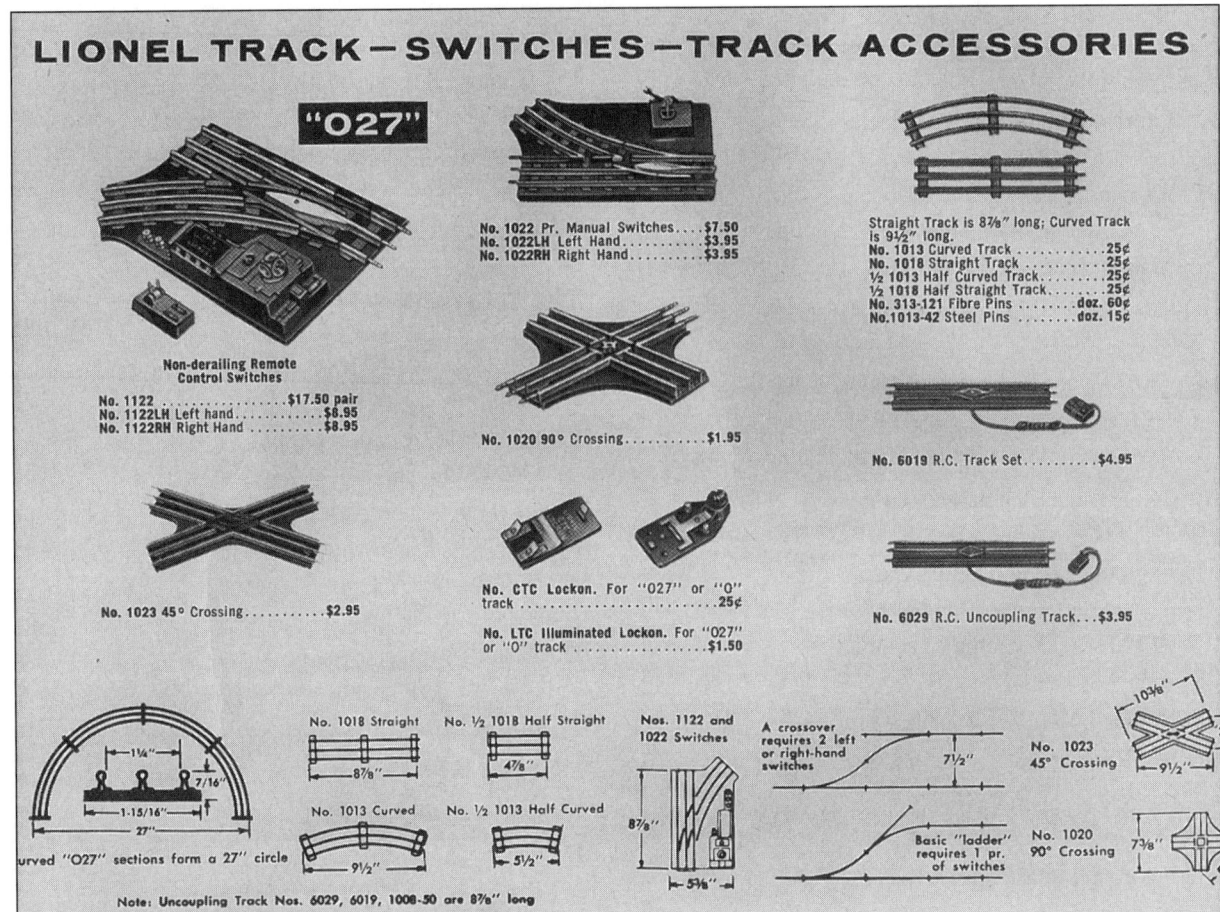

Various forms of track, switches and accessories as shown in the 1961 Lionel catalog.

	C6	C8	C10
987 Town Set, plastic, twenty-four pieces, 1962	10	25	33
988 Railroad Structure, sixteen pieces, 1962	10	25	33
HO-989 Track, HO scale, curved, 9", 18" radius, 1958	n/a	n/a	1
HO-990 90 Degrees Crossing, HO scale, 1958	3	5	7
1000 Passenger Car, 2-7/8" scale, motorized, 1904	1000	2000	4000
1000 Trailer Truck, standard scale, 100 series, 1910	840	1400	2800
1000 Trolley, standard scale, trailer, 1910	840	1400	2800
1001 Locomotive, O27 scale, 2-4-2, steam, w/1001T tender, 1948	15	25	50
1002 Gondola, O27 scale, 1948	4	7	14
1004 Boxcar, O27 scale, 1948	7	11	22
1005 Tank Car, O27 scale, 1948	4	7	13

	C6	C8	C10
1007 Caboose, O27 scale, 1948	3	4	8
1007 Platform and Background, O27 scale, 1936	30	45	60
1008 Uncoupling Track, O27 scale, each, 1957	n/a	n/a	2
1008-50 Automatic Uncoupling Track, O27 scale, each, 1961	n/a	n/a	2
1009 Manumatic Uncoupling Track Set, O27 scale, 1948	5	7	9
1010 Interurban Trolley, standard scale, 1910	1750	2625	3500
1010 Transformer, 35 watt, 1961	8	12	20
1010 Winner Locomotive, O27, scale, 0-4-0, electric, 1931	30	50	100
1011 Interurban Trolley, standard scale, motor car, 1910	1050	1750	3500
1011 Transformer, 15 watt, 1961	8	12	20
1011 Winner Pullman, O27 scale, 1931	9	15	30

	C6	C8	C10
1012 Interurban Trolley, standard scale, 1910	1050	1750	3500
1012 Transformer, 35 watt, 1950	7	9	19
1012 Winner Station Transformer, 1931	22	33	45
1013 Track, O27 scale, curved, 1934	n/a	n/a	1
1013 Track, O27 scale, curved, half-section, 1968	n/a	n/a	1
1013-17 Track Pins, O27 scale, steel, price per dozen, 1938	n/a	1	2
1014 Lockton, O27 scale, 1931	n/a	1	2
1014 Transformer, 40 watt, 1955	10	15	20
1015 Transformer, 45 watt, 1956	8	12	32
1015 Winner Locomotive, O27 scale, 0-4-0, steam, w/1016 tender, black, 1931	30	50	100
1016 Transformer, 35 watt, 1959	6	12	30
1016 Winner Locomotive, w/tender, black	30	50	100
1017 Lionel-Ives Transformer Station, 1933	22	34	45
1017 Winner Transformer Station, 1931	22	34	45
1018 Track, O27 scale, straight, half section, 1968	n/a	n/a	1
1018 Track, O27 scale, straight, 1934	n/a	n/a	1
1019 Track Set, O27 scale, remote control, 1938	5	8	10

	C6	C8	C10
1019 Winner Observation Car, O27 scale, 1931	7	13	25
1020 90 Degrees Crossing, O27 scale, 1955	1	2	6
1020 Winner Baggage Car, O27 scale, 1931	7	13	25
1021 90 Degrees Crossing, O27 scale, 1933	1	2	6
1022 Curved Tunnel, O27 scale, 1935	20	30	40
1022 Switch, O27 scale, manual, price per pair, 1955	8	12	25
1023 45 Degree Crossing, O27 scale, each, 1955	1	2	3
1023 Tunnel, O27 scale, straight, 1934	18	27	35
1024 Switches, O27 scale, manual, price per pair, 1935	5	8	11
1025 Bumper, O27 scale, 1946	6	10	15
1025 Transformer, 45 watt, 1961	12	18	30
1026 Transformer, 25 watt, 1963	5	7	12
1027 Transformer Station, 1934	20	30	40
1028 Transformer, 25 watt, 1935	3	4	5
1029 Transformer, 25 watt, 1936	3	4	5
1030 Transformer, 40 watt, 1936	4	6	12
1030 Winner Locomotive, O27 scale, 0-4-0, electric, orange w/green roof, 1932	30	50	100
1032 Transformer, 90 watt, 1948	30	40	60

Top row, left to right: No. 1107 Donald Duck hand car, $1,200; No. 1103 Peter Rabbit hand car, $1,000. Bottom row, left to right: No. 110 Mickey Mouse hand car, $1,000; No. 1005 Santa Claus hand car, $1,800.

	C6	C8	C10
1033 Transformer, 90 watt, 1948	40	55	75
1034 Transformer, 75 watt, 1948	28	35	55
1035 Transformer, 60 watt, 1947	12	18	25
1035 Winner Locomotive, O27 scale, 0-4-0, steam, w/1016 tender, 1932	30	50	100
1037 Transformer, 40 watt, 1941	10	15	20
1039 Transformer, 35 watt, 1938	10	15	20
1040 Transformer and Whistle Controller, 60 watt, 1938	12	18	25
1041 Transformer, 60 watt, 1940	12	18	25
1042 Transformer, 75 watt, 1942	12	18	25
1043 Transformer, 60 watt, 1953	10	15	20
1043 Transformer, 50 watt	12	20	35
1043-500FX Girls Train Transformer, 60 watt, ivory case, 1957	55	75	115
1044 Transformer, 90 watt, 1957	30	40	65
1045C Contactor, 1938	n/a	n/a	1
1045 Operating Watchman, nickel or brass sign, 1938	25	38	50
1046 Mechanical Gateman and Crossing, 1936	45	68	90
1047 Switchman, w/flat, 1959-1961	50	80	150
1050 Passenger Car, 2-7/8" scale, trailer, 1905	2000	3500	7500
1053 Transformer, 60 watt, 1956	30	45	60
1055 Locomotive, O scale, Alco A diesel, Texas Special, uncataloged, 1960	20	32	65
1060 Locomotive, O27 scale, Scout team, 2-4-2, w/1050T tender, uncataloged, 1960	12	20	30
1061 Locomotive, O27 scale, 2-4-2, steam, w/1061T tender, 1969	12	20	30
1062 Locomotive, O27 scale, 2-4-2, w/1062T tender, 1963	12	19	38
1063 Transformer, 75 watt, 1961	18	25	55
1065 Locomotive, O scale, Alco A unit only, diesel, Union Pacific, uncataloged	35	55	90
1066 Locomotive, O scale, Alco A unit only, diesel, Union Pacific, uncataloged	50	75	105
1073 Transformer, 60 watt, 1961	20	25	55

	C6	C8	C10
1100 Mickey Mouse Handcar, mechanical, wind-up, orange base, 1935	600	900	1200
1100 Mickey Mouse Handcar, green base, 1935	500	750	1000
1100 Mickey Mouse Handcar, red base, 1935	500	700	900
1100 Summer Trolley, standard scale, 1911	1050	1750	3500
1100 Trailer Trucks, standard scale, thirty-five series, 1924	3	5	10
1101 Locomotive, 2-4-2	15	25	50
1101 Trailer Trucks, standard scale, w/lights, thirty-five series, 1924	3	5	10
1103 Peter Rabbit Handcar, mechanical, wind-up, track operation, 1935	500	700	1000
1103 Peter Rabbit Handcar, floor operation, 1935	500	700	900
1105 Santa Claus Handcar, mechanical, wind-up, green base, 1935	900	1400	1800
1105 Santa Claus Handcar, mechanical, red base, 1935	800	1200	1600
1107 Donald Duck Rail Car, mechanical, wind-up, green roof, 1936	600	900	1200
1107 Donald Duck Rail Car, red roof, 1936	600	900	1200
1110 Locomotive, O27 scale, 2-4-2, scout steam, 1949	14	23	45
0-11-11 Fiber Pins, O scale, 1937	n/a	n/a	1
1120 Locomotive, O27 scale, 2-4-2, scout steam, 1950	15	25	50
1121 Switches, O27 scale, electric, remote control, pair, 1937	12	18	25
1122 Switches, O27 scale, remote control, 1952	17	26	35
1122-100 Switch Control, O27 scale, 1957	3	4	5
1122-234 Insulating Pins, O27 scale, 1957	n/a	n/a	1
1122-520 Adapter Kit, O27 scale, 1957	5	8	10
1130 Locomotive, O27 scale, 2-4-2, steam, w/1130T tender, 1953	16	13	35

No. 1536 Mickey Mouse Circus Train Outfit, $3,500. Photo courtesy Richard MacNary

	C6	C8	C10
1144 Transformer, 75 watt, 1968	22	33	45
1200 Trailer Truck, standard scale, ten series, 1923	4	6	12
1201 Trailer Truck, standard scale, ten series w/lights, 1923	4	6	12
1229 Transformer, 220 volts, 1938	50	75	100
1230 Transformer, 220 volts, 1938	50	75	100
1239 Transformer, 220 volts, 1941	50	75	100
1241 Transformer, 220 volts, 1941	50	75	100
1300 Trailer Truck, standard scale, 200 series, 1925	4	6	12
1301 Trailer Truck, standard scale, 200 series w/lights, 1925	4	6	12
1400 Trailer Truck, standard scale, 418 series, 1925	5	8	16
1401 Trailer Truck, standard scale, 418 series w/lights, 1925	5	8	16
1506 L.I. Locomotive, steam, mechanical, 1933	36	60	120
1506 Locomotive Outfit, mechanical, w/1509T Tender, 1515 tank and 1517 caboose, 1935	75	125	250
1506L Locomotive Outfit, mechanical, w/1502T tender, 1933	36	60	120
1506-8 Bulb, 1-1/2 volt, clear, 1935	n/a	n/a	1
1508 Locomotive Outfit, 0-4-0, mechanical, Vanderbilt-type, w/1509T tender, 1935	81	135	270
1511 Locomotive Outfit, 0-4-0, mechanical, Commodore Vanderbilt-type, black, w/1516 tender, 1936-1937	45	75	150

	C6	C8	C10
1511 Locomotive Outfit, 0-4-0, mechanical, red, w/1516 tender, 1936-1937	54	90	180
1512 Gondola, O27 scale, 1936	18	30	60
1512 L.I. Gondola, O27 scale, 1933	18	30	60
1512 Winner Gondola, O27 scale, 1931	18	30	60
1514 Boxcar, O27 scale, 1934	12	21	42
1514 L.I. Boxcar, O27 scale, 1933	7	11	22
1514 Winner Boxcar, O27 scale, 1932	9	15	30
1515 L.I. Tank Car, O27 scale, 1933	11	19	38
1515 Tank Car, O27 scale, 1934	19	32	64
1516T Tender, O27 scale, 1936	12	21	42
1517 Caboose, O27 scale, 1931-1937	11	18	36
1517 L.I. Caboose, O27 scale, 1933	9	15	30
1517 Winner Caboose, O27 scale, 1931	7	11	22
1520 Animal, 1935	60	100	200
1521 Locomotive Outfit, mechanical, w/1516T tender, 1937	180	300	600
1536 Mickey Mouse Circus Train Outfit, includes cardboard figures, circus facade, tickets and Mickey as barker; train loco 1508, 1509 red, 1536 dinner, 1536 band and 1536 animal car, w/original box	1500	2500	3500
1550 Switches-mechanical, remote control, price per pair, 1933	20	30	40
1551 90 Degrees Crossing, mechanical, 1936	2	3	4

	C6	C8	C10
1555 90 Degrees Crossing, mechanical, 1933	3	5	5
1560 Station, mechanical, 1933	15	22	30
1572 Lionel Jr. Telegraph Posts, mechanical, 1934	11	18	36
1573 Lionel Jr. Warning Signal, mechanical, 1934	8	12	16
1574 Lionel Jr. Clock, mechanical, 1934	5	8	16
1588 Locomotive Outfit, 0-4-0, mechanical, torpedo type, w/1588 or 1516 tender, 1936	66	110	220
1615 Locomotive, O27 scale, 0-4-0, w/1615T tender, switcher, 1955	85	145	200
1615E L.I. Locomotive, O27 scale, 0-4-0, electric, red cab, brown roof, 1933	75	125	250
1625 Locomotive, O27 scale, 0-4-0, steam, switcher, w/1625 tender, 1958	90	150	250
1630 Pullman, O27 scale, blue sides w/aluminum roof, 1938	20	33	65
1630 Pullman, O27 scale, blue sides w/gray roof, 1938	20	33	65
1631 Observation Car, O27 scale, blue sides w/aluminum roof, 1938	23	39	78
1640-100 Presidential Kit, 1960	80	90	100
1654 Locomotive, O27 scale, 2-4-2, steam, w/1654W tender, 1946	30	50	100
1655 Locomotive, O27 scale, 2-4-2, steam, w/6654W tender, 1945	45	75	150

	C6	C8	C10
1656 Locomotive, O27 scale, 0-4-0, steam, switcher, w/6403 tender, 1948	110	185	370
1661E L.I. Locomotive, O27 scale, 2-4-0, steam, glossy black, w/1661 Tender, 1933	39	65	130
1662 Locomotive, O27 scale, 0-4-0, steam, switcher, w/2203 tender, 1940	125	205	410
1663 Locomotive, O27 scale, 0-4-0, steam, switcher, 2201 tender, 1940	138	230	460
1664 or E Locomotive Outfit, O27 scale, 2-4-2, black or gunmetal gray, w/1689T, 1689W, 2666T or 2666W tender, 1938	60	103	205
1665 Locomotive, O27 scale, 0-4-0, steam, switcher w/2403B tender, 1946	125	210	420
1666 or E Locomotive Outfit, O27 scale, 2-4-2, black, w/2666T, 2666W, 2689T, 2689W or 1689W tender, 1938	39	65	130
1666 or E Locomotive Outfit, O27 scale, 2-4-2, gunmetal gray, w/tender, 1938	36	60	120
1668 or E Locomotive, O27 scale, steam, black, 2-6-2, w/1689T or 1689W tender, 1937	40	68	135
1668 or E Locomotive, O27 scale, 2-6-2, steam, gunmetal gray, 1937	42	70	140
1673 Coach, streamliner, mechanical, red, 1936	14	23	45

No. 1666 Locomotive Outfit 2-4-2, black, with 2666T, 2666W, 2689T, 2689W or 1689W tender, $130.

	C6	C8	C10
1674 Pullman, streamliner, mechanical, 1936	14	23	45
1675 Observation Car, streamliner, mechanical, 1936	14	23	45
1677 Gondola, O27 scale, 1934	12	20	40
1677 L.I. Gondola, O27 scale, 1933	12	20	40
1679 Boxcar, O27 scale, 1934	8	13	25
1679 L.I. Boxcar, O27 scale, 1933	12	20	40
1680 L.I. Tank Car, O27 scale, 1933	12	20	40
1680 Tank Car, O27 scale, 1934	13	21	42
1681 or E Lionel Jr. Locomotive, O27 scale, 2-4-0, steam, black, 1934	42	70	140
1681 or E Lionel Jr. Locomotive, O27 scale, 2-4-0, steam, red, 1934	48	80	160
1682 Caboose, O27 scale, 1934	6	10	20
1682 L.I. Caboose, O27 scale, 1933	9	15	30
1684 Locomotive, O27 scale, 2-4-2, steam, black, w/1689T, 1688T, 2689T or 2689W tender, 1942	45	78	155
1684 Locomotive, O27 scale, 2-4-2, steam, gunmetal gray, 1942	29	48	95
1685 Pullman, O scale, Ives transitional car, blue body w/silver roof, four-wheel trucks, uncataloged, 1933	120	200	400
1685 Pullman, O scale, red body w/maroon roof, four-wheel trucks, uncataloged, 1933	90	150	300
1685 Pullman, O scale, gray body w/maroon roof, six-wheel trucks, uncataloged, 1933	135	225	450
1686 Baggage Car, O scale, Ives transitional car, blue body w/silver roof, four-wheel trucks, uncataloged, 1933	120	200	400
1686 Baggage Car, O scale, red body w/maroon roof, four-wheel trucks, uncataloged, 1933	90	150	300
1686 Baggage Car, O scale, gray body w/maroon roof, six-wheel trucks, uncataloged, 1933	135	225	450
1687 Observation Car, O scale, Ives transitional car, blue body w/silver roof, four-wheel trucks, uncataloged, 1933	120	200	400
1687 Observation Car, O scale, red body w/maroon roof, four-wheel trucks, uncataloged, 1933	90	150	300
1687 Observation Car, O scale, gray body w/maroon roof, six-wheel trucks, uncataloged, 1933	135	225	450
1688 or E Locomotive, O27 scale, 2-4-2, steam, black, w/1689T tender, 1936	36	90	120
1688 or E Locomotive, O27 scale, 2-4-2, steam, gunmetal gray, 1936	60	100	200
1689E Locomotive, O27 scale, 2-4-2, steam, black, w/1689T tender, 1936	35	55	110
1689E Locomotive, O27 scale, 2-4-2, steam, gunmetal gray, 1936	39	65	130
1690 L.I. Pullman, O27 scale, red w/red or brown roof, 1933	15	25	50
1690 Pullman, O27 scale, red, w/red or brown roof, 1934	12	20	40
1691 L.I. Observation Car, O27 scale, red w/red or brown roof, 1933	12	20	40
1691 Observation Car, O27 scale, red w/red or brown roof, 1934	12	20	40
1692 Pullman, O27 scale, peacock body and roof, uncataloged, 1937	12	20	40
1693 Observation Car, O27 scale, peacock body and roof, uncataloged, 1937	12	20	40
1697 Locomotive, Tender and Transformer Outfit, O27 scale, 1937	45	75	150
1698E Locomotive, Tender and Transformer Outfit, O27 scale, 1936	60	100	200
1699E Locomotive, Tender and Transformer Outfit, O27 scale, 1936	60	100	200
1700 or E Power Car, O27 scale, diesel, streamliner, aluminum, red, marked "Lionel Jr.," 1935	66	110	220
1701 Coach, O27 scale, streamliner, aluminum, red or chrome, 1935	36	60	120
1702 Observation Car, O27 scale, streamliner, aluminum, red or chrome, 1935	36	60	120
1703 Front Coach, O27 scale, w/drawbar, streamliner, 1935	12	20	40
1717 Gondola, O scale, orange and tan or yellow and green, uncataloged, 1933	15	25	50
1719 Boxcar, O scale, peacock w/blue roof, orange doors, yellow and brown, uncataloged, 1933	13	23	45

	C6	C8	C10
1722 Caboose, O scale, orange or red body, uncataloged, 1933	18	30	60
1766 Pullman, standard scale, 1934	85	142	285
1767 Baggage Car, standard scale, 1934	90	150	300
1768 Observation Car, standard scale, 1934	105	175	350
1811 L.I. Pullman, O27 scale, 1933	22	36	72
1811 Pullman, O27 scale, 1934	22	36	72
1812 L.I. Observation Car, O27 scale, 1933	22	36	72
1812 Observation Car, O27 scale, 1934	22	36	72
1813 Baggage Car, O27 scale, 1934	18	30	60
1813 L.I. Baggage Car, O27 scale, 1933	18	30	60
1816 or W Power Car, diesel, streamliner, wind-up mechanical, marked "Silver Streak," 1935	42	70	140
1817 Coach, streamliner, mechanical, chrome and orange, 1935	10	16	32
1818 Observation Car, streamliner, mechanical, chrome and orange, 1935	10	16	32
1835E Locomotive, standard scale, 2-4-2, steam, w/1835T, 1835TW or 1835W tender, 1934	230	380	760
1862LT Locomotive, O27 scale, 4-4-0, steam, Civil War, w/1862T tender, marked "General," 1959	100	160	225
1865 Coach, O27 scale, Western & Atlantic, 1959	20	34	68
1866 Baggage Car, O27 scale, Western & Atlantic, 1959	30	50	100
1872 Locomotive, Super O scale, 4-4-0, steam, w/1872W tender, Civil War, marked "General," 1959	100	200	300
1875 Coach, Super O scale, Western & Atlantic, 1959	125	150	250
1875W Coach, Super O scale, Western & Atlantic, w/whistle, 1959	85	125	200
1876 Baggage Car, Super O scale, Western & Atlantic, 1959	36	60	120
1877 Flatcar, O27 scale, part of general set, w/six horses, 1959	30	50	80
1882 Locomotive, Super O scale, steam, Sears production, Civil War General, 4-4-0, also called Halloween General, uncataloged, 1959	200	300	500
1885 Coach, Super O scale, Sears production, Western & Atlantic, uncataloged, 1959	95	150	275
1887 Flatcar, O27 scale, Sears production, w/six horses, uncataloged, 1959	80	130	180
1910 Locomotive, standard scale, 0-6-0, electric, dark olive green, marked "New York, New Haven and Hartford," 1910	600	1000	2000
1910 Pullman, standard scale, dark olive green w/maroon doors, "1910 Pullman 1910," uncataloged, 1910	540	900	1800
1911 Locomotive, standard scale, 0-4-0, electric, dark olive, 1910	330	550	1100
1911 Locomotive, standard scale, 0-4-0, electric, maroon, 1910	300	500	1000
1911 Special Locomotive, standard scale, 0-4-4-0, electric, maroon, marked "New York, New Haven and Hartford" or "New York Central Lines," 1911	420	700	1400
1912 Locomotive, standard scale, 0-4-4-0, electric, dark olive green, 1910	660	1100	2200
1912 Locomotive, standard scale, 0-4-4-0, electric, marked "New York, New Haven and Hartford," 1910	720	1200	2400
1912 Special Locomotive, standard scale, 0-4-4-0, electric, all brass engine, 1911	1500	2500	5000
1917 Lionel Folder, 1917	8	13	25
1918 Lionel Folder, 1918	8	13	25
1919 Lionel Apology Folder, 1919	13	23	45
1919 Lionel Folder, 1919	8	13	25
1920 Lionel Folder, 1920	8	13	25
1921 Lionel Folder, 1921	8	13	25
1926-3 Lionel-Ives Bulb, 6 volt, 1933	n/a	n/a	1
1928 Dealer Display, large cardboard background showing power station, roundhouses, etc.	210	350	700
1930 Winner Folder, 1930	11	21	35

	C6	C8	C10
1931 Winner Folder, 1931	11	21	35
1932 Winner Folder, 1932	11	21	35
1946 Lionel Folder, 1946	12	20	40
2016 Locomotive, O27 scale, 2-6-4, steam, w/6026W tender, 1955	60	100	200
2018 Locomotive, O27 scale, 2-6-4, steam, w/6026W tender, 1956	60	85	120
2020 Locomotive, O27 scale, 6-8-6, steam, w/2020W, 2466WX or 6020W tender, 1946	100	140	210
2023 Color Variation, yellow body w/gray roof and gray nose	900	1500	3000
2023 Locomotive, O27 scale, UP Alco AA, diesel, yellow body w/gray roof or silver body w/gray roof, 1950	90	155	310
2024 Locomotive, O27 scale, Alco A, diesel, C&O, 1969	30	45	80
2025 Locomotive, O27 scale, 2-6-2, steam, w/6466WX or 6466W tender, 1947	70	100	175
2026 Locomotive, O27 scale, 2-6-2, steam, w/6466WX or 6466W tender, 1948	60	80	135
2026-58 Bulb, 18 volt, clear, 1950	n/a	n/a	1
2028 Locomotive, O27 scale, diesel, GP-7 PRR, Tuscan brown, 1955	140	375	500
2029 Locomotive, O scale, 2-6-4, steam, w/243W tender, 1964	70	90	125
2031 Locomotive, O27 scale, R.I. Alco AA, diesel, black body w/red middle stripe, 1952	150	275	410
2032 Locomotive, O27 scale, Erie Alco AA, diesel, black body w/yellow middle stripe, 1952	125	150	275
2033 Locomotive, O27 scale, U.P. Alco AA, diesel, silver body, 1952	155	200	350
2034 Locomotive, O27 scale, 2-4-2, steam, 1952	36	60	120
2035 Locomotive, O27 scale, 2-6-4, steam, w/2466W tender, 1950	65	95	190
2036 Locomotive, O27 scale, 2-6-4, steam, w/6466W tender, 1950	65	90	150
2037 Locomotive, O27 scale, 2-6-4, steam, w/6026W or 6026T tender, 1953	60	90	125
2037-500 Girl's Locomotive, O27 scale, 2-6-4, steam, pink, 1957	360	600	1200
2041 Locomotive, O27 scale, R.I., Alco AA, diesel, black body w/white stripe, 1969	60	85	120
2046 Locomotive, O27 scale, 4-6-4, steam, w/2046W tender, 1950	135	185	270
2055 Locomotive, O27 scale, 4-6-4, steam, w/1025W or 2046W tender, 1953	75	130	220
2056 Locomotive, O27 scale, 4-6-4, steam, w/2046W tender, 1952	105	175	250
2065 Locomotive, O27 scale, 4-6-4, steam, 2046W or 6026W tender, 1954	100	150	225
2200 Summer Trolley, standard scale, trailer, non-powered, marked "2200 Rapid Transit 2200," 1910	1050	1750	3500
2240 Locomotive, O27 scale, Wabash F-3 AB, diesel, gray and blue shell, single motor, 1956	400	600	800
2242 Locomotive, O27 scale, New Haven F-3 AB, diesel, checkerboard scheme, silver and black, single motor, 1958	500	800	1200
2243 Locomotive, O27 scale, Santa Fe F-3 AB, diesel, silver shell, red nose, single motor, 1955	300	400	495
2245 Locomotive, O27 scale, Texas Special F-3 AB, diesel red shell, single motor, 1954	300	400	700
2257 Caboose, non-illuminated, w/red plastic smokestack	175	300	400
2321 Locomotive, O scale, Lackawanna, diesel, double motor, gray, 1954	300	390	550
2321 Locomotive, O scale, Lackawanna, diesel, gray w/maroon roof, 1954	400	600	800
2322 Locomotive, O scale, Virginian, diesel, double motor, yellow w/blue roof, 1965	300	495	635
2328 Locomotive, O27 scale, Burlington, diesel, silver shell, 1955	200	300	435
2329 Locomotive, O scale, Virginian, electric, blue shell w/yellow striping, 1958	315	540	750
2330 Locomotive, O scale, New Brunswick Green, GG-I, electric, double motor, green w/five gold stripes, 1950	625	900	1550

No. 2333 Locomotive, $1,000. Photo courtesy Good Old Days Store; Bill Kaufman

	C6	C8	C10
2331 Locomotive, O scale, Virginian, diesel, double motor, yellow shell w/black stripe and gold lettering, 1955	720	1150	1400
2331 Locomotive, Virginian, diesel, yellow shell w/blue stripe and yellow lettering, 1955	600	900	1200
2331 Locomotive, Virginian, diesel, yellow w/black roof, 1955	720	1150	1500
2332 Locomotive, GG-I, electric, five silver stripes, 1947	900	1400	2000
2332 Locomotive, GG-I, electric, satin black w/five gold or silver stripes, 1947	510	850	1700
2332 Locomotive, New Brunswick GG-I, electric, single motor, green w/five gold stripes, 1947	320	450	880
2333 Locomotive, O scale, Santa Fe or NYC F-3 AA, diesel, silver w/red nose, 1948	425	750	1000
2333 Locomotive, O scale, NYC F-3 AA, diesel, gray, 1948	425	750	1000
2333 Locomotive, O scale, NYC F-3 AA, diesel, 1948	300	500	1000
2337 Locomotive, O27 scale, Wabash, GP-7, diesel, blue and gray body w/white striping, 1958	110	200	315
2338 Locomotive, O27 scale, Milwaukee Rd. GP-7, diesel, black and orange, 1955	150	200	260
2339 Locomotive, O scale, Wabash GP-7, diesel, blue and gray w/white striping, 1957	165	210	325
2340-1 Locomotive, O scale, GG-1, electric, maroon, double motor, Tuscan brown, w/five stripes, 1955	700	1000	1800
2340-25 Locomotive, O scale, New Brunswick, GG-1, electric, double motor, green w/five stripes, 1955	650	950	1700
2341 Locomotive, O scale, Jersey Central, diesel, double motor, orange body w/blue stripe, 1956	950	1300	2000
2343 Locomotive, O scale, Santa Fe AA, F-3, diesel, double motor, silver w/red nose, 1950	350	400	675
2343C Locomotive, O scale, Santa Fe, diesel, 1950	100	200	295
2344 Locomotive, O scale, NYC F-3 AA, diesel, double motor, gray, 1950	290	400	625
2344C Locomotive, O scale, NYC F-3 B, diesel, 1950	120	225	310
2345 Locomotive, O scale, Western Pacific F-3 AA, diesel, louvered roof, 1952	1100	1400	2075
2345 Locomotive, O scale, Western Pacific F-3 AA, diesel, double motor, silver and orange, screen roof, 1952	1100	1400	2075
2346 Locomotive, O27 scale, Boston and Maine GP-7, diesel, blue shell, black cab w/white trim, 1965	145	225	320
2347 Locomotive, O27 scale, C&O GP-7, diesel, Sears, blue shell w/yellow lettering, uncataloged, 1962	1350	2250	4500
2348 Locomotive, diesel, GP-9, M.St.L., O27 red shell w/blue roof, 1958	175	275	425
2349 Locomotive, O scale, diesel, GP-O, Northern Pacific, black shell, red striping w/gold lettering, 1959	200	295	415
2350 Locomotive, O scale, New Haven, electric, black shell w/orange and white striping, 1956	220	370	515
2351 Locomotive, O scale, electric, Milwaukee Rd., yellow shell w/black roof and red stripe, 1957	200	350	575
2352 Locomotive, O scale, diesel, PRR, Tuscan brown, 1958	225	375	615
2353 Locomotive, O scale, diesel AA, F-3, Santa Fe, double motor, silver w/red nose, 1953	270	400	640
2353C Locomotive, O scale, diesel, F-3, Santa Fe, 1954	120	200	400

	C6	C8	C10
2354 Locomotive, O scale, diesel, AA, F-3, NYC, double motor, gray, 1953	270	425	720
2354C Locomotive, O scale, diesel, B, F-3, NYC, 195480		133	265
2355 Locomotive, O scale, diesel, AA, F-3, Western Pacific, double motor, silver and orange, 1953	800	1300	1900
2356 Locomotive, O scale, diesel, AA, F-3, Southern RY, double motor, green, 1954	500	1100	1400
2356C Locomotive, O scale, diesel, B, F-3, Southern Ry, 1954	150	250	500

	C6	C8	C10
2357 Caboose, O scale, 1948	12	20	40
2358 Locomotive, O scale, Great Northern, electric, orange and green shell, yellow stripes, 1959	360	750	1200
2359 Locomotive, O27 scale, B&M GP-9, diesel, blue shell w/black cab and white trim, 1961	185	200	300
2360-1 Locomotive, GG-1, electric, double motor, single stripe, Tuscan brown, decal letters and numbers rubber stamped stripe, 1961	600	1050	1800
2360-1 Locomotive, GG-1, electric, heavy heat stamped letters and numbers, 1961	225	373	745

No. 2360-1 Locomotive, GG-1, $745.

No. 2352 Locomotive, $615.

	C6	C8	C10
2360-1 Locomotive, GG-1, electric, light pressed letters and numbers, rubber stamped stripe, 1961	600	1000	2000
2360-10 Locomotive, O scale, GG-1, electric, double motor, five stripes, Tuscan brown, heat-stamped letter and number, five rubber stamped stripes, 1956	750	1250	2500
2360-25 Locomotive, O scale, New Brunswick GG-1, electric, double motor, green, heat stamped letters and numbers, five rubber stamped stripes, 1956	575	1000	1300
2363 Locomotive, O scale, Illinois Central F-3 AB, diesel, double motor, brown shell w/orange stripe and yellow trim, 1955	450	900	1350
2365 Locomotive, O27 scale, C&O GP-7, diesel, blue shell, 1962	135	250	400
2367 Locomotive, O scale, Wabash F-3 AB, diesel, double motor, gray and blue shell w/white stripe and trim, 1955	400	800	1200
2368 Locomotive, O scale, B&O F-3 AB, diesel, double motor, blue shell w/black, white and yellow trim, 1956	800	1750	2500
2373 Locomotive, Super O scale, Canadian Pacific AA F-3, diesel, double motor, gray and maroon w/yellow trim, 1957	950	1500	2100
2378 Locomotive, O scale, Milwaukee Rd. F-3 AB, diesel, double motor, gray w/orange stripe, 1956	1000	1700	2400
2379 Locomotive, Super O scale, Rio Grande AB F-3, diesel, double motor, yellow body w/silver roof and stripe, 1957	600	800	1100
2383 Locomotive, Super O scale, Santa Fe AA, F-3, diesel, double motor, silver w/red nose, 1958	300	500	650
2400 Pullman, O27 scale, Maplewood, green shell w/gray roof and yellow trim, 1948	60	85	150
2401 Observation Car, O27 scale, Hillside, 1948	60	85	150
2402 Pullman, O27 scale, Chatham, 1948	60	85	150
2404 Vista Dome, O27 scale, Santa Fe, aluminum, blue lettering, 1964	30	50	70

	C6	C8	C10
2405 Pullman, O27 scale, Santa Fe, aluminum, blue lettering, 1964	30	50	70
2406 Observation Car, Santa Fe, aluminum, blue lettering, 1964	30	50	70
2408 Vista Dome, O27 scale, Santa Fe, aluminum, blue lettering, 1964	35	60	75
2409 Pullman, O27 scale, Santa Fe, aluminum, blue lettering, 1964	35	60	75
2410 Observation Car, Santa Fe scale, aluminum, blue lettering, 1964	35	60	75
2411 Flatcar, O27 scale, w/load of pipes, gray metal frame, 1946	50	70	90
2412 Vista Dome, O27 scale, silver, blue stripe through windows, illuminated, 1959	35	58	115
2414 Pullman, O27 scale, silver, blue stripe through windows, illuminated, 1959	35	58	115
2416 Observation Car, O27 scale, silver, blue stripe through windows, illuminated, 1959	27	45	90
2419 Wrecker Caboose, O27 scale, DL&W, gray metal frame w/gray cab, 1946	27	45	90
2420 Wrecker Caboose, O scale, DL&W, w/light, gray metal frame w/gray cab, 1946	40	70	100
2420-20 Bulb, 14 volt-clear, 1946	n/a	n/a	1
2421 Pullman, O27 scale, silver roof, no stripe, 1950	40	50	75
2421 Pullman, O27 scale, aluminum, gray roof w/black stripe, 1950	40	60	95
2422 Pullman, O27 scale, aluminum, gray roof w/black stripe, 1950	40	60	85
2422 Pullman, O27 scale, silver roof, no stripe, 1950	18	30	60
2423 Observation Car, O27 scale, aluminum, gray roof w/black stripe, 1950	40	60	100
2423 Observation Car, O27 scale, silver roof, no stripe, 1950	40	50	75
2426 WX Tender, O scale, 1946	87	145	290
2429 Pullman, O27 scale, aluminum, gray roof w/black stripe, 1952	50	85	120
2429 Pullman, O27 scale, silver roof, no stripe, 1952	50	85	120

	C6	C8	C10
2430 Pullman, O27 scale, sheet metal, blue w/silver roof, 1946	20	45	65
2431 Observation Car, O27 scale, sheet metal, blue w/silver roof, 1946	20	45	90
2432 Vista Dome, O27 scale, silver, red lettering reads "Clifton," 1954	24	40	80
2434 Pullman, O27 scale, silver, red lettering reads "Newark," 1954	24	40	80
2435 Pullman, O27 scale, silver, red lettering reads "Elizabeth," 1954	30	40	75
2436 Observation Car, O27 scale, silver, red lettering "Summit," 1954	25	42	85
2436 Observation Car, O27 scale, "Mooseheart," 1954	25	42	85
2440 Pullman, O27 scale, blue w/silver roof, 1946	21	35	70
2440 Pullman, O27 scale, green w/dark green roof, 1946	21	35	70
2441 Observation Car, O27 scale, blue w/silver roof, 1946	21	35	70
2441 Observation Car, O27 scale, green w/dark green roof, 1946	21	35	70
2442 Pullman, O27 scale, sheet metal, brown, 1946	36	60	120
2442 Vista Dome, O27 scale, aluminum, red window stripe, marked "Clifton," 1956	45	75	100
2443 Observation Car, O scale, sheet metal, brown, 1956	27	45	90
2444 Pullman, O scale, aluminum, red window stripe, 1956	45	75	140
2452 Gondola, O27 scale, "Pennsylvania," 1945	8	12	25
2452X Gondola, O27 scale, "Pennsylvania," 1946	11	19	38
2454 Boxcar, O27 scale, "Pennsylvania," 1946	60	100	160
2454 Boxcar, O27 scale, "Baby Ruth," 1946	9	15	30
2456 Hopper, O scale, Lehigh Valley, 1948	8	14	27
2457 Caboose, O scale, N5 type, "Pennsylvania," 1945	15	25	50
2458 Boxcar, O scale, automatic, double door, "Pennsylvania," 1945	20	33	65
2460 Operating Crane, O scale, Bucyrus Erie, 1946	35	50	85
2461 Transformer Car, O27 scale, metal, gray frame, 1947	36	60	120
2465 Tank Car, O27 scale, double dome, Sunoco logo, 1946	5	10	17
2472 Caboose, O27 scale, N5 type, "Pennsylvania," 1946	10	18	35
2481 Pullman, O27 scale, illuminated, yellow w/red stripes and gray roof, Anniversary Set, 1950	105	150	275
2482 Pullman, O27 scale, illuminated, yellow w/red stripes and gray roof, Anniversary Set, 1950	105	150	275
2483 Observation Car, O27 scale, illuminated, yellow w/red stripes and gray roof, Anniversary Set, 1950	85	125	230
2521 Observation Car, Super O scale, "Pres. McKinley," illuminated, extruded aluminum shell, gold stripe, 1962	80	125	180
2522 Vista Dome, Super O scale, "Pres. Harrison," extruded aluminum shell, illuminated, gold stripe, 1962	80	125	180
2523 Pullman, Super O scale, "Pres. Garfield," illuminated, extruded aluminum shell, gold stripe, 1962	80	125	185
2530 Baggage Car, O scale, Railway Express Agency, extruded aluminum shell, large door, 1956	250	400	550
2530 Baggage Car, O scale, small doors, 1956	125	175	225
2531 Observation Car, O scale, extruded aluminum shell, illuminated, marked "Silver Dawn," 1952	65	85	110
2532 Vista Dome, O scale, marked "Silver Range," 1952	65	85	115
2533 Pullman, O scale, marked "Silver Cloud," 1952	65	85	110
2534 Pullman, O scale, marked "Silver Bluff," 1952	75	100	140
2541 Observation Car, O scale, Penn., illuminated, extruded aluminum, brown stripes, marked "Alexander Hamilton," 1955	75	123	245
2542 Vista Dome, O scale, Penn., marked "Betsy Ross," 1955	75	123	245

No. 2628 Pullman, Manhattan, $245.

	C6	C8	C10
2543 Pullman, O scale, Penn., marked "William Penn," 1955	120	200	400
2544 Pullman, O scale, Penn., marked "Molly Pitcher," 1955	120	200	400
2550 Budd R.D.C. Mail Baggage Trailer, O scale, Baltimore and Ohio dummy to match motorized Budd 404, silver shell w/blue lettering, 1957	200	350	575
2551 Observation Car, Super O scale, extruded aluminum shell, illuminated, two brown stripes, top Canadian Pacific, bottom, name of car, "Banff Park," 1957	100	150	265
2552 Vista Dome, Super O scale, "Skyline 500," 1957	100	150	375
2553 Pullman, Super O scale, "Blair Manor," 1957	175	250	500
2554 Pullman, Super O scale, "Graig Manor," 1957	150	225	350
2555 Tank-One-Dome, O scale, 1945	17	28	55
2559 Budd Car Coach, O scale, Baltimore & Ohio, silver shell, blue lettering, dummy to match motorized 400 Budd, 1957	150	200	350
2560 Crane, O27 scale, marked "Lionel Lines," 1946	30	50	100
2561 Observation Car, O scale, extruded aluminum shell, marked "Santa Fe Set, Vista Valley," 1959	100	150	260
2562 Vista Dome, O scale, marked "Royal Pass," 1959	125	200	310
2563 Pullman, O scale, marked "Indian Falls," 1959	125	200	310
2600 Pullman, O scale, red body and roof, 1938	60	100	200

	C6	C8	C10
2601 Observation Car, O scale, red body and roof, 1938	60	100	200
2602 Baggage Car, O scale, red body and roof, 1938	60	100	200
2613 Pullman, O scale, green, 1938	84	140	280
2613 Pullman, O scale, Blue Comet, two-tone blue, 1938	81	135	270
2614 Observation Car, O scale, Blue Comet, two-tone blue, 1938	81	135	270
2614 Observation Car, O scale, green, 1938	84	140	280
2615 Baggage Car, O scale, Blue Comet, two-tone blue, 1938	81	135	270
2615 Baggage Car, O scale, green, 1938	120	200	400
2620 Floodlight, O scale, red frame on searchlight, 1938	23	38	75
2623 Pullman, O scale, Irvington, Bakelite, Tuscan brown, 1941	150	250	500
2623 Pullman, O scale, Manhattan, Bakelite, Tuscan brown, uncataloged, 1941	80	133	265
2624 Pullman, O scale, Manhattan, Bakelite, Tuscan brown, uncataloged, 1941	240	400	800
2625 Pullman, O scale, Madison, 1946	95	175	250
2625 Pullman, O scale, Irvington, Bakelite, Tuscan brown, 1946	95	150	220
2625 Pullman, O scale, Manhattan, 1946	112	188	375
2627 Pullman, O scale, Madison, Bakelite, Tuscan brown, 1946	95	150	220
2628 Pullman, O scale, Manhattan, Bakelite, Tuscan brown, 1946	95	150	245

	C6	C8	C10
2630 Pullman, O scale, light blue and silver or gray roof, 1938	30	50	100
2631 Observation Car, O scale, light blue and silver or gray roof, 1938	30	50	100
2640 Pullman, O scale, light blue w/silver roof, 1938	20	33	65
2640 Pullman, O scale, green w/dark green roof, 1938	20	33	65
2641 Observation Car, O scale, light blue w/silver roof, 1938	24	40	80
2641 Observation Car, O scale, green w/dark green roof, 1938	21	35	70
2642 Pullman, O scale, light blue w/silver or gray roof, 1941	24	40	80
2643 Observation Car, O scale, light blue w/silver or gray roof, 1941	15	25	50
2651 Flatcar, O scale, bright green w/lumber load, 1938	15	25	50
2652 Gondola, O scale, brown, 1938	18	30	60
2652 Gondola, O scale, yellow, 1938	18	30	60
2653 Hopper, O scale, light green, 1938	15	25	50
2653 Hopper, O scale, black, 1938	38	62	125
2654 Tank Car, O scale, aluminum, marked "Sunoco," 1938	20	33	65
2654 Tank Car, O scale, marked "Shell," 1938	21	35	70
2654 Tank Car, O scale, light gray, marked "Sunoco," 1938	18	30	60
2655 Boxcar, O scale, cream body w/maroon roof, 1938	18	30	60
2655 Boxcar, O scale, cream body w/Tuscan brown roof, 1938	20	34	68
2656 Cattle Car, O scale, light gray body w/red roof, 1938	38	63	125
2657 Caboose, O scale, red body w/red roof, 1938	12	20	40
2657 Caboose, O scale, red body w/brown roof, 1938	9	15	30
2659 Dump Car, O scale, green, black frame, 1938	12	23	45
2660 Crane, O scale, red roof, green boom, 1938	27	45	90
2672 Caboose, O27 scale, Pennsylvania N5 type, Tuscan brown, 1942	12	20	40

	C6	C8	C10
2677 Gondola, O27 scale, red w/black frame, 1940	11	18	36
2679 Boxcar, O27 scale, yellow w/maroon roof, 1938	9	15	30
2679 Boxcar, O27 scale, yellow w/blue roof, 1938	9	15	30
2680 Tank Car, O27 scale, aluminum, marked "Sunoco," 1938	8	12	25
2680 Tank Car, O27 scale, orange, marked "Shell," 1938	8	12	25
2680 Tank Car, O27 scale, gray, marked "Sunoco," 1938	8	12	25
2682 Caboose, O27 scale, red w/red roof, 1938	7	12	23
2682 Caboose, O27 scale, brown w/brown roof, 1938	7	12	23
2717 Gondola, O scale, orange and tan, uncataloged, 1938	37	63	125
2719 Boxcar, O scale, peacock and blue roof, uncataloged, 1938	37	63	125
2722 Caboose, O scale, red w/maroon roof, uncataloged, 1938	37	63	125
0-27-C1 Track Clip, O27 scale, 1949	n/a	2	3
2755 Tank Car, O scale, gray, marked "Sunoco," 1941	45	75	150
2757 Caboose, O scale, PRR-N5 type, Tuscan brown, 1941	12	20	40
2758 Boxcar, O scale, automobile, Tuscan body, marked "Pennsylvania," 1941	21	35	70
2810 Crane, O scale, yellow cab and red roof, 1938	74	123	245
2811 Flatcar, O scale, aluminum w/eight logs, 1938	36	60	120
2812 Gondola, O scale, bright green, 1938	21	35	70
2812 Gondola, O scale, dark green, 1938	21	35	70
2813 Cattle Car, O scale, cream body w/maroon roof, 1938	60	100	200
2814 Boxcar, O scale, light yellow body w/maroon roof, 1938	50	83	165
2814 Boxcar, O scale, orange body w/brown roof, 1938	120	200	400
2814R Refrigerator, O scale, white body w/brown roof, 1938	185	325	650

	C6	C8	C10
2815 Tank Car, O scale, silver, Sunoco, 1938	54	90	180
2815 Tank Car, O scale, orange, Shell, 1938	75	125	250
2816 Hopper, O scale, black, white rubber-stamped lettering, 1938	54	90	180
2816 Hopper, O scale, red, 1938	60	100	200
2817 Caboose, O scale, light red body and roof, 1938	31	53	105
2817 Caboose, O scale, red, Tuscan roof, white rubber-stamped lettering, 1938	29	48	95
2820 Floodlight, O scale, two searchlights, green base, plate-stamped lights, 1938	54	88	175
2820 Floodlight, O scale, green base, cast lights, 1938	90	150	300
2855 Tank Car, O scale, one-dome, black, S.U.N.X., 1946	62	103	205
2855 Tank Car, O scale, gray, 1946	59	98	195
2954 Boxcar, O47 scale, Tuscan brown, marked "Pennsylvania," 1940	105	175	350
2955 Tank Car, O72 scale, black, marked "S.U.N.X.," 1940	78	130	260
2956 Hopper, O72 scale, B&O, black, 1940	83	138	275
2957 Caboose, O72 scale, NYC, Tuscan brown, 1940	93	155	310
3300 Summer Trolley, standard scale, trailer, gold rubber-stamped, 3300 Electric Rapid Transit, 3300, non-powered, 1910	1200	2000	4000
3330 Flatcar, O scale, w/submarine, 1960	24	40	80
3330-100 Operating Submarine Kit, O27 scale, 1960	100	150	200
3349 Turbo Missile Firing Car, O scale, 1960	17	28	55
3356 Operating Horse Car, O scale, w/horses and corral, 1956	40	68	135
3356-100 Set of Nine Horses, O scale, black horses, 1956	6	10	20
3356-150 Horse Corral, O scale, white fencing, corral only, 1956	52	60	80
3356-2 Operating Horse Car, O scale, green, car alone, 1956	40	70	100
3357 Operating Cop and Hobo Car, O scale, blue boxcar w/hydraulic lift and figures, 1962	30	50	100
3359 Operating Dump Car, O scale, two gray dump bins, 1955	18	35	55
3360 Operating Burro Crane, O scale, yellow cab and boom, motorized, including track trips, 1956	150	265	340
3361 Lumber Car, O scale, operating, 1955	20	30	55
3362 Helium Tank Car, O scale, operating, green frame, 1961	20	32	64
3364 Log Dump Car, O scale, operating, green frame, 1966	18	33	65
3366 Circus Car, O scale, operating, white stock car, nine horses, white, and corral, 1959	125	150	250
3366-100 White Horses, O scale, set of nine, 1959	9	15	30
3370 Sheriff and Outlaw Car, O scale, operating, green stock car, 1961	25	43	85
3376 Giraffe Car, O scale, operating, green stock car, 1960	36	75	125
3376 Giraffe Car, O scale, operating, blue stock car, including track trips, w/teletails and poles, 1960	20	30	55
3410 Helicopter Launching Car, O scale, operating, blue flat w/helicopter, 1961	45	80	150
3413-150 Mercury Capsule Launching Car, O scale, red flat, gray platform, 1961	65	110	175
3419 Helicopter Launching Car, O scale, operating, blue flat w/helicopter, 1959	40	75	110
3424 Brakeman Car Set, O scale, operating, blue boxcar, set of track trips and teletails w/poles, 1956	30	50	80
3424-100 Low Bridge Warning Poles, O scale, w/track clips, set of two, 1956	15	25	30
3428 Mail Car, O scale, operating, red white and blue boxcar, man dumps mail bag, 1959	48	80	160
3429 U.S.M.C. Helicopter Car, O scale, olive frame, 1960	200	325	465
3434 Chicken Sweeper Car, O scale, brown stock car, man at door sweeps back and forth, 1959	50	75	105

	C6	C8	C10
3435 Aquarium Car, O scale, operating, green boxcar, gold letters marked "Tank 1" and "Tank 2," 1959	400	600	1000
3435 Aquarium Car, O scale, operating, green box w/four clear windows, fish move around on two spindles, 1959	100	175	250
3444 Animated Hobo Gondola, O scale, red gondola, cop chases hobo around freight load, marked "Erie," 1957	30	45	80
3451 Operating Lumber Car, O scale, operating, black die-cast base, black platform w/log stacks, 1946	14	23	45
3454 Merchandise Car, O scale, operating, silver boxcar, discharges five brown cubes, 1946	65	100	130
3456 Hopper Car, O scale, operating, black, "N&W," drops ore, 1950	17	28	55
3459 Dump Car, O scale, operating, die-cast frame, black, 1946	24	40	80
3459 Dump Car, O scale, operating, silver, 1946	93	155	310
3459 Dump Car, O scale, operating, green, 1946	25	43	85
3460 Piggyback Flatcar, O scale, red flat w/two trailer containers, 1955	22	45	65
3461 Lumber Car, O scale, operating, black die-cast frame, 1949	11	25	35
3461 Lumber Car, O scale, operating, green frame, 1949	17	30	55
3462P Milk Car Platform, O scale, 1952	8	15	75

	C6	C8	C10
3462 Milk Car Set, O scale, white boxcar, platform, green base, five cans, man discharges cans onto platform, 1947	20	40	55
3462-70 Milk Cans, set of five, 1952	6	8	10
3464 Boxcar, O scale, operating, NYC, brown shell, black doors, plunger mechanism opens door w/man, 1952	11	18	35
3464 Boxcar, O scale, operating, Santa Fe, orange shell, black doors, plunger mechanism opens door w/man, 1949	12	20	40
3469 Dump Car, O scale, operating, black die-cast frame, 1949	18	30	60
3470 Aerial Target Launching Car, O scale, blue flatcar, white top shell, blue balloon carriage, batter operation inflates balloons, 1962	30	50	75
3472 Milk Car Set, O27 scale, operating, white boxcar, five cans, man discharges cans onto platform, green base, 1949	20	35	60
3474 Boxcar, O27 scale, operating, W.P., silver box, yellow feather, plunger mechanism, 1952	27	45	90
3482 Milk Car Set, O scale, operating, white boxcar, man discharges cans onto platform, green base, five cans, 1954	24	40	80
3484 Boxcar, O scale, operating, Pennsylvania, Tuscan brown, plunger mechanism, 1953	18	35	60
3484-25 Boxcar, O scale, operating, Santa Fe, orange shell, orange doors, plunger mechanism, 1954	33	60	110

No. 3428 Mail Car, $160.

	C6	C8	C10
3494 Boxcar, O scale, operating, NYC Pacemaker, red and gray, red doors, plunger mechanism, 1955	40	75	110
3494-150 Boxcar, O scale, operating, MP, blue and gray, plunger mechanism, 1956	55	90	120
3494-275 Boxcar, O scale, operating, B.A.R., State of Maine, red, white and blue, plunger mechanism, 1956	55	90	130
3494-550 Boxcar, O scale, operating, Monon, maroon shell w/white stripe, plunger mechanism, 1957	125	225	400
3494-625 Boxcar, O scale, Operating, Soo Line, Tuscan brown, plunger mechanism, 1957	120	210	400
3509 Satellite Car, O scale, operating, green flat, black and silver satellite, yellow radar scope, manually operated, 1959	22	45	60
3510 Satellite Car, O scale, operating, red flat, 1959	45	90	155
3512 Fireman and Ladder Car, O scale, red frame and structure, black ladders, 1959	40	65	130
3512 Fireman and Ladder Car, O scale, silver ladders, 1959	83	138	275
3519 Automatic Satellite Car, O scale, remote track operated, 1961	20	30	55
3520 Searchlight, O scale, gray die-cast frame, orange generator, 1952	30	40	58
3530 G.M. Generator Car, O scale, blue boxcar w/white markings, transformer pole, remote searchlight, 1956	66	110	220
3535 AEC Security Car, O scale, red shell, white lettering, gray gun and gray rotating searchlight, one man, 1960	35	80	125
3540 Radar Scanning Car, O scale, operating, red flat, gray structure, yellow radar scope and silver radar antenna, revolving, 1959	39	85	135
3545 TV Monitor Car, O scale, operating, black base, blue structure, yellow camera and screen, two men, 1961	53	110	175
3559 Ore Dump Car, O scale, operating, black die-cast frame, 1946	15	28	45

	C6	C8	C10
3562 Barrel Car, O scale, operating, black, six wood barrels, 1954	75	100	180
3562-25 Barrel Car, O scale, operating, red lettering, 1954	150	250	500
3562-25 Barrel Car, O scale, operating, gray, blue lettering, 1954	25	40	55
3562-50 Barrel Car, O scale, operating, yellow, 1955	35	50	85
3562-75 Barrel Car, O scale, operating, orange, 1958	35	50	92
3619 Reconnaissance Helicopter Car, O scale, yellow shell, black double door, w/helicopter, 1962	38	63	125
3620 Searchlight, O scale, gray die-cast frame, orange generator, 1954	25	35	45
3650 Searchlight Extension Car, O scale, gray die-cast frame, gray generator, remote searchlight w/wire, 1956	40	50	80
3651 Operating Lumber Car, O scale, operating, black frame, nickel stakes, w/logs and bin, 1939	13	20	40
3652 Operating Gondola, O scale, operating, yellow, 1939	25	42	85
3656 Cattle Car, O scale, operating, orange stock car, set includes car, cattle and corral, white lettering reads "Armour," 1950	35	50	85
3656 Cattle Car, O scale, operating, black lettering, 1950	120	200	400
3656-150 Cattle Car Platform, O scale, green base, ivory fencing, 1952	45	55	75
3656-34 Cattle Set, O scale, black, set of nine, 1952	10	15	20
3657 Dump Car, silver w/brown bin, 1939	120	200	400
3659 Dump Car, O scale, operating, black frame, red hopper, 1939	20	33	65
3662 Operating, O scale, operating, white shell, brown roof, includes five cans and platform, 1955	30	50	70
3662-79 Milk Cans, O scale, set of five, 1955	6	9	12
3665 Minuteman Missile Car, O scale, operating, white shell, blue double door roof, w/missile, 1961	50	80	115

	C6	C8	C10
3666 Marine Missile Car, O scale, operating, Sears, white shell, blue double door roof, w/missile, 1960	170	350	535
3672 Bosco Boxcar, O scale, operating, yellow shell and brown roof, set includes seven Bosco cans and brown and yellow platform, 1959	120	265	430
3672-79 Bosco Cans, O scale, brown and yellow, set of seven, 1959	35	75	125
3811 Operating Flatcar, O scale, black frame w/lumber, 1939	18	30	60
3814 Merchandise Car, O scale, operating, Tuscan body and roof, discharges five cubes, 1939	48	80	160
3820 Submarine Car, O scale, operating, olive, "U.S.M.C.," gray, 1960	120	200	400
3830 Submarine Car, O scale, operating, blue, marked "Lionel," w/gray submarine, 1960	29	48	95
3854 Merchandise Car, O scale, operating, Tuscan brown, doors open and eject five merchandise cubes, 1946	200	400	600
3859 Dump Car, O scale, operating, black, 1938	25	41	82
3927 Track Cleaner Car, O scale, orange shell, motor-operated cleaning disk, includes two gray washol containers, 1956	60	80	120
3927-50 Track Cleaner Pads, O scale, package of twenty-five, 1956	5	10	25
4357 Caboose, O scale, Pennsylvania N5 type, electronic, metal, green and white, "Electronic Control" decal, red, 1948	68	112	225
4400 Summer Trolley, standard scale, trailer, 1910	1200	2000	4000
4452 Gondola, O scale, electronic, black, Pennsylvania, 1946	42	75	140
4454 Boxcar, electronic, Baby Ruth, P.R.R., orange w/brown doors, 1946	90	150	300
4457 Caboose, O scale, electronic, 1946	45	80	165
4671 Locomotive, O scale, 6-8-0, steam, electronic, 4671W tender, 1946	130	220	315

	C6	C8	C10
5100 Roadway, O scale, straight, 1963	n/a	n/a	1
5101 Roadway, O scale, straight, 1963	n/a	n/a	1
5102 Railroad and Roadway Crossway, O scale, 1963	n/a	n/a	1
5103 Roadway, O scale, straight, w/power connection, 1963	n/a	n/a	1
5104 Lane Change Over, O scale, 1963	n/a	n/a	1
5105 Roadway Intersection, O scale, 1963	n/a	n/a	1
5106 Inner Roadway, O scale, curved, 1963	n/a	n/a	1
5107 Inner Roadway, O scale, curved, 1963	n/a	n/a	1
5108 Outer Roadway, O scale, curved, 1963	n/a	n/a	1
5109 Outer Roadway, O scale, curved, 1963	n/a	n/a	1
5150 Banking Set, 1963	5	8	15
5151 Trestle Set, O scale, 1963	5	8	15
5152 Guard Rail and Flag Set, O scale, 1963	5	8	15
5154 Electric Lap Counter, O scale, 1963	5	8	15
5155 Pacesetter Timer, O scale, 1963	5	8	15
5156-24 Rail Clips, O scale, 1963	2	3	4
5157-34 Roadway Clips, O scale, 1963	2	3	4
5158 Barrels, 1963	2	3	4
5159 Lubrication Kit, 1963	3	4	5
5159-50 Lubrication Kit, 1968	3	4	5
5160 Official Viewing Stand, 1963	10	15	20
5163 Maintenance Kit, 1965	3	4	6
5200 Ferrari Racing Car, O scale, 1963	6	9	12
5201 "D" Jaguar Racing Car, O scale, 1963	6	9	12
5202 Corvette Racing Car, O scale, 1963	6	9	12
5210 Cooper Racing Car, O scale, 1963	6	9	12
5211 B.R.M. Racing Car, O scale, 1963	6	9	12

	C6	C8	C10
5222 Cooper Racing Car, O scale, 1964	6	9	12
5223 Corvette Racing Car, O scale, 1964	6	9	12
5230 Ferrari Racing Car, O scale, 1964	6	9	12
5231 B.R.M. Racing Car, O scale, 1964	6	9	12
5232 "D" Jaguar Racing Car, O scale, 1964	6	9	12
5233 Ford Racing Car, O scale, 1964	6	9	12
5234 Buick Racing Car, O scale, 1964	6	9	12
5235 Jaguar XKE Racing Car, O scale, 1964	6	9	12
5236 Buick Riviera Racing Car, O scale, 1964	6	9	12
5237 Buick Riviera Racing Car, O scale, 1964	6	9	12
5238 Ford Racing Car, O scale, 1964	6	9	12
5239 Ford Convertible Racing Car, O scale, 1964	7	11	15
5240 Ford Police Racing Car, O scale, 1964	7	11	15
5242 Conversion Kit, 1966	5	9	18
5300 Racemaster Power Pack, 1963	7	11	15
5302 Racemaster Power Pack, 1965	7	11	15
5304 HO Control Transformer, 1965	5	9	18
5310 Touch-A-Matic Speed Control, 1963	3	6	9
5320 Touch-A-Matic Speed Control, 1963	3	6	9
5321 Touch-A-Matic Speed Control, 1965	3	6	9
5322 Touch-A-Matic Speed Control, 1965	3	6	9
5400 Straight Roadway, HO scale, 1963	n/a	n/a	1
5401 Straight Roadway, HO scale, w/power connector, 1963	n/a	n/a	1
5402 Railroad and Roadway Crossing, HO scale, 1963	n/a	1	2
5403 Roadway Intersection, HO scale, 1963	n/a	1	2
5404 Lane Change Over, HO scale, 1963	n/a	1	2
5405 Roadway, HO scale, curved, 1963	n/a	n/a	1
5406 Roadway, HO scale, curved, 45 degree, 1963	n/a	n/a	1
5407 Inner Roadway, HO scale, curved, 90 degree, 1963	n/a	n/a	1
5408 Outer Roadway, HO scale, curved, 45 degree, 1963	n/a	n/a	1
5409 Inner Roadway, HO scale, curved, 45 degree, 1963	n/a	n/a	1
5410 Roadway, HO scale, straight, 1963	n/a	n/a	1
5411 Roadway, HO scale, straight, 1963	n/a	n/a	1
5412 Roadway, HO scale, straight, 1963	n/a	n/a	1
5415 Roadway, HO scale, straight, w/power connection, 1963	n/a	n/a	1
5421 Touch-A-Matic Speed Controller, HO scale, 1965	5	8	10
5422 Touch-A-Matic Speed Controller, HO scale, 1965	5	8	10
5425 Loop-the-Loop Kit, HO scale, 1960	10	15	20
5430 Universal Roadway Kit, HO scale, 1966	9	14	18
5431 Mystery Route Selector, HO scale, 1966	5	10	15
5433 Car Lane Controller, HO scale, 1965	6	9	13
5434 Car Lane Controller, HO scale, 1965	6	9	13
5450 Trestle Set, HO scale, 1963	4	6	8
5455 Car Lane Controller, HO scale, 1966	6	9	13
5457 Relay Kit, HO scale, 1966	10	15	20
5459 Dump Car, O scale, operating, electronic, black, "Lionel Lines," 1948	55	115	175
5478 Guard Rail and Flag Set, HO scale, 1966	10	15	20
5511 Tie-Jector, O scale, 1958-1961	51	85	170
5531 Buick Riviera Racing Car, HO scale, 1965	3	5	10
5532 Buick Patrol Racing Car, HO scale, 1965	3	5	10

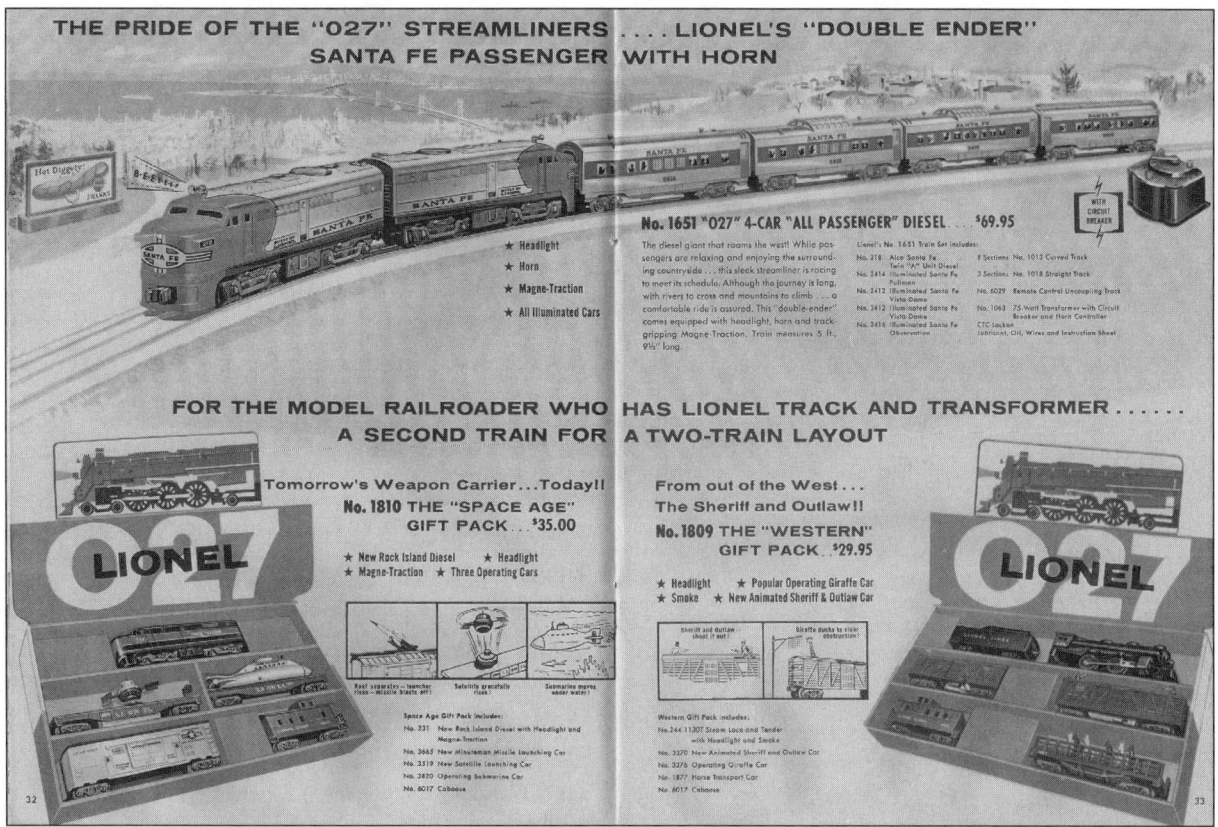

Top of page: No. 218 Locomotive, $170. Bottom of page: Space Age Gift Page, includes a No. 231 Locomotive, $2,000; No. 3665 Minuteman Missile car, $115; No. 3820 Submarine car, $400; No. 3665 Minuteman Missile car, $115; No. 6017 Caboose, $60. Photo courtesy 1961 Lionel catalog.

	C6	C8	C10		C6	C8	C10
5533 Ford Hardtop Racing Car, HO scale, 1965	3	5	10	6002 Gondola, O27 scale, NYC, 1949	5	9	18
5534 Ford Convertible Racing Car, HO scale, 1965	3	5	10	6004 Boxcar, O27 scale, Baby Ruth, P.R.R., 1950	4	7	13
5535 Ford Police Racing Car, HO scale, 1965	3	5	10	6007 Caboose, O27 scale, Lionel Lines, SP type, 1950	3	5	10
5537 Rolls Royce Racing Car, HO scale, 1965	3	5	10	6009 Remote Control Track, O27 scale, 1953	3	5	6
5538 Bentley Racing Car, HO scale, 1965	3	5	10	6012 Gondola, O27 scale, black, Lionel, 1955	3	4	8
5539 Jaguar XKE Racing Car, HO scale, 1965	3	5	10	6014 Boxcar, O27 scale, Air Ex., red, 1951	25	45	75
5540 Car Lane Control Car, HO scale, Thunderbird, 1965	4	6	12	6014 Boxcar, O27 scale, Air Ex., blue, 1951	15	25	50
5541 Car Lane Control Car, HO scale, Jaguar XKE, 1965	4	6	12	6014 Boxcar, O27 scale, white body, 1958	35	50	70
5542 Car Lane Control Car, HO scale, Thunderbird, 1965	4	6	12	6014 Boxcar, O27 scale, Frisco, 1957	4	6	8
5767-15 Valise Carrying Pack, HO scale, 1961	8	13	25	6014 Boxcar, O27 scale, Bosco, P.R.R., red or orange body, 1958	5	8	11

	C6	C8	C10
6014 Boxcar, O27 scale, Baby Ruth, P.R.R., 1955	5	8	10
6014 WIX, cream/white	80	120	175
6014-325 Boxcar, O27 scale, Frisco, 1964	7	11	22
6014-325 Frisco Savings Bank Car, O27 scale, 1963	7	11	22
6014-335 Boxcar, O27 scale, Frisco, 1965	7	11	22
6014-410 Boxcar, O27 scale, Frisco, 1969	7	11	22
6014-85 Boxcar, O27 scale, Frisco, 1969	7	11	22
6015 Tank Car, O27 scale, Sunoco, silver, one dome, 1954	5	8	15
6017 Caboose, O27 scale, Lionel, brown, 1951	3	5	10
6017-100 Caboose, B&M, light blue, 1959	15	25	50
6017-100 Caboose, B&M, dark blue, 1959	250	450	800
6017-185 Caboose, O27 scale, ATSF, gray, 1959	10	20	35
6017-200 Caboose, O27 scale, Navy, dark blue, 1960	35	50	85
6017-225 Caboose, O27 scale, ATSF, 1961	25	35	60
6017-50 Caboose, O27 scale, Marine, dark blue, 1958	20	30	55
6019 Remote Control Track, 1948	3	5	10
6024 Boxcar, O27 scale, RCA-Whirlpool, red, uncataloged, 1957	30	50	70
6024 Boxcar, O27 scale, Nabisco, 1957	12	20	28
6025 Tank Car, O27 scale, black, 1956	5	8	15
6025 Tank Car, O27 scale, Gulf, orange, 1956	9	15	29
6025 Tank Car, O27 scale, gray, 1956	11	18	36
6027 Caboose, O27 scale, Alaska, blue, 1959	25	45	80
6029 Uncoupling Track Set, 1955	3	5	6
6032 Gondola, O27 scale, black, "Lionel," 1952	2	4	6
6034 Boxcar, O27 scale, Baby Ruth, P.R.R., 1953	8	14	28

	C6	C8	C10
6035 Tank Car, O27 scale, gray, single dome, 1950	4	6	8
6037 Caboose, O27 scale, brown, marked "Lionel Lines," 1952	12	20	40
6042 Gondola, marked "Lionel," uncataloged	2	4	7
6044 Boxcar, O27 scale, Airex, light blue, uncataloged	12	20	40
6045 Tank Car, green, Cities Service	12	20	35
6047 Caboose, O27 scale, marked "Lionel Lines," 1962	2	4	7
6050 Savings Bank Car, O27 scale, Libby Tomato Juice, Libby promotional car, uncataloged, 1961	18	30	50
6050 Savings Bank Car, O27 scale, white and green, 1961	12	25	35
6050-100 Savings Bank Car, O27 scale, Swift's, red, 1963	22	38	75
6050-110 Savings Bank Car, O27 scale, Swift's, red, 1962	22	38	75
6057 Caboose, O27 scale, Lionel Lines, red, 1959	3	4	10
6057-50 Caboose, O27 scale, H.H., orange, 1962	12	15	25
6058 Caboose, O27 scale, C&O, yellow, 1961	15	25	45
6059-50 Caboose, O27 scale, M&StL, maroon, 1961	8	13	25
6059-60 Caboose, O27 scale, M&StL, shiny or flat red, 1969	5	8	15
6062 Gondola, O27 scale, glossy black, 1959	7	12	18
6076 Hopper, O27 scale, A.T.S.F., gray, 1959	10	15	22
6076-100 Hopper, O27 scale, Lionel, 1963	6	10	20
6076-75 Hopper, O27 scale, LV, gray or black or red, 1963	6	10	20
6110 Locomotive, O27 scale, 2-4-2, steam, 1951	15	25	50
6111 Flatcar, O27 scale, w/logs or pipes, 1955	8	13	25
6112 Gondola, O27 scale, w/canisters, blue, marked "Lionel," 1956	3	5	9
6112 Gondola, O27 scale, w/canisters, white, 1956	15	25	50

	C6	C8	C10
6112-25 Canisters, O27 scale, white or red, set of four, 1956	5	10	15
6119 Work Caboose, O27 scale, 1955	14	23	45
6119-100 Work Caboose, O27 scale, DL&W, 1963	12	24	28
6119-110 Work Caboose, O27 scale, DL&W, 1964	12	24	28
6119-25 Work Caboose, O27 scale, DL&W, 1957	10	15	30
6121 Flatcar, O27 scale, w/pipes, 1956	5	8	16
6130 Work Caboose, O27 scale, Santa Fe, 1965	10	20	34
6139 Uncoupling Track, O27 scale, remote control, 1963	4	6	8
6142 Gondola, O27 scale, w/canisters, 1963	3	5	7
6142-100 Gondola, O27 scale, w/canisters, 1964	3	5	10
6142-125 Gondola, O27 scale, 1964	3	5	10
6142-150 Gondola, O27 scale, 1964	3	5	10
6142-75 Gondola, O27 scale, w/canisters, 1963	3	5	10
6149 Uncoupling Track, O27 scale, remote control, 1964	3	5	10
6151 Range Patrol	40	80	120
6157 Caboose, O27 scale, brown, uncataloged	3	5	10
6162 Gondola, O27 scale, w/canisters, NYC, red, 1963	17	28	55
6162-100 Gondola, O27 scale, w/canisters, NYC, 1964	9	16	25
6162-110 Gondola, O27 scale, w/canisters, NYC, 1965	9	16	25
6162-25 Gondola, O27 scale, w/canisters, blue, 1959	5	9	12
6162-50 Gondola, O27 scale, w/canisters, Alaska, yellow, 1959	30	50	100
6167 Caboose, O27 scale, Lionel, 1963	4	6	12
6167-100 Caboose, O27 scale, Lionel, 1964	3	6	10
6167-125 Caboose, O27 scale, unlettered, 1964	3	6	10
6167-50 Caboose, O27 scale, D.R.W., 1963	3	4	5

	C6	C8	C10
6167-85 Caboose, O27 scale, U.P., 1969	10	15	30
6175 Rocket Car, O27 scale, red and white rocket, red or black frame, 1958	25	50	70
6176 Hopper, O27 scale, yellow, 1964	4	6	12
6176-50 Hopper, O27 scale, L.V., yellow, 1964	3	7	10
6176-75 Hopper, O27 scale, L.V., gray, 1964	3	7	10
6219 Work Caboose, O27 scale, C&O, blue cab, 1960	25	35	75
6220 Locomotive, O27 scale, diesel, SW2, NYC or Santa Fe, black, similar to 622, w/bell, 1949	150	180	360
6250 Locomotive, O27 scale, diesel, SW2, Seaboard, blue and orange, 1954	125	175	315
6257 Caboose, O27 scale, 1948	4	6	12
6257-100 Caboose, O27 scale, 1964	7	10	18
6257-25 Caboose, O27 scale, uncataloged	4	7	13
6257-50 Caboose, O27 scale, uncataloged	3	5	9
6262 Wheel Car, O scale, black or red frame w/eight set of wheels, 1956	30	50	65
6264 Forklift Accessory Flatcar, red frame, brown lumber rack	20	40	55
6311 Flatcar, O scale, brown, no load, 1955	23	38	75
6315 Tank Car, O scale, orange, three dome, marked "Gulf," 1956	22	36	72
6315-60 Chemical Car, O scale, orange, single dome tank, marked "Lionel Lines," 1963	11	19	37
6342 Culvert Car, O scale, red gondola, w/inclined rake for culvert pipes, 1957	11	18	36
6343 Barrel Ramp Car, O scale, red, gray ramp, 1961	15	25	47
6346 Covered Hopper, O scale, Alcoa, silver, 1956	17	28	55
6352 Refrigerator Car, O scale, for ice depot, Pacific Fruit Express, orange shell, door on roof for deposit of ice blocks, side door discharges, 1955	45	80	110

	C6	C8	C10
6356 Stock, O scale, NYC, yellow, 1954	16	27	53
6357 Caboose, O27 scale, maroon, red, Tuscan brown, 1948	7	11	23
6361 Timber Flatcar, O scale, green frame w/three lumber branches, 1960	25	50	83
6362 Rail Truck Car, O scale, orange frame w/three sets of trucks, 1955	20	40	60
6376 Circus Car, O scale, white stock car, 1956	30	50	80
6401 Flatcar, O scale, w/two vans, 1965	15	25	50
6402-50 Flatcar, O scale, w/cable reels, gray frame w/orange reels, 1964	22	38	75
6405 Flatcar, O scale, w/piggyback van, brown frame w/two trailer vans, 1961	12	25	40
6407 Flatcar, O scale, w/rocket, red frame, gray supports w/red and white rocket, blue nose, actually a pencil sharpener, 1963	125	300	425
6408 Flatcar, O scale, w/pipes, 1963	10	20	30
6409-25 Flatcar, O scale, w/pipes, 1963	10	20	30
6411 Flatcar, O27 scale, w/logs, gray die-cast frame, five logs, 1948	11	20	35
6413 Mercury Capsule Car, O scale, blue frame w/two gray Mercury capsules, 1962	70	110	140
6414 Evans Loader Car, O scale, red frame, black metal car rack w/four cars, 1961	40	70	100
6414-25 Autos, O scale, set of four, 1955	55	64	75
6415 Tank Car, O scale, Sunoco, silver, three dome, 1953	9	15	30
6415-60 Tank Car, O scale, Sunoco, 1969	9	15	30
6416 Four Boat Loader, O scale, red frame, black metal boat rack, 1961	80	150	200
6417 Caboose, O scale, P.R.R., 536417, N5C type, Tuscan brown, 1953	12	20	40
6417 Caboose, O scale, P.R.R., Lehigh Valley, gray, 1953	50	65	140

	C6	C8	C10
6417 Caboose, O scale, P.R.R., Tuscan, 1953	600	1000	2000
6418 Girder Flatcar, O scale, depressed center, gray die-cast frame w/two orange girder sections, four sets of trucks, 1955	45	75	100
6419 Wrecker Caboose, O27 scale, DL&W, gray cab, 1948	15	25	45
6419-100 Wrecker Caboose, O27 scale, N&W, light gray cab, 576419, 1954	45	75	135
6420 Wrecker Caboose, O scale, DL&W, dark gray, die-cast frame w/searchlight, 1949	35	65	105
6424 Twin Auto Car, O scale, black frame, two autos, 1956	16	30	45
6425 Tank Car, O scale, Gulf, silver, three dome, 1956	15	25	50
6427 Caboose, O scale, 64273, Tuscan brown, N5C type, 1954	14	23	45
6427-500 Caboose, O scale, Girl's train, 57, 6427, blue shell, white lettering, 1957	125	200	350
6427-60 Caboose, O scale, Virginian, 6427, blue shell, yellow lettering, N5C type, 1958	120	200	400
6428 Boxcar, O scale, U.S. Mail, red, white and blue, 1960	15	25	45
6429 Wrecker Caboose, O scale, gray die-cast frame, gray cab, 1963	125	200	310
6430 Flatcar, O scale, w/piggyback van, red frame w/two trailer vans, 1956	20	40	60
6434 Poultry Car, O scale, red stock car, gray doors, illuminated, 1958	40	60	80
6436 Hopper, O scale, N&W, red, 1955	12	20	40
6436-100 Hopper, O scale, L.V., 1957	14	24	48
6436-1 Hopper, O scale, L.V., black, 1956	15	25	50
6436-110 Hopper, O scale, L.V., 1963	23	38	75
6436-25 Hopper, O scale, L.V., maroon, 1956	15	25	50
6436-57 Hopper, O scale, L.V., girl's set, lilac, maroon lettering, 1957	75	150	225

EXCITING LIONEL LAND,

E MERCURY PROJECT CAPE CANAVERAL

F U.S. NAVY 3830   LI ON EL

B |6501 LI ONEL

Missile is hidden inside of car

A "Minuteman" Missile Launching Car — A real headline maker complete with Strategic Air Command markings! By remote control, roof of car separates and launching mechanism elevates to firing position . . . at this point missile blasts off automatically toward target. Missile will "shoot down" the Aerial Target Balloon and "explode" the Target Range Car.
No. 3665 $9.95

B New! Solid Fuel Motorboat Car —A twofold operation! Boat has a specially designed tank into which a pill is inserted. When placed in water, boat will accelerate at top speed as though it were jet-propelled. Boat is secured in its own cradle on the railroad flat car. Car is 11" long.
No. 6501 $6.95

C Operating Helicopter Launching Car — A favorite with everyone! After spring in the launching mechanism is wound, the "whirlybird" can be sent high into the air by remote control. A real delight to watch. Car 11" long.
No. 3419 $7.95

D New! Rocket Fuel Tank Car—No missile could be launched without its supply of essential rocket fuel! Brightly colored in white with red markings. A real "missile age" railroad accessory with minute detailing. Car is 9¼" long.
No. 6463 $4.95

34

Top row, left to right: No. 6413 Mercury Capsule car, $140; No. 3830 Submarine car, $95. Bottom: No. 6501 Flatcar with motorboat, $120. Photo courtesy 1962 Lionel catalog.

	C6	C8	C10
6437 Caboose, O scale, Pennsylvania, N5C, Tuscan brown, 1961	13	23	45
6440 Pullman, O27 scale, green sheetmetal body, dark green roof, 1948	20	30	45
6441 Observation Car, O27 scale, green sheetmetal body, dark green roof, 1948	20	30	45
6442 Pullman, O27 scale, brown sheetmetal body and roof, 1949	20	33	65
6443 Observation Car, O27 scale, brown sheetmetal body and roof, 1949	24	40	80
6445 Fort Knox Gold Car, O scale, silver w/four clear windows, showing gold bullion, 1961	60	100	140
6446-25 Covered Hopper, O scale, N&W, gray, 1956	23	38	75
6446-54 Covered Cement, O scale, N&W, black, 1954	17	28	55
6446-54 Covered Cement, O scale, N&W, gray, 1954	30	50	100
6447 Caboose, O scale, N5C type, Tuscan brown, 1963	125	200	350
6448 Expolding Target Range Car, O scale, red shell, white lettering, 1961	11	20	35
6454 Boxcar, O27 scale, NYC, brown, 1949	15	35	50
6454 Boxcar, O27 scale, Erie, brown, 1950	20	35	55
6454 Boxcar, O27 scale, Erie, SP, 1950	20	35	55
6454 Boxcar, O27 scale, P.R.R., Tuscan brown, 1948	60	130	200
6456 Hopper, O scale, maroon, black, gray, 1948	6	10	20
6456 Hopper, O scale, shiny red, yellow letters, 1948	48	80	160
6456 Hopper, O scale, white letters, 1948	200	350	500
6457 Caboose, O scale, brown or maroon, SP type, 1949	12	15	28
6460 Crane, O scale, black cab, 1952	23	40	75
6460 Crane, O scale, gray cab, 1952	25	40	75
6461 Transformer Car, O27 scale, gray die-cast frame, black transformer, 1949	32	53	105

	C6	C8	C10
6462-25 Gondola, O scale, NYC, black, bright red, green, 1954	5	8	15
6462C Gondola, O scale, NYC, 1949	4	6	12
6462-500 Gondola, O scale, Girl's train, pink, marked "NYC," 1957	65	110	170
6463 Rocket Fuel Tank Car, O scale, white shell, two dome, red lettering, 1962	23	38	75
6464-1 Boxcar, O scale, W.P., silver, 1953	35	60	88
6464-100 Boxcar, W.P., silver w/yellow feather, 1954	60	90	125
6464-100 Boxcar, W.P., orange w/blue feather, 1954	350	600	1000
6464-125 Boxcar, O scale, red and gray, marked "Pacemaker," 1954	40	80	130
6464-150 Boxcar, O scale, M.P., blue and gray, 1954	39	80	130
6464-175 Boxcar, O scale, R.I., silver, 1954	50	85	125
6464-200 Boxcar, O scale, P.R.R., Tuscan brown, 1954	70	100	140
6464-225 Boxcar, O scale, S.P., black, 1954	50	75	135
6464-25 Boxcar, O scale, G.N., orange, 1953	35	65	90
6464-250 Boxcar, O scale, W.P., orange w/blue feather, 1966	90	150	225
6464-275 Boxcar, O scale, red, white and blue, marked "State of Maine," 1955	50	75	100
6464-300 Boxcar, O scale, Rutland, green and yellow, 1955	40	70	125
6464-325 Boxcar, O scale, B&O, silver and aqua, "Sentinel," 1956	280	450	605
6464-350 Boxcar, O scale, M.K.T., maroon, 1956	115	205	290
6464-375 Boxcar, O scale, C.G., maroon and silver, 1956	45	85	120
6464-400 Boxcar, O scale, B&O, blue and orange, "timesaver," 1956	42	70	140
6464-425 Boxcar, O scale, N.H., black, 1956	30	50	75
6464-450 Boxcar, O scale, G.N., olive and orange, 1956	60	100	135
6464-475 Boxcar, O scale, B&M, blue, 1957	30	45	60

	C6	C8	C10
6464-50 Boxcar, O scale, M&StL, maroon, 1953	35	65	90
6464-500 Boxcar, O scale, Timken, yellow and white, 1957	60	100	130
6464-510 Boxcar, O scale, Girl's train, NYC, lilac, 1957	300	460	620
6464-515 Boxcar, O scale, Girl's train, M.K.T., yellow, 1957	260	430	600
6464-525 Boxcar, O scale, M&StL, red, 1957	30	50	77
6464-650 Boxcar, O scale, D.R.G.W., yellow and silver, 1957	50	90	130
6464-700 Boxcar, O scale, Santa Fe, red, 1961	50	90	130
6464-725 Boxcar, O scale, New Haven, black, 1962	30	50	65
6464-75 Boxcar, O scale, R.I., green, 1953	40	65	85
6464-825 Boxcar, O scale, Alaska, blue and yellow, 1959	111	185	370
6464-900 Boxcar, O scale, NYC, light green, 1960	50	85	120
6465 Tank Car, O27 scale, black, Lionel Lines, two dome, 1958	10	20	30
6465 Tank Car, O27 scale, orange, Lionel Lines, two dome, 1958	5	10	15
6465 Tank Car, O27 scale, Cities Service, green, two dome, 1960	12	15	30
6465 Tank Car, O27 scale, Gulf, black, two dome, 1958	25	50	75
6465 Tank Car, O27 scale, silver, two dome, marked "Sunoco," 1948	12	20	40
6466T W or WX Tender, O27 scale, 1948	30	50	100
6467 Bulkhead Car, O scale, red frame, two black bulkheads, 1956	18	35	50
6468 Automobile, O scale, B&O, blue, double door, 1953	20	40	60
6468 Automobile, O scale, B&O, brown, 1953	140	215	320
6468-25 Automobile, O scale, N.H., orange, double door, 1956	25	45	72
6469 Liquefied Gas Tank Car, O scale, red frame, white cylinder, 1963	75	125	150
6470 Exploding Boxcar, O scale, red w/white lettering, spring mechanism, 1959	12	28	40

	C6	C8	C10
6472 Refrigerator, O scale, white boxcar, 1950	18	28	38
6473 Horse Transport Car, yellow, two horse heads bob in and out, 1963	10	20	30
6475 Pickle Car, O scale, Heinz 57, 1960	n/a	n/a	n/a
6475 Pineapple Car, O scale, Libby, uncataloged, 1960	36	63	125
6476 Hopper, O scale, red, white letters, 1957	4	10	15
6476-25 Hopper, O scale, L.V., gray, black letters, 1963	3	5	10
6476-75 Hopper, O scale, L.V., red, white letters, 1963	4	7	10
6477 Pipe Car, O scale, red frame, two black bulkheads, w/sidestakes, 1957	24	40	80
6500 Beechcraft Bonanza Transport Car, O scale, black frame w/red and white plane, 1962	245	425	850
6501 Flatcar, O scale, w/motor boat, red frame w/white and brown boat, 1962	55	85	120
6502 Flatcar, O scale, w/girder, blue flat w/orange bridge, 1962	20	40	50
6511 Pipe Car, O scale, brown or red flat w/three aluminum colored pipes, 1953	15	25	50
6512 Cherry Picker Car, O scale, black or blue frame, gray ladder support, black ladder w/man, 1962	35	70	105
6517 Caboose, O scale, bay window, red, marked "Lionel Lines," 1955	30	50	70
6517 Caboose, O scale, Erie, bay window, red, uncataloged	180	250	465
6518 Transformer Car, O scale, gray die-cast frame, four sets of trucks, black transformer, 1956	45	80	120
6519 Allis Chalmers Car, O scale, orange car, gray reactor, 1958	27	45	90
6520 Operating Searchlight, O scale, orange or maroon generator, 1949	25	40	65
6520 Operating Searchlight, O scale, tan generator, 1949	200	350	500
6520 Operating Searchlight, O scale, gray die-cast base, green, 1949	132	225	450
6530 Fire Prevention Car, O scale, red shell, white lettering, 1960	40	60	75

	C6	C8	C10
6536 Hopper, O scale, M&StL, red w/white lettering, 1958	20	30	55
6544 Missile Firing Car, O scale, blue frame, gray launch platform, red firing control w/four white rockets, white console, 1960	45	80	110
6555 Tank Car, O scale, silver, single dome, metal tank, "Sunoco," 1949	18	30	60
6556 Stock, O scale, M.K.T., Katy, red shell, white lettering and doors, 1958	70	150	240
6557 Smoking Caboose, O scale, SP-type, Tuscan brown w/smoke unit, liquid type, marked "Lionel," 1958	85	150	250
6560 Crane, O scale, black frame, gray cab, marked "Bucyrus Erie," 1955	40	50	90
6560 Crane, O scale, red cab, "Bucyrus Erie," 1955	20	30	55
6560-25 Crane, O scale, black frame, red cab 6560-25, "Bucyrus Erie," 1961	45	65	110
6561 Cable Car, O scale, gray die-cast frame w/two orange or gray spools wrapped w/aluminum wire, 1953	20	65	110
6562 Gondola, O scale, NYC, gray, 1956	14	23	45
6562 Gondola, O scale, NYC, red, 1956	12	25	35
6562 Gondola, O scale, NYC, black, 1956	12	25	35
6572 Railway Express Reefer, O scale, green, 1958	45	70	90
6572 Railway Express Reefer, O scale, light green, 1958	45	70	90
6630 IRBM Missile Launcher Car, O scale, black frame, blue ramp, w/red and white missile, 1960	30	70	105
6636 Hopper, O scale, Alaska, black w/orange lettering, 1959	21	35	70
6640 U.S.M.C. Missile Launcher, olive frame, black ramp, w/white missile, 1960	85	150	225
6646 Stock, O scale, orange shell, black lettering, "Lionel Lines," 1957	17	29	58
6650 IRBM Missile Car, O scale, red frame, blue support, black ramp w/red and white missile, 1959	28	48	95

	C6	C8	C10
6650-80 Missile for 6650-0, five white missiles, 1959	5	8	16
6651 Marine Cannon Car, O scale, olive frame and cannon w/four cannon loads, uncataloged, 1960	63	110	210
6656 Stock, O scale, yellow shell, black lettering, 1950	8	13	26
6657 Caboose, O scale, D.R.G.W., SP type, yellow cab w/silver lower stripe, black lettering, 1957	50	83	165
6660 Flatcar, O scale, car w/boom, red flat, yellow crane, turn control, 1958	30	55	80
6670 Flatcar, O scale, car w/derrick, red flat, yellow crane, no turn control, 1959	20	50	70
6672 Refrigerator, O scale, "Santa Fe," white shell, brown roof, black lettering, 1954	25	50	80
6672 Refrigerator, O scale, blue lettering, 1954	25	50	70
6736 Hopper, O scale, Detroit & Mackinac, red shell, white lettering, 1960	17	30	70
6800 Flatcar, O scale, w/airplane, red frame w/black and yellow plane, 1957	75	125	175
6801 Flatcar, O scale, w/white boat, red flat, 1957	45	75	110
6801-50 Flatcar, O scale, w/yellow boat, red flat, 1957	45	75	110
6801-75 Flatcar, O scale, w/blue boat, red flat, 1957	48	80	160
6802 Flatcar, O scale, w/bridge, red flat w/black bridge, 1958	14	24	48
6803 Flatcar, O scale, w/tank and sound truck, red frame, two gray vehicles, 1958	70	140	205
6804 Flatcar, O scale, w/sound truck, red frame, two gray trucks, 1958	70	140	205
6805 Atomic Energy Car, O scale, red frame, two gray radioactivity containers, lights under containers, 1958	48	80	160
6806 Flatcar, O scale, w/radar and medical truck, red frame, two gray vehicles, 1958	70	125	175
6807 Flatcar, O scale, w/duck, amphibian boat, red frame, one gray boat, 1958	60	100	150

No. 6804 Flatcar with two gray trucks, $205. Photo courtesy Good Old Days; Photo by Bill Kaufman

	C6	C8	C10
6808 Flatcar, O scale, w/tank and searchlight, red flat w/two gray vehicles, 1958	100	175	250
6809 Flatcar, O scale, w/medical trucks, red frame, two gray vehicles, 1958	85	155	210
6810 Flatcar, O scale, w/piggyback van, red frame, one trailer container, "Cooper Jarretting," 1958	18	35	50
6812 Track Maintenance Car, O scale, red frame, gray, blue or yellow platform, w/two blue men, 1959	33	55	110
6814 First Aid Caboose, O scale, white frame, cab and tool boxes, two stretchers, oxygen tank and man, marked "Rescue Unit," 1959	37	63	125
6816 Flatcar, O scale, w/bulldozer, orange bulldozer, red flat, marked "Allis-Chalmers," 1959	200	320	450

	C6	C8	C10
6816-100 Bulldozer, O scale, 1959	75	125	250
6817 Flatcar, O scale, w/scraper, same as 6816, except bulldozer replaced by scraper, 1959	200	320	425
6817-100 Scraper, O scale, 1959	27	45	90
6818 Flatcar, O scale, w/transformer, red frame, black transformer, 1958	25	45	60
6819 Flatcar, O scale, w/helicopter, red frame w/gray helicopter, 1959	30	50	100
6820 Aerial Missile Car, O scale, blue frame, navy helicopter, 1960	90	150	300
6821 Flatcar, O scale, w/crates, red frame, tan crates, 1959	20	28	40
6822 Searchlight Car, O scale, red frame, gray searchlight, black housing w/blue man, 1961	20	30	45
6823 IRBM Missile Car, O scale, red frame, gray supports, two white missiles, 1959	25	45	75
6824 First Aid Caboose, O scale, olive frame, cab, tool boxes, w/two stretchers, oxygen tank and man, "Rescue Unit," 1960	63	105	210
6825 Flatcar, O scale, w/arch bridge, red frame, black bridge, or gray bridge, 1959	20	32	65
6826 Flatcar, O scale, w/trees, red frame w/bundles of life-like Christmas trees, 1959	50	90	145

Left to right: No. 616 Locomotive, $220; No. 6822 Searchlight car, $220. Photo courtesy 1961 Lionel catalog.

	C6	C8	C10
6827 Flatcar, O scale, w/power shovel, black frame, yellow and black steam shovel, 1960	65	100	175
6828 Flatcar, O scale, w/construction crane, black frame, yellow and black crane, 1960	45	70	140
6828-100 Construction Crane, O scale, 1960	80	130	180

	C6	C8	C10
6830 Submarine Car, O scale, blue frame, gray sub, marked "U.S. Navy," 1960	50	90	120
47618 Caboose, paper train, uncataloged, 1943	25	38	50
61100 Boxcar, paper train, uncataloged, 1943	25	38	50

Top row, left to right: No. 44 US Army Missile Launcher Locomotive, $240; No. 6844 flatcar. Middle row: No. 3419 Helicopter Launching car, $110. Bottom row, left to right: No. 6823 IRBM Missile car, $75; No. 6814 First Aid Caboose, $125. Photo courtesy Richard MacNary

MOVIES, RADIO & TELEVISION

Addams Family

	C6	C8	C10
Fester Puppet Doll, Ideal, 1964	30	65	80
Gomez Doll, Ideal, 1964	30	65	80
Lurch, Remco	100	150	200
Morticia, Remco, 1964	93	140	195
Morticia Doll, Ideal, 1964	30	60	80
Uncle Fester Hand Puppet, vinyl, 1960s	65	98	130

Amos and Andy

	C6	C8	C10
Amos and Andy in Car, glass, Victory Glass Co., 4-1/2" long	218	327	438
Amos Sparkler	500	750	1050
Amos Tin Wind-up, w/out moving eyes, Marx, 1930, 12" high	450	675	900
Amos Tin Wind-up, w/moving eyes, Marx, 1930, 12" high	493	740	985
Andy Panda, plush, Ideal, copyright 1960, 14" high	60	90	120
Andy Tin Wind-up, w/out moving eyes, Marx, 1930s, 12" high	450	675	900
Andy Tin Wind-up, w/moving eyes, Marx, 1930s, 12" high	485	725	970

Amos and Andy Amos Tin Wind-up, Marx, with original box, $1995 for the pair

Amos and Andy (Continued)

	C6	C8	C10
Dolls, wood jointed, pair, Jaymar, 6" high	300	450	600
Fresh-Air Taxi, tin wind-up, Marx, 1930s, 8" long	500	800	1185
Fresh-Air Taxi, cast iron, Dent, 6" long	600	950	1300

Left to Right: Amos & Andy Fresh Air Taxi, cast iron, Dent, $1300; Amos & Andy Tin Wind-ups, without moving eyes, $1800 for the pair; Amos & Andy Fresh Air Taxi Tin Wind-up, Marx, $1185; Amos & Andy Figures, cast iron, 4-1/4" high, $300; Amos & Andy Figures, chalkware, c. 1930, $800 for the pair.

Amos and Andy Fresh-Air Taxi, Marx, 1930s, $1185.

Beany & Cecil Ge-tar, Mattel, 1961, $155. Photo courtesy Brad Krewson

Leakin' Lena Pound-N' Pull (Beany & Cecil), Pressman, 1961, $95. Photo courtesy Brad Kewson

Leakin' Lena Toy Boat (Beany & Cecil), Irwin Toy, 1962, $150. Photo courtesy Brad Kewson

Beany & Cecil

	C6	C8	C10
Beany & Cecil Ge-tar, Cecil's eyes move, Mattel, 1961	78	115	155
Beany Doll, talking, Mattel, 1960, 17" high	62	93	125
Beany Doll, non-talking, Mattel, 1960, 15" high	45	68	90
Beany Halloween, Ben Cooper	35	52	70
Beany Hat, w/two propellers	35	52	70
Cecil Doll, non-talking, Mattel, 1960, 24" high	30	45	60
Cecil Doll, talking, Mattel, 1960, 29" high	90	135	180
Cecil Halloween Costume, Ben Cooper	37	56	75
Cecil Hand Puppet, talking, Mattel, 1961	32	48	65
Cecil Music Box, metal, plays show's theme song and Cecil pops up, Mattel, 1961	85	128	170
Cecil Soaky, 1950, 8" high	30	45	60
Colorforms Set, w/box, 1961	60	90	125
Dishonest John Hand Puppet, talks, Mattel, 1961	63	95	125

Beany & Cecil (Continued)

	C6	C8	C10
Leakin' Lena Pound-N' Pull, wooden, Pressman, 1961	48	72	95
Leakin' Lena Ship, wood, Pressman, 1960s	138	205	275
Leakin' Lena Toy Boat, plastic, Irwin Toy, 1962	75	112	150
Tea Set, six-place settings, Worcester, 1960	36	54	72

Ben Casey

	C6	C8	C10
Ben Casey Doll, 1962, 12" high	85	127	170
Ben Casey Play Hospital Set, Transogram	60	90	120

Betty Boop

	C6	C8	C10
Acrobat Wind-up, celluloid and metal, Japanese, 1930s	700	1100	1550
Betty Boop and Bunny Mechanical Toy	150	225	300
Doll, wood jointed, marked "1931," Jaymar, 3-3/4" high	90	135	180

Left to Right: Betty Boop Doll, c. 1930, $1300; Betty Booop Figure, celuloid, Japanese, $1200. Photo courtesy Christie's

Betty Boop (Continued)

	C6	C8	C10
Doll, wood and composition, jointed, c. 1930, 12" high	550	800	1300
Doll, jointed, 1930s, 9-1/2" tall	240	360	480
Figure, celluloid, head shakes, Japanese, 7" high	600	900	1200

Bozo the Clown

	C6	C8	C10
Bendee, Lakeside, 6" high	10	15	20
Bendem Doll, Knickerbocker, 9" high	11	16	23
Doll, Terrytoons, 1961, 15" high	80	120	160
Doll, talking type, Mattel	45	68	90
Doll, stuffed, Gund, 1970, 14" high	75	112	150
Flexie, Wham-O	8	12	17
Hand Puppet, Capital, 1962	15	22	30
Jumpkin, Kohner, 1960	25	38	50
Periscope, Lido, 1960s	8	12	16
Soaky, 11" high	22	33	44
Soaky	14	21	29
Squeeze Toy, 9"	60	90	120

Captain Kangaroo

	C6	C8	C10
Captain Kangaroo Badge, tin shield, 1960s	20	30	40
Captain Kangaroo Doll, talking type, Mattel, 1967, 20" high	21	32	42
Captain Kangaroo Hand Puppet, 1960s	22	33	45

Casper the Friendly Ghost

	C6	C8	C10
Casper the Talking Ghost, Mattel, 14"	65	98	130
Doll, stuffed w/beanbag body, 1960s, 11"	35	52	70
Hopper, Linemar, 1950s, 5" high	200	300	400
Soaky	16	24	33
Squeak Toy, 8" high	48	72	95
Turnover Tank Tin Wind-up, Linemar	150	225	300
Video Spaceport Play Set, Superior	250	375	500

Charlie Chaplin

	C6	C8	C10
Bell Toy, cast iron, c. 1912, 9-3/4"	300	450	600
Bicycle Rider String Toy, c. 1920s	350	525	700
Cymbal Player, tin litho, squeeze action, German, 6-3/4"	700	1050	1400
Dancing Charlie, cardboard	87	131	175
Doll, "Charlie's Back," Milton Bradley, 1971	35	52	70
Doll, composition and cloth, Louis Amberg, c. 1915, 14" high	75	113	150
Doll, steel, lead and cloth, ball-jointed w/movable arms, legs and feet, Boucher, 7-1/2" high	250	375	500

Left to Right: Charlie Chaplin Cymbal Player, tin German, $1400; Charlie Chaplin Wind-up Walker, composition and tin, French, $900; Charlie Chaplin Figure, composition, Mark Hampton Comany, $700; Charlie Chaplin Squeeze Toy, tin, Spanish, c. 1925, $1800; Charlie Chaplin Wind-up Walker, composition, cloth and metal, $1000; Charlie Chaplin Bell Toy, cast iron, c. 1912, $600; Charlie Chaplin Wind-up, composition, Ferguson Novelty Co., $2200.

Charlie Chaplin (Continued)

	C6	C8	C10
Figure, celluloid, 4" high	900	1350	1800
Figure, composition, marked, "CHAS. CHAPLIN," on base, Mark Hampton Company, 9" high	350	525	700
Squeeze Toy, tin litho metal ball, German, 7-1/4"	900	1350	1800
Squeeze Toy, tin litho, Spanish, c. 1925, 7-3/4" high	900	1350	1800
Tricycle Rider Tin Wind-up, c. 1930, 3-1/2"	900	1350	1800
Walker Wind-up, composition, cloth and metal, 11-1/2" high	500	750	1000
Walker Wind-up, composition, tin and cloth, French, 7" high	450	675	900
Walker Wind-up, composition, cloth and metal, Ferguson Novelty Co., 9" high	1100	1650	2200
Whistler Toy, wood, whistles "How Dry I Am," c. 1920, 13-1/4" high	1250	1875	2500
Wind-up, tips hat, CKO, pre-war, No. 256, Germany	150	225	300
Wind-up, flat tin litho, tips hat when string is pulled	110	165	220
Wind-up, tin and cloth, Boucher, 8-1/4" high	1000	1500	2000
Wind-up, tin, driving three-wheel vehicle, Paya	1100	1650	2200
Wind-up, tin, Schuco, 1920s	285	428	570
Wind-up, tin, w/spinning cane, 6-3/4" high	900	1350	1800

Charlie McCarthy

	C6	C8	C10
Charlie McCarthy and Mortimer Snerd Private Car, Marx	1000	1700	2265
Charlie McCarthy Doll, composition w/moving mouth, 1930s, 13" high	238	357	475

Charlie McCarthy Doll, Effanbee, $850. Photo courtesy Christie's East

Charlie McCarthy (Continued)

	C6	C8	C10
Charlie McCarthy Doll, rubber, Effanbee	45	68	90
Charlie McCarthy Doll, w/moving mouth and summer suit, Effanbee, 20" high	400	600	800
Charlie McCarthy Doll, w/moving mouth and tweed jacket, Effanbee, 20" high	425	638	850
Charlie McCarthy Doll, w/moving mouth, Effanbee, 20" high	308	462	615
Charlie McCarthy in his Benzine Buggy, Marx	463	695	925
Drummer Boy Tin Wind-up, Marx, 1938, 8" high	500	750	1000

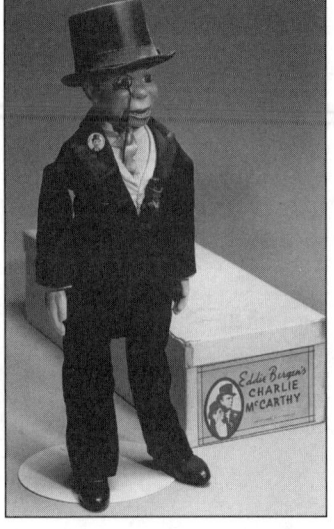

Charlie McCarthy Doll, Effanbee, $615. Photo courtesy Christie's East

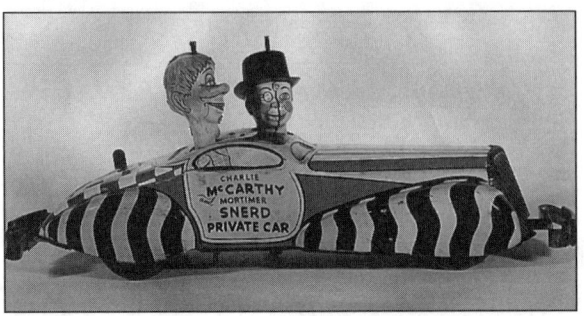

Charlie McCarthy and Mortimer Snerd Private Car, Marx, $2265. Photo courtesy Phillips, New York

Charlie McCarthy Drummer Boy Tin Wind-up, Marx, 1938, $1000. Photo courtesy Don Hultzman. Photo by Ron Chojnacki

Charlie McCarthy (Continued)	C6	C8	C10
Facemask, molded gauze, w/separate monocle	50	75	100
Figure, celluloid, 7-1/2" high	337	455	675
Hand Puppet, composition head, c. 1939	75	112	150
Paper Money	3	4	5
Puppet, cardboard, 1950s, 20" high	45	68	90
Tap Dancer, Marks Bros., 1938	125	188	250

Charlie McCarthy Paper Money, front, $5. Photo courtesy Toy Collector News

Charlie McCarthy Paper Money, back. Photo courtesy Rex and Richard Gray

Charlie McCarthy (Continued)	C6	C8	C10
Ventriloquist Doll, composition w/cloth body, ring pull in back of head activates lower jaw, 14-1/2" tall	600	900	1200
Ventriloquist Doll, Puppet Maker K&S, 33" tall	500	750	1000
Wind-up, tin, marked "Charlie McCarthy" on top hat, c. 1938, 8" high	185	278	370

Chipmunks	C6	C8	C10
Alvin Chipmunk Soaky	10	15	20
Simon Chipmunk Soaky	11	16	23
Theodore (Chipmunk) Soaky	10	15	20

Chitty Chitty Bang Bang	C6	C8	C10
Chitty Chitty Bang Bang, Corgi	125	188	250
Dick Van Dyke Doll, talking type, Mattel, 1967	125	188	250

Cisco Kid	C6	C8	C10
Cisco Kid Broomstick Horse, 1950s	35	53	70
Cisco Kid Neckerchief, w/nickel sombrero slide	50	75	100
Cisco Kid Western Outfit, 1950s	98	145	195

Daniel Boone	C6	C8	C10
Cannon, Remco, 1964	80	120	160
Canoe, vinyl, 18" long	15	22	30
Crime Lab, includes flashlight, signal gun, badge, handcuffs and fingerprint kit, 1955	90	135	180
Doll, Remco	40	60	80
Los Angeles Police Badge No. 714	10	15	20
Play Set, Grant exclusive, w/box	80	120	160
Police Set, includes gun, handcuffs and badge	35	52	70
Shoulder Holster and Pistol, 1950s	62	93	125
Talking Police Car, Ideal Toys, c. 1954	105	158	210
Water Pistol, No. 714 badge emblazoned on handle, c. 1955	25	38	50
Whistle, black plastic	6	9	12

Dr. Doolittle	C6	C8	C10
Dr. Doolittle Hand Puppet, talking type, Mattel, 1967	32	48	65
Dr. Doolittle Music Box, Gee-Tar, Mattel, 1967	40	60	80
Dr. Doolittle Pushmi Pullyu, 1965	43	65	87

Flintstones

	C6	C8	C10
Baby Pebbles, Ideal, 1963	65	100	130
Bamm-Bamm Doll, Ideal, 12-1/2" high	39	60	78
Bamm-Bamm Soaky	15	22	30
Barney Rubble Doll, vinyl, 1960, 10" high	36	48	72
Choo Choo Train Tin Wind-up, "Bedrock Express," Marx, 1950s, 13" long	188	280	375
Dino on Tricycle, Linemar, 1962, 4" high	500	750	1000
Dino the Dinosaur, Linemar, 1961, 9" long	188	280	375
Flintstone Flivver, friction type, Marx, 1962, 6-3/4" long	308	460	615
Flintstone Friction Cars, includes Fred, Barney, Wilma, etc., price for each, Linemar, 1962, 4" long	123	185	245
Flintstone Pals Wind-up, Barney and Dino, Linemar, 1962, 8" long	193	290	385
Flintstone Pals Wind-up, Fred on Dino, Linemar, 1962, 8" long	260	390	520
Flintstones Bedrock Express Handcar Wind-up, play set, Marx, 1962, 22" x 26"	225	338	450
Fred Flintstone Figure, hollow vinyl, 5-3/4" high	37	56	75
Hopping Barney Rubble Wind-up, Marx, 1962, 4" high	200	300	400
Hopping Dino, Linemar, 1962, 4" high	240	360	480
Hopping Fred Flintstone, Linemar, 4" high	200	300	400

Flintstones (Continued)

	C6	C8	C10
Mechanical Shooting Gallery, Marx, 1962, 13" long	48	72	95
Motorized Yacht	375	562	750
Paddy Wagon, Remco, 1961	100	150	200
Pebbles Doll, Ideal, 1964, 16"	75	100	160
Pebbles Doll, jointed, 7" high	60	90	120
Play Set, Marx	205	308	410
Tinykins, Marx	25	NPF	50
Turnover Tank Tin Wind-up, Linemar, 1950s, 4" long	310	465	620
Wilma Tricycle, Marx	240	360	480

Gleason, Jackie

	C6	C8	C10
Jackie Gleason, "Story Stage Theatre," Utopia Enterprises, copyright 1955	123	185	245
Jackie Gleason Bus, "Away, We Go," 13" high	450	675	900
Jackie Gleason Climbing toy	62	93	125
Jackie Gleason Doll, 1950s, 30" high	200	300	400

Green Hornet

	C6	C8	C10
Bendee, Lakeside, 1967	50	75	100
Car, die-cast, Corgi	192	280	385
Hand Puppet, Ideal	200	300	400
Hat with Flipdown Mask, Arlington Hat Co.	65	98	130
Raft	175	263	350
Signal Ray, Colorforms, 1966	300	450	600
Walkie Talkies, Remco	200	300	400

Gulliver's Travels

	C6	C8	C10
Gabby Doll, wood-jointed, Ideal, 10-1/2" high	300	450	600
King Little, jointed composition, Ideal, 12"	325	488	650

Flintstone Pals Wind-up, Linemar; Fred (left), $385; Barney (right), $520.

Jackie Gleason Bus, $900. Photo courtesy Don Coviello

Gumby

	C6	C8	C10
Gumby Bendee Figure	11	16	23
Gumby Hand Puppet, Lakeside, 1965	17	26	35
Gumby Wind-up, dated 1966, 4" high	50	75	100
Poky Bendee Figure	14	22	29
Poky Hand Puppet, Lakeside, 1965	24	36	47
Poky Jack-in-the-Box, Lakeside, 1965	16	24	32
Poky Wind-up, vinyl, dated 1966, 4" high	37	56	75

Harold Lloyd

	C6	C8	C10
Bell Toy, German, 6-1/2" high	300	450	600
Donkey Cart, tin litho, Spanish, c. 1929, 9-1/4" long	2200	3300	4500
Funny Face Wind-up Walker, Marx, 1929	400	600	800
Policeman Tin Wind-up, 12" high	375	562	750
Sparkler, tin litho, German	375	562	750

Left to Right: Harold Lloyd Bell Toy, German, $600; Harold Lloyd Funny Face Walker, Marx, 1929, $800; Harold Lloyd Parkler, German, $750. Photo courtesy Christie's East

Harold Lloyd Donkey Cart, Spanish, c. 1929, $4500. Photo courtesy Christie's East

Harold Lloyd Sparkler, German, $750. Photo courtesy James S. Maxwell and Virginia Caputo

Hopalong Cassidy

	C6	C8	C10
Automatic Television Set, Automatic Toy Co., 1950s, 5" square	150	225	300
Badge, tin, w/insert photo	27	41	55
Binoculars, plastic, c. 1950	78	115	155
Compass	105	158	210
Cowboy Outfit	200	300	400
Cowgirl Outfit	125	188	250
Dart Board, depicts stagecoach holdup and target practice, Toy Ent., 1950, 14" x 17"	110	165	220
Doll, 1930s-40s, 28" high	175	263	350
Field Glasses, metal, 1940	85	128	170
Flashlight Gun, plastic, marked w/Hoppy's name on side, 8" long	30	45	60
Hand Puppet, 1940s	200	300	400
Hopalong Cassidy Doll, Ideal, 1949	125	175	200
Hop-A-Long Cassidy Tin Wind-up, "Range Rider" rocker base, Marx, 9-1/2" high	315	472	630
Knife, c. mid-1940s, 3-1/2" long	80	120	160
Photo Ring, c. late 1940s	35	52	70
Picture Gun and Theater, Stephens Co., 1939, 12" x 8"	200	300	400
Rocking Horse, Topper	188	282	375
Shooting Gallery, Automatic Toy Co., 1950s, 18" long	170	255	340
Signet Ring, all metal, late 1940s	30	45	60
Spurs, leather and metal	110	165	220

Hopalong Cassidy (Continued)

	C6	C8	C10
Western Frontier Play Set, w/figures, stagecoach and buildings	300	450	600
Zoomerang Gun, shoots paper, Tigrett Enterprises, 1950, 9" long	100	150	200

Howdy Doody

	C6	C8	C10
Acrobat Tin Wind-up, Arnold, 1950s	205	308	410
Air-O-Doodle Circus Train Wind-up, Kagran, 1950s, 16" long	90	135	180
Airplane Squeeze Toy, Stahlwood	230	345	460
Clarabelle Clown Squeeze Action Cable, Kagran Corp., Linemar, 1950s, 6-1/2" high	188	280	375
Clarabelle Clown Wind-up, Kagran Corp., 1950s, 5" high	225	338	450
Clarabelle Hurdy Gurdy, Kagran Corp, FBA Industries, 1950s, 8" long	200	300	400
Clarabelle Marionette, Peter Puppet Playthings, 1950s	140	210	280
Clarabelle Playsuit, Wonderland Costumes	145	220	290
Clarabelle's Horn, 1950s	50	75	100
Dilly-Dally Marionette, Peter Puppet Playthings, 1950s	260	390	520
Flub-A-Dub Figure, plastic, 3-1/2" high	65	98	130
Flub-A-Dub Marionette, early 1950s	225	338	450
Flub-A-Dub Push Puppet, felt and wood, 5" high	50	75	100
Hand Puppets, rubber heads w/cloth bodies	25	38	50

Flub-A-Dub Push Puppet (Howdy Doody), $100.

Howdy Doody Tin Wind-up, Marx, c. 1950, $1100. Photo courtesy PB Eighty Four, New York

Howdy Doody (Continued)

	C6	C8	C10
Howdy Doody Doll, w/moveable jaws, Goldberger Dolls, 12" high	85	130	170
Howdy Doody Doll, Ideal, 1950s, 21" high	225	338	450
Howdy Doody Doll, wood-jointed, 13" high	175	263	350
Howdy Doody Doll, wood-jointed, holding NBC microphone, 5-1/2" high	200	300	400
Howdy Doody Doll, eyes close and mouth opens, w/plastic cloth clothes, 1950s, 7-1/2" high	312	468	625
Howdy Doody Marionette, composition head w/hands and feet, hand-painted features, 1950s, 16" high	145	220	290
Howdy Doody Marionette, composition head w/wooden arms and legs, 17" high	120	180	240
Howdy Doody Mask, rubber	12	18	24
Howdy Doody Push Puppet, plastic, w/NBC mike, Kohner, 4" high	85	128	170
Howdy Doody Squeeze Toy, 7" high	75	112	150
Howdy Doody Tin Wind-up, Howdy plays banjo and moves head, Marx, c. 1950, 5" high	240	360	480
Howdy Doody Tin Wind-up, Howdy does jig and Bob Smith sits at piano, Marx, c. 1950, 5-1/2" high	550	825	1100

Howdy Doody (Continued)

	C6	C8	C10
Howdy Doody Tin Wind-up, Howdy Doody and Bob Smith at the piano, Unique	680	1020	1360
Howdy Doody TV Set, w/paper filmstrips, Lego, 1950s	42	63	85
Howdy Doody Ventriloquist Dummy, 26" high	75	112	150
Howdy-Doody Jeep Wind-up, Marx	200	300	400
Life Preserver, plastic, shows Howdy, etc., Mr. Bluster, 1950s	21	31	42
Princess SummerFall WinterSpring Marionette, Peter Puppet	125	188	250
Puppet Set, plastic, w/levers in back of head of move mouths, includes Howdy, Bluster, Clarabelle, Princess, Dilly Dally, Tee-Vee Toys, the set, No. 549	70	105	140
Put-In-Head, similar to Mr. Potato Head, but w/Howdy characters: Howdy, Bluster, Clarabelle, Princess, the set	50	75	100
Sand Forms, molds of Howdy, Bluster, Flub-A-Dub, Clarabelle, w/shovel, 1952	43	65	85
Ukulele, plastic, Emenee, 1950s	55	82	110
Wall Walker Doll, 6" high	27	41	55
Zippy the Chimp Marionette, Peter Puppet Playthings, 1950s	550	800	1200

Huckleberry Hound

	C6	C8	C10
Aeroplane, tin friction, "Huckleberry Hound Yogi Bear," Linemar	425	638	850
Fireman Squeeze Toy, rubber, 1960s, 9" high	100	150	200

Huckleberry Hound Aeroplane, Linemar, $850. Photo courtesy Don Hultzman. Photo by Ron Chojnacki

Huckleberry Hound (Continued)

	C6	C8	C10
Huckleberry Hound Car Tin Wind-up, tin, Marx, 1962, 4" long	130	195	260
Huckleberry Hound Doll, stuffed, Knickerbocker, 1959, 18" high	27	41	55
Huckleberry Hound Hand Puppet, Knickerbocker, 1959	14	21	28
Huckleberry Hound Hopper Tin Wind-up, Linemar, 1962, 4-1/2" high	200	300	400
Huckleberry Hound Squeeze Toy, rubber, w/top hat, Dell, 1960s, 6" high	22	33	44
Huckleberry Hound Tricycle Wind-up, Linemar, 1961, 4" high	400	600	800

James Bond

	C6	C8	C10
007 attache case, includes code book, rifle, bullets, Code-O-Matic, billfold w/money, James Bond business cards and instructions, c. 1965, 11"	263	395	525
100 Shot Repeater Cap Pistol with Silencer, from Goldfinger, Lone Star Co., 1961, 9" long	88	132	175
Aston Martin, die-cast, No. 271, Corgi	105	158	210
Aston Martin, die-cast, No. 270, Corgi	98	150	195
Camera	138	205	275
James Bond Hand Puppet, A.C. Gilbert, 1965	140	210	280
Moonraker Shuttlecraft	38	57	75

Jetsons

	C6	C8	C10
Astro - the Jetsons' Dog Tin Wind-up, Marx, 1963, 5" high	212	318	425
George Jetson Squeeze Action Cable, Marx, 1963, 4" high	150	225	300
George Jetson Tin Wind-up, Marx, c. 1965, 4" high	190	275	380

Jetsons Express Choo Choo Train, Marx, 1960s, $500. Photo courtesy Don Hultzman

Jetsons Turnover Tank Tin Wind-up, Linemar, $410. Photo courtesy Don Hultzman

Jetsons (Continued)

	C6	C8	C10
Jetson Express Choo Choo Train, wind-up, Marx, 1960s, 13" long	250	375	500
Jetson's Turnover Tank Tin Wind-up, tin wind-up, Linemar	205	308	410

Laurel and Hardy

	C6	C8	C10
Oliver Hardy Bendy Doll, Knickerbocker, 1960, 9" high	27	41	55
Oliver Hardy Hand Puppet, Knickerbocker	25	38	50
Oliver Hardy Roly-Poly, plastic, 10-1/2" high	22	33	44
Oliver Hardy Sparkler, Isla, Spanish	1000	1500	2000
Oliver Hardy Wind-up, Lakeside, 1960s, 5" high	35	52	70
Stan Laurel, wind-up, Lakeside, 1960s, 5" high	35	52	70
Stan Laurel Bendem Doll, Knickerbocker, 1960, 9" high	22	33	45
Stan Laurel Doll, Dean	400	600	800
Stan Laurel Hand Puppet, Knickerbocker	24	36	48

Lone Ranger

	C6	C8	C10
Chuck Wagon Lantern	75	112	150
Deputy Badge, 1950s	9	13	18
Double Target Set, includes two-sided target, gun, two darts, Marx, 1939	125	188	250
Hat, white felt w/red trim, marked "Lone Ranger Hi! Yo! Silver!," 1940s	22	33	45

Lone Ranger (Continued)

	C6	C8	C10
Hat, 1930s	65	98	130
Lone Ranger and Silver Figure, composition, 4-1/2" high	88	132	175
Lone Ranger Bendy, No. 8705, Lakeside, 1967, 6" high	16	24	32
Lone Ranger Doll, composition, Dollcraft, 1938, 20" high	300	450	600
Lone Ranger Flashlight	80	120	160
Lone Ranger Hand Puppet, Ideal, 1966	25	38	50
Lone Ranger Hand Puppet, vinyl head, c. 1956	80	120	160
Lone Ranger Hand Puppet, cloth and vinyl, "Stringless Marionette"	120	180	240
Lone Ranger Harmonica, Magnus	40	60	80
Lone Ranger Official First-Aid Kit, tin litho, w/contents, 1938	105	158	210
Lone Ranger Official Outfit, M.A. Henry Co., 1942	70	105	140
Lone Ranger Official Outfit, includes mask, jail keys, badge, silver bullet, glow belt, and Lone Ranger buckle, shows Lee Powell and Chief Thundercloud on belt, 1939	62	93	125
Movie Viewer, Lone Ranger Rides Again, 1939	113	170	225

Left to Right: Lone Ranger Lone Ranger Doll, Dollcraft, 1938, $600; Lone Ranger Tonto Doll, Dollcraft,1938, $1000. Photo courtesy Christie's East

Lone Ranger (Continued)

	C6	C8	C10
Moviescope Set, includes four films-No. 1 Superman, No. 2 Lone Ranger, No. 3 Lone Ranger, No. 4 Lone Ranger, w/pop-up box, Acme, 1948	72	108	145
Picture Printing set, includes eight rubber stamps, 1939	75	112	150
Play Set, Ranch Set, series 500, Marx	250	375	500
Push Toy, w/wood base, Kohner, 1950s	42	63	85
Rodeo Play Set, w/metal bldgs., plastic figures, etc., No. 9392, Marx, 1950s	200	300	400
Signal Siren, w/silver bullet secret code, United States Electric Mfg. Co., 1950s	65	98	130
Silver Bullet Knife, 3" long closed	92	138	185
Strongbox, (coin bank), 1938	100	150	200
Target Game, Marx, 1938	52	78	105
Tonto Doll, composition head, hands, feet, Dollcraft, 1938, 20" high	500	750	1000
Tonto Hand Puppet, vinyl head, mid 1950s	48	72	95
Tonto Hand Puppet, Ideal, 1966	21	31	42
Wind-up, on "Range Rider" rocker base, Marx, 1938, 10-1/2" high	350	525	700
Wind-up, on "Range Rider" rocker, chrome version, Marx, 1938, 8-1/2" high from top of lariat	180	270	360
Wind-up, on "Range Rider" rocker, litho version, Marx, 1938, 8-1/2" high from top of lariat	193	290	385

Magilla Gorilla

	C6	C8	C10
Magilla Gorilla Doll, Ideal, 8" high	62	93	125
Magilla Gorilla Doll, Ideal, 1960s, 19" high	90	135	180
Magilla Gorilla Hand Puppet, Ideal, 1960s	24	36	48

Mortimer Snerd

	C6	C8	C10
Doll, composition and wire, Ideal, 13" high	338	505	675
Figure, celluloid, 5" high	200	300	400
Hand Puppet	75	112	150
Jack-in-the-Box, c. 1930s, 8" high	100	150	200
Teeth, plastic teeth, w/dental wax, c. 1950	15	22	30

Mortimer Snerd Doll, Ideal, $675. Photo courtesy Christie's East

Mortimer Snerd Wind-up, Marx, 1935, $900. Photo courtesy Christie's East

Mortimer Snerd (Continued)

	C6	C8	C10
Tricky Auto, Marx, 1939	370	555	740
Wind-up, tin, Mortimer's hat tips as he walks, Marx, c. 1939	300	450	600
Wind-up, tin, "Home Town Band," Marx, 1935	450	675	900

Mr. Magoo

	C6	C8	C10
Mr. Magoo Doll, Ideal, 1964, 15" high	45	68	90
Mr. Magoo Hand Puppet, vinyl, 1962	32	48	65
Mr. Magoo Soaky, 11" high	20	30	40

Munsters, The

	C6	C8	C10
Grandpa Hand Puppet, vinyl, 1960s	93	140	185
Herman Munster Doll, Mattel	88	132	175
Herman Munster Hand Puppet, vinyl, 1960s	95	140	190
Herman Munster Puppet, talking-type	200	300	400

Munsters, The (Continued)

	C6	C8	C10
Lily Munster Hand Puppet, 1960s	95	140	190
Munster Family Dolls, Ideal, 1966	30	65	80

Rin Tin Tin

	C6	C8	C10
Rin Tin Tin, Fort Apache Stockade, No. 3628, Marx, 1950s	190	285	380
Rin Tin Tin and Rusty knife, 1950s	60	90	120
Rin Tin Tin Bugle, w/banner	37	56	75
Rin Tin Tin Doll, stuffed, Ideal	37	56	75

Robin Hood

	C6	C8	C10
Robin Hood Bow and Arrow Set, Richard Greene, 1956	6	9	12
Robin Hood Money Pouch, w/six foreign coins, 1953-54	20	30	40
Robin Hood Money Pouch, w/fifteen foreign coins	20	30	40
Robin Hood Shield Badge, w/embossed Robin Hood and gem stone, c. 1956	25	38	50

Rocky and Bullwinkle

	C6	C8	C10
Rocky the Flying Squirrel Bendee Figure, Wham-O, 1960s	10	15	21
Rocky the Flying Squirrel Hand Puppet	25	38	50
Rocky the Flying Squirrel Soaky	20	30	40

Roy Rogers

	C6	C8	C10
Branding Iron Set	40	60	80
Bullet Doll, stuffed, c. 1955	40	60	80
Double R Bar Ranch Play Set, tin litho, ranch house, Marx, 1950s	175	263	350
Mineral City, tin, town includes hotel, music hall, café, bank, barber shop, and trade goods	185	278	370

Roy Rogers Stage Coach Wagon Train Wind-up, 1950s, $160. Photo courtesy Continental Hobby House

Roy Rogers (Continued)

	C6	C8	C10
Nellie Belle Jeep, metal	30	45	60
Pocket Flashlight	37	56	75
Quickshooter Hat with Secret Gun	90	135	180
Ranch Lantern, hurricane-type w/plastic chimney, No. 90, 1950s, 7-3/4" tall	78	115	155
Rodeo Ranch Play Set, Marx	125	188	250
Roy Rogers and Bullet Hobby Horse, No. 812, N.N. Hill Brass Co., 1950s, 19" long	200	300	400
Roy Rogers and Trigger Pocket Knife	75	112	150
Roy Rogers Bandanna, large	48	72	95
Roy Rogers Bobbin' Head Doll, 1962, 6" high	90	135	180

Roy Rogers Signal Flashlight, $190. Photo courtesy Gary J. Linden

Roy Rogers Fix-it Chuck Wagon, Ideal, 1950s, $245.

Roy Rogers (Continued)

	C6	C8	C10
Roy Rogers Buckboard, Ideal, 1950s, 16" long	65	98	130
Roy Rogers Fix-it Chuck Wagon, Ideal, 1950s, 13" long	123	185	245
Roy Rogers Fix-it Stagecoach, Ideal, 1950s, 13" long	90	135	180
Roy Rogers Horse Trailer and Jeep, Ideal, 1950s, 15" long	180	270	360
Roy Rogers Stage Coach Wagon Train Wind-up, plastic, 1950s, 14" long	80	120	160
Signal Flashlight	95	140	190
Telescope	40	60	80
Wagon Train, Marx	150	225	300
Western Town Play Set, Marx	125	188	250

Tom Corbett

	C6	C8	C10
Cosmic Vision Space Helmet, plastic, one-way vision, early 1950s	207	310	415
Polaris Rocket Ship Wind-up, depicts Tom, Astro and Rogers looking out of cockpit, Marx, 1952, 12" long	300	450	600
Space Academy Set, No. 7000, Marx	238	355	475
Space Cadet 2-Way Space Phone, Zimmerman	80	120	160
Space Cadet Field Glasses, three power, Herald, 5-1/2" long	60	90	120
Space Cadet Flashlight, metal, w/built-in signal siren, U.S. Alite Corp., 7" long	90	135	180
Space Cadet Molding and Coloring Set, Model Craft	55	82	110
Space Cadet Official Space Pistol, No. 105, Marx	180	270	360
Space Cadet Rifle, No. 0239, Marx	140	210	280
Space Hat, Lee	40	60	80
Space Station	325	490	650
Spurs, metal and leather, 1934	150	225	300
Tom Corbett Official Outfit, Yankiboy	92	138	185
Tom Corbett Space Cadet Atomic Rifle, Marx, 1950s, 24" long	150	225	300
Tom Corbett Space Cadet Official Space Pistol, Rockhill, 1950s, 9-1/2" long	105	158	210

Underdog

	C6	C8	C10
Underdog Doll, small	40	60	80
Underdog Doll, medium	50	75	100
Underdog Doll, large	62	93	125

Universal Monsters

	C6	C8	C10
Creature Soaky	55	83	110
Frankenstein Soaky	55	83	110
Wolfman Soaky	60	90	120

Universal Monters

	C6	C8	C10
Mummy Soaky	60	90	120

Wizard of Oz

	C6	C8	C10
Cowardly Lion Facemask, molded gauze	40	60	80
Dorothy and Toto Figure, Mego	19	28	38
Dorothy Doll, Ideal, 1940	200	300	500
Emerald City Play Set, Mego	80	120	160
Lion Figure, Mego, 1972, 15" long	15	22	30
Mayor Munchkin Figure, Mego	45	68	90
Munchkinland Figures, total of four, price of each	48	72	95
Munchkinland Play Set	65	98	130
Scarecrow Facemask, molded gauze	60	90	120
Scarecrow Figure, Mego, 1972, 8" high	14	21	28
Tinman Facemask, molded gauze	60	90	120
Tinman Figure, Mego, 1972, 8" high	15	22	30
Witch's Castle, Mego	175	262	350
Wizard Figure, Mego, 8" high	8	12	17
Wizard of Oz, four-headed hand puppet, talks, Mattel, c. 1967	105	158	210
Wizard of Oz Masks, set of five, Einson-Freement Co., Inc., 1939	138	205	275
Wizard of Oz Series Dolls, Ideal, 1984	20	30	45

Wyatt Earp

	C6	C8	C10
Wyatt Earp Play Set, Marx	275	415	550
Wyatt Earp U.S. Marshall Badge, Lone Star	18	27	36
Wyatt Earp U.S. Marshall Badge, 20th century, 1950s	14	21	28

Yogi Bear

	C6	C8	C10
Doll, stuffed, Knickerbocker, 1973, 7-1/2" high	45	68	90

Yogi Bear (Continued)

	C6	C8	C10
Friction Car, Marx, 1962	100	150	200
Go-Cart, Linemar	138	205	275
Hand Puppet, 1959	12	18	24
Jellystone National Park Play Set, Marx	350	525	700
Tricky Trapeze, 1967, 5" high	17	25	34
Yogi Bear Car, Marx, 1962, 4" long	100	150	200
Yogi Bear Hopper Wind-up, Linemar, 1962, 4" high	300	450	600

Miscellaneous

	C6	C8	C10
Abbott & Costello, price for each, 1984	30	65	80
Augie Doggie Soaky	27	41	55
Babalooie Doll, vinyl face, Knickerbocker, 14" high	30	45	60
Babalooie Soaky	15	22	30
Baby Huey (Paramount) Hand Puppet, Gund, late 1950s	24	36	48
Baby Sandy Pull Toy, Sandy & Goose, Gong Bell, 12-1/2" long	150	225	300
Bat Masterson Gun and Holster Set, w/cane and vest, Carnell, 1958	138	205	275
Beatles Figures, vinyl, Ringo, John, Paul, George, price for each, Remco, 1964, 5" high	45	68	90
Beatles Soakies, price for each each	62	93	125
Ben Hur Sword, scabbard and shield, Marx, 1959	142	213	285
Beverly Hillbillies Wind-up Car, Ideal, 1960s	270	405	540
Bob Burns Bazooka, brass kazoo-like toy, metal sliding tube, M.M. Pochapia Toys, 1930s, 13" long not extended	20	30	40
Bob Hope Hand Puppet, c. 1940	32	48	65
Bojangles Dances Again, tin litho and wood, tap button on base and he dances, 1930s	200	300	400
Buck Jones Rangers Chaps	90	135	180
Buffalo Bill Jr. Belt and Buckle, 1950s	25	38	50
Buster Keaton Sparkler, tin litho, w/moving arms and legs, Spanish, c. 1925, 7" high	1650	2475	3300

Miscellaneous (Continued)

	C6	C8	C10
Captain Gallant Foreign Legion Holster Outfit	80	120	160
Captain Gallant Play Set, Marx	400	600	800
Charley Weaver Nodder	112	188	225
Cheyenne Target Game, Mettoy, 1961	62	93	125
Clyde Beatty Hingees Set, 1944	25	38	50
Danny O'Day (Jimmy Nelson) Ventriloquist Doll	40	60	80
Davy Crockett and His Horse, Ideal, 1955	20	35	50
Deputy Dawg Doll, stuffed, Ideal, 1961, 14" high	37	56	75
Deputy Dawg Soaky	15	22	30
Doggie Daddie Doll, vinyl head, Knickerbocker	100	150	200
Ed Wynn Fire Chief, jointed wood, w/ax in hand	80	120	160
Fanny Brice (Baby Snooks) Doll, composition and wire, Ideal, 12" high	125	188	250
Farfel (Jimmy Nelson) Hand Puppet, Juro	85	127	170
Farmer Alfalfa (Terrytoons) Doll, stuffed body w/vinyl head and hands, c. 1950, 17-1/2" high	30	45	60
Flip Wilson Geraldine Doll, talking type, Shindana, 1970	25	38	50
Flying Nun, Hasbro, 1960s, 4-3/4"	25	38	50
Flying Nun Flying Toy, Rayline, 1970	25	38	50
Froggie the Gremlin Squeeze Toy, 10-3/4" high	170	255	340
Froggie the Gremlin Squeeze Toy, 6-1/2" high	34	51	68
Froggie the Gremlin Squeeze Toy, 9-1/4" high	40	60	80
Froggie the Gremlin Squeeze Toy, hollow rubber, Rempel, 1950s, 5" high	62	93	125
Gangbusters Target Game, Marx	55	83	110
Gene Autry Marionette, 1940s, 18" high	140	210	280
Gene Autry spurs	60	90	120
General Figure, (Wizard of Oz), Mego	45	68	90

The Box for Bat Masterson Gun and HolsterSet. The complete set, by Carnell, is valued at $275.

Beverly Hillbillies Wind-up Car, Ideal, 1960s, $540. Photo courtesy Don Hultzman. Photo by Ron Chojnacki

Buster Keaton Sparkler, Spanish, c. 1925, $3300. Photo courtesy Christie's East

Joe Penner Tin Wind-up, Marx ,c. 1930s, $700. Photo courtesy Sotheby's, New York

Jackie Coogan ("The Kidd") Walker Tin Wind-up, German, $1600.

W.C. Fields Doll, Effanbee, $850. Photo courtesy Christie's East

Miscellaneous (Continued)

	C6	C8	C10
Get Smart Spy Purse Kit, Miner Ind., 7" long...............	30	45	60
Gilligan's Island Floating Island Play Set	88	132	175
Glinda Figure, (Wizard of Oz), Mego, 1972, 8" high	19	28	38
Gomez Hand Puppet, (Addams Family)...............	70	105	142
Groucho Marx, "Ventriloquist Play Pal," Goldberger	40	60	80
Gulliver's Travels Boat, wooden, Paramount	110	165	220
Gulliver's Travels Drum, tin, Chein, 1939	25	38	50
Gulliver's Travels Musical top, Chein ..	30	45	60
Gulliver's Travels Sandpail, tin, Chein...............	45	68	90
Gumby's Jeep, metal, 1960s, 12"........	125	188	250
Gunsmoke Handcuffs and Badge, c. 1952	42	63	85
Henry Fonda Texas Ranger Sheriff Badge, The Deputy, 1951	17	26	35
Highway Patrol, "Highway Patrol Car," Broderick Crawford, 8" long.....	75	112	150
Highway Patrol Pistol Outfit, includes gun, holster, badge, handcuffs, ID, whistle, etc., Halco, 1956	125	188	250
Hoot Gibson Cowboy Outfit, Wornova Clothes, 1935	70	105	140
Hoot Gibson Lariat...............	40	60	80
Hoot Gibson Outfit, "Squaw style," Wornova Clothes, 1930s...............	60	90	120
Hugh O'Brian-Wyatt Earp, Dodge City Western Town, Marx, 1950s.....	450	675	900
I Spy Target Set...............	17	26	35
J. Fred Muggs Hand Puppet (Today show), 1954	41	62	82
J. Fred Muggs Pull Toy (Today show), Gong Bell	90	135	180
Jackie Coogan ("The Kidd") Walker Tin Wind-up, German, 7" high	800	1200	1600
Jackie Coogan Candy Container, glass, 5" high...............	800	1200	1600
Jackie Coogan Figure, celluloid, 1920s, 5-1/2" high...............	130	195	260

Miscellaneous (Continued)

	C6	C8	C10
Jerry Lewis/Dean Martin Hand Puppet, two-sided...............	150	225	300
Jerry Mahoney Ventriloquist Dummy.	115	173	230
Joe Penner Tin Wind-up, tin wind-up, tips hat, walks, marked "Wanna Buy a Duck?," Marx, c. 1930s, 8" high...............	350	525	700
Jungle Jim Play Set, Marx	500	800	1100
Kukla & Ollie Puppet theatre, cardboard, 1962...............	50	75	100
Lambchop Shari Lewis Hand Puppet.....	18	27	36
Man from U.N.C.L.E. Secret Print Putty, c. 1965	25	38	50
Mary Poppins Hand Puppet, Gund........	48	72	95
Matt Dillon (Gunsmoke) badge, U.S. Marshall	9	30	38
Men Into Space Space Helmet, retractable visor, space mike, made of fortiflex	65	98	130
Milton Berle Car, w/two large and two small wheels, "What the Hey," written on car, Marx, 1950s	215	323	430
Mr. Ed Hand Puppet, Mattel, 1962........	48	72	95
My Favorite Martian, "Martian Magic Tricks," magic set, Gilbert, 1964...............	115	175	230
Pink Panther Hand Puppet, cloth body, Gund, early...............	20	30	40
Pinky Lee Doll, vinyl, squeeze and his head pops up, 1950...............	90	135	180
Pinky Lee Pull Toy, Gong Bell	100	150	200
Quick Draw McGraw, "Quick Draw McGraw Hopper," Linemar, 1962, 4-1/2" high	200	300	400
Quick Draw McGraw, "Animal Airplane," Linemar, 1960s, 8-1/2" long w/9-1/2" wingspan	400	600	800
Quick Draw McGraw, Knickerbocker, 17-1/2" high............	105	158	210
Quick Draw McGraw Squeeze Toy, Dell, 9-1/2" high...............	100	150	200
Ramar of the Jungle Play Set...............	217	325	435
Rat Patrol Giant Action Battle Set.......	250	375	500
Rat Patrol Jeep, Marx	200	300	400
Ricochet Rabbit, Ideal	52	78	105
Rifleman (TV) Ranch, Marx	600	1000	1500

Miscellaneous (Continued)	C6	C8	C10
Rookies (TV) Official Police Car, Fleetwood, 1975	15	22	30
Rootie Kazootie Doll, Effanbee, 19" high	62	93	125
Rootie Kazootie Marionette, rubber head and hands, wooden shoes, 14" high	90	135	180
Scrappy & Margie Pull Toy, wooden, 13-1/2" long	165	248	330
Scrappy Doll, cloth and composition, (Columbia Pictures), E.D.&T.C. Co., c. 1935, 14-1/2" high	320	480	640
Secret Squirrel Soaky	37	56	75
Sgt. Bilko Holster Set, from CBS TV series "You'll Never Get Rich," contains leather holster and belt w/die-cast Army, arm patch and Sgt. Bilko hat w/Badge, Halco Brand, 1956	100	150	200
Shadow Crimefighter Detection Belt, w/pistol and handcuffs, Madison Ltd., 1978	15	22	30
Shadow Felt Hat, early 1940s	187	280	375
Shirley Temple playhouse	120	180	240
Sneak Facemask, (Gulliver's Travels), molded gauze, 1939	50	75	100
Soupy Sales Doll, Sunshine Doll Co., 1965, 5" high	90	135	180
Soupy Sales Marionette, Knickerbocker, 1966	37	56	75
Star Trek, Mr. Spock Vulcan Ears, 1976	7	11	15
Tales of the Texas Rangers Deputy Badge	12	18	24
Tarzan Bendy, Mego, 1972	25	38	50

Miscellaneous (Continued)	C6	C8	C10
Tennessee Tuxedo Soaky	17	26	35
Three Stooges as part of Jolly Theatre, 1930s	125	188	250
Three Stooges Hand Puppet, includes Moe, Curley, and Larry, price for each, 1959, 9-1/2" high	90	135	180
Tim Holt Litho Target, w/dart gun	70	105	140
Tim Mix on Tony, Arcor Rubber, 1930s	85	128	170
Tom Mix Rocking Horse, wooden, 1930s	175	263	350
Tom Mix Rodeo Rope, w/box and instructions, 1928	100	150	200
Topo Gigio (Ed Sullivan Show) Nodder	75	112	150
Topo Gigio Airplane, friction	75	112	150
Umbriago (Jimmy Durante) Hand Puppet, American Merchandise, 1945	45	68	90
Untouchable Detective Set, includes gun, holster, etc., Marx	112	168	225
Untouchable Tommy Gun, Marx, 1950s, 23" long	48	72	96
W.C. Fields Doll, w/movable mouth, Effanbee, 19" high	425	638	850
Wagon Train Play Set, Marx	213	320	425
Waterfront "Cheryl Ann" Tugboat, (TV series), 1950s, 21"	100	150	200
Wild Bill Hickok and Jingles Holster Set	50	75	100
Wild Bill Hickok Marshal Star Badge, w/picture of Hickok and Jingles in center	42	63	85
Yellow Submarine, Corgi	180	270	360

PEZ

PEZ candy dispensers first became available in the United States around 1950, although the candy was produced in Austria as far back as the 1930s. It wasn't until the late 1940s that the "box" or dispenser became available with the candy. The very first dispenser had no head (the aspect most of us associate with PEZ), making it resemble a Bic lighter. Soon thereafter, a Spacegun, a full-bodied Santa, a full-bodied Robot and many more dispensers appeared. Who can forget the fun of favorite cartoon friends tilting their heads back to offer a piece of PEZ candy?

Over the years PEZ dispensers have been manufactured in Austria, Yugoslavia, Hong Kong and the United States. Dispensers are usually marked with one of these five patent numbers—2,620,061; 3,410,455; 3,845,882; 3,942,683; or 4,966,305, which appears on items dated from 1992 to the present. It is virtually impossible to date a dispenser with any certainty, although the patent number can sometimes be a vague indicator. Neither the country of origin, the patent number, nor the age are necessarily tied to value. The bottom line on value is which head is on the dispenser.

Since their introduction in the United States, PEZ dispensers have been continuously available. As of late 1998, there were approximately 350 different PEZ dispensers known. This figure excludes color variation and other minor differences occurring on individual dispensers. Only the more valuable dispensers are found in these listings. Other companies—Totems, Yummies and Smarties—have copied the dispenser with head concept, but none have approached the universal acceptance of PEZ.

The years 1997 and 1998 were big years for PEZ collectors. It was not unusual to see prices rise 100 percent over the 1996 figures. The influence of the Internet, the large American market and increased foreign collector interest made PEZ one of the blue-chip collectibles of the late 1990s.

Prices given are for dispensers in Excellent to Mint condition. Defects such as missing pieces, melt marks, scuffs, excessive dirt and cracks decrease the value by a minimum of twenty percent. The condition of the stem that holds the candy does not affect value as much as the condition of the head. Exceptions to this rule apply in the cases of Regulars, Die-Cuts, Guns, Zorro A, Psychedelics and other dispensers in which the stem itself is an important part of the identity or appearance. Missing head pieces and facial melt marks can render most dispensers valueless. However, the heads alone are sometimes of value on the most expensive dispensers.

Contributor: David Welch, P.O. Box 714, Murphysboro, IL 62966. Welch is convinced he has spent more money on PEZ items than any other two people combined. He also claims the finest collection of PEZ-related advertising in the world. Welch has authored several books on PEZ dispensers and PEZ collecting—*Pictorial Guide to Plastic Candy Dispensers featuring PEZ* and *Collecting PEZ.*

	C10
Alpine, 1972 Olympics	1000
Arithmetic	650
Astronaut, white helmet	150
Astronaut, blue helmet	175
Astronaut, clear helmet	150
Astronaut, clear helmet w/"Cocoa Marsh" on side	200
Astronaut, small helmet, silver or white	600
Baseball Glove, w/ball	225

	C10
Baseball Glove, w/home plate and bat	600
Batman, w/cape	125
Betsy Ross	150
Bozo	200
Bozo Die-cut, w/"Bozo/Butch" on side	225
Bride, w/white veil	2000
Brutus, from Popeye	250
Bullwinkle	275

Left to Right: Astronaut with white helmet, $150; Astronaut with clear helmet, $150; Astronaut with small helmet, $600; Robot, $400. Photo courtesy Barry Koester

Left to Right: Little Orphan Annie, $160; Bullwinkle, $275; Brutus, $250; Olive Oyl, $250; Popeye, $150. Photo courtesy Barry Koester

Left to Right: Uncle Sam, $225; Wounded Soldier, $170; Betsy Ross, $150; Captain, $150; Daniel Boone with Coonskin Cap, $220. Photo courtesy Barry Koester

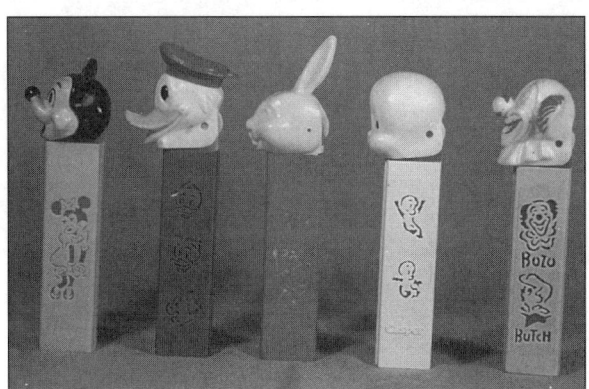

Left to Right: Mickey Mouse Die-cut, $175; Donald Duck Die-cut, $185; Easter Bunny Die-cut, $600; Casper Die-cut, $300; Bozo Die-cut, $25. Photo courtesy Barry Koester

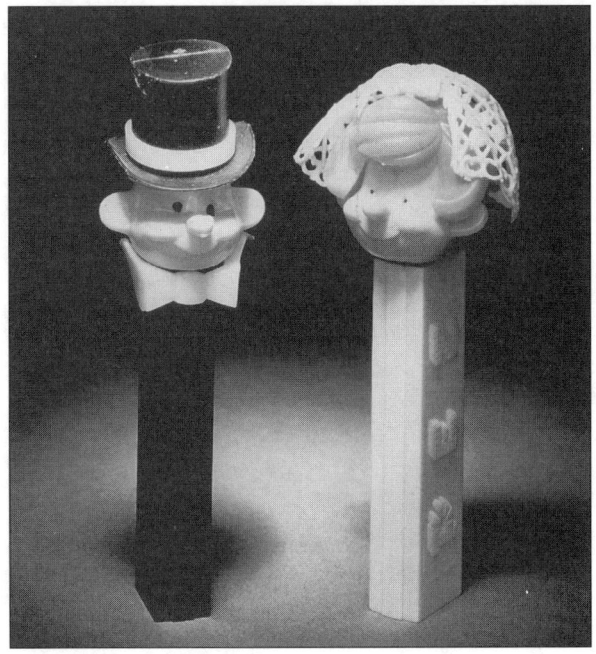

Left to Right: Groom, $500; Bride, $2000.

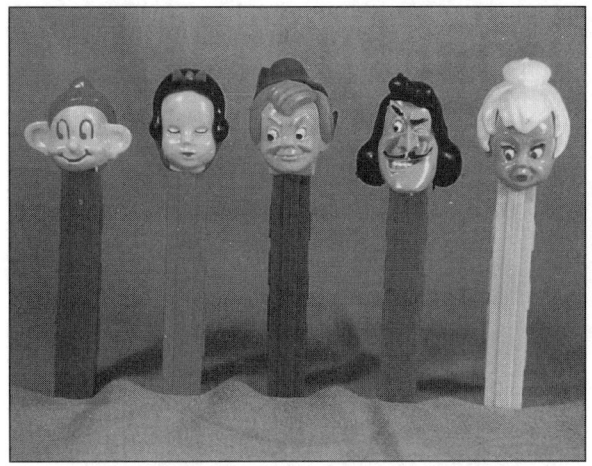

Left to Right: Dopey, $225; Snow White, $220; Peter Pan, $175; Captain Hook, $100; Tinkerbell, $250. Photo courtesy Barry Koester

	C10
Camel Whistle	50
Captain	150
Captain Hook	100
Casper	225
Casper Die-cut, "Casper" on side	300
Chick in Egg, without hat	100
Cow, w/large nose and circular ears	100
Cowboy	300
Creature from the Black Lagoon, green cartridge/head	300
Creature from the Black Lagoon, black head	200
Crocodile	120
Dalmatian Pup, foreign issue	50
Daniel Boone, w/coonskin cap	220
Doctor	130
Dog	40
Donald Duck Die-cut, w/three duck nephews on side	185
Dopey	225
Easter Bunny, with thin/straight ears	225
Easter Bunny Die-cut, w/bunny w/eggs on side	600
Football Player	150
Frankenstein	300

Gun, $425. Photo courtesy Barry Koester

	C10
Giraffe	200
Green Hornet	255
Groom, w/black top hat and hat band	500
Gun, Space, 1950s	425
Gun, handgun, mail-order premium	125
Gun, space, 1980s	125
Indian Brave	200
Indian Chief	125
Indian Woman	175
Joker (from Batman), soft head	175
Knight	325

Left to Right: Robot, $400; Frankenstein, $300. Photo courtesy Barry Koester

Gun, $125. Photo courtesy Barry Koester

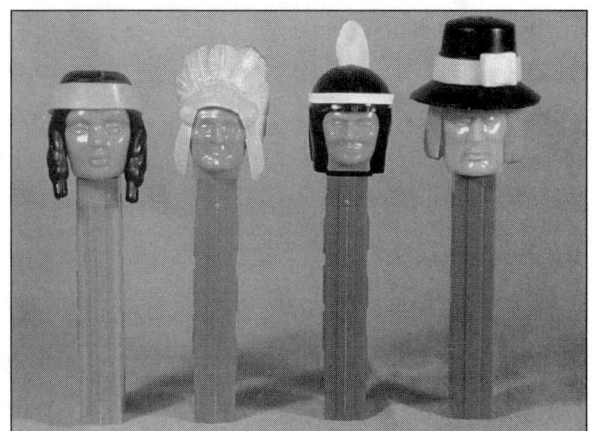

Left to Right: Indian Woman, $175; Indian Chief, $125; Indian Brave, $200; Pilgrim, $160. Photo Courtesy Barry Koester

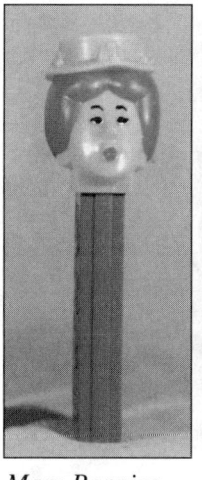

Mary Poppins, $1100. Photo courtesy Barry Koester

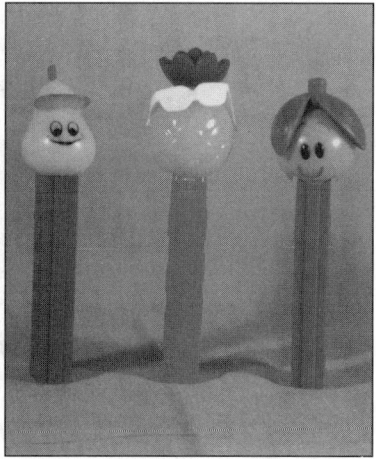

Pear, $1000. Photo courtesy Barry Koester

	C10
Koala whistle	35
Lion's Club Lion, stem inscribed, 1962	3000
Little Orphan Annie	160
Make-A-Face, similar to Mr. Potato Head w/seventeen face pieces, loose	2500
Make-A-Face, mint on card	3000
Mary Poppins	1100
Mickey Mouse Die-cut, w/"Minnie" on side	175
Monsters, soft heads, six varieties, price for each	175
Olive Oyl	250
Orange	200
Panther, blue head	200
Pear, w/visor	1000
Penguin (from Batman), soft head	175
Peter Pan	175

	C10
Pilgrim	160
Pineapple, w/sunglasses	2500
Pinocchio, old version, has eyes looking up, feather is part of hat	200
Popeye, old version, hat cannot be removed	150
Psychedelic Eye, hand holding eyeball (versions marked "©1967" or "1968" are 1998 reissues)	500

Make-A-Face, $3000. Photo courtesy Barry Koester

Left to Right: Psychedelic Eye, $500; Psychedelic Flower, $600

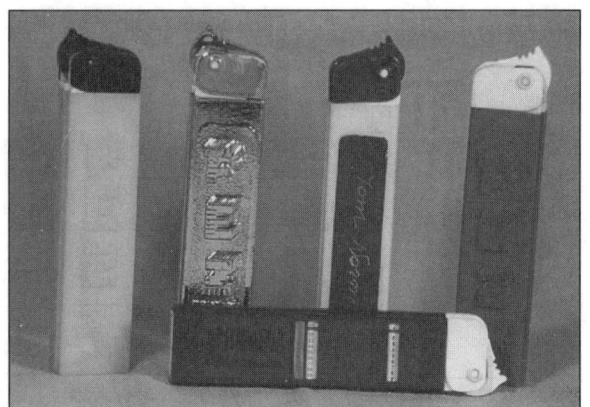

Left to Right: Regular, no markings, $150; Regular, Golden Glow with shiny gold finish, $150; Regular, personalized with paper label on side, $300; Regular, no markings. Front: Arithmetic, $650. Photo courtesy Barry Koester

	C10
Psychedelic Flower, eyeball in flower	600
Regular, personalized w/paper label on side	300
Regular, no markings	150
Regular, U.S. Zone Germany marking	200
Regular, Golden Glow w/gold shiny finish	150
Regular (no heads), Witch w/pictures of witches on side	3200
Rhino Whistle	25
Robot, full body, three colors	400

	C10
Sailor, full white beard w/blue hat	160
Santa, full body	225
Santa, face and beard same color	125
Santa, small head w/flesh face and white beard	125
Snow White	220
Snowman, w/arms, 1976 Olympics	475
Stewardess	225
Thor, helmet w/wings	325
Tinkerbell	250
Uncle Sam	225
Witch, w/one-piece orange head	300
Wolf, 1984 Olympics, Ski hat	775
Wolf, 1984 Olympics, bobsled hat	775
Wolf, 1984 Olympics, no hat	750
Wolfman	275
Wounded Soldier	170
Zorro, not marked "Zorro" on side	65
Zorro, marked "Zorro" on side	85

Left to Right: Santa, face and beard same color, $125; Santa, full body, $225; Santa, flesh face and white beard, $125. Photo courtesy Barry Koester

Left to Right: Wolfman, $275; Creature from the Black Lagoon, green cartridge/head, $300; Frankenstein, $300. Photo courtesy Barry Koester

PREMIUMS

Many radio premiums were nearly as free as the wonderful radio shows that advertised them. We did have to pay the electric bill (or our folks did) to run the radio, and to get the offered toys we did have to send in a box-top from the sponsor's product.

Sometimes it was only that, a proof of purchase. Orphan Annie and Captain Midnight were particularly generous in responding with gifts for inner labels or inner seals from Ovaltine drink mix. Other times, usually only a dime was required "to handle the cost of handling and mailing." (That's really all it did do—the cost of the premium itself came from the advertising budget.)

The lure of the premium for kids then and for grown-up kids who are now collectors is difficult to explain to those who never lived through the era themselves. The ring or badge was more than the toy itself; it was our tangible link to those magical friends on the other side of the speaker cloth.

Those voices were wonderful out there: The rumbling bass of Brace Beemer as the Lone Ranger; the slightly "country" sound of Curley Bradley as Tom Mix; Bret Morrison, whom we recognized even as children was "sophisticated" as Lamont Cranston (alias The Shadow). But they were bodiless and yes, a bit remote. It was the premium they offered, the same as the one they were using in the story, that put us in touch with them.

There were historic precedents for radio premiums. There were pictures of famous actresses in cigarette packages around the turn of the century, and early radio personalities, such as bandleader Vincent Lopez, offered their autographed pictures. Such footnotes to history aside, radio premiums began with Little Orphan Annie in 1931. The plucky little waif from the Sunday comics first gave away sheet music of her theme song ("Who's that little chatterbox with the pretty auburn locks?") and her own photo, but very shortly, she offered a drinking mug that could be used to shake up Ovaltine powder with milk to make something resembling a soda fountain milk shake.

The first significant radio premium, it was the only successful one that encouraged further use of the sponsor's product.

Many different models of the shake-up mug were offered by Annie and later by Captain Midnight (on both radio and TV). So successful were the offers, shake-up mugs are not rare or high in value. (The most sought after is the orange and blue, embossed—not decaled—Midnight mug.)

It was two years after Annie came to radio that the fledgling medium developed its classic adventure heroes. In 1933 there appeared the Lone Ranger, Tom Mix and Jack Armstrong. Unlike Annie, the two Westerners and the All-American Boy were still around until the 1950s, when television began driving out radio drama. In those nearly twenty years, the shows offered hundreds of give-away toys, which inspired similar premiums on dozens of other shows.

Any small toy that could be manufactured inexpensively might turn up as a premium. Those concerned with the great outdoors were popular. We had compasses, pedometers, telescopes, flashlights, pocket knives, signal mirrors, and portable telegraph sets.

Secret decoders and manuals of every size and description had special emblems and tokens. It is these and other paper items that have the greatest dollar value. They were the most easily lost or used up in the rush to adulthood. A Captain Midnight Secret Manual is worth more than the metallic decoder it accompanied.

The rarest paper item is the Lone Ranger Frontier Town, offered about 1947. To complete this model of a Western village, one had to get four different envelopes by mail, then augment this by buying several packages of Cheerios to cut out the model buildings from the packs. The complete set has been known to sell for hundreds of dollars and today might bring $4,000 for a Mint set.

Perhaps the most popular single type of premium was the ring. Rings let the listener show loyalty to the fraternity of his or her favorite hero, but in a less officious and more "grown-up" way than the badge (although they were also highly popular). Besides . . . the rings looked neat, and many of them could do things—some of them pretty incredible things.

As with radio premiums in general, the Tom Mix show (and Ralston cereal's premium manufacturer, the Robbins Company) blazed the trail with ingenious ring designs. In 1937 Tom Mix Straight Shooters could get a Signet Ring with their own initial on it. (Years later, Captain Midnight would offer a ring that would ink-stamp your initial.) By 1938, Tom had a ring that let you look in a peep-hole and see a magnified picture of himself and his horse, Tony. (Technology had progressed so much that by the fifties, Straight Arrow offered a similar ring that put your own photo, if supplied, alongside radio's great Indian hero.)

After World War II and the ease in metal rationing, Tom Mix offered a Magnet Ring. His spinning siren whistle ring was neat (but admittedly borrowed in design from Jack Armstrong's 1937 Egyptian Whistle Ring). Tom's Sliding Whistle Ring, which played different musical notes (about 1948), was unique, however. His Look-Around Ring concealed an inner mirror that let you see behind you (sort of), a design rustled for a later Tennessee Jed ring.

The final Tom Mix ring looked attractive, sporting a glowing cat's-eye, but the 1949 Tiger-Eye Ring was only lightweight plastic, a far cry from the well-crafted metal rings of a decade earlier. But then, the decade was nearly over, and so was the era, fading in the light of another glowing eye in the living room.

The Shadow's own Glow-in-the-Dark Ring (1939) had a band composed of two sculpted Shadow figures holding up a jagged blue stone—a proxy lump of his sponsor's product, Blue Coal. One of the very few Shadow premiums and the best-looking, this ring has sold for $950.

The identical mold for one glowing plastic ring was used for several different radio shows. The band had two crocodiles holding a setting in their mouths. The "stone" was black when it was Jack Armstrong's Dragon Eye Ring in 1940. It was green for "Terry and the Pirates" in the mid-1940s, but it was black for Carey Salt's Shadow ring in 1947 (not the rare Blue Coal model). The setting was red for Buck Roger's Ring of Saturn in 1945. It is black again in the slightly lumpy counterfeit being manufactured today. This ring is one of the handful of premiums of simple enough design to be faked for profit. The best way to authenticate these rings is by the accompanying paper instruction sheets naming the famous character whose prize it is.

These rings are worth whatever you will pay to possess them, as are all radio premiums. A fair average price is $60, with $300 a top price for very rare, complex and fragile items. Of course, many items are priced much higher. But anybody who is not familiar with the whole field should not pay more, even though $500 or more may be easier to come by today than a dime and a box-top were in those days of yesteryear.

Since 1992 there has been a radical change in the prices of radio and early TV premiums (and associated toys). For nearly twenty years there had been no appreciable rise in premium prices. In fact, premium prices had not even kept up with inflation. You could have bought a Tom Mix Magnet Ring for $35 in 1967 and bought the Magnet Ring for the same $35 in 1987. But now there has come a radical change in premium pricing, especially for rings. The Magnet Ring generally brought $150 in 1998.

Part of the reason is the unnatural influence of "investor" types who have manipulated the market, much as they did the old comic book market. The results have been mixed. Prices have risen, but the number of premium collectors and the number of premium objects is far smaller than their counterparts in the comic book field. As a result, most premiums have virtually disappeared from the market. Now is the time to buy, if premiums can be found. They may never be cheaper, and they may never be seen again.

Despite rarity, condition is still very important. No matter how rare, a premium that is battered, defaced or broken is virtually worthless. It may bring a token price of $5.

Stores of premiums newly found in attics no longer seem to be turning up, but older collectors are retiring from their occupations and, sadly, selling their collections for needed money. Some die, and survivors sell. These collectors and families know the value of collectibles and sell for top market value. The number of these "retiring" collectors is still fairly small and does not greatly affect the general state of rarity of premiums.

The items connected to once well-known characters (and those still famous) such as the Lone Ranger, Tom Mix, Buck Rogers, Buck Jones, and Gene Autry, have the highest prices. These prices are still on the rise. Even minor and nearly forgotten characters such as Scoop Ward and Speed Gibson are not being given away. Such once well-known characters will generally prevent a button from selling for less than $15, a badge for less than $25 or a ring for under $30.

Rings have a great appeal to many, and are the hottest ticket in the premium market. The rare ones are going up and up. The Shadow Blue Coal Ring, Green Hornet Seal Ring, and Captain Midnight Mystic Sun God have gone into the thousands of dollars.

Cereal boxes of the sponsors who offered the premiums, especially ones with premium offers on the boxes, have become valuable. Near the top of the line are complete boxes of the nine Lone Ranger Frontier Town Cheerios packs (about $200 each; the backs off the boxes with unassembled model buildings can go for $35). Tom Mix Ralston boxes from the late 1940s-1950s go for up to $400.

A few new authentic premiums have appeared in recent years. Boraxo offered a 20 Mule Team model in 1980 (similar to the Death Valley Days original of the 1930s, 1940s, and 1950s); Cheerios offered a Lone Ranger Deputy Kit in 1981 styled after the movie of that year but similar to earlier offers with mask, badge, etc.

In 1982 Ralston began a limited Tom Mix revival. Premiums offered included a set of four Mix Ralston cereal bowls, a wind-up wrist watch, a Straight Shooters membership kit, a Tom Mix photo, a Mix in-box miniature comic and a LP recording with old Mix radio episodes and one 1983 episode featuring Curley Bradley. In 1993-94, Ralston again showcased Tom Mix on their boxes, but offered only a chance for the customer to write in their memories of Tom. A full-color box came in 1996.

In 1987 Ovaltine resurrected their original formula in jars and instituted new premiums of their character, Captain Midnight of the Secret Squadron. The 1987 premium was a tee-shirt, in 1988 a Midnight digital watch was offered, and in 1989 an arm patch was available (apparently the last of the current revival). Dick Tracy premiums, such as the Quaker wrist radio, came with the new movie in 1990. Superman continued his fifty-year-plus association with Kellogg's cereals in 1994, appearing on the box and inside, with a mini-comic book for Kellogg's Cinnamon Mini-Buns. In 2000, Ovaltine ovvered decoder rings for two proofs of purchase and $2.50. Contrary to popular belief, Ovaltine nor any other radio sponsor has offered a code ring before.

Prices on these are already comparable to older premiums, topped by the Tom Mix watch at $300. The biggest premium news of the early 1990s was the sale of a Superman comic book premium ring for a record $18,000 and its resale for $43,000. But this event was really a part of the world of incredibly-priced Golden Age comic books. In effect, the ring was treated as another rare old comic book, not as the premium ring it was. This astonishing sale only raised the value of a real radio premium, the Superman Crusaders Club ring, from $65 to a less than overwhelming $250. Real radio and TV premiums from broadcast series have broken the $1,000 barrier, with the complete Lone Ranger Frontier Town and rings—Captain Midnight Mystic Sun God, Green Hornet Seal, Shadow Blue Coal and many others in a new and much changed market.

Contributor: Jim Harmon, 634 South Orchard Dr., Burbank, CA 91506. Harmon is the author of Radio & TV Premiums; Value and History from Tom Mix to Space Patrol

	C6	C8	C10
Admiral Television Studio Giveaway, paper punch-out TV Studio and characters, features Sky King, Flight to Mars, Walt Disney's Peter Pan and Three Little Pigs, 1953, 15" x 16"	65	131	262
Amos & Andy Pepsodent Giveaway, Amos' Wedding	48	72	95
Amos & Andy Puzzle	55	83	110
Archie Comics Club Button	5	10	20
Aunt Jemima Breakfast Club Badge, metal	12	18	30
Barney Baxter Junior Birdmen of America Wings, metal, c. late 1930s	12	18	25

	C6	C8	C10
Bendix Radio, WWII military figures, color photos w/stands—a.) Navy Lt. (jg); b.) Marine 1st Lt. (dress uniform); c.) Coast Guard Commander; d.) Army Air Force officer w/parachute harness; e.) 2nd Lt. W/modern Mae West; f.) Flier w/flying suit; g.) Army Air Force Capt.; h.) Air officer w/fur-lined jacket and helmet; price for each, c. 1944, 5-1/2"	5	10	15
Betty Boop Face Mask, theatre premium, 1931	27	41	63
Betty Boop Pin, "Roxy Theatre, New York," large	20	30	50

	C6	C8	C10
Bobby Benson Code Rule, cardboard decoder, 1935	40	75	150
Bobby Benson's Game Circus, 1934	50	97	195
Buck Jones Club Ring	60	110	220
Buck Jones Horseshoe Pin	25	50	100
Buck Jones Jr. Sheriff Badge	25	50	100
Buck Rogers, items given away for Cream of Wheat green triangle (also sold in stores) Buck Rogers Films for Projector	10	15	25
Buck Rogers Badge, enameled	83	125	165
Buck Rogers Chief Explorer Badge	45	90	180
Buck Rogers Flight Commander Whistle Badge	90	175	350
Buck Rogers Girl's Charm Bracelet	83	125	180
Buck Rogers Helmet	200	300	400
Buck Rogers Interplanetary Game	83	125	165
Buck Rogers Knife	83	125	165
Buck Rogers Lead Figures, solid, includes Cocomalt, Buck, Wilma, Killer Kane, price for each	30	60	120
Buck Rogers Lead Figures, hollow lead, Buck, Wilma, Huer, Robot, Kane, Ardala, price for each	200	300	400
Buck Rogers Lite Blaster Flashlight	30	60	100
Buck Rogers Morton Salt Punch-O-Bag, 1930s	42	63	85
Buck Rogers Morton Salt Spaceship, came in envelope	83	125	165
Buck Rogers Movie Projector	110	200	400

	C6	C8	C10
Buck Rogers Pendant	42	63	100
Buck Rogers Pinback Button, "Buck Rogers in the 25th Century," c. 1935	42	63	100
Buck Rogers Printing Set, twelve rubber stamps	48	72	150
Buck Rogers Repeller Ray Ring, seal ring	800	1550	3500
Buck Rogers Ring of Saturn, glows in the dark, w/red stone	250	375	575
Buck Rogers Ring of Saturn Instruction Sheet	63	125	250
Buck Rogers Solar Scouts Badge, all brass color	55	83	110
Buck Rogers Solar Scouts Spaceship Commander Badge, 1936 Cream of Wheat premium	55	83	110
Buck Rogers Solar Scouts Sweater Emblem	1000	2000	4000
Buck Rogers Space Ranger Kit, Sylvania	70	125	250
Buck Rogers Super Dreadnaught, balsa wood	310	625	1250
Buck Rogers Telescope	70	105	140
Buck Rogers Uniform	400	800	1600
Buffalo Bill Bamby Bread Horseshoe Badge, late 1930s	12	18	30
Buffalo Bill Jr. Brass Ring, Buffalo in relief on top, TV premium	30	50	90
Buster Brown Gang (Smilin' Ed) Ring	50	90	165
Buster Brown Gang Tab Pins, assorted, price for each	10	15	25
Butter-Nut Bread Premium, "Sail-Me" glider, c. 1930, 4-1/2" wingspan	6	10	25
Capt. Tim Ivory Club Pin, Ivory Soap, c. 1936	9	13	25
Captain America Sentinel of Liberty Badge	190	375	750
Captain Franks Air Hawks Ring	70	150	275
Captain Franks Air Hawks Wings, Post's 40% Bran Flakes premium, c. late 1930s	35	50	75
Captain Gallant Medal, w/an animal, c. 1950, dated 1939-1945	17	26	35

Buck Rogers Space Ranger Kit, $250. Photo Courtesy Toy Collector News

	C6	C8	C10
Captain Gallant Medal, cross w/GRI, 1950s	17	26	35
Captain Hawk Sky Patrol Propeller Badge, c. late 1930s	15	30	65
Captain Marvel Club Button, five styles	35	70	140
Captain Marvel's Magic Whistle, full-color picture of Captain Marvel on both sides, American Seed Co. ad on the inside, c. 1943, American Seed Co.	27	41	55
Captain Midnight 1941 Manual for Decoder	60	110	225
Captain Midnight 1942 Manual for Decoder	85	160	330
Captain Midnight 1945 Manual for Code-O-Graph	65	90	140
Captain Midnight 1946 Manual for Code-O-Graph	65	90	140
Captain Midnight 1947 Manual for Code-O-Graph	55	65	110
Captain Midnight 1948 Manual for Code-O-Graph	55	65	110
Captain Midnight 1949 Manual for Code-O-Graph	75	110	220
Captain Midnight 1956 Manual for Decoder Badge	125	250	500
Captain Midnight 1957 Manual for Silver Dart Decoder	110	220	335
Captain Midnight 3-Way Mystic Dog Whistle, 1942	25	50	100
Captain Midnight Aerial Torpedo Bomber, 1941	80	100	150
Captain Midnight American Flag Loyalty Badge, 1940	75	150	300
Captain Midnight Code-O-Graph, round, w/mirror, 1948	55	110	225
Captain Midnight Code-O-Graph, Key-O-Matic, w/key, 1949	110	135	275
Captain Midnight Code-O-Graph, works as a whistle, 1947	50	100	200
Captain Midnight Code-O-Graph Badge, w/photo of Captain Midnight, 1942	75	150	300
Captain Midnight Code-O-Graph Decoder Pin, eagle on top, 1941	60	120	225
Captain Midnight Code-O-Graph Magnifier, 1945	85	135	175

	C6	C8	C10
Captain Midnight Code-O-Graph Mirrormatic, 1946	125	175	250
Captain Midnight Detect-O-Scope, 1941	55	85	150
Captain Midnight Flight Commander Commission, 1956	35	50	100
Captain Midnight Flight Commander Flying Cross, 1942	50	100	200
Captain Midnight Flight Commander Ring, 1941	175	250	500
Captain Midnight Flight Commander Signet Ring, 1957	550	1050	2250
Captain Midnight Flight Patrol Wings Badge, 1942	48	72	95
Captain Midnight Flight Patrol Wings Badge	48	72	95
Captain Midnight Jumping Bean Target, 1939	75	150	300
Captain Midnight Magic Blackout Lite-Ups, 1942	125	250	500
Captain Midnight Marine Corps Ring, 1942	190	275	550
Captain Midnight Medal, brass, pictures of cast, secret word, spinner, 1940	15	23	30
Captain Midnight MJC-10 Plane Detector, distance finder, 1942	300	600	1200
Captain Midnight Mystic Eye Detector Ring, 1942	135	190	275
Captain Midnight Mystic Sun God Ring, 1946	1200	2250	4400
Captain Midnight Printing Ring, 1948	80	160	350
Captain Midnight Secret Squadron Decoder Badge, gold, 1956	110	165	275
Captain Midnight Secret Squadron Decoder Badge, silver, 1957	85	110	275
Captain Midnight Secret Squadron Insignia Transfer, 1949	20	30	40
Captain Midnight Service Ribbon Pin, 1944	60	115	225
Captain Midnight Spy Scope, 1947	53	80	105
Captain Midnight Surprise Package, 1942	27	41	55
Captain Midnight Trick and Riddle Book, Skelly Oil premium, sixty-four pages, 1939	15	25	50

	C6	C8	C10
Captain Midnight Weather Wings, predicts weather, 1940	42	63	85
Captain Midnight Whirlwind Whistling Ring, 1941	140	280	575
Captain Video Flying Saucer Ring	400	800	1650
Captain Video Rite-O-Lite	50	100	200
Captain Video Rocket Launcher and Ships, 1950s	110	165	220
Captain Video Secret Seal Ring, 1950s	150	325	650
Captain Video Space Fleet Ray Gun, TV premium, Powerhouse, 1952	138	210	275
Captain Video X-9 Rocket Balloon, 1950s	30	45	60
Chandu Boxed Set of Tricks	400	575	800
Chandu the Magician Galloping Coin Trick, 1930s	30	45	60
Chandu the Magician Hindu Cones, 1930s	30	45	60
Charlie McCarthy Puppet Doll, cardboard, Chase & Sanborn mailer, 21" high	25	50	100
Charlie McCarthy Radio Party Game, giveaway by Standard Brands, twenty-one cardboard figures, 1938	25	50	100
Cinnamon Bear Silver Star, annual Christmas show, c. 1940s	35	50	100
Cisco Kid and Pancho Face Masks, price for each, 1953	25	38	50
Cisco Kid Badge, western hat on chain, 1950s	17	26	35
Cisco Kid Cardboard Gun, Harvest Bread giveaway, clicker sounds when handle squeezed, 7" long	20	50	100
Cisco Kid Picture Ring, 1950s	40	75	150
Cisco Kid Secret Compartment Ring	225	450	900
Cisco Kid Triple S Club Kit	25	38	50
Coco Wheats Radio Club Badge, shape of microphone	22	33	45
David Harding Counterspy, Junior Agent Badge	37	56	75
Davy Crockett Goldplated Ring	12	15	25
Dick Tracy Air Detective Ring	130	375	750
Dick Tracy Badge, "Detective Club," secret money pouch in rear	38	75	150
Dick Tracy Badge, "Captain"	100	175	375

	C6	C8	C10
Dick Tracy Badge, "Crime Stoppers"	12	18	25
Dick Tracy Badge, "Detective," picture of Tracy and Junior	17	25	50
Dick Tracy Badge, "Inspector General"	200	410	825
Dick Tracy Badge, "Lieutenant"	50	100	200
Dick Tracy Badge, "A Republic Pictures"	50	100	200
Dick Tracy Badge, "Sergeant"	40	80	160
Dick Tracy Decoder, red, 1948	22	33	45
Dick Tracy Decoder, green, 1948	22	33	45
Dick Tracy Glider Airplane, 1938	40	75	175
Dick Tracy Portrait Ring, enameled	60	200	325
Dick Tracy Secret Compartment Ring	20	40	75
Dick Tracy Secret Service, second year member pin	50	100	200

Dick Tracy Badge, "Crime Stoppers," $25. Photo courtesy Jim Harmon

Dick Tracy Badges, top row, left to right: Lieutenant, $200; "Captain," $375; bottom row, left to right: "Sergeant," $160; "Inspector General," $825. Photo courtesy Jim Harmon

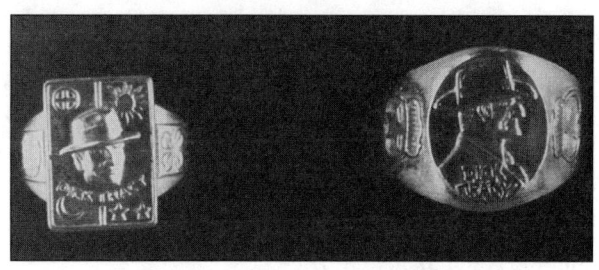

Left to Right: Dick Tracy Secret Compartment Ring, $35; Dick Tracy Portrait Ring, $325

	C6	C8	C10
Dick Tracy Secret Service Patrol Member Pinback, early 1940s	50	100	200
Dick Tracy's Secret Detective Methods & Magic Tricks, 1939 Quaker Oats, sixty-eight pages	30	60	120
Dionne Quints "All Aboard for Shut-Eye Town" Paper Dolls, Palmolive Soap	17	26	35
Don Winslow Decoder Torpedo	875	1750	3500
Don Winslow Honor Badge	75	125	250
Don Winslow Magic Slate Secret Code Book	35	75	150
Don Winslow Ring	350	700	1400
Don Winslow USN Secret Code Book, Oxydol giveaway, sixteen-pages, 1935, 7-3/4" x 4"	40	75	150
Donald Duck Playboard, comics giveaway, 1946, 9" high	50	100	200
Donald Duck Punch-out Figure, Donald Duck bread, c. late 1940s	50	100	200
Elsie the Cow, set of four figural buttons on color illustrated card, 1949	11	16	35
Fighting Devil Dogs Ring, w/bulldog head on top, Republic Pictures serial ring, 1938	110	220	425
Flash Gordon Ring, Post Toasties Corn Flakes, 1949	30	45	65
Fort Apache (Rin Tin Tin) Plastic Ring, TV premium, 1950s	15	25	35
Frank Buck Explorer's Sun Watch, post-WWII, offered by Jack Armstrong	53	80	105
Frank Buck Leopard Ring	850	1700	3500
G.E. Punch-out Circus, sixty-five pieces	65	98	130
G.E. Rodeo Punch-out, sixty-five pieces	65	98	130

	C6	C8	C10
Gabby Hayes Antique Cars, price for set, 1950s	40	80	160
Gabby Hayes Quaker Cannon Ring, 1950s	75	175	350
Gabby Hayes Western Gun Collection, six weapons, six pistols, six rifles, solid non-working, 1950s	37	56	75
Gabby Scoops Junior Press Club Card, Crackajack Comics, 1945	9	13	25
Gabby Scoops Press Card, Crackajack Comics, 1940-41	9	13	25
Gangbusters Pin	25	38	50
G-Man Badge	10	15	20
G-Man Official Signet Ring, metal, radio program premium, 1933-35	35	75	150
Goofy Playboard, comics giveaway, 1946, 9" high	17	25	35
Green Hornet Secret Compartment Ring, Hornet seal, glows in dark	450	900	1900
Gun, cardboard, giveaway from Theatorium in Lykens, Penn., Pat'd Dec. 1914 by Lexington, KY	5	10	15
H.C.B. Club Kit, contains badge, etc., early Cream of Wheat	22	33	45
Hop Harrigan Para-Plane, from Grape Nut Flakes plus two code signal blinders, cardboard plane, small parachute w/water container in tail of plane	250	490	975
Hop Harrigan Sun Dial Ring, unmarked	30	45	75
Hopalong Cassidy Bar 20 Compass Ring	65	140	275
Hopalong Cassidy Face Ring	50	100	185
Hopalong Cassidy Tin Badge, Post Raisin Bran giveaway, c. 1950s	17	26	35
Howdy Doody, Princess WinterSpring SummerFall, cardboard figure, 14"	17	26	35
Howdy Doody, flexible cardboard figure, Wonder Bread, 8"	32	48	65
Howdy Doody Climber, cardboard, w/string, Welch's Premium, 1950s	37	56	75
Howdy Doody Face Flashlight Ring, 1950s	60	125	250
Howdy Doody Flicker Key chain, three-dimensional picture of Howdy Doody flicks to Poll Parrot (Poll Parrot Shoes), 1950s	15	30	60

	C6	C8	C10
Howdy Doody Flicker Ring, flicks from Howdy to Poll Parrot, Poll Parrot premium	15	30	65
Howdy Doody Princess Dancing Puppet, moveable joints, Snickers premium, 1950s, 13"	17	26	35
Howdy Doody Puppet, cardboard, Mars Candy, 1950s, 15" high	37	56	75
I Am A Spy Smasher Button, Fawcett Comics, 1940	25	38	100
Indian Chief Tin Badge, Post Raisin Bran, c. 1950s	4	7	9
Indian Gum Chief's Head Ring, Goudey Gum card premium, silver, 1930s	10	15	20
Jack Armstrong, Secret Norden Bomb Sight, w/three bombs, paper target ships, c. WWII	150	300	650
Jack Armstrong 3-D Viewer, filmstrip	63	125	250
Jack Armstrong Big 10 Football Game	45	68	90
Jack Armstrong Crocodile Ring, glows in the dark, green stone	200	425	850
Jack Armstrong Explorer's Telescope	17	25	50
Jack Armstrong Flashlight	15	30	60
Jack Armstrong Hike-O-Meter	25	50	100
Jack Armstrong Magic Answer Box	37	75	150
Jack Armstrong Paper Airplane Models, many different, price per each	17	25	35
Jack Armstrong Paper Airplane Models, many different, reprints, price per each	5	8	10
Jack Armstrong Ped-O-Meter, blue or silver models	25	50	100
Jack Armstrong Secret Egyptian Coder Siren Ring, Wheaties, late 1930s	65	100	150
Jack Armstrong Secret Whistle Code Card for Secret Egyptian Coder Siren Ring	15	20	45
Jeff Paper Mask, Shell Oil, 1933	10	15	20
Jimmie Allen Colonial Gasoline Flying Cadet Wings, bronze, late 1930s	17	26	35
Jimmie Allen High-Speed Gasoline Flying Cadet Wings, bronze, late 1930s	20	30	40

	C6	C8	C10
Jimmie Allen Richfield Hi-Octane Flying Cadet Wings, c. 1930s	20	30	40
Jimmie Allen Richfield Hi-Octane Pilot's Identification Bracelet, metal, late 1930s	21	32	42
Jimmie Allen Skelly Oil Die-cut Airplane Cadet Wings, late 1930s	15	23	30
Jimmie Allen Skelly Oil Flying Cadet Wings, bronze, late 1930s	15	23	30
Joe E. Brown Pin	10	15	20
Junior G-Men Membership Kit, c. mid-1930s	50	100	200
Junior G-Men of America, gold-plated tin badge, late 1930s	22	33	45
Junior Texas Ranger Badge, 1936	17	26	35
Kellogg's Frogmen, add baking soda and they swim underwater, 1950s	10	15	35
Kellogg's Krumbles Around-the-World Paper Dolls, each cutout from box contains boy and girl; includes Italy, Mexico, France and Czechoslovakia, price for each	4	7	9
Kellogg's Nautilus Nuclear Submarine, 1950s	20	40	75
Kellogg's Pep Airplane Carrier, cut-out sheet w/airplane carrier and five planes, 3/4" wingspan, carrier 6-1/2" x 10"	37	56	75
Kellogg's Pep Warplanes, cardboard, price for each, c. 1944	7	11	20
Kellogg's Pep Warplanes, balsa, w/Superman ad on envelope, c. 1945	20	30	45
Little Orphan Annie Necklace, metal enamel figure of Annie on metal chain, c. 1936	63	125	250
Little Orphan Annie Pinback Button, Little Orphan Annie, Member Funny Frosty's Club, mid-1930s	21	32	42
Lone Ranger, brass star badge, A Republic Serial	88	175	350
Lone Ranger Atom Bomb Ring	75	125	175
Lone Ranger Blackout Kit, Kix cereal, glow-in-the-dark material (two pieces), glow-in-the-dark pledge to flag, glow-in-the-dark Lone Ranger Volunteers armband, includes instructions, 1942	52	90	125

	C6	C8	C10
Lone Ranger Bond Bread Safety Club Badge, 1938	22	40	50
Lone Ranger Chief Scout Badge, Silvercup Bread, early 1940s	75	112	150
Lone Ranger Clicker Pistol, black, movie giveaway, Lone Ranger on one side and ruby on other, non-moveable silver cylinder, 1939	83	125	200
Lone Ranger Deputy Shield, brass, w/secret compartment	40	60	100
Lone Ranger Flashlight Ring	42	63	95
Lone Ranger Frontier Town, full set	1000	2000	4000
Lone Ranger Glow-in-the-Dark Belt, 1941	85	140	175
Lone Ranger Hi-Yo Silver Pin, 1938	15	30	60
Lone Ranger Kix Air Base, w/cereal box cut-outs, plus map, precursor of Frontier Town	125	250	500
Lone Ranger Lucky Piece, advertises seventeenth anniversary, 1933-50	50	100	200
Lone Ranger Mask, back of black mask promotes a personal appearance by "The Long Ranger and Silver!," one of the last radio premiums, c. 1953 or 1954	20	35	75
Lone Ranger Movie Film Ring, Cheerios, late 1949-50	80	120	175
Lone Ranger Pedometer, Cheerios, 1948	15	23	30
Lone Ranger Rubber Band Gun, cardboard, 1938 Morton Salt giveaway, w/six different targets	100	225	450
Lone Ranger Safety Scout Badge, Silvercup Bread, 1935	22	33	65
Lone Ranger Secret Compartment Ring, w/picture of Lone Ranger and Silver	135	125	175

Lone Ranger Movie Film Ring, $175. Photo courtesy Jim Harmon

	C6	C8	C10
Lone Ranger Silver Bullet, secret compartment compass	35	50	100
Lone Ranger Silver Saddle Film Ring, Cheerios, late 1940s	80	115	160
Lone Ranger Silvercup Bread Safety Patrol, metal, silver and blue	25	40	75
Lone Ranger Six-Shooter Ring, gun ring w/plastic and metal gun attached to top, turn wheel and flint sparks	135	190	275
Lone Ranger Victory Corps Badge, Kix Cereal, 1942	32	48	65
Lone Ranger Weather Ring, color square stone on top w/litmus paper, no markings to identify as Lone Ranger	40	60	80
Magic Show Kit, General Mills, 1946	14	21	35
Magician's Book of Cigarette Tricks, Camel Cigarettes, 1933	9	13	30
Major Bowes Home Microphone	30	50	100
Maltex Health Club Pinback Button	4	7	9
Melvin Purvis Junior G-Man Corps Badge, late 1930s	30	40	85
Melvin Purvis Junior G-Man Corps Roving Operative Badge, late 1930s	30	40	85
Melvin Purvis Law and Order Patrol Lieutenant's Secret Operator Badge, mid-1930s	40	60	85
Melvin Purvis Law and Order Patrol Secret Operator Badge, late 1930s	40	60	80
Melvin Purvis Law and Order Ring	55	110	225
Melvin Purvis Secret Operator, Girl's Division	35	50	100
Mickey and Donald's Race to Treasure Island, Standard Oil giveaway, 1939, 12" x 25"	100	150	225
Mickey and Donald's Race to Treasure Island, map of U.S. in full color, Calco Gasoline giveaway, w/stamps, 1939, 20" x 27"	350	500	700
Mickey Mouse Club Pinback Button, "Copyright 1928-30 by W.E. Disney," 1-1/4"	60	185	125
Mickey Mouse Globe Trotters Map, NBC Bread, 1937, 28" x 20"	355	525	715
Mickey Mouse Globe Trotters Map, NBC Bread, w/all pictures pasted on, 28" x 22"	355	525	715

	C6	C8	C10
Mickey Mouse Globe Trotters Map, Pevely Milk premium, 1930s	355	525	715
Mickey Mouse Official Money, Mickey Mouse Cones dollar bills, one dollar denomination, each, 1930s	12	18	25
Mickey Mouse Playboard, comics giveaway, 1946, 9" high	27	41	55
Morton Salt "Bat-O-Ball," features The Shadow (cartoon), 1939	62	93	125
Myrt and Marge Recordings, platic, 1930s, 4"	20	30	40
My-T-Fine Grocery Store, folds into a full-color grocery store w/period products on the shelves, shoppers and workers, dated 1930, 8" x 3"	40	75	150
Nabisco Finger Puppet Rings, Slim Chants, horse Humbolt, gun, Prairie Mary, Tagalong Boswell, Cold Deck Charlie, Sam Spiel, price for each	2	3	5
Nabisco Santa Fe Twin Unit Diesel Train, includes engine, train, tracks, grounds, background, 1956	12	18	25
Nabisco Shredded Wheat Nabisco Flying Circus, designed by Wallace Rigby, series of twenty-four, price for each, 1948, 4" x 7" cards	5	8	10
Nabisco Sound-Jet Glider	15	18	25
Nabisco Trailblazers of America cards, six cards make up horse-drawn van and open van, 1956	5	8	10
Nebbs, The—Detroit Times series No. 27544, (comic strip)	7	11	15
New York World's Fair Children's World G-Man Badge, giveaway, three-color brass badge	30	40	60
Newsboy Brand Soups and Vegetables Official Booster Badge, late 1930s	4	7	9
Pep Pins, Popeye and Olive Oyl, price for each	7	11	15
Pep Pins, Superman	25	35	50
Pep Pins, The Phantom	10	15	25
Pep Pins, Dick Tracy	15	22	30
Pep Pins, Flash Gordon	15	22	30
Pep Pins, Little Orphan Annie	7	11	15
Pep Pins, Felix the Cat	5	8	10

	C6	C8	C10
Pep Pins, Others; includes Smitty, Harold Teen, Skeezix, Corky, Pop Jenks, Goofy, Spud, Andy Gump, Gravel Gertie, Punjab, Hans, Kayo, Smilin' Jack, Dagwood, B.O. Plenty, Mr. Bailey, Shadow, Moon Mullins, Flattop, Rip Winkle, Uncle Willie, Emma, Inspector, Chief Brandon, Vitamin Flintheart, Sandy, Uncle Bim, Sundown, Lillums, Tilda, Uncle Walt, Perry Winkle, Judy, Min Gump, Wilmer, Smoky Stover, Daisy, Ma Winkle, Tess Trueheart, Herbie, Mamie, Breezie, Pat Patton, Maggie, Barney Google, Fat Stuff, Chief Brandon, Toots, Nine, etc., average price for each	7	11	20
Pep Rings, Jack Kramer, Dennis O'Keefe, Burt Lancaster, Sitting Bull, Pocahontas, Pan American Clipper, Douglas F-3D Sky Knight, Republic XF91 Thundercepter, price for each	10	15	20
Pepsodent's Moving Picture Machine, shows Mickey Mouse, Donald Duck, Snow White and Seven Dwarfs, in color	350	500	750
Pillsbury-Farina Complete Tel-A-Phone Set, two holders, mouthpieces, ear phones and fifty feet of line, 1938	30	40	75
Pinocchio Playboard, Disney Comics subscription giveaway, 1946	30	40	60
Popeye the Sailor Man Button, theatre giveaway, copyright 1935, 3/4"	20	25	35
Popsicle Movie Star Coins, aluminum coins, includes Irene Dunne, Clark Gable, Marion Davies, Fredric March, Marie Dressler, Gary Cooper, c. 1930s	5	8	15
Porcelain Enamel & Mfg. Co. West Point Cadet, on card w/Pemco ad on back, 6" figure, 3" x 6" card	2	3	5
Post Cereal Rings, Perry Winkle, Winnie Winkle, Harold Teen, Skeezix, Lillums, Herbie and Smoky Stover, 1948	17	26	35
Post Cereal Rings, Dick Tracy, 1948	20	30	40
Post Grape Nuts Flakes Playing-Filling Station, c. 1950s	5	8	10

	C6	C8	C10
Post Grape Nuts Tin Rings, Little King, Phantom, Skeezix, Lillums, Harold Teen	20	30	40
Post Raisin Bran Sheriff Badge	10	15	20
Post Toasties Corn Flakes Comic Rings, Fritz, hans, Tillie the Toiler, Toots and Casper, 1949	17	26	35
Post Toasties Walt Disney Cut-out Figures on Box, Mickey the Traffic Cop, two types of Pinocchio, price for each, 1939	27	41	60
Post's Cereal Junior Detective Club Sergeant Badge, late 1930s	10	15	35
Post's Explorer Ring, plastic dome, includes compass, sun watch, sunset predictor and star finder, 1947	30	40	60
Radio Orphan Annie 1934 Manual	62	93	125
Radio Orphan Annie 1935 Decoder Manual	62	93	125
Radio Orphan Annie 1935 Decoder Pin	30	40	60

	C6	C8	C10
Radio Orphan Annie 1936 Decoder Badge	30	40	60
Radio Orphan Annie 1936 Decoder Manual	62	93	125
Radio Orphan Annie 1937 Decoder Badge	30	50	110
Radio Orphan Annie 1937 Decoder Manual	62	93	125
Radio Orphan Annie 1938 Decoder Badge	40	70	130
Radio Orphan Annie 1938 Decoder Manual	62	93	125
Radio Orphan Annie 1939 Decoder Badge	40	70	130
Radio Orphan Annie 1939 Decoder Manual	62	93	125
Radio Orphan Annie 1940 Decoder Badge	40	70	130
Radio Orphan Annie 1940 Decoder Manual	83	125	165
Radio Orphan Annie 1942 Decoder Manual, w/cardboard decoder	200	350	425

Front to Back: Radio Orphan Annie Decoder Manual, 1937, $125; Decoder Badge, 1937, $110. Photo courtesy Jim Harmon

Radio Orphan Annie Decoder Manual, 1938, $125. Photo courtesy Jim Harmon

*Radio Orphan Annie 1939 Decoder Badge, $130.
Photo courtesy Jim Harmon*

	C6	C8	C10
Radio Orphan Annie 3-Way Dog Whistle, 1940	25	50	100
Radio Orphan Annie Altascope Ring, fewer than fifteen known to exist	n/a	n/a	24,000
Radio Orphan Annie Annie and Joe Corntassel Button, 1931	150	300	600
Radio Orphan Annie Associated Membership Pin, 1934	10	25	50
Radio Orphan Annie Bandanna, 1934	20	40	80
Radio Orphan Annie Birthstone Ring, 1935	125	225	550
Radio Orphan Annie Capt. Sparks Aviation Trainer	250	375	500
Radio Orphan Annie Circus Cut-Outs, 1935	150	250	500
Radio Orphan Annie Code Captain Belt and Buckle, 1940	75	150	300
Radio Orphan Annie Code Captain Pin, 1939	25	50	100
Radio Orphan Annie Foreign Coins, 1937	25	38	50
Radio Orphan Annie Goofy Circus, 1939	188	375	750
Radio Orphan Annie Identification Bracelet, 1935	25	50	100
Radio Orphan Annie Identification Bracelet, 1934	25	50	100

	C6	C8	C10
Radio Orphan Annie Identification Tag, 1939	20	35	75
Radio Orphan Annie Magic Transfer Picture, 1937	20	40	85
Radio Orphan Annie Magic Transfer Pictures, 1935	20	40	85
Radio Orphan Annie Mask, 1933	60	80	125
Radio Orphan Annie Mystic Eye Ring, 1939	150	275	550
Radio Orphan Annie Package, includes Whirl-O-Matic Decoder, Whistle Badge, booklet, and order blanks, 1942	125	300	600
Radio Orphan Annie Pin, 1937	17	26	50
Radio Orphan Annie Portrait Ring, ring has head of Annie embossed on top, 1934	50	75	100
Radio Orphan Annie Punch-outs	120	180	240
Radio Orphan Annie Ring, 1934	50	75	100
Radio Orphan Annie Ring, 1935	50	75	100
Radio Orphan Annie Roller Skates, 1938	50	100	200
Radio Orphan Annie School Pin, 1939	20	40	75
Radio Orphan Annie Secret Egyptian Compass and Sundial, 1938	50	75	100
Radio Orphan Annie Secret Guard Clicker, 1942	25	50	100
Radio Orphan Annie Secret Society Silver Star Ring, 1936	100	200	400
Radio Orphan Annie Shake-up Game, 1931	25	50	100
Radio Orphan Annie Signet Ring, 1937	65	130	275
Radio Orphan Annie Silver Star Pin, 1935	48	72	95
Radio Orphan Annie Silver Star Pin, 1934	48	72	95
Radio Orphan Annie Silver Star Ring, 1937	100	200	400
Radio Orphan Annie Silver Star Ring, 1938	100	200	400
Radio Orphan Annie Treasure Hunt Game, 1933	75	150	300
Radio Orphan Annie Treasure Hunt Game, 1935	75	150	300

Ad for Roy Rogers Branding Iron Ring on Quaker Oats Box, price for ring $275. Photo courtesy Jim Harmon

Roy Rogers Deputy Badge, $20. Photo courtesy Jim Harmon

	C6	C8	C10
Roy Rogers Branding Iron Ring	80	130	275
Roy Rogers Deputy Badge	10	15	20
Roy Rogers Microscope Ring, Quaker Oats, 1947	65	95	150
Roy Rogers Paint Set, 1950s	12	18	25
Roy Rogers Signal Badge, w/mirror, secret compartment and whistle	40	88	175
Roy Rogers Silver Hat Ring	200	425	850
Roy Rogers Trigger's Lucky Horseshoe, full size, black rubber	12	18	35
Roy Rogers Tuck-A-Way Gun	15	20	40
Scoop Ward News of Youth Official Reporter Badge, Ward's Soft Bun Bread giveaway, late 1930s	10	15	20
Secret Three Badge, w/manual of secret codes	10	15	20
Sgt. Preston Distance Finder	45	65	95
Sgt. Preston Firefighting Set	45	65	95
Sgt. Preston Flashlight, signals has two filters	25	50	100
Sgt. Preston Klondike Land Pouch	25	38	50
Sgt. Preston Klondike Movie Film Viewer	60	120	250
Sgt. Preston Pedometer	15	30	65
Sgt. Preston Police Whistle, nylon cord, brass, 1950	27	41	55
Sgt. Preston Skinning Knife	125	250	300
Sgt. Preston Totem Pole Set	55	100	200
Sgt. Preston Trail Kit, the most complex of all premiums, rare	320	475	700

	C6	C8	C10
Range Rider & Dick West Button, Peter Pan bread, 1950s	37	56	75
Red Ryder Lucky Coin	7	11	15
Renfrew of Mounted Pinback	10	15	20
Rin Tin Tin "Ball-in-the-Hole" Games, sealed coin-size games of Rinty, Rip Masters, Fort Apache, etc., price for each	9	13	18
Rin Tin Tin Ring, plastic, 1950s	20	30	40
Rin Tin Tin Set of Plastic Dinosaurs, radio-TV, 1954	62	93	125
Rin Tin Tin Wonderscope, Telescope-Microscope-Compass w/"Rin Tin Tin" on face, radio-TV, 1954	30	45	100
Rip Masters (Rin Tin Tin) Plastic Rings, 1950s	25	35	45
Rocky Lane's Explorer's Sun Watch, Carnation Milk, 1951	20	40	75

	C6	C8	C10
Sgt. Preston Yukon Village	300	450	600
Shadow "Carey Salt" Ring, same as J. Armstrong Crocodile ring w/black stone, (this ring has been counterfeited; original is smoothly circular w/clean-cut design, requires identifying papers for C10 price)	300	550	1150
Shadow Ring, Glow in Dark, "blue coal" jewel on white ring	500	740	975
Shield G-Man Club Badge, Pep Comics premium, lithographed celluloid pinback, 1942	35	75	125
Skippy Compass, 1930s?	10	15	20
Skippy S.S.S.S. Captain, celluloid pinback button, 1930s	12	18	25
Sky Birds Propeller Ring, brass and silver, Goudey Gum premium, 1930s	12	18	25
Sky King Aztec Indian Ring	250	500	1000
Sky King Detecto Microscope	53	78	105
Sky King Detecto Writer	70	105	140
Sky King Electronic Television Ring	110	175	225
Sky King Magni-Glo Ring	110	175	225
Sky King Mystery Picture Ring	60	85	120
Sky King Navajo Indian Ring	135	200	275
Sky King Signal Scope	70	105	140
Sky King Small Plastic Statues, includes Sky King, Penny, Sky King's horse, Sky King's plane, The Songbird, Nabisco giveaways in Wheat Honey and Rice Honey, price for each, 1950s	15	22	30
Sky King Stamp Kit	48	72	95
Sky King Teleblinker Ring	135	200	275
Snow White Game, Tek Toothbrush	35	75	150
Space Patrol Binoculars, c. 1950s	120	175	225
Space Patrol Diplomatic Pouch, contains money, stamps, etc.	138	210	275
Space Patrol Goggles	53	78	105
Space Patrol Jet Glow Code Belt, 1951	138	210	275
Space Patrol Ring, w/secret powder compartment, c. early 1950s	145	225	300
Space Patrol Smoke Gun, 1950s	150	225	300
Space Patrol Space Helmet, c. 1950s	180	270	360

	C6	C8	C10
Space Patrol Space Ship, c. 1950s	88	132	175
Space Patrol Space-O-Phone, 1952	98	150	195
Speed Gibson's Flying Police Badge, Dreikorn's Bread	12	18	25
Staight Arrow Magic Cave Ring, w/original art, 1949	110	150	300
Staight Arrow Puppets and Props, Nabisco radio premium, 1949	30	45	60
Staight Arrow Target Game, lithographed tin target board, National Biscuit Company, copyright on the edge, 10" x 14"	37	56	75
Staight Arrow Tom-Tom, c. early 1950s	25	50	75
Staight Arrow Wrist Bracelet, w/secret compartment, c. early 1950s	35	75	150
Straight Arrow Face Ring, c. early 1950s	60	90	125
Sunbrite "Junior Nurse Corps" Brass Badge	4	7	9
Sunbrite "Junior Nurse Corps" Pinback Button, pictures of Dorothy Hart	3	5	7
Superman Crusader Ring	140	195	275
Superman Kellogg's Gy Rocket	50	100	200
Superman Kellogg's Silver Jet Airplane Ring, plane flies off	80	140	260
Superman Kellogg's Walkie-Talkie	37	56	75
Superman of America Button, pinback button, 1939 version, 1-3/8"	20	40	75
Superman Pin, "Read Superman Action Comics Magazine," 1940s	20	35	75
Superman Planes from Pep Cereal, set of eight, 1948	30	45	60
Superman Premium Club Set, certificate, button and decoder	200	400	800
Superman Tim Club Ring	3750	7500	15,000
Superman's Secret Code, c. 1939	24	36	63
Tarzan Gift Statues, Foulds, Tarzan, Jane, Kala, etc., price per set, 1930s	300	600	1100
Tarzan Jungle Map and Treasure Hunt Weston Biscuit, 1933	250	300	600
Tennessee Jed Lariat	37	56	75
Tennessee Jed Look Around Ring, 1940s	130	275	550

Mail-in form for Tarzan Gift Statues, price for set $1,100

	C6	C8	C10
Tennessee Jed Paper Gun, c. 1940s	21	32	42
Terry and The Pirates Glow-in-the Dark Ring, crocodiles on sides	40	60	80
Terry and The Pirates Gold Detector Ring	70	95	150
Texas Longhorn Tin Badge, Post Raisin Bran, c. 1950s	4	7	9
The Liberty Gun For Young America - McGrath's Big Store, w/photos of Charlie Chaplin, 7" cardboard	20	30	40
Tom Corbett Decoder, cardboard, 1950s	35	52	70
Tom Corbett Rings, Kellogg's twelve different rings, including-Space Cruiser, Rocket Scout, Space Academy, Space Suit, Space Helmet, Corbett-Space Cadet, Cadet Dress Uniform, Girl's Space Uniform, Parallo-Ray Gun, Strate-Telescope, Sound Ray Gun, price for each, 1950-55	20	30	40
Tom Corbett Space Cadet Badge, early 1950s	35	75	150
Tom Corbett Space Cadet Belt Buckle Decoder, early 1950s	75	150	300
Tom Mix 1941 Manual	50	80	160
Tom Mix 1944 Manual	50	80	140
Tom Mix 1946 Manual	40	60	115
Tom Mix Airplane and Parachute	100	150	200
Tom Mix Arm Patch, Tom Mix bar on ckeckerboard design, 1933, predominantly blue; 1947, predominantly red; 1983, predominantly black	20	35	75

	C6	C8	C10
Tom Mix Badge Ranch Boss	130	263	525
Tom Mix Bag of Marbles	20	30	40
Tom Mix Bandanna, has Tom Mix brand	50	100	200
Tom Mix Baseball	25	38	50
Tom Mix Baseball Bat	25	38	50
Tom Mix Baseball Cap	27	41	55
Tom Mix Belt Buckle with Secret Compartment, belt glows in the dark, offered only on cereal boxes after radio show ended	75	125	250
Tom Mix Blowdart Game	250	300	600
Tom Mix Branding Iron, w/Tom Mix brand	52	78	105
Tom Mix Bullet Flashlight	52	78	105
Tom Mix Bullet Telescope, w/bird-call device, 4" long	35	52	105
Tom Mix Catalog of Straight Shooter Premiums, wood gun, black and white sheet w/order form on reverse, desciptions and small pictures of premiums on the front, includes sheepskin vest, rodeo rope, leather cuffs, lucky spinner, etc., 8-1/2" x 11"	20	30	60
Tom Mix Charm Bracelet, charm steer head, gun, horseman, w/Tom Mix brand	75	150	250
Tom Mix Coloring Book, Ralston, c. 1949	20	30	40
Tom Mix Compass Magnifying Glass, silver color, (originals have "Japan" written on the back; imitations have the words "Comet-Japan" on the back), 1947	45	68	90
Tom Mix Compass Magnifying Glass, brass, 1939	50	100	200
Tom Mix Compass Magnifying Glass, plastic, glows in the dark, c. 1948	75	125	150
Tom Mix Cowboy Shirt	75	150	300
Tom Mix Cowboy Skirt	150	225	300
Tom Mix Cowboy Vest	82	125	165
Tom Mix Decoder Badge, moveable six-shooter points to symbols, 1940	110	160	275
Tom Mix Decoder Buttons Instruction Sheet, Ralston, 1946	20	30	50

	C6	C8	C10
Tom Mix Decoder Pin, "Curley Bradley"	15	30	60
Tom Mix Decoder Pins, Tony, Jane, Sheriff, Wash, price for each	20	30	50
Tom Mix Deputy Ring, chewing gum premium, 1934	2000	3500	7500
Tom Mix Glow-in-the-Dark Arrowhead, has compass and magnifying glass, 1946	75	125	150
Tom Mix Gold Ore Badge	25	50	100
Tom Mix Good Luck Spinner	27	41	55
Tom Mix Horseshoe Nail Ring, rounded point identifies original, 1933	25	50	75
Tom Mix Identification Bracelet	42	63	85
Tom Mix Initial Ring, 1935	110	175	225
Tom Mix Look-Around Ring, c. 1945	65	95	150
Tom Mix Lucky Wrist Band, Ralston premium, Tom Mix brand, metal, w/leather strap and buckle, 1936	50	100	200
Tom Mix Magnet Gun and Signal Arrowhead Bracelet, gun and arrowhead glow in the dark	50	80	165
Tom Mix Magnet Ring, 1945	60	80	160
Tom Mix Makeup Kit, two grease-paint model, plus five grease-paint model	300	450	600
Tom Mix Mask, cardboard	385	580	770
Tom Mix Mystery Picture Ring, w/"look-in" picture of Tom Mix and Tony, viewed through one side of the ring, 1939	175	275	400
Tom Mix Ore Charm, contains genuine gold ore under plastic dome, 1940	42	63	85
Tom Mix Parachute, Ralston premium, 1936	75	125	250
Tom Mix Periscope	75	125	250
Tom Mix Postal Telegraph Set, metal, blue, Ralston premium, 1938	45	75	150
Tom Mix Premium Enclosures and Correspondence, many picture postcards, letters on Straight Shooter stationery, etc.; sent out to listeners who wrote to the radio show; these and various coupons, instruction sheets, contest entries are offered by dealers and collectors	20	30	40

	C6	C8	C10
Tom Mix Ralston Straight Shooters Pocket Knife, 1940	40	80	175
Tom Mix RCA TV Set, shows photographs or comic strips, brown or reddish model	25	50	75
Tom Mix RCA TV Set, shows photographs or comic strips, gold	75	150	300
Tom Mix Secret Code Manual	25	50	100
Tom Mix Sharpshooters Medal, glows blue in the dark, copy	10	20	40
Tom Mix Sharpshooters Medal, glows green in the dark, original	83	125	165
Tom Mix Sheriff of Dobie County Siren Badge, Ralston, 1946	48	72	115
Tom Mix Signal Arrowhead, made of lucite w/magnifying glass and "whizzer" flute-type whistle, 1949	40	75	150
Tom Mix Signal Flashlight	40	75	150
Tom Mix Signature Ring, pre-WWII	140	200	275
Tom Mix Siren Ring, 1945	75	100	175
Tom Mix Six-Shooter, wooden, barrel breaks and cartridge drum spins, 1933	60	180	320
Tom Mix Six-Shooter, wooden, barrel spins, 1936	75	150	300
Tom Mix Six-Shooter, wooden, no moving parts, 1939	80	140	275
Tom Mix Spinning Rope, hemp w/wood handle, 1936	53	78	105
Tom Mix Spurs, metal, w/plastic glow-in-the-dark rowels	50	100	200
Tom Mix Square and Fair Spinner	37	56	75
Tom Mix Straight Shooters Campaign Medal, silver	42	63	85
Tom Mix Straight Shooters Campaign Medal, gold	42	63	85
Tom Mix Sundial Watch	45	75	150
Tom Mix Telegraph Set, red, uses batteries, 1940	140	210	280
Tom Mix Telephone Set	45	75	175
Tom Mix Telescope, Tom Mix brand on side	45	75	150
Tom Mix Tiger Eye Ring, Ralston, 1949	175	250	325
Tom Mix TM Brand Ring, c. 1933	100	115	160

	C6	C8	C10
Tom Mix Western Movie Viewer, shows scenes from Tom Mix films, 1935	75	125	250
Tom Mix Whistle Ring, 1945	75	100	150
Tom Mix Wrangler Badge, Ralston, 1936	40	80	175
Toonerville Trolley Cardboard Village, put out by Coca-Cola	88	132	175
Trigger Button, Post Grape Nut Flakes, 7/8"	12	18	25
Welch's Grape Juice Train, paper engine, box car, passenger car, caboose, price for each	3	5	7
Welch's Grape Juice Train, Complete set	12	18	25
Westinghouse, 1940	10	15	20
Wheaties Jogometer, 1960s	12	18	25
Wheaties Pedometer, late 1940s	10	15	20
Wild Bill Hickok Bunkhouse Set, cut-out pin-ups of Bill, Jingles, guns, ropes, etc.	15	25	50
Wild Bill Hickok Treasure Map and Guide, Kellogg's, 1952	48	72	95

Tom Mix Western Movie Viewer, $250. Photo Courtesy Jim Harmon

SCHOENHUT

The A. Schoenhut Company had a long history of toy manufacturing. Many items were produced, including animals, figures, moving pictures, Palmer Cox Brownies, children's musical instruments and dolls. This section covers some of the items in the Humpty Dumpty Circus.

The Humpty Dumpty items covered in this section span the years of 1903 to 1935. Glass-eyed animals and two-part head personnel, along with other rare examples, are priced higher than painted-eye animals and pressed-head figures produced later. Delavan items are generally priced lower than reduced-size figures.

In the past few years, the toys' popularity among toy collectors and folk art collectors has driven prices up. Particular interest in Teddy Roosevelt's Adventures in Africa series (produced from 1909 to 1911) has led the price increase.

Although this history is not all inclusive, it should help the collector identify age for some animals/figures.

1872	Produced the first toy pianos
1903	Began producing Humpty Dumpty Circus items
	Began producing glass-eyed animals, molded/two-part head personnel
1909/11	Produced Teddy Roosevelt figures
1910	Produced bisque head ring master, lady circus rider, lion tamer, lady/gent acrobats
1918	Produced painted-eyed animals, wooden-head personnel
1923	Began producing reduced-size circus
1927	Produced miniature set (donkey, elephant, clown)
1935	Company closed
1950	Nelson Delavan purchased manufacturing rights and produced several figures and animals

There are a few rules to keep in mind while collecting Schoenhut toys.

Condition determines price

Mint condition Schoenhut toys are virtually non-existent. Mint condition means the toy was never played with and demand higher prices. Boxes increase value, and Mint in Box items commands a sizable premium.

Glass-eyed animals, early figures with plaster faces, and rare animals demand high prices.

Bisque-headed figures and molded/two-part head figures generally demand a higher price than carved-face figures.

Condition on the majority of animals and figures found today is between C4 and C7.

Skillful restoration can increase value. Anyone selling an animal or figure with restored sections should indicate where restoration has occurred.

Prices in this guide have not been established for every style of animal and figure.

Because of the importance of condition and classification for the Schoenhut category of toys, the existing definitions of Schoenhut categories need to be explained.

Rating	Definition
C1	Bits and pieces of Schoenhut toys.
C2	Poor quality with no paint or with a "child's" effort to repaint, or missing a major part. Definitely needs repair.
C3	Fair with no missing major parts but with little paint; moisture/moth/animal damage and soiling. Needs repair.
C4	Good with play wear; soiled/worn clothing, damaged paint/chips, missing leather and/or other attachable parts.
C5	Very good with restored paint, clothes, and/or leather.
C6	Fine with good paint, new or worn leather and minor restorations. Could also have some soiling/wear/color loss and missing minor attached parts.
C7	Very fine with minor wear/color loss and fractional restoration.
C8	Almost perfect with no restoration but may have slight color loss.
C9	Perfect, meaning no damage or color loss of any kind. Almost new.
C10	Mint, meaning never played with and stored under ideal conditions. Factory new.

Note: Restringing is not considered restoration. If the restringing effort is not done properly, however, wood damage can occur and reduce the value of the piece. Additional information on Schoenhut figures or dolls can be obtained by joining the Schoenhut Collectors Club. For a membership application, please contact Pat Girbach, 103 West Huron Street, Ann Arbor, MI 48103.

Contributors: Jim and Patsy Carlson, 7939 Caberfare Trail, Clarkston, MI 48348-3708. The Carlson's purchased a partial Schoenhut circus in 1988 as a remembrance to a deceased parent. That remembrance has grown to include several specialized Schoenhut pieces. They are active members of the Schoenhut Collectors Club and Antique Toy Collectors of America. In addition to Schoenhut toys, they collect platform animals, American rocking horses, early squeak toys, folk art and American primitive folk art.

Circus Accessories (Regular and Reduced Size)

These items are most commonly found in "play wear" condition of C4 to C7 category. Not all accessories have been included.

	C2	C4	C6	C8
Ball, reduced	10	15	30	40
Ball	10	20	40	50
Barrel	2	4	6	10
Chair	2	4	6	10
Flexible Cage	75	175	525	675
Goblet	3	5	8	12
Hoop	10	15	25	40
Horizontal Bar	75	175	375	500
Ladder	2	4	6	10
Pedestal, tall	15	25	40	60
Pedestal, short	10	20	30	45
Table	15	25	40	65

Circus Accessories (Regular and Reduced Size) (Continued)

	C2	C4	C6	C8
Tent, 24" x 16" (small)	200	400	500	750
Tent, 24" x 36" (large)	700	1100	1400	2200
Tent, litho w/panels	2000	3000	6000	9000
Tub	10	20	35	50

Tent, C8 condition $2200. Photo courtesy Jim and Patsy Carlson

A group pf Schoenhut Humpty Dumpty Circus figures and accessories, $2000-$3000. Photo courtesy Christie's East

Left to Right: Tall pedestal, Short pedestal and Tub, all are painted wood with applied printed paper bands; all in C7 condition valued at $40-60, $30-45 and $35-50, respectively. Photo courtesy Jim and Patsy Carlson

Circus Accessories (Regular and Reduced Size) (Continued)

	C2	C4	C6	C8
Weights, 50/100/200 lbs..............	75	150	200	325
Whip, 4-1/2" shaft	10	20	30	45
Whip, 5-1/2" shaft	15	25	40	65
Wild Animal Cage Wagon	300	400	775	1200

Circus Animals: Glass-Eyed and Painted-Eyed (Regular Size)

Prices below are for the animals that are most frequently seen; not all animals have been included. Glass-eyed animals were made from 1903, when A. Schoenhut Company began to produce circus animals and performers, to about 1918. Painted-eyed animals were produced from about 1918 to 1933, when the A. Schoenhut Company closed.

	C2	C4	C6	C8
Alligator, painted eyes.................	75	125	250	385
Alligator, glass eyes	100	175	350	475
Brown Bear, glass eyes	175	325	425	600
Brown Bear, painted eyes............	75	120	250	375
Buffalo, painted eyes.................	100	200	300	450
Buffalo, glass eyes, cloth...........	100	200	325	500
Buffalo, glass eyes, curved........	200	400	750	1050
Bulldog, glass eyes, carved mane	200	350	850	1250
Bulldog, painted eyes	100	150	250	425
Burro, painted eyes....................	100	175	275	400
Camel, one hump, painted eyes...	95	120	250	375
Camel, two hump, glass eyes	200	475	950	1400

Brown Bear with glass eyes in C6 condition, $425. Photo courtesy Jim and Patsy Carlson

Circus Animals: Glass-Eyed and Painted-Eyed (Regular Size) (Continued)

	C2	C4	C6	C8
Camel, two hump, painted eyes...	95	135	275	400
Camel, one hump, glass eyes.....	100	150	300	425
Cat, glass eyes	500	1000	1600	2400
Cat, painted eyes........................	200	360	725	1100
Cow, painted eyes........................	50	125	250	385
Deer, glass eyes	200	300	575	875
Deer, painted eyes	175	325	425	600
Donkey, glass eyes	30	60	120	175
Donkey, painted eyes...................	20	30	50	75
Elephant, glass eyes....................	40	70	135	200
Elephant, glass eyes w/blanket..	125	325	450	700

Cat, glass eyes, C6 condition, $2400. Photo courtesy Jim and Patsy Carlson

Left to Right: Camel with one hump (Arabian), glass eyes and open mouth, C8 condition, $425; Camel with two humps (Bactrian), glass eyes, carved head and neck showing tool marks, C8 condition, $1400. Photo courtesy Jim and Patsy Carlson

Elephant with glass eyes, blanket and triangular-shaped headdress, the most sought-after of all elephants; C7 condition, $450-700. Photo courtesy Jim and Patsy Carlson

Gorilla with two-part head and leather ears, C7 condition, $2,300-3,000. Photo courtesy Jim and Patsy Carlson

Giraffe with glass eyes and open mouth, C6 condition, $350; Flexible Cage, C6 condition, $525. Photo courtesy Jim and Patsy Carlson

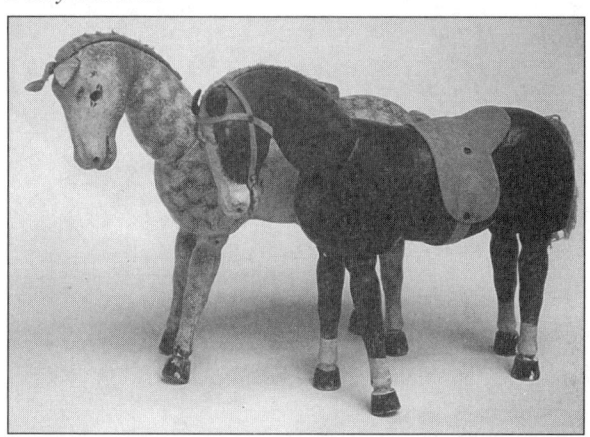

Left to Right: White horse with glass eyes, referred to as "Educated Horse," C8 condition, $275; Brown horse with glass eyes, leather saddle and bridle, C8 condition, $250. Photo courtesy Jim and Patsy Carlson

Circus Animals: Glass-Eyed and Painted-Eyed (Regular Size) (Continued)

	C2	C4	C6	C8
Elephant, painted eyes	30	50	100	150
Gazelle, glass eyes	400	1000	1600	2400
Gazelle, painted eyes	300	400	775	1200
Giraffe, glass eyes	100	175	350	500
Giraffe, painted eyes	75	120	250	350

Circus Animals: Glass-Eyed and Painted-Eyed (Regular Size) (Continued)

	C2	C4	C6	C8
Goat, painted eyes	50	150	225	300
Goat, glass eyes	75	200	275	350
Goose, painted eyes	75	150	350	475
Gorilla, molded ears	1000	1300	1600	2400
Gorilla, leather ears	1000	1700	2300	3000
Hippopotamus, glass eyes	100	275	550	800
Hippopotamus, painted eyes	75	120	250	375
Horse, brown, painted eyes	30	50	100	150

Circus Animals: Glass-Eyed and Painted-Eyed (Regular Size) (Continued)

	C2	C4	C6	C8
Horse, white, glass eyes	85	120	175	275
Horse, white, painted eyes	40	75	125	190
Horse, brown, glass eyes	75	100	160	250
Hyena, glass eyes	1400	1600	2200	3200
Hyena, painted eyes	400	500	950	1400
Kangaroo, glass eyes	400	500	2100	3000
Kangaroo, painted eyes	200	350	700	1000
Leopard, painted eyes	75	150	300	450
Leopard, glass eyes	100	275	550	825
Lion, painted eyes	95	175	375	525

Circus Animals: Glass-Eyed and Painted-Eyed (Regular Size) (Continued)

	C2	C4	C6	C8
Lion, glass eyes, carved mane	300	475	1050	1500
Lion, glass eyes, cloth mane	100	200	400	700
Monkey, black face	100	200	400	600
Monkey, white face	120	225	500	750
Ostrich, glass eyes	200	300	600	900
Ostrich, painted eyes	100	225	300	550
Pig, painted eyes	100	175	300	450
Pig, glass eyes	125	275	550	825
Polar Bear, painted eyes	250	350	575	875
Polar Bear, glass eyes	300	475	850	1275
Poodle, glass eyes, carved mane	100	225	400	675
Poodle, painted eyes	40	70	135	200
Rhinoceros, glass eyes	175	375	600	950

Left to Right: Monkey with black face, one-piece molded head, C6 condition, $400; Monkey with white face, C5 condition, $225-500. Photo courtesy Jim and Patsy Carlson

Left to Right: Lion, painted eyes, C8 condition $525; Lion, glass eyes, carved mane, C8 condition $1500. Photo courtesy Jim and Patsy Carlson

Tiger, with glass eyes, full ball-jointed neck and leather ears, C8 condition, $925. Photo courtesy Jim and Patsy Carlson

Wolf, painted eyes, C6 condition $1200. Photo courtesy Jim and Patsy Carlson

Zebra with glass eyes, closed mouth, head and neck in two sections leather strip mane and cord tail, C7 condition, $1200. Photo courtesy Jim and Patsy Carlson

Chinaman with two-part head, C6 condition, $325. Photo courtesy Jim and Patsy Carlson

Circus Animals: Glass-Eyed and Painted-Eyed (Regular Size) (Continued)

	C2	C4	C6	C8
Rhinoceros, painted eyes	125	300	400	600
Sea Lion, glass eyes	200	400	625	900
Sea Lion, painted eyes	125	225	450	700
Sheep, glass eyes	100	175	385	550
Sheep, painted eyes	75	135	275	400
Tiger, painted eyes	75	150	300	450

Clown with two-part head, Dresden "footprint" glued to front of suit and star collar, rare, C7 condition, $100-125. Photo courtesy Jim and Patsy Carlson

Circus Animals: Glass-Eyed and Painted-Eyed (Regular Size) (Continued)

	C2	C4	C6	C8
Tiger, glass eyes	100	275	650	925
Wolf, glass eyes	1000	1300	1600	2400
Wolf, painted eyes	300	400	775	1200
Zebra, glass eyes	175	425	725	1200
Zebra, painted eyes	150	325	425	600
Zebu, painted eyes	400	500	950	1400
Zebu, glass eyes	1200	1400	2100	3000

Performers Wooden/Pressed One-Part Head (Regular Size)

The manufacturing sequence for figures was plaster face two-part head/faces, bisque heads, and finally wooden/pressed one-part head. Not all figures have been included.

	C2	C4	C6	C8
Chinaman	100	200	325	450
Clown	20	65	100	125
Hobo	45	145	250	325

Performers Wooden/Pressed One-Part Head (Regular Size) (Continued)

	C2	C4	C6	C8
Lady Acrobat	65	150	275	375
Lady Rider	45	145	250	325
Lion Tamer	45	145	250	325
Negro Dude	100	200	325	450
Ring Master	65	150	275	375

Negro Dude, C6 condition $450. Photo courtesy Jim and Patsy Carlson

Left to Right: bisque-head performers—Lion Tamer, C6 condition, $250; Lady Rider, C6 condition, $250; Lady Acrobat, C6 condition, $275; Ringmaster, C6 condition, $275. Photo courtesy Jim and Patsy Carlson

Close-up of bisque-head Ringmaster. Photo courtesy Jim and Patsy Carlson

Reduced-Size Figures and Animals

Reduced-size figures and animals were first produced around 1927 by the A. Schoenhut Company to appeal to another market and as a last-ditch effort to save the company. Unfortunately, the company closed in 1933. Not all figures and animals have been included.

Animals Reduced

	C2	C4	C6	C8
Brown Bear	75	120	275	400
Buffalo	65	140	225	350
Camel, two humps	75	120	275	375
Donkey	20	30	40	50
Elephant	25	45	95	125
Giraffe	75	120	275	400
Hippopotamus	100	240	325	500
Horse, white	30	50	100	135
Horse, brown	30	50	100	135
Leopard	75	120	275	375
Lion	75	120	275	375
Ostrich	85	150	300	425
Pig	100	250	400	425
Poodle	75	120	275	400
Rhinoceros	85	150	300	425

Animals Reduced

	C4	C6	C8
Tiger	75	120	275	375
Zebra	150	325	450	600

Circus Figures, Reduced

	C2	C4	C6	C8
Clown	15	40	65	100
Hobo	55	130	280	410
Lady Rider	30	65	125	225
Negro Dude	65	140	370	500
Ring Master	30	60	120	200

Teddy Roosevelt's Adventures in Africa

These figures were produced in low volume from 1909 to 1911 and represent "rare" or "scarce" toys. Some of the animals were used in circus play toys produced with glass eyes until 1918.

Teddy Roosevelt Animals

	C2	C4	C6	C8
Alligator, glass eyes	100	175	350	475
Camel, glass eyes, one hump, closed mouth	100	150	300	425
Deer, glass eyes	200	300	575	875
Elephant, glass eyes	40	70	135	200
Gazelle, glass eyes	400	1000	1600	2400
Giraffe, glass eyes, closed mouth	175	350	475	650
Gorilla, leather ear	1000	1700	2300	3000
Hippopotamus, glass eyes	100	275	550	800
Hyena, glass eyes	1400	1600	2200	3200
Lion, glass eyes, carved mane	300	475	850	1500
Rhinoceros, glass eyes	175	375	600	950
Zebra, glass eyes, closed mouth	175	375	625	950
Zebu, glass eyes	1200	1400	2100	3000

Teddy Roosevelt Figures

	C2	C4	C6	C8
African Chief	650	900	1500	2200
African Drummer	950	1400	2400	3500
African Native	950	1400	2200	3200

Teddy Roosevelt Figures (Continued)

	C2	C4	C6	C8
Arab Chief	950	1400	1800	2700
Doctor	950	1400	1800	2700
Naturalist	950	1400	2200	3500
Photographer (Kermit)	850	1300	1700	2450
Teddy Roosevelt	750	1000	1300	2000

Miscellaneous

	C2	C4	C6	C8
Doll House, large	150	225	500	750
Doll House, medium	125	175	375	425
Doll House, small	100	150	250	375
Golfer, Man	125	175	350	425
Golfer, Girl	125	200	375	475
Milk Wagon, horses and driver	1250	2400	3000	4000
Piano, 14" x 10"	30	60	120	175
Railroad Station, large	125	175	350	475
Roly Poly, Black Clown	200	300	600	850

African Chief, C7 condition $2200. Photo courtesy Jim and Patsy Carlson

SHIPS

(See also Tin Wind-Ups, Paper)

A.C. Williams

	C6	C8	C10
Speed Boat, cast iron, blue, 4-3/4" long	120	180	240
Speed Boat, cast iron, 5-1/4" long	60	90	120
Speed Boat, cast iron, 4" long	45	68	90
Speed Boat, cast iron, w/rider, 4-3/4" long	120	180	240

Auburn Rubber

	C6	C8	C10
Battleship, No. 1582, c. 1940, 8-1/4" long	22	33	45
Dreadnaught, extremely rare, 1941, 9-1/8" long	30	50	70
Freighter, 1941, 9-1/4" long	22	33	45
Submarine, c. 1941, 6-1/2" long	20	30	40
Tugboat, plastic	37	56	75

Authenticast

	C6	C8	C10
French Warships, includes Richelieu, Algiers, Fantasque and others, price for each	17	26	35
German Warships, scale models including Narvik, Galster and others, price for each	22	33	44
Japanese Warships, includes Fuso, Kaga, Mogani and others, price for each	17	26	35
U.S. Scale Model Warships, WWII including Iowa, Enterprise, Sims and Farragut and submarine Sarge, each	17	26	35

Bing

	C6	C8	C10
Battleship, tin clockwork, 16"	800	1300	1800
Destroyer, tin clockwork, 22-1/2" long	1500	2400	3500

Freighter, Auburn Rubber, $45

Bing (Continued)

	C6	C8	C10
Ferry, clockwork, 16" long	800	1300	1800
Gunboat, hand-painted tin, 29" long	1800	3000	5500
Ocean Liner, tin keywind, c. 1925, 13-1/2" long	400	650	900
Torpedo Boat, 27-1/2" long	2000	3500	6500
Warship, clockwork, c. 1915, 19" long	500	800	1100

Warship, Bing, $1100. Photo courtesy Bill Bertoia Auctions

Torpedo Boat, Bing, $6500. Photo courtesy of Bill Bertoia Auctions

Ferry, Bing, $1800. Photo courtesy Bill Bertoia Auctions

Battleship, Bliss, $4300. Photo courtesy Lloyd Ralston Auctions

Battleship, Bliss, $4300. Photo courtesy Lloyd Ralston Auctions

49 LST, Buddy "L," $100. Photo courtesy Ed Poole

Bliss	C6	C8	C10
Admiral gunboat, gun shoots, 20"	260	390	520
Battleship, litho and wood, 36"	1800	3000	4300
Battleship New York, paper litho and stained wood, 1890, 36" x 22"	450	675	900
Conqueror, wood and paper litho, 20" long	900	1400	2000
Marguerite Sailing Schooner, 22" long	350	525	700
Rover Torpedo Boat, paper litho on wood, c. 1896, 20" long	850	1375	1900
St. Louis, litho on wood liner, c. 1895, 34-1/2" long	800	1300	1800
Union Ferry, sidewheel, c. 1900, 24" long	225	375	450
Vesuvius Gunboat, paper litho on wood, 25-1/2" long	1200	2000	2800

Buckman	C6	C8	C10
Steamboat, twin sidewheeler, steam engine, marked "Patented May 7, 1872," 11" long	2000	3500	5000
Steamboat, c. 1872, 11" long	1300	2000	3000

Buddy "L"	C6	C8	C10
49 LST, includes tank, 12" long	50	75	100
Tugboat, No. 3000, 1929-30, 28" long	5000	8500	13,500

Cass	C6	C8	C10
Tugboat, wood, c. WWII?, 15" long	37	56	75
Yacht, wood, c. WWII?, 15" long	37	56	75

Chein	C6	C8	C10
Sailboat, wheeled	112	168	225
Sailboat, Hercules "Peggy Jane," 23" long	252	375	505
Speed Boat "Peggy Jane," 14-1/2" long	115	175	235

Converse	C6	C8	C10
Battleship Indiana, litho on wood, c. 1900, 32" long	650	1100	1600
Battleship Oregon, tin litho and wood, c. 1900	500	750	1000

Dent	C6	C8	C10
Adirondack, cast iron, 15" long	1000	1700	2300
Battleship New York, largest cast-iron boat made, c. 1900, 21"	2000	3200	4350

Eldon	C6	C8	C10
Aircraft Carrier, 22" long	55	83	110
Freighter, 20" long	40	60	80
L.C.T. Landing Craft, 10" long	17	26	35
U.S. Coast Guard Patrol Boat, w/figures, 22"	37	56	75

Racing Boat "Baby," Hubley?, $120

Racing Boat "Baby," Hubley?, $120

Scull, varsity racing, Ideal, $4000. Photo courtesy Wilkinson Collection; Detroit Antique Toy Museum

Fallows

	C6	C8	C10
Riverboat "Jumbo," painted tin, w/sidewheel, mechanical walking beam, 1880, 14" long	1000	1500	2000
Volunteer IVL, 16" long	1800	2700	3600

Fleischmann

	C6	C8	C10
Battleship	2000	3000	4000
Ocean Liner, painted tin clockwork, 1930, 20-1/2" long	700	1350	1800
Ocean Liner, 7-1/2" long	80	120	160
Ocean Liner, 15-1/2" long	1000	1600	2250
Oil Tanker Esso, 20" long	600	1000	1350

Hubley

	C6	C8	C10
Motorboat "Sea Horse," cast iron	1750	2625	3500
Racing Boat "Baby," cast-iron, wheeled, c. 1930, 4-1/2" long	60	90	120
Speed Boat "Baby," cast iron	60	90	120

Ideal

	C6	C8	C10
Destroyer, plastic, 15" long	17	28	35
Fireboat, plastic, pumping w/siren, 1955	60	90	120
Houseboat, 5" long	12	18	25
Motorboat, Slo Motion VI, wind-up motorboat, 13" long	60	90	120
Phantom Raider	60	90	120
Pirate Ship, plastic, w/six pirates, 1953	75	112	150

Ideal (Continued)

	C6	C8	C10
Police Boat, Harbor Police	30	45	60
PT Boat	50	75	100
Scull, cast iron, Varsity Racing, eight rowers w/moving oars, coxswain, c. 1890, 14" long	2000	3000	4000
Submarine, plastic, w/torpedoes, 1950s	20	30	40
Torpedo Boat, plastic, sparking, wind-up, 12" long	50	75	100
Treasure Hunter, plastic	75	112	150

Ives

	C6	C8	C10
Merchant Marine Ship, tin keywind, 13" long	450	675	900
Ocean Liner New York, 13" long	500	800	1100
Speed Boat "Miss Liberty," steam-powered, 13-1/2" long	750	1125	1500
Speed Boat "Vim," 10-1/2" long	650	975	1300
Speed Boat "Vixen," 12" long	650	975	1300
Submarine, tin keywind, dives, c. 1910, 10" long	400	600	800
U.S. Merchant Marine Boat, painted pressed tin clockwork, 10-1/2" long	250	375	500

Keystone

	C6	C8	C10
Action Submarine	50	75	100
Aircraft Carrier, wooden, 12" long	50	75	100
Battleship, wooden, airplanes take off from a spring on deck of ship, 2' long w/guns	130	195	260
Battleship, early 1940s, under 2' length	64	96	128
Ferry, wooden, w/two cars and trucks, c. 1930s, 14" long	40	60	80
Fishing Boat, wooden, c. 1940s, 12" long	37	56	75

Scull, varsity racing, Ideal, $4000. Photo courtesy Wilkinson Collection; Detroit Antique Toy Museum

Aircraft Carrier, Keystone, $100

Keystone (Continued)	C6	C8	C10
Racing Sailboat, wood	30	45	60
Radar Rocket Ship	75	112	150

Liberty Playthings

Liberty Playthings was in business in the late 1920s and early 1930s in Niagara Falls, New York. All its toys, which were made of wood and metal, had names related to the word "Liberty," and all had nautical themes. Those advertised in 1929 were No. 2 Tug and Scow, No. 5 Freighter, No. 6 Airplane Carrier, No. 7 Fireboat, No. 8 Destroyer, and No. 22 Seaplane. The Carrier, which in the ad was called "Liberator," sold for $10. The "Libertania" Aircraft Carrier seems to be the same ship, or a slight variation.

	C6	C8	C10
Aircraft Carrier, "Libertania," wood and tin litho w/lead planes, 27-3/4" long	250	375	500
Cruiser or Battleship	225	338	450
Destroyer No. 8	225	338	450
Fire Boat, 23"	200	300	400
Runabout, wind-up	155	233	310

Lionel Craft	C6	C8	C10
Speed Boat, No. 44, wind-up	750	1100	1700
Speed Boat, No. 43, wind-up	290	435	580

Märklin	C6	C8	C10
Battleship, clockwork, 28" long	2500	4500	9000
Liner "Columbus," tin, electrified, 42" long	4000	8000	16,500
Riverboat "Priscilla," 30" long	5000	10,000	17,600
Sidewheeler "New York," tin and cast iron, w/five lead figures, 19-1/2" long	8000	15,000	30,000
Submarine, tin, clockwork, 9-1/2" long	288	430	575
Yacht, tin, steam, "Priscilla," 20-1/2" long	2000	3500	6000

Marx	C6	C8	C10
Luxury Liner "Caribbean," friction, sparkling, 15" long, 3-1/2" tall	42	63	85
Putt Putt Boat, Mosquito Fleet	55	83	110

Milton Bradley	C6	C8	C10
Tillicum Battle Fleet, No. 115, c. late 1920s	31	46	62
Tillicum Convoy Set, two destroyers, three freight boats, three ocean liners, two patrol boats, painted wood, c. 1940s, destroyers 5-1/2" long, others about 4-1/2" long	350	525	700
Tillicum Harbor Set	20	30	40
Tillicum National Defense Set	40	60	80

Multiple Products	C6	C8	C10
Patrol Boat, w/radar mast and accessories	27	41	55
Pirate Ship, plastic w/pirates	60	90	125

Orkin

Orkin, of Cambridge, Massachusetts, was founded by Samuel Orkin about the end of World War I. His metal ships were modeled after the real thing. They were big, ranging from about fifteen to thirty-five inches, but relatively inexpensive.

	C6	C8	C10
Battleship "Constitution," steel keywind, c. 1914, 25" long	500	750	1000
Battleship "Marcella," 18" long	600	900	1350
Battleship "Nevada," steel, keywind, c. 1914, 22" long	550	825	1100

Top row, left to right: "New Jersey," Orkin, $1,400; "Nevada," $1,100. Middle, left to right: "Pennsylvania," Orkin, $1,700; "New Mexico," Orkin, $1,000. Bottom row: "Constitution," Orkin, $1,000. Photo courtesy Christie's East

Chris-Craft Commuter Yacht, Kilgore, $6000. Photo courtesy Chic Gast

Orkin (Continued)

	C6	C8	C10
Battleship "New Jersey," tin and wood, c. 1920, 35" long	600	900	1400
Battleship "New Mexico," steel, keywind, c. 1914, 25" long	500	750	1000
Battleship "Pennsylvania," steel, keywind, c. 1914, 30" long	700	1100	1700
Battleship "Texas," steel, keywind, 30" long	1000	1800	3800
Battleship B2, pressed steel, 36" long	3000	5000	8000

Orkin Craft

Orkin Craft was owned by the president of the Waterman Pen Company. Manufacturing was done by Calwis Industries Ltd. of Beverly Hills, California. The pleasure boats sold by the firm were too expensive for the era (the price was in the $15-$20 range), which is probably why they failed about 1935 or 1936. All the boats were motor-driven. Some were all metal, and some had wooden decks.

Battleship B2, Orkin, $8000. Photo courtesy Sotheby's, New York

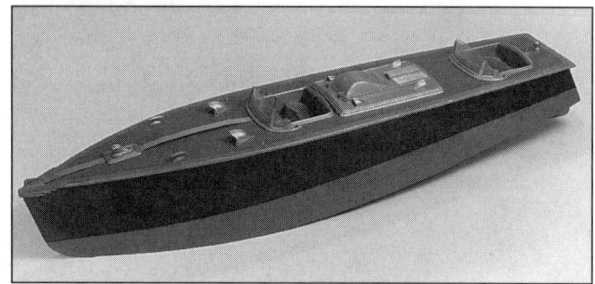

Speedboat, Orkincraft, $1450. Photo courtesy Mapes Auctioneers and Appraisers

Battleship Philadelphia, Reed, $880. Photo courtesy Bill Bertoia Auctions

	C6	C8	C10
Cabin Cruiser, 30" long	700	1200	1700
Speedboat, clockwork, 29" long	600	1000	1450

Reed

	C6	C8	C10
Battleship Philadelphia, paper litho on wood, 30" long	440	660	880
Clipper Ship, wood and paper litho, c. 1887, 36" long	550	800	1200
Freighter Ocean Wave, paper litho on wood, w/cargo, c. 1883, 35" long	650	1100	1500
Passenger liner St. Louis, paper litho on wood, 31" long	800	1300	1800
Riverboat "Ocean Queen," litho on wood, 23" long	750	1300	1800
Riverboat "Pilgrim," paper litho, 28-1/2" long	1000	1500	2000

Reed (Continued)

	C6	C8	C10
Sidewheeler "River Queen," litho on wood, c. 1895, 25" long	440	660	880
U.S.S. Maine, paper litho on wood	600	900	1200

Remco

	C6	C8	C10
Aircraft Carrier "Mighty Matilda," plastic, complete w/all accessories, 35" long	83	125	165
Barracuda Submarine, twenty-three man crew	75	112	150
Battleship Fighting Lady, No. 710, 31" long	115	172	230
Carrier, Mighty Magee Carrier	80	120	160
Roman Warship "Big Caesar," w/figures, 29" long	175	265	350
Roman Warship Gallant Gladiator, 17" long	60	90	120
Showboat Theater	75	112	150

Renwal

	C6	C8	C10
Cargo Ship, No. 139, 4" long	4	6	8
Drawbridge Set, w/bridge, twelve cars and boats	50	75	100

Renwal (Continued)

	C6	C8	C10
Ferry No. 140, 4" long	4	6	8
Ocean Liner	30	45	60
Panama Canal, No. 273, c. 1957, 29" x 11"	108	162	215
Speed Boat, No. 141, 4" long	4	6	8
Tugboat, No. 142, 4" long	4	6	8
Viking Ship, No. 245, 1955, 17" long	55	83	110

Schiebel

	C6	C8	C10
Battleship, friction motor, wood stacks and large wood guns and turrets, c. 1920	1250	1875	2500
Battleship, unpowered, c. 1927	1000	1500	2000

Thomas Toys

	C6	C8	C10
Aircraft Carrier, plastic, 5-1/2" long	12	18	25
Battleship, plastic, 5-1/2" long	12	18	25
Ferry, Hudson River, plastic, No. 481, w/sailboat, nine cars	12	18	25

Clipper Ship, Reed, $1200. Photo courtesy Bill Bertoia Auctions

Sidewheeler "River Queen," Reed, $880

Panama Canal, Renwal, $215. Photo courtesy Islyn Thomas

Viking Ship, Renwal, $110. Photo courtesy Islyn Thomas

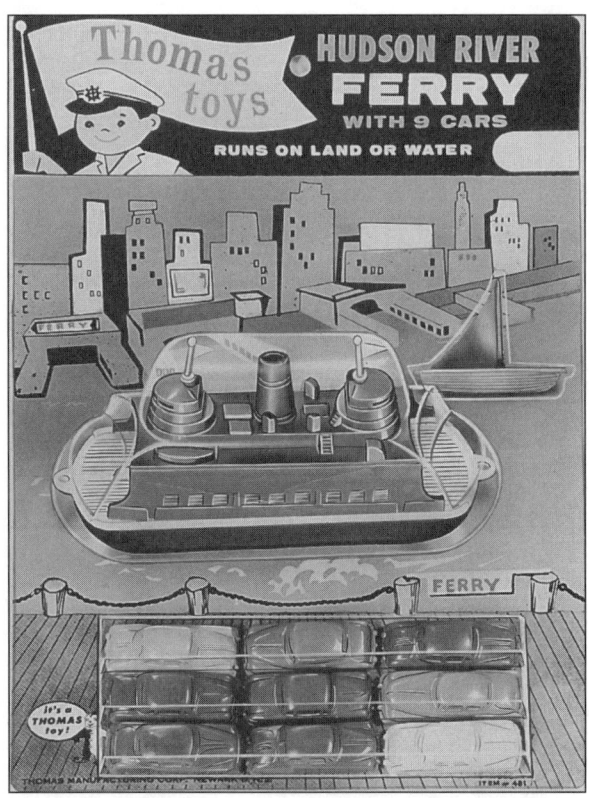

Hudson River Ferry, Thomas Toys, $25. Photo courtesy Islyn Thomas

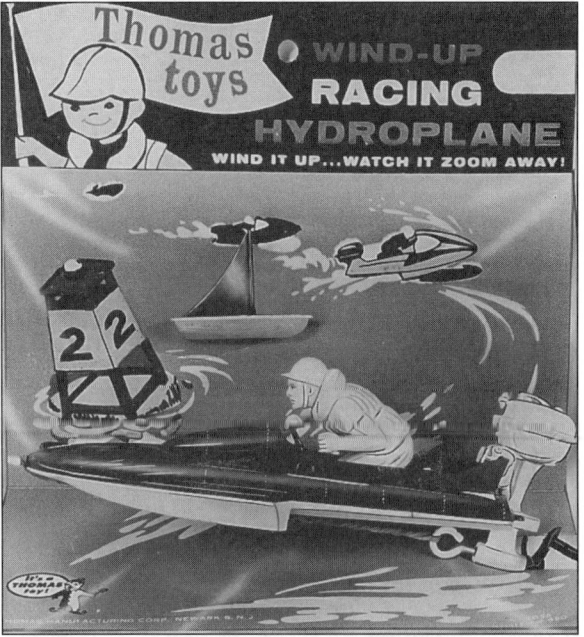

Racing Hydroplane, Thomas Toys, $25. Photo courtesy Islyn Thomas

Thomas Toys (Continued)

	C6	C8	C10
Freighter, plastic, 5-1/2"long	12	18	25
Queen Mary, plastic, 5-1/2" long	15	22	30

Swamp Buggy, Thomas Toys, $25. Photo courtesy Islyn Thomas

Thomas Toys (Continued)

	C6	C8	C10
Racing Hydroplane, plastic, No. 480	12	18	25
Swamp Buggy, plastic, motorized, No. 487	12	18	25
Tugboat, 8-1/4" long	15	22	30
Weekend Cruise Set, No. 339, w/boat trailer, 4-1/4" car, 4-1/2" boat	22	33	45

U.S. Hardware

	C6	C8	C10
Rowers, castcast iron, four-man crew and coxswain, large wheels, c. 1890	2000	3500	5200
Rowers, cast iron, eight-man crew and coxswain, large wheels, c. 1890, 14-1/2" long	1800	3000	4200
Scull, nine-man crew, wheeled, 14" long	1600	2400	3200

Wannatoys

	C6	C8	C10
Cruiser	25	38	50
Freighter	25	38	50

Wilkins

	C6	C8	C10
Battleship, cast iron	800	1400	2000
Riverboat, 5-3/4" long	135	205	270
Riverboat, cast iron, 10-1/2" long	450	675	900
Riverboat, cast iron, c. 1910, 7-1/2" long	250	375	500
Riverboat "City of New York," 15" long	800	1400	2035
Riverboat "Puritan," 10-1/2" long	600	1000	1400
Rowers, cast iron, big-wheeled boat, four-man crew and coxswain, c. 1890, 10" long	1250	1875	2500

Wolverine

	C6	C8	C10
Diving Submarine, 13" long	105	158	210
Ferry, tin and wood, Sandy Andy "Ferrygo," 11" long	150	225	300
Ferry, tin litho, "Sandy Andy Ferry," 13-1/2" long	75	113	150
Ocean Liner	125	188	250

Wyandotte

	C6	C8	C10
Aircraft Carrier	55	82	110
Pocket Battleship, tin litho, wheeled, 7" long	70	105	140
S.S. America, moves on metal wheels, 1930s, 7" long	50	75	100
U.S.S. Enterprise	80	120	160

Miscellaneous

	C6	C8	C10
Adirondack Sidewheeler, cast iron, 13" long	500	750	1000
Admiral Dewey Flagship, paper litho on wood, c. 1900, 30" long	300	450	600
Admiral Dewey's Flagship from the White Fleet, wood and paper, 6" long	100	150	200
Aeroplane Carrier, No. 372, Barclay	25	38	50
Aircraft Carrier, tin litho, "65," large, c. 1950s	50	75	100
Aircraft Carrier, friction, Cragstan, 8-1/2" long	60	90	120
Aircraft Carrier, plastic, Saunders, 12" long	32	48	65
Aircraft Carrier, steel, w/three jet planes that fire rockets, shell or drop bombs, Argo, 6" planes, 36" long	68	102	135
Amazon Sidewheeler, plastic and metal, Atwood Motors, California, c. 1950s	125	188	250
Atomic Submarine, Hasbro	32	48	65

Battleship, Hillclimber, $400. Photo courtesy Mapes Auctioneers and Appraisers

Miscellaneous (Continued)

	C6	C8	C10
Battleship, pressed steel, Hillclimber, 15" long	200	300	400
Battleship, painted pressed steel, friction, Ohio, 16" long	140	210	280
Battleship, pressed steel, hill climber, 18" long	300	450	600
Battleship, tin friction, c. 1920s, 9-1/2" long	200	300	400
Battleship, plastic, Banner, 4" long	15	22	30
Battleship, glass, candy container, approx. 3" long	60	90	120
Battleship, No. 373, Barclay	27	41	55
Battleship, cast iron, 14-1/2" long	400	600	800
Battleship, friction, Dayton, c. 1920, 16" long	200	300	400
Battleship Admiral, paper litho, 1890, 20" long	600	900	1200
Battleship Missouri, all wood and metal, radio control, w/three electric motors, Sterling "56" scale model	350	525	700
Battleship New York, cast iron, c. 1920s, 20"	375	565	750
Battleship Oregon, paper litho and wood, 25" long	700	1050	1400
Battleship Rover, paper litho and wood, 20" long	600	900	1200
B-LO Submarine, metal, pat. No. 1318048	75	113	150
Boat, tin friction, painted, early	150	225	300
Boat, tin with driver, Hot Air, 9" long	100	150	200
Boat, wood and brass, wind-up motor concealed within the rudder, controlled from the wheel in the circular cockpit w/a start-stop lever, marked "C.C. Jr," 14-1/2" long	90	135	180
Boat, tin friction, two smokestacks, four lifeboats, 13" long	90	135	180
Boat, tin friction, lithographed	100	150	200
Boat, Kingsbury, 10" long	100	150	200
Boat, cast iron, Freidag, c. 1920s	225	338	450
Boat, tin friction, painted, early	100	150	200
Boat, metal, pull motor	100	150	200
Bremen, tin keywind, Falk, c. 1920, 18" long	1300	2100	3000
Canoe, wood, 6" long	15	22	30

Miscellaneous (Continued)

	C6	C8	C10
Columbia side paddlewheeler, wood and paper litho, Bradley, c. 1890, 24" long	400	600	800
Destroyer, cast iron, w/wheels, 12" long	1000	1500	2000
Ferry "Ferry Go" Pull Toy, tin litho, w/twin paddlewheels, 14" long	125	185	250
Ferry and Cars, plastic, Pyro, 7" long	25	38	50
Fighting Fire Boat, Knickerbocker, 1950s, 13" long	40	60	80
Gee Whiz speedboat, painted sheet metal, heavy clockwork motor, bronze propeller, Boucher, 25" long	550	825	1000
Gunboat, two guns, two small stacks, two stories above deck, wheeled, friction, 1920s or earlier	300	450	600
Gunboat, tin friction, rocks back and forth on wheels, 10" long	250	375	500
Gunboat, friction, 19" long	400	600	800
Gunboat "Kearsage," cast iron, 13-3/4" long	700	1150	1700
Launch, steam-driven, 18" long	350	525	700
Life Boat, steel, simple design, c. late 1930s, 11" long x 5-1/4" wide	20	30	40
Motorboat, wind-up, Irwin	25	38	50
Motorboat "Sea Wolf," Fleetline, 16" long	112	168	225
Naval Base Play Set, No. 888, Cohn	180	270	360
Navy Gun Boat, cast iron, No. 9B, Big Bang, 8-1/4" long	125	200	250
Navy Ship "Tirpitz," Comet, 19" long	75	112	150
Ocean Liner, tin keywind, Arnold, c. 1930, 11-1/2" long	400	650	900
Pike Steam Launch, Buckman	2500	3800	5500
PT107	30	45	60
Pull For the Shore, litho paper on wood, W.S. Reed	3500	8000	12,000
Riverboat "Columbia," paper and tin litho and wood, working walking beam, c. 1890, 2' long	700	1100	1650
Riverboat "Atlantic," painted and stenciled tin, sidewheel, George Brown, 14" long	2250	3375	4500
Riverboat "Pacific," Althof-Bergmann, 14" long	900	2000	3500
Rowboat, tin, rubber band driver w/man rowing, 9" long	40	60	80

Miscellaneous (Continued)

	C6	C8	C10
Rowboat, cast iron, w/four men and oars, mechanical, 9" long	1250	1875	2500
Sea Raider, Payton, 34" long	20	30	40
Shore Patrol, tin, battery operated, 9" long	10	15	20
Showboat, cast iron, 11" long	1000	1500	2000
Showboat, cast iron, Arcade, 1929, 10-3/4" long	500	750	1050
Sidewheeler, cast iron, 10-1/2" long	150	225	300
Sidewheeler, tin, Barmwell-Smith, pat. 1872	2000	3500	5000
Sidewheeler, tin clockwork, 11" long	90	135	180
Sidewheeler, cast iron, approx. 5-1/2" long	100	150	200
Sidewheeler, cast iron, 8" long	188	275	375
Sidewheeler "America," painted tin, c. 1874, 20" long	7000	11,000	18,000
Sidewheeler "Betsy," Buffalo Toys, 26" long	350	525	700
Sidewheeler "Constitution" Fallows, 10" long	2000	3000	4000
Sidewheeler "New Orleans," cast iron, c.1895, 10-1/2" long	600	950	1400
Sidewheeler "New York," cast iron, 15" long	500	750	1000

Sidewheeler "New Orleans," $1400. Photo courtesy Mapes Auctioneers and Appraisals

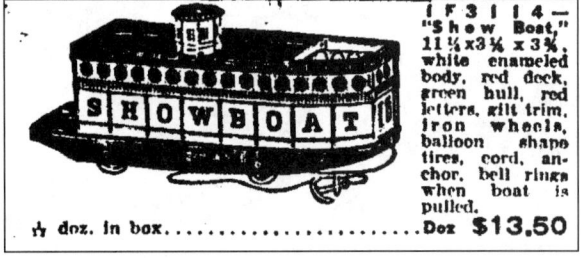

Showboat, Arcade, $1050

Steamship, $400. Photo courtesy Mapes Auctions and Appraisals

Miscellaneous (Continued)

	C6	C8	C10
Sidewheeler "Priscilla," paper litho on wood, 37" long	2000	3500	5800
Sidewheeler "Priscilla," cast iron, Dent or Wilkins, approx. 10" long	500	750	1000
Sidewheeler "Puritan," cast iron, 10-1/2" long	480	720	960
Sidewheeler Boat "The Star," tin, height w/stand 21", length 14-1/2"	3500	5200	7000
Sinking Battleship, rubber band torpedo strikes die on ship and sinks it, Walbert Mfg.	250	375	500
Speed Boat, cast iron, Kenton	90	135	180
Speed Boat, wood, rubber band propelled	40	60	80
Speed Boat "Johnson's Sea Horse," cast iron, w/figure, 10-1/2" long	1750	2625	3500
SS United States, tin friction, 6-1/2" long	50	75	100
Steamboat, live steam, 15" long	300	450	600
Steamboat, tin, self-propelled, 17" long	150	225	300
Steamboat "Dewey," c. 1900, 15-1/2" long	500	750	1000

Miscellaneous (Continued)

	C6	C8	C10
Steamboat Buckman, No. 55, c. 1870, 19" long	1500	2500	3500
Steamer, litho paper on wood, 39" long, 22-1/2" high	450	675	900
Steamship, alcohol burner, c. 1885, 19" long	200	300	400
Submarine, fires torpedo, 11-1/2" long	12	18	25
Submarine, tin litho, remote controlled, "575," c. 1960	40	60	80
Submarine, tin litho, remote control, automatic	40	60	80
Submarine, lead alloy, No. 79, Manoil	15	22	30
Submarine, steel, 6" long	40	60	80
Submarine and Dreadnought Naval War Toy, torpedo explodes ship, Pat. 4/6/15, Schoenhut	70	105	140
Tanker, Texaco	80	120	160
Turbo Boat, pressed tin, 10-1/2" long	40	60	80
U.S. Naval Base, Superior	60	90	120
U.S. Submarine, painted wood, fires torpedo for target set, 13" long	20	30	40
U.S. Wasp Carrier, wood, storage under deck for planes, 27" long	50	75	100
U.S.S. Narwahl Submarine, lead, 1930s, 7-1/2" long	20	30	40
U.S.S. New Mexico Battleship, lead, 1930s	20	30	40
Warship "Oregon," tin	400	600	800
Yacht, cast iron, Chris-Craft Commuter Yacht, Kilgore, c. 1930, 11" long	2000	3500	6000
Yacht-type Ship, spring wind motor, either Ives or Bing, 28" long	2000	3000	4000

SOLDIERS

The price of a toy soldier depends not only on its desirability, but on its condition. Mint condition means the item is in the condition in which it was originally issued—perfect, regardless of age, not the slightest blemish. Needless to say this is a fairly rare state of affairs, but enough soldiers exist in Mint condition to make it an employable term. Many people, hoping to dispose of toys, are tempted to term them Mint when they are really Near Mint, Very Good, or sometimes even just Good. Inevitably this can result in unhappiness all around and, not infrequently, in a canceled sale.

Very Good condition indicates a soldier that has obviously seen use. It has signs of wear and aging, but most of its paint remains and, in general, it has a freshness to its appearance that makes it seem attractive and collectible to all but the most discriminating.

Good condition signals a soldier that has seen considerable wear, but has at least one-half to one-third of its original paint, and is basically sound. Collectors will collect it, but they will often not be wholly satisfied with it as an example of their collection, and thus the price is well below that of the same item in Mint condition.

A condition below Good results in another drastic drop in price. Figures with missing parts, although otherwise in Excellent condition, will usually fall into this lower-priced category. At present, a Barclay soldier minus its tin helmet (signaled by a large round hole in the top of its head) is worth about half of what it would otherwise bring. On the cast-iron soldiers, even small spots of rust can seriously lower their price, as can repainting of any of the soldiers. Near Mint, Fine, Very Fine and similar terms denote conditions between Mint and Very Good, and are priced accordingly.

The key to grading is to avoid wishful thinking. Grading can sometimes be a problem for the uninitiated, but common sense will usually prevail, and when possible, a consultation with an expert in the field can often clear up lingering doubts. A toy in its original box is worth up to ten to twenty percent more if the box is in Mint condition, with the price dropping as condition lessens.

Contributor: Stan Alekna, Toy Soldiers Etcetera, 732 Aspen Lane. Lebanon, PA 17042-9073.

American Metal Toys

Until recently, these 3-1/4-inch dime-store soldiers were attributed to Chicago toy soldier maker J. Edward Jones. Though Jones did make many other figures, research has established that the following were produced by American Metal Toys, Inc. of Chicago. The president of the firm was Royce Reyff (1898-1986) and his equal partner was C. Raymond Pierson. Although the company was formally incorporated on October 24, 1939, they began in 1937 and went out of business in April 1942, when its supply of metal was cut off by the demands of World War II. The sculpting and diemaking were done by Henry Kasselowski.

	C6	C8	C10
Ammunition Carrier (AM18)	200	300	400
Bugler (AM25)	78	117	155
Charging, port arms (AM9)	125	188	250

American Metal Toys (Continued)

	C6	C8	C10
Cook with Chef's Hat, frying pan (AM17)	75	112	150
Cowboy Kneeling, with base, rare (AM33a)	NPF	NPF	NPF
Cowboy Kneeling (AM33)	40	60	80
Cowboy on Prancing Horse (AM39) ..	NPF	NPF	NPF
Cowboy on Rearing Horse, firing backward (AM31)	130	195	260
Cowboy Shooting, on foot (AM43)	60	70	95
Doctor with Bag (AM28)	40	60	125
Farmer (AM37)	9	15	25
Farmer's Wife (AM38)	9	15	25
Firing Machine Gun on Stump, No. 1 on pocket (AM10a)	100	150	200

American Metal Toys (Continued)

	C6	C8	C10
Firing Machine Gun on Stump (AM10)	40	60	80
Flagbearer (AM20)	120	180	240
German, charging w/rifle (AM2)	107	160	215
German, kneeling w/rifle (AM1)	95	142	190
German, kneeling w/short rifle (AM1a)	110	165	220
German, prone machine gunner (AM3)	71	106	143
Grenade Thrower, no weapons (AM11)	67	100	135
Indian Kneeling, shooting (AM35a)	59	70	85
Indian on Rearing Horse (AM34)	60	100	200
Indian with Bow, copy of Beton's (AM35)	NPF	NPF	NPF
Kneeling, firing rifle, no stand (AM23)	60	90	120
Kneeling, firing shorter rifle, no stand (AM23a)	75	112	150
Kneeling, firing anti-tank gun (AM16)	52	78	105
Kneeling, firing anti-tank gun w/barrel brace, "23" on wheel (AM16a)	50	75	100
Kneeling Horse, probably American Metal, copy of Barlcay's but shorter (AM42)	NPF	NPF	NPF
Kneeling with AA Gun (AM8)	60	95	125
Kneeling with Searchlight, "27," "Made in USA" on sides of stanchion (AM21a)	55	82	110
Kneeling with Searchlight (AM21)	62	93	125
Knight with Pennant, flat underbase (AM41)	64	95	128
Marching with Rifle (AM32)	57	85	115
Motorcyclist, w/machine gun mounted on motorcycle (AM19)	70	105	140
Nurse with Bag (AM27)	60	95	175
Observer with Binoculars and Rifle (AM4)	60	95	125
Officer in Greatcoat, pointing, holding pistol (AM13)	120	170	275
Prone, firing double-barreled machine gun (AM15)	78	117	155
Prone, body arched, firing machine gun (AM24)	60	90	120

American Metal Toys (Continued)

	C6	C8	C10
Prone with Rifle, trunk upraised (AM14)	70	105	140
Seated with Phone (AM22)	60	95	125
Seated with Rifle (AM12)	60	95	125
Soldier with Gas Mask, plunging rifle down, slightly smaller in size (AM26)	130	185	275
Soldier with Rifle, gassed or shot in neck (AM6)	170	255	340
Standing, firing rifle (AM29)	60	95	125
Stretcher-bearer (AM7)	80	110	155
Tramp (AM36)	9	18	25
Wire-cutter, prone (AM5)	225	338	450
Wounded Supine (AM30)	60	95	125

Auburn Rubber

Auburn (also Aub-Rub'r) was founded in 1913 in Auburn, Indiana, as the Double Fabric Tire Corporation to make auto tubes and tires for Model T Fords. They produced five soldiers in 1935—their first toys. The prototype was a Palace Guard that Auburn president and chief stockholder A.L. Murray obtained in England. The model was taken to a local pattern maker where original molds were made from lead. Sample toys were made and taken to an artist and decorated per Murray's instructions. They immediately caught on when presented to buyers.

The soldiers were molded in twenty-four-inch rubber presses, each containing forty to sixty soldiers. Once trimmed, the soldiers were dipped in a base lacquer and sent down a decorating conveyor where as many as twenty-four women, using small camel-hair brushes, added the finishing touches—painting the faces, shoes, belts, buttons, medals, and finally eyes. After drying, each toy was individually wrapped in waxed paper and packed three dozen to a chip-board carton and twelve dozen to a corrugated carton for shipment. Design of the soldiers was credited to freelance artist Edward McCandlish.

The soldiers sold well from the beginning. Shortly after the first soldiers were introduced, animals and wheeled vehicles (the first was a Cord automobile) were marketed, all successfully. Auburn produced no soldiers during the war and few after it, though they continued to make toys in great quantity. In 1960 the toys portion of Auburn was purchased by the town of Deming, New Mexico, where it remained until it went out of business in 1969.

Auburn's soldiers, all the standard 3-1/4-inch length, went through three stages. The first were frail-looking with long, thin bodies; the second, which emerged as early as September 1938, were stockier and larger-headed; and the third, introduced in 1941, were more well-proportioned and realistic. Unlike its competitors, Auburn produced no cowboys, Indians, sailors or civilians, except for baseball and football players and two farm workers. Auburn's infantry came in colors other than brown—the blue were meant to represent U.S. Marines; the white also were sold as Marines. It is thought that some Auburn Ethiopians remain to be discovered.

Auburn Rubber

	C6	C8	C10
200 U.S. Infantry Private (A2)	9	14	23
202 Bugler, U.S. Infantry (A4)	13	18	29
204 U.S. Infantry Officer (A9)	10	15	26
206 Stretcher Bearer (A16)	19	30	42
208 Wounded Soldier (A17)	19	30	42
214 & 218 Foreign Legion Private (A6)	17	28	40
216 Observer with Binoculars (A18)	13	18	29
222 Sniper, crawling, rifle over shoulder (A20)	45	65	85
224 Red Cross Doctor (A14)	22	35	48
226 Red Cross Nurse, white or khaki uniform (add 25% far khaki figure) (A15)	22	35	48
230 Machine Gunner (A13)	9	14	23
232 Officer on Horse (A12)	25	35	52
234 Bomb Thrower (A21)	30	40	57
236 Signalman (A19)	65	110	276
238 Charging Soldier with Tommy Gun (A11)	14	19	30
240 Motorcycle Soldiers with Sidecar (A24)	34	75	117
242 Anti-Aircraft Gun (A22)	19	25	37
250 Pitcher (A40)	20	40	59
252 Batter (A38)	20	41	60
254 Catcher (A41)	20	40	59
256 Fielder or Baseman (A39)	21	36	55
258 Baserunner (A37)	21	36	55
260 Lineman, football player (A45)	21	36	55
262 Backfieldman, football player (A44)	20	40	59

Auburn Rubber (Continued)	C6	C8	C10
264 Center, football player (A43)	20	40	59
266 Passer, football player (A46)	23	43	62
268 Carrier, football player (A42)	23	43	62
272 Plane Shooter (A29)	22	35	48
296 Trench Mortar (A32)	24	37	50
1546 Motorcycle Cop, blue or khaki as soldier (A23)	42	59	74
Aircraft Defender (A25)	30	40	56
Army Docter, khaki uniform (A14a)	NPF	NPF	NPF
Color Bearer (A26)	80	125	180
Cowboy, large, on wheeled horse (A48)	45	70	95
Ethiopian Bugler, only one known (A7a)	NPF	NPF	NPF
Ethiopian with Shield and Rifle, in robes, only one known (A7b)	100	200	300
Ethiopian with Shield and Rifle (A7)	100	200	300
Firing Soldier (A28)	23	38	57
Foreign Legion, also White Guard officer (A5)	12	18	24
Pilot Running, looking skyward, in pilot helmet and goggles (A35)	NPF	NPF	NPF
Searchlight (A31)	22	35	48
Sound Detector (A30)	19	28	43
Tank Defender (A33)	24	36	48
Tank Soldier, running w/box (A34)	19	29	39

Barclay

Barclay Mfg. Co. was the largest manufacturer of toy soldiers in the United States prior to World War II, selling millions of figures annually. The company, named after Barclay Street in West Hoboken, New Jersey, began in 1924 or late 1923, and was owned by Leon Donze (1865-1950) and by Michael Levy (c. 1895-1964). Around 1929, Levy took over the company, and he turned it into a major manufacturer. It grew from five employees in 1924 to a pre-war peak of 400 workers and moved several times to increasingly larger quarters.

Barclay's soldiers came in four styles prior to World War II. Soldiers from the first group, probably produced almost from Barclay's beginning, were small with moving arms on the mounted figures. The second group, approximately 3-1/4-inches high, seems to have debuted in 1935. These were designed and sculpted by Barclay employee Frank Krupp and had a separate tin helmet, which was subcontracted. These figures are rather stiff and are known by collectors as "short stride" because the marching figures' feet are close together. The third style, again by Krupp, also had a separate tin helmet, was more realistic and is known as "long stride." These were on sale as early as 1936. In 1937 or 1938, a clip was designed to hold on the tin helmets, as the formerly glued-on helmets frequently came off, drawing complaints from the chain stores, such as Woolworth's, that sold Barclay toys. The fourth style was introduced about 1939-1940 when Barclay moved from slush-casting to die-casting its soldiers. It was by freelance artist Olive Kooken (1904-1964) and is known as "cast helmet," as the soldiers featured helmets that were an integral part of the figure.

Barclay's soldiers were made of antimonial lead, consisting of about thirteen percent antimony and the rest lead. When slush-molding was done, only one mold was made of each figure. The lead would be poured into the mold, rocked, and immediately poured out, providing a hollow figure. Later, the die-cast molds produced a number of the same figure at the same time.

During World War II, Barclay laid off all but four of its employees and did subcontract work. The company was never as successful after the war and finally closed down in 1971. Although Barclay assigned numbers to its figures from the beginning for its own records, many of the soldiers themselves bore no numbers. Figures listed with a question mark after the number are based on the memory of longtime Barclay employee George Fall, whose memory, judged against known Barclay numbers, is accurate, but not infallible

Pre-1934

	C6	C8	C10
87? Mounted Officer, moving arm holding pistol, on cantering horse (Baa)	37	53	70
87? Mounted Officer, moving arm holding sword, on rearing horse (Ba)	49	62	75
87? Mounted Officer, moving arm holding bugle, on rearing horse (Bb)	49	62	75
186? Cavalryman mounted, no moving parts, modeled on French toy soldier (Bg)	19	31	40
200 Jockey on Horse (Bm)	20	28	38
486 Cavalryman, no moving parts (Bh)	19	31	46
486 Officer on Horse, smaller size, eight known (Bn)	12	21	38

Pre-1934 (Continued)

	C6	C8	C10
500 Santa Claus on Tin Skis,	30	43	56
88? Mounted Cowboy with Lasso (Bd)	NPF	NPF	NPF
89? Mounted Indian, moving arm holding rifle (Be)	52	76	93
90? Mounted Cowboy, w/moving arm, holding rifle (Bfa)	49	66	87
90? Mounted Cowboy with Pistol (Bf)	40	60	80
90? Mounted Indian, moving arm holding pistol (BeA)	NPF	NPF	NPF
Baseball Batter (Bk)	78	119	175
Baseball Fielder (Bi)	78	119	175
Baseball Pitcher (Bj)	78	119	175
Indian Brave on Foot, carrying rifle across stomach (Bfb)	NPF	NPF	NPF
Indian Chief on Foot, blue and red striped headdress (Bfa)	NPF	NPF	NPF
Mounted Indian on Rearing Horse (B1)	20	29	38

1934 and After

	C6	C8	C10
45 Machine Gunner and Driver (B153)	31	52	76
87 Officer on Horse, in cap, khaki or grey, larger black, grey or brown horse (B3A)	19	29	40
87? Mounted, in grey cap, intermediate size (B3)	41	68	86
87? Mounted in colored jacket and cap, might be Chinese or Japanese (BA)	25	37	49
89 Indian on Horse, on catalog sheet with Ethiopians (BAC)	27	38	50
89 Indian on Horse, Indian's head turned to right (B1-1)	35	47	59
89 Indian on Horse, two feathers (B1a)	31	44	57
90 Cowboy on Horse (BAD)	27	38	50
90 Cowboy on Horse, variation, no bullets in gunbelt (B2AA)	25	45	65
90 Cowboy on Horse, variation, thinner bullets in gunbelt, saddle not as long (B2A)	27	38	50
100 Masked Rider on Horse, facing forward (B2AAA)	350	525	700
100? Masked Rider with Lasso, horse's tail up (B2C)	150	225	350

1934 and After (Continued)

	C6	C8	C10
100? Masked Rider with Lasso, horse's tail down (B2B)	29	49	65
310 Army Motorcyclist (B93)	34	47	59
310 Army Motorcyclist, post-war, dot eyes or none at all, larger, motor variation (B93A)	32	45	57
310 Cop on Motorcycle (B93a)	36	49	61
310 Cop on Motorcycle, head lower (B93c)	37	50	62
310 Cop on Motorcycle, post-war, dot eyes or none at all, larger, motor variation (B93B)	36	49	69
310 Motorcyclist, head higher (B93b)	37	50	62
310 Motorcyclist, larger, markings on cycle, like B93A and B93B but cruder (B93d)	37	50	62
374 Army Motorcycle, w/sidecar (B152)	45	65	85
495 Man on Skis (B190)	16	23	29
496 Girl on Skis (B191)	16	23	29
497 Man on Sled (B192)	15	22	28
498 Girl on Sled (B193)	15	22	28
499 Santa Claus on Sled (B194)	31	42	55
500 Santa Claus on Lead Skis (B195)	32	45	58
500 Santa Claus on Skis, no skis poles and no holes for them (B195a)	75	115	148
510 One Horse Open Sleigh, includes sleigh, horse, seated man and woman (B198)	51	73	95
530 Man Pulling Children on Sled (B199)	31	42	65
535 Young Man Putting Skates on Girl Sitting on Bench (B200)	119	141	175
610 Woman Passenger, w/dog (B157)	11	19	23
611 Man Passenger, overcoat over arm (B158)	11	19	23
612 Conductor (B161)	11	19	23
613 Black Porter, w/whisk broom (B160)	12	20	25
614 Black Man in Red Cap, w/bags (B159)	12	20	25
615 Engineer (B162)	11	19	23
616 Boy (B163)	10	18	22
617 Girl (B164)	10	18	22

1934 and After (Continued)

	C6	C8	C10
618 Elderly Woman (B165)	12	19	23
619 Old Man (B166)	12	19	23
620 Minister Walking (B167)	41	62	83
621 Minister Holding Hat (B168)	11	18	25
621 Newsboy (B169)	10	18	22
622 Shoeshine Boy (B170)	19	31	44
623 Detective with Pistol (B171)	110	147	179
624 Burglar (B172)	110	147	179
625 Bride (B173)	11	19	28
626 Groom (B174)	11	19	28
627 Girl in Rocker (B175)	10	18	25
628 Boy Skater (B176)	8	12	20
629 Girl Skater (B177)	8	12	20
630-1/2 Man and Woman on Park Bench (B178)	18	29	43
635 Man Speed Skater (B180)	9	14	22
636 Girl Figure Skater (B181)	9	14	22
701 Flagbearer, cast helmet (B7)	11	16	22
701 Flagbearer, Cuban flag variation, painted for ten Woolworth's in Cuba, cast or pot helmet (B10)	NPF	NPF	NPF
701 Flagbearer, tin helmet, long stride (B6)	16	21	34
701 Flagbearer, tin helmet, short stride (B5)	12	21	42
701 Machine-Gunner, kneeling, short stride (B9)	12	18	27
702 Machine-Gunner, kneeling, cast helmet (B11)	11	17	26
702 Machine-Gunner, kneeling, long stride (B10)	12	18	27
703 Sniper, kneeling, firing, long stride, tin helmet (B13)	13	18	25
703 Sniper, kneeling, firing, short stride (B12)	14	19	26
703 Sniper, kneeling, firing, short stride, shorter rifle, fat portion of gun and thin portion of barrel about equal length (B12A)	19	29	42
704 Soldier on Parade, shoulder arms, long stride, tin helmet (B15)	12	19	26
704 Soldier on Parade, shoulder arms, short stride (B14)	14	21	28
705 Soldier at Attention, actually port arms (B16)	16	23	31

1934 and After (Continued)

	C6	C8	C10
705 Soldier at Attention, actually port arms, cast helmet (B17)	14	21	36
706 Soldier, charging, cast helmet (B21)	11	17	32
706 Soldier, charging, short stride w/shorter rifle, sling around hand, two known (B18a)	425	638	850
706 Soldier, charging, short stride (B18)	12	17	32
706 Soldier, charging, long stride, tin helmet (B20)	55	82	110
706 Soldier, tall, tin helmet, solid puttees (B19)	325	500	750
707 At Attention, cast helmet (B22)	13	21	29
707 Sharpshooter, standing, firing, short stride (B86)	14	21	30
708 Marine Officer, w/sword, cast helmet (B28)	39	60	85
708 Officer, w/sword, cast helmet (B27)	36	50	75
708 Officer, w/sword, short stride (B23)	14	21	30
708 Officer, w/sword, long stride, no chest strap, tin helmet (B25a)	85	125	250
708 Officer, w/sword, long stride, tin helmet (B25)	19	31	44
709 Bugler, short stride (B29)	15	22	35
709 Bugler, long stride, tin helmet (B30)	12	19	32
710 Drummer, long stride, tin helmet (B32)	19	30	41
710 Drummer, short stride (B31)	13	19	32
711 Drum Major, long stride, tin helmet (B34)	14	20	33
711 Drum Major, short stride (B33)	13	19	32
712 Knight, w/shield (B156)	11	15	25
712 Knight, w/pennant (B155)	13	17	27
714 Pirate (B154)	13	21	38
715 Cowboy, with tin hat brim, badges, stripes painted on vest (B94A)	NPF	NPF	NPF
715 Cowboy, w/tin hat brim (B94)	12	17	30
716 Indian Chief (B48)	9	15	24
717 Indian Brave, rifle across waist (B47)	10	16	25

1934 and After (Continued)

	C6	C8	C10
718 West Point Cadet, long stride (B38)	15	20	31
718 West Point Cadet, w/rifle, short stride (B37)	17	22	33
719 Sailor in White Uniform, in puttees (B52)	13	18	30
719 Sailor White Uniform, long stride, bell bottoms (B51)	12	17	29
719 Sailor White Uniform, marching, short stride (B49)	12	17	29
720 Sailor Blue Uniform, in puttees (B52a)	13	18	30
720 Sailor Blue Uniform, marching, short stride (B50)	13	18	30
720 Sailor Blue Uniform, long stride, bell bottoms (B51a)	15	20	31
721 Naval Officer, long stride (B56)	17	22	33
721 Naval Officer, short stride (B55)	12	18	32
721 Naval Officer, short stride, tin top to cap (B54)	55	80	120
721 Naval Officer in Blue, short stride, tin top to cap (B54a)	110	200	375
722 Marine, short stride, tin top to cap (B57)	60	81	120
722 Marine, short stride (B58)	12	21	38
722 Marine, long stride (B59)	19	27	40
722 Marine, long stride, white cap (possibly post-war) (B59a)	26	35	47
723 Marine Officer, w/sword, short stride (B24)	19	29	41
723 Marine Officer, w/sword, long stride, no chest strap, in blue, tin helmet (B25b)	85	125	275
723 Marine Officer, w/sword, cast helmet (B26)	51	72	95
724 Ethiopian Soldier (B39)	120	169	277
725 Ethiopian Officer (B40)	135	195	310
726 Italian Soldier (B42)	110	160	241
727 Italian Officer (B41)	110	170	275
728 Machine Gunner Lying Flat, cast helmet (B62)	13	19	31
728 Machine Gunner Lying Flat (B61)	14	20	32
728 Machine Gunner Lying Flat, lip of base extends under gun barrel, cast helmet (B63)	14	20	32

1934 and After (Continued)

	C6	C8	C10
729 Soldier with Binoculars, short binoculars (B114)	60	80	110
729 Soldier with Binoculars, long binoculars (B113)	19	25	37
730 Soldier Signal Man with Flag (B65)	16	24	39
731 Soldier Pigeon Dispatcher (B66)	17	30	40
732 Soldier Telephone Operator (B67)	14	20	32
733 Soldier Bullet Feeder, actually a shell (B68)	12	19	27
734 Soldier Ammunition Carrier (B69)	14	21	29
735 Soldier Range Finder (B70)	16	22	34
736 Soldier Sentry (B71)	16	22	34
737 Soldier Charging Machine Gunner, cast helmet (B73)	21	36	48
737 Soldier Charging Machine Gunner, tin helmet (B72)	13	20	28
738 Soldier Bomb Thrower (B74)	14	21	31

738 Soldier Bomb Thrower, Barclay, very rare. Photo courtesy Stan Alekna

1934 and After (Continued)

	C6	C8	C10
738 Soldier Bomb Thrower, rifle off ground, cast helmet (B77)	18	30	40
738 Soldier Bomb Thrower, rifle off ground, tin helmet (B76)	18	30	40
738 Soldier Bomb Thrower, tall, solid puttees, tin helmet (B75)	325	475	625
739 Soldier Fifer (B78)	14	21	31
740 Soldier French Horn (B79)	13	20	30
741 Aviator (B80)	14	21	31
743 West Point Officer, short stride (B35)	14	21	31
744 Nurse, hand on hip (B83)	14	21	31
744 Nurse in Blue, hand on hip (B83a)	68	90	150
745 Navy Doctor, in white, flat underbase (B81)	18	30	40
746 Army Doctor, in brown, flat underbase (B81a)	18	30	40
746 Doctor, in brown, concave base (B81A&B)	8	12	33
747 Sharpshooter, standing, firing, cast helmet (B88)	11	18	26
747 Sharpshooter, standing, firing, long stride, tin helmet (B87)	13	20	30
748 Soldier Running, w/rifle, cast helmet (B90)	19	26	36
748 Soldier Running, w/rifle, tin helmet (B89)	20	27	37
749 Soldier Gas Mask, charging w/rifle, tin helmet (B92)	17	24	34
749 Soldier Gas Mask, charging w/rifle, cast helmet (B91)	22	34	44
750 Soldier Crawling (B64)	15	22	32
751 Soldier Sharpshooter, prone position (B54)	16	23	33
752 Cowboy with Lasso (B95)	12	19	27
752 Cowboy with Lasso, post-WWII version, lasso goes directly through hands (B95a)	11	18	26
752 Masked Cowboy with Lasso (B95A)	14	21	29
753 Cowboy with Two Guns, pointing one (B96)	12	19	27
754 Indian Chief, tomahawk and shield (B97)	11	18	26
755 Indian with Bow and Arrow (B98)	10	17	25

1934 and After (Continued)

	C6	C8	C10
756 Indian Chief, long headdress, may only have been produced post-WWII (B99)	60	85	105
756 Sailor Flagbearer, long stride (B53)	22	34	44
757 Indian Brave, standing w/bow and arrow, may only have been produced post-WWII (B100)	21	29	39
757 Sailor with Signal Flags (B60)	18	30	40
757 Sailor with Signal Flags, flat underbase, minor variations in cap (B60a)	20	33	45
758 Camera Man, kneeling, tin helmet (B101)	22	31	48
759 Soldier Stretcher Bearer, closed hand (B102a)	15	21	33
759 Soldier Stretcher Bearer, open hand (B102)	95	125	165
760 Soldier Sitting Eating (B115)	20	31	40
760 Surgeon, w/strethoscope (B103)	19	25	38
761 Lying Wounded, tin helmet (B104)	14	20	32
762 Wounded, sitting, arm in sling (B85)	18	21	34
763 Raiding, in crouch, tin helmet (B105)	24	35	50
765 Bayoneting, no bayonet, cast helmet (B107a)	135	210	325
765 Bayoneting, although no bayonet, thrusting w/gun muzzle, tin helmet (B107)	41	51	75
766 Clubbing with Rifle, cast helmet (B109)	75	125	213
766 Clubbing with Rifle, tin helmet (B108)	32	58	70
767 Advance, raised rifle, tin helmet (B106)	16	22	35
767 Nurse, kneeling (B82)	16	22	33
769 Cook, egg-timer (B110a)	80	125	165
769 Cook, holding roast (B110)	20	28	40
770 At Mess, typist alone, apparently meant to sit at mess table (B151A)	14	21	39
771 Peeling Potatoes (B111)	16	23	31
774 Soldier with AA Gun, cast helmet (B118)	14	20	32
774 Soldier with AA Gun, tin helmet (B117)	20	27	37

1934 and After (Continued)

	C6	C8	C10
775 Wounded on Crutches (B119)	19	40	36
776 Officer Reading Orders (B116)	19	26	36
776 Standing at Searchlight, high seat, no rivets in front of left foot (B125)	21	42	68
776 Standing at Searchlight, high seat, two rivets in front of left foot (B124)	24	33	49
776 Standing at Searchlight, low seat, not connected to searchlight (B123)	17	23	34
776 Standing at Searchlight, smooth lens, elevation wheel (B120)	75	125	200
776 Standing at Searchlight, smooth lens, no elevation wheel (B120a)	75	125	200
776 Standing at Searchlight, ridges along base, ridged lenses (B121)	28	41	53
776 Standing at Searchlight, smooth base connected to searchlight, no elevation wheel, ridged lenses (B122)	28	41	53
777 Marching with Pack, cast helmet (B127)	18	26	45
777 Marching with Pack, tin helmet (B126)	14	24	35
778 Officer with Gas Mask, cast helmet (B128)	16	21	32
779 Firing from Behind Wall, cast helmet (B129)	41	62	78
780 Falling with Rifle, cast helmet (B130)	24	33	48
781 Digging, cast helmet (B131)	41	58	70
782 Leaning Out, w/field phone, antenna, cast helmet (B132)	41	69	88
783 Crouching with Binoculars, cast helmet (B133)	24	33	42
784 Parachutist Landing (B134)	16	21	38
785 Skier in Brown, no skis (B137)	39	61	74
785 Skier in White, w/separate metal skis, meant to be Finn, no left breast pocket, cast helmet (B135)	24	36	48
785 Skier in White, no skis (B136)	16	21	38
787 Diver with Axe (B135)	350	525	725
788 Soldier Marching with Gun Slung Behind Back, cast helmet (B140)	20	31	44
789 Soldier Shooting Triple-Barreled Gun, sitting, cast helmet (B141)	17	24	35

1934 and After (Continued)

	C6	C8	C10
790 Soldier Shooting Anti-Tank Gun, cast helmet (B145)	18	25	35
791 Soldiers with Mortar (B143)	26	35	44
792 Airplane Mechanic, prop spins, brace on back of engine bulges (B144)	29	42	65
793 Soldiers in Boat, cast helmets (B142)	65	81	98
802 Boy Scout Saluting (B183)	31	41	59
803 Boy Scout Signaling (B184)	31	41	59
804 Boy Scout Cooking (B185)	31	41	59
850 Policeman, arm raised (B186)	13	19	25
850 Policeman, figure eight base (B186a)	14	20	26
851 Fireman with Axe (B187)	20	31	44
852 Fireman with Hose (B188)	21	32	45
853 Postman (B189)	9	15	22
951 Soldier Wireless Operator (B147)	22	39	50
952 Soldier Dispatcher with Dog (B148)	41	75	98
953 American Legionnaire in Overseas Cap, tall, made for 1937 Legion convention in New York (B149)	175	285	400
954? American Legionnaire flagbearer, tall, cloth flag, made for 1937 Legion convention in New York, as above, five known (B150)	525	875	1500
960 Surgeon and Soldier (B146)	60	81	121
961 At Typewriter, w/typewriter and table (B151)	62	81	99
Chinese of Mongolian Rifleman, pronounced right breast pocket (B46)	90	135	213
Chinese or Mongolian Officer, in steel helmet (B45)	105	150	275
Fireman with Axe, flat underbase (B187a)	21	31	45
Japanese, charging w/rifle (B43)	80	110	160
Japanese Officer, this is the original Ethiopian officer, painted as a Japanese (B44)	120	165	245
Paint Your Own Army, Set No. 2003, boxed (BA)	175	250	400
Santa Claus Seated, bag of toys at side, made to ride in sleigh (B197)	110	165	295

1934 and After (Continued)

	C6	C8	C10
Santa Claus with Holly Sprig (B196)	50	70	95
West Point Cadet, w/rifle, short stride, w/line-and-dot eyes, white pants, white gloves (B37a)	20	30	40
West Point Cadet, w/rifle, short stride, but painted as wooden soldier, only four known (B37)	350	500	750

Barclay Podfoot Series

Made from c. 1950s to 1971, most podfoot soldiers came in khaki and later green. Add fifty percent to the price for a green example.

	C6	C8	C10
81 Two Soldier Crew at Radar Equipment (B219)	20	30	41
82 Three Soldier Crew at Range Finder (B220)	23	33	44
83 Two Soldier Crew at Searchlight (B221)	20	30	41
84 Two Soldier Crew at Mobile Cannon (B222)	21	31	42
85 Two Soldier Crew at AA Gun (B223)	21	31	42
187 Officer on Horse, w/pot helmet (B224)	62	89	121
188 Cowboy on Horse, w/lasso (B225)	25	35	46
189 Indian on Horse (B226)	18	28	39
190 Cowboy with Pistol on Horse (B227)	18	28	39
800 Black Knight with Sword and Shield (B228)	19	30	42
801 Knight with Red and Blue Shield and Sword (B229)	19	30	42

Barclay Podfoots in Red. Some collectors believe they were meant to represent the Korean War enemy.

Barclay Podfoot
Series (Continued)

	C6	C8	C10
802 Knight with Orange and Black Shield and Sword (B230) 19		30	42
803 Knight with Red and Green Shield and Sword (B231) 19		30	42
901 Soldier Flag Bearer (B232) 8		12	24
903 Soldier Sniper, in red (B233A) 62		81	134
903 Soldier Sniper, kneeling (B233) 6		10	19
906 Soldier Charging (B234A) 7		11	20
906 Soldier Charging, in red (B234) 62		81	134
908 Soldier Officer (B235) 8		12	21
908 Soldier Officer, in blue (B235A) ... 95		210	375
908 Soldier Officer, in red (B235B) 62		81	134
909 Soldier Bugler, in red (B236A) 62		81	134
909 Soldier Bugler (B236) 9		13	22
919 Sailor White Uniform (B237) 12		17	28
920 Sailor Blue Uniform (B238) 12		17	28
922 Marine (B239) 15		20	31
928 Soldier Machine Gunner Lying Flat (B240A) 9		13	22
928 Soldier Machine Gunner Lying Flat, in red (B240) 62		81	134
929 Soldier with Pistol Crawling (B241) 15		21	31
929 Soldier with Pistol Crawling, in red (B241A) 62		81	134
937 Soldier Charging Machine Gunner, in red (B242A) 62		81	134
937 Soldier Charging Machine Gunner, holding tommy gun (B242) 7		11	20
938 Soldier Bomb Thrower (B243) 11		17	27
938 Soldier Bomb Thrower, in red (B243A) 62		81	134
941 Aviator (B244) 12		16	26
941 Aviator, in red (B244A) 100		125	175
947 Soldier Marksman (B245) 5		11	20
947 Soldier Marksman, in red (B245A) 62		81	134
948 Soldier Running (B246) 6		12	21
948 Soldier Running, in red (B246A) .. 90		110	150
950 Cowboy with Pistol Shooting (B247) 26		38	50
951 Cowboy with Rifle (B248) 11		15	23

Barclay Podfoot
Series (Continued)

	C6	C8	C10
952 Cowboy with Lasso (B249) 11		15	23
953 Cowboy with Pistol, upraised (B250) 11		15	23
954 Indian with Shield and Tomahawk (B251) 7		12	19
955 Indian with Rifle (B252) 16		28	42
956 Indian with Knife and Spear (B253) 7		12	19
957 Indian with Bow and Arrow (B254) 7		12	19
960 Soldier Wounded with Crutches (B255) 18		24	31
960 Soldier Wounded with Crutches, in red (B255A) 125		160	195
961 Soldier Wounded Head and Arm (B256) 14		21	28
961 Soldier Wounded Head and Arm, in red (B256A) 125		160	195
962 Nurse (B257) 19		31	44
974 Soldier Anti-Aircraft Gunner, in red (B258A) 62		81	134
974 Soldier Anti-Aircraft Gunner (B258) 9		13	24
977 Soldier Under Marching Orders, in red (B259A) 62		81	134
977 Soldier Under Marching Orders, marching (B259) 7		14	22
988 Soldier Marching with Gun on Back, gun slung over shoulder (B260) 7		12	19
988 Soldier Marching with Gun on Back, gun slung over shoulder, in red (B260A) 62		81	134
990 Soldier with Bazooka (B261) 8		13	20
990 Soldier with Bazooka, in red (B261A) 62		81	134
991 Soldier Flame Thrower, in red (B262A) 62		81	134
991 Soldier Flame Thrower (B262) 8		13	20

HO-scale Figures
(1-1/2" tall)

	C6	C8	C10
350 Policeman (B275) 5		8	12
351 Man (B276) 5		8	12
352 Woman (B277) 5		8	12

HO-scale Figures
(1-1/2" tall) (Continued)

	C6	C8	C10
353 Conductor (B278) 5		8	12
354 Red Cap (B279) 5		8	12
355 Oiler (B280) 5		8	12
356 Brakeman (B281) 5		8	12
357 Engineer (B282) 5		8	12
358 Porter (B283) 5		8	12
359 Dining Steward (B284) 5		9	12
360 Hobo (B285) 5		8	12
361 Newsboy (B286) 5		8	12
362 Mailman (B287) 5		8	12
363 Fireman (B288) 8		12	20
366 Peg Legged Gateman (B289) 9		12	21
369 Woman Carrying Baby (B290) 6		12	16
370 Little Boy (B291) 5		11	15
371 Little Girl (B292) 5		11	15
372 Bride (B293) 10		16	22
373 Groom (B294) 8		12	22
Advancing with Rifle (B267) 49		70	105
Bugler (B264) 49		70	105
Cowboy with Pistol (B272) 40		65	85
Cowboy with Rifle (B271) 40		65	85
Firing Bazooka (B269) 49		70	105
Firing Tommy Gun (B270) 49		70	105
Flame Thrower, ... 49		70	105
Indian with Hatchet (B273) 40		65	85
Indian with Rifle (B274) 40		65	85
Marching, slung rifle (B268) 49		70	105
Officer with Binoculars (B265) 49		70	105
Talking on Field Phone (B266) 49		70	105
Walking Forward, rifle at side, pointing down (B270A) 49		70	105

Post-WWII

	C6	C8	C10
701 Flagbearer, pot helmet (B201) 16		21	34
703? Kneeling, firing rifle (B202) 40		65	79
705 Port Arms (B203) 14		20	31
707 Order Arms (B204) 14		20	31
708 Officer with Sword (B205) 15		20	31
720 Blue Sailor (B218a) 31		43	54
728 Prone Machine Gunner (B206) 14		20	31

Post-WWII (Continued)

	C6	C8	C10
723 Marine Officer, w/sword, short stride, in blue (B24) 16		24	32
737 Tommy Gunner (B207) 14		20	31
747 Standing Firing Rifle (B208) 14		20	31
774 AA Gunner (B209) 14		20	31
777 Marching at Slope (B210) 14		20	31
788 Marching, rifle slung (B211) 14		20	31
789 AA Gunner (B212) 16		22	36
Bugler (B215) 50		62	75
Bugler, buttons run down front of uniform (B215A) 52		65	78
Clarinetist (B216) 50		62	75
Cowboy, two pistols, one in air (B212a) 40		57	65
Drum Major (B213) 50		62	75
Drummer (B214) 50		62	75
Sailor, white (B218) 31		43	54
Tubist (B217) 50		62	75

Grey Iron

Founded as the Brady Machine Shop in Mount Joy, Pennsylvania in 1840, Grey Iron made the only 3-1/4-inch cast-iron soldiers. In 1881, the company was organized as the Grey Iron Casting Company, Ltd., and as early as 1903 it was manufacturing toy banks and stoves, cap pistols, wheeled toys and trains, as well as a number of non-toy items.

On August 14, 1917, the company was granted two patents for their 40mm solid cast-iron Grey Klip Armies, which they manufactured through 1941. The last of this series was made in 1938 as "Uncle Sam's Defenders" which were painted khaki rather than nickel-plated. The soldiers were not successful at first, but with the advent of a new distributor, the company was swamped with orders, and in January 1933, introduced a new line of thirty-five different cast-iron soldiers that were approximately three inches tall. Four Revolutionary War soldiers—an infantryman, a foot officer, a flagbearer, and a mounted officer—may have been introduced earlier, as they are numbered lower, but were not part of the 1933 announcement.

The figures tended to be slight and, while apparently successful, were superseded in July 1936 by Grey Iron's "Iron Men" series, slightly larger, more robust models that continued to be sold until World War II.

There were at least two designers for the soldiers—Edward Musser and Samuel S. Schmidt. The soldiers were hand-poured and then painted on an assembly-line basis, and were initially sold for a dime, while their competitors charged a nickel.

Grey Iron is still in business today as the John Wright division of Donsco, and has recently been producing, on an erratic basis, some unpainted soldiers from its old molds.

Grey Iron

	C6	C8	C10
1 Colonial Soldier (G1)	12	18	35
1A Colonial Foot Officer (G2)	12	18	35
1B Colonial Color-Bearer (G3)	275	450	900
1B Colonial Color-Bearer, 1950s version, w/rifle barrel drilled out for flag (G2)	22	39	72
1MA Colonial Mounted Officer (G4)	16	28	53
2 Cadet, early version (G5)	11	19	37
2 Cadet (G6)	11	19	37
2A Cadet Officer, early (G7)	11	19	37
2A Cadet Officer (G8)	11	19	37
3 U.S. Infantry, Shoulder Arms (G10)	9	15	27
3 U.S. Infantry, Shoulder Arms, early (G9)	7	13	23
3/1 U.S. Infantry, Port Arms (G11)	9	15	27
3A U.S. Infantry Officer, early (G12)	9	15	27
3A U.S. Infantry Officer (G13)	9	15	27
4 U.S. Infantry, Port Arms, early (G16)	9	15	27
4/1 U.S. Doughboy Signaling (G18)	15	27	46
4/2 U.S. Doughboy Combat Trooper (G19)	12	21	40
4/3 U.S. Doughboy with Range Finder (G20)	27	52	99
4/4 U.S. Doughboy Ammunition Carrier (G21)	37	69	130
4/5 U.S. Doughboy Sharpshooter (G22)	11	18	35
4/6 U.S. Doughboy with Bayonet (G23)	12	22	41
4A U.S. Doughboy Officer with Field Glasses (G17)	16	25	44
5 U.S. Infantry Charging, early (G24)	8	12	25
6 U.S. Doughboy, Port Arms, early (G25)	9	13	26

Grey Iron (Continued)

	C6	C8	C10
6 U.S. Doughboy, Shoulder Arms (G26)	8	12	25
6/1 U.S. Doughboy Charging (G29)	9	13	26
6/1F Foreign Legion Charging (G110)	15	29	57
6/2 U.S. Doughboy Sentry (G30)	11	19	39
6/3 Foreign Legion Bomber (G111)	19	35	67
6/3 U.S. Doughboy Bomber, crawling (G31)	12	19	35
6/4 U.S. Doughboy Grenade Thrower (G32)	16	31	61
6A U.S. Doughboy Officer (G28)	9	13	26
6A U.S. Doughboy Officer, early (G27)	9	13	26
6AF Foreign Legion Officer (G108)	19	34	65
6F Foreign Legion Shoulder Arms (G109)	18	32	60
7 U.S. Doughboy Charging, early (G33)	9	15	27
8/F Foreign Legion Cavalryman (G114)	36	70	125
8A/F Foreign Legion Cavalry Officer (G113)	36	70	125
8M U.S. Cavalryman, early (G34)	12	21	41
8M U.S. Cavalryman (G35)	13	24	47
8MA U.S. Cavalry Officer, early (G37)	15	28	54
8MA U.S. Cavalry Officer (G38)	14	27	51
9 U.S. Marine (G40)	9	16	30
9 U.S. Marine, early (G39)	10	18	35
10 Royal Canadian Police, early (G41)	9	15	32
10 Royal Canadian Police (G42)	12	22	40
11 Indian, w/hatchet, early (G45)	8	13	24
11 Indian Chief, w/knife (G46)	11	19	36
11/1 Indian Brave, shielding eyes (G47)	12	22	40
11/1M Indian Scout Mounted, firing pistol backwards (G51)	95	175	325
11/2 Chief Attacking, upraised tomahawk (G48)	34	65	125
11M Indian Mounted, early (G49)	16	30	58
11M Indian Mounted, lying on horse (G50)	22	40	78

Grey Iron (Continued)

	C6	C8	C10
12 Cowboy (G53)	10	15	28
12 Cowboy, early (G52)	9	14	27
12/1 Hold-Up Man (G54)	12	22	40
12/1M Masked Cowboy Mounted (G59)	150	265	410
12/2 Cowboy with Lasso (G55)	18	34	61
12/3 Bandit, surrendering (G56)	49	84	150
12M Cowboy Mounted, early (G57)	18	32	60
12M Cowboy Mounted (G58)	21	39	75
13 U.S. Machine Gunner (G61)	8	13	24
13 U.S. Machine Gunner, early (G60)	11	17	36
13/1 U.S. Machine Gunner (G62)	10	15	28
13F Foreign Legion Machine Gunner (G112)	19	35	60
14 U.S. Sailor, in blue, early (G63)	9	16	28
14 U.S. Sailor, in white, early (G64)	9	16	28
14 U.S. Sailor, in blue (G65)	9	17	29
14/1W U.S. Sailor Signalman (G71)	12	23	42
14A U.S. Naval Officer, in blue (G69)	9	17	29
14A U.S. Naval Officer, early, in blue (G67)	9	17	30
14AW U.S. Naval Officer, in white (G70)	9	17	29
14AW U.S. Naval Officer, early, in white (G68)	9	16	30
14W U.S. Sailor, in white (G66)	9	17	29
15/1 Boy Scout Saluting, early (G72)	12	23	42
15/2 Boy Scout Walking, early (G73)	14	23	42
16/1 Pirate Boy (G74)	14	26	45
16/2 Pirate Chief (G75)	12	22	41
16/3 Pirate with Dagger (G76)	12	22	41
16/4 Pirate with Hook (G77)	12	22	41
16/5 Pirate with Sword (G78)	12	22	41
17/1 Legion Drum Major (G80)	9	17	31
17/1 Legion Drum Major, early (G79)	18	34	63
17/2 Legion Bugler (G82)	8	15	29
17/2 Legion Bugler, early (G81)	9	16	31
17/3 Legion Drummer, early (G83)	10	18	34
17/3 Legion Drummer (G84)	9	16	31
17/4 Legion Color Bearer (G85)	13	23	43

Grey Iron (Continued)

	C6	C8	C10
18/1 Ethiopian Tribesman (G86)	23	42	79
18/2 Ethiopian Chief (G87)	24	43	84
18/3 Ethiopian Soldier, Shoulder Arms (G88)	23	42	80
18/3A Ethiopian Officer (G89)	24	43	84
18/5 Ethiopian Soldier Charging (G90)	24	43	84
19 Knight in Armor (G93)	13	25	47
20 Red Cross Doctor (G94)	13	25	47
21 Stretcher Bearer (G95)	15	28	52
21 Stretcher with Patient (G96)	14	26	49
22/1/Wounded Sitting (G97)	25	48	97
22/2 Wounded on Crutches (G98)	21	39	77
23 Red Cross Nurse (G99)	10	19	36
25 Aviator, non-soldier (G100)	27	49	97
75 Radio Set, Operator and Aerial (G103)	112	210	410
75 Radio Set, Operator Only (G103A)	49	74	98
D26 Nurse and Wounded Soldier (G104)	70	130	240
D27 Doughboy Supporting Wounded Soldier (G105)	78	148	283
Greek Evzone (G102)	41	78	153
Italian or English Desert Infantryman (G91)	75	140	270
Italian or English Desert Officer (G92)	78	150	280
Ski Trooper, w/original skis (G101)	25	46	86
U.S. Cavalry Officer, earliest version (G106)	65	115	220
U.S. Cavalryman, earliest version (G107)	60	110	215

American Family Series

All American Family figures are approximately 2-1/4-inch high

	C6	C8	C10
Boy Flying Kite, w/original kite (H-3)	10	18	35
Colored Cook (H-7)	10	19	37
Colored Man Digging (H-8)	10	18	35
Delivery Boy (H-10)	8	15	28
Dog (H-12)	6	10	18

This Grey Iron American Family at Home set is one of only two known.

American Family at Home (Continued)

	C6	C8	C10
Garageman (H-9)	8	15	28
Girl Skipping Rope, w/orignal rope (H-4)	10	18	35
Lawn Seat (H-13)	5	8	15
Man with Watering Can (H-1)	8	12	22
Milkman (H-11)	8	15	22
Old Man Sitting (H-5)	5	8	15
Old Woman Sitting (H-6)	5	8	15
Woman with Basket (H-2)	8	12	22

American Family on the Beach

	C6	C8	C10
Bench (B-13)	5	8	14
Boy in White Summer Suit (B-3)	19	37	73
Boy with Ball (B-8)	19	37	73
Boy with Life Preserver (B-6)	19	37	73
Girl Catching Ball (B-9)	19	37	73
Girl in Slacks (B-4)	19	37	73
Girl with Sand Pail (B-7)	19	37	73
Life Boat (B-12)	19	37	73
Life Guard (B-10)	19	37	73
Life Guard's Chair (B-11)	19	37	73
Man in Bathing Suit (B-1)	19	37	73
Old Man Sitting, white suit (B-5)	19	37	73
Woman in Bathing Suit (B-2)	19	37	73

American Family on the Farm

	C6	C8	C10
Calf (F-7)	6	10	18
Cow (F-6)	6	10	18

American Family on the Farm (Continued)

	C6	C8	C10
Dog (F-12)	6	10	18
Farmer (T-1)	7	12	22
Farmer's Wife (F-2)	7	12	22
Fence (F-14)	7	12	21
Gate with Post (F-13)	9	17	32
Girl (F-3)	7	12	22
Goat (F-10)	6	10	18
Goose (F-11)	6	10	18
Hired Man Digging (F-4)	8	14	24
Horse (F-5)	6	10	18
Pig (F-8)	6	10	18
Sheep (F-9)	6	10	18

American Family on the Ranch

	C6	C8	C10
Boy in Cowboy Suit (R-4)	19	37	73
Bucking Bronco (R-8)	19	37	73
Burro (R-10)	19	37	73
Calf (R-11)	19	37	73
Colt (R-9)	19	37	73
Cowboy Rider (R-2)	19	37	73
Cowboy Squatting (R-3)	19	37	73
Cowboy with Lasso (R-1)	19	37	73
Cowgirl Rider (R-6)	19	37	73
Girl in Riding Suit (R-5)	19	37	73
Rooster and Chickens (R-15)	20	38	75
Stallion (R-7)	19	37	73
Three Ducks (R-16)	20	38	75

American Family Travels

	C6	C8	C10
Boy in Traveling Suit (T-3)	6	10	18
Conductor (T-5)	6	10	18
Engineer (T-6)	6	10	18
Girl in Traveling Suit (T-4)	6	10	18
Man in Traveling Suit (T-1)	6	10	18
Newboy (T-10)	7	11	20
Old Colored Man Sitting (T-12)	11	19	35
Policeman (T-8)	6	10	18
Porter (T-7)	6	10	18
Postman (T-9)	6	10	18
Preacher (T-11)	7	11	20

American Family Travels

	C8	C10
Seat (T-13) 5	8	14
Woman in Traveling Costume (T-2) 6	10	18

Greyklip Armies

	C6	C8	C10
Set 1/Company A, at attention, consists of bugler, officer, flagbearer, drummer, rifleman (rifleman vallued at C6 $3, C8 $4, C10$5), price for each (GA) 2		4	6
Set 2/Company B, marching, consists of bugler, officer, flagbearer, drummer, rifleman (rifleman valued at C6 $3, C8 $4, C10 $6), price for each (GB) 2		4	6
Set 3/Company C, charging, consists of bugler, officer, flagbearer, drummer, rifleman (C6 $3, C8 $4, C10 $5), price for each (GC) 2		4	6
Set 4/Troop D, consists of four mounted troopers, one mounted officer with sword on shoulder, price for each (GD) 3		5	8
Set 5/Aviator Corps, consists of pilot (two of the same figure in set) and plane w/detachable wing, price for set (GG) 45		85	160
Set 5/Battery E, two-piece set, led by officer from Troop D, second piece is a gun limber w/four horses, several attached soldiers, price for second piece (GF) 9		16	30
Set 6/Battery E, consists of shell stack, loader bending, loader standing, gunner, cannon, price for each, shell stack is double (GE) 4		7	12
Uncle Sam's Defenders, consists of charging rifleman, machine gunner, charging officer, rifleman at attention, flagbearer, officer saluting, price for each (double the price on saluting officer and ten times the price on flagbearer) (GH) 5		9	16

Manoil

Manoil began production of toy soldiers in 1935. It was in business as early as 1927 under the name Jack Manoil. The company changed its name to Man-O-Lamp Corporation on July 11, 1928 and was owned by Maurice Manoil (1893-1974) and Jack Manoil (1902-1955), two brothers who had emigrated from Romania in the early 1900s. The final name change to Manoil Manufacturing Co., Inc. took place on July 7, 1934.

Manoil advanced into toy making in 1934 manufacturing seven vehicles. The company moved to other addresses as it grew, leaving Manhattan in 1937 for Brooklyn, and moving to Waverly, New York in June 1940 and employed 225 people at its peak.

With the onset of World War II, Manoil shut down, but resumed production of soldiers in a fine-grained composition (employing sulfur) in January 1944. The pieces were brittle and ultimately unsuccessful, and their manufacture stopped by the end of the year.

After the war the company introduced several new lines of soldiers, but they were no longer distributed as widely.

In 1953, the firm moved to a smaller location in Waverly, changing its name to Jack Manoil Specialty Company, but went out of business shortly after his death. Jack Manoil and sculptor Walter Baetz were both keenly interested in the company's soldiers and would work late into the night as they collaborated on ideas for them. One of Baetz's continuing concerns was to design the molds so that there was no structural weakness in the soldiers as a result of air bubbles. For this reason many of Manoil's soldiers were redesigned a number of times with sometimes subtle, and sometimes broad, variations.

Manoil's soldiers have a distinctive jauntiness to them, at times veering on caricature, the latter trait becoming more pronounced as the years wore on.

	C6	C8	C10
7 Flag Bearer, hollow base version (M1) 50	50	75	102
7 Flag Bearer, third version (M2) 18	18	25	40
7 Flag Bearer, second version (M3) 15	15	20	33
8 Parade, stocky version (M5) 10	10	20	30
8 Parade, campaign cap straight on head (M6) 25	25	35	51
8 Parade, fifth version (M8) 11	11	18	26
8 Parade, hollow base version (M4) 40	40	65	86
8 Parade, number on back (M6) 85	85	105	125
9 Officer, hollow base version (M9) 50	50	65	90
9 Officer, second version (M10) 12	12	21	33
10 Bugler, hollow base version (M11) 50	50	72	97
10 Bugler, second version (M12) 12	12	20	32
11 Drummer, hollow base version (M13) 50	50	72	97
11 Drummer, stocky version (M14) 15	15	30	44

A page from the 1939 Manoil catalog.

Manoil (Continued)

	C6	C8	C10
11 Drummer, vertical drum (M15)	26	42	59
12 Machine Gunner (Prone), no aperture, pack on back (M20)	14	26	36
12 Machine Gunner (Prone), no aperture between hands and gun (M19)	11	17	26
12 Machine Gunner (Prone), grass on base (M16)	16	25	37
12 Machine Gunner (Prone), flat base, no grass (M17)	15	22	38
12 Machine Gunner (Prone), spaces under body (M18)	35	65	90
13 Cadet, hollow base, no buckle on belt (M21)	36	52	73
13 Cadet, second version (M22)	14	24	34
14 Sailor, hollow base (M23)	32	52	74
14 Sailor, in blue (M23a)	32	52	74
15 Marine, second version (M26)	14	20	39
15 Marine, hollow base (M25)	50	72	97
16 Ensign (M27)	13	20	34

Manoil (Continued)

	C6	C8	C10
16 Ensign, hollow base (M27a)	42	65	91
17 Signal Man, hollow base version (M28)	26	37	58
17 Signal Man, second version (M29)	24	40	55
18 Cowboy, hollow base version (M30)	24	40	55
18 Cowboy, second version (M31)	12	17	29
18A Cowboy with Hands Up (M32)	13	20	35
18A Cowboy with Hands Up, subtle variation (M33)	13	21	36
20 Doctor, white (M34)	13	20	35
20K Doctor, khaki (M35)	18	28	42
21 Nurse, no hem in skirt, shorter (M36a)	19	35	53
21 Nurse (M36)	11	19	31
22 Indian, w/knives (M38)	13	20	35
22 Indian, w/knives, right toes off base (M38a)	15	22	37
23 Machine Gunner Sitting, markings under base (M40)	14	21	36
23 Machine Gunner Sitting, seated on four pillows, bullets feed from ammo box (M39)	14	21	30
24 Cannon Loader (M42)	10	19	33
25 Sniper (kneeling), folding rifle (M44)	140	285	425
25 Sniper (kneeling), longer, thicker rifle (M46)	14	31	42
25 Sniper (kneeling), short thin rifle (M45)	15	25	34
26 Sniper, folding rifle (M47)	140	285	425
26 Sniper, shorter rifle, angle different on underside of rifle (M48a)	40	55	75
26 Sniper (M48)	12	26	35
27 Tommy Gunner, bloated version (M49)	22	32	48
27 Tommy Gunner, second version (M50)	12	20	36
28 Observer (M51)	16	29	42
29 Wounded Soldier Walking (M52)	14	21	36
30 Wounded Soldier Lying (M53)	10	17	28
30 Wounded Soldier Lying, number on back, shorter head (M54)	15	21	37

Manoil (Continued)	C6	C8	C10
31 Bomb Thrower, three grenades in pouch (M55)	16	24	36
31 Bomb Thrower, two grenades in pouch (M56)	17	25	37
32 Stretcher Carrier, medical kit (M58a)	14	21	33
32 Stretcher Carrier, medical kit, number on back, buttons on uniform, different pockets and collar from above (M58)	40	80	125
32 Stretcher Carrier, no medical kit (M57)	13	20	36
33 Sitting Soldier (M59)	22	32	47
34 Aviator (M60)	20	35	60
35 Hostess, in green	31	55	79
35 Hostess, in white (M61)	85	180	275
35 Hostess in Khaki (M61a)	125	225	300
36 Soldier with Bayonet Charging (M62)	24	42	65
37 Soldier with Gun Charging (M63)	30	49	67
38 Soldier with Gun Butting (M64)	33	52	73
39 Soldier with Bayonet Jabbing (M65)	30	50	75
40 Soldier Kneeling with Bayonet (M66)	40	55	80
41 Soldier Crouching with Hand Grenade (M67)	34	60	80
42 Field Doctor Crawling (M68)	45	75	90
43 Officer Lying Down, Shooting Revolver (M69)	28	46	70
44 Crawling Scout with Gun, left leg high when right leg on ground, only three known (M70)	95	210	300
44 Crawling Scout with Gun, left leg lower (M71)	27	46	55
45 Observer with Periscope (M72)	19	40	58
46 Anti-Aircraft Gunner, barrel of gun drops below arm (M73)	14	20	36
46 Anti-Aircraft Gunner, barrel of gun ends at arm (M74)	14	20	36
47 Anti-Aircraft Searchlight, like No. 47 number on back, helmet looks as if it was adapted to look like WWII helmet (M75b)	21	43	62
47 Anti-Aircraft Searchlight (M75)	15	21	37
47 Anti-Aircraft Searchlight, w/tin lens (M75a)	125	200	310

Manoil (Continued)	C6	C8	C10
48 Navy Gunner (M76)	14	24	44
49 Policeman, slightly larger (M78)	12	24	36
49 Policeman (M77)	11	20	32
50 Bicycle Dispatch Rider (M79)	19	30	41
51 Motorized Machine Gunner (M80)	39	70	93
52 Motorcycle Rider (M82)	21	39	52
52 Motorcycle Rider, number over rear wheel, grass base (M81)	28	51	67
53 Sitting Soldier without Gun (M93)	16	29	42
54 Sitting Soldier Eating (M84)	26	40	60
55 Sitting Soldier at Table with Phone and Map (M85)	18	29	57
56 Paymaster (M86)	75	120	210
57 Camouflage Sharpshooter Lying Down (M87)	12	22	40
58 Parachute Jumper (M88)	16	30	61
59 Soldier Writing Letter (M89)	24	48	80
59 Soldier Writing Letter, foot not curled up, pencil is flat, helmet rounder, fuller (M89a)	26	53	85
60 Cook's Helper with Ladle, helmet looks as if it was adapted to look like WWII helmet (M91)	49	95	180
60 Cook's Helper with Ladle, normal helmet (M90)	20	39	68
61 Soldier with Camera (M92) 28		49	86
62 Soldier with Gas Mask & Gun (M93)	12	19	37
63 Soldier with Gas Mask with Flare Pistol (M94)	13	21	40
64 Soldier Playing Banjo (M95)	39	75	136
65 Deep Sea Diver, w/"65" on chest (M97)	13	20	37
65 Deep Sea Diver (M96)	13	20	37
66 Soldier with Gun on Parade with Overseas Cap (M98)	29	49	85
67 Soldier with Gun and Pack Marching (M99)	11	20	39
68 Soldier Boxing (M100)	29	54	105
77 Lineman and Telephone Pole, pole comes w/two different-shaped bases, oval or diagonal (M101)	40	68	125
78 Anti-Tank Gun, wooden wheels (M104)	25	46	89

Manoil (Continued)	C6	C8	C10
78 Anti-Tank Gun, squared shield (M103)	15	28	55
78 Anti-Tank Gun, round shield, all variations based on Vickers 2.95 mountain gun (M102)	17	30	57
79 Soldier Marching with Gun Slung at Angle (M105)	49	93	185
80 Anti-Aircraft Machine Gunner (M106)	11	19	34
81 Machine Gunner and Helper, aperture between hand and machine gun (M107)	15	28	52
81 Machine Gunner and Helper, no aperture (M108)	15	28	52
82 Anti-Aircraft with Range Finder (M109)	11	19	36
83 Soldier Trench Mortar (M110)	12	20	38
84 Soldier with Shell (M111)	15	28	47
85 Aviator Holding Bomb (M112)	12	22	42
86 Aviator Mechanic with Propeller, away from head (M113)	165	285	500
86 Aviator Mechanic with Propeller, orange prop, flat lower hand (M114)	48	88	175
86 Aviator Mechanic with Propeller Orange prop, curved lower hand (M114b)	48	88	175
86 Aviator Mechanic with Propeller Silver Prop (M114a)	48	88	175
87 Aviator Carrying Bomb Sight (M115)	16	30	58
88 Radio Operator Standing (M116)	26	47	90
89 Radio Operator Lying Down (M117)	20	38	73
90 Soldier Digging Trench (M118)	20	38	72
91 Soldier with Barbed Wire (M120)	19	36	69
91 Soldier with Barbed Wire, wide-faced version (M119)	19	36	69
92 Fire Fighter, in gray (M121)	40	75	140
92 Fire Fighter, in white (M121a)	38	70	130
93 Soldier on Guard Duty (M122)	35	60	110
94 Soldier Running with Cannon, thin face, wooden wheels (M124)	21	40	76
94 Soldier Running with Cannon, marked "Manoil USA," "1," cannon slants to right when looked at from above (M123)	18	31	58

Manoil (Continued)	C6	C8	C10
94 Soldier Running with Cannon, no markings, cannon straight from above, face narrower (M123a)	21	33	58
99 Finn with Skis (M125)	31	53	98
100 Finn Machine Gunner (M126)	27	47	86
101 Soldier Jumping with Chute (M127)	37	65	120
102 Soldier Jumping with Machine Gun (M128)	34	63	118
Aviator Holding Bomb, hand variation (M112a)	15	22	30
Indian, w/hatchet (M37)	49	90	175
Machine Gunner Sitting, squarer-looking, markings near right leg (M41)	13	21	36
Sailor, second version (M24)	10	18	29
Soldier with Camera, thinner arm (M92a)	32	58	100

Happy Farm Series	C6	C8	C10
41/1 Bench (M129)	6	10	18
41/10 Farmer Sowing Grain (M138)	11	18	33
41/11 Man Carrying Sheaves Under Arm (M139)	11	18	33
41/12 Darky Eating Watermelon (M142)	32	59	105
41/12 Scarecrow with Top Hat (M140)	11	18	33
41/13 Farmer Carrying Pumpkin (M141)	11	18	33
41/15 Scarecrow with Straw Hat (M143)	11	18	33
41/16 Watchman Blowing Out Lantern (M144)	12	19	35
41/17 Hod Carrier with Bricks (M145)	13	25	44
41/18 Man Chopping Wood (M146)	11	18	33
41/19 Mason Laying Bricks (M147)	13	25	44
41/2 Girl (M130)	6	10	18
41/20 Man Dumping Wheel Barrow (M148)	12	20	50
41/21 Old Man Fixing Shoe (M149)	15	26	50
41/22 Blacksmith with Wheel (M150)	11	18	33
41/23 Carpenter Carrying Door (M151)	21	39	74

Happy Farm Series (Continued)

	C6	C8	C10
41/24 Hound (M152)	11	18	33
41/25 Carpenter Sawing Lumber (M153)	11	19	36
41/26 Carpenter with Square (M154)	21	39	75
41/27 Shepherd with Flute (M155)	21	39	75
41/28 Lady with Pie (M156)	11	18	33
41/29 Lady with Child (M157)	11	18	33
41/3 Young Man (M131)	6	10	18
41/30 School Teacher (M158)	17	31	58
41/31 Girl Watering Flowers (M159)	11	18	33
41/32 Woman Lifting Hen From Nest (M160)	11	18	33
41/33 Woman with Butter Churn (M161)	11	18	33
41/34 Woman Laying Out Wash on Grass (M162)	11	18	33
41/35 Woman Sweeping with Broom (M163)	11	18	33
41/36 Man Juggling Barrel (M164)	22	39	76
41/36 Man Juggling Barrel, in khaki (M164a)	27	49	88
41/37 Man Planting Tree (M165)	19	35	68
41/38 Girl Picking Berries (M166)	18	34	67
41/39 Farmer at Water Pump (M167)	11	18	33
41/4 Man Carrying Sack on Back (M132)	11	18	33
41/40 Boy Carrying Wood (M168)	11	18	33
41/41 Stacks of Sheaves (M169)	11	18	33
41/5 Farmer Pitching Sheaves (M133)	11	18	33
41/6 Farmer Sharpening Scythe (M134)	11	18	33
41/7 Blacksmith Making Horseshoes (M135)	11	18	33
41/8 Farmer Cutting with Scythe (M136)	11	18	33
41/9 Farmer Cutting Corn (M137)	11	18	33
Boxed Happy Farm Set, no standard contents, ten pieces (M169a)	110	225	425

Manoil Composition

	C6	C8	C10
Firing Camouflaged AA Gun (MC4)	19	39	75
Motorcyclist, minor variation of above (MC3A)	27	49	95

Manoil Composition (Continued)

	C6	C8	C10
Motorcyclist (MC3) 27		49	95
Prone Machine-gunner (MC1)	19	39	75
Seated Machine-gunner (MC2)	19	39	75

My Ranch Corral Series

	C6	C8	C10
C01 Fence (M219)	8	10	18
C02 Large Ranch Fence, gate (M211)	40	60	75
C12 Blanket Over Fence Section (M212)	50	70	85
C14 Brahma Bull (M217)	12	20	29
C18 Small Calf (M213)	9	13	19
C19 Cow feeding (M215)	10	18	25
C20 Bull, head turned (M214)	10	18	25
C22 Horse for Mounted Cowboy (M221)	15	25	40
C22 Horse for Mounted Cowgirl (M222)	15	25	40
C23 Cowboy Rider (M207)	10	18	25
C24 Cowgirl Rider (M208)	10	18	25
C25 Small Horse (M220)	12	20	30
C26 Large Cactus (M218)	15	30	45
C28 Short Cactus (M216)	15	30	45
C29 Mounted Cowboy (M209)	35	62	75
C30 Mounted Cowboy Shooting (M210)	35	62	75
Small Gate (M223)	19	30	40

Postwar

The following were the first new post-World War II series, and were produced only for a limited time. On a trial basis, early production was also sold unpainted.

	C6	C8	C10
45/10 At Attention, present arms (M180)	14	26	48
45/11 Sniper (M181)	16	28	54
45/12 Tommy Gunner (M182)	14	26	48
45/13 Soldier with Bazooka Cannon, some marked "45/18" (M183)	14	26	48
45/14 Soldier with Shell for Bazooka, some marked "46/14" (M184)	14	26	48
45/15 General, some "46/15" (M185)	49	95	180
45/16 Mine Detector, some "46/16" (M186)	14	26	48

Postwar (Continued)	C6	C8	C10
45/6 Parade, thin (M176)	13	24	45
45/7 Flag Bearer (M177)	14	27	52
45/8 Parade (M178)	13	24	45
45/9 Combat (M179)	14	27	52
521 Flag Bearer, all 500s (M187)	15	28	53
522 Parade (M188)	13	24	45
523 Soldier in Poncho (M189)	15	28	53
524 Combat (M190)	15	28	53
525 Aviator Holding Bomb (M191)	16	30	55
526 Observer (M192)	28	38	48
527 Aircraft Spotter (M193)	28	38	48
528 Soldier with Bazooka (M194)	28	38	48
529 Motorcycle Rider (M195)	45	60	70
530 Machine Gunner, lying (M196)	28	38	48
531 Machine Gunner, sitting (M197)	28	38	48

Postwar (Continued)	C6	C8	C10
532 Sniper, kneeling (M198)	28	38	48
533 Soldier, w/gas mask w/flare pistol (M199)	28	38	48
534 Sniper (M200)	28	38	48
535 Soldier Throwing Hand Grenade (M201)	28	38	48
536 Anti-Aircraft Gunner (M202)	28	38	48
537 Soldier, w/tommy gun (M203)	28	38	48
538 Soldier Firing Up (M204)	28	38	48
539 Stretcher Bearer (M205)	90	125	150
540 Wounded Soldier, lying (M206)	100	150	175
Flag Bearer, thin (M170)	20	30	40
Machine Gunner Lying, thin (M174)	75	100	125
Machine Gunner Sitting, thin (M173)	65	90	115
Sniper, thin (M175)	40	50	60
Tommy Gunner, thin (M172)	40	50	60

TIN WIND-UPS

Today's toys may be durable, but most are made of plastic, which just doesn't hold the charm and nostalgia of yesterday's tin creations. Those tin toys, made in large numbers mainly before World War II, are among the priciest collectible toys today.

The advent of chromolithography changed the way most toys were produced. Chromolithography was actually developed late in the nineteenth century. The technique allowed multicolor illustrations to be printed on flat tin plates which were molded tin toys.

Starting in the 1920s, lithographed tin toys began to dramatically change toy production. American manufacturers could produce these colorful toys more inexpensively than the classic European toys that had dominated the toy market until this time.

With mass production came mass appeal. New tin mechanical toys were based on the characters and celebrities that were popular at the time. Newspaper comic strips and Walt Disney movies provided already popular subject matter for toy marketers.

Among the most well-known makers of mechanical tin toys were Marx, Chein, Lehman and Strauss.

Others include Courtland, Girard, Ohio Art, Schuco, Unique Art and Wolverine.

Many of these manufacturers had business relationships with each other. Over the years, some would be found working together, producing toys for others, distributing others' toys or being absorbed by other companies. There even appeared to be some pilfering and reproducing others' ideas.

One of the advantages of lithography was that it allowed old toys to be recycled in many ways. When a character's public appeal began to wane, a new image could be printed on the same body to produce a new toy. Or when a toy company was absorbed by another, older models could be dusted off and dressed up with new lithography. Many of the mechanical tin wind-up toys show up in surprisingly similar versions with other manufacturer's name on them.

Remember, the better the condition, the better the value, especially with tin. Those with the original box are true treasures. Tin robots have virtually become an endangered species. Those that are on the market generally command premium prices.

Contributor: Scott Smiles, 157 Yacht Club Way Apt. 112, Hypoluxo, FL 33462-6048, ssmiles664@aol.com, 561-582-6016

Animate Toy Co.

In 1918 this firm was located at East 17th Street in New York City, and its president was L.T. Savage. By 1931 it had moved to 30 North 15th Street in East Orange, New Jersey and employed ten men and forty women. In 1934 the president-vice president was George V. Turnbull and the secretary-treasurer was George H. Webb. Five men and eleven women made up the work force.

	C6	C8	C10
Climbing Tractor, Animate Toy Co., 1929, 9" long	100	150	200
U.S. Baby Tank, Animate Toy Co., pat. 6/20/16, 1918, 2-1/2" long	40	60	80

Automatic Toy Co.	C6	C8	C10
Alpine Express, Automatic Toy Co., 1940s	75	112	150

Automatic Toy Co. (Continued)	C6	C8	C10
Auto Speedway, Automatic Toy Co., c. 1930	125	175	225
Cross-Over Trolley Set, Automatic Toy Co., 1940s	90	135	180
Dizzy Liz, No. 180, Automatic Toy Co., 1940s, 5" long	125	175	225
Jungle Pete, No. 175, Automatic Toy Co., 15" long	90	135	180
Magic Crossroads Track, w/two wind-up cars, Automatic Toy Co., c. 1950	130	195	260
Mystery Alpine Express, Automatic Toy Co., 1940s, 20" long, 14" wide, 2" high	100	150	200
Operation Airlift, two plastic planes, Automatic Toy Co., 1950s	80	120	160

Automatic Toy Co. (Continued)

	C6	C8	C10
Rocket Space Ship, No. 305, sparks, Automatic Toy Co., 1940s, 8-1/2" long	100	150	200
Space Shooting Range, Automatic Toy Co., 1950s, 15" long	150	225	300
Speedway, w/two race cars and garage, Automatic Toy Co., 1930s	175	262	350

Chein

	C6	C8	C10
Alligator, w/native on its back, Chein, 1930s	150	200	300
Army Drummer, plunger-activated, Chein, 1930s, 7" high	125	200	250
Barnacle Bill in a Barrel, Chein, 1930s, 7" high	275	375	500
Barnacle Bill the Sailor, punching a bag, Chein, 7-1/2"	275	375	475
Barnacle Bill the Sailor, Chein, 1930s	250	350	475
Bass Drummer, Chein	150	225	300
Bear, w/hat, pants, shirt, bow tie, Chein, c. 1938	65	90	115
Cabin Cruiser, Chein, 1940s, 9" long	65	98	130

Chein Ferris Wheel, 1930s, $525.

Chein (Continued)

	C6	C8	C10
Chick, brightly colored clothes and polka-dot bow tie, Chein, 4" high	50	75	100
Chicken Pulling Wheelbarrow, Chein, 1930s, 6" x 3-1/2"	50	75	100
Clown, w/umbrella, Chein	125	200	275
Clown in Barrel, Chein, 1930s, 8" high	300	375	575
Clown Puncher, Chein	375	562	750
Dan-Dee Dump Truck, Chein	200	300	400
Doughboy, Chein, 1920s, 6" high	175	262	350
Drum Major, Chein, 1930s, 8-1/2" high	225	325	425
Drummer Boy, w/shako, Chein, c. 1930s, 9" high	100	150	200
Duck, long-beaked, in orange sailor suit, not Donald Duck, but similar, waddles, Chein, 1930s, 6" high	125	175	225
Duck, waddles, Chein, 1930, 4" high	75	100	125
Ferris Wheel, six compartments, ringing bell, Chein, 1930s, 16-1/2" high	275	400	525
Greyhound Bus, Chein, 9" long	85	130	175
Handstand Clown, Chein, 1940s, 6" high	65	100	125
Indian in Headdress, Chein, 1930s, 5-1/2" high	110	175	225
Jumping Rabbit, Chein, 1925, 5" long	120	180	240
Marine, hand on belt, Chein, 1950s, 6" high	120	180	240
Mark I Cabin Cruiser, Chein, 1957, 8-1/2" long	50	75	100
Mechanical Aquaplane, No. 39, boat-like pontoons, no insignia, Chein, 1932, 8-1/2" long, 7-1/2" wingspan	200	300	400
Mechanical Aquaplane, post-WWII insignia, Chein	200	300	400
Mechanical Aquaplane, pre-WWII insignia, Chein	150	250	350
Mechanical Fish, Chein, 1940s, 11"	50	75	100
Mechanical Frog Man, Chein, 1950s, 11" long	100	150	200
Mechanical Rocket Ride, No. 400, Chein, 1950s, 18" high	500	800	1100
Melody Player, No. 135, 4 rolls, Chein, 1930s, 6-3/4" high	100	150	200
Musical Aero Swing, Chein, 1940s, 10" high	283	425	565

Chein Rabbit in Shirt and Pants, c. 1938, $105. Photo courtesy Scott Smiles

Chein Roller Coaster, 1950s, $400. Photo courtesy Don Hultzman; photo by Ron Chojnacki

Chein Roller Coaster, 1938, $500. Photo courtesy Don Hultzman; photo by Ron Chojnacki

Chein (Continued)

	C6	C8	C10
Navy Frog Man, No. 122, Chein, 1950s, 12" long	100	150	200
Pan-Am Clipper, pontoons, Chein, 1930s, 11" wingspan	400	600	775
Peggy Jane Boat, Chein, 13" long	62	93	125
Penguin in Tuxedo-type Jacket, Chein, c. 1940	75	100	125
Pig, Chein, 1940s, 4-1/2" high	50	75	100
Playland Merry-Go-Round, Chein, 1930s, 9-1/2" high	400	600	800
Playland Whip, No. 340, four bump cars, driver's head wobbles, Chein	450	675	900
Rabbit, w/wheelbarrow, Chein	75	125	150
Rabbit in Shirt and Pants, Chein, c. 1938	53	78	105
Rabbit Pulling Cart, Chein	48	72	95
Race Car #52, Chein, 1930s, 6-1/2" long	80	120	160
Racer #3, Chein, 1920s, 6-1/2" long	150	225	300
Ride-A-Rocket, Chein	300	450	600
Rocket Ride, No. 400, four rockets, Chein, 18" high, 11" diameter base	455	685	910
Roller Coaster, w/two cars, Chein, 1950s	200	300	400
Roller Coaster, w/two cars, Chein, 1938	250	375	500
Santa Elf, Chein, 1920s, 6" high	220	330	440

Chein (Continued)

	C6	C8	C10
Ski Boy, No. 157, Chein, 1940s, 7-3/4" long, 5-1/4" tall	150	235	310
Skin Driver, No. 122, Chein, 1950s, 12" long	75	100	125
Ski-Ride, No. 320, Chein, 19" long	225	350	475
Space Ride, No. 205, Chein, 1950s, 10" high	500	750	1000
Space Ride, lever action, Chein, 1940s, 9" high	425	650	850
Spirit of St. Louis Airplane, Chein, 1930s, 8" long, 8" wingspan	250	375	500
Taxi, Chein, 1920s, 7" long	200	300	400
Toy Town Helicopter, Chein, 1950s, 13" long	65	98	130
Turtle, w/native on back, Chein	250	375	525
U.S. Army Sergeant, No. 153, Chein, 1950s, 5-1/2" high	105	158	210
Walking Pelican, Chein, 1930s, 5" high	100	150	200

Courtland Mfg. Co. Circus Elephant and "Monkeys" Cart, $700. Photo courtesy Joe and Sharon Freed

Courtland Mfg. Co.

	C6	C8	C10
Circus Elephant and "African Lions" Cart, No. 400, Courtland Mfg. Co., 11-5/8" long, 3" wide, 3-1/2" high....	250	450	700
Circus Elephant and "Circus Band" Cart, No. 500, Courtland Mfg. Co., 11-5/8" long, 3" wide, 3-1/2" high....	350	550	850
Circus Elephant and "Monkeys" Cart, No. 300, Courtland Mfg. Co., 11-5/8" long, 3" wide, 3-1/2" high....	250	450	700
Easter Rabbit and Trailer, No. 200, Courtland Mfg. Co., 11-5/8" long, 3" wide, 3-1/2" high	75	125	200
Mechanical Parking Meter and Bank, No. 7500, Courtland Mfg. Co., base 6" x 6", 24-1/2" high	150	225	300
Mechanical Rocking R Ranch See-Saw, No. 8000, Courtland Mfg. Co., 17-3/4" long, 2-1/8" wide, 6" high....	125	175	225

Girard

C.G. Wood founded Girard Model Works in Girard, Pennsylvania, in 1906 and his son Frank joined the firm a few years after its inception. Originally the company made patterns, models and special machinery, but in 1918 they began making toys for an unidentified large firm in New York. It was in 1920 that they began making toys under the name Wood's Mechanical Toys. By 1931 Louis Marx was associated with Girard, and during the Depression Marx took over the firm. The last Girard toys seem to have been produced in 1975, though the firm remained in business until 1980. Many of Marx's and Girard's toys are interchangeable.

	C6	C8	C10
Air Mail Bipane, three-engine, Girard..	600	900	1200
Airways Express Plane, Girard, 13" wingspan	175	275	350
Bi-Wing Monoplane, Girard, 1918, 12" long, 14" wingspan (Wood's)	150	225	300

Girard (Continued)	C6	C8	C10
Bus, w/driver, Girard, 1930s, 12-1/2" long	200	300	400
Coolie & Pushcart, Girard	150	200	275
Farm Boy Walking, w/shovel and rake, (Wood's), Girard, 1920, 6"	450	675	900
Fire Chief Siren Coupe, Girard, 1930s, 14" long	250	400	525
Flasho the Mechanical Grinder, Girard, 1920s	200	275	325
Goble the Gobbling Goose, Girard	125	175	250
Man Pushing Wheelbarrow, Girard, 1920s, 5-1/2"	225	325	450
Monoplane, high wing, one-engine, Girard, 1921-22, 13" long	350	525	700
Monoplane, high wing, one-engine, pilot, Girard, 9" long	275	395	550
Pierce-Arrow Coupe, green, orange and cream, Girard, c. 1932, 14" long..	225	338	450
Race Car #2, Girard, 8" long	300	450	600
Railroad Handcar, Girard	200	300	400
Spirit of St. Louis, Girard, 9" long	400	600	800
Tri-Motor Air Lines, Girard, 1920s	175	275	350
Whiz Sky Fighter, biplane, Girard, 7" wingspan	313	470	625

Kingsbury	C6	C8	C10
Ambulance, Kingsbury, 7" long	500	750	1000
Artillery Launcher, Kingsbury	100	150	200
Biplane, single engine, rubber wheels, Kingsbury, c. 1925, 16" long	450	700	950
Bi-Wing Airplane, w/cast-iron pilot, Kingsbury, 1918, 16" long, 17" wingspan	400	600	800
Borden's Milk Truck, Kingsbury	250	375	500
Convertible, w/rumble seat, electric headlamps, hard rubber wheels, Kingsbury, 12-1/2" long	180	270	360
Fireman's Ladder Truck, driver, hard rubber wheels, Kingsbury, 23-1/2" long	200	300	400
Monoplane, high wing, single engine, wind-up wheels and spins prop via rubber band, Kingsbury, 1930s, 11" long	300	450	600
Roadster, electric headlamps, Kingsbury, 12-1/2" long	250	375	500

Kingsbury (Continued)

	C6	C8	C10
Station Wagon, Kingsbury, 1920s.......	150	225	300
Streetcar, No. 782, Kingsbury, 1930s, 9" long..............	200	300	400
Transatlantic Air-Go-Round, Kingsbury........................	250	375	500

Lehmann

	C6	C8	C10
Adam the Porter, Lehmann, 1920s, 9" high................................	400	800	1200
Aha Delivery Van, No. 550, Lehmann, 1907-1935, 5-1/2" long....	500	750	1000
Ajax Warrior, No. 659, w/two clubs, Lehmann, 1914-1944	1000	1500	2200
Alabama Coon Jigger, No. 685, Lehmann, 1912	500	700	900
Am Pol, No. 681, Amundsen driving, figure behind w/umbrella, map of North Pole, Lehmann, 1910-1935...	1800	2700	3750
Anxious Bride Nanni, No. 470, chauffeur on tricycle, woman in car, Lehmann, 1901-1935	800	1300	1965
Autobus, No. 590, Lehmann, 1907-1945	700	1300	2000
Autohutte Garage, No. 771, Lehmann, 1934-1941, 6" long	450	675	900
Baker & Chimney Sweep, No. 450, Lehmann, 1900-1935	1500	2600	4000
Baldur Limousine, No. 739, Lehmann, 1920-1935, 10" long	700	1100	1800
Balky Mule, Lehmann, 1930s, 7-1/2" long	250	350	475
Berolina Car, Lehmann, 1914	1500	2400	3500
Bucking Bronco, No. 625, Wild West, Lehmann, 1909-1945, 6-1/2" long	475	675	925
Climbing Miller, No. 230, cardboard blades, Lehmann, 1890-1945............	300	500	675
Crawling Beetle, The, No. 431, Lehmann, 1848-1935, 4" long	150	225	300
Crocodile, No. 442, Lehmann, 1948-1945	200	300	400
Dancing Sailor, No. 535, Lehmann, 1904-1948, 7-1/2" high	400	600	800
Daredevil Zebra Cart, Zikra, No. 752, Lehmann, 1924-1935	400	600	800
Duo, rooster pulling rabbit, Lehmann, 1918-1945	750	1100	1400
Echo Motorcycle, No. 725, Lehmann, 1917-1935, 8-3/4" long..................	1000	1500	2500

Lehmann (Continued)

	C6	C8	C10
EHE & Co., No. 570, open bed, Lehmann, 1907-1935	325	500	650
EPL I Dirigible, No. 651, Lehmann, 1910-1941	400	600	800
EPL II Dirigible, No. 652, Lehmann, 1912-1958	500	700	1000
Express, No. 140, porter pulling cart, Lehmann, 1888-1918, 6" long	300	400	500
Galop Racer, No. 760, w/garage, Lehmann, 1934-1941	800	1200	1600
Galop Zebra Cart, No. 852, Lehmann, 1954-62	175	250	325
Going to the Fair, Lehmann.................	800	1300	1800
Heavy Swell, No. 525, dude-it-up man, Lehmann, 1904-1918	850	1400	1975
Ito Sedan, No. 679, Lehmann, 1914-1935, 6-1/2"	500	700	900
Kadi, No. 723, two Chinese men carrying tea chest, Lehmann, 1917-27	600	950	1400

Lehmann Kadi, 1917-27, $1400. Photo courtesy Sotheby's, New York

Lehmann Express, 1888-1918, $500. Photo courtesy Sotheby's, New York

Lehmann (Continued)

	C6	C8	C10
Lana Auto, No. 776, Lehmann, 1930-1936	1200	2000	2800
Lehmann's Autobus 590, No. 590, Lehmann, 1907-1945	1000	1800	2400
Li La Hansom Cab, No. 520, early car w/two excited women passengers, driver in top hat and dog w/turning head, Lehmann, 1903-1935, 5-1/2"	1000	1850	2500
Lo & Li, No. 769, clown and ring master, Lehmann, 1924-38	5000	7500	10,000
Lo Lo, No. 540, early car, driver, Lehmann, 1906-1918	500	750	1100
Lu-Lu Bird, Lehmann	100	150	200
Lu-Lu Delivery Truck, No. 763, Lehmann, 1922-1938, 7-1/4" long	1500	2500	4000
Mandarin, No. 565, two coolies carrying Chinese in sedan chair, Lehmann, 1905-41	1500	2500	3700
Mars Cycle, No. 471, Lehmann, 1901-35	450	675	900
Masuyama, No. 773, coolie pulling rickshaw, Lehmann, 1927-1938	800	1400	2000
Mensa Delivery Van, No. 688, Lehmann, 1912-1941	1200	2100	3000
Mikado Family, No. 350, Lehmann, 1894-1918, 6-1/2" long	650	1100	1500
Mixtum, No. 775, African-American driver, Lehmann	1000	1500	2000

Lehmann Paddy Pig, 1903-1935, $1750. Photo courtesy Sotheby's, New York

Lehmann (Continued)

	C6	C8	C10
Mixtum, No. 775, white driver, Lehmann	800	1350	1800
Motor Car Kutsche, Lehmann, 1897-1935, 5-1/2" long	350	575	750
Na-Ob, No. 680, man driving horse cart, wheels marked w/elf, Lehmann, 1917-1938, 6" long	250	350	450
Naughty Boy, No. 495, Lehmann, 1904-1935	800	1300	1800
New Century Cycle, No. 345, Lehmann, 1895-1938, 5" long	400	600	800
Nu-Nu, No. 733, Lehmann, 1924-1938, 4-1/2" long	600	950	1400
Oh My, No. 690, Lehmann, 10" high	450	625	800
OHO, No. 545, patented 1903, Lehmann, 1906-1916	400	600	800
Onkel, Lehmann	375	562	750
Paak-Paak, No. 645, ducklings in cart pulled by duck, Lehmann, 1910-1935	350	450	550
Paddy Pig, No. 500, Lehmann, 1903-1935, 6" long	750	1250	1750
Pao Pao Peacock, Lehmann, 10" long	250	375	500
Performing Sea Lion, The, No. 445, Lehmann, 1899-1935, 7" long	100	150	200
Peter, three-wheeled car, Lehmann	1200	1900	2700
Power Carriage, Lehmann	360	540	720
Quack-Quack, mother duck pulling cart w/three small ducks, Lehmann	300	450	600
Rad-Cycle, Lehmann, c. 1927, 5" long	650	1180	1575
Rollo Chair, Lehmann	1000	1700	2400
Sedan, No. 765, Lehmann, 1927-41, 5-1/2" long	300	400	550
Skirolf, No. 781, skier, Lehmann, 1930-1941	1200	2200	3000
Taku Battleship, No. 671, Lehmann, 1913-1935	450	650	850
Tap Tap, No. 560, man pushing wheelbarrow, Lehmann, 1907-1945	200	275	350
Terra, Lehmann	550	950	1385
Tom, No. 385, climbing monkey, Lehmann, 1895-1945, 8" long	100	150	200
Tut-Tut, No. 490, man in car w/horn, Lehmann, 1903-1935, 6-3/4" long	700	1000	1400
Tyras Walking Dog, No. 432, Lehmann, 1898-1935, 6" long	400	550	750

Lehmann (Continued)

	C6	C8	C10
Uhu, No. 555, amphibious car, Lehmann, 1907-1938	800	1400	2000
Walking Down Broadway, No. 260, strolling couple, Lehmann, 1890-1895	2000	3000	4200
Wild West, No. 625, Lehmann, 1909-1945	400	600	825
Zig Zag, No. 640, Lehmann, 1910-1945, 5" long	750	1125	1500
Zikra, No. 752, Lehmann, 1924-35, 7" long	800	1300	1800
Zulu, No. 721, black man in cart pulled by ostrich, Lehmann, 1918-1938	500	800	1100

Lindstrom

	C6	C8	C10
American Railway Express Truck & Trailer, Lindstrom, 16" long	375	550	725
Baby Wee Speedboat, Lindstrom, 10-1/2" long	40	60	80
Betty, shako walker, Lindstrom, 1930s, 8" tall	175	263	350
Bird, Lindstrom	100	150	200
Bumper Car, Lindstrom, 6-1/2" long	112	168	225
Dancing Dutch Boy, Lindstrom, 1930s, 8" high	125	188	250
Dancing Lassie, shako, Lindstrom, 1930s, 8" tall	100	150	200
Delfine 7 Motorboat, Lindstrom, c. 1930	175	275	350
Ferry Boat, lithographed, Lindstrom, approx. 8-1/4"	100	150	200
Flyer, Lindstrom, 14"	100	150	200
Johnny the Dancing Clown, No. 122, Lindstrom, 1930s, 8" tall	200	300	400
Katrinka, Lindstrom, 1930s, 8" tall	100	150	200
Mammy, shako walker, Lindstrom, 1930s, 8" tall	300	450	600
Miss America Speedboat, Lindstrom	125	175	225
Parcel Post No. 2 Truck, Lindstrom	200	300	400
Racing Car, Lindstrom, 1930s, 6"	175	263	350
Skeeter Bug, bumper car, Lindstrom, 1930s, 9" long	100	150	200
Speedboat, Lindstrom, 7" long	50	75	100
Speedboat, Lindstrom, c. 1950, 18-1/2" long	163	245	325

Lindstrom (Continued)

	C6	C8	C10
Sweeping Betty, Lindstrom	120	180	240
Sweeping Mammy, No. 1750, shako walker while sweeping, Lindstrom, 1930s, 8" tall	212	318	425

Louis Marx Toy Co.

By the 1950s Louis Marx was the largest manufacturer of toys in the world; his empire included six large factories in the United States and ownership of interest in factories in seven other countries. Marx, born in Brooklyn in 1896, worked for "Toy King" Ferdinand Strauss during his teens, and by the age of twenty his energy and enterprise had made him a director of that company. A falling out with Strauss persuaded Marx to go into business for himself, and in 1921 he and his brother began making their own toys, including some adaptations of items by the now-defunct Strauss.

Although Marx made almost every type of toy (with the exception of dolls), his tin wind-up toys are probably the most favored by toy collectors.

	C6	C8	C10
1st Batt. F.D. Chief's Car, siren, battery headlights, Marx Toy Co., 16"	300	450	600
Acrobatic Marvel, monkey on 13" spring and 7-1/2" rocking base, Marx Toy Co., 1930s	118	175	235
Alligator, Marx Toy Co.	75	110	150
Ambulance, w/siren, Marx Toy Co., 1930s, 14-1/2"	350	525	700
Ambulance, "M.D. War Dept.," Marx Toy Co., 1930s	450	675	900
American Tractor, w/implements, Marx Toy Co., 1920s, 10" long	200	300	400
Armored Trucking Co., Marx Toy Co.	150	225	300
Army Dive Bomber No. 482, Marx Toy Co.	150	225	275
Army Staff Car, litho steel, Marx Toy Co., 1930s	250	375	500
Army Staff Car, w/flasher and siren, W-601158, Marx Toy Co., 1940s, 11" long	135	200	300
Army Truck, cloth cover, Marx Toy Co., 1930s, 10"	300	450	600
Automatic Car Wash, w/wind-up car, Marx Toy Co., 6"	200	300	400

Marx Toy Co. (Continued)

	C6	C8	C10
Automatic Fire House, Fire Chief Car, 7-1/2" long; Volunteer Fire Dept. Garage, 19" long, Marx Toy Co., 1950s, 7-1/2" long, 19" long	200	300	400
Automatic Reversing Road Roller, Marx Toy Co., 1925, 9" long	200	300	400
Balky Mule, No. 425, Marx Toy Co., 1897-1938, 8" long	350	450	650
Balky Mule, pre-war, Marx Toy Co....	125	165	250
Be Bop—The Jivin' Jigger, Marx Toy Co., 1948, 10"	210	325	425
Bear Cyclist, Marx Toy Co., 1930s, 6" long..........	163	245	325
Beat it the Komikal Kop, Marx Toy Co., 1930s	475	625	875
Big Lizzie Car, Marx Toy Co., early 1930s, 7-1/4"	150	225	300
Big Parade, w/moving vehicles, soldiers, tin airplane, etc., Marx Toy Co., 1929, 24" long	300	475	650
Big Silver, Mack Dump Truck, Marx Toy Co.	250	375	500
Big Three Aerial Acrobats, Marx Toy Co., 1920..........	200	300	400
Boy on Trapeze, Marx Toy Co...........	100	150	200
Bulldozer Climbing Tractor, caterpillar type, Marx Toy Co., c. 1950s, 10-1/2" long	150	225	300
Bumper Auto, streamlined, large bumpers, front and rear, Marx Toy Co., c. 1939	150	225	300
Busy Bridge, vehicles on bridge, Marx Toy Co., 1935..........	350	525	700
Busy Delivery, Black Pinocchio, Marx Toy Co., 1930s, 9" long, 8" high	675	1000	1200
Busy Miners, includes 2-1/4" tin litho miner's car, Marx Toy Co., 1930s, 16-1/2" long	200	300	425
Busy Parking Station, Marx Toy Co., 1930s, 17" long, w/2" tin race car.....	200	300	400
Butter & Egg Man, Marx Toy Co., 1930s, 8" high	525	775	1000
Cadillac Coupe, Marx Toy Co., 1931	500	750	1150
Cadillac Roadster, trunk w/tools on luggage carrier, Marx Toy Co., 1930, 13" long..........	250	375	500

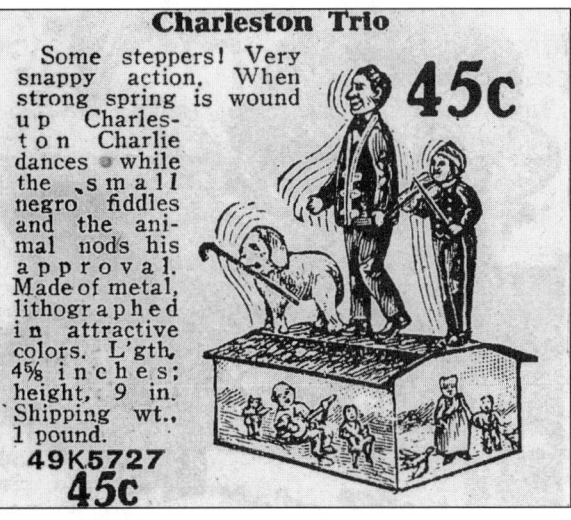

Advertisement for Charleston Trio from the Marx Toy Co.

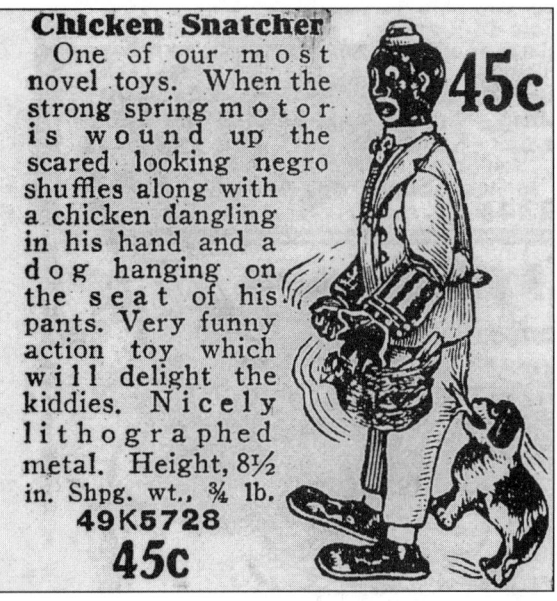

Advertisement for Chicken Snatcher from the Marx Toy Co.

Marx Toy Co. (Continued)

	C6	C8	C10
Car Carrier, three racers, Marx Toy Co., 22-3/4" long..........	600	900	1500
Careful Johnnie, Marx Toy Co., 1950s, 5-1/2" long..........	100	150	200
Caterpillar Climbing Tractor, Marx Toy Co., c. 1950s, 10" long	100	150	200
Charleston Trio, one Black adult, Black child dancer and dog, Marx Toy Co., 1921..........	500	750	1000
Chicken Snatcher, black holding chicken, dog biting at the seat of his pants, Marx Toy Co., c. 1927..........	650	950	1250

Marx Toy Co. (Continued)

	C6	C8	C10
Climbing, Fighting Tank, Marx Toy Co.	125	188	250
Climbing Fireman, Marx Toy Co., 1930s	200	325	425
Climbing Tractor, sparkling, Marx Toy Co., 1960s, 8-1/2" long	112	168	225
Coast Defense, circular, w/three cannon, revolving airplane, Marx Toy Co., 1929	450	685	925
Coast to Coast Greyhound Bus, Marx Toy Co., 1930s	500	850	1200
Coke Coal City Coal Co. Truck, Marx Toy Co.	500	800	1150
Construction Tractor, Marx Toy Co.	300	450	600
Coo Coo Car, Marx Toy Co., 1920s, 7-1/2" long	300	425	550
Cowboy Rider, cowboy w/lariat on dapple or black horse, Marx Toy Co., c. 1941	175	250	350
Crazy Dora nodder head, (also "Dan"), Marx Toy Co.	100	150	200
Cross-Country Flyer, Zeppelin and Airplane fly around 18" hangar tower, Marx Toy Co., 1920	400	600	800
Dan Dipsy Car, plastic nodder, Marx Toy Co., 1950s, 5-1/2" long	200	300	400
Dapper Dan Coon Jigger, Marx Toy Co., 1910	600	900	1300
Dare Devil Flyer, new in 1928, Marx Toy Co., 1920s	400	600	800
Daredevil Motor Drome, w/2" wind-up car, Marx Toy Co., 1930s, 5-1/2" high, 9" diameter	100	150	200
Deluxe Delivery Truck, Marx Toy Co., 1950s, 11"	100	150	200
Deluxe Tractor, six wheels, four in treads, Marx Toy Co.	250	375	500
Dipsy Doodle Bug Dodgem cars, Dan or Dora, Marx Toy Co., 6" high (pair)	262	395	525
Donkey Pulling Cart, w/rider, Marx Toy Co., 1950s, 10" long	110	165	220
Dora Dipsy Car, plastic nodder, Marx Toy Co., 1950s, 5-1/2" long	100	150	200
Dottie the Driver, Marx Toy Co., 1950s, 6-1/2"	100	150	200
Doughboy Tank, two side turrets, w/top turret, soldier w/gun pops out, Marx Toy Co., 1930, 9-1/4" long	175	250	325

Marx Toy Co. (Continued)

	C6	C8	C10
Doughboy Tank, no side turrets, Marx Toy Co.	125	175	250
Driver Training Car, Marx Toy Co., 1950s, 6" long	75	110	150
Drive-UR-Self Car, Marx Toy Co., 1950s, 11" long	325	488	650
Dump Truck, Marx Toy Co., 1950s, 13" long	375	475	575
Fire Dept. Chief, Marx Toy Co., c. 1950s, 11" long	150	200	250
Firemen Joe, Marx Toy Co., 1930s, 8" tall	125	200	300
Firewater Boat, Marx Toy Co., 1920, 9" long	350	525	700
Flipo the Jumping Dog, See Me Jump, on hind legs, Marx Toy Co., c. 1940, 3-1/2" x 4"	150	200	250
Flying Fortress 2095 sparkling aeroplane, Marx Toy Co., 1940s	225	350	450
Funny Face, new in 1928, Marx Toy Co.	500	750	1000
Funny Flivver, Marx Toy Co., c. 1925	325	490	650
George the Drummer Boy, No. 881, w/stationary eyes, Marx Toy Co., 1930s, 9" tall	125	175	225
George the Drummer Boy, w/moving eyes, Marx Toy Co., 1930s, 9" tall	150	225	300
Ghee Whiz Auto Racer, four 2" long tin cars, Marx Toy Co., 1930s, 13" diameter	450	700	1000
Giant King Racer, marked "711," Marx Toy Co., c. 1930s	150	225	300
Giant Reversing Tractor Truck, w/tools, "Hauling," Marx Toy Co., c. 1950s, 14" long	140	210	280
G-Man Pursuit Car, Marx Toy Co., 1930s	355	525	710
Golden Pecking Goose, hops along pecking at ground, dated July 8, 1924, Marx Toy Co., 9-1/2" long	100	150	200
Hauling Tractor Truck, six-wheel, Marx Toy Co.	200	300	400
Hee-Haw Balky Mule, six-color litho, goes backward, forward and rears, farmer and his dog on seat and five milk cans in cart, Marx Toy Co., 1929, 10-3/4" long	200	300	400

Marx Toy Co. Doughboy Tank, $250.

Advertisement for the Honeymoon Express from the Marx Toy Co.

Marx Toy Co. (Continued)

	C6	C8	C10
Helicopter Skyport, two plastic copters, Marx Toy Co., 1950s, 9" x 11"	100	150	200
Highboy Climbing Tractor, Marx Toy Co., c. 1950s, 10-1/2" long	75	125	150
Highboy Tractor, sparkles, Marx Toy Co., c. 1950s, 10" long	100	150	200
Honeymoon Cottage, Marx Toy Co., 1950s	125	175	250
Honeymoon Express, circling train and plane, Marx Toy Co., c. 1940, 9-3/8" diameter	125	200	250
Honeymoon Express, steamlined train on circular track, Marx Toy Co., 1947, 9-3/8"	85	125	175
Honeymoon Express, Marx Toy Co., c. late 1930s	100	150	200
Hoppo the Waltzing Monkey with Cymbals, Marx Toy Co., 1930s, 9-1/2" high	200	300	400

Marx Toy Co. (Continued)

	C6	C8	C10
Ice Man, Marx Toy Co.	300	450	600
Jalopy Pickup Truck, Marx Toy Co., 7"	100	125	150
Jazzbo Jim, Marx Toy Co., 1920s, 9" high	275	400	550
Jolly Joe Jeep, plastic helmet, Marx Toy Co., 1950s, 6" long	175	275	350
Joy-Rider 1929, College Boy driver w/bag, wording on car "goes backward, forward, circles and rears" head moves, Marx Toy Co., 8" long	310	475	625
Jumpin' Jeep, Marx Toy Co., c. WWII, 6"	135	210	275
King Racer, Marx Toy Co., 1930s, 8-1/2" long	325	490	650
Let sthe Drummer Boy Play, Marx Toy Co., 1930s, 8-1/2" high	450	650	825
Light Duty Climbing Tractor, Marx Toy Co., 1930s	150	225	300
Limping Lizzie Car, Marx Toy Co.	200	300	400
Looping Plane, No. 182, Marx Toy Co.	200	300	400
Looping Plane, No. 382, Marx Toy Co.	200	300	400
Lucky Stunt Flyer, Marx Toy Co.	200	300	400
Mack Dump Truck, City Coal Co., Marx Toy Co., 1930s, 13" long	350	525	700
Main Street, moving vehicles, traffic cop, etc., Marx Toy Co., 1929	350	525	700
Mammy's Boy, Marx Toy Co., 1930s, 11" tall	500	750	1000
Mechanical Airplane, Marx Toy Co.	200	300	400
Mechanical Roadster, Marx Toy Co., 1950s, 11"	100	150	200
Mechanical Speed Racer, Marx Toy Co., 1930s, 9" long	100	150	200
Mechanical Speedway Racer, Marx Toy Co.	75	125	175
Mechanical Station Wagon, Marx Toy Co.	125	175	225
Mechanical Taxi Cab, Marx Toy Co., 1950s, 11"	80	120	160
Mechanical Tractor, Marx Toy Co., c. 1930s, 6"	100	150	200
Mechanical Tractor with Earth Grader, Marx Toy Co., c. 1950s, 21-1/2" long	100	150	200

Marx Toy Co. (Continued)

	C6	C8	C10
Merrymakers, four mice, three in band and one dancer, w/marquee, Marx Toy Co., 1929	750	1250	1725
Merrymakers, four mice, three in band and one dancer, without marquee, has conductor with baton, Marx Toy Co., 1929	500	825	1175
Merrymakers, four mice, three in band and one dancer, without marquee, has violinist, Marx Toy Co., 1929	600	950	1300
Midget Climbing Fighting Tank, Pat. No. 1334539, Marx Toy Co., c. 1935, 5-1/2" long	70	100	130
Midget Climbing Tractor, Marx Toy Co., c. 1950, 5-1/2" long	75	115	150
Midget Racer, plastic, Marx Toy Co., 1950s, 6"	50	75	100
Midget Special Race Car No. 2, driver in old headgear and goggles, Marx Toy Co., 1930s, 5" long	75	100	150
Midget Special Race Car No. 7, driver in old headgear and goggles, Marx Toy Co., 1930s, 5" long	75	100	150
Monkey Cyclist, Marx Toy Co., 1930s	100	150	200
Moon Creature, (Japan), Marx Toy Co., 1950s, 5-1/2" high	100	125	175
Motor Squad, sidecar, Marx Toy Co.	240	360	480
Motorcycle Trooper, Marx Toy Co., 1935	212	318	425

Marx Toy Co. Mechanical Speed Racer, 1930s, $200. Photo courtesy Don Hultzman; photo by Ron Chojnacki

Marx Toy Co. (Continued)

	C6	C8	C10
Mountain Climber, Japan, Marx Toy Co., 1960s, 32" long, 4" car	80	120	160
Mysterious Kitty Kat, Marx Toy Co., 1950s, 8"	90	135	180
Mystery Police Cycle, Marx Toy Co., 1930s, 4-1/2"	125	175	250
Mystery Tunnel, Marx Toy Co.	60	90	120
Mystic Motorcycle, Marx Toy Co., c. 1930s	150	225	300
New Flivver, Marx Toy Co., 1920s, 7" long	200	300	400
New Rocket Racer, Marx Toy Co., 1930s, 16"	200	300	400
New York, circular, w/train and tin airplane, new in 1928, Marx Toy Co., 9-1/2" diameter	600	900	1200
Nodding Goose, Marx Toy Co.	75	120	150
North American Van Lines Inc. Long Distance Moving Truck, Marx Toy Co.	125	188	250
Old Jalopy, post-WWII, Marx Toy Co.	150	225	300
Old Jalopy, college boys, post-WWII, Marx Toy Co.	125	225	300
P.D. Motorcyclist, Pat. No. 2001625, Marx Toy Co., 4" long	165	240	325
P.D. Police motorcycle, w/sidecar, on-off lever, wood wheels, Marx Toy Co., 1930s, 3-1/2" long	165	240	325
Parade Drummer, marked "Let the Drummer Boy Play While You Swing and Sway," Marx Toy Co., 1930s	400	600	800
Parcel Post U.S. Mail, Marx Toy Co., early, 8-1/2" long	225	338	450

Marx Toy Co. Old Jalopy, $300. Photo courtesy Scott Smiles

Advertisement for Pinched Roadster from the Marx Toy Co., c. 1927, $650.

Marx Toy Co. (Continued)

	C6	C8	C10
Peter Rabbit, eccentric car, Marx Toy Co.	300	450	600
Piggy, Marx Toy Co., 4" high	50	75	100
Pike's Peak Mountain Climber, Marx Toy Co., 1930s, 3-1/2" car, 30" long	300	450	600
Pinched Roadster, motorcycle cop in circular track, Marx Toy Co., c. 1927, 9-1/2" x 9-1/2"	325	488	650
Play-Away-Piano, w/songbook, Marx Toy Co., 1930s, 9" x 9"	60	90	120
Police Patrol, motorcycle w/sidecar, Marx Toy Co., 1935	300	450	600
Police Precinct Police Patrol Armored Truck, Marx Toy Co., c. early 1930s, 10-1/2"	1800	2800	3800
Police Siren Motorcycle, Marx Toy Co., 1930s, 8" long	200	300	400
Police Squad, motorcycle cop w/sidecar, Marx Toy Co., 8-1/2" long	275	400	550
Power Snap Caterpillar Climbing Tractor, Marx Toy Co., 1950s, 8" long	112	168	225
Prone WW I Soldier, Marx Toy Co., 1925, 8" long	100	150	200
Racer no. 2, Marx Toy Co., 1930s, 5" long	75	110	150
Racer No. 3, Marx Toy Co., 1930s, 5" long	75	110	150

Marx Toy Co. (Continued)

	C6	C8	C10
Racer No. 4, Marx Toy Co., 1930s, 5" long	75	110	150
Racer No. 5, Marx Toy Co., 1930s, 5" long	75	110	150
Racer No. 7, Marx Toy Co., 1930s, 5" long	75	110	150
Racing Car, litho, two-man team, Marx Toy Co., c. 1940, 12"	110	165	220
Racing Car, plastic driver, lithographed, Marx Toy Co., c. 1950, 16" long	125	188	250
Racing Car "27," plastic driver, lithographed, Marx Toy Co., c. 1950	100	150	200
Range Rider, Marx Toy Co., 1940s, 10-1/2" high on rocker base	200	300	400
Range Rider, Marx Toy Co., 1940s, 8-1/2" high	150	225	300
Red Cap Porter, Marx Toy Co.	350	550	750
Red Devil Stunt Auto, Marx Toy Co., 1930s, 12" long ramp w/2-1/2" tin racer	150	225	300
Reversible Coupe, marked "The Marvel Car," Marx Toy Co., c. 1938, 16-3/4" long	248	372	495
Reversing Road Roller, Marx Toy Co.	135	202	270
Reversing Tank, Marx Toy Co., 1930s	65	98	130
Reversing Tractor, Marx Toy Co.	275	412	550
Rex Mars Planet Patrol, pastel colors, Marx Toy Co., 1950s, 9-1/2" long	250	375	500
Rex Race Car, Marx Toy Co., 1920s	162	243	325
Ride 'Em Cowboy, Marx Toy Co.	120	180	240
Ring-A-Ling Circus, early ringmaster and circus animals, green base, Marx Toy Co.	550	825	1280
Ring-A-Ling Circus, early ringmaster and circus animals, pink base, Marx Toy Co.	550	850	1300
Road Roller, w/driver, Marx Toy Co., c. 1930, 8-1/2" long	375	562	750
Rocket Fighter, complete w/tail fin and sparking mechanism, Marx Toy Co., c. 1950s	225	350	475
Rocket Racer, Marx Toy Co., 1930, 16-1/2" long	225	350	475

Marx Toy Co. (Continued)

	C6	C8	C10
Rodeo Joe, Marx Toy Co., 1933	200	300	400
Roll Over Cat, Marx Toy Co.	65	98	130
Roll Over Plane, Marx Toy Co., c. 1920s	150	200	275
Rollover Tank, Marx Toy Co.	75	100	125
Rookie Cop, w/siren, Marx Toy Co., 1930s, 8-1/2"	250	350	475
Rookie Pilot, No. 77, Marx Toy Co., c. 1940, 7" long	295	445	590
Rooster Pulling Wagon, Marx Toy Co., 1930s	60	90	120
Royal Bus Line, Marx Toy Co., 10" long	275	410	550
Royal Coupe, Marx Toy Co., 1920s, 9" long	350	525	700
Royal Van Co., reads "We Haul Anywhere," Marx Toy Co., 9" long..	375	562	750
Running Scottie, Marx Toy Co., 1940s, 5-1/2" long	115	172	230
Sam, the Gardner, includes six plastic tools, Marx Toy Co., 1950s, 8" tall...	125	175	235
Sand and Gravel Truck-Builders Supply Co., Marx Toy Co., 1920......	100	150	200
Scenic Express Train Set, Marx Toy Co., c. 1950s	90	135	180
Sheriff Sam & His Whoopee Car, Marx Toy Co., 1960s, 6" long	200	300	400
Single Track Speedway, eight track sections, Marx Toy Co., 1938, 4" long wind-up car	70	105	140
Sky Hawk Airport Tower, No. 333, two planes, Marx Toy Co., tower 7-1/2" high	175	263	350
Skybird Flyer, c. 1927, Marx Toy Co.	187	280	375
Skyscraper Go-Round, monoplane, Zeppelin, Marx Toy Co., 1930s, 13-1/2" high	400	600	800
Smoky Sam the Wild Fireman, Marx Toy Co.	138	210	275
Snoopy and Gus Hook and Ladder, Marx Toy Co., 8" x 7-1/4"	700	1100	1550
Soap Box Derby Racer No. 3, Marx Toy Co., 5-1/2" long	100	150	200
Soldier, prone, firing rifle, WWI helmet, Marx Toy Co.	90	135	180
Space Mobile, (Japan), Marx Toy Co., 1960s, 32" long, 4" long car......	120	180	240

Marx Toy Co. (Continued)

	C6	C8	C10
Space Satellite with Launching Station, Marx Toy Co., 1950s, 9" x 12" base and plastic accessories..........	70	105	140
Sparkling Climbing Bulldozer Tractor, later, Marx Toy Co.	187	280	375
Sparkling Climbing Fighting Tank, cannon recoils, Marx Toy Co.	125	188	250
Sparkling Climbing Tank, Marx Toy Co., 1939	85	128	170
Sparkling Climbing Tractor, Marx Toy Co., c. 1950s, 8-1/2" long	88	135	175
Sparkling Climbing Tractor, Marx Toy Co., 1940s	93	140	185
Sparkling Climbing Tractor and Trailer, Marx Toy Co., c. 1950s, 16" long	130	195	260
Sparkling Heavy Duty Bulldog Tractor with Road Scraper, Marx Toy Co., c. 1950s, 11"......................	115	162	230
Sparkling Luxury Liner, Marx Toy Co., 1950s, 14" long...........................	85	128	170
Sparkling Mountain Climber Train Set, tin loco and car, Marx Toy Co., 1950s, 9" long	100	150	200
Sparkling Mountain Climber Train Set, Marx Toy Co., 1930s, 11" tall ...	500	750	1000
Sparkling Rocket Fighter Ship, Marx Toy Co.	425	638	850
Sparkling Soldier, crawls, Marx Toy Co., 7-3/4" long	150	225	300
Sparkling Soldier Motorcycle, Marx Toy Co., c. 1940, 11"	350	500	675
Sparkling Space Tank, Marx Toy Co..	187	280	375
Sparkling Super Power Tank, Marx Toy Co., c. 1950s, 9-1/2" long	115	172	230
Sparkling Tank, Marx Toy Co., 4" long	95	142	190
Sparkling Tractor, tractor w/plow blade, Marx Toy Co., 1939	140	210	280
Sparkling Tractor and Trailer Set, "Marbrook Farms," Marx Toy Co., c. 1950s, 21" long...........................	100	150	200

Marx Toy Co. Sparkling Soldier, $300.

Marx Toy Co. Speed Boy Delivery Motorcycle Delivery, 1930s, $600. Photo courtesy Don Hultzman

Marx Toy Co. (Continued)

	C6	C8	C10
Sparkling Turn Over Tank, Marx Toy Co.	50	75	100
Sparkling Warship, same as U.S.S. Washington, Marx Toy Co., 14" long	90	135	180
Speed Boy Delivery Motorcycle Delivery, battery-operated light, Marx Toy Co., 1930s, 9-3/4" long	350	475	600
Speed Boy Delivery Motorcycle Delivery, no lights, Marx Toy Co., 1930s, 9-3/4" long	300	400	550
Speed King Racer, Marx Toy Co., 1930s, 16" long	425	638	850
Speedway Coupe, battery to be inserted for headlights, Marx Toy Co., 8" long	312	468	625
Spic and Span the Hams What Am, drummer and dancer, Marx Toy Co., 1924	1000	1600	2250
Spic Coon Drummer, Marx Toy Co., 1924, 8-1/2" high	900	1400	2000
Streamline Speedway, two wind-up cars w/tin figure-eight track, Marx Toy Co., 1938, 31" long	118	175	235
Streamlined Coupe, Marx Toy Co.	225	338	450
Subway Express, w/plastic tunnel, Marx Toy Co., 1950s, 9-3/8" diameter	90	135	180
Super Streamline Racer, Marx Toy Co., 1950s, 17" long	138	207	275
Tidy Tim Streetcleaner, pushing wagon, Marx Toy Co., 1933, 7-1/2" high, 8-1/2" long	350	500	700
Tom Tom Jungle Boy, Marx Toy Co.	100	150	200

Marx Toy Co. (Continued)

	C6	C8	C10
Toto Acrobat, Marx Toy Co.	100	150	200
Tower Aeroplane, Marx Toy Co., 1940s, two 3" tin airplanes, 7-1/2" high	200	300	400
Toy Town Dairy, horsedrawn cart, Marx Toy Co., 1930s, 10-1/2" long	150	225	300
Toyland Farm Products, milk wagon, Marx Toy Co., 1930s, 10-1/2" long	295	450	590
Tractor, Marx Toy Co., early 1940s	105	158	210
Tractor and Trailer, Marx Toy Co., c. 1950s, 16-1/12" long	150	225	300
Trans-Atlantic Zeppelin, rear propeller, Marx Toy Co., 1930s, 10" long	250	375	500
Tricky Fire Chief, Marx Toy Co., 1925, 4" car on 6" x 10" base	200	300	400
Tricky Motorcycle, non-fail action, Marx Toy Co., 1930s, 4-1/4" long	150	225	300
Tricky Taxi, Marx Toy Co., 4-1/2" long	100	140	200
Tricky Taxi on a Busy Street, Marx Toy Co.	175	262	350
Trolley, headlight, bell, Marx Toy Co., 9" long	170	255	340
Tumbling Monkey, on two chairs, Marx Toy Co., 1930s, 5" high	125	175	225
Tumbling Monkey on Trapeze, Marx Toy Co., 1920s, 6" high	100	150	200
Turn Over Tank, No. 3, Marx Toy Co.	105	158	210
TWA-U.S. Main-990, Marx Toy Co., c. 1941, 5"	120	180	240
U.S. Army Bomber, two-engine, post-war, Marx Toy Co., 1940s	162	243	325
U.S. Army Fighter Plane, Marx Toy Co., 1940, 8" wingspan	185	280	370
U.S. Mail-TWA Biplane, Marx Toy Co., 1930s, 15" long, 18" wingspan	400	600	800
U.S. Main Truck, Marx Toy Co., 9-1/2" long	450	680	975
U.S.S. Washington Battleship, Marx Toy Co.	65	98	130
Vacationland Express, Marx Toy Co.	75	100	125
Wacky Taxi, Marx Toy Co.	125	175	225
Walking Clancy, Marx Toy Co.	400	600	800

Marx Toy Co. Whoopee Car, 1929, $400. Photo courtesy Scott Smiles; photo by Mark Adams

Marx Toy Co. (Continued)

	C6	C8	C10
Walking Drummer Boy, marked "Let The Drummer Boy Play While You Swing and Sway," Marx Toy Co., c. 1939	350	525	700
Wee Scottie, also called Running Scottie, Marx Toy Co., 5" long	88	130	175
Whoopee Car, "Yale-Princeton" pennants on wheels, Marx Toy Co.	350	525	700
Whoopee Car, laughing cows on wheels, driver looks like cowboy, Marx Toy Co., 1929	200	300	400
Whoopee Car with Flappers, Marx Toy Co., 7-1/2" long	250	375	500
Wonder Cyclist, Marx Toy Co., 1930s, 9" high	170	255	340
Xylophonist, Marx Toy Co., 5"	100	150	200
Yellow Cab-LMN 52, Marx Toy Co., 1940s, 6-1/2" long	150	225	300
Zeppelin, Marx Toy Co., 10" long	175	250	325
Zeppelin, Marx Toy Co., 1930s, 27" long	200	300	400
Zeppelin, propeller on front, Marx Toy Co., 1925, 11" long	175	263	350
Zeppelin TransAtlantic, Marx Toy Co., 10" long	175	250	325
Zippo the Climbing Monkey, Marx Toy Co., 1930s, 9-1/2" long	100	150	175

Ohio Art

	C6	C8	C10
Automatic Airport, Ohio Art, 1940s, 9" high	90	135	180
Boat, Ohio Art, 14" long	80	120	160

Ohio Art (Continued)

	C6	C8	C10
Cabin Cruiser, Ohio Art, 1950s, 15" long	60	90	120
Circus Shooting Gallery, Ohio Art, 1950s, 12" high, 17" long	60	90	120
Coast Guard Seaplane, Ohio Art, 1950s, 10" wingspan	75	125	175
Commando Joe, Ohio Art, 1950s, 8" long	125	175	235
Giant Ride Ferris Wheel, Ohio Art, 1950s, 16" high	275	375	500
Hot Job Floatplane, Ohio Art	100	150	175
Injun Chief, Ohio Art, 1950s, 8" long	80	120	160
Jungle Eyes Shooting Gallery, Ohio Art, 1950s, 18" long, 14" high	90	135	180
Mechanical Sea Plane, Ohio Art	100	150	200
Musical Sail Away Ride, Ohio Art	200	300	400
Sea Patrol Seaplane, Ohio Art, 10" wingspan	90	135	180
Switch and Dump Train, Ohio Art, 1950s, 28" long	100	150	200
Traffic Control, Ohio Art, 1950s, 3-1/2" long, base 19" x 13"	60	90	120

Schuco

Schuco was founded in 1912 by Heinrich Muller and Herr Schreyer as Schreyer and Co. They later adopted the name "Schuco" as its trademark. Schuco toys were produced from the 1930s to the 1950s and were marked either "Germany" or "U.S. Zone-Germany." Toys with other markings are reissues.

	C6	C8	C10
Akustico 2002, Schuco, 1940s, 5-1/2" long	100	130	175
Anno 2000, Schuco, 1940s, 5-1/2" long	80	120	160
Beer Drinker, Schuco, 1950s, 5-1/2" high	100	150	200
Buick, No. 5311, Schuco, 9" long	200	300	400
Cadillac DeVille Convertible 5505, plastic, Schuco, 1960s, 11" long	90	135	180
Charly 1005, motorcycle w/driver, Schuco, 1950s, 3-1/2" long	400	550	700
Clown Juggler, No. 965, Schuco, 1950s, 5" high	300	450	600
Combination 4003, w/wind-up horn, Schuco, 1950s, 7-1/2" long	175	263	350

Schuco (Continued)

	C6	C8	C10
Commando Auto, No. 2000, responds to whistle, Schuco, 1950s, 5-3/4" long	150	225	300
Curvo 1000, Schuco, 1950s, 5" long	150	200	275
Dalli 1011, tin car w/plastic driver, Schuco, 1950s, 6-1/2" long	175	250	325
Disneyland Alweg Monorail, play set, Schuco, 1950s	300	450	600
Electro Ingenico, No. 5311/61, Schuco, 1950s, 8-1/2" long car	600	900	1200
Electro Submarine, No. 5552, Schuco, 1950s, 13" long	100	150	200
Elektro Ingenico 5311, remote control, Schuco, 1950s, 8-1/2" long	180	270	360
Examico 4001, five-speed BMW, Schuco, 1950s, 6" long	75	125	175
Fernlenk Auto, No. 3000, part of play set, Schuco, 1950s, 4-1/4" long	160	240	320
Fex 1111, Schuco, 1950s, 6" long	100	150	200
Fire Engine, w/remote control, Schuco, 1950s, 11-1/8" long	1000	1500	2000
Fox and Goose, No. 969, Schuco, 1950s, 4-1/4" high	800	1200	1600
Gas Station 3054, Schuco, 1950s, 8" long	60	90	120
Grand Prix Racer 1070, Schuco, 1950s, 6"	100	150	200
Hegi-Fipsi 110, glider airplane kit, Schuco, 1950	70	100	150
Hopsa, Schuco, 1950s, 4" high	120	180	240
Ingenico 5311/56-MK, part of play set, Schuco, 1950, 8-1/4" long car	500	750	1000
Ingenico 5335 MK, play set, Schuco, 1950s, 8" long car	700	1050	1400
Jaguar 1250, Schuco, 1940s, 5-1/2" long	175	250	325

Schuco Examico 4001, 1950s, $175. Photo courtesy Don Hultzman; photo by Ron Chojnacki

Schuco (Continued)

	C6	C8	C10
Kommando Anno 2000, Schuco, 1940s, 5-1/2" long	100	150	200
Latso 3042 Truck, Schuco, 1950s, 4-1/2"	60	90	120
Magico Alpha Romeo, No. 2010, Schuco, 1950s, 9-1/2" long	600	900	1200
Magico Auto 2008, responds to blowing, Schuco, 1950s, 5-1/2" long	300	450	600
Magico Car and Garage, Schuco, 1950s, 6"	120	180	240
Mercedes 190SL, No. 2095, Schuco, 1950s, 8"	225	350	450
Mercedes TYP SSK 1928, Schuco, 1950s, 4" long	100	150	200
Mercer Auto 1225, Schuco, 1950s, 7-1/2"	100	150	200
Micro Racer 101, Porsche style, Schuco, 1950s, 3-1/2" long	100	150	200
Micro Racer 102, Indy style, Schuco, 1950s, 3-1/2" long	100	150	200
Micro Racer 1036, Schuco, 1950s, 4-1/2"	100	150	200
Micro Racer 1040, Schuco, 1950s, 4" long	75	112	150
Micro Racer 1041, Schuco, 1950s, 4" long	75	110	150
Micro Racer 1042, Schuco, 1950s, 4" long	100	150	200
Micro Racer 1043, Schuco, 1950s, 4" long	100	150	200
Micro Racer '57 Ford 1045, Schuco, 1950s, 4" long	100	150	200
Micro Racer Apha Romeo 1048, Schuco, 1950s, 4" long	100	150	200
Micro Racer Go Kart 1035, Schuco, 1950s, 4" long	100	150	200
Micro Racer Hot Rod 1036, Schuco, 1950s, 4" long	90	135	180
Micro Racer Mercedes-Benz 1038, Schuco, 1950s, 4" long	100	150	200
Micro Racer Mercedes-Benz 1044, Schuco, 1950s, 4" long	110	165	220
Micro Racer Mercer 1036/1, Schuco, 1950s, 4" long	100	150	200
Micro Racer Porsche 1047, Schuco, 1950s, 4" long	110	165	220

Schuco (Continued)

	C6	C8	C10
Micro Racer Rally 1034, eight three-lane tracks, Schuco, 1950s, 10' 6" long	60	90	120
Micro Racer Stake Truck 1049, Schuco, 1950s, 4" long	100	150	200
Micro Racer Volkswagen 1046, Schuco, 1950s, 4" long	100	150	200
Micro Racer Volkswagen Polizei 1039, Schuco, 1950s, 4" long	100	150	200
Micro-Jet 1030 Thunderjet, Schuco, 1950s, 5" wingspan, 5-1/2" long	80	120	160
Micro-Jet 1031 Magister 170R, Schuco, 1950s, 5" wingspan, 5-1/2" long	80	120	160
Micro-Jet 1032 Super Sabre F 100, Schuco, 1950s, 5" wingspan, 5-1/2" long	90	135	180
Micro-Jet 1033 Douglas F4 D-1, Schuco, 1950s, 5" wingspan, 5-1/2" long	80	120	160
Mikifex 922, non-fall action mouse, Schuco, 1950s, 3-1/2" long	40	60	80
Mirakocar 1001, non-fall action, Schuco, 1950s, 4-1/2" long	75	100	125
Mirakomot 1012, non-fall action, Schuco, 1950s, 5-1/4" long	300	450	600
Mirako-Peter, No. 1013, rare, Schuco, 1950s, 5" long	1000	1500	2000
Monkey Car, orange-black, smiling monkey, Schuco, 1930s, 6" long	1400	2100	2800
Motodrill 1006, circular action, Schuco, 1950s, 5" long	300	450	600
Motodrill Clown 1007 Motorcycle, composition head, rare, Schuco, 1950s, 5" long	1000	1500	2000
Mystery Car 1010, non-fall action, Schuco, 1950s, 5-1/2" long	100	150	200
Patent Motorcar, Schuco, 1950s, 4-1/2" long	100	150	200
Pick-Pick, No. 905, Schuco, 1950s, 4-1/2" long	100	150	200
Porsche Formel II-1037, Schuco, 1950s, 4-1/2" long	80	120	160
Racing Boat 1015, non-fall action, Schuco, 1950s, 5" long	90	135	180
Radio 4012 Musical Car, Schuco, 1950s, 6"	200	300	400
Sonny 2005, mouse w/balloon in BMW, Schuco, 1950s, 5-1/4" long	300	450	600

Schuco (Continued)

	C6	C8	C10
Spirit of St. Louis Plane, Lindbergh figure, rare, Schuco, 1920s, 4" long	800	1200	1600
Station Car 3118, Schuco, 1950s, 4-1/2" long	60	90	120
Studio Racer 1050, includes tools, Schuco, 1950s, 5-1/2" long	125	188	250
Submarine 3007, has some plastic parts, Schuco, 1950s, 12" long	113	170	225
Synchromatic 5700, resembles Packard Hawk, Schuco, 1950s, 11" long	500	750	1000
Telesteering 3000 Limo, Schuco, 1950s, 4" long	75	100	125
Tippy, No. 990, Scotty, Schuco, 1950s, 4" long	80	120	160
Trip-Trap, dog, Schuco, 1950s, 7" long	400	600	800
Turn Miki Clown, Schuco, 1950s, 3-3/4" high	200	300	400
Varianto 3010, two-car play set, Schuco, 1950s, cars are 4-1/2" long	100	150	200
Varianto 3010 Super, service station, Schuco, 1950s, w/two 4-1/2" cars	170	225	340
Varianto 3010/0, truck and garage, Schuco, 1950s, 4-1/2" long	75	100	125
Varianto 3041 Limo, Schuco, 1950s, 4" long	100	150	200
Varianto 3064, all plastic, Schuco, 1950s, 8" long	30	45	60
Varianto Box 3010/30, includes tin garage and 3041 Limo, Schuco, 1950s, 4-1/2" long	135	200	250
Varianto Bus 3044, Schuco, 1950s, 4" long	70	105	140
Varianto Electro 3112, truck, Schuco, 1950s, 4" long	75	100	125
Varianto Electro 3112u, truck, Schuco, 1950s, 4-1/2" long	75	100	125
Varianto Lasto, No. 3042, truck, Schuco, 1950s, 4-1/4" long	80	120	160

Strauss

Ferdinand Strauss emigrated to the United States from Alsace, France. He worked as a toy importer in the early 1900s and by 1914 had four New York toy shops. When World War I disrupted imports, he began to manufacture toys himself. In 1918 his company was located in East Rutherford, New Jersey, and was staffed by fifty employees. Eventually Strauss was known as "The Founder of the Mechanical Toy Industry in America." Evidently Strauss was wholly or partially out of business in the late 1920s, but later resumed production of wind-ups and other toys until at least 1941-42. He is also famous for having employed the very young Louis Marx.

Strauss

	C6	C8	C10
Air Devil Monoplane, Strauss	300	450	600
Alabama Coon Jigger, Strauss, 9-3/4"	400	575	750
Alabama Coon Jigger—Tombo, Strauss, 1918, 10-1/2" high, 3" x 5" base	425	600	775
Aluminum Flying Airship LA 1017, Strauss, 1930s, 9" long	275	362	550
Big Show Circus Truck, Strauss, 9-1/2" long	600	950	1400
Big Trixo Climbing Monkey, Strauss, 10" long	150	225	300
Billiards Player, Strauss, 1920s	300	450	600
Black Porter Pulling Wheelbarrow, Strauss, 6-1/4"	150	225	300
Bus Deluxe, Strauss, 1920s, 12" long	550	825	1250
Check-A-Cab, Strauss, 8-1/2" long	500	750	1025
Chicago Zeppelin, Strauss, 1930s, 9" long	400	600	800
Circus Wagon, containing lion and tamer, no engine compartment, Strauss, 8-1/2" long	420	630	840

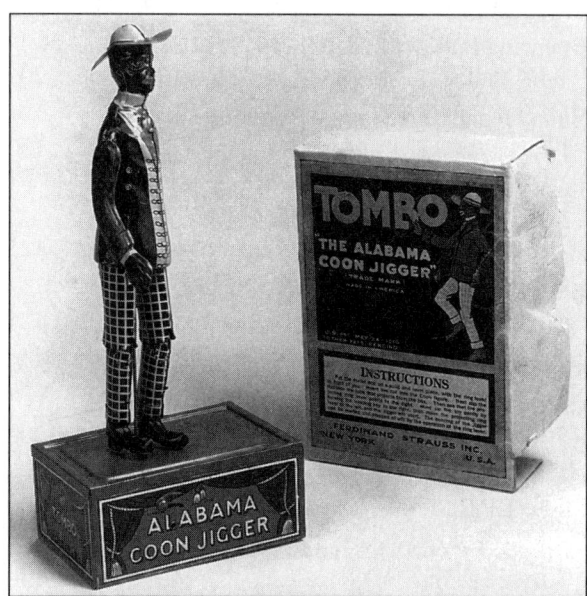

Strauss Alabama Coon Jigger—Tombo, 1918, $775. Photo courtesy Mapes Auctioneers and Appraisers

Strauss (Continued)

	C6	C8	C10
Circus Wagon, w/engine compartment, Strauss, 10" long	1100	1700	2500
Dandy Jim, copyright 1921, Strauss, 1920s	500	750	1200
Dizzie Lizzie, Strauss	250	375	500
Flying Airship Dirigible, Strauss	200	300	400
Ham and Sam the Minstrel Team, piano player and banjoist, Strauss, 1921, 6-1/2" long	600	850	1250
Haul Away Truck, No. 22, dump body, Strauss	240	360	480
Hooligans Hack, Strauss	300	450	600
Interstate Double Decker Bus, Strauss, 1920, 10-1/2" long	500	750	1000
Jackee the Hornpipe Dancer, No. 51, Strauss, 8-1/2" long	500	800	1150
Jazzbo Jim the Dancer on the Roof, Strauss, 1910, 10" high	375	550	725
Jenny the Balky Mule, No. 55, six-color litho, goes backward, forward and rears, farmer holding extended tin grain pail from his seat in front of mule's face to keep him moving, vegetables in cart, Strauss, 1920s, 10" long	250	350	450
Jitney Bus, Strauss, 1920s, 9-1/4" long	225	350	425
Jocko the Golfer, Strauss, 1920s	300	400	500
Knock-Out Prize Fighters, No. 52, Strauss, c. 1910, 7" high	325	450	575
Kraka Jack Car, Strauss, 1920s, 5-1/2" long	150	225	300
Leaping Lena, Strauss	300	450	600
Long Haulage Truck, Strauss	350	525	700

Strauss Jenny the Balky Mule, 1920s, $450. Photo courtesy Scott Smiles

Strauss (Continued)

	C6	C8	C10
Lux-A-Cab, Strauss, 8-1/2" long.........	500	800	1200
Mailplane, Strauss, 1930s....................	225	350	475
Miami Sea Sled, Strauss, 1920s, w/4" dinghy attached, 10" long	250	375	500
Monkey Driving Three-wheel Cart Bulled by Bulldog, Strauss, 1930s, 4-1/2" high	280	420	560
Old Jalopy, The, w/four college kids, Strauss..	100	150	200
Play Golf, Strauss, 1920s, 7" x 12" base w/5" high golfer	275	412	550
Red Flash Racer, Strauss.....................	400	550	750
Red-Cap Porter, porter pushing a large trunk, Strauss	300	450	600
Rollo Chair, black man pushing boardwalk chair, marked "Stock, DRGM, December 6, 1921," Strauss...	500	800	1100
Santee Claus, in sleigh w/two reindeer, Strauss, 1921, 6" high	1000	1500	2000
Speedwagon, Strauss...........................	200	300	400
Standard Oil Truck, "73," Strauss.......	325	488	650
Tip Top Dump Truck, Strauss.............	500	750	1050
Tip Top Man with Wheelbarrow, Strauss..	80	120	160
Tip Top Porter, No. 40, Strauss, 1920s, 6" long	275	400	525
Tippy Canoe, Strauss...........................	175	250	350
Tom Twist, Strauss, 1920s, 8-1/2" tall	450	675	900
Travel Chiks, chickens on railroad car, Strauss, 1930s	400	550	675
Trikauto, No. 53, Strauss.....................	200	300	425
Water Sprinkle Truck, Strauss	450	675	900
What's It? Car, No. 53, Strauss, 1923, 9-1/2" long	600	900	1200
Yell-O Taxi, Strauss, 8-1/2" long........	400	600	800

T.P.S.

T.P.S. is the trademark of Toplay, Ltd., founded in 1956 and noted for its most unusual and unique mechanical toys. More T.P.S. toys are listed in Battery Operated section.

	C6	C8	C10
Animal Barber Shop, T.P.S., 1950s, 5" high..	300	400	500

T.P.S. Big League Hockey Player, 1950s, $475. Photo courtesy Don Hultzman

T.P.S. (Continued)

	C6	C8	C10
Animals Playland, T.P.S., 1950s, 9-1/4"...	225	300	375
Ball Playing Giraffe, T.P.S., 1950s, 8-1/2" tall	200	300	400
Bear Golfer, T.P.S., 1950s, assembled 7-1/2" long.....................	175	225	300
Bear Playing Ball, T.P.S., 1950s, 19" long, 4" high	250	300	375
Big League Hockey Player, T.P.S., 1950s, 6" tall	275	375	475
Bo Bo the Juggling Clown, T.P.S., 1950s, 6"	400	500	700
Bouncing Ball Dolly, T.P.S., 1950s, 5-1/4" tall	125	150	200
Bunny Family Parade, T.P.S., 1950s, 13".......................................	100	125	150
Busy Choo Choo, T.P.S., 1950s, 5-1/2" x 9-1/4" base, w/2-1/4" tin locomotive...	75	100	125
Busy Mouse, T.P.S., 1950s, 6" x 9" base, w/3-1/4" tin mouse....................	75	100	125
Calypso Joe, T.P.S., 1950s, 6" tall	300	400	500
Candy Loving Canine, T.P.S., 1950s, 5-1/2" high	125	150	200
Champ on Ice—Bear Skater Trio, rare, T.P.S., 1960s, 9" long	500	700	900
Circus Acrobatic Seal and Ball, T.P.S., 1950s, 5" high	100	125	150
Circus Bugler, w/trombone, T.P.S., 1950s, 7" tall	325	425	525

T.P.S. (Continued)	C6	C8	C10
Circus Clown and Monkey, T.P.S., 1950s, 5" high	150	225	300
Circus Clown on Ball, T.P.S., 1950s, 5-1/2" high	150	225	300
Circus Cyclist, T.P.S., 1950s, 6-1/2" tall	450	600	750
Circus Parade, T.P.S., 1950s, 11-1/2" long	200	300	400
Circus Parade—Juggling Duck and Friends, T.P.S., 1950s, 9" long	150	225	300
Circus Seal, w/plastic ball on nose, T.P.S., 1960s, 6-1/2" high	75	100	125
Cleo Clown—The Dogs, T.P.S., 1950s, 4-1/2" high	200	300	400
Climbing Panda, all plastic, T.P.S., 1970s, 6" high	40	60	80
Climbing Pirate, string climber, T.P.S., 1960s, 6" long	140	180	220
Climbo the Climbing Clown, string climber, T.P.S., 1960s, 6" long	180	230	300
Clown Jalopy Cycle, friction, T.P.S., 1960s, 9" long	325	425	525
Clown Juggler with Ball, T.P.S., 1950s, 6" tall	300	400	500
Clown Juggler with Monkey, T.P.S., 1950s, 9-1/2" tall	500	700	900
Clown Making the Lion Jump Thru the Flaming Hoop, T.P.S., 1960s, 4-1/2"	180	270	360
Clown on Rollerskates, T.P.S., 1950s, 5-3/4" tall	175	250	300
Clown Trainer and His Acrobatic Dog, T.P.S., 1960s, 4-1/2" high	150	225	300
Cock-A-Doodle, T.P.S., 1960s, 8" long	50	75	100
Combat Tank on Battle Front, T.P.S., 1960s, 6-1/4" x 15" base, w/2-1/4" tank	125	175	200
Comical Clara, T.P.S., 1960s, 5-1/2" tall	300	375	450
Coney Island Scooter, T.P.S., 1960s, 10" square w/2-1/2" bumper car	150	200	250
Dancing Couple, T.P.S., 1960s, 5-1/2" tall	100	125	150
Dreamland Airport, T.P.S., 1960s, 6-1/2" x 12" base w/3-1/2" tin helicopter	125	150	175
T.P.S. (Continued)	C6	C8	C10
Drive Tester, T.P.S., 1960s, 7" x 10-1/2" base and two 2" cars	150	200	250
Duck Amphibious Taxi, T.P.S., 1960s, 6-1/2" long, 4-3/8" high	500	600	700
Duck Family Parade, T.P.S., 1950s, 12" long	100	125	150
Duck the Mailman, Turn-N-Go action, T.P.S., 1960s, 4-1/2" high	500	600	700
Educational Pet Pooch, T.P.S., 1960s, 4" high	100	150	200
Fairyland Taxi, similar to "Wagon Fantasyland," T.P.S., 1950s, 11" long	200	250	350
Family Giraffe Loco, locomotive w/three cars called "Kiddy," "Mammy," and "Pappy," T.P.S., 1960s, 11" long	150	225	300
Fishing Bear, T.P.S., 1950s, 7-1/2" high	175	225	275
Fishing Monkey on Whale, T.P.S., 1950s, 9" long	225	300	375
Flying Birds with Voice, includes two birds, T.P.S., 1960s, 4" diameter base	150	175	225
Gay 90s Cyclist, T.P.S., 1950s, 7" high	225	300	375
Girl Skipping Rope, T.P.S., 1960s, 12" long, 6" high	150	225	300
Girl with Chickens, T.P.S., 1960s, 6" tall, 5" long	250	325	400
Happy Caterpillar, T.P.S., 1950s, 13" long	80	120	160
Happy Hippo, brown, T.P.S., 1950s, 5-1/2" long	350	450	600
Happy Skaters, rabbit w/solid pants, T.P.S., 1950s	250	325	425
Happy Skaters, bears, T.P.S., 1950s, 6-1/2" tall	225	300	375
Happy Skaters, monkey, T.P.S., 1950s, 5-1/2" tall	250	375	500
Happy Skaters, rabbit w/plaid pants, T.P.S., 1950s, 5-1/2" tall	300	375	500
Happy the Violinist, striped pants and black shoes, T.P.S., 1950s, 9" tall	150	200	275
Happy the Violinist, bowtie, red jacket and red shoes, T.P.S.	250	325	450
Hapy Hippo, gray, T.P.S., 1950s	400	525	675

T.P.S. Happy Skaters, 1950s, $500. Photo courtesy Don Hultzman; photo by Ron Chojnacki

T.P.S. Happy the Violinist, 1950s, $275. Photo courtesy Don Hultzman; photo by Ron Chojnacki

T.P.S. Jolly Wiggling Snake, 1960s, $175. Photo courtesy Don Hultzman; photo by Ron Chojnacki

T.P.S. Juggling Clown with Apples, 1950s, $650. Photo courtesy Don Hultzman; photo by Ron Chojnacki

T.P.S. (Continued)	C6	C8	C10
Hockey Player, T.P.S., 1950s, 6" tall	175	275	375
Hungry Whale, No. 1960s, T.P.S., 1950s, w/3" long small whale or fish, 5" long	50	75	100
Joe the Acrobat, clown, T.P.S., 1950s, 5-1/2" high	450	625	750
Joe the Xylophone Player, T.P.S., 1950s, 5" tall	300	375	450
Jolly Wiggling Snake, T.P.S., 1960s, 7-1/2" long	100	125	175
Juggling Clown with Apples, T.P.S., 1950s, 8-1/2" tall	400	500	650
Ladder Truck, T.P.S., 1950s, 2" tin fire engine on 5-1/2" x 9-1/4" base	80	120	160
Lady Bug & Tortoise with Babies, T.P.S., 1960s, 7" long	60	90	120

T.P.S. (Continued)	C6	C8	C10
Lady Bug Family Parade, T.P.S., 1950s, 12" long	60	75	100
Lucky Monkey Playing Billiards, includes plastic balls, T.P.S., 1960s, 6" long	225	275	350
Magic Choo Choo, T.P.S., 1960s, 5-1/2" x 9-1/4" base w/2-1/4" tin locomotive	75	100	125
Magic Circus, includes tin seal and monkey, T.P.S., 1960s, 6" high	125	150	175
Magic Cross Road, T.P.S., 1960s, 5-1/2" x 9-1/4" base w/2-1/4" tin locomotive	75	100	125
Magic Tunnel, T.P.S., 1960s, 6" x 9" base w/2" tin "Dreamland Bus"	150	200	250
Mama Kangaroo with Playful Baby in Her Pouch, T.P.S., 1960s, 6" tall	125	175	225
Midget Lady Bug, T.P.S., 1960s, 7-1/2" tall	50	75	100
Missile Robot, T.P.S., 1960s, 6" high	80	120	160
Monkey Basketball Player, T.P.S., 1960s, 7" high	225	300	400

T.P.S. (Continued)

	C6	C8	C10
Monkey Golfer, T.P.S., 1960s, assembled 7-1/2" long	225	275	325
Monkey on Whale, T.P.S., 1950s, 4" long, 3-3/4" high	250	400	500
Mountain Climber, string climber, T.P.S., 1960s, 6-1/2" long	175	225	300
Mounted Cavalryman with Cannon, T.P.S., 1960s, 5-1/2" high, w/2-1/2" long tin cannon	275	425	550
Mouse Race Cat, T.P.S., 1960s, 10" x 10"	100	125	150
Mr. Caterpillar, T.P.S., 1960s, 12" long	100	125	150
Oscar the Seal, w/ball on nose, T.P.S., 1950s, 6-1/2" high	125	150	175
Oscar the Seal, w/flour-bladed plastic propeller on nose, T.P.S., 1950s	100	125	150
Pango Pango, T.P.S., 1950s, 6" tall	150	225	300
Performing Seal and Monkey with Fish, T.P.S., 1960s, 4-1/2" tall	300	425	575
Plane the Loop Pilot, w/remote control, T.P.S., 1950s, 6" high	150	225	300
Playland Scooter, T.P.S., 1960s, 6" x 9" base w/2" tin car	100	125	175
Police Patrol, T.P.S., 1950s, 5-1/2" x 9-1/2" base and 2" tin police car	80	120	160
Pop Eye Pete, T.P.S., 1960s, 5-1/2" tall	300	400	525
Pussy Cat Chasing Butterfly, T.P.S., 1960s, 4-1/2" high	150	200	250
Rabbit and Bear Playing Ball, T.P.S., 1950s, 19" long, 5" high	200	300	425

T.P.S. (Continued)

	C6	C8	C10
Samson the Strongman, T.P.S., 1960s, 6" tall	550	650	825
Satellite Fleet, T.P.S., 1960s, 12" long	150	225	300
Seal and Monkey with Fish, rare, T.P.S., 1950s, 5" high, 4" long	250	375	500
Shuttle Zoo Train, T.P.S., 1960s, 5-1/2" x 9-1/4" base and two-piece tin train	100	150	200
Skating Chef, African American, T.P.S., 1950s, 6"	325	450	525
Skating Chef, white, T.P.S., 1950s, 6" tall	200	275	350
Skip Rope Animals, T.P.S., 1960s, 8" long	110	165	220
Skippy the Tricky Cyclist, T.P.S., 1950s, 6" tall	150	225	300
Slim the Seal and Friends, w/four-bladed propeller on nose, T.P.S., 1960s, 10" long	300	400	500
Sports Car Race, w/four plastic racers, T.P.S., 1960s, 8" x 14" base	100	150	200
Susie the Ostrich, rare, T.P.S., 1960s, 5-1/2" high	500	700	900
Susy Bouncing Ball, T.P.S., 1960s, 5-1/2" tall	100	125	150

T.P.S. Two Gun Tex, $375. Photo courtesy Don Hultzman; photo by Ron Chojnacki

T.P.S. Satellite Fleet, 1960s, $300. Photo courtesy Don Hultzman

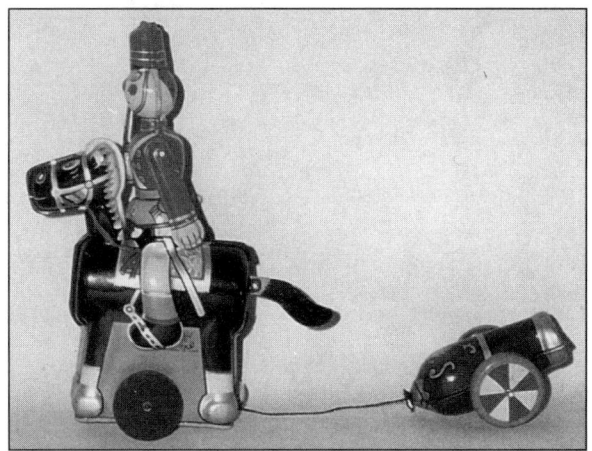

T.P.S. Mounted Cavalryman with Cannon, 1960s, $550. Photo courtesy Don Hultzman

T.P.S. (Continued)

	C6	C8	C10
Take-off Airport, T.P.S., 1960s, 5-1/2" x 9-1/2" base w/3" tin airplane	125	150	200
Tippy Toy Train, gravity action, T.P.S., 1960s, 6" diameter, 4" high	60	90	120
Touchdown Pete, T.P.S., 1950s, 5" tall	250	325	450
Tricycle Tot, T.P.S., 1960s, 5-1/2" long	125	175	225
Trombone Player, black hair, T.P.S., 1950s, 5-1/4" tall	200	275	325
Tumbling Chimp, T.P.S., 1950s, 4-1/2"	150	225	300
Two Gun Tex, T.P.S., 11" long	200	300	375
Violinist, T.P.S., 1950s, 5-1/4" tall	200	250	325
Wagon Fantasyland, T.P.S., 1960s, 11" long	200	250	350
World Champion Auto Racer, T.P.S., 1960s, 5-1/2" x 9-1/2" base, 2-1/4" tin car	100	125	150

Technofix

The Technofix Co., founded in Nuremberg, Germany, by Gebruder Einfalt, was engaged in German military technology during World War II. After the war, Technofix diverted its expertise to toy manufacturing. Among their toys were impressively large, three-dimensional, platform toys. These colorful items were made from stamped tin blanks and highlighted with delicate relief features that duplicated realistic outdoor-recreational themes. In the late 1950s vacuform plastic took the place of tin, and, as a result, quality declined and sales dropped. Later many Technofix toys carried the Ohio Art trademark.

	C6	C8	C10
Alpine Express No. 300, (Ohio Art No. 614), Technofix, 1950s, 6-1/2" x 32" long extended, two 3" tin cars	120	180	240
Cable Car No. 303, Technofix, 1950s, 7-3/4" x 18-1/2" long, two 1-3/4" long tin cars	220	330	440
Coney Island No. 290, Technofix, 1950s, 14" x 21" long, two 3" long tin cars	125	175	250
Grand Prix, Technofix, 1950s, 14" x 21" long, three 3" tin cars	150	200	275
Holiday Camp No. 304, Technofix, 1950s, 9" x 28-1/2" long, two 3-1/2" cars	400	600	800
International Airways No. 309, Technofix, 1950s, 9" x 28" base, 5" long plastic jet airplane	300	450	600
Lift Garage No. 308, Technofix, 1950s, 10-1/2" x 15" long base, three 1-3/4" tin cars	100	200	300
Motorcycle and Sidecar No. 225, Technofix, 1950s, 7" long, 4-3/4" high	200	300	400
Mystic Station No. 306, Technofix, 1950s, 17" x 8" base	100	125	150
Rallye, plastic base and four tin cars, Technofix, 1950s, 15" x 18"	300	450	600
Rocket Express, includes two tin cars, Technofix, 1950s, 14-3/4" long	220	330	440
Silver Mine Express, Technofix, 1950s, 23" x 6" base, w/3" long tin car	90	135	180
Toboggan No. 290, Technofix, 1950s, 14" x 21" long base, two 3-1/2" tin cars	150	225	300

Technofix Cable Car No. 303, 1950s, $440. Photo courtesy Don Hultzman

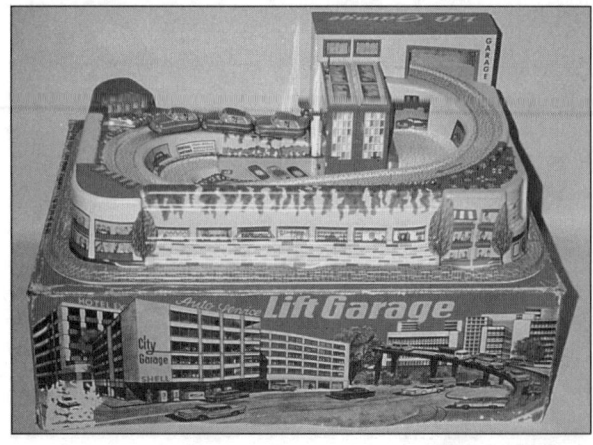

Technofix Lift Garage No. 308, 1950s, $300. Photo courtesy Don Hultzman

Technofix Trick Motorcycle, 1950s, $600. Photo courtesy Don Hultzman; photo by Ron Chojnacki

Technofix (Continued)	C6	C8	C10
Touchdown Chimp, Technofix, 1950s, 3-1/2" high	140	210	280
Traffic Control, Technofix, 1950s, 13" x 19" long base, three 3-1/2" tin cars	50	75	100
Traffic Crossing with Police Control, Technofix, 1950s, two 3" tin cars	100	150	200
Trick Motorcycle, Technofix, 1950s, 7" long	300	450	600

Unique Art Mfg. Co.

Unique Art Mfg. Co. began producing toys in 1916 when it introduced its Merry Juggler and Charlie Chaplin. In 1931 it was located at Waverly and Peshine Avenues in Newark, New Jersey. Its president was Wm. Marbe. In a 1946-47 directory the address was 200 Waverly Avenue in Newark, and the president was Samuel Burger.

	C6	C8	C10
Artie the Clown in his Crazy Car, Unique Art Mfg. Co.	300	450	600
Bombo the Monk, two-piece, Unique Art Mfg. Co., 1930s, tree 9-1/2" high, monkey 5-1/2" long	100	150	200
Capitol Hill Racer, Unique Art Mfg. Co., 1930s, 17-1/2" long, w/2" racing car	100	150	200
Casey the Cop, Unique Art Mfg. Co., early	500	800	1200
Dandy Jim Dancer, Unique Art Mfg. Co., 1921	500	750	1000
Daredevil Motor Cop, Unique Art Mfg. Co., 1940s, 8-1/2" long	300	450	600
Finnegan, w/cardboard luggage, Unique Art Mfg. Co., 1930s, 14" long	200	300	400
Flying Circus, elephant supports flying plane and flying clown, Unique Art Mfg. Co.	450	675	900

Schuco Motodrill Clown 1007 Motorcycle, 1950s, $2000. Photo courtesy Don Hultzman

Unique Art Mfg. Co. (Continued)	C6	C8	C10
G.I. Joe and His Jouncing Jeep, post-WWII, Unique Art Mfg. Co., 7"	200	275	400
G.I. Joe and the K-9 Pups, Unique Art Mfg. Co., c. 1941, 9" high	150	225	300
Gertie the Galloping Goose, Unique Art Mfg. Co., 1930s, 9-1/2" long	145	220	290
Hee Haw donkey Pulling Milk Cart, Unique Art Mfg. Co., 10" long	150	225	300
Hillbilly Express, three pieces, Unique Art Mfg. Co., 1930s, 3-1/4" tin locomotive, 18" long	100	150	200
Hobo Train, dog biting pants of hobo atop train, Unique Art Mfg. Co., 1920s, 8-1/2"	300	450	600
Hott an' Tott Musical Band, Unique Art Mfg. Co., 1920s	500	800	1200
Jazzbo Jim—The Dancer on the Roof, Unique Art Mfg. Co., 1920s, 10" high, base 5" x 3" x 3"	250	375	500
Kiddy Cyclist, steers figure-eight pattern and rings bell, Unique Art Mfg. Co., 1930s, 8-3/4" tall	300	400	500
Kid-Go-Round Plastic Horsemen and Boat, Unique Art Mfg. Co.	150	225	300
Krazy Kar, new in 1921, Unique Art Mfg. Co.	300	450	600
Lincoln Tunnel, moving vehicles, cop, Unique Art Mfg. Co., 1935, 24" long	200	300	400
Motorcycle Cop, Unique Art Mfg. Co., 1930s, 9" long	300	400	500

Unique Art Mfg. Co. Kiddy Cyclist, 1930s, $500. Photo courtesy Scott Smiles

Unique Art Mfg. Co. Rodeo Joe Crazy Car, $300.

Unique Art Mfg. Co. (Continued)

	C6	C8	C10
Musical Sail-way Carousel, w/three kids in spinning plastic boats, Unique Art Mfg. Co., 9" tall	170	255	340
Pecking Goose, Witch and Cat, Unique Art Mfg. Co.	350	525	700
Rap and Tap, boxers in ring, Unique Art Mfg. Co., 1921	500	750	1000
Rodeo Joe Crazy Car, Unique Art Mfg. Co.	150	225	300
Rollover Motorcycle Cop, Unique Art Mfg. Co., 1935	300	400	500
Sky Rangers Plane and Zeppelin, revolving from tower, Unique Art Mfg. Co., 1933	200	300	400

Wolverine

	C6	C8	C10
Acrobat, Wolverine, 1940s	125	175	225
Acrobatic Monkeys, No. 810, Wolverine, 1930s, 10" diameter base	200	300	400

Wolverine (Continued)

	C6	C8	C10
Autolift, includes 2-1/2" tin car w/four sections of track, Wolverine, 1930s, 10-1/4" high	225	300	400
Drum Major, No. 27, pat. 1892546, Wolverine, 1930s, 13-5/8" tall on rectangular 4-1/2" x 6-1/2" base	200	300	400
Drummer Boy, Wolverine, 1930s, 14" high	150	250	300
Farm Wagon, plastic, Wolverine, 1950s, 10" long	25	40	50
Jet Roller Coaster and Small Car, Wolverine, 21" long extended	155	233	310
Loop-A-Loop, includes small car, No. 30, Wolverine, 1930s, 19"	175	262	350
Luxury Liner, Wolverine	100	150	200
Mechanical Man on the Flying Trapeze, Wolverine, 1930s, 8-1/2" high	120	180	240
Merry-Go-Round, No. 31, includes four tin-litho flags, Wolverine, 1930s, 11" diameter, 12" high	275	400	525
Neck & Neck, horse-racing game, Wolverine, 1940s, 36" long	70	105	140
Pontiac Mystery Car, Wolverine	100	150	200
S.S. Wolverine, Wolverine, 14-1/2" long	100	150	200
Sandy Andy Caterpillar Tractor-Trailer, Wolverine, 21" long	500	750	1000
Sandy Andy Circus, dancing toy, Wolverine	150	225	300
Sandy Andy Tank, Wolverine, 14" long	90	135	180
Zilotone, w/six interchangeable records, Wolverine, 1930s	400	550	725

Woodhaven

Research has established that in the 1930s Herman Joerger bought Animate Toy, and about the same time, Ranger Toys. He sold the business to his son, Herman, Jr., who in turn sold it to his son, Kurt. The firm made toys until at least 1939. It was located in Woodhaven, New York, and is now called Woodhaven Telesis Corporation, making sheet metal parts to order.

	C6	C8	C10
Robot Bus with the Mechanical Brain, Woodhaven, 1940s, 13-1/2" long	78	115	155

Woodhaven Tractor, $130. Photo courtesy John Monteleone

Wyandotte Hoky-Poky, $275. Photo courtesy Scott Smiles

Woodhaven (Continued)

	C6	C8	C10
Tractor, marked "1916" but produced and sold much later, Woodhaven	65	100	130

Wyandotte

	C6	C8	C10
Acrobatic Monkeys, Wyandotte, 1930s	200	300	400
Carnival, Wyandotte, 16" x 11"	425	650	850
Carousel, Wyandotte, 5-1/4" high	150	225	300
Chicken Pulling Chick in Cart, Wyandotte, 7-1/2" long	75	100	125
Duck Pulling Tin Easter cart, litho, wooden wheels, Wyandotte, 15" long	50	75	100
Ducky Ducklings, Wyandotte	90	135	180
Hoky-Poky, handcar w/two clowns, Wyandotte	150	200	275

Wyandotte (Continued)

	C6	C8	C10
Man on the Flying Trapeze, Wyandotte, 1930s, 9" high	100	150	200
Mechanical Handcar, Wyandotte, 1935, 6-1/2" long	200	300	400
Red Ranger Ride 'Em Cowboy, No. 515, Wyandotte, 6-1/2" high	140	210	280

Yone

Yone was a Japanese manufacturer of tin wind-up and friction toys in the early to mid-1960s.

	C6	C8	C10
Bears Seesaw, Yone	130	195	260
Chef, Japanese, Yone, c. 1960s	90	135	180
Pirate, Japanese, Yone, c. 1960s	115	172	230
Soldier, Japanese, Yone, c. 1960s	100	150	200

VEHICLES

Modern man has always had a love affair with machines that move. Partial evidence of this is the amazing number of toy vehicles that have been produced in the twentieth century. In fact, it could be reasonably argued that toy vehicles are collected more than any other type of toy.

With the dawn of the modern industrial age, the mass production of full-size automobiles and their toy counterparts seemed to go hand-in-hand. As cars rolled off assembly lines, their miniature replicas were not far behind.

The earliest toy automobiles came along soon after their big daddy originals in the late nineteenth century and were produced in cast iron. But it wasn't until World War I that toy production really began to hit its stride.

The Early Days

Firms such as Arcade and Hubley are among the most well-known and sought-after manufacturers of early cast-iron vehicles.

Cars, trucks and buses produced by Arcade Manufacturing of Freeport, Illinois are highly valued to toy vehicle collectors. Arcade actually began producing toys in the late 1800s, but it wasn't until around 1920 when the company reportedly issued its first toy vehicle, a replica of a Chicago Yellow Cab. After that came more realistic models of actual cars, trucks and buses. The company's slogan was "They Look Real."

Hubley is another name associated with quality toy vehicles. This Pennsylvania company began manufacturing cast-iron toys in the 1890s, mostly horse-drawn wagons, trains and guns. By the 1930s, Hubley was producing the cast-iron cars that became their most well-known products. Many were patterned after actual automobiles of the day, while others were apparently looser interpretations of reality. Some of the Hubley vehicles also included company names, and some of the most interesting pieces had separate nickel-plated grilles.

One of the more skilled makers of smaller scale cast-iron vehicles was A.C. Williams. The Ohio company began producing toys in the late 1800s. The smaller cars and airplanes produced by A.C. Williams were intended for the five-and-dime market of the time. Williams toys are difficult for the novice collector to identify since the toys bear no markings.

Steel Takes Over

One of the most famous manufacturers of toy cars and trucks was Buddy "L." These large pressed-steel toys were not the kind of toys bought for display or quiet play on the living room floor. These were big trucks (around two feet long) designed for tough play.

Buddy "L" toys grew out of the Moline Pressed Steel company of Moline, Illinois. The company was named for the son of the company's owner, reportedly for whom the first toys were produced. The Buddy "L" toys most sought by collectors were produced in the 1920s and 1930s and were of very heavy-duty construction. Starting in the early 1930s, the company began to use lighter-weight materials.

The Buddy "L" name has remained, but its post World-War II toys are not considered in the same league as its early issues, which command high collector prices today.

Buddy "L" is best remembered for its heavy-duty trucks, but another name that was synonymous with trucks was Smith-Miller. Founded by Bob Smith and Matt Miller, the company specialized in "famous trucks in miniature." Smith-Miller was later known as Miller-Ironson Corporation, but is more commonly referred to as Smitty Toys. They produced large cast-metal and aluminum trucks.

Because of their outstanding quality, some of the Mack trucks made by Smith-Miller are very highly regarded among toy collectors. The Smith-Miller name continues today, with new limited-edition trucks produced for collectors.

Wyandotte is another company associated with pressed steel vehicles. Known as either Wyandotte Toys or All Metal Products, this Michigan company produced several large steel vehicles with baked enamel finishes in the 1930s. Not all Wyandotte toys are marked, which tends to cause some confusion among collectors, but the vehicles can often be identified by their art-deco styling and wooden wheels.

Another company that produced large steel toys was Structo. The company originally produced metal construction sets, but developed a line of vehicles in the 1920s.

Slush Molds

Slush casting was a process simple enough to be done in tiny factories and even in home industries during the Depression. A few large manufacturers made toys in this way—most notably Barclay, Manoil, Savoye, Kansas Toy and Novelty and others, but many were made by anonymous, small, unidentifiable, local operations, using molds made and marketed by a few firms. Many slush-cast toys are of very little value today, but there are exceptions. Foremost among these were dealer promotional replicas of real cars, made by Banthrico and National Products. Other very accurate and detailed slush models, similar in size and scale to the contemporary Tootsietoys, can be valuable. Most notable among these are certain nicely cast models of the Reo Victoria, Packard, Chrysler Imperial, Cord coupe (late 1920s), Buick and Model A Ford. Lincoln White Metal Works made these, and others made with an extra mold part resulting in detailed radiator grilles. Tommy Toy made other small accurate replicas, with the names cast on the door sides.

Rubber Toy Vehicles

The Auburn Rubber Company of Auburn, Indiana was not the first to introduce rubber toys to the American market, but they were no doubt the largest and had the greatest impact on the toy field. After introducing some toy soldiers in 1935, Auburn brought out its first vehicle in 1936—a beautiful coffin-nosed Cord sedan. Today, the Auburn Cord is one of the most highly prized rubber toys and is seldom seen offered for sale.

Auburn followed the Cord with a wealth of vehicles, including trucks, farm tractors and implements, motorcycles, racers, fire engines, military vehicles, aircraft, ships, and trains. It seems that 1952 was Auburn's last year of marketing rubber toys exclusively. The 1953 Auburn catalog contained a vinyl motorcycle, believed to be their first vinyl toy. By 1955 their toy line was mostly vinyl with a few rubber varieties hanging on. The 1956 catalog was exclusively vinyl, except for two rubber fire engines, the last rubber toys to be marketed by Auburn.

The Sun Rubber Company of Barberton, Ohio, was the second largest producer of rubber toys. Like Auburn, they produced a full line of toys in addition to vehicles, including dolls, balls and baby squeak toys. Sun Rubber's 1936 catalog contains a large selection of cars, trucks and racers. In later years, they added a few airplanes and military. Among the most famous of the Sun Rubber vehicles are the Walt Disney characters—Mickey Mouse and Donald Duck driving a tractor, firetruck, roadster or airplane. By 1955, Sun's catalog line largely consisted of athletic balls, and the Disney toys were included as the only vehicle toys.

Auburn and Sun made the vast majority of rubber toys we see today, but there were a significant number of rubber toys made by other companies, mostly prior to World War II. Several companies from the rubber industry produced rubber toy vehicles, including Firestone, Seiberling, Barr and Rainbow. All of the Rainbow, Barr and Seiberling toys appear to have been made from 1935-1936, or at least based on real cars from those years. Most of the Seiberling or Barr toys are 1935 Fords; the Firestone toys include a 1935 Ford, a 1936 Ford and a 1939 Mercury. Rainbow's vehicles seem to be based on the 1935 Oldsmobile. Some of these toys were mass-marketed through dime stores, just like Auburn and Sun toys; although, some were sold or given away at expositions and exhibits. All of the Firestone toys seem to be marked with some significant event, like the Texas Centennial in 1936.

Many rubber toys were produced as promotionals for the automobile industry and are not marked to indicate who manufactured them. A number of Chrysler, DeSoto, Dodge and Plymouth promotionals were produced during the mid-1930s and are highly prized as collectibles.

A few rubber vehicles were produced as very inexpensive toys, perhaps sold in sets, and can take the form of either a solid rubber or hollow vehicle. These toys often had the wheels molded into the body, so they could not turn. Many of these solid rubber toys are two-dimensional and are referred to as "flat" toys. Although they were originally sold as inexpensive toys, they are actively sought by collectors and constitute a small, but important, segment of the field.

Die Cast

Other popularly collected vehicles are smaller die-cast models, generally three to six inches long. Probably the leading producer of this type of toy was Tootsietoy.

Although few toys were produced by Tootsietoy before 1920, it was during the 1920s when the name Tootsietoy began to appear regularly. By the 1930s, the company was producing a wide line of toys, many of which are highly prized by collectors today. Tootsietoy's Federal vans from the 1920s are among the most sought-after toys, particularly those with company logos.

Being mass produced and economically priced, Tootsietoys were widely available in the five-and-dime arena. The success of these products no doubt led to several competitors.

One of the competitors was Barclay, which also produced die-cast vehicles, although most were generally considered of lesser quality than Tootsietoys. The first Barclay vehicles had metal tires, but in the mid-1930s, white rubber tires on wooden axles were introduced. Metal axles soon replaced the wood, and black tires replaced white after World War II.

Another competitor soon emerged from Europe—Dinky Toys were manufactured from 1933 through the 1970s in England and France. Their vehicles were high quality die cast, at least until the mid-1960s, generally in 1:43 scale.

Another competitor in this classification of small die-cast vehicles is Corgi, which came on the scene in the late 1950s. Corgi was the trade name for the die-cast toys which were produced by England's Mettoy Company.

One of the best known series of toy cars today is Matchbox. These die-cast beauties are roughly three-inches in length. However Lesney, the company that produced them, did manufacture several larger scale cars before it began the Matchbox line. Some of these early Lesney vehicles are valued at up to $2,000 each.

Matchbox vehicles were immensely popular, so much so that in the United States, Mattel introduced a similar line called Hot Wheels. The California-based company gave its cars a California-type appeal, focusing on colorful hot rods that appealed to youngsters.

In the head-to-head battle that followed, Lesney at one time was producing 5.5 million toys a week.

Eventually, Lesney lost the battle and went into receivership. Matchbox was restructured and sold twice, eventually landing with Tyco Toys. In 1996, Mattel purchased Tyco, bringing Matchbox cars into their company.

Tips on Grading

Demand and desirability are affected by a number of factors, one of which is nostalgia. As a guide to other factors affecting desirability, there are a few broad, easy clues. Accuracy of scale and proportion, the use of many different cast parts, cast-in or decal logos and details and hand-painting (by the original maker, but not by some later child or collector) all enhance the value. In most cases, a four-inch roadster with a separate chassis, separate nickel-plated radiator and headlights, and a separate cast figure will be worth much more than a two-piece vehicle with the halves riveted together. While any imperfections or scratches always lessen a vehicle's value, such things are more likely to deflate prices on vehicles such as Hot Wheels or Matchbox cars. On the latter two, any defect will bring the value down about twenty-five percent.

Reproductions are usually easy to spot once one has gained a little experience. They are usually held together by a long screw, which is threaded all the way to the head. Only a few genuinely old toys are assembled with a screw rather than a long peaned rivet, and the few screws used often had only about a quarter-inch threaded at the tip (the Hubley Packard is an important exception). Modern axles are usually a hollow rolled piece of sheet metal, much like a long shear pin, though a few are rods with threaded ends and sheet metal acorn nuts. The castings themselves are the most dependable giveaway, but require a little experience. The old castings are thinner, lighter and smoother, the modern ones being gritty, thick and coarse of detail

A.C. Williams

A.C. Williams was founded in 1886 when Adam Clark Williams bought the J.W. Williams Company from his father. After a fire in 1893, the firm moved from Chagrin Falls, Ohio, to Ravenna. Toy production began about this time. Small cast-iron toys were Williams' specialty, with banks, cars, and aircraft predominant. A.C. Williams retired in 1919, but the firm continued to make toys until 1938, after which it continued in business in a non-toy capacity. Williams marked few, if any, of its toys. Two clues to an A.C. Williams toy are turned steel hubs and starred axle peens.

	C6	C8	C10
Car, four-casting nickeled radiator car, 4" long	75	112	150
Car Carrier, w/three Austins, 1920, 12-1/2" long	450	675	900
Coupe, two-piece body, 1936, 3" long	95	145	190
Coupe, cast iron, rumble seat, side mounts, rubber tires, 1930, 6-3/4" long	155	225	310
Delivery Van, 8" long	350	525	700

A.C. Williams (Continued)

	C6	C8	C10
Dump Truck, 6-1/4" long	195	292	390
Laundry Truck, 8" long	400	600	800
Lincoln Touring Car, 7" long	312	470	625
Mack Gas Tank Truck, 3-3/4" long	122	185	245
Mack Gas Tank Truck, 5-1/8" long	100	150	200
Mack Gas Tank Truck, 7-1/4" long	350	525	700
Mack Stake Truck, 3-1/2"	45	68	90
Mack Stake Truck, 4-1/4"	80	120	160
Mack Stake Truck, 5-1/8"	112	170	225
Mack Stake Truck, 7" long	150	225	300
Mack Stake Truck, 8-1/2"	200	300	400
Mack Truck, 3-1/2" long	45	68	90
Mack Truck, 4-3/4" long	95	140	190
Mack Truck, 6-3/4" long	100	150	200
Model T Coupe, 6" long	180	270	360
Moving & Storage Truck, 3-1/2" long	112	168	225
Racer, boattailed, 6-1/2" long	262	395	525
Sedan, 5" long	75	112	150
Sedan, cast iron, streamlined rear fender, c. 1930, 6-1/2" long	175	265	355
Sedan, cast iron, interchangeable body, c. 1931, 6-3/4" long	350	525	700
Stake Truck, "C to C Co.," two pieces, 7" long	200	300	400
Steam Roller, 1930s, 5-1/2"	95	145	190
Studebaker, two-tone sedan, c. 1933-34, approx. 4" long	110	165	220
Tank, 4" long	73	110	145
Taxi, 5-3/4" long	182	275	365
Touring Car, w/driver, 5"	100	150	200
Touring Car, cast iron, 9-1/2" long	475	712	950
Willys Knight, cast iron, w/driver, 1920s, 8" long	120	180	240
Wrecker, 6-1/2" long	250	375	500

All American Toy Company

All American was founded by Clay Steinke in Salem, Oregon, in 1948. It continued until 1955, with its location in the Jorgenson Building on Ferry Street. At its peak, it employed forty-two people. In total, it sold 26,000 toys. And despite the formidable 1950 price of $20, All American's most popular toy was

The Cargo-Liner, Timber Toter and Utility Truck were some of the new offerings from All-American in 1953. Photo from 1953 All-American catalog

the Timber Toter. Collectors should note that toy vehicles made by All American had air-horn steering and Goodyear tires.

Patrick Russell purchased All American Toy Company in 1992. Available now are parts and new limited edition vehicles.

	C6	C8	C10
C-5 Cattle Liner, 38" long	500	800	1150
CL-8 Cargo Liner, 38" long	470	705	940
D-3 Dyna-Dump, 20" long	295	445	590
Hay Feed and Grain	275	410	550
HD-7 Play-Dozer, 9" long	338	505	675
HH-9 Heavy Hauler, 38" long	475	710	950
L-2 Timber Toter, w/logs, 38" extended length	275	415	555
LJ-4 Timber Toter, Jr., w/lumber, 20" long	212	318	425
MS Midget Skagit, battery-powered, 18" long	300	450	600

All American Toy
Company (Continued)

	C6	C8	C10
S-1 Scoop-A-Veyor, 16" long	237	355	475

American Metal Toys

	C6	C8	C10
Mack Truck, "Giant," 26-1/2" long	800	1400	2000
Packard Coupe, steerable front wheels, 1920s, 54" long	3000	5000	7000
Pedal Car, Velie, c. 1918	1600	2500	3400
Pedal Car, dump truck, tin, "Juvenile Auto," red and yellow, 57" long	2000	3500	5000
Tank, throwing flame, flame touching hull	40	60	80
Tank, throwing flame, flame not touching hull	45	67	90
Tank, No. 25, throwing flame	60	90	120
Tank, "22" on side	50	75	100

Arcade

In 1869, a foundry in Freeport, Illinois, was organized as a two-man partnership under the name of Novelty Iron and Brass Foundry. It was dissolved in 1885 when a new, larger factory was incorporated under the name of Arcade Manufacturing Co.

Arcade made industrial castings and household items, but no toys. After a disastrous fire in 1892 and management changes in 1893, toys began to appear in its catalog, and by the early 1900s the line had become so extensive that a fifty-page catalog was issued showing a large line of notions and novelties, small stoves, banks and a few trains, including a unique pile-driver. But it was not until an enterprising young lawyer married the daughter of one of the officers and joined the firm in 1919 that the firm rapidly became one of the major makers of cast-iron toys.

Struck by the large numbers of Yellow Cabs in the streets of Chicago, the young man approached the Yellow Cab Company with a novel proposition: in return for the sole right to make toy replicas of the cab, the Yellow Cab Company would have the exclusive right to use the toy in its advertising. Success was instantaneous.

In the booming 1920s, the company's sales swelled so much that a new and larger plant was built in 1927. Two years later, the stock market crash heralded the Great Depression, and hard times hit the small car business just as it did the large ones.

Cheap competition and dwindling demand for toys costing more than a dime had brought the company to the brink of bankruptcy by 1933. Management gave the firm new life with an exclusive arrangement to provide souvenir replicas of the fairground buses made by G.M.C. for the Chicago Century of Progress.

As with most toy compaies, Arcade stopped making toys during Warold War II

After the war, the company returned to making industrial and household hardware and a few toys, but cheaper toys eclipsed the more expensive cast-iron toys. In 1946 the firm was sold to the Rockwell Manufacturing Co. of Pittsburgh. Arcade is no longer in business.

Arcade toys were meant to be played with and are extremely rare in Mint condition. The year listed is the year the toy was introduced.

Contributor: Michael W. Curran, Illinois Antiques, P.O. Box 545, Hampton, IL 61256, 309-496-9426.

	C6	C8	C10
A.C.F. Bus, 1927, 11-1/2" long (AR1)	1700	2700	4100
Ambulance, No. 188, 1932, 6" long (AR7)	370	550	740
Ambulance, No. 187, 1932, 7-3/4" long (AR6)	400	700	1200
Austin Autocrat Road Roller, No. 291, 1928, 7" long (AR10)	300	475	675
Austin Delivery Truck, No. 173, 1932, 3-3/4" long (AR11)	50	75	100
Austin Racer, No. 175X, 1932, 3-3/4" long (AR12)	50	90	135
Austin Roadster, No. 174, 1932, 3-3/4" long (AR13)	125	200	275
Austin Roll-A-Plane, 8"long (AR14)	500	900	1400
Austin Stake Truck, No. 176X, 1932, 3-3/4" long (AR15)	125	200	300
Austin Wrecker, No. 177X, 1932, 3-3/4" long (AR16)	125	200	300
Borden's Milk Bottle Truck, No. 2640X, 1936, 6-1/4" long (AR19)	1000	1600	2400

Left to Right: Arcade Manufacturing Company A.C.F. Bus, 1927, 11-1/2" long, $4100; Arcade Manufacturing Company Yellow Parlor Coach Bus, 1926, 13" long, $2200. Photo courtesy Bill Bertoia Auctions

Arcade Manufacturing Company Austin Wrecker, No. 177X, 1932, 3-3/4" long, $300

Arcade Manufacturing Company (Continued)

	C6	C8	C10
Brinks Express Truck, 1932, 11-3/4" long (AR20)	8000	15,000	20,000
Buick Opera Coupe, 1927, 8-1/2" long (AR21)	2500	4400	6250
Bus, No. 317, Double-Decker, "Chicago Motor Coach" stamp, 1936, 8-1/4" long (AR24)	400	675	950
Car Carrier, No. 238, Ford AA truck w/5" Ford Model A cars or three 6" Ford Model A cars, 1930, 24-1/2" long (AR26)	2000	3500	5000
Car Transport, No. 2977, holds two sedans and two trucks, 1937, 11-1/2" long (AR28)	427	640	900
Car Transport, No. 3107, came w/two No. 1501 sedans, No. 1502 stake truck and No. 1503 wrecker, 1937, 18-1/2" long (AR27)	900	1350	1800
Carry Car Truck and Trailer Set, No. 2970, carries three Austins, 1934, 14-1/4" long (AR29)	650	1000	1650
Century of Progress Bus, No. 3220, 1933, 10-1/2" long (AR37)	175	275	425

Arcade Manufacturing Company Brinks Express Truck, 1932, 11-3/4" long, $20,000. Photo courtesy Bill Bertoia Auctions

Arcade Manufacturing Company Checker Cab, No. 157, 1932, 9-1/4" long, $62,000. Photo courtesy Bill Bertoia Auctions

Arcade Manufacturing Company (Continued)

	C6	C8	C10
Century of Progress Bus, No. 3210, 1933, 12" long (AR36)	200	325	450
Century of Progress Bus, No. 3250, 1933, 14-1/2" long (AR35)	250	375	525
Century of Progress Bus, No. 3230, 1933, 7-5/8" long (AR38)	100	175	250
Century of Progress Yellow Cab, 6-3/4" long (AR38B)	1000	2000	3200
Checker Cab, No. 157, came w/and w/o "Checker" on visor, 1932, 9-1/4" long (AR40)	15,000	20,000	62,000
Chevrolet Coupe, No. 1150X, rumble seat, 1934, 4-3/8" long (AR42)	150	250	350
Chevrolet Coupe, No. 121X, 1929, 8-1/4" long (AR41)	700	1200	1800
Chevrolet Panel Delivery Truck, No. 2620X, 1936, 4" long (AR43)	125	175	275
Chevrolet Sedan, No. 1170X, 1934, 4-1/4" long (AR45)	70	110	180

Arcade Manufacturing Company Chevrolet Coupe, No. 121X, 1929, 8-1/4" long, $1800. Photo courtesy Virginia Caputo

Arcade Manufacturing Company Chevrolet Superior Sedan, 1925, 7" long, $1050. Photo courtesy Bill Bertoia Auctions

Arcade Manufacturing
Company (Continued)

	C6	C8	C10
Chevrolet Sedan, No. 122X, 1929, 8-1/4" long (AR44)	900	1500	2200
Chevrolet Superior Roadster, 1925, 7" long (AR48)	1000	1700	2500
Chevrolet Superior Sedan, 1925, 7" long (AR49)	450	700	1050
Chevrolet Superior Touring Car, 1925, 7" long (AR50)	700	1250	2000
Chevrolet Utility Coupe, 1925, 7" long (AR51)	750	1300	1950
Chevrolet Wrecker Truck, No. 2630X, 1936, 4-1/4" long (AR52)	150	225	325
Chief Fire Chief Coupe, No. 1240, 1934, 5" long (AR54)	500	800	1400
Chief Fire Chief Coupe, No. 1230, 1934, 6-3/4" long (AR53)	1500	2500	3500

Arcade Manufacturing Company Chevrolet Superior Touring Car, 1925, 7" long, $2000. Photo courtesy Bill Bertoia Auctions

Arcade Manufacturing
Company (Continued)

	C6	C8	C10
Coast to Coast GMC Transcontinental Bus, No. 4378X, 1937, 9" long (AR55)	200	325	475
Coupe, no 1922 date on spare (AR60)	850	1250	1750
Coupe, No. 109, no Arcade markings, rumble seat opens, 1932, 6" long (AR61)	300	450	650
Coupe, "1922" on spare tire, 9" long (AR59)	1500	2500	4000
Deluxe Sedan, No. 1590X, same as Yellow Cab No. 1590Y, but w/top lights and sun roof ground off, 1941, 8-1/2" long (AR62)	500	825	1250
DeSoto Sedan, No. 1460X, 1936, 4" long (AR63)	150	225	325
Double Decker Bus, No. 3180, 1939, 8" long (AR64)	425	625	900
Dump Truck, No. 2320, 1936, 4-1/2" long (AR65)	90	130	200
Express Truck, No. 214X, 1929, 5" long (AR71)	150	250	400
Express Truck, No. 207X, 1929, 8" long (AR69)	450	650	1000
Fageol Bus, 1925, 12" long (AR72)	375	550	800
Fire Chief Car, 1941, 5-5/8" long (AR78A)	160	300	450
Fire Engine, No. 6990, 1941, 13-1/2" long (AR83)	700	1150	1650
Fire Engine, pumper, 1923, 7-1/2" long (AR79)	225	375	525
Fire Engine, No. 1740, pumper, 1936, 9" long (AR80)	475	775	1250
Fire Ladder Truck, No. 1820, 1936, 7" long (AR84)	200	300	450

Arcade Manufacturing Company Fire Engine, No. 6990, 1941, 13-1/2" long, $1650. Photo courtesy Bill Bertoia Auctions

Arcade Manufacturing Company Fire Trailer Truck, No. 1940, 1934, 16-1/4" long, $1200. Photo courtesy Bill Bertoia Auctions

Arcade Manufacturing
Company (Continued)

	C6	C8	C10
Fire Trailer Truck, No. 1940, 1934, 16-1/4" long (AR85)	600	900	1200
Ford Coupe, No. 1610X, rumble seat opens, 1934, 6-3/4" long (AR89)	200	350	500
Ford Dump Truck, No. 219X, 1929, 7-1/2" long (AR91)	285	425	700
Ford Express Truck, No. 210X, 1929, 8-1/4" long (AR92)	1000	1650	2400
Ford Model A Coupe, No. 116X, rumble seat, 1928, 5" long (AR161)	300	450	550
Ford Model A Coupe, No. 106, rumble seat, 1928, 6-3/4" long (AR162)	550	950	1400
Ford Model A Wrecker, No. 215, w/"weaver" host, 1929 (AR106)	550	850	1400
Ford Model A Wrecker, No. 218, 1930, 4-1/2" long	125	200	300
Ford Model T Coupe, 1923, 6" long (AR87)	175	300	450
Ford Model T Coupe, 1924, 6-1/2" long (AR88)	290	435	750
Ford Model T Fordor Sedan, removable chauffeur, 1924, 6-1/2" long (AR93)	250	350	650

Arcade Manufacturing Company Ford Model T Fordor Sedan, 1924, 6-1/2" long, $650. Photo courtesy Bill Bertoia Auctions

Arcade Manufacturing
Company (Continued)

	C6	C8	C10
Ford Model T Stake Truck, 1927, 5-3/4" long (AR167)	175	250	350
Ford Model T Stake Truck, No. 2010X, 1934, 7" long (AR101)	300	600	950
Ford Model T Stake Truck, 1925, 8-3/4" long (AR99)	800	1100	1600
Ford Model T Touring Car, 1923, 6-1/2" long (AR102)	450	650	900
Ford Model T Touring Car Bank, 1923, 6-1/2" long (AR103)	1000	1500	2250
Ford Model T Wrecker, 1927, 11" long (AR168)	700	1200	2000
Ford Sedan, "Century of Progress," 1934, 4-3/4" long (AR97A)	200	600	900
Ford Sedan, No. 1620X, 1933, 6-7/8" long (AR95)	350	600	850

Arcade Manufacturing Company Ford Dump Truck, No. 219X, 1929, 7-1/2" long, $700. Photo courtesy Bill Bertoia Auctions

Arcade Manufacturing Company Ford Model T Touring Car, 1923, 6-1/2" long, $900. Photo courtesy Bill Bertoia Auctions

Arcade Manufacturing Company Greyhound Cruiser Coach Bus, No. 4400, 1941, 9-1/8" long, $450. Photo courtesy Sotheby's, New York

Arcade Manufacturing Company International Delivery Truck, No. 226, 1932, 9-3/4" long, $1300. Photo courtesy Bill Bertoia Auctions

Arcade Manufacturing Company (Continued)

	C6	C8	C10
Ford Sedan, "Century of Progress," 1934, 6-7/8" long (AR96)	900	1500	2500
Ford Sedan with Trailer, No. 1970, "Covered Wagon," 1937, 12" long, trailer 5-1/2" long (AR98)	650	1200	1700
Ford Truck, cab, one ton, 1923, 8-1/2" long (AR105)	800	1000	1700
Greyhound Cruiser Coach Bus, No. 4400, 1941, 9-1/8" long (AR112)	200	325	450
Greyhound Lines Bus, No. 3850 SP, 1937, 7-3/4" long (AR113)	175	275	400
Greyhound Lines Great Lakes Exposition, No. 437, 1936, 11" long (AR114)	450	700	1000
Greyhound Lines Great Lakes Exposition, No. 436, 1936, 6-3/4" long (AR115)	350	475	725
Greyhound Super Coach, No. 4380, 1937, 9" long (AR116)	275	425	600
Ice Truck, No. 1933, circa 1941, 6-3/4" long (AR117)	275	375	575

Arcade Manufacturing Company (Continued)

	C6	C8	C10
International Delivery Truck, No. 3020, 1936, 9-1/2" long (AR119)	1800	2900	4200
International Delivery Truck, No. 226, 1932, 9-3/4" long (AR118)	500	800	1300
International Dump Truck, No. 3030, 1936, 10-1/2" long (AR121)	1000	1600	2350
International Dump Truck, No. 7100, 1941, 11-1/8" long (AR124)	600	900	1400
International Dump Truck, No. 1670, chassis and dump box are steel, 1940, 11-5/8" long (AR123)	650	1000	1650
International Dump Truck, No. 3710, 1937, 9-1/2" long (AR122)	450	700	1000
International Pickup Truck, No. 7000, 1941, 9-1/2" long (AR126)	500	750	1100
International Stake Truck, No. 7090, 1941, 11-1/2" long (AR130)	950	1450	2100
International Stake Truck, No. 237-0, 1931, 12" long (AR127)	700	1100	1700
International Stake Truck, No. 3090, 1936, 12" long (AR128)	900	1500	2300

Arcade Manufacturing Company Greyhound Lines Great Lakes Exposition, No. 436, 1936, 6-3/4" long, $725. Photo courtesy John Gibson

Arcade Manufacturing Company International Dump Truck, No. 1670, 1940, 11-5/8" long, $1650. Photo courtesy Tim Oei

Arcade Manufacturing
Company (Continued)

	C6	C8	C10
International Stake Truck, No. 2600, 1937, 9-1/2" long (AR129)	850	1450	2800
International Wrecker, No. 1650, wrecker crane body and crane are steel, 1940, 13" long (AR131)	500	800	1200
Ladder Truck, No. 1700, w/ladders, 1936, 12-1/2" long (AR132)	475	725	1000
Ladder Truck, No. 2350, 1936, 4-3/4" long (AR133)	90	150	200
Mack Chemical Truck, No. 245R, fire engine, has ladders, 1928, 15" long (AR136)	2000	3500	5500
Mack Dump Truck, 1925, 12" long (AR139)	1400	2400	3400
Mack Dump Truck, No. 248X, 1929, 8-1/2" long (AR140)	600	950	1600
Mack Fire Apparatus Truck, No. 242, ladder truck, 1929, 21" long (AR143)	850	1200	1600
Mack High Dump Truck, No. 244X, 1931, 10" long (AR141)	900	1600	2300
Mack High Dump Truck, No. 259X, 1931, 8-1/2" long (AR142)	700	1150	1700
Mack Hoist Truck, No. 198, 1932, body 8" long (AR144)	900	1500	2200
Mack Ice Truck, No. 257, w/driver, glass "ice" and tongs, 1932, 10-3/4" long (AR147)	1600	2800	4200
Mack Ice Truck, No. 257, w/driver, glass "ice" and tongs, 1930, 10-5/8" long (AR145)	375	600	1000
Mack Stake Truck, No. 253, 1929, 8-3/4" long (AR150)	950	1500	2250

Arcade Manufacturing Company Mack Tank Truck, 1925, 13-1/4" long, $2800. Photo courtesy Bill Bertoia Auctions

Arcade Manufacturing Company National Trailways Bus, No. 3870, 1937, 9-1/4" long, $1800. Photo courtesy Bob Smith

Arcade Manufacturing
Company (Continued)

	C6	C8	C10
Mack Tank Truck, No. 241, sheet metal tank, marked "Gasoline" and "Mack," 1930, 13" long (AR154)	1100	1900	2800
Mack Tank Truck, 1925, 13-1/4" long (AR151)	1000	1600	2800
Mack Tank Truck, "American Gasoline," 1925, 13-1/4" long (AR152)	1200	1850	2800
Mack Tank Truck, "Lubrite," 1925, 13-1/4" long (AR153)	1200	1800	2800
Mack Wrecker, No. 255, 1930, 12-1/2" long (AR155)	1900	3200	4700
Nash Wrecker, 1936, 4-1/2" long (AR169)	225	400	575
National Trailways Bus, No. 3870, 1937, 9-1/4" long (AR170)	750	1300	1800
New York World's Fair Bus, No. 3780, 1939, 10-1/2" long (AR171)	450	650	950
New York World's Fair Bus, No. 3750, 1939, 7" long (AR173)	150	200	325
New York World's Fair Bus, No. 3770, 1939, 8-1/2" long (AR172)	300	450	675
New York World's Fair Tractor-Train, No. 7290, w/three cars, 1939 (AR175)	450	675	900
New York World's Fair Tractor-Train, No. 7270, tractor and one car, 1939, tractor 3-1/4" long, car 4-1/4" long (AR174)	200	350	525
Pierce Silver Arrow, 1934, 7-1/4" long	300	450	750
Plymouth Coupe, No. 1340, 1933, 4-3/4" long (AR181)	400	800	1100

Arcade Manufacturing Company (Continued)

	C6	C8	C10
Plymouth Sedan, No. 1330, 1933, 4-3/4" long (AR182)	350	550	775
Plymouth Stake Truck, No. 1840, 1933, 4-3/4" long (AR183)	250	325	450
Plymouth Wrecker, No. 1830, 1933, 4-3/4" long (AR184)	175	250	350
Pontiac Sedan, No. 1350, 1935, 4-1/4" long (AR185)	150	250	375
Pontiac Sedan, 1935, 6-1/2" long (AR186)	350	525	800
Pontiac Stake Truck, No. 2780, 1936, 4-1/4" long (AR188)	150	250	350
Pontiac Wrecker, No. 2000, 1936, 4-1/4" long (AR189)	125	188	250
Racer, No. 1457, 1937, 5-3/4" long (AR196)	100	150	225
Racer, No. 137, 1932, 5-5/8" long (AR194)	120	180	240
Racer, No. 138, 1931, 6-3/4" long (AR192)	200	300	450
Racer, No. 139, Bullet Racer, 1931, 7-5/8" long (AR191)	950	1500	2300
Red Baby Dump Truck, No. 2, 1923, 10-3/4" long (AR197)	600	900	1500
Red Baby Dump Truck, No. 1, 1923, 10-3/4" long (AR198)	600	900	1500
Red Baby Weaver Wrecker, 1929, 12" long (AR199)	900	1500	2300
Reo Coupe, 1931, 7-1/2" (AR201)	1000	1700	3000
Reo Coupe, No. 1247, 1932, 9-3/8" long (AR200)	1000	2000	3000
Sand Loading Shovel, No. 298 later No. 299, 1932 (AR202)	500	800	1250

Arcade Manufacturing Company Red Baby Weaver Wrecker, 1929, 12" long, $2300. Photo courtesy Bill Bertoia Auctions

Arcade Manufacturing Company (Continued)

	C6	C8	C10
Scraper, No. 287, 1929, 8-1/4" long (AR203)	50	100	200
Sedan, No. 1501X, 1937, 4-3/4" long (AR204)	90	150	200
Sedan and Trailer, No. 1497X, 1937, car 5-5/8" long, trailer 2-1/2" long (AR205)	300	500	900
Side Dump Trailer, No. 290, fastens to trucks or tractors, 1932, 7" long (AR206)	100	200	350
Stake Trailer Truck, No. 233, 1931, 11-5/16" long (AR208)	325	550	750
Stake Truck, No. 1502, 1937, 4-1/4" long (AR212)	125	200	300
Steam Shovel, No. 292, Industrial Derrick, 1932, body 6" long (AR213)	750	1125	1600
Texas Centennial Bus, 1936, 10-3/4" long (AR217)	1500	2500	4000
Transport Trailer Truck, No. 1800, 1934, 7-1/2" long (AR232)	385	580	770

Arcade Manufacturing Company Red Baby Dump Truck, No. 2, 1923, 10-3/4" long, $1500

Arcade Manufacturing Company Reo Coupe, No. 1247, 1932, 9-3/8" long, $3000. Photo courtesy Harris Auctions

Arcade Manufacturing Company White Bus, No. 319, 1928, 13-1/4" long, $7750. Photo courtesy Bill Bertoia Auctions

Arcade Manufacturing Company (Continued)

	C6	C8	C10
W&K Truck Trailer, 1923, 8-1/2" long (AR233)	100	150	225
White Bus, No. 319, 1928, 13-1/4" long (AR235)	2800	5500	7750
White Tank Truck, No. 254, "Gasoline," 1931, 14-1/8" long (AR240)	1000	1500	2200
Wrecker, No. 225, no Arcade markings, 1932 (AR242)	500	850	1350
Wrecker, No. 1493, 1937, 6-1/2" long (AR244)	150	250	350
Wrecker, No. 2020, 1934, 7" long (AR243)	600	950	1500
Wrecker, No. 217, 1929, body 8" long (AR241)	450	700	1100
Yellow Baby Dump Truck, 1923, 10-1/2" long (AR246A)	600	1050	1650
Yellow Baby Wrecker, 1929, 12" long (AR247)	650	1100	1600

Arcade Manufacturing Company Yellow Cab, No. 1, 1927, 9" long, $1500. Photo courtesy Sotheby's, New York

Arcade Manufacturing Company Yellow Cab Bank, 1923, 8" long, $1500. Photo courtesy Bill Bertoia Auctions

Arcade Manufacturing Company (Continued)

	C6	C8	C10
Yellow Cab, No. 1350, 1935, 4-1/4" long	200	300	450
Yellow Cab, No. 3, 1925, 5-1/4" long (AR253)	500	800	1200
Yellow Cab, Ford Sedan, 1934, 6-7/8" long (AR254)	1300	2000	3000
Yellow Cab, No. 2, 1922, 8" long (AR249)	500	800	1200
Yellow Cab, No. 2, 1925, 8" long (AR252)	600	900	1400
Yellow Cab, No. 1590Y, 1941, 8-1/2" long (AR256)	225	300	600
Yellow Cab, No. 5, 1927, 8-1/2" long (AR251)	500	800	1000
Yellow Cab, No. 1580Y, 1936, 8-1/4" long (AR255)	1700	2800	4250
Yellow Cab, No. 1, 1927, 9" long (AR248)	600	900	1500
Yellow Cab Bank, "Flat Top," 1927 (AR258)	1800	4500	9200
Yellow Cab Bank, 1923, 8" long (AR257)	700	1100	1500
Yellow Cab Panel Delivery Truck, w/driver, 1925, 8-1/4" long (AR259)	1000	1700	2700
Yellow Coach Double-Decker Bus, 1925, 14" long (AR260)	1750	3250	4800
Yellow Parlor Coach Bus, 1926, 13" long (AR261)	800	1400	2200
Yellow Parlor Coach Bus, 1926, 9-1/2" long (AR262)	325	550	750

Auburn Rubber

For more than twenty years, American kids and moms loved rubber toys—children thought they were fun, and moms liked the fact that these toys wouldn't scratch furniture and floors. Then, almost as suddenly as they appeared on the market, the toys disappeared.

The Auburn Rubber Company of Auburn, Indiana, was not the first to introduce rubber toys to the American market, but it was no doubt the largest and had the greatest impact on the toy market. After producing toy soldiers in 1935, Auburn introduced its first vehicle in 1936—a beautiful coffin-nosed Cord Sedan. Today, the Auburn Cord is one of the most prized rubber toys and is seldom seen for sale.

Auburn followed the Cord with a wealth of vehicles, including trucks, farm tractors and implements, motorcycles, racers, fire engines, military vehicles, aircraft, ships and trains. The following listing consists of approximately ninety varieties of Auburn Rubber vehicles.

According to catalogs, 1952 was the final year Auburn Rubber exclusively marketed rubber vehicles. By 1955, Auburn's line was mostly vinyl with a few rubber toys left in the line. What appears to be the last rubber toys to be marketed by Auburn were two fire engines shown in the 1956 catalog.

Auburn continued in the toy business in Auburn, Indiana, and later Deming, New Mexico, until going out of business in 1969.

Note: The numbers in parentheses coincide with the numbers in Dave Leopard's book *Rubber Toy Vehicles*.

Contributor: Dave Leopard, 2507 Feather Run Trail, West Columbia, SC 29169-4915. Leopard, a retired United States Air Force Colonel now employed by the State of South Carolina, is a collector of small, American-made toy cars and trucks. He is considered an expert in on the subject of rubber toys and self-published *Rubber Toy Vehicles*, a definitive work in this field.

	C6	C8	C10
'35 Ford, two-door slantback sedan, 4" long (AA09)	27	41	55
'35 Ford Coupe, 4" long (AA08)	27	41	55
'36 Cord, four-door coffin-nose sedan, w/rounded bumper, minor variations, 6" long	25	35	50
'36 Cord, four-door coffin-nose sedan, 6" long (AA01)	65	100	150
'37 International Cabover Stake Truck, 3-3/4" long (AT05)	20	30	40

Auburn Rubber '37 International Cabover Stake Truck, 4-1/4" long, $100. Photo courtesy Dave Leopard's book, Rubber Toy Vehicles

Auburn Rubber (Continued)	C6	C8	C10
'37 International Cabover Stake Truck, 4-1/4" long (AT03)	20	30	40
'37 International Cabover Stake Truck, milk version, 4-1/4" long (AT07)	60	80	100
'37 International Cabover Stake Truck, khaki, w/rounded bumper, minor variations, 4-1/4" long (AT04)	20	30	40
'37 International Cabover Stake Truck, khaki, 4-1/4" long (AT03A)	20	30	40
'37 International Cabover Stake Truck, "US Army" decal, khaki, 5-3/8" long (AT01A)	30	40	55
'37 International Cabover Stake Truck, 5-3/8" long (AT01)	22	55	45
'37 Olds, four-door sedan, 4-1/2" long (AA02)	25	35	50
'38 GMC Cab/Open Squared-off Trailer, 9" long (AT15)	42	63	85

Auburn Rubber '37 Olds, 4-1/2" long, $50. Photo courtesy Dave Leopard's book, Rubber Toy Vehicles

Auburn Rubber '38 GMC Cab/Open Squared-off Trailer, 9" long, $85. Photo courtesy Dave Leopard's book, Rubber Toy Vehicles

Auburn Rubber '47 Chevy Cab Forward Box Truck, 5-3/4" long, $45. Photo courtesy Dave Leopard's Rubber Toy Vehicles

Auburn Rubber (Continued)

	C6	C8	C10
'38 GMC Carry Car Auto Transport, 11-1/2" long (AT14)	50	70	110
'38 Olds, four-door sedan, 5-3/4" long (AA03)	30	50	70
'39 Plymouth, two-door trunk back sedan, 4-1/4" long (AA12)	25	35	50
'40 Olds, four-door sedan, fender skirts, 6" long (AA05)	25	38	50
'40 Olds, four-door sedan, open fenders, 6" long (AA04)	27	41	59
'46 Lincoln convertible, two-door, round headlights, 4-1/2" long (AA13)	20	30	40
'46 Lincoln convertible, two-door square headlights, 4-1/2" long (AA13)	20	30	40
'47 Chevy Cab Forward Box Truck, 5-3/4" long (AT11)	22	33	45
'48 Buick, two-door sedanette, fastback, 7-1/4" long (AA06)	40	70	100

Auburn Rubber (Continued)

	C6	C8	C10
'50 Cadillac, four-door sedan, 7-1/4" long (AA10)	40	60	100
'50 Pickup Truck, open fenders, 4-1/2" long (AT12c)	20	30	40
'50 Pickup Truck, fender skirts, 4-1/2" long (AT13c)	20	30	40
Ahrens-Fox Fire Engine, 5-1/2" long (AE01)	75	112	150
Cab-Forward Box Truck, smooth sides, futuristic, 5-1/2" long (AT09)	22	33	45

Auburn Rubber '48 Buick, 7-1/4" long, $100. Photo courtesy Dave Leopard's Rubber Toy Vehicles

Auburn Rubber '39 Plymouth, 4-1/4" long, $50. Photo courtesy Dave Leopard's book, Rubber Toy Vehicles

Auburn Rubber '50 Cadillac, 7-1/4" long, $100. Photo courtesy Dave Leopard's book, Rubber Toy Vehicles

*Auburn Rubber Cab-Forward Box Truck, 5-1/2"
long, $45. Photo courtesy Dave Leopard's book,*
Rubber Toy Vehicles

*Auburn Rubber Trailer, 4-3/4" long, $45. Photo
courtesy Dave Leopard's book,* Rubber Toy Vehicles

Auburn Rubber (Continued)	C6	C8	C10
Cabover Box Truck, smooth sides, futuristic, 4-1/8" long (AT10)	20	30	40
Carry Car Transport (Updated), cab changed, trailer same, 11-3/4" long (AT16)	45	65	95
Fire Engine, hose and ladders, c. 1940s, 7-3/4" long (AE02)	27	41	55
Fire Engine, ladders, no hose, c. 1940s, 7-3/4" long (AE04)	27	41	55
Late 40s Futuristic Sedan, fin down back, 5" long (AA15)	20	30	40
Open Racer, short, tapered tail, large tires, 10-1/2" long (AR03)	40	60	80
Open Racer, V-6, low fin, 10-1/2" long (AR02)	45	65	85
Open Racer, V-6, high fin, 10-1/2" long (AR01)	55	82	110
Open Racer, boattail, 4-3/4" long (AR05)	30	45	60

Auburn Rubber (Continued)	C6	C8	C10
Open Racer, boattail, no side pipes, 4-3/4" long (AR09)	25	35	50
Open Racer, no fenders, low fin, long back, 5-1/4" long (AR08)	20	30	40
Open Racer, short, boattail, 6-1/2" long (AR04)	30	45	60
Open Racer, small fin, 6-1/4" long (AR06)	30	45	60
Pumper, boiler, c. 1940s, 7-3/4" long (AE03)	27	41	55
Side-Cutter Sickle Bar Mower, David Bradley, 3-3/4" long (AI07)	20	30	40
Tank, Marmon-Harrington, 3-1/4" long (AM02)	20	30	40
Tank, Marmon-Harrington, 4-1/2" long (AM01)	25	35	50
Trailer, four wheel, Graham-Bradley, 4-3/4" long (AI02)	22	33	45
Trailer, two wheel, Graham-Bradley, 5-3/4" long (AI01)	22	33	45

Banner

Emanuel M. Pressner and Bernard Schiller founded banner in 1944. Pressner had been a toy importer, and in 1938, he bought interest in Columbia Protektosite, which cast Beton's plastic toy soldiers. Schiller was eventually edged out.

In 1950, Banner moved from 150 Buckner Blvd., Bronx, New York, to 80 Beckwith Ave., Paterson, New Jersey, where it remained.

Banner manufactured small plastic cars and trucks and specialized in plastic tea sets and metallic plastic forks, knives and spoons. Banner used "off-falls"— blanks formed when holes were cut in steel for car windows and television tubes—to produce their stamped-steel toys.

*Auburn Rubber Open Racer, 10-1/2" long, $110.
Photo courtesy Dave Leopard's book,* Rubber Toy
Vehicles

The company, which at its peak had up to 200 employees, went into Chapter 11 bankruptcy in 1965. They rebounded for a few years, only to be sold in 1967 to Tal-Cap, a toy conglomerate in Minnesota.

Contributor: John Taylor, P.O. Box 63, Nolensville, TN 37135-0063.

Banner

	C6	C8	C10
Aeriel Ladder Fire Truck, No. 1143, pressed metal wheels, 20" Long	125	175	250
American Express Truck, tin, 10" long	75	150	225
Army Ambulance, tin and plastic, 6" long	12	25	40
Car Transport, w/two cars, lithographed trailer, 16" long	125	200	275
Cross Country Express, rubber tires, late 1940s-early 1950s, 12" long	125	200	275
Dodge, plastic, 1950, 4" long	8	15	25
Dump Truck, plastic, 5-1/4" long	10	15	20
Fair Lawn Dairy Truck, pressed metal wheels, 1940, 11-1/2" long	125	175	250
Garbage Truck, plastic, Ford, 1954, 4" long	8	15	30
Grocery Service Truck, pressed metal wheels, 13" long	125	200	275
Hi-Way Emergency Truck, w/tools and two spare tires, 1940, 12" long	150	225	325
International Harvester Metro 1950 Van, plastic, 4" long	8	12	25
Jewel Tea Van	175	275	375
Kellog's Express Truck, six wheels, pressed metal wheels, dual metal axles, 1940, 13" long	250	400	550
LaFrance Fire Truck, plastic, 1950, 4" long	8	12	25

Banner Kellog's Express Truck, 1940, 13" long, $550. Photo courtesy John Taylor

Banner Sand and Gravel Dump Truck, No. 1142, 13" long, $225. Photo courtesy John Taylor

Banner (Continued)

	C6	C8	C10
North American Van Lines Truck and Trailer, 15" long	100	175	225
Sand and Gravel Dump Truck, No. 1142, pressed metal wheels, 13" long	100	175	225
Service Station, cardboard, w/three plastic trucks, c. late 1940s-early 1950s	22	35	50
Side Dump Truck, plastic, 1950s, 5-1/4" long	10	20	30
Stake Truck, plastic, GMC, 4" long	12	18	25
Station Wagon, plastic, Oldsmobile, 1948, 4" long	16	24	32
Tractor, plastic, wheelhorse, 3" long	14	21	28
Trailer Steamshovel, 6-3/4" long	15	25	35
Wonder Bread Truck, tin litho, c. 1950s, 11" long	75	125	175

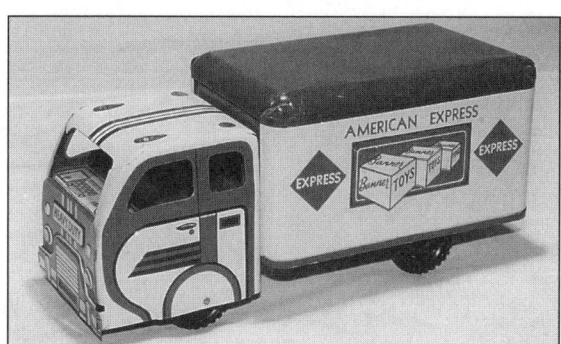

Banner American Express Truck, 10" long, $225. Photo courtesy Bob Smith

Banner Trailer Steamshovel, 6-3/4" long, $35

Barclay

Barclay, named after Barclay Street in West Hoboken, New Jersey, began in 1924 or late 1923, and was owned by partners Leon Donze (1865-1950) and by Michael Levy (c.1895-1964). In 1929, Levy took over the company and turned it into a major toy manufacturer. Under his guidance, it grew from five employees to a prewar peak of 400 workers and moved several times to increasingly larger quarters.

While known for its toy soldiers, Barclay was the largest producer of lead-alloy vehicles in the 1930s and early 1940s. The most popular vehicle was the tiny No. 53 racer.

World War II was a difficult time for all toy manufacturers and Barclay was no exception. Forced to lay off all but four of its employees, Barclay moved in the direction of subcontract work. Unfortunately, the firm was never able to regain its prewar success and closed its doors in 1971.

	C6	C8	C10
Ambulance, No. 194, small cross, 3-1/2" long (BV1)	26	39	52
Ambulance, No. 194, large cross, 3-1/2" long (BV2)	20	30	40
Ambulance, No. 50, 5" long (BV3)	55	82	110
Anti-Aircraft Gun Truck, No. 198, shown in 1931 Barclay catalog, 3-1/8" long (BV16)	20	30	40
Anti-Aircraft Gun Truck, No. 48, one man, 4" long (BV19)	22	33	45
Anti-Aircraft Gun Truck, No. 48, two men, 4" long (BV20)	16	24	32
Armored Army Truck, No. 152, 2-7/8" long (BV6)	8	13	17
Army Oil Truck, c. 1968, approx. 2" long (BV106)	9	13	18
Army Tank Truck, No. 197, c. 1935-36, 3-1/8" long (BV7)	11	16	22

This ad is the first known appearance of Barlcay vehicles in the 1931 Butler Brothers catalog

Barclay Vehicles Build and Paint Set, No. 2004, early, $360. Photo courtesy Perry Eichor

Barclay Vehicles (Continued)

	C6	C8	C10
Army Tractor, (Minneapolis-Moline "Jeep"), 2-3/4" long (BV9)	14	21	28
Army Truck, open bed, c. 1968, approx. 2" long (BV105)	7	11	15
Army Truck with Anti-Aircraft Gun, No. 151, 2-1/2" long (BV5)	10	15	21
Army Truck with Gun, No. 151, 2-3/4" long (BV4)	13	19	27
Auburn Speeder, No. 58, c. 1931 (BV139)	17	26	35
Austin Coupe, No. 43, c. 1931, 2" long (BV10)	30	45	60
Auto Transport Set, No. 330, two 1950s cars, 4-1/2" long (BV11)	36	55	73
Beer Truck, No. 377, w/barrels (BV13)	35	52	70
Beer Truck, No. 376, w/wood barrels, c. 1940, 4" long (BV12)	27	41	55
Buick Sedan, 1929, 3" long (BV118)	27	41	55

Barclay Vehicles Convertible, $100

Left to Right: Barclay Vehicles Cord Front Drive Coupe, No. 40, c. 1931, 3-5/8" long, $50; Golden Arrow Racer, 1930s, 4-1/2" long, $40; Parcel Delivery Truck, No. 45, 1930s, 3-5/8" long, $130

Barclay Vehicles (Continued)	C6	C8	C10
Build and Paint Set, No. 2004, truck, coupe, sedan, parts, paints, early (BV90)	180	270	360
Bus, futuristic, "Made in U.S.A.," 3" long (BV14)	34	51	68
Bus, Coast to Coast, No. 405, die-cast, two-piece, "Barclay Toy," 2-7/8" long (BV24)	42	63	85
Cannon Car, battery-powered headlight, first appeared in 1935 catalog, 3-1/2" long (BV18)	80	130	225
Cannon Car, slight casting differences from headlight version, 3-1/4" long (BV17)	19	28	38
Cannon Car, gunner low, 3-5/16" long (BV15)	13	21	27
Cannon Truck, moveable cannon, 4" long (BV83)	37	56	75
Cannon Truck, w/moveable cannon, 4" long (BV21)	20	30	40
Car Carrier, two small cars, early 1930s (BV114)	25	38	50
Chief Police Car, approx. 2" long (BV97)	5	8	10
Chrysler Airflow, c. 1936, 4" long (BV23)	30	45	60

Barclay Vehicles (Continued)	C6	C8	C10
Chrysler Airflow Sedan, No. 1703, large, 1935 (BV127)	17	26	35
Convertible, w/vacationers (BV88)	50	75	100
Cord Front Drive Coupe, No. 40, c. 1931, 3-5/8" long (BV31)	25	38	50
Coupe, No. 361, Streamline (BV112)	17	26	35
Coupe, c. 1935, 2-1/2" long (BV26)	50	75	100
Coupe, No. 51, c. 1931, 2-3/16" long (BV132)	17	26	35
Coupe, two-piece, "Barclay Toy," 1930s, 2-7/8" long (BV28)	42	63	85
Coupe, "Made in U.S.A.," 1930s, 3" long (BV25)	12	18	25
Coupe, No. 301, Streamline, 3-1/4" long (BV123)	50	75	100
Coupe, 200 series (?), cast rear tire, c. 1935, 3-1/8" long (BV145)	21	31	42
Coupe, removable spare tire, 1935, 4-1/2" long (BV146)	30	45	60
Coupe, 1934, 4-1/4" long (BV27)	40	60	80
Delivery Truck, No. 309, 2-15/16" long (BV33)	15	23	30
Delivery Truck, No. 309, c. 1936, 3-1/2" long (BV136)	12	18	25
Delivery Truck, No. 206, "Bakery Fine Cake Pies," c. 1934, 3-1/8" long (BV131)	70	105	140
DeSoto Airflow, 1935, 5-3/16" long (BV113)	17	26	35
Double Decker Bus, No. 56, c. 1931, 3-1/4" long (BV138)	22	33	45
Double Decker Bus, 4" long (BV34)	60	90	120
Double Transport Set, No. 440, four cars on upper and lower racks, hinged for unloading, 1939-1963, 4-1/2" long (BV157)	72	109	145

Barclay Vehicles Coupe, 1930s, 3" long, $25

Barclay Vehicles Double Transport Set, No. 440, 1939-1963, 4-1/2" long, $145. Photo courtesy Craig Clark

Barclay Vehicles (Continued)

	C6	C8	C10
Dump Truck, spring action, ratchet, 1935, 4" long (BV147)	20	30	40
Dump Truck, c. 1960s, approx. 2" long (BV94)	7	11	15
Express Stack Truck, 1930s, 2-15/16" long (BV37)	30	45	60
Field Kitchen, 2-1/4" long (BV39)	35	52	70
Fire Engine, No. 390?, moveable ladder, c. 1950s (BV38)	15	22	30
Fire Engine, No. 41, two firemen, black metal wheels, 1930s, 2-3/4" long (BV40)	17	26	35
Fire Engine, No. 209, c. 1934, 3-1/8" long (BV134)	25	38	50
Fire Engine, French-looking, 4" long (BV41)	17	26	35
Fire Truck, No. 50, c. 1931, 2-3/8" long (BV137)	22	33	45
Fire Truck, No. 210, c. 1934, 3-1/8" long (BV133)	25	38	50
Fire Truck, No. 368, "Fire Dept. No. 99," 1930s, 5-3/4" long (BV126)	20	30	40
Ford, 1931, 2-1/4" long (BV42)	15	22	30
Gas Truck, 200 series, four tanks on top, c. 1935, 3" long (BV144A)	25	38	50
Gasoline Truck, small, three tank on top, c. 1931, 2-5/16" long (BV144)	30	45	60
Golden Arrow Racer, 1930s, 4-1/2" long (BV43)	20	30	40
Hook and Ladder, No. 208, 1935, 3" long (BV122)	16	24	32
Hospital Truck, c. 1968, 2" long (BV104)	9	13	18
Imperial Chrysler Coupe, No. 39, c. 1931 (BV129)	15	22	30
Log Truck, c. 1960s, approx. 2" long (BV93)	7	11	15
Mack Pickup Truck, 3-1/2" long (BV44)	15	22	30
Milk & Cream Truck, No. 377, stamped, white rubber tires, 3-5/8" long (BV45)	81	122	163
Milk Truck, No. 567, in shape of bottle (BV84)	162	243	325
Milk Truck, No. 377, black rubber tires, 3-5/8" long (BV45A)	22	33	45

Barclay Vehicles Moving Truck (three different trucks show decal variants), c. 1960s, approx. 2" long, $18. Photo courtesy Stan Alekna

Barclay Vehicles (Continued)

	C6	C8	C10
Milk Van Truck, bottle on side, 2-7/8" long (BV85)	20	30	41
Motorcycle with Flat Rider, No. 55, full-dimensional sidecar, 2-3/4" long (BV46)	47	70	95
Moving Truck, c. 1960s, approx. 2" long (BV161)	8	13	18
Officer's Car, w/megaphone on top, 2-1/2" long (BV86)	22	33	44
Oil Truck, c. 1960s, approx. 2" long (BV99)	9	13	18
Oil-Fuel Truck, No. 308, c. 1936, 3-9/16" long (BV47)	12	18	25
Open Coupe with Driver in Cab, early 1930s (BV110)	15	22	30
Parcel Delivery Truck, No. 45, slush lead, 1930s, 3-5/8" long (BV48)	65	98	130
Pepsi-Cola Truck, 1960s, 2" long (BV100)	9	13	18
Police Car, 2" long (BV96)	5	8	10
Police Car, No. 317, die-cast, 3-5/8" long (BV49A)	15	22	30
Race Car, 3" long (BV50)	12	18	24
Race Car, open, driver, 4" long (BV150)	70	105	140
Racer, No. 306, 1936 (BV120)	15	22	30

Barclay Vehicles Oil Truck with Yoo-Hoo, Pepsi-Cola Truck and Coca-Cola decals, c. 1960s, approx. 2" long, $18. Photo courtesy Stan Alekna

Barclay Vehicles (Continued)

	C6	C8	C10
Racer, No. 5, 1931 (BV130)	15	22	30
Racer, two passengers, 4-1/4" long (BV54)	55	82	110
Racer, No. 303, streamline, 4-3/8" long (BV121)	15	22	30
Racer, closed cockpit, 5-1/2" long (BV51)	17	26	35
Racer, closed cockpit, c. 1939, 7" long (BV52)	30	45	60
Racer, No. 53, early slush lead, 1920s-30s, approx. 2" long (BV53)	24	36	48
Racer with Tail Fin, "Made in U.S.A.," 3-1/2" long (BV55)	17	26	35
Racing Car, large, raised exhaust pipe, driver, appeared in the 1935 catalog (BV149)	17	26	35
Racing Car, No. 37, large, 1930s, 14-1/4" long (BV115)	16	24	32
Racing Car, c. 1968, approx. 2" long (BV95)	5	8	10
Racing Car, no fenders, c. 1968, approx. 2" long (BV101)	5	8	10
Renault Tank, No. 47, c. 1937, 4" long (BV56)	22	33	45
Searchlight Truck, second version (BV57A)	87	130	175
Searchlight Truck, white rubber tires, c. 1940, 4-1/16" long (BV57)	87	130	175
Sedan, No. 311, c. 1936 (BV135)	21	32	43
Sedan, No. 362, streamline, large, 1935 (BV125)	41	61	82
Sedan, c. 1934 (BV140)	37	56	75
Sedan, two-door, 1960s, 1-5/8" long (BV108)	2	3	5
Sedan, No. 401, die cast, two-piece, two-door, "Barclay Toy," 1930s, 2-7/8" long (BV60)	42	63	85

Barclay Vehicles Sedan and Tourist Trailer, 1930s, 6-1/2" long, $70

Barclay Vehicles Steam Shovel, 4" x 1-3/4", $500. Photo courtesy Fred Maxwell

Barclay Vehicles (Continued)

	C6	C8	C10
Sedan, two-door, rubber wheels, c. 1935, 3-1/8" long (BV59)	37	56	75
Sedan, four-door, possibly a Chrysler, c. 1936, 5" long (BV58)	17	26	35
Sedan and Tourist Trailer, "Made in U.S.A.," 1930s, 6-1/2" long (BV61)	35	52	70
Side Dump, 1-1/2" long (BV87)	7	11	15
Silver Arrow Race Car, 5-1/2" long (BV62)	22	33	45
Sport Coupe, removable spare tire, 1935, 2-7/8" long (BV148)	32	48	65
Stake Truck, No. 207, 1935 catalog, 3-1/8" long (BV124)	39	58	78
Stake Truck, 1935, 4-3/8" long (BV151)	36	54	72
Station Wagon, No. 404, die-cast, two-piece, "Barclay Toy," 1930s, 2-15/16" long (BV63)	37	56	75
Steam Shovel, no number, known as Panama Shovel, built w/Mack truck chassis with steam engine body with tin shovel hinged on a derrick, w/driver, metal disc wheels, vertical hood louvers, no windshield, 4" x 1-3/4"	150	250	500
Steam-Roller, No. 44, slush lead, w/tin roof, traction type, c. 1931, 3-1/4" long (BV64)	30	45	60
Streamline Coupe, Large, 1930s (BV143)	15	22	30
Streamline Coupe, Large, No. 363, appeared in 1935 catalog, 6-7/8" long (BV143)	45	68	90
Streamline Sedan, No. 302, c. 1936, 3-1/8" long (BV32)	25	38	50

Barclay Vehicles Streamline Sedan, No. 302, c. 1936, 3-1/8" long, $50

Barclay Vehicles (Continued)

	C6	C8	C10
Tank, based on U.S. M2 light tank, 2-1/4" long (BV70)	20	31	41
Tank, "4562," one man in turret, 3-7/8" long (BV66)	17	26	35
Tank T41, 4-1/2" long (BV68)	15	22	30
Taxi, c. 1940s, 3-1/4" long (BV71)	14	21	28
Taxi, No. 318, die-cast, 3-1/4" long (BV71A)	50	75	100
Tow Car, No. 205, appeared in 1935 catalog, 3-1/16" long (BV141)	20	30	40
Tow Truck, No. 1105, "Towing Service," large (BV117)	82	124	175
Tow Truck, No. 312, "Towing," appeared in 1936 catalog, 3-3/8" long (BV119)	17	26	35
Tractor, No. 203, peg hitch, 2-1/8" long (BV109)	11	16	22
Trailer Truck variously "Railway Express," or w/other moving company name, c. 1950s (BV74)	5	8	10
Transport Set, No. 330, w/two cars, 1960s, 4-1/2" long (BV75)	25	40	75
Transport Set, two car, 4-3/4" long (BV152)	42	63	85

Barclay Vehicles Tow Car, No. 205, 3-1/16" long, $40

Barclay Vehicles (Continued)

	C6	C8	C10
Truck, "Esso Gas," 1930s, 5" long (BV111)	20	30	40
U.S. Army Truck, c. 1968, 2" long (BV103)	7	11	15
U.S. Army Truck, wire or peg hitch, white rubber wheels, 2-1/2" long (BV77)	12	18	25
U.S. Army Truck, No. 204, no hitch, red wood hubs, 2-1/2" long (BV76)	19	28	38
U.S. Mail Truck, 1960s, 2" long (BV91)	10	17	24
U.S. Motor Unit Truck, three versions-no hitch, wire hitch, peg hitch, white rubber tires, c. 1940, 3-1/4" long (BV78)	17	26	35
Van, no number, embossed "Moving Van," horizontal grille pattern, no windshield, vertical stripes on van body, metal disc wheels, dual rear axles, 4"	100	150	200
Van, "White Horse" van (some have sticker reading "Welcome I.C.MA. Compliments the White Motor Co."), approx. 03" long (BV156)	55	82	110
Vintage Car, approx. 2" long (BV98)	15	22	30
Volkswagen, 1960s, approx. 2" long (BV102)	12	18	24
Wheel-A-Rific speedway track, two lead racers, black rubber wheels, 10' of plastic track, c. 1970 (BV79)	17	26	35
Wrecker, No. 403, die cast, two piece, "Barclay Toy," 1930s, 2-7/8" long (BV82)	42	63	85
Wrecker, No. 46, c. 1931, 3-1/2" long (BV80)	22	33	45

Barr Rubber

Barr Rubber was located in Sandusky, Ohio. The following list and the code numbers in parentheses, was compiled by Dave Leopard. Vehicles are broken down by type.

Contributor: Dave Leopard, 2507 Feather Run Trail, West Columbia, SC 29169-4915.

	C6	C8	C10
'35 Ford Army Truck, 4-3/4" long (BT03)	32	48	65
'35 Ford Coupe, 4" long (BA01)	27	41	55

Left to Right: Barr Rubber '35 Ford Two-door Slantback Sedan, 4" long, $55; '35 Ford Coupe, 4" long, $55. Photo courtesy Dave Leopard's book, Rubber Toy Vehicles

Barr Rubber '35 Ford Panel Truck/Ambulance, 4-1/4" long, $55. Photo courtesy Dave Leopard's book, Rubber Toy Vehicles

Barr Rubber (Continued)

	C6	C8	C10
'35 Ford Panel Truck/Ambulance, 4-1/4" long (BT02)	27	41	55
'35 Ford Stake Body Truck, 4-3/4" long (BT01)	27	41	55
'35 Ford Two-door Slantback Sedan, 4" long (BA02)	27	41	55

Beaut Mfg. Co.

Beaut Mfg. Co., North Bergen, New Jersey, was founded in 1946 by Eugene Buhler and Irving Reader (former machinist and salesman, respectively) for Barclay Mfg. Co. The company put out five toys—a taxi cab, a police car, a fire engine, a sedan and a child's wagon. The company was successful at first, selling to Woolworth's and many overseas buyers. Beaut ceased toymaking activities around 1950 because of competition from plastic toys, although they continued until 1982 as a general machine shop.

	C6	C8	C10
Fire Car, No. 4, approx. 3-3/4" long	10	15	20
Police Car, approx. 3-3/4" long	10	15	20
Sedan, approx. 3-3/4" long	10	15	20
Taxi, approx. 3-3/4" long	10	15	20

Best Toy & Novelty Factory

Best Toy, founded by John M. Best in Manhattan Kansas in the 1930s, started as a family hobby for Best's children, relatives, friends and neighbors. From a hobby it grew into a respectable business, supplying toy distributors and dime stores. After several years of operation it was sold in 1939 to Ralstoy, a Ralston, Nebraska, company. Best toys are still found in today's toy markets.

At this point we are not certain when Best started or what number in the series was his first molding. In 1933, Best took over production from the toy line of Kansas Toy & Novelty of Clifton, Kansas. It's not known whether he introduced any new patterns, although with his experience it is likely that he did. Regardless, it was an important chapter in the story of those wandering molds. Best Toy and Novelty, along with the Kansas Toy molds, were acquired by Ralstoy of Ralston, Nebraska in 1939.

Best Toy reproductions can usually be distinguished by the rubber wheels and the marking "Made in USA." However, some of their toys used the metal wheels of the Kansas Toy originals or the later wood hubs with rubber tires. It is also possible that Best modified or rebuilt his molds to create variations.

For more information, see *O'Brien's Collecting Toy Cars & Trucks*.

Contributors: Fred Maxwell, 4722 N. 33 St., Arlington, VA 22207. Maxwell, a collector and occasional author, has been collecting antique aircraft and vehicle toys for over twenty-five years. He founded the Auto Collectors Club twenty-five years ago to promote interest in the central Atlantic states region.

Perry R. Eichor, 703 North Almond Drive, Simpsonville, SC, 29681. Captain Eichor has been collecting aircraft toys since he was a young officer in the Air Force; his twenty-one years as an Air Force officer only served to deepen his interest in the subject. Today when he is not collecting, researching or writing about aeronautical toys, he works as a criminal justice administrator as well as an appraiser and auctioneer.

	C6	C8	C10
Cab Unit, No. 101, International (?), sleeper cab, slanted grille, hood cap, Motometer or ornament, two open windows, rare, 3-1/4" long (BEV15)	40	60	80
Coupe, No. 98 (BEV12)	15	30	40
Coupe, apparently same car as No. 91, grid pattern grille, two open windows, 3-1/2" long (BEV10)	20	45	50

Best Toy & Novelty Factory Cab Unit, No. 101, 3-1/4" long, $80

Best Toy & Novelty Factory

	C8	C10
Coupe, Dodge (?), chopped top, Brewster-like heart-shaped grille, hood cap, Motometer or ornament, long streamlined front fenders, 3-3/4" long (BEV6) 20	30	40
Coupe, No. 93, Cadillac?, Streamlined, hood similar to No. 91, grid pattern grille, two open windows, hard rubber wheels, 3-5/8" long (BEV7) 16	24	32
Coupe, Pontiac (?), streamlined, hood cap, Motometer or ornament, rearmount, 4" long (BEV13) 25	45	70
Oil Transport, No. 102, streamlined "Gasoline" semi-trailer to No. 101, four tanks, four storage compartments, total length of cab-trailer, 6-3/4", 4" long (BEV16) 47	70	95
Racer, No. 85, record car w/large square fin, driver, hood cap, Motometer or ornament, vertical grille pattern, twelve exhaust ports, wooden hubs, rubber tires, 4" long (BEV1) 10	15	20
Racer, No. 97, Bluebird record car, driver, large fin, twelve exhaust port, faired, hard rubber wheels, 4-1/2" long (BEV11) 10	15	20
Sedan, No. 87, Brewster (?) (BEV3) 15	25	35

Left to Right: Best Toy & Novelty Racer, No. 76; Racer, No. 85, 4" long, $20. Photo courtesy Perry Eichor

Best Toy & Novelty Factory

	C8	C10
Sedan, No. 90, two door, airflow, hood reaches front bumper w/no grille, four open windows, hard rubber wheels, 3-1/2" long (BEV4) 25	40	70
Sedan, No. 91, Cadillac (?), two door airflow, high style vee grille, faired front fenders, 3-1/2" long (BEV5) 25	40	70
Sedan, No. 95, two door, airflow, similar to No. 94 w/three headlamps, four open windows, trunk, hard rubber wheels, Chrysler-Briggs show car (?), 3-1/2" long 30	40	55
Sedan, No. 95, two door, airflow, similar to No. 94, w/three headlamps, four open windows, trunk, hard rubber wheels, w/"Police Dept." shield on doors, centered headlamp may be a siren, one version has "Police" painted on roof, 3-1/2" long (BEV9b) 35	45	60
Sedan, No. 100, Pontiac, streamlined, two door, hood open, horizontal grille pattern, four open windows, trunk, 4" long (BEV14) 20	30	40
Sedan, No. 86, Lincoln (?), two-door fastback, clanted grille w/grid pattern, horizontal hood louvers, divided windshield, rear wheel skirts, 4" long (BEV2) 20	30	50
Sedan, No. 94, two door, airflow, similar to No. 90, four open windows, taxi lamp on roof, 4-1/2" long (BEV8) 35	45	70

Buddy "L"

Buddy "L" toys, named after owner Fred Lundahl's son, Buddy, were first maufactured by the Moline Pressed Steel Company of Moiline, Illinois in 1921. Lundahl started the company eight years earlier in order to maufacture car and truck parts. The toys, originally made as special items for his son, caught the attention of other children and their fathers.

Buddy "L" toys are large, averaging twenty-one to twenty-six inches in length. The original toys were made of heavy steel and could support a grown man's weight, but lighter material was adopted in the 1930s. Wooden toys were produced during World War II when steel was in short supply.

Lundahl relinquished control of the company to J.W. Bettendorf in 1930 and died later that year. The named of the company has changed many times over the years, yet continues to make toys at the present time.

Because the early Buddy "L" toys were almost indestructible, fifty percent of the items found are either rusty or have been repainted which lowers the value considerably.

Contributors: John Taylor, P.O. Box 63, Nolensville, TN 37135-0063.

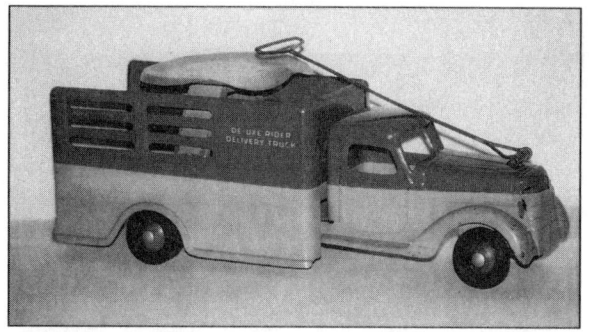

Buddy "L" Delivery Truck (Post-1932), No. 803, 1945-48, 22-3/4" long, $650. Photo courtesy Joe and Sharon Freed

Buddy "L" Post-1932	C6	C8	C10
Allied Van Lines, No. 910	600	1000	1500
Allied Van Lines Moving Van, No. 366, 31" long	340	600	950
Army Signal Corps Truck, 1941-42, 12" long	140	225	300
Army Tank, wood, 1943, 13" long	50	95	150
Army Transport Truck, six-spoke wheels, 1954-57	225	350	475
Army Truck, No. 506, 20-1/2" long	150	200	300
Automatic Tail-Gate Loader, w/steering handle	200	325	475
Baby Ruth/Butterfinger Curtiss Candies Tandem Truck, International-style cab, late 1930s-40s	750	1500	2000
Baggage Truck, No. 11, 1933, 26-1/2" long	225	350	550
Big Show Circus Truck, No. 484, wood, 1947, 25-1/2" long	750	1000	1500
City Baggage Dray, No. 439, 1934-37, 19" long	175	275	550
City Baggage Dray, No. 839, 1938, 20-3/4" long	125	200	325
Coca-Cola Truck, No. 5536, 1955-56, 15" long	200	350	400
Coca-Cola Truck, No. 5426, 1960-61	150	250	400

Buddy "L" Post-1932 (Continued)	C6	C8	C10
Coca-Cola Truck, No. 5646, 1957-59	200	300	450
Concrete Mixer, No. 832, w/motor sound, 1950-51, 10-3/4" long	250	400	575
Concrete Mixer with Truck, No. 54, 1937, 34-1/2" long	300	200	450
Country Squire Station Wagon, No. 53051, 1963-64, 15" long	100	150	250
Dairy Truck, No. 2002, (Junior Line), 1930-32, 24" long	1100	1800	2700
Dandy Digger, No. 33 and 2025, 1931-37	75	100	150
Delivery Truck, No. 803, Deluxe Rider, 1945-48, 22-3/4" long	225	400	650
Double Hydraulic Self-Loader-N-Dump Truck, No. 5892, 1956-57, 29" long	75	125	225
Dump Truck, No. 434, 1936, 20" long	225	325	425
Dump Truck, No. 634, 1948, 22-1/2" long	150	250	375

Buddy "L" Big Show Circus Truck (Post-1932), No. 484, 1947, 25-1/2" long, $1500

Buddy "L" Excavator Truck and Shovel Set (Post-1932), No. 948, 1940, 27-1/2" long, $600. Photo courtesy John Taylor

Buddy "L" Greyhound Bus with Bell (Post-1932), No. 481, 1948-49, 18-1/2" long, $1000. Photo courtesy Bill Bertoia Auctions

Buddy "L" Sand & Gravel Truck (Post-1932), No. 3312, 13-1/2", $225. Photo courtesy Bill Bertoia Auctions

Buddy "L" Post-1932 (Continued)	C6	C8	C10
Emergency Auto Wrecker, No. 3317 ..	100	200	275
Engine, No. 29, 1933-34, 25-1/2" long	200	250	525
Excavator Truck and Shovel Set, No. 948, 1940, 27-1/2" long	275	400	600
Express Trailer Truck, No. 35, 1933-34 ..	475	650	950
Fire Chief's Car with Siren, No. 483, wooden, 1949, 19-1/2" long	475	750	1100
Fire Ladder Truck, semi, rounded trailer fenders, 1960	100	150	200
Greyhound Bus, winds up, 1938-40, 16" long	300	325	500
Greyhound Bus with Bell, No. 481, wooden, 1948-49, 18-1/2" long	450	675	1000
Hook and Ladder Truck, No. 859, wooden, 21-1/2" long	250	375	550
Hose Truck, No. 38, 1933, 21-3/4" long	125	225	325
Hydraulic Aerial Truck, No. 27, 1933-34, 40" long w/ladders down ...	800	1000	1400
Hydraulic DumpTruck, No. 10, 1933-34, 24-3/4" long	300	500	600
Ice Truck, No. 12, 1933-34, 26-1/2" long	600	1000	1750

Buddy "L" Ice Truck (Post-1932), No. 12, 1933-34, 26-1/2" long, $1750. Photo courtesy Tim Oei

Buddy "L" Post-1932 (Continued)	C6	C8	C10
International Delivery Truck, No. 51, 1935, 24-1/2" long	200	300	500
Merry-Go-Round Truck, No. 5429	75	125	200
Mister Buddy Ice Cream Van, 1964-65 ..	125	200	325
Railway Express Truck, No. 480, wooden, 1947, 16-1/4" long	300	450	700
Railway Express Truck, No. 763, 1952, 25" long	600	1000	2000
Riding Academy Truck, No. 5455, w/three horses	65	85	125
Robotoy Dump Truck with driver, operates on remote control	500	1000	1250
Sand & Gravel Truck, No. 3312, 13-1/2" ..	100	150	225
Scarab, No. 211, no wind-up mechanism, 1941, 10-1/2" long	200	300	400
Scarab, No. 711, wind-up, 1936-40, 10-1/2" ..	250	400	550
Service Truck, No. 5409, 1960	120	180	300
Siren Pull-n-Ride, No. 3722, 1953	100	160	240
Steam Shovel, No. 30, mechanical, 1935, 17-1/2" long, 13-1/2" high	175	275	400
Steam Shovel and International Truck, No. 16, 1937, 29-1/2" long, 36" extended	150	250	375
Tank Truck, No. 438, "Shell," 1935, 19-1/4" long	450	750	1200
Tank Truck, No. 938, 1941, 21-1/2" long ..	200	300	450
Texaco Tanker, No. 5603, promo sold at gas stations, 25" long	150	225	300
Traveling Zoo, No. 5420, 1965-66	100	175	250
Utility Delivery Truck, No. 946, 1941-42, 25" long	75	125	200

Buddy "L" Wrigley's Spearmint Railway Express Truck (Post-1932), No. 435, 1935, 23-1/8" long, $2200

Buddy "L" Post-1932 (Continued)

	C6	C8	C10
Victory Jeep and Cannon, No. 353, wood	100	150	250
Wrecker, No. 3667, "Repair-It," 1953, 24" long	150	225	300
Wrecker, No. 937, two-tone slant, 1939, 25-1/4" long	150	250	350
Wrecker, No. W37, 1939, 25-1/4" long	150	225	300
Wrecker, No. 503, 1940, 1941-42, 19-1/4" long	175	275	375
Wrecker, No. 437, 1934-37, 24" long	375	527	750
Wrecker, No. 13, 1933-37, 31" long	850	1500	3000
Wrecker, No. 37, 1933, 24" long	200	350	450
Wrigley's Spearmint Railway Express Agency Truck, No. 953, 1940	800	1350	2250
Wrigley's Spearmint Railway Express Truck, No. 435, headlights light up, 1935, 23-1/8" long	700	1400	2200

Construction Equipment

	C6	C8	C10
Aerial Tramway, No. 360, 1929-30	1500	2400	3700
Concrete Mixer, No. 280, 1926-30	500	750	1000
Dredge, No. 270, (Clamshell), 1926-30	800	1200	1500
Heavy Shovel, No. 220AB, (on Treads), 1929-30	2500	4000	7000
Heavy Steam Shovel, No. 220A, 1929-30	400	600	800
Hoisting Tower, No. 350, 1929-31	500	900	1250
Large Derrick, No. 241, 1922-31	275	375	600
Mixer, No. 280A, (on Treads), 1929-31	1100	1700	2600

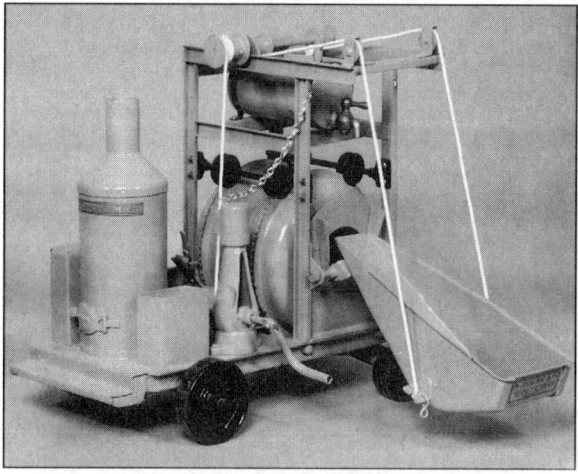

Buddy "L" Concrete Mixer (Construction Equipment), No. 280, 1926-30, $1000. Photo courtesy Bill Bertoia Auctions

Construction Equipment (Continued)

	C6	C8	C10
Overhead Crane, No. 250, 1924-27	700	1100	1750
Pile Driver, No. 260, 1926-28	750	1125	1600
Road Roller, No. 290, 1929-31	2100	3700	5280
Sand Loader, No. 230, 1925-31	175	250	350
Sand Screener, No. 300, 1929-30	700	1100	1700
Small Derrick, No. 240, 1922-31	300	450	625
Steam Shovel, No. 220, 1921-31	250	375	600
Tractor Dredge, No. 270A, (on Treads), 1929-30	2500	5000	8000
Trencher, No. 400, 1928-31	1800	2700	4200

Fire Trucks

	C6	C8	C10
Aerial Ladder, No. 205B, w/three ladders, 1926-30	750	1400	2200
Hook & Ladder, No. 205, 1923-32	800	1250	1950
Insurance Patrol, No. 205C, 1925-30	1500	2500	3500
Water Tower Truck, No. 205D, (Working), 1929-32	2500	4500	7250

Buddy "L" Pumper (Fire Trucks), No. 205A, 1925-30, $3000. Photo courtesy Bill Bertoia Auctions

Top to Bottom: Buddy "L" Baggage Truck (Large Trucks), No. 203B, 1927-32, $3500; Buddy "L" Auto Wrecker, No. 209, 1928-31, $4500. Photo courtesy Bill Bertoia Auctions

Large Trucks

	C6	C8	C10
Auto Wrecker, No. 209, 1928-31	1750	2750	4500
Baggage Truck, No. 203B, 1927-32	1400	2300	3500
Coach, No. 208, light green motorbus w/gold stripes, 1928-31	2000	3000	4800
Coal Truck, No. 202, 1926-32	2500	4000	6500
Dump Truck, No. 201, (Ratchet), 1923-29, 25"	500	750	1250
Express Truck, No. 200, 1921-31	1000	1600	2500
Hydraulic Dump Truck, No. 201A, 1926-31	600	1100	1700

Buddy "L" Oil Truck (Large Trucks), No. 206A, 1925-30, $2200. Photo courtesy Calvin L. Chaussee

Large Trucks (Continued)

	C6	C8	C10
Ice Truck, No. 207, 1926-31	600	750	1250
Lumber Truck, No. 203A, 1925-30	1500	2500	4000
Moving Van, No. 204, 1924-30	750	1250	2000
Oil Truck, No. 206A, 1925-30	900	1500	2200
Railway Express, No. 204A, 1926-31, 25"	1000	1600	2500
Sand & Gravel Truck, No. 202A, 1926-32	1500	2500	3500
Stake Truck, No. 203, 1921-24, 1926-28	750	1350	1900
Street Sprinkler Truck, No. 206, 206B, 1924-31	1200	1800	3200

Model T Series

	C6	C8	C10
Flivver Coupe, No. 210B, 1924-30	400	700	1200
Flivver Roadster, No. 210A, 1924-26	500	750	1250
Flivver Truck, No. 210, 1924-30	900	1400	1900
Ford Dump Cart, No. 211, 1926-30	800	1550	2750
Ford Dump Truck, No. 211A, 1926-30	1100	1700	2650
Ford Express Truck, No. 212, 1927-30	1400	2300	3225
One-Ton Ford Delivery Truck, No. 212A, 1927-30	2000	3500	5000

C.A.W. Novelty Company

Charles A. Wood, founder of C.A.W. Novelty Company, not only ran a substantial operation but made some of the finest replica toys in the slushmold industry. Founded about 1925, Wood's company was active until about 1940, when lead casting came to a halt due to World War II.

All of Wood's output showed artistry, ingenuity and meticulous craftsmanship. The toys are smooth and crisp, with detailed moldings and extra touches such as open windshields and multiple colors. Early products had metal disk wheels with painted black tires or metal-spoked wheels. Other details included, open V-shaped, divided windshields; drivers inside cabs; and tri-motored aircraft with the outboard engines mounted on the landing gear struts. Wood once told a reporter that it sometimes took three or four years to make a mold—just one example of how much pride Wood took in his work.

Charles Wood was born in 1891. He lived and worked in Topeka, Kansas and in nearby Clifton before moving to Clay Center. He was known for his civic boosterism and good works. After he helped establish the local airport, he built and operated his own aircraft maintenance hangar. A master machinist, he produced all of his toy molds, production tools, toy parts, and even plastic wheels.

The C & H Mfg. Co., formed in 1940 by Rod Hemphill, the last C.A.W. employee, and Howard Clevenger, made toys using original C.A.W. molds. These reproductions are heavier than C.A.W.'s and have black rubber wheels.

The seldom found C.A.W. trademark, consists of unique, lead blind hubs fitted over a wire axle. They are sometimes found with ordinary nail axles piercing the hubs.

Contributors: Fred Maxwell, 4722 N. 33 St., Arlington, VA 22207.

Perry R. Eichor, 703 North Almond Drive, Simpsonville, SC, 29681.

C.A.W. Novelty Company

	C6	C8	C10

Air Drive Coach, No. 25, blimp-like bus w/fin and rear propellor drive, twelve open windows, white soft rubber disc wheels w/unique fitted hubs with cap hidden axles, there is also a version w/o propellor, 3-7/8" long (CWV5) 30 45 60

DeSoto Sedan, No. 32, airflow, divided windshield, BOW, horizontal louvers, vertical grille pattern, hood cap, white soft rubber wheels, 3-7/8" long (CWV9) 40 50 60

Dump Truck, no number, Ford (?), hinged dump body, divided open windshield, two open windows, horizontal grille, metal disc wheels, 3-1/8" long (CWV13) 20 30 40

C.A.W. Novelty Company Dump Truck, 3-1/8" long, $40

C.A.W. Novelty Company Fuel Tanker, 3-3/4" long, $80

C.A.W. Novelty Company

	C8	C10

Fuel Tanker, Ford (?), cab w/driver inside, no windshield, horizontal grille pattern, three tanks, hose compartment, metal open-spoke wheels, 3-3/4" long (CWV4) 40 60 80

New Design Racer, No. 38, streamlined coupe, rounded tail, driver visible through two oval open windows, hood cap loop (stringpull?), white soft rubber wheels w/hubs, 3-3/8" long (CWV10).. 30 40 50

Overland Bus, no number, Fageol (?), Yellow line (?) tour bus, horizontal grille pattern, no headlamps, twelve windows, shallow observer deck, metal disc wheels, left sidemounted spare, 3-3/4" long (CWV3) 20 40 50

Racer, No. 39, transparent winshield, Indy FWD two-man racer, vee-shaped vertical grille, dual exhausts, boattail, unique hubs as on No. 25 (also WRW), not complete if divided plastic windshield is missing, 3" long (CWV11) 25 50 75

Sport Roadster, Buick?, no windshield, plain grille, vertical louvers, rearmount spare tire/wheel, right sidemounted spare, metal disc wheels, also version w/metal-spoked wheels, 3-1/2" long (CWV2).. 30 40 50

C.A.W. Novelty Company New Design Racer, No. 38, 3-3/8" long, $50

C.A.W. Novelty Company Overland Bus, 3-3/4" long, $50. Photo courtesy Gary Franson

C.A.W. Novelty Company Streamline Coupe, No. 30, 3" long, $75. Photo courtesy Perry Eichor

C.A.W. Novelty Company Tank Truck, 3-3/16" long, $45. Photo courtesy Gary Franson

C.A.W. Novelty Company

	C8	C10

Sport Roadster, open Buick, driver w/cap (gilt or silver), no windshield, horizontal grille, vertical louvers, no headlamps, rear-mount, metal disc wheels, 3-1/2" long (CWV1) 30 45 60

Streamline Coupe, No. 30, Airflow, vee pattern grille, hood cap, four open windows, small rear fin, small winged design on rear-wheel skirts, metal disc wheel also white soft rubber wheels, bottom pan goes over rear axle, 3" long (CWV6).......... 25 50 75

Tank Truck, no number, gasoline semi-trailer, two tanks, cab w/divided windsheild and open windows shows it is part of a set (CWV15) 30 40 60

Tank Truck, no number, Ford (?), three fuel tanks, hinged dump body, divided open windshield, two open window, horizontal grille pattern, metal disc wheels, unusual body connected by rear axle, 3-3/16" long (CWV14) 25 35 45

C.A.W. Novelty Company Sport Roadster, 3-1/2" long, $50. Photo courtesy Gary Franson

C.A.W. Novelty Company

	C8	C10

Three Auto Set, No. 40, includes: (a) Midget coupe racer, no number, horizontal grille pattern, horizontal hood louvers, divided open windshield, two open windows, two colored body ventilators, 2-1/16" long; (b) Midget racer, no number, gilt driver, vertical hood louvers, horizontal grille pattern, metal disc wheels (easily confused w/ Barclay No. 53), 2-1/8" long; (c) Austin Bantam, no number, two-door sedanette, five open windows, hood louvers, plain grille, rearmount spare tire/wheel, metal disc wheels (easily confused w/other makers' Bantams), 2" long; value per each (CWV12) 20 30 40

Wonder Special, No. 33, airflow coupe, three windshield companion to No. 30 Streamline Coupe, vertical grille, four open windows, white soft rubber wheels, front wheel skirts, pan goes over front axle, 3-3/8" long (CWV7) 25 50 75

Wonder Special, No. 33, airflow coupe, three-wheeled companion to No. 30 above, vertical grille pattern,, four open windows, white soft rubber wheels, front wheel skirts, pan goes over front axle, 3-3/8" long (CWV7) 25 50 75

C.A.W. Novelty Company Wonder Special, No. 33, 3-3/8" long, $75. Photo courtesy Gary Franson

Champion

	C6	C8	C10
Car, four casting nickeled radiator car, approx. 4" long	175	262	350
Coupe, Reo type, 7-1/2" long	212	318	425
Gas and Motor Oil Truck, cast iron, c. 1930s, 8" long	380	570	760
Mack Dump Truck, c. 1930s, 7" long	183	275	365
Mack Stake Truck, c. 1930, 4-1/2" long	90	135	180
Mack Stake Truck, 7-1/2" long	175	265	350
Motorcycle and rider, "Champion," 4-3/4" long	150	225	300
Panel Delivery, 7-3/4" long	495	745	990
Policeman on Motorcycle, rubber tires, 7" long	235	355	470
Race Car, w/two riders, 5-1/2"	125	188	250
Race Car, cast iron, removable driver, 6" long	150	225	300
Race Car, c. 1930s, 9" long	250	375	500
Sedan, 5-1/4" long	112	188	225
Wrecker, cast iron, "Champion," 7-1/2" long	308	463	615

Champion Mack Dump Truck, c. 1930s, 7" long, $365. Photo courtesy Harry Wolf; Detroit Antique Toy Museum

Champion Panel Delivery, 7-3/4" long, $990. Photo courtesy Bill Bertoia Auctions

Champion Wrecker, 7-1/2" long, $615

Chein

Chein (pronounced chain) was founded in 1903 by Julius Chein. The New Jersey company specialized in lithographed metal toys, the majority of them mechanical. In 1918, it was located at 310 Passaic Ave., in Harrison, New Jersey, with 250 employees. In 1934, it had 147 employees. In a 1946-47 directory, it listed 148 male and 132 female employees. Chein made toys until 1979, and is still in business today in Burlington, New Jersey.

Chein Hercules "C" Cab Mack Trucks

Chein introduced the Hercules series vehicles in 1925, the first model being the Dump Truck. It was made entirely of lightweight stamped-steel (heavy-gauge tin). Chein made at least fourteen different Hercules models, the smallest being seventeen inches long and stretching to thirty inches (with the C-Cab Bull Dog Mack mobile clam truck, including boom). These toys generally retailed between one dollar and $1.25. They were manufactured until the middle 1930s.

Contributor: Bob Smith, The Village Smith, 62 West Ave., Fairport, NY 14450-2102.

Chein

	C6	C8	C10
Army Truck, tin, cannon on back, early, 8-1/2" long	135	202	270

Chein Hercules Fire Pumper, No. 650, 1926, 18" long, $1600

Chein Hercules Racer No. 8, 20" long, $2200

Chein (Continued)	C6	C8	C10
Dan-Dee Dump Truck, wind-up..........	200	300	500
Greyhound Bus, wind-up, 9" long.......	120	200	400
Hercules Coal Truck, black cab, chassis, green bed, tin coal chute, chute door opens, 20" long	550	900	1600
Hercules Crane, 1925, 23" long	225	300	550
Hercules Fire Pumper, No. 650, 1926, 18" long..............................	650	1150	1600
Hercules Mack Army Truck, brown w/canvas cover, 19-3/4" long............	450	750	1500
Hercules Mack Crane Truck, No. 1100, 18" long..................................	750	1250	1800
Hercules Mack Dump Truck, black cab, chassis, red dump body, tailgate opens, 20" long.....................	350	650	375
Hercules Mack Motor Express, tin litho, black cab, orange stake bed, 19-1/2" long	550	900	1450
Hercules Mack Oil Tanker Truck, black and orange, c. 1928, 19" long..	600	1100	1700

Chein (Continued)	C6	C8	C10
Hercules Racer No. 8, w/driver, spare tire mounted on rear, red w/yellow trim, 20" long	700	1500	2200
Hercules Ready-Mix Concrete Truck, deluxe model, orange and black, lithographed, rotating drum, 17" long...	750	1300	2000
Hercules Roadster, red and black, rumble seat, luggage rack, 18" long..	475	800	1200
Hercules Royal Blue Line Pullman Bus, 18" long.................................	500	750	1350
Hercules Wrecker Truck, open cab, 18" long	500	750	1350
Junior Oil Tank Truck, 1920s, 8-1/2" long..	125	250	475
Junior Truck, 1920s	125	225	400
Limosine, tin wind-up, 1930s, 7" long ...	225	375	550
Mack Army Truck, open bed, 8-1/2" long..	200	300	450
Mack Ice Truck, 8-1/2" long	225	325	550
Mack Moving and Storage Van...........	400	650	750
Playland Whip, No. 340, four bump 'em cars, wind-up..............................	400	600	800
Racer No. 3, wind-up, 1920s, 6-1/2" long..	150	250	350

Chein Hercules Mack Crane Truck, No. 1100, 18" long, $1800. Photo courtesy Bob Smith

Chein Hercules Roadster, 18" long, $1200

Chein Racer No. 52, 6-1/2" long, $275. Photo courtesy Bob Smith

Chein Rapid Delivery Truck, No. 10, $600. Photo courtesy Bob Smith

Chein (Continued)

	C6	C8	C10
Racer No. 52, tin wind-up, 6-1/2" long	90	150	275
Rapid Delivery Truck, No. 10, tin wind-up	275	425	600
Roadster, tin lithographed, 1925, 8-1/2" long	250	475	675
Sedan, tin wind-up, six-window, c. 1920s, 8-1/2" long	250	475	675
Taxi, wind-up, 1920s, 7" long	185	325	450
Touring Car, tin litho, 7" long	250	375	500
Truck, "Junior Oil Tank," 1920s, 8-1/2" long	62	93	125
Woodie Sedan, tin wind-up, 5-1/4" long	48	72	95
Woodie Station Wagon, wind-up	100	150	200

Converse

Beginning in 1878, Converse helped make Winchendon, Massachusetts, "Toy Town U.S.A." It made wooden, tin and steel toys and was felled in 1934 by the Depression. It was originally owned by Morton E. Converse.

	C6	C8	C10
Auto with fringe on top, pressed steel, three-seat, painted, clockwork, rubber tires, 1905	600	900	1200
Fire Engine Ladder Truck, bell, wooden headlight, 1915, 10" long	1250	1875	2500
Parcel Post Van, 1920s, 15" long	1500	2500	3700
Pick-up Truck, very early, open cab	500	750	1000
Roadster, wind-up, open cab, 1908, 15-1/2" long	1100	1600	3000
Touring Auto, pressed steel, canvas roof, 1910	900	1400	2300
Transitional Taxi, clockwork, 10-1/2" long	525	770	1050

Cor-Cor

According to Margaret E. Holland (as reported by Ross Hermann in the July 27, 1992 *Antique News*), the granddaughter of Cor-Cor founder Louis A. Corcoran, this Washington, Indiana firm began on 21st Street in 1925, then expanded to East 3rd and Vantress. After a fire, Cor-Cor built its final plant on Front Street. At this latter location the company changed its name to Corcoran Metal Products. At its height, the firm employed up to 590 people. Corcoran retired in 1941 because of failing health, and died in 1945. His toys are marked "Cor-Cor" on the wheels.

	C6	C8	C10
Airflow, wind-up, electric lights, 16" long	1000	1700	2265
Bus, 23" long	425	638	850
Dump Truck, dumps back or side to side, 23" long	225	338	450
Graham Paige Sedan, electric, 20" long	900	1450	1950
Van, painted metal, c. 1928, 23" long	363	445	725

Courtland

	C6	C8	C10
Checker Cab Car, No. 4000, green and yellow, tin wind-up, 7-1/4" long, 3-1/4" wide, 2-3/4" high	200	225	350
Checker Cab Car, No. 4000, green and white, 7-1/4" long, 3-1/4" wide, 2-3/4" high	200	225	350
City Meat Market Delivery Sedan, No. 4000, tin wind-up, 7-1/4" long, 3-1/4" wide, 2-3/4" high	75	150	175

Courtland Checker Cab Car, No. 4000, 7-1/4" long, 3-1/4" wide, 2-3/4" high, $350

Courtland City Meat Market Delivery Sedan, No. 4000, 7-1/4" long, 3-1/4" wide, 2-3/4" high, $175

Courtland Mechanical Black Diamond Coal Truck, No. 5100, 10-1/2" wide, 3" wide, 3-3/8" high, $300. Photo courtesy Joe and Sharon Freed

Courtland (Continued)	C6	C8	C10
Country Produce Pickup, No. 4500, tin wind-up, 7-1/4" long, 3-1/4" wide, 2-3/4" high	75	125	175
Courtland Side Dump Tractor-Trailer, No. 1200, 13" long, 3" wide, 3-1/4" high	100	150	200
Courtland Tractor-Trailer, same tractor as No. 2000 except marked, "Loft-Fresh Candies"	350	550	850
Dump Truck, w/dual rear wheels, 10-1/2" long, 3" wide, 3-3/8" high	250	350	475
Easter Greetings Rabbit Truck, No. 800, 9" long	325	525	750
Express and Hauling Truck, No. 900, 1946, 9" long, 3" wide, 2-3/4" high	100	175	275
Express Service Pickup, No. 4500, tin wind-up, 7-1/4" long, 3-1/4" wide, 2-3/4" high	75	125	175
FBI Riot Squad Car, No. 4050, similar to No. 7600 FBI Riot Squad Car	100	125	150
FBI Riot Squad Car, No. 7600, 7-1/4" long, 3-1/4" wide, 2-3/4" high	100	150	200
Fire Chief Car, No. 4000, red and white, tin wind-up, 7-1/4" long, 3-1/4" wide, 2-3/4" high	100	125	175

Courtland (Continued)	C6	C8	C10
Fire Chief Car, No. 4000, red, tin wind-up, 7-1/4" long, 3-1/4" wide, 2-3/4" high	100	125	150
Fire Department with Automatic Darage Door, No. 9050, nonpowered fire chief car w/the Courtland Toy Co., Phila. Pa., markings,, 7-3/4" x 10-1/8" x 6-3/4"	75	125	175
Fire Patrol No. 2 Truck, No. 900, 1946, L 9", W 3", H 2-3/4"	100	175	275
Ice Cream Truck, No. 900, 1946, 9" long, 3" wide, 2-3/4" high	125	200	300
Log Truck Tractor-Trailer, No. 620, 1946, 13" long, 3" wide, 3-1/4" high	150	225	350
Mechanical Automatic Ladder Fire Truck, No. 1400, tin wind-up, 9" long, 3" wide, 2-3/4" high	175	250	350
Mechanical Black Diamond Coal Truck, No. 5100, tin wind-up, 10-1/2" wide, 3" wide, 3-3/8" high	150	225	300
Mechanical Chromed Trimmed Tow Truck, No. 8500, tow boom shows detail, tin wind-up, 8" long, 3-1/4" wide, 3-1/2" high	75	175	225

Courtland Mechanical Emergency Rescue Squad Tractor-Trailer, 13" long, 3" wide, 3-1/4" high, $250

Courtland (Continued)

	C6	C8	C10
Mechanical Chromed Trimmed Tow Truck, No. 8500, tow boom is solid color, tin wind-up, 8" long, 3-1/4" wide, 3-1/2" high..............................	175	300	350
Mechanical Combination Steam Shovel Carried by Low-boy Tractor-trailer, No. 5300, tin wind-up, 15-1/2" long, 3-7/8" wide, 10-1/2" high	350	550	775
Mechanical Dump Truck, No. 1600, tin wind-up, 7" long, 3" wide, 2-3/4" high	65	100	135
Mechanical Dump Truck, No. 3100, tin wind-up, 7" long, 3" wide, 3-1/4" high	65	100	135
Mechanical Emergency Rescue Squad Tractor-Trailer, tin wind-up, 13" long, 3" wide, 3-1/4" high	150	200	250
Mechanical ESSO Gasoline Tractor-Trailer, No. 2000, tin wind-up, 13" long, 3" wide, 3-1/4" high.................	250	350	450
Mechanical Express and Hauling Truck, No. 1300, tin wind-up, 9" long, 3" wide, 2-3/4" high.................	125	200	275
Mechanical Fire Chief Car, No. 7000, w/siren, tin wind-up, 7-1/4" long, 3-1/4" wide, 2-3/4" high	150	200	250
Mechanical Fire Chief Car with Siren, No. 7500, 7-1/4" long, 3-1/4" wide, 3-1/4" high..............................	150	200	250

Courtland Mechanical Heavy Duty Sand and Gravel Tractor-Trailer, No. 2375, 13" long, 3" wide, 3-1/4" high, $275

Courtland (Continued)

	C6	C8	C10
Mechanical Fire Patrol No. 2 Truck, No. 1300, tin wind-up, 9" long, 3" wide, 2-3/4" high...............................	125	200	275
Mechanical Freight Haulers Tractor-Trailer, No. 2600, tin wind-up, 13" long, 3" high, 3-1/4" wide	150	250	325
Mechanical Gasoline Tractor-Trailer, No. 2000, tin wind-up, 13" long, 3" wide, 3-1/4" high.................	150	250	325
Mechanical Gulf Gasoline Tractor-Trailer, No. 3875, 13" long, 3" wide, 3-1/4" high.................	225	350	475
Mechanical Heavy Duty Sand and Gravel Tractor-Trailer, No. 2375, tin wind-up, 13" long, 3" wide, 3-1/4" high	175	225	275
Mechanical Hook and Ladder Tractor-Trailer, No. 2100, tin wind-up, 13" long, 3" wide, 3-1/4" high	100	150	175

Courtland Mechanical Fire Chief Car, No. 7000, 7-1/4" long, 3-1/4" wide, 2-3/4" high, $250. Photo courtesy Joe and Sharon Freed

Courtland Mechanical Hook and Ladder Tractor-Trailer, No. 2100, 13" long, 3" wide, 3-1/4" high, $175

Courtland Mechanical Logging Tractor-Trailer, No. 2200, 13" long, 3" wide, 3-1/4" high, $250

Courtland Mechanical Road Roller Truck, No. 3000, 9" long, 3" wide, 3-1/4" high, $450

Courtland (Continued)	C6	C8	C10
Mechanical Ice Cream Scooter, No. 6500, tin wind-up, 6-1/2" long, 3" wide, 4-1/2" high	200	300	400
Mechanical Ice Cream Truck, No. 1300, tin wind-up, 9" long, 3" wide, 2-3/4" high	150	200	250
Mechanical Lawn Mower, No. 21, tin wind-up, 12" wide, 29" high, 5" wheels	65	85	110
Mechanical Logging Tractor-Trailer, No. 2200, tin wind-up, 13" long, 3" wide, 3-1/4" high	150	200	250
Mechanical Military Gun Car, lithographed gun shield, 7-1/2" long, 3-1/4" wide, 2-1/2" high	100	175	250
Mechanical Milk Tractor-Trailer, No. 2050, "American Dairies," tin wind-up. Note: 1951 catalog shows Milk Trailer markings that read the same as above except "Approved" is used in the place of "Vitamin D." This variation is not known to have been produced, 13" long, 3" wide, 3-1/4" high	150	250	325
Mechanical Moving and Storage Truck, w/No. 130 litho on the sides of the truck bed, tin wind-up	175	250	375
Mechanical No. 51 Steam Shovel, No. 5200, tin wind-up, 15-1/2" long, 3-3/4" wide, 9-1/2" high	150	200	250
Mechanical Open Van Tractor-Trailer, No. 2300, tin wind-up, 13" long, 3" wide, 3-1/4" high	75	125	175
Mechanical Operation No. 51 Crane Turck, No. 5000, tin wind-up, 13" long, 3-5/8" wide, 5" high	225	325	400
Mechanical Power Lawn Mower, No. 25, tin wind-up, 12" wide, 29" high, 5-3/4" wheels	75	100	125

Courtland (Continued)	C6	C8	C10
Mechanical Road Roller Truck, No. 3000, tin wind-up, 9" long, 3" wide, 3-1/4" high	250	350	450
Mechanical Side Tipper Tractor-Trailer, No. 2700, tin wind-up, 13" long, 3" high, 3-1/4" wide	200	300	375
Mechanical Side Tipper Tractor-Trailer, No. 3900, "Black Diamond Coal Company-340," tin wind-up, 13" long, 3" high, 3-1/4" wide	300	400	500
Mechanical Stake Bed Truck, No. 3200, tin wind-up, 7" long, 3" wide, 3-1/4" high	125	150	175

Courtland Mechanical Truck Set, No. 500, $600. Photo courtesy Joe and Sharon Freed

Courtland Pop-Up Ladder Fire Truck, No. 5450, 13" long, 3" wide, 3-1/4" high, $450

Courtland (Continued)

	C6	C8	C10
Mechanical State Police Car, No. 7500, w/siren, tin wind-up, 7-1/4" long, 3-1/4" wide, 2-3/4" high	165	225	275
Mechanical Tractor, w/tin wheels, w/o scraper, 7-1/2" long, 4-3/4" wide, 4-1/2" high	250	350	450
Mechanical Trailer Tow Truck, No. 2400, tin wind-up, 13" long, 3" wide, 3-1/4" high	225	325	400
Mechanical Truck Set, No. 500, w/box, includes four trucks: Nos. 2000, 2100, 2200, 2300	150	300	600
Mechanical Truck Terminal Set, No. 600, two trucks	450	750	1100
Modern Bakery Delivery Sedan, No. 4000, tin wind-up, 7-1/4" long, 3-1/4" wide, 2-3/4" high	100	150	175
Modern Decorators Pickup, No. 4500, tin wind-up, 7-1/4" long, 3-1/4" wide, 2-3/4" high	100	125	150
Moving and Storage Truck, No. 900, 1946, 9" long, 3" wide, 2-3/4" high	150	225	350
Pop-Up Ladder Fire Truck, No. 5450, 13" long, 3" wide, 3-1/4" high	250	350	450
Private Garage with Automatic Door, No. 9075, nonpowered car w/Courtland Toy Co., Phila. Pa. Markings, 7-3/4" x 10-1/8" x 6-3/4"	75	125	175
Side Dump Tractor-Trailer, No. 700, 1946, 13" long, 3" wide, 3-1/4" high	100	150	200
Space Rocket Patrol Car, No. 4060, 1952, 7-1/4" long, 3-1/4" wide, 2-3/4" high	150	200	250
Woody Sedan, No. 4000, blue and tan, stamped "A Walt Reach Toy by Courtland Toy Co. Philadelphia, PA. Made in U.S.A.," 7-1/4" long, 3-1/4" wide, 2-3/4" high	65	75	100

Craftoys

Craftoys, a small Omaha, Nebraska, firm, had a brief career casting slush-mold vehicles before World War II when the need for lead brought the pot metal era to a long halt. Craftoys acquired some of the molds when Ralstoy was reorganizing in 1940.

Contributor: Fred Maxwell, 4722 N. 33 St., Arlington, VA 22207.

Perry R. Eichor, 703 North Almond Drive, Simpsonville, SC, 29681.

	C6	C8	C10
Cement Mixer, No. 78, two open windows, "Made in USA," 3-3/4"	8	12	16
Fire Truck, No. 101, hose truck or insurance patrol, four open windows, 4-1/2" long	40	60	80
Freight Train, No. 3600, "Locomotive, 0-6-4, 4-1/2," "KT&N RR," "Made in USA," price per car, 16-1/2", cars 3-1/4", caboose 2-3/4"	6	9	12
Oil Truck, No. 104, 1938 International, tanker, COE, two open windows, marked "Gas" and "Oil," 3-3/4" long	45	70	80
Racer, no number, Indy type, driver, removable tin hood, slanted nose, available as reproduction, 3-3/4" long	30	40	60
Racer, No. 81, Miller FWD Indy racer, "Made in USA," 4-1/2"	10	15	20
Racer, No. 81, Miller FWD Indy, marked "Made in USA," 4-1/2" long	20	40	60
Racer, No. 100, Indy type, driver, removable tine hood, rounded nose, available as reproduction, 4-1/2" long	20	40	60
Sedan, No. 92, streamlined two-door sedan, four open windows, screen pattern grille, 4" long	20	40	60

Craftoys Oil Truck, No. 104, 3-3/4" long, $80. Photo courtesy Fred Maxwell

Top to Bottom: Craftoys Racer, No. 100, 4-1/2" long, $60; Craftoys Racer, 3-3/4" long, $60. Photo courtesy Perry Eichor

Craftoys Speed Car, No. 103, 4-1/4" long, $85. Photo courtesy Perry Eichor

Craftoys Tanker, No. 102, 6-3/4" long, $80. Photo courtesy Ferd Zegel

Craftoys (Continued)	C6	C8	C10
Speed Car, No. 103, streamlined closed racer, body trimmed in fantasy streamlines, available as reproduction, 4-1/4" long	45	70	85
Tanker, No. 102, International K-Line (?), semi-trailer, two open windows, marked "Gasoline," 6-3/4" long	40	60	80
Tractor, No. 17, "Fordson," "Made in USA," farm tractor, driver, rear wheels larger, visible engine, 2-1/2"	8	12	16

Dayton Friction Works	C6	C8	C10
Armored Car, sheet metal, flywheel drive, red and gold, 1909, 11"	250	450	600
Coal and Ice Truck, tin, friction, c. 1920	200	300	400
Coupe, c. 1920, 12-1/2" long	600	900	1200

Dayton Friction Works Armored Car, 1909, 11", $600. Photo courtesy Bob Smith

Dayton Friction Works (Continued)	C6	C8	C10
Coupe, tine friction, 17" long	500	650	900
Dayton Friction, pressed steel, rubber tires, 1920s, 14-1/4" long	250	375	500
Dump Truck	200	300	400
Fire Ladder Truck, 18" long	275	365	550
Fire Pumper, sheet metal construction, flywheel drive, white/gold, 1909, 14-3/4" long	500	750	1000
Ladder Truck, 1920s	350	525	700
Touring Car, unpowered, 13-1/2" long	350	525	700
Touring Car, friction motor, 13-1/2" long	500	750	1000
Touring Car, seven passenger, open, w/driver, flywheel drive, red and gold, patent date April 2, 1909, 13-1/4" long	150	225	300

Dayton Friction Works Coupe, 17" long, $900

Dayton Friction Works Touring Car, seven passenger, 13-1/4" long, $300

Dent Hardware Company

Dent, of Fullerton, Pennsylvania, was in business from 1895-1973. Henry H. Dent, with four partners, was the owner. Dent is known for particularly fine castings in its vehicles. It was also one of the first manufacturers to try (with little success) aluminum toys (in the 1920s). Toys seem to have been phased out during the Depression. Dent toys are difficult to identify due to the fact that few, if any, of its toys are marked.

	C6	C8	C10
American Oil Co. Truck, cast-iron, 10-1/2" long	800	1250	1750
Bus, 10-1/2" long	500	800	900
Bus, cast iron, 6-1/4" long	350	500	750
Bus Line, 9" long	450	600	1250
Coast to Coast Bus, 10" long	300	450	650
Coast to Coast Bus, c. 1925, 15" long	1100	1700	2500
Coast to Coast Bus, 7-1/2" long	125	175	275
Contractors Mack Dump, open cab, 10-1/2" long	100	2000	3000

Dent Hardware Company Freeman's Dairy Truck, 6" long, $1750

Dent Hardware Company

	C8	C10
Coupe, 5" long 125	175	250
Express J & B Stakebed Truck, driver, 1915, 14-1/2" long 500	800	1250
Fire Ladder Truck, w/driver, 8-1/2" long 400	625	925
Fire Truck, cast iron, w/ladder and men, 18" long 800	1250	1900
Fire Truck, cast iron, 7" long 125	500	325
Freeman's Dairy Truck, sliding doors, milkman, 6" long 650	1150	1750
Hose Reeler, cast iron, w/men, large 450	700	1100
Interurban Bus, cast iron, 9" long 225	350	550
Ladder Truck, two drivers, 10" long 225	350	550
LaSalle, 4-1/2" long 425	700	975
Mack Dump Truck, iron wheels, c. 1925, 4-1/2" long 50	75	125
Model T Sedan, two door, iron wheels, c. 1925 125	187	250
Patrol, c. 1920s, 6-1/2" long 125	187	250
Police Patrol, 8-3/4" long 700	1125	1650
Public Service Bus, c. 1926, 13-1/2" long 1750	3000	4750
Sedan, spare tire, has stop and go light, full bumpers on front, 7-1/2" ... 900	1350	1800
Steam Roller, cast iron, 6" long 40	70	90
Touring Car, driver and passenger, 12" long 450	700	1100
Valley View Dairy, 8" long 500	900	1500
Yellow Cab, approx. 7-3/4" long 800	1250	1800

Dinky

Dinky toys were first made in England in 1932 under the name "Modeled Miniatures," later "Meccano Miniatures," and in 1934, "Dinky," which in England means "fetching."

	C6	C8	C10
014c Coventry Fork Lift	35	75	100
023h Ferrari Racer	15	20	40
025c Flat Truck	85	125	175
027f 1948 Plymouth Station Wagon	75	150	200
029c Double Decker Bus	75	115	150
030r Fordson Truck	40	60	80
032c/576 Panhard Esso	60	90	120

Dinky (Continued)

	C6	C8	C10
033 AN Simca Bailly	55	110	150
034 Royal Mail Van	40	55	90
036b Bentley	95	145	190
036c Humber, 1936	100	150	200
036d Rover	85	127	170
038d Alvis	115	160	225
038c Lagonda	95	150	195
039c Lincoln Zephyr	140	225	275
040a Riley 4DS	90	130	175
045 45 Vauxhall Victor	15	20	40
097 Euclid Truck	15	20	40
106 Thunderbird 2 Space	45	95	125
112 Triumph Purdey	40	55	85
130 Ford Consul Corsair	40	55	90
134 Triumph Vitesse	30	42	65
135 Triumph 2000	20	30	40
137 Plymouth, 1963	50	75	95
151 Austin Devon	17	26	35
154 Ford Taurus	17	26	35
157 Jaguar XK 120	65	130	165
168 Ford Escort	15	25	50
170 Ford Sedan, 1950	35	55	75
172 Studebaker Land Cruiser	55	80	110
174 Hudson Hornet Sedan	65	115	155
181 Volkswagen MBD	50	100	135
197 Morris Mini	55	110	145
198 Rolls Royce Phantom V	40	80	105

Dinky Hudson Hornet Sedan, No. 174, $155

No. 13 Dinky Toys Catalog

Dinky (Continued)

	C6	C8	C10
200 Matra 630	15	20	40
201 Plymouth Rally, 1976	15	20	40
207 Triumph TR7 Leyland	15	20	40
227 Beach Buggy	15	20	40
241 Austin Taxi	25	40	50
252 1968 Pontiac RCMP Police Car	40	80	100
254 Austin Taxi	45	85	110
261 Telephone Service Truck	65	130	165
267 Bedford Dump	30	45	75
267 Dodge Fire Rescue	30	45	75
308 Leyland Tractor	30	40	60
344 Estate Car	30	40	60

Doepke "Model Toys"

Charles Wm. Doepke Mfg. Co., Inc., also known as Doepke, was located in Rossmoyne, Ohio. Each of their toys was an authorized replica of the actual vehicle, right down to the decals. The exception was the manufacturer's own Model Toys design. Doepke "Model Toys" advertised their toys as outlasting all others—three to one.

Of the Doepke "Model Toys" that were mass produced, several had variations in their basic construction. Usually these changes were an elimination of the more intricate operating procedures and had little or no effect on the toy's overall appearance.

Doepke accepted orders to make models of actual vehicles for various companies, but the toys with the most allure, playability, feasible mass production design, and greatest entertainment value were mass produced. The others, those that would not withstand rough handling by young hands or were too expensive, were only manufactured in low numbers, some-times only one. This is no doubt the explanation for the number gaps between the marketed items.

At the end of World War II, Doepke hit the market with five models, the first in a line of heavy-duty metal operating replicas employing metal tread or authentic miniature tires. The tires were either Good-year or Firestone, with authentic tread and name and tire sizes. The first five numbers in the toy series were 2000, 2001, 2002, 2006, 2007. Following is a list of the Doepke vehicles.

Doepke "Model Toys"	C6	C8	C10
No. 2000, Wooldridge H.D. Earth Hauler, 25" long	225	300	425
No. 2001, tracks, Barber-Greene High-capacity Bucket Loader, 13" high	430	510	625
No. 2002, Jaeger Concrete Mixer, 15" long	225	310	450
No. 2006, Adams Diesel Road Grader, 26" long	210	295	395
No. 2007, Unit Mobile Crane, 11-1/2" long	225	300	400
No. 2008, American LaFrance Aerial Ladder Truck	245	325	400
No. 2009, Euclid Earth Hauler Truck, 27" long	250	300	400

Doepke Wooldridge H.D. Earth Hauler, No. 2000, 25" long, $425. Photo courtesy Calvin L. Chausee

Doepke Jaeger Concrete Mixer, No. 2002, 15" long, $450. Photo courtesy Calvin L. Chausee

Doepke "Model Toys" (Continued)	C6	C8	C10
No. 2011, Heiliner Earth Scraper, 29" long	295	300	375
No. 2013, high-capacity bucket loader, wheels, Barber-Greene Mobile, 22" long	325	400	525
No. 2014, American LaFrance Aerial Ladder Fire Truck, 23" long	290	375	450
No. 2015, Clark Airport Tractor and Baggage Trailers	375	450	550
No. 2015, MG, 1954, 15" long	360	450	525
No. 2018, Jaguar, 1955	450	550	650
No. 2020, American LaFrance Pumper Fire Truck, 18" long	200	300	400
No. 2023, American LaFrance Improved Aeriel Searchlight Truck, 1955	950	1650	2100

Dunwell

Dunwell was the trade name given to its toys by Metal Products Co. of Clifton, New Jersey. Its trucks seem to have been sold from 1953-1958. Dunwell vehicles resemble the Tonka line, and are rare.

Dunwell	C6	C8	C10
Auto Transport	162	243	325
Dump Truck	100	150	200
Log Truck	110	165	220
Red Star Express Lines Truck	300	450	600
Snowcrop Refrigerator Semi	350	525	700
Steel Carrier Co. Semi	17	255	340
Wrecker	168	254	335

Dunwell Auto Transport, $325. Photo courtesy Roy Bonjour

Dunwell Log Truck, $220. Photo courtesy Tim Oei

Dunwell Steel Carrier Co. Semi, $340. Photo courtesy Tim Oei

Dyna-Model Products Company

Dyna-Model Products Co. may have pioneered the scale model industry of today's markets with their "Dyna-Mo" brand of HO toys. They produced pot-metal toys, identified by their method of assembling body parts (clamping axles between small posts) and by the standardized appearance of the undersides of the whole line.

Produced in the 1930s, and perhaps into the post-war era, the toys were made by a coarse die-casting process. The earlier vintage cars were made in two to five parts, exclusive of wheels and axles, to be pinned, clamped or glued together, including body, frame, steering wheel, top and windshield. Some were packaged as kits with instructions printed on the box. The toys were factory painted in as many as four colors.

Contributors: Fred Maxwell 4722 N. 33 St., Arlington, VA 22207.

Perry R. Eichor, 703 North Almond Drive, Simpsonville, SC, 29681.

	C6	C8	C10
Convertible, Cadillac two-door Sedan, late 1930s, 2-3/8" (D16)	6	9	12
Delivery Van, Pontiac, open windshield and door windows, late 1930s, 2-3/8" (D21)	4	6	8
Dump Truck, open windows, hinged body w/realistic load of coal, three-piece, two colors, dual rear wheels, 2-3/4" (D24)	6	9	12
Limousine, Cadillac, open windows, late 1930s, 2-1/2" (D20)	9	6	12
Pickup Truck, GMC?, one-piece, open windows, one color, 1930s, 2" (D25)	4	6	8
Pickup Truck, Mack?, "US Army," Air Corps star decals, two-piece body, two colors, late 1930s, 2" (D26)	4	6	8

Dyna-Model Products Company (Continued)

	C6	C8	C10
R-26 HO Buick Convertible 55c, open, two-door sedan, top down, one-piece body, solid cast windshield, disc wheels, late 1930s, 2-3/8" (D13)	6	9	12
R-26 HO Surrey, horseless carriage, tiller steering, three colors, three-piece body, kit, 1-3/4" (D1)	4	6	8
R-61 HO Model T Ford 1914 Touring with Top, one-piece body, top up, three colors, "cut plastic windshield to fit, darken edges w/ink or paint and glue top and windshield in place, in slots provided," 1-5/8" (D6)	4	6	8
Roadster, Buick (?), open, right-hand steering, four-piece, three colors, 1-7/8" (D4)	4	6	8
Roadster, Packard, top up, rumble seat, one-piece body, glued windshield, spoked wheels, three colors, 2" (D9)	6	9	12
Roadster, Model A Ford (?) top down, open rumble seat, disc wheels, one-piece body, unpainted, 2" (D11)	2	3	4
Sedan, Buick, open windshield and windows, two colors, 1930s, 2" (D12)	4	6	8

Dyna-Model Products Company. Top Row, Left to Right: Sedan, 2-3/8", $12; Limousine, late 1930s, 2-1/2", $12; Sedan, 1930s, 2", $8; Sedan, late 1930s, 2-3/8", $12. Middle Row, left to right: Taxi, Buick, late 1930s, 2-3/8", $12; Taxi, Cadillac, late 1930s, 2-3/8", $12; Delivery Van, late 1930s, 2-3/8", $8. Bottom Row, left to right: Pickup Truck, late 1930s, 2-1/2", $8; Wrecker, late 1930s, 2-3/4", $12; Dump Truck, 2-3/4", $12

Dyna-Model Products Company (Continued)

	C6	C8	C10
Sedan, Buick two-door airflow, open windshield and windows, 2-3/8" (D14)	6	9	12
Sedan, Cadillac two-door, open windshield and windows, late 1930s, 2-3/8" (D17)	6	9	12
Sedan, Pontiac four-door airflow, open windshield and windows including rear, 2-3/8" (D19)	6	9	12
Speedster, Antique Mercer, right-hand steering, four colors, three-piece, 2" (D3)	4	6	8
Taxi, Cadillac sedan, open windshield and windows including rear, two colors, late 1930s, 2-3/8" (D18)	6	9	12
Taxi, Buick sedan, open windshield and windows, two colors, late 1930s, 2-3/8" (D15)	6	9	12
Touring, Packard, top down, rumble seat, one-piece body, glued windshield, spoked wheels, three colors, 2" (D10)	6	9	12
Touring Car, 1914 Ford, top down cast in one-piece body, glued windshield, three colors, 1-3/4" (D7)	4	6	8
Touring Car, realistic folded top attachable w/hinge pins, left hand steering, five-piece, two colors, 1-7/8" (D5)	4	6	8
Touring Car, Stanley Steamer, open tonneau, right-hand steering, four colors, four-piece, 2" (D2)	4	6	8
Truck, Mack (?), tarpaulin-covered, two-piece body, 2" (D27)	4	6	8
Wrecker, GMC (?), open windows, three-piece, four colors, late 1930s, 2-3/4" (D23)	6	9	12

Erie (Parker White Metal)

According to James Apthrope, Erie toys were made by Parker White Metal Company, which apparently began in Erie, Pennsylvania, but moved to Fairview in the early 1960s. However, according to company officials, the firm made toys only prior to World War II. It printed no catalogs.

Contributor: Dave Leopard, 2507 Feather Run Trail, West Columbia, SC 29169-4915.

Erie Champion Coal Truck, 1935, 5" long, $95. Photo courtesy John Taylor

	C6	C8	C10
Cabover Truck, no tailgate, c. 1937, 3-1/4" (EV15)	20	25	35
Cabover Truck, tailgate, updated, c. 1937, 3-1/4" long (EV16)	20	25	35
Champion Coal Truck, 1935, 5" long	40	55	95
Coupe, futuristic, no chassis, c. 1939, 4-1/4" long (EV19)	30	40	50
Ford Ice Truck, "Pure Ice Co.," 1935, 5" long (EV13)	50	65	85
Ford Pickup Truck, high sides, small rear window, 1935, 5" long (EV12)	40	55	70
Ford Pickup Truck, low sides, painted, 1935, 5" long (EV09)	45	60	75
Ford Pickup Truck, high sides, large rear window, 1935, 5" long (EV11)	40	55	70
Ford Pickup Truck, low sides, plated, 1935, 5" long (EV10)	45	60	80
Ford Tow Truck, "Servel Body," 1935, 5" long (EV14)	50	65	80
Lincoln Zephyr Sedan, plated, 1936, 3-1/2" long (EV04)	35	40	55
Lincoln Zephyr Sedan, painted, 1936, 3-1/2" long (EV03)	25	30	40
Lincoln Zephyr Sedan, painted, 1936, 5-1/2" long (EV01)	40	50	70
Lincoln Zephyr Sedan, plated, 1936, 5-1/2" long (EV02)	45	55	75
Packard Roadster, plated, 1936, 3-1/2" long (EV08)	35	40	50
Packard Roadster, painted, 1936, 3-1/2" long (EV07)	25	30	40
Packard Roadster, plated, 1936, 6" long (EV06)	50	70	100
Packard Roadster, painted, 1936, 6" long (EV05)	45	65	95
Sedan, futuristic, fin on trunk, no chassis, c. 1939, 4-1/4" long (EV18)	30	35	50

Erie (Continued)

	C6	C8	C10
Sedan, sharknose, no chassis, c. 1939, 4-1/4" long (EV20)	30	35	50
Tow Truck, no chassis, c. 1939, 4-1/4" long (EV17)	30	40	50

Ertl

Ertl was begun by Fred Ertl Sr., in 1945, working out of his Dubuque, Iowa, home. As business expanded, the firm moved to Dyersville, Iowa. Ertl learned about using sand molds in his native Germany; very early in the company's history, he began working directly from the original blueprints to make his toy tractors, trucks and other wheeled toys. Ertl's specialty is farm toys, with rights obtained from such manufacturers as International Harvester and John Deere. Today, Ertl is the largest manufacturer of toy-farm equipment in the world; in addition, it makes a number of other toys, such as cars, trucks and airplanes.

Ertl was purchased by Racing Champions in 1998 and now go by the name Racing Champions-Ertl.

	C6	C8	C10
Conoco Tanker	75	120	175
Ertl Van Lines Pup Trailer, white	100	150	225
Fleetstar Dump Truck, ten wheel, red	125	185	250
Fleetstar Hi-side Dump Truck, red and white	125	185	250
Fleetstar Ten-wheel Dump Truck, red	85	128	170
Fleetstar Tilt Bed, green	125	185	250
GE Truck, white	15	22	30
GMC Dump	100	150	200
Hydraulic Dump Truck, No. 1645	20	30	40
International Dump	100	150	200

Ertl Ertl Van Lines Pup Trailer, $225

Ertl Fleetstar Dump Truck, $250

Ertl Fleetstar Tilt Bed, $250

Ertl (Continued)

	C6	C8	C10
International Scout, maroon or blue	85	135	195
Iron Horse Van	35	52	70
Loadstar Box Van, lavender and white	200	375	575
Loadstar Dump Truck	132	198	265
Loadstar Tilt Bed, green/gray	85	128	170
Loadstar Tow Truck, white/red	100	150	200
Mary Kay Cosmetics Trailer Truck	75	112	150
Mobile Tanker	42	63	85
Tilt Bed	92	138	185
Transtar Rowe Furniture Truck	27	41	55
Transtar Texaco Tanker	45	68	90
Velveeta Semi	25	38	50

Firestone

The following list and the numbers in parentheses, was compiled by David Leopard

	C6	C8	C10
'35 Ford Two-door Humpback Sedan, 4-7/8" long (FA02)	75	100	150
'36 Ford Two-door Humpback Sedan, 4-7/8" long (FA03)	75	100	150

Firestone (Continued)

	C6	**C8**	**C10**
'39 Mercury Fastback Four-door Sedan, 4-3/4" long (FA01)	100	125	165

Freidag

	C6	**C8**	**C10**
Bus, cast iron, 6-3/4" long	225	338	450
Coupe, cast iron, 5-3/4" long	290	435	580
Double-Decker Bus, 9-1/4" long	850	1400	2100
Panel Delivery Truck, 7-1/2" long	1200	2200	3200
Pickup Truck, 7-1/2" long	500	750	1000
Racer, driver and passenger, 6-1/2" long	550	900	1300
Roadster, w/driver and passenger, 6-1/2" long	400	600	800

Freidag Double-Decker Bus, 9-1/4" long, $2100. Photo courtesy Bill Bertoia Auctions

Left to Right: Freidag Panel Delivery Truck, 7-1/2" long, $3200; Freidag Pickup Truck, 7-1/2" long, $1000

Freidag Roadster, 6-1/2" long, $800. Photo courtesy Bill Bertoia Auctions

Girard Fire Chief Siren Coupe, 14" long, $600

Girard

Girard Model Works was founded by C.G. Wood in 1906, in Girard, Pennsylvania. His son Frank was soon made a partner. In 1918, they began making mechanical toys for an unidentified New York firm. In 1920, they sold them under their name "Wood's Mechanical Toys." The business eventually passed into other hands and had 1,000 employees in 1931. During the Depression, Girard laid off its salesman, Louis Marx, who stalled Girard customers as he tried to get a plant of his own in business. Since Marx was better known to buyers than the people at Girard, he emerged triumphant, and in 1934, Marx took over the firm. Girard remained in business till 1980.

	C6	**C8**	**C10**
Coupe, battery-operated headlights, 14" long	350	525	700
Fire Chief Car, 15" long	260	300	400
Fire Chief Siren Coupe, wind-up, 14" long	275	450	600
Fire Truck, 1920s, 12" long	50	75	100
Pierce-Arrow Coupe, wind-up, green, orange and cream, 1932, 14" long	250	350	500
Pump Truck, battery-operated, headlights, 10" long	100	150	200
Roadster, electrified, 14-1/2" long	212	318	425
Side Dump, 11-1/2" long	150	225	300

Girard Pierce-Arrow Coupe, 1932, 14" long, $500

Girard Wrecker Truck, 1930s, 10" long, $600

Girard (Continued)

	C6	C8	C10
Stake Truck, electric, headlights, 10" long	150	225	300
Tank Truck, wood wheels, 11-1/2" long	92	138	185
Touring Bus, painted tin, c. 1920, 12" long	150	225	300
Truck with Trailer, 1930s, 17" long	100	150	200
Wrecker Truck, mechanical boom, 1930s, 10" long	275	450	600

Grey Iron

	C6	C8	C10
Convertible Midget, 1-1/2"	20	30	40
Coupe Midget, 1-1/2" long	20	30	40
Delivery Truck, Midget, 1-1/2" long	20	30	40
Ford Coupe, 8-3/8" long	475	715	950
Racer, Midget, 1-1/2" long	20	30	40
Sedan, 1927, 9" long	1000	1500	2000
Sedan Midget, older, 1-1/2" long	20	30	40
Sedan Midget, airflow type, 1-1/2" long	20	30	40

Grey Iron Midget Vehicles, $40, each. Photo courtesy Stan Alekna

Hess Promotional Toys

The Hess Service Stations first staked a claim in the toy world in the mid-1960s, collaborating with the Louis Marx Co., in producing a $1.29 Christmas-time toy that would promote the East-coast service station chain. The B-Line Mack Tanker, with battery-operated lights, inaugurated a series that would become a mainstay of the collecting world. Hess released a new model yearly, usually a tanker truck or tractor-trailer. It varied the line in 1966 with the Voyager tanker ship, in 1970 with an American LaFrance fire pumper truck, and in 1980 with the GMC Motorhome Training Van. Emergency vehicles reurned in 1986 and became a mainstay of the line-up into the 1990s. Race-car transporters became part of the line in 1988. Since collectors emphasize Mint-in-Box toys almost to the exclusion of played-with toys, the following prices are for C10 examples.

	C10
1964-5 B-Line Mack Tanker Truck, white trailer, made in Hong Kong	2000
1966 Voyager Tanker Ship, made in Hong Kong	2400
1967 Tanker Truck, green and white trailer, red velvet box, made in United States	2400
1968-69 Tanker Truck, green and white trailer, made in Hong Kong	650
1969 Tanker Truck, Amerada Hess, made in Hong Kong, never sold to the general public **replica alert**	2500
1970 Pumper Fire Truck, Amerada Hess, made in Hong Kong by marx	695
1971 Pumper Fire Truck, red, made in Hong Kong by Marx, marked "Season's Greetings"	3000
1972-74 Amerada Hess Tanker Truck, split window, (reissue of 1968 model)	350
1975 Tractor-Box Trailer, w/oil barrels, paper labels, made in both Hong Kong and United States	200

Hess 1966 Voyager Tanker Ship, $2400. Photo courtesy John and Suzanne Adivari

Hess 1971 Pumper Fire Truck, $3000. Photo courtesy John and Suzanne Adivari

Hess 1975 Tractor-Box Trailer, $200. Photo courtesy John and Suzanne Adivari

Hess (Continued)   C10

1976 Tractor-Box Trailer, w/oil barrels, no labels, made in Hong Kong 200

1977 Tanker Truck, large rear label, made in Hong Kong 150

1978-79 Tanker Truck, small rear label, made in Hong Kong 95

1980 GMC Training Van, made in Hong Kong 250

1982-83 "First Hess Truck" '34 Chevy Tanker, made in Hong Kong 65

1983-85 "First Hess Truck" '34 Chevy Tanker Bank, made in Hong Kong 65

1984-85 Tanker Truck Bank 65

1986 Ladder Truck, made in Hong Kong 75

1987 Tractor-Box Trailer Bank, w/oil barrels, made in Hong kong and China 50

1988 Race Car Transporter, made in Hong Kong...... 50

1989 Ladder Fire Truck, white, made in Hong Kong 35

1990 Tanker Truck, w/"Hess 1990" license plate, made in China.. 30

1991 Race Car Transporter, made in China.............. 50

Hess 1980 GMC Training Van, $250. Photo courtesy John and Suzanne Adivari

Hess (Continued)   C10

1992 Tractor-Box Trailer, w/window and Porsche, made in China.. 35

1993 Patrol Car, white and green w/siren 20

1993 Tanker Truck, limited edition "New Premium Diesel," not sold to general public, given as gift to bulk diesel fuel dealers 1500

1994 Fire Rescue Pickup Truck 15

1995 Helicopter Transporter 35

1996 Emergency Ladder Truck.................................. 25

1997 Tractor-Box Trailer, w/two race cars 25

1998 Mini Hess Tanker Truck 30

1999 Flatbed Truck with Space Shuttle and Satellite.. 30

2000 Fire Truck, w/working headlights and taillights 20

Hess 1972-74 Amerada Hess Tanker Truck, $350. Photo courtesy John and Suzanne Adivari

Hess 1993 Tanker Truck, $1500. Photo courtesy John and Suzanne Adivari

Hot Wheels

It all started in 1968 when Mattel issued the original sixteen metallic colored toy cars. Today, most toy discount stores will have at least a four-foot section of space devoted to Hot Wheels.

Redlines, so called sue to the red line around the tires, are some of the most valuable Hot Wheels on the secondary market. Other vintage, non-readline Hot Wheels can also be quite valuable. The Beach Bomb with surfboards in the back is probably the most valuable Hot Wheels known. In 2000, a collector paid close to $$$$ for a pink Beach Bomb. Believed to be a prototype, it was the most paid for one Hot Wheels toy.

Contributors: Reid Covey, Box 2D Highmarket Rd., Constableville, NY, 13325, e-mail: sullivan@north-net.org. Covey lives in New York with his wife Melissa, and works for B.O.C.E.S. as a computer technician. An avid collector, Covey boasts of a collection that includes more than 2,500 Hot Wheels, 200 Matchbox cars and a vast collection of Jeff Gordon items. His wife's collection of #97 Chad Little items complements Covey's items and her 300-plus salt-and-pepper shakers.

Hot Wheels

	C8	C10
'31 Doozie, No. 6949, orange, blackwall, 1977	8	15
'31 Doozie, No. 9649, orange, redline, 1977	15	60
'56 Hi Tail Hauler, No. 9647, orange, blackwall, 1977	10	30
'56 Hi Tail Hauler, No. 9647, orange, redline, 1977	15	60
'57 Chevy, No. 9638, red, redline, 1977	20	85
'57 Chevy, No. 9638, red, blackwall, 1977	10	30
Alive '55, No. 9210, chrome, redline, 1977	15	55

Hot Wheels Alive '55, No. 6968, 1973, $110

Hot Wheels (Continued)

	C8	C10
Alive '55, No. 9210, chrome, blackwall, 1977	15	30
Alive '55, No. 6968, green, 1973	50	110
Alive '55, No. 6968, assorted, 1973	125	600
Alive '55, No. 6968, blue, 1974	90	350
Ambulance, No. 6451, assorted, 1970	30	50
American Hauler, No. 9118, blue, 1976	25	65
American Victory, No. 7662, light blue, 1975	20	60
AMX/2, No. 6460, assorted, 1971	40	150
Aw Shoot, No. 9243, olive, 1976	15	25
Backwoods Bomb, No. 7670, light blue, 1975	40	125
Backwoods Bomb, No. 7670, green, redline or blackwall, 1977	30	120
Baja Bruiser, No. 8258, yellow, magenta in tampo, 1974	300	1200
Baja Bruiser, No. 8258, blue, redline or blackwall, 1977	25	85
Baja Bruiser, No. 8258, yellow, blue in tampo, 1974	300	1200
Baja Bruiser, No. 8258, orange, 1974	30	75
Baja Bruiser, No. 8258, light green, 1976	400	1300
Beatnik Bandit, No. 6217, assorted, 1968	15	45
Boss Hoss, No. 6407, assorted, 1971	125	300
Boss Hoss, No. 6499, chrome, Club Kit, 1970	50	160
Brabham-Repco FL, No. 6264, assorted, 1969	20	65

Hot Wheels Carabo, No. 6420, 1970, $80

Hot Wheels Classic Nomad, No. 6404, 1970, $150

Hot Wheels (Continued)

	C8	C10
Bronco 4-Wheeler, Toys R Us, 1981	75	150
Bugeye, No. 6178, assorted, 1971	30	75
Buzz Off, No. 6976, assorted, 1973	110	500
Buzz Off, No. 6976, blue, 1974	30	90
Buzz Off, No. 6976, gold plated, redline or blackwall, 1977	15	30
Bye Focal, No. 6187, assorted, 1971	125	400
Bywayman, No. 2509, Toys R Us, 1979	75	150
Bywayman, No. 2196, blue, red interior, 1989	60	120
Captain America, No. 2879, white, Scene Machine, 1979	40	100
Carabo, No. 7617, yellow, 1974	500	1400
Carabo, No. 7617, light green, 1974	35	100
Carabo, No. 6420, assorted, 1970	35	80
Cement Mixer, No. 6452, assorted, 1970	30	60
Chapparal 2G, No. 6256, assorted, 1969	20	45
Chevy Monza 2+2, No. 9202, light green, 1975	200	800
Chevy Monza 2+2, No. 7671, orange, 1975	40	110
Chief's Special Cruiser, No. 7665, red, 1975	30	75
Chief's Special Cruiser, No. 7665, red, redline, 1977	25	65

Hot Wheels (Continued)

	C8	C10
Chief's Special Cruiser, No. 7665, red, blackwall, 1977	10	20
Circus Cats, No. 3303, white, 1981	75	150
Classic '31 Ford Woody, assorted, 1969	20	90
Classic '32 Ford Vicky, No. 6250, assorted, 1969	30	95
Classic '36 Ford Coupe, No. 6253, blue, 1969	20	60
Classic '36 Ford Coupe, No. 6253, assorted, 1969	20	60
Classic '57 T-Bird, No. 6252, assorted, 1969	30	100
Classic Caddy, No. 2529, red/white/blue, Museum Exhibit car, 1992	15	35
Classic Nomad, No. 6404, assorted, 6404, 1970	55	150
Cockney Cab, No. 6466, assorted, 1971	50	160
Continental Mark III, No. 6266, assorted, 1969	20	60
Cool One, No. 9120, plum, blackwall, 1977	20	40
Corvette Stingray, No. 9506, chrome, blackwall set only, 1977	55	70
Corvette Stingray, No. 9241, red, 1976	30	80
Corvette Stingray, No. 9506, chrome, 1976	20	50
Custom AMX, No. 6267, assorted, 1969	100	225
Custom Barracuda, No. 6211, assorted, 1968	80	400
Custom Camaro, No. 6208, white enamel, 1968	400	2500
Custom Camaro, No. 6208, assorted, 1968	100	450

Hot Wheels Chapparal 2G, No. 6256, 1969, $45

Hot Wheels Custom Charger, No. 6268, 1969, $250

Hot Wheels Deora, No. 6210, 1968, $375

Hot Wheels Custom Fleetside, No. 6213, 1968, $250

Hot Wheels (Continued)

	C8	C10
Custom Charger, No. 6268, assorted, 1969 ...	100	250
Custom Corvette, No. 6215, assorted, 1968.....	90	300
Custom Cougar, No. 6205, assorted, 1968.......	80	275
Custom El Dorado, No. 6218, assorted, 1968..	40	140
Custom Firebird, No. 6212, assorted, 1968	50	250
Custom Fleetside, No. 6213, assorted, 1968....	60	250
Custom Mustang, No. 6206, assorted, 1968	80	425
Custom Mustang, No. 6206, assorted w/open hood scoops or ribbed windows, 1968	400	1200
Custom Police Cruiser, No. 6269, assorted, 1969	55	200
Custom T-Bird, No. 6207, assorted, 1968	50	165
Custom Volkswagen, No. 6220, assorted, 1968	30	125
Datsun 200SX, No. 3255, maroon, Canada, 1982	75	175
Demon, No. 6401, assorted, 1970	20	50
Deora, No. 6210, assorted, 1968	60	375
Double Header, No. 5880, assorted, 1973	120	450
Double Vision, No. 6975, assorted, 1973	110	400
Dune Daddy, No. 6967, assorted, 1973	110	400
Dune Daddy, No. 6967, light green, 1975	25	75
Dune Daddy, No. 6967, orange, 1975.............	225	600
El Rey Special, green, 1974	40	75
El Rey Special, No. 8273, dark blue, 1974	225	900
El Rey Special, No. 8273, light blue, 1974....	300	1200
El Rey Special, No. 8273, light green, 1974....	75	175

Hot Wheels Double Header, No. 5880, 1973, $450

Hot Wheels (Continued)

	C8	C10
Emergency Squad, No. 7650, red, 1975...........	15	65
Evil Weevil, No. 6471, assorted, 1971.............	75	150
Ferrari 312P, No. 6973, red, 1974....................	40	80
Ferrari 312P, No. 6417, assorted, 1970............	30	60
Ferrari 312P, No. 6973, assorted, 1973..........	300	1100
Ferrari 512-S, No. 6021, assorted, 1972...........	75	250
Fire Chief Cruiser, No. 6469, red, 1970...........	15	45
Fire Engine, No. 6454, red, 1970	25	60
Ford J-Car, No. 6214, assorted, 1968..............	20	70
Ford MK IV, No. 6257, assorted, 1969............	15	60
Formula 5000, No. 9511, chrome, 1976...........	30	65
Formula 5000, No. 9119, white, 1976.............	20	50
Fuel Tanker, No. 6018, assorted, 1971.............	75	200
Funny Money, No. 7621, magenta, 1974.........	60	150
Funny Money, No. 7621, gray, blackwall, 1977...	20	65
Funny Money, No. 7621, gray, redline, 1977 ..	60	150
Funny Money, No. 6005, gray, 1972	60	325
GMC Motorhome, No. 9645, orange, redline, 1977	400	1200

Hot Wheels Custom Mustang, No. 6206, 1968, $425

Hot Wheels (Continued)

	C8	C10
GMC Motorhome, No. 9645, orange, blackwall, 1977	10	25
Grass Hopper, No. 7622, light green, no engine, 1975	90	350
Grass Hopper, No. 7621, light green, 1974	40	100
Grass Hopper, No. 6461, assorted, 1971	45	100
Gremlin Grinder, No. 9201, chrome, blackwall, 1977	20	40
Gremlin Grinder, No. 7652, green, 1975	35	75
Gun Bucket, No. 9090, olive, 1976	25	60
Gun Bucket, No. 9090, olive, blackwall, 1977	25	60
Gun Slinger, No. 7664, olive, blackwall, 1976	25	50
Gun Slinger, No. 7664, olive, 1975	25	50
Hairy Hauler, No. 6458, assorted, 1971	20	65
Hammer Down, red set only, 1980	125	n/a
Heavy Chevy, No. 7619, light green, 1974	200	750
Heavy Chevy, No. 6408, assorted, 1970	25	55
Heavy Chevy, No. 9212, chrome, redline or blackwall, 1977	40	120
Heavy Chevy, No. 6189, chrome, Club Kit, 1970	50	175
Heavy Chevy, No. 7619, yellow, 1974	90	200
Hiway Robber, No. 6979, assorted, 1973	75	250
Hood, No. 6175, assorted, 1971	25	110
Hot Bird, blue, 1980	60	12
Hot Bird, brown, 1980	90	200
Hot Heap, No. 6219, assorted, 1968	20	65
Human Torch, No. 2881, black, 1979	20	40
Ice T, No. 6980, light green, 1974	25	75

Hot Wheels Hiway Robber, No. 6979, 1973, $250

Hot Wheels King Kuda, No. 6411, 1970, $300

Hot Wheels (Continued)

	C8	C10
Ice T, No. 6980, yellow w/hood tampo, 1974	200	525
Ice T, No. 6980, light green, blackwall, 1977	20	35
Ice T, No. 6184, yellow, 1971	40	200
Ice T, No. 6980, assorted, 1973	200	650
Incredible Hulk Van, No. 2850, white, Scene Machine, 1979	75	125
Indy Eagle, No. 6263, gold, 1969	75	240
Indy Eagle, No. 6263, assorted, 1969	15	40
Inferno, No. 9186, yellow, 1976	30	60
Jack Rabbit Special, No. 6421, white, 1970	10	55
Jack-in-the-Box Promotion, No. 6421, white, Jack Rabbit w/decals, 1970	300	n/a
Jet Threat, No. 6179, assorted, 1973	45	160
Jet Threat II, No. 8235, magenta, 1976	35	80
Khaki Kooler, No. 9183, olive, 1976	15	30
King Kuda, No. 6411, assorted, 1970	25	100
King Kuda, No. 6411, chrome, Club Kit, 1970	75	300
Large Charge, No. 8272, green, 1975	25	60
Letter Getter, No. 9643, white, redline, 1977	175	550
Letter Getter, No. 9643, white, blackwall, 1977	8	15
Light My Firebird, No. 6412, assorted, 1970	35	75
Lola GT 70, No. 6254, assorted, 1969	20	60
Lotus Turbine, No. 6262, assorted, 1969	15	30
Lowdown, No. 9185, light blue, 1976	30	75
Lowdown, No. 9185, gold plated, redline or blackwall, 1977	15	30
Mantis, No. 6423, assorted, 1970	15	40
Masterati Mistral, No. 6277, assorted, 1969	50	125
Maxi Taxi, No. 9184, yellow, blackwall, 1977	20	60

Hot Wheels Masterati Mistral, No. 6277, 1969, $125

Hot Wheels (Continued)

	C8	C10
Maxi Taxi, No. 9184, yellow, 1976	25	60
McClaren M6A, No. 6255, assorted, 1969	10	40
Mercedes 280SL, No. 6962, assorted, 1973	100	450
Mercedes 280SL, No. 6275, assorted, 1969	10	40
Mercedes C-111, No. 6978, red, 1974	40	90
Mercedes C-111, No. 6169, assorted, 1972	80	250
Mercedes C-111, No. 6978, assorted, 1973	300	1200
Mighty Maverick, No. 7653, blue, 1975	50	100
Mighty Maverick, No. 6414, assorted, 1970	40	130
Mighty Maverick, No. 9209, chrome, blackwall, 1977	25	50
Mighty Maverick, No. 9209, light green, 1975	300	750
Mod-Quad, No. 6456, assorted, 1970	20	60
Mongoose, No. 6970, red/blue, 1973	400	1400
Mongoose Funny Car, No. 6410, red, 1970	50	160
Mongoose II, No. 5954, metallic blue, 1971	75	350
Mongoose Rail Dragster, No. 5952, blue, two pack, 1971	75	600
Monte Carlo Stocker, No. 7660, yellow, blackwall, 1977	55	70
Monte Carlo Stocker, No. 7660, yellow, 1975	45	90

Hot Wheels Mongoose Rail Dragster, No. 5952, 1971, $600

Hot Wheels Mutt Mobile, No. 5185, 1971, $175

Hot Wheels (Continued)

	C8	C10
Motorcross I, No. 7668, red, 1975	100	200
Motorcross Team Van, No. 2853, red, Scene Machine, 1979	50	125
Movin' On, white set only, 1980	125	n/a
Moving Van, No. 6455, assorted, 1970	50	125
Mustang Stocker, No. 7664, white, 1975	400	1200
Mustang Stocker, No. 9203, chrome, 1976	40	90
Mustang Stocker, No. 9203, yellow w/red in tampo, 1975	300	900
Mustang Stocker, No. 7664, yellow w/magenta tampo, 1975	90	300
Mustang Stocker, No. 9203, chrome, redline or blackwall, 1977	40	90
Mutt Mobile, No. 5185, assorted, 1971	75	175
Neet Streeter, No. 9510, chrome, blackwall set only, 1977	40	n/a
Neet Streeter, No. 9510, chrome, 1976	20	40
Neet Streeter, No. 9244, blue, blackwall, 1977	15	30
Neet Streeter, No. 9244, blue, 1976	20	60
Nitty Gritty Kitty, No. 6405, assorted, 1970	25	65
Noddle Head, No. 6000, assorted, 1971	40	150
Odd Job, No. 6891, assorted, 1973	100	600
Odd Rod, No. 9642, plum, blackwall or redline, 1977	200	400
Odd Rod, No. 9642, yellow, redline, 1977	30	50

Hot Wheels Olds 442, No. 6467, 1971, $800

Hot Wheels Pit Crew Car, No. 6183, 1971, $350

Hot Wheels (Continued)

	C8	C10
Odd Rod, No. 9642, yellow, blackwall, 1977 ..	20	40
Old Number 5, No. 1695, red, no louvers, 1982	10	20
Olds 442, No. 6467, assorted, 1971	400	800
Open Fire, No. 5881, 1972	100	400
Paddy Wagon, No. 6966, blue, 1973	30	120
Paddy Wagon, No. 6966, blue, blackwall, 1977	10	20
Paddy Wagon, No. 6402, blue, 1970	15	30
Paramedic, No. 7661, yellow, 1976	30	50
Paramedic, No. 7661, yellow, blackwall or redline, 1977	25	45
Paramedic, No. 7661, white, 1975	25	55
Peepin' Bomb, No. 6419, assorted, 1970	20	50
Pepsi Challenger, No. 2023, yellow funny car, 1982	20	25
Pit Crew Car, No. 6183, white, 1971	30	350
Poison Pinto, No. 9508, chrome, blackwall set only, 1977	50	65
Poison Pinto, No. 9240, light green, 1976	25	65
Poison Pinto, chrome, 1976	20	40
Poison Pinto, No. 9240, green, blackwall, 1977	15	30
Police Cruiser, No. 6963, white w/blue light, 1977	30	65
Police Cruiser, No. 6963, white, 1974	45	125
Police Cruiser, No. 6963, white, blackwall, 1977	25	45
Police Cruiser, No. 6963, white, 1973	200	500
Porsche 911, No. 9206, chrome, redline or blackwall, 1977	35	70
Porsche 911, No. 7648, black, six pack blackwall, 1977	175	350

Hot Wheels (Continued)

	C8	C10
Porsche 911, No. 7648, yellow, 1975	40	75
Porsche 911, No. 6972, orange, 1975	25	65
Porsche 917, No. 6416, assorted, 1970	25	65
Porsche 917, No. 6972, red, 1974	175	500
Porsche 917, No. 6972, orange, 1974	40	75
Porsche 917, No. 6972, orange, blackwall, 1977	15	25
Porsche 917, No. 6972, assorted, 1973	300	950
Power Pad, No. 6459, assorted, 1970	30	80
Prowler, No. 6965, assorted, 1973	200	1000
Prowler, No. 6965, light green, 1974	500	1000
Prowler, No. 9207, chrome, blackwall, 1977	35	70
Prowler, No. 6965, orange, 1974	35	75
Python, No. 6216, assorted, 1968	20	75
Race Ace, No. 2620, white, 1986	15	30
Racer Rig, No. 6194, red/white, 1971	100	375
Ramblin' Cruiser, No. 7659, white w/o phone number, 1977	15	25
Ramblin' Wrecker, No. 7659, white, 1975	10	20
Ramblin' Wrecker, No. 7659, white, blackwall, 1977	10	20
Ranger Rig, No. 7666, green, 1975	20	65
Rash I, No. 7616, green, 1974	50	75
Rash I, No. 7616, blue, 1974	300	800
Rear Engine Mongoose, No. 5699, red, 1972	200	600
Rear Engine Snake, No. 5865, yellow, 1972	200	600
Red Baron, No. 6964, red, blackwall, 1977	15	25
Red Baron, No. 6964, red, 1973	30	200
Red Baron, No. 6400, red, 1970	15	40
Rescue Squad, No. 3304, red, Scene Machine, 1982	70	125
Road King Truck, No. 7615, yellow set only, 1974	600	1200

Hot Wheels Racer Rig, No. 6194, 1971, $375

Hot Wheels (Continued)

	C8	C10
Rock Buster, No. 9088, yellow, 1976	20	35
Rock Buster, No. 9507, chrome, 1976	15	30
Rock Buster, No. 9088, yellow, blackwall, 1977	10	15
Rock Buster, No. 9507, chrome, blackwall set only, 1977	45	n/a
Rocket Bye Baby, No. 6186, assorted, 1971	60	200
Rodger Dodger, No. 8259, magenta, 1974	40	90
Rodger Dodger, No. 8259, blue, 1974	200	550
Rodger Dodger, No. 8259, gold plated, blackwall or redline, 1977	30	80
Rolls-Royce Silver Shadow, No. 6276, assorted, 1969	25	45
S.W.A.T. Van, No. 2854, blue, Scene Machine, 1979	70	125
Sand Crab, No. 6403, assorted, 1970	20	60
Sand Drifter, No. 7651, green, 1975	150	375
Sand Drifter, No. 7651, yellow, 1975	35	75
Sand Witch, No. 6974, assorted, 1973	125	400
S'Cool Bus, No. 6468, yellow, 1971	175	750
Scooper, No. 6193, assorted, 1971	100	325
Seasider, No. 6413, assorted, 1970	60	135

Hot Wheels S'Cool Bus, No. 6468, 1971, $750

Hot Wheels Seasider, No. 6413, 1970, $135

Hot Wheels Sky Show Fleetside (Aero Launcher), No. 6436, 1970, $850

Hot Wheels (Continued)

	C8	C10
Second Wind, No. 9644, white, blackwall or redline, 1977	35	75
Shelby Turbine, No. 6265, assorted, 1969	20	55
Short Order, No. 6176, assorted, 1971	50	125
Show Hoss II, No. 9646, yellow, redline, 1977	300	600
Show Hoss II, No. 9646, yellow, blackwall, 1977	40	75
Show-Off, No. 6982, assorted, 1973	140	400
Sidekick, No. 6022, assorted, 1972	80	200
Silhouette, No. 6209, assorted, 1968	20	90
Sir Rodney Roadster, yellow, blackwall, 1977	40	70
Sir Sidney Roadster, No. 8261, light green, 1974	325	650
Sir Sidney Roadster, No. 8261, orange/brown, 1974	375	700
Sir Sidney Roadster, No. 8261, yellow, 1974	25	65
Six Shooter, No. 6003, assorted, 1971	75	225
Sky Show Fleetside (Aero Launcher), No. 6436, assorted, 1970	400	850
Snake, No. 6969, white/yellow, 1973	600	1500
Snake Funny Car, No. 6409, assorted, 1970	60	300
Snake II, No. 5953, white, 1971	60	275
Snorkel, No. 6020, assorted, 1971	90	200
Space Van, No. 2855, gray, Scene Machine, 1979	70	150
Special Delivery, No. 6006, blue, 1971	45	150
Spider-Man, No. 2852, black, 1979	15	35
Spider-Man Van, No. 2852, white, Scene Machine, 1979	50	125
Splittin' Image, No. 6261, assorted, 1969	15	50
Spoiler Sport, No. 9641, light green, blackwall, 1977	10	20

Hot Wheels Staff Car, No. 9521, 1977, $850

Hot Wheels (Continued)

	C8	C10
Spoiler Sport, No. 9641, light green, redline, 1977	25	50
Staff Car, No. 9521, olive, blackwall, 1977	500	750
Staff Car, No. 9521, olive, redlines, 1977	600	850
Steam Roller, No. 9208, chrome w/seven stars, 1977	100	300
Steam Roller, No. 8260, white, 1974	25	70
Steam Roller, No. 9208, chrome, redline or blackwall, 1977	25	55
Steam Roller, No. 8260, white w/seven stars, 1974	100	300
Street Eater, No. 7669, black, 1975	40	60
Street Rodder, No. 9242, black, blackwall, 1977	30	50
Street Rodder, No. 9242, black, 1976	40	85
Street Snorter, No. 6971, assorted, 1973	110	400
Strip Teaser, No. 6188, assorted, 1971	65	200
Sugar Caddy, No. 6418, assorted, 1971	45	120
Super Chromes, No. 9505, chrome, blackwall six-pack, 1977	375	n/a
Super Van, No. 7649, black, blackwall, 1977	15	25
Super Van, No. 7649, blue, 1975	650	NPF
Super Van, No. 7649, Toys-R-Us, 1975	100	350
Super Van, No. 7649, plum, 1975	90	250
Super Van, No. 9205, chrome, 1976	20	40
Superfine Turbine, No. 6004, assorted, 1973	400	1100
Sweet 16, No. 6007, assorted, 1973	125	650
Swingin' Wing, No. 6422, assorted, 1970	25	75
T-4-2, No. 6177, assorted, 1971	50	175
Team Trailer, No. 6019, white/red, 1971	95	225
Thing, The, No. 2882, dark/blue, 1979	20	50

Hot Wheels T-4-2, No. 6177, 1971, $175

Hot Wheels (Continued)

	C8	C10
Thor, No. 2880, yellow, 1979	15	30
Thrill Driver Torino, No. 9793, red/white, blackwall, set of two, 1977	275	n/a
TNT-Bird, No. 6407, assorted, 1970	60	125
Top Eliminator, No. 7630, blue, 1974	50	165
Top Eliminator, No. 7630, gold plated, redline or blackwall, 1977	30	50
Torero, No. 6260, assorted, 1969	15	60
Torino Stocker, No. 7647, red, 1975	35	70
Torino Stocker, No. 7647, gold plated, redline or blackwall, 1977	35	70
Tough Customer, No. 7655, olive, 1975	25	55
Tow Truck, No. 6450, assorted, 1970	30	80
Tri-Baby, No. 6424, assorted, 1970	20	55
T-Totaller, No. 9648, black, Red Line, six-pack only, 1977	500	1000
T-Totaller, No. 9648, brown, blackwall, 1977	15	40
T-Totaller, No. 9648, black, blackwall, 1977	15	40
Turbofire, No. 6259, assorted, 1969	15	50
Twinmill, No. 6258, assorted, 1969	15	50
Twinmill II, No. 8240, orange, blackwall, 1977	10	25

Hot Wheels Team Trailer, No. 6019, 1971, $225

Hot Wheels Volkswagen Beach Bomb, No. 6274, 1969, $300

Hot Wheels (Continued)

	C8	C10
Twinmill II, No. 9509, chrome, 1976	20	45
Twinmill II, No. 8240, orange, 1976	10	35
Vega Bomb, No. 7658, green, 1975	250	800
Vega Bomb, No. 7654, orange, blackwall, 1977	40	75
Vega Bomb, No. 7658, orange, 1975	40	85
Volkswagen, No. 7620, orange w/bug on roof, 1974	30	60
Volkswagen, No. 7620, orange w/stripes on roof, 1974	100	400
Volkswagen Beach Bomb, No. 6274, surfboards in rear window, 1969	7000	n/a
Volkswagen Beach Bomb, No. 6274, surfboards on side raised panels, 1969	115	300
Warpath, No. 7654, white, 1975	50	110
Waste Wagon, No. 6192, assorted, 1971	90	325
What-4, No. 6001, assorted, 1971	50	150
Whip Creamer, No. 6457, assorted, 1970	25	60
Winnipeg, No. 7618, yellow, 1974	90	300
Xploder, No. 6977, assorted, 1973	100	500
Z Whiz, No. 9639, blue, 1982	20	55
Z Whiz, No. 9639, white, redline, 1977	1500	n/a
Z Whiz, No. 9639, gray, blackwall, 1977	15	25
Z Whiz, No. 9639, gray, redline, 1977	15	25

Hubley

The Hubley Manufacturing Company was founded in 1892 by John Hubley. It made iron toys from the start at its plant in Lancaster, Pennsylvania. In the beginning, all toys were cast iron, and some early toys included coal ranges, circus wagons and mechanical banks. Hubley's cast-iron toys were popular almost from the start, and have long been collector's items because they were well made and attractive.

By 1940, however, the cast-iron toy, due to the increased cost of freight and foreign competition, was slowly becoming a thing of the past. At this time, when Hubley was the largest producer of cast-iron toys and cap pistols in the world, it began to introduce die-cast zinc alloy toys.

After the World War II, Hubley manufactured die-cast toys and plastic toys exclusively. In 1952, Hubley manufactured 9,763,610 toys and 11,184,878 cap pistols, about ten times the amount of toys and pistols it produced in 1930, but with a line of toys eighty percent smaller than in 1930. It is the combination of the relative scarcity (and multiplicity) of the older toys, plus the preference by collectors for cast-iron over die-cast zinc alloy and plastic toys that makes the prewar toys the most attractive to collectors. Hubley was acquired by Gabriel Industries in late 1965.

	C6	C8	C10
Air Compass Truck, c. 1950s, 7" long	50	75	100
Airflow-type Car, "Hubley U.S.A.," c. 1937, approx. 3-1/2" long	20	30	40
Army Motor Truck, No. 807, w/driver, 15" long	1100	1700	2500
Auto, die-cast, black plastic wheels, c. 1950s	12	18	25
Auto Carrier, w/three cars and one pickup truck, c. 1939, 10" long	262	395	525
Auto Express, cast iron, 9"	900	1450	2000
Auto Transport, plastic, marked "Hubley Transport," 13" long	125	188	250
Bell Telephone Truck, w/derrick and windlass, auger, trailer w/10" pole, three digging tools, and two loose ladders, 1931, 10"	550	950	1300
Bell Telephone Truck, w/tools, 12" long	500	800	1100

Hubley Bell Telephone Truck, 5-1/4" long, $450

Hubley Bus, "Coast to Coast," 1927, 13" long, $2200. Photo courtesy Bill Bertoia Auctions

Hubley (Continued)	C6	C8	C10
Bell Telephone Truck, 1940s, 12-1/2" long	75	115	150
Bell Telephone Truck, just ladders as equipment, 13" long	250	375	500
Bell Telephone Truck, 5-1/4" long	200	320	450
Bell Telephone Truck, 7" long	600	1000	1400
Bell Telephone Truck, tools and ladders, 8-1/4" long	425	638	850
Bell Telephone Truck, implements, 9" long	600	1000	1400
Black & White Cab, 1920s	1200	2000	3000
Bulldozer, die-cast, front scoop, rubber treads, c. 1950, 10-1/4"	80	100	155
Bus, futuristic type, c. 1935, 3-1/2" long	50	75	100
Bus, rubber wheels, c. 1938, 5-1/2" long	50	75	100
Bus, "Coast to Coast," cast iron, 1927, 13" long	1000	1600	2200
Car and House Trailer, No. 2278 and No. 2279, c. 1939	150	225	300
Cement Mixer, Jaeger	475	715	950
Champion Stake Truck, white rubber tires, 1930s, 8-1/2" long	140	210	280
Chemical Truck, w/ladders, 13" long	200	300	400
Chevrolet 1932 Coupe Kit	25	38	50
Chevrolet 1932 Phaeton kit, 1960s	40	60	80

Hubley Coal Truck, c. 1922, 9-1/2" long, $875. Photo courtesy Christie's East

Hubley (Continued)	C6	C8	C10
Chevrolet 1932 Roadster kit, 1960s	25	38	50
Chrysler Airflow, take-apart body, 4-1/2" long	117	175	250
Chrysler Airflow, electrified, white rubber tires on wood hubs, 8" long	900	1200	2000
Chrysler Airflow Racing Car, c. 1938	100	150	200
Coal Truck, cast iron, w/driver, 16-3/4" long	1200	1800	2500
Coal Truck, cast iron, c. 1922, 9-1/2" long	438	655	875
Compressor Truck, Ingersoll Rand, 8-1/4" long	2500	4500	7000
Corvette, 13-1/2" long	255	380	510
Coupe Roadster, rumble seat, rubber tires, 11" long	200	290	390
Crane, wooden wheels, 1940s	67	100	135
Crash Car, three-wheel motorcycle, chrome wheels, 11-1/2" long	2400	4200	6365

Hubley Chrysler Airflow, 8" long, $2000

Hubley Compressor Truck, 8-1/4" long, $7000. Photo courtesy Bill Bertoia Auctions

Hubley Corvette, 13-1/2" long, $510

Hubley (Continued)

	C6	C8	C10
Crash Car, white rubber tires, c. 1937, 4-3/4" long	100	150	200
Delivery Van, 1932, 4-1/2" long	700	1300	1800
Digger, Mack, general, 10" long	450	700	1000
Duesenberg Town Car, build-it model, 9" long	30	45	60
Dump Truck, Mack, six tires, 1930s, 10-3/4" long	1000	1800	2800
Dump Truck, c. 1938, 7-1/2" long	295	442	590
Fire Engine, die-cast, white rubber tires w/wooden rims, c. 1941	112	168	225
Fire Engine, No. 526, c. 1936, 10-1/2" long	175	263	350
Fire Engine Pumper, No. 504, early	350	525	700
Fire Engine Pumper, cast iron, driver, boiler-tender, black rubber tires, c. 1920, 12-1/2" long	350	525	700
Fire Ladder Truck, two wood ladders, c. 1920, 15-1/2" long	300	450	600
Fire Ladder Truck, 19-1/2" long	600	950	1450
Fire Ladder Truck, early, 7-1/2" long	130	195	260
Fire Ladder Truck, early, 8-1/2"	350	525	700
Fire Truck, w/searchlight, white rubber tires w/wooden rims	55	82	110

Hubley Delivery Van, 1932, 4-1/2" long, $1800

Hubley Fire Ladder Truck, 7-1/2" long, $260. Photo courtesy Rod Carnahan

Hubley Flatbed Truck, No. 506, $235. Photo courtesy Harvey Raines

Hubley (Continued)

	C6	C8	C10
Flatbed Truck, No. 506, all metal	118	177	235
Ford Model A Coupe Kit, 1960s	25	38	50
Ford Model A Phaeton Kit, 1960s	32	48	65
Ford Model A Pickup Kit, 1960s	32	48	65
Ford Model A Station Wagon Kit, 1960s	37	56	75
Ford Model A Town Car Kit, 1960s	32	48	65
Ford Model A Victoria Kit, 1960s	40	60	80
Fordson Front-End Loader, cast iron, early 1930s, 9" long	800	1400	2000
Hook & Ladder Truck, No. 463	28	42	56
Hook & Ladder Truck, cast iron, 19-1/2" long	200	300	400

Hubley Kiddie Toy Dump Truck, 8" long, $150

Hubley Kiddie Toy Motorcycle, 5" long, $30. Photo courtesy Kent M. Comstock

Hubley Mack Gasoline Truck, 10-3/4" long, $1800. Photo courtesy Bill Bertoia Auctions

Hubley (Continued)	C6	C8	C10
Huber Road Roller, 13" long	25	3850	5000
Huber Road Roller, 4-1/2" long	110	165	220
Huber Road Roller, tractor-like, 7-3/4" long	257	385	515
Hubley Life Saver Truck, small hole in rear	400	600	800
Hubley Road Grader, 12" long	60	90	120
Kiddie Toy Dump Truck, No. 510 series	125	188	250
Kiddie Toy Dump Truck, plastic cab w/metal dump, 8" long	50	75	150
Kiddie Toy MGTD Roadster, No. 432, 6" long	110	165	220
Kiddie Toy Motorcycle, plastic, 5" long	15	22	30
Kiddie Toy Patrol Stake Truck, c. 1937	30	40	55
Kiddie Toy Racer, No. 457, die-cast, rubber tires, 6-1/2" long	46	69	92
Ladder Truck, 1930s, 10" long	110	165	225
Ladder Truck, c. 1940, 13-1/2" long	350	525	700

Hubley (Continued)	C6	C8	C10
Ladder Truck, late 1930s, 5" long	45	68	90
Ladder Truck, Terraplane front, 1930s, 6" long	312	468	625
Life Saver Truck, hole in rear is large enough to hold pack of Life Savers, c. 1930, 4-1/4" long	675	1100	1650
Lincoln Zephyr, 7-1/4" long	240	360	480
Lincoln Zephyr and House Trailer, cast iron, 14" overall	400	600	800
Log Truck, No. 469	55	83	110
Log Truck, die-cast, w/five chained logs, black rubber tires, approx. 19" long	138	205	275
Low Boy Truck, trailer, tractor	200	300	400
Mack Dump Truck, w/driver, 11-1/2" long	650	1100	1600
Mack Gasoline Truck, 10-3/4" long	800	1350	1800
Mack Truck Steam Shovel-Digger, nickel wheels and scoop, c. 1920, 7" long	1300	2200	3200
Merchants Delivery, 1920s, 6" long	400	600	800

Hubley Life Saver Truck, c. 1930, 4-1/4" long, $1650. Photo courtesy Bill Bertoia Auctions

Hubley Merchants Delivery, 1920s, 6" long, $800. Photo courtesy Bill Bertoia Auctions

Hubley Milk Cream Truck, 1930s, 3-1/2" long, $525.
Photo courtesy Mapes Auctioneers and Appraisers

Hubley (Continued)	C6	C8	C10
Milk Cream Truck, cast iron, embossed "Milk Cream," white rubber tires, 1930s, 3-1/2" long	265	395	525
Monarch Tractor, 5-1/2" long	600	900	1200
Motor Express Tractor and Trailer, 500 series, black rubber tires, approx. 19" long	95	143	190
Motorcycle, policeman, "Cop," 1920s, 4" long	50	75	100
Motorcycle, Harley-Davidson, w/policeman, white rubber wheels, 5-1/2" long	275	363	550
Motorcycle, Harley-Davidson, Police, w/sidecar and rider, 5-1/4" long	250	350	500
Motorcycle, has light in front and place for battery, 6" long	300	450	600
Motorcycle, "Harley-Davidson," civilian rider, 6-1/4" long	382	575	775
Motorcycle, Harley-Davidson, w/policeman, swivel head, small wheels near feet, 1930s, 7-1/4" long	700	1200	1600
Motorcycle, armored, w/sidecar and removable riders, 9" long	1200	2000	2750
Motorcycle, two-cylinder Indian, w/sidecar, two cops, 9" long	600	900	1200
Motorcycle, "U.S. Air Mail," 9-1/2" long	1100	2000	2700
Motorcycle, Parcel Post Delivery, w/two-wheel cart, 9-1/4" long	1300	2200	2900
Motorcycle, Indian, policeman rider, nickel-plated cylinder, 9-1/4" long	800	1300	1800
Motorcycle "Traffic Car," four cyclinder Indian w/stake sides on two-wheel cart, 11-1/2" long	1500	2500	3500

Hubley (Continued)	C6	C8	C10
Motorcycle and Rider, 4" long	110	165	220
Motorcycle Hill Climber, No. 649, 1936, 6-3/4" long	400	600	800
Motorcycle with Removable Cop, cast iron, "Made in USA," c. mid-1930s, 4-1/4" long	60	90	120
Motorcycle with Sidecar, battery-operated headlight, cop driver, passenger, 8" long	1150	1900	2650
Motorcycle with Sidecar, No. 46-F, two removable policemen, 8-1/2" long	700	1200	1600
Motorized Steam Pumper, c. 1930s, 4" long	50	75	100
Nite Coach, metal wheels, went on Nucar carrier, 1930s, 3-1/2" long	30	45	60
Packard, "Phaeton" kit, 1930	50	75	100
Packard, fifteen parts, straight eight, 1929, 11" long	6000	12,000	16,000
Packard Roadster Kit	50	75	100
Panama Digger, Mack, 13" long	800	1400	2100
Panama Digger, 3-1/2" long	162	243	325
Panama Digger, 9-1/2" long	800	1300	1800
Parcel Post Motorcycle and Sidecar, Harley-Davidson, 9-1/2"	1600	2800	4000
Patrol, driver, policeman, 15-1/2" long	1400	2100	2800
Pipe Truck, No. 803, c. 1950s, 9-1/2" long	35	52	70
Power Shovel, 14"	105	160	210
Pumper, c. late 1930s	115	175	230
Pumper, Terraplane front, 1930s, 6-1/4" long	150	225	300
Racer, die-cast, black rubber tires, 4" long	80	120	160

Hubley Packard, 1929, 11" long, $16000. Photo
courtesy Bill Bertoia Auctions

Hubley Racer, 5", $200. Photo courtesy Bill Kaufman

Hubley (Continued)

	C6	C8	C10
Racer, marked "1790," 5"	100	150	200
Racer, two passengers, 1930s, 5-1/2" long	130	195	260
Racer, cast iron, exhaust stacks, white rubber tires, wodden hubs, tail fins, marked "1791" on driver and "2233" on cast iron, 6" long..............	150	200	250
Racer, driver, large tail fin, 7" long.....	165	248	330
Racer, animated exhaust stacks, driver, 8" long	600	1000	1400
Racer No. 1, 8" long.............................	250	375	500
Racer No. 22, aluminum and cast iron, 7-3/8" long...............................	100	150	200
Racer No. 5, hood opens, painted and nickeled iron and aluminum, 9-1/2" long	900	1600	2300
Racer No. 629, 1936, 6-3/4" long	145	225	290
Railway Express Truck, rubber tires, 5" long..	150	225	300
Road Roller, w/driver, late 1920s, 8" long	300	450	600
Road Scraper, No. 481	60	90	120
Say it with Flowers, 10-1/2" long	6000	12,000	18,000
Sedan, two-door, rubber wheels, looks like Ford, c. 1938, 3-1/2"	70	105	140

Hubley Racer No. 5, 9-1/2" long, $2300. Photo courtesy Christie's East

Hubley Railway Express Truck, 5" long, $300

Hubley Road Roller, late 1920s, 8" long, $600. Photo courtesy Mapes Auctioneers and Appraisers

Hubley (Continued)

	C6	C8	C10
Sedan, cast iron, 1920, 7" long............	100	150	200
Service Car, cast iron, including wheels, 5" long...................................	200	300	400
Sport Car, No. 485.................................	70	105	140
Stake Bed Struck, cast iron, marked "10 ton," 7" long	300	525	700
Stake Bed Truck, cast iron, 3-1/2" long..	25	38	50

Hubley Stake Bed Struck, 7" long, $700. Photo courtesy Bill Bertoia Auctions

Hubley Streetsweeper, 1931, 8" long, $4400

Hubley Wrecker, 1940, 6" long, $200. Photo courtesy Mapes Auctioneers and Appraisers

Hubley Yellow Cab, 1920, 7-3/4" long, $1200. Photo courtesy Sotheby's, New York

Hubley (Continued)	C6	C8	C10
Stake Bed Truck, 7" long	100	150	200
Stake Truck, No. 614, c. 1930s	75	115	150
Stake Truck with Trailer, No. 927, two-piece, 21" long	100	150	200
Stake-type Truck, No. 452, black, rubber tires, post WWII	55	82	110
Station Wagon, c. 1940s, 1950s, 8-1/2" long	75	112	150
Steam Shovel, "General," 15" long	450	700	1000
Steam Shovel, "General," 7" long	240	360	580
Steam Shovel, "General," rubber tires on hubs, 9" long	375	565	750
Streetsweeper, cast iron, "The Elgin," 1931, 8" long	1550	2800	4400
Studebaker Roadster, frame and body separate	300	450	600
Tow Truck, cast iron, c. 1930s, 8-3/4" long	180	270	360
Tractor Loader, No. 501, 1950s, 11" long	80	115	155
Tractor Trailer and Road Scraper, No. 506	100	150	200
Transitional Fire Patrol, cast iron, driver, firemen, 1920, 12"	800	1300	2000
Truck, "5 Ton Truck," eight wooden barrels, c. 1920, 17" long	700	1150	1800
Truck, Milk Cream Truck, cast iron, white rubber tires, 1930s, 3-1/2"	400	600	800
Truck, "Borden's Milk Cream," standard version, 6" long	475	720	950
Truck, "Borden's Milk Cream," deluxe version, clicker, rubber tires, 7-1/2"	2000	3500	5500

Hubley (Continued)	C6	C8	C10
Truck and Trailer, No. 2287, "Motor Express," 8" long	162	243	325
Wrecker, chrome wheels, service car	45	70	100
Wrecker, rubber wheels, 1930, 4-1/2" long	65	100	150
Wrecker, white wheels on large hubs, c. 1940, 6" long	65	98	130
Wrecker, white wheels on large hubs, 1940, 6" long	100	150	200
Wrecking Truck, cast iron, rubber tires, 1930, 7-1/2" long	150	225	300
Yellow Cab, 1920, 7-3/4" long	550	850	1200
Yellow Cab, c. 1939, 8" long	650	1150	1600

Ideal	C6	C8	C10
American LaFrance Fire Truck	75	110	145
Barracuda Coupe, plastic, 1964, 4" long	15	25	30
Cadillac, plastic, four-door, 1948, 4" long	25	40	50
Car Trailer, plastic, four cars, 27" long	40	60	80
Car Trailer, plastic, c. 1945, 3" long	20	30	40

Ideal Cattle Truck, 13" long, $50. Photo courtesy Terry Sells

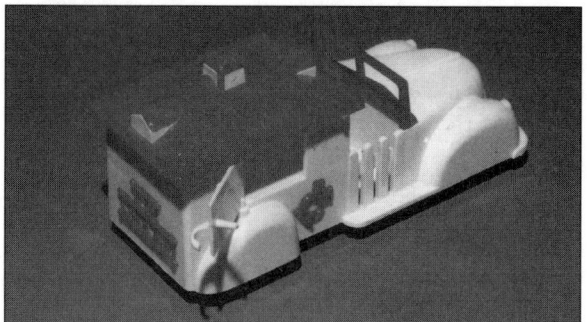

Ideal Ice Cream Truck, 1948-54, 5-1/2" long, $100. Photo courtesy Bob and Alice Wagner

Ideal (Continued)

	C6	C8	C10
Cattle Truck, 13" long	25	38	50
Dream Car Convertible, metal, 16" long	200	300	400
Fix-it Convertible	65	100	130
Ford Sunliner, plastic, friction, 9"	90	135	175
Ice Cream Truck, plastic, 15" long	45	65	90
Ice Cream Truck, 1948-54, 5-1/2" long	30	60	100
Jaguar Roadster, 6" long	35	50	70
Jeep, plastic, 1945	40	60	80

Ideal Jeep, 1945, $80. Photo courtesy Terry Sells

Ideal Rocket Cycle, 6-1/2" long, $200. Photo courtesy Terry Sells

Ideal Rolls Royce, 8" long, $25. Photo courtesy Ron Fink

Ideal Sanitation Truck, 5-1/2" long, $50. Photo courtesy Terry Sells

Ideal (Continued)

	C6	C8	C10
Mercedes Sedan, plastic, 9" long	35	50	70
Pickup Truck, plastic, Ford, 1940, 4" long	20	30	40
Pickup Truck, plastic, American, 1948, 4" long	6	10	14
Rocket Cycle, 6-1/2" long	100	150	200
Rolls Royce, plastic, 8" long	12	18	25
Sanitation Truck, plastic, 5-1/2" long	20	35	50
Sedan, plastic, 9-1/4" long	20	35	50
Semi, 12" long	35	50	70
Shell Oil Truck, plastic, 12-1/2" long	25	38	50

Ideal Steam Shovel, 7-1/2" long, $45. Photo courtesy Dave Leopard

Ideal Turbo-Jet Car, No. 4867, $120. Photo courtesy Tim Oei

Ideal XP-600 Fix-It Car of Tomorrow, 16" long, $170. Photo courtesy Terry Sells

Ideal (Continued)	C6	C8	C10
Steam Shovel, plastic, 7-1/2" long	22	33	45
Tow Truck, plastic and metal, 17" long	50	75	100
Truck, "Television Repair"	50	75	100
Turbo-Jet Car, No. 4867	60	90	120
XP-600 Fix-It Car of Tomorrow, 16" long	85	128	170

Jane Francis Toys Gulf Service Station, $750. Photo courtesy Barbara Fancis Vanyo

Jane Francis Toys

Jane Francis Toys operated in Wilkinsburg, Pennsylvania, from 1942-1946 and in Somerset, Pennsylvania, from 1947-1949. Starting as a stuffed-toy maker, the company introduced a line of die-cast cars in 1945. The last Jane Francis toys were manufactured in 1949.

	C6	C8	C10
Gulf Service Station, eight pieces	400	575	750
Gulf Truck, No. 447, tin cover, 5" long (JF05)	30	45	75
Pickup Truck, No. 447, 5" long (JF03)	20	25	30
Pickup Truck, No. 347, 5" long (JF02)	20	25	30
Pickup Truck, 6-1/2" long (JF01)	30	40	50
Sedan, fastback, futuristic, w/wind-up motor, 6-1/2" long (JF07)	30	40	50
Sedan, fastback, futuristic, 6-1/2" long (JF06)	25	30	40
Service Station, "Gulf Truck Service," Jane Francis	500	750	1000
Tow Truck, No. 447, 5" long (JF04)	30	40	65

Japanese Tin Vehicles

Tin toy cars have been manufactured since the first horseless carriages roamed the streets of the United States and Europe. They ranged in size and price from the tiny one-inch penny toy to the twenty-eight-inch Eldorado that sold for ten dollars. Although there are German, Spanish and French toy cars listed here, this chapter concentrates on the 1950s—the Golden Era of Japanese tin toy cars. These examples are popular today and prices continue to rise.

Contributor: Ron Smith, 33005 Arlesford, Solon, OH, 44139, 440-248-7066, fax 440-519-0906. Smith has always loved toy cars and planes, he can still show you his first Dinky Toy his aunt bought him at Fred Harvey's Toy Store in Cleveland's Terminal Tower Building. Smith has collected die-cast cars, trucks and planes, cast-iron toys and plastic promotional cars, but for the past fifteen years he has specialized in tin-plate cars and planes. Smith lives in Ohio with his wife Joan and their two cats, T-2 and Bogart.

Japanese Tin Vehicles	C6	C8	C10
Dream Car, friction, "Y" Co., 17" (J278A)	600	800	1500
Electrospecial No. 21, battery-op, "Y" Co., 10" (J290)	300	600	1200
Midget Special No. 6, friction, "Y" Co., 7" (J291)	300	500	1000
1930s DeSoto, friction, Masudaya, 8" (J81)	300	400	800
1949 Ford Sedan, wind-up, Guntherman, 11" (J93)	150	300	400
1950 BMW 600 Isetta, friction, Bandai, 9" (J16)	150	300	500
1950 BMW Isetta (three wheels), friction, Bandai, 6-1/2" (J17)	75	125	200
1950 Cadillac, friction, Marusan, 11" (J19)	300	500	850

Japanese Tin Vehicles, Dream Car, 17", $1500. Photo courtesy Ron Smith

Japanese Tin Vehicles, Electrospecial No. 21, 10", $1200. Photo courtesy Ron Smith

Japanese Tin Vehicles, 1950 Champion No. 15 Racer, 18", $1500. Photo courtesy Ron Smith

Japanese Tin Vehicles (Continued)	C6	C8	C10
1950 Cadillac, battery-op, Marusan, 11" (J18)	400	800	1800
1950 Champion No. 15 Racer, friction, German, 18" (J289)	500	750	1500
1950 Champion No. 42 Racer, friction, German, 18" (J288)	500	750	1500
1950 Chrysler, friction, Guntherman, 11" (J70)	100	400	800
1950 Daihatsu Midget, friction, Kokyu Shokai, 5" (J270)	75	100	250
1950 Ford Good Humor Ice Cream Truck, friction, KTS, Japan, 10-3/4" (J95)	100	400	800
1950 Volkswagen Convertible, friction, T.N., 9-1/2" (J258)	100	150	225
1950s Agajanian Racer No. 98, friction, "Y" Co., 18" (J286)	500	1000	2000
1950s Atom Car, Yonezawa, 17" (J284)	200	400	900
1950s Atom Jet Car, friction, "Y" Co., 30" (J283)	300	500	1100
1950s Buick Futuristic LeSabre, friction, Yonezawa, 7-1/2" (J276)	200	300	500
1950s Champion No. 98 Racer, friction, "Y" Co., 18" (J287)	500	800	1100

Japanese Tin Vehicles, 1950s Agajanian Racer No. 98, 18", $2000. Photo courtesy Ron Smith

Japanese Tin Vehicles, 1950s Mazda Auto Tricycle, 8", $250. Photo courtesy Ron Smith

Japanese Tin Vehicles (Continued)

	C6	C8	C10
1950s Daihatsu Auto Tricycle, friction, Nomura, 11" (J275)	100	150	350
1950s Daihatsu Midget, friction, Yonezawa, 7" (J269)	75	100	250
1950s Divco Dugans Bakery Truck, friction, 7-1/2" (J80)	200	400	500
1950s Dream Car Buick Phantom, friction, Tipp & Co., 12" (J278)	300	400	800
1950s International Cement Mixer, friction, SSS, 19" (J152)	300	600	1000
1950s International Grain Hauler, friction, SSS, 23" (J153)	300	600	1000
1950s Lotus Elite, friction, Bandai, 8-1/2" (J170)	25	35	60
1950s Mazda Auto Tricycle, friction, Bandai, 8" (J274)	75	125	250
1950s Mazda Auto Tricycle K360, friction, Bandai, 6"	75	125	250
1950s Mercedes Limousine, friction, Tipp & Co., 14" (J172)	500	800	1000
1950s Mercedes-Benz 300 SL, battery-op, Cragstan, 9" (J185)	65	95	125
1950s Mercedes-Benz 300 SL, friction, Bandai, 8" (J186)	65	95	150
1950s Mercedes-Benz 300 SL, battery-op, T.N., 11" (J183)	125	150	200
1950s Mercedes-Benz 300 SL, battery-op, KS, 7" (J184)	45	65	85
1950s Mercedes-Benz Racer, friction, Linemar, 9-1/2" (J173)	95	150	185
1950s Mercedes-Benz Racer W196, battery-op, Marusan, 10" (J174)	150	200	400
1950s Mitsubishi Auto Tricycle, friction, Bandai, 11" (J272)	100	150	300

Japanese Tin Vehicles (Continued)

	C6	C8	C10
1950s Mitsubishi Auto Tricycle Leo, friction, Bandai, 5" (J271)	75	150	300
1950s Nash, battery-op, MSK, 8" (J206)	40	70	90
1950s Opel Sedan, battery-op, Yonezawa, 11-1/2" (J217)	70	90	150
1950s Orient Auto Tricycle, friction, Yonezawa, 9" (J273)	75	150	300
1950s Pontiac Dream Car, friction, Mitsubishi, 10" (J282)	100	200	600
1950s Porsche Speedster, battery-op, Distler, 10-1/2" (J235)	200	300	600
1950s Record Racer NSU, friction, Bandai, 18" (J285)	100	150	300
1950s Volkswagen Bus, battery-op, Tipp & Co., 9" (J257)	250	375	450
1950s Volvo, wind-up, Sweden, 11" (J265A)	600	1000	2000
1950s Zuendapp Janus, friction, Bandai, 8" (J267)	200	400	700
1951 Ford Sedan, wind-up, Guntherman, 11" (J94)	150	300	400
1952 Cadillac, battery-op, T.N., 13" (J21)	100	250	500
1952 Cadillac, friction, Alps, 11-1/2" (J20)	250	400	800
1952 MG TF, friction, unknown manufacturer, 8-1/2" (J198)	50	75	100
1952 Oldsmobile, friction, "Y" Co., 11" (J207A)	150	350	500
1953 Buick, friction, Marusan, 7" (J3)	50	100	200
1953 Chevrolet Corvette, friction, Bandai, 7" (J37)	100	200	400
1953 Chrysler, friction, Yonezawa, 10" (J70B)	100	225	350

Japanese Tin Vehicles, 1953 Packard Convertible/Sedan, 16", $1600. Photo courtesy Ron Smith

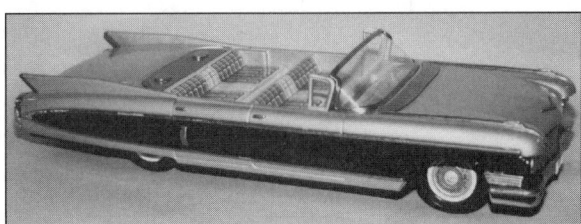

Japanese Tin Vehicles, 1954 Cadillac, 12", $450. Photo courtesy Ron Smith

Japanese Tin Vehicles, 1954 Chevrolet, 11", $1500. Photo courtesy Ron Smith

Japanese Tin Vehicles, 1955 Buick Roadmaster, 11", $500. Photo courtesy Ron Smith

Japanese Tin Vehicles (Continued)	C6	C8	C10
1953 Packard Convertible/Sedan, friction, Alps, 16" (J222)	500	800	1600
1954 Buick Station Wagon, battery-op, unknown manufacturer, 8" (J4)	75	150	200
1954 Cadillac, battery-op, Joustra, 12" (J23)	100	200	450
1954 Cadillac, friction, Gama, 12" (J22)	100	200	450
1954 Chevrolet, friction, Marusan, 11" (J49)	300	800	1500
1954 Lincoln, friction, unknown manufacturer, 12" (J162)	175	275	375
1954 Mercury Hardtop, battery-op, Rock Valley Toys, 9-1/2" (J192)	100	150	250
1954 MG TD, friction, SSS, 6-1/2" (J199)	35	65	80
1954 Pontiac, Minister, friction, Minister, 11" (J218A)	10	20	30
1954 Pontiac Star Chief, friction, Asahi, 11" (J218)	250	350	700
1954 Studebaker, friction, Yoshiva, 9" (J243)	150	200	375
1955 Buick Roadmaster, friction, Yoshiya, 11" (J5)	125	250	500
1955 Chevrolet, battery-op, Marusan, 10-3/4" (J50)	300	800	1500

Japanese Tin Vehicles (Continued)	C6	C8	C10
1955 Chrysler, friction, Yonezawa, 8" (J71)	100	200	300
1955 Ford Ambulance, friction, Bandai, 12" (J98)	150	200	250
1955 Ford Convertible, friction, Bandai, 12" (J100)	200	400	700
1955 Ford Panel Truck, "Flowers," friction, Bandai, 12" (J99)	200	400	600
1955 Ford Panel Truck, friction, "Standard Coffee," Bandai, 12"	600	800	1500
1955 Ford Pickup, friction, Bandai, 12" (J96)	150	250	300
1955 Ford Station Wagon, friction, Bandai, 12" (J97)	150	250	300
1955 Ford Thunderbird, friction, Bandai, 7" (J126A)	75	100	150

Japanese Tin Vehicles, 1955 Ford Convertible, 12", $700. Photo courtesy Ron Smith

Japanese Tin Vehicles, 1955 Lincoln Sedan, 12", $1200. Photo courtesy Ron Smith

Japanese Tin Vehicles, 1956 Ford Convertible, 11-1/2", $900. Photo courtesy Ron Smith

Japanese Tin Vehicles (Continued)	C6	C8	C10
1955 Lincoln Sedan, friction, Yonezawa, 12" (J163)	250	600	1200
1955 MG TF, friction, Bandai, 8" (J200)	95	125	150
1956 Chevrolet Convertible, friction, Bandai, 9-1/2" (J53)	100	150	225
1956 Chevrolet Pickup, friction, Bandai, 9-1/2" (J52)	75	125	175
1956 Chevrolet Station Wagon, friction, Bandai, 9-1/2" (J51)	60	120	180
1956 Ford Convertible, friction, Haji, 11-1/2" (J102)	400	600	900
1956 Ford Hardtop, friction, Yonezawa, 12" (J101)	300	500	950
1956 Ford Sedan, friction, Marusan, 13" (J103)	500	1000	3000
1956 Ford Thunderbird, friction, T.N., 11" (J127)	200	300	400
1956 Ford Thunderbird, battery-op, T.N., 11" (J129)	200	300	400
1956 Ford Thunderbird Hardtop Clear Top, friction, T.N., 11" (J128)	200	300	400
1956 Ford Wagon, friction, Nomura, 10-1/2" (J104)	100	150	300
1956 GM's Gas Turbine Powered Firebird II, friction, Ashahi, 8-1/2" (J281)	100	200	400

Japanese Tin Vehicles, 1956 Ford Thunderbird, 11", $400. Photo courtesy Ron Smith

Japanese Tin Vehicles, 1956 Mercury Hardtop, 9-1/2", $1400. Photo courtesy Ron Smith

Japanese Tin Vehicles, 1956 Oldsmobile Sedan, 10-1/2", $600. Photo courtesy Ron Smith

Japanese Tin Vehicles (Continued)	C6	C8	C10
1956 Lincoln, friction, Ichiko, 16-1/2" (J165)	150	250	375
1956 Lincoln Continental Mark II, friction, Linemar, 12" (J164)	600	1200	2500
1956 Mercury Hardtop, friction, Alps, 9-1/2" (J193)	600	800	1400
1956 Nash Ambassador, friction, Sankei Gangu, 8" (J207)	100	125	150
1956 Oldsmobile Sedan, friction, Ichiko/Kanto, 10-1/2" (J208)	200	400	600
1956 Oldsmobile Super 88 Sedan, friction, Masudaya, 16" (J209)	200	300	500
1956 Plymouth Hardtop, friction, unknown manufacturer, 8-1/2" (J224)	150	200	400
1956 Plymouth Hardtop, battery-op, Alps, 12" (J225)	300	400	600
1957 Chrysler New Yorker, friction, Alps, 14" (J72)	500	700	1500
1957 Ferrari 250 G. Convertible, friction, A.T.C., 9-1/2" (J147)	150	300	750
1957 Ford Fairlane Sedan, friction, Ichiko, 10" (J105)	100	200	300
1957 Ford Hardtop, friction, T.N., 12" (J106)	100	200	300

*Japanese Tin Vehicles, 1957 Ford Hardtop, 12",
$300. Photo courtesy Ron Smith*

*Japanese Tin Vehicles, 1958 Buick Century, 12",
$1500. Photo courtesy Ron Smith*

*Japanese Tin Vehicles, 1958 Chevrolet Corvette,
9-1/2", $600. Photo courtesy Ron Smith*

Japanese Tin Vehicles (Continued)	C6	C8	C10
1957 Ford Panel Truck, friction, "Standard Coffee," Bandai, 12"	600	900	1800
1957 Ford Sedan/Convertible/ Wagon/Pickup, friction, Bandai, 12" (J108)	200	250	300
1957 Ford Sedan/Convertible/ Wagon/Pickup, friction, Joustra, 12" (J107)	200	250	300
1957 Ford Station Wagon, friction, Nomura, 7-1/2" (J109)	60	80	100
1957 Mercedes-Benz 300 SL, friction, Marusan, 8-1/2" (J187)	100	200	300
1957 MGA, friction, A.T.C., 10" (J201)	175	250	500
1957 Packard Hawk Convertible, battery-op, Schuco, 10-3/4" (J223)	300	400	900
1957 Plymouth Fury Hardtop, friction, "Y" Co., 11-1/2" (J226)	300	400	600
1958 Buick Century, friction, Bandai, 8" (J7)	80	100	150
1958 Buick Century, friction, Yonezawa, 12" (J6)	400	650	1500
1958 Chevrolet Convertible, friction, Bandai, 8" (J56)	60	125	275
1958 Chevrolet Corvette, friction, Yonezawa, 9-1/2" (J38)	200	300	600

*Japanese Tin Vehicles, 1957 Packard Hawk
Convertible, 10-3/4", $900. Photo courtesy
Ron Smith*

Japanese Tin Vehicles (Continued)	C6	C8	C10
1958 Chevrolet Pickup Truck, friction, Bandai, 8" (J55)	50	65	90
1958 Chevrolet Red Cross Ambulance, friction, Bandai, 8" (J54)	20	50	100
1958 Chevrolet Sedan, friction, Bandai, 8" (J58)	75	125	175
1958 Chevrolet Station Wagon, friction, Bandai, 8" (J57)	50	65	125
1958 Chrysler, battery-op, unknown manufacturer, 13" (J73)	300	400	800
1958 Dodge Sedan, friction, T.N., 11" (J82)	300	400	800
1958 Edsel, friction, Yonezawa, 10-1/2" (J92)	300	600	1200
1958 Edsel Ambulance, friction, Haji, 11" (J88)	200	250	400
1958 Edsel Convertible/Sedan, friction, Haji, 10-1/2" (J86)	300	500	1000
1958 Edsel Hardtop, friction, Toy Nomura, 8-1/2" (J90)	100	150	250
1958 Edsel Hardtop, friction, Asahi, 10-3/4" (J91)	100	200	350
1958 Edsel Station Wagon, friction, T.N., 11" (J89)	150	200	300

Japanese Tin Vehicles, 1958 Edsel Convertible/Sedan, 10-1/2", $1000. Photo courtesy

Japanese Tin Vehicles, 1959 Buick, 12", $350. Photo courtesy Ron Smith

Japanese Tin Vehicles, 1959 Cadillac Convertible, 12", $185. Photo courtesy Ron Smith

Japanese Tin Vehicles (Continued)	C6	C8	C10
1958 Edsel Wagon, friction, Haji, 10-1/2" (J87)	200	300	600
1958 Ferrari, battery-op, Bandai, 11" (J148)	90	150	350
1958 Ford Country Squire Station Wagon, friction, Bandai, 8" (J112)	60	80	125
1958 Ford Fairlane Hardtop/Convertible, friction, Sankei Gangu, 9" (J114)	90	115	125
1958 Ford Fairlane Hardtop/Convertible, friction, Bandai, 8" (J113)	60	80	125
1958 Ford Retractable Top, battery-op, T.N., 11" (J111)	80	100	165
1958 Ford Retractable Top, friction, K. Japan, 10" (J110)	80	100	165
1958 Mercury Hardtop, friction, Yonezawa, 11-1/2" (J195)	250	325	400
1958 Mercury Station Wagon, friction, Bandai, 8" (J194)	60	80	100
1958 Oldsmobile Sedan, friction, A.T.C., 12" (J210)	200	300	400
1958 Oldsmobile Sedan, friction, "Y" Co., 16" (J212)	300	400	700
1958 Oldsmobile Super 88 Sedan, friction, A.T.C., 13" (J211)	250	325	425
1958 Plymouth Fury, friction, Bandai, 8" (J227)	75	90	165

Japanese Tin Vehicles (Continued)	C6	C8	C10
1959 Austin Healey 100 Six Convertible, friction, Bandai, 8" (J2B)	50	100	200
1959 Austin Healey 100 Six Coupe, friction, Bandai, 8" (J2A)	50	100	200
1959 Buick, battery-op/friction, Ichiko, 12" (J9)	100	275	350
1959 Buick, friction, T.N., 11" (J8)	90	150	300
1959 Cadillac Convertible, friction, Bandai, 12" (J25)	50	100	185
1959 Cadillac Sedan, friction, Bandai, 12" (J24)	50	100	185
1959 Chevrolet Sedan/Convertible/ Wagon, friction, SY, 11-1/2" (J59)	200	400	800
1959 Chrysler Imperial Convertible, friction, Bandai, 8" (J74)	50	100	175
1959 Chrysler Imperial Sedan, friction, Bandai, 8" (J75)	50	100	175

Japanese Tin Vehicles, 1958 Mercury Hardtop, 11-1/2", $400. Photo courtesy Ron Smith

Japanese Tin Vehicles, 1959 Dodge Pickup, 18-1/2", $1200. Photo courtesy Ron Smith

Japanese Tin Vehicles, 1959 Lincoln Continental Mark III Convertible, 12", $175. Photo courtesy Ron Smith

Japanese Tin Vehicles (Continued)	C6	C8	C10
1959 Dodge Pickup, friction, unknown manufacturer, 18-1/2" (J84)	350	500	1200
1959 Dodge Truck, friction, unknown manufacturer, 24" (J83)	350	500	1000
1959 Ford Fairlane Skyliner, friction, Sankei Gangu, 9" (J115)	90	115	125
1959 Ford Retractable, friction, T.N., 11" (J117)	80	100	165
1959 Ford Station Wagon, friction, T.N., 12" (J116)	100	150	200
1959 Ford Thunderbird Convertible, friction, Bandai, 8" (J131)	50	80	125
1959 Ford Thunderbird Sedan, friction, Bandai, 8" (J130)	50	80	125
1959 Lincoln Continental Mark III Convertible, friction, Bandai, 12" (J166)	90	125	175
1959 Lincoln Continental Mark III Sedan, friction, Bandai, 12" (J167)	90	125	175
1959 Oldsmobile Sedan, friction, Ichiko, 12-1/2" (J213)	75	125	175
1959 Plymouth Convertible, friction, A.T.C., 10-1/2" (J229)	250	400	600
1959 Plymouth Hardtop, friction, A.T.C., 10-1/2" (J228)	200	400	600
1960 Buick, friction, Ichiko, 17-1/2" (J10)	150	300	800

Japanese Tin Vehicles, 1959 Oldsmobile Sedan, 12-1/2", $175. Photo courtesy Ron Smith

Japanese Tin Vehicles, 1960 Citroen DS 19 Sedan, 12", $900. Photo courtesy Ron Smith

Japanese Tin Vehicles (Continued)	C6	C8	C10
1960 Cadillac, friction, Yonezawa, 18" (J27)	100	150	300
1960 Chevrolet, friction, Marusan, 11-1/2" (J60)	200	400	800
1960 Chrysler Valiant, friction, Bandai, 8" (J76)	20	30	60
1960 Citroen 2 CV, friction, Daiya, 8" (J69A)	100	150	250
1960 Citroen DS 19 Convertible, friction, Bandai, 12" (J67)	300	600	900
1960 Citroen DS 19 Sedan, friction, Bandai, 12" (J68)	300	600	900
1960 Citroen DS 19 Station Wagon, friction, Bandai, 12" (J69)	300	600	900
1960 DKW 1000 Convertible, friction, Bandai, 8" (J78)	90	125	250
1960 Ferrari Super America Coupe, friction, Bandai, 12" (J149)	100	200	350
1960 Ford, friction, Haji, 11" (J119)	125	200	350
1960 Ford Gyron, battery-op, Ichida, 11" (J280)	75	150	250
1960 Jaguar XK150 Hardtop Convertible, friction, Bandai, 9-1/2" (J154)	75	125	225
1960 Lincoln Hardtop/Convertible, friction, Yonezawa, 11" (J168)	100	150	300
1960 Porsche 911, battery-op, Bandai, 10" (J234)	65	95	125
1960 Renault, friction, Bandai, 7-1/2" (J241)	95	150	200
1960 Rolls Royce, friction, T.N., 10-1/2" (J239)	200	300	500

Japanese Tin Vehicles, 1960 Rolls Royce Silver Coupe Convertible, 12", $300. Photo courtesy Ron Smith

Japanese Tin Vehicles (Continued)	C6	C8	C10
1960 Rolls Royce Silver Coupe Convertible, friction, Bandai, 12" (J236)	100	150	300
1960 Volkswagen Karmann-Ghia, friction, Bandai, 7" (J252)	100	150	300
1960s Aston-Martin DB5 (James Bond), friction, Gilbert, 11-1/2" (J1)	75	150	350
1960s Aston-Martin DB6, friction, Asahi Toy Co., 11" (J2)	200	400	600
1960s Cadillac, friction, Bandai, 17" (J26)	125	175	375
1960s Chevrolet Corvair, friction, Bandai, 8" (J43)	30	50	80
1960s Datsun Bluebird 1200, friction, Bandai, 8" (J79)	60	100	200
1960s Dream Car Firebird III, friction, Alps, 11" (J279)	100	200	400

Japanese Tin Vehicles, 1960 Volkswagen Karmann-Ghia, 7", $300. Photo courtesy Ron Smith

Japanese Tin Vehicles, 1960s Aston-Martin DB5 (James Bond), 11-1/2", $350. Photo courtesy Ron Smith

Japanese Tin Vehicles, 1960s Jaguar XKE Convertible, 10-1/2", $250. Photo courtesy Ron Smith

Japanese Tin Vehicles (Continued)	C6	C8	C10
1960s Ferrari Super America Conventible, friction, Bandai, 12" (J150)	100	200	350
1960s Fiat 600 Sedan, friction, Bandai, 8" (J151)	50	70	100
1960s Ford Falcon, friction, Bandai, 8" (J118)	20	30	50
1960s Ford GT, battery-op, Bandai, 10" (J146)	65	85	125
1960s Ford Taunus 17M, friction, Bandai, 8" (J145)	20	40	60
1960s Jaguar 3.4 Convertible, friction, Bandai, 8" (J160)	50	60	135
1960s Jaguar 3.4 Sedan, friction, Bandai, 8" (J159)	50	60	135
1960s Jaguar XK 140, friction, Bandai, 9-1/2" (J157)	75	125	225
1960s Jaguar XKE, battery-op, Bandai, 10" (J158)	90	125	200
1960s Jaguar XKE Convertible, friction, T.T., 10-1/2" (J155)	75	100	250
1960s Jaguar XKE Coupe, friction, Lendolet Auto, 10-1/2" (J156)	75	100	125
1960s Land Rover "88" Station Wagon, friction, Bandai, 8" (J171)	30	40	80
1960s Mercedes, friction, Ichiko, 12-1/2" (J175)	100	150	175
1960s Mercedes-Benz 219 Convertible, friction, Bandai, 8" (J177)	50	80	120
1960s Mercedes-Benz 219 Sedan, friction, Bandai, 8" (J176)	50	80	120
1960s Mercedes-Benz 230 SL, battery-op, Modern Toys, 15" (J178)	175	210	250

Japanese Tin Vehicles (Continued)

	C6	C8	C10
1960s Mercedes-Benz 230 SL, battery, Alps, 10" (J179)	65	75	95
1960s Mercedes-Benz 230 SL, battery-op, Yanoman, 14-1/2" (J180)	125	155	185
1960s Mercedes-Benz 250 S, friction, Daiya, 14" (J182)	110	155	175
1960s Mercedes-Benz 250 SE, battery-op, Ichiko, 13" (J181)	110	140	185
1960s Mercedes-Benz 600, friction, unknown manufacturer, 10" (J188)	95	125	175
1960s Mercedes-Benz Taxi, battery-op, Bandai, 10" (J189)	75	100	125
1960s Messerschmitt Four-wheel Convertible, friction, Bandai, 8" (J204)	200	250	450
1960s Messerschmitt Four-wheel Sedan, friction, Bandai, 8" (J205)	200	250	450
1960s MG Magnette Mark III Convertible, friction, Bandai, 8" (J203)	95	125	165
1960s MG Magnette Mark III Sedan, friction, Bandai, 8" (J202)	95	125	165
1960s Rambler Rebel Station Wagon, friction, Bandai, 12" (J240)	60	90	150
1960s Rolls Royce, w/electric lights, battery-op, Bandai, 12" (J238)	150	300	600
1960s Rolls Royce Silver Coupe Sedan, friction, Bandai, 12" (J237)	100	150	250
1960s Saab 93B, friction, Bandai, 7" (J244)	50	70	90
1960s Studebaker Avanti, friction, Bandai, 8" (J242)	125	175	350
1960s Subaru 360, friction, Bandai, 7" (J245)	100	225	450
1960s Toyopet Crown, friction, Bandai, 9" (J248)	100	200	400

Japanese Tin Vehicles, 1960s Rambler Rebel Station Wagon, 12", $150. Photo courtesy Ron Smith

Japanese Tin Vehicles, 1960s Rolls Royce Silver Coupe Sedan, 12", $250. Photo courtesy Ron Smith

Japanese Tin Vehicles, 1960s Studebaker Avanti, 8", $350. Photo courtesy Ron Smith

Japanese Tin Vehicles (Continued)

	C6	C8	C10
1960s Toyota, friction, Ichiko, 16" (J249)	75	100	150
1960s Triumph TR-3 Convertible, friction, Bandai, 8" (J246)	50	80	175
1960s Triumph TR-3 Coupe, friction, Bandai, 8" (J247)	50	80	175
1960s Vespa, friction, Bandai, 9" (J251)	80	125	200
1960s Volkswagen, battery-op, Bandai, 10-1/2" (J263)	25	50	75
1960s Volkswagen, battery-op, Bandai, 11" (J264)	25	50	75
1960s Volkswagen, friction, Bandai, 8" (J262)	25	45	60
1960s Volkswagen Bus, friction, A.T.C., 12" (J253)	125	175	350
1960s Volkswagen Bus, friction, Bandai, 8" (J255)	50	60	100
1960s Volkswagen Bus, battery-op/friction, Bandai, 9-1/2" (J256)	75	125	200
1960s Volkswagen Convertible, battery-op, Taiyo, 10-1/2" (J261)	25	40	80
1960s Volkswagen Convertible, battery-op, Bandai, 11" (J260)	110	145	200
1960s Volkswagen Convertible, battery-op, Bandai, 7-1/2" (J259)	40	60	80

Japanese Tin Vehicles, 1960s Volkswagen Convertible, 11", $200. Photo courtesy Ron Smith

Japanese Tin Vehicles (Continued)

	C6	C8	C10
1960s Volkswagen Pickup Truck, friction, Bandai, 8" (J254)	50	60	100
1960s Volkswagen with or without Sun Roof, friction, Bandai, 15" (J265)	60	90	125
1960s Willys Jeep FC-150 Pickup, friction, T.N. Toy Nomura, 11" (J266)	50	75	95
1961 Buick, friction, T.N., 11" (J11)	100	150	250
1961 Buick Emergency Car, friction, T.N., 14" (J12)	50	95	125
1961 Cadillac 60, friction, unknown manufacturer, 9" (J28)	95	125	150
1961 Cadillac Fleetwood, friction, SSS, 17-1/2" (J29)	100	200	350
1961 Chevrolet Impala Convertible, friction, Bandai, 11" (J63)	100	150	300
1961 Chevrolet Impala Sedan, friction, Bandai, 11" (J62)	100	150	300
1961 Ford Country Sedan, friction, Bandai, 10-1/2" (J120)	125	150	250
1961 Ford Thunderbird Retractable, battery-op, remote control, Yonezawa, 11" (J132)	80	150	200
1961 Oldsmobile Convertible, friction, Yonezawa, 12" (J214)	75	125	200

Japanese Tin Vehicles, 1961 Cadillac Fleetwood, 17-1/2", $350. Photo courtesy Ron Smith

Japanese Tin Vehicles, 1961 Chevrolet Impala Convertible, 11", $300. Photo courtesy Ron Smith

Japanese Tin Vehicles, 1961 Oldsmobile Convertible, 12", $200. Photo courtesy Ron Smith

Japanese Tin Vehicles (Continued)

	C6	C8	C10
1961 Plymouth Sedan, friction, Ichiko, 12" (J230)	150	300	550
1961 Plymouth Station Wagon, friction, Ichiko, 12" (J231)	150	250	500
1961 Plymouth T.V. Car, battery-op, Ichiko, 12" (J232)	125	350	700
1962 Cadillac, friction, Yonezawa, 22" (J30)	100	250	350
1962 Chevrolet, friction, unknown manufacturer, 11" (J65)	125	250	350
1962 Chevrolet Corvette, friction, Bandai, 8" (J39)	50	75	150

Japanese Tin Vehicles, 1961 Plymouth T.V. Car, 12", $700. Photo courtesy Ron Smith

*Japanese Tin Vehicles, 1962 Chrysler Imperial, 16",
$2200. Photo courtesy Ron Smith*

*Japanese Tin Vehicles, 1964 Ford Hardtop, 13",
$700. Photo courtesy Ron Smith*

*Japanese Tin Vehicles, 1964 Ford Thunderbird
Hardtop, 12", $400. Photo courtesy Ron Smith*

Japanese Tin Vehicles (Continued)	C6	C8	C10
1962 Chevrolet Secret Agent, battery-op, unknown manufacturer, 14" (J64)	50	75	150
1962 Chrysler Imperial, friction, black, red (white: add 20% to value), Asahi Toy Co., 16" (J77)	600	1200	2200
1962 Ford Country Sedan, friction, Asahi, 12" (J121)	200	350	700
1962 Ford Thunderbird Retractable, battery-op, Yonezawa, 11" (J133)	80	150	200
1962 Mercedes-Benz, battery-op, SSS, 12" (J190)	150	200	300
1963 Buick Wildcat, friction, Ichiko, 15" (J13)	200	400	800
1963 Cadillac, friction, Bandai, 17" (J31)	100	200	350
1963 Chevrolet Corvair, friction, Bandai, 8" (J44)	50	65	125
1963 Chevrolet Impala, friction, Bandai (?), 18" (J66)	200	300	400
1963 Corvair Bertone, battery-op, Bandai, 12" (J277)	75	150	250
1963 Ford Thunderbird Retractable, battery-op, Yonezawa, 11" (J134)	80	150	200
1964 Chevrolet Corvette, battery-op, Ichida, 12" (J41)	150	225	350
1964 Ford Convertible, friction, Rico, 17" (J124)	200	300	400

Japanese Tin Vehicles (Continued)	C6	C8	C10
1964 Ford Hardtop, friction, Rico, 17" (J123)	200	300	400
1964 Ford Hardtop, friction, Ichiko, 13" (J122)	200	450	700
1964 Ford Thunderbird, friction, Ichiko, 16" (J137)	100	200	400
1964 Ford Thunderbird Convertible, friction, Asahi, 12-1/2" (J135)	150	200	400
1964 Ford Thunderbird Hardtop, friction, Asahi, 12" (J136)	150	200	400
1964 Lincoln, friction, unknown manufacturer, 10-1/2" (J169)	90	175	275
1964 Plymouth Fury Hardtop, friction, Kusama, 10" (J223)	30	60	90
1965 Cadillac, friction, Asahi Toy Co., 17" (J32)	125	250	425
1965 Cadillac, friction, Ichiko, 22" (J33)	300	400	600
1965 Chevrolet Corvette, friction, Bandai, 8" (J40)	50	75	125
1965 Ford Galaxie Hardtop, friction, MT, 11" (J125)	125	150	300
1965 Ford Mustang (FBI), friction, Bandai, 11" (J141)	100	200	400
1965 Ford Mustang Convertible, battery-op, Yonezawa, 13-1/2" (J142)	90	125	200

*Japanese Tin Vehicles, 1963 Buick Wildcat, 15",
$800. Photo courtesy Ron Smith*

Japanese Tin Vehicles, 1966 Ford Mustang Fastback, 17", $325. Photo courtesy Ron Smith

Japanese Tin Vehicles, 1967 Pontiac Firebird, 15-1/2", $900. Photo courtesy Ron Smith

Japanese Tin Vehicles, 1968 Ford Torino, 16", $600. Photo courtesy Ron Smith

Japanese Tin Vehicles (Continued)

	C6	C8	C10
1965 Ford Mustang Fastback, friction, Bandai, 11" (J139)	45	65	90
1965 Ford Mustang Hardtop/Convertible, friction/battery-op, Bandai, 11" (J140)	75	125	150
1965 Ford Thunderbird Hardtop, friction, Bandai, 10-3/4" (J138)	60	90	175
1965 Jaguar XKE120, friction, Alps, 6-1/2" (J161)	90	150	350
1966 Buick LeSabre, friction, Asahi Toy Co., 19" (J14)	100	150	300
1966 Ford Mustang Fastback, friction, T.N., 17" (J143)	120	200	325
1966 Oldsmobile Toronado, battery-op, Bandai, 11" (J215)	65	110	150
1967 Cadillac, friction, K.O., 10-1/2" (J34)	100	150	250
1967 Cadillac, friction, unknown manufacturer, 10-3/4" (J35)	75	100	125
1967 Cadillac El Dorado, friction, Ichiko, 28" (J36)	200	400	800
1967 Chevrolet Camaro, friction, Modern Toys, 11" (J47)	25	50	75
1967 Chevrolet Camaro, friction, Taiyo, 9-1/2" (J45)	10	20	25
1967 Chevrolet Camaro, battery-op, T.N., 14" (J46)	100	150	300
1967 Ford Mustang, battery-op, Bandai, 13" (J144)	45	65	100

Japanese Tin Vehicles (Continued)

	C6	C8	C10
1967 Mercury Cougar Hardtop, battery-op, Taiyo, 10" (J196)	25	45	90
1967 Mercury Cougar Hardtop, friction, Asakusa Toys, 15" (J197)	200	400	800
1967 Pontiac Firebird, w/wipers, battery-op, Bandai, 9-1/2" (J221)	40	55	100
1967 Pontiac Firebird, friction, Akasura, 15-1/2" (J219)	200	400	900
1967 Pontiac Firebird, friction, Bandai, 10" (J220)	30	55	100
1967 Toyota 2000 GT, friction, A.T.C., 15" (J250)	125	250	350
1968 Buick Sportswagon, friction, Asakusa, 15" (J15)	150	200	300
1968 Chevrolet Corvette, battery-op, Taiyo, 9-1/2" (J42)	20	40	80
1968 Dodge Yellow Cab, friction, T.N., 12" (J85)	100	200	500

Japanese Tin Vehicles, 1967 Mercury Cougar Hardtop, 15", $800. Photo courtesy Ron Smith

Japanese Tin Vehicles, 1971 Chevrolet Camaro Rusher, 9-1/2", $25. Photo courtesy Ron Smith

Japanese Tin Vehicles (Continued)

	C6	C8	C10
1968 Ford Torino, friction, S.T., 16" (J126)	175	300	600
1968 Oldsmobile Toronado, friction, Ichiko, 17-1/2" (J216)	300	400	500
1970 Mercedes-Benz, friction, Ichiko, 24" (J191)	125	150	200
1971 Chevrolet Camaro Rusher, battery-op, Taiyo, 9-1/2" (J48)	10	20	25

The Judy Company

The Judy Company of Minneapolis made educational toys, including a farm set called Happy's Farm Family (patented in 1945) that included a solid rubber car, pick-up truck, and tractor, along with human and animal figures.

Contributor: Dave Leopard, 2507 Feather Run Trail, West Columbia, SC 29169-4915.

	C6	C8	C10
Pickup Truck, solid rubber, two dimensional, (part of set), 5-1/4" long (JT01)	15	20	25
Sedan, solid rubber, two dimensional, (part of set), 5-1/4" long (JA01)	15	20	25

Kansas Toy & Novelty Company

Arthur Haynes, an auto mechanic, began molding toys in his Clifton, Kansas, shed for local stores in 1923. With clever hands and an artist's eye, he charmed his friends and local townspeople with his bright-colored toys. He made his patterns from advertising pictures, from local vehicles and probably from other makes of toys, such as Tootsietoy. He made his own production tools. His range was diverse, for he made miniatures of aircraft, autos, trains, farm equipment, zeppelin and a few animals, novelties and charms.

Haynes believed that he invented the hollow-casting of metal toys, so he must have started with solid toys. One day, he dropped his full mold, spilling its hot metal. To his delight he had a perfect, hollow toy vehicle, with promise of savings of metal and shipping costs.

This was a town enterprise from the beginning. Jess Foster, news editor, helped with alloy mixtures; Mr. Hadsell, Union Pacific agent, suggested they send samples to Woolworth's in New York. Clayton D. Young, a traveling salesman, saw the toys, joined the company and built a profitable business with the chain stores, including Kress, Kresge and Sears-Roebuck; he later became a partner. At its peak of international sales in the late 1920s, the firm employed as many as sixty-five in two shifts during the Christmas-order season.

During its good years, Kansas Toy & Novelty created more designs and produced more toys than any producer of white-metal toys except Barclay. Young withdrew his share and retired around 1930. With the loss of these assets and the onset of the Depression, the company went downhill. George Hoeffer reorganized the company and moved the factory down the road, but this effort lasted only a few months. An era was coming to an end. This later history is scanty, but there is evidence that Haynes kept trying until toy No. 100 in 1935.

High-numbered toys are rare. Changes of wheel types suggest that Haynes was having problems. Perhaps he had always overreached, for looking back at the diversity of his toys and novelties, it is remarkable from a few mechanics in a small Midwest town.

Contributor: Fred Maxwell, 4722 N. 33 St., Arlington, VA 22207.

Perry R. Eichor, 703 North Almond Drive, Simpsonville, SC 29681.

	C6	C8	C10
Coupe, No. 8, convertible, landau iron, vertical hood louvers, horizontal grille pattern, windshield visor, string-pull knob in handcrank area, rearmount spare tire/wheel, metal simulated wire wheels, no hood cap, motometer or hood ornament, no headlamps, enamel finish, also un-numbered versions w/"Chrysler," headlamps and hood cap, motometer or hood ornament, or metal disc solid spokes, 3-1/8" long (KTV7)	20	30	40
Coupe, No. 66, streamlined three-wheeler, six open windows, metal simulated wire wheels, 3-1/2" long (KTV51)	60	80	100
Coupe, convertible, landau iron, vertical hood louvers, horizontal grille pattern, windshield visor, string-pull knob in handcrank area, metal disc solid spokes, lacquer, 2-7/8"	30	45	60
Coupe, crude, slant roof, shallow rear body, no fenders, hood similar to first racer above, lacquer; possibly the first "hoopie" or stripdown made?, rare, 3-1/8" long (KTV4)	32	48	64

Kansas Toy & Novelty (Continued)

	C6	C8	C10
Coupe, No. 35, convertible, landau iron, vertical hood louvers, horizontal grille pattern, hood cap, motometer or hood ornament, rearmount spare tire/wheel, metal simulated wire wheels, also an un-numbered version, 2-1/4" long (KTV26)	20	30	40
Dirt Tumble, No. 64, adjustable dumping scoop, 1-1/2" wide on same frame as No. 62, six pieces, four colors, 4" long (KTV49)	50	75	100
Dump Truck, No. 42, Ford?, driver, no cab, diamond emblem on hinged body, horizontal grille pattern, string-pull knob in handcrank area, metal simulated wire wheels, 3-1/2" (KTV33)	30	45	60
Indy Racer, No. 10, driver, boattail, exhaust right, vertical hood louvers, horizontal grille pattern, hood cap, motometer or hood ornament, string-pull knob in handcrank area, metal open-spoke wheels or metal simulated wire wheels, also un-numbered version, 3-1/8" (KTV14)	20	30	40
Locomotive-Tender, No. 36, "KT & N RR," six metal open-spoke wheels, four metal disc wheels, 0-6-4, 4-3/8" long (KTV27)	20	30	40
Midget Racer, No. 31, driver, torpedo tail, vertical hood louvers, horizontal grille pattern, hood cap, motometer or hood ornament, metal simulated wire wheels, lacquer, also un-numbered version, 2-1/8" (KTV24)	14	21	28
Midget Racer, No. 67, driver, torpedo-tail, vertical hood louvers, horizontal grille pattern, hood cap, motometer or hood ornament, metal disc wheels, smaller version of No. 31, also an un-numbered version, 1-1/2" long (KTV52)	25	45	55
Midget Racer, no driver, torpedo tail, hood cap, motometer or hood ornament, string-pull knob in handcrank area, vertical hood louvers, horizontal grille pattern, 5/8" metal disc wheels w/simulated lug nuts, lacquer finish, 3" long (KTV1)	20	30	40

Kansas Toy & Novelty Overland Bus, No. 9, 3-1/2" long, $45. Photo courtesy Fred Maxwell

Kansas Toy & Novelty (Continued)

	C6	C8	C10
Midget Racer, no number, torpedo tail, w/driver, plain metal disc wheels, lacquer; easily confused w/another maker's copy, 3" long (KTV2)	70	105	140
Overland Bus, "Fageol," nine male passengers, driver and "baggage" cast-on windows, horizontal grille pattern, rearmount spare tire/wheel, metal disc wheels, also an un-numbered version w/various family passengers on windows, 3-1/2" (KTV13)	35	50	70
Overland Bus, No. 9, "Fageol," solid windows, 3-1/2" long (KTV12)	25	35	45
Racer, No. 46, 1929 Golden Arrow record car, driver, large tail fin, metal simulated wire wheels, 2-7/8" long (KTV35)	25	35	45
Roadster, No. 14, open, "Chrysler," solid windshield, plain grille, hood cap, motometer or hood ornament, vertical hood louvers, string-pull knob in handcrank area, rearmount spare tire/wheel, metal disc, solid spokes, 3-1/8" long (KTV15)	20	30	45
Roadster, No. 54, Buick, driver w/cap, rumble seat, external trunk, plain hood and grille, no headlamps, sidemounted spare, metal simulated wire wheels, also an un-numbered version, 2-3/8" long (KTV39)	30	50	70

Kansas Toy & Novelty Roadster, No. 54, 2-3/8" long, $70. Photo courtesy Fred Maxwell

Kansas Toy & Novelty (Continued)

	C6	C8	C10

Roadster, No. 54, Buick, driver w/cap, rumble seat, external trunk, plain hood and grille, no headlamps, no trunk, sidemounted spare, metal simulated wire wheels, also an un-numbered version, 2-1/4" long (KTV40)... 60 75 100

Sedan, No. 60, 1930 Reo Royale? or Chrysler two-door Brougham, plain hood, vee-vertical grille pattern, square rear deck, metal disc wheels, metal disc wheels, sidemounted spare, also an un-numbered version w/metal simulated wire wheels and metal simulated wire wheels, sidemounted spare, 3-1/2" (KTV45)... 30 45 60

Sedan, "Chevrolet," six windows, landau iron, windshield visor, vertical hood louvers, string-pull knob in handcrank area, rearmount spare tire/wheel, metal simulated wire wheels, 2-7/8" long (KTV10) 20 30 40

Sedanette, No. 58, Austin Bantam, unique fighting cock on door panels, four open windows, horizontal hood louvers, vertical grille pattern, rearmount spare tire/wheel, mettal simulated wire wheels, three piece molded grille, 2-1/4" long (KTV43) 25 35 45

Steam Road Roller, No. 43, driver, string-pull knob in handcrank area, boiler, wooden rollers, 3-1/4" (KTV34).. 30 45 60

Tour Bus, No. 59, 1928 Pickwick COE double-deck night-coach, screen grille, larger version of No. 49 above, also an un-numbered version-w/dual wheels, 3-3/8" long (KTV44).. 75 125 150

Kansas Toy & Novelty Truck, No. 20, 3-1/8" long, $80. Photo courtesy Fred Maxwell

Kansas Toy & Novelty Warehouse Tractor, No. 48, 3" long, $50. Photo courtesy Fred Maxwell

Kansas Toy & Novelty (Continued)

	C6	C8	C10

Truck, No. 20, Ford (?), solid windshield, two open windows, three tanks, vertical hood louvers, horizontal grille pattern, rear faucet, metal simulated wire wheels, versions w/ and w/o driver, also an un-numbered version, 3-1/8" long (KTV20) 40 60 80

Warehouse Tractor, No. 48, "Caterpillar," "Whoopee," driver, vertical hood louvers, horizontal grille pattern, hood cap, motometer or hood ornament, string-pull knob in handcrank area, tow loop, metal simulated wire wheels, also an un-numbered version, 3" long (KTV36)... 25 38 50

Kansas Toy Transitional Vehicles

	C6	C8	C10

Coupe, No. 80, convertible, top up, landau iron, two open windows, vertical grille pattern, external trunk, metal simulated wire wheels, w/metal simulated wire wheels, sidemounted spare, three-piece molded grille, 3-1/2" long (KTV67) ... 30 45 60

Racer, No. 76, Auburn speedster, low driver, headrest fairing, string-pull knob in handcrank area, horizontal grille pattern, slanted louvers, large oval fin, kickplates, wooden hubs, rubber tires, 4-1/4" long (KTV63) 25 38 50

Roadster, No. 77, open short Duesenberg, windshield down, driver, vertical grille pattern, slanted louvers, sidemounted spare, external trunk, 4" long (KTV64)......... 25 38 50

Sedan, No. 79, two-door, Graham-like, four open windows, vertical grille pattern, horizontal hood louvers, rearmount spare tire/wheel, wooden hubs, rubber tires w/five removable tires, found both w/ and w/o bottom pan, 4-1/4" long (KTV66).................... 20 30 40

Kenton

Kenton Lock Manufacturing Co., was incorporated in May 1890, in Kenton, Ohio. In November of 1894 it became the Kenton Hardware Manufacturing Co. Around this period, it began producing toys. In 1903, it brought out its first toy vehicle line, calling them the Red Devils, since most cars in those days were painted red. The firm was a guild. In 1930, L.S. Bixler, of Jones & Bixler, was its president. Cast iron was its material.

	C6	C8	C10
Ambulance, cast iron, 7" long	700	1200	1800
Army Motor Truck 807, cast iron, 14" long	600	950	1400
Boattail Cut-Down Speedster, 1910, 7" long	120	180	260
Buckeye Ditcher, 9" long	500	750	1200
Bus, "Coast-to-Coast"	350	525	700
Bus, 1920s, 10-3/4" long	375	525	750
Bus, double-decker, 1920s, 6" long	312	470	625
Bus, double-decker, 1920, 7-1/4" long	1100	1650	2200
Bus, double-decker, 9-1/2"	650	1050	1550
Cement Mixer, Jaeger, 6-1/2" long	365	545	730
Cement Mixer, Jaeger, 8" long	1100	1700	2500

Kenton Ambulance, 7" long, $1800. Photo courtesy Sotheby's, New York

Kenton Bus, 9-1/2", $1550. Photo courtesy Sotheby's, New York

Kenton Dump Wagon, 9-3/4" long, $1000. Photo courtesy Sotheby's, New York

Kenton (Continued)	C6	C8	C10
Cement Mixer, cast-iron, Jaeger, 9" long..	1000	2000	3000
Circus Truck, 10" long	1300	2000	2700
Coal Dump Truck, 8-1/2" long............	300	450	600
Coupe, 1926, 10" long.......................	3000	5500	9500
Coupe, 8" long..................................	700	1100	1600
Dump Truck, 6" long..........................	340	500	675
Dump Wagon, cast iron, "Contractors," 9-3/4" long	500	750	1000
Emergency Truck, black rubber tires, c. 1930s	180	270	360
Fire Pump Truck, early w/driver, 10" long..	220	330	440
Fire Pumper, 1920s, 14-1/2" long	800	1200	1600
Fire Pumper, w/gong, c. 1920s, 18" long..	350	525	700
Fire Truck, w/pumper, 15" long	1200	2000	2800
Franklin, air-cooled, 8-1/2"	1300	1950	2600
Hose Truck, open cab, green, driver, rider, hose, ladders, c. 1920s, 6-3/4" long..	285	430	570

Kenton Overland Circus Cage Truck, 7-1/2" long, $2000

Kenton Runabout Auto, 1908, 6-1/2" long, $1400. Photo courtesy Christie's East

Kenton Touring Car, No. 1923, 9" long, $1300. Photo courtesy Bill Bertoia Auctions

Kenton (Continued)	C6	C8	C10
Ice Truck, tongs and glass ice, 7-1/2" long	1000	2000	3000
Ladder Truck, pressed-steel ladders, 16" long	500	850	1100
Ladder Truck, 17-1/4" long	750	1200	1700
Ladder Truck, cast iron, approx. 7-1/2" long	300	450	600
Overland Circus, w/lion, 9" long	800	1300	2000
Overland Circus Cage Truck, w/driver, 7-1/2" long	800	1300	2000
Patrol Wagon, marked "Patrol" on side, w/driver and three fireman, c. 1920s-30s, 9" long	650	1100	1600
Pickwick Nite Coach, cast iron, 14" long	1500	2500	3800
Racer, cast iron, early, 9" long	600	1000	1400
Red Devil, w/driver, 6" long	200	300	400
Road Grader, cast iron, nickel-plated movable blade, rubber tires, 7-1/2" long	212	318	425
Road Roller, "Galion Master," 7" long	150	225	300

Kenton (Continued)	C6	C8	C10
Roadster, driver, c. 1908, 6" long	300	450	600
Runabout Auto, 1900, 5" long	170	255	340
Runabout Auto, cast iron, w/driver, 1908, 6-1/2" long	700	1050	1400
Sedan, rubber tires, take-apart body, late 1930s, 7" long	1200	2000	2800
Sprinkler Truck, early, 8"	425	638	850
Stake Truck, "Speed," c. 1927, 5-1/2" long	410	615	825
Stake Truck, "Speed," 9/1/8" long	450	850	1250
Steam Roller, "Galion Master," 6-1/2" long	225	340	450
Steam Shovel, Marion, 7-1/4"	600	900	1200
Touring Car, open, driver and passenger, 8-1/2" long	650	975	1300
Touring Car, No. 1923, open, w/driver and passenger, 9" long	650	975	1300
Tow Auto, 1920s, 9-1/2" long	1100	1800	2700
Yellow Cab, 1950s, 6-3/8" long	470	705	940

Keystone

Keystone of Boston had an odd assortment of products—movie projectors, steel trucks, wooden boats and pressed-wood forts and garages. Founded in 1922 or 1923 by Chester Rimmer and Arthur Jackson, it was first located in a small shop in Malden, Massachusetts under the name Jacrim, using parts of partners' last names. Rimmer retired in 1958 and sold out to various companies. The address in Boston was 288 A Street.

	C6	C8	C10
No. 41 Dump Truck, 26-1/2" long	500	750	1100
No. 43 American Railway Express, 26" long	1000	1700	2500
No. 44 Truck Loader, 17-3/4" high	500	800	1100

Kenton Stake Truck, 9-1/8" long, $1250. Photo courtesy Bill Bertoia Auctions

Keystone Dump Truck, No. 41, 26-1/2" long, $1100.
Photo courtesy Joe and Sharon Freed

Keystone American Railway Express, No. 43, 26"
long, $2500. Photo courtesy Joe and Sharon Freed

Keystone (Continued)

	C6	C8	C10
No. 45 U.S. Mail Truck, 26" long	900	1450	2100
No. 46 Steam Shovel, 26" long when arm is extended	425	650	800
No. 47 Steam Shovel, 34-1/2" long when arm is extended	250	375	500
No. 48 U.S. Army Truck, 26" long	500	800	1200
No. 49 Fire Truck, 27-1/2" long	700	1000	2100
No. 51 Police Patrol, 27-1/2" long	800	1400	1900
No. 52 Fire Truck, 27-1/2" long	645	1000	1300
No. 53 Sprinkler Truck, tank 12" long	1000	1600	2400

Keystone Fire Truck, No. 49, 27-1/2" long, $2100.
Photo courtesy Joe and Sharon Freed

Keystone Moving Van, No. 58, 26" long, $1850.
Photo courtesy Mapes Auctioneers and Appraisers

Keystone (Continued)

	C6	C8	C10
No. 54 Koaster Truck, w/skids, hoist cable, windlass, 26" long when skids retracted	800	1300	1800
No. 55 Koaster Truckw/o skids and windlass,	500	720	1000
No. 56 Water Pump Tower, 29" long	700	1100	1600
No. 57 Chemical Pump Engine, 27-1/2" long	1000	1550	2100
No. 58 Moving Van, 26" long	750	1300	1850
No. 60 Riding Steam Roller	300	450	600
No. 62 Hydraulic Dump Truck, 26" long	500	800	1100
No. 73 military, Ambulance, 27" long	800	1400	1950
No. 78 Wrecking Car, 27" long	850	1400	1950
No. 79 Aerial Ladder, 30-1/2" long	700	1100	1550

Kilgore

Kilgore, of Westerville, Ohio, appears to have begun toy making in the 1920s. Its toys were cast iron and low priced, with cap pistols its most popular line. But it also did well with a number of attractive trucks, fire engines and cars, as well as scattered aircraft and ships. Some subsidiary manufacturing was done in Lancaster, Pennsylvania and Canada. In 1937, Kilgore began making plastic cars, trucks, planes and buses, and later added plastic cap pistols, placing it among the first companies to produce plastic toys. Kilgore remained in business until 1978.

	C6	C8	C10
Auto, "LF 1300A," w/driver	180	270	360
Bus, plastic, advertised in 1937, 4" long	20	25	30
Convertible, w/rumble seat, w/driver, early 1930s, 7" long	160	240	320

Kilgore (Continued)

	C6	C8	C10
Coupe, plastic, streamlined, advertised in 1937, 4" long	25	35	45
Double-Decker Bus, c. 1930, 6" long	450	675	900
Dump Truck, cast iron, c. 1934, 5-3/4" long	160	240	320
Dump Truck, 1930s, 7" long	175	265	350
Dump Truck, cast iron, c. 1934, 8-1/2" long	450	675	900
Fire Chief Sedan, plastic, advertised in 1937, 4" long	25	35	45
Fire Truck, w/ladders, 1929, 6-3/4" long	190	285	375
Motorcycle, single rider, 4"	115	175	250
Motorcycle, "Special Delivery," 4-1/4" long	150	225	350
Police Car, plastic, 1937, 4"	25	35	45
Pontiac, cast iron, 1930, 10"	1200	1800	2700
Roadster, driver, rumble seat, 6" long	250	375	500
Roadster, Pierce-Arrow, take-apart body, 6-1/8" long	250	375	500
Sedan, 3-1/4" long	70	100	150
Sedan, Packard Luxury, take-apart body, 8-1/4" long	800	1400	1600
Stutz Roadster, thirteen parts	1200	1800	2700
Taxi, plastic, 4" long	25	35	45
Truck, plastic, "Express," advertised in 1937, 4" long	25	35	45
Truck, "Toy Town Delivery," 6-1/8" long	445	668	890
Truck, "Arctic Ice Cream Truck," 8" long	800	1300	1800

Kingsbury Cannon Truck, c. 1939, 15" long, $275

Kilgore (Continued)

	C6	C8	C10
Truck, "Arctic Ice Cream Truck," 9" long	500	750	1000

Kingsbury

Kingsbury had its origins in 1886 in Keene, New Hampshire. Its owner was Harry T. Kingsbury, who bought the Wilkins Toy Co., apparently not phasing out that firm's name until 1919. Steel and spring motors characterized Kingsbury's toys, with cars, fire engines, farm equipment and racing cars its primary output. Kingsbury is still in business, but gave up toy production in 1942.

	C6	C8	C10
Aerial Ladder Truck, presed steel, wind-up, ladder rises automatically to height of 38" when the truck runs into any obstruction, fireman on ladder climbs up and down by turning crank at base of ladder, c. 1905	450	700	1000
Aerial Ladder Truck, pressed steel, wind-up, ladder rises automatically to height of 38" when the truck runs into any obstruction, fireman on ladder climbs up and down by turning crank at base of ladder, c. 1941, 24" long	250	375	625
Airflow, pressed steel, rubber tires, c. 1934, 14" long	310	465	620
Airflow, clockwork, 14" long	500	750	1060
Auto, steel, wind-up, very early, 9-3/4" long	325	525	750
Bluebird Racer, 18" long	1000	1500	2100
Brougham Sedan, pressed steel, wind-up, 13" long	1100	1700	2425
Bus, pressed steel, 18" long	400	590	800
Cannon Truck, very early, clockwork, 11" long	225	325	450
Cannon Truck, wind-up, c. 1939, 15" long	125	190	275
Car, wind-up, curved dash, driver, 9" long	225	340	450
DeSoto, pressed steel, wind-up, c. 1938, 14-1/2" long	225	350	450
Dump Truck, tin, w/driver, 10" long	450	675	900
Dump Truck, clockwork, early 1930s, 16" long	350	525	700
Fire Chief Coupe, 1930s, 14" long	325	450	675

Kingsbury Wrecker, late 1920s, 14" long, $950.
Photo courtesy John Taylor

Kingsbury (Continued)

	C6	C8	C10
Fire Pumper, clockwork iron and steel, clockwork, very early, 11" long	365	550	750
Fire Pumper, 1920s, 23" long	600	800	1200
Ford Sedan & House Trailer, pressed steel, 1937, 23" long	450	675	900
Golden Arrow Racer, pressed steel wind-up, 20" long	600	1000	1375
Greyhound Bus, wind-up, 18" long	275	400	550
Ladder Truck, No. 225, pressed steel, wind-up, 1930s, 15" long	275	375	475
Ladder Truck, steel, driver, 22" long	200	300	400
Ladder Truck, c. 1930, 35" long	1200	2100	3100
Ladder Wagon Fire Truck, tin, rubber tires, 23-1/2" long	165	250	330
Lincoln Zephyr and Travel Trailer, 1936, 22-1/2" long	325	500	700
Phaeton Auto, rubber slip tires, 1900, 9-1/2" long	1400	2700	3500
Rack Truck, pressed steel, wind-up, 16" long	350	525	700
Roadster, No. 242, electric headlights, spring motor, luggage rack, 13" long	375	565	750
Sunbeam Racer, sheetmetal, red w/rubber tires on steel wheels, clockwork motor, 19" long	800	1300	1725
Truck, tin, w/C cap, 10" long	175	265	350
Truck with Crane, 1930s, 20" long	175	300	500
Wrecker, pressed steel, wind-up, 13" long	1000	1600	2300
Wrecker, pressed steel, wind-up, late 1920s, 14" long	550	750	950

Lansing Slik-Toys

Lansing Slik-Toys were made in Lansing, Iowa, and sometimes bear the name "Kipp," in addition to the "Lansing" and "Slik-Toy" trademarks. Most Slik-Toys are made of aluminum in a single casting, but some were made of hard plastic. It seems that all Slik-Toys have a four-digit number beginning with "9." If a toy bears such a number, even if it has no other markings, it is almost surely a Slik-Toy.

Contributor: Dave Leopard, 2507 Feather Run Trail, West Columbia, SC 29169-4915.

	C6	C8	C10
Fire Truck, No. 9700, 3-1/2" long	25	35	45
Fire Truck, No. 9706, plastic, 4" long	20	25	30
Fire Truck, No. 9606, 6" long	20	30	40
Metro Van, No. 9618, 5" long	25	30	40
Open Stake Truck, No. 9602, 7" long	23	35	50
Pickup Truck, No. 9703, plastic, 4" long	20	25	35
Pickup Truck, No. 9605, 6" long	20	30	40
Pickup Truck, No. 9601, 7" long	25	35	50
Roadster, No. 9701, 3-1/2" long	25	35	45
Sedan, No. 9702, plastic, 1949 Buick, 4" long	20	25	35
Sedan, No. 9604, four-door, 6" long	20	30	40
Sedan, No. 9600, fastback, 7" long	30	45	60
Sedan, No. 9600, fastback, taxi version, 7" long	30	45	60
Stake Truck, No. 9616, 6" long	25	30	40
Stakebody Truck, No. 9500, 11" long	45	60	75
Station Wagon, No. 9704, plastic, 4" long	20	25	35
Tank Truck, No. 9705, plastic, 4" long	20	25	35
Tank Truck, No. 9607, 6" long	20	30	40
Tank Truck, No. 9603, 7" long	40	50	60
Tractor/Trailer Rig, No. 9613, flatbed trailer, 8" long	25	35	50
Tractor/Trailer Rig, No. 9611, grain trailer, 8" long	25	35	50
Tractor/Trailer Rig, log trailer, 8" long	25	35	50
Tractor/Trailer Rig, No. 9610, milk tanker, 8" long	30	40	55
Wrecker, No. 9617, 5" long	20	25	35

Lincoln White Metal Works

This company, located in Lincoln, Nebraska, was formed by Clayton E. Stevenson, the manufacturer of many high-quality slush-mold vehicles. Stevenson made toys out of his home for many years and, as a salesman for Western Diecasting Co., even sold molds to Kansas Toy & Novelty company, Tip Top Toy Co. and others. His specialty was the three-piece mold, there is even some speculation that he was the inventor of this complex mold.

Stevenson's was a remarkably long toy-making career, about fifteen years, through the Great Depression. An auto mechanic, Stevenson was born in 1896 and raised in Axtell, Kansas. He and his wife, Esther, moved to Lincoln in 1931 where they began selling toys in his name. His new business grew rapidly, and he made upwards of 800,000 toys in three months. As his business grew, he moved to a larger facility at 2204 Y Street and in 1935 the company address was listed as 3433 J Street.

Lincoln White Metal Works toys were sold across the United States at Woolworth, Kress, Kresge and Schwartz Paper Co. stores, some were even abroad.

After nine years of production, the factory was sold in 1940 due to shortages of lead and rubber and the rising costs of labor. It is not certain who aquired the remaing molds and inventory, although many indications point to Ralstoy.

A variety of toys were made, including airplanes, midget racers, larger speed sedans, small coupes, tri-motor plane models and miniature sawmills. Most range in size from three-to-seven-inches in length. Stevenson designed his molds using photographs from magazines as guides. The midget racer was based on a Miller special, and the sedan is a replica of the front-drive Cord. A Nash was the basis for Lincoln White Metal's coupe.

Lincoln White Metal toys had a few distinct characteristics—early toys had metal wheels and tin propellers with patterned bottom-pans; later toys had rubber wheels. These distinctions can assist collectors in identifying their toys.

The following list is incomplete because of the rarity of these cars.

Contributors: Fred Maxwell, 4722 N. 33 St., Arlington, VA 22207.

Perry R. Eichor, 703 North Almond Drive, Simpsonville, SC, 29681

Lincoln White Metal Works	C6	C8	C10
Brougham, Graham?, vertical vee-grille, SM, four open windows, T, from three-piece mold, 3-1/2" long (LWV21)	40	60	80
Bus, Overland, hood cap, ornament or Motormeter, horizontal grille pattern, ten open windows, 3-1/2" long (LWV27)	25	40	65
Coupe, slanted hood, rearmount hub for rubber tire, slanted grille (see Tootsie Graham), 4-1/2" long (LWV19)	40	60	80
Fire Engine, steam pumper, two-man crew, hose real compartment, hood cap, ornament or Motormeter, 3-1/4" long (LWV12)	25	50	75
Fire Engine Pumper, w/fireman on rear step, Graham-like grille, fenders faired bumper to bumper, patterned pan, sides embossed "Patrol 79," marked "Made in USA," 3-3/4" long (LWV9)	75	100	125
Railcar, Streamline, marked "Union Pacific" with shield symbol, two open windows in cab, eighteen open windows in passenger section, hidden rubber wheels, patterned pan, marked "Made in USA," 4-1/2" long	80	110	140
Sedan, DeSoto (?), two-door, hood cap, ornament or Motometer, horizontal grille pattern, four open windows, sreamlined airflow rear (LWV35)	40	60	80

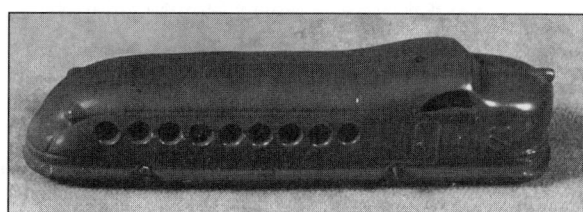

Lincoln White Metal Works Railcar, Streamline, 4-1/2" long, $140. Photo courtesy Perry Eichor

Lincoln White Metal Works Fire Engine Pumper, 3-3/4" long, $125. Photo courtesy Perry Eichor

Lincoln White Metal Works Sedan, $80. Photo courtesy Bob Ackerly

Lincoln White Metal Works Speed Car, 4" long, $110. Photo courtesy John Taylor

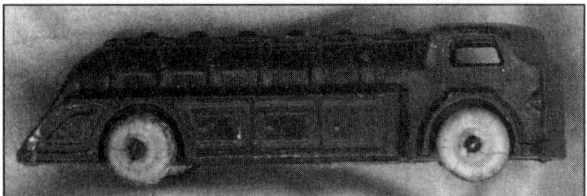

Lincoln White Metal Works Tanker Truck, 3-3/4" long, $100. Photo courtesy Fred Maxwell

Lincoln White Metal Works Wrekcer, 3-1/2" long, $80. Photo courtesy Perry Eichor

Lincoln White Metal Works

	C8	C10
Sedan, Pierce-Arrow Silver Arrow, vertical vee-grille, headlamps and front fenders faired, six open windows, divided windshield, plain pan, 3-1/2" long (LWV5) 40	60	80
Speed Car, Bluebird record car, driver, V-8 engine w/intake ports, triangular fin w/wing design, 4" long (LWV3) 55	85	110
Speed Car, A V-12 version of Bluebird w/triangular fin, Lincoln?, 4-5/8" long (LWV4) 60	90	120
Stake Truck, slanted grille w/horizontal patten, divided windshield, two open windows, open stakes, rounded pan, 3-1/2" long (LWV22) 20	30	40
Tanker Truck, COE, two open windows, eight companrtments, patterned pan, marked "Made in the USA," 3-3/4" long (LWV10) 60	80	100
Wrecker, high style w/chopped top, Graham-like grille, two open windows, fenders faired bumper to bumper, solid crane w/grid pattern marked "Made in the USA," 3-1/2" long (LWV8) 40	60	80

Lindstrom

The Lindstrom Tool & Toy Company made wind-up toys of light pressed steel, as well as tin. Located in Bridgeport, Connecticut, and Lindstrom began making toy cars about 1913. It seems to have ceased production in the 1940s.

	C6	C8	C10
Cabin Racer	12	18	25
Lumber Truck, No. 160, tin, steerable front wheels, w/driver, 10" long	125	187	250
Racer, 2-3/4" long	10	15	20
Steam Roller, No. 181, mechanical, 12" long	50	75	100

Manoil

Manoil was owned by two brothers, Jack and Maurice Manoil. Its sole sculptor was Walter Baetz, the man responsible for Manoil's seven early vehicles, which were Manoil's first toys, debuting in 1934. The firm, originally located in Manhattan, then Brooklyn, and finally in Waverly, New York, closed down about 1955.

	C6	C8	C10
Armored Car with Anti-Aircraft Gun	27	41	55
Armored Car with Anti-Tank Gun	22	33	45
Armored Car with Siren, siren cast separately	25	38	50
Armored Car with Siren, siren cast w/vehicle	34	51	68
Chemical Truck	11	16	23
Coupe, futuristic	70	100	135
Five Barrel Gun on Wheels	12	18	25
Gasoline Truck	10	15	20
Large Shell on Truck	11	16	22
Pontoon on Wheels	22	33	45
Roadster, futuristic, Pat. No. 95791	54	80	100

Manoil (Continued)

	C6	C8	C10
Rocket, futuristic bus-like vehicle, Pat. No. 95793	60	90	120
Sedan, futuristic	50	75	100
Sedan, futuristic	60	85	115
Sedan, futuristic, Pat. No. 95792	45	68	98
Shell Carrier with Soldier on Shell Box	10	15	20
Shell Carrier with Soldier on Shell Box, has loop	12	18	24
Soup Kitchen, large number	9	15	20
Soup Kitchen, small number	9	13	18
Tank11		16	22
Torpedo on Wheels	10	15	20

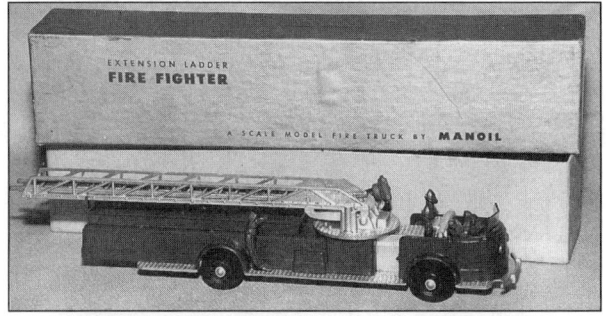

Manoil Aerial Ladder with box (top), $400; Ariel ladder with ladder extended (bottom), (Post-War Vehicles), $400. Photos courtesy Old Toy Soldier Magazine

Manoil (Continued)

	C6	C8	C10
Water Wagon, large number	10	15	20
Wrecker, futuristic	80	120	160

Manoil Plastic Vehicles

	C6	C8	C10
Dump Cart	12	18	25
Pick-Up	12	18	25
Road Scraper	12	18	25
Roadster	12	18	25
Sedan	12	18	25
Towing Truck	12	18	25

Manoil Post-War Vehicles

	C6	C8	C10
Aerial Ladder	200	300	400
Bus	12	18	24
Commerical Truck	10	15	20
Convertible	10	15	20
Convertible, hard top	25	38	50
Fire Engine	18	28	38
Oil Tanker	13	20	27
Pumper	200	300	400
Ranch Wagon	10	15	20
Roadster, vertical radiator	50	75	100
Roadster, horizontal radiator	27	41	54
Sedan	10	15	20
Sedan	31	46	62
Sport Car	10	15	20
Towing Truck	10	15	20

Marx

By the 1950s, Louis Marx Toy Co. was the largest manufacturer of toys in the world—six large factories in the United States and ownership of interest in factories in seven other countries.

Marx, born in Brooklyn in 1896, was working for the so-called toy king Ferdinand Strauss when he was in his teens. By the age of twenty, his energy and enterprise had made him a director of that company. A falling out with Strauss persuaded him to go into business for himself. In 1921, he and his brother began making their own toys, including some adaptations of items by the now-defunct Strauss. Marx's watchword seems to have been quality at the lowest possible price, and he was such a favorite with toy buyers that he had virtually no need for salesmen or advertising.

Marx made virtually every type of toy, with the exception of dolls. In April 1972, he sold his company to the Quaker Oats Company, who, in 1976, sold it to Europe's largest toy manufacturer, Dunbee-Combex-Marx. The company went into bankruptcy in 1980. Marx died in 1982, at the age of 85.

In 1982, American Plastics bought much of the Marx assets; in 1990, it began producing toys from the original molds. Marx eventually ended up in the hands Jay Horowitz, the current president. Horowitz produces Marx action figures based on the original molds and has licensed Jim and Debby Flynn to produce new tin-lithographed trains. For more information on Marx trains, see *O'Brien's Collecting Toy Trains.*

Contributors: Michael W. Curran, Heritage America Company, P.O. Box 545, Hampton, IL 61256, 309-496-9426.

John Taylor, P.O. Box 63, Nolensville, TN 37135-0063.

Marx Brake Kar, $210. Photo courtesy Continental Hobby House

Marx Bus, 1940, 4-1/2" long, $180. Photo courtesy Richard MacNary

Marx Toy City Sanitation Dept. Help Keep Your City Clean Truck Train, c. 1940, 12-3/4" long, $350. Photo courtesy Calvin L. Chaussee

Marx Toy Co.	C6	C8	C10
Air Force Truck, canvas top, 20"	105	158	210
Air Force Truck, No. 3290, "Air Defense Group," ride'm toy, 32"	125	188	250
Ambulance, "M.D. War Dept.," 1930s	475	715	1000
Ambulance, No. 8500, 1930s, 14" long	200	325	500
Ambulance, No. 8600, 1930s, 14" long	240	360	480
American Railroad Express Agency Inc., Truck Train, open cab, early 1930s, 7" long	150	200	250
American Truck Co. Moving Truck, No. 65, friction	65	98	130
Army Corps of Engineers, canvas top, 20" long	125	190	250
Army Jeep with Searchlight Trailer, steel	100	150	250
Arrow Special Delivery Truck, 1940s, 13" long	125	175	225
Auto Transport, w/two tin litho cars, 1950s, 34" long	175	205	350
Brake Kar, w/screeching noise	105	157	210
Bud Bowman's Milk Express Truck	175	250	350
Bus, 1940, 4-1/2" long	90	135	180
Candy Truck, plastic, "Fanny Farmer"	100	150	200
Cannon Truck, plastic, "Big Shot," fires cap-loaded missile, 22" long	75	112	150
Car Carrier, No. T-50447B, "Auto Transwalk," 1930s truck w/three cars	200	300	400
Car Carrier, Big Boss, 42" long	90	135	180
Carousel Truck, marked "1967," 8" long	50	75	100
Chief-Fire Dept. No. 1, friction drive, c. 1948	90	135	180
City Sanitation Dept. Help Keep Your City Clean Truck Train, c. 1940, 12-3/4" long	150	250	350
Cloverdale Farms Milk Truck, 11-1/2" long	100	150	200
Coal Truck, electric motor and lights, early	280	420	565
Coast to Coast Delivery Truck, 1930s, 6" long	75	100	150

Marx Toy Coca-Cola Truck, late 1940s to early 1950s, 20" long, $450

Marx Toy Coca-Cola Truck, 10-1/2" long, $350. Photo courtesy Terry Sells

Marx Toy Co. (Continued)

	C6	C8	C10
Coca-Cola Truck, plastic, 10-1/2" long	175	263	350
Coca-Cola Truck, stamped steel, Sprite decal, late 1940s to early 1950s, 20" long	185	250	450
Coca-Cola Truck, tin, Linemar, friction, 3" long	50	75	100
Coca-Cola Truck Shelf Sidecases, shelf sidecase, 1950s	200	300	450
Corvette Coupe, plastic, friction, 8"	45	65	85
Crane, Lumar Contractors	120	180	240
Cunningham Drug Stores Truck, plastic, scarce, 1950s	30	45	75
Curtiss Candy Truck, plastic	10	20	30
Dairy Stake Truck, No. E-271, three-color, c. 1941	100	150	200
Delivery Truck, Pet Shop, 1950s, 10"	80	120	160
Deluxe Coupe, wind-up, electric lights, 15" long	450	650	950
Deluxe Delivery Truck	100	175	225
Deluxe Delivery Truck, 13" long	100	175	225
Dump Truck, No. 962, Lumar Contractors	480	720	960
Dump Truck, No. 1084	30	45	60
Dump Truck, No. T751, two-color, c. 1930s	85	130	175
Dump Truck, No. 695B, 17" long	120	180	240

Marx Toy Coca-Cola Truck Shelf Sidecases, 1950s, $450. Photo courtesy Don Hultzman

Marx Toy Dump Truck, c. 1940, 4-1/2" long, $140. Photo courtesy Bob Smith

Marx Toy Easter Dump Truck, late 1930s, 6" long, $300. Photo courtesy John Taylor

Marx Toy Co. (Continued)

	C6	C8	C10
Dump Truck, c. 1940, 4-1/2" long	50	95	140
Easter Dump Truck, late 1930s, 6" long	150	225	300
Easter Stake Truck, 1938, 10-1/2" long	190	275	380
Easter Stake Truck, w/coal chute, 1940, 7" long	162	243	325
Electrically Lighted Truck and Trailer Set Truck and Trailer, No. T-5715, c. 1930s, 15"	150	225	300
Falcon, w/plastic bubble top, black rubber tires	145	218	290
Fix-It Jaguar, plastic, 12" long	75	100	150
Gang Buster Car, No. 7200, 1930s, 14" long	550	825	1100

Marx Toy Ice Truck, $525. Photo courtesy Terry Sells

Marx Toy Magnetic Crane Truck, 1940s, 8-1/2" long, $850. Photo courtesy Bob Smith

Marx Toy Siren Police Car, No. 8300, 1930s, 14" long, $400

Marx Toy Siren Fire Chief, c. 1930, 15" long, $750

Marx Toy Co. (Continued)	C6	C8	C10
Gold Star Transfer Company Trailer Truck	150	225	325
Grader, Lumar Power	35	52	70
Gravel Truck, 13" long	115	175	225
Gravel Truck, 9" long	70	110	140
High-Boy Climbing Tractor, No. 950, 10-1/2" long	100	150	200
Hi-Way Express Truck	125	200	300
Ice Truck, w/tongs and ice	275	400	525
Lazy-Day Dairy Farm Truck and Trailer, 22" long	115	175	230
Lifesavers Truck, plastic, 9-1/2" long	75	100	150
Lonesome Pine Trailer and Convertible Sedan, 1930s, 13" long	350	525	700
Lumar Scoop-A-Dump	150	225	300
Machinery Moving Truck, No. 1016	275	400	550
Magnetic Crane Truck, 1940s, 8-1/2" long	425	640	850

Marx Toy Co. (Continued)	C6	C8	C10
Mammoth Truck Train, No. T-50-12345, truck w/five trailers, c. 1930s	175	262	350
Marx Doughboy Tank, World War II pot helmet, c. 1950	130	195	260
Mechanical Coupe, tin, wind-up, 1933, 8" long	275	400	575
Merchants Transfer Truck, tin, wind-up, 1929, 10" long	275	400	700
Mystery Taxi, press down to operate, c. 1930s	100	150	275
Navy Jeep, No. 1078	65	98	130
Navy Jeep with Searchlight Trailer	100	150	200
Nutty Mad Cars, friction, price for each, c. 1965, 4" long	150	225	300
Pepsi-Cola Truck, 1950s, 11" long	50	125	200
Pickup Truck, electric lights, 11" long	100	175	225
Power Grader, No. 1759, black or white wheels, 17-1/2" long	40	60	80
Pure Milk Dairy Truck, pressed steel, w/glass bottles, tin wheels, c. 1940	100	150	200
REA Express Truck, No. 1021	325	488	650
Roadster, nickel-plated tin, convertible, 1930s, 11" long	200	300	400
Rocker Dump, No. 1752, 17-1/2"	110	165	220

Marx Toy Tricky Taxi, 4-1/2", $160

Marx Toy U.S. Mail Truck, 14" long, $250

Marx Toy Co. (Continued)	C6	C8	C10
Sand & Gravel Dump Truck, 1940s, 10" long	60	90	120
Siren Fire Chief, "F.D. 1st. Batt.," c. 1930, 15" long	375	550	750
Siren Police Car, No. 8300, 1930s, 14" long	200	300	400
Sparkling Hot Rod Racer, plastic, wind-up, 1950s, 8" long	40	60	75
Sports Coupe, 1930s, 15" long	200	300	400
Stake Truck, c. 1941, 15" long	100	125	175
Steam Shovel, Lumar Contractors	115	200	275
Trailer and Convertible Sedan, Lonesome Pine, 1930s, 19" long	465	700	950
Tricky Taxi, friction, 4-1/2"	75	120	160
Truck, steel, Sinclair Fuel	200	325	475
Truck, No. 4488, Guided Missile	220	330	440
Truck, Grocery, 1950s, 14-1/2"	62	93	125
U.S. Army Truck with Searchlight Trailer, 1950s, 27" total length	150	200	300
U.S. Mail Truck, 14" long	125	188	250
U.S. Navy Jeep with Searchlight Trailer, 1950s, 21" total length	140	200	275
Willys Jeep, steel, hood opens, windshield folds down, c. 1938, 12"	90	135	180
Willys Jeep and Trailer, c. 1940s	133	200	265

Marx Toy Co. (Continued)	C6	C8	C10
Willys Jeepster, plastic, wind-up	75	112	150
Wrecker, "Cities Service," Linemar, 4-1/2"	65	100	130
Wrecker and Convertible, "Fix-All," set	125	188	250
Wrecker Truck, No. T-16, c. 1930s	150	225	300
Wrecker Truck, 1920s, 10" long	100	150	200

Matchbox

Matchbox Toys grew out of a company begun in 1947 by two Navy friends, Leslie Smith and Rodney Smith (no relation). Manufacturing toys was not even planned at this point. On June 19, 1947, the two partners combined portions of their first names, and the name Lesney was born. In 1948, Lesney Products produced their first toy, a 4-1/2-inch Aveling Barford Road Roller. Encouraged by the brisk sales, three other toys were produced that year—a 4-1/2-inch Caterpillar Bulldozer, a 3-1/8-inch Caterpillar Tractor and a 3-3/4-inch Cement Mixer. It was decided to package the toys in a matchbox-type box, and thereafter the toys would be known as Matchbox. Value on these rare early Lesney toys today is near $1,000.

These small vehicles quickly became very popular. These first small vehicles had metal wheels, but were shortly changed to plastic. These early wheels are known to collectors as regular wheels, not to be confused with the Superfast wheels that were introduced in 1969.

It is not uncommon to find slight color and style variations for the same vehicle. These variations were often due to paint or part shortages, and are now highly sought-after by collectors.

The year 1956 saw the introduction of the Models of Yesteryear line. The king-size line was first developed and marketed in 1957 and was known as Major Packs. Matchbox toys were first marketed in the United States in 1958; by the early 1960s, they became a household standard. The year 1993 marked the 40th anniversary of Matchbox toys, and these small vehicles are rapidly gaining popularity and value among collectors. Listed are all of the basic models and some important variations.

Contributor: Reid Covey, Box 2D Highmarket Rd., Constableville, NY 13325, e-mail: sullivan@north-net.org.

	C6	C8	C10
No. 01 Aveling Barford Road Roller, 1964	17	26	39

Matchbox (Continued)

	C6	C8	C10
No. 01 Diesel Road Roller, 1953	20	40	90
No. 01 Dodge Challenger, 1976	4	6	8
No. 01 Mercedes Benz Lorry, 1968	6	11	18
No. 01 Mod Rod, 1971	8	12	20
No. 02 Dumper, 1953	25	40	90
No. 02 Hot Rod Jeep, 1971	5	7	12
No. 02 Hovercraft, 1976	5	7	12
No. 02 Mercedes Trailer, 1968	5	10	15
No. 02 Muir-Hill Dumper, 1962	10	15	25
No. 03 Bedford Ton Tipper, 1961	10	15	20
No. 03 Cement Mixer, 1953	25	35	50
No. 03 Mercedes Benz Ambulance, 1968	7	15	20
No. 03 Monteverdi Hai, 1973	5	8	15
No. 03 Porsche Turbo, 1978	5	10	15
No. 04 '57 Chevy, 1981	5	10	15
No. 04 Gruesome Twosome, 1971	3	6	10
No. 04 Massey Harris Tractor, 1954	25	45	80
No. 04 Pontiac Firebird, 1976	5	10	15
No. 04 Stake Truck, 1967	10	20	30
No. 04 Triumph Motorcycle and Sidecar, 1959	25	45	80
No. 05 London Bus, 1954	20	30	65
No. 05 Lotus European Sports Car, 1969	10	20	25
No. 05 Seafire, 1976	3	7	10
No. 05 U.S. Mail Truck, 1981	5	10	15
No. 06 Euclid Ten-Wheel Quarry, 1964	20	30	50
No. 06 Ford Pickup, 1969	8	15	20
No. 06 Mercedes Tourer, 1974	5	8	12
No. 06 Quarry Truck, 1955	20	35	75

Matchbox (Continued)

	C6	C8	C10
No. 07 Ford Anglia, 1961	15	25	35
No. 07 Ford Refuse Truck, 1967	7	10	15
No. 07 Hairy Hustler, 1971	5	8	12
No. 07 Horse Drawn Milk Cart, 1955	25	40	80
No. 07 VW Golf, 1976	4	6	9
No. 08 Caterpillar Tractor, 1955	25	40	75
No. 08 De Tomaso Pantera, 1975	15	22	35
No. 08 Ford Mustang Fastback, 1966	10	15	25
No. 08 Wildcat Dragster, 1971	7	12	16
No. 09 Boat and Trailer, 1967	5	10	15
No. 09 Dennis Fire Engine, 1955	20	35	75
No. 09 Ford Escort RS2000, 1978	3	5	7
No. 09 Javelin, 1972	5	9	11
No. 09 Merryweather Marquis Fire Engine, 1959	20	25	35
No. 10 Mechanical Horse and Trailer, 1955	30	45	75
No. 10 Pipe Truck, 1967	10	15	20
No. 10 Piston Popper, 1973	5	10	15
No. 10 Plymouth "Gran Fury" Police Car, 1980	3	4	7
No. 10 Sugar Container Truck, 1961	25	35	75
No. 11 Car Transporter, 1977	5	8	10
No. 11 Flying Bug, 1972	5	10	15
No. 11 Jumbo Crane, Taylor, 1964	7	12	17
No. 11 Petrol Tanker, Esso decal, 1955	25	35	75

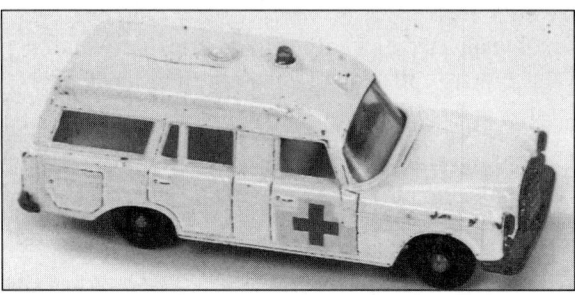

Matchbox No. 03 Mercedes Benz Ambulance, 1968, $20

Matchbox No. 09 Merryweather Marquis Fire Engine, 1959, $35. Photo courtesy Gary Linden

Matchbox No. 12 Land Rover, 1953, $40. Photo courtesy Gary Linden

Matchbox No. 14 Bedford Lomas Ambulance, $60. Photo courtesy Gary Linden

Matchbox (Continued)	C6	C8	C10
No. 11 Petrol Tanker, green body, no number on bottom	140	200	350
No. 11 Scaffolding Truck, Mercedes, 1969	10	15	25
No. 12 Big Bull, 1975	5	8	11
No. 12 Citroen CX, 1981	5	7	12
No. 12 Land Rover, 1953	15	25	40
No. 12 Safari Land Rover, 1965	11	18	30
No. 12 Setra Coach, 1971	7	10	15
No. 13 Baja Buggy, 1971	8	10	15
No. 13 Bedford Wreck Truck, 1955	25	35	65
No. 13 Dodge Wreck Truck, BP Label, yellow cab, green body, 1961	18	23	35
No. 13 Dodge Wreck Truck, green cab, yellow body (rare)	300	490	750
No. 13 Snorkel Fire Engine, 1977	4	5	6
No. 13 Thames Wreck Truck, MB Garages, 1959	10	25	50
No. 14 Bedford Lomas Ambulance	20	40	60
No. 14 Daimler Ambulance, 1955	15	25	40
No. 14 Iso Grifo Sports Car, 1968	5	10	15
No. 14 Mini Ha Ha, 1975	5	10	15
No. 15 Dennis Refuse Truck, 1963	15	20	30
No. 15 Fork Lift Truck, 1972	5	7	11
No. 15 Prime Mover, 1955	25	35	50
No. 15 Volkswagen 1500 Saloon, 1968	8	17	27
No. 16 Badger, 1974	5	8	13

Matchbox No. 15 Dennis Refuse Truck, 1963, $30. Photo courtesy Gary Linden

Matchbox (Continued)	C6	C8	C10
No. 16 Case Tractor Bulldozer, 1969	6	11	18
No. 16 Low-Loading Trailer, six wheels, 1955	15	20	40
No. 16 Low-Loading Trailer, eight wheels, 1955	20	25	45
No. 16 Pontiac, 1981	2	4	6
No. 16 Scammel Mountaineer Dump with Plow, 1961	15	25	35
No. 17 Austin Taxi, 1960	25	45	70
No. 17 Bedford Removal Van, 1955	35	65	110
No. 17 Eight-Wheel Tipper "Hoveringham," 1964	7	15	25

Matchbox (Continued)

	C6	C8	C10
No. 17 Horse Box "Ergomatic Cab," 1969 5	5	8	15
No. 17 Londoner, 1973 10	10	15	20
No. 18 Caterpillar Bulldozer, 1955 20	20	24	46
No. 18 Field Car, 1969 7	7	10	20
No. 18 Field Car, green plastic tires (rare) 55	55	100	165
No. 18 Hondarora, 1975 5	5	10	20
No. 19 Aston-Martin F.I., 1961 30	30	45	100
No. 19 Cement Truck, 1976 5	5	7	9
No. 19 Lotus Racing Car, 1965 6	6	8	15
No. 19 MG Midget Sports Car, 1955 25	25	45	75
No. 19 MGA Sports Car, 1959 30	30	50	100
No. 19 Road Dragster, 1971 4	4	6	10
No. 20 E.R.F. Lorry Truck, 1955 30	30	50	75
No. 20 Lamborghini Marzel, 1969 8	8	10	15
No. 20 Police Patrol, 1975 4	4	6	10
No. 20 Taxi Cab, Chevrolet Impala, 1965 15	15	25	35
No. 21 Commer Milk Truck, 1961 30	30	49	58
No. 21 Foden Concrete Truck, 1969 8	8	12	18
No. 21 Long Distance Coach "London to Glasgow," 1955 24	24	39	55
No. 21 Road Roller, 1973 6	6	8	14
No. 22 Blaze Buster, 1975 4	4	6	10
No. 22 Freeman Inter City Commuter, 1970 6	6	9	14
No. 22 Pontiac "Grand Prix" Sports Coupe, 1964 10	10	15	25

Matchbox (Continued)

	C6	C8	C10
No. 22 Vauxhall Cresta, 1955 35	35	45	55
No. 23 Atlas, 1975 5	5	7	12
No. 23 Caravan Trailer, 1956 10	10	15	20
No. 23 House Trailer Caravan, 1967 15	15	20	35
No. 23 Volkswagen Camper, 1970 5	5	10	15
No. 24 Diesel Shunter, 1979 3	3	5	7
No. 24 Excavator, 1956 15	15	20	30
No. 24 Rolls Royce Silver Shadow, 1967 5	5	15	25
No. 24 Team Matchbox, 1973 8	8	13	19
No. 25 B.P. Tanker, 1960 10	10	15	25
No. 25 Bedford Dunlop Van, 1956 20	20	30	55
No. 25 Flat Car & Container, 1979 3	3	5	7
No. 25 Ford Cortina G.T., 1968 5	5	10	15
No. 25 Mod Tractor, 1972 10	10	15	20
No. 25 Volkswagen 1200 Sedan, 1958 40	40	60	100
No. 26 Big Banger, 1972 4	4	6	9
No. 26 GMC Tipper Truck, 1968 5	5	10	15
No. 26 Ready Mix Concrete Truck, 1956 18	18	26	36
No. 26 Site Dumper, 1976 3	3	5	8
No. 27 Bedford Low-Loader, 1956 30	30	40	75
No. 27 Bedford Low-Loader, metal wheels (rare) 200	200	300	415
No. 27 Cadillac Sedan, 1960 35	35	45	75
No. 27 Lamborghini Countach, 1974 5	5	7	10

Matchbox No. 19 MG Midget Sports Car, 1955, $75. Photo courtesy Gary Linden

Matchbox No. 28 Bedford Compressor Truck, 1956, $50. Photo courtesy Gary Linden

Matchbox No. 32 Jaguar XK 140 Coupe, 1956, $75

Matchbox No. 36 Lambretta and Sidecar, 1960, $75

Matchbox No. 36 Opel Diplomant, 1966, $20

Matchbox (Continued)	C6	C8	C10
No. 30 Ford Perfect with Towbar, 1956	30	42	55
No. 30 German Crane Truck, 1961	25	39	50
No. 30 Swamp Rat, 1977	4	6	8
No. 31 Caravan, 1977	4	6	8
No. 31 Ford Customline Station Wagon, 1956	25	40	90
No. 31 Ford Fairlane Station Wagon, 1959	25	40	90
No. 31 Lincoln Continental, 1964	10	15	20
No. 31 Volks Dragon, 1971	5	7	10
No. 32 Excavator, 1981	10	15	25
No. 32 Jaguar XK 140 Coupe, 1956	25	40	75
No. 32 Leyland Tanker, 1968	16	24	34
No. 33 Datsun 126X, 1973	5	8	12
No. 33 Ford Zephyr 6 MKIII, 1963	20	25	40
No. 33 Ford Zodiac MKII, 1956	25	35	50
No. 33 Lamborghini Muira P400, 1969	10	15	25
No. 33 Police Motorcyclist, 1977	4	6	8
No. 34 Chevy Pro Stocker, 1981	2	4	6
No. 34 Formula 1 Racing Car, 1971	7	11	15
No. 34 Vantastic, 1976	4	7	15
No. 34 Volkswagen Camper, 1961	14	21	35
No. 34 Volkswagen Microvan Matchbox Express, 1956	30	44	75
No. 35 Fandango, 1975	5	7	10
No. 35 Marschall Horse Box, 1956	40	65	90
No. 35 Merryweather Marquis Fire Engine, 1970	5	10	14
No. 35 Sno-Trac Tractor, 1961	15	20	35
No. 36 Austin A50, w/towbar, 1956	20	30	40
No. 36 Formula 5000, 1975	4	6	8
No. 36 Hot Rod Draguar, 1971	5	8	20

Matchbox (Continued)	C6	C8	C10
No. 27 Mercedes Benz 230SL, 1965	10	15	22
No. 28 Bedford Compressor Truck, 1956	20	35	50
No. 28 Lincoln Continental, 1980	10	15	20
No. 28 Mack Dump Truck, 1968	5	10	15
No. 28 Mack Ten Jaguar, 1964	35	40	75
No. 28 Stoat, 1974	5	10	20
No. 28 Thames Compressor Truck, 1959	20	30	60
No. 29 Austin A55 Cambridge, 1961	20	30	50
No. 29 Bedford Milk Delivery Van, 1956	20	30	50
No. 29 Fire Pumper Truck, 1965	10	20	30
No. 29 Racing Mini, 1971	5	10	15
No. 29 Shovel Nose Tractor, 1976	5	10	15
No. 30 Articulated Truck, 1981	4	6	8
No. 30 Beach Buggy, 1971	5	10	15
No. 30 Favin Crane, eight-wheel, 1965	11	16	25

Matchbox (Continued)

	C6	C8	C10
No. 36 Lambretta and Sidecar, 1960.....	30	55	75
No. 36 Opel Diplomant, 1966	8	13	20
No. 36 Refuse Truck, 1981	3	5	8
No. 37 Cattle Truck, Dodge, 1967	10	15	20
No. 37 Coca-Cola Truck, 1956	45	62	100
No. 37 Skip Truck, 1976	4	6	8
No. 37 Soopa Coopa, 1973.....................	5	7	11
No. 38 Armored Jeep, 1976	5	10	15
No. 38 Camper, 1981	3	5	7
No. 38 Darrier Refuse Collector	25	40	75
No. 38 Honda Motorcycle with Trailer, 1968.......................................	11	16	22
No. 38 Stingeroo, 1973	6	8	11
No. 38 Vauxhall Estate, 1963................	11	20	27
No. 39 Clipper, 1973	6	8	12
No. 39 Ford Zodiac Convertible, 1956	30	40	95
No. 39 Pontiac Convertible, 1962	35	51	65

Matchbox No. 38 Darrier Refuse Collector, $75. Photo courtesy Gary Linden

Matchbox No. 37 Coca-Cola Truck, 1956, $100

Matchbox (Continued)

	C6	C8	C10
No. 39 Rolls-Royce Silver Shadow MKII..	4	6	8
No. 40 Bedford Seven-Ton Tipper, 1956..	25	35	65
No. 40 Guildsman, 1971.........................	5	8	12
No. 40 Hay Trailer, 1967........................	4	8	12
No. 40 Horse Box, 1977	4	6	8
No. 40 Leyland "Royal Tiger" Coach/Long Distance, 1961	11	18	26
No. 41 "D" Type Jaguar Racing Car, 1956...	80	115	150
No. 41 Ambulance, 1978........................	4	6	8
No. 41 Ford G.T. 40, Sports Racer, 1965...	14	21	30
No. 41 Siva Spyder, 1972.......................	5	10	15
No. 42 Bedford "Evening News" Van, 1956...	30	45	60
No. 42 Container Truck, 1977	4	6	8
No. 42 Iron Fairy Crane, 1969................	7	11	18
No. 42 Iron Fairy Crane, spoke wheels, 1970......................................	30	45	60
No. 42 Studebaker Lark Wagonaire, 1965...	10	20	30
No. 42 Tyre Fryer, 1972	5	10	15
No. 43 Aveling-Barford Shovel, 1962...	10	20	30
No. 43 Dragon Wheels, 1972	5	7	10
No. 43 Hillman Minx, 1957	30	45	75
No. 43 Pony Trailer, 1968	10	15	20
No. 43 Steam Loco, 1978	4	6	8
No. 44 Boss Mustang, 1972	3	5	8
No. 44 Passenger Coach, 1978	3	5	7
No. 44 Refrigerator Truck, GMC, 1967...	10	15	20
No. 44 Rolls-Royce Silver Cloud, 1957...	20	30	50
No. 45 BMW, 1976	5	8	11
No. 45 Ford Corsair with Green Boat, 1959...	11	15	20
No. 45 Ford Group Six, 1970	6	9	11
No. 45 Vauxhall Victor, 1957	15	25	40
No. 46 Mercedes-Benz 300SE, 1968	6	11	16
No. 46 Morris Minor 1000, 1957	35	50	80
No. 46 Pickfords Removal Van, 1960...	20	35	60

Matchbox No. 46 Morris Minor 1000, 1957, $80. Photo courtesy Gary Linden

Matchbox No. 47 Trojan Brooke Bond Van, 1957, $75. Photo courtesy Gary Linden

Matchbox No. 54 Army Saracen Personnel Carrier, 1959, $50

Matchbox (Continued)

	C6	C8	C10
No. 46 Stretcha Fetcha, 1972	5	9	15
No. 47 Beach Hopper, 1973	5	7	10
No. 47 Daf Tipper Container Truck, 1968	8	12	16
No. 47 Neilson Ice Cream Van, 1963	30	46	60
No. 47 Pannier Loco, 1980	3	5	7
No. 47 Trojan Brooke Bond Van, 1957	30	55	75
No. 48 Dodge Dumper Truck, 1967	11	16	25
No. 48 Pi-Eyed Piper, 1973	4	6	10
No. 48 Sambron Jack Lift, 1977	4	6	8
No. 48 Sports Boat & Trailer, 1957	30	40	80

Matchbox (Continued)

	C6	C8	C10
No. 49 Army Half Track MKIII, 1958	20	30	55
No. 49 Chop Suey, 1973	10	15	20
No. 49 Chop Suey, chrome handle bar	30	45	70
No. 49 Crane Truck, 1976	3	5	8
No. 49 Mercedes Unimog Truck, 1967	11	18	24
No. 50 Articulated Truck, 1973	6	11	16
No. 50 Commer Pickup Truck, 1958	20	30	50
No. 50 Ford Kennel Truck, 1969	10	15	20
No. 50 Harley Davidson Motorcycle, 1981	2	3	5
No. 51 Albion Truck "Portland Cement," 1958	15	25	35
No. 51 Citroen SM, 1972	5	7	10
No. 51 Eight-Wheel Tipper Truck, 1969	10	15	20
No. 52 BRM Racing Car, 1965	10	15	20
No. 52 Dodge Charger MKIII, 1970	5	10	15
No. 52 Maserati 4 CLT, 1958	35	45	65
No. 52 Police Launch, 1976	3	5	7
No. 53 Aston-Martin DB2/4, 1959	19	26	35
No. 53 C.J. 6 Jeep, 1977	4	6	8
No. 53 Ford Zodiac MKIV, 1968	10	15	20
No. 53 Mercedes-Benz 220SE, 1968	15	25	40
No. 53 Tanzara, 1972	3	7	10

Matchbox (Continued)

	C6	C8	C10
No. 54 Army Saracen Personnel Carrier, 1959	20	30	50
No. 54 Cadillac Ambulance, 1965	16	25	35
No. 54 Ford Capri, 1971	4	7	9
No. 54 Mobile Home, 1981	3	5	7
No. 54 Personnel Carrier, 1976	5	7	10
No. 55 D.U.K.W., Army Amphibian, 1959	25	35	65
No. 55 Ford Cortina, 1980	5	9	11
No. 55 Ford Police Car, 1963	50	75	100
No. 55 Hell Raiser, 1975	4	6	8
No. 55 Mercury Parkland Police Car, 1969	15	20	25
No. 55 Mercury Police Car, Station Wagon, 1970	5	10	15

Matchbox No. 56 Fiat 1500, 1965, $20. Photo courtesy Gary Linden

Matchbox No. 55 Ford Police Car, 1963, $100. Photo courtesy Gary Linden

Matchbox (Continued)

	C6	C8	C10
No. 56 BMC 1800 Pininfarina, 1970	7	10	15
No. 56 Fiat 1500, 1965	9	12	20
No. 56 Hi Trailer, 1975	5	10	15
No. 56 London Trolley Bus, 1959	35	45	80
No. 56 Mercedes 450SEL, 1980	4	6	8
No. 57 Chevrolet Impala, 1966	25	35	50
No. 57 Eccles Caravan, 1970	5	10	15
No. 57 Wild Life Truck, 1973	7	9	15
No. 57 Wolseley 1500, 1959	20	25	35
No. 58 British European Airways Coach, 1959	25	35	75
No. 58 DAF Girder Truck, 1968	9	12	16
No. 58 Drott Excavator, 1963	25	30	55
No. 58 Faun Dumper, 1976	5	9	15
No. 58 Woosh-N-Push, 1972	5	10	15
No. 59 Fire Chief Car, 1966	35	45	80
No. 59 Ford "Singer" Van, 1959	45	60	100
No. 59 Ford Fairlane Fire Car, 1964	30	45	90
No. 59 Planet Scout, 1975	15	20	30
No. 59 Porsche 928, 1981	5	7	9
No. 60 Holden Pickup, 1977	8	11	15
No. 60 Lotus Super Seven, 1971	6	9	12
No. 60 Morris Omnitruck J2 Pickup	17	26	35
No. 60 Truck with Site Office, 1967	10	15	20
No. 61 Alvis Stalwart, 1967	20	30	45
No. 61 Blue Shark, 1971	4	6	10

Matchbox No. 59 Ford "Singer" Van, 1959, $100. Photo courtesy Gary Linden

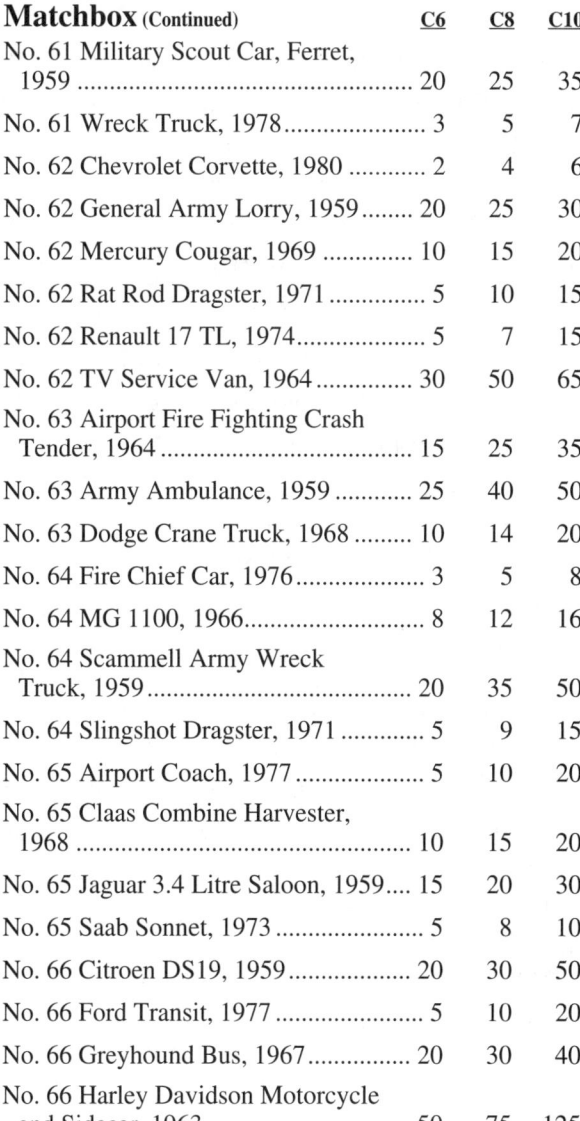

Matchbox No. 64 Scammell Army Wreck Truck, 1959, $50. Photo courtesy Gary Linden

Matchbox No. 69 Commer 30 Cwt. Van "Nestle's," 1959, $50. Photo courtesy Gary Linden

Matchbox (Continued)	C6	C8	C10
No. 61 Military Scout Car, Ferret, 1959	20	25	35
No. 61 Wreck Truck, 1978	3	5	7
No. 62 Chevrolet Corvette, 1980	2	4	6
No. 62 General Army Lorry, 1959	20	25	30
No. 62 Mercury Cougar, 1969	10	15	20
No. 62 Rat Rod Dragster, 1971	5	10	15
No. 62 Renault 17 TL, 1974	5	7	15
No. 62 TV Service Van, 1964	30	50	65
No. 63 Airport Fire Fighting Crash Tender, 1964	15	25	35
No. 63 Army Ambulance, 1959	25	40	50
No. 63 Dodge Crane Truck, 1968	10	14	20
No. 64 Fire Chief Car, 1976	3	5	8
No. 64 MG 1100, 1966	8	12	16
No. 64 Scammell Army Wreck Truck, 1959	20	35	50
No. 64 Slingshot Dragster, 1971	5	9	15
No. 65 Airport Coach, 1977	5	10	20
No. 65 Claas Combine Harvester, 1968	10	15	20
No. 65 Jaguar 3.4 Litre Saloon, 1959	15	20	30
No. 65 Saab Sonnet, 1973	5	8	10
No. 66 Citroen DS19, 1959	20	30	50
No. 66 Ford Transit, 1977	5	10	20
No. 66 Greyhound Bus, 1967	20	30	40
No. 66 Harley Davidson Motorcycle and Sidecar, 1963	50	75	125

Matchbox (Continued)	C6	C8	C10
No. 66 Mazda RX500, 1972	5	8	10
No. 67 "Saladin" Armored Car, 1959	20	30	40
No. 67 Datsun 260Z, 1978	4	6	8
No. 67 Hot Rocker, 1973	4	6	9
No. 67 Volkswagen 1600 T.L., 1968	10	15	20
No. 68 Army Austin MKII Radio Truck, 1959	15	20	30
No. 68 Cosmobile, 1975	8	10	15
No. 68 Mercedes Coach, 1965	20	25	40
No. 68 Porsche 910, 1970	7	10	15
No. 69 Chevrolet Van, 1980	12	18	26
No. 69 Commer 30 Cwt. Van "Nestle's," 1959	25	40	50
No. 69 Hatra Tractor Shovel, 1965	20	25	40
No. 69 Rolls-Royce Silver Shadow, 1970	10	20	25
No. 69 Turbo Fury, 1973	6	8	12
No. 69 Wells Fargo Security, 1978	5	10	15
No. 70 Atkinson Grit-Spreading Truck, 1965	10	15	20
No. 70 Dodge Dragster, 1971	7	11	16
No. 70 Ferrari, 1981	2	3	6
No. 70 Ford Thames Estate Car, 1959	20	30	40
No. 70 S.P. Gun, 1977	3	6	10
No. 71 Army Water Truck, 1959	15	25	50
No. 71 Cattle Truck, 1976	4	6	10
No. 71 Ford Heavy Wreck Truck, amber windows, light and white bumper	20	30	40

Matchbox (Continued)

	C6	C8	C10
No. 71 Ford Heavy Wreck Truck, 1968	10	20	35
No. 71 Jeep Pickup Truck, 1964	20	40	55
No. 71 Jumbo Jet, 1973	3	5	10
No. 72 Bomag Road Roller, 1980	4	6	10
No. 72 Fordson Tractor, Power Major, 1959	20	30	45
No. 72 Hovercraft SRN6, 1972	4	8	10
No. 72 Standard Jeep, 1967	10	15	20
No. 73 Ferrari Racing Car, 1963	15	27	36
No. 73 Mercury Station Wagon, Commuter, 1969	10	15	20
No. 73 Model "A" Ford, 1981	4	6	8
No. 73 RAF Ten-Ton Pressure Refueler Tanker, 1959	22	32	45
No. 73 Weasel, 1974	5	10	15
No. 74 Cougar Villager, 1978	4	6	8
No. 74 Daimler Bus, 1966	15	20	30
No. 74 Mobile Refreshment Bar, Canteen, 1959	24	40	55
No. 74 Toe Joe, 1972	4	6	10
No. 75 Alfa Carabo, 1971	6	9	13
No. 75 Ferrari Berlinetta, 1965	11	16	22
No. 75 Ford Thunderbird, 1959	50	75	125
No. 75 Helicopter, 1976	4	6	9

Models of Yesteryear

	C6	C8	C10
Y-01 1911 Model "T" Ford, 1964	14	22	30
Y-01 1925 Allchin 7 N.H.P. Traction Engine, 1955	25	35	45

Matchbox No. 73 RAF Ten-Ton Pressure Refueler Tanker, 1959, $45. Photo courtesy Gary Linden

Models of Yesteryear (Continued)

	C6	C8	C10
Y-01 1936 Jaguar SS100, 1977	14	22	32
Y-02 1911 "B" Type London Bus, 1955	50	75	100
Y-02 1911 Renault Two-Seater, 1963	10	20	30
Y-02 Prince Henry Vauxhall, 1970	10	15	25
Y-03 1907 London "E" Class Tramcar, 1955	55	90	115
Y-03 1910 Benz Limousine, 1965	10	25	30
Y-03 1934 Riley MPH, 1972	10	15	20
Y-04 1905 Shank-Mason Horse-Drawn Fire Engine, 1960	75	100	125
Y-04 1909 Opel Coupe, 1966	15	30	45
Y-04 1930 Dusenberg Model J, 1976	15	25	35
Y-04 Sentinel Steam Wagon, 1955	55	75	100
Y-05 1907 Peugeot, 1968	17	29	36
Y-05 1927 Talbot Van, 1978	20	30	40
Y-05 1929 LeMans Bentley, 1955	50	65	90
Y-05 1929 Supercharged 4-1/2 Litre Bentley, 1960	16	25	33
Y-06 1913 Cadillac, 1967	15	20	30
Y-06 1916 A.E.C. "Y" type Lorry Truck, 1955	25	30	45
Y-06 1920 Rolls-Royce Fire Engine, 1978	18	29	44
Y-06 1926 Type "35" Bugatti, 1961	22	33	44
Y-07 1912 Rolls-Royce, 1967	25	39	48
Y-07 1913 Mercer Raceabout Sportcar, 1961	25	35	45
Y-07 1914 4-Ton Leyland, 1955	30	40	50
Y-08 1914 Stutz Roadster, 1968	15	20	30
Y-08 1914 Sunbeam Motorcycle with sidecar, 1962	20	35	45
Y-08 1926 Morris Cowley "Bullnose," 1955	40	50	60
Y-08 1945 MC TC Sports Car, 1978	7	11	15
Y-09 1912 Simplex, 1967	25	41	56
Y-09 1924 Fowler "Big Lion" Showman Engine, 1955	30	40	55
Y-10 1906 Rolls-Royce Silver Cloud, 1968	12	17	25
Y-10 1908 Grand Prix Mercedes Racing Car, 1957	40	60	80
Y-10 1928 Mercedes-Benz 36/220, 1963	24	38	50

Matchbox Y-14 1931 Stutz Bearcat (Models of Yesteryear), 1972, $20. Photo courtesy Gary Linden

Models of Yesteryear (Continued)	C6	C8	C10
Y-11 1912 Packard Landaulet, 1963	19	29	37
Y-11 1920 Aveling and Porter Steam Roller, 1957	39	57	76
Y-11 1938 Lagonda Drophead Coupe, 1972	15	22	32
Y-12 1899 Horse-Bus, London, 1957	81	113	150
Y-12 1909 Thomas Flyabout, 1967	22	33	44
Y-12 1912 Model "T" Ford, 1979	12	19	25
Y-13 1862 American 4-4-0 Locomotive	33	49	66
Y-13 1911 Daimler, 1965	17	26	32
Y-13 1918 Crossley Truck, 1972	20	33	40
Y-14 1903 Duke of Connaught Locomotive, 1957	85	122	159
Y-14 1911 Maxwell Roadster, 1965	25	38	54
Y-14 1931 Stutz Bearcat, 1972	10	15	20
Y-15 1907 Rolls-Royce "Silver Ghost," 1960	20	35	45
Y-15 1930 Packard Victoria, 1969	10	15	25
Y-16 1904 Spyker Veteran Auto, 1961	30	45	60
Y-16 1928 Mercedes SS, 1971	10	15	25
Y-17 1938 Hispano Suiza, 1972	11	15	25
Y-18 1937 Cord 812, 1979	8	10	12
Y-19 1935 Auburn 851, 1980	5	8	11
Y-20 1938 Mercedes 540K, 1981	6	8	10
Y-21 1929 Woody Wagon, 1981	7	12	20

Metal Cast Products Company

Metal Cast Products was formed when S. Sachs was reorganized in 1925. The producer of slush molds for small business and hobbyists, Metal Cast's molds were used by so many different franchises it is difficult to identify the actual makers unless they engraved their names on the model, Fred Green Toys was one such maker. Metal Cast objective was to offer any or all support materials and services to slush-mold entrepreneurs.

A variety of wheels may be found on Metal Cast vehicles—metal disk wheels, metal spoke wheels, wood wheels with rubber tires, and white or black rubber wheels.

Contributor: Fred Maxwell, 4722 N. 33 St., Arlington, VA 22207.

Perry R. Eichor, 703 North Almond Drive, Simpsonville, SC 29681.

	C6	C8	C10
Fire Engine, similar to No. 65 w/o watercannon, 3-3/8"	6	10	14
Fire Engine, No. 61, hook and ladder truck, crew of two, 4-1/2"	25	50	60
Open Rack Truck, No. 01-04, COE cab, stake semi-trailer, 6"	15	25	35
Packard Convertible, No. 41, two-door, top down, 5-1/4"	20	30	40
Streamline Sedan, No. 60, rubber tires, DeSoto? Airflow, eight open windows, spoke wheels, 4"	20	30	40
Tank Truck, No. 01-03, same COE cab, semi-fuel tanker, "FRED GREEN TOYS," "Made in U.S.A.," 6"	20	30	40
War Tank, No. 08, early heavy Sherman Tank, 4"	30	50	65

Metal Cast Company Streamline Sedan, No. 60, 4", $40. Photo from Metal Cast catalog

Metal Cast Products Packard Convertible, No. 41, 5-1/4", $40. Photo from Metal Cast catalog

Metal Masters

Contributor: Dave Leopard, 2507 Feather Run Trail, West Columbia, SC 29169-4915.

	C6	C8	C10
Bus, c. 1938, 7-1/4" long (MM02)	25	38	50
Fire Truck, removable ladders, c. 1940, 10" long (MM12)	50	65	85
Fire Truck, ladders, wind-up motors, c. 1940, 10" long (MM13)	60	90	120
Fire Truck, version of pickup, c. 1938, 7" long (MM04)	35	55	75
Jeep, c. 1947, 5-1/2" long (MM06)	20	30	55
Pickup Truck, c. 1938, 7" long (MM03)	25	38	50
Roadster, c. 1938, 7" long (MM01)	25	38	50
Station Wagon, wind-up motor, c. 1940, 8-1/2" (MM08)	45	55	75
Station Wagon, ambulance version, c. 1940, 8-1/2" (MM09)	45	55	75
Station Wagon, c. 1940, 8-1/2" (MM07)	40	55	65
Tow Truck, wind-up motor, c. 1940, 10" long (MM11)	55	80	110
Tow Truck, "ABC Towing Service," c. 1940, 10" long (MM10)	50	75	100
Tow Truck, version of pickup, c. 1938, 7" long (MM05)	35	45	50

Metalcraft

Metalcraft, of St. Louis, Missouri, began producing its pressed-steel trucks in 1931. About a million were sold, most as advertising toys. In 1937, defeated by the Depression, Metalcraft closed. According to a collector-researcher, Al Korte was the designer of all of the firm's trucks and worked there from 1931 to 1936.

Contributor: John Taylor, P.O. Box 63, Nolensville, TN 37135-0063.

	C6	C8	C10
Acme Stores Truck, heart-shaped grille, 1935, 13" long	200	300	500
Bunte Candies Truck, 1933, 12-1/2" long	200	375	450
Clover Farm Stores Truck	450	675	900
Coca-Cola Truck, ten bottles in racks, "Every Bottle Sterilized," c. 1928, 11" long	450	650	875

Metalcraft Plee-Zing Quality Products, 1928, 11" long, $500. Photo courtesy Mapes Auctioneers and Appraisers

Metalcraft (Continued)

	C6	C8	C10
Coca-Cola Truck, pressed steel, ten bottles in rack, "Every Bottle Sterilized," rubber tires, early 1930s, 11" long	450	700	1000
Coca-Cola Truck, ten bottles, long nose, stamped metal, late 1930s, 12" long	450	675	1000
CW Coffee Dump Truck, 1928, 11" long	225	400	525
Decker's Iowana Truck, heart-shaped grille, 1935	500	700	1000
Delivery Truck Van, steel, 1928, 11" long	200	300	450
Drink Smile Truck, w/electric lights and spare tire, 1933, 12-1/2" long	300	450	650
Goodrich Silvertone Tires Wrecker, w/three spare tires, 1931, 12" long	225	375	450
Heinz Truck, spare tire, electric lights, "Baked Beans," "Bottled Vinegar," "Rice Flakes," c. 1932, 12" long	250	350	425
Kroger Food Express Truck, open w/food packages, 10" long	300	450	600
Kroger Food Express Truck, closed, 1929, 11" long	325	450	650
Krug Bakery Truck, 1933, 12-1/2" long	450	675	935
Machinery Hauling Truck, 14-1/2" long	500	700	900
Meadow Gold Butter Truck, battery-operated lights, 1935, 13" long	425	552	750
Plee-Zing Quality Products, 1928, 11" long	250	375	500
Pure Oil Truck, 1935	500	700	1100

Metalcraft Pure Oil Truck, 1935, $1100. Photo courtesy Bob Smith

Metalcraft Sand-Gravel Dump Truck, No. 150, 1928, 11" long, $375. Photo courtesy Bob Smith

Metalcraft Shell Motor Oil Truck, 1933, 12" long, $900. Photo courtesy Bob Smith

Metalcraft (Continued)

	C6	C8	C10
Sand-Gravel Dump Truck, No. 150, 1928, 11" long	175	275	375
Shell Motor Oil Truck, eight barrels, 1933, 12" long	325	600	900
St. Louis Truck, c. 1930, 11" long	250	400	550
Steam Shovel, No. 4, 8"	115	150	200
Sunshine Biscuits Truck, 1933, 12-1/2"	250	400	550
Towing & Repairs, 1928, 11-1/2"	250	425	550
Toy Town Grocery	275	425	550
Waldorf Lager, white	400	600	900
Waldorf Logan Truck, heart-shaped grille, 1935	300	500	700

Metalcraft (Continued)

	C6	C8	C10
Werks Tag Soap Truck	300	450	600
Weston's Biscuits	250	375	500
White King Delivery Truck, 12" long	300	400	500

Midgetoy

Contributor: Mark Rich, P.O. Box 971, Stevens Point, WI 54481-0971.

Chevrolet Tractor-Trailer Series, 8" Vehicles

	C6	C8	C10
Auto Transporter with Loading Ramp, 1962	12	20	27
Hook and Ladder Aerial Fire Truck, 1963	12	20	30
Kenworth Sleeper Cab, 1980	2	4	8
Oil Tanker, "Midgetoy Oil Co."	12	20	30
Oil Tanker Trailer, 1962	12	20	30
Shipping Van, "Midgetoy Van Lines, Inc."	12	20	30
Shipping Van Trailer, 1962	12	20	30

Jumbo Series, 6" Vehicles

	C6	C8	C10
American La France Pumper Truck, black rubber tires	11	18	27
Cadillac Four-Door Convertible, black rubber tires	10	17	25
Mobile Artillery, black rubber tires, 1957	10	17	25
Oil Tanker, black rubber tires, 1957	10	17	25

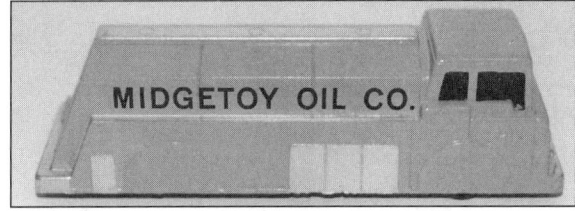

Midgetoy Oil Tanker (Jumbo Series, 6" Vehicles), 1957, $25

Midgetoy American La France Pumper Truck (Jumbo Series, 6" Vehicles), $27

*Midgetoy Scenicruiser Bus (Jumbo Series, 6"
Vehicles), late 1950s, $30*

Jumbo Series,
6" Vehicles (Continued)

	C6	C8	C10
Oil Tanker, "Midgetoy Oil Co."	10	17	25
Scenicruiser Bus, late version, "Midgetoy Bus Line"	NPF	NPF	NPF
Scenicruiser Bus, black rubber tires, late 1950s	12	20	30
Utility Truck	10	17	25

Junior Series, 2-1/2" to
3-1/2" Vehicles

	C6	C8	C10
American LaFrance Pumper, open cab, black rubber tires, late 1950s	6	9	13
Army Amphibious "Battle Bug," 1949?	8	14	22
Army Howitzer, black plastic tires	2	5	7
Army Howitzer, black plastic tires, 1949?	2	5	7
Army Jeep, black rubber tires, 1950	4	7	10
Cadillac Convertible, black rubber tires, 1949	6	11	17
Corvette Convertible, black rubber tires, late 1950s	5	8	10
Ford Hot Rod, br, 2-1/2"	5	8	12
Ford V-8 Hot Rod, black rubber tires, 1948	8	14	22
Ford V-8 Hot Rod, black plastic tires	5	9	12
Ford Wrecker Truck, black rubber tires, late 1950s	5	8	12
Greyhound Bus, black rubber tires, 1955	6	10	15
MG Sports Roadster, black rubber tires, 1958	6	9	13
Open Cockpit Indy Curtis Craft Race Car, black rubber tires, 1950	8	14	22
Sunbeam Racer, black plastic tires	5	8	12
Sunbeam Racer, black rubber tires, 1950	8	14	22

Junior Series, 2-1/2" to
3-1/2" Vehicles (Continued)

	C6	C8	C10
Volkswagen Beetle, black plastic tires, 1960	6	9	15

King-Size Series,
4" Vehicles

	C6	C8	C10
American La France Pumper, black rubber tires, early 1950s	8	14	22
Army Half-Track, black rubber tires, late 1950s	8	15	20
Army Personnel Carrier, black rubber tires, late 1950s	8	15	20
Army Tank, black rubber tires, late 1940s or early 1950s	8	15	20
Cadillac Four-door Sedan, military, black rubber tires	8	13	18
Cadillac Four-door Sedan, black rubber tires, late 1950s	10	15	20
Cadillac Two-door Coupe, black rubber tires, early 1950s	11	18	24
Chrysler-style Convertible Roadster, black rubber tires	10	16	22
Ford Pickup Truck, black rubber tires, late 1950s	10	16	22
Ford Pickup Truck, black rubber tires, early 1950s	13	20	26
Oil Tanker Truck, military, black rubber tires	10	15	20
Oil Tanker Truck, black rubber tires, late 1950s	12	18	24
Van-style Streamlined Ambulance, Red-Cross, black rubber tires, late 1950s	8	12	16
Van-style Streamlined Station Wagon, black rubber tires, late 1950s	8	12	16

New Junior Series (1970),
2-1/2" to 3" Vehicles

	C6	C8	C10
'68 Corvette L88 Stingray, 1971	2	3	4
Cadillac Ambulance, 1971	5	8	12
Ford 1971 Pickup Truck	2	4	5
Ford Mark IV, 1971	2	4	5
Ford Mustang	1	2	3
Ford Ranchero Pickup	2	3	4
Ford Torino, 1971	1	2	3
Ford Torino Fire Chief Car, 1971	2	4	6
Ford Torino Police Car, 1971	2	4	6

New Junior Series (1970), 2-1/2" to 3" Vehicles (Continued)

	C6	C8	C10
Ford Wrecker Truck, 1971	3	5	7
Jaguar XKE, 1971	3	5	8

Pee-Wee Series (1969), 2" Mini Vehicles

	C6	C8	C10
American LaFrance Fire Truck	1	2	3
Jeep, race cars, sports cars and hot rods	n/a	1	2
MG Sports Roadster	1	2	3

Sets

	C6	C8	C10
1860 Western Train, "Train That Won the West," black plastic tires	8	14	25
1860 Western Train	6	12	25
1920 Passenger Train, black plastic tires	8	14	25
1920 Passenger Train	6	12	25
1940 Diesel Train	6	12	25
1940 Diesel Train, late version, "Amtrak," black plastic tires	8	14	25
1950 Freight Train, black plastic tires	8	14	25
1950 Freight Train	6	12	25
Dixie Chargers, three-car set, 1981	5	8	12
Interchangeable Truck Set	12	25	45

Neff-Moon Toy Company

William Moon and Charles Neff owned neff-Moon, of Sandusky, Ohio. Production of its pressed-steel toys began in 1923. The firm, which was located above a grocery, was apparently an early victim of the Depression.

	C6	C8	C10
Groceries Van	300	450	600
Taxi, 12" long	350	525	700
Tow Truck, c. 1925, 16" long	200	300	400

Nylint

The Nylint Tool and Manufacturing Company was formed in 1937 by Bernard C. Klint and David Nyberg (thus its name) in Rockford, Illinois. Toy production began in the spring of 1946. Since 1951, the firm concentrated on the production of heavy-duty scale reproductions, in steel, of earth-moving equipment and over-the-road trucks.

Nylint closed in 2000.

Nylint American Oil Emergency Truck, No. 6000, 11-1/4" long, $250. Photo courtesy Bob Smith

	C6	C8	C10
Airport Courtesy Van, No. 6900, "Holiday Inn," 12" long	300	375	600
Amazing Car, No. 600, wind-up, 1946-49, 13-3/4" long	125	200	350
Ambulance, No. 6700, 12" long	150	175	250
American Oil Emergency Truck, No. 6000, 11-1/4" long	125	175	250
Army Ambulance, No. 7300, 12" long	100	150	175
Bronco, No. 8200, 12-1/2" long	100	150	200
Bulldozer, No. 4200, 14" long	90	125	175
Camper on Pickup, No. 4400, 13-1/2" long	100	150	175
Construction Four-Wheel Platform Dump, No. 4600, 15-3/4" long	100	150	225
Countdown Rocket Launcher, No. 3500, 1959-61, 21" long	150	225	275
Custom Camper on Pickup Truck, No. 5300, 12-1/2" long	100	150	200
Custom Camper on Pickup Truck with Boat, No. 5400, 23-1/2" long	150	200	275
Deliverall, No. 1000, wind-up, 1948-51, 10" long	300	475	625
Dump Truck, No. 5100, 13-1/2"	100	150	200
Dump Truck with Cement Mixer, No. 5000, 20-1/2" long	150	200	300
Electronic Cannon, No. 2400, has no radar antenna, 1956	125	175	250
Electronic Cannon, No. 2400, w/radar antenna, 1956, 22-1/2" long	100	150	200
Elgin Street Sweeper, No. 2300, battery-operated version, closed cab, 1956-57	150	200	250

Nylint (Continued)

	C6	C8	C10
Elgin Street Sweeper, No. 1100, wind-up, 1950-52, 8-1/4" long	250	400	525
Ford Econoline Van, No. 5800, 12" long	75	125	150
Ford Pickup & U-Haul Box Trailer, No. 4100	150	180	250
Ford Platform Tilt Truck, No. 3900, 15-3/4" long	125	200	275
Ford Rapid Delivery, No. 3600, 18-1/4" long	175	250	350
Ford Sales & Service, No. 3800, 13-5/8" long	150	225	300
Ford Speedway Truck with Racer, No. 4000, 24-3/4" long	125	200	265
Ford U-Haul Rental Fleet, No. 4300, three pieces	200	275	375
Fun on Farm Econoline Truck, No. 7100, twenty-nine pieces, 11-1/4" long	100	150	200
Grader-Loader, No. 3000, 1959-61, 23-3/4" long	100	150	200
Guided Missile Carrier, No. 2800, later (through 1960), cone of missile fires	75	125	175
Guided Missile Carrier, No. 2800, first version (1958), nose cone of missile doesn't fire, 15-1/2" long	150	250	350
Happy Acres Truck with Horses, No. 4700, 14" long	75	100	150

Nylint Elgin Street Sweeper, No. 2300, 1956-57, $250

Nylint Electronic Cannon, No. 2400, 1956, $250. Photo courtesy Calvin L. Chaussee

Nylint (Continued)

	C6	C8	C10
Highway Emergency Unit, 1959-63, 18-5/8" long (3400)	75	125	150
Horse Van, No. 6300, 23-1/2"	90	125	175
Jack Hammer, No. 2900, w/box, 1958-60, 19-1/2" long	150	250	325
Jalopy, No. 6800, 9-5/8" long	30	50	75
Kennel Truck with Dogs, No. 6200, 11-1/2" long	100	150	200
Lift Truck (fork lift), No. 700, wind-up, 1947-49	75	125	175
Michigan Shovel, No. 2200, 1955-65, 31-1/2" long	100	125	175
Missile Launcher, No. 2600, 1957-60, 31-1/2" long	125	200	275
Mobile Home, No. 6600, semi-type, 1964, 30" long	150	200	275
Payloader, No. 1600, dark green, 1958	125	175	250
Payloader, No. 1600, yellow, 1958	140	200	260
Payloader, No. 1600, light green, 1956-57	125	175	250
Payloader, No. 1600, tan, 1955	150	200	275
Payloader, No. 1600, red, 1951-54, 18" long	100	125	175
Payloader Tractor-Shovel, No. 3100, 1959-61, 17-5/8" long	125	175	250
Pepsi Truck, No. 5500, 16-1/2"	150	200	275
Pickup Truck, No. 5200, Econoline, 11-1/4" long	100	150	280
Pony Farm Van, No. 8000, seven piece set, 11-1/4" long	150	200	300
Power & Light Lineman Truck, No. 3200, 1959-61, 35-3/4" long	175	250	350
Power & Light Posthole Digger, No. 3300, 1959-61, 35-3/4" long	175	250	350

Nylint Michigan Shovel, No. 2200, 1955-65, 31-1/2" long, $175

Nylint Pepsi Truck, No. 5500, 16-1/2", $275. Photo courtesy Bob Smith

Nylint Ranch Truck, No. 4500, 14" long, $175

Nylint Tournarocker, No. 1300, 1951-52, 18" long, $150

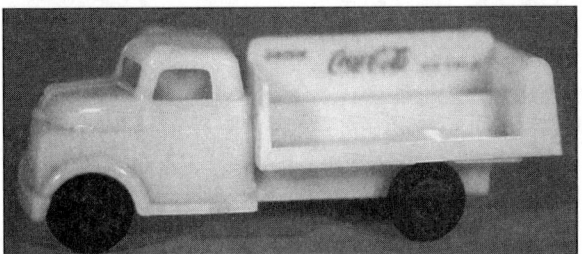

Pyro Coca-Cola Truck, 5-1/2" long, $150. Photo courtesy Terry Sells

Nylint (Continued)

	C6	C8	C10
Pumpmobile, No. 1200, wind-up, 1950-52, 8-5/8" long	150	200	275
Ranch Truck, No. 4500, 14" long	100	125	175
Road Grader, No. 1400, larger wheels, 1952-58	100	125	175
Road Grader, No. 7900, 15" long	75	100	150
Road Grader, No. 1400, small wheels, 1951, 19-1/4" long	75	100	150
Scootscycle, No. 800, wind-up, 1948-50, 7-1/4" long	250	350	450
Speed Swing, No. 2000, 1955-58, 19" long	125	175	250
Street Sprinkler Truck, No. 3700, 18" long	150	225	300
Suburban Fire Pumper, No. 8100, 12-1/2" long	125	175	225
Telescoping Crane, No. 2500, 1957-60, 27" long	150	200	275
Texaco Service van, No. 8300, 12" long	175	250	350
Tournadozer, No. 2100, 1956-59, 20" long	125	180	250
Tournadozer, No. 1700, 1953-56, 30-1/4" long	100	125	175
Tournahopper, No. 1500, 1951-56, 22-1/2" long	200	275	275

Nylint (Continued)

	C6	C8	C10
Tournaractor, No. 1900, 1954-55, 14-3/4" long	175	250	325
Tournarocker, No. 1300, open tractor w/driver, 1951-52, 18" long	75	100	150
Tournarocker, No. 1300, closed cab, no driver, 1953-57, 18" long	115	175	225
Traveloader, No. 1800, 1953-55, 30" long	125	200	250
U-Haul Cube Van, No. 8400, 1965, 22" long	100	150	200
U-Haul Trailer, No. 4800, 8" long	75	100	150
U-Haul Trailer, No. 4900, 9" long	75	100	150
U-Haul Truck, No. 8411, Chevy, 1975	100	125	175
U-Haul Truck & Trailer, No. 8410, 1974, 22" long	100	150	200
Uranium Hauler, No. 2700, 1958-59, 22-1/2" long	150	200	275

Pyro

Pyro began in 1939 in Pyro Park, Union City, New Jersey. The owner was William Lester. At its height, the company had 400 employees.

	C6	C8	C10
Car, cast iron, 9" long	235	352	470
City Builders Truck, 5-1/2" long	NPF	NPF	NPF
Coca-Cola Truck, 5-1/2" long	75	112	150

Pyro Design-A-Car Set, $75. Photo courtesy Terry Sells

Pyro Ice & Coal Truck, 5-1/2" long, NPF. Photo courtesy Terry Sells

Pyro (Continued)

	C6	C8	C10
Design-A-Car Set, builds fourteen models	35	55	75
Ice & Coal Truck, 5-1/2" long	NPF	NPF	NPF
Race Car, 4" long	20	30	40
Range Patrol Truck	15	20	25
Road Roller	12	18	25
U.S. Army Truck	9	13	20
U.S. Navy Truck	10	15	20
U.S.M.C. Truck	10	15	20

Rainbow

Contributor: Dave Leopard, 2507 Feather Run Trail, West Columbia, SC 29169-4915.

	C6	C8	C10
'35 Oldsmobile Coupe, 3-3/4"	35	55	70
'35 Oldsmobile Four-door Sedan, 3-1/4" long	35	55	75
'35 Oldsmobile Four-door Sedan, 5" long	50	75	100
'35 Studebaker (?) Stake Side Pickup, 5-1/4" long	45	65	85
Open Racer, tapered tail, 4" long	25	38	50

Rainbow '35 Studebaker (?) Stake Side Pickup, 5-1/4" long, $85. Photo courtesy Dave Leopard's book, Rubber Toy Vehicles

Rainbow Open Racer, 4" long, $50. Photo courtesy Dave Leopard's book, Rubber Toy Vehicles

Ralston Toy & Novelty Co. (Ralstoy)

Ralston Toy & Novelty Co., also known as Ralstoy, was formed in July of 1939, by Dr. Felix Despecher, former Mayor of Ralston, Nebraska, A.M. Erickson, and Henry C. Nestor. These three men acquired the molds of Best Toy Co. of Manhattan, Kansas and the surviving molds of Kansas Toy Co. Included in the acquisition was the temporary services of John M. Best, his molder Conrad Morsch and about 140 molds from these pioneering slush mold companies. Located in a building formerly occupied by the American Legion, they continued a low-cost toy line that had been familiar to collectors since Kansas Toy was founded in 1923.

With the death of founder Dr. Despecherin in 1940, the young company was forced into reorganization. Lawyer Paul Massey took over control but was forced to give up the use of pot metal item due to the need for lead during World War II. To survive, Ralstoy turned to making wooden toys, including a replica of an Army Jeep, selling almost two million through dime stores such as Woolworth and Kresge. Other wooden toys included an Army tank and a Navy PT boat.

After World War II, Ralstoy turned to die-cast toys and novelties. As the business expanded it moved to 5707 So. 77th St., where it is today producing a well-known line of promotional trucks under Art Massey.

Ralstoy did label a few of its toys. The bottom pans, introduced by Best Toy, provided a surface to emboss with "Ralstoy" and "Made in USA." Unlike other slush-mold toys, wheels are not a good clue.

Contributors: Fred Maxwell, 4722 N. 33 St., Arlington, VA 22207.

Perry R. Eichor, 703 North Almond Drive, Simpsonville, SC 29681.

Ralston Toy & Novelty Company (Ralstoy)

	C6	C8	C10
Army Jeep, wooden, WWII issue (RAV10)	20	30	40
Army Tank, wooden, "USA W356," "Ralstoy" on bottom, WWII issue (RAV11)	37	56	75
Army Tank, "US Army," two-gun turret, entirely different tank than Kansas Toy No. 74, 74, 2-1/4" (RAV3)	13	20	26
Army Tank, "US Army," two gunturret, larger version of No. 74 above, also version w/black rubber wheels, wood grooved 3/4" track-laying wheels, 107, 3-1/8" (RAV7)	13	20	26
Ford Tractor, w/trailer, overall, 1948, 9" long	30	45	60
Gun Truck, Large, "US Army Anti-Aircraft Unit," three axle carrier, AA gun, searchlight and crew of three, 5-5/8" (RAV6)	28	42	56
Mayflower Moving Van	20	30	40
Railway (?) Gun, version of No. 23 muzzle-loading cannon on wheeled platform w/hook and loop connectors, perhaps addition to No. 3600 toy train, 108, 3-1/4"	12	18	25

Ralston Toy & Novelty Army Tank, 107, 3-1/8", $26. Photo courtesy Fred Maxwell

Ralston Toy & Novelty Army Tank, $75. Photo courtesy Ed Poole

Ralston Toy & Novelty Sedan, 5-5/8", $75. Photo courtesy Fred Maxwell

Ralston Toy & Novelty Company (Ralstoy) (Continued)

	C6	C8	C10
Sedan, die-cast, large, "2R," Cadillac?, "Ralstoy," "Made in USA," four open vent windows, divided open windshield, three open rear windows, long fenders, rear-wheel skirts, bumper guard, black rubber wheels, early postwar issue (?), 5-5/8" (RAV12)	37	56	75
Tanker Truck, "Ralstoy," International (?) Sleeper cab, two open windows, vertical grille w/"Gasoline" semi-trailer, "No. 102," four tanks, storage compartments, 102, entire length: 6-3/4" sleeper cab length: 3-3/8" (RAV4)	30	45	60
Transporter, large, "Ralstoy" cab unit in RAV4 above, steel semi-trailer w/No. 74 tank, No. 34 muzzle-loading cannon and No. 32 aircraft, olive drab color, not known if Ralstoy issued them as a set (some stamped No. 108, some No. 101), 9" (RAV5)	40	60	80

Renwal

The Renwal Manufacturing Company, founded in 1939 by either Irving Rosenblum or Irving Lawner (accounts vary), began by manufacturing a glass knife, later to be replaced by a plastic knife. It was this plastic knife that lead to the production of plastic toys in 1945.

Chein purchased Renwal's tooling when Renwal went out of business in the 1970s, Chein, in turn sold them to Revell.

	C6	C8	C10
Cadillac Convertible, No. 174, w/driver, top goes up and down, 1953, 5-1/2" long	20	30	50
Cement Mixer Truck, No. 56, mixer revolves, rear cap comes off, tank rises, 1948, 7-1/2"	62	93	125

*Renwal Cement Mixer Truck, No. 56, 1948, 7-1/2",
$125. Photo courtesy Terry Sells*

*Renwal Fire Truck, No. 57, 1948, 7" long, 8" high
when ladder extended, $95. Photo courtesy Bill and
Alice Wagner*

*Renwal Gasoline Truck, No. 49, $100. Photo
courtesy Bill and Alice Wagner*

*Renwal Sedan, two door, No. 90, 1949, 6-1/2" long,
$85. Photo courtesy Bob Alice Wagner*

*Renwal Steam Shovel Truck, No. 86, 1949, 19" long,
$90. Photo courtesy Terry Sells*

Renwal (Continued)	C6	C8	C10
Coal-Coke Dump Truck, w/driver. Doors open, body raises, 1948, 7-1/2" long	50	75	100
Convertible Sedan, No. 39, w/driver, doors open, top slides back, trunk opens, 1948, 6-1/2"	30	45	60
Fire Truck, No. 57, plastic, w/three fireman, 1948, 7" long, 8" high when ladder extended	48	72	95
Gasoline Truck, No. 49, plastic, w/driver	50	75	100
Gasoline Truck, No. 8008, die-cast, 1955, 6" long	30	40	55
Racer, No. 173, w/driver, 9-1/2"	85	128	170
Sedan, two door, No. 90, w/driver, doors and trunk open, 1949, 6-1/2" long	45	60	85
Steam Shovel Truck, No. 86, w/truck driver and cran operator, doors open, cab swings, shovel can be raised, 1949, 19" long	45	70	90
TV Truck, No. 260, w/camera, mike, working spotlight, 18" long	75	112	150

Rubber Vehicles
(Unknown Manufacturers)

The following list, with its number codes, was compiled by Dave Leopard. Vehicles are broken down by types. The gaps in the numbering indicate vehicles that have been identified since the list was compiled.

Contributor: Dave Leopard, 2507 Feather Run Trail, West Columbia, SC 29169-4915.

Rubber Vehicles '35 Chrysler Two-door Airflow Sedan, 5-1/8" long, $115. Photo courtesy Dave Leopard's book, Rubber Toy Vehicles

Rubber Vehicles '46 Nash Two-door Fastback Sedan, 4" long, $25. Photo courtesy Dave Leopard's book, Rubber Toy Vehicles

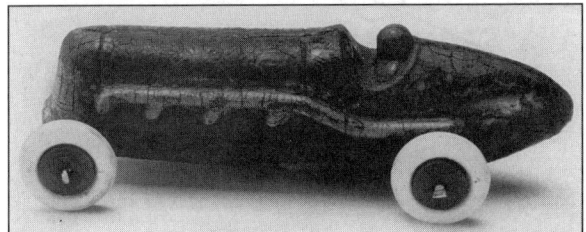

Rubber Vehicles Open Racer, 4" long, $60. Photo courtesy Dave Leopard's book, Rubber Toy Vehicles

Rubber Vehicles (Unknown Manufacturers) (continued)

	C6	C8	C10
'35 Chrysler Two-door Airflow Sedan, 5-1/8" long (UA08)	60	80	115
'35 DeSoto Four-door Airflow Sedan, 5" long (UA06)	60	80	115
'36 Plymouth Four-door Trunkback Sedan, 4-7/8" long (UA09)	75	115	150
'37 Plymouth Four-door Trunkback Sedan, 4-7/8" long (UA10)	75	115	150
'46 Nash Two-door Fastback Sedan, hollow, molded tires, 4" long (UA11)	12	18	25

Rubber Vehicles (Unknown Manufacturers) (continued)

	C6	C8	C10
Open Racer, solid rubber, left side header pipes, 3-1/2" long (UA01)	20	35	50
Open Racer, V-8, solid, large tires on wood hubs, 4" long (UA02)	25	40	60

Savoye Pewter Toy Company

Savoye was incorporated August 1930. In 1931, Savoye Pewter Toy Co., manufacturer of pewter toys (pewter was often the word used for lead alloy or pot metal) was listed in a directory at 69 Paterson Plank Road in North Bergen, New Jersey, with six male and three female employees. The names of the owners may have been Selma and Joseph Wigh. In 1934, at the same address, the workforce was seven males and two females. Slush-mold toys were probably its only product. Savoye was in the 1936 phone book but not in the February 1937 directory.

Collectors identify vehicle toys as Savoye if they have a somewhat coarse appearance, heavy slush-mold body, and white rubber tires on oversized red wooden hubs that are smooth on the outside surface (no axle showing); but whether this is simply lore is not known at present. The son of one of the owners of Tommy Toy Co. thinks some Savoye-looking vehicles were made by Tommy Toy. If so, it's possible Savoye sold its molds to nearby Tommy Toy.

Contributor: Fred Maxwell, 4722 N. 33 St., Arlington, VA 22207.

Perry R. Eichor, 703 North Almond Drive, Simpsonville, SC 29681.

	C6	C8	C10
Bus, Cross-Country, partial upper deck, twelve open windows, rearmount spare, 3-3/8" (SA8)	20	30	40
Bus, Heavy 5th Ave. Sight-Seeing, open overhanging upper deck, twelve open windows, gilt or silver trim, 4-3/4" (SA7)	62	93	125

Savoye Pewter Toy Bus, 3-3/8", $40. Photo courtesy Al Lane

Savoye Pewter Toy Milk Grade A Van, 3-1/4" long, $40. Photo courtesy Al Lane

Savoye Pewter Toy Pickup Truck, No. SA22, $40

Savoye Pewter Toy Company (Continued)

	C6	C8	C10
Coupe, (Graham like), two open windows, silver vertical grille, vertical louvers, 3-3/8" long (SA3)	20	30	40
Coupe, similar to above, slanted louvers, fantasy grille and large black rubber wheels, 3-3/8" long (SA4)	14	21	28
Fire Truck, driver and steersman w/high style gilt helmets, bell on hood, two glued ladders, oversized wheel wells w/oversized tires, 4-1/4" long (SA15)	30	50	70
Milk Grade A Van, two open windows, sidemounts, 3-1/4" long (SA5)	20	30	40
Moving Van, six wheels, 3-7/8" long	105	158	210
Pickup Truck, No. SA22	20	30	40
Roadster, (reminiscent of Tootsietoy Graham), driver, open rumble seat, silver vertical grille, vertical louvers, 3-1/2" long (SA1)	20	35	50
Tank Car Set, tow cab: 3-1/4", two tank cars: 3-1/2"; marked "Oil" "Cap. 80000" (RR type), not known whether Savoye sold these as a set; no known Savoye train, either, overall length: 10-1/4" (SA20)	40	60	80

Savoye Pewter Toy Company (Continued)

	C6	C8	C10
Truck, stake body, 4-1/2" long (SA11)	12	18	24
Truck, heavy "Beer Truck," six wood barrels set in cast depressions, 4-3/8" long (SA10)	40	60	80
Van, "Police Patrol," policeman on rear step, six open windows, gilt trim, sidemounts, 4" long (SA6)	30	50	75

Schieble Toy & Novelty Co.

William E. Schieble was a partner in D.P. Clark & Co. for nearly ten years. In 1909, after some disagreements with Clark, he broke up the partnership and became the sole owner. At this time, Schieble changed the name of the company to Schieble Toy & Novelty. Things went well during the 1920s, but as did many manufacturing companies, Schieble declared bankruptcy in 1931.

Contributor: Bob Smith, The Village Smith, 62 West Ave., Fairport, NY 14450-2102.

	C6	C8	C10
Fire Ladder Truck, 1920s, 20" long	325	475	650
Fire Ladder Truck, w/small driver, flywheel drive, white and red, 1909, 21-1/2" long	300	450	650
Fire Ladder Truck, large drive, flywheel drive, white and red, 1909, 21-1/2" long	400	600	800
Fire Truck, flywheel drive, red and gold, 1917, 11-1/2" long	300	450	650
Mack Semi Dump truck, chein look-a-like, c. 1925, 22" long	425	700	900

Schieble Toy and Novelty Fire Truck, 1917, 11-1/2" long, $650. Photo courtesy Bob Smith

Schieble Toy and Novelty Mack Semi Dump truck, c. 1925, 22" long, $900. Photo courtesy Bob Smith

Schieble Toy and Novelty (Continued)

	C6	C8	C10
Racer, team, steel wind-up, c. 1910, 12" long	450	675	900
Roadster, spare tire on back, 18-1/4" long	400	600	850
Sedan, 17" long	500	775	850
Touring Car, c. 1909, 14" long	375	575	725

Seiberling Rubber

	C6	C8	C10
'35 Ford two-door slantback sedan, 4" long (GA2)	27	41	55
'35 Ford two-door slantback sedan, 5" long (GA1)	32	48	65

Sharon

Founded in 1933 on the campus of Eastern Mennonite School (what is now Eastern Mennonite University) in Harrisburg, Virginia, Sharon was, at the time, the only maker of cast aluminum toys in the United States.

Started by Earnest G. Gehman, A.D. Wenger, and E.C. Shank, the company was designed to give employment to students attending the school during rough financial times. Jacob N. Brubaker, a Lancaster County, Pennsylvania minister who was also a designer for Hubley, designed the toys.

Sharon was forced out of business in late 1934 because the National Recovery Administration regulations forced the company to sell their products at a price not competitive with other toys.

Because Brubaker was the designer, many of the toys are mistaken as Hubley, but each Sharon toy is unique unto itself and only the method of construction was similar. Besides cars and trucks, Sharon also produced numerous novelty items and developed a design for a streamlined train to be constructed from Campbell's Soup cans. Unfortunately, Campbell's rejected the idea.

For some time, the toys have been mistakenly labeled "Sharron" with an extra R, but examination of actual documents from the company show the name to be Sharon.

Sharon Pierce Arrow-type Sedan, No. 10S, $150. Photo courtesy Perry Eichor

Most vehicles were sold with a paper tag that read, "This is a Genuine Cast Aluminum Toy light—Strong—durable." The other side read, "Cast Aluminum Toys, Will not CRUSH if accidentally stepped on. Will not BREAK when dropped on cement. Will not INJURE little toes, polished floors. Will not CUT—no sharp or jagged edges. Will not RUST—so will not stain clothes."

One of their prototypes was a long cast aluminum racer with a very powerful barrel spring, that when compressed would propel the racer across the floor. There is no record of it ever being put in to production.

Contributors: Perry R. Eichor, ASAF (retired), 703 North Almond Drive, Simpsonville, SC, 29681.

Dave Leopard, 2507 Feather Run Trail, West Columbia, SC 29169-4915.

	C6	C8	C10
Mack Dump Truck, No. 13SD, side-dump, 4" long	100	175	250
Open Racer, 6" long (SV003)	80	100	130
Pierce Arrow-type Sedan, No. 20S	75	125	200
Pierce Arrow-type Sedan, No. 10S	50	100	150
Pierce Arrow-type Silver Arrow, 1933, 6" long (SV001)	125	175	225
Racer, unnumbered, spring loaded, 12" long	NPF	NPF	NPF
Racer, No. 11R, two-man, twelve cylinder, 5-3/4" long	75	145	225
Rohr, 1934, 5" long (SV002)	100	150	200
Trolley Car (SV004)	NPF	NPF	NPF

Smith-Miller

Smith-Miller trucks entered an already competitive market in 1945. These cast-metal and aluminum trucks, produced in Santa Monica, California, should have failed—who would've thought that a new toy vehicle company could compete with such toy giants as Buddy "L," Structo, Marx and Hubley. Despite the stiff competition, Smith-Miller Toys stayed on the market for a full ten years outclassing virtually all toy trucks.

Their first trucks had two different classes, expensive replicas or smaller, no-name trucks that looked like half-breed Fords. During their last year they changed their profile from Mack Trucks to Auto-Car diesels with opening doors and working steering wheels.

Smith-Miller is once again in operation using original and new parts.

Contributors: John Taylor, P.O. Box 63, Nolensville, TN 37135-0063.

Smith-Miller Toys

	C6	C8	C10
Aerial Ladder Semi, No. 410, six-wheel tractor and four-wheel trailer, "SMFD," 36" long	450	850	1500
Arden Milk Truck, No. 204-A, twelve milk cans, four cases, four wheels, 14" long	350	550	800
B Mack Jr. Fire Truck, warning light, battery-operated, four wheels	1400	2650	3950
B Mack Orange Dump, ten wheels	950	1850	2800
B Mack P.I.E., eighteen wheels	400	625	850
Bekins Van, No. 406, six-wheel tractor and four-wheel trailer, 29" long	325	495	750
Bekins Vanliner, No. 208-B, fourteen wheels, 22-1/2" long	325	500	850
Blue Diamond, No. 408, ten-wheel dump truck, 18-1/2" long	650	1100	1600
B-Mack Lumber Truck, No. 404, 19"	375	560	750
Chevy Bekins Van, fourteen wheels, plain tires, hubcaps, 1945-46	200	300	400
Chevy Coca-Cola, four wheels, plain tires, early, 1945-46	450	675	900

Smith-Miller Toys (Continued)

	C6	C8	C10
Chevy Flatbed Tractor-Trailer, fourteen wheels, unpainted wood trailer, plain tires, hub caps, early, 1945	200	300	450
Chevy Milk Truck, four wheels, plain tires, hub caps, early, 1945-46	300	500	950
Coca-Cola Truck, twenty-four plastic bottles in six cases, four wheels, 1954-55	275	400	550
Coca-Cola Truck, No. 206-C, sixteen Coca-Cola cases, four wheels, 14" long	450	675	900
Dump Truck, No. 402, 11-1/2"	250	350	500
Ford Bekins Van, fourteen-wheeler, plain tires, hub, possibly earliest Smith-Miller, 1944	350	450	650
Ford Coca-Cola, four wheels, wood soda cases, early, 1944	600	1000	1400
GMC Bank of America, No. 404-B, lock and key, four wheels	200	400	500
GMC Be Mac T-Trailer, fourteen wheel, 1949	265	350	650
GMC Coca-Cola, No. 306-C, four wheels, sixteen Coca-Cola cases	425	875	1925
GMC Drive-O Steerable Dump, six wheels, cable w/hand control, 1946	325	550	925

Smith-Miller GMC Lyon Van Tractor-Trailer, No. 407-V, $700. Photo courtesy Bob Smith

Smith-Miller B Mack Orange Dump, $2800. Photo courtesy Tim Oei

Smith-Miller GMC Drive-O Steerable Dump, 1946, $925. Photo courtesy Bob Smith

Smith-Miller Toys (Continued)

	C6	C8	C10
GMC Furniture Mart Pickup, four wheels	250	350	500
GMC Heinz Grocery Truck	200	300	400
GMC Hi-Way Freighter Tractor-Trailer, No. 310-H, fourteen wheels	250	350	500
GMC Kraft Foods, No. 304-K, four wheels	275	475	550
GMC Lumber Tractor-Trailer, No. 406-L, fourteen wheels, eight timbers	250	350	500
GMC Lyon Van Tractor-Trailer, No. 308-V, fourteen wheels	375	575	800
GMC Lyon Van Tractor-Trailer, No. 407-V, ten wheels	350	500	700
GMC Machinery Hauler, No. 408-H, thirteen wheels	300	450	600
GMC Machinery Hauler, ten wheeler	200	300	450
GMC Marshall Field & Company Tractor-Trailer, ten-wheel T-Trailer	400	650	1000
GMC Material Truck, No. 402-M, four barrels, two timbers	250	350	500
GMC Materials Truck, No. 302-M, four barrels, three timbers	250	350	500
GMC Mobilgas Tanker, No. 409-G, fourteen wheels, two hoses	270	400	750
GMC P.I.E., No. 412-P, fourteen wheels	250	375	500
GMC P.I.E. Tractor-Trailer, No. 312-P	300	450	600
GMC Peoples First National Bank and Trust Company armored Truck, lock and key, 1951	225	400	525
GMC Rack Truck, No. 303-R, six wheels	250	350	500
GMC Rack Truck, No. 403-R, six wheels	225	380	550
GMC Redwood Logger Tractor-Trailer, No. 307-L, three logs	500	800	1100
GMC Rexall Drug, four wheels	475	815	1550
GMC Searchlight Truck, "Hollywood Film Ad" w/trailer, 1953	550	900	1600
GMC Silver Streak Express Tractor-Trailer, No. 311-E, fourteen wheels	212	318	425
GMC Silver Streak Tractor-Trailer, No. 411-E, fourteen wheels	185	350	475

Smith-Miller Toys (Continued)

	C6	C8	C10
GMC Super Cargo Tractor-Trailer, No. 309-S, fourteen wheels, ten barrels	250	350	500
GMC Transcontinental Tractor-Trailer, No. 410-F, 14 wheels	250	350	550
GMC Triton Oil, No. 405-T, six wheels, three drums	250	400	500
GMC Triton Oil, No. 305-T, three drums	175	263	350
GMC U.S. Treasury Truck, armored truck, w/lock and key, 1952	250	375	500
GMC Wrecker, No. 301-W, four-wheeler	250	350	500
GMC Wrecker, No. 401-W, six wheels	350	525	700
Heinz Grocery Truck, No. 203-H, six wheels, 14" long	250	400	675
L Mack Aerial Ladder, "SMFD," eight wheels	440	660	880
L Mack Army Materials Truck, three barrels, two boards, one large crate, one small crate, ten wheels	460	690	925
L Mack Army Personnel Carrier, ten wheels	460	690	925
L Mack Bekins Van, all white, ten wheels	750	1200	1800
L Mack Blue Diamond Dump, ten wheels	800	1300	1800
L Mack International Paper Co., ten wheels	700	1000	2100
L Mack Lyon Van, six wheels	550	875	1200
L Mack Material Truck, two barrels, six timbers, six wheels	350	550	750
L Mack Merchandise Van, six wheels	475	775	1200
L Mack Merchandise Van and Trailer, twelve wheels	850	1400	2500

Smith-Miller GMC Silver Streak Express Tractor-Trailer, No. 311-E, $425. Photo courtesy Bob Smith

Smith-Miller Toys (Continued)

	C6	C8	C10
L Mack Mobil Tandem Tanker, twelve wheels	800	1300	1800
L Mack Orange Hydraulic Dump, ten wheels	750	1650	2950
L Mack Orange Material Truck, three barrels, two boards, one large crate, one small, ten wheels	650	950	1200
L Mack P.I.E., fourteen wheels	450	800	1050
L Mack Sibley's Van, six wheels, rare	600	900	1500
L Mack Tandem Timber, eighteen or twenty-four timbers, six wheels	420	630	950
L Mack Telephone Truck, six wheels	600	1000	1400
L Mack West Coast Transport, six wheels	800	1300	1800
Lumber Trailer, No. 404-T, 17"	200	300	400
Lumber Truck, No. 201-L, sixty boards, six wheels, 14" long	300	400	550
Material Truck, No. 202-M, three barrels, three cases, eighteen boards, four wheels, 14" long	450	675	900
MIC Aerial Ladder	375	565	750
MIC Fruehauf Road Star Tractor-Trailer, fourteen wheels	400	600	950
MIC House Trailer	380	550	750
MIC Hydraulic Dump, ten wheels	500	850	1250
MIC Lift-O-Matic, two barrels, six wheels	500	800	1100
MIC Lincoln Capri (for MIC House Trailer), steerable	425	700	950
MIC P.I.E. Tractor-Trailer, fourteen wheels	375	600	850
MIC Teamsters Hydraulic Dump, ten wheels	500	850	1250

Smith-Miller MIC Lift-O-Matic, $1100. Photo courtesy Bob Smith

Smith-Miller Toys (Continued)

	C6	C8	C10
MIC Teamsters Tractor-Trailer, fourteen wheels	750	1100	1700
MIC Tow Truck, "Official Tow Car," six wheels	500	800	1200
MIC Tow Truck, unpainted, polished, six wheels	400	775	1025
MIC Tractor-Trailer, polished aluminum trailer, no decals, fourteen wheels	375	600	850
NEC Lumber Truck, nine timbers, six wheels	600	1000	1450
Oil Truck, No. 205-P, four drums, six wheels, 14" long	275	415	550
Red Ball, No. 212-R, fourteen wheels, 23-1/2" long	250	350	500
Scoop Dump, No. 403, 14" long	275	325	550
Searchlight Truck, No. 407, "Hollywood Film ad," 18-1/2" long	800	1500	2500
Silver Streak, No. 405, six-wheel tractor, 28" long	170	255	440
Stake Truck, No. 210-S, fourteen wheels, 23-1/2" long	250	375	500

Smith-Miller Searchlight Truck, No. 407, 18-1/2" long, $2500. Photo courtesy Bob Smith

Smith-Miller MIC Tow Truck, $1200. Photo courtesy Tim Oei

Smith-Miller Toys (Continued)

	C6	C8	C10
Sunkist Special, No. 211-L, fourteen wheels, 23-1/2" long	250	350	500
Timber Giant, No. 209-T, three logs, fourteen wheels, 23-1/2" long	260	350	550
Tow Truck, No. 401, 15" long	350	550	800

Steelcraft

	C6	C8	C10
Army Truck, Mack, c. 1930, 22" long	650	1000	1450
Bloomindale's Delivery Truck, 25" long	450	600	900
City Fire Dept. Ladder Truck, early	500	800	1200
City Milk Co. Truck, 18" long	400	600	800
Coca-Cola Truck, twelve bottles on side	400	600	800
Cream Crest Truck, 18" long	270	400	550
Dump Truck, Airflow	1500	2500	3500
Dump Truck, Mack, 26" long	450	700	1300
Fire Truck, 25" long	750	1100	1500
Fro-Joy Ice Cream Truck, c. 1930s	400	600	800
GMC Scissor Dump Truck	550	850	1400
Inter City Bus, 24" long	500	800	1100
Little Jim Fire Truck	600	900	1200
Little Jim Mack Dump Truck, red and black, c. 1928	600	900	1400

Steelcraft New York Trucking Co., 1930, 23-1/4" long, $1400. Photo courtesy John Gibson

Steelcraft Little Jim Mack Dump Truck, c. 1928, $1400. Photo courtesy Bob Smith

Steelcraft (Continued)

	C6	C8	C10
Model T Roadster Pedal Car, license No. 65-287, 50" long	450	675	900
New York Trucking Co., Headlights work, 1930, 23-1/4" long	800	1100	1400
Railway Express Truck, 26" long	1100	1600	2600
Sheffield Farms Truck, 1930s, 21" long	500	800	1300
Shell Motor Oil Truck, w/oil barrels	300	450	600
Steam Shovel, 26" long	225	350	450
Tank Truck, sheet metal, 25-1/2" long	650	1100	1500
U.S. Mail Truck, c. 1928, 27-1/4" long	1150	1725	2300

Structo

Structo of Freeport, Illinois, was founded in 1908 by brothers Louis and Edward Strohacker, and C.C. Thompson. They initially manufactured Erector Construction Kits, and in 1919 they started making toy vehicles. In 1935, J.G. Cokey bought a majority of the business, and when he died in 1975, the toy patents and designs were taken over by the Ertl Company.

Contributor: Randy Prasse, 916 Hayes Avenue, Racine, WI 53405, 414-637-0620.

	C6	C8	C10
Aerial Fire Truck, No. 902	100	150	200
Army Ambulance, No. 416, 17" long	175	263	350
Army Truck, w/canvas top, 21" long	125	200	300
Army Van, No. 415, pressed steel and canvas, 17-1/2" long	170	255	340
Auto Transport Trailer, No. 706, w/cars, 1953-54	115	175	250
Barrel Truck, No. 609, early 1950s	115	175	225
Barrel Truck, No. 811, wind-up, early to mid-1950s	115	175	225

Structo Barrel Truck, No. 811, early to mid-1950s, $225. Photo courtesy Randy Prasse

Structo Machinery Truck, No. 607, early 1950s, $250. Photo courtesy Randy Prasse

Structo (Continued)	C6	C8	C10
Bearcat Racer, clockwork, 12-1/4" long	400	600	800
Camper, w/cloth top, 12" long	55	82	110
Cattle Trailer, No. 708	100	125	175
Cement Mixer, c. 1950s, 20" long	100	150	350
Communications Center Truck, 21" long	175	265	350
Coupe, convertible, c. 1920s	350	545	760
Delivery Truck, tin, electric lights	150	225	300
Dump Truck, early, Mack type	200	300	400
Fire Dept. Emergency Patrol Truck, red bubble light, 1950s, 12" long	55	82	110
Garbage Truck, "Sanitation Dept."	110	160	225
Garbage Truck, 21" long	75	115	175
Gasoline Truck, No. 912, 1950s, 13" long	75	112	150
Gasoline Truck, No. 866, wind-up, steerable front axle, Structo 66 decals, red cab w/red body, early 1950s, 13-1/2" long	150	200	300
Grain Trailer, No. 704, early and mid-1950s	115	175	225
Guided Missile Launcher, No. 906, w/plastic launcher, missiles made of wood and vinyl, 13" long	70	105	140
Guided Missile Launching Truck, truck metal, plastic missiles, rubber tires	60	75	110
Hi-Lift Dump, No. 844, wind-up, early 1950s	110	165	220
Machinery Truck, No. 607, early 1950s	125	195	250
Motor Express Stake Truck, No. 601, also known as Freeport Motor Express Truck, early 1950s	55	83	110
Moving Van, No. 427, open cab, c. 1920, 16" long	175	265	350

Structo (Continued)	C6	C8	C10
Overland Freight Trailer, No. 704, early 1950s	100	150	200
Package Delivery, No. 603, early 1950s	100	160	200
Packard Dump Truck, No. 405, c. 1930, 18" long	600	950	1400
Police Patrol Truck, No. 426, 17" long	375	590	800
Renault Tank, clockwork, green w/red turret	260	400	520
Roadster, clockwork, 1920s, 16" long	600	1000	1400
Sand Loader, c. 1928, 12" high	100	150	200
Searchlight Truck, metal, light and generator plastic, uses batteries, has rubber tires	75	125	175
Shovel Dump, No. 605, also known as Structo Excavating Company, early 1950s	100	150	200
Stake Truck, lights work, 1930s, 21" long	250	600	900
Steam Shovel, 14" x 11"	75	150	200
Steam Shovel, 16"	57	87	115
Steam Shovel, 21" x 18" 95		140	190
Steel Cargo Trailer, No. 702, early to mid-1950s	125	175	225
Tank, No. 48, 11" long	225	338	450
Tank, olive drab w/orange turret, ten metal wheels, 12-1/2"	300	450	600
Transport Trailer, No. 700, early 1950s	90	135	180
Truck, "Structo Telephone Co.," c. 1948, 12" long	38	56	75
Truck Assortment No. 317, Dump Truck, blue, Stake Truck, Lumber Truck, heavy gauge metal, rubber wheels, original box folds to form garage, price per set, 1920s, each 9" long, 3-1/2" wide, 3-1/2" tall	175	250	400
U.S. Mail Delivery Truck, No. 428, 17" long	225	338	450
Whippet Tank, No. 48, heavy spring clockwork motor enameled green, red and black, may read "Patented 1920," 1929, 12"	200	300	400
Wrecker, "Toyland Garage"	50	75	125
Wrecker, No. 822, "Toyland Garage," wind-up, early to mid-1950s	100	135	200

Sturditoy Coal Dump Truck, 1920s, 25" long, $2900. Photo courtesy Tim Oei

Sturditoy Traveling Store, 26" long, $4200. Photo courtesy Bill Bertoia Auctions

Sturditoy

The Sturdy Corporation of Providence and Pawtucket, Rhode Island, manufactured its steel toy trucks from about 1929 to 1933.

	C6	C8	C10
Ambulance, open cab, c. 1929, 26" long	2000	3500	5000
American Railway Express Truck, c. 1920s, 26" long	1000	1800	2750
Coal Dump Truck, 1920s, 25" long	1200	2000	2900
Dump Truck, 1920s, 25" long	800	1300	1900
Dump Truck, 1920s, 26-1/2"	600	950	1300
Pumper, c. 1930, 26" long	1100	1800	2500
Sturditory Oil Company Truck, c. 1929, 27" long	1100	1800	2500
Traveling Store, 26" long	1800	2900	4200
U.S. Mail Screenside Truck	1200	2500	3500
Water Tower	1500	2500	3500
Wells Fargo Armored truck, c. 1927, 24" long	2200	3700	5500
Wrecker, 30" long	1000	1650	2750

Sun Rubber

Sun Rubber of Barberton, Ohio, was founded in 1923. Toy making started in 1924 and vehicles were introduced in April 1935. The owner was Tom W. Smith Jr.

Sun Rubber Art Deco Housetrailer, No. 1025, 4-3/8" long, $250. Photo courtesy Dave Leopard's book, Rubber Toy Vehicles

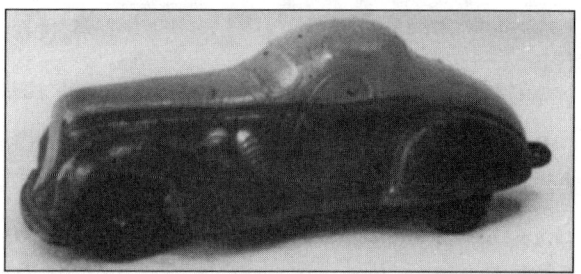

Sun Rubber Coupe, No. 515, 1936, 4" long, NPF. Photo courtesy Dave Leopard's book, Rubber Toy Vehicles

Contributor: Dave Leopard, 2507 Feather Run Trail, West Columbia, SC 29169-4915.

	C6	C8	C10
'34 DeSoto Airflow, No. 500, four-door sedan, 4" long (SA02)	25	35	50
'40 Dodge, No. 12001, four-door sedan, 4-1/2" long (SA03)	25	35	50
Ambulance, No. 12006, late 1930s, 3-3/4" long (ST07)	25	35	50
Art Deco Housetrailer, No. 1025, fits Teardrop Sedan, 4-3/8" long (SA05)	60	80	250
Coupe, No. 515, external exhaust pipes, 1936, 4" long (SA01)	25	35	50
Open Racer, No. 505, two drivers, 1936, 4-3/8" long (SR01)	25	35	50
Open Racer, No. 1000, full fenders on rear, 1936, 6-1/2" long (SR02)	40	60	80
Open Racer, No. 12012, boattail, "Super" racer, 6-3/4" long (SR03)	30	45	65
Pickup Truck, No. 510, stake sides, streamlined, 4-1/2" long (ST01)	25	35	55
Scout Car, No. 12014, four gunners, 1946, 6" long (SM02)	45	65	100
Tank, No. 12015, revolving turret and gunner, 1946, 6" long (SM01)	50	75	100
Teardrop Sedan, No. 1010, c. 1936, 5-1/2" long (SA04)	25	40	65
Town Car, No. 1015, Brewster-type limo, exposed driver, 5-3/8" (SA06)	40	60	95

Sun Rubber White Bus, No. 520, 1936, 4-1/2" long, $50. Photo courtesy Dave Leopard's book, Rubber Toy Vehicles

Sun Rubber (Continued)

	C6	C8	C10
Tractor/Trailer, No. 12013, one piece, three axles, futuristic, 5-1/8" long (ST03)	25	35	55
Truck, No. 12003, open, futuristic, 4-1/2" long (ST04)	25	35	50
Truck, No. 1005, open, stake side, streamlined, 5-1/4" (ST02)	35	45	55
Truck, No. 12111, open, "Master," futuristic, 5-5/8" long	25	35	55
White Bus, No. 520, streamlined, 1936, 4-1/2" long (ST07)	20	30	50
Woody Station Wagon, No. 12007, mid-1930s, 3-3/4" long (SA07)	20	30	50

Thomas Toys

Thomas Toys was founded by Islyn Thomas in 1944. Located at 80 Clinton Strett, Newark, New Jersey, at its peak it had 350 employees. The company's first toys were plastic jeeps, planes and vinyl dolls. Thomas sold the firm to Banner in 1960.

	C6	C8	C10
Buick Torpedo Sedan, No. 133, plastic, 11" long	20	30	40
Harley-Davidson, w/removable rider, 3" long	75	112	150
Jeep with Trailer, w/yellow driver wearing GI helmet, 1954, 8-3/8" long	14	16	18
Loudspeaker Van, No. 140, plastic, 4" long	20	25	30
Wrecker, 4-1/2" long	12	18	24

Tip-Top Toy Co.

Tip-Top toys were realistic, crisply detailed, and often unique. Wheels were either metal disks or Tootsietoy-like with lug bolts, metal hubs with rubber tires and rubber wheels. This progression helps to date the issues. Windshields and windows were open. Except where noted, cars and trucks were without bumpers.

Tip Top Toy 1923 Dodge (?) Coupe, 3-1/8", $32. Photo courtesy Ferd Zegel

Tip Top Toy Stake Truck, 4-5/8" long, $125. Photo courtesy Ferd Zegel

Contributors: Fred Maxwell, 4722 N. 33 St., Arlington, VA 22207.

Perry R. Eichor, 703 North Almond Drive, Simpsonville, SC 29681.

	C6	C8	C10
1923 Dodge (?) Coupe, 1923 Dodge, 3-1/8" (TTTV01)	16	24	32
Overland Bus, die-cast, thirteen windows, 3-3/8" long (TTTV05)	25	40	60
Stake Truck, four- or six-wheel versions, body cast separately and fastened to chassis, 4-5/8" long (TTTV13)	75	100	125
Tow Truck, 3-5/16" long	16	24	32

Toledo Metal Wheel Company

The Toledo Metal Wheel Company was located in Toledo, Ohio, during the early and late 1920s. It manufactured a large range of pedal cars, as well as toy trucks. Its trade name for its products was "Blue Streak."

	C6	C8	C10
Bull Dog Coal Truck, No. 50, 25" long	800	1350	1875
Bull Dog Dump Truck, No. 46, 26-1/2" long	600	1000	1475

Toledo Metal Wheel Company (Continued)

	C6	C8	C10
Bull Dog Moving Van, No. 48, 26" long	550	1050	1550
Bull Dog Sprinkler Truck, No. 47, 27-1/2" long	600	1100	1510
Bull Dog Truck, No. 45, open cab, 26" long	500	1000	1500
Fire Pumper Pedal Car, red, painted, 59" long	1250	1875	2500

Tommy Toy

Tommy Toy, 131 Palisade Ave., Union City, New Jersey, had its first sale on Nov. 13, 1935. Its principal owners were Dr. Albert Greene and Charles E. Weldon. It seems to have gone out of business between August 1938 and May 1939.

Some Tommy Toy vehicles resemble Metal Cast, Savoye, and other makers' vehicles. However, since slush molds did tend to change hands, production of a vehicle by one company would not preclude later manufacture of the same toy by another company. American Alloy is known to have produced copies of Tommy Toy's soldiers, using new molds. The only vehicle known to bear the Tommy Toy trademark is the No. 810 Cord.

	C6	C8	C10
Aerial Ladder Truck, (like Savoye), late 1920s type (TTV1)	20	30	40
Airflow-type Auto, like Savoye, c. 1935 (TTV2)	32	48	65
Ambulance, like Kansas Toy, late 1920s-early 1930s type (TTV3)	16	24	32
Cannon Truck, like Barclay; Barclay's had wooden hubs, mid-1930s (TTV5)	17	25	34
Convertible, 1935 Oldsmobile, w/driver, mid-to-late 1930s (TTV7)	10	15	20
Convertible, no driver, mid to late 1930s (TTV6)	18	27	36
Cord, No. 810, 1935 (TTV8)	40	60	80
Coupe, Packard, mid-1930s (TTV21)	17	26	35
Delivery Truck, "Delivery Deluxe," like Savoye, late 1930s (TTV9)	18	27	36
Double-Decker Bus, closed top, early 1930s (TTV10)	16	24	32
Double-Decker Bus, open top, extended hood, like Savoye, late 1920s (TTV11)	35	52	70

Tommy Toy (Continued)

	C6	C8	C10
Double-Decker Bus, open top, no hood, like Barclay, late 1930s (TTV12)	16	24	32
Dump Truck, resembles Kansas Toy, Best Toy, Manhattan Toys, late 1930s (TTV13)	16	24	32
Ladder Truck, mid-1930s (TTV15)	20	30	40
Police Patrol, solid windows, late 1920s-early 1930s type (TTV23)	35	52	70
Police Patrol, open windows, late 1920s-early 1930s type (TTV22)	70	105	140
Pumper, large, red hubs, late 1930s (TTV25)	11	16	22
Pumper, mid-1930s (TTV24)	12	18	25
Pumper, small, late 1930s (TTV26)	8	12	16
Racing Car, large, c. mid-1930s (TTV27)	16	24	32
Racing Car, small, c. mid-1930s (TTV28)	12	18	25
Sedan, four-door, c. 1935 (TTV29)	17	26	35
Sedan Towing "Tourist" Trailer, c. 1936-37 (TTV30)	40	60	100
Towing Car Coupe, like Savoye, early 1930s type (TTV31)	16	24	32
Truck, "General Trucking," late 1930s (TTV14)	12	18	25
Truck, "Milk Truck," grilled window, c. late 1930s (TTV17)	20	30	40
Truck, "Milk Truck," smooth window, c. late 1930s (TTV18)	20	30	40
Truck, "Milk," late 1930s (TTV16)	20	30	40
Truck, "Oil," "Cap 80000" (like Metal Cast, which has different capacity number), attaches to Tommy Toy Towing Car Coupe, 1930s (TTV20)	8	12	16
Truck, "Beer Truck," w/wooden barrels, late 1930s (TTV4)	14	21	28
Wrecker, late 1930s (TTV33)	10	15	20

Tonka

Tonka was incorporated in Mound, Minnesota, in September 1946. The firm had secured the tooling for a steam shovel and crane and clam from Streator Industries, which had unsuccessfully introduced these toys at the 1946 toy Fair. In 1948, Tonka introduced a forklift with trailer, and in 1949 premiered its line of trucks, including a dump and wrecker.

Contributors: Don Desalle, 5106 Knollwood, Anderson, IN 46011, 800-392-8697. DeSalle and his wife, Barb, are nationally-known authorities and collectors of Tonka trucks. The DeSalles are the authors of the Hasbro-licensed book, *Collector's Guide to Tonka Trucks 1947-1963*. Through the knowledge they have acquired at the antique shows the promote and attend, the DeSalles have an excellent knowledge base for the market value of Tonka trucks. The DeSalles are licensed to reproduce replacement parts for antique Tonka Trucks. These parts are available through Julian Thomas, Thomas Toy Parts, Fenton, Michigan. Please see the Collectors and Dealers section for more information.

John Taylor, P.O. Box 63, Nolensville, TN 37135-0063.

1947

	C6	C8	C10
No. 050 Steam Shovel, 20-3/4" long...	135	200	350
No. 150 Crane and Clam, 24" long	135	200	350

1948

	C6	C8	C10
No. 200 Power Lift Truck and Trailer.................................	200	350	600

1949

	C6	C8	C10
No. 100 Steam Shovel Deluxe, 22" long	100	250	400
No. 140 Tonka Toy Transport Van, 22-1/4" long	150	300	500

Tonka Power Lift Truck and Trailer, No. 200, 1948, $600. Photo courtesy Don and Barb DeSalle

1949 (Continued)

	C6	C8	C10
No. 180 Dump Truck, 12" long...........	100	175	375
No. 250 Wrecker Truck, 12-1/2" long.	125	250	375

1950

	C6	C8	C10
No. 145 Steel Carrier Semi, 22" long..	125	200	350
No. 175 Utility Hauler, 12" long	100	150	300

1951

	C6	C8	C10
No. 400 Allied Van Lines Semi, 23-1/2" long	175	260	400

1953

	C6	C8	C10
Wrecker	125	200	350
No. 575 Logger Semi, wood flat bed ..	125	180	350
No. 575 Logger Semi, 22-1/4"	125	180	350
No. 600 Road Grader, 17" long.............	50	75	100
No. 650 Green Giant Transport Semi, 22-1/4" long	150	300	500
No. 675 Trailer Fleet Set, two tractors, five interchangeable trailers, price per set	450	680	975

1954

	C6	C8	C10
Utility Truck	110	275	425
Wrecker	100	300	500
No. 145 Steel Carrier Truck	100	185	380
No. 580 Pickup Truck..........................	125	188	250
No. 700 Aerial Ladder Semi Fire Truck, 32-1/2" long..........................	175	260	450
No. 725 Minute Maid Delivery Van, 14-1/2" long	250	575	950
No. 725 Star Kist Van, 14-1/2"	250	575	950
No. 750 Carnation Milk Step Van, 11-3/4" long	200	400	600
No. 750 Parcel Delivery Van, 11-3/4" long..	200	300	500
No. 775 Road Builder Set, five-piece set, Road Grader, semi, T&T crane, and dump truck.................................	350	525	900

Tonka Utility Truck, 1954, $425. Photo courtesy Don and Barb DeSalle

Tonka Minute Maid Orange Juice Van, No. 725, 1955, $950. Photo courtesy Don and Barb DeSalle

Tonka Stake Truck, No. 860, 1955, $500. Photo courtesy Don and Barb DeSalle

Tonka Dump Truck, No. 180, 1956, 13" long, $350. Photo courtesy Don and Barb DeSalle

Tonka Gasoline Truck, 1957, 15" long, $1000. Photo courtesy Don and Barb DeSalle

1955

	C6	C8	C10
Allied Van Lines	150	275	500
Dump	100	150	350
Freighter	90	135	280
Hook and Ladder	100	300	450
Loboy and Shovel	150	300	450
Rescue Van	200	450	800
Wrecker	100	150	200
No. 065 Trailer, stake side	30	45	60
No. 600 Grader	75	125	200
No. 725 Minute Maid Orange Juice Van	275	650	950
No. 750 Carnation Milk Delivery Van	200	400	600
No. 850 Lumber Truck, six wheels	175	260	400
No. 860 Stake Truck, six wheels	175	360	500
No. 880 Pickup Truck	125	280	450

1956

	C6	C8	C10
Green Giant Semi Reefer	155	350	600
Rescue Squad Van, 11-3/4"	225	400	850
No. 120 Shovel and Carry-All (Loboy), 33" long total	188	280	475

1956 (Continued)

	C6	C8	C10
No. 180 Dump Truck, 13" long	100	150	350
No. 600 Road Grader, 17" long	75	125	200
No. 700 Aerial Ladder, 32-1/2" long	150	300	450
No. 880 Pickup Truck, 13-3/4"	150	350	650
No. 950 Pumper, 17" long	150	275	450
No. 980 Hi-Way Dump Truck, 13" long	130	280	395
No. 990 Suburban Pumper, 17"	175	262	350
No. 991 Farm Stake Truck, 13" long	150	250	460
No. 992 Aerial Sand Loader Set, includes Loader and Dump Truck	225	338	450
No. 994 Sand Loader Set, includes Loader and Dump Truck	90	135	180
No. 996 Wrecker, white, AAA, rare, 12" long	390	525	800
No. 998 Lumber Truck, 18-3/4" long	80	120	160

1957

	C6	C8	C10
Aerial Ladder Truck	200	300	500
Big Mike Dual Hydraulic Dump Truck, 14" long	325	595	1000

1957 (Continued)

	C6	C8	C10
Gasoline Truck, 15" long	350	525	1000
Hook and Ladder	150	225	300
Parcel Delivery Van, 12" long	200	350	500
Pickup with Stake Trailer, 20-1/2" long	150	250	400
Stake Trailer	30	45	75
Stock Rack Truck with Animals, 16-1/4" long	175	365	650
Three-in-One Hi-Way Service Truck, w/two snowblades, 13" long	275	400	700
Thunderbird Express Semi, 24" long	150	400	600
Wrecker	100	300	500

1958

	C6	C8	C10
No. 002 Pickup Truck	100	150	300
No. 003 Utility Truck	100	150	300
No. 005 Sportsman Pickup with Topper, 12-3/4" long	150	225	450
No. 006 Dump Truck	100	150	300
No. 012 Road Grader	75	112	150
No. 018 Wrecker Truck	100	250	450
No. 020 Hydraulic Dump Truck	125	175	275
No. 028 Pickup with Stake Trailer and Animal	125	175	275
No. 029 Sportsman Truck with Box Trailer	150	225	400
No. 032 Stock Rack Truck	175	300	500
No. 033 Gasoline Truck, hinged back door, hose and nozzle	350	500	900
No. 034 Deluxe Sportsman with Boat Trailer, 22-3/4" long	150	325	750
No. 036 Livestock Van	175	250	450
No. 037 Thunderbird Express	150	300	400
No. 039 Nationwide Moving Van, 24-1/2" long	250	475	800
No. 041 Hi-Way Service Truck	100	200	400
No. 043 Shovel & Carry-All Trailer	200	300	500
No. 045 Big Mike Dual Hydraulic Dump Truck with Snow Plow	375	675	1000
No. 046 Suburban Pumper	175	225	450
No. 048 Hydraulic Aerial Ladder	100	250	450

1959

	C6	C8	C10
Sanitary Truck, square back	450	700	1000
No. 001 Service Truck, 12-3/4"	100	150	350

1959 (Continued)

	C6	C8	C10
No. 005 Sportsman	100	175	350
No. 014 Dragline, 20" long	100	175	375
No. 016 Air Express	350	425	700
No. 022 Deluxe Sportsman	150	325	500
No. 030 Tandem Platform Stake, 28-1/4" long	240	450	800
No. 036 Tandem Air Express, w/trailer, 24-3/4" long	225	338	450
No. 040 Car Carrier	85	128	170
No. 041 Boat Transport, 38"	175	263	350
No. 042 Hydraulic Land Rover, 15" long	350	525	700
No. 044 Dragline & Trailer, 26-1/4" long	150	275	400

1960

	C6	C8	C10
Tonka Ford Falcon, from set	50	75	100
Tonka Jolly Green Giant Special, white, green stake racks	375	450	850
Tonka Standard Oil Company Wrecker Special	250	375	500
No. 001 Service Truck	100	150	350
No. 002 Pickup	100	200	375
No. 005 Sportsman	100	275	400
No. 006 Dump Truck	75	125	290
No. 008 Logger	150	225	300
No. 018 Wrecker, white sidewalls	150	225	300
No. 020 Hydraulic Dump	75	150	375
No. 022 Deluxe Sportsman	100	250	400
No. 028 Pickup and Trailer	100	150	300
No. 037 Thunderbird Express	150	350	550
No. 040 Car Carrier	100	225	450
No. 041 Boat Transport, 38" long	250	450	850
No. 046 Surburban Pumper	100	250	350
No. 048 Aerial Ladder	125	250	350
No. 100 Bulldozer, plated roller wheels only in 1960, 8-7/8"	75	125	200
No. 105 Rescue Squad, 13-3/4" long	100	250	450
No. 110 Fisherman Pickup with Sportsman Cover, 14" long	100	175	375
No. 115 Power Boom Loader, 1960 only, 18-1/2" long	300	650	1000
No. 120 Cement Mixer, 15-1/2" long	100	150	300

1960 (Continued)

	C6	C8	C10
No. 125 Loboy & Bulldozer, 26-1/4" long ... 190		375	675
No. 130 Deluxe Fisherman, also new boat and trailer ... 150		350	550
No. 135 Mobile Dragline ... 100		250	450
No. 140 Sanitary Truck ... 350		550	900
No. 145 Tanker, first Tonka w/major use of plastic, 28" long ... 100		250	450

1961

	C6	C8	C10
No. 002 Pickup ... 100		190	320
No. 005 Sportsman ... 100		150	375
No. 006 Dump Truck ... 75		100	250
No. 012 Road Grader, yellow ... 75		100	200
No. 014 Dragline, yellow ... 100		150	250
No. 018 Wrecker ... 100		250	400
No. 020 Hydraulic Dump ... 75		110	250
No. 022 Deluxe Sportsman ... 100		200	450
No. 039 Allied Van ... 120		250	450
No. 040 Car Carrier ... 100		250	450
No. 041 Boat Transport Truck ... 150		300	650
No. 048 Aerial Ladder ... 125		200	450
No. 116 Dump Truck with Sandloader, 23-1/4" long ... 100		175	395
No. 117 Boat Service Truck, 1961 only ... 100		250	450
No. 118 Giant Dozer, 12-1/2" long ... 70		100	250
No. 120 Cement Mixer ... 100		150	300
No. 130 Deluxe Fisherman ... 150		350	550
No. 134 Grading Service Truck, Trailer and bulldozer, 25-1/2" long ... 100		150	350
No. 135 Mobile Dragline ... 100		250	450
No. 136 Houseboat Set, 29" long total ... 200		400	800

Tonka Cement Mixer, No. 620, 1962, $300. Photo courtesy Don and Barb DeSalle

1961 (Continued)

	C6	C8	C10
No. 142 Mobile Clam, 27-1/4" long ... 100		250	450
No. 145 Tanker ... 100		250	350

1962

	C6	C8	C10
No. 200 Jeep Dispatcher, 9-3/4" long ... 50		75	100
No. 201 Serv-I-Car, 9-1/8" long ... 75		125	200
No. 249 Jeep Universal ... 75		125	175
No. 300 Bulldozer ... 50		75	100
No. 301 Utility Dump, rervised Golf Club Tractor, 1961 only, 12-1/2" long ... 100		150	300
No. 302 Pickup ... 95		150	250
No. 308 Stake Pickup, 12-5/8" long ... 50		100	200
No. 350 Jeep Surrey, fringe top, 10-1/2" long ... 75		125	200
No. 402 Loader, yellow and green ... 40		60	80
No. 405 Sportsman ... 75		100	200
No. 406 Dump Truck ... 75		150	275
No. 410 Jet Delivery Truck, 1962 only, 14" long ... 200		350	850
No. 420 Airlines Luggage Service, 16-5/8" long ... 100		250	400
No. 512 Road Grader ... 45		68	90
No. 514 Dragline ... 150		225	300
No. 516 Jeep Runabout, Trailer and Boat, 25-5/8" long ... 75		175	350
No. 518 Wrecker ... 75		175	350
No. 520 Hyraulic Dump ... 75		100	220
No. 524 Dozer Packer, Packer has eleven tires, sold only in 1962, 18-1/4" long ... 100		250	400
No. 528 Pickup and Trailer ... 50		75	150
No. 530 Camper, 14" long ... 75		150	250
No. 616 Dump Truck and Sand Loader ... 75		125	240
No. 618 Giant Dozer ... 100		150	200
No. 620 Cement Mixer ... 85		150	300
No. 739 Allied Van ... 125		250	350
No. 834 Grading Service Truck ... 70		100	150
No. 840 Car Carrier ... 100		150	300
No. 926 Pumper Truck ... 100		150	300
No. 942 Mobile Clam ... 100		150	320
No. 1348 Aerial Ladder ... 100		150	350

Tonka Jeep Pumper, No. 425, 1963, 10-3/4" long, $400. Photo courtesy Don and Barb DeSalle

Tonka Dump Truck and Sand Loader, No. 616, 1963, $235. Photo courtesy Don and Barb DeSalle

1963	C6	C8	C10
No. 050 Mini-Tonka Jeep Pickup, 9-1/4" long	35	52	70
No. 056 Mini-Tonka Stake Truck, 9-1/4" long	35	52	70
No. 060 Mini-Tonka Dump, 9-3/4" long	30	50	75
No. 068 Mini-Tonka Wrecker, 9-1/2" long	30	50	75
No. 070 Mini-Tonka Camper, 9-5/8" long	75	112	150
No. 201 Servi-I-Car	55	82	110
No. 251 Military Jeep Universal, 10-1/2" long	25	38	50
No. 300 Bulldozer	55	82	110
No. 302 Pickup	35	52	70
No. 308 Stake Pickup	50	95	150
No. 350 Jeep Surrey	50	75	100
No. 352 Loader	40	60	80
No. 354 Style-Side Pickup, 14" long	40	60	125
No. 406 Dump Truck	45	68	90
No. 422 Back Hoe, 17-1/8" long	100	175	350
No. 425 Jeep Pumper, 10-3/4" long	100	175	400
No. 514 Dragline	60	90	120
No. 516 Jeep Runabout, Trailer and Boat	75	150	300
No. 518 Wrecker	45	75	150
No. 520 Hydraulic Dump Truck	45	68	90
No. 524 Dozer Packer, yellow	200	300	400
No. 530 Camper	25	38	50
No. 536 Giant Dozer	110	160	225
No. 616 Dump Truck and Sand Loader, yellow	100	150	235

1963 (Continued)	C6	C8	C10
No. 620 Cement Mixer	75	125	175
No. 625 Stake Pickup and Horse Trailer, 21-3/4" long overall	75	125	175
No. 640 Ramp Hoist, red and white, 19-1/4" long	175	350	550
No. 720 Terminal Train, fifteen suitcases, 33-5/8" long total	105	175	300
No. 739 Allied Van	118	175	235
No. 840 Car Carrier	42	63	85
No. 926 Pumper	60	90	120
No. 942 Mobile Clam	75	112	150
No. 1001 Trencher & Loboy, 28-1/2" long	75	112	150
No. 1348 Aerial Ladder Truck	100	150	200
No. 2100 Airport Service Set	150	225	300

1964	C6	C8	C10
No. 077 Mini-Tonka Mixer, 9"	30	50	75
No. 086 Mini-Tonka Van, 16"	36	54	72
No. 096 Mini-Tonka Car Carrier, two cars, 18-1/2" long	50	75	100
No. 250 Military Tractor, black seat	55	70	100
No. 251 Military Jeep Universal	35	55	75
No. 304 Jeep Commander, canvas top, 10-1/2" long	30	50	75
No. 315 Dump Truck, 13-1/2"	40	60	90
No. 375 Jeep Wrecker, 11"	75	130	200
No. 380 Troop Carrier, 14"	70	100	150
No. 384 Military Jeep and Box Trailer, 19-3/8" overall	50	75	150
No. 404 Stake Truck, red	70	120	170
No. 425 Jeep Pumper, black steering wheel	100	150	275
No. 504 Stake Pickup & Trailer, 21-5/8" long	50	75	185

Tonka Ramp Hoist, No. 640, 1964, $900. Photo courtesy Don and Barb DeSalle

1964 (Continued)

	C6	C8	C10
No. 525 Jeep & Horse Trailer, two horses, 19-1/4" long total	45	68	135
No. 616 Dump Truck and Sandloader, orange and yellow	75	125	175
No. 640 Ramp Hoist, park green and white, very rare	300	650	900
No. 739 Allied Van Lines, black knob on door	75	125	175
No. 900 Mighty Tonka Dump Truck	65	100	230
No. 942 Mobile Clam, yellow	50	75	100
No. 998 Aerial Ladder, two auxiliary ladders	50	75	100

Tootsietoy

Tootsietoy is one of the best-known names in the world of the toy collecting, and for good reason.

The toys, products of a Chicago concern that now has a century of manufacturing behind it, have long appealed to parents because of their cheap price, and to kids because of their high play value. The Tootsietoy line through the years has included toy cars, trucks, trains, dollhouse furniture, airplanes and toy soldiers. During the company's heyday, roughly from the 1930s through 1960s, a person would have had to search long and hard to find a child with no knowledge of the trademark.

Dowst and Company started in 1876 in the publishing trade, and moved into manufacturing after the 1893 Columbian World Exposition in Chicago, where the new die-casting technology was introduced to the public. By then named Dowst Brothers, the company released its first die-cast-body, free-axle toy car in 1911, the generic Limousine. The first specific-model car, the Model T Ford touring car, followed in 1914. The name Tootsietoy was adopted in the early 1920s and was registered in 1924 as the company's trademark.

Theodore Dowst, who joined the firm in 1906, is generally seen as the guiding force behind the growth of toy production at Dowst Brothers. He remained with the company even after its purchase by Nathan Shure in 1926, until 1945. For most collectors, the toys of the Ted Dowst period are the most noteworthy.

High points in the world of Tootsietoy collecting include the 1933 Graham series, notable for its use of three-piece construction, with separately die-cast bodies, chassis and radiator grilles, and the 1935 LaSalles, which used four-piece construction, adding a casting for the rear bumpers. Collectors also avidly seek the 1932-33 Funnies series cars, which featured such comic figures as Andy Gump, Uncle Walt and Moon Mullins.

Interest seems to be growing in the various advertising toys Tootsietoy produced through the years, ranging from the 1932 Wrigley's Railroad Express truck to more recent U-Haul and Coast-to-Coast vehicles. Collector demand for postwar toys remains stable at a fairly low level; and it may not grow stronger any time soon, given the heavy contemporary interest in detailed scale models as opposed to made-for-play toys. On the other hand, interest in the post-Vietnam toys is inching upward, reflecting the maturing of the later Baby Boomers.

Contributors: Mark Rich, P.O. Box 971, Stevens Point, WI 54481. Rich is a toy collector and writer. A columnist for *Toy Shop* and *Toy Cars & Models*, he is also the author of *100 Greatest Baby Boomer Toys* (Krause Publications).

John Gibson, 9713 Pleasant Gate Lane Potomac, MD 20854.

Miniature Ships

	C6	C8	C10
No. 0127 Destroyer, 4" long	9	12	15
No. 0128 Submarine, 4" long	9	12	15
No. 0129 Tender, 4" long	10	15	20
No. 0130 Yacht, 4" long	18	24	30
No. 0196 Battleship	4	6	8
No. 1035 Cruiser, 5-1/2" long	15	20	25
No. 1036 Aircraft Carrier, 6" long	14	21	28
No. 1037 Transport, 6" long	15	20	25
No. 1038 Freighter, 5-1/2" long	15	20	25
No. 1039 Tanker, 5-1/2" long	15	20	25
No. 1405 Fleet, nine-piece carded battleship assortment: USS Idaho, USS Indiana, USS Tennessee, USS Texas, USS New Mexico, USS Maryland, USS Arizona, USS New York, USS Pennsylvania, 1941	50	75	100
No. 1408 Naval Defense, fourteen-piece carded assortment, 1941	70	105	140
No. 1612 Cruiser	3	4	6
No. 1613 Destroyer	3	4	6

Miniature Ships (Continued)

	C6	C8	C10
No. 1614 Submarine, smaller	2	3	4
No. 1618 Submarine	3	4	6
No. 1619 Destroyer	3	4	6
No. 1620 Aero Carrier	4	6	8
No. 1638 Battleship	4	6	8
No. 1811 Sea Champions, five-piece carded set contains two No. 1638 battleships, one No. 1618 submarine, one No. 1619 destroyer, and one No. 1620 aero carrier, 1946	30	45	60
No. 4519 Battleship	8	12	16
No. 4538 Tugboat	2	3	4
No. 4539 Speedboat	2	3	4

Prewar

	C6	C8	C10
Ford Model A Delivery Van, "US Mail," sold in sets only, 1931	38	56	75
No. 0023 Racer with Driver, 1927	35	60	80
No. 0230 LaSalle Sedan, 3" long	15	20	30
No. 0231 Chevy Coupe, 3" long	15	20	30
No. 0232 Buick Roadmaster Touring Coupe, 3" long	15	20	30
No. 0233 Boattail Roadster, 3" long	15	20	30
No. 0234 GMC Box Truck, 3" long	15	20	30
No. 0235 Oil Tank Truck, 3" long	13	18	25

Tootsietoy Roamer House Trailer (Prewar), No. 1044, 1937, $200. Photo courtesy John Gibson

Tootsietoy Wrigley GMC Box Truck (Prewar), No. 1010, 1940, $110. Photo courtesy John Gibson

Prewar (Continued)

	C6	C8	C10
No. 0236 Hook and Ladder Fire engine, 3" long	20	30	40
No. 0237 Insurance Patrol Fire Engine, 3" long	15	25	35
No. 0238 Hose Wagon Fire Engine, 3" long	20	30	40
No. 0239 '38 Ford Paneled Station Wagon, 3" long	30	40	50
No. 1010 Wrigley GMC Box Truck, 1940, 4" long	55	80	110
No. 1043 Small Ford Sedan or Coupe 111 or 112, and Camping Trailer, 1937	35	53	70
No. 1044 Roamer House Trailer, w/door and tin bottom, 1937	150	175	200
No. 1046 Paneled Station Wagon, 1940, 4" long	43	64	85
No. 4528 Limousine, 1911	24	32	40
No. 4570 Ford Model T Tourer, 1914	35	50	65
No. 4610 Ford Model T Pickup, 1916	35	50	70
No. 4629 Sedan, "Yellow Cab", 1923	15	25	60
No. 4634 Army Supply Truck, 1939, 4" long	33	50	65
No. 4635 Armored Car, 1938, 4" long	33	50	65
No. 4636 Buick Coupe, 1924	23	34	45
No. 4641 Buick Touring Car, 1925	28	42	55
No. 4642 Army Long-Range Cannon, 1931	13	18	25
No. 4647 Renault Tank with treads, 1931, 3" long	23	34	45
No. 4648 Steamroller, 1931, 3" long	65	95	125
No. 4651 Fageol Safety Coach, 1927	30	45	65
No. 4652 Hook & Ladder Fire Engine, 1927	39	52	75
No. 4653 Water Tower Fire Engine, 1927	38	56	75

Tootsietoy Ford Model T Tourer (Prewar), No. 4570, 1914, $65. Photo courtesy David Richter

Prewar (Continued)

	C6	C8	C10
No. 4654 Huber Star Farm Tractor, 1927	40	65	95
No. 4655 Ford Model A Coupe, 1928	20	30	40
No. 4665 Ford Model A Sedan, 1929	20	30	40
No. 4666 Bluebird Dayton Record Car, 1932, 4" long	30	45	55
No. 4680 Overland Bus Lines, 1929	45	65	95

5091 Funnies Series (1932)

	C6	C8	C10
No. 5101 Andy Gump Roadster, mechanical	225	340	450
No. 5101 Andy Gump Roadster	175	265	350
No. 5102 Uncle Walt Roadster, mechanical	225	340	450
No. 5102 Uncle Walt Roadster	175	265	350
No. 5103 Smitty Motorcycle, mechanical	225	340	450
No. 5103 Smitty Motorcycle	175	265	350
No. 5104 Moon Mullins Police Wagon, mechanical	225	340	450
No. 5104 Moon Mullins Police Wagon	175	265	350
No. 5105 Kayo Ice Wagon, mechanical	240	320	400
No. 5105 Kayo Ice Wagon	150	225	300
No. 5106 Uncle Willie Rowboat, mechanical	240	320	400
No. 5106 Uncle Willie Rowboat	135	210	275

Camelback Delivery Van Series (1937), 3" Vehicles

	C6	C8	C10
No. 0123 Lewis's	195	260	325
No. 0123 McLeans	280	380	475
No. 0123 Miller & Rhoads	300	400	500

Camelback Delivery Van Series (1937), 3" Vehicles (Continued)

	C6	C8	C10
No. 0123 Shepards	285	380	475
No. 0123 Special Delivery	30	40	55
No. 0123 Wieboldt's	285	380	475

Depression-Years Miniatures (1931)

	C6	C8	C10
No. 0101/4656 Buick Marquette Coupe, 1931	10	15	20
No. 0102 Buick Marquette Roadster, 1932?	13	19	25
No. 0103/4657 Buick Marquette Sedan, 1931	10	15	20
No. 0104/4658 Mack Insurance Patrol Fire truck, 1931	25	35	45
No. 0105 Mack Tank Truck, 1932	25	40	55
No. 0106 Low Wing Monoplane, w/prop, tin wings, 1932	35	55	70
No. 0107 High Wing Monoplane, w/prop, tin wings, 1932	35	55	70
No. 0108 Caterpillar Tractor, w/tread, 1932	23	34	45
No. 0109 Ford Stake Truck, 1932	20	30	40
No. 0110 Bluebird Dayton Racer, 1932	25	40	55

Federal Delivery Van Series (1924)

	C6	C8	C10
No. 4630 Grocery	35	55	85
No. 4631 Bakery	50	80	105
No. 4632 Market	35	60	75
No. 4633 Laundry	45	65	95
No. 4634 Milk, most common in series	25	40	55
No. 4635 Florist, rarest in series	95	175	225

Tootsietoy Kayo Ice Wagon (5091 Funnies Series, 1932), No. 5105, $300. Photo courtesy John Gibson

This No. 4630 Grocery Van is embossed with "Emil Kraus State at 18th." Emil Kraus was an Erie, Pennsylvania store

Tootsietoy Florist (Federal Delivery Van Series, 1924), No. 4635, $225. Photo courtesy John Gibson

Tootsietoy '35 Wrecker (Ford V8 Series, 1935, 3" Vehicles), No. 0113, $65

Ford V8 Series (1935), 3" Vehicles	C6	C8	C10
No. 0111 '34 Sedan	30	45	60
No. 0111 '35 Sedan	15	23	30
No. 0112 '34 Coupe	33	49	65
No. 0112 '35 Coupe	18	26	35
No. 0113 '34 Wrecker	38	56	75
No. 0113 '35 Wrecker	33	49	65
No. 0114 '34 Convertible Coupe	40	60	80
No. 0114 '35 Convertible Coupe	30	45	60
No. 0115 '34 Convertible Sedan	40	60	80
No. 0115 '35 Convertible Sedan	30	45	60
No. 0116 '35 Roadster	23	34	45
No. 0117 '35 Roadster Fire Chief Car	50	75	100
No. 0118 DeSoto Airflow Sedan, 1935, 3" long	27	40	55

GM Series (1927)	C6	C8	C10
No. 6-02 No-Name Coupe	55	83	110
No. 6-03 No-Name Brougham	55	83	110
No. 6-04 No-Name Sedan	55	83	110
No. 6-05 No-Name Touring Car	75	113	150
No. 6-06 No-Name Screenside Delivery Truck	65	95	125
No. 6-01 No-Name Roadster	55	83	110
No. 6001 Buick Roadster	30	45	60

Tootsietoy No-Name Screenside Delivery Truck (GM Series, 1927), No. 6-06, $125

Tootsietoy No-Name Touring Car (GM Series, 1927), No. 6-05, $150

Tootsietoy Cadillac Touring Car (GM Series, 1927), No. 6105, $120. Photo courtesy John Gibson

GM Series (1927) (Continued)	C6	C8	C10
No. 6002 Buick Coupe	28	41	55
No. 6003 Buick Brougham	28	41	55
No. 6004 Buick Sedan	28	41	55
No. 6005 Buick Touring Car	50	75	100
No. 6006 Buick Screenside Delivery Truck	35	53	70
No. 6101 Cadillac Roadster	40	60	80
No. 6102 Cadillac coupe	40	60	80
No. 6103 Cadillac Brougham	40	60	80
No. 6104 Cadillac Sedan	40	60	80
No. 6105 Cadillac Touring Car	60	90	120
No. 6106 Cadillac Screenside Delivery Truck	48	71	95

GM Series (1927) (Continued)	C6	C8	C10
No. 6201 Chevrolet Roadster	33	50	65
No. 6202 Chevrolet Coupe	33	50	65
No. 6203 Chevrolet Brougham	33	50	65
No. 6204 Chevrolet Sedan	33	50	65
No. 6205 Chevrolet Touring Car	55	83	110
No. 6206 Chevrolet Screenside Delivery Truck	35	53	70
No. 6301 Oldsmobile Roadster	38	55	75
No. 6302 Oldsmobile Coupe	35	53	70
No. 6303 Oldsmobile Brougham	35	53	70
No. 6304 Oldsmobile Sedan	35	53	70
No. 6305 Oldsmobile Touring Car	55	83	110
No. 6306 Oldsmobile Screenside Delivery Truck	45	68	90

Graham Series (1933), 4" Vehicles	C6	C8	C10
Bild-A-Car Coupe, four wheels	65	95	130
Bild-A-Car Roadster, four wheels	85	130	175
Bild-A-Car Sedan, four wheels	65	95	130
Commercial Tire & Supply Co. Van	112	168	225
Commerical Tire & Supply Co. Van	75	110	150
No. 0511 Roadster, five wheels	80	125	165
No. 0512 Coupe, five wheels	70	110	145
No. 0513 Sedan, five wheels	70	110	145
No. 0514 Convertible Coupe, five wheels	120	160	200
No. 0515 Convertible Sedan, five wheels	80	120	160
No. 0516 Towncar, five wheels	88	130	175
No. 0611 Roadster, six wheels	120	160	200
No. 0612 Coupe, six wheels	72	110	145
No. 0613 Sedan, six wheels	70	110	145

Graham Series (1933), 4" Vehicles (Continued)	C6	C8	C10
No. 0614 Convertible Coupe, six wheels	80	120	160
No. 0615 Convertible Sedan, six wheels	80	120	160
No. 0616 Towncar, six wheels	75	110	150
No. 0806 Wrecker	75	110	150
No. 0808 Tootsietoy Dairy Delivery Van	120	160	200
No. 0809 Army Ambulance	75	110	150

Jumbo Series (1936), 6" Vehicles	C6	C8	C10
No. 1016 Auburn Torpedo Roadster	23	34	45
No. 1017 Torpedo Coupe	20	30	40
No. 1018 Torpedo Sedan	20	30	40
No. 1019 Torpedo Pickup truck	20	30	40
No. 1026/1045 Torpedo Cross-Country "Greyhound" Bus	25	55	80
No. 1027 Torpedo Wrecker	23	34	45
No. 1045 Greyhound Bus, w/tin bottom	25	50	70
No. 1045 Trans-America Bus, sold only in sets, 1941	90	130	175

LaSalle Series (1935), 4" Vehicles	C6	C8	C10
No. 0180 Zephyr and Roamer House Trailer, wind-up	660	880	1100
No. 0180 Zephyr and Roamer House Trailer	555	740	925
No. 0712 Coupe	115	180	240
No. 0713 Sedan	115	180	240
No. 0714 Convertible Coupe	125	205	265
No. 0715 Convertible Sedan	125	205	265
No. 0716 Briggs-Lincoln prototype, "Doodlebug"	75	95	125

Tootsietoy Commercial Tire & Supply Co. Van (Graham Series, 1933, 4" Vehicles), $225. Photo courtesy John Gibson

Tootsietoy Briggs-Lincoln prototype (LaSalle Series, 1935, 4" Vehicles), No. 0716, $125. Photo courtesy John Gibson

Tootsietoy City Fuel Company Coal Truck (Mack Delivery Trucks and Vans, 1933, 4" Vehicles), No. 0804, 1933, $150. Photo courtesy John Gibson

Tootsietoy Tootsietoy Dairy Tanker (Mack Tractor-Trailers 1:43-scale, 1931), No. 0192, 1935, $150. Photo courtesy Phillips

LaSalle Series (1935), 4" Vehicles (Continued)

	C6	C8	C10
No. 6015 Zephyr, wind-up version	240	365	485
No. 6015 Zephyr	165	245	325
No. 6016 Wrecker, wind-up version ...	350	525	700
No. 6016 Wrecker	150	230	350

MackDelivery Trucks and Vans (1933), 4" Vehicles

	C6	C8	C10
No. 0804 City Fuel Company Coal Truck, ten-wheel, 1933	75	115	150
No. 0804 City Fuel Company Coal Truck, four-wheel, 1937	60	95	130
No. 0807 Delivery Motorcycle, (1933 adaped from 5103)	85	125	175
No. 0810 Railway Express Co., Wrigley's Gum, two-piece cab	75	115	165
No. 0810 Railway Express Co., Wrigley's Gum, one-piece cab, 1935	70	105	150
No. 1040 Hook and Ladder	35	50	70
No. 1041 Hose Car	35	55	75
No. 1042 Insurance Patrol, w/ladder and rear fireman	35	55	75
No. 1042 Insurance Patrol, open end	30	45	60

Mack Tractor-Trailers 1:43-scale (1931)

	C6	C8	C10
Auto Transport, trailer holds three 1940s Buicks in tilted position, 1941	275	415	550
No. 0190 Auto Transport Four-car Hauler, w/101-103 Buicks and 109 Ford, 1933	115	170	225

Tootsietoy Domaco tank Semi-Trailer (Mack Tractor-Trailers 1:43-scale, 1931), No. 0802, $150. Photo courtesy John Gibson

Tootsietoy Long Distance Hauling (Mack Tractor-Trailers 1:43-scale, 1931), No. 0803, 1933, $175. Photo courtesy John Gibson

Mack Tractor-Trailers 1:43-scale (1931) (Continued)

	C6	C8	C10
No. 0190 Auto Transport Three-car Hauler, w/101-103 Buicks, 1931	105	140	175
No. 0191 Contractor Set, w/Mack AC hauling three spoke-wheeled tipper trailers, 1933......................................	105	140	175
No. 0192 Tootsietoy Dairy Tanker, one-piece cab, three trailers, 1935	75	115	150
No. 0192 Tootsietoy Dairy Tanker, two-piece cab, three trailers, 1933	120	160	200
No. 0198 Auto Transport, two-piece cab, three '35 Fords...........................	150	250	350
No. 0198 Auto Transport, one-piece cab, three '35 Fords...........................	125	200	275
No. 0801 Express Stake Semi-Trailer, two-piece cab	80	105	135
No. 0801 Express Stake Semi-Trailer, one-piece cab, 1933.............................	55	80	105
No. 0802 Domaco Tank Semi-Trailer, two-piece cab	90	120	150
No. 0802 Domaco Tank Semi-Trailer, one-piece cab, 1933................	60	90	120
No. 0803 Long Distance Hauling, Semi-Trailer, 1933	85	130	175
No. 0805 Tootsietoy Dairy Semi-Trailer, single tires	60	90	120
No. 0805 Tootsietoy Dairy Semi-Trailer, dual tires, 1933	70	105	140

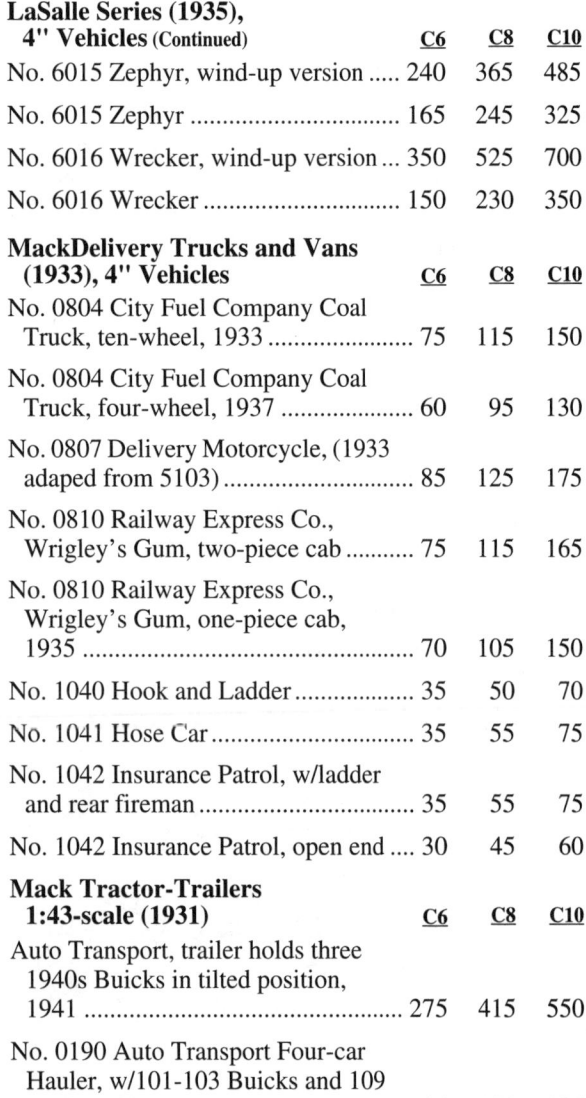

Tootsietoy Tootsietoy Dairy Semi-Trailer (Mack Tractor-Trailers 1:43-scale, 1931), No. 0805, 1933, $140

Mack Trucks 1:72-scale (1925)

	C6	C8	C10
No. 0170 Interchangeable Truck Set, 1925-31	50	65	80
No. 4638 Stake Truck, 1925, revised 1928	23	34	45
No. 4639 Coal Truck, 1925, revised 1928	23	34	45
No. 4640 Tank Truck, 1925, revised 1928	23	34	45
No. 4643 Anti-Aircraft Gun Army Truck, 1931	25	38	50
No. 4644 Searchlight Army Truck, 1931	65	95	130
No. 4645 US Mail Air Mail Service, 1931	35	55	75
No. 4670 A&P Trailer Truck, 1929	100	150	200
No. 4670 American Railway Express Trailer Truck, 1929	115	170	225

Midget Series/Cracker Jacks (1936), 1" Vehicles

	C6	C8	C10
No. 0120 Oil Tank truck, 1936, 3" long	23	34	45
No. 0121 Ford Pickup Truck, 1936, 3" long	18	26	35
No. 0510 Boxed Set, (ten-piece)	90	130	175
No. 0510 Boxed Set, (eight-piece)	75	100	150
No. 0610 Boxed Set, (twelve-piece, 1941?)	100	150	200
No. 1628 Bus	6	9	12
No. 1629 Wrecker	7	10	14
No. 1630 Racer	5	7	10
No. 1631 DeSoto Airflow Sedan	5	7	10
No. 1632 Zephyr Railcar	7	10	14
No. 1634 Fire Engine	7	10	14
No. 1635 Delivery Van	6	9	12
No. 1666 Army Tank	4	6	8
No. 1667 Armored Car	6	9	12

Reo Oil Truck Series (1938), 6" Trucks

	C6	C8	C10
No. 1006 Standard	35	55	80
No. 1007 Sinclair	35	55	80
No. 1008 Texaco	35	55	80
No. 1009 Shell	40	60	90

Postwar

	C6	C8	C10
'31 Ford B Hot Rod, 1961, 3" long	8	12	20
'38 Buick Y Experimental Convertible, 4" long	20	30	40
'40 Ford Special Deluxe Convertible, 1960, 6" long	20	30	40
'40 Ford V-8 Hot Rod, 1960, 6" long	15	22	30
'41 Chrysler Windsor Convertible, 4" long	20	30	40
'41 International Army Ambulance, 4" long	24	34	50
'41 International K1 Panel Truck, 4" long	22	32	45
'41 White Army Half Track, 4" long	10	16	25
'42 Chrysler Thunderbolt Experimental Roadster, 6" long	22	34	45
'46 International K11 Oil Tanker, Shell, 6" long	25	40	65
'46 International K11 Oil Tanker, Sinclair, 6" long	25	35	55
'46 International K11 Oil Tanker, Texaco, 6" long	25	40	65
'46 International K11 Oil Tanker, Standard, 6" long	25	35	55
'47 Chevrolet Fleetmaster Coupe, 4" long	13	19	25
'47 Hudson Streamlined Pickup, 4" long	22	32	45
'47 Kaiser Sedan, 6" long	28	37	50
'47 Mack L-Line Dump Truck, 6" long	14	25	35
'47 Mack L-Line Fire Pumper, 6" long	35	55	70
'47 Mack L-Line Stake Truck, 6" long	22	32	45
'47 Mack L-Line Wrecker, 6" long	20	30	40
'47 Offenhauser Race Car, 4" long	13	19	25
'47 Offenhauser Race Car, on trailer, 4" long	15	22	30
'47 Studebaker Champion Coupe, rare, 3" long	25	35	55

Postwar (Continued)

	C6	C8	C10
'48 Buick Super Estate Wagon, 6" long	27	42	65
'48 Cadillac 60 Special Four-door Sedan, 6" long	18	26	35
'48 GMC 3751 Greyhound Diesel Bus, 6" long	25	35	55
'48 Willys Jeepster, 3" long	10	15	20
'49 American La France Pumper, 3" long	10	15	25
'49 Buick Roadmaster Four-door Sedan, 6" long	22	34	45
'49 Chevrolet Deluxe Panel, 4" long	14	21	28
'49 Ford Custom Convertible, 3" long	10	15	25
'49 Ford Custom Four-door Sedan, 3" long	10	15	25
'49 Ford F1 Pickup, 3" long	10	15	25
'49 Ford F6 Oil Tanker, 4" long	13	19	25
'49 Ford F6 Oil Tanker, Texaco, 6" long	25	35	55
'49 Ford F6 Oil Tanker, Standard, 6" long	25	35	55
'49 Ford F6 Oil Tanker, Sinclair, 6" long	25	35	55
'49 Ford F6 Oil Tanker, Shell, 6" long	25	35	55
'49 Ford F6 Stake Truck, 4" long	15	22	30
'49 Indianapolis No. 3 Race Car, 3" long	10	15	25
'49 Mercury Fire Chief Sedan, 4" long	22	32	45
'49 Mercury Four-door Sedan, 4" long	15	24	35
'49 Oldsmobile 88 Convertible, 4" long	20	30	40
'49 Twin Coach Bus, 3" long	12	21	30
'50 Chevrolet Army Ambulance, 4" long	15	24	35
'50 Chevrolet Deluxe Panel Truck, 3" long	10	15	25
'50 Chevrolet Fleetline Deluxe Two-door Sedan, 3" long	10	15	25
'50 Chrysler Windsor Convertible, 6" long	70	95	125
'50 Civilian Jeep, 3" long	5	7	14
'50 Dodge Pickup, 4" long	15	22	30

Postwar (Continued)

	C6	C8	C10
'50 Jeep CJ3 Army, 4" long	9	15	22
'50 Plymouth Special Deluxe Four-door Sedan, 3" long	10	15	25
'50 Pontiac Cheftain Deluxe Coupe Sedan, 4" long	20	30	40
'50 Pontiac Fire Chief Chieftain Sedan, 4" long	22	32	45
'51 Buick Le Sabre Experimental Roadster, 6" long	25	38	55
'52 Ford Mainline Four-door Sedan, 3" long	12	21	32
'52 Lincoln Capri Two-door Hardtop, 6" long	28	37	50
'52 Mercury Custom Four-door Sedan, 4" long	15	22	30
'53 Chrysler New Yorker Four-door Sedan, 6" long	18	28	45
'54 Buick Century Estate Wagon, 6" long	20	34	45
'54 Buick Special Experimental Coupe, 6" long	23	38	50
'54 Cadillac 62 Four-door Sedan, 6" long	20	30	40
'54 Ford Ranch Wagon, 3" long	8	12	20
'54 Ford Ranch Wagon, 4" long	15	24	35
'54 Jaguar XK120 Roadster, 3" long	8	12	20
'54 MG Roadster, 3" long	8	12	20
'54 MG Roadster, 6" long	10	20	30
'54 Nash Metropolitan Convertible, 3" long	32	50	70
'54 Volkswagen 113, 6" long	10	20	30
'54-55 Chevrolet Corvette Roadster, 4" long	15	22	30
'55 Chevrolet Bel Air Four-door Sedan, 3" long	8	12	20
'55 Ford C600 Oil Tanker, 3" long	8	12	20
'55 Ford Customline V-8 Two-door Sedan, 3" long	8	12	20
'55 Ford Thunderbird Coupe, 3" long	7	11	18
'55 Ford Thunderbird Coupe, 4" long	20	30	40
'55 Mack B-Line Cement Mixer, 6" long	22	32	45
'55 Mack B-Line Cement Mixer, axle-driven drum, 6" long	30	40	55

Postwar (Continued)

	C6	C8	C10
'55 Mack B-Line Stake Truck, w/"Tootsietoy" tin cover, 1958, 6" long	50	75	100
'55 Oldsmobile 98 Holiday Two-door Hardtop, 4" long	15	24	35
'56 Austin-Healey 100-5 Roadster, 6" long	20	30	40
'56 Caterpillar Bulldozer, 6" long	23	38	50
'56 Caterpillar Road Scraper, 6" long	18	26	35
'56 Chevrolet Cameo Pickup, 4" long	13	19	25
'56 Dodge D100 Panel Truck, 6" long	23	38	50
'56 Ferrari Racer, 6" long	18	28	45
'56 Jaguar XK140 Coupe, 6" long	15	22	30
'56 Lancia Racer, 6" long	18	27	45
'56 Mercedes 190SL Coupe, 6" long	10	20	30
'56 Packard Patrician Four-door Sedan, 6" long	28	37	50
'56 Porsche Spyder Roadster, 6" long	10	20	30
'56 Triumph TR3 Roadster, 3" long	7	11	18
'57 Ford F100 Styleside Pickup, 3" long	5	7	14
'57 Ford Fairlane 500 Convertible, 3" long	8	12	20
'57 GMC Greyhound Scenicruiser Bus, 6" long	22	32	45
'57 Jaguar Type D, 3" long	8	12	20
'57 Plymouth Belvedere Two-door Hardtop, 3" long	8	12	20
'59 Ford Country Sedan Station Wagon, 6" long	10	20	30
'59 Oldsmobile Dynamic 88 Convertible, 6" long	14	25	35
'59 Pontiac Star Chief Four-door Sedan, 4" long	10	16	25
'60 Chevrolet El Camino Pickup, 6" long	12	22	30
'60 Chevrolet El Camino Pickup with Camper and Boat, 6" long	17	32	50
'60 Chrysler Windsor Convertible, 4" long	13	19	25
'60 Ford Country Sedan Station Wagon, 3" long	8	12	20
'60 Ford Falcon Two-door Sedan, 3" long	5	8	15

Postwar (Continued)

	C6	C8	C10
'60 International Metro Van, rare, 6" long	100	125	150
'60 Jeep CJ5, 6" long	9	18	25
'60 Jeep CJ5 with Snow Plow, 6" long	25	35	55
'60 Rambler Super Cross-Country Wagon, 4" long	15	24	35
'60 Studebaker Lark Custom Convertible, 3" long	9	16	22
'60 Volkswagen Bug, 3" long	7	11	18
'62 Ford C600 Oil Tanker Truck, 6" long	20	30	40
'62 Ford Country Sedan Station Wagon, 6" long	8	18	25
'62 Ford Econoline Pickup, 6" long	20	30	40
'69 Ford LTD Two-door Hardtop, last of the larger-size die-cast Tootsietoys, 4" long	13	19	25
Army Cannon, four-wheel, 4" long	10	15	25
Army Cannon, six-wheel, 4" long	12	21	30
Retaurant Trailer, 6"	32	50	70
U-Haul Trailer, 3" long	4	6	8
U-Haul Trailer, 4" long	5	10	15

'47 International K5 Tractor-Trailers

	C6	C8	C10
Auto Transporter, scaled to match 6" long series	30	42	55
Machinery Hauler, scaled to match 6" long series	30	42	55
Shipping Van, Tootsietoy Trucking, scaled to match 6" long series	27	37	50
Utility Truck, scaled to match 6" long series	27	37	50

'47 Mack L-Line Tractor-Trailers (1954)

	C6	C8	C10
Hood and Ladder, 1954, scaled to match 6" long series	35	55	75
Log Hauler, scaled to match 6" long series	35	55	75
Machinery Hauler, scaled to match 6" long series	35	55	75
Oil Tanker, Tootsietoy Line, scaled to match 6" long series	50	75	125
Oil Tanker, scaled to match 6" long series	32	50	70

'47 Mack L-Line Tractor-Trailers (1954) (Continued)

	C6	C8	C10
Pipe Truck, scaled to match 6" long series	35	55	75
Shipping Van, Tootsietoy Coast to Coast, scaled to match 6" long series	37	57	80
Shipping Van, Tootsietoy Line, scaled to match 6" long series	32	50	75
Stake Truck, closed sides, scaled to match 6" long series	35	55	75
Stake Truck, open sides, scaled to match 6" long series	50	70	115

'55 Mack B-Line Tractor-Trailers (1960)

	C6	C8	C10
Auto Transport, 1960, scaled to match 6" long series	30	42	65
Boat Transport, scaled to match 6" long series	28	40	60
Hook and Ladder, scaled to match 6" long series	28	40	60
Log Hauler, scaled to match 6" long series	28	40	60
Machinery Hauler, scaled to match 6" long series	28	40	60
Oil Tanker, Tootsietoy Line, scaled to match 6" long series	40	60	80
Oil Tanker, Mobil, scaled to match 6" long series	28	40	60
Pipe Truck, scaled to match 6" long series	28	40	60
Shipping Van, scaled to match 6" long series	28	40	60
Stake Truck, closed sides, scaled to match 6" long series	28	40	60
Utility Truck, scaled to match 6" long series	25	35	55

'58 International RC180 Tractor-Trailers (1962)

	C6	C8	C10
Auto Transport, plastic trailer, scaled to match 6" long series	24	32	45
Auto Transport, metal trailer, 1962, scaled to match 6" long series	42	65	85
Boat Transport, scaled to match 6" long series	24	32	45
Machinery Hauler, scaled to match 6" long series	25	35	55

'58 International RD180 Tractor-Trailers (1962)

	C6	C8	C10
Shipping Van, Dean Van Lines, plastic trailer, scaled to match 6" long series	40	60	80

'59 Chevrolet Tractor-Trailers (1965)

	C6	C8	C10
Auto Transport, 1965, scaled to match 6" long series	50	75	125
Hook and Ladder, scaled to match 6" long series	50	75	125
Log Hauler, scaled to match 6" long series	45	70	100
Machinery Hauler, scaled to match 6" long series	45	70	100
Oil Tanker, scaled to match 6" long series	45	70	100

Classic Series (1960)

	C6	C8	C10
1907 Stanley Steamer Runabout	8	12	18
1912 Ford Model T Touring Car	8	12	18
1919 Stutz Bearcat, 1919	8	12	18
1921 Mack Dump Truck	10	15	25
1929 Ford Model A Coupe	8	12	18

HO Pocket Series (1960)

	C6	C8	C10
Cadillac	8	15	20
Dump Truck	10	15	22
Ford Sunliner Convertible with Boat Trailer	10	18	30
Ford Sunliner Convertible with Midget RacerTrailer	12	22	35
Ford Wrecker Truck	10	15	22
Metro Van, Sunnydale Milk	32	50	70
Metro Van, US Mail	18	35	55
Metro Van, Railway Express	18	35	55
Rambler Station Wagon with U-Haul Trailer	10	18	30
Township School Bus	10	18	30

Little Toughs/Midget Series (1970)

	C6	C8	C10
American La France Aerial Ladder Truck	5	8	12
American La France Ladder Truck	4	6	10
Auto Transport Semi-Cab and Trailer	12	17	25
Cement Truck	6	8	12
Coast to Coast Shipping Semi-cab and Van	12	17	25

Little Toughs/Midget Series (1970)

	C8	C10
Dump Truck 6	8	12
Heavy Duty Hydraulic Crane 8	12	17
Logging Semi-cab and Trailer 6	8	12
Mobil Semi-cab and Tanker 10	15	20
Shipping Semi-cab and Van 6	8	12
Shuttle Truck, 1967 2	3	4

Reo Oil Truck Series (1938), 6" Trucks

	C6	C8	C10
No. 1006 Standard 35	55	80
No. 1007 Sinclair 35	55	80
No. 1008 Texaco 35	55	80
No. 1009 Shell 40	60	90

Turner, John C.

Contributor: Bob Smith, The Village Smith, 62 West Ave., Fairport, NY 14450-2102.

	C6	C8	C10
Ahrens Fox Ladder Truck, 1920, 15" long 500	750	1080
Bulldog Mack Dump Truck, red and green, 23" long 325	600	875
Crane, 22" long 300	450	600
Dump Truck, friction, c. early 1930s, 15-1/2" long 625	1000	1500
Dump Truck, C-cab, 22" long 400	600	800
Dump Truck, 26" long 415	620	800

Turner Bulldog Mack Dump Truck, 23" long, $875. Photo courtesy John Taylor

Turner Ahrens Fox Ladder Truck, 15" long, $1080. Photo courtesy Rodney A. Aeesacker

Turner, John C. (Continued)

	C6	C8	C10
Dump Truck, Dodge, 28" long 200	325	450
Fire Engine Pumper, 15" long 750	1400	1800
Hook and Ladder, c. 1930s, 15" long .. 225	338	450
Lincoln Sedan, 26" long 2000	3500	5000
Packard (?) Roadster, friction, 26" long 900	1500	2200
Packard Roadster, 1920s, 16-1/2" long 600	950	1300
Speedster, c. late 1920s, early 1930s, 17" long 500	750	1000
Steam Shovel 75	125	150
Water Truck with Copper Tank 150	225	300

VINDEX

Contributor (motorcycles): Kent M. Comstock, 532 Pleasant St., Ashland, OH 44805, 419-289-3308, 800-443-TOYS.

	C6	C8	C10
Coast to Coast Bus, cast iron, c. 1929, 12" long 1250	1875	2500
Motorcycle with Package Truck, "Henderson PDQ Delivery," w/removable blue rider, red or green, 9" long (VM3) 1800	2500	3500

Vindex Motorcycle with Removable Cop, 9", $3500. Photo courtesy Kent M. Comstock

Vindex Coast to Coast Bus, c. 1929, 12" long, $2500. Photo courtesy Bill Bertoia Auctions

Vindex (Continued)

	C6	C8	C10
Motorcycle with Removable Cop, "Henderson," red or green, 9" (VM1)	1800	2500	3500
Motorcycle with Sidecar, two removable cops, "Henderson," red or green, 9" long (VM2)	1200	1800	3000
P&H Power shovel, cast iron, wheels in caterpillar base, handle revolves rig, 12", 17" extended	2700	4100	8000
Racer No. 2, cast iron, c. 1920s, 11-1/2" long	1000	1600	2500

Wilkins Toy Company

Wilkins, of Keene, New Hampshire, was begun by James S. Wilkins as the Triumph Wringer Company. But the tiny model Wilkins produced to promote his product proved so intriguing to prospective customers and their children, that requests for them poured in. The real thing was quickly forgotten as Wilkins turned to toy making. Its toys were generally cast iron and steel. The firm was acquired in 1894 by Kingsbury, which is still in business, though now as a tool and die maker.

	C6	C8	C10
Aerial Ladder Truck, wind-up, 1910, 18" long	300	450	600
Automobile Racer, light pressed steel, silver, clockwork motor, 10" long	750	1100	1700
Dray, driver, barrels, tiller	400	600	800
Fire Engine, w/driver, steam boiler, c. 1900, 9" long	550	850	1200
Hook and Ladder Open Truck, steel, wind-up motor, 9-1/4" long	175	250	325

Wilkins Automobile Racer, 10" long, $1700. Photo courtesy Bob Smith

Wilkins (Continued)

	C6	C8	C10
Olds, curved dash, wind-up, 1904, 10"	400	600	800
Truck, open cab, very early, clockwork, 11" long	450	675	900

Wolverine

Wolverine, of Pittsburgh, Pennsylvania was founded in 1903 by B.F. Bain. The company got its name from Bain's Michigan hometown. In later years, Wolverine became a subsidiary of Spang Industries. In 1970, it moved to Boonville, Arkansas. The Sandy Andy, in all its variations, was probably Wolverine's most successful and famous toy.

	C6	C8	C10
Dump Truck, white, 12"	55	85	110
Mystery Car, press down to make car move, c. 1938, 13" long	150	225	300
Mystery Car and Trailer, press down to operate, 27" long	200	300	400
Mystery Taxi, 33200		300	400
Speeding Bus, tin litho, driver and occupants, marked "5 Via Main St" and "19302," press down on rear to move, 14" long	100	150	200
U.S.A. Transport Army Truck	150	225	300
White Mustang Dump Truck, 14" long	75	115	150

Wyandotte

Wyandotte was formed in the fall of 1921 with toy pistols being its main product. But by 1935 the Wynadotte, Michigan, firm became known for its simple, streamlined, Art Deco steel cars and trucks with woodrn wheels. During World War II, Wyandotte made clips for the M-1 rifle and after the war moved the company to Piqua, Ohio.

In an attempt to diversify, it bought Hafner Train line, but went out of business in 1965. Wyandottes' heavy-gauge steel toys with baked enamel finish also include aircraft, doll buggies, misical toys, wagons and games.

Wolverine Mystery Car and Trailer, 27" long, $400. Photo courtesy Calvin L. Chaussee

Contributor: John Taylor, P.O. Box 63, Nolensville, TN 37135-0063.

Brian Seligman, 11004 S. W. 37th Manor, Davie, Florida.

Wyandotte	C6	C8	C10
Air Speed Coupe, No. 309, flat grille, white rubber tires, 1934-37, 6" long ...	70	85	110
Ambulance, No. 224, flat nose, black wood wheels, side ports, inset front grille, 1939, 6-3/8" long	35	50	105
Auto Transport, No. 455, cab over, black rubber tires, plastic cab and lithographed trailer, marked "#455" "Auto Transport," "Wt.714," "Cap.4," and "Tires.90-20," 1952, 10" long	35	50	95
Auto Transport, shaded windshield, yellow wood wheels, green cab and black trailer w/four vehicles, electric lights, 1932, 21-5/8" long	85	175	300
Baggage Truck, shark nose, black metal wheels, marked "Baggage," 1953, 11-1/2" long	40	70	135
Bank Truck (also called Bus Bank), No. 375, rooster comb, black wood wheels, green, red and orange, four portholes on each side, 1936-40, 6-3/8" long	40	65	115

Wyandotte (Continued)	C6	C8	C10
Bus, No. 377, rooster comb, black wood wheels or white rubber tires, green, red, orange and yellow, eight windows on each side and rear panel w/two windows and embossed spare tire, sealed chassis, 1936-40, 6-3/8" long	40	70	115
Cadillac, plastic, plastic wheels, many colors, used on auto transports, 1952-54, 5-5/8" long	30	50	95
Cement Truck, cab over, black rubber tires, "Cement Mixer / Sell / Rent," may have had attached mixer, 1940-50, 5" long	20	40	65
Circus Truck, No. 503, rooster comb, embossed wood wheels, two-piece, red cab and lithographed double trailers w/swing down rear ramps, reads "Greatest Show On Earth," cardboard animals on metal stands, 1936, 19-1/4" long	200	750	1200
Contractor Truck, No. 434C, long nose, black wood wheels, marked "Contractor Truck," 1941, 11-1/4" long	45	70	105
Coupe, two-door, shaded windshield, white rubber tires w/red hubs, no light, 1933, 8-1/4" long	45	90	135

Wyandotte Bus, No. 377, 1936-40, 6-3/8" long, $115. Photo courtesy Brian Seligman

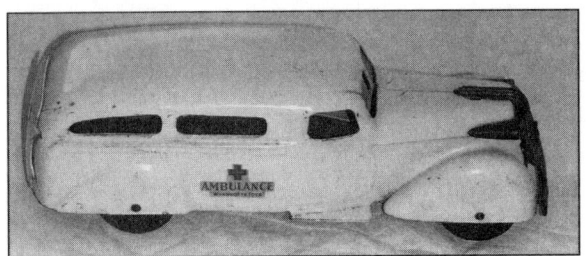

Wyandotte Ambulance, No. 340, 1936-38, 11-1/4" long, $125. Photo courtesy Brian Seligman

Wyandotte Coupe, two-door, 1933, 8-1/4" long, $135

Wyandotte Circus Truck, No. 503, 1936, 19-1/4" long, $1200. Photo courtesy Brian Seligman

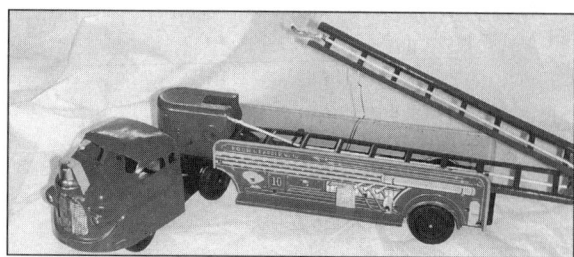

*Wyandotte Fire Truck, No. 1004, 1940-41, 27-1/2"
long, $250. Photo courtesy Brian Seligman*

*Wyandotte Lumber Truck/Log Hauler, 1952, 10-1/4"
long, $105. Photo courtesy Brian Seligman*

*Wyandotte Indy Racer, 7" long, $125. Photo
courtesy Brian Seligman*

Wyandotte (Continued)	C6	C8	C10
Dairy/Milk Truck, No. 805, plastic yellow body and metal red frame, panel van, black rubber tires, "Sunshine Dairy," friction, 1952, 4-7/8" long	20	35	95
Delivery Truck, No. 353, red plastic body/metal chassis, panel van, black rubber tires, "Toy Town Delivery" and "Super Service," lithographed grille and dashboard, opening side and rear doors, 1952, 11-1/2" long	50	75	110
Dump Truck, No. 352, plastic cab, cab over, yellow metal wheels, tailgate, 1952, 11" long	50	65	105
Dump Truck, No. 315, shaded windshield, white rubber tires, w/grille, green or red, 1934-36, 5-1/4" long	40	65	85
Fire Truck, No. 1004, cab over, six black wood wheels, "Hook and Ladder No. 10," 29" expanding ladder, hood bell, 1940-41, 27-1/2" long	65	125	250
Fire Truck, No. 157, plastic, cab over, black rubber tires, 1952, 5-1/2" long	65	80	110
Fire Truck, No. 308R, open cab, white rubber tires, red body w/three green ladders, 1932, 6" long	65	80	110

Wyandotte (Continued)	C6	C8	C10
Garbage Truck, No. 332, cab over/square cab, black rubber tires, dump action and rear loading sliding gate, marked "Metropolitan Department of Public Service" and "Help Keep our City Clean," 1956-57, 17" long	70	110	140
Ice Cream Cart, plastic, sliding lid and bell, 1953, 4-1/2" long	30	50	100
Ice Truck, No. 123, sleepy eye/checker board, lithographed metal wheels, lithographed body, marked "Igloo Ice Company," one ice cube and one pair of ice tongs, 1954, 10-1/4" long	50	75	110
Indy Racer, black rubber tires, lithographed body w/attached head of driver, marked "Wyandotte" and "7," also "Jet Streak" version, 7" long	45	65	125
La Salle Land Cruiser, No. 385, white rubber tires, hood opens, electric lights, 1939, 15" long	75	130	210
Lumber Truck/Log Hauler, sleepy eye, black and white metal wheels, lithographed cab, flat bed has four plastic posts, marked "Lumber Supply," four logs included, 1952, 10-1/4" long	45	60	105
Oil/Gas Tanker, No. 225, rooster comb, black wood wheels, four embossed top hatches and fold down rear hatch, sealed chassis, 1939, 6-3/8" long	30	55	110
Pickup Truck, plastic, black rubber tires, 1950s, 7-7/8" long	10	40	65
Racer, boattail, yellow wood wheels, red w/electric lights, 1933, 8-5/8" long	75	105	195
Racer, boattail, No. 333, white rubber tires, green and red, electric lights, 1934, 8-5/8" long	60	105	155

Wyandotte Semi-Tractor Trailer, 1953, 7-3/4" long, $105. Photo courtesy Brian Seligman

Wyandotte Tow Truck, 1953, 9" long, $110. Photo courtesy Brian Seligman

Wyandotte (Continued)	C6	C8	C10
Railway Express Truck, cab over, black rubber tires, REA lithographed, "Nation Wide," "Air, Rail Service" and "Railway Express Agency," late 1940s-52, 12-1/2" long	60	90	135
Rocket Racer, No. 319, white rubber tires or black wood wheels, wood rear wheel, 1935-36, 6-1/4" long	60	75	135
Sedan, four door, No. 425, pressed metal wheels, touring sedan (Nash style), 1939, 11" long	65	105	205
Sedan, four door, No. 311, rounded windshield, white rubber tires, w/grille, trunk mounted rear spare, 1934-37, 4-1/2" long	35	60	95
Sedan, four door, No. 344, long nose, lithographed metal wheels w/black rubber tires, enclosed chassis, 1938, 9" long	65	80	120
Semi-Tractor Trailer, No. 390, cab over, black rubber tires, "Green Valley Stock Ranch," lithographed cab marked w/"Wyandotte" and "W" in a dot on cab, 1950s, 17-1/2" long	80	95	165
Semi-Tractor Trailer, cab over, black rubber tires, "Produce Van," "Refrigerated Cargo" and "Coast to Coast," 1953, 7-3/4" long	50	70	105

Wyandotte (Continued)	C6	C8	C10
Soap Box Derby Racer, No. 226, soap box racer, red version w/red wood wheels and blue version w/black wood wheels, marked "Soap Box Derby" and "Thunderbird 226," 1941, 6" long	75	150	195
Speedster, No. 378, black wood wheels, w/lithographed driver and passenger, 1937-38, 6-3/4" long	50	100	200
Stake Truck, No. 426, cab over, metal wheels, 1940-45, 12-1/4" long	40	65	105
Stake Truck, No. 352, shaded windshield, wood wheels, w/ and without electric lights, 1933-34, 15" long	60	95	150
Tow Truck, No. 365, long nose, black rubber tires, lithographed grille, "Service + Wrecker," "Toy Town Only 24 hr Service," 1941, 17-1/2" long	50	90	140
Tow Truck, sleepy eye, lithographed metal wheels, "Wyandotte Automobile Society," "Towing and Repairs" and "Towing Service Nite and Day," rear crank operated hoist, 1953, 9" long	45	70	110

WOODEN TOYS

Toy companies did not use plastic, or man-made material for toys of this type until the late 1930s, so items covered in this chapter are from the period 1920 through 1940.

Made primarily of wood, they were shaped by a simple turning on a lathe or by jigsaw. Their form rises from combining these simple shapes using nails, glue, rubber cords and springs in clever ways to achieve amusing actions when played with by a child.

The wooden characters were often mounted on metal platforms to make pull toys. Workers then painted the toys primarily with the aid of stencils and stamps.

Hundreds of companies made these types of toys. Some of the important makers of these popular toys include—The Toy Tinkers of Evanston, Illinois; Rich Made Toys of Sterling, Illinois; Hyker Toy Co. of Highland Park, Illinois, and The Toy-Kraft Co. of Wooster, Ohio.

Contributor: Jim and Judy Sneed, Hollywood, South Carolina. The Sneeds began collecting wooden pull toys about five years ago and now have a collection of over 150 of these toys. They maintain a Web site at www.old-woodtoys.com where information seekers may find photos, company histories, want lists and price guides. They can be contacted through this Web site.

Hustler Toy Company

In 1920, the Frantz Manufacturing Company of Sterling, Illinois began making toys. These early toys were marked "Frantz" and included the very popular baseball and football games.

In 1924, responding to rumors that Frantz was getting out of the hardware business, he created the Hustler Toy Company as a subsidiary. Toys of this transition period can be found with a Hustler decal over a Frantz logo. In the late 1920s, they took over the Toylander Corporation, a toy manufacturer in Sterling, Illinois. Some of the goose pull toy and possibly other toys are marked Hustler while others are marked Toylander.

The chief designer was Clare A. Wetzel, and his name appears on almost all Frantz and Hustler patents.

Hustler Toy Company made wood toys well into the 1930s and seemed to have stopped by 1939. After that, the Hustler name appears only on metal strap-on roller skates until about 1970. Frantz Manufacturing is still in business making bearings and steel balls in Sterling, Illinois.

A C6 grade indicates noticeable playwear but still an attractive sample. A C9 grade indicates a sample that has not seen play but may have one or more handling or storage flaws such as a paint chip but is otherwise indistinguishable from new. Mint pieces are almost impossible to find and command premium prices especially with their original boxes. Names and spellings are those of the Hustler Toy Co.

	C6	C9
Action Builder, canister full of parts, 12" high canister	50	90
Aerorace Shooter, airplane game, 8" x 15"	NPF	NPF
Auto Caravan Truck, w/four trailers, 8" long	60	100
Auto Transport Truck, w/four autos, 21" long	150	280
Aviator Clown Riding Torpedo Airplane	80	180
Baby Hustler Crib Doll, girl, 6"	25	65
Baseball, lithographed playing surface w/pegs	100	175
Beads, glass jars, three sizes	25	45
Beads, metal cans, three sizes	45	70
Bell-Hop, black bell hop, bags, 8"	85	190
Betty Roll Duck, three-wheel, ivory or yellow	25	45
Betty Roll Duck, four-wheel, fixed ivory, blue, or pink	25	45
Big Joe Hustler, giant version of Joe Hustler	NPF	NPF
Big Pete Hustler, giant version of Peter Hustler, 23"	NPF	NPF
Big Sambo, giant version of Sambo Hustler	NPF	NPF

Action Builder, Hustler Toy Company, $90. Photo courtesy Jim and Judy Sneed

Left to Right: Billy Hustler, $125; Watch Dog; Larry Hustler, $90; Betty Roll Duck, $45; Pup, $75. Photo courtesy Jim and Judy Sneed

Doc, Hustler Toy Company, $180. Photo courtesy Jim and Judy Sneed

Hustler Toy Company (Continued)	C6	C9
Bildkraft Erector, set-type	NPF	NPF
Billy Hustler, dog pulling wagon and driver, 15"	75	125
Block Engine, colorful blocks, cylinders, 10"	NPF	NPF
Bobby Beach Duck, green or yellow flat base, duck head	25	45
Camel, w/blanket walker, 11" long	40	85
Circus Pony, push-pull toy, bell on back, 13"	55	110
Circus Train, loco and four circus wagons, 30"	NPF	NPF
Clown Car, clown driving jalopy, from patent	NPF	NPF
Color Boat, colored funnels on boat, 12" long	40	85
Crew, four oarsmen in boat, 10"	45	90
Doc, black base, old style auto, 14"	90	180
Doc, green base, newer syled auto, 14"	90	180
Doc Stork, stork on delivery bike, 14"	NPF	NPF
Doll Carriage, giant horse, wagon, 18"	NPF	NPF

Hustler Toy Company (Continued)	C6	C9
Dolly Tinkle Hustler, push toy, doll w/bell, 21"	NPF	NPF
Duck Duck, w/litho wagon, 13"	50	90
Ducky Racer, duck driving car, 12"	150	325
Easter Bunny Bunny, w/egg box on back, 8"	NPF	NPF
Elephant, walker, red, hard rubber feet, 11" long	45	80
Elephant and Trainer, trainer and elephant, 14"	NPF	NPF
Elephant Parade, elephant and baby elephant, 14"	NPF	NPF
Floaty Duck, duck on water, bucket, 12"	NPF	NPF
Football, lithographed field and stadium	90	165
Fran-zell Walking-Barking Dog, black and white dog, collar, 8"	35	70
Gardener, driver and horse, large wagon, 23"	130	270
Golf Game, golfer puts into tray, 18"	NPF	NPF
Hiram Hustler, farmer driving horse, 11" long	90	150
Horse Shoe Players, two players w/rings	45	80
Jack Rabbit, rabbit holding carrot, 12"	NPF	NPF

Jimmie Mouse, Hustler Toy Company, $400. Photo courtesy Jim and Judy Sneed

Poncho Hustler, Hustler Toy Company, $225. Photo courtesy Jim and Judy Sneed

Hustler Toy Company (Continued)

	C6	C9
Jimmie Mouse, mouse driving red auto, 11"	250	400
Joe Hustler, litho bucket, four wheels, 11"	90	170
Joe Hustler Transfer, wood,bucket, four wheels, 11"	80	150
Jungle Pals, red lion driven by dog	125	280
Kids, Joe and Pete on tricycle wagon, 14"	75	180
Kitty, cat pushing ball, 11" long	NPF	NPF
Larry Hustler, boy riding horse, 8"	40	90
Limber Jack, man on truck pushing with hands, 15"	150	280
Movie in Felt, animal show play set	NPF	NPF
Nok-Out Bench, mallet and blocks, 12"	15	35
Peppy Pup, roll over pup, hand control	50	90
Peter Hustler, litho bucket, tricycle, 11"	90	170
Peter Hustler Transfer, wood bucket, tricycle, 11"	85	150
Play-Learn, letters and pictures learning game	NPF	NPF
Poncho Hustler, clown, dog riding mule, 17"	125	225
Pup, Hustler walking barking dog, 8"	35	75

Hustler Toy Company (Continued)

	C6	C9
Pup with Blanket, pup with blanket on back, 8"	NPF	NPF
Questor, fortune telling game, 9" x 14"	NPF	NPF
Racer, race horse and jockey, 8" high	90	180
Rastus and Rachel, two characters, dog, mule drawn, 20"	225	400
Red Cap, white face porter, 8"	NPF	NPF
Ring Toss, girl, numbered balls, 15"	60	90
Rolls-right, rights itself	15	25
Sam Hustler Transfer, man driving mule, 21"	NPF	NPF
Sambo Hustler, black driver, horse head, 11"	85	135
San Duck, duck head with bucket, 15"	50	90
San Fish, fish with bucket on back, 16"	NPF	NPF
Sand Box, shovel, box, 6" x 10"	30	65
Sand Cart, shovel, cart, 7" x 11"	35	55
Sand Sprinkler, sand sprinker system, shovel, 14"	NPF	NPF
Scotty Hustler, dog barks at frog, 14"	NPF	NPF
Speed Boat, man and two children in boat, 12"	NPF	NPF
Surf-rider, man on surf board, 8"	NPF	NPF
Swimmer, arms on wheels, 9"	34	90
Target Game, cowboy on target, dart gun, 28"	NPF	NPF
Terry Hustler, push-pull toy, walking dog, 11"	55	90
Tulip Peg Board, teaching tool	25	50
Twins, two dancing girls, green base, 7"	75	150

The Ted Toy-lers

The Ted Toy-lers began toy production in 1925 in New Bedford, Massachusetts. The founder and chief designer was Edwin V. Babbitt of Fairhaven, Massachusetts.

The Ted Toy-lers (also spelled as Toylers) reached its peak in about 1928 shipping more than 50,000 toys a week all over the world. In 1929, International Toy Company took over, or merged with The Ted Toy-lers. Toy labels of this period say "The Ted Toylers an International Toy Co." At this time, probably to increase sales, the company made smaller and cheaper versions of its best selling toys. For example, oilcloth belts and hat plumes were replaced with painted representations. In 1930, The Ted Toy-lers ceased operations and Edwin V. Babbitt started a new toy company making dollhouses.

Their toys were of the highest quality, made of birch wood and painted with a durable lacquer. Early toys used braided cord for arms and legs, but in 1927, springs or wires running through wooden arm and leg beads replaced the cords.

Toys marked International Toys were produced in 1929, and possibly 1928 and 1930.

A C6 grade indicates noticeable play wear but still an attractive sample. A C9 grade indicates a sample that has not seen play but may have one or more handling or storage flaws such as a paint chip but is otherwise indistinguishable from new. Mint pieces are almost impossible to find and command premium prices especially with their original boxes. Names and spellings are those of The Ted Toylers. Toys are pull toys unless otherwise described.

The Ted Toy-lers

	C6	C9
Acrobat klown, beaded legs, four wheels	95	170
Acrobat klown, corded legs, three wheel	85	180
Aeroplane, white plane, two heads, pull toy, 16"	125	225
Blue Sailor Doll, corded arms and legs, 6"	35	70
Dapple Horse, black and white horse, beaded legs, 5"	50	125
Galloping Jockey, dapple horse bifurcated horse legs	60	135
Galloping Jockey, dapple horse, 7"	75	155
Galloping Jockey, black horse, 7"	60	145
Giant Galloping Jockey, klown on dapple horse, 13-1/2"	150	350
Giant Horse, black and white, beaded legs, 11"	100	210
Giant Klown Doll, yellow suit, beaded arms legs, 17"	85	180
Giant Marching Soldier, wood rifle, red body, yellow legs, 19"	125	280

The Ted Toy-lers (Continued)

	C6	C9
Giant Roaring Racer, yellow race car, two heads, 17-1/2"	100	225
Giant Soldier Doll, red suit, beaded arms legs, 16" high	100	170
Giant Ted Toy Express, two horses pulling wagon, 20"	NPF	NPF
Giant Walking Sailor Doll, blue suit, beaded arms legs, 19"	90	150
Hobby, beaded arms and legs	90	190
Hobby, corded arms and wood stick legs	90	190
Locomotive, red and yellow, 7" long	35	90
Marching Soldier, cord arms, 10"	65	135
Marching Soldier, beaded arms	75	145
Marching Soldier Squad, five marching soldiers, 11"	250	550
Racer, one head, 5" long	20	50
Racing Jockeys, two horses w/jockeys, 6"	45	85
Red Soldier Doll, beaded arms, red suit, 8" high	35	75
Roaring Racer, yellow race, two drivers	80	155

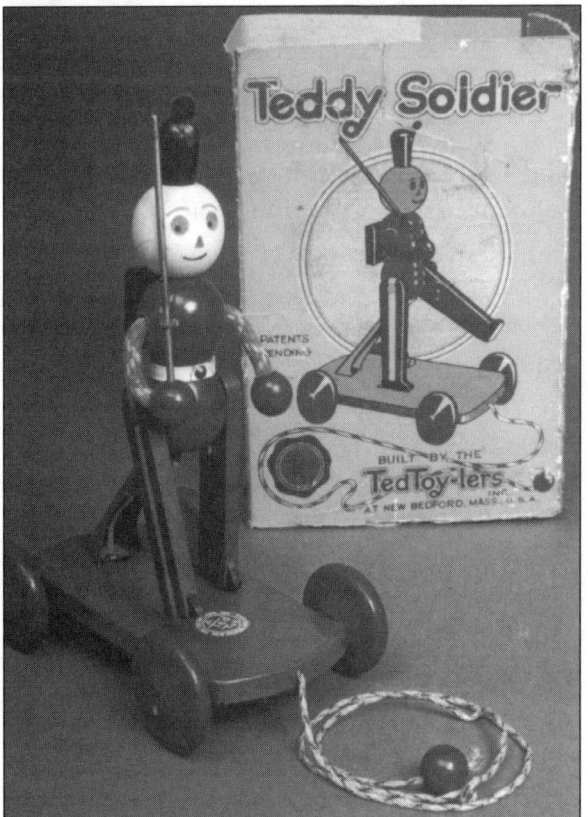

Marching Soldier, The Ted Toy-lers, $135. Photo courtesy Jim and Judy Sneed

A group of Tedo Toy-lers toys, including two versions of the Galloping Jockey. Photo courtesy Jim and Judy Sneed

Marching Soldier, The Ted Toy-lers, $145. Photo courtesy Jim and Judy Sneed

Racing Jockeys, The Ted Toy-lers, $85. Photo courtesy Jim and Judy Sneed

The Ted Toy-lers (Continued)

	C6	C9
Sailboat, two sails, two heads, 12" long	NPF	NPF
Sea Skooter, catamaran boat, two heads, 13"	NPF	NPF
Ted Toy Army Bowling Game, w/five 8" soldiers	180	350
Ted Toy Express, two horses pulling wagon, 12"	60	125
Toy Crafter, builder set in 4" x 10" x 2" box	35	65
Train Loco, w/three cars, 28" long	100	185
Waddling Duck, yellow duck, metal legs and tail, 6"	25	65
Waddling Duck, waddling duck pull toy	65	110
Walking Sailor, beaded arms, wood legs	60	120
Walking Sailor, cord arms and legs	55	100
White Sailor Doll, corded arms and legs, 6"	35	80
Yellow Klown Doll, beaded arms and legs, 7"	55	90

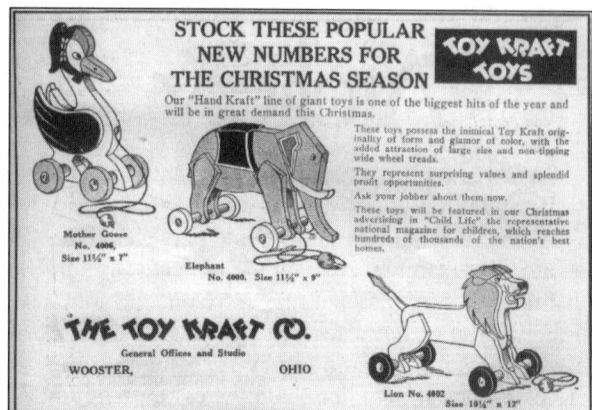

Bunny and Wagon, The Toy Kraft Co., $180. Photo courtesy Jim and Judy Sneed

The Toy Kraft Co.

The Toy Kraft Co. of Wooster, Ohio began toy making in 1916 and continued until 1950. Early toy was made of high quality but by the 1940s cheapened its line by introducing cardboard materials into its products.

Today, a Wooster company is reproducing a few of Toy Kraft's early toys.

	C6	C9
Bunny and Wagon, bunny pulling wagon	90	180
Bunny Duck Cart, Bunny pushing two ducks cart	NPF	NPF
Bunny Team and Wagon, two bunnies pulling wagon	NPF	NPF
Circus Horse and Rider, flat rider on horse pull toy	NPF	NPF
Circus Wagon, w/various animals	110	225
Ducky Cart, two ducks pulling wagon	NPF	NPF
Elephant, pull toy, 11-1/2" x 9"	55	100
Elephant Push Cart, elephant pushing cart	NPF	NPF
Flower Wheelbarrow, cart w/blue flower on side	NPF	NPF
Lion, pull toy, 10-1/4" x 12"	55	100
Mother Goose, pull toy, 11-1/2 x 7	45	95
Pup, dog pull toy	55	100
Puss-in-boots Cart, pulling cart, 1933	NPF	NPF

Appendix A

MUSEUMS

ART INSTITUTE OF CHICAGO,
THORNE MINIATURE ROOMS
111 S. Michigan Ave.
Chicago, IL 60603
Phone: 312-443-0849
e-mail: webmaster@artic.edu
Web page:www.artic.edu/aic/
firstpage.html

ANTIQUE TOY MUSEUM
Exit 230, I-44
P.O. Box 175
Stanton, MO 63079
Phone: 314-927-5555

AUBURN-CORD-DUSENBERG
MUSEUM
Auburn, IN 46706
Auburn toys and Cord and Dusenberg
automobiles

BAUER TOY MUSEUM
Donald A. Bauer
233 E. Main
Fredericksburg, TX
Phone: 512-997-9394

CRAYOLA HALL OF FAME, BINNEY
& SMITH, INC.
Two Rivers Landing
30 Centre Square
Easton, PA 18042-774
Phone: 423-515-8000
e-mail: crayola@crayola.com
Web page: www.crayola.com

DAISY MANUFACGUN MUSEUM
211 South 8th St.
P.O. Box 220
Rogers, AR 72757
e-mail: djohnson@daisy.com
Web page: http:www.Daisy.com
The world's most complete collection
of air rifles, dating from the
18th century

DELAWARE TOY & MINIATURE
MUSEUM
P.O. Box 4053
Route 141
Wilmington, DE 19807
Phone: 302-427-8697
e-mail: toys@thomes.net
Web page: thomes.net/toys

DENVER MUSEUM OF MINIATURES,
DOLLS & TOYS
1880 Gaylord St.

Denver, CO 80206-1221
Phone: 303-322-1053
e-mail: idsbc@aol.com
Web page: www.sni.net/start/dmmdt

EUGENE FIELD HOUSE & TOY
MUSEUM
634 So. Broadway St.
St. Louis, MO 63102
Phone: 314-421-4689

FAWCETT'S TOY MUSEUM
P.O. Box 1156
3506 Atlantic Highway
Waldoboro, ME 04572

HOBBY CITY DOLL & TOY
MUSEUM
1238 South Beach Blvd.
Anaheim, CA 92804
Phone: 714-527-2323

ISLIP TOWN MUSEUM
Montauk Highway
Oakdale, NY

LAWRENCE SCRIPPS WILKINSON
COLLECTION
c/o Detroit Antique Toy Museum
6325 West Jefferson
Detroit, MI 48209
Phone: 383-843-9775
Available only for traveling exhibitions

THE LONDON TOY & MODEL
MUSEUM
23 Craven Hill
London, England

MARGARET WOODBURY STRONG
MUSEUM
One Manhattan Square
Rochester, NY 14607

MUSEUM OF CHILDHOOD
8 Broad Street
Greensport, NY

MUSEUM OF THE CITY OF
NEW YORK
5th Avenue and 103rd Street
New York, NY

NASHVILLE TOY MUSEUM
2613 McGavok Pike
Nashville, TN
Next to Opryland USA

NATIONAL FARM TOY MUSEUM
1110 16th Ave. SE
Dyersville, IA 52040
319-875-2727

REMEMBER WHEN TOY MUSEUM
Box 226A
Canton, MO 63435
Phone: 314-288-3995 or 288-3176

SAN FRANCISCO INTERNATIONAL
TOY MUSEUM
2801 Leavenworth Street
San Francisco, CA

SMITHSONIAN INSTITUTION
Public Inquiry Mail Service - MRC010
1000 Jefferson Drive SW
Washington, DC 20560
Phone: 202-357-1300

THE STERLING COLLECTION
Stone Castle
804 North Third Street
Bardstown, KY

THE STRONG MUSEUM
1 Manhattan Square
Rochester, NY 14607
Phone: 716-263-2700
Web page: www.strongmuseum.org

SULLIVAN-JOHNSON MUSEUM
223 North Main Street
Kenton, OH
Kenton Toys exhibit

TOY & MINIATURE MUSEUM OF
KANSAS CITY
5235 Oak St.
Kansas City, MO 64112-2877
Phone: 816-333-2055
e-mail: bergr@umkc.edu
Web page: www.unkc.edu.tmm

THE TOY MUSEUM
42 Bridge St. Row
Chester, Cheshire
England

TOY TRAIN MUSEUM
Paradise Lane
Strasburg, PA

WASHINGTON DOLL'S HOUSE &
TOY MUSEUM
5236 44th Street NW
Washington, DC 20015

Appendix B

AUCTION HOUSES

These are established firms experienced in auctioning large collections of toys.

REX & KATHY BARRETT (MAIL)
P.O. Box 254
Medinah, IL 60157

BILL BERTOIA AUCTIONS
2413 Madison Ave.
Vineland, NJ 08360
Phone: 609-692-1881
Fax: 609-692-8697
Web page: www.BertoiaAuctions.com

BLOCK'S BOX
Bob Block
P.O. Box 51
Trumball, CT 06611
Phone: 206-926-8448

JEFF BUB
1658 Barbara Drive
Brunswick, OH 44212
Phone: 216-225-1110

BUTTERFIELD & BUTTERFIELD
220 San Bruno Ave.
San Francisco, CA 94109
415-861-7500
e-mail: info@butterfields.com
Web page: www.butterfields.com

CHICAGO ANTIQUE TOY AUCTION
by Just Right, Inc.
6582 RFD
Long Grove, IL 60047
Phone: 708-949-0059

CHRISTIE'S EAST
219 East 67th Street
New York, NY 10021
Phone: 212-606-0400
Web page: www.christies.com

COLLECTORS AUCTION SERVICES
RR 2 Box 431
Oakwodd Road
Oil City, PA 16301
Phone: 814-677-6070
Fax: 814-677-6166
e-mail: manderton@mailusachoice.net
Web page: www.caswel.com

CONTINENTAL AUCTIONS (MAIL)
P.O. Box 193
Sheboygan, WI 53082

DEBBIE & MARTY KRIM'S NEW
ENGLAND AUCTION GALLERY
(MAIL)
Box 2273-T
West Peabody, MA 01960
Phone: 508-535-3140
Fax: 508-535-7522

DOLL EXPRESS
P.O. Box 367
Reamstown, PA 17567

DUNNING'S AUCTION SERVICE
755 Church St.
Elgin, IL 60123-9302
Phone: 708-741-3483
Fax: 708-741-3589

GARTH'S AUCTIONS
2690 Stratford Rd.
Delaware, OH 43015
Phone: 614-362-4771
e-mail: info@garths.com
Web page: www.garths.com

GUERNSEY'S
108 East 73rd Street
New York, NY 10021
Phone: 212-794-2280
e-mail: catalogues@gurnseys.com

HAKE'S AMERICANA &
COLLECTIBLES
P.O. Box 1444N
York, PA 17405
Phone: 717-848-1333
e-mail: hake@hakes.com
Web page: www.hakes.com

HENRY/PIERCE AUCTIONEERS
1525 S. Arcadia Dr.
New Berlin, WI 53151
Phone: 414-797-7933

RANDY INMAN AUCTIONS
P.O. Box 726
Watersville, ME 04903
Phone: 207-872-6900
e-mail: inman@inmanauctions.com
Web page: www.inmanauctions.com

JACKON'S AUCTIONEERS &
APPRAISERS
James L. Jackson
2229 Lincoln St.
Cedar Falls, IA 50613

Phone: 319-277-2256
Fax: 319-277-1252
e-mail: jacksons@jacksonsauction.com

JAMES D. JULIA AUCTIONEERS,
INC.
Rt. 201 Skowhegan Rd.
P.O. Box 830
Fairfield, ME 04937
Phone: 207-453-7125
Fax: 207-453-2502

HENRY KURTZ, LTD.
163 Amsterdam Ave. Suite 136
New York, NY 10023
Phone: 212-642-5904
Fax: 212-874-6018

LEWIS & LAMBRIGHT, INC.
112 N. Detroit St.
LaGrange, IN 46761
Phone: 413-549-3775

JOY LUKE AUCTION GALLERY
300 E. Grove St.
Bloomington, IL 61701-5232
Phone: 309-828-5533
Fax: 309-829-2266

MAPES AUCTIONEERS & APPRAISERS
1600 Vestal Parkway West
Vestal, NY 13850
Phone: 607-754-9193

TED MAURER
1003 Brookwood Dr.
Pottstown, PA 19646
Phone: 215-323-1573 or 367-5024

McMasters Doll Auctions
P.O. Box 1755
Cambridge, OH 43725
Phone: 800-842-3526
e-mail: mcmasters@jadeinc.com
Web page: www.macmastersauctions.com

MID-HUDSON AUCTION GALLERIES
One Idlewild Avenue
Croton-On-Hudson, NY 12520

NOEL BARRETT ANTIQUES &
AUCTIONS
P.O. Box 300
Carversville, PA 18913

PHILIPS NEW YORK
406 E. 79th St.
New York, NY 10021
Phone: 212-570-4830
Web page: www.phillips-auctions.com

LLOYD W. RALSTON
173 Post Road
Fairfield, CT 06430
Phone: 203-255-1233
Web page: www.lloydralstontoys.com

RICHARD OPFER AUCTIONEERING,
INC.
1919 Greenspring Drive
Timonium, MD 21093
Phone: 410-252-4053
e-mail: info@opferauction.com
Web page: www.opferauction.com

SKINNER, INC.
357 Main St.
Bolton, MA 01740-1104
Phone: 508-779-6241
Fax: 508-779-5144
Web page: www.skinnerinc.com

SMITH HOUSE (MAIL)
P.O. Box 336
Eliot, ME 03903
Phone: 207-439-4614

SOTHEBY'S
1334 York Avenue
New York, NY 10021
Phone: 212-606-7000
Web page: www.sothebys.com

TOY LOCATERS (MAIL)
5821 Diana Lane
Lake View, NY 14085
Phone: 716-627-5840

TOY SCOUTS, INC.
137 Casterton Ave.
Akron, OH 44303
Phone: 330-836-0668
Fax: 330-869-8668
e-mail: info@toyscouts.com
Web page: www.toyscouts.com

WALLIS & WALLIS
West Street Auction Galleries
Glenn Butler
Lewes
East Sussex BN7 2NJ
United Kingdom
Phone: 01273-480208
Fax: 01273-476562

WITHINGTON, INC.
RD 2 Box 440
Hillsboro, NH 03244
Phone: 603-464-3232

Appendix C

COLLECTORS AND DEALERS

It is suggested that, when writing to any of the following, you enclose a stamped, self-addressed envelope.

STAN ALEKNA
732 Aspen Lane
Lebanon, PA
Phone: 717-228-2361
Fax: 717228-2362
Toy soldiers

STEVE BALKIN
Burlington Antique Toys
1082 Madison Avenue
New York, NY 10028
Toy soldiers including Warren

CHARLES W. BEST
11523 Pine Valley Drive
Franktown, CO 80116
e-mail: budbest@aol.com
Old toy pistols, etc.

BOB LOWE'S TOONERVILLE
JUNCTION
7 E. Church Street
Bethlehem, PA 18018
Phone: 215-691-6736
Classic American and
European Toys

BOSSEN IMPLEMENT, INC.
300 Washington Ave.
Hwy. 187 S.
Lamont, IA 50650
Phone: 319-924-2880
Web page: www.bossenimp.com
Farm toys

BLYSTONE'S
2132 Delaware Ave.
Pittsburgh, PA 15218
Phone: 412-371-3511
Fax: 412-244-8028
Specialists in books on toys

RAYMOND V. BRANDES
1844 Mt. Cello Rd.
Marianna, FL 32448-5365
e-mail: rvb@ray-vin.com
Web page: www.ray-vin.com
Big Bang cannons collector/dealer

LARRY BRUCH
P.O. Box 121
Mountaintop, PA 18707
Phone: 717-474-9202
Old toys wanted & for sale

BUDDY K TOYS
Buddy "L" Toys, etc.
RD 9 Box 322
Bingen Road
Bethlehem, PA 18015

JIM BUSKIRK
c/o TGCA
3009 Oleander Avenue
San Marcos, CA 92069
Spring-Air BB guns, cast iron pistols

JIM & PATSY CARLSON
7939 Caberfae Trail
Clarkston, MI 48348-3708
Schoenhut collectors

ROD CARNAHAN
541 El Paso
Jacksonville, TX 75766
Buy, sell, trade old toys

CALVIN L. CHAUSSEE
Box 22
Calhan, CO 80808
Phone: 719-347-2000
Fax: 719-347-2780
Antique toy buyer—any quantity

CLASSIC TOYS
69 Thompson St.
New York, NY 10012
New and old toys; military, vehicles,
zoo, etc.

CLASSIC ANTIQUES—TOYS
537 El Paso Street
Jacksonville, Texas 75766-2532
Phone: 903-586-1355
e-mail: rodcarnahan_toys@tyler.net
Web page: www.antique-
center.com/classic.htm

KENT M. COMSTOCK
532 Pleasant Street
Ashland, OH 44805
Phone: 419-289-3308
Motorcycles, all types

CONTINENTAL HOBBY HOUSE
P.O. Box 193
Sheboygan, WI 53082
Toys and trains,
regular catalogs

REID COVEY
Box 2D Highmarket Rd.
Constableville, NY 13325
Phone: 315-397-8026
e-mail: sullivan@northnet.org
Matchbox, Hot Wheels

DARROW'S FUN ANTIQUES
1101 1st Ave.
New York, NY 10021
Phone: 212-838-0730
e-mail: george@fun-antiques.com
Website: www.fun.antiques.com
Vintage toys, dolls, radios, penny
banks, autographs, animation art,
games, toy soldiers

ROBERT A. DECENZO
P.O. Box 2266
Framingham, MA 01701
Marbles, tin wind-ups, paper litho,
games, trains

DUTKINS' COLLECTABLES
1019 W. Route 70
Cherry Hill, NJ 08002
Phone: 609-428-9559
Tin toys, soldiers, etc.

ECCLES BROTHERS
R.R. 1, Box 253-D
Burlington, IA 52601
Toy soldiers, comic figures and vehi-
cles from original molds,
catalog $3.00

PERRY R. EICHOR
703 North Almond Dr.
Simpsonville, SC 29681
Aircraft toys and literature

JOHN FAWCETT
P.O. Box 1156
Waldoboro, ME 04572
Disney, Lone Ranger,
Character Toys

EXCALIBUR HOBBIES LTD
63 Exchange Street
Malden, MA 02148-5523
Phone: 617-322-2959
Toy soldiers, all types

JUDY IZEN
P.O. Box 623
Lexington, MA 02173
e-mail: jizenres@aol.com
Idal dolls, paper dolls

JOE FREEMAN—TIN TOY WORKS
1313 North 15th Street
Allentown, PA 18102
Phone: 610-439-8268
Fax: 610-439-1288
Repairs, parts made for tin toys

DANNY FUCHS
209-80 18th Avenue
Bayside, NY 11360
Superman toys, games, etc.

RAY FUNK
826 East 8th St.
Upland, CA 91786
Toys, bicycles

JOHN GIBSON
P.O. Box 40054
Washington, DC 20016
Phone: 301-527-0076
Tootsietoy restoration, parts and ser-
vices

BARRY GOODMAN
P.O. Box 218
Woodbury, NY 11797
Phone: 516-338-2701
G.I. Joes, Barbie, Robots and all
1950s-60s character toys

TERRY GRAHAM
3083 Crescent Street
Long Island City, NY 11102
Phone: 718-956-3382
Dealer in toy guns

TONY AND JACKI GRECCO
P.O. Box 3490
Poughkeepsie, NY 12603
Phone: 914-462-8829
Toy soldiers and related items

A. (GUS) HANSEN
4645 Lilac Avenue
Glenview, IL 60025
Mignot, Dimestore, Britains, etc.

RAY HARADIN
Toys of Yesteryear
1039 Lakemont Drive
Pittsburgh, PA 15243-1817
Phone: 800-349-8009 (Call for detailed
catalog)
Mechanical banks, toy soldiers

JIM HARMON
634 S. Orchard Dr.
Burbank, CA 91506
Radio premiums and tapes, comic
books and strips

W S (BILL) HARRISON III
223 Boa Vista St.
Punta Vista, FL 33983-5644

BILL HELLIE
All American Toy Company
P.O. Box 4266
Salem, OR 97302
American Toy Company parts and lim-
ited editions; buy sell, restore antique
toys

JEFFREY L. HUBBARD
1770 4th Street South
Naples, FL 33940-7502
Doepke, Nylint collector

INSURANCE FOR COLLECTIBLE
TOYS
Debbie Riley
Reeves & Melvin
P.O. Box 229
Millville, NJ 08332
Phone: 800-298-4318

BRAD KREWSON
588 Lindford Drive
Bay Village, OH 44140
Beany & Cecil toys

BILL LANGO
127 74th Street
North Bergen, NJ 07047
Barclay vehicles, animals and soldiers
from original and new molds; send for
flyer

RICHARD LEACH
26146 Redfield Rd.
Edwardsburg, MI 49112
Old steam engine toys, literature

STEVE LEONARD
Box 127T
Albertson, LI, NY 11507
Phone: 516-742-0979
Antique mechanical toys, etc.

DAVID M. LEOPARD
2507 Feather Run Trail
West Columbia, SC 29169-4915
Old toy cars and trucks

CARL LOBEL
Box 74A
Warren, VT 05674
Phone: 802-496-4025
Toys of all eras

LONDON BRIDGE COLLECTOR'S
TOYS
East Penn Plaza
1325 Chestnut Street
Emmaus, PA 18049
Phone: 215-967-6887
Britains soldiers, etc. and Britains
replacement parts

RICHARD MACNARY
4727 Alpine Drive
Lilburn, GA 30247
Marx trains, Coca-Cola vehicles,
wood, cardboard, paper toys, soldiers

MARBLE COLLECTORS SOCIETY OF
AMERICA
P.O. Box 222
Trumbull, CT 06611

JOHN D. (JACK) MATTHEWS
13 Bufflehead Dr.
Kiawah Island, SC 29455
World War II toys, etc.

FRED MAXWELL
4722 No. 33 Street
Arlington, VA 22207
Collector/researcher; slush mold cars,
planes, novelties, literature, toys

K. WARREN MITCHELL
1008 Forward Pass
Pataskala, OH 43062
Soldiers of all types, regular lists at no
charge

MONUMENTAL COLLECTIBLES
Tom Gordon III
P.O. Box 295
Reistertown, MD 21136
Character toys, Disney, PEZ

JOHN MURRAY
Box 29
Eden, NY 14057
Fisher-Price

NEW ERA TOYS
P.O. Box 10
Lambertville, NJ 08530
Phone: 609-397-2113
Restorations service for pressed steel
toy, pedal cars

BARBARA & JONATHAN NEWMAN
The Paper Soldier
8 McIntosh Lane
Clifton Park, NY 12065
Paper toys, old and new

TIM OEI—OEI ENTERPRISES, LTD.
241 Rowayton Ave.
Rowayton, CT 06853-1227
Phone: 203-866-2470
Buys, sells, trades, restores old toys

DON PIELIN
1009 Kenilworth
Wheeling, IL 60090
Toy soldiers

PLYMOUTH ROCK TOY CO.
P.O. Box 1202
Plymouth, MA 02362
Phone: 508-746-2842 or 508-830-1180
Fax: 508-830-0364
Toy pistols, etc., all eras

EDWARD K. POOLE
926 Terrace Mtn. Drive
Austin, TX 78746
Toy soldiers, 1:36-scale ID vehicles
and old wooden military vehicle kits

HARVEY K. RAINESS
Rustic Ridge - N13
289 Mount Hope Avenue
Dover, NJ 07801
Phone: 201-366-4677
Dealer in vehicles, tin, soldiers

MARK RICH
P.O. Box 971
Stevens Point, WI 54481
Tootsietoy, Baby-Boomer-era toys

LEO RISHTY
Toydoc
2563 Jardin Lane
Weston, FL 33327
TOY1DOC@aol.com

SALUNGA (DON ECKEL)
P.O. Box 369
Talmage, PA 17580
Phone: 717-656-4857
Cast-iron parts for toys

PHIL SAVINO
Rt. 2, Box 76
Micanopy, FL 32667
Mail auctions in various toy categories,
send SASE

CONRAD SCHWAGER
10321 N. Trails Edge Dr.
Peoria, IL 61615
Arcade, Buddy L, Metalcraft

SECOND CHILDHOOD
283 Bleecker Street
New York, NY
Antique toys

RONALD L. SIMKOFF
5171 Mayfield Rd.
Lyndhurst, OH 44124
Phone: 216-461-2660
Holgate toys

JOHN K. SNYDER, JR.
Diamond International Galleries
1966 Greensprig Dr., Ste. 401
Timonium, MD 21093
Comic characters

SCOTT SMILES
Mechanical Toys
157 Yacht Club Way, Apt. #112
Hypoluxo, FL 33462-6048
Phone: 561-582-6016
e-mail: ssmiles@aol.com
Tin wind-ups, battery-operated toys,
friction;
Toy Appraisals—call for details

BOB SMITH
62 West Ave.
Fairport, NY 14450
Phone: 716-377-8394
Sells toys of all types, Toy Show

RON SMITH
33005 Arlesford
Solon, OH 44139
Phone: 216-248-7006
Tin plate cars and planes, plastic pro-
motional cars

MARK SUOZZI
Box 102
Ashfield, MA 01330
Phone: 413-628-3241
Antique penny banks & toys

FRED THOMPSON
Smith-Miller Inc.
P.O. Box 139
Canoga Park, CA 91305
New designs of
Smith-Miller vehicles

TRADER FRED'S
Fred Berecz
Rt. 132 Box 65
Thetford, VT 05075
Doepke trucks

MARCIE TUBBS
6405 Mitchell Hollow Rd.
Charlotte, NC 28277
Dollhouses and Miniature
Furniture

DAVID WELCH
P.O. Box 714
Murphysboro, IL 62966
Phone: 618-687-2282
PEZ, Cereal boxes, model kits, TV,
Disney, premiums

RANDY WELCH
Raven' Tiques
27965 Peach Orchard Drive
Easton, MD 21601
Phone: 410-822-5441
Ramp walkers, tin wind-ups, and spar-
klers

CHARLES FRANCIS WILDING
Secretary, Capitol Miniature Auto Collectors Club
10207 Greenacres Dr.
Silver Springs, MD 20903

FRED & MARGARET WILHELM
W & F Collectibles
Box 2054
Leucadia, CA 92024
Disney, Popeye, comic, Barclay, Man-
oil soldiers

FERDINAND ZEGEL
P.O. Box 589
Ft. Belvoir, VA 22060
Antique toys, postwar, Corgi, Dinky

Appendix D

RECOMMENDED READING

Periodicals

A.C. Gilbert Heritage Society Newsletter. Quarterly. Marion Designs, 594 Front St., Marion, MA 02738.

Antique Toy World. Monthly. Dale Kelley, P.O. Box 34509, Chicago, IL 60634.

Old Toy Soldier Newsletter. Bimonthly. Steve Sommers, 209 North Lombard, Oak Park, IL 60302.

Toy Cars & Models. Monthly. Krause Publications, 700 E. State Street, Iola, WI 54990.

Toy Farmer. Monthly. Toy Farmer, 7462 106 Ave. SE, LaMoure, ND 58458-9404

Toy Shop. Biweekly. Krause Publications, 700 E. State Street, Iola, WI 54990.

Toy Gun Collectors of America Newsletter. 16-page quarterly. Jim Buskirk, 3009 Oleander Avenue, San Marcos, CA 92069.

Toy Soldier Review. Vintage Castings Inc., 127-74th Street, North Bergen, NJ 07047.

Books

101 Greatest Baby Boomer Toys. Mark Rich. Krause Publications, 700 E. State St., Iola, WI 54490

Arcade Toys by Al Aune. 1990. Robert F. Mannella, 4441 Shari Ann Lane, Brooklyn Park, MN 55443

Barclay Catalog Book, The. Early Barclay catalogs, drawings, photos, etc. Richard O'Brien. (Out of print)

Big Bang Cannons. Raymond V. Brandes. Ray-Vin Publishing, 2964-R Brookshire Way, Duluth, GA 30136.

Cast Iron Toy Guns and Capshooter by Samuel H. Logan and Charles W. Best. Heavily illustrated book. $55. Sam Logan, 1200 Harvard Drive, Davis, CA 95616

Collector's Guide to PEZ. Shawn Peterson. Krause Publications, 700 east State Street, Iola, WI 54990

Collecting American-Made Soldiers. Richard O'Brien. Krause Publications, 700 East State Street, Iola, WI 54990.

Collecting Foreign-Made Soldiers. Richard O'Brien. Krause Publications, 700 East State Street, Iola, WI 54990.

Collecting PEZ by David Welch. $43.95 in U.S., 350 pages. P.O. Box 714, Murphysboro, IL 62966. (618) 687-2282, FAX (618) 684-2243.

Collecting Toy Cars & Trucks, 2nd Edition. Richard O'Brien. Krause Publications, 700 East State Street, Iola, WI 54990.

Collecting Toy Cars & Trucks, 3rd Edition. Elizabeth A. Stephan, editor. Krause Publications, 700 East State Street, Iola, WI 54990.

Collecting Toy Trains, 5th Edition. Elizabeth A. Stephan, editor. Krause Publications, 700 E. State St., Iola, WI 54490

Encyclopedia of Marx Action Figures, The. Tom Heaton. Krause Publications, 700 E. State St., Iola, WI 54490

Fisher-Price 1931-1963. 1991 edition. Krause Publications, 700 East State Street, Iola, WI 54990.

Maloney's Antiques & Collectibles Resource Directory. David J. Maloney, Jr. Antique Trader Books, A Division of Krause Publications, 700 E. State St., Iola, WI 54490

Marbles: Price and Identification Guide. Robert Black. P.O. Box 222, Trumbull, CT 06611.

Pictorial Guide to Weeden Steam Toys. Richard B. Leach. $10. 26146 Redfield Road, Edwardsburg, MI 49112.

Plastic Figure & Playset Collector. Bimonthly. Specialty Publishing Company, P.O. Box 1355, LaCrosse, WI 54602-1355,

Plastic Toys. Bill Hanlon. All-color, 288 pages. Schiffer Publishing, 77 Lower Valley Road, Atglen, PA 19310.

Radio Mystery and Adventure. Jim Harmon. McFarland & Company, Inc., Jefferson, North Carolina & London.

Rubber Toy Vehicles. Dave Leopard. Dave Leopard, 2507 Feather Run Trail, West Columbia, SC 29169-4915.

The Second Catalog Book. Reprints of catalogs by Manoil, Barclay, Warren, All-Nu, Authenticast, Belton, Grey Iron. $16. Richard O'Brien, 705 Greene Street, Beaufort, SC 29902.

The Story of American Toys by Richard O'Brien. 1990. Abbeville Press. (Out of print)

Today's Hottest Die-Cast Vehicles. Elizabeth A. Stephan, editor. Krause Publications, 700 E. State St., Iola, WI 54490

Toy Shop's Action Figure Price Guide. Elizabeth A. Stephan, editor. Krause Publications, 700 E. State St., Iola, WI 54490

Toys A to Z. Mark Rich. Krause Publications, 700 E. State St., Iola, WI 54490

Toys & Prices. Sharon Korbeck, Elizabeth A. Stephan, editors. Krause Publications, 700 E. State St., Iola, WI 54490

Vintage Toys. Jim Bunte, Dave Hullma, Heinz Mueller. Antique Trader Books, A Division of Krause Publications, 700 E. State St., Iola, WI 54490